THE FREE AND THE BRAVE

By HENRY F. GRAFF PROFESSOR OF HISTORY COLUMBIA UNIVERSITY

Teacher's Edition · Annotated

Introduction by Henry F. Graff

Teacher's Guide with Tests
by John A. Davitt

Counselor, Merritt College
Formerly, Teacher of Social Studies
Roosevelt Junior High School
San Francisco, California

INTRODUCTION TO TEACHER'S EDITION

The essence of good history is good story—full of magnetic people, dramatic interest, and clear relevance to the present. Young people especially need good history, for it can light their path with confidence as they make their way in a stubbornly unpredictable world.

A few years ago, however, when my older daughter was an eighth-grader, I became fascinated by—and alarmed at—how unreal and remote she and her friends found the American history they were studying, despite their skillful teacher. Very humbly, but with increasing absorption, I undertook to write a modern textbook for their age-group.

I knew at first hand that for such a book to be accepted by young people, it would have to be marked at the very least by unfaked frankness, a sincere respect for the student, and a quality of writing appropriate for a very knowing generation. It would have to talk about an America that young Americans can recognize as their own—the one in which they lead their lives. In a word, I had to explain persuasively the development of the America that is emerging as we enter the last third of the century. It is an America increasingly proud of how it governs itself by the democratic process, increasingly urban and suburban in outlook, increasingly attentive to injustices of the past and present toward large groups of its own people, increasingly dependent on its technological genius, increasingly aware of its abundant artistic heritage, and increasingly involved with the other cultures of the world.

This book, which has been written to fulfill these aims, is being published just as my younger daughter is entering the seventh grade. I trust that she and her contemporaries will read and enjoy it for its own sake because it tells a thrilling tale that no other people on earth can match and because it is a beautiful example of the bookmaker's craft. More than anything else, though, I hope that they will come away from its pages with a well-founded pleasure in knowing what it is to be an American today, going forward in the great line of "the free and the brave."

HENRY F. GRAFF

June 1, 1966

CONTENT AND OBJECTIVES

The Free and the Brave was written to help prepare young Americans to live responsibly in a rapidly changing country and world. To cope with the present, people need to know the conditions and changes in the past that have contributed to the situations of today and that will bear on those of tomorrow. In his chronological organization of this narrative history, the author concentrated on these objectives:

1. To help students understand and appreciate the nature of their own complicated *culture*—way of life—and to see how important aspects of it developed.
2. To impress the fact that American culture is plural—that many individuals and many groups have contributed to it in the past, and many more continue to do so.
3. To show how democracy—an outstanding characteristic of American life—first took root and has continued to evolve.
4. To demonstrate how Americans have created an advanced technology—another significant feature of their culture.
5. To explain how the United States, once a relatively rural, agricultural country, has become a large, highly industrialized one in which most people live in urban areas.
6. To describe the important problems Americans have faced both at home and abroad and the solutions they arrived at, and to make clear what problems they are confronting today and what they are doing about them.
7. To make it plain that *free, democratic* people have the ability and the means to solve their own problems.
8. To inspire faith in the future, based on a knowledge of American achievements against great odds in the past.
9. To provide help in the development of the critical-thinking and study skills and techniques required in a challenging, very competitive society and time.

Part One (Chapters 1, 2, 3)

American history began when human beings first began living in what Europeans later called the New World—not when seamen of western Europe set out to find new trade routes to the East. The author tells the circumstances of the arrival of the first Americans from Asia and uses his account to introduce the concepts of technology and technological change. He goes on to discuss the people who descended from the Indians—the first Americans—and he explains "culture," illustrating its meaning by describing the cultures of two important groups in North America, the Eastern and the Oasis Indians.

After noting Indian contributions to later Americans, the author narrates the story of the Vikings' journeys to Greenland and North America and of their impermanent settlements. He then explains what motivated Christopher Columbus to undertake the voyage west across the Atlantic, which resulted in his landfall in the West Indies.

The account of the Spanish exploration and conquest of large areas in the New World—with the help of a technology superior to that of the Indians—follows. It ends with a summary of the rich heritage the Spanish created in the Americas.

Finally, the French explorations of the St. Lawrence Valley, the Great Lakes region, and the Mississippi Valley are recounted. The extensive French claim to land is contrasted with the limited nature of the French settlements. Continuing to develop the concept of culture, the author strongly emphasizes the lasting contributions the French, in spite of their relatively few numbers, were able to make to the culture of present-day eastern Canada.

Part Two (Chapters 4, 5, 6)

The English establishment of colonies along the Atlantic seaboard is described chronologically in Part Two. The author starts with the beginning of Virginia and ends with the settlement of Georgia. He includes accounts of the Dutch and Swedish colonies, since both lay along the Atlantic coast and since both were eventually absorbed by the English.

Running through the chapters in this part is the continuous story of how primarily English culture—with its technology, which was advanced for the time, its language, and its religions—became fixed in our own culture. The early plural nature of American culture is exemplified in the story of Pennsylvania, the most successful English colony; and the contributions of various peoples to American life—for example, the log cabin of the Swedes—are noted.

The English settlers' early relations with the mother country are touched on, but the focus is, as in Part One, on the American scene and its effect on the colonists. Although the motives of the settlers, the early conditions they faced, their problems, and the solutions to those problems are special concerns, major emphasis is placed on certain aspects of colonial life which took root in American culture. Among these are the beginnings of democracy—self-government in Virginia, Plymouth, and elsewhere; the establishment of religious freedom in Rhode Island, particularly, and in a more limited sense, in Maryland; and the initiation of public education in Massachusetts.

Further, the author calls special attention to the relationships among colonial characteristics which came in a later day to be considered "typically American." The settlers everywhere were business-minded, they were self-made, and they were a hopeful people. *A man's position in life was not fixed*—it could change, depending on his ability. (See page 122.) The qualities of the Pilgrims were those we like to ascribe to ourselves when we are at our best (see page 84).

Because of these various emphases, the colonial period is seen to be an important formative one in American history. The settlers are shown to have established certain American institutions and to have begun to shape, so far as is possible, a basically American set of characteristics.

Part Three (Chapters 7, 8, 9, 10)

In the first chapter of Part Three, the author breaks his chronological account in order to consider the colonies as a whole about 1700, before they became involved in the English struggle with the French or in their own contest with England. He describes the various groups of people in the colonies and the way they lived, keeping the emphasis on the fact that all the people—except the slaves—could rise in position. Education is stressed as the best means of advancing, and early colleges in America are discussed in some detail.

The chronological narrative is resumed as the competing interests—in part, business—of the English in the Ohio Valley are described. The English colonists are seen as involved with the mother country in the war that followed a British effort to dislodge the French. The end of the war left Britain and Spain supreme in the New World and led to a changed British policy toward the colonies.

Both the reasons for the change and the colonial reaction to it are presented. Evidence of the growing spirit of independence among the colonists and of their insistence on the *right to self-taxation* is kept in the foreground as events leading to an open break in 1775 are unfolded.

The spirit of the colonists, the leadership of Washington, and the help of foreign allies are shown to have been decisive in the American victory in the War for Independence. The results were that independence, so nobly justified in the Declaration of Independence, was recognized and that the new United States stretched from the Atlantic to the Mississippi. With only limited experience in working together but with a *common Western heritage, excellent resources,* and the *will to succeed,* the newly independent Americans faced a future all their own. Britain held what is now Canada, and Spain remained the only other important European power in the New World.

Part Four (Chapters 11, 12, 13, 14)

The struggle to win their independence over, Americans faced new difficulties. But before he discusses them, the author names the legal and social changes the American Revolution brought, among them a destruction of "aristocratic ways," the beginning of the separation of church and state in the new country, and a new tendency of the people to pick up and move—west.

After a description of the difficulty the new states had in agreeing on a form of central government, the division of powers within the one decided upon and its weakness are discussed. Nevertheless, the enduring achievement of the government set up under the Articles of Confederation—the arrangement for governing and settling western land—receives very strong emphasis.

The major portion of Part Four of the book is devoted to the circumstances that led to the writing of the United States Constitution, to a description of the "supreme law of the land" and the federal system of government it created, and to its operation in the republic it created. The Bill of Rights is spoken of as assuring Americans of *"rights necessary to all people who call themselves free."*

Significant precedents—for instance, the establishment of the Cabinet—are emphasized. Hamilton's plan to strengthen the new government and the disputes it aroused are centered on. The rise of political parties is shown to be a natural result of the reaction to the plan. Also, the contrast between Hamilton's ideal of an industrialized America and Jefferson's ideal of an agricultural country is used to sharpen the focus of the disputes.

The United States in the late 1790's and early 1800's is shown to be involved in differences with Spain, France, and Britain. Because of Euro-pean rivalries America obtained Florida and the huge Louisiana Purchase, a vast new West—and new responsibilities. But also because of European difficulties the United States, as a neutral country, found itself in trouble over its shipping on the Atlantic.

Attempts of Jefferson and Madison to avoid war failed, and the indecisive War of 1812 followed. Though neither Britain nor the United States won a clear-cut victory, Americans saw the need for greater unity among themselves. A new national feeling was expressed—for example, by the Monroe Doctrine, a cornerstone of American foreign policy. Sectionalism appeared, but the spirit of compromise, especially over the extension of slavery into the Louisiana Purchase, prevailed.

In Part Four the author continues to help students develop their concept of democracy. He makes clear what Jeffersonian democracy means and how Jefferson's ideas and dreams affected America.

Part Five (Chapters 15, 16, 17, 18)

The author uses Henry Clay as the subject of the essay beginning Part Five because he stood for friendship among the sections in the period of growing sectionalism before the Civil War. Jackson's first administration was marked by the nullification crisis. His handling of the matter and, above all, the concept of democracy he held and shared with fellow countrymen are shown to have had a lasting effect on Americans.

The period in which "Jacksonian democracy" flourished is described as a time when merchants and cities were greatly influencing American life, when new enterprises and material things were unusually attractive, when people were not bound by the past, and when new ways of carrying on politics developed. The author not only builds up the students' idea of American democracy but also shows clearly how American life was changing with the passage of time.

Americans' interest in business enterprises in the years covered is seen to be largely northern and in part the result of certain inventions, which speeded the shift from work at home to factory work. Mass production—a characteristic of American industry—is carefully explained. The effects of the factory system upon factory "hands" and these people's early efforts at unionizing are set forth.

Achievement of needed reforms in factory life led to reform movements of other kinds, among them the antislavery movement. The spread of slavery, which accompanied the expansion of cotton production in the South, is treated in some detail. Sectional differences between the North and the South widened as southerners specialized in growing cotton and northerners built factories and railroads and welcomed immigrant workers.

A new period of expansion, which saw the acquisition of the Oregon Country and of Texas and California and the territory between them as well as the settlement of some of these areas, is described in detail. The Mexican War is shown as a part of the expansion movement.

The migrations of people westward are seen as logically leading to the desire of settlers to organize new states and to the reopening of the difficulty between the North and the South over the extension of slavery into the territories. The views of the various leaders of the day are clearly presented to give an understanding of the time and people. The ambitions of Douglas are shown to have been responsible for upsetting the peace effected by Clay in 1850, and the escalating difficulties and violence after the Kansas-Nebraska Act are emphasized.

The freedom of Americans to form new political parties whenever they wish is described as a privilege of democracy, exercised when the Republican party was formed over the issue of the extension of slavery into the territories. The position of American newspapers—a free press—in the period is also brought out.

This part closes with an analysis of the situation in the country just before the election of 1860, when Americans had reached the "point of no compromise." The division among Democrats is seen as paving the way for the victory of the Republican candidate, which led to secession in the South and to Lincoln's resolve to save the Union.

Part Six (Chapters 19, 20)

The author makes Lincoln's idea of the importance of saving the Union the keynote of Part Six, which deals with the Civil War and reconstruction. Although he gives an account of military operations in the war, he incorporates material which enriches students' understanding of what went on, and above all, he describes developments which were speeded up during the war and which endured in or affected American life afterward.

Among these developments was the accelerated growth of industry in the North because of inventions and discoveries (which are described). Possessing industry and good means of transportation and communication (again, through technology) is seen as an advantage of the North—an advantage later extended to the whole country. The assets and liabilities of the South are also summed up.

The terrible cost of war to both sides is stressed in various ways—in heads, in statistics, and otherwise in accounts of significant battles or campaigns (as in the story of Sherman's march). It is also brought out in the description of conditions in the South during the war and of the situation afterward (see pages 441–442, 449–450).

The course of the war is made more understandable by the outline of Union strategy which is presented. The human side of the war is kept uppermost through details given about colorful and heroic individuals.

An account of the assassination of Lincoln follows that of the ending of the war, and a quotation from the President's second inaugural address dramatically summarizes an attitude toward the South not shown by later leaders. The No. 1 problem of both the South and the North is identified as being what to do about the southern Negroes, whose situation needed careful attention from both northerners and southerners. The fact that finding a solution involved reaching agreement among leaders who disagreed violently is brought out. Efforts to solve the problem were also made a part of reconstruction policies, which were, above everything, a subject of dispute.

The Thirteenth, Fourteenth, and Fifteenth amendments were added to the Constitution, and certain legislation was enacted to protect and aid the Negro during this period. Nevertheless, a complete and lasting solution to his problem was lost sight of in the difficulties that led to the impeachment of Johnson, to the forming of the Ku Klux Klan, to "Grantism," to a long depression, and to an end of reconstruction in the Compromise of 1877. The author closes Part Six by mentioning the coming years of discrimination against Negroes and by pointing out that the unfinished Statue of Liberty in 1876 seemed to suggest that the work of building democracy was unfinished.

Part Seven (Chapters 21, 22, 23, 24, 25)

In Part Seven of the book, the author discusses the great changes in American life brought about by the continuing growth of population, development of industry, and movement of people to cities. In the period covered, the transformation of the United States—once an agricultural country—into an industrialized nation was accomplished.

The author describes the growth of heavy industry after the Civil War and the work of important businessmen and inventors. The country was knit together even more closely than before by telephones and was cemented by transcontinentals. The author also takes occasion to speak of the improved American standard of living resulting from the growth of industry and the rapid technological change (see page 480).

Miners, cattlemen, and finally farmers are seen as having come to the previously unsettled mountain areas and Great Plains in successive waves. The arrival of the last two of these three groups, especially, is shown as being related to the building of the transcontinentals and to the tragic outcome for western Indians.

The author next describes the difficulties of the Great Plains farmers—their problems with a new environment and their complaints about the railroads. The former are solved in part through technology and the latter to some extent through the efforts of the federal government. It is pointed out that the government's acceptance of responsibility for just treatment of citizens by private business was an important change in American life. Nevertheless, workingmen's problems and their efforts to handle them through strikes did not at first meet with much sympathy, though laboring men formed national organizations, whose histories and aims are described in detail.

American cities, the homes of many workingmen and the refuge of numerous people who were part of the "new immigration," are described, and features—good and bad—of city life are brought out. *The point is emphasized that problems of the cities,* like those of workingmen, were not solved in part because American leaders had *rural backgrounds and viewpoints.* Further, the nation generally was not ready to be concerned with the personal problems of people. The 1870's, 1880's, and early 1890's are characterized as "dull, do-nothing days of politics."

In 1896 there was a change. Within two years the United States fought the Spanish-American War, gaining overseas possessions. The author carefully gives the background for the development of imperialism (see page 540), relating it in part to the growth of industry. The role of newspapers is also stressed.

Though Theodore Roosevelt is shown as extending the role of the United States in world affairs, by building the Panama Canal, for example, the chief emphasis in the account of his years in the White House—and of Wilson's early years there—is on the reform of social evils, a result of the efforts of the progressives. The conditions requiring reform and the reforms themselves are described in detail.

Reforming is said to have reached a peak under Wilson, affecting the tariff, the control of money and banking, and big business, among other things. In a summary of the reform years, the progressives are characterized as having helped Americans through the years in which the *rural United States* became *industrialized.*

Part Eight (Chapters 26, 27, 28, 29, 30)

In this final section the complete involvement of the United States in world affairs is described as having been a gradual, step-by-step process of turning from isolationism to a new relationship with other countries, partly because of American trade and the growth of nationalism. Americans became deeply involved especially in Latin America, Europe, and Asia.

Nevertheless, though Americans had fought in the First World War to help destroy an enemy, assist allies, and "help make the world safe for democracy," they are shown as having been unwilling in 1918 to accept the responsibilities of world leadership they might have won. They turned to cars and planes and to movies, sports, and the radio after the war.

The author is careful to show the effects on American life of twentieth-century technological improvements and of new popular interests. Further, he describes a new wave of intolerance (caused by fear) of minorities (see page 616) and some results. Attention is called to the firing of the first liquid-fuel rocket in 1926—unnoticed then, but highly significant later.

As he discusses the election of 1928 and the Great Depression that followed, the author continues to stress the fact that more and more Americans were living in cities. In contrasting the actions of Hoover and Franklin D. Roosevelt, he makes it clear that Hoover did not believe that the *federal government* ought to give *direct relief,* as the Roosevelt administrations did. He emphasizes, further, that reform laws of the New Deal permanently changed American life. Some of them dealt with old problems in new forms. The Social Security Act receives special attention.

In keeping with his practice of centering on democracy, the author discusses Franklin Roosevelt's contributions to it—especially his *faith in its ability to solve problems* and guide Americans in a threatening world.

The aggressions (a word used and explained) of Italy, Germany, and Japan in the 1930's and 1940's made the world threatening, and Americans again reluctantly faced involvements. Their reluctance is shown to have ended quickly when Pearl Harbor was attacked. How the Allies, including the United States, overcame the dictatorships in Europe and Africa is described, as is the conquest of Japan in the Pacific. Truman's tribute to the American spirit of liberty as being a main reason for the ultimate victory in East Asia is quoted.

The author calls attention to the fact that the cold war loomed soon after the Second World War ended. He makes clear the goal and ways of Communists (see page 674) and shows how the United States has undertaken—by foreign aid, by decisive acts of Presidents, and by military action—to stop

Communist aggression wherever it has threatened. This has been true in both Democratic and Republican administrations.

The rivalry between the United States and the U.S.S.R. is seen as affecting the United Nations and the space race as well as world affairs. In spite of their grave commitments abroad, Americans are shown to be undertaking improvements in their lives at home. The civil rights revolution is identified as part of their effort. Discrimination against Negroes is called a blot on American democracy.

After describing President Johnson's efforts to build the Great Society and his view of future needs, the author concludes by saying that Americans in the years ahead will require the courage Americans have had in the past. Nevertheless, young people can look for unknown new triumphs and can hope to contribute their own glorious achievements to the future of their country.

TESTS

The following tests for Chapters 1–30 of the book may be reproduced for class use. The tests for all the chapters in each of the eight parts of the book may be used together as a test for a part. Directions for students taking each kind of test included are as follows:

MULTIPLE-CHOICE
Fill in each blank with the letter appearing before the best choice.

TRUE-FALSE
Write *T* or *F* before each statement.

COMPLETION
Write the correct answers in the blanks.

MATCHING
Before each item in the first column, write the letter that identifies the matching item, which appears somewhere in the second column.

An answer key follows the tests for each of the chapters.

CHAPTER 1

MULTIPLE-CHOICE

_____1. Columbus would have been even more fearful of sailing on the Atlantic Ocean than he was without: A.–firearms; B.–the steam engine; C.–sails; D.–the compass.

_____2. The first Americans traveled to North America in the Ice Age by: A.–Strait of Magellan; B.–Bering Strait; C.–Strait of Anian.

_____3. Technological change was very slow among the first Americans partly because they: A.–were not very intelligent; B.–had no neighbors from whom to learn; C.–were not interested in inventions.

_____4. The Oasis Indians lived in what is now the American: A.–Southwest; B.–Great Plains; C.–Southeast.

_____5. Sedentary agriculture is evidence of cultural progress compared with: A.–cattle raising; B.–truck farming; C.–nomadic living.

_____6. Maize was an important New World crop because it: A.–supported a large population; B.–was easy to grow; C.–could be grown over a wide area.

_____7. The practical use of the wheel shows the level of a people's culture because: A.–only a clever people could have developed it; B.–it enabled people to move about quickly; C.–it meant that animals could be used more efficiently.

_____8. The Vikings were long not given credit for their discovery of America because they: A.–did not make it widely known; B.–found it by accident; C.–were not sure it was important.

_____9. The place the Vikings first reached in their westward journeys was: A.–Newfoundland; B.–Greenland; C.–Vinland.

_____10. The principal value of *The Book of Ser Marco Polo* was that it: A.–aroused the curiosity of Europeans about China; B.–led to European colonization of China; C.–helped Columbus find China.

_____11. Columbus figured incorrectly the distance Asia lies west of Europe because maps of the day did not show: A.–Africa; B.–the Pacific Ocean; C.–China.

_____12. The person who proved there is an all-water route to India around Africa was: A.–Dias; B.–Da Gama; C.–Cabral.

___13. The lands actually discovered by Columbus are those bordering the: A.—Atlantic Ocean; B.—Caribbean Sea; C.—Pacific Ocean.

TRUE-FALSE

___1. Columbus quickly realized that he was nowhere near the lands Marco Polo had described.

___2. By the time Columbus died in 1506, Portugal had found a route to Asia.

___3. The American Indians developed the wheel but had no beasts of burden to use with it.

___4. As they arrived in the New World, Columbus and his men first sighted Cuba.

___5. When Columbus reached the New World, the natives he found were very unfriendly.

___6. The first inhabitants of the American continents arrived from Europe.

___7. The Spanish called the Oasis groups of Indians the Pueblos.

___8. Squash, tomatoes, and chocolate are examples of Indian contributions to Europeans and to us.

___9. Toscanelli's map accurately showed the world as we know it today.

___10. Fourteenth-century Europeans had little knowledge of the world except for their own immediate environments.

COMPLETION

1. The two main groups of Indians in North America can be called the ___ and ___.

2. The Strait of ___ was the name given the hoped-for waterway connecting the Atlantic Ocean with the body of water that would lead to China.

3. The homeland of the Vikings was ___.

4. Three elements of European civilization not present in the New World were ___, ___, and ___.

5. The Ice Age began ___ years ago.

MATCHING

___1. the Pinzóns   A. Viking explorer
___2. Prince Henry   B. four voyages
___3. Lucky Leif   C. sailed with Columbus
___4. sedentary   D. reached India, 1498
___5. pueblo   E. had a school for navigators
   F. Indian home
   G. opposite of nomadic

KEY FOR CHAPTER 1 TESTS
Multiple-Choice: 1-D/2-B/3-B/4-A/5-C/6-B/ 7-C/8-A/9-B/10-A/11-B/12-B/13-B. *True-False:* 1-F/2-T/3-T/4-F/5-F/6-F/7-T/8-T/9-F/10-T. *Completion:* 1—Oasis, Eastern/2—Anian/ 3—Norway/4—metal tools, practical use of wheel, beasts of burden/5—between one and two million. *Matching:* 1-C/2-E/3-A/4-G/5-F.

CHAPTER 2
(See instructions, page 8.)

MULTIPLE-CHOICE

___1. The first countries to explore the New World were: A.—Spain and Portugal; B.—France and England; C.—England and Spain.

___2. The chief advantages of Cortés in conquering the Aztecs were: A.—a fine army and a fleet; B.—horses and superior weapons; C.—Marina's help and the loose Aztec political organization.

___3. Viceroys ruled the: A.—viceroyalties of New Spain and Peru; B.—land in South America; C.—West Indies.

___4. Negroes became the main workers on West Indian sugar plantations because: A.—the Spanish disliked Indians; B.—Negroes needed the work; C.—Negroes were skilled farmers who used tools.

___5. Vespucci's name was given to all of the New World when: A.—Waldseemüller used his name to refer to it; B.—Columbus was wrong; C.—the entire New World was an island.

___6. The two cultures that influenced the New World most were: A.—Portuguese and Spanish; B.—Indian and Spanish; C.—Spanish and English.

___7. Two main accomplishments of Magellan were: A.—rounding southern Africa and naming the Ladrones; B.—proving the earth is round and finding a route from the Atlantic to the Pacific; C.—putting down a mutiny and reaching Brazil.

___8. Two forces that influenced Spanish exploration in America were: A.—rivalry with England and France; B.—a desire to outdo Portugal; C.—the wish to convert the heathen and find gold and silver.

___9. A lasting reminder of Magellan's voyage was Spanish colonization of: A.—

South America and the Hawaiian Islands; B.—South Africa and the East Indies; C.—the Philippine Islands.

_____10. Lasting remains of Spanish culture in the New World are: A.—cities and towns; B.—forts and residences; C.—the Roman Catholic religion and the Spanish language.

TRUE-FALSE

_____1. Spain made no effort to plant its culture in the New World.

_____2. All the Spanish who came to the New World were conquerors seeking gold.

_____3. De Soto explored a good deal of what is now the southeastern part of the United States.

_____4. In 1494 the world was divided between Spain and Portugal, and Spain got the New World except part of what is now Brazil.

_____5. Peoples sometimes develop immunity to a particular disease after long contact with it.

_____6. Pizarro traveled to southern South America to conquer Peru.

_____7. Europeans greatly influenced the New World, and Americans greatly influenced Europe.

_____8. Vespucci claimed that the lands he discovered were additional islands off the coast of China.

_____9. We can find many examples of a Spanish heritage in California and other states of the Southwest.

_____10. Indian artists made drawings of the coming of Cortés to Mexico.

COMPLETION

1. The two greatest Spanish discoveries of gold were made in present-day _____ and _____.
2. The oldest European settlement in the present United States is the city of _____.
3. Balboa called the ocean he discovered the _____ Sea, and it was later renamed the _____ Ocean by Magellan.
4. The leader of the Aztec empire conquered by

Cortés was _____, and the leader of the Incas was _____.
5. A bad effect of Spanish rule in the West Indies was the introduction of _____.

MATCHING

_____1. John Cabot
_____2. Vasco Nuñez de Balboa
_____3. *asiento*
_____4. Estevanico
_____5. Bartolomé de Las Casas
_____6. Grand Canyon
_____7. Mississippi River
_____8. Cuzco
_____9. Franciscans
_____10. viceroyalty
_____11. *Victoria*
_____12. Quivira
_____13. Great Plains
_____14. Andes Mountains
_____15. Crusades

A. Inca capital
B. tried to protect the Indians
C. explored North American coast for England
D. map-maker
E. crossed Isthmus of Panama
F. labor contract
G. most famous Negro explorer of New World
H. discovered by De Soto
I. discovered by Coronado's men
J. taught Europeans new war skills
K. crossed by Pizarro in travels through South America
L. Spanish friars
M. aided Cortés
N. Magellan's ship
O. seen by Coronado and his men
P. object of Coronado's search
Q. a division of Spain's colonial empire

KEY FOR CHAPTER 2 TESTS
Multiple-Choice: 1-A/2-B/3-A/4-C/5-A/6-C/ 7-B/8-C/9-C/10-C. *True-False:* 1-F/2-F/3-T/ 4-T/5-T/6-F/7-T/8-F/9-T/10-T. *Completion:* 1—Mexico, Peru/2—St. Augustine, Florida/3—South, Pacific/4—Montezuma, Atahualpa/5—slavery. *Matching:* 1-C/2-E/3-F/4-G/5-B/6-I/7-H/8-A/ 9-L/10-Q/11-N/12-P/13-0/14-K/15-J.

CHAPTER 3

(See instructions, page 8.)

MULTIPLE-CHOICE

_____1. France hoped to open a route to the East by sailing: A.—south around Africa; B.—west around South America; C.—west through the northern part of the New World.

_____2. Verrazano is thought to be the first European to view the present site of: A.—Philadelphia; B.—New York City; C.—Boston.

3. Champlain's greatest accomplishment was: A.—discovering the St. Lawrence River; B.—proving the St. Lawrence River was not the Northwest Passage; C.—establishing a permanent French colony in America.

4. Richelieu was important because he: A.—realized that colonies could increase the mother country's wealth through trade; B.—was one of France's strongest kings; C.—was a powerful general.

5. La Salle claimed for France: A.—the St. Lawrence Valley and Great Lakes area; B.—Texas and the Gulf of Mexico; C.—the Mississippi River, its tributaries, and the land drained by them.

6. New France was weak because it lacked: A.—enough settlers; B.—good transportation routes; C.—sufficient land.

TRUE-FALSE

1. In New France there was an attempt to separate one class of people from another.

2. Champlain's major settlement in New France is not the city of Montreal.

3. Verrazano explored the major part of what is now our Atlantic coast.

4. France relied heavily upon the Jesuits to civilize the Indians and keep them peaceful.

5. Grants of land in New France were given on the basis of a person's skill as an organizer.

COMPLETION

1. The prosperity of New France mainly depended on the "Three F's," ____, ____, and ____.

2. The fur traders of New France were known as the ____ and ____.

3. Two main cities of present-day Canada which were settled by the French are ____ and ____.

4. Most French settlers lived along the ____ River.

5. The man known as the Father of New France is ____.

6. France based its claims to North America upon the voyages of ____.

7. The French left in eastern Canada a heritage of French ____, ____, and ____.

8. Two fur-trading routes the French used were ____ and ____.

9. Quebec was not attractive to settlers because ____.

10. The French protected the land they claimed by means of ____.

MATCHING

____1. Port Royal
____2. Étienne Brulé
____3. Jacques Cartier
____4. Guadeloupe
____5. Jesuits
____6. habitants
____7. *intendant*
____8. Algonkian
____9. seigneurs

A. Indians allied with Champlain
B. representative of the king in New France
C. founded Quebec
D. French colony in West Indies
E. governor of New France
F. discovered the St. Lawrence River
G. first French settlement in America
H. French tenant farmers
I. Catholic missionaries in America
J. French explorer who perhaps reached Lake Superior
K. nobles who owned land in New France

KEY FOR CHAPTER 3 TESTS

Multiple-Choice: 1-C/2-B/3-C/4-A/5-C/6-A. *True-False:* 1-T/2-F/3-T/4-T/5-F. *Completion:* 1—fish, furs, farming/2—*coureurs de bois, voyageurs*/3—Quebec, Montreal/4-St. Lawrence/ 5-Champlain/6-Cartier/7-laws, language, Roman Catholic religion/8-Ottawa and Mattawa rivers; past Forts Frontenac, Niagara, Pontchartrain (Detroit), and Michilimackinac to Green Bay/9-the St. Lawrence froze over about half the year/ 10-forts. *Matching:* 1-G/2-J/3-F/4-D/5-I/6-H/ 7-B/8-A/9-K.

CHAPTER 4

(See instructions, page 8.)

MULTIPLE-CHOICE

_____ 1. Establishing colonies and finding new trade routes were important for England because they: A.—were a means of rivaling Sweden; B.—provided adventure for British citizens; C.—helped England find markets for its growing industry.

_____ 2. The defeat of the Spanish Armada was important because it: A.—showed that the British were better sailors than the Spanish; B.—encouraged Britain to challenge Spain in America; C.—prevented Spain from establishing colonies in North America.

_____ 3. In a joint-stock company the: A.—king kept control; B.—merchants held the most power; C.—stockholders had control.

_____ 4. The Northwest Passage refers to a route: A.—around northern North America; B.—in the area of what is now the Panama Canal; C.—around the southern tip of South America.

_____ 5. Raleigh sent colonists to America to: A.—trade with the West Indies; B.—find gold and the Northwest Passage and be gentlemen of leisure; C.—keep the Spanish from the Atlantic coast.

_____ 6. In American history the Pilgrims stand for: A.—the virtues and steady habits Americans like to think they have at their best; B.—the beginning of religious tolerance in America; C.—the establishment of Thanksgiving Day.

_____ 7. Plymouth was not a success because: A.—the stockholders expected too much and the settlers would not coöperate with them; B.—its soil was infertile, its harbor poor, furs scarce, and people scarce; C.—the climate was bad, disease common, and housing poor.

_____ 8. Dissenters were people who differed with the king on the question of: A.—the church they should attend; B.—ownership of land along the frontier; C.—payment of taxes.

_____ 9. The Puritans: A.—sympathized with the Catholics; B.—wished to purify the Church of England; C.—persecuted the Pilgrims.

_____ 10. A very important provision of the land grants to the London and Plymouth companies was that they: A.—overlapped; B.—were north of 34° N.; C.—extended west indefinitely.

TRUE-FALSE

_____ 1. The Englishman Frobisher made three voyages in search of the Northwest Passage.

_____ 2. The Plymouth colony is in the present state of Connecticut.

_____ 3. Gilbert made and published a very early map of New England.

_____ 4. John Smith established the requirements for people who followed him to America.

_____ 5. Raleigh's two colonies were on Roanoke Island.

_____ 6. The Pilgrims were more successful in their relations with the Indians than were the settlers at Jamestown.

_____ 7. Towns were important in the Virginia colony.

_____ 8. Indentured servants were the same as slaves.

_____ 9. The London Company tried to establish manufacturing in Virginia.

_____ 10. At first each settler in Virginia received 3 acres of land, and later each family received 50.

COMPLETION

1. Virginians discovered that when they faced great dangers, they could take care of them through _____.

2. A big problem for the first English settlers in America was _____.

3. The main crop of Virginia was _____.

4. Two early landmarks on the road to self-government in America were the _____ and the _____.

5. The Virginia Company was a _____ company.

6. A charter was an _____.

7. Some early products of Plymouth were _____ and _____.

8. Two important developments in sixteenth-century England were that it became _____ and _____.

9. The Pilgrims first settled in _____ because it offered religious freedom.

10. A royal colony was governed by _____.

MATCHING

_____ 1. stock   A. military leader of
_____ 2. frontier   Pilgrims

_____3. John Rolfe
_____4. Miles Standish
_____5. East India Company
_____6. William Bradford
_____7. Church of England
_____8. John White
_____9. Massasoit
_____10. Ferdinando Gorges

B. English trading company
C. businessman in Plymouth group of Virginia Company
D. Indian friend of Pilgrims
E. governor and artist in Roanoke's "lost colony"
F. Pilgrim governor
G. leader in Jamestown
H. introduced tobacco into England
I. edge of settlement

J. shares in joint-stock company
K. the Protestant church established in England

KEY FOR CHAPTER 4 TESTS
Multiple-Choice: 1-C/2-B/3-C/4-A/5-B/6-A/7-B/8-A/9-B/10-C. *True-False:* 1-T/2-F/3-F/4-T/5-T/6-T/7-F/8-F/9-T/10-T. *Completion:* 1–self-government/2–lack of workers/3–tobacco/4–House of Burgesses, Mayflower compact/5–stock/6–official permit to set up a colony in America/7–oak timbers, furs/8–Protestant, a manufacturing country/9–the Netherlands/10–the king. *Matching:* 1-J/2-I/3-H/4-A/5-B/6-F/7-K/8-E/9-D/10-C.

CHAPTER 5
(See instructions, page 8.)

MULTIPLE-CHOICE

_____1. Massachusetts Bay Colony was established within the territory: A.—granted to the Council of New England; B.—given earlier to the Pilgrims; C.—occupied by the Pequot Indians.

_____2. Maryland was founded: A.—to develop fishing and fur trading north of Virginia; B.—as a refuge for persecuted Catholics; C.—as a home for displaced farmers from England.

_____3. In Massachusetts Bay Colony the right to vote was given to: A.—men who owned property; B.—all Protestant adults; C.—only members of the Massachusetts Bay Company.

_____4. The settlements that became part of Connecticut were founded to obtain: A.—fishing rights in New Haven Sound; B.—better land for farming; C.—religious freedom.

_____5. Massachusetts was less dependent on England than other colonies because: A.—its company and charter were transferred to America; B.—its settlers were harder to handle; C.—many Puritans were rich.

_____6. Early settlements made in what is now New Hampshire are: A.—Windsor, Hartford, and Wethersfield; B.—Rye, Exeter, and Dover; C.—New Haven, Salem, and Newton.

_____7. The Act of Toleration extended religious tolerance to: A.—Jews and Catholics; B.—all Christians; C.—Protestants and Jews.

_____8. Maryland was a successful colony because: A.—it was well located, it inherited cleared land, and other colonies helped it; B.—its religious policy, cash crops, and independence benefited it; C.—its leaders, government, and education were superior.

_____9. The town meeting was an important development because: A.—the king allowed the townspeople to decide all important questions; B.—it preserved the towns for the proprietors; C.—it gave the colonists experience in self-government.

_____10. One difficulty in the relations of Indians and Englishmen was that: A.—the English did not become as friendly with the Indians as the French; B.—the English were cruel to Indians; C.—Indians did not understand that an individual could fully own a piece of land.

TRUE-FALSE

_____1. The kind of farming in which no surplus is produced is called subsistence farming.

   2. The New England colonies found it easy to grow cash crops.

   3. Connecticut, Maine, and Rhode Island can be called offshoots of Massachusetts Bay Colony.

   4. New England colonies had little trouble with Indians.

   5. A proprietary colony was supervised directly by the king.

   6. Most New England towns were built around commons.

   7. A theocracy is a government in which religion plays a major role.

   8. Early New England towns were 10 miles square.

   9. Religious belief helped determine the right to vote in Maryland and Rhode Island.

   10. Maryland was laid out in huge estates of thousands of acres.

COMPLETION

1. The first colony to emphasize education was _____.

2. For years Maine was part of _____.

3. Massachusetts was established on a grant of land between the _____ and _____ rivers.

4. The crossing to America in 1630 by over a thousand Puritans is called the _____.

5. The document drawn up by the General Court to describe Connecticut's government is called the _____.

6. In Plymouth and Massachusetts the churches people organized in which control was left to each congregation were called _____ churches.

7. A basic principle of the community Roger Williams founded was _____.

8. Sir Ferdinando Gorges had a part in establishing settlements in _____.

9. In Massachusetts farmland was assigned in _____.

10. The first settlement in Maryland was _____.

MATCHING

   1. Anne Hutchinson
   2. Thomas Hooker
   3. Salem
   4. Annapolis
   5. tobacco
   6. King Philip
   7. Cecilius Calvert
   8. John Winthrop
   9. Leonard Calvert
   10. John Davenport

A. banished from Massachusetts Bay Colony

B. first governor of Massachusetts Bay Colony

C. cash crop of Maryland

D. leader in settling Connecticut

E. governor of the New Haven community

F. Protestant town in Maryland

G. founded Maryland

H. oldest town in Massachusetts Bay Colony

I. received charter for Maryland

J. led settlers to Hartford

K. leader of Wampanoag

KEY FOR CHAPTER 5 TESTS

Multiple-Choice: 1-A/2-B/3-C/4-B/5-A/6-B/ 7-B/8-A/9-C/10-C. *True-False:* 1-T/2-F/3-T/ 4-F/5-F/6-T/7-T/8-F/9-F/10-T. *Completion:* 1—Massachusetts Bay Colony/2—Massachusetts/ 3—Merrimack, Charles/4—Great Migration/ 5—Fundamental Orders/6—Congregational/7—religious freedom/8—Maine/9—strips/10—St. Marys. *Matching:* 1-A/2-D/3-H/4-F/5-C/6-K/7-I/8-B/ 9-G/10-E.

CHAPTER 6

(See instructions, page 8.)

MULTIPLE-CHOICE

   1. The seventeenth-century rivalry between the Dutch and the English arose chiefly over: A.—land in Europe; B.—gold in the New World; C.—markets for manufactured goods.

   2. Few people settled in New Netherland because: A.—taking part in the government was forbidden and taxes were high; B.—there was little reason to leave the homeland; C.—Indians were dangerous.

   3. England disliked the Dutch colony because: A.—it drove a wedge between the English colonies; B.—the Dutch were rivals in trade; C.—the Dutch were more prosperous than the English.

   4. New Jersey was formed from land: A.—the English had bought from the Dutch; B.—the Swedes had taken from the English; C.—the English had taken from the Dutch.

   5. Charles II gave land to Penn: A.—to pay off a debt; B.—to get the Quakers out of

England; C.—to fill in the Atlantic coastline.

6. New Netherland surrendered to the English because: A.—there was little fight in the burghers and little ammunition in the colony; B.—the Dutch disliked Stuyvesant and Gustavus Adolphus; C.—the English offered religious freedom and democratic government.

7. The proprietors of Georgia became discouraged because: A.—few people settled there; B.—plans to raise citrus fruits and silkworms failed; C.—slavery was established.

8. North Carolina differed from South Carolina because it: A.—depended on slaves; B.—became a refuge for many Europeans; C.—raised tobacco as a main crop.

9. Georgia's settlement was planned to: A.—prevent French expansion from the east; B.—prevent Spanish expansion from the south; C.—provide excellent harbors for trade.

10. Common characteristics of the English colonists were: A.—hopefulness and lack of snobbery; B.—pride and self-reliance; C.—wisdom and trust.

TRUE-FALSE

1. The Dutch introduced a democratic way of landholding in New Netherland.

2. The real rulers of New Netherland were the burghers.

3. Oglethorpe took some American Indians to England.

4. The first permanent settlement in New Netherland was Fort Amsterdam.

5. Penn's colony showed how good relations with the Indians could be set up.

6. The present state of Delaware traces its history to the colony of New Sweden.

7. New Netherland suffered from being the only Dutch colony then in the New World and was thus difficult to defend.

8. The chief South Carolina crop was rice.

9. Pennsylvania was a most prosperous English colony.

10. The principal product of Pennsylvania and New York was naval stores.

COMPLETION

1. Two Dutch painters were ——— and ———.

2. The ———, ———, and ——— were three non-English groups that settled in Pennsylvania.

3. The Quakers refused to bear arms and believed in the equality of ——— and ———.

4. The principal settlements in South Carolina were near the city of ———.

5. The Navigation Acts provided that ——— and ———.

6. The Swedes contributed the ——— to American life.

7. The first settlements in New Sweden were located near what is now the city of ———.

8. Henry Hudson's voyage to America resulted in Dutch trading along the ———.

9. The colony of New Sweden was absorbed by ———.

10. The first planned city in America can be said to be ———.

MATCHING

1. Rensselaerswyck
2. William Kieft
3. Peter Minuit
4. Peter Stuyvesant
5. James Oglethorpe
6. Berkeley and Carteret
7. Duke of York
8. patroon
9. Huguenots
10. Dutch West India Company

A. purchased Manhattan Island
B. founded New Netherland
C. created colony of New Jersey
D. headed New Sweden
E. largest, most successful patroonship
F. proprietor of New Netherland after the English take-over
G. harsh director general of New Netherland
H. founded Georgia
I. caused trouble between the Dutch and the Indians
J. French Protestant settlers in Carolina
K. Dutch settler assigned land in New Netherland

KEY FOR CHAPTER 6 TESTS

Multiple-Choice: 1-C/2-B/3-B/4-C/5-A/6-A/ 7-B/8-C/9-B/10-A. *True-False:* 1-F/2-T/3-T/ 4-F/5-T/6-F/7-T/8-T/9-T/10-F. *Completion:* 1—Rembrandt, Frans Hals/2—Scotch-Irish, Welsh, Germans/3—men, women/4—Charleston/5—colonial products could be sold only in England, only English ships could carry on colonial trade/6—log cabin/7—Wilmington/8—Hudson River/9—New Netherland/10—Philadelphia. *Matching:* 1-E/2-I/ 3-A/4-G/5-H/6-C/7-F/8-K/9-J/10-B.

CHAPTER 7

(See instructions, page 8.)

MULTIPLE-CHOICE

_____1. Old World differences between classes of people broke down in America because: A.—workers were scarce; B.—people were less snobbish here; C.—land was plentiful.

_____2. The democratic idea in America that one man is as good as another was based on the: A.—early development of self-government; B.—fact that people could improve their situations; C.—many schools.

_____3. The force attracting the most immigrants to America during the colonial period was the: A.—desire to Christianize the Indians; B.—search for a better living; C.—desire for self-government.

_____4. The wealth of the aristocrats in the southern colonies was based upon: A.—trade with other colonies; B.—town business; C.—plantation crops for export.

_____5. In the English colonies a man's place in society was often the result of: A.—where he was born; B.—who his ancestors were; C.—his success in acquiring an education.

_____6. Pioneers made an important contribution to American life because they: A.—farmed better than most other settlers; B.—helped push the frontier west and prepared the way for later settlers; C.—developed superior farm tools.

_____7. Indentured servitude was important in the development of the English colonies because it: A.—prevented slavery from becoming established; B.—helped bring thousands of factory workers to the colonies; C.—enabled large numbers of settlers to come to the colonies who otherwise would not have been able to.

_____8. Negroes were desirable in the English colonies because they: A.—had good farming skills; B.—could be easily enslaved; C.—had few people to fight for their rights.

_____9. Practically all the schools in the English colonies were operated: A.—to teach skills; B.—to train apprentices for future work; C.—to increase religious knowledge and devotion.

_____10. Unlike other Americans, slaves: A.—could have no hope or ambition; B.—had generally poor living conditions; C.—worked very hard.

TRUE-FALSE

_____1. By 1700 the frontier of the English colonies had been pushed west about 200 miles.

_____2. The first college in the southern colonies was the College of William and Mary.

_____3. The first college established in the English colonies was Yale.

_____4. Among the slaves were skilled craftsmen.

_____5. Most English colonists could be called rural people.

_____6. Shipbuilding, trading, and fishing were important in the middle colonies, for example, Pennsylvania and New York.

_____7. Most colonists lived in the area called the tidewater because it was fertile and convenient for transportation.

_____8. The "aristocrats" in both the northern and the southern colonies rarely tried to imitate the aristocrats of Europe but developed their own styles and customs.

_____9. Voters were required to own property in the English colonies in the 1700's.

_____10. The English colonists early developed good mechanical skills.

COMPLETION

1. In 1700 the most populous colony was _____ and the second most populous, _____.
2. The emphasis on learning was greatest in the _____ colony.
3. The _____ system trained artisans and educated poor boys and girls.
4. Many pioneers were called _____ because they simply settled on unclaimed land.
5. The _____ was considered socially superior to the artisan because he was more independent.
6. Two feelings linking the farmers and artisans were _____ and _____.
7. Two groups of English migrants who kept pushing west were the _____ and the _____.
8. Prominent planters and traders entered _____.
9. _____ architecture became popular among colonists in the eighteenth century.
10. The first Negroes arrived in the colonies in _____, the same year that the House of Burgesses first met.

MATCHING

_____1. pewter   A. Pennsylvania's
_____2. Jesuits   leading citizen
_____3. Rainbow Row   B. row of houses in
_____4. pioneers   Charleston

16

_____5. William Tucker
_____6. Log Cabin
_____7. indenture
_____8. plantation
_____9. Williamsburg, Virginia
_____10. Benjamin Franklin

C. where first American theater was established
D. large farm in South
E. colonial silversmith
F. people who first settled an area
G. first Negro born in present-day United States
H. established Maryland's first schools
I. school in Pennsylvania

J. contract of indentured servant
K. combination of metals used to make dishes

KEY FOR CHAPTER 7 TESTS
Multiple-Choice: 1-A/2-B/3-B/4-C/5-C/6-B/7-C/8-A/9-C/10-A. *True-False:* 1-T/2-T/3-F/4-T/5-T/6-T/7-T/8-F/9-T/10-T. *Completion:* 1–Virginia, Massachusetts/2–Massachusetts/3–apprentice/4–squatters/5–farmer/6–the hope to own property, respect for work/7–fur traders, farmers/8–politics/9–Georgian/10–1619. *Matching:* 1-K/2-H/3-B/4-F/5-G/6-I/7-J/8-D/9-C/10-A.

CHAPTER 8
(See instructions, page 8.)

MULTIPLE-CHOICE

_____1. A French advantage during the French and Indian War was that France had: A.—a strong king who tightly controlled the colony; B.—a large French population in North America; C.—Indian allies.

_____2. The main cause of the French and Indian War was: A.—a quarrel over fur-trading privileges with the Iroquois; B.—rival land claims in the Ohio Valley; C.—trouble over the Jesuit missionaries.

_____3. The most important reason for English victory in the French and Indian War was: A.—Braddock's ability; B.—the leadership of Pitt; C.—British naval supremacy.

_____4. The Proclamation of 1763: A.—brought an end to the French and Indian War; B.—proved that setting up the Albany Plan was a poor way to defend the colonies; C.—aimed to keep colonists east of the Appalachians.

_____5. One effect of the French and Indian War on the colonists was that: A.—the colonists acquired military know-how; B.—the French had to give up the St. Lawrence Valley; C.—Spain received French lands west of the Mississippi River.

_____6. The French hoped to defend the large area they claimed in America by: A.—building forts along its rivers and lakes; B.—relying on control of the seas; C.—depending on the large French population in New France.

_____7. The struggle between the French and English: A.—was limited to North America; B.—took place chiefly on the seas; C.—took place in many other parts of the world, too.

_____8. The location of Fort Duquesne was important because it: A.—was on an excellent harbor; B.—controlled the head of the Ohio River; C.—was easily defended.

_____9. England could not be sure of winning a war with France in America because the: A.—English colonists did not see alike and were not used to acting together; B.—French had strong defenses; C.—English made a bad start.

_____10. The Albany Plan failed because the: A.—colonists distrusted Benjamin Franklin; B.—colonies were not ready to give any of their powers to a central organization; C.—plan itself was poor.

_____11. The Navigation Acts were intended to: A.—regulate colonial trade to suit better the needs of Britain; B.—give the colonies greater freedom of trade; C.—prevent the colonies from growing prosperous.

_____12. England passed laws restricting the amount of manufacturing in the colonies because: A.—there was a shortage of raw materials; B.—colonial manufacturing would rival that of Britain; C.—the British could manufacture better than the colonists.

TRUE-FALSE

_____1. During the early years of the French and Indian War, the French seemed to be winning.

2. The construction of Fort Ticonderoga appeared to the French as a threat to their control of the St. Lawrence Valley.

3. England valued the food-producing colonies more than the staple producers.

4. Whaling supported the people of Nantucket Island and New Bedford.

5. After the French and Indian War England believed the colonies could take care of themselves.

6. Major activities of the New England colonies were shipbuilding, trade, and making rum.

7. The middle colonies produced much wheat.

8. The Sugar Act was aimed at illegal colonial trade with the West Indies.

9. The colonists traded with each other, with England, and with the West Indies.

10. The Grand Banks are near Savannah.

COMPLETION

1. In 1763 Britain gave back Cuba and the Philippines in exchange for _____.
2. The land between the Mississippi and the Rockies was called _____.
3. The capture of _____ in 1758 gave the English control of the mouth of the St. Lawrence.
4. The Molasses Act placed heavy duties on goods coming from the French _____.
5. Three sources of wealth in the colonies were _____, _____, and _____.
6. The idea of federalism is that _____.
7. France gave up _____ to the English in 1763.
8. French strength in the New World lay in the regions of the _____ River and the _____.
9. Pitt's foreign policy became known as the _____ policy.
10. Operating private vessels to prey on enemy trade is called _____.
11. Tar, resin, turpentine, and pitch are referred to as _____.

12. After the French and Indian War only _____ and _____ held large areas in America.

13. Foundries were located near resources of _____ and _____.

MATCHING

_1._ Lord Loudoun
_2._ Charles Willson Peale
_3._ Sam Adams
_4._ William Pitt
_5._ Louis Montcalm
_6._ Edward Braddock
_7._ Pontiac
_8._ James Wolfe
_9._ Lord Amherst
_10._ Robert Dinwiddie

A. English military leader
B. sent young Washington on mission to the French
C. artist who painted Washington
D. succeeded Braddock as English commander
E. defeated at Battle of the Wilderness
F. led Indian attack on English forts
G. English leader killed in Battle of Quebec
H. colonist who wanted American independence
I. Great Commoner
J. French general at Battle of Quebec
K. a college

KEY FOR CHAPTER 8 TESTS
Multiple-Choice: 1-C/2-B/3-B/4-C/5-A/6-A/7-C/8-B/9-A/10-B/11-A/12-B. *True-False:* 1-T/2-F/3-F/4-T/5-F/6-T/7-T/8-T/9-T/10-F. *Completion:* 1–Florida/2–Louisiana/3–Louisbourg/4–West Indies/5–farming, trade, manufacturing/6–a central government shares power with local governments/7–New France/8–St. Lawrence, Great Lakes/9–"blue-water"/10–privateering/11–naval stores/12–England, Spain/13–iron ore, oak trees. *Matching:* 1-D/2-C/3-H/4-I/5-J/6-E/7-F/8-G/9-A/10-B.

CHAPTER 9
(See instructions, page 8.)

MULTIPLE-CHOICE

_1._ Britain's policies toward its colonies after 1763 were influenced by: *A.*—a new, strict English king; *B.*—the difficulties in the area west of the Appalachians and the feeling that the colonists should help pay the cost of the war with France; *C.*—the smuggling of the New England colonists.

_2._ The Sugar Act angered the colonists, since: *A.*—they had to pay taxes they did not vote for; *B.*—it regulated their trade; *C.*—it raised revenue.

_3._ The Stamp Act was repealed because: *A.*—it was a direct tax; *B.*—Franklin's presence in London influenced Parliament; *C.*—the colonists boycotted British goods and caused stamp agents to resign.

4. Those of the Townshend acts which aroused the colonists most: A.—laid taxes on tea, paper, lead, and paint; B.—allowed writs of assistance and suspended the New York legislature; C.—provided that the colonists support the British officials and army.

5. John Adams defended a British commander whose soldiers shot five colonists because he: A.—thought the British were innocent; B.—needed money; C.—believed it more important to protect the innocent than to punish the guilty.

6. Britain punished Boston in 1774 by: A.—closing the port and placing soldiers in the colonies to prevent violence; B.—passing the Quebec Act; C.—stopping elections in Massachusetts.

7. Many colonists thought Britain had a right to: A.—raise revenue for defense; B.—raise revenue for any purpose; C.—regulate trade.

8. The First Continental Congress decided: A.—to break with England completely and become independent; B.—not to import from England or export to it and to disobey the "Intolerable Acts"; C.—to store arms and ammunition to fight England.

9. By 1774 the colonists wanted to: A.—be recognized as being equal to Englishmen; B.—elect representatives to Parliament; C.—return to their earlier relations with Britain.

10. After the First Continental Congress met, Britain wished to: A.—divide and weaken the colonies; B.—make an example out of Sam Adams; C.—put down the rebellion in the colonies.

TRUE-FALSE

1. As early as 1765, most Americans supported the idea of independence from Britain.

2. At first the Boston Tea Party was criticized by Americans.

3. Members of the First Continental Congress were poor men for the most part.

4. Minutemen met the British at Concord and Lexington but lost all their ammunition.

5. The colonists sent help to Boston after the "Intolerable Acts."

6. The British ship *Gaspée* was burned by the colonists.

7. Paul Revere gave notice that the British were headed toward Lexington by signaling from the North Church in Boston.

COMPLETION

1. The colonists who supported the colonial side against Britain were called ——.

2. One way in which the colonists coöperated in the late 1760's was in joining in ——.

3. A leading group of colonists who opposed British policies was made up of ——.

4. In 1770 Parliament repealed all Townshend taxes except the one on ——.

5. The Stamp Act Congress met in —— and was attended by delegates from —— (number) colonies.

6. Sam Adams was a master of ——, the definite effort to influence opinion.

7. The earliest instance of violence in the colonists' struggle with Britain involved two ships, the —— and the ——.

8. The colonies formed —— to exchange ideas about protecting themselves against British actions.

9. The Boston Tea Party was caused by Britain's desire to help the —— Company.

10. Gage marched toward Lexington to capture —— and —— and to Concord to seize colonial ——.

11. The First Continental Congress met in the city of —— in the year ——.

12. The most influential person at the First Continental Congress was ——.

MATCHING

1. Patrick Henry
2. John Hancock
3. John Adams
4. John Dickinson
5. Crispus Attucks
6. Thomas Preston
7. Thomas Hutchinson
8. John Parker
9. Paul Revere
10. Thomas E. Gage

A. represented Massachusetts at First Continental Congress
B. Negro killed at "Boston Massacre"
C. wrote *Letters from a Farmer in Pennsylvania*
D. British commander in chief in colonies in 1774
E. Paul Revere's companion
F. sounded the alarm that the British were coming
G. Boston merchant who opposed British policies

H. English commander at "Boston Massacre"
I. commander of minutemen at Lexington
J. Virginia patriot orator
K. acting governor of Massachusetts

CHAPTER 10

(See instructions, page 8.)

MULTIPLE-CHOICE

——1. After the Declaration of Independence was approved, Americans could: A.—trade with anyone they wished and refuse to pay British taxes; B.—form state governments and seek foreign aid; C.—tear down a statue of George III.

——2. Besides having France on their side, the colonists had the help of: A.—Spain and the Netherlands; B.—Spain and Portugal; C.—the Netherlands and Russia.

——3. Two New Jersey victories of Washington's army were at: A.—Fort Ticonderoga and Germantown; B.—Brandywine and Germantown; C.—Trenton and Princeton.

——4. One explanation of the shame of Valley Forge is that: A.—the home front failed the troops; B.—food was scarce throughout the colonies; C.—merchants were selling goods to the British.

——5. The American army held together because Americans: A.—had spirit, Washington, and the help of foreigners; B.—were fighting to win their independence; C.—wanted to get revenge on the British.

——6. The opening campaigns of the Revolution were in: A.—the South, New England, and New York City; B.—New England, the middle colonies, and the West; C.—the West, the South, and Canada.

——7. The campaign to capture Canada failed because: A.—the Americans were betrayed by Benedict Arnold; B.—the French residents of Quebec were uninterested; C.—the British were too strong.

——8. The governing body in the colonies during the Revolution was the: A.—House of Burgesses; B.—Second Continental Congress; C.—New York assembly.

——9. The colonists had allies in Europe because: A.—many countries were sympathetic with the colonists' desire to win independence; B.—England had enemies; C.—Washington offered land to those helping the colonists.

——10. The most important part of the Treaty of Paris of 1783 was that: A.—United States boundaries were set up; B.—American independence was recognized; C.—the British were pushed out of North America.

TRUE-FALSE

——1. Many Negroes served in the American army in the American Revolution.

——2. The man who did most to win French help for the colonists was John Adams.

——3. In the back country the English relied on the help of Indians.

——4. Burgoyne tried to cut off the South from the middle colonies.

——5. Herkimer died fighting to defend the Mohawk Valley.

——6. The "Swamp Fox" was Francis Marion.

——7. Parliament accepted the Olive Branch Petition.

——8. The Battle of Monmouth greatly cheered Washington.

——9. John Barry was the hero of Guilford Courthouse.

——10. The Liberty Bell is now in Independence Hall.

COMPLETION

1. Most Loyalists were drawn from the ranks of ——.

2. The first battle of the American Revolution, ——, took place in the year ——, and the last, ——, occurred in the year ——.

3. The colonists declared themselves independent in the year ——.

4. France signed the Treaty of ——— with America after the Battle of ———.

5. One of the outstanding naval battles in the Revolution was between the ——— and the ———.

6. Patriots carried on ——— warfare in the South.

7. Four American ports captured by the British were ———, ———, ———, and ———.

8. In the Treaty of Paris, Spain received ———.

9. In the same treaty, the western boundary of the United States was the middle of the ———; the southern one was at ———.

10. Americans learned how to drill from ———.

MATCHING

———1. Ethan Allen
———2. Benedict Arnold
———3. Thomas Paine
———4. Thomas Jefferson
———5. Charles Cornwallis
———6. François de Grasse

A. commander of American forces in South
B. American leader who led campaigns in old Northwest
C. leader of American naval forces in Revolution
D. British leader defeated at Battle of Saratoga

———7. Nathanael Greene
———8. John Paul Jones
———9. George Rogers Clark
———10. John Burgoyne

E. commander of French fleet in America
F. leader of Green Mountain Boys
G. British general who surrendered at Yorktown
H. American hero at Kings Mountain
I. wrote Declaration of Independence
J. American who became a traitor
K. American who wrote *Common Sense*

KEY FOR CHAPTER 10 TESTS
Multiple-Choice: 1-B/2-A/3-C/4-A/5-A/6-A/ 7-C/8-B/9-B/10-B. *True-False:* 1-T/2-F/3-T/ 4-F/5-T/6-T/7-F/8-T/9-F/10-T. *Completion:* 1–the wealthy/2–Bunker Hill, 1775, Yorktown, 1781/3–1775/4–Alliance and Friendship, Saratoga/5–*Bon Homme Richard, Serapis*/6–guerrilla/ 7–New York, Philadelphia, Savannah, Charleston/ 8–Florida/9–Mississippi, 31°N./10–Steuben. *Matching:* 1-F/2-J/3-K/4-I/5-G/6-E/7-A/8-C/ 9-B/10-D.

CHAPTER 11

(See instructions, page 8.)

MULTIPLE-CHOICE

———1. The Northwest Ordinance was a major achievement because it: A.—opened the Northwest to settlement; B.—removed the British from the Great Lakes region; C.—has served as the basis for admitting new states to the Union.

———2. One problem under the Articles of Confederation was that: A.—some of the states never accepted the Articles; B.—the Congress was controlled by New England merchants; C.—the central government was practically powerless.

———3. The Constitutional Convention was called officially to: A.—revise the Articles of Confederation; B.—write a new Constitution; C.—discuss the possibility of reunion with Britain.

———4. Men such as Sam Adams and Patrick Henry opposed the Constitution because it: A.—gave too little power to the central government; B.—did not protect individual liberties; C.—allowed the large states to control Congress.

———5. The Great Compromise settled the dispute over the: A.—war claims of the Loyalists; B.—basis for representation in Congress; C.—sale of western lands.

———6. The work of the Constitutional Convention showed that: A.—most of the delegates lacked experience in government; B.—many compromises were necessary in order to achieve the final result; C.—no major changes were made in the Articles of Confederation.

———7. *The Federalist* was important because it: A.—had the largest circulation of any newspaper in Virginia; B.—clearly stated the arguments for ratification of the Constitution; C.—upheld the value of the Articles of Confederation.

———8. Among the results of the Revolutionary War were: A.—steps toward separation of church and state; B.—the ending of slavery in the South and the spread of primogeniture in the North; C.—state control of private business and temporary limits on individual freedom.

____ 9. The Articles of Confederation provided for a weak government because: *A.*—they were drawn up hurriedly in wartime; *B.*—the only purpose of the government was to carry on relations with other countries; *C.*—after the break with England, most Americans distrusted strong government in any form.

____ 10. Paper money holds its value as long as: *A.*—the public feels that there is sufficient gold and silver to back it up; *B.*—no other kind of money is available; *C.*—the government issues it in large quantities.

____ 11. A major dispute with Britain concerned: *A.*—control of fur-trading posts; *B.*—payment of debts to Americans; *C.*—use of the Mississippi River.

TRUE-FALSE

____ 1. People who favored ratification of the Constitution were called Federalists.

____ 2. The Land Ordinance of 1785 outlawed slavery in the western lands.

____ 3. The Annapolis and Mt. Vernon conferences followed the Constitutional Convention and were called to discuss ratification.

____ 4. Virginia and New York were among the first states to ratify the Constitution.

____ 5. According to the Virginia Plan, the size of a state's population would determine the number of representatives it had in Congress.

____ 6. From the beginning the new Constitution contained a clearly stated Bill of Rights.

____ 7. Many delegates at the Convention were afraid to let the people choose the President.

____ 8. In a federal system most power is held by the central government, and only a few small tasks are left to the states.

____ 9. All Constitutional Convention meetings were open to the public so that everyone could be aware of the proceedings.

____ 10. The Constitutional Convention placed no limits on the number of times a person could be elected President.

COMPLETION

1. The adoption of the Articles of Confederation was delayed until all states had given up their claims to ____.

2. The Articles of Confederation could be amended only if ____ states agreed to the change.

3. To discourage American expansion, ____ blocked American shipping on the Mississippi.

4. Chairman of the Constitutional Convention was ____.

5. The Constitution provided that ____ of a states' slaves be counted as population in determining representation in the House.

6. The Constitution provided that the federal government would be made up of three branches: ____, ____, and ____.

7. The only one of these three branches that existed under the Articles was the ____.

8. The Northwest Territory was surveyed into ____, each consisting of 36 square miles of land.

9. The author of the Virginia Statute of Religious Freedom was ____.

10. ____ and ____ were the first two areas west of the Appalachians to receive large numbers of settlers after the Revolutionary War.

MATCHING

____ 1. Edmund Randolph

____ 2. Daniel Shays

____ 3. Alexander Hamilton

____ 4. Robert Morris

____ 5. James Madison

____ 6. John Dickinson

____ 7. John Adams

____ 8. John Sevier

A. leader of early settlers in Tennessee

B. delegate from New York who wrote many of *The Federalist* papers

C. Pennsylvanian who authored the Articles of Confederation

D. chairman of the Constitutional Convention

E. leader of an uprising of Massachusetts farmers

F. negotiated with the Spanish over the use of the Mississippi

G. Superintendent of Finance under the Articles

H. American minister to England

I. introduced the Virginia Plan

J. Virginian who kept careful notes on Constitutional Convention proceedings

KEY FOR CHAPTER 11 TESTS

Multiple-Choice: 1-C/2-C/3-A/4-B/5-B/6-B/
7-B/8-A/9-C/10-A/11-A. *True-False:* 1-T/
2-F/3-F/4-F/5-T/6-F/7-T/8-F/9-F/10-T.
Completion: 1-western lands/2-all/3-Spain/
4-George Washington/5-3/5/6-legislative, executive, judicial/7-legislative/8-townships/9-Thomas
Jefferson/10-Kentucky, Tennessee. *Matching:*
1-I/2-E/3-B/4-G/5-J/6-C/7-H/8-A.

CHAPTER 12

(See instructions, page 8.)

MULTIPLE-CHOICE

_____1. The Virginia and Kentucky resolutions of 1798 mark the beginning of the struggle over: A.—the Bank of the U.S.; B.—state rights; C.—the tariff.

_____2. The group that would seem to benefit most from Hamilton's financial program was made up of: A.—farmers in the South; B.—businessmen in the North; C.—land speculators in the West.

_____3. The Alien and Sedition Acts were intended to: A.—protect the country from traitors; B.—limit the strength of Jefferson's Republicans; C.—prepare Americans for war against Britain.

_____4. Washington's Proclamation of Neutrality was aimed at: A.—keeping the United States out of European wars; B.—improving relations with Spain; C.—ending the impressment of American seamen.

_____5. Washington is considered to be one of our greatest Presidents because: A.—in his administration more legislation was passed than in any other administration; B.—he started the two-term tradition; C.—under his guidance the new government was successfully launched.

_____6. Hamilton's program was designed to win foreign respect and to: A.—embarrass Jefferson; B.—build business opportunities; C.—prepare the way for his election.

_____7. Hamilton and Washington showed the power of the federal government by taking strong action in putting down: A.—Shays' Rebellion; B.—the X Y Z affair; C.—the Whisky Rebellion.

_____8. In his Farewell Address Washington warned against: A.—the rising cost of government; B.—the danger of permanent foreign alliances; C.—the threat of large armies and navies.

_____9. Jay's treaty of 1794: A.—prevented war with Spain; B.—angered the Federalists, who wanted close ties with France; C.—won little except a British promise to leave the northwest fur posts.

_____10. The election of 1800 was unusual in that: A.—its outcome was decided by the House of Representatives; B.—only one candidate ran for the presidency; C.—four states cast no electoral votes.

_____11. The bill to charter the Bank of the United States: A.—raised the issue of whether or not Congress had implied powers; B.—was vetoed by President Washington; C.—was contrary to Hamilton's financial program.

_____12. Hamilton's plan to have the federal government pay state debts: A.—decreased the taxes paid by farmers; B.—was originally opposed by Madison and Jefferson; C.—resulted in the founding of the Federalist party.

TRUE-FALSE

_____1. No provision is made in the Constitution for the President's Cabinet.

_____2. Hamilton claimed that all Americans should share in the payment of debts incurred in the fight for independence.

_____3. The Federalists wanted the United States to aid France in its war against England.

_____4. Jefferson believed in the strict construction of the Constitution.

_____5. The Alien and Sedition Acts protected freedom of speech and freedom of the press.

_____6. Jefferson became President in 1800 because Hamilton supported him over Burr.

_____7. John Adams and Thomas Jefferson belonged to the same political party.

_____8. John Adams did not favor the use of the Alien and Sedition Acts.

_____9. People on the frontier strongly supported the Federalist party.

_____10. Hamilton believed that a tariff was necessary to protect American industries from European competition.

COMPLETION

1. The refusal of Pennsylvania farmers to pay a federal excise tax became known as the _____.

2. As a result of _____ treaty, the Mississippi River was opened to American shipping.

3. Because of a political bargain, the _____ of the United States is located on the Potomac.

4. Jefferson's political followers were known as _____.

5. _____ is the name given to the procedure by which a foreigner becomes a citizen.

MATCHING

_____1. Thomas Jefferson

_____2. John Adams

_____3. Henry Knox

_____4. Aaron Burr

_____5. Alexander Hamilton

_____6. Anthony Wayne

_____7. Thomas Pinckney

_____8. John Jay

A. first chief justice of the Supreme Court

B. Secretary of State who became leader of the Republicans

C. Secretary of the Treasury who wanted the United States to develop industry

D. negotiated a treaty with the Spanish

E. second president of the United States

F. leader in the Battle of Fallen Timbers

G. Secretary of War under President Washington

H. poet who was editor of the *National Gazette*

I. became Vice-President after losing out in the election of 1800

KEY FOR CHAPTER 12 TESTS

Multiple-Choice: 1-B/2-B/3-B/4-A/5-C/6-B/ 7-C/8-B/9-C/10-A/11-A/12-B. *True-False:* 1-T/ 2-T/3-F/4-T/5-F/6-T/7-F/8-T/9-F/10-T. *Completion:* 1-Whisky Rebellion/2-Pinckney's/3-capital/4-Republicans/5-Naturalization. *Matching:* 1-B/2-E/3-G/4-I/5-C/6-F/7-D/8-A.

CHAPTER 13

(*See instructions, page 8.*)

MULTIPLE-CHOICE

_____**1.** By 1800 the Federalists had lost control of the government because: *A.*—they lacked experienced leaders; *B.*—they did not organize the voters so as to win elections; *C.*—their beliefs no longer represented the thinking of most Americans.

_____**2.** Before the War of 1812, both France and England were guilty of: *A.*—seizing American ships; *B.*—impressing American seamen; *C.*—inciting Indian raids on the frontier.

_____**3.** The case of *Marbury* v. *Madison* was significant because it helped establish the principle that: *A.*—the Supreme Court can declare an act of Congress unconstitutional; *B.*—the states cannot tax an agency of the federal government; *C.*—the Supreme Court can refuse to listen to a case brought before it.

_____**4.** Some people used Jefferson's own idea of the strict construction of the Constitution to oppose his: *A.*—repeal of the tax on whisky; *B.*—use of money for the Lewis and Clark expedition; *C.*—purchase of the Louisiana Territory.

_____**5.** Jefferson believed firmly that England and France would be forced to respect American rights if the United States:

A.—threatened to attack Canada; *B.*—built up the strength of its army; *C.*—cut off all its foreign trade with them.

_____**6.** During Jefferson's administration the United States was involved in warfare against: *A.*—England; *B.*—Tripoli; *C.*—France.

_____**7.** The people who were damaged the most by the Embargo Act and the Nonintercourse Act were: *A.*—American shippers, merchants, and planters; *B.*—British merchants; *C.*—molasses producers in the French West Indies.

_____**8.** In their route westward Lewis and Clark generally followed: *A.*—the Mississippi and Missouri rivers; *B.*—the Missouri and Columbia rivers; *C.*—the Missouri and Arkansas rivers.

_____**9.** Napoleon probably sold Louisiana because: *A.*—he wanted to deprive Spain of its New World possessions; *B.*—he wanted to concentrate on crushing the uprising on Santo Domingo; *C.*—he wanted money and American goodwill during the coming struggle with England.

_____**10.** Unlike Hamilton, Secretary of Treasury Gallatin made his main object: *A.*—increasing excise taxes and tariff duties;

B.—reducing the national debt; C.—issuing bonds to raise money for the army and navy.

TRUE-FALSE

_____1. The Embargo Act resulted in the end of impressment.

_____2. Madison's election in 1808 was a clear rejection by the voters of Jefferson and his party.

_____3. The decision in *Marbury* v. *Madison* increased the influence of the judicial branch of the government.

_____4. As President, Jefferson found that he could not put all his political ideas into practice.

_____5. Jefferson's behavior as President was less formal than that of Washington and Adams.

_____6. Lewis and Clark took their expedition beyond the lands purchased from France.

_____7. After the British fired on the *Chesapeake*, Jefferson asked Congress to declare war.

_____8. After their defeat in the election of 1800, the Federalists tried to maintain control of the judicial branch.

_____9. President Madison controlled Congress more forcefully than Jefferson had.

_____10. Many Americans wanted to attack Canada in order to punish England for violating American rights.

_____11. The Supreme Court's power to decide whether or not laws are constitutional is not specifically stated in the Constitution.

_____12. The Nonintercourse Act was less severe in its restrictions on trade than the Embargo Act had been.

COMPLETION

1. The Louisiana Purchase was acquired from _____.

2. Jefferson believed that ownership of _____ was necessary to good citizenship.

3. One aim of the Lewis and Clark expedition was to find an overland route to the _____, an area rich in furs.

4. The western Congressmen who wanted to declare war on England were known as _____.

5. Originally Jefferson expected to buy only _____ and _____, not all of Louisiana.

6. The Barbary pirates operated in the _____ Sea.

7. The _____ was an American naval vessel attacked off the Virginia coast by the British.

8. The word _____ was applied to the British practice of seizing seamen and forcing them to serve in the British navy.

9. Jefferson's term as President covered the years _____ to _____.

10. As a result of the case of *Marbury* v. *Madison*, the Supreme Court's right of _____ was established.

MATCHING

_____1. James Madison

_____2. Henry Clay

_____3. Toussaint L'Ouverture

_____4. Zebulon Pike

_____5. John Marshall

_____6. William Henry Harrison

_____7. Meriwether Lewis

_____8. James Monroe

A. explored the Louisiana Purchase

B. led a rebellion on Santo Domingo

C. one of the leading War Hawks

D. chief justice of the Supreme Court

E. explored parts of Arkansas, Oklahoma, and Colorado

F. defeated Indians at Tippecanoe

G. captain of the *Chesapeake*

H. helped to negotiate the Louisiana Purchase

I. one of the "midnight judges"

J. President when the War of 1812 began

KEY FOR CHAPTER 13 TESTS

Multiple-Choice: 1-C/2-A/3-A/4-C/5-C/6-B/7-A/8-B/9-C/10-B. *True-False:* 1-F/2-F/3-T/4-T/5-T/6-T/7-F/8-T/9-F/10-T/11-T/12-T. *Completion:* 1-France/2-land/3-Oregon Country/4-War Hawks/5-New Orleans, West Florida/6-Mediterranean/7-*Chesapeake*/8-impressment/9-1801, 1809/10-judicial review. *Matching:* 1-J/2-C/3-B/4-E/5-D/6-F/7-A/8-H.

CHAPTER 14

(See instructions, page 8.)

MULTIPLE-CHOICE

_____1. As a result of the Missouri Compromise: A.—Missouri was admitted as a free state; B.—Maine was admitted as a free state; C.—slavery was prohibited in the entire Louisiana Territory except in Missouri.

_____2. An economic development which was spurred on by the War of 1812 was: A.—rapid increase in foreign trade; B.—rapid increase in manufacturing; C.—decline in Negro slavery.

_____3. During the War of 1812, the war on the Canadian frontier led to: A.—an American victory; B.—a clear English victory; C.—a stalemate.

_____4. After the War of 1812, the greatest desire of westerners was: A.—a high tariff; B.—better transportation; C.—a second Bank of the United States.

_____5. In 1816 the Jeffersonians reversed one of their old positions by: A.—paying off the national debt; B.—lowering the tariff; C.—rechartering the Bank of the United States.

_____6. The Monroe Doctrine is: A.—now part of the national Constitution; B.—a part of international law; C.—a statement on foreign policy by the President.

_____7. The people that most opposed the War of 1812 were the: A.—Federalists; B.—Republicans; C.—War Hawks.

_____8. The Treaty of Ghent, which ended the War of 1812: A.—settled most of the questions that had caused the war; B.—gave the United States a small part of Canada; C.—made no mention of the causes of the war.

_____9. The War of 1812 was important because it: A.—gave many Americans an increased pride in their country; B.—showed that Americans were still better fighters than the English; C.—proved the effectiveness of the Monroe Doctrine.

_____10. The purpose of the Hartford Convention was to: A.—protect the interests of New England; B.—eliminate the Federalist party from national politics; C.—force President Madison to resign.

_____11. The first transportation project which involved federal funds was the: A.—Erie Canal; B.—Cumberland Road; C.—Baltimore and Ohio Railroad.

_____12. The election of 1824 showed clearly the increase in what could be called: A.—nationalism; B.—sectionalism; C.—Americanism.

_____13. The Monroe Doctrine warned European nations to: A.—give up all their colonies in the New World; B.—respect American rights on the high seas; C.—give up any plans for establishing new colonies in the New World.

_____14. The election of 1820 showed that: A.—no major issues divided the American people; B.—Monroe had a great personal following in all parts of the country; C.—the Federalists were on the verge of new power.

TRUE-FALSE

_____1. The Erie Canal connected the Ohio River and Lake Erie.

_____2. From a military and financial standpoint, the United States was in a poor position to fight the War of 1812.

_____3. By the close of the War of 1812, many state banks had issued large quantities of bank notes without enough backing.

_____4. The United States acquired Florida in the Treaty of Ghent.

_____5. The Battle of New Orleans had no influence on the writing of the peace treaty that ended the War of 1812.

_____6. The Federalist party was held in disgrace because of the Hartford Convention.

_____7. The Missouri Compromise opened more land to slavery than it closed to it.

_____8. John Quincy Adams had an unsatisfactory administration partly because of the constant attacks of the Jackson men.

COMPLETION

1. The outstanding American naval vessel in the War of 1812 was _____, which became a symbol of America.

2. The two largest cities in the United States in the early 1800's were _____ and _____.

3. Privately owned toll roads known as _____ were built in the East during the early 1800's.

4. As a result of the _____ Compromise, slavery was prohibited in the Louisiana Purchase north of _____ N. latitude.

5. Fear of the possibility that Spain would try to regain its New World colonies led to the pronouncement of the _____ in a presidential message.

6. The election of 1824 was decided by the _____ because no candidate had a majority of the electoral votes.

7. After the election of 1824, Jackson's supporters started calling themselves _____, which became the name of members of a major political party.

8. The Panic of 1819 was a business slump which today would be called a _____.

MATCHING

_____1. Samuel Slater
_____2. James Madison
_____3. De Witt Clinton
_____4. James Tallmadge
_____5. Francis Scott Key
_____6. James Monroe
_____7. John Quincy Adams
_____8. Oliver Hazard Perry
_____9. Andrew Jackson
_____10. Henry Clay

A. Secretary of State whose appointment aroused charges of corruption

B. father of the American factory system

C. largely responsible for the building of the Erie Canal

D. an able Secretary of State who was elected President in 1824

E. English prime minister during the War of 1812

F. inventor of the first successful steamboat

G. author of our national anthem

H. defeated a British squadron on Lake Erie

I. became a hero because of his victory at New Orleans—later elected President

J. President who warned European nations to stay out of affairs of the New World

K. Congressman who tried to keep slavery out of Missouri

L. President during the War of 1812

KEY FOR CHAPTER 14 TESTS
Multiple-Choice: 1-B/2-B/3-C/4-B/5-C/6-C/ 7-A/8-C/9-A/10-A/11-B/12-B/13-C/14-B. *True-False:* 1-F/2-T/3-T/4-F/5-T/6-T/7-F/8-T. *Completion:* 1—the *Constitution*/2—New York, Philadelphia/3—turnpikes/4—Missouri, 36°30′/ 5—Monroe Doctrine/6—House of Representatives/ 7—Democrats/8—depression. *Matching:* 1-B/2-L/ 3-C/4-K/5-G/6-J/7-D/8-H/9-I/10-A.

CHAPTER 15
(See instructions, page 8.)

MULTIPLE-CHOICE

_____**1.** The "Tariff of Abominations" and the tariffs following were important because they raised the question of: A.—nullification; B.—abolition; C.—secession.

_____**2.** The Webster-Hayne debates brought before the American people the basic conflict between: A.—manufacturing development and agricultural growth; B.—state power and national supremacy; C.—slaveholding and individual liberty.

_____**3.** The Whigs were held together by their: A.—opposition to Jackson; B.—belief in a protective tariff and a national bank; C.—faith in Henry Clay's leadership.

_____**4.** The Whig leaders disliked President Tyler because he: A.—carried out most of Harrison's political goals; B.—destroyed the second Bank; C.—rejected most of Clay's Whig proposals.

_____**5.** Calhoun was the first Vice-President to: A.—die in office; B.—become President; C.—resign from office.

_____**6.** The Peggy Eaton affair: A.—resulted in attacks on Jackson's wife; B.—caused Jackson to bitterly dislike Calhoun; C.—prevented Van Buren from being re-elected President.

_____**7.** In the election of 1832, Clay underestimated the support the people were giving Jackson because of his stand: A.—in the nullification crisis; B.—in favor of the spoils system; C.—against the Bank of the United States.

_____**8.** Compromise to end the nullification crisis was brought about by: A.—Calhoun; B.—Clay; C.—Jackson.

_____**9.** The Specie Circular: A.—touched off controversy over the Bank of the United States; B.—encouraged the spread of the spoils system; *C.*—resulted in a shortage of gold and silver.

_____10. Van Buren's actions during the depression of 1837: *A.*—showed his belief that the government should not get involved in the business affairs of individuals; *B.*—marked the beginning of firm government action to halt economic suffering; *C.*—increased the power of the federal government at the expense of the states.

_____11. The political campaign in the election of 1840 was important because it marked: *A.*—the first large-scale use of slogans and ballyhoo to sway people's votes; *B.*—a break in the two-term tradition; *C.*—the first time that slavery was a main presidential-election issue.

_____12. Jackson opposed the Bank of the United States because: *A.*—Clay and Calhoun supported it; *B.*—he was suspicious of all banks and believed that the Bank of the United States favored a small group of eastern businessmen; *C.*—he believed in strict construction and thought the Bank was unconstitutional.

TRUE-FALSE

_____1. Jackson created the Independent Treasury system to receive the funds which he had taken from the Bank of the United States.

_____2. The age of Jackson, it could be said, encouraged Americans to place great value on material things.

_____3. The national nominating convention in time replaced the caucus as the means of choosing presidential candidates.

_____4. Jackson placed little emphasis upon formal training for holding government jobs.

_____5. By the age of Jackson, American life was influenced increasingly by cities and merchants.

_____6. The Whigs chose Harrison as their candidate in 1840 because he had taken a definite stand on the important issues of the day.

_____7. Calhoun felt that the Union was more important than liberty itself.

_____8. Webster explained that liberty and union were inseparable.

_____9. Martin Van Buren had never wanted the presidency but ran for the office as a favor to Jackson.

_____10. Abraham Lincoln was at one time a Whig politician.

COMPLETION

1. The practice of replacing previously appointed officeholders with one's own political supporters is known as the _____.

2. Because the South wished to exchange its raw materials for European manufactured goods, it opposed the _____, which was designed to benefit northern manufacturers.

3. The state banks in which Jackson placed government money withdrawn from the Bank of the United States were known as _____.

4. The attempts by outside people to influence lawmakers to pass or to kill certain bills is called _____.

5. _____ agriculture is the type of farming in which people raise enough food for themselves and their families but have very little or nothing to market.

6. Members of Jackson's political party were known as _____. By 1836 his opponents had organized the _____ party.

7. A leading Whig politician of the 1830's and 1840's whose political ideas came nearest to those of Alexander Hamilton was _____.

8. A catchy but meaningless Whig campaign slogan in 1840 was _____.

9. By the practice of _____, lawmakers help each other by agreeing to vote for each other's bills.

10. Certain supporters of state rights believed that a state could _____ a federal law, that is, declare it of no effect within the state.

MATCHING

_____1. Henry Clay
_____2. Martin Van Buren
_____3. William Henry Harrison
_____4. John C. Calhoun
_____5. Andrew Jackson
_____6. Daniel Webster
_____7. John Tyler
_____8. Nicholas Biddle

A. first Vice-President to move up to the White House because of the death of the President

B. wrote a paper saying a state could declare an act of Congress unconstitutional

C. elected President because he was the hero of Tippecanoe

D. frontiersman who ridiculed Martin Van Buren's handling of the presidency

E. Vice-President who later became President because of Jackson's backing

F. president of the Bank of the United States

G. first politician to take part in logrolling

H. leader of the Whigs who had run unsuccessfully for President in 1832

I. Senator from Massachusetts who by his speaking ability stirred people's feelings in support of the Union

J. intended to use force if necessary to prevent nullification

KEY FOR CHAPTER 15 TESTS
Multiple-Choice: 1-A/2-B/3-A/4-C/5-C/6-B/ 7-C/8-B/9-C/10-A/11-A/12-B. *True-False:* 1-F/ 2-T/3-T/4-T/5-T/6-F/7-F/8-T/9-F/10-T. *Completion:* 1–spoils system/2–protective tariff/ 3–pet banks/4–lobbying/5–Subsistence/ 6–Democrats. Whig/7–Henry Clay/ 8–"Tippecanoe and Tyler, too"/9–logrolling/ 10–nullify. *Matching:* 1-H/2-E/3-C/4-B/5-J/ 6-I/7-A/8-F.

CHAPTER 16
(See instructions, page 8.)

MULTIPLE-CHOICE

——1. Most of the immigrants who entered the United States during the middle years of the nineteenth century: A.—went to the old Northwest and the Great Plains; B.—settled on small farms in the South; C.—settled in the North.

——2. The factory system developed much more rapidly in the North than in the South because: A.—the North had better port facilities; B.—northerners were willing to invest money in manufacturing; C.—southerners were afraid of placing slave labor in factories.

——3. Early American labor unions: A.—were formed primarily by skilled craftsmen; B.—were usually established during depressions but lost members in times of prosperity; C.—were encouraged by the federal government.

——4. Early coöperative societies such as Brook Farm were based on the idea that: A.—men of learning should work with their hands; B.—men could create perfect communities; C.—the world was evil and men could not change it.

——5. The development of the cotton gin: A.—resulted in the spread of cotton growing into new areas; B.—decreased the demand for slave labor; C.—caused factories to be established in the South.

——6. As the antislavery movement grew strong in the North, southerners began to speak of slavery as the: A.—peculiar institution; B.—regrettable necessity; C.—servant problem.

——7. By the 1830's farming had decreased in New England because: A.—the best farmland had been used up by rapidly growing towns and cities; B.—New England grain could not compete with that produced by new farms in the old Northwest; C.—European countries began to buy their farm products from Canada.

——8. The mass production of goods in factories became possible after: A.—cheap labor became plentiful; B.—coal replaced wood as the main factory fuel; C.—interchangeable parts were used.

——9. A major effect of the spread of railroads was: A.—the growth of factories to take advantage of larger markets; B.—increased cotton production in the South; C.—increased government control over business life.

——10. Nat Turner's revolt: A.—started a whole series of rebellions throughout the lower South; B.—won the majority of northerners to the antislavery cause; C.—made many southerners fearful of further slave revolts.

TRUE-FALSE

——1. By the 1840's most southern families owned at least one slave each.

——2. By the 1830's the majority of northerners supported the abolitionist efforts of men such as William Lloyd Garrison.

——3. Most early labor unions were unsuccessful in bringing about important reforms in working conditions and wage rates.

——4. Most of the Irish immigrants who came

to America in the 1840's were escaping from political persecution at home.

_____ 5. Production was more efficient and more easily supervised under the factory system than under the "homework" system.

_____ 6. The leading abolitionists favored the gradual freeing of the slaves and payment to their owners.

_____ 7. Railroad mileage was much more extensive in the North than in the South.

_____ 8. The Waltham system was begun to attract New England farm girls to factory work.

_____ 9. Southerners came to believe that England was dependent on them because of its need for cotton.

_____ 10. On large plantations the overseer had more to do with the slaves than did the plantation owner.

COMPLETION

1. The opening of the _____ in 1825 made it convenient to ship farm products from the old Northwest to eastern markets.

2. At the height of slavery, only _____ (fraction) of southern families owned slaves.

3. Great waves of immigrants came to the United States around 1850 from the countries of _____ and _____.

4. The railroad became an important form of transportation when _____ rather than horses began to be used to move trains.

5. _____ was the name of a place set up by New England reformers as a perfect community.

6. The religious group whose members were known as _____ led the antislavery movement in its early years.

7. The first passenger railway in the United States was the _____.

8. The area of the United States that came to be known as the North was made up of parts of the middle Atlantic states, _____, and the _____.

MATCHING

_____ 1. Eli Whitney
_____ 2. Horace Mann
_____ 3. Dorothea Dix
_____ 4. Harriet Tubman
_____ 5. William Lloyd Garrison

A. helped slaves to freedom by means of the underground railroad

B. German refugee who founded New Harmony

C. invented the cotton gin

D. sought better treatment for the mentally ill

E. presidential candidate of the Liberty party

F. abolitionist who published *The Liberator*

G. urged free public education

KEY FOR CHAPTER 16 TESTS

Multiple-Choice: 1-C/2-B/3-A/4-B/5-A/6-A/ 7-B/8-C/9-A/10-C. *True-False:* 1-F/2-F/3-T/ 4-F/5-T/6-F/7-T/8-T/9-T/10-T. *Completion:* 1–Erie Canal/2–one-fourth/3–Ireland, Germany/ 4–steam engines/5–Brook Farm/6–Quakers/ 7–Baltimore and Ohio/8–New England, old Northwest. *Matching:* 1-C/2-G/3-D/4-A/5-F.

CHAPTER 17

(See instructions, page 8.)

MULTIPLE-CHOICE

_____ 1. The main cause of the Mexican War was: A.—the attack on the Alamo; B.—American attempts to take over California; C.—a dispute over the southern boundary of Texas.

_____ 2. The Oregon question was finally settled by a: A.—war with Mexico; B.—treaty with England; C.—revolt of settlers.

_____ 3. In the Treaty of Guadalupe Hidalgo, Mexico gave the United States: A.—Texas and Florida; B.—the Gadsden Purchase; C.—California, New Mexico, and the Rio Grande boundary.

_____ 4. American claims to the Oregon Country were based on: A.—activities of John Jacob Astor's men; B.—explorations by the Hudson's Bay Company; C.—the voyages of George Vancouver.

_____ 5. The annexation of Texas was accomplished by a: A.—treaty approved by the Senate; B.—purchase agreement with Mexico; C.—joint resolution of Congress.

_____ 6. During his election campaign, Polk had urged the: A.—annexation of Texas and California; B.—conquest of New Mexico and purchase of Florida; C.—annexation of both Texas and Oregon.

7. Those most opposed to the annexation of Texas were: A.—abolitionists; B.—manufacturers; C.—Whigs.

8. The first Americans to be seriously interested in Oregon were: A.—fur traders and missionaries; B.—wheat farmers and gold seekers; C.—New England shippers and land speculators.

9. The Mormons moved to Utah because: A.—they had been persecuted in Missouri and Illinois; B.—gold had been discovered near Great Salt Lake; C.—they were specially skilled in the raising of crops by irrigation.

10. An important result of the California gold rush was: A.—the loss of workers in eastern cities; B.—hard feelings and eventually war with Mexico; C.—prosperity for settlers in Oregon and Utah.

11. After 1829 Americans in Texas became alarmed when the Mexican government: A.—abolished slavery; B.—restricted foreign trade; C.—prohibited private ownership of land.

TRUE-FALSE

1. Most Americans favored the annexation of Texas immediately after the Battle of San Jacinto.

2. Americans had little desire to acquire California until the discovery of gold in 1848.

3. Supporters of the Lone Star Republic and the Bear Flag Republic hoped to keep their lands free and independent of American rule.

4. Polk, Calhoun, and Tyler all held about the same views on the question of Texan annexation.

5. Abraham Lincoln opposed American entrance into the Mexican War.

COMPLETION

1. Americans first became interested in New Mexico as a result of trade on the ——— Trail.

2. The tragedy that overcame the ——— party indicates the hardships of traveling by wagon train on the western trails.

3. In 1853 the United States paid Mexico ten million dollars for the ———, the Gila River region.

4. An early name for the present state of Utah was ———.

5. As a result of a treaty signed in 1846, the United States accepted the 49th parallel of latitude as its boundary with ———.

6. Two American generals in the Mexican War who were regarded by some as future presidential candidates were ——— and ———.

7. A little-known candidate who was not thought to have a chance for the nomination at the beginning of a convention is a ———.

8. The capital of Mexico, captured by Scott, is ———.

9. The siege at the ——— stirred Texans to get revenge as well as to achieve victory in their fight for independence.

10. The gold discovery which started the rush to California was on land belonging to ———.

MATCHING

_1._ Zachary Taylor
_2._ Marcus Whitman
_3._ Sam Houston
_4._ James K. Polk
_5._ Brigham Young
_6._ Junípero Serra
_7._ John Tyler

A. President who had Texas annexed
B. founder of the California missions
C. conquered New Mexico
D. "hero of Buena Vista"
E. leader of the Texas revolt
F. leader of the Mormons
G. opened the Santa Fe Trail
H. President during the Mexican War
I. missionary to Oregon

KEY FOR CHAPTER 17 TESTS

Multiple-Choice: 1-C/2-B/3-C/4-A/5-C/6-C/ 7-A/8-A/9-A/10-C/11-A. *True-False:* 1-F/2-F/ 3-F/4-T/5-T. *Completion:* 1—Santa Fe/2—Donner/ 3—Gadsden Purchase/4—Deseret/5—Canada/ 6—Scott, Taylor/7—dark horse/8—Mexico City/ 9—Alamo/10—Sutter. *Matching:* 1-D/2-I/3-E/ 4-H/5-F/6-B/7-A.

CHAPTER 18
(See instructions, page 8.)

MULTIPLE-CHOICE

1. The Dred Scott decision was important because it: A.—allowed the extension of slavery into the territories; B.—was a victory for abolitionists; C.—prevented slavery in Kansas and Nebraska.

2. Southern members of Congress supported the Kansas-Nebraska Act because it: *A.*—admitted Kansas as a slave state; *B.*—was proposed by John C. Calhoun; *C.*—provided a chance for slavery to go north of the 36° 30′ line.

3. The Democratic party split apart in 1860 because: *A.*—southerners would not accept Douglas and popular sovereignty; *B.*—northerners refused to uphold the Compromise of 1850; *C.*—Congress had not admitted Kansas as a slave state.

4. The major result of the Compromise of 1850 was that: *A.*—the South received an advantage in the number of slave states; *B.*—slavery was banned from California and New Mexico; *C.*—the Union was saved from breakup for a time.

5. The man who made an eloquent plea for the Compromise of 1850 in order to save the Union was: *A.*—Calhoun; *B.*—Lincoln; *C.*—Webster.

6. The basic aim of the Republican party was to: *A.*—abolish slavery everywhere; *B.*—prevent the expansion of slavery; *C.*—settle the slavery issue by popular sovereignty.

7. The Lincoln-Douglas debates had the effect of: *A.*—assuring Douglas' reelection to the Senate; *B.*—making Lincoln nationally known; *C.*—gaining Douglas the presidential nomination in 1860.

8. The Presidents of the 1850's could be described as: *A.*—strong leaders willing to tackle the major problems of the day; *B.*—strongly antislavery in their policies; *C.*—weak men unwilling to take strong stands on the major issues.

9. "Bleeding Kansas" proved that: *A.*—concern for the Union could unite deeply divided people; *B.*—popular sovereignty would not work without strong military or police support; *C.*—the Dred Scott decision was the most practical solution to the slavery problem.

10. John Brown's raid and his later execution had the effect of: *A.*—dividing the South on the Fugitive Slave Law; *B.*—giving the North a "martyr" for the antislavery crusade; *C.*—endangering the passage of the Compromise of 1850.

11. The election of 1860 showed clearly that: *A.*—the nation's voters were solidly behind Lincoln's program; *B.*—a majority of the voters were influenced by sectional feelings; *C.*—the Whig party was no longer a force in national politics.

TRUE-FALSE

1. An old rule of American politics is that no politician can further his career by attacking a President who belongs to his party.

2. Lincoln felt that slavery was morally wrong, but he was not an abolitionist in 1860.

3. Douglas' answer to Lincoln at Freeport proved that popular sovereignty and the Dred Scott decision were the same thing.

4. In addition to taking a stand on slavery, the Republicans favored a higher tariff and a transcontinental railroad.

5. Lincoln received numerous votes in both the North and the South in the election of 1860.

COMPLETION

1. The two men who were Lincoln's political heroes were _____ and _____.

2. According to the Compromise of 1850, _____ was admitted to the Union as a free state.

3. Violence and open warfare between pro- and antislavery people occurred in the territory of _____.

4. The book _____, written by Harriet Beecher Stowe, stirred northern feeling against slavery as no politician had been able to do.

5. The idea that the voters who lived in a territory should decide whether it would be slave or free was called _____.

6. John Brown staged his most famous raid at the town of _____, which was located in the state of _____.

7. The three great Senators who argued for the last time over proposals for the Compromise of 1850 were _____, _____, and _____.

8. The Republican party ran a presidential candidate for the first time in the election of _____.

9. Between the 1830's and the rise of the Republican party in the 1850's, the two leading political parties in the United States were the _____ and the _____.

MATCHING

_1. John C. Breckinridge

_2. Henry Clay

_3. Zachary Taylor

A. President who intended to bring in Kansas as a slave state

_____4. John C. Calhoun

_____5. James Buchanan

_____6. William H. Seward

_____7. Charles Sumner

_____8. Stephen A. Douglas

B. Chief Justice at time of Dred Scott decision

C. Senator who was beaten unconscious by a Congressman

D. elected President in 1860

E. brought about Compromise of 1850

F. Senator from South Carolina who opposed what became Compromise of 1850

G. proposed the Kansas-Nebraska Bill

H. Whig President who died in office

I. a leading prospect for the Republican presidential nomination in 1860

J. candidate of the southern Democrats in 1860

KEY FOR CHAPTER 18 TESTS
Multiple-Choice: 1-A/2-C/3-A/4-C/5-C/6-B/ 7-B/8-C/9-B/10-B/11-B. *True-False:* 1-T/2-T/ 3-F/4-T/5-F. *Completion:* 1–Jefferson, Clay/ 2–California/3–Kansas/4–*Uncle Tom's Cabin*/ 5–popular sovereignty/6–Harpers Ferry, Virginia/ 7–Clay, Calhoun, Webster/8–1856/9–Whigs, Democrats. *Matching:* 1-J/2-E/3-H/4-F/5-A/ 6-I/7-C/8-G.

CHAPTER 19
(*See instructions, page 8.*)

MULTIPLE-CHOICE

_____1. The Emancipation Proclamation: A.— freed all the slaves; B.—made slavery unconstitutional; C.—freed only the slaves in states at war with the Union.

_____2. The importance of the victory at Vicksburg was that: A.—it robbed the South of an important industrial area; B.—a large southern army was destroyed there; C.—it cut the South in two.

_____3. The "anaconda policy" was to: A.—destroy southern transportation and communication; B.—capture Richmond, hold the border states, split and blockade the Confederacy; C.—free the slaves and stop work in the South.

_____4. The capture of Fort Sumter was important because: A.—a Union fort surrendered to Confederates; B.—General Beauregard won fame as a commander; C.— the North united behind Lincoln.

_____5. The North had a definite advantage in the Civil War because of its: A.—man power and industry; B.—railroads and generals; C.—victory at the outset.

TRUE-FALSE

_____1. European countries recognized the Confederacy, and Britain aided it.

_____2. The Confederacy fought a generally defensive war like that fought by the colonists in the American Revolution.

_____3. At his inauguration Lincoln stated his aim of abolishing slavery.

_____4. The Civil War began as a war to save the Union.

_____5. The capture of Vicksburg gave the North control of the Tennessee River.

_____6. Confederate civilian leaders were poor.

_____7. Buchanan offered weak leadership in the crisis caused by secession.

_____8. No Negroes served in the Union army.

_____9. The Gettysburg Address expresses what the United States stands for and what the Civil War was fought to preserve.

_____10. Telegraph companies and express lines helped link the United States together by the 1860's.

COMPLETION

1. The South felt that England would break the Union blockade because it depended upon southern _____.

2. Lincoln was able to issue the Emancipation Proclamation after the Battle of _____.

3. Perhaps the South's _____ problem was its most serious wartime one.

4. The first state to secede was _____.

5. The English language was the weapon _____ used best.

6. Vicksburg was captured by _____.

7. A famous battle off the Atlantic coast took place between the Confederate _____ and the Union _____.

8. The four border states were _____, _____, _____, and _____.

9. The leaders of the Confederacy believed in _____, not necessarily in slavery.

MATCHING

_____1. Gail Borden
_____2. Frederick Douglass
_____3. Pierre G. T. de Beauregard
_____4. George E. Pickett
_____5. George H. Thomas
_____6. Charles Goodyear
_____7. George B. McClellan
_____8. "Stonewall" Jackson
_____9. Joseph E. Johnston
_____10. Cyrus McCormick
_____11. David G. Farragut
_____12. Elias Howe
_____13. James Longstreet
_____14. William H. Seward
_____15. Jefferson Davis

A. opened fire on Fort Sumter
B. Confederate general killed at Chancellorsville
C. Lincoln's Secretary of State
D. Lee's cavalry leader
E. president of the Confederacy
F. led a famous charge at Gettysburg
G. Confederate general in the Peninsula campaign
H. patented the process of evaporating milk
I. developed the sewing machine
J. Union general called Rock of Chickamauga
K. Union commodore who captured New Orleans
L. credited with inventing the reaper
M. discovered how to vulcanize rubber
N. hero of Battle of Gettysburg
O. general in chief of Army of the Potomac
P. distinguished ex-slave

KEY FOR CHAPTER 19 TESTS

Multiple-Choice: 1-C/2-C/3-B/4-C/5-A. *True-False:* 1-F/2-T/3-F/4-T/5-F/6-T/7-T/8-F/9-T/10-T. *Completion:* 1–cotton/2–Antietam/3–financial/4–South Carolina/5–Lincoln/6–Grant/7–*Merrimac, Monitor*/8–Kentucky, Missouri, Maryland, Delaware/9–state rights. *Matching:* 1-H/2-P/3-A/4-F/5-J/6-M/7-O/8-B/9-G/10-L/11-K/12-I/13-D/14-C/15-E.

CHAPTER 20

(See instructions, page 8.)

MULTIPLE-CHOICE

_____1. Radical Republicans in Congress in December, 1865, would not accept southern members because: *A.*—Negroes had not been taken care of, and Democrats might soon control Congress; *B.*—the southerners had not been properly elected; *C.*—Johnson opposed the southerners' return.

_____2. The Congressional plan of reconstruction required: *A.*—that all the southern states be divided into military districts with military commanders; *B.*—that each ex-Confederate state draw up an acceptable state government and that the new legislature ratify the Fourteenth Amendment; *C.*—that Negroes hold government positions.

_____3. The Fifteenth Amendment: *A.*—gave the states the right to make local laws about who should vote; *B.*—gave women the right to vote; *C.*—said no citizen can be kept from voting because of his race or color.

_____4. After the Civil War corruption broke out: *A.*—only in Radical state governments; *B.*—throughout the United States;

C.—in large cities.

_____5. The Grant administration is remembered particularly for: *A.*—many reforms in the civil service; *B.*—a constant campaign against graft and corruption; *C.*—many scandals involving government officials close to Grant.

_____6. The Compromise of 1877: *A.*—brought withdrawal of the last federal troops from the South; *B.*—enabled Grant to leave office without having the scandals of his administration revealed; *C.*—brought Hayes support from both political parties.

_____7. Northerners failed to complete the Negro's emancipation because: *A.*—the Democratic party revived; *B.*—the Freedmen's Bureau was disbanded; *C.*—Radicals died out and new leaders arose.

_____8. The Democrats' two issues in 1876 were: *A.*—the Force and Ku Klux Klan acts; *B.*—corruption and the depression; *C.*—the smashing of the Tweed Ring and self-rule in the South.

_____9. The lasting results of Radical reconstruction are: *A.*—the Fourteenth and Fifteenth amendments; *B.*—railroads and public schools built in the South; C.—the dying out of sectionalism.

_____ **10.** The real reason for Johnson's impeachment was that he: A.—broke a law the Senate had passed; B.—aimed to reconstruct the seceded states by himself; C.—was a poor President.

_____ **11.** The Radicals were unwilling to seat southerners in Congress in 1865 because: A.—they feared they themselves might lose control; B.—Johnson favored seating them; C.—Stevens wished to punish the ex-Confederates.

COMPLETION

1. Leaders in the Radical state governments were the _____ and the _____.

2. Johnson was impeached by the _____ and tried by the _____.

3. An organization formed to frighten Negro voters was the _____.

4. Johnson's plan of reconstruction resembled _____ more than that of Congress.

5. The Homestead Act granted _____ acres of western land free to a _____.

6. The _____ was set up during the Civil War to aid Negroes.

7. The _____ of the Constitution says that all citizens of the United States are entitled to equal protection of the laws.

8. A new system of farming that developed in the South after the Civil War was _____.

9. The _____ banished slavery forever in the United States.

10. Immediately after the Civil War southern governments enacted what were called _____ to control activities of freedmen.

11. Lincoln's plan of reconstruction was called the _____.

MATCHING

_____ *1.* Rutherford B. Hayes

_____ *2.* Ben Wade

_____ *3.* Blanche Bruce

_____ *4.* Carl Schurz

_____ *5.* Thaddeus Stevens

_____ *6.* "Boss" Tweed

_____ *7.* Samuel J. Tilden

_____ *8.* Hiram R. Revels

_____ *9.* Alexander Graham Bell

_____ *10.* Horace Greeley

_____ *11.* Salmon P. Chase

A. Democratic presidential candidate, 1876

B. Radical Republican leader from Ohio

C. Liberal Republican leader

D. invented telephone

E. Chief Justice who presided at Johnson's trial

F. Negro minister and Congressman

G. greatest Negro politician in reconstruction years

H. became President in 1877

I. New York politician famous for graft

J. Liberal Republican presidential candidate in 1872

K. Radical Republican leader from Pennsylvania

L. President Grant's Secretary of State

KEY FOR CHAPTER 20 TESTS

Multiple-Choice: 1-A/2-B/3-C/4-B/5-C/6-A/7-C/8-B/9-A/10-B/11-A. *Completion:* 1–scalawags, carpetbaggers/2–House of Representatives, Senate/3–Ku Klux Klan/4–Lincoln's/5–160, farmer/6–Freedmen's Bureau/7–Fourteenth Amendment/8–sharecropping/9–Thirteenth Amendment/10–codes/11–10-percent plan. *Matching:* 1-H/2-B/3-G/4-C/5-K/6-I/7-A/8-F/9-D/10-J/11-E.

CHAPTER 21

(*See instructions, page 8.*)

MULTIPLE-CHOICE

_____ **1.** After 1860 the greatest mining development occurred in: A.—Colorado and Nevada; B.—Colorado and California; C.—Idaho and Arizona.

_____ **2.** Among the reasons why John D. Rockefeller was so successful was the fact that he: A.—believed in competition; B.—bought out his competitors or drove them out of business; C.—gave so much of his money to charity.

_____ **3.** One factor which aided the development of manufacturing in the United States was: A.—a government-sponsored low tariff; B.—strong labor unions; C.—a ready supply of money to invest.

_____ **4.** The Indians were removed as an obstacle to the westward movement because they: A.—were poor fighters; B.—could not stop the building of the railroads; C.—could not compete with the power of the United States government.

_____ **5.** Among the new industries that developed after the Civil War were: A.—

petroleum refining and the electrical industry; B.—steelmaking and textile processing; C.—gold mining and weapons manufacturing.

____6. Both Carnegie and Rockefeller: A.—gained their greatest wealth by investing their money in many different industries; B.—came into their chosen industries after some success in other businesses; C.—received help from government loans in getting started.

____7. One result of the surging growth of industry after the Civil War was that: A.—Americans became used to rapid technological change; B.—the nation's coal and iron-ore resources were almost exhausted by 1900; C.—interest in foreign trade fell off as the United States became self-sufficient.

____8. The importance of such things as the telephone and the railroad was that they: A.—industrialized the country; B.—helped make Americans more national in their outlook; C.—brought great returns to stockholders.

____9. The railroads helped the growth of the West by: A.—charging cheap rates; B.—encouraging people to settle on land along the railroads; C.—giving valuable mining lands to the government.

____10. The Cattle Kingdom suffered hard times in the late 1880's because: A.—people cut down on eating meat; B.—railroad prices were too low to attract stockholders; C.—drought and hard winters killed much of the stock.

____11. During the latter part of the nineteenth century, many Americans felt that: A.—farming was the only worthwhile means of making a living; B.—only light manufacturing should be permitted; C.—manufacturing offered a quicker path to wealth than farming.

TRUE-FALSE

____1. The first transcontinental railroad to be completed followed a southern route in order to win support from southern Congressmen.

____2. The government aided the building of many railroads by the granting of lands and loans.

____3. The Cattle Kingdom developed primarily in the region known as the Great Plains.

____4. In the mining states a town's growth and survival usually depended completely on the amount and value of ores nearby.

____5. The coming of farmers to the Great Plains closed off lands to the Cattle Kingdom.

COMPLETION

1. The _____ and the _____ were the two companies that built the first transcontinental railroad.

2. _____, coal burned without oxygen, is a necessary fuel in the making of high-grade steel.

3. The _____ was the name of a rich silver strike in Nevada.

4. The destruction of the _____ was one of the main reasons for the defeat of the Plains Indians.

5. The movement of cattle from Texas northward to railroad points was known as the _____.

6. Rockefeller created the _____ Company, which was organized in the form of a _____.

7. In 1901 Carnegie sold his business to a group that had formed the _____ Corporation, which is still the nation's largest producer.

8. The Sioux went on the warpath when the government allowed gold seekers to pour into the _____, territory that had been promised to the Indians.

9. To encourage the building of the transcontinental railroads, the government gave the companies _____ and _____.

10. The _____ industry was created to arouse in people a desire for goods that they either had not known about or had not known they wanted.

MATCHING

____1. John D. Rockefeller
____2. Alexander Graham Bell
____3. Samuel F. B. Morse
____4. E. L. Drake
____5. James J. Hill
____6. Andrew Carnegie
____7. Thomas Edison

A. invented the electric-light bulb
B. invented the telephone
C. leader of the oil industry
D. leader of the steel industry
E. discovered the Comstock Lode
F. established the telegraph
G. built the Great Northern Railroad

H. forced the Plains
Indians to surrender
I. drilled the first
successful oil well

CHAPTER 22

(See instructions, page 8.)

MULTIPLE-CHOICE

_____ 1. The famous Pullman Strike came to an end when: A.—the Interstate Commerce Commission was created; B.—government troops were sent in; C.—the Haymarket affair occurred.

_____ 2. The Homestead Strike of 1892 involved: A.—farmers; B.—miners; C.—steelworkers.

_____ 3. The Knights of Labor organized: A.—skilled workers only; B.—immigrants without skills; C.—all wage earners, skilled or unskilled.

_____ 4. Among the improvements that were most important to the early farmers on the Great Plains were: A.—the telegraph and the waterwheel; B.—barbed wire and the windmill; C.—electricity and the gasoline engine.

_____ 5. The Homestead Act was a disappointment to some because: A.—the price of government land was still too high; B.—the railroads took over most of the best land; C.—money as well as land was required to establish a farm on the Great Plains.

_____ 6. The Haymarket affair was damaging to the labor-union movement because: A.—the demands of the demonstrators were unjust; B.—many Americans came to believe that all labor unions were violent; C.—it brought on the depression of 1893.

_____ 7. Among the problems farmers on the Great Plains had to face were those resulting from both: A.—water shortages and insect pests; B.—uncleared land and buffalo herds; C.—barbed-wire fences and reckless cowboys.

_____ 8. In the late 1800's the Plains farmers suffered greatly because: A.—agricultural prices were going down at a time when farm costs were going up; B.—the government refused to continue the Homestead Act; C.—frequent railroad strikes kept their crops from getting to market.

_____ 9. Granger laws attempted to regulate the: A.—cattle industry; B.—meat-packing plants in the East; C.—railroads.

_____ 10. The Interstate Commerce Commission was very important because it: A.—encouraged the growth of labor unions; B.—marked the first attempt of the federal government to regulate a privately owned business; C.—committed the federal government to try to prevent depressions such as those of 1873 and 1893.

_____ 11. Abuses resented by many working people in the late 1800's included: A.—the truck system and unhealthy working conditions; B.—rebates and arbitration; C.—blacklists and regulatory commissions.

TRUE-FALSE

_____ 1. The American Federation of Workers organized a national political party in the 1860's in order to get laws favorable to labor.

_____ 2. Most presidential administrations seemed to favor labor unions during the last quarter of the nineteenth century.

_____ 3. If American farmers could have found the means to increase agricultural production, many of their problems would have been solved.

_____ 4. The Knights of Labor and the AFL were different both in particular aims and in organization.

_____ 5. During the nineteenth century most Americans felt that government should not interfere with the freedom of businessmen.

_____ 6. One of the main reasons why railroads charged Plains farmers such high rates was that their products had to be shipped long distances to market.

COMPLETION

1. An organization that took in workers from one craft only was known as a _____.
2. Many houses and other structures on the Great Plains were built of _____ because of the shortage of wood.
3. Businesses run for profit by private individuals who invest their own money are called _____.
4. The AFL tried to help workers and avoid strikes by arranging _____, or agreements on wages, hours, etc., with employers.
5. A secret workers' organization that terrorized the Pennsylvania coalfields in the 1870's was called the _____.
6. Trade that crosses state lines is referred to as _____ commerce.
7. The method whereby two opposing groups agree to let a third one settle their dispute is known as _____.
8. The practice of cultivating soil in such a way as to preserve as much moisture as possible is known as _____.
9. In the late 1800's _____ and _____, along with the United States, became major wheat-producing nations.
10. The _____ land run was the rush of settlers into an area of the southwestern United States that had once been reserved for Indians.

11. Workers were often forced to buy the goods they needed at a _____ store, one owned by the employer, because they were paid in coupons not good anywhere else.

MATCHING

_____1. Oliver Hudson Kelley
_____2. Terence Powderly
_____3. Joseph F. Glidden
_____4. George Pullman
_____5. Samuel Gompers

A. owner of company where strike resulted in nationwide railroad tie-up
B. created the Grange
C. wrote *Progress and Poverty*
D. leader of the Knights of Labor
E. founded the Molly Maguires
F. founded the AFL
G. invented barbed wire

KEY FOR CHAPTER 22 TESTS

Multiple-Choice: 1-B/2-C/3-C/4-B/5-C/6-B/ 7-A/8-A/9-C/10-B/11-A. *True-False:* 1-F/2-F/ 3-F/4-T/5-T/6-F. *Completion:* 1–trade union/ 2–sod/3–private enterprises/4–contracts/5–Molly Maguires/6–interstate/7–arbitration/8–dry farming/9–any two: Canada, Australia, Argentina, Russia/10–Oklahoma/11–company. *Matching:* 1-B/2-D/3-G/4-A/5-F.

CHAPTER 23
(*See instructions, page 8.*)

MULTIPLE-CHOICE

_____1. Cities changed old ways of family living by: A.—providing spectator sports and other amusements; B.—increasing the mother's importance and reducing the size of houses; C.—making school attendance compulsory.

_____2. Immigrants enriched American culture by: A.—seeking political freedom; B.—working in many jobs; C.—bringing with them various outlooks and ways of doing things.

_____3. An important result of Garfield's death was that: A.—Arthur became President; B.—it proved Roscoe Conkling could not be trusted; C.—it focused public attention on the evils of the spoils system.

_____4. Cleveland's election in 1884 was important politically because he was: A.—a vetoing President; B.—the first Democratic President after the Civil War;

C.—the first President married in the White House.

_____5. Late nineteenth-century cities created departments of public health because: A.—there were sanitation problems in the cities; B.—the life expectancy was lower in the country than in the cities; C.—there were dangers from the rapid pace of city life.

_____6. During the Harrison administration: A.—the President showed great courage; B.—Congress passed the high McKinley Tariff; C.—Republicans controlled Congress completely.

_____7. Coxey proposed that: A.—veterans receive bonuses; B.—the tariff rate be reduced; C.—the unemployed be put to work on public-works programs paid for by the federal government.

_____8. Cleveland showed courage in: A.—opposing a law favored by the Grand

Army of the Republic; *B.*—providing aid for people hurt by the depression of 1893; *C.*—pushing the "Good Roads bill."

___9. Arthur is given credit for: *A.*—being an outstanding President; *B.*—redecorating the White House; *C.*—rebuilding the navy.

___10. In Garfield's administration: *A.*—the President appointed many Democrats to office; *B.*—there was fighting within the President's party; *C.*—Conkling led the Half-Breeds.

___11. Immigration rose steadily: *A.*—between 1870 and 1890; *B.*—between 1890 and 1900; *C.*—between 1860 and 1890.

COMPLETION

1. The most important cause of the growth of American cities was the increase in _____.
2. Cities greatly strengthened Americans' spirit of _____.
3. People of the "old immigration" came from _____ and _____ Europe; those of the "new" came from _____ and _____ Europe.
4. Most Presidents in the late 1800's had _____ or _____ backgrounds.
5. Immigrants often received help from _____.
6. In 1883 Congress passed a law creating a _____.
7. The Grand Army of the Republic was an organization of _____.
8. Two new types of stores developed in the last half of the nineteenth century were _____ and _____.
9. The Columbian Exposition (world's fair) was held in the city of _____ in the year _____.
10. The Sixteenth Amendment to the Constitution gives Congress the power to _____.
11. Cleveland believed tariff rates should be _____.

MATCHING

___1. Roscoe Conkling
___2. Thomas Nast
___3. John L. Sullivan
___4. Chester A. Arthur
___5. Grover Cleveland
___6. "Lemonade Lucy" Hayes
___7. James A. Garfield
___8. James G. Blaine
___9. Montgomery Ward
___10. Jacob S. Coxey
___11. Benjamin Harrison

A. elected Republican President in 1888
B. Republican President shot in 1881
C. Republican presidential candidate in 1884
D. opened earliest mail-order house
E. led an army of the unemployed to Washington
F. disappointed office seeker
G. nineteenth-century political cartoonist
H. first modern heavyweight champion
I. leader of Stalwarts, who opposed Garfield
J. elected Democratic President in 1884
K. Vice-President succeeding Garfield
L. wife of Rutherford B. Hayes

KEY FOR CHAPTER 23 TESTS
Multiple-Choice: 1-B/2-C/3-C/4-B/5-A/6-B/ 7-C/8-A/9-C/10-B/11-A. *Completion:* 1—farm production/2—freedom/3—northern, western; southern, eastern/4—rural, small-town/5—city machines/6—Civil Service Commission/7—Union veterans/8—department stores, mail-order houses/ 9—Chicago, 1893/10—tax incomes/11—lowered. *Matching:* 1-I/2-G/3-H/4-K/5-J/6-L/7-B/8-C/ 9-D/10-E/11-A.

CHAPTER 24

(*See instructions, page 8.*)

MULTIPLE-CHOICE

___1. Among the proposals in the Populist program in 1892 were those for: *A.*—lower mortgage and shipping rates; *B.*—unlimited coinage of silver and the government ownership of railroads; *C.*—supports for farm prices and direct election of Senators.

___2. Populists supported Bryan in 1896 because: *A.*—he was a popular candidate; *B.*—many Populists had been Democrats;

C.—he agreed with them on the silver issue.

___3. American imperialism was encouraged by: *A.*—European examples and American trade; *B.*—the Monroe Doctrine and a new attitude toward race; *C.*—yellow journalism and Theodore Roosevelt.

___4. Cleveland halted a treaty to annex Hawaii because: *A.*—many Americans opposed it; *B.*—he disliked the way the Hawaiian government was overthrown;

C.—Hawaii was to be made a state immediately.

_____ 5. Among the reasons for the increase in newspaper reading among Americans in the 1890's were the: A.—growth of advertising and the increase in leisure time; B.—invention of a new way to print photographs and the excitement of the times; C.—low cost of newsprint and the invention of the press.

_____ 6. As a result of the peace treaty with Spain in 1898, the United States: A.—gained Hawaii and Puerto Rico; B.—acquired Guam, Puerto Rico, the Philippines, and Cuba; C.—began a new period of imperialism.

_____ 7. The Republican victory in 1900 showed: A.—public approval of imperialism; B.—the personal popularity of the President; C.—the appeal of continuing prosperity and leaving things as they were.

_____ 8. Americans were attracted to the Pacific Ocean area in the second half of the nineteenth century because: A.—it was a good place in which to convert Christians and develop trade; B.—sugar was grown there; C.—the Panama Canal made travel to it easier.

_____ 9. Americans were upset by the Cuban revolt against Spain since: A.—the leaders had lived and traveled in the United States; B.—the rebels caused suffering; C.—American trade was upset.

_____ 10. American naval strategy in the Spanish-American War was to: A.—attack the Philippines and capture the Spanish fleet in the Caribbean; B.—guard the Panama Canal; C.—reinforce the troops.

_____ 11. In the Spanish-American War Americans suffered not only from casualties but also from: A.—being so far from home; B.—diseases like malaria and yellow fever; C.—lack of supplies.

COMPLETION

1. McKinley had the support of both _____ and _____ in the election of 1896.

2. Alaska was purchased from _____ in the year _____.

3. In 1899 the Samoan Islands were divided between _____ and the _____.

4. Newspapers that practiced _____ helped stir up Americans in the 1890's.

5. Two serious events leading to the Spanish-American War were the publication of the _____ and the sinking of the _____.

6. In the Spanish-American War, Theodore Roosevelt was a member of the _____ and took part in the Battle of _____.

7. The Spanish-American War was fought in two parts of the world, _____ and the _____.

8. Among the Americans opposing imperialism was the author _____.

9. The United States granted Cuba _____.

10. McKinley was the _____ President to be assassinated in a little over _____ years.

11. The United States bought the Danish West Indies from _____ in the year _____ and renamed them the _____.

MATCHING

_____ 1. William Seward

_____ 2. William Jennings Bryan

_____ 3. Dupuy de Lôme

_____ 4. George E. Dewey

_____ 5. William B. McKinley

_____ 6. James B. Weaver

_____ 7. Pascual Cervera

_____ 8. William T. Sampson

_____ 9. Emilio Aguinaldo

_____ 10. Liliuokalani

_____ 11. Matthew C. Perry

A. Populist presidential candidate in 1892

B. commander of Asian squadron of United States Navy

C. last ruler of Hawaii

D. Republican President elected in 1896 and 1900 and shot in 1901

E. Secretary of State who arranged purchase of Alaska

F. led rebel Filipinos after Spanish-American War

G. Democratic presidential candidate in 1896

H. Spanish diplomat who wrote critical letter about McKinley

I. American who opened Japanese ports to American trade

J. Spaniard in charge of putting down the Cuban rebellion

K. admiral in charge of Spanish fleet

L. American admiral in charge of Atlantic fleet

CHAPTER 25

(*See instructions, page 8.*)

MULTIPLE-CHOICE

_____**1.** Theodore Roosevelt's special concern as President was: A.—difficulties created by the Spanish-American War; B.—problems caused by the growth of industry after the Civil War; C.—conservation.

_____**2.** The progressive movement refers to: A.—muckrakers; B.—attempts to improve American life through private and governmental activities; C.—reform laws.

_____**3.** Wilson was elected in 1912 because: A.—he was a scholarly candidate; B.—he proposed to reduce the control over big business; C.—the Republicans were split.

_____**4.** Among President Wilson's accomplishments were: A.—a lowered tariff and a new banking system; B.—laws to control child labor and graft in city government; C.—the manufacture of cigars in tenement houses and the Clayton Antitrust Act.

_____**5.** "T. R." sometimes attacked big business by: A.—settling strikes; B.—warning big businessmen; C.—breaking large businesses into smaller ones.

_____**6.** The writers who told about social evils were important because they: A.—told Roosevelt what was going on; B.—forced Congress to enact a tremendous amount of reform legislation; C.—made the people as a whole aware of some of the serious problems of the day.

_____**7.** Included in the Wisconsin idea were: A.—the initiative and the recall; B.—the state primary election and regulation of railroads; C.—the right of women to vote and the secret ballot.

_____**8.** The United States was able to arrange a treaty to build the Panama Canal by: A.—recognizing the independence of Panama after its hasty rebellion; B.—paying money to Colombia; C.—negotiating with a French company.

_____**9.** Taft was not a popular President because: A.—Theodore Roosevelt opposed him; B.—he had never served in a public office before; C.—he made mistakes and was unable to please all his party.

_____**10.** The chief accomplishment of the progressives was: A.—changing the viewpoint of courts; B.—obtaining new health laws; C.—helping Americans through the years in which the rural United States became industrialized.

_____**11.** One of the most important actions a President ever took in a labor dispute was: A.—Wilson's in the Oregon case; B.—"T. R.'s" in the strike in the hard-coal industry; C.—Taft's in the Northern Securities case.

COMPLETION

1. Conservation means the _____ of _____.

2. One reform in some cities was hiring a _____ instead of electing a _____.

3. "T. R.'s" party in 1912 was nicknamed the _____ party.

4. The Pure Food and Drug Act was passed to control the distribution of _____ and _____.

5. The Seventeenth Amendment to the Constitution provided for the _____ of _____.

6. There were two possible routes for a canal between the Atlantic and Pacific, across the _____ and across _____.

7. The only man who has been both President and Chief Justice is _____.

8. Wilson's name for his program was the _____.

9. The Federal Reserve Act divided the United States into _____ (number) banking districts.

10. Theodore Roosevelt gave the control of forest lands to the _____.

11. The United States became interested in a canal between the Atlantic and Pacific after it gained islands in the _____ and in the _____.

MATCHING

_____*1.* Jacob Riis

_____*2.* Robert La Follette

A. leader in wiping out malaria and yellow fever

41

_____3. Edward M. House
_____4. Jane Addams
_____5. William Howard Taft
_____6. Upton Sinclair
_____7. Woodrow Wilson
_____8. William C. Gorgas
_____9. Samuel Jones
_____10. Lincoln Steffens
_____11. Louis D. Brandeis

B. Republican elected President in 1909
C. helped found the NAACP
D. wrote *The Jungle*
E. Democrat elected President in 1912
F. wrote *The Shame of the Cities*
G. a Texan who was Wilson's adviser
H. governor of Wisconsin associated with reform idea
I. led in establishing Hull House to help the poor of Chicago
J. lawyer defending Oregon's law about women in laundries
K. reform mayor of Toledo, 1897–1904
L. wrote *How the Other Half Lives*

KEY FOR CHAPTER 25 TESTS

Multiple-Choice: 1-B/2-B/3-C/4-A/5-C/6-C/ 7-B/8-A/9-C/10-C/11-B. *Completion:* 1–wise use, natural resources/2–city manager, mayor/ 3–Bull Moose/4–foods, medicines/5–direct election, Senators/6–Isthmus of Panama, Nicaragua/7–Taft/8–new freedom/9–twelve/ 10–Department of Agriculture/11–Caribbean, Pacific. *Matching:* 1-L/2-H/3-G/4-I/5-B/6-D/ 7-E/8-A/9-K/10-F/11-J.

CHAPTER 26

(See instructions, page 8.)

MULTIPLE-CHOICE

_____1. Americans long believed they needed no alliances with other peoples because: A.—they had a strong army and navy; B.—their location made them safe; C.—no country would think of attacking the United States.

_____2. Isolation began to appeal less to Americans as: A.—they acquired Puerto Rico and the Philippines; B.—the Panama Canal was built; C.—nationalism and international trade developed.

_____3. The open-door policy meant that: A.—anyone could join the League of Nations; B.—more Asian immigrants could come to America; C.—each nation with trading privileges in China would allow others equal trading privileges there.

_____4. United States concern about troubles in Mexico came to an end when: A.—Wilson convinced Mexicans that they should choose better officials; B.—problems in Europe forced Wilson to turn away from Mexican troubles; C.—American troops settled matters in Mexico.

_____5. Some Latin Americans said that Theodore Roosevelt had changed the Monroe Doctrine to: A.—allow European nations to establish new colonies in the New World; B.—allow the United States to police Mexico; C.—give the United States the right to interfere in Latin American affairs.

_____6. Theodore Roosevelt won the Nobel Peace Prize because he: A.—helped end the Russo-Japanese War; B.—established the open-door policy; C.—gave Cuba its independence.

_____7. Congress declared war on Germany on April 6, 1917, because: A.—the Germans had just sunk the *Lusitania*; B.—Germany would no longer promise not to sink unarmed vessels; C.—Wilson had been hotheaded in dealing with Germany.

_____8. The Senate turned down the Treaty of Versailles because: A.—Americans distrusted the Big Four; B.—Wilson had had a stroke; C.—Americans wanted to keep away from the responsibilities of world leadership.

_____9. Wilson differed at first from the French and British leaders after the First World War in: A.—not wanting Germany punished; B.—favoring the Treaty of Versailles; C.—not gaining support at home.

_____10. Wilson's chief aim in going to Paris was to: A.—win honor at home; B.—create a League of Nations; C.—win some of Germany's possessions.

_____11. Many of Wilson's friends wanted him to: A.—go on a speaking tour to promote the League of Nations; B.—drop the Fourteen Points; C.—agree that the United States would not go to war as a member of the League unless Congress approved.

COMPLETION

1. When the First World War broke out, Wilson urged Americans to be ———.
2. Wilson won reelection in 1916 with the slogan ———.
3. Three places where Americans fought in the First World War were ———, ———, and ———.
4. Wilson's peace plans were summed up in his ———.
5. Russia fought in the First World War on the side of the ———.
6. The chief coaling station the United States acquired from Cuba became ———.
7. The eastern half of Hispaniola is occupied by the ———.
8. President Taft's administration was known for "——— diplomacy."
9. Austria started the First World War by declaring war on ———.
10. An armistice that brought an end to the fighting in the First World War was signed on ——— of the year ———.
11. American soldiers in the war were known as ———.

MATCHING

———1. Charles Evans Hughes
———2. John J. Pershing
———3. Georges Clemenceau
———4. David Lloyd George
———5. Arthur Zimmermann
———6. Henry Cabot Lodge
———7. Edward M. House
———8. Franz Ferdinand
———9. Pancho Villa
———10. Victoriano Huerta
———11. George M. Cohan

A. Wilson's chief adviser
B. Austrian archduke murdered in Bosnia
C. wrote the song "Over There"
D. Mexican bandit who killed 17 Americans
E. French member of the Big Four
F. Republican presidential candidate in 1916
G. American commanding general in First World War
H. British prime minister; one of Big Four
I. German official who sought German alliance with Mexico
J. Senator from Massachusetts who opposed Treaty of Versailles
K. French commander in First World War
L. Mexican dictator

KEY FOR CHAPTER 26 TESTS
Multiple–Choice: 1-B/2-C/3-C/4-B/5-C/6-A/ 7-B/8-C/9-A/10-B/11-C. *Completion:* 1–neutral/ 2–"He kept us out of war."/3–any three: Cantigny, Château-Thierry, Belleau Wood, St. Mihiel, Argonne Forest/4–Fourteen Points/5–Allies/ 6–Guantánamo naval base/7–Dominican Republic/ 8–dollar/9–Serbia/10–November 11, 1918/ 11–doughboys. *Matching:* 1-F/2-G/3-E/4-H/ 5-I/6-J/7-A/8-B/9-D/10-L/11-C.

CHAPTER 27
(*See instructions, page 8.*)

MULTIPLE-CHOICE

———1. The automobile changed America, increasing: *A.*—the sale of gasoline and rubber; *B.*—crime and the building of highways; *C.*—federal legislation and interest in tourist centers.

———2. The main reason for the strength of the prohibition movement was the: *A.*—increase in drinking; *B.*—attack on saloons; *C.*—organization of its supporters.

———3. *The Birth of a Nation* was unfortunate because it: *A.*—damaged race relations in the United States; *B.*—was a poor example of technological change; *C.*—caused the rise of wild movie stars.

———4. The election of Harding in 1920 showed that most Americans wanted the President to: *A.*—let them alone so that they could lead their own private lives; *B.*—give strong leadership in international affairs; *C.*—work for better treatment of minority groups.

———5. The new Ku Klux Klan: *A.*—worked against all foreigners; *B.*—opposed Negroes, Catholics, and Jews; *C.*—crusaded against immigrants from northern Europe.

———6. The Sacco-Vanzetti case showed that: *A.*—there were many anarchists in America; *B.*—all Americans were prejudiced; *C.*—the rest of the world was much interested in United States affairs.

———7. The best evidence of the general prosperity in the 1920's was that: *A.*—the quantity of goods and services being produced greatly increased; *B.*—people bought on the installment plan; *C.*—amusements flourished.

8. The price of a "Model T" Ford: *A.*—made it a car for the wealthy only; *B.*—rose steadily; *C.*—dropped astonishingly.

9. From the beginning, planes were clearly valuable for: *A.*—crossing the continent; *B.*—military use; *C.*—crossing the Atlantic.

10. Teapot Dome involved a scandal dealing with: *A.*—the taking of bribes by the Attorney-General; *B.*—the acceptance by President Harding of a bribe; *C.*—the secret lease to private companies of certain lands containing oil reserves.

11. As members of American families seemed less dependent on each other: *A.*—the divorce rate rose; *B.*—they enjoyed more leisure; *C.*—people ate more canned foods.

COMPLETION

1. Henry Ford applied to the manufacture of automobiles the principle of ——.

2. An outstanding baseball player, famous for his output of home runs, was ——.

3. The first radio station, KDKA, came on the air in the year —— in time to broadcast the election returns.

4. Congress created the —— to regulate radio stations.

5. The main reason for the laws passed to cut down on immigration in the 1920's was ——.

6. A person who believes all government should be destroyed is called an ——.

7. Prohibition seems to have encouraged ——.

8. Warren G. Harding opposed the —— and talked of ——.

9. Coolidge was President from the year —— into the year ——.

10. The —— first flew an airplane, at ——, in the state of ——.

11. The first transcontinental air route was created in the year ——.

MATCHING

——**1.** Gertrude Ederle
——**2.** Rudolph Valentino
——**3.** Amelia Earhart
——**4.** W. C. Handy
——**5.** Albert B. Fall
——**6.** Lee De Forest
——**7.** Richard E. Byrd
——**8.** Ransom E. Olds
——**9.** James H. Doolittle
——**10.** Robert H. Goddard
——**11.** Charles A. Lindbergh

A. first person to fly across North America in one day
B. popular crooner of the 1920's
C. made first solo flight across Atlantic
D. manufactured Oldsmobiles from 1899 on
E. fired the first liquid-fuel rocket
F. movie idol in 1920's
G. patented first vacuum tube, on which radio transmission is based
H. "father of the blues"
I. member of Harding's Cabinet involved in Teapot Dome scandal
J. first woman to swim across English Channel
K. accomplished woman flier
L. one of first two men to fly over North Pole

KEY FOR CHAPTER 27 TESTS

Multiple-Choice: 1-B/2-C/3-A/4-A/5-B/6-C/7-A/8-C/9-B/10-C/11-A. *Completion:* 1—mass production/2—Babe Ruth/3—1920/4—Federal Radio Commission/5—intolerance/6—anarchist/7—lawlessness/8—League of Nations, "normalcy"/9—1923, 1929/10—Wright brothers, Kitty Hawk, N.C./11—1930. *Matching:* 1-J/2-F/3-K/4-H/5-I/6-G/7-L/8-D/9-A/10-E/11-C.

CHAPTER 28
(*See instructions, page 8.*)

MULTIPLE-CHOICE

——**1.** The Great Depression is said to have begun in 1929 when: *A.*—Hoover took office; *B.*—the stock market crashed; *C.*—Britain stopped trading with the United States.

——**2.** As their difficulties increased, Americans put the blame for the depression on: *A.*—the poor money policies of their country; *B.*—businessmen and employers; *C.*—Hoover.

——**3.** The election of 1928 showed: *A.*—the strength of the Democratic party in cities; *B.*—that Americans feared a depression; *C.*—that Americans were strongly isolationist.

——**4.** The NRA allowed businessmen to set up codes to: *A.*—lower the minimum age for employment; *B.*—increase the length of the workday; *C.*—establish fair prices and minimum wages.

——— **5.** The Supreme Court declared the NRA unconstitutional because it: *A.*—took money from one group to benefit another; *B.*—gave businessmen the right to make laws about wages and hours; *C.*—violated the Sixteenth Amendment.

——— **6.** The TVA's accomplishments are: *A.*—controlling floods and providing electric power; *B.*—eliminating the "dust bowl" by planting trees; *C.*—restoring public buildings and building parks.

——— **7.** The Wagner Act: *A.*—insured deposits in banks; *B.*—made sure that employees can bargain collectively with employers; *C.*—provided unemployment insurance.

——— **8.** An important change in labor's place in American life was marked by the: *A.*—formation of the CIO; *B.*—CIO's split with the AFL; *C.*—refusal of state and federal governments to use force to end sit-down strikes.

——— **9.** "F. D. R." tried to appoint new Justices in the Supreme Court because: *A.*—some Justices were old; *B.*—he feared the Court would declare many New Deal laws unconstitutional; *C.*—there was a large number of Justices.

——— **10.** "F. D. R.'s" main contributions were: *A.*—convincing Americans that democracy could solve our problems and guide us in a threatening world; *B.*—his personal courage and strength in spite of polio; *C.*—the NYA and the FDIC.

COMPLETION

1. Members of the CCC were given temporary work conserving ——— and ———.

2. The ——— brought Franklin D. Roosevelt in closer touch with more people than any other President had ever been.

3. Al Smith was handicapped in the presidential election of 1928 because he was a ——— and represented the ———.

4. In the Great Depression ——— of people were thrown out of work.

5. "F. D. R." differed from Hoover in believing in ——— relief for the unemployed.

6. The "Bonus Marchers" were ——— of the First World War.

7. Some of the laws of the New Deal were ——— measures, and the others were ———.

8. "WPA" stands for ———, and "NYA" for ———

9. The AAA granted a ——— to farmers to cut down their production of certain farm products.

10. Two dams built in the West during the 1930's were the ———, on the ——— River, and the ———, on the ——— River.

11. The Social Security Act applied the word conservation to protecting ———.

12. The Twentieth Amendment changed the inauguration date of the President from ——— to ———.

MATCHING

——— *1.* Walter Reuther
——— *2.* Frances Perkins
——— *3.* Alfred M. Landon
——— *4.* Henry A. Wallace
——— *5.* Lou Henry Hoover
——— *6.* Harry Hopkins
——— *7.* Robert F. Wagner
——— *8.* Eleanor Roosevelt
——— *9.* Cordell Hull
——— *10.* John L. Lewis
——— *11.* William Henry Hastie

A. "F. D. R.'s" wife, who acted as a reporter for him
B. head of the United Mine Workers
C. wife of President Herbert Hoover
D. Senatorial spokesman for labor
E. created the CWA
F. first woman Cabinet member
G. "F. D. R.'s" Secretary of Agriculture
H. Republican presidential candidate in 1936
I. first Negro federal judge
J. labor leader of United Automobile Workers
K. carried out "F. D. R.'s" direct-relief program
L. "F. D. R.'s" Secretary of State

KEY FOR CHAPTER 28 TESTS

Multiple-Choice: 1-B/2-C/3-A/4-C/5-B/6-A/ 7-B/8-C/9-B/10-A. *Completion:* 1–land, forests/ 2–radio/3–Roman Catholic, cities/4–millions/ 5–direct/6–unemployed veterans/7–recovery, reforms/8–"Works Progress Administration," "National Youth Administration"/9–subsidy/ 10–Hoover, Colorado, Grand Coulee, Columbia/ 11–human resources/12–March 4, January 20. *Matching:* 1-J/2-F/3-H/4-G/5-C/6-K/7-D/8-A/ 9-L/10-B/11-I.

CHAPTER 29

(See instructions, page 8.)

MULTIPLE-CHOICE

_____ 1. In the 1930's Americans hoped to stay out of another war through: *A.*—heeding the isolationists; *B.*—neutrality laws; *C.*—joining in collective security.

_____ 2. Hitler's troops first invaded and overcame: *A.*—the Soviet Union, Poland, France; *B.*—Austria, Switzerland, Poland; *C.*—Austria, Czechoslovakia, Poland.

_____ 3. The Atlantic Charter contained plans: *A.*—for the postwar world; *B.*—for lend-lease; *C.*—to invade Europe.

_____ 4. The Allies first invaded: *A.*—North Africa, France, Germany; *B.*—North Africa, Italy, France; *C.*—Italy, France, Germany.

_____ 5. An unfortunate mistake made in the invasion of Germany was in: *A.*—letting Hitler commit suicide; *B.*—bombing Cologne; *C.*—letting the Soviets reach Berlin before us.

_____ 6. The victory over Germany brought out in the open the: *A.*—terrible massacre of the Jews; *B.*—difficulty with the Soviets; *C.*—divided feelings in Germany.

_____ 7. The American campaign to push back the Japanese in the Pacific turned out to consist of: *A.*—dropping atomic bombs; *B.*—shelling islands, landing on them, and fighting the enemy; *C.*—invading Japan.

_____ 8. President Truman said that American strength came from: *A.*—superior weapons; *B.*—a strong navy and army; *C.*—the spirit of liberty.

_____ 9. Hitler and Mussolini kept their power by: *A.*—punishing those among their own people who criticized them; *B.*—making conquests abroad; *C.*—building strong armies.

_____ 10. Before entering the Second World War, the United States aided the Allies: *A.*—with a peacetime draft law; *B.*—by taking a stand against Germany; *C.*—by the Lend-Lease Act.

TRUE-FALSE

_____ 1. In 1940 "F. D. R." became the first third-term President in history.

_____ 2. The code name for the invasion of Italy was Operation OVERLORD.

_____ 3. America decided to destroy Japanese power before attacking Europe.

_____ 4. United States marines captured Iwo Jima.

_____ 5. The Japanese surrendered aboard the *Missouri*.

_____ 6. The Japanese captured American, English, and Dutch possessions in the Pacific.

_____ 7. Roosevelt was elected three times.

_____ 8. Ethiopia was the victim of Italy's first conquest.

_____ 9. The war aim of the Allies was unconditional surrender.

_____ 10. Hitler tried to invade Britain after the fall of France.

COMPLETION

1. Hitler broke the Treaty of Versailles in 1936 by _____ to the Rhineland.

2. Many people believed the way to stop Hitler was through _____.

3. Japan invaded _____ in 1931 and seized _____.

4. The _____ party ruled in Germany, and the _____ party in Italy.

5. In June, 1940, Germany conquered _____, and the British were caught in a trap at _____.

6. The first atomic bomb was dropped on the city of _____, in _____.

7. The most costly American victory of the war was the conquest of the island of _____.

8. The United States entered the Second World War after the attack on _____, on _____ of the year _____.

9. The Battles of the _____ and _____ stopped the Japanese advance in the Pacific.

10. The attempt of Germans to stop the Allied invasion of their country was called the _____.

MATCHING

_____1. Winston Churchill

_____2. George C. Marshall

_____3. Benito Mussolini

_____4. Saburo Kurusu

_____5. Wendell L. Willkie

_____6. Anthony C. McAuliffe

_____7. Jonathan Wainwright

_____8. Harry S Truman

_____9. Douglas MacArthur

_____10. Charles de Gaulle

A. American commanding general in Pacific

B. Japanese special ambassador to United States

C. American general in Battle of the Bulge

D. American general who was taken prisoner in Philippines

E. senior United States general in Washington

F. leader of "Free French" movement

G. Republican presidential candidate in 1940

H. dictator of Italy in Second World War

I. prime minister of Japan

J. became President in 1945

K. British prime minister in Second World War

CHAPTER 30

(*See instructions, page 8.*)

MULTIPLE-CHOICE

_____1. The Soviet Union did not carry out an agreement it made at Yalta to: A.—help the Allies in the Pacific against Japan; B.—permit free elections in countries of eastern Europe; C.—establish a pathway to Berlin through the Soviet zone in Germany.

_____2. Truman's plan to "contain" the Communists meant: A.—stopping their aggression wherever it occurred; B.—stamping out communism; C.—giving foreign aid.

_____3. The Marshall Plan provided a program of aid for: A.—all Europe; B.—Greece and Turkey; C.—all Europe except the Soviet Union and its satellites.

_____4. The Soviet Union blockaded Berlin in order to: A.—push the Allies out or force them to give up the idea of a West Germany; B.—force the Allies to pay to use Soviet highways and railroads; C.—stop East Berliners from going to West Berlin.

_____5. The Berlin blockade caused the United States and the countries of western Europe to: A.—set up an airlift; B.—form NATO; C.—withdraw from the city.

_____6. Truman removed MacArthur from his command in 1951 in order to: A.—keep Red China out of the Korean War; B.—stop American defeats; C.—keep civilian control over military decisions.

_____7. When the Korean War ended: A.—the Communists left North Korea; B.—North and South Korea were set up, divided generally along the 38th parallel; C.—the United Nations had won.

_____8. In the Cuban missile crisis, Kennedy: A.—called for help from United States alliances for collective security; B.—demanded that the Soviets remove the missiles from Cuba; C.—decided to use patience.

9. Johnson's program for creating the Great Society included: A.—"Medicare" and much aid to education; B.—the Peace Corps and foreign aid; C.—ending war.

10. Perhaps the greatest contrast between the Johnson administration and the administrations of the nineteenth century is that Johnson: A.—became President through an assassination; B.—became involved in foreign affairs; C.—faced urban problems.

11. In *Brown* v. *Board of Education of Topeka*, the Supreme Court declared unconstitutional: A.—the Civil Rights Act of 1964; B.—separate schools for Negroes and whites; C.—OAS.

COMPLETION

1. The aim of Communists is to ———.

2. The Security Council of the United Nations corresponds to the ——— branch of our government.

3. The rivalry between the United States and the Soviet Union after the Second World War came to be called the ———.

4. Except in special circumstances, the Twenty-second Amendment limits a man to being elected President ———.

5. Two events that strengthened world communism in 1949 were the ——— and the Soviets' announcement about the ———.

6. The Soviet Union gained the right to occupy northern Korea at the ——— Conference.

7. The Nationalist Chinese government took up its position on the island of ———.

8. In 1961 a group of Cubans trained by Americans tried to invade Cuba at an inlet named the ———.

9. In 1963 the United States and the Soviet Union signed a ——— treaty.

10. Communist aggression in South Vietnam was encouraged by ———.

11. From the 1950's on, organized Negroes and whites carried on a ——— movement.

MATCHING

———1. Nikita Khrushchev

———2. Chiang Kai-shek

———3. Fidel Castro

———4. John H. Glenn, Jr.

———5. Joseph R. McCarthy

———6. Alger Hiss

———7. Robert C. Weaver

———8. Dean Rusk

———9. Martin Luther King

———10. Mao Tse-tung

———11. Adlai E. Stevenson

A. Secretary of State under Kennedy and Johnson

B. Communist leader of China

C. American official convicted of lying about giving secret documents to Soviets

D. leader of the Negro civil rights movement

E. first Negro Cabinet member

F. Soviet dictator replacing Stalin

G. leader of Nationalist China

H. defeated Democratic presidential candidate in 1952, 1956

I. Senator who made many unproved charges of communism in our government

J. Communist leader of Cuba

K. Chinese ambassador to the United States

L. first American to orbit the earth

KEY FOR CHAPTER 30 TESTS
Multiple-Choice: 1-B/2-A/3-C/4-A/5-B/6-C/ 7-B/8-B/9-A/10-C/11-B. *Completion:* 1—control the world/2—executive/3—cold war/4—twice/ 5—fall of China, atomic bomb/6—Yalta/7—Taiwan/ 8—Bay of Pigs/9—limited nuclear test-ban/10—Red China/11—civil rights. *Matching:* 1-F/2-G/3-J/ 4-L/5-I/6-C/7-E/8-A/9-D/10-B/11-H.

The quotation, from a poem in <u>Leaves of Grass</u>, suggests pride in the rich variety among Americans which has been a source of our country's strength.

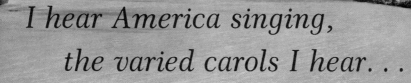

I hear America singing,
the varied carols I hear. . . .

— WALT WHITMAN

This picture of the historic Mississippi River was taken at Clarksville, Missouri, north of St. Louis.

The title of this book was inspired by words in "The Star-Spangled Banner." The cover design was also suggested by the national anthem.

The picture at the right is an impression from the original die of the Great Seal of the United States, on a commission given George Washington in 1782.

The Free

Henry F. Graff is coauthor of The Adventure of the American People (with John A. Krout) and The Modern Researcher (with Jacques Barzun). He is author of Bluejackets with Perry in Japan and is a frequent contributor to the New York Times Magazine. (See also Who's Who in America.)

THE STORY OF THE AMERICAN PEOPLE

HENRY F. GRAFF

PROFESSOR OF HISTORY « COLUMBIA UNIVERSITY

Rand McNally & Company « Chicago

ACKNOWLEDGMENTS

Grateful acknowledgment is made to publishers or organizations for the use of materials not acknowledged elsewhere as follows:

Introductory page, Jack Zehrt; Title page, Library of Congress; Dedication page, United States Capitol Historical Society, National Gallery of Art, Index of American Design; Contents, Houston Chamber of Commerce, Bill Barnes, Phil Palmer from FPG, Kerwin B. Roche from Monkmeyer, Hutchinson from FPG.

Page 1, John Carter Brown Library, Brown University, Archives des France, Paris, Giraudon, Paris, Pigafetta, *Premier voyage autour du monde*, Paris, 1801 (New York Public Library); page 2, Church of the Ognissanti, Florence, Italy (Alinari), Library of Congress; page 3, Justin Windsor, *Narrative and Critical History of America*, Houghton Mifflin and Company, 1886; page 4, Grant Heilman, Smithsonian Institution, Ewing Krainin from APA, *Codex Mendosa* (American Museum of Natural History), Denver Art Museum; page 5, Field Museum of Natural History, Arizona State Museum; page 24, Florida State News Bureau, Museum of the American Indian, Spencer Collection, New York Public Library, Giraudon, Paris, Arthur Griffin, *Retratos de los Españoles ilustres* . . . , Madrid, 1791 (New York Public Library); page 25, Staatliche Museen Zu Berlin, Jose Y. Bermudez; page 44, Ohio Historical Society, Marc de Villiers (ed.), *Les Raretés des Indes*, Paris, 1930 (Quebec Provincial Archives), George Hunter, Samuel de Champlain, *Les Voyages*, 1632 (Newberry Library), New York Historical Society, *Vallard Atlas* (Henry E. Huntington Library); page 45, Duhamel du Monceau, *Traité général des pesches*, Paris, 1772 (New York Public Library), Bibliothèque Municipale, Rouen, France; page 61, Essex Institute, Butterworth, *Rise of Industrial Arts* (New York Public Library), Diderot and D'Alembert, *Encyclopédie* (New York Public Library), Alexander Anderson Collection, New York Public Library, *The Book of Trades, or Library of the Useful Arts*, London, 1807 (Warshaw Collection), Essex Institute; page 62, Virginia State Library; page 63, John Smith's Map of Virginia, 1612 (Library of Congress); page 64, British Museum, Jamestown Foundation, Theodorus Tabernaemontanus, "Neuw Kreuterbuch," Frankfurt, 1588 (Massachusetts Horticultural Society), 1607, Inc., Jamestown, Plimouth Plantation, Pilgrim Society; page 65, Pena, Pierre, and Matthias de l'Obel, "Stirpium Adversaria Nova," London, 1570 (Arents Collections, New York Public Library); page 86, Samuel Chamberlain, Silver Collection of the First Church in Boston, on loan to the Museum of Fine Arts, Boston (Photo by David F. Lawlor), Maryland Historical Society (2 illustrations), Library of Congress, Essex Institute; page 87, National Gallery of Art, Index of American Design, Massachusetts Art Commission (Photo by George M. Cushing, Jr.); page 104, Philadelphia Museum of Art, Penn Mutual Life Insurance Company Collection, Historical Society of Pennsylvania, Museum of the City of New York, North Carolina Museum of History, National Gallery of Art, Gift of Edgar William and Bernice Chrysler Garbisch; page 105, Charleston Museum; page 125, Corning Museum of Glass, Corning, New York, New York Public Library, *The Book of Trades, or Library of the Useful Arts*, London, 1807 (Warshaw Collection), Smithsonian Institution, Westfield Athenaeum (2 illustrations); page 126, City of Boston, on loan to the Museum of Fine Arts, Boston, William Vincent Wells, *Samuel Adams*, Boston, 1866 (New York Public Library); page 127, Eastern National Park & Monument Association; page 128, New York Historical Society, Fogg Art Museum, Harvard University (2 illustrations), Colonial Williamsburg, Independence National Historical Park Collection; page 129, *New York Magazine*, May, 1790 (New York Historical Society), Newark Museum; page 148, Roman J. Burkiewicz Stamp Shop, Isaac Hutton Albany Map, 1794 (Albany Institute of History and Art), Quebec Provincial Archives, Martin House, Swansea, Massachusetts (Photo by John L. Eddy), Essex Institute, Maryland Historical Society; page 149, Maryland Historical Society; page 170, Eric Sanford, Minute Man National Historical Park Project, Concord Antiquarian Society (2 illustrations), Weston Kemp; page 171, *Pennsylvania Journal and Weekly Advertiser*, October 31, 1765 (New York Public Library); page 190, Independence National Historical Park Collection (3 illustrations), Yale University Art Gallery, Indiana Bureau of Natural Resources; page 191, Historical Society of Pennsylvania, Westfield Athenaeum; page 217, Vermont Historical Society, Missouri Historical Society, Illinois State Museum, Library of Congress, Smithsonian Institution (2 illustrations); page 218, Collection of Albert E. Leeds, Philadelphia, *James Madison Papers* (New York Public Library); page 219, United States Department of State; page 220, William Penn Memorial Museum, American Numismatic Society, Missouri Historical Society, Kentucky Historical Society, Lincoln's New Salem Enterprises, Petersburg, Illinois; page 221, National Archives; page 246, Penn Mutual Life Insurance Company Collection, National Gallery of Art, Index of American Design, Mount Vernon Ladies' Association (3 illustrations), Independence National Historical Park Collection; page 247, Art Color Card Distributors, Camden, New Jersey; page 270, Kentucky Department of Parks, Louisiana State Museum, Allan P. Kirby Collection, Lafayette College, Easton, Pennsylvania, Alderman Library, University of Virginia, Thomas Jefferson Memorial Foundation (2 illustrations); page 271, Historical Paintings Collection, Continental Insurance Company; page 292, New York Historical Society, Old Print Shop (2 illustrations), Fort McHenry National Monument and Historic Shrine, Historical Society of Pennsylvania; page 293, National Gallery of Art, Index of American Design; page 319, Howard Tilton Memorial Library, Tulane University, Collection of I. S. Seidman, New York, Smithsonian Institution (3 illustrations), New York Central Railroad; page 320, Henry Clay Memorial Foundation, Kentucky Historical Society; page 321, Smithsonian Institution; page 322, Chicago Historical Society, Collection of I. S. Seidman, New York (2 illustrations), Trustees of Dartmouth College (Hopkins Center Art Galleries), Ladies' Hermitage Association, Phelps Stokes Collection, New York Public Library and the United States Capitol Historical Society; page 323, American Antiquarian Society, Collection of I. S. Seidman, New York; page 344, Collection of Mr. and Mrs. Samuel J. Henry, Washington, D. C. (Francis G. Mayer), William J. Barbee, *The Cotton Question*, New York, 1866 (South Caroliniana Library, University of South Carolina), Collection of Edgar William and Bernice Chrysler Garbisch; page 345, Illinois State Historical Library, Collection of I. S. Seidman, New York; page 366, Thomas M. Iverson, Collection of Hall Park McCullough, Bennington, Vermont (Marshall B. Davidson, LIFE IN AMERICA, Houghton Mifflin Company, 1951), Alexander Forbes, Esq., *California: A History of Upper and Lower California*, London, 1839 (Newberry Library), Chicago Historical Society, Jack Zehrt; page 367, Texas Highway Department, Society of California Pioneers; page 388, Abby Aldrich Rockefeller Folk Art Collection, Museum of the City of New York, Chicago Historical Society, Illinois State Historical Library, Illinois Information Service, Schomburg Collection, New York Public Library; page 389, Museum of the City of New York; page 413, History Room, Wells Fargo Bank, San Francisco, International Harvester Company, Clarence P. Hornung, *Handbook of Early American Advertising Art*, Dover Publications, 1953, Chicago Museum of Science and Industry, Borden Company; page 414, Chicago Historical Society, Illinois State Historical Library; page 415, Clarence P. Hornung, *Handbook of Early American Advertising Art*, Dover Publications, 1953; page 416, Library of Congress, Chicago Historical Society, Cooper Union Museum, Illinois State Historical Library, Confederate Museum (2 illustrations); page 417, J. Doyle De Witt Collection of Political Americana; page 448, Kennedy Galleries, New York State Department of Commerce, Rutherford B. Hayes Library (2 illustrations), Kiplinger Collection, United States Capitol Historical Society; page 449, Collection of Mrs. James Ward Thorne (Art Institute of Chicago); page 469, Chicago Museum of Science and Industry (3 illustrations), American Telephone and Telegraph Company, Sperry Rand Corporation, Edison National Historic Site; page 470, Chicago Historical Society (2 illustrations); page 471 Library of Congress; page 472, American Museum of Natural History, Tropico Gold Camp Museum, Rosamond, California, Woolaroc Museum, Bartlesville, Oklahoma, National Gallery of Art, Index of American Design (2 illustrations), Putnam County Historical Society; page 494, David A. Howe Public Library, Wellsville, New York, Kansas State Historical Society, Deere & Company, Chicago Museum of Science and Natural History, American Museum of Natural History; page 495, J. H. Beadle, *The Undeveloped West*, Philadelphia, 1873; page 514, Art Institute of Chicago, Chicago Historical Society (2 illustrations), Atwater Kent Museum (2 illustrations), David F. Lawlor; page 515, Metropolitan Museum of Art, Bequest of Moses Tanenbaum, 1937; page 534, Norfolk Museum of Arts and Sciences, Cowlitz County Historical Museum (2 illustrations), Hawaii Visitors Bureau, Charles Johnson Post Collection—Courtesy LIFE © 1958 by Time, Inc., Chicago Historical Society; page 535, United States Department of the Navy, Index of American Design, National Gallary of Art; page 556, Panama Canal Company, Katharine Tweed from Underwood & Underwood, Sears, Roebuck and Co., Underwood & Underwood, United States Food & Drug Administration, Lillian Nassau, New York; page 579, National Aeronautics and Space Administration (3 illustrations), Boeing Company, International Business Machines Corp., University of Illinois Medical Center, Chicago, Ford Motor Company, Orlando R. Cabanban; page 580, UPI; page 581, Eastern National Park & Monument Association; page 582, United States Naval Academy Museum, UPI, Library of Congress; page 583, UPI (2 illustrations); page 602, Chicago Historical Society, Ford Motor Company, UPI; page 603, UPI; page 624, Metropolitan Museum of Art, Fletcher Fund, 1941 (Francis G. Mayer), Franklin D. Roosevelt Library, National Recovery Administration Collection, National Archives, Bob Amft, Wide World; page 625, Herbert Hoover Presidential Library, Kansas Department of Economic Development; page 646, UPI, Columbia University, Franklin D. Roosevelt Library (3 illustrations); page 647, UPI; page 672, Wide World (2 illustrations), United Nations, UPI; page 673, Harry S. Truman Library, Wide World, Fred J. Maroon.

Page 592, quotation from "OVER THERE" by George M. Cohan, /Copyright 1917/ Copyright Renewal 1945 Leo Feist Inc., New York, N. Y. Used by permission of Copyright Proprietor; pages 634-635, quotation from Eleanor Roosevelt's *This I Remember*, with the permission of Harper & Row, Publishers, Inc., New York, © 1949; page 663, quotation from Bedell Smith's *Eisenhower's Six Great Decisions*, with the permission of David McKay Co., Inc., New York, © 1956; page 669, quotation from Major General Courtney Whitney's *MacArthur, His Rendezvous with History*, with the permission of Time, Inc., New York, © 1955; page 683, quotation from Dwight D. Eisenhower's *The White House Years: Mandate for Change, 1953-1956*, © Dwight D. Eisenhower, 1963, with the permission of Doubleday & Co., Inc., New York.

The map on page 8 was adapted from Map 2 of Harold E. Driver's *Indians of North America*, with the permission of the University of Chicago Press, Chicago, © 1961.

Credits shown here are those not appearing elsewhere in the book.

This book is dedicated to the memory of
Harry James Carman, my beloved teacher.
By his example in the classroom he inspired young Americans
to learn the stirring history of their country.

A gate made in Connecticut using instruments that recall America's agricultural beginnings.

The consultants include three well-known American historians and seven classroom teachers. These people brought a wealth of knowledge and a rich diversity of experience to the book.

Consultants

JOHN A. KROUT
Professor Emeritus of History
Columbia University
Visiting Professor of American History
Arizona State University

EDGAR A. TOPPIN
Professor of History
Virginia State College

C. VANN WOODWARD
Sterling Professor of History
Yale University

PAUL B. BUCAR
Teacher of American History
Norwin Junior High School West
Irwin, Pennsylvania

JOHN A. DAVITT
Counselor
Merritt College
Formerly, Teacher of Social Studies
Roosevelt Junior High School
San Francisco, California

MRS. GEORGE F. GRAY
Teacher of Social Studies
Edison Junior High School
Port Arthur, Texas

MARY E. HYNES
Teacher of Social Studies
Weeks Junior High School
Newton Center, Massachusetts

LORAINE C. ORME
Teacher of Social Studies
Washington Irving School
Oak Park, Illinois

CARROLL W. RUPP
Teacher of Social Studies
Westview Junior High School
Miami, Florida

CORNELIA TONGUE
Teacher and Chairman of
Social Studies Department
William G. Enloe High School
Raleigh, North Carolina

STUDENT ACTIVITIES WRITTEN BY:

JOHN A. DAVITT

The picture here--of downtown Houston, Texas--and others on pages following bear out the fact that the United States is largely urban today. Its change from being an agricultural country to becoming a nation of cities is an important theme of this book.

THE CONTENTS

This textbook contains eight parts and thirty chapters, all named here.

PAGE

The city seen here is Atlanta, Georgia. Many of the buildings shown have been erected since 1960, and others will soon be put up in this southern metropolis.

The photograph below is a view of San Francisco, California, showing part of the Bay area. Coit Tower rises high in the right background, and below it part of the Golden Gate Bridge may be seen.

APPENDIX

The maps and graphs in this text were made especially for it by Rand McNally cartographers.

Maps and Graphs

Part One: FACING THE AMERICAS

Philadelphia, Pennsylvania, seen from the steps of the Art Museum, is the subject of the photograph below. No American city is more closely tied to American history than this eastern one.

Part Two: NEWCOMERS ON THE SEABOARD

Part Three: THE STRUGGLE FOR LIBERTY

A part of the downtown area of Chicago, Illinois, photographed at night, is seen here. Once a small fort, this city has become the center of one of the largest metropolitan areas in the United States.

Part Four: SHAPING A NATION

Part Five: SECTIONAL SQUABBLING

Part Six: BROTHERS IN CONFLICT

Activities to help students develop desirable skills in using maps and graphs may be found in the chapter Workshops.

Part Seven: THE TESTING OF DEMOCRACY

Part Eight: IN DEFENSE OF FREEDOM

Certain words are pronounced within the text itself. A key to pronunciation appears at the beginning of the Index.

The captions for the pictures on the first page of the Part One opening (opposite) appear below. In every other instance the captions and pictures for a part opening appear on the same page. All illustrations in the openings show aspects of the development of American technology.

Daring men, long experienced at sailing the seas, found the New World.
(a) Before the days of ocean-going vessels,
European sailors used "rowboats" called galleys, like this one.
(b) A later type of European boat was guided by one oar,
as seen on the seal of a city in Belgium.
(c) A still later European ship was steered by a hinged rudder at the back,
as shown on the seal of an English seaport.
(d) Columbus and other seamen of his day carried compasses like this
to tell direction: the needle always points north.
(e) Small seagoing vessels – called caravels –
were commonly used at the time of Columbus:
clumsy and slow, they depended on the undependable winds.

The ability to build seagoing vessels was an achievement that enabled western Europeans to explore the world and to discover America. The compass, an important aid to navigation, had been used by both the Chinese and the Mediterranean sailors since 1000 or 1100 A.D.

(a)

(c)

(b)

(d)

(e)

(e)

The Free and the Brave

Part One: FACING THE AMERICAS

Technology, one of the major themes of this book, is featured in every part opening and in other places as well. Every culture has a technology--ways of working and using the environment. In American culture-- a branch of Western culture--technology is so advanced that it has brought about exceedingly rapid changes. Among them are the growth of cities and new and improved means of transportation and communication. The story of the development of American technology is an important part of the content of The Free and the Brave.

Part One: FACING THE AMERICAS

A time line precedes each part in this book. Acquaint the class with this one. Time lines help students develop a sense of time and chronology--a social-studies skill--and the concept of time and change. Students should often refer to this and other time lines.

A FANTASTIC IDEA: A NEW WORLD!

By a twist of fate, in the same year—1454—Amerigo Vespucci was born and the first dated printing appeared in Europe. Both of these events eventually changed the life of every human being on earth.

The printing press made it possible for information to be multiplied without limit. Vespucci's work gave mankind the knowledge of a new world and, therefore, a glorious new subject to print books about—and to stir men's minds and hearts about.

Vespucci came into the world in the beautiful city of Florence, Italy. The wealth

Time and Change

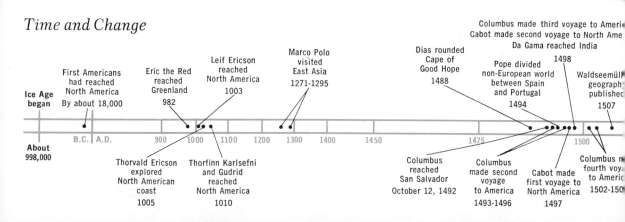

Ice Age began

About 998,000

First Americans had reached North America By about 18,000

Eric the Red reached Greenland 982

Leif Ericson reached North America 1003

Marco Polo visited East Asia 1271-1295

Dias rounded Cape of Good Hope 1488

Columbus made third voyage to America
Cabot made second voyage to North America
Da Gama reached India 1498

Pope divided non-European world between Spain and Portugal 1494

Waldseemüller geography published 1507

B.C. A.D. 900 1000 1100 1200 1300 1400 1450 1475 1500

Thorvald Ericson explored North American coast 1005

Thorfinn Karlsefni and Gudrid reached North America 1010

Columbus reached San Salvador October 12, 1492

Columbus made second voyage to America 1493-1496

Cabot made first voyage to North America 1497

Columbus fourth voyage to America 1502-150

that its leading family—the Medicis—had piled up helped support some of the most gifted artists who have ever lived. Vespucci himself entered the service of the Medicis. They sent him to Spain in 1492 to look after their interests.

But Vespucci was lured by exploration. Sailing for the king of Spain and then for the king of Portugal, he became the first European to set eyes on the Amazon River. And all in all, he explored about six thousand miles of "new" coastline.

Appreciating what he had seen, Vespucci wrote to his old employers, the Medicis: "We arrived at a new land which, for many reasons . . . we observed to be a continent."

A fantastic idea: a new world! Columbus and other explorers had also talked of having found a new world, but they had meant simply that they had come upon a new part of Asia, one not previously known to exist. Vespucci meant, on the other hand, a "new" hemisphere, another half of the earth.

Before Amerigo Vespucci died in 1512, a well-known geographer had named the "new" continent for him. "America" then joined Europe, Asia, and Africa as a fourth major portion of the earth's land area. The printing press would place its name on every map and in time on every tongue.

For all its artistic magnificence, Florence, like any city of Europe, offered a chance to rise in life to only a very, very few. One day Amerigo's America would stand for something more beautiful than the noblest statue or most wonderful painting. It would mean in every language of the globe "individual freedom and opportunity for the many."

A biographical sketch or essay by the author appears at the beginning of each part. The subject is a key person in the period of history to be covered. Vespucci was chosen for this one because he especially well linked the Old and the New worlds, he explored parts of America, and America was named for him.

The rich coat of arms of Spain, the European country that ambitiously supported the bold voyages of Columbus and the first explorations of Vespucci.

The last paragraph introduces a fundamental concept about the United States and American democracy. Discuss the meaning of the words in quotation marks, especially "individual freedom."

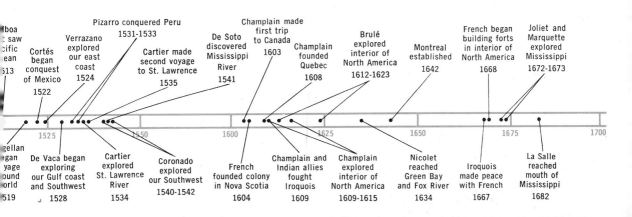

Balboa saw Pacific Ocean 1513

Cortés began conquest of Mexico 1522

Verrazano explored our east coast 1524

Pizarro conquered Peru 1531-1533

Cartier made second voyage to St. Lawrence 1535

De Soto discovered Mississippi River 1541

Champlain made first trip to Canada 1603

Champlain founded Quebec 1608

Brulé explored interior of North America 1612-1623

Montreal established 1642

French began building forts in interior of North America 1668

Joliet and Marquette explored Mississippi 1672-1673

Magellan began voyage round world 1519

De Vaca began exploring our Gulf coast and Southwest 1528

Cartier explored St. Lawrence River 1534

Coronado explored our Southwest 1540-1542

French founded colony in Nova Scotia 1604

Champlain and Indian allies fought Iroquois 1609

Champlain explored interior of North America 1609-1615

Nicolet reached Green Bay and Fox River 1634

Iroquois made peace with French 1667

La Salle reached mouth of Mississippi 1682

1525 1550 1600 1625 1650 1675 1700

(c)

(d)

(e)

(a) Ruins of Mesa Verde Pueblo, dwelling of Oasis Indians in southwestern Colorado.
(b) An Indian drawing of a doll (a sun worshiper) made for children of Oasis Indians.
(c) Machu Picchu, an ancient Indian city in Peru, South America, discovered in 1911.
(d) An early-sixteenth-century Indian drawing of a hero in a Mexican legend.
(e) A gold-leaf mummy mask created by a talented Indian artist in Peru about 1500 A.D.

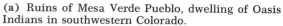

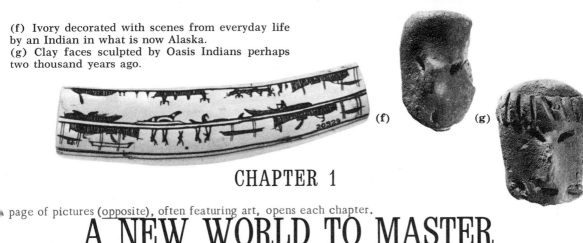

(f) Ivory decorated with scenes from everyday life by an Indian in what is now Alaska.

(g) Clay faces sculpted by Oasis Indians perhaps two thousand years ago.

(f) **(g)**

CHAPTER 1

A page of pictures (opposite), often featuring art, opens each chapter.

A NEW WORLD TO MASTER

Use the page of pictures to let students "discover" further the content of the chapter. Discuss the meaning of "Western" and "non-Western" worlds. In this introduction the author emphasizes three ideas: (1) the passage of time, which is best understood through the study of history; (2) the continuous nature of history; and (3) the contributions of both peoples and individuals.

HAVE you ever pictured to yourself what it was like to be alive in North America when your grandparents were young people? When Abraham Lincoln was President? When the American Revolution was going on? When the first colonists were arriving? When only Indians lived here? When—— ?

Everybody has a favorite time in the past. Which is yours? Do you choose it because you like the way people of those days dressed? Or is it that their era was especially exciting and you can see yourself playing a role in it?

Actually all bygone times should be interesting to us. History is like some mighty river, fed by many, many small streams, each having its own currents and appearance. From the time that these streams flow into the larger body of water, they can never again be separately identified. Their content, though, is evermore a part of the mainstream.

So it is that no past era is ever lost to the present. We who live in what we call the Western world are indebted in one way or another to all the Western—and non-Western—men and women who have gone before us. And the ways of life of people coming after us will be affected by whatever we feed into the river of history.

Americans have already contributed significantly to that great river. Above all they have shown that a free people can advance the public welfare and human happiness more than any other people. #

Because of this contribution, the American stream has changed the river of history more than any other of the countless streams that have entered it. Our aim is to understand this American stream by studying the springs that formed it.

#Another important concept about life in the United States--a free country.

Wanderers Arrive from the East

We are not sure who the first American was, and we shall certainly never discover his name. We are fairly certain only that his ancestors lived in the Old World. We are also convinced that by the time he arrived in the New World, he was physically and mentally much as we know him today. Only now are we beginning to understand how he probably reached here and where he came from.

5

Crossing the Bridge

The first immigrants began to slip from northeastern Asia into what we call Alaska thousands of years ago. These earliest Americans crossed Bering Strait during the period of time known as the Ice Age, which began between one and two million years ago.

We now believe that the snow and ice of the Ice Age tied up much of the water of the world. The result was that the oceans were probably 100 feet lower than they are today. The earliest immigrants, therefore, came from Asia to America across a bridge of land that is under water today, but was once dry.

Armed with a spear. Nimble and strong, the first Americans were wandering hunters who had no fixed dwelling places but followed animal trails wherever they led. They chased such Ice Age game as bison, camels, mammoths, mastodons, giant ground sloths, and primitive horses. The men and women of those days lived short lives full of natural dangers. Before entering America, they had developed the spear, which was their only weapon against the hazards they had to face.

The first model of the spear must have been a crudely fashioned piece of jagged flint, or rock. Held in the palm of the hand, it was like a human claw, useful in hacking an animal to death.

Later—who knows how much later, perhaps thousands of years—the spear was improved. The flint was attached to a shaft of wood so that the weapon could be hurled at an animal from a distance, with greater force and safety.

Still later the new spear was attached to another stick of wood, about 2 feet long. This spear-thrower made it possible for the early hunters to propel the weapon a much greater distance and with even greater force.

Today Americans look every year for new and improved models of cars, refrigerators, hair dryers, and many other conveniences. The first Americans, on the other hand, possibly waited a thousand years or more for the bettering of the single instrument on which their very lives depended.

Technological change. When people apply scientific principles—in the case of the Ice Age people, simply shrewd observations—to the making of useful tools and instruments, they are practicing *technology*. We call changes in tools and instruments *technological change*.

The rate of technological change is one important measure of human progress. In the Ice Age, human progress was so slow that changes took place only over thousands of years.

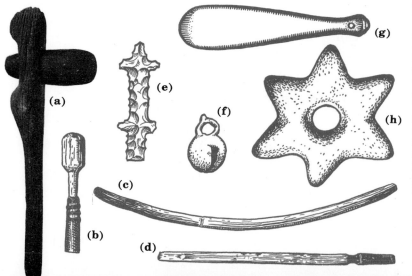

Implements of early Americans: **(a)** A stone celt, used for throwing at objects and as an ax without a handle. **(b)** A blunt stone point on a handle, used to stone animals, found in Texas. **(c)** A curved throwing-stick used as a weapon, also dug up in Texas. **(d)** A spear-thrower discovered in Texas. **(e)** A flint found in Illinois. **(f)** A copper bell from Arizona. **(g)** A stone club used in California. **(h)** A mace-head in which a handle was inserted to form a weapon—found in Peru.

People on the move. In meeting the dangers they faced, the men and women who first reached America were simply coping with their environment, just as we do. They probably were not more venturesome or any braver than we are. Very likely they had no sense of doing anything remarkable, and they had no knowledge that they had reached a new continent. They were merely looking for more favorable homesites—even as we might.

The first Americans seemed to follow animal trails southward along the east side of the Rocky Mountains into our present-day Southwest and eventually into the southernmost part of South America. This southward migration is understandable. *Geologists,* scientists who study the formation of the earth, say that at different times during the Ice Age parts of North America were free of ice for several thousand years.

How long did it take the Ice Age hunters to spread throughout North and South America? We do not know. There had to be time for the migrants to adapt to the changing conditions they met as they moved southward. There had to be a large enough increase in numbers to permit descendants of the earliest arrivals to begin widely scattered settlements.

The migrations must have taken a very long time. One scientist thinks they could not have taken less than twenty-five thousand years.

Unsolved mysteries. For convenience and because they knew no better, the Spanish who came to the New World in 1492 called descendants of the people who had crossed over from Asia "Indians." Actually we do not know what the earliest spear-throwing people called themselves or the land of the New World or its rivers, lakes, and mountains. All of those names are lost to us forever in the mists of the American beginnings.

We must accept the fact that we shall always be without knowledge of the men and women who were the earliest American heroes and heroines. We shall not know how many or what kind of communities flourished, because few remains have been found. Works of art, styles of language, and ways of living and playing also existed about which we shall never have any information.

You can see here how close Asia is to North America at the place where Asians crossed to our continent, beginning new lives as Americans.

Routes of the First Americans

0   200   400   800   1200   miles at equator

—— Known routes
—— Probable route
—— Extent of ice

© RMⒶN & CO.

The map shows how close northern Asia, northern Europe, and northern North America are. Call attention to the area once covered by ice. Review latitude and longitude. The map grid helps students visualize the extent of the migrations. It also helps the class to relate history and geography.

7

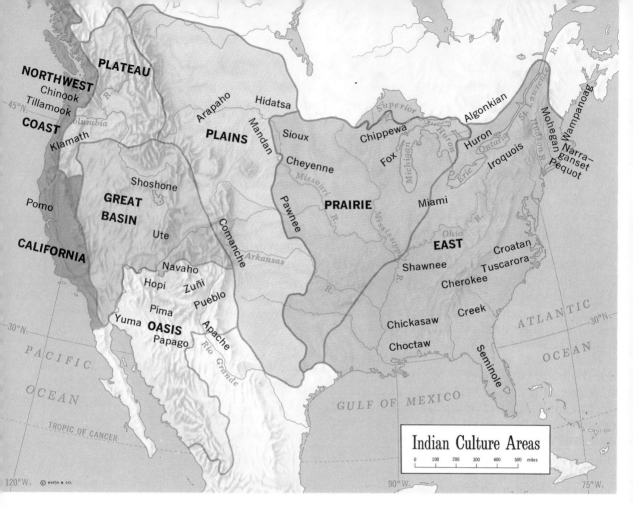

The areas shown are those in which important Indian cultures existed about the time Europeans came to America. Later on, the tribes named within the culture areas moved, died out, or were transferred elsewhere.

Ways of Indian Life

We can, though, consider some of the *cultures*, or ways of life, that later flourished on the land now occupied by the United States. Two of them, those of what are called today the Oasis and the East peoples, are especially interesting to us. It was with them that the Europeans first came into contact.

The Oasis peoples. The Oasis group of tribes dominated most of what was to become Arizona and New Mexico (as well as parts of northern Mexico). Because they lived amid the dryness of desert climate, they established their settlements near oases or other sources of water.

Some of the Oasis tribesmen lived in villages or towns. After the Spanish came, they were commonly called Pueblo Indians, *pueblo* being the Spanish word for village. The Pueblo Indians were less affected than some other tribes by the westward movement in the United States. To this day they keep many of their old teachings and customs.

Mostly, oasis-type Indians were farmers, and their chief crop was corn. Meat made up only a small part of their diet because large game was scarce. The animal they ate most commonly was the rabbit. Fish

Eight distinct culture areas--where eight different ways of life developed--are shown on the map above, two of which are discussed by the author. Students should compare this map with the one on pp. 542-543 and tell why each culture area appearing here received its name.

was not an important food because rivers and streams were few.

The Oasis peoples were the only Indians who wore cotton clothing before the coming of Europeans. Men wore cotton kilts fastened around the waist. Women wore cotton dresses which did not go over the head but were wrapped around the body and fastened at one shoulder. Both men and women kept their hair long in the back and in bangs in the front.

Most families lived in rectangular rooms with flat roofs. Because these rooms were built one next to another and one on top of another, the villages looked from a distance something like modern apartment houses. Each village, or pueblo, was governed by committees of its inhabitants.

The East peoples. The East group of Indians, as you see on the map, lived in the region bounded roughly by the St. Lawrence River in the North and the Gulf of Mexico in the South. They occupied the land from what is now the southern part of New England westward to present-day Texas. Some of the famous tribes in this group were the Iroquois in New York and the Civilized Tribes of the South—the Cherokee, Choctaw, Chickasaw, Creeks, and Seminole.

Farming folk. The East group of Indians, like the Oasis group, had long ago discovered the value of *sedentary* agriculture. That is, they stayed in one place and farmed. They raised corn, squashes, beans, pumpkins, and tobacco—products which they were to teach the first European settlers how to grow.

The coats of the large furry animals of the region provided winter clothing for these Indians, who in cold weather sometimes wore whole hides as robes, or mantles. In warmer weather the men wore buckskin breechcloths and the women buckskin skirts. Both men and women used leggings, and the men and sometimes the women wore moccasins.

A woman kept her hair long and braided. A man shaved his head except for a lock of hair he allowed to grow from the middle of the scalp.

The Iroquois, best known of the East Indians, had achieved remarkable success in self-government. If it had not been for the coming of the Europeans, they might have taken important steps to unite other tribes with themselves to make a nation.

The permanent Iroquois villages were impressive. Each was made up of a series of houses solidly built and surrounded by a low earthen wall. On or inside the wall a wooden stockade was constructed.

Clearing the land. The Indians made some of their farm tools from the bones of

Iroquois Indians (Seneca) about 1500 A.D. in a community in what is now western New York State. Men at the left are beginning to build a longhouse, the typical Iroquois dwelling. Women in front of the storage building at the right are busy preparing food.

Rochester Museum of Arts and Sciences

Denver Art Museum

Above, left: Indian artists of Peru fashioned thousands of plants from metal before the Europeans arrived and melted them down. This one of maize is in bright copper.
Above, right: Fishhooks made by Indians of South America and California.
Below: This baked-clay toy crocodile, found in Mexico, proves that American Indians knew the wheel even if they made no practical use of it.

The picture at the far left shows how any people's art reflects its culture.

deer and others from seashells and stones. They had no iron implements. Not knowing that they suffered a serious lack, they learned to clear land by girdling trees. That is, they would cut a groove into the bark all around the trunk of a tree in order to kill it. When it was dead, they pulled it down.

An area that had been cleared would be planted to vegetable crops. Such a clearing might serve for ten or twelve years. Then, as its yield of food grew smaller and piles of refuse rose higher and higher, the tribe would move on and repeat the clearing process. The first Europeans who came to America occupied some of these abandoned Indian "old fields," as they were called.

Ask what varieties of corn we use today.

Clearly American
How?

It is important to understand the differences between the life of the Indians we have been discussing and that of the uncivilized people who, about ten thousand years ago, were the chief inhabitants of Europe. Possibly the most telling difference was that in the Americas the good-tasting and nourishing food called corn—or, often, maize—was available.

We do not know when or where maize first appeared, but it seems to have been grown as far back as several thousand years B.C., that is, before Christ was born. Easily raised, it supported a large population, and it was an ideal plant for people who had to depend on crude farming implements.

Missing elements. On the other hand, three things on which Old World men and women depended were lacking in America. One was work animals. A second was metal tools. A third, unbelievable as it may seem, was the wheel, or at least the practical use of it.

It seems safe to say that if there had been beasts of burden in the New World,

Talk about the three missing elements: Ask how each element has contributed to the development of American culture in our day. Discuss "B.C." and "A.D." Call attention to their use, pp. 2-3. Students should think of the fishhooks as examples of technology.

Algonkian Indians constructing birch-bark canoes from the covering of
birch trees, like those seen at the right. The shelters—
at the left—were also neatly covered with the white bark

the development of the wheel would have taken place. Only with the help of the wheel can animals be used to advantage in pulling heavy loads. The llama, to be sure, served the Indians in Peru, but it is a frail animal and particularly unsuitable for use in mountainous country. The dog drew sleds in snow country but could do little more.

The horse had once existed here in the New World but had disappeared by the end of the Ice Age. We do not know why. Perhaps an insect pest was responsible. We can only tease our imagination by thinking how different the New World would have appeared to Columbus if the horse had survived here.

To sum up, it is a mistake to assume that when the first Europeans arrived they met the same kind of Indians everywhere they went. It is wrong, too, to think that the Indians lacked ability or were foolish. Their technology was merely inferior to that of the Europeans, and their rate of technological change was slow.

Heavy debt. Americans today, mainly descendants of the peoples of Europe and Africa, should feel eternally grateful to the Indians. They made possible our ancestors' own adjustment to this wonderfully rich continent. Besides maize, they gave them turkeys and popcorn, buckwheat cakes and maple syrup, root beer and strawberries, chocolate and sarsaparilla, tomatoes and potatoes, chicle (for making chewing gum) and black walnuts, pumpkins and pineapples, vanilla and blueberries, rhubarb and tobacco, and peanuts. And the complete list would be many times longer.

Moreover, the Indians perfected means for getting about in the forests and on the inland waterways. They invented moccasins, snowshoes for travel in winter, and the canoe.

In its basic design, the canoe has never been improved upon since the Europeans saw it five hundred years ago. The design of the American whaling ships which first carried the American flag into the ports of the world was mainly modeled on the canoe.

Our language is rich in Indian words— *cigar*, *Tammany*, *hominy*, and *tuxedo*, to name only a few. And hundreds of place names, including the names of many states, are Indian in origin.

1. From where did the first Americans come? In what period? 2. With what two Indian cultures did Europeans mainly come in contact? 3. What three elements did the Indians lack? 4. For what are we indebted to the Indians?

The contributions of Indians to American culture today are emphasized for their own sake and also to help overcome the idea that the various Indian cultures Europeans came in contact with were necessarily inferior because they were <u>different</u> from European culture.

11

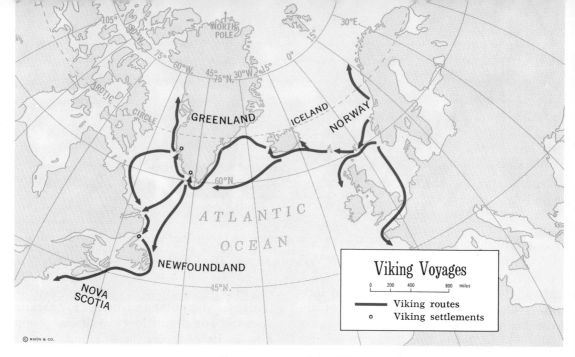

It was as natural for Vikings to discover coastal lands west and southwest of their homeland as it was for Columbus to find later the West Indies, lying across the Atlantic southwest of Spain.

Europeans Find the Earth Is Bigger

How does it happen that *we* are the people who share in the Indian cultures and combine man's advances elsewhere with those taking place in America? The answer is to be found in a set of circumstances that can only be described as wonderful historical luck.

Viking Voyages

Our story begins in an unpromising way in northern Europe about 1000 A.D. A Norwegian known by the name of Eric the Red —a man of terrible temper—committed a crime. As punishment he was banished to Iceland, an island first reached by Norsemen in the ninth century and later colonized by them.

Deciding to travel westward across the Atlantic, Eric eventually reached, in 982, a land which he called Greenland. Settling there on the southwestern coast, in a few years he persuaded several hundred Icelanders to join him and found a colony. This was really the first European colony in the New World.

Lucky Leif. One of Eric's four children was Leif, who, in the custom of Norway, took his last name from his father's first, becoming therefore Leif Ericson. Leif went to Norway when he was a young man. He received from King Olaf a command to introduce Christianity into Greenland on his return there. This fact shows that Leif was recognized to be a responsible person.

Another Norwegian, by the name of Bjarni Herjulfsson, set out from Iceland, about 986, to join his father (who had followed Eric to Greenland). Sailing a great distance, he and his crew reached the coast of a flat, forested country not at all like the Greenland—with its mountains of ice—

which they were looking for.

Not being inquisitive people, and certainly not as adventurous as they must have thought themselves to be, they sailed away, finally reaching Greenland. There Bjarni was happy to be reunited with his father. One wonders if it ever occurred to this young man or to his sailors that they had "discovered" the continent of North America.

Bjarni was soon telling Leif Ericson, a restless and energetic man full of daring and spirit, of the journey he had made. Leif seems to have made up his mind to "see for himself." About the year 1003, with a crew of thirty-five sailors, he sailed from Greenland to the west. After many days at sea, Leif and his men probably touched at what is now Newfoundland and, later on, at what is now Nova Scotia. Then they sailed in a southwesterly direction, again sighting land.

Going ashore there, the men decided to avoid the stormy season on the ocean and remain for the winter. The description they later gave of the region—that grapes were growing and that cattle grazed all winter—suggests that they may have been as far south as present-day Massachusetts.

Vinland. The abundance of wild grapes which Leif is said to have stowed into the hold of his ship led the explorers to name the country Vinland (Wineland). In the milder weather of the following spring, he and his men returned home to Greenland. Like someone just returned from outer space, Leif had a remarkable story to tell.

No one seems to have been more excited by Leif's report than Leif's brother Thorvald. In 1005 Thorvald borrowed Leif's ship and set out to continue Leif's explorations. He may have taken the vessel along the coasts of what are now Connecticut, New York, New Jersey, Delaware, and Maryland. Tragically, though, the Norsemen under Thorvald's leadership were attacked by people who traveled in canoes. The Norsemen called them "Skrellings"— the screeching people, that is, the war whoopers.

Thorvald suffered a fatal wound. After burying him, his men took the ship back to Greenland, and the inhabitants there heard new tales about Vinland.

Further expeditions. Now still another of Leif's brothers, Thorstein Ericson, was stirred to visit Vinland. He set sail for the new land with a party of twenty-five, in-

The carefully carved head of a wooden stem like those at the bows of Viking ships after about 800 A.D.

British Museum

A modern painting of a brightly colored Viking ship of the kind used after the eighth century.

Jefferson Field House, Chicago Park District (Photo by Bob Amft)

cluding his wife, Gudrid. But when he died on the way, his ship turned about and returned home. Leif offered Gudrid lodging in his own home. There she met and fell in love with a Norseman just arrived in Greenland, Thorfinn Karlsefni.

Thorfinn and Gudrid were married, and about the year 1010 A.D. they set out from Greenland with the largest expedition yet —sixty-five people, including four women besides Gudrid. The party reached Vinland safely and was welcomed by the Skrellings, with whom they were soon busily trading. Probably they were exchanging cloth for skins. It is said that a baby boy, Snorri, was born to Gudrid—the first child of European parents to be born in America.

National Museum of Antiquities of Scotland

Vikings by no means spent all their time fighting and exploring: their artists carved these chessmen from walrus ivory about 1200 A.D.

Weaving gay threads, Viking artists of the twelfth century showed a Viking soldier on horseback.

Kunstindustrimuseet, Oslo, Norway

Norsemen and Skrellings

Although the Norsemen and the Indian people they found in Vinland were friendly at first, they fell more and more into conflict. The Norsemen, like the Indians, relied chiefly on bows and arrows. They knew how to make iron, but they had not yet turned this skill to the manufacture of deadly weapons.

Breaking off contact. It was not yet possible, therefore, for the Europeans to defeat the Indians overwhelmingly. That kind of effort would have to await the increased power that gunpowder provided a few hundred years later. Nevertheless there was growing resistance to Karlsefni's expedition. It returned to Greenland after about three years.

The on-and-off contact between Greenland and Vinland may have continued until about the middle of the fourteenth century. Around that time, we are fairly sure, the Greenland colony died out.

Possibly the cause was related to the terrible plague that swept Europe in the fourteenth century, in some places wiping out as much as two-thirds of the population. For those who survived, competition to make a living must have become less keen. Doubtless fewer men cared to seek opportunity far from home, at the end of a dangerous sea voyage.

Through new eyes. What had the Vikings accomplished? Today we realize that they had traveled by sea on a reliable ship, carrying efficient tools to a land area reached thousands of years earlier by men who had crossed Bering Strait. The differences in the ways these two peoples faced the awesome new land reflect the differences in their cultures before their arrivals.

At the time of Leif Ericson's journey, Europeans had a well-developed agriculture, domesticated animals, and the opening stages of manufacturing. They also #

#Some of the characteristics of Western culture are named here. Another one--Christianity-- was named on p. 12.

A Viking ax head
and two swords.

National Geographic Society © 1963

Scientists in 1963 dug up the remains (seen enclosed here) of Viking buildings in Newfoundland on a site shown on the map on page 12.

had the Christian and Jewish religions, the beginnings of national government, and a start in understanding the natural world.

With their background the Viking travelers must have looked at the new continent with a viewpoint different from that of those wanderers from Asia. Furthermore, whereas the first arrivals across Bering Strait greeted a land covered in large part by ice, the Norsemen gazed at an inviting and fruitful one. Those two # words, *inviting* and *fruitful,* continue to characterize America for Europeans.

Meaning of discovery. A claim of discovery depends on who is the discoverer and who is discovered. Those people who ## watched the Norse ships arrive on the American shore discovered the Norsemen just as certainly as the Norsemen discovered them. We must keep in mind, too, that the Skrellings were neither lost nor waiting for visitors. Europeans were just finding out for the first time about the Skrellings and about the huge area of unmapped American land.

The Skrellings were probably terrified by the Vikings and their long ships. They must have been glad to see the intruders leave at last.

The Norsemen made no international claim to the area they had reached, and they made no permanent settlements. All traces of their visits to North America apparently disappeared. These facts explain why the Norsemen do not usually get credit for "discovering" America. Not until 1963 did remarkable excavations in Newfoundland turn up the remains of a Viking community.

It is fascinating to imagine what our country might have been like if the Norsemen had colonized permanently. They would have brought European civilization to this continent five hundred years earlier than it actually was introduced. Besides, how different the history of Europe might have been if Norway had been enriched by possessions in the New World!

1. By what path did Norsemen reach North America? 2. What parts may they have explored? 3. What facts explain why the Norsemen usually get no credit for discovering America? 4. What proof is there of Viking settlement on the continent?

#Another addition to the concept of what life in the United States is like.
##The author presents an American point of view here. Usually only the European one is given.
The questions here and elsewhere inside chapters are to help students review main facts only.

15

Columbus Unlocks the Atlantic Ocean

The knowledge of what the Norsemen had accomplished was either unknown or forgotten in most of Europe because other Europeans had no particular interest in wild grapes or colonization. They were interested in gold and spices and in doing the work of the Christian church—the work of saving souls. The idea of the world that most Europeans held did not include any land areas except Europe, Asia, and northern Africa.

Be sure "fifteenth century" is clear.

The Chinese Magnet

What the people of Europe knew about regions outside their own was exceedingly limited, and if their ideas were not simply wrong, they were somehow unbelievably vague in detail. For instance, as late as the middle of the fifteenth century, the king and queen of Spain believed that China was still ruled by the Khan kings of Mongolia. In fact, the Ming rulers had replaced them during the fourteenth century.

Communication from one distant area to another was entirely dependent on the occasional traveler and often took years to complete. It was so difficult that for any practical purpose parts of the world were not in touch with each other.

Immortal Marco. The principal ideas that educated people in Europe held about China were fashioned from *The Book of Ser Marco Polo*, which appeared at the end of the thirteenth century. In it Marco Polo, a man from Venice, told of a fabulous journey in his youth. With his father and uncle, who were merchants, he had traveled overland across Asia to both China and Japan.

Marco Polo's story was widely circulated in many versions. (Bear in mind that the trip took place about one hundred fifty years before the printing press was invented.) Undoubtedly it is the most influential adventure tale ever told.

The view Marco presented of untold wealth to be had in the East has never really left the minds of Western man. Marco talked not only of the accumulated treasures of the Grand Khan but also of an island that he called Cipangu (actually Japan), which, he said, contained a palace roofed with gold. He also described spice-producing islands rich beyond compare.

The dream of traveling to the East ever afterward inspired venturesome men, and many were sure it would be possible to go by sea. We shall never know how many and what kinds of schemes were thought up in order to reach the story lands of Marco Polo.

To reach the East, Marco Polo and his relatives took a long land route *east* across the vastness of Asia.

Several views of the Rand McNally Geophysical Globe are used in this book. This view shows the difficulty of overland routes to the East and the vast distances involved in traveling there by either land or sea.

The gatherers shown may have been people of India, who are dark-skinned Caucasians.

A picture from a French book about Marco Polo's travels: the artist showed Polo with Asian pepper gatherers as he imagined they might look.

Bibliothèque Nationale, Paris

How the world looked. We can, however, picture the map of the world that most western Europeans had in mind as the basis for their dreams. First of all, of course, the map did not contain the two American continents. Second, the map did not show the Pacific, and probably Europeans could not imagine an ocean twice the size of the Atlantic. Third, the map clearly showed that if one traveled westward from Spain, only a few islands would lie across the path to China—or, as it was called, Cathay. (Sailors of that day generally believed that the Atlantic was filled with dangerous and angry sea serpents which would make a voyage across it an unendurable torment.)

Of one thing European geographers of the fifteenth century were certain: the earth was shaped like a ball. This shape meant that, in theory, a ship sailing west might reach the fabulous East—an idea that grew and grew in its fascination for adventurous people.

In time men would want to test the belief by actually sailing west to find China and Japan. The results of the voyages would be enormous. Unknowingly these sailors would be raising the curtain on modern American history. In this period American Indians would have to make room, and then make way, for a new and mighty stream of immigrants.

Ho! for the East! By the middle of the fifteenth century the idea of an all-water route to the East was fascinating the monarchs of western Europe completely. Italian merchants who met Asian traders at the eastern end of the Mediterranean held the rich trade in Asian goods in their hands. These Italians made large profits by distributing to Europe the many products which wealthy European customers demanded from the East—silks, spices, and jewels.

The kings of the European nations bor-## dering the Atlantic envied the Italians and were resolved to buy the goods direct from the Asians. They wanted to send out their own ships and bypass the Italians.

European geographers of the fifteenth century believed that there were two ocean routes for reaching the East, which then meant India, China, and the East Indies. One ran southward along the west coast of Africa. It was assumed that if mariners could reach the southern tip of Africa, they could then sail eastward and reach India.

Henry the Navigator. Early in the fifteenth century Prince Henry of Portugal —known in history as the Navigator—began encouraging and supporting voyages in African waters. In 1488 the Portuguese seaman Bartholomeu Dias sailed around the Cape of Good Hope. But it was not until 1498 that a Portuguese navigator, Vasco

#The idea--often presented--that people of the 1400's believed the earth was flat is false.
##Use a globe or a world map to show how far these European nations were from the eastern end of the Mediterranean. See also the view of the Geophysical Globe on the next page.

17

Dias and Da Gama, unlike Marco Polo, tried to reach the East—in their case, India—by traveling *southward* around Africa.

Relate Portugal's early explorations to the fact that it has African possessions today.

when they sailed fairly close to the shore-line, as Da Gama's little fleet did. Of the 170 men who set out with Da Gama, only 44 lived to see their homeland again. The banks of the Tagus River, in Portugal, from which so many men departed never to return, became known as the shore of tears.

The fact that seamen called the Atlantic the Sea of Darkness tells us something of their feelings about sailing on it. Nevertheless, the challenge it offered overcame many brave men.

A Giant Italian

The desire to find China by traveling across the Atlantic attracted one Christopher Columbus, the son of a weaver in Genoa, Italy. He had read Marco Polo's book. Marco's journey overland, two centuries earlier, had taken over three years to make. Columbus decided that a trip by sea would be much shorter.

By 1474 a learned Italian physician, Paolo Toscanelli, had made a map which showed Asia to be only a few weeks' sail from Europe. According to it, Lisbon was about five thousand miles from the coast of China. (Actually, the distance by air is

da Gama, sailed from Lisbon and reached the port of Calicut, in India.

The Sea of Darkness. The other route to India was thought to lie due west from Portugal. Portuguese sailors had already traveled westward about a thousand miles into the Atlantic and had found the Azores. But nobody, so far as we know, had dared to continue onward into unknown waters.

Ocean voyagers lived dangerously even

The significant Mediterranean region from which the seafarers Dias, Da Gama, and Columbus set out on historic voyages to the East.

Modern Italian models of Columbus' fleet. *Left to right:* the *Niña,* the *Pinta,* and the *Santa Maria.*

about eleven thousand miles!) Finding out about this map, Columbus excitedly wrote to Toscanelli for more details. Toscanelli sent Columbus another of his maps and encouraged him to sail according to it.

At the Spanish court. But who would put up the money for an expedition to sail by such uncertain guides as Toscanelli's maps? The people Columbus approached in his native city turned him down, as did the king of Portugal. Columbus, whose wife had died, thereupon went to Spain with his five-year-old son. There he hoped to persuade King Ferdinand and Queen Isabella to approve and finance his grand plan.

Being absolutely certain that he was right, Columbus felt frustrated and angry when he was forced to wait six years for a definite decision. He had already headed for France in order to interest the French king in the project when the Spanish court called him back and gave him his opportunity. That decision turned out to be one of the supreme turning points in the history of man.

Anchors aweigh. Soon there was much activity in the tiny town of Palos, on the southern coast of Spain. There Columbus was assembling and equipping a fleet of three caravels, the *Niña,* the *Pinta,* and the *Santa Maria.* When it became known that he wanted to sail the Atlantic, he found it very hard to collect a crew. But a well-known, experienced sailor, Martín Alonso Pinzón, signed on. Then two of Pinzón's brothers agreed to come along.

As word spread that the Pinzóns were going to take a chance with Columbus, others joined, too. Gradually, a crew of ninety was assembled. Before dawn on August 3, 1492, the courageous and tense men weighed anchor and were on their way— into the Sea of Darkness.

The start of the voyage was not attended by public fanfare. The ships departed practically unnoticed. If the sailors were afraid, we do not know it. In any case, they were soon too busy to brood very much.

The little fleet made first for the Canary Islands, where it had to remain four weeks for repairs. Then it was off again, sailing briskly westward with favorable winds.

In those days it was impossible to do more than guess at the distances covered in a day. Columbus kept two records, a secret one for himself and one for his men to read. In this second record he understated the number of miles traveled, lest the men become discouraged and insist on returning home.

Days of doubt. As the days at sea grew in number, the impatience of the men increased. On at least one occasion a sailor shouted "Land, Ho!" and Columbus ordered all on board to give thanks to God on bended knees. But the "land" proved to be

#Use a globe to show the vast extent of the Atlantic and Pacific oceans. Let the class use the scale to measure Lisbon's distance <u>west</u> of the coast of China. Students should see how much this differs from Toscanelli's estimate. Columbus had a globe--without the Americas.

19

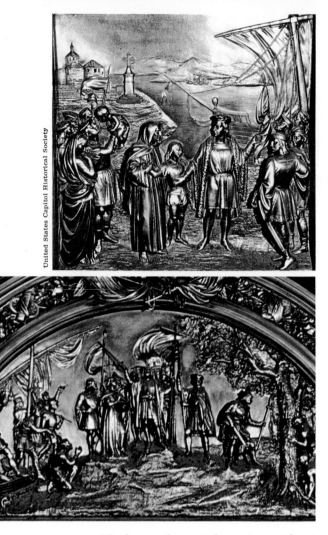

The bronze doors at the main east front entrance to our Capitol, in Washington, D.C., were designed by the American artist Randolph Rogers. The three scenes from the "Columbus doors" shown here are Columbus departing from Palos, his claiming of the new American land, and his return to Spain.

only imaginary in the sunlight, and the voyage continued. You can guess the questions that were now arising: Had Columbus been wrong from the first? Had the ships passed Cipangu without his being aware of it?

Columbus himself turned anxious and irritable, not only because his calculations seemed off but also because there was muttering among some of his men. They put pressure on him to turn back. They even threatened to throw him overboard.

Land! Land! On October 11 signs indicated that the ships were approaching land: branches of trees and shrubs could be observed floating in the water. The discontent quickly ceased. No one slept that night because the queen of Spain had offered a large reward to the first man who sighted land. His shout came at two o'clock on the morning of October 12, from aboard the *Pinta:* "Tierra! Tierra! Land! Land!"

The land was a little wooded island, with tropical trees. Later, amid shouts of joy and "Hallelujah," Columbus called it San Salvador—"Holy Savior."

Of course the people of San Salvador # had not been waiting for visitors to give *their* island a name. For nobody knows how long, they had been calling it "Guanahani." But the newcomers in time would overwhelm the people to whose land they were coming, and they would make the new name stick. Moreover, their historians would say that the men from Europe had discovered San Salvador.

As Columbus explored the island, his disappointment because he could find no Asians was very great. He recorded, though, that the people of the island, being friendly, could be taught the Gospel—and ## be made to work for the Europeans! Hoping still that the land would somehow turn out to be the Indies, he called the people Indians.

Disappointment. Columbus took several of the "Indians" with him to serve as

#Again, an American viewpoint is given.
##Another reference to the important fact that the Spaniards aimed to spread Christianity.

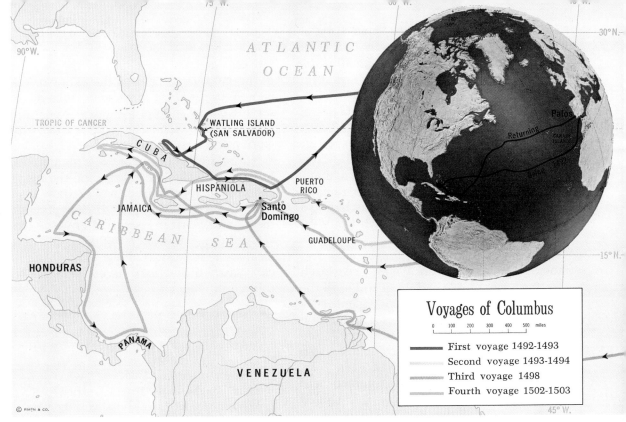

In *his* search for the East, Columbus turned *westward*, finding
a strange new world across the Atlantic Ocean.

guides to the area. They led him to the island now called Cuba. Here, as at San Salvador, Columbus was moved by the beauty
of the scenery. But his disappointment
deepened: he saw no brocades, no golden
rooftops, no ornaments of pearl, no precious jewels. In short, nothing matched
Marco Polo's description of China. For
three months Columbus searched the region—in vain, of course—looking for
signs that he had reached Asia.

Columbus concluded that he had found
the outlying islands of the continent of
Asia. He then set sail for the return trip
to his home port. On the way, one mishap
after another befell the expedition, and it
was forced to put in at the Portuguese port
of Lisbon.

At Lisbon Columbus half expected to be
imprisoned so his great secret would not
reach Spain. But the news had already arrived there.

Before long Columbus sailed into Palos,
laden with presents and remarkable tales
for Ferdinand and Isabella. They bestowed
on him the proud title "Admiral of the
Ocean Sea."

Other journeys. In the years following,
Columbus made three more voyages to the
New World. None could equal the first—
how could it?

On the four voyages Columbus had
found Cuba, Hispaniola, Puerto Rico, Jamaica, and portions of what are now Vene-
zuela, Honduras, and Panama. These
lands he declared until his dying day were
"another world," a part of China lying off
its shores.

Measuring the man. Privately Columbus'
sense of failure must have been keen.
He had never gazed upon the land he had
dreamed of seeing. Yet he regarded himself
as the greatest explorer who ever lived.
Considering his skill as a navigator, his

unyielding belief in the idea of an all-water route to the East, and the wide range of his travels, can anyone dispute him?

After Columbus, the grand hope of finding a way across the Atlantic to China persisted. Even though later explorers gradually outlined the map of the New World, unknown coasts long remained. Navigators continued to believe that one of the gaps in the outline surely was hiding a break in the mass of land which would be the road to China.

There was even a name for the gateway: the Strait of Anian (ăn ī′ ăn). The search for the Strait of Anian did not end until the last years of the eighteenth century—about the time that George Washington was serving as first president of the United States. By then the western and eastern coasts of North America had been fully mapped, and the first explorers had pushed across what is now the United States, reaching the Pacific Ocean.

Making a new America. In the three hundred years between 1492 and 1789, people from almost every country of west-ern Europe tried their luck in the forests, in the mountains, and on the plains of the New World. Their aims were mixed: to serve God, to enlarge the possessions and fame of their monarchs, and, not least, to glorify and enrich themselves.

Stimulated by these powerful motives, Europeans found the energy and the inspiration to adapt themselves to the new land they had happened upon. In the process, they—and Africans soon afterward—developed new habits, new outlooks, and new ideals. The result was a new kind of American, vastly different from any yet seen on this continent.

1. What man aroused special European interest in the East? How?   2. What caused western European kings to seek a new route to the East?   3. What seamen sought one around Africa?   4. Who succeeded?   5. What was the purpose of Columbus' first voyage?   6. Name parts of America he found then and later.

The Workshop

The Workshops in this text encourage thinking and the development of social-studies skills.

Many thought questions may be answered in a number of ways. Try to involve everybody.

The Shapers of Our World

Identify each of the following people and tell how each helped make the New World known to the Old World:

Eric the Red
Lucky Leif
Bjarni Herjulfsson
Bartholomeu Dias
Vasco da Gama
Thorvald

the Pinzóns
Ferdinand and
    Isabella
Toscanelli
Prince Henry
Marco Polo

Adding to Your Vocabulary

Be sure you know the meaning of the words at the top of the next column.

technology
geologists
Ice Age
culture

pueblo
sedentary
Strait of
    Anian

Thinking Things Through

After reviewing the chapter with the help of the boxed exercises within it, see if you can answer these questions:

1. Why was the beast of burden essential for human progress?

2. Why was technological change slower among Indians than among Europeans?

3. Why did Marco Polo's book stimulate interest in exploration?

Always ask students to identify the people named under "The Shapers of Our World" by relating eac to a major idea in the chapter. For example, it is as important to know that Marco Polo aroused new European interest in the East as that he traveled overland to East Asia, returning by sea.

4. Why were the Vikings probably the Europeans best suited to make their way to the unknown world?

5. Why did Portugal seem uninterested in Columbus' plan?

ortugal had found a new route to the East.

Geography and History

1. None of the Italian merchants from Venice and neighboring places took part in the exploration race of the fifteenth and sixteenth centuries. Why not?

2. Portugal was the first country to develop the southern route to the East. Why?

3. Most of the explorers who followed Columbus in examining the New World sailed up each river they came upon. Why?

4. Two large areas in Africa that remain possessions of Portugal are current topics in the news. Study a modern map of Africa and then name these colonies and explain how Portugal came to claim them.

The Research Center

Use the library or other sources of reference material to locate information called for below.

1. Tell about the civilization of the Vikings, especially their relations with western Europe. Why might the average citizen of England or France have refused to believe the Vikings even if they had told about their discoveries?

2. Report to the class about the Moslem conquest of Spain in the eighth century and the Spanish efforts to expel the Moors. Why was Spain unable to send out explorers earlier? How did the marriage of Ferdinand and Isabella mark the beginnings of the Spanish nation?

3. Divide the class into sections. Let each one choose a different group of North American Indians and describe its culture. Why were its members unable to resist the Europeans? Did they count too much on force of arms? Does the coming together of the Indian and European cultures in America hold any lessons for us today?

4. Prepare a meal in coöperation with your home economics teacher, using foods developed by the North American Indians.

5. Illustrate various aspects of Indian culture that helped the European newcomers. Make a bulletin-board display by drawing items that suggest aspects of European culture the Indians learned. Compare these with what the Indians taught the Europeans.

6. Read the description of the voyage of Columbus. Imagine that you were the official diarist of the journey. Choose one or more of the days listed below and write entries in your journal for that day. Relate the date to what was probably happening on board the *Santa Maria*.

   a. August 3, 1492
   b. August 24, 1492
   c. September 24, 1492
   d. October 11, 1492
   e. October 12, 1492

7. Much of what fifteenth-century Europeans thought about Asia was based on the stories of Marco Polo. Yet it was difficult for Columbus to recruit a crew because of the fears of a journey across the Atlantic.

Pretend you are a recruiter for Columbus and are asked to write an article for the local paper which will be read by prospective sailors. Tell the advantages of joining such an exciting undertaking.

The head "The Research Center" appears in many Workshops in the book in order to give students many opportunities to carry on the research they are capable of. Before assigning activities, be sure students are familiar with the methods and techniques called for. Dull reports kill interest fast.

23

(a)

(b)

(c)

(d)

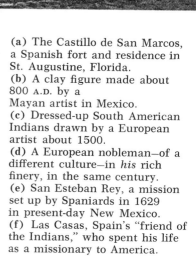

(e)

(f)

(a) The Castillo de San Marcos, a Spanish fort and residence in St. Augustine, Florida.
(b) A clay figure made about 800 A.D. by a Mayan artist in Mexico.
(c) Dressed-up South American Indians drawn by a European artist about 1500.
(d) A European nobleman—of a different culture—in *his* rich finery, in the same century.
(e) San Esteban Rey, a mission set up by Spaniards in 1629 in present-day New Mexico.
(f) Las Casas, Spain's "friend of the Indians," who spent his life as a missionary to America.

(g)

(h)

CHAPTER 2

UNDER THE SPANISH FLAG

ONE day we Earth people will make our way to another planet. It could be that this event will occur within our own lifetimes. The thrill and satisfaction for those who achieve this feat will be unimaginable. Possibly only then shall we appreciate the excitement and sense of novelty which western Europeans, and especially the Spanish, experienced because of their discoveries in the sixteenth century.

Mariners Reach Around the World

For several centuries after Columbus visited America, there was such ambitious exploration and adventuring on land and sea as had never been seen before. Behind the frenzied activity lay powerful forces.

The Push to America

One of the forces influencing exploration was the duty of introducing the Indians to Christianity. This work of "saving souls" was expected of faithful Catholics. The kings of Europe who sent out expeditions to the New World regarded converting the heathen as a personal obligation.

The second force was a fierce search for gold and silver. The same monarchs who were Christianizing the Indians thought that a country's power was measured by the amount of precious metals in its treasury. They hoped to be enriched by the mines of America. Furthermore, gold and silver were needed to pay for the products from the East because there was nothing else the Asians wanted from Europe.

We shall never know how many young people as well as grown-ups prayed, planned, and schemed to be the first to find the gold which no one doubted existed in the New World. So the kings in western Europe and their subjects alike wanted the joy and glory of discovery.

The navigators and explorers the monarchs employed were not all mere imitators of Columbus. Many had their own interesting theories and ideas about how to reach the "Indies," their name for the New World. (People did not begin to call it the

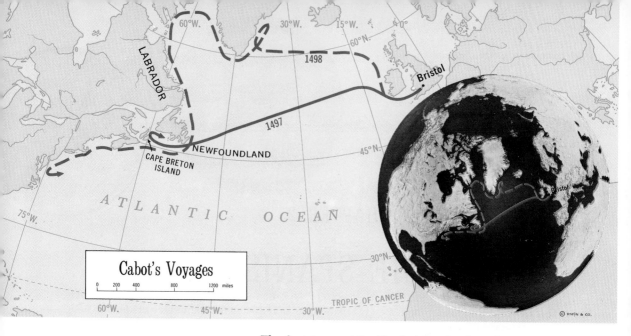

The first to cross the North Atlantic after the Vikings, Cabot gave England a claim to America, though Arctic ice doomed his hopes.

New World until the early part of the sixteenth century.) As they tested their notions, they widened man's knowledge of the earth.

Cabot's voyages. One of the seamen with an independent mind was John Cabot, like Columbus a native of Genoa, Italy. As a young man Cabot had worked in the spice trade in the city of Venice. He seems to have concluded that by sailing in a more

A map showing the eastern coast of North America made by Sebastian Cabot in 1544 and redrawn later. Cabot called the Atlantic the Oceanus Occidentalis—the "Western Sea."

J. G. Kohl, "History of the Discovery of Maine," Portland, 1869

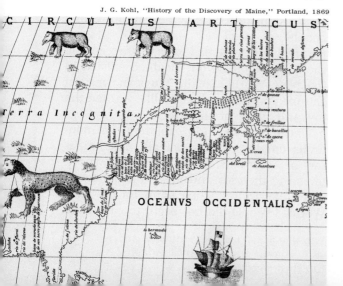

northwesterly direction than had Columbus, he could reach the source of the spices —the East Indies—cheaply and directly.

Cabot went to England, where he undertook a voyage of exploration for King Henry VII. Cabot persuaded the merchants of the seaport of Bristol that by putting them in direct touch with the spice markets of the East, he could make them rich. Cabot therefore joined together the merchants' interest in trade with King Henry's desire for gold.

A "newefounde" land. Accompanied by eighteen men, Cabot set sail aboard the little ship *Mathew* in the late spring of 1497. We do not know for certain where, or even if, he finally set foot on the west shore of the Atlantic. Some think he may have landed at Labrador, although possibly it was Newfoundland, for the British claimed it as their "newefounde land."

Cabot was a boastful fellow, but he never wrote about his discoveries. In the year 1498 he sailed again to North America. This time he was accompanied by his son Sebastian. The father never returned to Europe. Apparently he went down with his ship.

Students should compare Cabot's map with the one on pp. 542-543. He gave England claim to the East Coast.

So it happened that two Italian mariners —Columbus and Cabot—reached American soil, one on behalf of the king of Spain and one on behalf of the king of England. They were only the first of a long line of men who carried the Spanish and English banners to America. They had taken giant steps toward making the Spanish and English cultures, the Spanish and English ways of life, dominant in the new land.

We wondered in the last chapter what America would be like if the Norsemen had created permanent colonies (see page 15). We may also want to imagine what the history of the Western world might have been if Italians had settled in America first and had made American history an offshoot of Italian history.

Amerigo Vespucci. It was an Italian who gave a name—his own—to the new land. He was Amerigo Vespucci, of the city of Florence. Vespucci was sent to Seville, Spain, in 1492 as an agent for a banking firm. There he met many of the men directly involved in Columbus' voyages to the New World. He soon was aroused by the voyages of discovery, and he himself became an explorer.

A brilliant man, Vespucci found out on one of his voyages that what we call South America was in fact a new continent, not merely a part of Asia. In the year 1507 a German named Martin Waldseemüller published a little 52-page geography book. In it he wrote of three parts of the world: Europe, Asia, and Africa. Then he added:

Now another fourth part has been discovered by Amerigo Vespucci . . . and therefore I see no reason why we should not call it Amerige [that is, America] after its discoverer Amerigo.

But much remained to be learned about America. Waldseemüller, following the information he had learned from Vespucci, included a map in his book which showed South America as an island!

South America, the main scene of Vespucci's travels, was the continent first called America.

Balboa's Sea

Ask what new explorations Vespucci made.

Slowly the size of the New World was revealed. And people also learned how far from Asia it lay. The story of these revelations has many strands. Each is more dramatic than the next. One of the most important had a very unpromising beginning.

A redheaded stowaway. A group of Spaniards who settled on Hispaniola (today divided between Haiti and the Dominican Republic) sought gold on the coast of what is now Colombia. They not only found none but also had to send back for help: they were starving. A relief expedition of two ships was organized and set sail for South America. Aboard, hiding in a barrel as a stowaway, there was a redhaired Spanish planter who had settled on Hispaniola. This man, broke and in debt, was named Vasco Núñez de Balboa.

A few days out, Balboa announced his presence. The commander of the expedition at first threatened to abandon him on a lonely island but then generously forgave him. The vessels proceeded to what is now

Ask students why the "fourth part" of the world was not named Columbia or Vinland instead of America. Let them judge from the globe on this page what special contribution Vespucci made which justified at least in part the honoring of his name.

27

Balboa and his men, possibly at Darien, quarreling over gold objects— no doubt like those pictured on page 29— brought to them by the luckless Indians.

Theodore DeBry, "India Occidentalis," 1590 (New York Public Library)

Colombia, where they picked up the unfortunate colonists.

On the return trip the commander decided to head for the Isthmus of Panama in order to found a colony and to look around for the gold he had heard was there. (Does it have to be said that there was always a new rumor that this or that was *the* place to find gold?)

Deviltry at Darien. At the site of the new colony, Darien, the ungrateful Balboa seized the commander, clapped him into irons, and took over the expedition. Balboa, really a gentle man in a harsh age of history, got along well with the Indians, who became his good friends.

When Balboa told the Indians of his keen love for gold, they thought he was mad. But they told him where he could find it in quantities that would blind his eyes and sink his vessels. Pointing in the direction of what is now called Peru, they said the place could be reached by crossing the Isthmus of Panama at its narrowest point. They also told him of a "great sea" on the other side of the Isthmus. Balboa could not easily control his excitement, nor could one of his men, named Francisco Pizarro, whom we shall meet again shortly.

Across the Isthmus of Panama. In a very brief time Balboa fitted out an expedition and was on his way to Peru. With numerous Indian guides he made a 60-mile march across the Isthmus of Panama. The way was unimaginably difficult because of wild animals, strange fevers, rugged mountains, and dark jungles. Balboa made

Use the scale to find Balboa's mileage in crossing the Isthmus of Panama—chiefly a jungle.

Balboa's Travels
1501-1513

Relate the part of the New World Balboa explored to the location of the Panama Canal and the difficulties encountered in building it. Call attention to the closeness of the equator. Only areas of high elevation escape the heat.

his journey the story of a determination to conquer.

Despite the fact that his men died like flies, Balboa pressed on toward his goal. When he faced Indian enemies on the way, he turned on them the dozen ferocious dogs he had brought along. They could tear a man limb from limb and needed little encouragement in their work, which they performed often.

On the morning of September 25, 1513, Balboa and his companions climbed a hill, and suddenly for the first time, Europeans gazed upon the Pacific Ocean. (They called it the South Sea, because it lay south of the spot where they stood.) A few days later the trudging ended, and the weary, bedraggled explorers stood in a blazing sun on the shore of the vast ocean.

A sight never to be forgotten. Balboa put on his armor, fastened his buckler, and marched into the cool blue water up to his knees. Unfurling the banner of Spain, which he had carried with him for this heroic moment, he laid a claim for his country. In the name of his king, he took possession of "these seas and lands and coasts and ports and islands of the south . . . both now and in all times, as long as # the world endures, and unto the final day of judgment of all mankind."

What could Balboa's private thoughts have been? Do you think he believed that at last he had found the secret, that *this* was the sea that would lead to China— only a few days' journey away?

And what of the gold? Balboa never reached it. A few years later while preparing an expedition to Peru, Balboa was suddenly arrested on a charge of treason, convicted, and beheaded.

Magellan's Feat

#A typically extravagant claim.

Nations once reckoned their naval power on the basis of their ability to control the seaways. Consequently, in the late four-

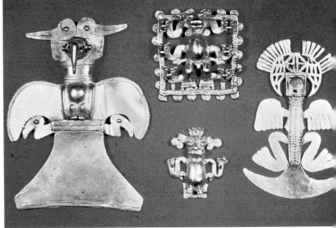

Museum of the American Indian

Indian artisans of what are now Colombia and Panama created these gold ornaments before 1492.

teenth century and in the fifteenth, maps of new routes across the oceans were carefully guarded lest they fall into the hands of a rival. Only a few selected navigators were allowed to see these charts and to study the sailing directions they contained.

In Portugal one of the favored seamen was Ferdinand Magellan. Tough and fearless, he had an astounding plan.

Westward to the East. Magellan had concluded that one could reach the East by sailing westward across the Atlantic and then across Balboa's ocean, too. Beyond that, if one were to continue traveling westward he could arrive at the coast of Africa, round it, and return to Portugal. In a word, it seemed possible to travel completely around the earth.

Calculations and miscalculations. We know Magellan was counting especially on a strait—a narrow water passageway—in the South American continent. Such a strait would allow him to sail easily from the Atlantic to the Pacific. Second, he was assuming that the distance across the Pacific was about six hundred miles.

Actually, from the west coast of South America to the Spice Islands (now the Moluccas), in the East Indies, it is almost twenty times six hundred miles. Mistaken ideas like Magellan's were corrected only by experience. Until they were tested, though, they sounded reasonable.

Ask how Magellan's idea was a development of the one Columbus had. What similar mistake did both men make? The class should measure a distance of 600 miles west of the west coast of South America and compare that distance with the true distance across the Pacific.

29

Magellan had a falling-out with the king of Portugal, who thereupon refused to support his plans for an expedition to sail westward. Not one to be put off, Magellan took his proposal and his knowledge to Portugal's rival, Spain. King Charles V of Spain gave him 5 ships and 270 men.

Magellan therefore switched loyalty in the great "cold war" of that day, between Portugal and Spain. (In 1494, shortly after the existence of the New World was discovered, Portugal and Spain by a treaty divided the world between themselves. They followed the recommendation of the reigning Pope. The map on page 39 shows that Spain acquired practically all of the New World. Portugal got Africa and India.)

With anxious hearts. The little fleet set forth on September 20, 1519. It was made up of not very good vessels manned by not very good sailors (mainly prisoners released to risk their lives on the oceans). It sailed first to the Canary Islands and then to the coast of Brazil. There it searched for the strait Magellan expected would lead into the Pacific.

Follow Magellan's route south around South America into the East Indies—after he crossed the Pacific—and the *Victoria*'s route southwest around Africa and then northwest back toward Spain.

Each day the voyagers failed to find the strait, they grew more anxious and fierce. Finally they decided to winter in what they later called Patagonia. The nervous strain among the men was building up nearly to the breaking point.

Outraged at Magellan and terrified that they might never return home, some of the crew organized a mutiny that was not smashed until Magellan had two of the ringleaders killed. He punished a third by leaving him behind when the ships took up the journey again in the spring.

In October some of Magellan's men discovered the strait which now bears his name. It took about five weeks for the vessels to wend their way through its dangerous, uncharted waters.

One ship, led by a man who was sure that Magellan did not know what he was doing, withdrew from the expedition and headed back to Spain. This departure endangered the entire undertaking, because the deserting ship carried most of the supplies for the other vessels, including food.

Suffering at sea. Nothing, though, could bend Magellan's iron courage. He refused to turn back, as many were now urging him to do. The only encouragement was that, after all, he had reached—and named —the Pacific, "the calm sea."

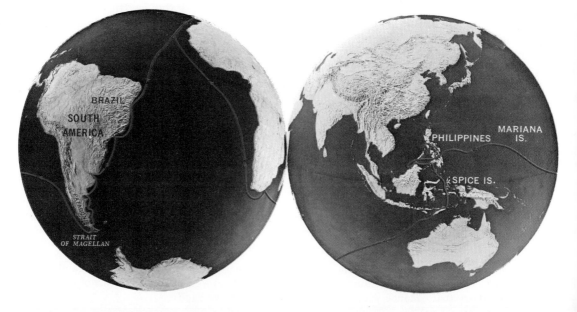

BRAZIL

SOUTH AMERICA

STRAIT OF MAGELLAN

PHILIPPINES

MARIANA IS.

SPICE IS.

A drawing of the Ladrones by one of Magellan's men. In the boat are Magellan and the artist.

The confidence of Magellan's crew was completely shattered as they sailed the Pacific. They sighted no land for two months, and for an even longer period they took on no new provisions. Their suffering both in mind and in body was intense. The drinking water spoiled, and food ran out. Many of the sailors became ill of scurvy— a disease caused by a lack of vitamin C— and hunger, and many died. The survivors were reduced to eating rats and the leather from the ship's rigging.

Finally the expedition reached the group of islands now called the Marianas. There the inhabitants stole so much of the sailors' equipment that they called the place the Ladrones—"the Islands of Thieves." Ten days later, on March 16, 1521, the crew reached the Philippines. There, the following month, Magellan was killed by some of the islanders in a battle that he had begun.

Success. Before Magellan died, he had the satisfaction of knowing that the Spice Islands—the object of all his struggle—lay only a few hundred miles to the south. The voyage continued without him, but his had been the skill and the merciless determination that assured its final success.

One vessel, the *Victoria*, leaking at every seam, finally returned to Spain in September, 1522. It bore the 18 survivors of the 270 men who had commenced this first voyage around the world. Its cargo of spices was so profitable it paid for the expenses of the whole trip.

History's applause. Magellan's contributions to our knowledge were immense, but they can be named simply. First of all, he established by actual experience that the earth is round. Second, he was able to show roughly the way in which the earth's surface is divided between land and water. Third, he found the route from the Atlantic into the Pacific.

---

1. Name two reasons for the continuing exploration of America after its discovery. 2. What was the result of Cabot's first voyage? 3. How did America get its name? 4. What did Balboa achieve? 5. Describe Magellan's route. 6. What did he accomplish?

Have the class sum up what Europeans knew about the world in 1515 which was unknown before.

Indian Empires Fall to the Invaders

The range of European sailors had now become worldwide. They found many lands and islands all over the earth, and in getting to know them and their inhabitants, they opened a new era for all human beings. Our principal concern is with America, where by far the most exciting events of all took place.

Cortés and His Horsemen

The earliest voyages of exploration had added to man's knowledge of some of the coastlines of the New World. Where, though, was the gold? Where indeed! A group of Spaniards who had raided Yuca-

refer students to the discussion of Indian cultures in the New World in Chapter 1. Ask what disadvantages the Indians would have in meeting the invasions of the Europeans. An important one is the Indians' lack of metal tools or weapons; another is the lack of horses.

31

tan, on the coast of what is now Mexico, turned up a clue. Upon returning to Cuba, they reported that they had seen Maya Indians wearing gold objects. The governor of Cuba, stirred by the possibility of large amounts of gold, took steps to go after it.

On the road to fame. The man the governor chose to win all of Mexico for Spain was Hernando Cortés, a thirty-four-year-old soldier and politician. Cortés could not know that he would earn undying fame as the greatest of the Spanish conquistadors, that is, the Spanish conquerors.

In February, 1519, Cortés, with only 700 men and 16 horses, set sail from Cuba on his mighty mission to the land of the Aztecs. The geographical obstacles—mountains, deserts, and tropical jungles—were forbidding, and they tested the Spaniards'

The Spaniards advanced over difficult country without good roads and without communications.

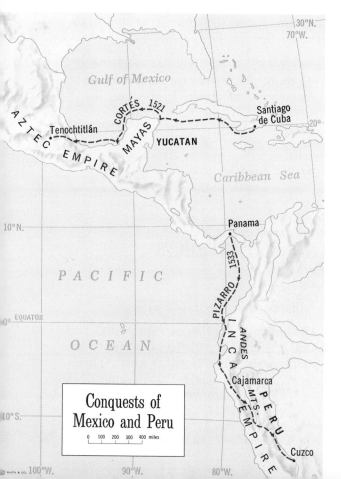

Conquests of
Mexico and Peru

0 100 200 300 400 miles

endurance. But the fearless Cortés provided leadership worthy of the challenge.

When the conquistador landed on the coast of Mexico on Good Friday in 1519, his mind and energies were focused on the gold he hoped to find. He drove himself as hard as he drove his men. He had the good luck to pick up a Spaniard named Aguilar. He had been cast away in Mexico seven or eight years before and had learned the tongue of the neighboring Mayas. Aguilar proved himself an excellent interpreter.##

Advantages. But Cortés' greatest assets were his horses and the superiority of his weapons. Can you picture the scene when the Spaniards thundered into sight? They were riding the first horses the Mayas had ever seen, firing cannons, and wearing armor that turned the Indians' arrows as if they were toothpicks. Cortés himself wrote: ". . . it seems to me that the Indians are terrified at the horses and may think they and the cannon make war on them by themselves."

The Spanish force was joined by an Indian princess, named Marina, who knew both the Aztec and the Mayan languages. She was able to translate Aztec into Mayan, and Aguilar, the interpreter, would then put the Mayan into Spanish. In this way, communication was carried on.

Return of the gods. Cortés had another extraordinary advantage serving him. The Aztecs believed that, long before, their land had been ruled over by a fair-skinned god called Quetzalcoatl (kĕt säl' kô ä' tl), who, although kind and good, had been driven out. At the time he sailed away, Quetzalcoatl prophesied he would return to punish the country in the first year of one of the 52-year subdivisions of the Mexican calendar. The year 1519 was such a year!

The Aztec king, Montezuma, was overcome with fright at the news of the arrival of the strangers. They must surely be the god Quetzalcoatl and his companions! Montezuma sent artists to sketch pictures of the newcomers. Cortés made sure that his horses were always mounted when the artists were about. He wanted Montezuma to hear that some of the visitors had the head and shoulders of a man and the body of a four-legged animal.

Montezuma's fears increased by the minute as he thought about the arrival of the "gods." But many Mexicans were overjoyed and looked to Cortés to liberate them # from Montezuma's tyranny. Before long Indians in large numbers were flocking in to join Cortés in an attack on the capital city, Tenochtitlán (tä nŏch tē tlän′). Tenochtitlán is now Mexico City.

Capture of Montezuma. By a trick in which he made believe he was a friend, Cortés took Montezuma prisoner. Montezuma still seems to have thought that Cortés and his men were gods. But some of the Indians became aware of the truth. In fact, one of the "divine" horses was killed and its body seized.

As the Aztec warriors gathered threateningly about Cortés' army, Cortés forced Montezuma to address them in order to calm them down. Montezuma's own people now saw that their king was a fool, and they stoned him to death. Having thus disposed of one source of misery, they attacked the Spaniards and drove them off.

But the Aztecs had not reckoned with Cortés. He reorganized his forces outside the city, gained new followers among the Indians, and returned to lay siege to the town. Finally, exhausted and starved, the Aztecs surrendered to Cortés, and in triumph he entered Tenochtitlán on August 13, 1521.

Some explanations. Naturally one asks, How did a mere handful of invaders so easily inflict such a defeat on the Indians and

Right: Drawings of the coming of Cortés to Mexico by Indian artists of the time. *Top:* Montezuma, seated at left, meets Cortés. *Middle:* Spaniards attack Montezuma's Great Temple. *Bottom:* Europeans—in gray—fight Aztecs.

"Codex Lienzo de Tlaxcalla" (American Museum of Natural History)

#The Aztecs ruled neighboring tribes which they had been able to conquer. The feelings of these tribes might be compared with those of eastern Europeans today who would like to win their freedom from the Soviet Union.

take over the country? The most important reason was that the Spanish weapons were enormously superior.

But there is another explanation, too. The very loose political organization of the Aztec people made them weak. The Aztecs lived in a group of quarreling city-states. One city, Tenochtitlán, became more powerful than the others in the early fifteenth century, but it never succeeded in bringing its rivals under tight control.

The Spanish conquered Mexico because its people had neither the means to fight back nor the leadership to persuade them to try. In a short time the fabulous riches Cortés was shipping home to Spain lured other countrymen to seek fame and fortune in the area of the Gulf of Mexico.

Pizarro Against the Incas

In the whole story of the Spanish explorations of the New World, no one was more bent on finding gold than Francisco Pizarro. An ignorant man, he had dreamed of little else since his days with Balboa, when he had first heard of the Inca Indians in Peru. He organized two expeditions to reach them and each time failed. Then in 1531 he set out once again from Panama with 3 ships, 180 men, and 27 horses.

In the Andes. After reaching Peru, Pizarro slowly made his way through the Andes Mountains. He was permitted to do so because he declared himself to be a friend anxious to help the Incas establish good relations with the king of Spain. At last he arrived at the home of the emperor, Atahualpa (ä′ tä wäl′ pä). As the Spaniards gazed down from the mountains at the teeming army of the Incas, they realized that to triumph over these people required the capture of their emperor.

A tricked emperor. Atahualpa, having agreed to visit Pizarro for a conference, was carried on a golden throne into the Spaniard's presence. It appeared that only a Spanish priest and an Indian interpreter were there to greet the Inca emperor and the four thousand men who accompanied him. But hiding all about were Pizarro and his greedy followers.

At a prepared signal Pizarro's men rushed out, cannons booming and horses' hooves flying. In a little while, as the Spaniards charged, swords in hands, hordes of Inca warriors lay dead, and Atahualpa was the prisoner of Pizarro. Not a single Spanish soldier had been lost! In this way the Spanish conquered the Inca capital, Cuzco, in 1533. They then fanned out over the countryside, seizing all the gold they could locate. They did not have

These illustrations strengthen the concept of the importance of technology.

European technology helped conquer the American Indians. *Left:* Cortés, splendid in armor, as the Indians of Mexico may have seen him. *Right:* Cortés' own gun, used against the Aztecs.

Justin Winsor, "Narrative and Critical History of America," Houghton Mifflin and Co., 1886

United States Naval Academy Museum

far to look, for the mines of Peru had been well worked by the Incas and were easily found.

Pizarro even turned Atahualpa into gold, so to speak. He conceived the idea of asking the Inca people to ransom their ruler by providing enough gold to fill the large room where the emperor was imprisoned. Atahualpa's countrymen responded nobly, and the gold flowed in a torrent into Spanish hands. In modern money it was worth untold millions of dollars.

The end of Atahualpa. But the conquerors were still not satisfied. Accusing Atahualpa of conspiring to influence his supporters to revolt, Pizarro put him on trial for his life and had him killed.

Why? Although the Indians continued from time to time to resist the Spanish conquerors, only the most hopeful among them believed that the invaders would soon go away. No other such great, well-run empire had ever been taken in so short a time, with so little struggle.

One explanation is that the empire was gravely weakened in the year 1527 by a dispute over who should be ruler. The empire may have been paralyzed by this crisis just at the moment when Pizarro was approaching. The paralysis was exceedingly bad luck or good luck, depending on whether you see it from the Spanish or the Inca point of view.

Moreover, as in the conquest of the Aztecs, Inca arms were no match for the Spanish. There is reason to think, also, that smallpox was partly responsible for the collapse of the Inca Empire, since an epidemic was raging about the time Pizarro arrived. (Europeans had already developed some immunity to the disease.)

North of the Rio Grande

After the Norsemen, the first European known to have set foot on what still later arrivals would call the United States was a Spanish official named Juan Ponce de León. As governor of Puerto Rico, where he made a fortune in gold and slaves, he heard from the Indians of a fabulously rich island to the north called Bimini.

Florida. Deciding to make Bimini his own, De León sailed north from Puerto Rico on March 3, 1513. A few weeks later he landed on the Florida peninsula near where the town of St. Augustine now stands. Because it was the Easter season, he named the land *Pascua Florida,* the Spanish words for Easter.

After exploring the area, De León returned to Puerto Rico. He then journeyed to Spain, where the king authorized him to conquer and colonize Florida. After a number of delays he reached Florida again, only to be killed by Indians. Little could anyone know that when the Spanish began to build St. Augustine in 1565, it would ## one day be the United States' oldest city.

A fountain of youth. Originally Ponce de León had been persuaded to seek Bimini by a tale he had heard. According to the story, a spring whose waters made eternally young all those who drank them flowed through Bimini. De León was the first of millions of people who have arrived on American shores thinking they might find a way to start their lives all over again.

Cabeza de Vaca. Another royal official tempted by the area north of Mexico was Cabeza de Vaca. He arrived in Florida from Spain in 1528 as a member of an exploring expedition. After several of its ships had been lost in the Gulf of Mexico, Cabeza de Vaca found himself shipwrecked on the coast of present-day Texas.

Setting out overland, the Spaniard probably traveled through what are now New Mexico, Arizona, and Texas. Then he turned and proceeded to Mexico City. In 1537 he sailed back to Spain. He was the first Spaniard to cross the continent of North America—a distance of three thousand miles.

Students should turn to the map on p. 37 as they read about each explorer mentioned in this section.   35
See also Exercise 5 under "Sharpening Your Map Skills" on p. 43.
Refer to picture <u>a</u> on p. 24.   A student might report on the history of St. Augustine.

Cabeza de Vaca, home at last, kept anyone who would pay attention—and listeners were not hard to find—wide-eyed with stories of the huge continent he had explored. He must have awed them with his accounts of the buffalo he had seen and the Indian pueblos he had examined. He probably also bragged that gold no doubt could be found in abundance—although he had found none.

The "Seven Cities." One of those aroused to organize an expedition was Hernando de Soto, who had been with Pizarro in Peru. He had been given permission by the king of Spain to explore what was called Florida —which at that time meant the huge area that is today roughly the southeastern part of the United States.

Below, top: Cabeza de Vaca may have seen pueblos like these of our time at Taos, New Mexico. *Bottom:* The earliest drawing of an American buffalo, done by a European for Europeans.

New Mexico State Tourist Bureau

Louis Hennepin, "Voyage de L'Amerique," London, 1697 (Chicago Historical Society)

De Soto was sure he could find the place that was holding the rapt attention of Spaniards in Spain. These were the so-called Seven Cities of Cibola (sē′ bŏ lä). Probably the tales of their existence grew out of exaggerations of Cabeza de Vaca's account of the pueblos.

The "Seven Cities," the legend had it, had been founded centuries before by seven Portuguese bishops who had fled to the New World when their country was overrun by invaders. The exiles were believed to have settled on an island. In time rumor spread that they were not situated on an island after all but were somewhere in the vast land north of Mexico.

The quest for the "Seven Cities" was a strong spur to the exploration of what is now the American Southwest. Among the conquistadors the talk about the "Seven Cities" raised the hope of finding another Indian kingdom like Peru or Mexico. The only requirements for taking its "golden" cities would be energy and zeal.

De Soto's river. Landing in 1539 probably at present-day Tampa Bay, Florida, De Soto set out to discover gold, silver, and jewels. In his long and fruitless search he was in what are now Georgia, the Carolinas, Tennessee, and Alabama.

In 1541, in his wild quest, De Soto crossed the Mississippi River (probably not far south of what became Memphis, Tennessee). He and his men were likely the first Europeans to set eyes on the incomparable Father of Waters. But they were not interested: they could hardly wait to get to the other side.

Onward De Soto and his men pressed, up the Arkansas River and into present-day Oklahoma. But—no luck. Discouraged at not finding the "Seven Cities," they returned to the Mississippi, where De Soto died. He was buried in the mighty river he had regarded simply as a great obstacle.

Coronado's march. A brave and ambitious Spaniard, Francisco Vásquez de Coro-

The map labels:
GRAND CANYON, GREAT PLAINS, Kansas R., Arkansas R., Mississippi R., Rio Grande, De Soto Died, Wreck with Narváez, Tampa Bay, FLORIDA, St. Augustine 1565, ATLANTIC OCEAN, GULF OF MEXICO, TROPIC OF CANCER, CUBA, HISPANIOLA, PUERTO RICO, GUADELOUPE, PACIFIC OCEAN, Mexico City, 70°W, 60°W, 30°N, 20°N, 10°N, 110°W, 100°W, 90°W, 80°W

The Spanish Turn North

0 100 200 300 400 500 miles

—— De León 1513   - - - De Vaca 1536
—— Coronado 1542   —— De Soto 1542

Cabeza de Vaca accompanied Narváez.

By exploring land now part of the United States, the Spanish widened a claim to the New World which they held for centuries.

nado, undertook in 1540 to lead another expedition to conquer the "Seven Cities." Nattily dressed in bright velvets, Coronado's men set out from Mexico with high hopes. They soon learned the truth: the heat and hardships of the journey would fade the colors and tear the clothes, and the "few days' journey" would stretch into years.

An explorer named Estevanico (Little Stephen), a Negro, guided Coronado's advance party. Estevanico had been on the expedition of Cabeza de Vaca years before. After sending reports to Coronado as he neared what he thought were the "Seven Cities," he was killed by the Indians. Although he became the most famed Negro explorer of the New World, he was not the only one. Negroes accompanied Balboa, De León, Cortés, and Pizarro.

The fabled cities proved, of course, to be the pueblos of the Zuñi Indians of present-day New Mexico. It was no comfort and of little interest to Coronado that some of his men had gazed at the awesome Grand Canyon. (It is one of the most spectacular sights in the world.)

Coronado wintered on the banks of the Rio Grande. During this layover he met a slave of the Pueblo Indians—a man the Spanish nicknamed the Turk because of his appearance. The Turk told Coronado that the "Seven Cities" were in fact in his country, a place called Quivira.

In Quivira, the Turk reported, a chief lord took his afternoon nap under a great tree on which were hung little gold bells. They put him to sleep as, tinkling, they swung in the air. The Turk added that, of course, everyone in the country ate out of golden bowls and drank from golden jugs.

On the way to Quivira, with hopes high again, Coronado and his men gazed upon the vast herds of buffalo that inhabited the Great Plains. Each herd consisted of thousands, maybe hundreds of thousands, of animals. For miles and miles the explorers could see "nothing but cows and sky." Of course, they were struck by the grandeur of the landscape. "When a man sits down," they said, "the horizon surrounds him all around at a distance of a musket shot."

At Quivira. Alas, when the Spaniards reached Quivira, it proved to be nothing

#The term "Great Plains" occurs again and again in American history. Make sure that students know it is the sloping plateau about 400 miles wide bordering the eastern base of the Rockies, extending from inside Canada into Mexico. Too dry to be forested, it is an area of short grass.

37

Ask students to point out the mistakes on this map. These mistakes were important, because people believed them.

Even after Coronado found out the truth about the "Seven Cities," people clung to the story. Count the cities on this 1578 map of Spanish possessions in what is today the United States.

more than a collection of huts thatched with grass, on what is now called the Kansas River. The chief of the Indians who had built the huts wore around his neck a large plate, not of gold but of copper. Little did Coronado and his men know that in this region they had had a look at what would become part of the richest wheat-growing region in the world. They turned wearily back to Mexico City, which they reached in 1542.

Put yourself in the place of the Spaniards and you, too, would probably have regarded the region as worthless. The thought of the effort required to make this area habitable must have sunk the explorers' spirits. There simply were not enough Spaniards to occupy such a vast land and make it valuable.

1. For what event is Cortés remembered? 2. What Indians were involved? 3. What territory did Cortés win? 4. What other benefits did he bring Spain? 5. What area did Pizarro acquire for Spain? How? 6. What lands did the Spanish claim as a result of the explorations of De León? Of Cabeza de Vaca? Of Coronado?

Museum of the American Indian

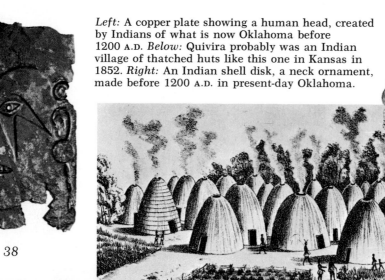

Left: A copper plate showing a human head, created by Indians of what is now Oklahoma before 1200 A.D. *Below:* Quivira probably was an Indian village of thatched huts like this one in Kansas in 1852. *Right:* An Indian shell disk, a neck ornament, made before 1200 A.D. in present-day Oklahoma.

Museum of the American Indian

Smithsonian Institution

38

New Spain Creates a Rich Heritage

After 1543, that is, after Coronado's great journey, the Spanish continued to explore the New World. But the novelty of exploration was beginning to wear off. Besides, the Indians were becoming acquainted with Spanish ways and were beginning to resist the invaders.

Earlier, when Cortés left behind an injured horse at one point on his march, the Indians respectfully fed it flowers. After it died, they worshiped a statue of it. Yet within thirty years, horses were roaming wild in ever increasing numbers. Their use by the Indians tended to make the rivalry with the Spanish less unequal.

Controlling the Conquered

Facing often hostile Indians and lacking man power, the Spanish found it difficult to explore and settle the huge areas of land they claimed. Their domain, called New Spain, is shown on the map on this page. As you see, it extended from what is now the central part of the United States along almost the entire west coast of South America. This vast empire was ruled by two viceroys—that is, representatives of the king. One headed the Viceroyalty of New Spain (its capital was Mexico City), and the other, the Viceroyalty of Peru (its capital was Lima).

But despite the vastness of the empire, two things encouraged further exploration and settlement. The first was the discovery of precious metals in the mountains of North America, beginning in the 1530's. The effect was that frenzied searchers eagerly went into what seemed to be out-of-the-way and unattractive regions to look for valued gold and silver.

The second was the zeal of missionaries, which spread Spaniards into the interior of

the New World. In the sixteenth and seventeenth centuries Roman Catholic leaders in Europe began a new crusade—a vigorous movement—to save souls.

The friars. Courageously and unceasingly, friars of the Jesuit, Dominican, and Franciscan religious orders took Christianity even to the outer edge of Spanish areas. Sometimes they paid for their religious devotion with their lives. Nevertheless, they established the Roman Catholic faith permanently in parts of America.

Mining the precious ores and building the missions that conversion to Christianity seemed to require called for huge quantities of labor. Sufficient workers, however, were just not available. The burden on the Indians was very heavy.

Unfree men. The Indians must have had

New Spain was safely in the area assigned to Spain by the Pope in 1494. What part of the New World fell to Portugal?

Spanish Viceroyalties

0   500   1000 miles

mixed feelings about the Spanish invaders. They must have wished sometimes with all their hearts that the Europeans would go away. On the other hand, the Indians wanted some of the things the newcomers could provide, particularly items like iron, steel, mules, and horses. The price they had to pay for them, though, was often being forced to play the everlasting role of underdog.

Of course, the Spanish contribution in return was very considerable. There is no question that the Spanish aimed to "civilize" the Indians as well as profit from them. Yet "civilizing" the Indians too often meant merely getting them to work.

The encomenderos. Spanish *encomenderos* (ĕn' kŏ mĕn dā' rōs), or royal favorites, were given charge of large groups of Indians—between fifty and a hundred per group. These Spanish lords were responsible for teaching the Indians the Catholic faith and putting them to work.

The labor the Indians had to perform changed their way of life greatly. While working for months at a time in the mines or on the building of roads or on the clearing of land, they were separated from their families. Moreover, in giving up their own ways of farming in order to work for the Spanish, the Indians became more or less dependent on the Europeans.

Infants died at a very high rate, and in general the death rate among Indians rose. Epidemics, particularly of smallpox and measles, carried off large numbers.

The Spanish were affected by their contact with the Indians, too. They fell into the habit of refusing to work with their hands—a usual vice of conquerors. It was said that the Indians "do work so cheape that poore young men that go out of Spain to get their living are not set on worke." Bad feeling developed between the workers and those who looked on as masters.

The great Las Casas. One of the greatest Spanish missionaries, though, was also one of history's greathearted humanitarians. He was Bartolomé de Las Casas, known as the Apostle of the Indies. Beginning in 1514, he was trying to improve the treatment of the Indians. He devoted almost all of his long life to this cause.

As early as 1501, when the Indian population declined as a result of a variety of hardships, the Spanish began to import African slaves to do the work. After the mines in the West Indies were played out, the Negroes became the labor force operating the sugar plantations which the Spanish developed there.

Africans proved useful in agriculture. Unlike the Indians, Africans had had experience with metal tools and weapons for centuries. African men themselves were skilled farmers, not leaving this important work to the women.

The asiento. Between 1550 and 1750 at least three thousand slaves a year were imported under a contract called an *asiento*, awarded by the Spanish king. The *asiento* was a valuable right hotly competed for. The death rate of the Africans was very high, not only on the ocean crossing but after landing, too.

Slavery never became widespread in Spanish possessions outside the sugar islands in the Caribbean. Elsewhere in Spanish colonies the owning of slaves was chiefly a mark of luxury, enjoyed by the well-to-do.

Slavery. Despite the harshness of slave life, a Spanish slave could, if he wanted to, seek to persuade another Spaniard to purchase him—possibly one who was kinder than his present master. He could choose his own wife, buy his freedom at the lowest going price for a slave, and buy his wife and children. He could sue in the courts of law.

But there is no intention to paint a rosy picture of conditions under Spanish slavery. Physically the slaves were often neglected. It has sometimes been said a

Spaniard was more concerned with how—or if—his slaves said their prayers than with whether they had enough food and clothing.

The Spaniards were, it would turn out, only the first to wrestle with the problem of finding a supply of labor in the New World. They never found a way of getting enough hands for their undertakings. We shall see that the English and French found solutions that were different.

Crisscross of Cultures

The Spanish took the first steps in Europeanizing America. They did more than merely take advantage of the Indians. # They taught them the Spanish language and literature, Roman Catholic prayers, and the Roman Catholic catechism, and they showed them how to farm in European fashion.

Missions. The training was carried on in mission establishments in a vast region extending from what are now California and Texas on the north to present-day Chile on the south. A *mission* was an educational, religious, and social center. Sometimes it was useful for defense purposes, too. Missions often began as little chapels in the wilderness, conducted by friars wearing sandals and sackcloth gowns. Some of these humble structures later were added to or rebuilt to become architectural masterpieces.

As each mission expanded its work, it became the center around which a Spanish village grew. A new mission was then built at the edge of the wilderness, and the same slow, tiresome process was repeated. In this way the Indian culture, inch by inch, it seemed, gave ground to the Spanish.

The people of New Spain. Life in New Spain was based from the start on *inequality*—a result of the way in which the region was conquered and settled. The Spanish Empire contained Americans of Spanish ancestry, Americans of African ancestry, and descendants of the Indians. For centuries those of European origin would maintain themselves as the rulers and masters of the others.

A lasting heritage. So the Spanish placed the deep stamp of their culture on the New World. It can be seen in California, in our Southwest, and in the vast area south of what is now the United States—known as Latin America. Whatever changes come to pass in Latin America now or in the future

Directly below: Franciscan friars preaching and teaching, baptizing infants, and hearing confessions in Central America about 1650. *Left:* An early drawing of the Mission San Carlos, still in existence on the central coast of California.

Cordoba y Salinas, "Coronica de la religiosissima provincia de los doze apostoles del Peru . . . ," Lima, 1651 (New York Public Library)

Alexander Forbes, Esq., "California: A History of Upper and Lower California," London, 1839 (Newberry Library)

will be built on strong foundations established by the Spaniards.

The intertwining of history. From the first instant that the Spaniards arrived in the New World, America and Europe were destined to be altered by each other. The two streams of history they represented would never flow separately again.

The slow linking of the various parts of the world had long been going on. Major events in this process, but only one example, were the Crusades. These were the "holy wars" in the Middle East fought by European Christians to free Jerusalem from followers of Mohammed's teachings. These struggles took place on and off from the eleventh century to the thirteenth.

The Crusades taught the Spaniards and other Europeans new skills at waging war. The crusaders learned methods of attack which few other people in the world—possibly only the Japanese—could match. So it was that the history of Europe and the Middle East affected the way in which conquistadors, wearing armor and carrying destructive halberds (two-handed swords), faced American Indians.

In similar fashion the influence of America affected Europe and Asia. Within a century the introduction of new American foods like maize, white potatoes, and sweet potatoes helped bring about a growth of population in both places. And the flow of much American gold and silver to Europe raised prices there, while wages, which were fixed by age-old custom, remained unchanged.

Consequently, not only was the number of Europeans growing, but also for many of them dissatisfaction with life was increasing. Such people no longer had to be without hope. The New World, inviting and fruitful, seemed to beckon to them. #

#The author adds to the concept of America.

---

1. Describe the extent of New Spain. Who ruled New Spain? 2. What contributions did the Spanish make to the Indians of America? 3. What disadvantages did the Spanish conquest bring to Indians? 4. When were Negroes first brought to America? Why? 5. What were missions? 6. What lasting heritage did the Spanish leave behind them in America?

The Workshop

conquer large parts of it, and transplant their culture to it. Each person listed should be seen as a link between the Old and New worlds.

The Shapers of Our World

Each of the following helped to link the Old World and the New World. Identify and explain the significance of:

Cabot
Balboa
Magellan
Victoria
Cortés
Pizarro
Coronado
conquistador

Montezuma
Atahualpa
De León
St. Augustine
Cabeza de Vaca
De Soto
"Seven Cities
    of Cibola"

encomendero
asiento
mission
Aguilar
Quivira
Waldseemüller

Las Casas
Marina
viceroyalty
Quetzalcoatl
Spice Islands

Thinking Things Through

After reviewing by means of the boxed exercises in the chapter, explain the whys of history called for here:

1. Why did the Indians usually tell a Spanish explorer that the object of his

Activities to help students learn how to do research were introduced in the first Workshop. Activities to help them develop two other social-studies skills are introduced in this one--map skills (being able to use map scales and to compare maps) and discussion skills.

search was just a few miles farther on? How does this practice help account for the wanderings of the Spanish explorers?

2. Why is trade the "mother of exploration"? Show how the Crusades, the journey of Marco Polo, and the voyages of Columbus and Cabot are all part of the same story.

3. Why did Columbus not receive credit for the discovery of the New World? What geographical feature of the New World tied Vespucci's name to two continents?

4. In only one large country of South America is the official language not Spanish, but Portuguese. Why?

##5. The sixteenth century is called Spain's Golden Age. Why?

6. Although the conquistadors explored great areas of the New World, it is often said that the real heroes of Spanish colonization of the New World were the "priest and the private." Why?

Sharpening Your Map Skills

1. Referring to the map on page 21 and the maps in this chapter showing Spanish explorations, tell approximately in what latitudes—north and south—the Spanish claims in America lay. What geographical conditions made Spanish settlement of their land difficult?

2. Compare the map on page 37 with a map of the United States today. Through what present-day states did each explorer pass?

3. Also, compare the map on page 39 with a map of modern Latin America. List the independent countries today that were formed from each of the viceroyalties.

4. In what way did Magellan's voyage fulfill the dream of Columbus? How can Soviet Yuri Gagarin's feat in April, 1962, be compared with Magellan's?

5. Using the scale on the map on page 37, figure about how far De Soto and Coronado traveled in North America. Considering the facts that they moved by foot and on horseback and that the land covered was wilderness, what do you conclude about the men's ambitions and strength?

The Art of Discussion

1. The Spanish were responsible for a number of firsts in the New World. Choose one of these firsts and use the library to prepare a report on it for the class. Remember to keep the report interesting to the listeners. Perhaps you can find some means to illustrate it. Tell about one of these:
   a. The first hospital
   b. The first university
   c. The first printing press
   d. The first city government
   e. The first Negro slaves

2. The missions helped bring Spanish culture to the Indians. A group of students might present to the class a discussion of the California missions. One student might collect pictures of the missions, another might build a model of a typical mission, and another might display samples of mission farm products. Possible topics for oral presentation are:
   a. Junípero Serra
   b. Mission education
   c. Mission agriculture
   d. Mission architecture
   e. Mission Indians
   f. The romance of the missions
      (the swallows at San Juan Capistrano, the book *Ramona*, etc.)

##It was the period when American gold was enriching Spain. The famous Spanish artists--El Greco, Murillo, and Velásquez--were painting their pictures, and the king built his new royal residence, the Escorial. Without the gold Spain would have had no Golden Age.

(a) A stone pipe (the mouthpiece is on the head) made by Indians about two hundred years ago in what is now Ohio, land once French.

(b) An American beaver, the delight of fur traders, sketched by a French artist.

(c) Quebec today, overlooking the St. Lawrence River, where Frenchmen settled in 1608 and where French is now a native language.

(d) The even earlier French colony of Port Royal, in what is now Nova Scotia, as drawn by one of the settlers.

(e) An astrolabe, an astronomical instrument that was part of the technology of European navigators. This one was lost in America by Champlain and was not found until 1867.

(f) A drawing of the arrival of Cartier—the earliest French explorer of America—and his companions, printed on a map in 1546.

(g) French fishermen sailed to America to catch codfish.
(h) La Salle, a French explorer of North America, as seen by an artist of his own time.

(h)

(g)

CHAPTER 3

THE FRENCH EXPERIMENT

This chapter is shorter than the preceding one, because French influence on America--especially on the part that became our country--was not as great as Spanish. French culture has survived chiefly in the province of Quebec, Canada. Before beginning this chapter, review the extent of Spanish claims in both North and South America and in the Caribbean.

BEFORE the fifteenth century ended, modern European nations began to form and rivalries among them developed. Their rivalries were sometimes between jealous monarchs, sometimes between their merchants, and occasionally even between their artists and sculptors. Gradually the race to gain wealth in America became the most important of all the contests. It was something like the race in our own day to reach the moon or the planets ahead of one's rivals.

Let the class study the pictures on this and the opposite pages. Ask what is suggested.

King Francis Points Toward America

France lagged only a little bit behind Spain, Portugal, and England in sending explorers to the New World. Under the leadership of the bold, fun-loving King Francis I, who was crowned in 1515, the French found themselves in the thick of the race.

A picture of the Verrazano bridge could introduce this section.

Verrazano and Cartier

France's mariners came from two
French coastal towns in particular: Dieppe and St. Malo. There, as at Genoa or Bristol or along the Tagus River, men looked out on the sea. They enjoyed dreams which took them to new lands and to new opportunities on the other side of the horizon.

Newfoundland fisheries. Some of the fishermen of the French towns became active along the fishing banks of Newfoundland shortly after Cabot first went there. In time Newfoundland codfish became an important part of France's food supply. Consequently, the French turned their attention more and more to the New World. They soon became aware of the possibilities which lay inland.

Off the coast of North Carolina. One remarkable event always seems to suggest another to match or surpass it. Not long

#These places are shown on the map, p. 47. Call attention to the fact that France, like Spain and Portugal, was a seagoing western European nation which was not content to buy Eastern goods through Italian merchants or to see rival countries getting rich in America.

45

#The influence of Pigafetta's account will recall the influence of Marco Polo's stories. Call attention to the fact that scientific discoveries today are based on other, earlier ones.

New York Historical Society

A bust of Verrazano, the first European to see the site of New York City, whose longest bridge today bears his name.

now call North Carolina. Later he wrote to Francis that he had viewed a region "never before seen by anyone, ancient or modern." Nevertheless, his mind was fixed on reaching China. He hoped to find a strait through the "new" land he had found which would take him to Asia.

New York Harbor. Sailing northward, Verrazano arrived at last at a beautiful harbor that made him and his men breathless as they stared upon it. They had reached the mouth of what we know as the Hudson River, leading to one of the magnificent river valleys of the world. Of course, they could not foresee there the great port of New York City, graced by the Statue of Liberty.

Following the shoreline of the Atlantic Ocean northward, Verrazano saw Cape Cod and sailed to Newfoundland along what we call the New England coast. From there he headed back to France. When he arrived home, he was full of talk—and deceit. He stoutly maintained that Pamlico Sound was the "Oriental Sea" which would lead to China.

The Gulf of St. Lawrence. Despite Verrazano's failure to find the road to China, the French persisted. Another of Francis' explorers—who unknowingly was to open the way to a New World empire—was a man who was French by birth. He was Jacques Cartier, a sailor from St. Malo. Francis backed him with 2 vessels and 61 men. Cartier's expedition set sail April 20, 1534. The aim was by now familiar: to see ## if there was a northern route to Asia.

Cartier reached the coast of Newfoundland and sailed into the Gulf of St. Lawrence. He, too, had found one of the picturesque gateways into the continent. But his disappointment was complete when he realized he was blocked at the western end.

Cartier explored what is today New Brunswick and also the Gaspé Peninsula, where he set up a wooden cross to mark his claim of all the new land for France. He

after Magellan's men returned (see page 31), a man named Antonio Pigafetta, who had served as the historian on that memorable voyage, turned up at the French court. He had come to present a copy of his # account of the trip. This valuable work must have been read and discussed with lively interest as it went from hand to hand among the people at the palace.

Possibly influenced by the book or by the enthusiasm it kindled among his advisers, Francis became eager to open a direct northern route to the East. Threatened by enemies, particularly by Spain, he believed that the wealth that would soon be his could pay for the wars France would wage.

In the little coastal town of Dieppe, Francis found the man to head his expedition. He was Giovanni da Verrazano, an Italian.

Verrazano's crossing of the Atlantic early in 1524 was uneventful, and in seven weeks he landed on the coast of what we

 ##Emphasize that France was not thinking of setting up colonies in America--it was seeking a route to the treasures of the East, just as Columbus was. Without good maps, such a search meant exploring every opening in the eastern coast of North America.

sailed along the coast of Labrador, too. When he returned to France, the king sent him back, for Francis was fascinated by the thought that the Gulf of St. Lawrence *did* contain a strait leading to Asia.

Hochelaga. On the second voyage, in 1535, Cartier had three ships. Of course he never came upon the strait, but he found out more about the St. Lawrence Valley. He learned, also, that the Indians called it "Canada." On a trip up the river, he wintered at the Indian town of Stadacona, (now Quebec). There he heard about the Indian city of Hochelaga, farther up the St. Lawrence. Visions played before his eyes of a rich kingdom, maybe even a part of China.

Hochelaga finally turned out to be only a poor village. Cartier must have felt as let # down as De Soto and Coronado felt a few years later, elsewhere on the American continent. Today the city of Montreal stands near where Hochelaga once was.

Champlain's New France

Cartier's pioneering efforts broke important new paths in America. Yet a greater explorer came in his footsteps. He was Samuel de Champlain, the founder of New France.

First visit. Champlain was born in 1567 in a little seaport on France's western coast. He must early have acquired his curiosity about the lands that lay beyond the ocean. In 1598, after completing service as a French army officer, he went to Spain. Deeply desiring to visit the New World, he obtained passage aboard a Spanish ship early the next year. His travels in Mexico and the Caribbean aroused his ambition to create a French empire in America.

With Pontgravé. Champlain returned to France and in 1603 went on an expedition to Canada which lasted three months. The leader of this expedition was a happy-go-lucky sailor known in history as Pontgravé (pôn grä vä'). Champlain made an alliance with the Algonkian Indians (see page 8), which later would be important in the settling of Canada by Frenchmen.

On a trip up the St. Lawrence River, Champlain heard from the Indians of the Great Lakes and Niagara Falls. Knowledge of these great natural wonders of the earth was no longer the Indians' alone.

The Sieur de Monts. Returned to France once more, Champlain published an ab-

Observe how closely Cartier followed the path of Cabot (see page 26) in an area which both Britain and France wanted to hold.

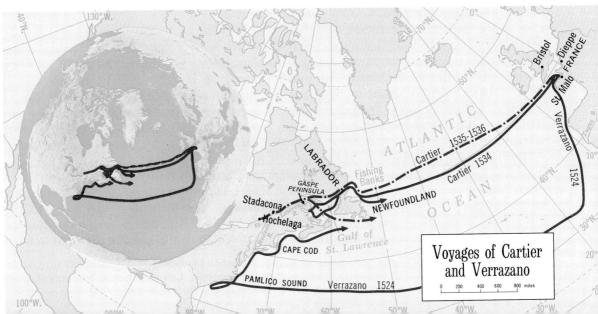

Voyages of Cartier and Verrazano

Bacqueville de la Potherie, "Historie de l'Amerique Septentrionale," Paris, 1753 (New York Public Library)

Champlain, the "Father of New France," and Brulé explored the interior of the continent by following the ways of the Indians—using their canoes and speaking their languages. Snowshoes were helpful, as the French American seen at the left shows.

sorbing account of his voyage. Immediately, his friends and other Frenchmen regarded him as an expert on America. He had no difficulty, therefore, in obtaining a place in the expedition of Pierre, Sieur de Monts (syoer' də mõn'). In 1604 that energetic French nobleman departed on still another trip to the New World. The aim # was to create a colony based on religious tolerance—and hard work. The colony also would have the sole right to trade with the Indians for furs.

Accompanying the Sieur de Monts and Champlain was Champlain's former associate, Pontgravé. The expedition, against the best advice of Champlain, chose for its settlement the mouth of the St. Croix River, on the Bay of Fundy rather than on the banks of the St. Lawrence. The seventy-nine pathetic colonists faced a fearful first winter, when thirty-five perished. Those who did not die of cold died of scurvy.

Port Royal. By the summer of 1605 the colony was joined by a new group of settlers, and it was moved to Port Royal (now Annapolis Royal). In 1613 the governor of Virginia sent a fleet from Jamestown in an attempt to destroy it (see page 74). Old World rivalries were being transferred to the New World and kept alive in the American forest!

Champlain returned to France in 1607, his head spinning with new plans and projects. The Sieur de Monts had obtained the king's permission to create another colony, which would acquire the right to trade

#Stress that although Cartier established a claim to the St. Lawrence Valley, Champlain and Brulé extended and clinched it by their explorations of the upper St. Lawrence and the Great Lakes and by the establishment of a French colony. Discuss "religious tolerance."

for furs. Would Champlain agree to lead the undertaking? Would he! The following spring he set sail with his old comrade, Pontgravé. Together they reached the St. Lawrence, and in 1608, at a choice site beneath cliffs, founded the city of Quebec.

The colonists being transplanted from France underwent terrible suffering in the first winter, but by the summer some of them seem to have taken root. So well were things going that Champlain left the colony in July to join his allies, the Algonkian and Huron Indians, in a war against the Iroquois.

Defeating the Iroquois. Champlain and his allies traveled in pursuit of the enemy from what is now the area of Lake Champlain to the present site of Fort Ticonderoga. There they finally met the Iroquois, who were quickly overwhelmed by French weapons.

The "Western Sea." For Champlain, Quebec was a springboard. From it he might "penetrate inland as far as the Western Sea, and thence at some future day to reach even to China." He guessed that the "Western Sea" was nearby—about 1250 miles away. What he knew of it was really a report about Lakes Ontario and Huron, which afterward he had occasion to visit (see the map on the opposite page).

Coureurs de bois **and** *voyageurs.* Although the French learned only slowly about the map of the new country, they learned quickly how to get along in the woods. Two new types of Frenchmen appeared: the *coureurs de bois* (kōō rûr′ də bwä′), who traded and hunted in the Canadian forests, and the *voyageurs* (vwà yà-zhoer′), who traveled in search of furs even beyond the wooded areas, onto the plains.

Both types of men, who often married Indian women, mingled freely with the Indians, treated them with respect, and learned their languages. In so doing, they carried French influences as far west as

the Rockies, as far north as Hudson Bay, and as far south as the Gulf of Mexico. These men helped France extend its claims of empire far out of proportion to the number of Frenchmen here.

Brulé. The first of the *coureurs de bois* was a young Quebec settler named Étienne Brulé—a friend of Champlain's and Pontgravé's. He was sent to live among the Huron Indians, learn their tongue, and become acquainted with the lay of the land. He practically became a Huron (later he was cooked and eaten by them), and he made the French familiar with the St. Lawrence Valley. Brulé also traveled beyond Lake Huron, perhaps reaching as far as Lake Superior.

One of the most impressive of Brulé's journeys took him through what is now western New York, past the headwaters of the Susquehanna, and on to Chesapeake Bay. Brulé thus was the first European to travel across what became Pennsylvania.

By the year 1620 the French had become acquainted with the river systems of north- # eastern North America, from the St. Lawrence to the Great Lakes and south to Chesapeake Bay. Still, at that time there were only 50 Frenchmen living in Quebec. Neither Champlain nor the authorities in Paris were satisfied with the way their col- ## ony had developed. They had spread French energies courageously but too thinly over the new land.

Pressure from the south. There was another reason for the slow growth of Quebec. English and Dutch traders to the south were severely undermining the French position. Both had been supplying trading goods to the Indians at much lower prices than the French. This meant that the trade in furs was being increasingly shifted from the Ottawa and St. Lawrence rivers to the shorter ones that run into the Atlantic. France's rivals controlled these.

The French found out that they were at a terrible military disadvantage, too. In

##Point out that fur trading did not encourage large groups of settlers. The French had covered a large expanse of territory, but they held it only by establishing trading posts here and there. Their failure to settle the interior would cost them later.

49

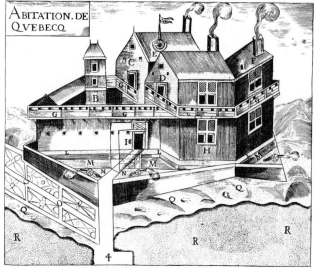

ABITATION·DE QVEBECQ

Samuel de Champlain, "Les Voyages," 1632 (Newberry Library)

Champlain himself drew these buildings at Quebec, using letters to identify their parts. For example, *C, D,* and *F* are lodgings for workmen. *H* marks Champlain's rooms, *Q* is the garden, and *R* is the St. Lawrence.

1629, when England was at war with # France, British warships sailed up the St. Lawrence and forced Champlain to surrender his beloved Quebec. (The pilot for the English vessels was none other than Étienne Brulé, who had changed his allegiance.) On his arrival in England as a prisoner, Champlain learned that the war was over. He was released and allowed to return to France.

In 1632, in accordance with the treaty ending the war, New France was restored to its mother country, and the next year Champlain returned to the scene of his pathbreaking adventures in America. The

"Abitation" (l'habitation) was a place where a habitant (French settler) lived.

Indians welcomed him back with rejoicing.

Nicolet. Champlain's own days as an active explorer and colonizer were done, but younger men could follow some of the paths he had marked out. In 1634 one of them, Jean Nicolet, traveled westward to Lake Michigan and followed the shores of that "sweet-water sea" to Green Bay (north of present-day Chicago).

Further travels brought Nicolet to the Fox River. What was he looking for so far from his home base? Perhaps there is a clue in the handsome cloak he took along. It was a robe "of China damask, all strewn with flowers and birds of many colors."

Doubtless the fancy garment was something for Nicolet to slip into in case a few more miles or a few more days of travel westward should bring him to fabled Cathay. At least he might arrive at the outskirts of Asia. Of course, he reached neither. For another century China continued to be imagined on every path and on every stream in America.

---

1. What first attracted French attention to the New World? 2. Explain the purpose of Verrazano's voyage. 3. Which parts of America did France claim because of Cartier's voyages? 4. Who is called the founder of New France? 5. How did he get the name? 6. How far into North America had French explorers gone by 1620?

#Difficulties in Europe have affected people in America since Europeans settled in the New World. In this case Britain and France were involved, as they were later, in 1756-1763.

Canadian Forests Lure Immigrants

Even as Champlain's career was ending (he died in 1635), the French were making efforts at home to put New France on a firmer footing. When the brilliant Cardinal Richelieu became the chief French minister in 1624, he hoped to see his country lead all others in establishing colonies.

Richelieu asserted bluntly: "No land is so well situated as France to be mistress of the seas or so rich in all the things necessary to achieve this goal." He persuaded the king to cancel the trading privileges granted earlier. He urged the creation in their place of a huge company able to rival

Some students may know that a cardinal is an important official in the Roman Catholic church. France was and is a Catholic country and, like the Spanish, the French brought the Roman Catholic religion to the area they settled. It is part of the French heritage in Quebec today.

in business the Englishmen and Dutchmen in the New World.

The Company of New France

＃ The Company of New France was therefore organized in 1627 to trade and colonize in America. It was also known as the Company of One Hundred Associates, because the investors who supported it were limited in number to one hundred. None of these people would ever travel to the New World, but they expected to profit from the labors of those who did.

Seigneurs and seigneuries. The Company of New France tried to duplicate here in America the kind of rule that existed in France itself. Richelieu had even provided in the company's charter for an order of titled noblemen to be created for Canada.

To influence the *seigneurs* (sēn yûrs'), or nobles, to go to live in America, the company gave them *seigneuries* (sēn' yə rĭs), or grants, along the lakes and riverfronts of New France. The grants were usually ＃＃ only 768 feet wide at the waterfront and 1920 feet deep. Tenants who were to do farm work, when they were available at all, lived on the seigneurs' grants, but farther back from the water.

Because the French established good relations with the Indians, there was relatively little fear of Indian attacks. The settlers, therefore, did not have to fortify their villages. Nevertheless, the fearful loneliness of the colonists and people's natural desire to live close together led the French to locate themselves near one another.

The French arrangements had an impractical side, too. Land was plentiful in the New World: Why should a tenant pay dues to a seigneur? Why should a tenant be forced to use a lord's gristmill? Why must he work on a lord's roads for six days a year or give the lord one fish out of every eleven he caught? All these were among the requirements the settlers had to meet.

Habitants. In practice, the requirements were rarely carried out to the letter. Each farm tenant, or *habitant*, paid an annual rental in grain or poultry. It amounted to about six chickens or a bushel of wheat for every 50 or 60 acres worked. The presenting of this payment—not really a very burdensome one—was a festive occasion for the women as well as the men.

May Day morning gave the habitants another public occasion for celebrating and being social. They were required to erect a Maypole in front of the seigneur's house and dance about it in his honor. This duty they did not fail to perform, because the next move was the seigneur's: providing refreshments for all.

Students should compare this grouping with pictures of Spanish buildings in Chapter 2.

A stockade enclosed some buildings in this seigneury of New France in 1671. The numbers, in order, indicate the mill, the priest's house, the church, a residence, a barn, palisades, and fortified places.

Désiré Girouard, "LeVieux Lachine et le Massacre du 5 aout 1689," Montreal, 1889 (New York Public Library)

＃＃Long, narrow farms can still be seen in Quebec.

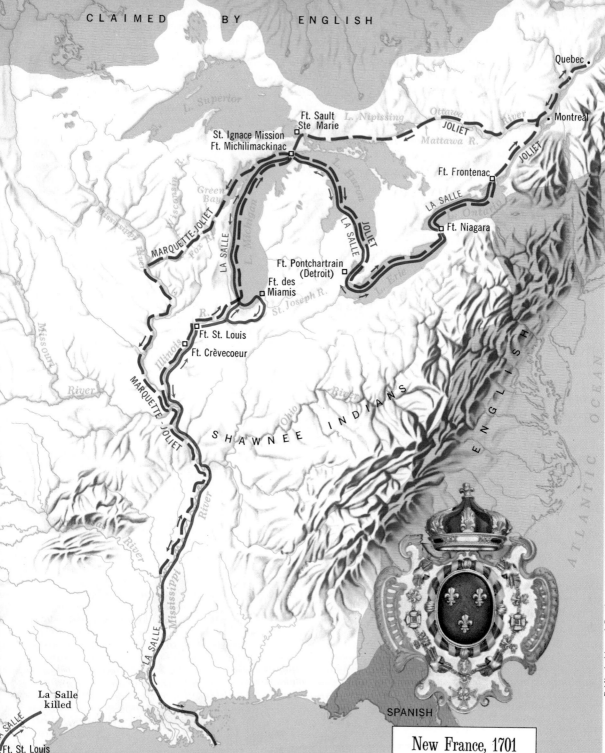

CLAIMED BY ENGLISH

L. Superior

Ft. Sault Ste Marie

L. Nipissing

Ottawa River

Quebec

Montreal

JOLIET

Mattawa R.

St. Ignace Mission
Ft. Michilimackinac

Wisconsin R.

Green Bay

Fox R.

MARQUETTE-JOLIET

LA SALLE

Mississippi River

L. Michigan

L. Huron

LA SALLE

JOLIET

Ft. Frontenac

LA SALLE

Ontario

JOLIET

Ft. Niagara

Ft. Pontchartrain
(Detroit)

Ft. des
Miamis

St. Joseph R.

L. Erie

Missouri River

Illinois R.

Ft. St. Louis

Ft. Crèvecoeur

MARQUETTE-JOLIET

Ohio River

SHAWNEE INDIANS

Wabash River

ENGLISH

ATLANTIC OCEAN

Missouri River

Mississippi River

LA SALLE

La Salle
killed

LA SALLE

Ft. St. Louis

Matagorda Bay

GULF OF MEXICO

SPANISH

New France, 1701

0   50   100   200 miles

Public Archives of Canada

RMEN & CO.

52   As the eighteenth century opened, France held the heart of North America
and one of its main water gateways. New France's proud coat of arms,
Call attention to the forts.   shown here, was designed by a Quebec artist.

Discuss why it is that people living in new settlements apart from older, established communities tend to accept people for what they are or can do, not for what they have.

We can see that the rigid lines separating one class of people from another in France tended to break down here in America. Shortly, the very idea of meeting the seigneurs' demands in the New World would seem ridiculous.

A scattered population. Moreover, a Frenchman's way of making a living in the New World depended on the supply of furry animals. This fact in the long run tended to scatter the population of New France. In 1650 the population of Quebec, the largest city in the St. Lawrence Valley, was only about 500.

The most densely populated French settlements were in the islands of the Caribbean. By the middle of the seventeenth century, 7000 Frenchmen were living there. The island of Guadeloupe (see the map, page 21), at that time producing vast amounts of sugar, was considered the single most important colony held by any European power.

Nevertheless, Quebec was the apple of the French eye. It sat like a guardian over an entranceway to the interior of North America, where the furs were. It was seemingly a fortress so strong that no foreign army would dare to challenge it. It was connected with the work of Champlain, France's greatest explorer.

Drawbacks. Of course, we realize today that the French enthusiasm for Quebec was overdone. The truth is that Quebec was not ideally suited for the methods of transportation and the military equipment of the day.

\# Most important, the St. Lawrence, because of ice, cannot be navigated during the winter months. The freezing over of the water meant idleness for the people of Quebec for about half the year and, worse, terrible isolation from the rest of the world. As a result, Quebec was not attractive to settlers.

A wrong emphasis. Look at the map on page 52 and you can see why Quebec was at the mercy of the English in the event of war. The British had a powerful fleet, growing stronger all the time, which controlled the North Atlantic coast.

Further, the French interest in furs and in saving souls far outstripped the interest in farming. By 1663 only 3333 acres of New France had been cleared, that is, stripped of trees and brush and made ready for farming. Successful colonizing in the New World required large numbers of farmers to occupy and develop the land.

Although land grants in New France were generously made, they were given on the basis of a man's noble background rather than his likely skill as an organizer. A seigneur was expected to recruit men and women who would work his land and build a mill for grinding their grain. Before they produced a crop, they had to break the wilderness by felling trees, removing stumps, and turning the soil—all with wooden tools.

Of course, some of the seigneurs colonized successfully by gathering people they knew would work loyally and effectively. Others were less energetic: they always had to invent new excuses for failing to develop their grants of land.

Many seigneurs came to New France and then complained constantly that the arrivals from home were too few or too lacking in skill. By 1712 only about ninety seigneuries had been created—not many.

Wives for bachelors. Most of the habitants and all of the soldiers who came to New France were single. Unmarried women had constantly to be encouraged to come to New France. At one time the chief French official in America wrote home asking for a shipment of between 150 and 200 female immigrants to be wives in Canada.

The colony grew gradually, possibly encouraged by generous bounties for large families. Parents of ten children or more received pensions. Generous dowries were presented to girls who married before they

\#The St. Lawrence Seaway is closed during the winter months for the same reason. Use the content in Column 2 to establish clearly what made a colony a success: settlement by families. Observe that in France people were not accepted for what they could do.

were sixteen. Boys who became husbands before they were twenty also received special help. By 1641 the population of New France was 240. By 1663 it was 2500. By 1680 it was 9719, and by 1698 it was 15,355.

The work of the Jesuits. Although the French simply failed to settle in America in sufficient numbers to occupy all the land they claimed, they left their influence on what became Canada. They gave to its eastern part the French language and laws and the Roman Catholic religion. French Jesuit missionaries were chiefly responsible for this success in transplanting French culture.

The French Jesuits were eager to convert the Indians to Christianity. And although the Jesuits' first aim was to serve Christ, they also aided France's interest.

The Jesuit missionaries found that they could do their work best by persuading the Indians to coöperate with the French traders. In this way the French Jesuits became the advance agents of France's trading empire, based on animal furs and skins.

Reaching Southward

New France was regarded at home as the proud symbol of a worldwide empire. To extend its boundaries was the goal of those who truly served the French king. In 1661 the greatest of France's kings, Louis XIV, a forbidding monarch with supreme power, came to the throne. He wanted Canada firmly under his royal thumb.

The great Louis. The France that Louis ruled was the greatest nation in Europe—a leader in the arts, in fashion, and in the science of waging war. Its population was larger than Spain's and three times the size of England's. Its army of 500,000 men was the largest the world had seen since the days of ancient Rome. A country like this would not willingly allow Spain to be unchallenged in the New World.

The royal intendant. Louis XIV appointed a representative—an *intendant*—to carry out his wishes in New France. An intendant (ĕn tän dôn′) was subject only to the king himself. Jean Talon, the first one, kept his mind always on increasing French profits from the fur trade.

Down the Mississippi. Talon worked closely with the Jesuit missionaries. By the beginning of the 1670's, the Jesuits were busy in the northeastern part of the triangle made by Lake Superior, Lake Huron, and Lake Michigan. They had already heard from the Indians much about a "great river named Messipi." If *coureurs de bois* had already visited it, we do not know, but no European had yet written of a journey upon it.

Joliet and Marquette. In the keen contest that raged between the Jesuits and the *coureurs de bois* to lead the Indians, the command of the Mississippi River was important. To explore the Mississippi, Talon in 1672 chose a trader, Louis Joliet, who may already have traveled near the river. Father Jacques Marquette, a Jesuit, obtained Talon's permission to go along on the expedition.

Despite Indian tales about monsters living in the river's waters and of unbearable southern heat, the men were not put off. And on June 17, 1673, Marquette wrote "we safely entered the Missisipi . . . with a joy that I cannot express."

The wide Missouri. Wide-eyed at the scenery and also at the many fur-bearing animals they saw, the men floated on. One disturbing note: the river seemed to keep flowing to the south. While traveling on it, though, they were severely jolted suddenly by a mighty torrent of water rushing at them from the west. They had, of course, come upon the Missouri River.

The thought that must have surely crossed their minds was, *This* is the water route to the Pacific. But they decided to postpone to some other time the explora-

##To an extent unknown in New Spain, French Jesuits were explorers as well as missionaries. Relate this account to the map on p. 52. Students should observe where the men were when they saw the Missouri River. Call attention to the main tributaries of the Mississippi.

The Mississippi Valley is not all flat, by any means. Bluffs border the river in a number of places.

La Salle, standing, and his men—after a successful hunt along the upper Mississippi River.

Louis Hennepin, "Nouvelle de Couverte," Amsterdam, 1704 (Chicago Historical Society)

tion of that huge river. For the moment they were going to settle once and for all what they were fairly sure of: that the Mississippi flowed into the Gulf of Mexico.

Short of the goal. Just north of where the Arkansas River enters the Mississippi, Joliet and Marquette stopped to inquire of the Shawnee Indians how far from the Gulf they were. The friendly Shawnee answered them and also warned them that they were heading into enemy country and risking death or imprisonment at the hands of the Spaniards.

The explorers knew now what they had set out to discover. "Beyond a doubt," they wrote, "the Missisipi River discharges into the Florida or Mexican Gulf, and not to the east in Virginia . . . or to the west in California." To fall into Spanish hands would only keep knowledge of the important fact from the French. The men turned back.

Important news. On the return trip, near the Ohio River, Father Marquette came upon friendly Indians to whom he entrusted a letter in Latin about himself and the expedition. Possibly he hoped thus to put himself in touch with the Spanish Jesuits to the south or even with the Jesuits in Maryland (see page 100).

The letter finally found its way into the hands of an Englishman on the Atlantic seaboard, who sent it across the ocean to England. In ways like this new geographical information sometimes became known.

The excitement Marquette and Joliet created when they returned to New France quickly spread to the mother country. The French were delighted: they had a water route from Quebec to the Gulf of Mexico.

The French in Europe were too busy to take advantage of their gain—wars here and wars there exhausted their money and men. The Jesuits grew less active, too, when public support for their missionary labors fell off near the end of the century. The work of spreading French influence fell to ambitious individuals.

Frontenac. One of these was Louis, Comte de Frontenac, who succeeded Talon in 1672. Frontenac carried instructions which included mention of urgent business in New France. They said: "After the increase of the colony of Canada, nothing is of greater importance for that country and for the service of his Majesty than the discovery of a passage to the South Sea." #

Frontenac saw, though, that the mother country was out of touch with things. A peace treaty with the Iroquois in 1667 had opened the way for a more immediately practical exploration.

La Salle. Under Frontenac's guidance a memorable journey was taken by Robert Cavelier, Sieur de La Salle. In January, 1682, with a party of fifty-four, only

In 1672 the king of France was still thinking about finding a passage to the sea that would lead to the East and to riches--not about making New France a stronger colony and one more attractive to settlers. On arriving in New France, Frontenac saw how out of touch the king was.

twenty-three of whom were Frenchmen, he set forth to travel the Mississippi.

La Salle had planned to sail down the river in an armored ship weighing 40 tons. But when the hull was only partially completed, he and his party left it on the Illinois River. He had decided to chance the trip by a fleet of canoes.

After a nerve-racking voyage, La Salle and his men reached their goal, the mouth of the Mississippi, in April: ". . . with all possible display, we performed the ceremony of planting the cross and raising the flag of France." In the name of the king of France, La Salle "took possession" of a

\# huge area. He claimed the river and the land washed by all rivers that enter it and all the country watered by them. He named the region Louisiana in honor of Louis XIV.

Settlement in Texas. La Salle had a grand plan. He wanted to take advantage of the failure of the Spaniards to link up their settlement in Florida with their settlements in Mexico. Returning to France, he obtained men and money to establish a colony above the mouth of the Mississippi.

In 1684 La Salle sailed into the Gulf of Mexico, but he unhappily missed the mouth of the Mississippi. Going ashore instead at Matagorda Bay, in Texas, the party tried to create a permanent home.

The colony was a dreadful failure. By the beginning of 1687, all kinds of misfortune had struck the struggling band of settlers. Disease and starvation had badly reduced their ranks, and La Salle himself was killed in a fight that followed.

The Busy Beavers

People in the vast land of furry animals in North America concentrated on obtaining beaver skins. The desire for beaver

\#\# skins became a craze in Europe after the beginning of the seventeenth century. Hats and coats for the well-to-do were every-

where made of the extremely adaptable furs of beavers. So widespread were the trapping and selling of beaver skins that the worth of a beaver pelt became the unit of value for the entire fur trade.

Paths of trade. In time the city of Montreal, established in 1642, became the base of operations of the French fur country. In general there were two pathways for the trade in skins. One followed the Ottawa and Mattawa rivers.

You can see from the map on page 52 that this route crosses an area through which furs had to be carried overland—a serious handicap. But it was a route fairly free from attacks by Indian enemies—particularly the Iroquois. It was far enough from English America to be safe from English interference, also.

The other route ran past Frontenac, Niagara, and Detroit and on to Michilimackinac or to Green Bay. This was the main avenue of the fur trade and the easier of the two to use because it was almost entirely a water route. But it could be attacked by both enemy Indians and the English.

Defending the trade. The furs themselves were found in areas north, west, and south of the Great Lakes. Look at the map on page 52 and observe where the French built their forts. In 1668 forts went up at Sault Ste Marie and at Michilimackinac, then in 1673 at Cataraqui (this was Fort Frontenac), in 1679 at Niagara, and in 1701 at Detroit. These forts together were a protective barrier for the French fur trade, which reached deep into the American wilderness.

You see from those dates that within the span of a very few years the French took big steps to gain a hold on the heart of North America. This was the area washed by the St. Lawrence River, the Great Lakes, and the Mississippi River. The reward was the power to control the Indians of this region. The tribesmen were encouraged to turn their skills and physical strength to

56   \#\#Hats were not made from the skin--just from the fur, which was clipped off the skin and made into fine, long-wearing felt. Even today some beaver felt is made. Let the class follow the fur-trade routes on the map on p. 52. Indians traded at the forts.

hunting animals whose coats could be exchanged for trinkets and brandy.

When the beavers were finally gone, French power was also gone. The Indians remained, greatly weakened by new and often bad habits and unable easily to find a new way of making a living.

A different technology based on iron plows would later strip the French land of its natural vegetation and turn it into very productive farmland. But at that time all that counted was getting the beaver skins.

The drama of the trade. The fur trade had a dramatic and beautiful side which did much to brighten the dull life of the wilderness. Every spring, all along the routes of trade, the *coureurs de bois* would move far into the woods and begin to assemble the Indians and their piles of furs. (The animals caught during the winter had very thick coats. And their pelts could be preserved more easily than in the warmer seasons.)

Annual flotilla. The Indians and the *coureurs* gathered in the regions of Michilimackinac and Green Bay and gradually formed an enormous flotilla of bark canoes. Sometimes one of these flotillas numbered as many as four or five hundred canoes. The canoes might contain over a thousand Indians and a cargo of pelts worth hundreds of thousands of dollars in French money.

This huge water train slowly wended its way toward Montreal. As it approached, the French people greeted it with such cheers as formerly had been reserved for the arrival of ships from France. The governor would come down from Quebec in his dress uniform, which included a scarlet cloak and a plumed hat, to welcome the Indians and smoke the peace pipe with them.

The waiting merchants. On the banks of the river the merchants of Montreal would spread out their wares. There was a large assortment of goods made of metal—kettles and knives, needles and nails, muskets and spoons. There were baubles of bone and glass and cheap cloth—like combs and necklaces, brooches and bracelets, blankets and dresses. The merchants also had on hand large quantities of liquor which usually turned these annual occasions into loud brawls.

After about two weeks the exciting bazaar was over and the Indians returned. Many had far less to show for their hunting efforts than they should have had.

The pressure of rivals. Even though New France never had a large population, its presence was felt by both the Spanish to the south and the English to the east. It was as if a giant wedge was being driven ## into the center of the continent, exerting pressure in every direction.

From roughly 1670 on, a bloody rivalry

Quebec about 1700 in summertime, when ships can navigate the St. Lawrence. Compare this picture with the one on page 50.

for the control of the central portion of the American continent went on. The French forts became busy, and their occupants hoped to be strong enough to defend them.

The Changing Challenge

The North American continent has presented various faces to mankind. Each has been a different challenge.

Responses. To the first arrival twenty thousand years or so ago, North America was a region that, hopefully, had a better climate and more food than Asia. To the Norsemen, it was a faraway land of sweet grapes, to be visited on rare occasions.

\#   To the Spanish, America was at first an immense roadblock in the way of China, and later it was a source of treasure for the king of Spain. To the French, it was a fascinating preserve in which to hunt animals, and later it was a glorious sign to the world of France's strength.

Another possibility. Men are often blind or unwilling to see when they face the truly golden opportunities historical luck places at their feet. America could be something else than simply a huge arena in which the kings of Europe might compete for power.

It is hard to believe that at the start of Europe's contact with America, no one seemed to think the new land might offer the richest prize in all the world: freedom for the individual. The work of discovering this treasure fell to the English. The result of their efforts, carried on in still another portion of the New World, produced a pattern of life never experienced in New Spain or New France.

---

1. What two methods did the French use to make France foremost among European nations in colonizing the New World? 2. Name some requirements French tenant farmers had to meet. 3. What were Quebec's drawbacks as a colony? 4. On what group of people did a successful colony depend? 5. Who had the biggest role in spreading French influence in North America? 6. Describe the two pathways of the fur trade. 7. How did the French protect their trade?

Review the chapter with the help of the facts questions and the lists of names and words given here.

The Workshop

The part workshop (p. 60) contains activities that help summarize the contents of Part One.

The Shapers of Our World

Identify the following people and tell how they helped establish a French claim in North America:

Verrazano	Brulé
Francis I	Nicolet
Pigafetta	Louis XIV
Cartier	Jesuits
Pontgravé	Frontenac
Champlain	La Salle
Sieur de Monts	Talon
Cardinal Richelieu	Joliet
Marquette	

Adding to Your Vocabulary

Be sure you know the meaning of the following terms:

well-to-do	*voyageurs*
coureurs de bois	*intendant*
flotilla	religious tolerance
mariners	seigneurs
habitants	seigneuries

Thinking Things Through

After reviewing the chapter with the help of the boxed exercises, see if you can answer the following:

A good test of what was learned in this chapter would be to ask the class to look back at the pictures on p. 44 and describe the parts of the history of New France that are suggested by them. This would give students a chance to try to organize answers to an essay type of test.

1. Why did the French value Guadeloupe so highly? What does their attitude tell you about the value of colonies in the eyes of the Europeans?

2. If New France could have been fully developed, why would the discoveries of Marquette, Joliet, and La Salle have been extremely important?

3. How do Marquette and Joliet as a team illustrate the growth of New France into a "giant wedge driven into the center of the continent"?

4. Although France took pride in the enormous empire created out of a wilderness in North America, its size was its main handicap. Why?

5. The fur trade was New France's greatest source of wealth. How was it also the cause of a great problem?

Geography and History

1. Study the map on page 52, showing New France in 1701. Compare it with the map of the present-day United States on pages 542–543 and tell what states or parts of states are included in the former French land. What cities, rivers, or lakes have names showing a French heritage?

2. Look at the map of New Spain on page 39 and that of New France on page 52. Draw the boundaries of both these empires on an outline map of North America. What areas were left for the English? Why would the English have felt trapped? Why was the French area poorly located for purposes of defense? What problem do you see as a cause of future trouble between France and England?

3. France explored and held the mouths of the two largest water gateways to North America. Name them. What great seaports are now located at or near these mouths? What is the origin of each of their names?

4. In Canada today one can see in the province of Quebec, near the St. Lawrence River, land that is laid out in long, narrow strips. How did such a method of dividing land begin?

The Research Center

Develop the library habit by using reference books as well as the books listed in the part workshops. Report orally to the class on Item 1 or 2, and write on one of the subjects described in 3 and 4.

1. What characteristics did the Algonkian, Huron, and Iroquois tribes have in common? How did they differ? Why were the French attracted to the first two and enemies of the third?

2. Tell what parts of the early lives of Champlain and Marquette helped to fit them for their places in history.

3. Imagine that you are a Jesuit missionary in New France writing to your superior in France. Describe conditions in the forest and the problems you face in your work with the Indians.

4. Imagine that you are Governor Frontenac writing to the king of France. In your letter, outline for the king the problems that New France faces and the remedies that you see for them.

Ideas for Drawing and Listening

1. Draw your impression of a giant fur-trading flotilla moving down the river toward Montreal or of the yearly party when the habitants came to pay their rent to the seigneur.

2. Using such materials as magazines and travel literature, choose as many pictures showing examples of French culture in the United States as you can find. Mount these pictures on a poster for display purposes.

3. Bring to school the recording of Victor Herbert's *Naughty Marietta*. In addition to playing the recording, tell the class the background story, emphasizing its description of life in New France.

e the test for Part One in the Introduction to the Teacher Edition. Another good test for the
rt would be to give students outline maps of the New World and ask them to show on the maps
e areas explored, claimed, and settled by the Spanish and the French.   59

Two kinds of activities are consistently found in the part workshops: One kind is under the head "Time and Change," always used above the time lines in the book. The other kind encourages students to relate the past to the present so that they can see how our past history is related to what is going on today. Both kinds help students see the content of the part as a whole, not as a discussion of a jumble of people and events.

#This is a good test of the knowledge of Part One and its significance.

Part One Workshop

##Questions 2 and 3 will help students understand current problems and possible solutions

Time and Change

Review the chapters in Part One and study the time line on pages 2–3.

1. How many centuries A.D. are included? The age of European exploration discussed in Part One covers what years? How many centuries?

2. List the dates and events which relate to (*a*) Europeans learning the makeup of the world, and (*b*) Europeans becoming acquainted with the geography of North America.

3. Using three outline maps of the world, date them (*a*) 1400, (*b*) 1498, and (*c*) 1524. Show how knowledge of the world exploded at an amazing rate by marking on each map the areas of the earth that were known to Europeans in the year concerned.

4. Certain events in the New World led to changes in Spain's position in the Old World. Consult your time line and find major changes in the New World discussed in Part One. What events caused each one?

5. How did Europeans change when they came to the New World? What changes in the life of the Indians took place because of European settlement in the Americas?

Reaching to the Present

Groups of students might choose one of the following exercises, study it, and report the results of their inquiries.

1. What problems make it hard for democratic governments to survive in many Latin American countries? How are the people trying to meet their problems? Choose one Latin American country and study its history, geography, and people. How have we helped in that country? Can we help more? How?

2. What problem does present-day Canada face because it has both a French and an English heritage? How is the Canadian government trying to solve this problem? Can you name other parts of the world trying to work out the same problem Canada has? Why is it so difficult to solve?

3. What problems do Indians in the present-day United States have? Where and how do most of the Indians live? How are their problems being solved?

The Book Shelf

Blacker, Irwin R., and eds. of *Horizon* Magazine. *Cortes and the Aztec Conquest.* Consultant, Gordon Eckholm. New York: American Heritage Publishing Co., Inc., 1965. (How the Spanish overcame Mexico.)

Craig, Gerald E. *Canada, Neighbor to the North.* Chicago: Rand McNally & Co., 1967. (Traces the history of Canada.)

Donovan, Frank R., and eds. of *Horizon* Magazine. *The Vikings.* Consultant, Sir Thomas D. Kendrick. New York: American Heritage Publishing Co., Inc., 1964. (About the Viking explorations.)

Driver, Harold E. and Wilhelmine. *Indian Farmers of North America.* Chicago: Rand McNally & Co., 1967. (Describes eastern and southwestern farming.)

Hibben, Frank C. *Earliest Hunters of North America.* Chicago: Rand McNally & Co., 1967. (The first Americans.)

Judson, Clara Ingram. *Admiral Christopher Columbus.* Chicago: Follett Publishing Co., 1965. (Life of Columbus.)

"The Book Shelf" does not include older books, however good they are. Libraries already have them, and teachers are familiar with them. For this reason, newer books are listed here. They are geared to the students' reading level and provide enrichment material.

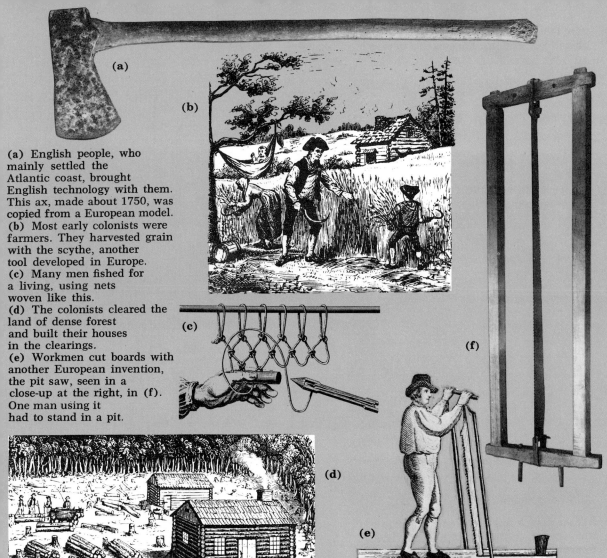

(a) English people, who mainly settled the Atlantic coast, brought English technology with them. This ax, made about 1750, was copied from a European model.
(b) Most early colonists were farmers. They harvested grain with the scythe, another tool developed in Europe.
(c) Many men fished for a living, using nets woven like this.
(d) The colonists cleared the land of dense forest and built their houses in the clearings.
(e) Workmen cut boards with another European invention, the pit saw, seen in a close-up at the right, in **(f)**. One man using it had to stand in a pit.

Part Two:
NEWCOMERS ON THE SEABOARD

The beginnings of American technology--based on European, or Western, technology--are illustrated here. Point out the use of metal, something the Indians were not familiar with.

The tools shown were ones the pioneers in the New World needed first in building homes and obtaining food. Call attention to the broad-leaved forest shown, a characteristic of the Atlantic seaboard and all the land east of the Mississippi. Areas of broad-leaved forest make good farmland. Ask what natural resources are suggested by the pictures and what technology is shown but not named in <u>d</u> (well apparatus, harness).

Part Two begins the account of English colonization. Examine the contents in class.

Part Two:
NEWCOMERS ON THE SEABOARD

Ask the class to find some entries on the time line which are related to heads shown in the contents. Ask them what years Part Two covers (as dates on the time line indicate). Discuss "refuge" and "tracts."

MORE LIVES THAN A CAT

No tale ever created by a writer of fiction compares in excitement with the story of the settling of America by the peoples of western Europe. One of the most powerful characters in the drama was Captain John Smith (1580–1631), an English soldier and adventurer.

Who can say that John Smith arrived on the colonial scene with too little experience of personal danger? When he was a very young man, he fought bravely (by his own admission!) in a war against the Turks and was taken prisoner in battle. His captors sent him

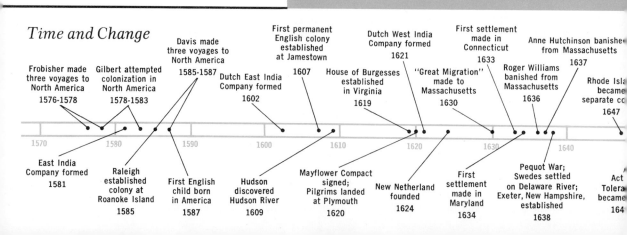

Time and Change

Frobisher made three voyages to North America
1576-1578

Gilbert attempted colonization in North America
1578-1583

Davis made three voyages to North America
1585-1587

First permanent English colony established at Jamestown
1607

Dutch East India Company formed
1602

House of Burgesses established in Virginia
1619

Dutch West India Company formed
1621

"Great Migration" made to Massachusetts
1630

First settlement made in Connecticut
1633

Roger Williams banished from Massachusetts
1636

Anne Hutchinson banished from Massachusetts
1637

Rhode Isla became separate co
1647

East India Company formed
1581

Raleigh established colony at Roanoke Island
1585

First English child born in America
1587

Hudson discovered Hudson River
1609

Mayflower Compact signed; Pilgrims landed at Plymouth
1620

New Netherland founded
1624

First settlement made in Maryland
1634

Pequot War; Swedes settled on Delaware River; Exeter, New Hampshire, established
1638

Act Tolera became 164

1570   1580   1590   1600   1610   1620   1630   1640

as a present to the wife of the ruler of Turkey. She fell in love with him. Shipped off to her brother for safekeeping, Smith was made a slave.

The Captain escaped from captivity, however, and returned to his homeland just as a band of fellow Englishmen was about to head for the Virginia coast. Joining the expedition, he soon was its leader, instilling in those scared people his own spirit of never-say-die.

In his hazardous work Smith revealed that he had more lives than a cat. He gradually became a perfect symbol of Virginia, which earlier had teetered on the brink of failure. His greatest skill lay in managing the relations between the Indians and the English. As a result, the colonists learned how to survive and then to prosper.

Having been forced to return to England, Smith later was back in America again, this time exploring in New England. His map of the region, published in 1616, helped to make the name "New England" stick.

Near the end of his remarkable career, Smith wrote books about Virginia and New England and described them fondly as "my children." Moreover, he said, "were there not one Englishman remaining in those places (as God be thanked there is some thousands) I would yet begin again with as small means as I did at first."

Smith's high achievement was that he set the requirements for the millions upon millions of people who would come to the New World after him. These qualifications #would be strong faith in final success, strict self-control, and, above all, a stout heart.

The coat of arms of Virginia, showing the motto of the   # English Order of the Garter, the highest badge of knighthood.

John Smith was chosen as the subject of this biography because he was the kind of person who could make a success of English colonization in the New World. He did, in fact, save the first colony. He symbolizes all the immigrants who have come to America.

#The motto is: "Shame to him who evil thinks."

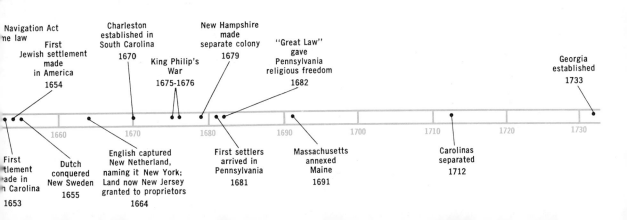

Navigation Act ne law

First Jewish settlement made in America
1654

Charleston established in South Carolina
1670

King Philip's War
1675-1676

New Hampshire made separate colony
1679

"Great Law" gave Pennsylvania religious freedom
1682

Georgia established
1733

First tlement ade in n Carolina
1653

Dutch conquered New Sweden
1655

English captured New Netherland, naming it New York; Land now New Jersey granted to proprietors
1664

First settlers arrived in Pennsylvania
1681

Massachusetts annexed Maine
1691

Carolinas separated
1712

1660   1670   1680   1690   1700   1710   1720   1730

(a) The Englishmen quickly were involved with American Indians. One of the first colonists, John White, painted this Algonkian village.

(b) Jamestown settlers crossed the ocean in the *Discovery*, the *Godspeed*, and the *Susan Constant*, seen here, left to right, in full-scale reproduction.

(c) People in Europe, who had never seen corn, could tell what the plant looked like by studying this drawing, which appeared in a book published in 1588.

(d) An artist of our time painted the Jamestown fort as it was described by the settlers and as it is reproduced near the James River today.

(e) The buildings of the Pilgrims' colony, seen in part here, have been reconstructed to appear as they probably did in 1627.

(f)

(g)

CHAPTER 4

FOOTHOLDS ON THE SHORE

..k the class to look carefully at the pictures above and on page 64 to see what they can "discover": the ..mes and the palisades of the Algonkians, all of wood; the winter weather; the wooden homes of the Pil-..ims; the kind of ships; the differences between corn then and now; the emphasis on religion among the ..lgrims and on tobacco among the Virginians.

B ECAUSE Englishmen lived on an island off the continent of Europe, they were a part of Europe yet also separate from it. They had always felt themselves to be different from other Europeans. After the opening of America, they sensed that as an island people they might be able to play a role on the sea.

English ships had traded with the Span-ish colonies in the New World almost from the beginning. Furthermore, English sailors had traveled north of Florida along the Atlantic coast and had observed the possibilities it offered for settlement. Many Englishmen were early relishing the idea of competing with the Spanish in the building of an empire. The Spaniards were their old enemies.

Englishmen Try and Try Again

During the sixteenth century, while Spain and France were planting their flags in America, Englishmen were chiefly busy at home. They brought about new developments that gave special qualities to their efforts in the New World—which began as the seventeenth century was opening.

New Conditions

The first of the developments made England a Protestant country. This meant that the English were officially separated from the Roman Catholic church. Further, the English king himself, rather than the Pope, became the religious head of the country. The newly organized church was called the Church of England.

The second development was that England was becoming a manufacturing country. The production of iron and steel and coal was not yet changing English life entirely. Yet the future was being hinted at. Not only was the manufacture of iron and steel, glass, lead, and ships increasing enormously, but also new industries were

Review the activities of the Spanish, relating them to the sixteenth century (see pp. 2-3). Empha-
..ze the difference in the time of Spanish and English activities.
‡Be sure students understand the developments, since they greatly influenced English colonies.

Off the coast of England, the Spanish Armada—right—faces the English fleet that shattered Spain's ambition to rule the seas.

appearing. These were producing paper, soap, copper, and brass, to name only a few items. Older businesses, such as wool-manufacturing, goldsmithing and silver-smithing, and the buying and selling of grain, were also prospering.

Growing prosperity. As a result of the activity in manufacturing and business, the number of English merchants was growing and the towns of England were becoming places in which a man might get ahead. Each year the pace of life seemed to pick up a little more.

English products found markets in ports throughout the world. Englishmen came to be as commonly seen on the maritime trading routes as Dutchmen and Spaniards were.

The defeat of the Armada. Being people of a little country, Englishmen learned early that, for them, achieving great results sometimes meant taking great risks. The daring with which, in 1588, they defeated and scattered the Spanish Armada—that brave enemy fleet—was just such a bold action. It immediately made Englishmen feel "chestier" and taller. As a distin-

guished historian phrased it: "It . . . led them to say to one another, 'What we have done once, we can do again.'"

The victory over Spain persuaded many Englishmen that they might enjoy further triumphs of seamanship. Many wondered whether the time had not now come to challenge Spain in New World activities, too.

The joint-stock company. England had already developed a form of business organization for overseas undertakings. It was known as the *joint-stock company.* Such a company was under the management of a board of directors. Its money, or capital, for investment was obtained by selling shares—called *stock.*

A joint-stock company was usually formed by a group of English merchants in order to carry on trade in certain parts of the world. For example, the Russia, or Muscovy, Company traded in Russia. The Levant Company traded with Turkey. ("The Levant" was the name used then for the eastern shore of the Mediterranean and nearby areas, where Turkey is located.)

The Barbary Company controlled the

#Relate joint-stock companies, described, to business companies today that sell stock to people w receive profits from the investment of their money. Emphasize that English manufacturing led to increased trade, to a larger number of merchants, and to joint-stock companies.

trade along the North African coast. The Guinea Company concentrated on the northwestern coast of Africa.

The greatest of the trading companies was the East India Company, formed in 1599. Englishmen created it as an anti-Spanish step. Spain had acquired Portugal in 1581, together with Portugal's long-standing spice trade in the East Indies. One way to weaken Spain, therefore, was to enter this valuable trade and seek to make it English.

Discuss "project."

Grand Projects

In addition to following worldwide commercial interests, Englishmen—like their neighbors in Europe—wanted to find a northwest passage to China. In 1576 a close friend and admirer of Queen Elizabeth's, Sir Humphrey Gilbert—a shareholder in the Muscovy Company—published a little book on the subject. He insisted in this work that the Americas were an island. By sailing around them, he maintained, people could find the path to China.

A northwest passage. One of the ablest of English mariners, Martin Frobisher, made up his mind to test Gilbert's theory. Possibly Frobisher was egged on by Gilbert's words: "This discovery hath bene reserved for some noble prince or worthie man, thereby to make himselfe rich, and the world happie."

Frobisher made three voyages. The first of them, in 1576, brought him to what is today called Frobisher Bay. He discovered also what is now Baffin Island and the Eskimos living along its southern shores. There he found some ore he was positive contained gold. When he returned to England, experts backed up his opinion.

The English for the moment became

Magellan had found a "southwest passage" around America. Frobisher and Davis, following Viking paths, hoped to go northwest around it.

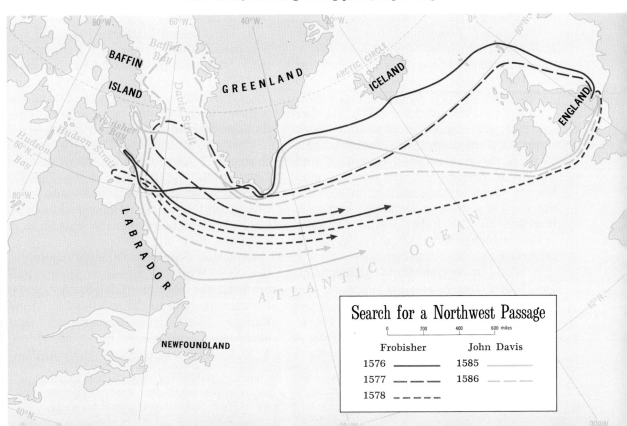

Search for a Northwest Passage

Frobisher	John Davis
1576 ————	1585 ————
1577 —— ——	1586 ——— ———
1578 —— —— ——	

Above: Real gold ore.
Below: "Fool's gold" like
this misled Frobisher.

A seventeenth-century London publication showed Frobisher hunting
birds in North American waters and a man, possibly one of
those who accompanied him, looking at Eskimos.

more interested in mining than in exploration—and the work of finding the Northwest Passage was postponed. Elizabeth herself invested a large amount of money in Frobisher's second expedition.

Only after Frobisher's third trip, in 1578, from which he brought back over a thousand tons of ore, was it discovered that his precious cargo was merely iron pyrite. This was the so-called fool's gold.

In the next decade John Davis, another splendid sea captain, commanded two expeditions in Frobisher's footsteps. He explored the area between Greenland and the Arctic Archipelago. He and his men learned much about surviving in cold climates. They were constantly bothered, however, by the icebergs and ice floes against which wooden ships could not be protected.

A colony in Newfoundland. Although no one found the Northwest Passage, the search for it spurred men to settle in the New World. It was the main reason for establishing an English colony. A settlement could be a way station on the northwestern

route to Asia. If the settlement could be made at Newfoundland, the English fishermen in the waters there would have a place of shelter and safety when they needed it.

In 1578 Queen Elizabeth I granted Gilbert permission to create such a colony. He twice attempted to succeed. The first time, in 1578–1579, an ill wind blew him into the West Indies. He had a hard time explaining to the Spanish what he was doing there and getting out of their clutches.

The second time, in 1583, Gilbert, in charge of 5 vessels and 260 men, reached Newfoundland. The bleak scene immediately discouraged the immigrants, and Gilbert and some of his people set out to return home. Their ship sank, though, and they lost their lives.

Exploring Virginia. Gilbert's rights in the New World now passed to his half brother, Sir Walter Raleigh. A special favorite of Queen Elizabeth's, in 1584 Raleigh, like Gilbert, was granted royal permission to settle in the New World. A little more foresighted than Gilbert,

#

#Students should not confuse this reason with the one for establishing Virginia or Plymouth.
This sentence refers to the attempt to set up a colony at Newfoundland, which did not succeed. A "way station" would have been like a naval base used today to supply our ships.

...aleigh's clothing in the picture is typical of that ...orn by English gentlemen of the time.

Raleigh sent men to explore the American coast in 1584 before sending off colonists in the following year. The land they found they named Virginia in honor of the Virgin Queen, Elizabeth.

Raleigh himself was interested in discovering gold. Some of his associates, who shared that interest, wanted to find the Northwest Passage, too. Yet all of them wanted to set up here in America a way of life like England's: they, of course, would be the gentlemen of leisure! They soon learned what settling in the New World would *really* be like.

Roanoke Island. Raleigh's first colony was established in 1585 on Roanoke Island, at the northern end of Pamlico Sound. The colonists unfortunately made enemies of the Indians, probably because Ralph Lane, their leader, was tactless. Furthermore, in a short time the struggling settlers were near starvation.

They were lucky, though, that they were Englishmen. Just finishing a highly profitable raid on Spanish shipping in 1586, Sir Francis Drake decided to go see the colonists before going home. In low spirits, they persuaded him to take them back to England. Drake, of course, traveled in triumph, they in disappointment.

The failure at Roanoke was a keen challenge to Raleigh. How could he make a colony stick? In 1587 one hundred fifty new adventurers set out for the New World, but this time the ranks included women—seventeen of them. Already the English were adjusting to the situation they found in America. They were beginning to see that family farming might be the basis on which an English colony could succeed there.

A "lost colony." Raleigh's new group went forth with more knowledge of what it would have to face than any previous one had. The governor was John White. He had been in the first expedition to Roanoke and had made sketches of the Indians and of American animal and plant life.

...f these three purposes for establishing a colony, ...ne was realized.
‡An important concept: farmers were true settlers.

The Granger Collection
Raleigh, seen here in a painting by an artist of his day, had one main hope for America: "I shall yet live to see it an English nation."

Where the English first tried to colonize and where Raleigh's hope died.

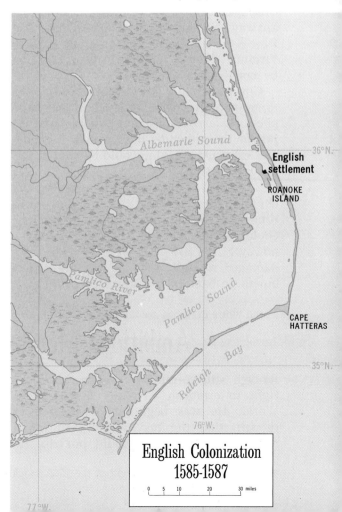

Albemarle Sound

English settlement

ROANOKE ISLAND

36°N.

Pamlico River

Pamlico Sound

CAPE HATTERAS

35°N.

Raleigh Bay

76°W.

English Colonization 1585-1587

0   5   10   20   30 miles

Through John White's eyes we can see an American "land crab" and a "box turtle" of 1585.

Among the colonists was White's daughter, Eleanor, who was married to Ananias Dare, one of White's assistants. Mrs. Dare was expecting a baby.

The settlers ignored Raleigh's wishes to avoid Roanoke because of the fierce storms there and to land instead somewhere along Chesapeake Bay. They settled at Roanoke anyway. Shortly after their arrival, the Dare baby was born. Appropriately named Virginia, she was the first English child to be born in the New World.

Governor White left almost immediately to go back to England for additional supplies. He arrived, as luck would have it, just as the attack by the Spanish Armada was expected. No ship could be spared for his return trip.

But through Raleigh's influence White obtained two vessels after only a short time and set out for Virginia again. He could not escape the Spanish warships, however: his two craft were attacked and damaged so badly that he had no choice but to go back to England. Not until two years later, in 1590, did he finally return to Roanoke Island. His dismay and grief were complete. The band of settlers, including his daughter and granddaughter, had disappeared—where to, we still do not know.

Possibly the "lost colony" was absorbed by Indian tribes or killed by unfriendly ones. White found the letters CRO cut into the bark of a tree and CROATOAN carved in a post. The unfortunate Englishmen may have been trying to tell whoever came to find them that Croatan Indians knew their whereabouts.

1. Name two developments in England in the sixteenth century. 2. What were their effects? 3. How did the English defeat of the Spanish Armada affect American history? 4. Name the greatest trading company, and tell why it was formed. 5. What relationship was there among Gilbert, Frobisher, and Davis? 6. In what two places in America did the English first try to colonize?

The John White drawings are the best possible examples of art of the period being discussed.

Ambitious Merchants Plant Virginia

Raleigh still continued to claim the sole right to establish a colony in the New World. He was beginning to find out, though, that the task would cost more money than one man could put up. In 1589 he offered trading privileges to a group of London businessmen and a chance to invest in the colony he was stubbornly planning to establish.

However, Raleigh made no further at-

#Raleigh naturally thought of the joint-stock companies organized in England to carry on trade.

tempts to plant a settlement in the New World. Moreover, in 1603 he was accused of treason against the queen, and he lost his privilege to colonize.

Meanwhile, the leaders of a number of joint-stock companies were eyeing the New World. After all, they must have reasoned, if profits can be found in the Levant, in Russia, and in the East Indies, why not in America also?

Along the James River

In 1606 the businessmen Raleigh had been approaching organized a joint-stock company, the Virginia Company. Its purpose was to create an American colony whose products could be sold profitably. The stockholders obtained from King James I a *charter*, that is, an official permit, to establish settlements in America.

The arrangements. The king made two grants of land. To one group of the stockholders—known as the London group—he gave the land lying between the 34th and 41st parallels of north latitude. To another group—known as the Plymouth group—he gave the land lying between the 38th and 45th parallels. Although the grants, as you can see on the map at the right, overlapped 3 degrees, neither group could occupy land within a hundred miles of a settlement already made by the other.

A very important provision of the grants was that they extended westward indefinitely. One day this provision would have an important bearing on the establishment of the United States of America.

Ashore. The London group was first to try its luck. Late in December, 1606, three ships filled by a little more than a hundred men, commanded by Captain Christopher Newport, sailed from London, England.

Within the land grants shown here were made the English settlements which were the start of what became our own country—the United States.

The old seal of the Virginia colony.

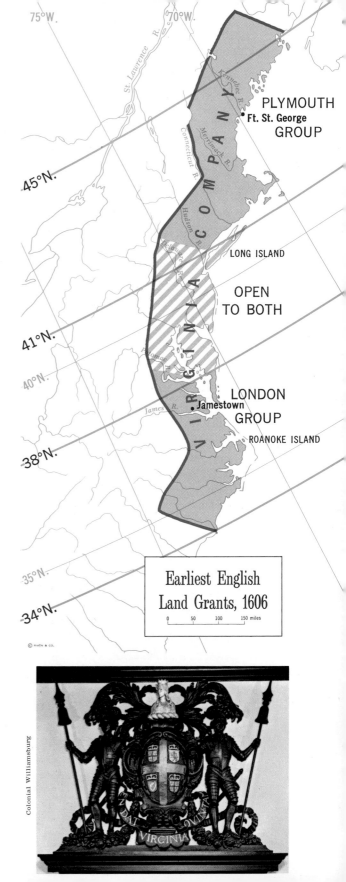

PLYMOUTH
● Ft. St. George
GROUP

LONG ISLAND

OPEN
TO BOTH

VIRGINIA COMPANY

LONDON
● Jamestown
GROUP

ROANOKE ISLAND

Earliest English Land Grants, 1606

0   50   100   150 miles

Colonial Williamsburg

EN DAT VIRGINIA QVINTA

VIRGINIA

Bound for the New World, their aim was adventure quite as much as the creation of homes in the American forest.

Not until nearly the middle of May did the expedition reach the New World—just in time to be greeted by the warm fragrance of springtime in what is now Virginia. The countryside was alive with flowers, and strawberries were ready for the picking.

Though exhausted, the men were excited by what they saw. Unfortunately, they went ashore in a low, swampy place about fifty miles up a river. They called the place # Jamestown in honor of their king, and they named the river the James.

False hopes. Captain Newport returned home full of enthusiasm and exaggeration. He told the London businessmen (the London group) that the New World mountains were rich in gold and copper—although, of course, he could not know that this was so. He reported also that the Indians had pointed out to him some beds of mussels—freshwater shellfish—rich in pearls. (His big talk was not going to help the settlers, of whom too much was already expected.)

Officials at home were delighted. Along with basic supplies they sent additional men, including six tailors and a perfumer (this, after all, was going to be a settlement of gentlemen). They also sent men able to judge the quality of precious metals, a jeweler, two gold refiners, and two goldsmiths. A tragic story was beginning to unfold.

The new arrivals quickly busied themselves digging what came to be referred to as gilded dirt. They might better have turned their hand to getting ready for the following winter. The "gilded dirt" proved to be just that—iron pyrite, "fool's gold."

Already the first settlers were suffering intensely. By August one of them was writing: "There were never Englishmen left in a foreign country in such a misery as we were in this new discovered Virginia."

Definite orders. Despite the suffering of the bewildered settlers, the stockholders in London showed no mercy. They ordered the captains of the supply ships they sent to Jamestown not to return without gold nuggets.

The stockholders also directed the colonists to set up an iron factory, a glass ## factory, and a saltworks. Further, the company insisted that the colonists raise silkworms. Word had reached England that mulberry trees, on whose leaves silkworms feed, grew in Virginia. The experiment in silk culture was a failure.

These men are demonstrating how the Jamestown settlers built their houses. Working as the colonists did, they first made frames out of logs hewn from tall trees and fastened the logs together with wooden pegs. Now they are weaving green sticks to make walls, which will next be covered with clay.

1607, Inc., Jamestown

If the stockholders seemed stubborn and demanding, remember first of all that communication across the Atlantic was slow and unreliable. The people back home could not keep up from day to day with news of how things were going.

Second, the company had no way of really knowing what to expect of the colonists or what the hardships would be. The Spanish, the only ones who had built colonies previously, had settled, for the most part, in a much warmer climate.

Third, the men in London had invested their money, and they hoped to make a profit on it. They had received no financial help from the king.

Relief from home. The bad luck the Jamestown colony experienced sometimes seemed endless. In 1609 a relief expedition of 9 ships and 600 passengers was sent from London. (We can imagine the tales of the good life in Virginia which lured these people away from their homeland.)

The flagship, the *Sea Venture*, having aboard it all the leaders of the expedition, apparently disappeared in a hurricane which struck the little fleet. One other ship sank, and all aboard went down with it.

Captain John Smith. When the surviving passengers landed at Jamestown late in 1609, they proved too numerous for the colony to take care of. Moreover, the head of the Jamestown settlement, Captain John Smith, was already losing patience with some of the settlers, who would neither work nor obey.

Smith was himself a coarse and rough man, but he was often able to get the best out of people. He also succeeded in making friends with the Indians. The story goes that when he had a disagreement with Powhatan, a local Indian chief, who then wanted to kill him, he was saved by Pocahontas, Powhatan's daughter. Whether true or not, the tale adds to the colorful legend that still surrounds the Captain's name.

John Smith, "The General Historie of Virginia, New England, and the Summer Isles," London, 1624 (Newberry Library)

The boastful Captain Smith wrote a book about Virginia in which these pictures appeared. Besides examples of his bravery with Indians, you can see his rescue by Pocahontas.

Despite his faults, Smith was a firm and skillful leader. When he was seriously injured in a gunpowder explosion, the colony was in for trouble. He had to return to England for treatment, and no leader arose to take his place. Besides, the new arrivals had brought no food and quickly became a burden to the other colonists. The Indians would not supply provisions.

The weakened colonists, afraid of the Indians, refused to go outside their stockade in search of food. By the middle of the winter of 1609–1610, some of them burned as fuel parts of the houses they lived in. So desperate were they that they even engaged in cannibalism. One man not only murdered his wife but also ate her.

A glorious surprise. When the spring came at last and the "starving time" was over, only sixty out of several hundred settlers were alive. The bedraggled colonists were discouraged beyond belief. Suddenly over the horizon one day loomed two ships, brilliantly named the *Deliverance* and the *Patience*.

The ships had been built out of timbers from the *Sea Venture*, which miraculously had not disappeared after all. It had been swept by the hurricane to the Bermudas, in the warm Caribbean. Not a soul aboard had been lost, and in fact the lucky people had found fruit and animals to eat.

You no doubt can imagine the newcomers' reaction to the starving Virginians. Taking one look, Sir Thomas Gates, the leader, decided to move the poor wretches. He thought the English fishing fleet at Newfoundland, to the north, could provide shelter and food.

As the grateful Virginians sailed down the James River, fate came to their aid again. Virginia's new governor, Lord Delaware, was arriving with a relief expedition of three ships. He ordered the fleeing colonists to return, which they did. Fortunately, they had been persuaded not to burn the Jamestown stockade as they left. The property of the London Company, it had been saved because one day it might be needed again.

A Land of Golden Tobacco

Time and experience provided the necessary key to making the colony stick. One John Rolfe, who became well known in Virginia because he married Pocahontas, deserves credit for showing the way. He obtained some West Indian tobacco, grew # and cured a small crop of it, and sent it to England in 1614, where people received it enthusiastically.

The first American tobacco to reach Europe had been of unpleasant taste. Rolfe's was regarded as being as "pleasant, sweet, and strong" as any "under the sunne."

Acres to till. Within a very few years the raising of tobacco changed the outlook of the entire colony. The governor of Virginia had early arranged for every settler to receive 3 acres of land to cultivate as his own. In return, he would pay rent and give

By piecing together over two hundred pieces found in excavations in Jamestown, scientists restored this baking oven to its appearance of three centuries ago. Hot stones usually heated the oven, though sometimes it was placed directly on the smoldering remains of a fire.

Colonial National Historical Park

74 ##This kind of tobacco was also grown in South America. King James hated the smell of tobacco and vainly forbade its use in England.
See Exercise 3, col. 2, p. 85. The letter to the Jamestown park should be written now.

Planters oversee Negroes packing tobacco leaves to be shipped to Europe, perhaps on ships docked along the coast in the far background.

services to the London Company.

Soon the terms were made even more generous. In 1618 it was decided that every man who brought himself and his family to America would receive 50 acres for each person (including servants).

Immigrants from Africa. The following year a passing Dutch man-of-war from the African coast sold twenty Negroes to the Virginians. The Negroes and their children were able to obtain land and full freedom when they had "worked off" their cost. Yet, as we shall see, with these arrivals Negro slavery was in the making in America.

Shipment of wives. Just about the same time that the Negroes landed, women began to come to Virginia in numbers. Ninety arrived in one shipment—"young women to make wives . . . handsome and honestly educated maids."

The condition of the women was not as romantic as it has sometimes been made out in novels to be. They were simply taking a chance that their life in America would be an improvement over their life in England. They had to travel on crowded, uncomfortable ships, fearing all the while drowning on the way. And there was always the possibility of starving after arrival or, worst of all, proving unacceptable to men in the New World.

In royal hands. Despite much personal sacrifice in America, the Virginia Company itself never made money. The early trials and discouragements of the Jamestown settlement were followed by poor management and disputes among the stockholders. Finally, in 1624 the English king canceled the Virginia Company's charter, and Virginia became a *royal* colony—one governed by the king.

The House of Burgesses. A permanent contribution of the Virginia Company was the House of Burgesses—the earliest representative assembly to meet in America. Consisting of twenty-two men (two from each of the eleven settlements which had been made), it first came together in 1619 to write laws for Virginia. Its members were elected by the men of Virginia, all of whom could vote. Its meeting place was the little church at Jamestown.

Most of the settlers could never have owned any land in England or in the rest of Europe.
#The establishment of the House of Burgesses was the beginning of local government in America.
n 1619 also the first Negroes arrived--the beginning of what is now an important minority.

Careful digging has resulted in uncovering this foundation of the meeting place of the first House of Burgesses in Virginia.

The establishment of the House of Burgesses opened the long road to *democratic* government in America. By this system of rule, the people themselves make decisions on questions of general public concern or elect spokesmen responsible to the public.

Within a few years the Virginia settlements looked far different from what the original leaders had planned. The American environment was giving an unexpected twist to the way colonists had to live.

The spread westward. The raising of tobacco changed the hope that people would live close by one another in towns. Tobacco quickly wore out the settlers' land. After a particular piece of ground was used to grow tobacco a few seasons, the tobacco plants yielded weak stalks and only small leaves. The grower then was forced to look for better land. Gradually the planters spread out over a wide area. The creeks and rivers were lined with tobacco farms.

Towns never became important in Virginia. Jamestown, of course, was the capital of the colony, and it had a few public buildings. But even it did not become an important port, because the more prosperous farmers built wharves on the rivers that ran near their places. Vessels from Europe came directly to them.

Indian relations. The settlers' relations with the Indians were affected by the spreading out of the colony. The alarm felt by the tribesmen at the swift occupying of their land was great, and they turned their feeling into fearful action.

The Englishmen had been lulled into feeling secure against Indian attacks. Many thought the marriage of John Rolfe to Pocahontas would insure peace. Some people compared it with one of those great royal matches that sometimes linked together rival European countries.

But the Indians had other thoughts. They organized to drive the colonists—the invaders of their hunting grounds—out of Virginia and into the sea. On Good Friday ## in 1622, they took the settlers by surprise, killing 347 of those who lived on the outlying farms. The warfare that thus began did not end for two years.

As protection against the tribesmen, the House of Burgesses arranged for the building of a palisade (a huge fence) 6 miles

#The author here introduces a most important concept. Ask why he speaks of a "long road." (Virginia became a royal colony in 1624; democratic government developed slowly in America.)
##Note the reference to the day when Christ was crucified--the Virginians were Christians.

long. Behind this wall many of the remaining settlements could be safe. But by the time it was completed in 1630, the settlements were spilling outside its reach.

Another fierce Indian uprising took place much later—in 1644—when once again the most outlying of the farms were attacked. This time the counterattack of the settlers was successful. The Indians, driven westward, ended their fighting.

Indentured servants. Although a legend was later created about the aristocratic backgrounds of the first Virginians, the truth is that there were very few people of noble birth among them. Most of the settlers came as *indentured servants*. That is, they were under obligation to work for from four to seven years in order to pay for their transportation. At the end of that time, they became free men and women, and many finally acquired considerable land and frequently their own servants.

Indentured servants tended to speed up the westward movement of the settlers as a whole. In general, while they were servants they had little or no interest in helping to preserve the fertility of the soil they tilled. Their lack of care in working the soil tended to wear out the land fast.

On the frontier. When indentured servants had completed their obligation and became free, they were presented with the well-situated land to which they were entitled. Generally they quickly sold their acres and took up farming on the cheaper land at the *frontier*, or the edge of settlement. They became frontiersmen.

Frontier farmers usually moved westward in the fall. Finding land they could see was fertile, they girdled the trees in Indian fashion (see page 10). With axes they then chopped down the weakened trees and prepared the timber needed for crude houses.

By springtime it was possible to grow a crop of corn amid the stumps of the trees. The Indian corn and English turnips and beets were the chief vegetables. In addition, hogs usually were raised, often puny and scrawny in the first year or so—or until the corn crop could be shared with them.

By the second year it became possible to grow a crop of tobacco. This was the so-called cash crop. When the tobacco was eventually sold in England, it provided the small amount of money the frontiersman needed for the goods he could not produce himself. These included sugar, tea, and iron nails.

Usually, after a few years the frontier farmer would sell out, move westward, and

Some of these important relics from the site of the Jamestown colony show plainly how European culture was brought to America. *From left to right:* An earthenware vessel put together from pieces found at Jamestown and probably made there. A pitcher that had been brought to the colony from England. A brass buckle and an earthenware cup. A square bottle that had come to Jamestown from the Netherlands. A bone-handled knife. A clay pipe, possibly like the one seen in the picture on page 75. Thousands of pipes have been dug up at the site of Jamestown.

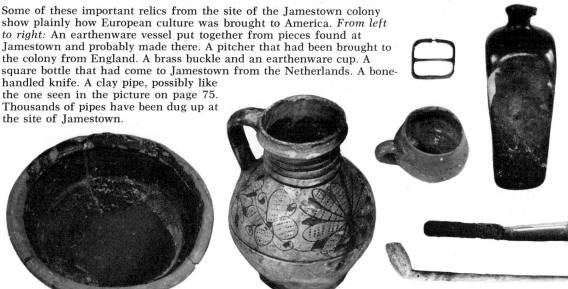

Colonial National Historical Park

start over again. In a lifetime he might do this two or even three times.

The death rate of settlers in Virginia remained shockingly high for a long time. It has been estimated that only one in every five of the newcomers survived the first year. Many had been prisoners in England (not usually criminals, but debtors and victims of political enemies), and their health may already have been weakened. In America they had to face the danger of malaria. This disease claimed numerous victims until quinine, made from Peruvian bark, came into use as medicine in the middle of the seventeenth century.

The conditions in the New World changed in innumerable ways the outlook of the settlers. Even their firm ideas about religion were altered. For example, the Church of England, the officially recognized church in the mother country, was established as the sole religious body in Virginia. All who did not belong—called *dissenters*—were, according to the law, supposed to be expelled. Yet it was so hard to find hands to do the work that few cared to expel a man solely for the way he worshiped God.

Achievements. As Virginia grew—and by 1650 the population was more than 18,000 —the accomplishments of the inhabitants there stood out for all to see. First, they had proved that European families could be transplanted to the New World and support themselves. Second, they had shown that colonists could produce a crop useful in the trade of the mother country. Third, they had established that people who were "failures" in Europe could be "successes" in America. Fourth, they had discovered that even when they faced great dangers, self-government could make possible effective solutions.

---

1. Why was the Virginia Company formed? 2. What two grants did it receive? 3. Account for the London Company's demands on its colonists. 4. How did John Smith contribute to his colony's success? 5. Name a lasting contribution of the Virginia Company to the American people. 6. Upon what crop did Virginians come to depend? How did it affect settlement of the colony? 7. How did indentured servants also affect settlement? 8. Name four achievements of Virginians.

Pilgrims Seek Refuge in New England

The people who settled New England brought to America experience and ideas different from those of the men and women who colonized Virginia. Men and women found in New England a setting of soil and climate that was different, too. The type of colony they created, therefore, had its own characteristics.

A Charitable Grant

The Plymouth group of the Virginia Company was indirectly responsible for the first successful effort to colonize in New England. In August, 1607, an expedition it sent out landed at the mouth of the Kennebec River, in present-day Maine. The forty-four men left behind there at Fort St. ## George suffered fearfully in the bleak cold of the winter that soon closed in on them. The undertaking was a failure.

Sir Ferdinando Gorges. One of the businessmen active in the Plymouth group was Sir Ferdinando Gorges. Determined eventually to plant a colony in America, he directed many expeditions to the coast of

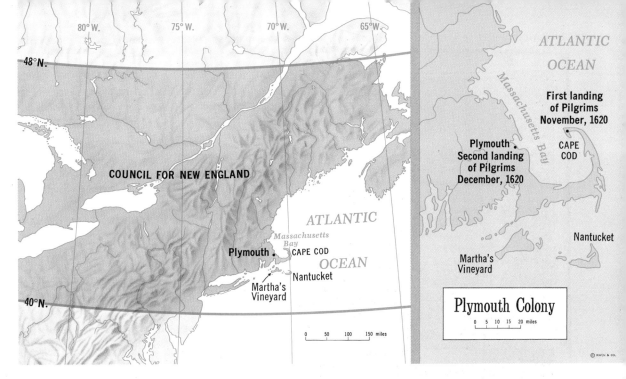

Pilgrim Society

The Plymouth colony—seen in the close-up at the right—was founded on land of the Council for New England in an area now a famous tourist attraction.

The seal of the Plymouth colony.

New England. Bad luck dogged his efforts, and his ships repeatedly ran into trouble even before they were out of sight of the mother country.

In 1620 Gorges and some of the other members of his group obtained a new charter and set themselves up as the Council for New England. They were granted the territory—for the first time called New England—lying between 40° and 48° north latitude and stretching indefinitely westward.

The experience of the Virginians was already well known. It taught that a successful colony required a large amount of money and enthusiastic backers. Neither was easily found. After all, the London Company had never made a profit on its investment. Furthermore, Virginia's "starving time"—already famous in England—did not inspire people to leave their homes, however much they longed for a change.

The Council made many land grants to individuals and to groups. The first of these grants was made in 1620, to a group of Englishmen known as Puritans. They were then living in the Netherlands.

The Puritan view. The story of the Puritans really began shortly after England broke away from the Roman Catholic # church. A considerable number of people felt that the ceremonies of the Church of England ought to be simplified—*purified* was the word they used. Furthermore, they saw no reason why they could not interpret for themselves the Word of God as revealed in the Bible, rather than having the

#Review these facts: Before the middle of the 1500's, all Europeans were Roman Catholic. The form of Prostestantism called Lutheranism began in Germany and spread generally through northern Europe. The Puritans were members of the Protestant Church of England in England.

79

that they were increasingly out of place in church and different from most of their fellow citizens. A small group of them living in Scrooby, England, having become convinced that they could not "purify" the Church of England, decided to emigrate to the Netherlands. These people were called *separatists* because they had ## separated from the Church.

In the town of Leyden in 1609, the separatists settled down and were soon joined by other separatists, for the Dutch welcomed any Christians. They lived there for twelve years, "knit together as a body in the most strict and sacred bond and covenant of the Lord."

Still dissatisfied. But no matter how they tried, the separatists could not escape the pressures of the world about them. In the Netherlands they were free to worship as they pleased, but their children were taking on Dutch ways. They themselves could find work only as day laborers. Besides, the Netherlands' war with Spain seemed to threaten life in their adopted land.

The separatists, therefore, made a fateful decision. They would pull up their roots once again and go to America. There they would establish an English community of their own, far from European control or trouble. They became pilgrims—wanderers in search of an agreeable homeland.

The Pilgrims, as the separatists were called, were poor people, unlike most other Puritans, who were usually successful businessmen. They knew they would have to find a way to pay the expense of their trip. They hit upon a plan.

The Pilgrims' plan called for going to Virginia in the service of a group of English merchants. There they would create a colony and work as a team for seven years to make it succeed. Afterward they would divide the profits with the investors in England and be on their own. They hoped, of course, to live at some considerable distance north of the Jamestown settlement.

Above: A page from Governor Bradford's Bible, which had been published in England in 1592. *Below:* The Pilgrim's signature.

Pilgrim Society

clergy do it for them.

The Puritans regarded lavish showiness either in religious displays or in their personal lives as sinful. They denied themselves dancing and public entertainment. Hard work was good for a man, they said, and it ought to be his delight.

Man, the Puritans said, has two main duties in the world: one is to serve God # and the other is to work hard at a chosen calling in life, whatever it may be. They took personally the majestic words of the Bible (Proverbs 22:29), "Seest thou a man diligent in his business? he shall stand before kings."

To the Netherlands. The Puritans felt

##Students should understand that the separatists were Puritans who gave up reforming the Church of England. Later they were called Pilgrims--"travelers." Their problems in the Netherlands were those of any immigrants in a foreign land who do not wish to change their ways.

After entering into a partnership with London investors, the Pilgrims set out from the Netherlands August 15, 1620, on a worthless vessel, the *Speedwell*. They had received the promise of King James I that "he would . . . not molest them [that is, interfere with them], provided they carried themselves peaceably."

The voyage across. The *Speedwell* was to sail to England. There it would join a somewhat larger ship, the *Mayflower*, whose passengers included still other separatists.

The travelers were as poorly equipped as any Englishmen who ever ventured across the Atlantic. They were strengthened, though, by their incomparable courage.

The trip began with a serious hitch: the *Speedwell* sprang a leak, and its passengers had to be transferred to the *Mayflower*. On September 16 the *Mayflower*, carrying about a hundred people, finally put to sea from Plymouth, England.

Leaders. Three of the Pilgrims were especially outstanding: William Brewster, the elder of the group; Miles Standish, who became their military leader; and William Bradford, who became their governor. Bradford also wrote the group's history and had a large part in helping the Pilgrims hold together.

When the *Mayflower* at last left port, the  # time was past for a smooth, warm-weather crossing of the Atlantic. After a hard voyage the prospective colonists came to what is now Provincetown, on the tip of Cape Cod, in the latter part of November. In the chilly weather a landing party led by Miles Standish went ashore to find a suitable place for a settlement. How different was the bleak scene from the first glimpse of America the people of Virginia had had!

While these scouts were away, the *Mayflower* rolled in the surf. The excitement and anxiety aboard must have been at high pitch.

The crowding on the ship had set the people's nerves on edge. Also, there was snow on the ground, and many rumors were circulating as to the dangers ahead.

The hold of the ship must have been a noisy place, too: there were thirty children aboard. During the crossing a boy had been born, named appropriately "Oceanus." And a girl had been born while the ship rode at anchor. She was named "Peregrine," which is the Latin form of *pilgrim*.

The scouts returned with a decision.

About two hundred years after the Pilgrims landed in America, an artist painted his idea of the event. He added Indians, though none had met the Europeans, and he incorrectly portrayed the *Mayflower* (background).

Collection of Mrs. Robert Bowler, Plymouth (Pilgrim Society)

The Pilgrims, seen here on their way to church, attended two
Sunday services, one in the morning and one in the afternoon.

They would remain there instead of going southward to Virginia.

The brave band of people went ashore. Bradford later wrote: "It was winter, and they that know the winters of the country know them to be sharp and violent. . . . What could they [the Pilgrims] see but a hideous and desolate wilderness. . . ?"

The Mayflower Compact. Arrangements had not been made for the governing of the colony. But circumstances forced the Pilgrims to act. When it became clear that they were going to settle in New England rather than in Virginia, a number of men declared they would not obey the leaders. Authority over them, they said, was based on arrangements with the London backers, which had called for a Virginia colony.

To avoid difficulties, forty-one men signed a *compact*, or agreement, while the *Mayflower* lay in Provincetown Harbor. By its terms they agreed to form a government and make "just and equal laws . . . unto which we promise all due submission and obedience."

The Mayflower Compact stands as one of the landmarks on the long road to self-government. As we have seen, the men of Virginia had recently laid a milestone of their own (page 75).

A Home in the Wilderness

The location of the colony was poor. So the Pilgrims decided upon another site, which they called Plymouth, after the name of their port of departure from England. It was located directly across the bay from the place they had first selected. Plymouth had a good harbor, and some of the land had been cleared and planted in corn by Indians.

Patient suffering. Gathering food and building shelter were, of course, the chief tasks. The men did not have a minute to lose. Eighteen of them had brought their wives with them, unlike the men of Virginia, who had traveled as bachelors.

The suffering that quickly overcame Plymouth was horrifying: the lack of adequate housing and food brought on disease that spread through the colony like a brush fire. Sometimes only a handful of the settlers were able to care for their fallen fellows. But they faithfully cared for the ill.

Brewster was to write: ". . . be it spoken, [they] spared no pains, night or day, but with abundance of toil and hazard of their own health, fetched them wood, made them fires, drest their meat, made their beds, washed their loathsome clothes,

#Ask the class to compare the step toward self-government the Pilgrims took with that taken by the Virginians. No such steps were taken in the Spanish settlements. English culture included some self-government--Spanish culture did not.

cloathed and unclothed them . . . and all this willingly and cheerfully, without any grudging in the least."

Indian friends. At first, out of fear, the settlers shunned the Indians. The colonists did not then know that a terrible epidemic of either smallpox or influenza had practically wiped out the tribes in the region shortly before the landing. When spring came, an Indian by the name of Samoset surprised the settlers by introducing himself in a friendly fashion, in broken English. He had, he said, learned English words from fishermen working in American waters.

Samoset left and returned, as he had promised he would, with another Indian, Squanto. Squanto spoke even better English than Samoset, because he had for a number of years been a captive in the mother country.

Four or five days later, Chief Massasoit appeared, having traveled 40 miles to visit the colonists. The governor and Massasoit smoked a pipe of peace. Then they made a "treaty." It provided that the Indians would not injure the Pilgrims and that the Pilgrims would not harm the Indians.

Squanto stayed on after Massasoit left, and, Brewster wrote, he "became a special instrument sent of God. . . ." He showed the Pilgrims how to plant corn and where to catch fish and guided them to unknown places. He never left them until he died.

When the *Mayflower* sailed back to England, not one of the colonists returned with it. The temptation must have been great, though, for that winter thirteen of the eighteen wives and many others had died.

Thanksgiving. But the settlement had a good summer. In June, 1621, the Council for New England gave the colony a generous land grant. When fall came, the people had confidence that they were going to be able to survive as a colony. In November the Pilgrims gathered for the first Thanksgiving, enjoying a feast of wild ## duck, venison, fish, clams, corn bread, and other good foods.

Soon the settlers discovered the advantages of the fur trade. The commerce in skins became a mainstay in their struggle to make a living. One historian has said that the chief supports of the Plymouth colony were the Bible and the beaver. When the ship *Fortune*—sent by the London backers—arrived shortly after Thanksgiving, the Pilgrims were able to fill it with oak timbers and valuable furs.

However, the London merchants never received the profits they expected. In 1627 Governor Bradford finally negotiated a settlement with the London partners. He agreed to buy out their investment by paying them off in nine annual installments.

Plymouth, despite the skills and hard work of the Pilgrims, never really flourished. First of all, the soil was not fertile

Our national festival in the fourth week of November recalls the Pilgrims' thanksgiving for their first rich harvest.

What foods can be identified? What signs of friendship?

enough for raising good crops. Second, the harbor at Plymouth was not large enough to receive the bigger vessels engaged in trade. Third, fur-bearing animals soon disappeared from the immediate vicinity. Fourth, since the colony was not on a river, it was out of reach of other areas. Finally, there were not enough people back in England who would join the colony and in that way increase its strength.

What the Pilgrims stand for. By 1637 the Pilgrims numbered a mere 549. Nevertheless, the Pilgrim Fathers, as historians have sometimes called these hardy souls, had shown that it was possible to survive in New England. In time they would be recalled as symbols of the virtues and steady habits we Americans like to think all of us possess when we are at our best.

The people who settled in Virginia and Plymouth did not find wealth lying on the surface, to be had for the taking, as had been the Spanish experience. But they learned that the trade in tobacco, furs, and fish could also be richly rewarding.

A big problem for Englishmen was the shortage of labor—hands—to do the work of taming the wilderness and *making* it productive. They never were able to force the Indians to work for them, as the Spanish had, and the Indians did not adopt their culture. But even before the problem of finding a labor supply had been solved, the two English footholds on the Atlantic seaboard were joined by others.

---

1. Describe the land grant given the Council for New England. 2. What were the views of the Puritans? 3. For what three reasons did the separatists leave the Netherlands? 4. In what did the English colonists trade? 5. How can you explain why Plymouth was not a successful colony? 6. What do the Pilgrims stand for?

The Workshop

Observe that the English were not as interested in missionary work among the Indians as the Spanish and the French were. Neither was there a blending of English and Indian cultures in the United States like the blending of Spanish and Indian cultures in Mexico, for example.

The Shapers of Our World

Identify each of the following, and tell how each helped the English establish a foothold in North America.

Gilbert
Frobisher
Raleigh
Virginia Dare
James I
Pocahontas
Mayflower Compact

John Rolfe
Miles Standish
Bradford
Squanto
House of
  Burgesses
Spanish Armada

Adding to Your Vocabulary

Be sure you can use each of these terms correctly:

joint-stock
  company
charter
palisade
man-of-war
royal colony
indentured
  servant

democratic
frontier
cash crop
debtors
dissenters
Puritans
Pilgrims
separatists

Thinking Things Through

After carefully reviewing the boxed-in questions within the chapter, answer the following:

1. Why did the defeat of the Spanish # Armada help open the path for English colonization overseas?

2. Why did the growth of industry in

#Students need to remember that Spain earlier controlled the Atlantic Ocean and also the Pacific coasts of the Americas. Sir Francis Drake challenged this control. Until the Spanish Armada was defeated, the English could not freely carry on trade and colonize.

y to involve all students in activities in "The Research Center." They are designed in such a way that everybody can participate--everybody can feel his talents are being used.

the British Isles lead to colonization overseas?

3. Why, in your opinion, did men like Gilbert and Raleigh badly misjudge conditions in the New World when they were planning colonies?

4. Why could the House of Burgesses and other legislatures that developed in the colonies be referred to as schools for independence?

5. Why were cash crops considered necessary for the success of the American colonies?

6. What was the chief difference between Puritans and separatists in Europe? When the Puritans came to America, they, too, were separatists. Why?

7. How did what the Pilgrims and the settlers at Jamestown found in the New World compare with what they expected to find?

Sharpening Your Map Skills

1. Every map in this book has a scale. What is the purpose of the scale? The one used for making the insert in the map on page 79 is different from the one for the rest of the map. Why? Which part of the map was made on a small scale? On a large scale?

2. King James I gave the London and Plymouth groups land grants that were located by degrees of north latitude. What is #north latitude? Find maps in Chapter 1 in which both north and south latitude are shown. Longitude may be either west or east. Why? In which did the two English land grants lie?

3. It was said that when Britain's foreign possessions—or empire—were most widespread, the sun never set on the British flag. What did this mean?

The Research Center

Use some of these activities to test your skill at carrying on research and presenting information.

1. Find out the sizes of some of the ships that brought colonists to America. Make a graph comparing the sizes of those ships with sizes of some modern ocean liners. Make another graph comparing the length of time it took to make a sea voyage in colonial times with the time it takes to make both a sea voyage and a transocean flight today.

2. In 1957 Queen Elizabeth II and her husband visited Jamestown, Virginia. Imagine that you were her speech writer. Compose a brief address that she might have given as she stepped aboard the reconstructed *Godspeed* on the James River.

3. The Jamestown and Plymouth areas have both been restored as national historical parks. Request illustrative material from both. Arrange it in poster form and report to the class on the restorations.

4. Have a group write and present to the class a brief playlet, using both historical facts and imagination. Perhaps some students could make scenery and others costumes. Possible subjects for the plays are: (*a*) the last days of Raleigh's lost colony, (*b*) the departure of the Pilgrims from Plymouth, and (*c*) the signing of the Mayflower Compact.

5. Collect samples of the kinds of food that women of the Plymouth colony served at the first Thanksgiving. Arrange a display of them, possibly with pictures of Indians and Pilgrims.

6. Write the kind of letter a Virginia settler of 1625 might have sent to a relative in England explaining to the relative why he should come to live in America.

*By examining many map scales, students can see that <u>large</u> areas are shown on <u>small</u> scales and <u>small</u> areas on <u>large</u> scales. Be sure they understand why.
#Of course, latitude is numbered north-south of the equator and longitude east-west of Greenwich.

(a) A minister's home—the Parson Capen House—built in Massachusetts in 1638, restored in 1913.

(b) The Puritan John Winthrop gave this silver Communion cup to the first church in Boston.

(c) The richly garbed Cecilius Calvert and his grandson display a map of Maryland, the colony the grandfather founded. At the left is a Negro slave.

(d) Both sides of a coin, showing a likeness of Calvert and a symbol of the mother country.

(e) Youngsters in Massachusetts learned the alphabet from hornbooks, like this. Transparent layers of horn covered the frames, which students held by the handles.

(f) Perhaps the oldest timepiece in America, this sundial belonged to John Endecott, who led settlers to Massachusetts in 1628.

(g) A Puritan woman of the seventeenth century embroidered this elaborate Asian design, which traders may have brought to England.

(h) The seal used by the Massachusetts Bay Colony featured an Indian saying, "Come over and help us."

(g)

(h)

k what the pictures on
86 and above suggest
ligion, slavery, education, trade).

CHAPTER 5

A SECOND WAVE OF SETTLEMENTS

uis B. Wright's <u>The Atlantic Frontier</u> is an excellent reference book for your use. Before beginning this apter, review the accounts of the first two English colonies given in Chapter 4. What lessons did the lonists there learn?

As the Pilgrims struggled to make their way in the New World, other Puritans were making strong efforts at home to "purify" the Church of England. They hoped, however, to remain within it rather than become separatists.

James I was no longer as unfriendly to Puritans as he had seemed to be when he threatened to drive them out of the country. But James died in 1625, and his son Charles I, who then became king, quickly aroused the Puritans again. He supported a group of churchmen who had determined to crush them.

his is the story of a second wave of Puritan settlers. The first were the Pilgrims.

Puritans Cross Over and Dig In

Puritans more and more became fearful that they would be the victims of "the generall callamitie" they said the new king's conduct would bring. They decided to seek a home elsewhere. Because many of the Puritans were rich, they could afford the cost that such a venture would involve.

Under Winthrop's Wing

By the late 1620's the Puritans, like other Englishmen, had heard firsthand stories about life in America. It is safe to guess that by then hundreds of traders and fishermen had visited the shores of the colonies. At least they had seen colonists'

houses outlined against the sky.

In the summer of 1629 John Winthrop, a Puritan lawyer, decided to go to America. He wanted to escape not only the religious and political intolerance of the day but also the burden of personal debts. He soon had a following of others who held ideas like his—although not all were in debt. Almost miraculously arrangements for their colony were made.

In 1628 a group of Puritans obtained from the Council for New England a grant of land between the Merrimack and Charles rivers. Possibly through the influence of a friend of the king's they obtained a charter to establish a royal colony

#

Students will readily understand religious intolerance from their previous study of American his- ory. It appeared in England when certain people wished to crush the Puritans. Political intoler- nce showed itself in the way the king treated the Puritans.

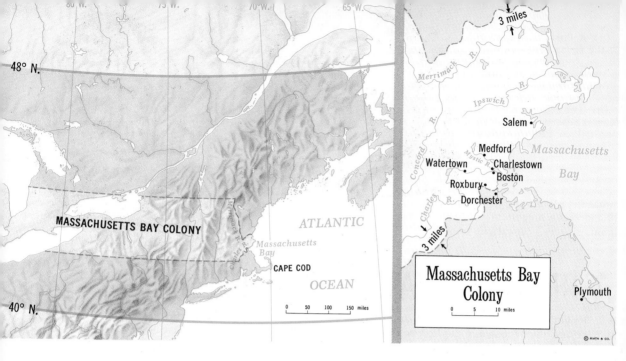

Massachusetts Bay Colony

American Numismatic Society

Above: The beginnings of Massachusetts are seen in the close-up at the right. Salem, the oldest town, was called Naumkeag by the Indians. *Left:* This pine-tree shilling, about the size of our quarter but worth only about half as much, was issued by the first colonial mint, opened in Boston in 1652.

there. The next year a group was formed called the Massachusetts Bay Company. "Massachusetts," meaning "near the great hill," was the name of an Indian tribe that once lived in the Massachusetts Bay area. The company immediately sent a small party to America to prepare the way for a larger band to follow.

The "Great Migration." In March, 1630, more than a thousand people were ready to cross the Atlantic. The people of this Great Migration, as it is called, sailed on eleven vessels. By summer's end they had been transported to the Puritan colony—the largest single group of emigrants from Europe so far.

The colonists were also the first people of considerable wealth to come to the New World. One of them, for example,

was Winthrop's brother-in-law Emmanuel Downing, for whose son Downing Street in London was later named. Another was Richard Saltonstall, the first of a long line of Saltonstalls who have played an important part in the affairs of Massachusetts. These men were well educated and used to a life of comfort. In fact, servants even accompanied some of them to America.

The most important figure in the colony was John Winthrop, the first governor. Vigorous, God-fearing, used to giving orders, he never doubted that he would be able to create a lasting Puritan community in America.

A setback. But when the first group of "Great Migration" emigrants landed at Salem on June 12, 1630, their jaws sagged in dismay. They learned that a quarter of the advance party of colonists had died during the winter. Many others were weak and ailing and would not last much long-

Map: The lines drawn 3 miles north of the Merrimack R. and 3 miles south of the Charles mark the exact boundary lines of the Bay Colony's land grant (right). The boundaries of the grant of the Council of New England are shown at the left. The Bay Colony was plainly inside it.

er. Two hundred of the fresh arrivals immediately decided to return home in the vessel which had brought them!

Winthrop had the foresight to see that supplies would be needed quickly if the venture was to have a chance of success. The returning ship, the *Lyon*, carried word to England to send provisions as soon as possible. These did not arrive quickly enough, however, to prevent much suffering: before the next year two hundred of the settlers had perished.

Winthrop and his people settled at Charlestown, along the coast south of Salem. One of the first tasks he set was the building of a meetinghouse, which was accomplished even while the settlers were living in tents.

The toll of winter. The freeze came late that year. But when it did come—about Christmastime—it quickly left its mark. Food was hard to find, and some of the people simply could not eat corn. Scurvy and homesickness also took a heavy toll.

Nevertheless, not everything was discouraging. Some of the women, for instance, successfully braved the weather to dig clams and other seafood. Some of the men made their way to Plymouth for aid.

When the *Lyon* came back to America in February, 1631, there was rejoicing. It brought not only food that was familiar but also lemons—a cure for scurvy. An early spring also helped. But Winthrop's words to his son back home stated the facts clearly: "People must come well provided and not too many at once."

Boston. Shortly Winthrop saw that the water supply of Charlestown was too small for such a large group. He decided to locate in Boston. Situated favorably along the coast, it gradually became the central city of the colony.

All was not yet well, but John Winthrop had written his wife in 1630: "I thanke God, I like so well to be heer, as I doe not repent my comminge. . . . I never fared better in my life, never slept better, never had more contente of minde . . . we have not the . . . meanes of . . . comforts heer which we had in England, but the Lord is allsufficient, blessed be his holy name."

Governing the Bay Colony. The problem of what kind of government should be established arose almost immediately. Au-

Seven hundred Puritans made the long voyage to the Bay Colony on the four ships in Boston Harbor painted here. The *Arabella*—center—carried Winthrop.

Collection of Walter B. Ellis, Alexandria, Virginia

thority in the colony rested with the officers of the Massachusetts Bay Company. In August, 1629, the stockholders had agreed to either migrate to the colony or sell their stock. The company and its charter and governing power were transferred to America. The result was that Massachusetts was less dependent on England than other colonies. Fewer than twenty of the two thousand settlers there by the end of 1630 were members of the company. In October of that year over one hundred men petitioned # to be made members, or *freemen*. That is, they asked to be allowed to vote when decisions were made.

Maintaining control. The petition was granted, but the difficult question of who should vote remained under discussion. A

In both Plymouth and Massachusetts, churches were organized in which the control was left to each congregation. This church in Massachusetts today calls to mind the Puritans who built it as a Congregational church.

Massachusetts Department of Commerce and Development

colony as weak as Massachusetts required a firm central leadership. To open the vote to all might take from the Puritans the control of the colony, since not all the settlers were Puritans.

Yet if the number of freemen was not increased, some of the settlers might just go off and join the Pilgrims at Plymouth. The Pilgrims, who were struggling to grow in numbers, would have welcomed them with open arms. Or as we shall soon see, Massachusetts Bay settlers might go to Maine or New Hampshire, where they could also make a home.

People continued to insist on being allowed to take part in the government of Massachusetts. For a long time, though, only members of Puritan congregations could become freemen.

The charter provided that the freemen meet four times a year as a "General Court" to make laws. Betweentimes the colony was to be managed by a governor and a lieutenant governor (or magistrates, as they were called) and a board of "assistants" elected annually by the freemen.

As the power of the magistrates and the assistants grew, the freemen objected. Yet it would have been impossible for the freemen to participate in government as directly as they wished. They were too many by then, and too widely scattered.

Consequently, it became the custom for each town to send two representatives, or deputies, to the General Court. By 1644 a government of two houses had developed. The lower was made up of the deputies from the towns, and the upper consisted of the governor and the board of assistants.#

The clergy in charge. Being religious men, the freemen tended to choose magistrates approved by the clergy. For fifty years the magistrates and the ministers managed to control the Massachusetts Bay Colony.

So far as the pious Puritans of Massachusetts were concerned, the government they had created was perfect. It was a

heocracy" comes from the Greek words <u>theos</u>,
aning "God," and <u>kratein</u>, "to rule."

theocracy, that is, it was a government run according to God's word, as they understood it. They believed, as their beloved John Winthrop wrote, "that God hath provided this place, to be a refuge for manye, whom he means to save out of the General Destruction."

Discuss "pious" and "refuge."

Troublemaking Preachers

The affairs of Massachusetts were thrown into confusion between 1634 and 1637. A brilliant but unyielding man and an equally remarkable, argumentative woman were the causes of the trouble.

Roger Williams. The man was Roger Williams, a young minister who had studied at Cambridge University in England. (He had arrived in the colony aboard the *Lyon* when it made its return trip bringing the lemons that ended the suffering from scurvy.) Williams' views of religion were somewhat different from those of most of the people who came to Massachusetts. He did not believe, as the Puritans did, that the Church of England could be "purified." He believed that a complete separation from it was needed.

"Dangerous" views. A brilliant man, Williams nevertheless came soon to be regarded as being "very unsettled in judgemente." For one thing, he wanted to cut the ties of the Massachusetts churches to the Church of England. For another, he declared that the land of New England rightfully belonged to the Indians.

Moreover, Williams denied that government had the right to exercise any authority over an individual's religious beliefs. He even denied that it had the right to punish people who broke the Sabbath.

Williams, a personal friend of Winthrop's, was a lovable man. Some people found him to be the kind of minister they would follow wherever he might choose to lead them. However, even his faithful congregation at Salem grew fright-

Charles A. Goodrich, "A History of the United States of America....,"
H. F. Sumner & Co., 1833 (New London County Historical Society)

On this early American woodcut, an artist showed the departure of Roger Williams—in foreground—from the Bay Colony. Friends appear to be accompanying him.

ened at the turn his ideas were taking.

Banished. Massachusetts officials decided in 1635 to banish Williams from the colony, that is, throw him out. The authorities agreed to allow him to remain through the winter, provided he did not "go about to draw others to his opinions." When he failed to keep silent, the General Court moved to ship him back to England. He never gave the authorities a chance to catch him. On a cold January day he fled to Narragansett Bay, where the Indians gave him shelter.

Years later Williams told a friend in a letter, "That ever honored Governor, Mr. Winthrop, privately wrote to me to steer my course to Narragansett Bay and Indians. . . . I steered my course from Salem (though in winter snow, which I feel yet) unto these parts." "These parts" were Providence, now a city in Rhode Island, where he would help build a colony based on his views.

Freedom of religion. Roger Williams made "liberty of conscience," that is, free-

Emphasize that the Puritans wanted religious freedom for themselves but were unwilling to give it
o others. Let the class discuss what they think the Puritans--who felt their religion was the true
ne--should have done with Roger Williams and Anne Hutchinson (next page).

Above: This drawing of the emigration to Connecticut appeared in the first complete history of our country. Written by George Bancroft, it was published in 1834.

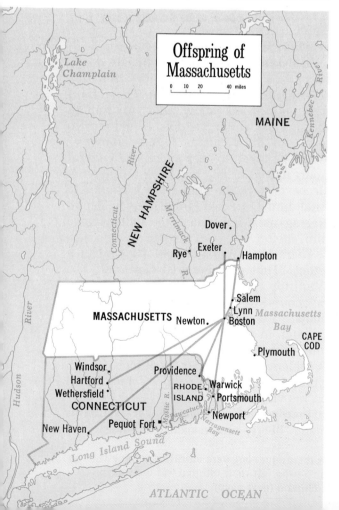

Offspring of Massachusetts

0   10   20   40 miles

Left: As Virginia has been called the Mother of Presidents, so Massachusetts can be called the Mother of Colonies.

<u>Map:</u> Call attention to the English names: Dover, Exeter, Windsor, Warwick, for example.

#The author adds another element to the st[u]dents' concept of American democracy.

dom to worship God in one's own fashion, a basic principle of the community he founded. Eventually this freedom would be a foundation stone of American democracy and a shining example to men everywhere.

"Mistress Anne." Anne Hutchinson, like Williams, easily made friends. She had arrived in Massachusetts Bay Colony in 1634 accompanied by her husband, William—"a man of very mild temper . . . and wholly guided by his wife."

All we know about Anne Hutchinson was written by those who criticized or hated her. Yet her good character shines through all these reports. She was the kind of person welcomed in a community that suffers loneliness and boredom. She gossiped, comforted the sick, and enjoyed thinking and talking about the meaning of the ministers' sermons.

"Mistress Anne," as she was called, each week held a meeting of a small group in her home—a familiar custom of the day. Her purpose was to discuss the sermon delivered the previous Sunday. She quickly attracted a following because she had a reputation as a midwife and because of the force and charm of her manner.

Mrs. Hutchinson argued that doing good deeds could not get one into Heaven. She said that if the Holy Spirit was within a person, he would go to Heaven no matter what he did, good or bad.

Mrs. Hutchinson's teachings raised serious questions. Among them was this one: How could the Puritan colony, dependent on maintaining strictly moral personal behavior, stand for such preaching? Although the ideas she presented were upsetting to the ministers and officials, you can understand their appeal to ordinary men and women.

To Portsmouth. The authorities decided

to act. Mrs. Hutchinson was brought to trial in Newtown, convicted, and sentenced to be banished in the fall of 1637. Her banishment was postponed over winter because she was expecting a baby. In the spring of 1638, she went to Portsmouth, in what is now Rhode Island.

Offspring of Massachusetts

An unexpected result of these troubles in Massachusetts was the establishment of new colonies. These would no doubt soon have developed anyway. But they would not necessarily have been offshoots of the Bay Colony.

Rhode Island. Portsmouth had been settled in 1638 by a group of eighteen persons led by a friend of Mrs. Hutchinson's. People from Portsmouth later established the village of Newport. The town of Warwick was organized by settlers from both Providence and Portsmouth. As the communities multiplied, they became like building blocks to be used in a new colony.

In 1643 Roger Williams was sent to the mother country by the community of Providence and by the other settlements to obtain a charter from King Charles I. In England war had recently broken out among the people. Before it ended, the king was beheaded. For a time Parliament took over complete management of British affairs. As it was controlled by Puritans, it granted the charter Williams wanted—in 1644.

Three years later the voters of Providence, Newport, and Portsmouth formed a union under the charter, and Warwick was admitted to it. So Rhode Island became a separate colony.

Liberal arrangements. Rhode Island's government *in form* was closely modeled on that of Massachusetts. There were a governor, a board of four assistants (one from each of the colony's communities), and an assembly consisting of representatives of each of the communities.

An important difference from Massachusetts was that a man did not have to be a church member to vote. Furthermore, the towns could propose laws for passage by the legislature, and the towns could accept or reject laws passed by the legislature.

The government of Rhode Island was, therefore, a very different kind of government *in spirit* from the one that Massachusetts had established. Life in America was weakening the stern ways of the Massachusetts leaders.

Into Connecticut. The colonists who left Massachusetts not only disagreed on religious matters but also were seeking better homes. Very early, Massachusetts people discovered fertile land in the Connecticut River Valley. In 1633 some of the people from Plymouth made a settlement at what is now Windsor, Connecticut. Others followed them. In the summer of 1636 three entire church congregations left Massachusetts and resettled at Windsor, Wethersfield, and Hartford.

Hooker of Hartford. Hartford was settled by a congregation that came from Newtown, Massachusetts. Its minister was the Reverend Thomas Hooker. He and his followers—one hundred in all—traveled the hundred miles to their new location in Hartford driving their cattle before them. Hooker, who, like Roger Williams, had disagreed with Governor Winthrop, must have felt like Moses leading his people into the Promised Land.

The younger Winthrop. The Connecticut settlers were living on land a group of Puritans had obtained from the Council for New England. In the fall of 1635 these Puritans had sent over to America Winthrop's son, John Winthrop, Jr. The younger Winthrop was to be "governor of the river Connecticut, with the places adjoining thereunto."

In May, 1637, the citizens of Windsor, Hartford, and Wethersfield formed a self-governing colony. They established a General Court made up of six assistants and nine representatives, three from each of the three towns.

The Fundamental Orders. The settlers were drawing on their experience in Massachusetts. But they were more generous. In a document describing their government, drawn up by their General Court and adopted in 1639, the vote was granted even to men who were not church members. The document is called the Fundamental Orders.

New Haven. Gazing in the direction of Rhode Island and Connecticut, the faithful of Massachusetts may have wondered what kind of wickedness surrounded them. The only neighboring settlement that gave them pleasure was the one at New Haven. That town, on Long Island Sound, was settled by a group of Puritans under the direction of their minister, John Davenport, and a wealthy London businessman, Theophilus Eaton.

Davenport and Eaton had arrived in Boston at about the time that the fight was raging over Anne Hutchinson and her teachings. Distressed by the commotion they heard, they had led fifty families to the other side of the Connecticut River. There the Puritans had "purchased" from the Indians the land they settled on.

Being severe and very religious people, the settlers organized their community according to the practices in the Massachusetts Bay Colony. In order to vote, a man had to be a church member. Unlike any other colony, New Haven did not have trial by jury.

Davenport was a strong governor. As new settlers created towns near New Haven, he brought them under his control. Consequently, two colonies with somewhat differing views of life developed within Connecticut—one was governed by John Winthrop, Jr., and the other by Davenport.

The king's grant. In 1662 John Winthrop, Jr., a warm and friendly man, trav-

eled to England. He persuaded the king to grant to Connecticut all the land from the southern border of Massachusetts to Long Island Sound. Westward the colony was to extend to the Pacific! By a later agreement with Rhode Island, the Pawcatuck River was made its eastern boundary.

The king permitted the colony to continue the government it had established under the Fundamental Orders. Because New Haven was included in the royal grant, it became a part of Connecticut, although this made some of its people unhappy.

The younger Winthrop was elected governor of Connecticut for eighteen terms in a row. Perhaps his numerous reelections tell us something of the kind of affection and respect he inspired. The liberal charter he obtained for Connecticut will always be a reminder of a son who almost equaled his father in influence on New England.

Gorges and Mason. Meanwhile the Council for New England had granted to Sir Ferdinando Gorges and Captain John Mason practically all of what are now the states of Maine and New Hampshire. The men organized several settlements in their territory. In 1629 these adventurers divided the region between themselves.

Founding New Hampshire. As dissatisfaction with conditions in Massachusetts continued, towns were also begun in New Hampshire. One was started by Anne Hutchinson's brother-in-law, the Reverend John Wheelwright. He had been banished from Boston for taking her side in the famous disagreement. After spending a winter with the Indians just outside the Massachusetts line with thirty-five of his followers, he established Exeter, New Hampshire, in 1638.

In the same year a group which had left the church at Lynn, Massachusetts, founded the town of Hampton, also in New Hampshire. The towns of Rye and Dover had been settled a few years earlier by members of the Church of England.

Emphasize that in spite of certain differences between the New England colonies, all provided for considerable control by the people and little control by the king. For these reasons the New England colonies became seedbeds of American independence.

The picture illustrates how this book uses art as a means of helping students understand the culture of the people. See Exercise 3 under "Understanding Pictures," p. 103.

Three young Puritans, David, Joanna, and Abigail Mason, posed in their Sunday best for an unknown artist in Boston about 1670.

Collection of Nathaniel Hamlen, Boston
(Photo by David F. Lawlor)

Because the New Hampshire settlements differed from one another in their religious views, they were not able to join together easily to form a single government. Nevertheless, they drew up a compact to live by.

The towns immediately north of Massachusetts came under the influence of the Bay Colony. For many years they were represented in the Massachusetts General Court. In 1679, however, New Hampshire's claim to be a separate colony was recognized in England, and it received its own charter from the king.

Maine's struggle. Maine's history, like New Hampshire's, is a story of a relatively weak collection of settlements. Before 1640 there were only a few communities on the eastern side of the boundary line between Maine and New Hampshire. The population of Maine never grew sufficiently to fulfill Gorges' lofty hopes for his colony.

Massachusetts, meanwhile, had laid claim to the Maine settlements, and it annexed them one by one between 1652 and 1658. In 1691 Massachusetts received a new charter. Maine was included in it and disappeared as a separate colony. It did not reappear until 1820, under circumstances which no one in the seventeenth century could have foreseen (see page 311).

Indian Neighbors

The reference is to the Missouri Compromise.

During the time when the Massachusetts settlements produced others in Connecticut, Rhode Island, New Hampshire, and Maine, the Indians grew alarmed. The # towns growing along the Connecticut River and Narragansett Bay seemed to threaten the Indians living in between. The most distressed were the Pequot, who had only recently been pushed into the area (see the map on page 92) as a result of wars with the Iroquois.

The Pequot War. In the summer of 1636 a trader from Boston was killed. The Massachusetts leaders blamed the Pequot, although they were not responsible for the murder. Cruel fighting broke out the following year.

Discuss the problem the Indians had in trying to keep their farmland in the face of increasing 95
umbers of settlers from Europe. Ask for suggestions about how the Indians' rights might have
een preserved better by Englishmen--rights that actually were disregarded.

The Englishmen were able to win the Mohegan Indians over to their side. Moreover, Roger Williams played an important part in keeping his old friends, the Narraganset, out of the fight.

An army of Englishmen and Mohegan skillfully outwitted the Pequot and surprised them in their fort on the Mystic River. In the following attack, the colonists and their Indian allies almost destroyed the whole tribe. Later many of the re-

maining Pequot—including women and children—were slain or made slaves.

The tribesmen's complaint. The Indians did not understand the European idea that an individual could acquire complete title to, that is, full ownership of, a piece of land. They thought of land as being owned by the whole community and of all individuals as being able to use it.

So-called purchases of land from the Indians, therefore, never meant the same to the tribesmen as to the Englishmen. When an Indian chief placed his mark on a "treaty," the English took it to mean that he had given up forever the rights of his people to use the territory. The Indian, on the other hand, was merely agreeing to allow the Englishmen to share in the use of an Indian community's property.

The solid settlements of the English ter-

Charles A. Goodrich, "Stories on the History of Connecticut . . . .,"
D. F. Robinson & Co., 1829 (New London County Historical Society)

A seventeenth-century artist drew the pictorial map—below—of the attack on the Pequot fort. You can see burning homes inside the fort and also in the picture at the left. On the map Indians and Englishmen carry on hand-to-hand fights outside the palisade.

John Underhill, "Newes from America . . . .," London, 1638 (New York Public Library)

rified the Indians. The tribesmen's very ability to make a living seemed threatened. The colonists appeared either unaware of the Indians' fears or indifferent to them.

King Philip on the warpath. In 1675 the Wampanoag Indians burst forth in a fierce attack on New England settlers, led by King Philip, their chief.

Before long the entire frontier in New England was aflame with war. As the fighting spread, other tribes became involved. The ferocious attacks by the Indians on lonely settlements were avenged by the English, who seemed bent on destroying the tribesmen. The colonists burned crops and murdered captives, as the Indians themselves had.

Although the New Englanders lacked good military leaders and had too few soldiers, they were more numerous than the Indians. Their population was about four times that of the Indians, and their supplies were more abundant.

Peace at last. In 1676 the colonists were able to make headway against their enemies and end most Indian resistance. Yet fighting continued in parts of Maine and New Hampshire before a treaty was finally signed in 1678.

The power of the Indians had been broken. Some of the Indian captives were slain and others were sold into slavery as far away as the West Indies. These tragic victims included Philip's wife and nine-year-old son—a grandson of Massasoit. The Indians, who sustained frightful casualties, had been cleared off the New England frontier.

Heavy cost. The loss of life among the English was also enormous. Not a settler was left in one community in Maine. Sixteen towns in Massachusetts and four in Rhode Island were completely destroyed. More than 6 percent of the men of military age were killed—about six hundred in all.

The colonists at least had the satisfaction of discovering that they were able to overcome their enemies without crying to the mother country for help. In short, they were gaining self-confidence.

Forming New Towns

As the Indians retreated, the regions they abandoned were often taken over by the Englishmen. Scores and scores of new villages and towns sprang up during the last part of the seventeenth century. Most of them were along the seaboard, as you see on the map on page 88. The push to the west, however, was also under way.

The town system. An important reason for the success of the New England colonies was the town system, which began in Massachusetts. It made settlement orderly and attractive. A group of prospective settlers would petition the General Court to be allowed to form a new town. After authorities had convinced themselves that the petitioners were true believers and that the land in question was fertile and could be defended, they would make a grant.

Dividing the site. The officials of the new town, or proprietors, as they were called, would be given control of a 6-mile square of land. This they were expected to divide up and sell or give away in portions to people they could attract to their site. The proprietors were expected to build a church and obtain a minister to serve it. They also had the duty of laying out a village green around which the community buildings would be erected. The buildings had to include a school, a meetinghouse (often the same as the church), a gristmill, a sawmill, and a blacksmith's shop.

Large fields nearby were to be cleared and assigned in strips. When one field was cultivated, the clearing of another would be started. It, too, would be assigned in strips. After a time, therefore, a freeman would own strips in various parts of the town. By swapping, he usually could assemble a large, single plot of land. Often

The strips are indicated on the diagram on the next page. Assigning land in strips assured fair stribution of good and poor land--nobody got all good or all poor land. This was a practice llowed in Europe, and the English settlers naturally transplanted it here.

#Another idea to help students build a concept of democracy. See Exercise 1, Col. 1, p. 103.

severe conflicts developed between the proprietors, who controlled the undivided lands, and the freemen, who wanted some control—and a share—in these lands.

The common. The town officials retained authority over a common field, or common, available for the use of all. Generally it served for the grazing of animals.

A push into newer country. Another group of townspeople were those who worked as laborers and lived on the scrubby, undesirable land. They sometimes joined with the freemen in protests against the proprietors. Usually the officials were victorious in these struggles, which were settled in courts they were able to control. The effect was to push the freemen and the laborers farther west. They sought towns whose officials would be more generous.

The town meeting. The town dwellers came together more or less regularly at their meetinghouses to discuss, argue about, and decide important business. Included was the choosing of representatives to the General Court.

The town meetings helped establish the democratic idea that people ought to have an active part in making decisions affecting themselves. Through these gatherings thousands gained the experience required for effective self-government.

Schools. One of the public questions that# particularly concerned New Englanders was schooling for young people. Even though there was so much physical work to do, Puritans believed it was absolutely necessary that everyone be able to read the Bible. They maintained that the chief work of the devil was "to keep man from a knowledge of the Scriptures."

From the earliest days of settlement, schools were established voluntarily in many towns. In 1647 Massachusetts passed a law *requiring* every town containing fifty families to maintain an elementary school. If there were a hundred families, the town had to have, in addition, a

Charles Carleton Coffin, "Building the Nation," Harper Brothers, 1883
(New London County Historical Society)

Above: A New Englander speaks his mind in a town meeting being held in a town hall, just as New Englanders do today.
Below: If you could have flown over an early Massachusetts town, you would have seen a pattern on the ground much like this.

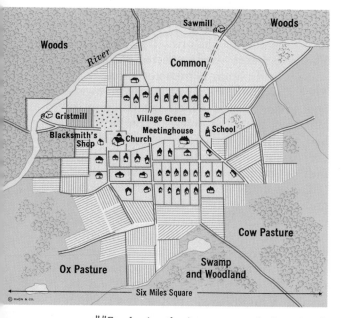

##Emphasize the importance of education for people who govern themselves. Why is it vital for them? The 1647 law was the first compulsory school-attendance law in America. The class should find out what kind of law governing school attendance their own state has today.

school to prepare young men for college. This provision, it was hoped, would insure a supply of ministers.

The arrangements for schools made by Massachusetts were generally copied throughout New England. In trying to insure an informed body of citizens, the people of New England, without knowing it, were helping lay another foundation stone of democracy.

Use of the land. New Englanders never found really rich soil or a staple crop—like tobacco—on which they could concentrate completely. Generally they grew enough cereals and vegetables to supply their families and the handful of craftsmen who did not raise food for themselves. This kind of farming, which produces no surplus for export, is called *subsistence farming*. It does not lead to wealth, but it helped to build tightly knit communities in New England.

---

1. What led to the settlement of Massachusetts? 2. Identify the "Great Migration." 3. Describe the government of Massachusetts. 4. Name four offspring of the colony. 5. What was the root of the colonial trouble with the Indians? 6. Name the advantages of the town system.

Catholics Make a Home in Maryland

The way a man worshiped God was important, also, in the settlement of Virginia's neighbor, Maryland. There, as in New England, the wilderness was tamed by men of strong faith.

Maryland was established in 1634—twenty-seven years after the first Englishman came ashore at Jamestown. Note the year: it tells us that those who settled Maryland could learn from the experiences of both the Virginians and the people of Massachusetts.

The Baltimores

The land north of the Potomac River was granted to Sir George Calvert. He was a good friend of the king's and for a number of years was an official at the royal court. When in 1625 Calvert announced that he had accepted the Roman Catholic faith, he had to resign his position. But Calvert and King James remained on good terms, and James made him Baron of Baltimore, or Lord Baltimore.

Trial in Newfoundland. Interested in becoming a colonizer in the New World, Calvert took his family to Newfoundland, where he had been given a royal grant of land. He aimed to make a go of living there, but it was a poor place.

After a winter of discouragement, Calvert decided to move southward to a warmer climate. He tried to obtain land in Virginia, but he was turned down because he refused to take an oath recognizing King James as head of the church.

The hand of the king. Lord Baltimore now went back to England, where in 1632 he received from the new king, Charles I, a grant of land that took in the northern part of Chesapeake Bay. As you can see on the map on page 71, it lay within the grant of the Virginia Company. Because Lord Baltimore died before he received the charter, it was issued to his son Cecilius Calvert, the second Lord Baltimore. The new colony was named Maryland by King Charles, in honor of the English queen, Henrietta Maria.

Cecilius Calvert now was known as Lord Proprietor of Maryland. "Lord Proprietor"

emphasize that each religious group settling in America sought to found its own colony--not to join another religious group already established. This fact benefited England, whose colonies were beginning to fill in the Atlantic coastline.

99

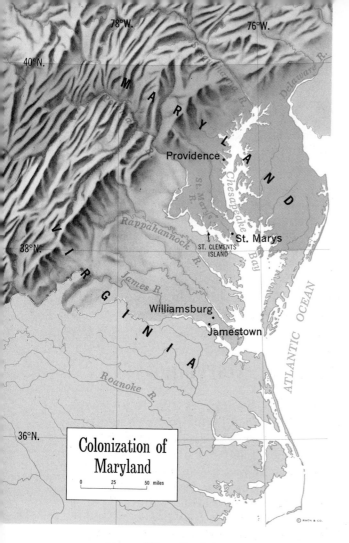

Colonization of
Maryland

0   25   50 miles

Above: When Englishmen made homes in Jamestown, their neighbors were Indians. Marylanders had fellow Englishmen.

Below: The seal of the Calverts, carrying an English symbol.

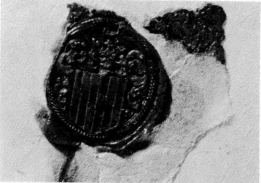

#The proprietor held the colony's charter and controlled its government.

was the title of any individual who received a royal grant to start a colony in America. The settlements of such persons were often called *proprietary colonies.*

Calvert quickly recruited several hundred colonists. The reports being heard from the Virginians and the Pilgrims were making it easier than it had been in Sir Humphrey Gilbert's day to get people to move to America.

There were still many frightening tales about the New World, to be sure. But there were solid facts to go on, too. The chief one was that though life was demanding in America, the rewards could be great.

Off to America. Calvert decided to stay home in England and defend his charter rights from the attacks of some members of the old Virginia Company. He named one of his brothers, Leonard, governor of the colony, and Leonard sailed for America in December, 1633.

The following March, Leonard Calvert and his party reached the Potomac River. Landing there on a small island which they called St. Clements, they heard one of their members, Father Andrew White, a# Jesuit, celebrate Mass.

A glorious country. The immigrants shortly sailed into what is now the St. Marys River, a branch of the Potomac. A few miles above its mouth they made their settlement, naming it St. Marys. Soon they believed that if they had not found paradise itself, they could scarcely come any closer. Father White wrote: "We cannot set down a foot without but tread on strawberries, raspberries, fallen mulberry vines, acorns, walnuts, sassafras, etc., and those in the wildest woods."

Religious disputes. Cecilius Calvert had been interested in establishing religious freedom for fellow Catholics, but he had also wanted his colony to survive physically. He, therefore, had encouraged Protestants as well as Catholics to join his settlement. Also, he had told his brother to try

##Some students may not know the word mass, and they may require an explanation. Discuss the advantages of the location of Maryland as a colony. Students can see the advantages of the closeness to Virginia and the ease of water transport.

to prevent any unnecessary disputes over religion from arising among the settlers. But trouble developed anyhow.

The Catholics even quarreled among themselves. Difficulties arose with the Virginians, too, who tried to stir the Indians up against the new settlers.

Nevertheless, the colony caught hold. Catholics made St. Marys their center, and Protestants established themselves around a town they first called Providence and later renamed Annapolis.

Some luck. Several reasons explain the colony's success. First, its location seems to have been more healthful than Virginia's. Second, the settlers of Maryland inherited from the local Indians, who were moving out, sufficient cleared land to start agriculture quickly. (The Indians also sold the settlers the corn they could not carry with them as they departed.)

Third, the settlers could obtain both supplies and information from the Virginians and from the colonists of New England. Knowledge of tobacco-growing, particularly, they learned from the Virginians. Think

what it meant to be *told* how to clear land, raise corn and tobacco, and live in the wilderness instead of having to learn everything by hard experience.

The Marylanders acquired something else, too: the spirit of independence their Virginia neighbors had already developed. The strict control which the Calverts had expected to exercise over settlers became impossible to establish.

The Calverts had laid out their colony in huge estates of thousands of acres to be run by friends and relatives. The Baltimores were to receive an annual payment from each of the planters among whom the estates would be divided. These arrangements did not last long in the American # forest, where fertile land was plentiful and willing hands few.

Lord Baltimore had also thought he would make whatever laws his colony required. Within fifteen years after the settlement began, the local assembly—which Baltimore had thought would merely advise him—was in fact making the laws of the colony.

Compare this with a picture of Baltimore today. Note the absence of evidence of a planned community like those in New England.

Baltimore, Maryland, looked like this in 1752. On the hill above the town is the Protestant St. Paul's Episcopal Church. The wheat field at the right, the boats, and the fishermen suggest Baltimore's future. The people would support themselves by fishing and shipbuilding and by exporting grain and tobacco to England.

Maryland Historical Society

Act of Toleration

Within a comparatively short time the Catholics were afraid that the large number of Protestants entering the colony might threaten their freedom of religion. They feared that the angry dispute at home between Catholics and Protestants over the break with Rome (see page 65) would be carried to America and continued.

\#   To protect the Catholics, the assembly passed in 1649 the so-called Act of Toleration. It granted freedom of religion to all who believed in Christ. In time this law came to be regarded as still another foundation stone of American democracy.

As the seventeenth century drew near its close, the New England colonies and the tobacco colonies of Virginia and Maryland were well launched. Who could have known in the year 1606, when those venturesome London investors planned on some quick profits, that their calculations were all wrong? Who had thought that, as the New Englanders discovered, families rather than gangs of men were required to make colonies flourish? Who had dreamed that, as the colonists in the South learned, the cultivation of tobacco, "this stinking weed of America," was the clue to financial success?

Shortly frontiersmen in both parts of English America would be pushing westward over the mountains. They were still Englishmen and were not yet calling themselves American. Nevertheless, their ways of life were vastly different from the ones they or their parents and grandparents had left behind in the old country.

---

1. What religious groups settled in Maryland? 2. Account for the colony's success. 3. What was the purpose of the Act of Toleration? 4. On what did the financial success of Maryland depend?

The Workshop

Review the early development of the English colonies studied so far. Compare them with the Spanish and French colonies.

On outline maps of the eastern coast of the present-day United States, let the class locate the English colonies and name them

The Shapers of Our World

Identify the following and tell how each contributed to establishing the British in the New World.

John Winthrop   Father Andrew White
Roger Williams   John Winthrop, Jr.
Anne Hutchinson Sir George Calvert
Thomas Hooker   Cecilius Calvert
John Davenport   Ferdinando Gorges
John Mason   Charles I

Adding to Your Vocabulary

Show your understanding of important ideas in this chapter by using the following words:

emigrants
"Great Migration"
freemen
theocracy
scurvy
Sabbath
cereals

subsistence
   farming
proprietary
   colony
toleration
town meeting

The Seeds of Democracy

1. Why was the transfer of the charter of the Massachusetts Bay Company to the New World so important for the growth of self-government in the New World?

2. Study the Massachusetts General Court. Tell why direct democracy—in which all the people personally take part in making the decisions in their govern-

ment—often develops into representative democracy.

3. Review the lives of dissenters such as Roger Williams and Anne Hutchinson. What is the role of dissent in a democracy?

4. Prove that Rhode Island was a more tolerant place to live in than some of its neighbors.

5. The extension of the right to vote has been a part of the development of democracy in America. How were the Fundamental Orders a stepping-stone in this development?

6. Compare the amount of religious freedom settlers enjoyed in Massachusetts, Rhode Island, and Maryland. Why was the Act of Toleration so important?

The Research Center

1. The class should prepare to take part in a town meeting. Let it do this by choosing and becoming well informed on a topic that would have been discussed at a typical seventeenth-century New England town meeting. It might consider, for example, the Indian problem, how to finance a "public" school required under the Massachusetts law, and the behavior of Roger Williams or Anne Hutchinson.

Divide the students into two groups, representing freemen and laborers, in order to carry on the discussion. When the meeting is concluded, have a group of students write a letter to the royal governor of their colony expressing the feeling of the townspeople about what was said.

2. Collect pictures from back magazines showing typical New England scenes. Relate them to the town buildings discussed in the chapter.

3. Imagine that you speak for a group of proprietors who are preparing to establish a New England town. To attract inhabitants, make a drawing of your proposed settlement. Include the following: principal streets, public buildings, strip fields, and a common.

4. Use library books or other reference materials to find out the relationship between the following Old World and New World developments. Report to the class.

   a. Arguments over religion in England and the settlement of Puritans in Massachusetts.

   b. The coming of the Industrial Revolution to England and the arrival of farmers in America.

   c. The position of the Catholics in sixteenth-century England and the colonization of Maryland.

Understanding Pictures

1. Look at the painting of Cecilius Calvert on page 86. What do his clothes tell you about his station in life? What does the presence of a slave mean?

2. What two religious groups are represented by the pictures of Calvert and the Communion cup on the same page?

3. Compare the Sunday-best clothing of the youngsters seen in the picture on page 95 with the clothing of children today dressed in their best. What differences are there? In your opinion, what helps account for them?

4. Study the picture on page 101. What ## proof can you find there that Marylanders carried out their Act of Toleration? What natural resources can you identify in the picture?

*#There are several churches--one a Catholic church (with the cross). The others are no doubt
Protestant churches.
Use the technique of picture study begun here to study pictures in other parts of the book.

(a)

(b)

(a) The German settlers of Pennsylvania colorfully decorated their housewares. The earthenware dish dates back to 1780.
(b) William Penn's Bible—printed in Latin—and his prayer book, bound together.
(c) Wampum, made of beads pierced and strung together, was used as money by the Indians. William Penn received this piece.
(d) A windmill and typical Dutch houses tell that Netherlanders settled New Amsterdam, which looked like this in 1653. Settlers tried hard to copy the appearance of the old country.
(e) The front of a coin used in Carolina.
(f) The Swedes who came to America already knew the kind of house that is called a log cabin. Pennsylvanians, here having a bee, or party, and other frontiersmen adopted the log cabin.

(c)

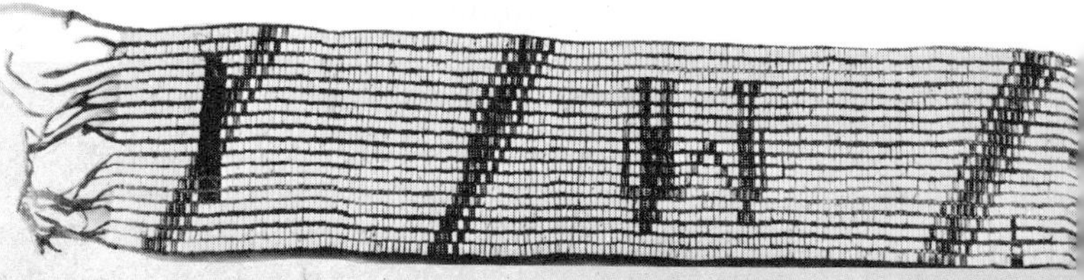

GOD: PRESERVE: CAROLINA: AND THE: LORDS: PROPRIETORS 1694

(e)

(f)

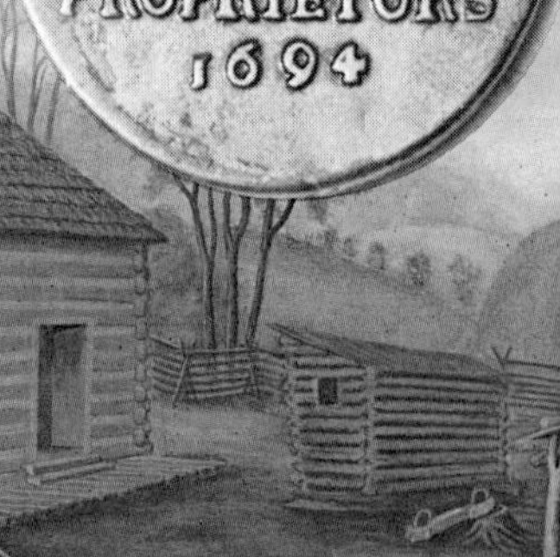

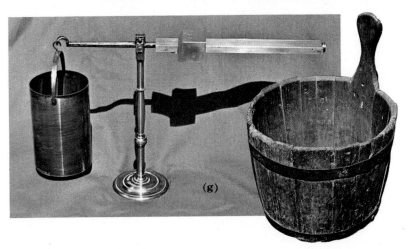

(g) A wooden tub called a piggin, used on Carolina rice plantations for holding the grain, and a scale for measuring it.

What things in the pictures on the opposite page suggest that settlers in America both clung to European ways and adopted new ways?

CHAPTER 6

FILLING IN THE COASTLINE

efore beginning this chapter, review the founding of the English colonies in Virginia, New England, and Maryland. This chapter discusses the last group of colonies to be founded along the Atlantic seaboard. It also takes up the rivalry between the Dutch and the English.

THE settlement of the eastern seaboard continued to be influenced by events taking place in western Europe. The colonists felt keenly the effects of Europe's struggles for power. This was so because as modern nations began to rise on the European side of the Atlantic Ocean, they developed furious jealousies of each other.

In contesting for prestige and power, western European countries recognized that a sure way to achieve both was by becoming wealthy. Wealth could pay for armies and navies and, above all, overseas colonies.

The Netherlands furnishes another example of the shift in European power after 1500 from the countries of the Mediterranean to those of the Atlantic coast.

The Dutch and English Bid for Power

In the seventeenth century an especially important struggle took place between England and the Netherlands for the markets of the world. Both countries traded energetically on the seven seas, and each was determined to triumph over the other.

Traders and Sailors

In the first half of the seventeenth century, it looked for a long time as if the Dutch were going to win the contest. They had succeeded in freeing their country of Spanish control. They had entered the very profitable trade in spices in the East Indies. They had built the largest fleet of merchant ships ever seen. With boundless energy they had made their capital, Amsterdam, a center of seaborne trade in lumber and herring.

The superior Dutch textile workers wove woolens from fleece imported raw from England and sold them at high profits. Every now and then the Dutch would also pounce on the Spanish treasure ships and loot them.

Compare and contrast the colonial activities of the Netherlands and England. Note how these two small countries relied on sea power, trade, and industry to bring themselves prosperity and power. Point out the areas of the world that were once part of the Dutch empire.

In the expressive faces of these Dutchmen, painted by Frans Hals in 1641, we see something of the vigor the Dutch brought to America.

Rembrandt's people. Look sometime into the faces of the men and women Rembrandt and Frans Hals painted and you will see what seventeenth-century Dutch people looked like. Vigorous, orderly, and purposeful, they seemed to combine zeal for hard work with the shrewdness that can make dangerous competitors.

Henry Hudson. The Dutch were in America almost as early as the English—looking for that road to Asia. In 1602 the Dutch government chartered the Dutch East India Company to control Dutch trade in the East Indies. The directors of the company, like other Europeans before them, had decided to seek a shorter passage to the East.

The directors hired an Englishman, Henry Hudson, to sail for them on a mission of discovery. Already Hudson had been searching for a northeastern passage to the East Indies. Twice, sailing under his own country's flag into the frozen regions of the North, he had failed to find the route he was looking for.

In 1609 Hudson, doubtless thinking to change his luck, sailed from the Netherlands in command of a small Dutch ship, the *Half Moon*. Accompanied by a crew of twenty, he headed northeastward with marvelous confidence. But stopped by contrary winds and ice, he gave up the effort and turned westward across the Atlantic. Without difficulty the *Half Moon* reached Newfoundland. Then it sailed southward.

A beautiful river valley. In September, 1609, the *Half Moon* entered the harbor now used by New York. Hudson and his crew were the first visitors there from Europe since Verrazano, eighty-five years earlier. They sailed up the river now known by Hudson's name to the present site of Albany.

Anyone who has admired the beauty of the Hudson River Valley in the autumn knows what the members of the expedition saw. But the river does not lead to the Pacific!

The Indians, however, were very friendly, even coming on board the ship. They had furs to offer—beaver, otter, and mink —in exchange for some trinkets and beads and a few knives and hatchets. The *Half Moon* was quickly well supplied.

Hudson, like the English and French explorers before him, sought a route to the East in the northern latitudes. Notice that he went both northeastward and northwestward in his search. In sailing up the Hudson River, he hoped to find an ocean passage.

The scattered settlements of New Netherland
lay uncomfortably close to land
claimed by the English.

Before returning home, Hudson sailed
into Chesapeake Bay. There he and his
men probably gazed upon the struggling
settlement at Jamestown.

When news of Hudson's trading with
the Indians reached the Netherlands, there
was considerable excitement. There was
also strong feeling in London: the English
insisted that Hudson must sail thereafter
under his own country's flag.

The Dutch followed up vigorously their
first contact with the Indians. Within a
year they were trading regularly for furs
along the Hudson. But they made no permanent settlement immediately.

New Netherland

In 1621 the Dutch chartered the Dutch
West India Company to carry on all trade
in the New World. The company founded
New Netherland, making a permanent settlement finally at Fort Orange, near
present-day Albany, in 1624. It also located settlers in a few other places.

Spread-out settlers. The first colonists
consisted altogether of only thirty families.
They were divided into small groups so
they would occupy as large an area as possible. Most of them settled at Fort Orange,
but some were sent to the Delaware River,
where they created a tiny settlement called
Fort Nassau. A few were assigned to hold
Manhattan Island.

The Dutch West India Company sent
the colonists food and other necessities to
enable them to survive. Their struggle to
establish themselves, however, was not
much easier than that of the Virginians or
of the New Englanders.

A tiny capital. By the fall of 1626 a
blockhouse, or fort, had been built at the
southern tip of Manhattan Island. Called

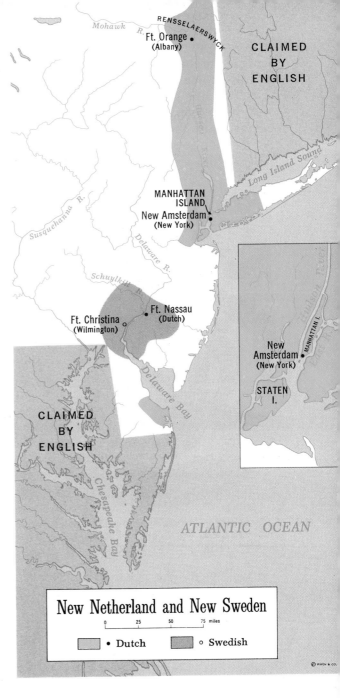

New Netherland and New Sweden

0   25   50   75 miles

■ • Dutch   ■ o Swedish

Fort Amsterdam, it guarded forty houses
constructed of felled trees. The houses
formed a town known as New Amsterdam,
later the capital of New Netherland.

The people of New Netherland did not
participate in the political affairs of their
colony. They were regarded simply as

Have students give examples of town, area, and street names that suggest the Dutch heritage of
New York City and the Hudson Valley area. Note the origin of the name Wall Street (see
page 109). Brooklyn was originally a Dutch settlement named Breuckelen.   107

being in the employ of the company. When they had come across the ocean, they had # agreed to live for six years on the land assigned to them. Their tasks and even the kinds of crops they raised were assigned by the director general and the council that assisted him.

Museum of the City of New York

In 1654 New Amsterdam adopted this seal, featuring the Dutch colors and the beaver, whose pelts supported the settlement's early trade.

Peter Minuit. The first director general was a slippery but capable fellow named Peter Minuit. One of the early steps he took was to "purchase" Manhattan Island —about 22,000 acres—for trinkets worth, it has been said, only twenty-four dollars.

Minuit, in general, maintained good relations with the Indians. He also made friends with the Pilgrims at Plymouth. But he had enemies at home who finally brought about his recall.

The home scene. The colony was a victim, in a way, of the prosperity of the homeland. Unlike England, where many poor people—even beggars—were eager

for a home in America, the Netherlands provided plenty of opportunities for making a living at home.

Furthermore, the Dutch government had long offered religious toleration to all religious groups. (You recall that the Puritans had been given a refuge in the Netherlands.) The need to escape religious persecution never moved the Dutch from the Old World to the New—as it did many thousands of Englishmen.

The patroons. The shortage of people in New Netherland directly affected the way in which the land was distributed there. The scheme hit upon was called the patroonship system. It seems to have originated as a suggestion of Kiliaen Van Rensselaer, a director of the Dutch West India Company and a wealthy diamond and pearl merchant.

The company would offer the rank of *patroon* to any man who within four years could persuade fifty people over fifteen years of age to come to America. A patroon had to settle on and farm portions of land assigned to him in New Netherland. His piece of land would extend 16 miles along one side of a navigable river or 8 miles along each of its sides. It would reach as far inland as it was possible for him to establish control. The island of Manhattan was reserved for the company.

The largest and most successful patroonship was Rensselaerswyck, owned by Van Rensselaer. Located on both sides of the Hudson near what is now Albany, it was so vast that it covered most of three present-day New York counties. Rensselaer himself never came to America, but he hoped anyhow to enjoy the advantages of a feudal lord.

Van Rensselaer's rules for the running of his patroonship and for the control of his lonely and often terrified settlers were strict. He even expected that every vessel passing his territory would pay him a tax. Although Rensselaerswyck enjoyed suc-

Contrast the conditions in England and the Netherlands in the seventeenth century. (Use the contrast to review why many Englishmen came to America.) In what ways were the situations of New Netherland and New France similar? Compare patroons and seigneurs.

cess, the rest of the patroonships were out-and-out failures. Some of the patroons never were able to acquire more than four or five families as tenants.

The burghers. The real rulers of the Dutch colony in the long run were not the patroons but the merchants who were engaged in trade along the shores of Manhattan Island. These men were the *burghers,* or town dwellers. Their warehouses in time bulged with furs, with goods from the Netherlands, and with tobacco from Virginia.

The burghers succeeded as well as they could in making their adopted land look like their native land—even building windmills. Their houses, filled with the best china, pewter, and furniture money could provide, came to be built after a while like those in the home country.

Brick and tile, favorite building materials, were plentiful in New Netherland almost from the beginning. These products served as ballast in empty ships. That is,

they supplied the weight required in the holds of vessels returning to America from Europe practically empty after dropping # off cargoes of furs and tobacco.

Kieft and the Indians. Yet the burghers' relations with the local Indians constantly reminded them of a difference between the Old World and the New. Indian trouble, which began in 1640, was largely the fault of the Dutch director general, William Kieft. Kieft often angered the tribesmen needlessly.

Before Kieft's time in office was over, the Indians as far north as Albany were on the warpath against the Dutchmen, and their war whoops were heard even in New Amsterdam itself. In fact, farms and homes along the southern tip of Manhattan Island were raided so often that Kieft had a stockade, or wall, built to protect the cattle that remained. That structure is remembered to this day, for the place where it stood became Wall Street, famous throughout the world.

Why were the ships almost empty--except for ballast?

A very small part of the land that once belonged to Rensselaer, near Albany, seen here in 1792. In the distance boats sail on the Hudson.

Swedes on the Delaware. The Dutch also found themselves increasingly on bad terms with other neighbors—fellow Europeans. One group of these were Swedes.

In 1638 a Swedish trading company sent out an expedition to settle along the Delaware River. The Swedes took advantage of the fact that the Dutch had not expanded the foothold they had earlier established there. By luck the Swedes obtained the services of Peter Minuit to head the settlement. This was the first effort at colonization commanded by a man with a previous record of success in America.

The course of New Sweden's history was like that we have now seen unfold in other places. On arrival at the Delaware, the weary but hopeful travelers built a stockade at the present site of the city of Wilmington. They named it Fort Christina in honor of the queen of Sweden, then twelve years old.

Christina's father, Gustavus Adolphus, had had plans to build an American colony as the "jewel of his kingdom." Yet Swedish settlements remained only tiny fur-trading posts, and the settlers, including some Finns, never numbered more than four hundred. The Swedish people were no more willing to leave the comforts of the homeland than the French or the Dutch.

The trade in furs that the Swedes established, however, was extensive enough to irritate the Dutch. Director General Kieft, of New Netherland, warned New Sweden it occupied land belonging to the Dutch. Before Kieft could take action, he had been removed from his post.

"Old Silver Nails" Stuyvesant. The new director general of New Netherland was Peter Stuyvesant. He had arrived in New Amsterdam in 1647. Although he was only about thirty-seven years old, he had already been governor of an island in the West Indies, where he had lost his right leg in battle.

Equipped now with an artificial wooden leg decorated with silver bands and nails, "Old Silver Nails" let the burghers know that he would tolerate no nonsense. He quickly showed what he meant. When a board of nine men he had named to help advise him proposed to report their grievances to the authorities at home, he dismissed the board.

He threatened: "It may during my administration be contemplated to appeal; but if anyone should do it, I will make him a foot shorter, and send the pieces to Holland and let him appeal in that way."

In brief, Stuyvesant was a harsh tyrant. When the Dutch government decreed that New Amsterdam ought to have the privilege of governing itself, Stuyvesant interfered. He took every step he could to keep control in his own hands. The burghers were outraged.

The acquiring of New Sweden. Stuyvesant showed little tact and little sympathy toward the Swedes, and in 1655 he sent men to attack New Sweden. When the Dutch vessels sailed up the Delaware carrying five or six hundred soldiers and sailors, the Swedes, owning only one round of ammunition, were unable to resist. Without the firing of a shot, the tiny colony surren-

The United States Post Office issued a stamp —left—in 1938 to honor the founding of Wilmington, Delaware, and one—below—in 1924 to call to mind some of the settlers of New Netherland.

Roman J. Burkiewicz Stamp Shop

New Sweden became part of New Netherland but in 1664 the whole area was taken by the British.

dered. The Swedes and Finns there in time were merged with the Dutch and English populations.

The Swedes' contribution to American life could long be seen on the frontier: the humble log cabin. The notching together of tree trunks to make a tight, secure dwelling until something better could be built had been learned in the forests of Scandinavia. In time, the log cabin became a symbol of brave pioneers in many parts of the American wilderness.

An open door. By the beginning of the 1660's the population of New Amsterdam had grown to about twenty-five hundred souls. Of all the towns on the Atlantic seaboard, only Boston was more impressive in size and in activity. People from many other places in America and, indeed, from all over the world put into New Amsterdam.

One day in the late summer of 1654, for example, twenty-three Jews from Brazil arrived in New Amsterdam—to create the first organized Jewish community in America. Stuyvesant requested them "in a friendly way to depart." But he was overruled by the Dutch West India Company, which granted them the rights of settlers.

Take-over

Englishmen also entered the domain of New Netherland. Energetic and numerous, they were not going to be absorbed easily.

Vigorous rivalry. The English had chartered a company called the Royal Adventurers to Africa to take charge of all trade between the New World and Africa. One of its chief purposes was to compete with the Dutch West India Company. To direct the organization, later renamed the Royal African Company, King Charles II chose his brother, James, Duke of York.

The rivalry between the Dutch and the English showed itself in a number of other ways, too. There were disputes over where the boundary lines between New Nether-

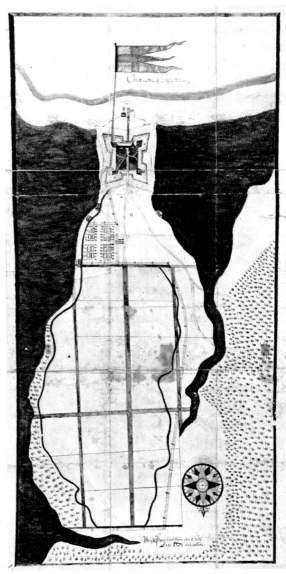

Riksarkivet, Stockholm

The Swedes' own map of their settlement on the Delaware. The flag of Sweden flies over Fort Christina, the site of the present city of Wilmington.

land and New England ran. The English, furthermore, were entering the Connecticut Valley and Long Island, which the Dutch claimed as their own.

Nevertheless, the admiration and envy that Dutchmen had for the privileges the New Englanders enjoyed may have weakened the hold of Dutch authority over the burghers. New England's town meetings

Emphasize how European countries competing for colonies often struggled throughout the world. The English challenged the Dutch in Africa and in Asia as well as in America. Similarly, the later conflict between the English and the French was worldwide.

111

and regular elections must have seemed very attractive to the Dutch colonists.

The Navigation Acts. The increasing commercial competition of the Dutch and the English throughout the world was having an effect on colonial life. The English Parliament, beginning in 1651, passed the so-called Navigation Acts, aimed at the Dutch. These laws declared that English colonial products could only be sold in England. They also provided that only English ships could carry on trade with the colonies.

The Navigation Acts were made even stronger as the years passed. The Dutch were stubborn competitors, and English merchants grew more and more hostile to them.

A call for surrender. In 1664 the English arranged a plan to reduce Dutch power. A fleet of four ships was sent to strike at New Netherland, the valuable outpost of the irritating Dutch West India Company. Charles named his brother, the Duke of York, to be proprietor of New Netherland and other lands around it.

Toward the end of August, 1664, the English vessels appeared off New Amsterdam and anchored there. The commander of the expedition, Colonel Richard Nicolls, called upon Governor Stuyvesant to surrender to him.

Stuyvesant at first refused, shouting, "I'd rather be carried a corpse to my grave!" But he quickly saw that there was no fight in his people, particularly the burghers he had so often outraged.

Moreover, just as New Sweden had had practically no gunpowder when the Dutch arrived to subdue it, so now the Dutch were almost out of ammunition. Finally, Stuyvesant's position was weakened by the fact that many Englishmen were living in the Dutch colony. They naturally preferred English rule.

Change of name. So it happened that on September 8, 1664, Stuyvesant surren-dered New Netherland without the firing of a single shot. The territory, now a possession of the English, became New York, in honor of the new proprietor.

The victors granted generous terms to the Dutch. Stuyvesant returned to the Netherlands the following year to explain before officials his failure to defend the colony. Then he came back to Manhattan to his farm and magnificent house. There he lived under the English flag until his death in 1672, at the age of eighty. He witnessed the skill of Governor Nicolls, who gradually introduced English-type laws and local government, to the satisfaction of Dutchmen and Englishmen alike.

New Jersey. The grant made to the Duke of York included the land between the Hudson and the Delaware rivers. This handsome area he turned over in 1664 to two loyal, old friends, John Lord Berkeley and Sir George Carteret. They created their own colony, calling it New Jersey.

Although the land was already occupied here and there by Swedes, Dutchmen, Englishmen, and Finns, the colony needed settlers. The proprietors announced that they would welcome immigrants. To these they would extend freedom of religion, land on generous terms, and participation in the government through a representative assembly.

---

1. In what products did the Dutch trade in the seventeenth century? 2. Describe the purpose of Hudson's voyage for the Netherlands. 3. What result did it have? 4. How was land distributed in New Netherland? 5. How is the history of New Netherland joined to that of New Sweden? 6. What did the Swedes contribute to American life? 7. In what way did English-Dutch rivalry affect colonial life? 8. How did New Netherland become New York? 9. What attracted settlers to New Jersey?

Ask the class to comment on whether or not the Dutch made mistakes in governing New Netherla Why were the English wise to grant generous terms to the defeated Dutch settlers? (People alway. resent harsh, unfair rule.)

Penn Designs a Place for Quakers

Another friend of the king's and of the Duke of York's was granted the opportunity to found what became Pennsylvania. He was William Penn, a man of strong religious faith and unusual skill in managing affairs. Penn stands in history as the greatest of all the colonial proprietors.

A Debt Repaid

Penn was the son of Admiral Sir William Penn, a favorite of the king's. The admiral, who was rich, tried to give his son the best of everything, including an education at Oxford University. But the father was disappointed because of the son's religious views. Penn had become a Quaker—a member of the Society of Friends.

The Society of Friends. The Quakers, or Friends, had developed in seventeenth-century England under the leadership of their founder, George Fox. They went farther than any other group which separated from the Church of England.

The Friends preached that no minister and no ceremony were required to be links between man and God. Each man could be guided only by his own "inward light."

The Friends, practicing a simple Christianity, addressed one and all with *Thee* and *Thou*, words hitherto used only in talking to servants and other "inferiors." They declined to remove their hats in the presence of their "superiors," expressed a belief in the equality of men and women, refused to bear arms, and opposed slavery.

Many Quakers preached openly on the streets, a practice almost unheard-of at that

tudents might find out bout the lives of Quakers today.

Quakers, wearing their typical clothing, attend a meeting in 1770. Notice that the men and women do not sit together.

Quaker Collection, Haverford College Library

William Penn at twenty-two years of age, wearing armor as a soldier in Ireland. He had not yet become a Quaker.

time. And the most extreme leaders trembled or quaked while offering their messages—whence the name "Quaker."

The Quakers refused to give money to the king or to the Church of England, and the jails of England were, in consequence, filled with Quakers. Penn himself had spent time in prison.

A grant in America. When Penn was thirty-six years old, his father died. Despite the younger Penn's religious views, he was able to maintain good relations with the king.

Moreover, King Charles II was ready to honor a debt of many thousand pounds he had owed Admiral Penn by paying it to the son. But Charles preferred to pay with a grant of land in America rather than with money. Penn immediately saw the opportunity such a grant presented: he could create a refuge for fellow Quakers.

Note that Penn's land grant had western limit
Compare the Pennsylvania and Virginia grant

The size of the area Charles gave to Penn in 1681 showed both the king's ignorance of America and the warmth of his friendship for the Penns. The grant extended from the Delaware River 5 degrees of longitude westward and from the 40th degree to the 43rd degree of north latitude. This was an area larger than England and Wales combined!

In 1682 the grant was made even larger. Disturbed because his colony had no seaport, Penn obtained from the Duke of York the land west of Delaware Bay (it later became the state of Delaware).

Named for father. The king named the grant Pennsylvania, that is, Penn's Forest. Penn himself, who thought the name indicated pride and vanity unbecoming a Quaker, protested. "It is not you but your father I honor," the king is reported to have replied.

Penn was quickly busy in day-and-night work to make ready for his vast undertaking. He had to find settlers (an old problem of colonizers by now), provide ships to carry them, and locate his settlements precisely. He also had to prepare what was called the Frame of Government.

Practicing Brotherly Love

More carefully than any who had come before him, Penn selected the site for his chief city. It would stand at the junction of the Schuylkill and Delaware rivers. He sent a surveyor to lay out the city with the utmost care.

A planned city. Named Philadelphia, "brotherly love," the city may well be regarded as the earliest example of a *planned* community in American history. For the first time streets were laid out in a checkerboard pattern. Provision was made for sparing from the ax particularly handsome trees. Streets Penn named for trees in time became world famous: "Walnut," "Chestnut," and "Pine."

#Have students bring to class detailed maps of their own community. Are the streets or roads laid out in a pattern? What things seem to influence the pattern? If your community has a city planner, ask students to find out about his activities and proposals.

This is a map of Philadelphia.

Above: Pennsylvania gained land from Maryland, as is seen here. But it lost to New York, in 1785–1787, the land between 42° and 43° north latitude.

\# *Below:* A map of part of Penn's colony, published in London in 1717.

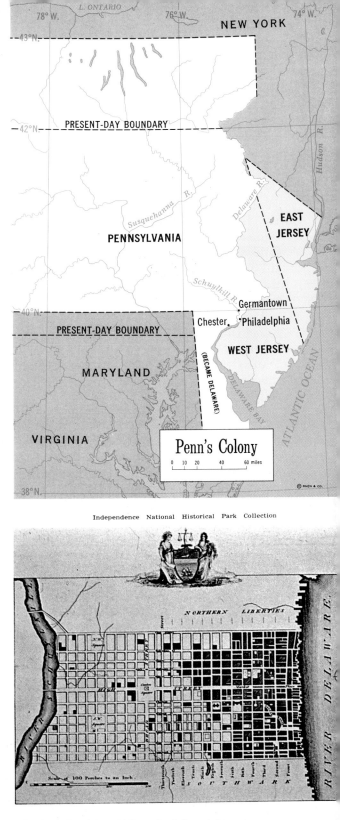

Penn's Colony

0   10   20   40   60 miles

Independence National Historical Park Collection

The Frame of Government. From its beginning Pennsylvania had features unusual for the day. Penn himself wrote the Frame of Government. It provided that although he, the proprietor, was governor, a deputy might serve in his absence. The governor or the deputy would be assisted by a council to be elected by the freeholders, that is, men who owned their land.

The "Great Law." The governor and the council would propose laws to a popular assembly to be chosen by the freeholders. The assembly, called in 1682 at what is now Chester, Pennsylvania, passed what has ever since been known as the Great Law. It granted to all Christians freedom of worship.

Treaty with the Indians. Penn's relations with the Indians were also a model of good planning. Before he left England, he arranged for special gifts of hats and other clothing for the chiefs. There is a legend that Penn and the Indians drew up and agreed upon a "great treaty" in a meeting under an elm tree in Philadelphia. Even if the details of this story cannot be proved, it suggests the excellent relations between the Quakers and the Indians.

Penn had written ahead to the Indians: "I have a great Love and Regard toward you, and I desire to win and gain your Love and Friendship by a kind, Just and Peaceable Life." For the first time Indians were treated by Englishmen like men, rather than as savages of the forest.

Steady growth. Pennsylvania grew rapidly. Within ten years the population of Philadelphia reached 4000—it was larger than New York's. It continued its remarkable growth for the next century. In fact, in 1776, when the Declaration of Indepen-

Compare William Penn's plans with those of the Calverts for Maryland (p. 101) and of the eight proprietors for the Carolinas (pp. 118-119). What besides Penn's policies helped make Pennsylvania a success?

dence was written in Philadelphia, it was the second largest city in the British Empire. Only London was bigger. Few of the lowly Quakers would have dreamed of such rapid growth or of the personal prosperity they were going to enjoy. The "starving time" for newcomers in America now seemed done.

Personal disappointments. Sad to say, Penn himself was not personally successful. He spent his fortune trying to make Pennsylvania take root. As a result, he landed in debtor's prison despite his powerful friends. His son, who was a spendthrift, disappointed him—as he himself had disappointed his father.

Furthermore, Penn became involved in a hot dispute over the location of the boundary line between Maryland and Pennsylvania. For a time it appeared that the line might even place Philadelphia itself in Maryland.

This dispute was not settled until 1767, when the proprietors of the two colonies accepted a line established by two surveyors, Charles Mason and Jeremiah Dixon. # The Mason-Dixon line placed the southern boundary of Pennsylvania where it is today. Later its extension westward also settled a boundary dispute with Virginia.

Penn became so absorbed in defending himself and his colony in England that he did not return to America until another fifteen years had passed. He reached Pennsylvania again in December, 1699. However, shortly learning that a move was afoot in England to place proprietary colonies (see page 100) under the king, he went home to fight. He never came back.

A mixed population. From the time the first settlers arrived in 1681, Pennsylvanians included a variety of Europeans, not just Englishmen. You will remember that long before Penn arrived, Swedes, Finns, and Dutchmen were living along the Delaware. After Pennsylvania's establishment, other non-English settlers began to arrive.

In part, no doubt, the newcomers were attracted by the generosity shown dissenting religious groups, of which there were many on the European continent. In part, also, they were attracted by the skillful advertising campaign carried on by Penn throughout western Europe.

Among the non-English the Welsh were numerous. They arrived from Wales and settled west of Philadelphia. For a long time they tried to maintain their language. But in the end, as every small group was sooner or later to learn, they could not do so. Their descendants spoke the tongue of their English neighbors.

The German Quakers have maintained their identity until the present day. Their

Note the number of different groups in Pennsylvania. Discuss the problems and advantages resulting from a variety of peoples.

Robert's Old Mill, built in 1683, the first flour mill in Germantown, Pennsylvania. Water running on the waterwheel provided power for grinding the grain.

Germantown Historical Society

What is the artist trying to say about Pennsylvania?

A nineteenth-century painter tried to express the spirit of Penn's "Holy Experiment" by picturing Penn at peace with the Indians, wild animals lying down together, and children showing no fear.

leader was capable Francis Daniel Pastorius, whose hometown had been Frankfurt, Germany. He attracted among others the devout, downtrodden people who lived in the Rhine River Valley. He brought eighty settlers to the New World aboard what he called his Noah's Ark, a vessel named *America*.

Germantown. In 1683 Pastorius officially established Germantown. Laid out like Philadelphia, a two hours' walk away, it was a fertile area in which its industrious people could find ample reward for their labors. Other German immigrants joined these original arrivals.

In the early part of the eighteenth century a second wave of Germans came. These were followed shortly by Scotch Presbyterians who had moved previously from Scotland to Ireland. They are usually known as Scotch-Irish.

More than any other colony, Pennsylvania was the symbol of how men and women might *systematically* remake their lives amid abundance and freedom. Pennsylvania's location and growing opportunities, both cultural and commercial, made it the leading settlement in America. By the middle of the eighteenth century, its greatest citizen, Benjamin Franklin, had become the first American to be known everywhere in the Western world.

1. How were Quakers distinguished from other separatists? 2. Pennsylvania included what land? 3. How did Penn practice brotherly love? 4. Name the satisfactions Penn obtained from his colony. 5. What non-English people settled in Pennsylvania? 6. Of what was Penn's colony a symbol?

The movement of Germans and Scotch-Irish to Pennsylvania illustrates that people pull up their roots and move not only because of the attraction of a new place but also because of troubles they wish to leave. Have students find out about conditions in the German states in the 1700's.

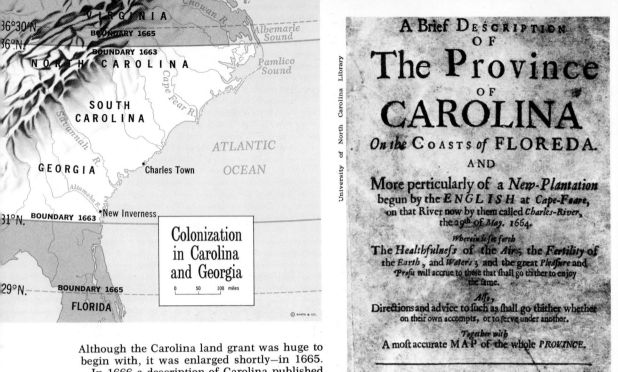

A Brief Description

OF

The Province

OF

CAROLINA

On the Coasts of FLOREDA.

AND

More perticularly of a New-Plantation
begun by the ENGLISH at Cape-Feare,
on that River now by them called Charles-River,
the 29th of May. 1664.

Wherein is set forth

The Healthfulness of the Air; the Fertility of
the Earth, and Waters; and the great Pleasure and
Profit will accrue to those that shall go thither to enjoy
the same.

Also,

Directions and advice to such as shall go thither whether
on their own accompts, or to serve under another.

Together with

A most accurate MAP of the whole PROVINCE.

London, Printed for Robert Horne in the first Court of Gresham-
Colledge neer Bishopsgate street. 1666.

Although the Carolina land grant was huge to begin with, it was enlarged shortly—in 1665. In 1666 a description of Carolina published in London said the colony was "on the coasts of Florida." The map above explains why.

Review the Spanish settlements in Florida (St. Augustine, etc.). The Spanish also attempted to settle the areas of Georgia and the Carolinas. Why did the English encourage settlement in this region?

Tracts to the South Draw Settlers

The spirit of restlessness that helped move many thousands of people from Europe to America also propelled men and women
\# within the New World. This free movement of people accounts for the settlement of Carolina.

The Carolinas

Carolina was named for Charles I, who had granted the vast area between 31° and 36° north latitude to a favorite, his attorney general. When that lucky fellow failed to create settlements on it, Charles II, now
\#\# on the throne, took it back and gave it to eight of *his* friends. Two of the eight were John Lord Berkeley and Sir George Carteret, who were the proprietors of New Jersey.

The eight proprietors were given the power to create titles of nobility. (Already the existence of such titles went against the grain of colonists in America, who were developing a growing respect for the worth of the individual.) The eight were permitted to grant freedom of conscience even to those who did not accept the Church of England.

Experienced colonists. A permanent settlement in Carolina had been made ten years before King Charles granted the charter to the eight proprietors. In 1653 some Virginians, looking to improve their lives, had built homes along the Chowan River in the region of Albemarle Sound, in what became North Carolina. But their settlement grew slowly.

As you can tell from the map above, rivers flowing from west to east cut up the region. Their courses made it difficult

118   \#An important point: These colonies received settlers who were already experienced
in living in America.
\#\#Have some students look up the results of the English Civil War and its aftermath in America.

to build uninterrupted roads running from north to south. Moreover, the swampy area between the Chowan River and Virginia made the settlement unattractive because it was isolated.

Another group—this time, of New Englanders—settled along the Cape Fear River in 1662. Their location, though, did not offer sufficient protection from Indian attacks.

Huguenots. Other bands of hopefuls made successful efforts. Among them were French Huguenots, who in 1691 came from Virginia to settle along the Pamlico River. Additional Huguenots steadily joined them, for in 1685 the special protections they had enjoyed in France had been taken away.

Charleston. All these efforts at colonization had not been made with the assistance of the North Carolina proprietors, yet the proprietors had not been idle. They had attempted to recruit settlers at home. One of their advertisements had even declared that the use of fat from the bears of Carolina made the hair grow!

In 1669 three well-equipped vessels set out from England, carrying prospective colonists. The expedition sailed first to the West Indies, where it stopped to pick up some recruits.

After first settling near present-day Charleston and finding that the location did not meet their needs, the voyagers moved to what is now Charleston Harbor in the spring of 1670. Their early experience tested their courage, but they had help from fellow Englishmen in Virginia and the West Indies. The settlement at Charleston (then called Charles Town) became Carolina's capital after 1680. Situated on a splendid, well-protected harbor, Charleston proved to be, in time, the most important southern port on the Atlantic coast.

Wrong hopes. The proprietors had expected that Carolina would serve as a place to which planters and workers from the West Indies might migrate. There they would produce commodities not grown at home. Silk, almonds, grapes, olives, and # wax were among the items anticipated. Instead, it proved necessary to raise crops for food. The main one was rice.

Carolina, in short, did not meet the expectations of the proprietors. The colony could not provide the goods from which profit was expected. In addition to rice, only pitch and tar from the pine forests of Carolina were shipped from Charleston's beautiful harbor.

Divided in two. Until 1691 the northern ## and southern portions of Carolina were governed separately. That year a single governor served both portions of the province. But they became unhitched again in

xplain the term Huguenot.
hy did the Huguenots not
ttle in France?

The British flag shows prominently in this scene in Charleston Harbor painted in the early 1700's. From this port in South Carolina, plantation products went to England.

Colonial Williamsburg

1712, when a separate governor was appointed for North Carolina.

South Carolina gradually made the cultivation of rice through the use of slaves its chief activity. North Carolina raised tobacco and took advantage of its pine forests to obtain lumber and naval stores. It turned for trade to its sister colonies to the north and had less contact with South Carolina.

Georgia

No other colony had a beginning like Georgia's. This fertile land, lying between the Savannah and Altamaha rivers, stretched westward to the Great South Sea. It was granted by the Carolina proprietors in 1717 to a Sir Robert Montgomery. He was to have the title of "Margrave" (the Carolina men had a special fondness for such titles). His domain was to be known as the Margravate of Azilia.

Azilia. In order to hold the land, Montgomery was expected to colonize it. When he failed to do so, Azilia became a part of Carolina again. And when North and South Carolina became crown colonies in 1729, a new phase of its history began.

James Oglethorpe. The land of Azilia, early described as the "fairest, fruitfullest, and pleasantest of all the world," became the scene of a unique undertaking by James Edward Oglethorpe. Educated at Oxford, he had become a distinguished soldier. Then, serving as a member of Parliament, he underwent an experience which changed his very way of looking at life.

Debtors in jail. Oglethorpe took part in an investigation of prison conditions in England. This service brought home to him the awful fate that befell the poor soul who owed debts he could never pay. In an age when humanitarian sentiments—feelings of sympathy for fellow men—were just beginning to be widespread, Oglethorpe became a humanitarian.

Oglethorpe had the idea of making it possible for unfortunate prisoners to start life over again—in the New World. He also felt keenly the need to help distressed Protestants on the continent of Europe.

A military purpose. When Oglethorpe approached King George II about the idea of using for his high purpose the land of Azilia, the monarch showed keen interest. The new colony could provide also an ideal protective "wall" against the Spanish, who were pressing upon South Carolina from Florida.

A princely area. To Oglethorpe and twenty associates, the king in 1732 gave the land between the Savannah and the Altamaha for settlement (formerly part of Carolina). The grant was for a period of twenty-one years. At the end of that time, Azilia was to become a royal colony. Parliament, moreover, made a large gift of money to help the project become a success. Charitable individuals also contributed generously.

Oglethorpe sought out the most deserving debtors he could find in the prisons as well as among poor people outside prisons. He also put himself in touch with persecuted Protestants in Catholic countries of Europe.

A two-hundred-ton ship, *Anne*, was made ready. Aboard it Oglethorpe himself sailed late in 1732, in company with over 120 hopeful settlers. Their destination had a new name, Georgia—in honor of the king.

Savannah. Two months out of London, the *Anne* put in at Charleston to restock its supplies. Sailing southward, Oglethorpe put his mind and experience to choosing a site for his first town, which he founded in 1733, naming it Savannah. He laid out the town with the kind of care that had been used in planning Philadelphia fifty years earlier.

A refuge. Georgia grew rapidly because Europe was in new turmoil and the knowledge that America was a reliable refuge for

Since the founding of Georgia completed England's colonization of the Atlantic coast, students might review the names of the original thirteen colonies. Indicate that Maine and Plymouth were absorbed by Massachusetts in 1691.

When Oglethorpe paid a visit to London in 1734, he took with him a group of American Indians who had sold him land and had promised to be friendly. Here he introduces them to Englishmen who had also contributed to the colony.

Europeans was now general. At Ebenezer a settlement was made by Lutherans who had fled persecution in Salzburg, a town in the Austrian Alps. Before Georgia was ten years old, over a thousand people were living there.

In the first summer of Georgia's existence, a group of forty Portuguese Jews arrived. They were accepted by Oglethorpe despite instructions from the trustees to expel them. One of their number was a medical doctor, whose services were quickly in demand.

Oglethorpe returned to England in 1734 and gave an enthusiastic progress report. Scotch highlanders now joined the wave of settlers, founding the town of New Inverness. Also John and Charles Wesley—some years later the founders of Methodism—brought their crusading zeal and high ideals to the colony.

Despite the promising start, the land proved less fertile than had been guessed. Moreover, the proprietors forbade the in-troduction of Negro slaves, an order which handicapped Georgians in competing with South Carolinians for settlers. Many Georgians, as a result, moved to South Carolina, where slaves were plentiful.

Experiments that failed. When well-tended experiments to raise citrus fruits and silkworms did not succeed, the proprietors grew discouraged. In 1751 they gave up to the king their rights in Georgia. #

The establishment of Georgia proved to be the last of the fresh starts of English colonization on the Atlantic coastline. The subdivision of the seaboard into permanent political units—later to be the first of the fifty United States—already had been begun.

Each of the New World colonies had been started under special circumstances. If, however, you had gone from colony to colony, by the beginning of the eighteenth century you would have been impressed by the common characteristics of the people.

Point out that by 1750 most of the North American colonies had been brought under the king's control. The only colonies that were not royal colonies by that time were Connecticut, Rhode Island, Pennsylvania, Maryland, and Delaware.

One day these qualities would be regarded as "typically American."

First of all, the colonists everywhere were business-minded. The need to be self-supporting had turned them toward commerce almost from the moment they arrived. Whether they were merchants or farmed or sailed ships, they were aware of the value of trade and the need for profits.

Second, the colonists wore the air of men who were self-made. They were sure of their abilities and were hard-working. Colonial experience had made it clear that a man's position in life need not be fixed forever. In America a man could fail at one enterprise and then try another. People who had been "nobodies" in the old country could become "somebodies" here. More than ever before in history, native ability seemed to shape a man's life.

Third, the colonists were a hopeful people. They looked forward to the future rather than backward to the past. In part this was because they especially put their trust in young people, who had the energy and enthusiasm necessary to make the new land bloom. Unlike worn-out Europe, America, the colonists knew, was going to be better tomorrow than it had been yesterday or was today.

Finally, the colonists everywhere had the glow of self-confidence. It came as naturally to them as the rising sun. And why not? To people who had a hand in the brave work of settling the New World, *nothing* would ever again seem impossible or beyond their strength.

---

1. Who created the first permanent settlement in Carolina? Where?   2. What other settlements had been established?   3. How did Carolina disappoint its proprietors?   4. Upon what crops or products did North and South Carolina depend?   5. What two purposes was Georgia to serve?   6. Name groups of refugees who settled there.   7. Identify four common characteristics of the colonies.

The Workshop

As students work on the questions and activities, have them bear in mind that most of the colonies discussed in this chapter were founded much later than Virginia or Massachusetts Bay. Discuss how the time difference explains certain situations in these later colonies.

The Shapers of Our World

Test your knowledge of the chapter by telling how each of the following contributed to the filling in of the Atlantic coastline with new European settlement.

Henry Hudson
Dutch West
  India Company
Peter Minuit
Peter Stuyvesant

Duke of York
Berkeley
Carteret
William Penn
James Oglethorpe

Adding to Your Vocabulary

Use the following words to help show your understanding of this chapter.

fleece
patroons
burghers
Quakers
Scotch-Irish

systematically
Huguenots
debtors
humanitarian
Mason-Dixon line

Thinking Things Through

Review the boxed-in exercises in the chapter and prepare to hold discussions on the following:

1. Compare the religious toleration in colonies such as Pennsylvania and Georgia with that in earlier ones, such as Virginia and Massachusetts. Why do you think policies changed?

2. In governing a colony, flexible rule—

In discussing matters raised in "Thinking Things Through," encourage creative thinking but stress that a historian checks out his ideas against the evidence. Nearly every historical problem has more than one answer, and the difficulty is in separating truth from half-truths.

that is, rule that can be changed—is often best. Why? How would you describe *policy*? Can you name any country today that has colonies? How does it govern them?

3. The beliefs of Quakers were often strongly opposed by seventeenth-century kings. Why?

4. How was it an advantage for Charles II to pay the Penn debt with land for a colony rather than with money?

5. In what ways did Penn show himself to be a wise proprietor? How might the events of 1664 have been different if Stuyvesant had followed the same policies as Penn?

6. The United States has been called the land of plural cultures. What does this mean? How was Pennsylvania the first colony to fit such a description?

7. How could the settlement of Georgia be called the final act in a play entitled *The English Conquest of the Atlantic Coast*?

Sharpening Your Map Skills

Consult the maps in the chapter and then carry out the following activities:

1. What do you notice about the locations of all the Dutch and Swedish settlements? Account for these locations.

2. Oglethorpe expected that olives could be grown in Georgia, but he was disappointed. In what places in the world are olives grown? Look at a world map to find the latitude of those places, and compare their approximate latitude with that of Georgia. What mistake did Oglethorpe make?

3. Choose settlements from the maps in this chapter to show the relationship among inland waterways, the ocean, and the locations of settlements.

Expressing Ideas to the Class

Use the following activities to learn how to express your ideas or opinions. First, be sure to research the topic. Then prepare to make an oral report. Try to learn both sides of the question so that you can disagree in an informed way with other members of the class.

1. Organize a meeting that might have been called in New Amsterdam in 1664 to discuss what course of action should be taken if English ships appeared in the harbor. Assign class members to be patroons, burghers, tenant farmers, and Englishmen in the colony. Establish a speaking order so that each person has a turn at talking about the problem. Then have an open discussion of it.

2. Have students represent Peter Stuyvesant, William Penn, and James Oglethorpe. Let each of these students have ten minutes to tell how he would organize a colony. Be sure to consider these questions: How will settlers be obtained? What will make the colony prosperous? How will the colony benefit the mother country? How should the colony be governed? The class should vote to decide which person should receive a charter on the basis of his report.

3. Collect and display pictures of New York City today that show the remains of Dutch influence there. Do the same for Philadelphia, showing Quaker and German influences, and for Charleston, showing French influence. Report to the class on the displays.

4. Many large cities across the nation are involved in what is called urban renewal (rebuilding the worn-out sections of a city). Interview your own city's urban-renewal director or city planner, or write to the office of urban renewal in a nearby city. What is involved? Report to the class on the activities being carried out. If possible, use pictures to illustrate your report.

Show in what ways city planning today is similar to that in Penn's own Philadelphia. How is it different? What are some new ideas in designing cities?

Part Two Workshop

Reaching to the Present

Let committees of students each select one of the following exercises and report to the class what their research reveals.

1. Who looked for a northwest passage after Frobisher and Davis? What part has the United States played in the search in our own day? When was a northwest passage finally found? How? Of what value is the passage? (A map of the area discussed should be used in the report.)

2. In the time of Cecilius Calvert (see page 86), there was a vast difference between the dress of rich people and poorer ones. Is the same thing true today? Why?

3. The leaders of the Massachusetts Bay Colony did not allow dissenters to live in the colony. Are dissenters permitted to express their ideas in our country? Why?

4. In parts of New England today, all the voters of a town can attend an annual town meeting in which they may express their opinions and vote on matters brought up. The citizens are their own legislature. Who laid the groundwork for this *direct democracy?* How?

5. A detailed map of the Hudson Valley today shows these Dutch names: Peekskill, Poughkeepsie, Catskill. Try to find out what the names mean. The Swedish names Swedesboro and Christiana appear near Wilmington, Delaware, on a detailed map. Can you find out what those names mean?

Time and Change

1. Some of the pictures on page 61 show work being done by hand. What has replaced the scythe on American farms today? How are logs hauled today? How do most farmwives obtain water today? Who does most of the building of houses today? How are logs cut? How have the changes come about?

2. Look at the time line on pages 62–63. What English colonies were established in America between 1607 and 1733? What colonies had other Europeans set up?

3. Within those years what two colonies granted religious freedom to settlers?

4. Which colony did not have this kind of freedom?

5. Which colonies established either self-government or the beginning of self-government?

The Book Shelf

DeGering, Etta. *Christopher Jones, Captain of the Mayflower.* New York: David McKay Co., Inc., 1965. (The life of the Pilgrims' shipmaster.)

Dolson, Hildegarde. *William Penn; Quaker Hero.* New York: Random House, Inc., 1961. (A biography of the great Quaker colony builder.)

Fishwick, Marshall W., and eds. of *American Heritage* Magazine. *Jamestown, First English Colony.* New York: American Heritage Publishing Co., Inc., 1965. (A history of the founding of Virginia.)

Tunis, Edwin. *Colonial Craftsmen; and the Beginnings of American Industry.* Cleveland: The World Publishing Co., 1965. (How American industry got its start.)

———. *Colonial Living.* Cleveland: The World Publishing Co., 1957. (The beginnings of American culture.)

Ziner, Feenie, and eds. of *American Heritage* Magazine. *Pilgrims and Plymouth Colony.* New York: American Heritage Publishing Co., Inc., 1961. (The story of the first New England colony.)

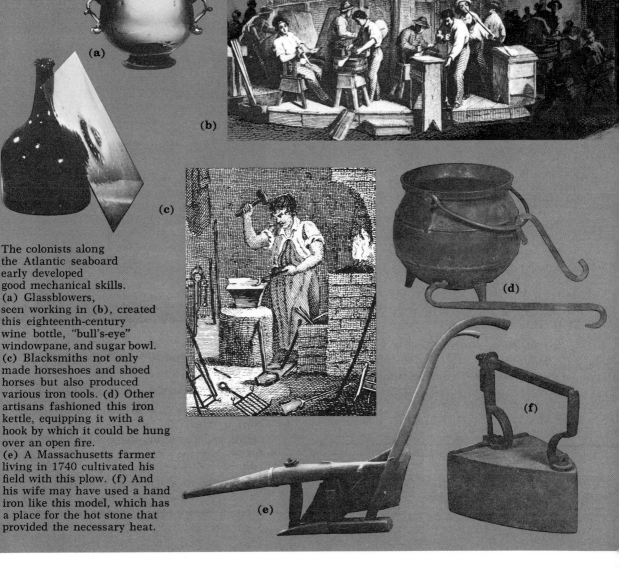

The colonists along the Atlantic seaboard early developed good mechanical skills. (a) Glassblowers, seen working in (b), created this eighteenth-century wine bottle, "bull's-eye" windowpane, and sugar bowl. (c) Blacksmiths not only made horseshoes and shoed horses but also produced various iron tools. (d) Other artisans fashioned this iron kettle, equipping it with a hook by which it could be hung over an open fire. (e) A Massachusetts farmer living in 1740 cultivated his field with this plow. (f) And his wife may have used a hand iron like this model, which has a place for the hot stone that provided the necessary heat.

Part Three:
THE STRUGGLE FOR LIBERTY

Are the skills and objects pictured above in widespread use today? How have they been changed or improved? Such questions help students understand the past and grasp the importance of change in American life.

Samuel Adams

THE HARVEST WAS SPLENDID

Samuel Adams (1722–1803) must have been born a rebel. But an experience in his life seems to have strengthened his natural tendency. His father was a prosperous brewer and merchant who lost his money while Sam was a student at Harvard College.

Ever afterward Sam Adams blamed English policies for his father's financial troubles.

Time and Change   Have students notice how colonial conflicts with England increased after 1763.

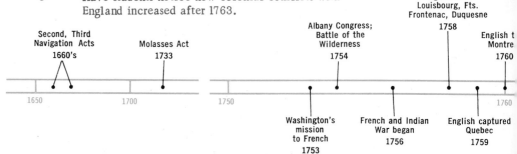

Second, Third
Navigation Acts
1660's

Molasses Act
1733

Albany Congress;
Battle of the
Wilderness
1754

English took
Louisbourg, Fts.
Frontenac, Duquesne
1758

English t
Montre
1760

1650   1700   1750   1760

Washington's
mission
to French
1753

French and Indian
War began
1756

English captured
Quebec
1759

The British government became the target of his fierce rebelliousness. He never took his eyes off this enemy.

After graduation in 1740, Adams began the study of law but gave it up. He started a business for himself but soon lost it. When his father died and left him an inheritance, he used it up in a few years.

By the 1760's Sam Adams, who could not support his own wife and children, had become the center of a storm of opposition to the mother country. His cousin, John, said of him, "He is too attentive to the public, and not enough to himself and his family."

Even in the periods of calm when trouble seemed to be dying down, Sam Adams was forever writing and speaking in the cause of American rights. He was a genius at recognizing how to take advantage of Britain's mistakes. In the starting of the American Revolution, he acted as both director and producer.

Adams drove steadily toward his goal of independence. His policy, he said, was one of waiting "till the Fruit is ripe." In the end the harvest was splendid.

Upsetter of a government, Adams did not have the talent to help create a new and better one. His lack of tact made him out of place in politics after his chosen work of cutting America loose from Britain had been done.

To the last, though, Adams remained faithful to the main theme of his life. "From my Youth," he wrote in his final years, "my mind has been strongly impressed with the Love of Mankind; and tho' I am old, the lamp still burns."

The first American flag, called for by an act of the Congress in 1777, during the American Revolution.

Consider the career of Sam Adams in light of the saying "Extraordinary men seldom lead ordinary lives."

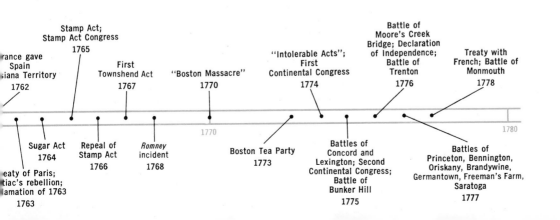

France gave Spain Louisiana Territory 1762

Treaty of Paris; Pontiac's rebellion; Proclamation of 1763 1763

Sugar Act 1764

Stamp Act; Stamp Act Congress 1765

Repeal of Stamp Act 1766

First Townshend Act 1767

Romney incident 1768

"Boston Massacre" 1770

1770

Boston Tea Party 1773

"Intolerable Acts"; First Continental Congress 1774

Battles of Concord and Lexington; Second Continental Congress; Battle of Bunker Hill 1775

Battle of Moore's Creek Bridge; Declaration of Independence; Battle of Trenton 1776

Battles of Princeton, Bennington, Oriskany, Brandywine, Germantown, Freeman's Farm, Saratoga 1777

Treaty with French; Battle of Monmouth 1778

1780

(a) The artist of the Revolution, Charles Willson Peale, began this portrait of his own family—and pet—in 177. He put himself in—leaning over his seated brother.
(b) The earliest picture of the gifted Benjamin Franklin made in 1748 when he was a printer in Pennsylvania.
(c) Carter's Grove, handsome plantation house built in eighteenth-century Virginia, still stands, a fine example of Georgian architecture.
(d) A fire mark, a metal plate fastened to a colonial house to show it was insured against fire.
(e) Earliest existing drawing of the oldest college in our country—Harvard College, now a part of Harvard University.

(f) New York's first college was King's College—now part of 'olumbia University. It looked like this in 1790.
g) A gleaming silver tankard—a large drinking cup—made in New York in the late 1700's.

(f)

(g)

:an students find similarities in the uildings pictured on p. 128-129?

CHAPTER 7

THE SHAPE OF COLONIAL WAYS OF LIFE

phasize that so far students have studied, mainly, how Europeans founded and settled the colonies. Now y will study how the colonists lived in the eighteenth century.

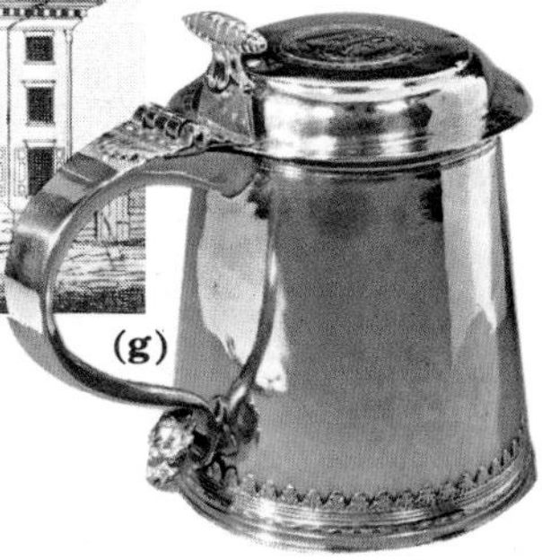

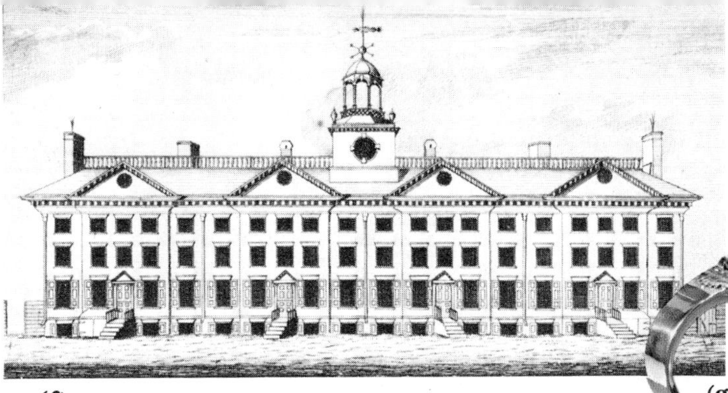

THE patterns of life that the seventeenth-century settlers created remained the chief ones in the developing American culture almost until the end of the eighteenth century. The colonists were in fact trying their very best to reconstruct on this side of the Atlantic the civilization of western Europe. In the area that later became the United States, it was, of course, English culture that took root.

Plantations and Towns Produce Native Leaders

By the opening of the eighteenth century, the frontier, or edge of settlement, of the colonies along the Atlantic seaboard had been pushed inland about two hundred miles. Westward lay a trackless expanse of wilderness that could be bleak and gray in the wintertime and was deeply shaded on sunny days in the summertime.

Two groups of migrants were, however, pushing into the virgin forest. One was made up of fur trappers, constantly searching for a richer supply of the animals whose furs gave them their living. The other was made up of farmers who built their homes along the frontier. They were often on the move, constantly seeking natural clearings in the thick woods which would save them the enormous labor of chopping down trees and uprooting stumps.

Variety in the Colonies

For the most part, though, Americans preferred to live close to the rivers and within what Virginians called the *tidewater*. This is the area inland from the ocean whose rivers are affected by the ebb and flow of the tides. Most of the colonists were simply not quite ready to cut them-

'he colonies differed greatly in population, area, and time of settlement. This section suggests er differences among the colonies.

selves off from easy reach of the Atlantic. Besides, settlements were spread out so thinly over the twelve colonies that few people felt it necessary to look for new dangers and uncertainties farther west.

\# **The population.** In 1700 probably no more than two hundred fifty families lived in the town of Charleston. Philadelphia probably contained not over seven hundred, and New York only around a thousand. The entire population of the colonies in 1700 was about 275,000.

A quarter of the total number of people lived in Virginia, the most heavily populated colony. Slightly fewer lived in Massachusetts, which had the second largest number of people. (About half the settlers lived in these two colonies.) The smallest colony was Delaware, with 2470 people. Next was South Carolina, containing only slightly more than 5000 inhabitants.

A range of riches. Mere numbers cannot begin to describe, though, the kind of *society*—that is, the organized community of people—which was developing in the new land. Some people became rich, some remained poor, and there were many variations in between.

The relationship that existed among the people affected colonial life greatly. There were quickly several standards of living. A few people lived elegantly, a greater number lived modestly, and a group lived in poverty. But regardless of wealth, all the inhabitants of a colony were closely dependent on each other.

Old World differences between classes of people broke down here in America. Colonists who became rich, for example, often had a hard time finding employees. They soon learned that they could not attract people to work for them if they maintained a stiff and unfriendly manner. Besides, a man who was an employee one year might be an employer the next. This fact often made people sympathetic to those who worked for them.

Colonial "Aristocrats"

The "aristocratic" group in the colonies remained small. Those who were considered to be members of it were the owners of large tracts of land, the wealthiest merchants, and the political leaders. These people did not do manual work—that is, they did not work with their hands.

The "aristocrats" of the land. The sharpest difference between the "aristocrats" and the colonists who were less powerful was found by 1700 in Virginia, Maryland, and South Carolina. Large landed estates were beginning to appear in those colonies. Robert Beverly, in Virginia, for instance, owned about 37,000 acres, and William Byrd I over 15,000 acres.

The landowner, or planter, who held the most land, was "King" Robert Carter, also a Virginian. He possessed 333,000 acres of land and seven hundred slaves. Carter earned his nickname because of his haughty manner toward those he considered inferior to him.

Virginia planters based their prosperity on the raising of tobacco. The cultivation of rice on large plantations was a source of wealth in South Carolina.

The way of life of some planters was lavish. William Fitzhugh, for example, who arrived in Virginia in 1670, was able on one occasion to provide violinists, an acrobat, and a tightrope dancer to entertain some unexpected guests.

The dwellings that planters built for themselves and their families often were called great houses or manor houses. Their owners sometimes imagined themselves to be lords like those in Europe.

Usually planters acquired over a period of time the possessions which marked men of means on the other side of the ocean. These might include pewter dishes, showpiece cabinets turned out by master craftsmen, and sterling-silver tableware. They might also include highly colored rugs or

\#Have students compare the population of their community or state with that of the colonies in 1700. (See Appendix pp. 729-730.) Does population alone determine the importance of a community? Ask students to explain their answers.

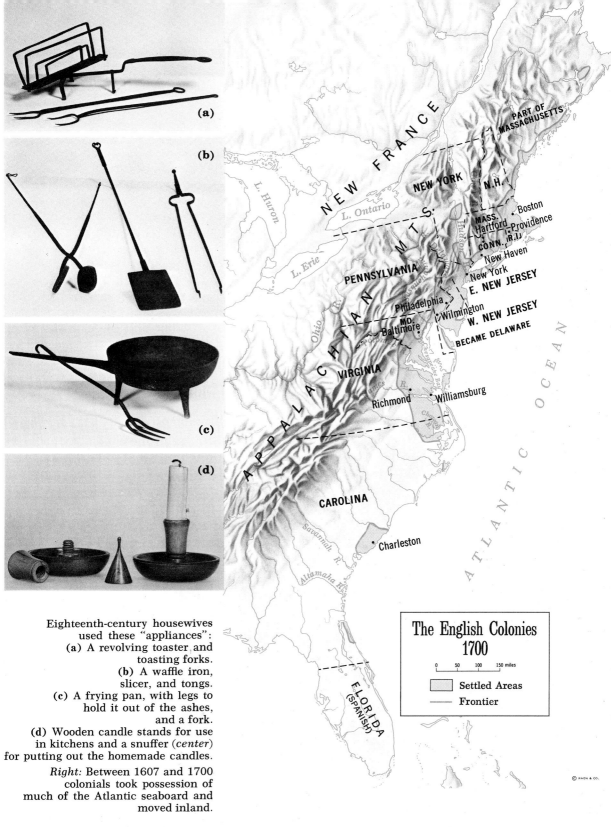

Eighteenth-century housewives
used these "appliances":
(a) A revolving toaster and
toasting forks.
(b) A waffle iron,
slicer, and tongs.
(c) A frying pan, with legs to
hold it out of the ashes,
and a fork.
(d) Wooden candle stands for use
in kitchens and a snuffer (*center*)
for putting out the homemade candles.

Right: Between 1607 and 1700
colonials took possession of
much of the Atlantic seaboard and
moved inland.

The English Colonies 1700

0   50   100   150 miles

▨ Settled Areas

— Frontier

© RAND & CO.

tapestries, linen or lace tablecloths, and possibly painted portraits of ancestors.

Planters also showed off their position by the way they dressed. They had their clothing made abroad. They wore linen shirts with metal buttons, wigs, shoes with buckles of silver or brass, broadcloth coats, and waistcoats often of bright colors.

The ladies. The planters' wives and daughters also were adorned brilliantly. Their calico dresses were of the best imported quality. The ladies used ornamental fans, perhaps to help suggest that the hands which carried them did not have to do manual work. On festive occasions they wore gowns made of silk.

Moreover, the ladies wore jewelry—gold bracelets or rings or silver brooches and earrings—that became heirlooms as they were handed down from mother to daughter. Today some of them are prizes of antique collectors.

The "aristocrats" of the marketplace. Outside of the South the "aristocrats" also lived lavishly. In New York, families like the Schuylers, the Van Cortlandts, the Beekmans, and the Van Rensselaers owned very large estates. An important difference between them and their fellow "aristocrats" in the South was that they tended to invest their extra money in trade rather than in land.

The great New York fortunes were built chiefly on the sale of furs in the European market. Other fortunes were established or increased by the lending of money—sometimes at rates of interest that today seem much too high.

As the "aristocrats" of the North, like those elsewhere, increased their holdings, they built finer houses. In the middle of the eighteenth century one New Yorker, William Walton, was proud of "a brick edifice, fifty feet in front and three stories high, built with Holland bricks." It had a doorway of Greek-style columns and a tile-covered roof. Inside, the sturdy walls were covered with expensive wooden paneling.

For the most part, New York "aristocrats" were never able to obtain enough tenants to farm their land—which lay largely uncultivated. Strongly influenced by the Dutch ideal of thriftiness, most of them lived somewhat less luxuriously than

Perhaps in their homes some students have pewter dishes which they will bring to class.

Many colonists ate and drank from pewter ware, made out of a combination of metals, but mainly tin. It was beautiful, as these samples show, and also less expensive than silver.

Henry Francis du Pont Winterthur Museum

Which of the items shown in the picture may have come from Europe?

Benjamin Franklin was among the visitors at the Van Cortlandt home on the Hudson River in New York, and he may have eaten in this handsome dining room, which displays the choice china and silver a rich colonist might own.

Sleepy Hollow Restorations,
Tarrytown, New York

the southern "aristocrats." But like the southerners, they tended through marriage ties to maintain tight control over their property and to strengthen the family links on which aristocracy thrives.

The merchants of Boston and Philadelphia also became prosperous from trade. The largest oceangoing vessels brought products of all the world to their cities.

The Quakers of Pennsylvania long remained known for their plain dress and simple home furnishings. Nevertheless, by the eighteenth century many of their houses, like the dwellings of other merchants, could only be described as elegant. Some even contained furniture made in England by Thomas Chippendale and other celebrated cabinetmakers.

Self-made men. A man in the colonies that engaged mainly in trade, to a somewhat greater extent than in the southern plantation colonies, could rise in the world from a low position. Benjamin Franklin of Philadelphia, for example, rose from being a humble printer's devil to being a diplomat and statesman of great fame. Some of Franklin's friends in Philadelphia also began life in lowly stations. Franklin wrote about them many years later in his *Autobiography*, saying:

William Parsons, bred a shoe-maker, but, loving reading, had acquir'd a considerable share of mathematics, which he first studied with a view to astrology, that he afterwards laught at it. He . . . became surveyor general. . . .

One William Coleman, . . . a merchant's clerk, about my age, who had the coolest, clearest head, the best heart, and the exactest morals of almost any man I ever met with. He became afterwards a merchant of great note, and one of our provincial judges.

Another example of how hard work could do wonders for a man not well born, that is, not born into a prosperous family, is the life of John Hull. The son of a blacksmith, Hull arrived in America as a child in 1634. At first he helped his father with farm chores, but soon he became a goldsmith's apprentice and learned to fashion precious metals. Becoming a master craftsman, he developed a profitable business, selling his products in Boston.

As Hull's profits mounted up, he invested in businesses of considerable variety.

According to Franklin, what helped Parsons and Coleman rise in the world? By what means do people seek to rise today? Analyze what Americans mean by "rising in the world."

Rich South Carolinians of the late 1700's lived in these houses in Charleston along Rainbow Row, so named because of the delicate colors of the buildings.

He was involved in the wine and sugar trades, the tobacco trade, and the textile trade. His business connections put him in touch with many parts of the world: Virginia, the West Indies, the Madeira Islands, Ireland, and Spain. He even had a farm in the West Indies where he raised and sold horses profitably.

Hull was able to provide his daughter Hannah with a handsome dowry when she married Samuel Sewall, a distinguished judge of colonial Massachusetts. A popular tale was that Hannah received her weight in shillings, coins her father had produced as the mintmaster for the colony.

The Look of Things

\# Dependence on English customs and tastes was typical of all the colonial "aristocrats," northern or southern, landed or merchant. In Charleston, where easygoing planter living was combined with the hus-

##Do people today try to make their homes distinctive and attractive? How?

tle and bustle of a tightly knit trading community, this fact could be seen best.

Splendid architecture. Charleston, whose leaders had grown rich on raising rice, also developed an "aristocratic" life based \# on owning beautiful houses. These were often the scene of fancy-dress balls and fine dinners. The brick houses were stuccoed in light blue, pink, yellow, and green.

Later, as the eighteenth century wore on, townspeople who had seen the city of London developed a liking for Georgian architecture, then the rage across the ocean. This stately style had several variations. In America it could be seen in basic red-brick buildings with white stone decorations and wood trimmings painted white.

Ambitious and eager to own the best of everything (and maybe even show off a little), "aristocrats" purchased from England the products they required—both luxuries and necessities. They also imported fashionable books and magazines from the mother country. Consequently, the people of means in every colony transplanted to America the culture in which wealthy Englishmen grew up.

Stylish entertainment. Nevertheless, the general community life in which the colonial "aristocrats" took part tended to vary from one section to another. In the South for instance, the stage was an important part of public entertainment.

In Williamsburg, Virginia, was established the first theater in the English colonies in America. There some of the best examples of eighteenth-century drama were shown—as well as many of Shakespeare's plays.

In Boston, music halls and plays—indeed, all public entertainment—were forbidden. They were regarded as contrary to God's will. A traveler reported from there in 1740, however, that the people did not "seem to be dispirited nor moped for want of them." "The ladies here," he wrote, "visit, drink tea and . . . neglect the affairs of

\#Why do colonists often copy the styles of their mother country? Colonists also develop styles o their own. Why? Discuss whether most American colonists considered themselves Englishmen or Americans.

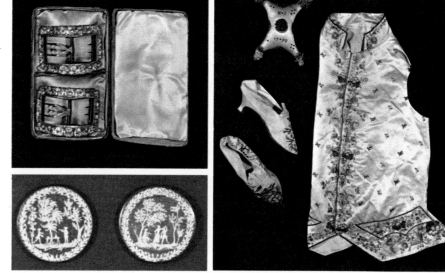

Far right: A wealthy colonist's satin vest, embroidered in silk. A pincushion, dated 1798. Wedding slippers worn in 1785 by a bride in Massachusetts. *Near right:* Shoe buckles set with rhinestones, owned by a Benjamin Joy, of Boston (1757–1829). Glass buttons, in which cut paper designs were mounted over blue silk.

their family with as good a grace as the finest ladies in London."

The wealthy people, then, were developing a way of life that imitated England's aristocratic life but that had characteristics relating to the special features of the American environment. Their life set a model for other men and women.

An open society. Moreover, new members of the "aristocracy" were constantly being created. These were ambitious people who had been born poor but acquired fortunes. In short, the road to high social position and honors in America was not closed to newcomers as it was in most places in Europe. This fact, which early characterized life in America, became a basis for the growth of the democratic idea that, regardless of his origin, one man is as good as another.

Colonial politics. Men who won prominence as planters or business leaders almost automatically entered politics and became government officials. Each colony had a governor as its executive, or administrator, whose tasks and duties were similar to those of state governors today.

A governor was advised by a council or a board of assistants whose members were men of wealth. Because these councillors usually held office for life, their influence and power were very great.

In each colony the work of writing laws fell to an assembly. Its members were elected for fixed terms.

In the eighteenth century "aristocrats" in America believed that a man ought not to be allowed to take part in politics unless he owned some property—preferably land. As a result, there was a property qualification, or requirement, for holding each colonial office.

There was also a property qualification for voting, but a great part of the population could meet it because land was very cheap. The right to vote, therefore, was not limited only to rich people, although it was not generally exercised.

1. What two groups of people led in the westward movement of colonists? 2. Where did most of the settlers live? Why? 3. What two colonies had the most people? 4. Which colonists made up the "aristocratic" group in the colonies? 5. Describe the "aristocrats'" way of life. 6. Name two men whose lives showed that men of low position could advance in America. 7. In what important way did life in America differ from life in Europe? 8. Name the chief government officials in the colonies.

Aore men can share in government when there are few restrictions on voting and officeholding d when most officials are elected for fixed terms instead of appointed for life. Have students ok up major changes in voting laws in the past few years.

Men Who Work with Their Hands Play Their Parts

People whose circumstances were meager did not *always* move ahead into the ranks of society's leaders even when they were very diligent. But many were able in one generation to move into the middle class of people, chiefly made up of artisans and farmers.

Artisans and Farmers

Artisans were craftsmen who possessed skills as carpenters, pewterers, weavers, blacksmiths, millers, cabinetmakers, coopers (that is, barrel-makers), shipwrights, glassblowers, or any of a great many other kinds of "mechanics." They lived in the # towns, often running one-man shops in their homes.

Almost everywhere farmers were regarded as being considerably superior to the artisans. Possibly this idea existed because the artisan was dependent on the rest of the community. The farmer, on the other hand, took pride in believing that he was self-reliant.

A love of property. Two attitudes held in common by farmers and artisans linked these people together. Both looked forward to raising their standing through acquiring property and by improving their education. Because they had to work with their hands, they respected a life of labor and urged it on their children. They had a high regard for themselves and a keen sense of the widening opportunity they were sure they and their children would enjoy.

High hopes. American farmers and artisans of the early eighteenth century must have known that they were different from people like themselves in Europe. In America they could hope someday to enjoy the advantages of life formerly open only to "aristocrats." They became the foundation of the present-day American middle class, a firm backbone of American life.

Pioneers

In addition to the "aristocrats," the farmers, and the artisans, there were people of little or almost no standing. These were the "inferiors," or the "meaner sort." America owes a great deal to them for their daring and their strength, even

Compare this picture with the ones on pages 133 and 134. What do the pictures reveal about different ways of life in colonial America?

The pioneers lived in a way very different from the style of the well-to-do colonists. They worked hard in an environment that could be harsh and cruel.

Lewis Collins, "History of Kentucky," 1874 (New York Public Library)

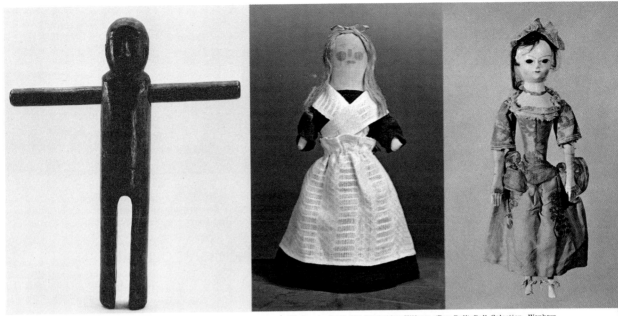

Which of these dolls might have been made in a pioneer home in the wilderness?

Some little girls played with clothespin dolls like the one at the left. Others owned rag dolls made of corncobs covered with cloth and having faces painted on with fruit juices (*center*). Still others played with more realistic and fancily dressed ones made in England (*right*).

though we do not recall many of them by name.

Among the "inferiors" was a less-settled kind of farmer than the ones mentioned earlier. Sometimes, in kind moods, historians have called them *pioneers*, the people who first enter or settle an area. In less sympathetic moods they have spoken of them as *squatters*. They were actually small-scale speculators who squatted on the land they worked. They never legally owned it, but after a few years they sold the improvements they had made on it to the next comer. He might hold the full title to it, that is, own it legally. "Improvements" were the removing of trees and the turning of the soil—necessary and back-breaking work.

A simple life. Since most of the pioneers owned few items besides their farm implements and cooking utensils, they found it fairly convenient to move. Their life remained simple, as they spent a large portion of their time hunting and fishing. Usually they were unable to provide schooling for their children, and they lacked also various comforts possessed by people who were better situated.

Close to nature. The pioneers lived their lives just out of the reach of government, churches, and other benefits of community life. In common with fellow Americans, though, they drew inspiration and strength—and hope for tomorrow—from a natural environment which seemed to be endlessly abundant.

People Without Skills

In towns and villages also lived people considered inferiors. These were the unskilled workers, who might be farmhands

ress the contribution of the squatter in extending the frontier to the west. Was the aristocratic
anter merely an earlier, more successful squatter?

How did each group mentioned in the caption contribute to the prosperity of the city?

The waterfront of Philadelphia in 1754, one of the flourishing colonial ports that owed its rapid development to the merchants, artisans, indentured servants, unskilled workers, and farmers living around it.

or handymen or dockhands. Occasionally some of these people were able, by saving a little money, to enter one of the trades or even to make a start in business. The pattern varied from one colony to another.

At sea. In New England, where the shipping industry took a great many unskilled men to sea, the opportunities to own land were not great. Moreover, the letdown among sailors when they came ashore after a long period at sea resulted often in quick spending of wages rather than in thoughtful saving.

The unskilled were, of course, not necessarily short of physical energy. They did hard manual labor at a time when machines were only beginning to come into everyday use. As yet nothing had changed the age-old fact that most men had to earn their bread in the sweat of their brows.

An uncertain living. Usually unskilled people were the first to be laid off in slack times and the ones least likely to be properly housed. It is probable (although there are no reliable figures) that their death rate was higher than that of the rest of the population.

For the most part these people could, at best, only read and write a little. They were ignorant of the politics of the day, and if they had opinions at all, they tended to agree with the views of their employers.

Indentured Servants

Still other "inferior" people were the indentured servants (see page 77). These made up the largest single portion of the total colonial population in the seventeenth century. Indentured servitude did not end until the early part of the nineteenth century.

Their passage. A man and his family wishing to come to America might agree while still in England to work for a number of years in return for payment of their passage. Some made arrangements with ship captains to carry them across the ocean. These contracts, or *indentures*, providing that the newcomers would work for a period of time, were sold to a master. After a term of service, the indentured servants became freemen.

A typical indenture tells us of the arrangement made by those who signed it:

> THIS INDENTURE made the _____ day of _____ in the _____ year of our sovereign lord King Charles, etc. between _____ of the one party and _____ of the other party, Witnesseth, that the said _____ doth hereby covenant, promise, and grant, to and with the said _____ his executors and assignes, to serve

#Remember, "indentured servant" referred in part to a legal status and in part to a social one. The existence of such a degree of social rank helps explain colonial society, but the term "indentured servant" reveals little about any individual to whom it applied.

him from the day of the date hereof, until his first and next arrival in Maryland; and after for and during the term of _____ years, in such service and employment, as he the said _____ or his assignes shall there employ him, according to the custom of the country in the like kind. In consideration whereof, the said _____ doth promise and grant, to and with the said _____ to pay for his passing, and to find him meat, drink, apparel and lodging, with other necessaries during the said term; and at the end of the said term, to give him one whole year's provisions of corn and fifty acres of land, according to the order of the country. In witness whereof, the said _____ hath hereunto put his hand and seal, the day and year above written.

Sealed and delivered in the presence of

Their treatment. Indentured servants in America endured a hard experience—although their situations varied from place to place and master to master. But American circumstances softened their treatment. The shortage of people to work in the colonies made it natural for a master to extend a comforting hand to the man who labored for him. Moreover, the ranks of the indentured servants included men trained in all kinds of trades that were needed—from carpentry to medicine and from upholstering to wigmaking.

In Maryland a law was passed in 1715 which established penalties for any master who mistreated his indentured servants. Such a master was defined as one who did not provide "sufficient meat, drink, lodging and clothing, . . . or [would] . . . beat or abuse [his people], or give them more than ten lashes for any one offense."

Nevertheless, indentured servants were sometimes harshly handled. Word would spread, often in a newspaper advertisement, that a group of men, women, and children was on its way and that its indentures were up for sale.

The "soul drivers." When the ship carrying such a group had docked, men known as soul drivers herded together the indentured servants on board. Then they would "drive them through the country like a parcel of sheep" until they could sell them at a profit. Sometimes children as young as ten years of age would be prodded from town to town in this way.

Indentured servants, in short, had an unhappy introduction to American life. Their sense of being unjustly treated must have been keen, because many were people of ability and even education.

It appears that as more poorly trained indentured servants began to come here at the beginning of the eighteenth century, the treatment of indentured servants worsened. They were respected less. Many were commonly referred to as thieves and lazy louts and were treated accordingly. One Elizabeth Sprigs wrote from Maryland of "toiling day and night . . . and of being . . . whipped to that degree you would not beat an animal, scarce anything but Indian corn and salt to eat. . . ."

It is a safe bet that indentured servants did not make the best employees. Frequently they ran away, becoming tired of their treatment or simply impatient to obtain their freedom.

Youthful Labor

Young people who did not go to college often were apprenticed so they could learn trades. The apprentice system was a method of training a new generation of artisans and of educating poor boys—and girls.

The apprentice system. Apprentices were expected to serve their masters faithfully, remain sober, avoid grumbling, and learn their craft or skill well. One apprentice agreement involved a pledge to instruct a

The apprentice system is still in use today. Have a student who is interested in labor unions compare the apprentice system today with the one followed in colonial times. See Activity in "The Research Center" (page 147).

139

girl in "house-wifery, knitting, spinning, sewing, and such like exercises as may be fitting and becoming her sex."

You must not conclude that children in the New World were roughly or unfeelingly treated. Remember that adults came here in order to enjoy a better life, one that offered better opportunity. They included their children, of course, in their hopes and dreams.

A helpful birth rate. Children not only were symbols of a better future. They were useful, indeed necessary, additions to the working force. Marriages took place at an early age. It was not uncommon for a girl to be wed by the time she was fourteen or fifteen. This meant that children were usually numerous.

Sarah Hext, of South Carolina, to give one example out of thousands, married Dr. John Rutledge when she was only fourteen. By the time she was twenty-five, she had borne seven children. One of them, Edward, was among the South Carolinians who later was to sign the Declaration of Independence.

Yet naturally children felt keenly the harshness of daily life in the colonies.
\# The death rate for youngsters was very high. It was not unusual for a family in which ten or twelve babies were born to see only a few grow up to be adults.

Emphasize the difference between slavery and

The Slave
servitude.

At the bottom of the labor force was the Negro slave. He was dragged from Africa to mingle his blood and sweat with that of Europeans in taming the American land.

The earliest arrivals. The first Negroes were shipped to America—to Jamestown —in 1619, the year before the *Mayflower* arrived. They had Spanish names like Antony, Isabella, and Pedro. There were twenty altogether.

Why the Dutch man-of-war carrying the Negroes stopped at Jamestown we do not

know. It probably had robbed a Spanish vessel going to the West Indies. In the robbery the Dutch removed the precious human cargo—the first of millions of Africans who were transported toward these shores in the next two hundred years.

Antony, one of the arrivals in Jamestown, fell in love with Isabella and they were married. In 1624 their child was born and named William Tucker for a local planter. He was the first Negro child born in an English colony in America.

Negro indentured servants. We should keep in mind that the first Negroes were not slaves, bound to masters. Taking advantage of the indenture system, captains of vessels bringing Negroes to English colonies sold them as indentured servants. The Africans were freed when the period of work agreed upon was over.

Just as some indentured servants had been practically kidnapped on the streets of English cities, so had these Negroes been taken against their wishes in Africa. Some came from western and central Africa, some were from the southern part of the continent, and others were from eastern Africa. The result was that Africans in America differed as much as Europeans.

The slip into bondage. At first the indentured servants from Europe seem to have worked side by side with those from Africa without feeling any prejudice. But circumstances handicapped the Negroes.

First of all, Negroes who ran away could easily be caught and returned to their masters. They could be readily identified.

Second, Negroes brought with them agricultural know-how which was badly needed. Consequently, they were taken to plantations, where they had little chance to avoid slavery. European indentured servants, being often artisans, were usually put to work at their trades, generally in towns.

Third, the constant turnover of workers who started as indentured servants made

Indentured servants were bound, often voluntarily, for a fixed term of service. Slaves were bound, involuntarily, for life. Servants also had a kind of protection in law that slaves seldom had.

life very uncertain for the planter. He could partially solve his problem of finding people to work by keeping some of his servants—the Negroes—permanently. In short, he could make them slaves.

The labor problem could not be solved by the use of Indians. Attempts to enslave them usually failed because, knowing the forest, they escaped into it easily. Besides, putting a large number of them into bondage would have meant having to fend off their fellow tribesmen in endless warfare. The Negro was caught: he had no one to fight to keep him free, and he could not fight for himself.

Legal developments. By the 1660's Maryland and Virginia were making important legal changes that established slavery for the first time. Negroes were to be servants for life. Their children were to inherit the condition of their mothers. That is, they would be either slave or free according to whether their mothers had been slave or free.

By 1700 slavery had become a way of life for thousands. A steady loss of personal dignity was the lot of the captured Negro from the time he left his homeland. # More often than not, death, violent death, awaited him sooner than he thought.

The terrible crossings. An eyewitness to the slave-trading that became common by the end of the seventeenth century described life for the Negroes aboard the slave-transport vessels: "The sense of misery and suffocation was so terrible in the 'tween-decks—where the height sometimes was only eighteen inches . . . that the unfortunate slaves could not turn round. . . . In their frenzy some killed others in

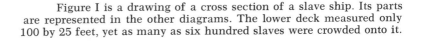

Figure I is a drawing of a cross section of a slave ship. Its parts are represented in the other diagrams. The lower deck measured only 100 by 25 feet, yet as many as six hundred slaves were crowded onto it.

Peabody Museum

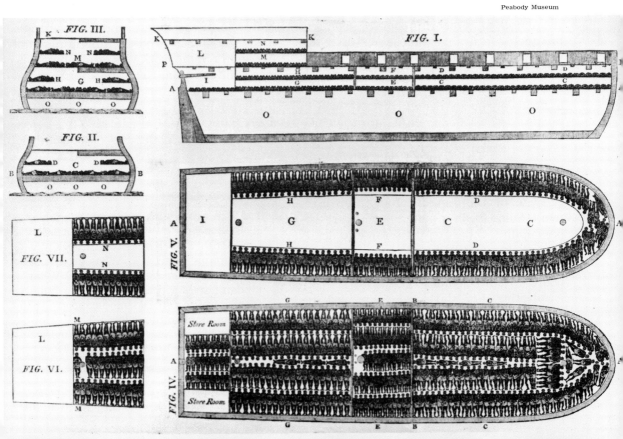

TO BE SOLD on board the Ship *Bance-Ifland*, on tuefday the 6th of *May* next, at *Afbley-Ferry*; a choice cargo of about 250 fine healthy

NEGROES,

juft arrived from the Windward & Rice Coaft. —The utmoft care has already been taken, and fhall be continued, to keep them free from the leaft danger of being infected with the SMALL-POX, no boat having been on board, and all other communication with people from *Charles-Town* prevented.

Auftin, Laurens, & Appleby.

N. B. Full one Half of the above Negroes have had the SMALL-POX in their own Country.

In the mid-1700's Negro slaves were considered property in both North and South: newspaper advertisements of slave sales were common.

the hope of procuring more room to breathe. Men strangled those next to them, and women drove nails into each other's brains."

The dead would be thrown overboard— as food for the sharks which were said to escort every slave ship on its grim journey across the ocean. The stench of a slave vessel was so intolerable that its owners were likely to burn it to the water line after a single voyage.

Some of the Negroes fought enslavement. Some died on African shores, resisting capture. Others tried to starve to death aboard ship and had to be forcibly fed by special devices. Still others jumped overboard to sure death.

Adapting. For slaves who survived the passage, normal life was impossible. Men greatly outnumbered women. Tribal ways which at home had given them a settled kind of life could not be practiced.

Slavery was not confined to the South. For a time it existed in the North--in farming, trades, etc.

Unlike Europeans, who saw America as a land of opportunity, Negro slaves found out that here they had to give up their own ways of living. They had to part with even their own names and be made over. Upon arrival Negroes would be taken in hand and trained by a handful of reliable slaves. These showed the newcomers how to do the work, taught them the English words they would require to obey orders, and drilled into them obedience to the master.

Underdogs. For the slave there were self-made entertainment and pleasures in the sparse and sometimes bleak slave quarters. But in general he was forced to face life without hope.

Unlike the farmers, who also tilled the soil and labored from dawn to dusk, the slaves could feel no ambition for themselves or their children. They were permanent underdogs in the country they, too, were helping to build.

Despite handicaps, some slaves became skilled workers, forming the bulk of artisans in the South before the Civil War. Slaves built the homes and furniture and made the utensils and clothing in much of the South. Some work was crude, but some was skillfully done. The finest example of slave craftsmanship is seen in the beautiful wrought-iron decoration on balconies, doors, lampposts, and gates in Charleston, New Orleans, Mobile, and other southern cities.

1. What two groups made up the middle class of people? Which was considered superior? 2. What two attitudes did both groups hold? 3. What groups of people were considered inferiors? What kinds of lives did they lead? 4. What three circumstances handicapped Negroes brought to the colonies? 5. How did the life of Negro slaves in America differ from the life of Europeans?

Students might like to speculate on how southern farming might have developed without slavery. How would a work force have been found? (Remember that slavery is a human institution; there is nothing natural about its development.)

The Schoolroom Holds Promise for All

One way in which the English colonists made sure that the gains of one generation would be handed down to and improved upon by the next was by educating their children. And the chief way a man rose on the ladder of success regardless of his birth was by acquiring an education. Families in northern cities had a special advantage: they lived close together and their children could easily attend local schools.

The Yankee Example

New England colonies led all the others in emphasizing the importance of learning. As early as 1635 the people of Boston set up a school modeled on the grammar schools of the mother country.

These schools were created for boys, not girls. Girls attended boarding schools, or they were taught in a home by a tutor or a mother who took in neighborhood girls.

To read the Bible. The simple fact was that in Massachusetts, where the emphasis on learning to read was keenest, the great concern was the ability to read the Bible. The settlers did not want Satan to "keep men from the knowledge of the scriptures ... by keeping them in an unknown tongue."

In New Amsterdam, schools did not develop until long after those in New England were established. As late as 1658 the burghers were asking the Dutch West India Company to send them a Latin teacher so that they could create a school.

To train ministers. The nature of education was similar everywhere: there was an emphasis on religion and the training of ministers. In Pennsylvania one of the best-known schools was set up by William Tennent at Neshaminy and was generally known as the Log College.

The Jesuits' contribution. Maryland's first schools were established by the Jesuits. Later, as Protestants outnumbered Roman Catholics, the Church of England helped organize education. But again the aim was unchanged: "to make learning a handmaid to [religious] devotion."

Tutoring in the South. South of Maryland the wealthier planters engaged tutors for their sons—or they sent them to England or, less frequently, to France. Charleston had a number of private schools, and the legislature of South Carolina in the early years of the eighteenth century passed laws creating a free school. That is, it was open to all children who were not the offspring of slaves.

For a long time, though, only the children of wealthy colonists could have much education beyond reading, writing, and ciphering (as arithmetic was then called). Their parents did not need them to work at home. Moreover, they looked forward as a

The Log College, founded in Pennsylvania in 1726, was supported by men who later became trustees of the College of New Jersey, now Princeton.

Princeton University Archives

143

matter of course to service as government officials or as clergymen—for which they would require an education.

Creating Colleges
Were these public or private schools?

Colleges were established—slowly. The colonies needed them to prepare people for
political or religious careers.

"One Mr. Harvard." The first and by far the most distinguished of the colleges was Harvard, created in Massachusetts in 1636. As an early New Englander said, "One of the first things we longed for and looked after was to advance learning... dreading to leave an illiterate ministry to

Yale University Art Gallery

In 1755 a friend gave Elihu Yale this silver snuffbox on which Yale's picture appears. Snuff is powdered tobacco which snuffers inhale through their nostrils.

A hard-working Harvard student studies his lesson as he cooks his meal in what we would call light-housekeeping rooms.

N. Hayward, "College Scenes," 1850 (Harvard University Library)

the churches when our present ministers shall lie in the dust." Then he added:

And as we were thinking and consulting how to effect this great work, it pleased God to stir up the heart of one Mr. Harvard... to give the one half of his estate [that is, property]... towards the erecting of a college, and all his library.... The college was by common consent appointed to be at Cambridge (a place very pleasant...) and is called (according to the name of the first founder) Harvard College.

By the end of fifteen years, about fifty students were enrolled at Harvard. From the start anybody could attend. By the end of the century, students were coming to Harvard from other colonies, although not yet from New York or places farther south.

William and Mary. The first college in the South was the College of William and Mary, created in 1693. The law which established it approved a tax on tobacco to provide money for its support. Aimed at training ministers, the school also encouraged young men of Virginia to stay at home instead of going off to Europe for their education.

Mr. Yale's generosity. Sometimes personal ambition had a part in the founding of a college. In 1701 a college was founded

The pursuit of knowledge in spite of difficulties is strikingly exemplified in the case of those students who board themselves.

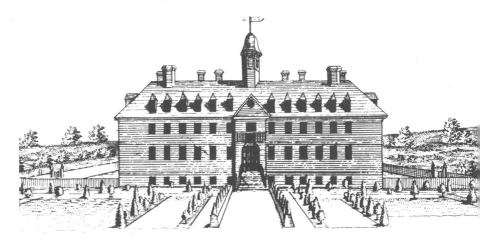

Wren Hall, shown here, is a college building still in use.

Southern members of the Church of England established the College of William and Mary—named for the English king and queen—in Williamsburg, Virginia. The main building is shown here.

Colonial Williamsburg

by a Massachusetts clergyman, Cotton Mather, who was angry when he failed to become president of Harvard. He turned his energies to building up the college which was located in New Haven, Connecticut. A first step was the writing of a letter in January, 1718, to Elihu Yale, a wealthy official of the East India Company, who had been born in New England.

Mather hinted that if Yale gave enough to the struggling college, its leaders would rename it for him. Six months later Yale sent to New Haven three bales of goods, a portrait of George I, and some books. The gift was to be the largest private contribution made to a college until the nineteenth century.

The College of New Jersey. Colleges were also founded in other colonies. But not all enjoyed the luck of Yale or possessed determined leaders like those who established Harvard. All these new colleges grew out of a need to train ministers.

Princeton originated because of a call for American-trained Presbyterian clergymen—that is, ministers of the branch of Protestantism that had begun in Scotland. Called the College of New Jersey at the time of its creation in 1746, Princeton soon was sending forth a steady stream of ministers. These men were well trained not only in religious matters but also in Latin and Greek.

King's College. In New York the need for a college became keener as the eighteenth century advanced. The result was the chartering of King's College in 1754—renamed Columbia later. After a fierce fight over its control between Presbyterians and members of the Church of England, an agreement was reached. The president was always to be a member of the Church of England.

However, the board of trustees included representatives of a number of Protestant groups, and before many years a rabbi was a trustee, also. This apparent coöperation between religious groups reflected the mixed makeup of New York's population. It also showed the need for differing religious groups to work together. (Clearly it would have been difficult for each of them to create its own college.)

The charter of King's College provided that no rules could be made that would shut out "any person of any religious denomination whatever from equal liberty and advantage of education . . . on account of his . . . religion."

Other colleges. Four other colleges established in the colonial period were Benjamin Franklin's Academy (later the University of Pennsylvania), in 1751; Rhode Island College (later Brown University), in 1764; Queen's College (later Rutgers), in 1766; and Dartmouth College, in 1769. But they did not have great influence until the nineteenth century.

The colleges mentioned in this section are now among the leading universities in the country. Have students look up the beginnings of some of the outstanding colleges in their state or region.

Professional training. Throughout the colonies, professional schools for the training of lawyers and doctors were either lacking or woefully poor. Would-be lawyers generally learned their profession through serving as apprentices in the offices of practicing lawyers. For the most part, youths entered the medical field in a similar fashion, working at the side of men already in practice.

The College of Philadelphia (later connected with the University of Pennsylvania) taught medicine from 1765 on, and King's College also had a medical school before the 1760's were over. But the training these provided could not be compared with what was available in the European medical schools—which, in general, was not very good either.

The ways of life that had developed in the colonies by the eighteenth century could not have been imagined by the first settlers a century and a half earlier. But already some were glimpsing an even more fascinating future.

A few colonists were thinking of how grand it would be if the boundaries and barriers between colonies and colonists could become less important. In the 1760's Christopher Gadsden, a leader of South Carolina, was writing, "There ought to be# no New England men, no New Yorkers, etc., known on the continent, but all of us Americans. . . ." This was a new idea. Carrying it out became the task of the next generation of colonists.

---

1. What was the chief means of rising in the world in the colonies? Which families possessed a special advantage concerning that means? 2. What was the main aim of most colonial schools? 3. Name nine colleges established in the colonies before 1770. What are their names today?

Words in "Adding to Your Vocabulary" might be used in answering questions in "Thinking Things Through."

The Workshop

Adding to Your Vocabulary

Be sure you know the meaning of these words:

tidewater	pioneer
society	squatter
aristocrat	indenture
standard of	bondage
living	apprentice

Thinking Things Through

Review the boxed-in exercises within the chapter. Then carry out the following:

1. Compare the way the "aristocrats" of the southern colonies made their fortunes with the way those of the northern and middle colonies made theirs. How did they differ in the way they spent their money?

2. Frontier people had few class or social distinctions. Why? What happens to a classless group of people as it becomes more established? Why?

3. Why were success stories such as that of John Hull important in attracting settlers to the colonies? How did the American path to success usually differ from the European?

4. Every society has certain *values*—highly regarded beliefs, ideals, or ways of looking at things. From your reading of this chapter, can you name any values or attitudes held by Americans today which date back to colonial times?

##Gadsden's words serve as an introduction to the topics of the next three chapters: the problems that brought the colonists together and made them think of themselves as Americans. Point out that the idea of union had early beginnings.

5. Why do you suppose education was generally considered more necessary for the people in the New England colonies than in the southern ones?

6. Squatters were never discouraged by colonial governments. Can you tell why? Review what Chapter 3 says about the inhabitants of New France. How might encouragement of squatters have changed the story of New France in North America?

Graphs Tell a Story

1. Make a pie graph showing by colonies the distribution of population in what became the United States. The populations of four colonies can be shown as percentages of the total population. One part of the "pie" can be labeled "Other colonies."

2. Make a bar graph showing a comparison of the populations of the two largest and two smallest colonies in 1700 with the present populations of the four states they became.

Which of the four has grown by the largest percentage? Which has grown the least?

How do Virginia and Massachusetts rank among the states today in size of population? Which two states are most populous? Which two are least populous?

The Research Center

1. Use reference books to obtain information about the War on Poverty program of the 1960's. What problem was it planned to help solve? Why was there no such program in colonial times? What colonial people might have benefited from it? What kind of instruction would you have provided for in a colonial program?

2. Find out the requirements for owning a union card in a major trade in your area. What are the requirements for being journeymen and apprentices? What similarities to the colonial system do you see?

3. Organize a class debate around the subject "*Resolved*, That only property owners should vote."

4. Report to the class on one of the major Negro civilizations of ancient Africa. What were some of its accomplishments? Why did it collapse? Compare some of these cultures with those of Mexico and Peru.

5. Obtain a present-day catalog of a school that was established in colonial days. Compare the subject offerings in the curriculum today with those in the eighteenth century.

6. If there are examples of Georgian architecture in your city, let the class visit them. Or one student might take pictures of the buildings and report to the class on this particular style of architecture.

7. Obtain a copy of *Poor Richard's Almanack*. On your school bulletin board post a new quotation from this book each day. Discuss its meaning for life today.

The Seeds of Democracy

1. In colonial America a person was more likely to be considered the equal of any other person than he would have been in Europe. Why? Why has it always been easier for a man or woman to rise in his station in life in America than in Europe? By what methods could a colonist "move up"? How can Americans today improve their situations?

2. The situation of one group of people in the colonies was a blot on the democracy that had begun to develop in America. Who were these men and women? What rights or privileges enjoyed by other colonists were denied them?

Creating a democracy is a continuing process. Use the "Seeds of Democracy" section to emphasize how democracy developed gradually in America and how it continues to grow. Let students
discuss whether or not democracy is broader than the enjoyment of purely political freedoms.   147

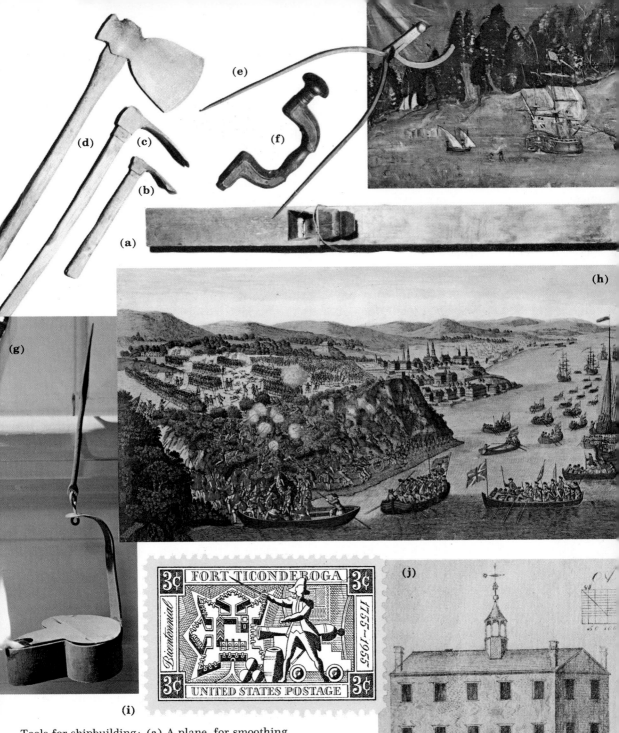

Tools for shipbuilding: (a) A plane, for smoothing wood. (b), (c), (d) Various axes. (e) A caliper, for measuring distance and drawing circles. (f) A brace, for holding a bit, used in boring holes.
(g) A whale-oil lamp of colonial days. (h) British troops, from ships on the St. Lawrence, climbed the heights of Quebec and took that French city.
(i) An American stamp issued in 1955 recalled one of the French forts the British took from their enemy.
(j) In this courthouse, in Albany, New York, Benjamin Franklin first proposed a union of the colonies.

(k)

(k) Colonial artisans built and repaired ships in shipyards along the Atlantic coast, like this one, located on a wooded inlet of Chesapeake Bay. All these ships fly the British flag.

CHAPTER 8

THE EXPULSION OF THE FRENCH

Use the pictures on pp. 148-149 to introduce topics in this chapter: the struggle between France and England, the importance of colonial trade and industry, the unity of the colonies, and the relations between the colonies and England.

As the eighteenth century began, most of the English colonies had been established in North America. The eyes of the colonists were no longer constantly turned toward the ocean, scanning it for ships which might be bearing news from home. By now America had become home, and eyes turned toward the west, toward unopened lands that seemed to stretch endlessly in the direction of the setting sun.

The English in America, who had been gradually moving inland since the first days of Jamestown, had reached the Appalachian Mountains in considerable numbers. Shortly they would spill over on the other side, where they would have to meet new kinds of dangers and new kinds of problems.

Be sure that students recall the position of New France in America (refer to the map on p. 52).

Trouble Brews Across the Appalachians

The most important fact the colonists faced was that the land beyond the mountains was claimed by the French. The French there were already pushing to the south. You can see on the map on page 52 that the English-Americans, many of whom were pressing westward, were going to collide with the French-Americans.

By the middle of the eighteenth century, the prize was clear. It was the great region shaped roughly like a triangle lying between the Ohio River, the Mississippi, the Great Lakes, and the St. Lawrence River. Control of this triangle was the key to possession of the great Mississippi Valley, a huge part of the interior of North America.

Competing Hopes

Look again at the map on page 52. You can see that the French built a number of forts in the interior of the continent to guard the outside limits of their empire.

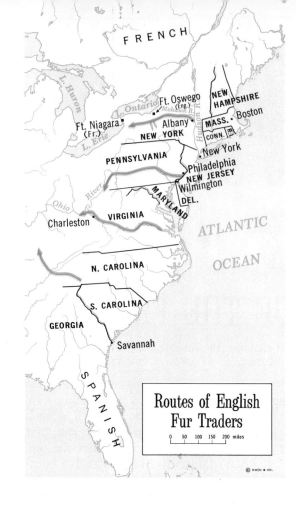

Routes of English
Fur Traders

0 50 100 150 200 miles

© RMSN & CO.

Their search for furs took English traders into French territory, where ambitious Englishmen were unwelcome.

Royal Ontario Museum

#Show how the French hoped to defend their lands by maintaining control of important rivers.

The British seemed to build forts in order to keep watch on the French forts.

French handicaps. If the French had defended their frontier less loosely and had concentrated their strength in the Ohio Valley, they might have slowed down the westward advance of the English. But they never had the man power to halt entirely the pressure of their rivals.

The Frenchmen in the seventeenth century had courageously ranged far and wide in the area west of the Appalachians. We recall the brave ventures of Frenchmen like Champlain, Brulé, and Marquette and Joliet (see pages 47–50 and 54–55).

English interests. The name of no Englishman who explored the region comes quickly to mind. The best energies of the English went into strengthening their settlements along the Atlantic. They worked hard to make the colonies producers of raw materials for the markets of Europe.

A leading product was fur. This fact meant that English interests extended deep into the frontier on the western side of the Appalachian Mountains. There the fur trade was the chief concern.

The fur trade was in the hands of four groups of traders. One group operated out of Albany, New York, in the area along the Mohawk River and the eastern Great Lakes. The French built Fort Niagara to help stop the advance of fur traders from Albany.

A second group came from Pennsylvania and conducted its hunting and trapping in the Ohio Valley. A third group, working out of Virginia, made its chief source of supply the southern and western parts of the Ohio Valley. A fourth group, largely Carolinians, conducted fur-trading business far to the west—in the Mississippi Valley.

The fur traders were bent on finding the furry animals from which they made their# livelihood. As they went west, they constantly broke into new wilderness.

Traders sought the furs and the skins of many animals: beaver, otter, bear, deer, fox, and others.

Behind the English fur traders came English settlers, not in hordes, but in a steady stream. Often they followed the paths of the fur traders themselves. Sometimes they established their own pathways into the wilderness. Like the fur traders, they made the French feel uneasy and threatened.

Non-English people—Scotsmen, Irishmen, and Germans—were also arriving on American shores in steadily growing numbers. They swelled the population of the backwoods regions, where they were usually friends of the English.

A growing rivalry. By the 1740's Frenchmen and Englishmen were in an increasingly keen rivalry for the land beyond the Appalachians. The effects were important not only in the colonies but also in the mother country.

Many Britons at home were directly concerned with the way things were going on the American frontier. They might not have had clear pictures in their minds of how the land in the New World looked. Perhaps they did not have even the faintest idea of what it meant to live on the frontier. Nevertheless, as bankers or manufacturers or merchants, they knew they would feel it in their pocketbooks if the expansion of the English colonies was suddenly dammed up. Besides, what kind of Englishmen would they be if they permitted the French to expel them from the immensely promising region in the heart of North America?

The land companies. One of the things the English tried in order to strengthen their claim to the region was the creation of land companies. These companies were very much like the ones that had originally settled some of the colonies (see pages 66 and 88). They aimed to encourage settlers to cross the Appalachians and make their homes on the frontier.

The Ohio Company and the Loyal Company, established in the 1740's, were organized by Virginians, although the Ohio Company had a royal grant. The directors of the companies hoped to find settlers for the hundreds of thousands of acres in the upper Ohio Valley which were placed under their control.

The French recognized the threat that the land companies represented to their own plans to make the land a glorious addition to New France. They built forts to strengthen their position. The man who led New France in its movement of self-protection was the Marquis Duquesne, who was the governor-general.

The French, as we have seen (page 54), had never been able to attract a large number of their countrymen to New France. # They had neither enough settlers nor, as it turned out, enough soldiers to man their forts. So they did the next best thing in the difficult predicament they faced: they leaned heavily on their allies and friends, the Indians.

Showdown

The relations between the French and the English came to a breaking point in the 1750's. The immediate cause was the desire to control the place where the Allegheny and Monongahela rivers join, the head of the Ohio River. Look for a minute at the map on page 153, and you will see that control of that point was the key to the entire trans-Appalachian region.

The French made the first move in 1753 to control the point by founding Fort Presqu'Isle (on the southern shore of Lake Erie) and Fort Le Boeuf (immediately southwest). The next year they built Fort Venango.

Aims. The British authorities were outraged at the French action and gave orders to the colonists to use force if necessary to drive the "invaders" out. The British officials said that their patience was at last at an end.

Claims to a region in the New World meant little without settlement. Remember that many of the **151** nglish colonies claimed the Ohio region as part of their original land grants, which often extended from sea to sea," presumably from the Atlantic to the Pacific.

It seemed to the British that, after all, the French were seeking the destruction of # British power throughout the world—in India, in Africa, and now in America. The time had arrived, they thought, to put an end to such insolence. French authorities were drawing the same conclusions about British movements—and were also puffing up their muscles.

George Washington's mission. In October, 1753, the lieutenant governor of Virginia, Robert Dinwiddie, acting on instructions from Britain, sent a message to the commander of the new French forts. The dangerous mission of delivering this message Dinwiddie gave to a young Virginian only recently turned twenty-one—George Washington.

Washington was instructed to tell the French commanding officer about the English king's "Concern and surprize" that the French were there. This was a polite way, of course, of telling them to get out. Furthermore, Washington was to "inquire into the numbers and force of the French on the Ohio and the adjacent country; [and] how they are likely to be assisted from Canada. . . ."

Washington knew the frontier well, for he had already had a number of years of experience there as a surveyor of land. He proceeded as far as Fort Le Boeuf and Fort Venango, but his mission was unsuccessful: the French refused to leave.

Fort Duquesne. Before Washington returned home, a number of Virginians, sensing future danger, started building a fort at the place where the Allegheny and Monongahela rivers join. They were driven out by the French, though, who finished the fort and named it Duquesne for the French governor-general.

Left: The earliest painting of Washington by Charles Willson Peale, showing him in the uniform of colonel in the Virginia regiment.
Below: Close-ups of the throat armor, the sword, and one of the uniform buttons seen in the painting.

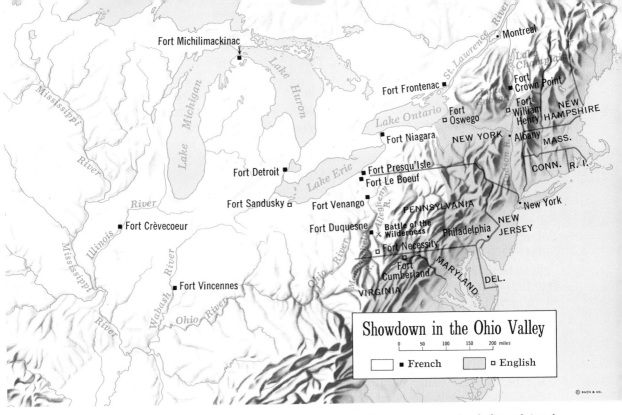

Observe how the French tried to protect the land they claimed and especially how they sought to defend the head of the Ohio.

hich of the place names
ove are still used today?

Fort Necessity. Meantime Washington had returned to Virginia. Almost immediately Governor Dinwiddie sent him out again with a few soldiers to protect the fort—not knowing it was already lost.

On the way Washington and his troops were waylaid by a French unit and were forced back. They tried to protect themselves in a hastily constructed fortification, which they called Fort Necessity. But this makeshift quickly fell to French troops from Fort Duquesne.

On July 4, 1754, Washington surrendered. He and his men were permitted to march away, but the long-awaited showdown between the English and the French was at hand.

The outlook. Even though the English-speaking colonists far outnumbered the French in North America, that fact could not guarantee a victory in war. First of all, the English-Americans did not all have the same outlook. Some disliked the French because they were Roman Catholics. Others, like Dinwiddie himself, were interested in land speculation. These speculators wanted to get the French out of the area assigned to the Ohio Company (in which Dinwiddie himself had invested) in the hope of profiting personally.

Second, the English colonies were not # yet accustomed to acting together. Each one was interested in protecting what it regarded as its portion of the back country, not the back country as a whole. Third, there simply was no organized military force to cope with a well-trained enemy army and its powerful Indian allies.

The Albany Plan of Union. The lack of unity among English colonists had already been observed by many of them and by the English at home. As a result, leaders

Be sure that students understand why the colonies had no central government or organized army.
ack of unity and military weakness also created problems during the American Revolution.

from Pennsylvania, Maryland, New York, and the New England colonies came together at Albany, New York, in 1754. Their purpose was to see if they could make an alliance with the Iroquois Indians (the Six Nations).

Besides making an agreement with the Iroquois, the colonial leaders considered and approved a plan of union prepared by Benjamin Franklin, of Pennsylvania. It called for the establishment of a council, or body of representatives, from all the colonies. This council would have power to collect taxes in the various colonies, regulate Indian matters, raise armies, and pass laws applying to all the colonies.

But the Albany Plan came to nothing. # The colonial legislatures were not ready yet to give up some of their powers—even though some responsibilities affecting all could be handled better centrally.

In a word, the colonies were not ready to accept the idea of *federalism*. They were unprepared to accept the principle of a central government which would share power with the governments of the separate colonies. Federalism, as we shall see, became a key idea in the development of the government of the United States.

Discuss the meaning of federalism.

Cannons and Muskets

In 1755 the mother country, greatly concerned over its hold on the Ohio Valley, sent to America two regiments of soldiers, with General Edward Braddock as their commander in chief. Braddock's first campaign was a move against Fort Duquesne.

Braddock on the march. Landing in Virginia, Braddock started out from Fort Cumberland with 450 Virginia militiamen, for whom he had no respect, and 1400 British regulars. He began to trudge overland toward Fort Duquesne. (Measure on the map on page 153 the distance between the two places.)

Braddock traveled with wagons and pack animals. The pace was so slow (because a road had to be built) that Braddock feared he was giving the French time to reinforce their garrison at the fort.

What Braddock badly needed was a number of friendly Indians to guide him in the fighting ahead. However, he got very little Indian help. He knew only how to fight by European rules of warfare, though physical conditions in the American wilderness were quite different from those in Europe.

On the way, however, Braddock finally took the advice of George Washington and sent back unnecessary baggage the armies had brought. (Washington was serving under him as commander of the militiamen). After that Braddock and his men approached Fort Duquesne somewhat more rapidly.

Along the way Washington had been suddenly taken with a fever. Despite his protests that he could go on, Braddock insisted on his remaining behind, although promising not to attack the fort until Washington had rejoined the army.

When Washington—lying on a pillow—was later reunited with Braddock, he saw a sight that must have stayed with him the rest of his life. The general's magnificently trained and uniformed troops crossed the Monongahela River as the fife and drum corps played the "Grenadiers' March."

Within minutes, though, the tuneful scene changed to one of blood and death. Nine hundred or more Frenchmen and Indians had come to meet the English about 7 miles from Fort Duquesne. The Battle of the Wilderness followed, July 9, 1755.

Disaster. Braddock's lines of troops were brutally cut to pieces as the enemy poured deadly fire on them from protected positions behind trees. The surprised Britons, wearing their scarlet coats, which made splendid targets, died like flies—by the hundreds. Braddock himself was critically wounded and died a few days later.

##Braddock's defeat showed the difficulty of using European rules of warfare in the American wilderness. Do problems of supply and movement often hamper even a well-equipped modern army?

mment on how the
tish uniforms and
apons aided the
emy.

Braddock, defeated
and fatally injured,
is taken from the
scene of the Battle
of the Wilderness by
his men and members
of the Virginia militia.

Chicago Historical Society

The survivors of Braddock's forces were a mournful group as they fled to Fort Cumberland. Washington, returning home, could still not understand what had happened and how. He told a friend, "We have been beaten, by a handful of men, who only intended to molest and disturb our march. Victory was their *smallest* expectation. But see the wondrous *works* of Providence, the uncertainty of human things!"

For the next two years, it appeared that English ambitions to control the Ohio Valley were doomed to disappointment. Indians, who assumed that the French were unbeatable, boldly attacked English settlers along the frontier. The efforts of the British against the French did not pick up again until 1756, when the French and Indian War began.

New generals. As England kept on losing, it sent Lord Loudoun to America to be the new commander in chief. However, Loudoun received little support from the colonies in either men or goods. In the meantime, the French had sent over in 1756 a first-rate commanding officer, Louis Montcalm.

Montcalm and his Indian allies captured and destroyed Fort Oswego, on Lake Ontario, in 1756 and Fort William Henry, on Lake George, the following year. The destruction of Fort William Henry was marked by a cruel slaughter of the English troops by Montcalm's Indian allies, although he had promised protection to the captives.

These victories gave control of the whole Great Lakes country to the French. And because success tends to breed further success, more Indians became allied to the French cause.

The emergence of Pitt. Big, important changes were now taking place in England. Distressed with the way the war was going, Parliament chose a new prime minister in 1757, William Pitt. Because Pitt relied on popular approval—he was the first Western leader to do so—he was beloved by the English public. He was often called the Great Commoner.

Pitt had a great vision he hoped to realize. He would make England into a mighty empire by capturing, through war if necessary, the trade of the world. He pursued what became famous as a "blue-water policy"—England would become a power on the seas and turn that power into wealth and glory.

ess the psychological as well as the military importance of the Battle of the Wilderness:
er Braddock's defeat the colonists were less awed by British military power. Why was
s important?

155

Pitt tied to this new and bold idea of England's role in the world an unusual ability to select military leaders capable of leading—which usually means capable of winning. One was Major General Jeffrey Amherst.

A change in fortunes. The first of Amherst's triumphs was the capture, on July 26, 1758, of the French fortress of Louisbourg, on Cape Breton Island at the mouth of the St. Lawrence. This successful military operation raised English spirits and put into English hands control of the entrance to the river.

A month later, an English unit seized Fort Frontenac, on Lake Ontario, sealing off the western end of the St. Lawrence. British soldiers also attacked Fort Duquesne so successfully that the French destroyed it and withdrew. The British soon rebuilt the fort and named it Fort Pitt, in honor of their inspiring leader. (On its site was later founded the city of Pittsburgh.)

As the year 1759 began, the French no longer controlled the Mississippi and Ohio valleys. The aims of the English now were to take Forts Niagara, Crown Point, and Ticonderoga. These operations went almost as planned, and when the three strong points passed into English hands, only Quebec and Montreal remained to be captured.

Wolfe and Montcalm. The work of taking Quebec fell to another of Pitt's fine appointees, James Wolfe. Wolfe, Amherst's second-in-command, was one of the heroes of the Battle of Louisbourg. Amherst rewarded him with the honor of attacking the French fortress at Quebec—a military operation Wolfe himself favored. Young— he was only thirty-two in 1759—personally unattractive, and ailing much of the time, Wolfe nevertheless had rare military skills which he put to work at Quebec.

Situated on high, steep cliffs, Quebec could not be taken by an assault from the front. The French soldiers could have made mincemeat of any British who tried to climb the rocky approach to the city. And in addition to their splendid position, the French troops also had a brilliant general, Louis Montcalm. But Montcalm and his men had not reckoned with the talent of General Wolfe.

Because winter was approaching, Wolfe had to make his move before the St. Lawrence River froze and trapped his ships in the ice. One night in September, 1759, he led his troops ashore a few miles north of the city. The British managed to scale the forbidding cliffs along a path guarded poorly by the French. When daybreak came, Montcalm faced his threatening enemy west of Quebec, on an expanse of level land called the Plains of Abraham.

In 1758 the British had tried hard to take Fort Ticonderoga from the French. Montcalm and his soldiers had vigorously defended the fort and pushed the British back. Here the French leader— center—praises his victorious troops.

Fort Ticonderoga Museum

Locate Fort Ticonderoga on the map on p. 157. Show its strategic value.

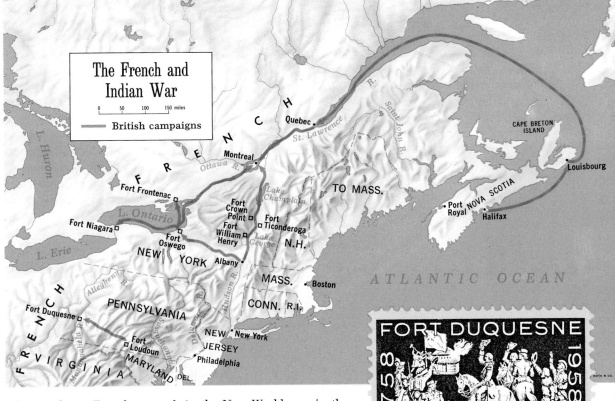

The French and Indian War

0   50   100   150 miles

British campaigns

Above: French strength in the New World was in the St. Lawrence Valley and the eastern Great Lakes. There the British struck, and there the French lost their priceless lands in North America. *Right:* The United States stamp which in 1958 honored the British seizure of Fort Duquesne two centuries earlier.

FORT DUQUESNE 1758 1958 U.S. POSTAGE 4¢

Roman J. Burkiewicz Stamp Shop

Montcalm attacked quickly, and the battle was on. But almost immediately the French line began to give way (Wolfe, probably unknowingly, had struck Montcalm at his weakest side). This was the beginning of the end of the long English-French struggle in America.

The fall of Quebec. It was the fate of both Wolfe and Montcalm to be fatally wounded in the fighting. Neither lived to see the fortress pass from French to English hands. Quebec surrendered on September 18, 1759. English forces then began to move on the city of Montreal, which fell to General Amherst in 1760.

In the same year George II died. He was succeeded by his grandson, who came to the throne as George III. The new king wanted peace. Pitt, on the other hand, wanted the war to continue until France

had been utterly destroyed and all its colonies everywhere in the world taken.

In fact, Pitt was anxious to declare war on Spain, too. After all, although France had been defeated in North America, its strength was great in Europe still. Besides, with Spain as its ally, France might become a threat again.

Pitt did not have his way. The new king distrusted him, and a new prime minister soon replaced him. Nevertheless, Spain did enter the war—only to share defeat with the French.

The Treaty of Paris, 1763. Under the terms agreed to in 1763—contained in the Treaty of Paris—the English acquired # Canada and all French land in North America east of the Mississippi (except New Orleans). France had been practically ## expelled from this continent.

Have students refer to the map on p. 158 for an idea of the immense area England gained as result of the French and Indian War.

Consider how the future development of the Mississippi Valley was to be affected by this.

The following text labels appear on the map:

UNEXPLORED

ENGLISH

CLAIMED BY HUDSON'S BAY CO.

SPANISH

NEWFOUNDLAND
MIQUELON (FR.) → ST. PIERRE (FR.)
CAPE BRETON ISLAND

L. Superior
L. Michigan
L. Huron
L. Ontario
L. Erie

Mississippi River

Rio Grande

PACIFIC OCEAN

ATLANTIC OCEAN

40°N.
30°N.
TROPIC OF CANCER
20°N.
10°N.

GULF OF MEXICO

CUBA (SP.)

HISPANIOLA

PUERTO RICO (SP.)

GUADELOUPE (FR.)

JAMAICA (ENG.)

HAITI (FR.)

Santo Domingo (SP.)

DOMINICA (ENG.)

MARTINIQUE (FR.)

CARIBBEAN SEA

ST. VINCENT (ENG.)
GRENADA (ENG.)

TOBAGO (ENG.)

North America, 1763

0 100 200 400 600 miles

Spanish   English   French

© RMcN & CO.

After 1763 only two European countries held large areas of land in North America—England and Spain. France, badly beaten in the French and Indian War, was left with only small island possessions.

Britain returned Cuba and the Philippines to the Spanish in exchange for Florida. It gave back to the French the sugar islands of Guadeloupe and Martinique, half of Hispaniola (Haiti), and two small islands, Saint Pierre and Miquelon, in the St. Lawrence (see the map above). Britain gained several West Indian islands.

To make up for the Spanish loss of Florida, France through a separate treaty gave Spain the area known as Louisiana. This was the vast area between the Rockies and the Mississippi.

Although many Englishmen thought the treaty too generous to the enemy, common sense led them to support it. They saw that an end to war could lower their taxes and that generosity to the defeated French might help begin a long period of peace.

Pitt, suffering from gout and other ailments, grew more irritable in his opposition to the king's policies. He criticized the king and the king's ministers for agreeing to the Treaty of Paris. He was, however, no longer in office.

Some consequences. The French and Indian War had many significant effects on English America. First, the barrier to the colonists' westward advance was shattered. Threatening Frenchmen were re-

#A student might report on the Seven Years' War, the name by which this conflict was known elsewhere. What did the Treaty of Paris provide concerning areas other than America? What new problems might have resulted had England demanded more of France?

moved and their Indian allies were given a lesson. Speculation—trade in hope of a quick profit—in western lands now increased enormously.

Second, the need of the colonies to respond to calls from the mother country for help increased colonial military know-how. It also introduced the colonials to the useful art of *privateering*—operating private vessels to prey on enemy trade on the sea.

Third, the British were made aware that the sprawling American colonies required closer governing. Further, colonial defense had been costly. The hour had come, it seemed to many in England, to take tighter control of the colonies and possibly to make them help pay the costs of the war.

> 1. Identify the American region which both the French and the English wished to control. 2. How did each side seek to protect its claims? 3. What mission was given Washington in 1753? What was its outcome? 4. For what three reasons was a British victory in war uncertain? 5. Give the main facts about the Battle of the Wilderness. 6. What British victories preceded the attack on Quebec? 7. What ·explains Wolfe's capture of Quebec? 8. Name the provisions of the Treaty of Paris. 9. How did France reward Spain? 10. State three effects the French and Indian War had on English America.

Colonists Test Ties of Trade and Loyalty

British soldiers who had been stationed in America had noticed the increasing wealth of the colonies. We can be sure that when they returned home, their accounts to friends and relatives of what North America was like made a deep impression. (Of course, a great many of the redcoats liked what they saw so well that they stayed!)

Sources of Wealth

One of the most significant facts the British troops had noticed was that in America there already were wealthy people looking for ways of investing their money. It is estimated that in 1700 American fortunes between $75,000 and $225,000 (in the approximate value of today) were not uncommon. By mid-century the yearly income of a very rich man might run as high as from $30,000 to $45,000.

Land. The chief source of wealth in the colonies was land. Its value rose from the day its first tree was removed or the first bridge thrown across one of its streams.

The activities of merchants. But there were sources of wealth other than land, as merchants early found out. A merchant might, for example, lend to his colonial government—at interest—money made in trading. Or he might obtain valuable government contracts for supplying the militia, or the like. Merchants, therefore, like land speculators, relied on close and friendly relations with the colonial political leaders.

Manufacturing. Another source of money## beginning to be significant by the mid-eighteenth century was manufacturing. Its development was based on the abundant natural resources available.

This included handwork done in homes.

Products of Forest and Ocean

Lumbering was the simplest and perhaps the most widespread kind of colonial manufacturing, involving the raiding of what must have seemed like limitless forest reserves. The earliest sawmills—we might call them lumberyards today—were cre-

ringing the colonies under tight control was to be difficult for a number of reasons. Review
w the colonies were founded with little government help and developed with little govern-
ent direction. Explain that as a result the colonists resented the change in British policy.

159

What industries besides shipbuild-ing depended on forests?

In this reproduction of an early Virginia shipyard, some men are working on a hull— the frame of a ship— one is sawing logs, and another is planing, or smoothing, the lumber.

Mariners Museum, Newport News, Virginia

ated in the very first years of the colonial settlements. The growing local market for lumber depended on the building of houses and the manufacturing of products like furniture, barrels, and spinning wheels. Gradually the market extended overseas.

Ships' masts. Almost from the time Jamestown was settled, British leaders recognized the importance of the American woodlands for the English navy. They sent agents to mark with broad arrows for future use as ships' masts the tallest and strongest pines in the forest.

The colonists often disregarded these royal arrows as they cut trees for other purposes. These purposes might include, among very many others, the production of *naval stores*—tar, resin, turpentine, and pitch.

Naval stores. Although the mother country once had had to obtain naval stores from Scandinavia, it acquired them from its New World colonies as the American settlements developed. In fact, Parliament in 1705 began to offer a *bounty*, or special sum of money, to the colonies for each ton of the various kinds of naval stores they manufactured.

The pine forests of North Carolina and South Carolina especially produced naval stores. The result was that thousands of Carolinians became dependent on the growth of the English navy and merchant marine.

Ships. New Englanders also depended heavily on their forest land and the mother country's seafaring needs. By the late colonial period, that is, by the 1760's, about a third of all England's ships were being made by Yankee (New England) hands. It was said that colonial shipwrights built vessels at from one-half to two-thirds the cost of those made in the mother country.

In the earlier part of the colonial period, every river along the Atlantic coast was the scene of shipbuilding. But aside from the hulls, most of the equipment for the ships, including sails, ropes, and iron fittings, had to be brought from England.

In time the various skills required in shipbuilding were found more and more in or near the larger colonial towns. Boston, Portsmouth, Salem, and Newport became the centers of the shipbuilding industry.

Other cities, such as Philadelphia, New York, and the port towns of Virginia and the Carolinas, also built ships. But New England held the lead for a long time. In Virginia and the Carolinas men often invested their profits in slaves and land. So these southern colonies lagged in shipbuilding and other industries.

Rum. Another branch of manufacturing that played a large part in New England's business life was rum-making. Many kinds of alcoholic beverages were made in the home, but only rum was produced commercially in colonial days.

#Point out that some groups in the colonies benefited directly from their position in the British empire. Not only did those that produced naval stores receive bounties, but also American tobacco growers were protected within the empire against competition from foreign tobacco.

Rum, made from West Indian molasses (the boiled-down juice of sugarcane), was widely sold to Indians, fishermen, and African slave-traders. The amount of American-made rum was never sufficient to satisfy the demand, however, and much rum was imported from the West Indies.

Iron. Some eighteenth-century Americans made money from the manufacture of iron. The first ironworks was established in Virginia in 1620, in the neighborhood of Jamestown. The Virginia Company provided about 150 skilled men to run the iron furnace. But they were all killed and the plant was destroyed in an Indian massacre.

In time, hundreds of furnaces and "bloomeries," that is, furnaces hardly larger than blacksmiths' forges, were operated throughout the colonies, but particularly in Pennsylvania. All the colonies contained some workable iron ore. But successful ironworks were in places that were favorably located.

Foundries were considered well situated if there were stands of oak trees nearby. (Because burning oak wood gave off high heat, it was much preferred to pine wood for firing the furnaces.) Also, some ores were better than others. Pennsylvania had both superior ores and oak trees and a heavy German immigration which included some experienced ironworkers. The village of Valley Forge, in southeastern Pennsylvania, for example, took its name from its chief nonagricultural activity.

Fish. Still another source of livelihood in the colonies was fishing. The Grand Banks of Newfoundland offered regularly a bumper crop of cod, mackerel, herring, halibut, bluefish, and other kinds of fish. Even before the seventeenth century was over, some six hundred vessels and almost five thousand men were engaged in the work of the fishing industry.

Fishing, often carried on in thick fogs and under threat from icebergs, was extremely dangerous. Morever, it could be exhausting and boring. But a ready market for fish in the West Indies and southern Europe spurred the toilers on. The codfish helped make Massachusetts rich—a fact kept alive by the gilded codfish that even today hangs over the speaker's desk in the statehouse in Boston.

Whales. Still more dangerous than fishing was whaling, which supported people of Nantucket Island and Massachusetts towns like Provincetown, Marblehead, and New Bedford by the 1770's. Whalers ran their vessels farther and farther from home each year in pursuit of the huge sea animals—to the Arctic, to the shores of Africa, and later into the Pacific.

The users of the whale products were everywhere. They included the housewives

These drawings show how the Saugus ironworks, built near Boston, Massachusetts, looked in 1650. *Left:* The three main buildings. *Right:* Men pouring liquid iron into casts to make cast-iron pots and kettles.

First Iron Works Association, Saugus, Massachusetts

Above: Whale-hunting was dangerous work. This painting was made from a sketch drawn by one of the men who served on the whaling ship seen in the background and who lost an arm during the voyage. *Left:* You can see the whale oil and the wicks carrying it to the flames in the lamp shown here. On the wall is a sample of the first embroidery work done by a twelve-year-old girl.

of mammals were great and voyages sometimes lasted two or three years, the whalers kept at the work.

Products of Plantations and Farms

Despite the beginnings of manufacturing, agriculture provided the main living for colonists. In the southern colonies it centered on plantations, and in the northern colonies, on family farms.

Tobacco and rice. Tobacco, grown on plantations, found its chief market in England. From there it reached consumers throughout Europe. Rice was grown on plantations along the Georgia and Carolina coasts. Coastal swamplands, which were periodically flooded by the flow of the rivers, were ideal for its cultivation.

Indigo. Indigo, a plant which provided an important violet-blue dye, was also grown in the South, especially in South Carolina and Georgia. Its cultivation fitted well with that of rice because it could be raised on high land. Slaves could care for it when not working in the rice fields below.

When the textile industry developed in England after the mid-eighteenth century, the need for indigo became greater than before, and Parliament provided a bounty to encourage its cultivation. Raising indigo in the colonies probably would not have

who used candles made from the oil and waxy substances of whales. Also, there were the well-dressed women desiring whalebone for stays in their clothing or perfume made from ambergris (a waxy secretion of the whale). And there were all the people who lighted houses and other buildings with whale-oil lamps.

While the largest share of the profits of a whaling voyage went to the shipowner, some proceeds were divided among all the members of the ship's crew. Consequently, although the dangers in chasing the largest

#Franklin estimated that 90 percent of the colonies made their living by farming. Review the difference between farm crops produced for a market and those produced mainly for the farm family's own use.

been profitable without this help.

Wheat. Wheat was grown in all the colonies but in greatest abundance in the middle colonies. Wheat was exported by New Jersey, New York, Pennsylvania, and Delaware because their fields were near rivers reaching ports from which wheat could be shipped overseas.

The wheat was frequently made into hard biscuits, or hardtack, which kept well in tropical climate and at sea. American wheat, therefore, found its way into the diets of people living in southern Europe, on islands off the west coast of Africa, and in the West Indies. Moreover, it helped feed thousands of sailors aboard the merchant vessels of the colonies.

The Lifelines of Commerce

From the end of the seventeenth century on, the colonies were engaged in a vigorous coastwise trade with one another and with foreign countries. This commerce steadily expanded.

Most of the trade across the sea was with the mother country, but it was unevenly divided among the colonies. England produced its own food and imported none from the New England and middle colonies, which raised more food than they could eat.

Virginia and Maryland, on the other hand, shipped tobacco to England. In fact, except for a little tobacco that was smuggled into the continent of Europe, all of the American exports of the "weed" went to England. We have seen also that the southern colonies, chiefly the Carolinas and Georgia, shipped staple products, such as indigo, rice, and naval stores, to England.

Staple-producers and food-producers. As a result of the shipment of the staple products, the southern colonies exported far more than those in the North. The mother country considered the staple-producers more valuable than the food-producers—

mainly the northern colonies. This was because the northern colonies provided few articles that England could not obtain elsewhere.

To the West Indies. Nevertheless, all the colonies, northern as well as southern, provided an excellent and expanding market for the various products of England's industries. Now the question naturally arises, If northern colonies could not sell as much in England as southern colonies, where did they obtain the money to purchase manufactured goods? The answer is, In good part they obtained it in the trade they carried on with the West Indies.

From 1750 on, the colonies of the North, that is, north of Maryland, shipped fish, corn, wheat (as hardtack and flour), lumber, and livestock to the West Indies. In return, the northern colonies imported much sugar, ginger, rum, and molasses.

The rum was swapped for furs in the trade with the Indians and for Negroes in the trade with the slave dealers of Africa. Both of these detestable trades were tied closely, therefore, to the busy sea traffic which ran from New England and the middle colonies to the sugar islands.

The flourishing grain-growing and fishing which New England and the middle colonies enjoyed would have been far less prosperous without the West Indian trade. Codfish, hardtack, and rum were, therefore, strangely linked together in helping to connect the northern colonies with other parts of America and the world. Even though the northern colonies did not have outstanding products that the mother country needed keenly, they had good sources of income.

Smuggling. But the sources of income available did not enable New Englanders to buy the variety of goods they needed and wanted from the mother country. The result was that the resourceful Yankees were soon engaging in illegal trading— that is, in smuggling.

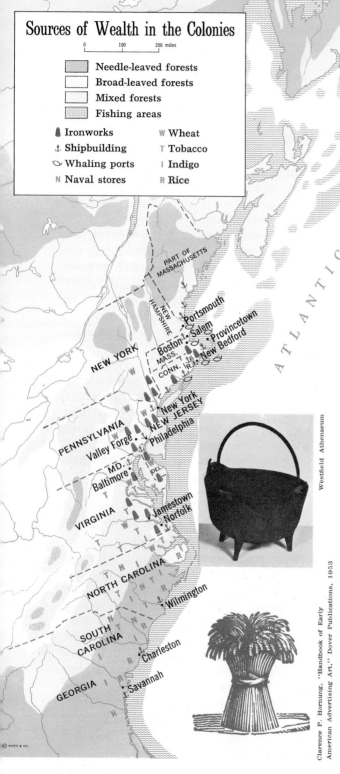

Sources of Wealth in the Colonies

0   100   200 miles

- ▨ Needle-leaved forests
- ☐ Broad-leaved forests
- ▨ Mixed forests
- ▨ Fishing areas

▮ Ironworks	W Wheat
⚓ Shipbuilding	T Tobacco
◡ Whaling ports	I Indigo
N Naval stores	R Rice

GRAND BANKS

ATLANTIC OCEAN

PART OF MASSACHUSETTS

NEW HAMPSHIRE

Portsmouth
Salem
Boston · Provincetown
MASS. · New Bedford
CONN. · R.I.

NEW YORK

NEW JERSEY
New York
PENNSYLVANIA
Valley Forge · Philadelphia
MD. · DEL.
Baltimore

VIRGINIA
Jamestown
Norfolk

NORTH CAROLINA
Wilmington

SOUTH CAROLINA
Charleston

GEORGIA
Savannah

© RMN & CO.

Westfield Athenaeum

Clarence P. Hornung, "Handbook of Early American Advertising Art," Dover Publications, 1953

"The Book of Trades, or Library of the Useful Arts," London, 1807 (Warshaw Collection)

Ways of making a living in the colonies depended on the available natural resources. Fertile land was a main resource, producing wheat—see the sheaf at the lower left—and other crops. Mines contributed iron for household products like the cast-iron pot also shown at the left. Pines and oaks were the best trees for making boards, shingles, and staves, which are narrow, shaped pieces of wood used in barrels. Above, a cooper fastens staves together.

The Navigation Acts. Through smuggling the New England colonists and other colonists as well violated long-standing laws designed to make the colonies suit England's needs more fully. Some of these laws, which were called Navigation Acts, had been passed by Parliament in the 1650's and 1660's and had been put into complete form in 1696. The Navigation Acts had been passed, of course, without anyone's consulting the colonists.

The first act had provided that all seaborne trade between England and its colonies and between them and other countries must employ ships built in the mother country or in the colonies. This law had been intended to keep Dutch ships from carrying products of the English colonies (see page 112). The aim, of course, was to protect the shipbuilding industry on both sides of the Atlantic.

#This indicates that the Navigation Acts were protective as well as restrictive. (See the annotation at the bottom of p. 160.)

The second act, in 1660, had repeated the provision of the first one. It had also listed, or *enumerated*, certain commodities which had to be shipped first to England or some English possession before they could be sold elsewhere. That is, they could not be sent direct to foreign countries for sale.

The list, which was added to from time to time, at first included tobacco, wool, sugar, indigo, and raw cotton. (Later, naval stores, rice, and furs were included.) The mother country hoped through enumeration to assure itself of the profits from the resale of these valuable colonial products.

The third Navigation Act, enacted in 1663, had required that most things imported by the colonies from Europe be sent to England first, for reshipment to America. This act aimed to guarantee to the mother country the handsome profits of the middleman. The Navigation Act of 1696 was planned to improve the enforcement of the earlier laws. It also gave customs officers in the colonies power to seize illegal goods.

Restrictions from the mother country. Parliament also enacted laws forbidding the colonists to develop industry on a scale large enough to rival that in England. The number of new ironworks that could be built was very severely limited. The colonists were forbidden to manufacture certain articles for export—beaver hats and woolen yarn and cloth—although they might manufacture these goods and sell them locally.

Now we see the nature of the problem faced by New Englanders. They could not compete with England in manufacturing. They did not raise a staple crop sorely needed in Europe. Yet they thirsted for the goods produced by the mother country. Where was the money for these English goods to be found? The answer was, In smuggling—that is, in violating the Navigation Acts.

The usefulness of the French West Indies. This is how the New Englanders smuggled: People in the French West Indies (see page 158) paid well for fish, bread, and lumber produced in New England and the middle colonies. Therefore, Yankee— New England—skippers took the products to the islands. They sold the goods there —a violation of the Navigation Acts.

In return, the New Englanders bought sugar and molasses at prices lower than the British planters asked. The French colonies were somewhat more successful producers of sugar than the English islands, partly because the French land had been worked for fewer years and had not yet been worn out.

Also, the British plantations in the West Indies were controlled by absentee landlords who lived in England. The French owners, on the other hand, usually lived on their sugar plantations and were able to give them constant personal attention.

#Explain the meaning of absentee ownership.

A Tightening of Control

The absentee English landlords greatly resented the trade between the French planters and the New Englanders. Because these landlords had great influence in Parliament, they quickly acted to protect their interests.

The Molasses Act. In 1733 the absentee landlords brought about the passage of the Molasses Act. This law put a very high *duty*—a tax on an import—on molasses and sugar shipped into the colonies from the French and Spanish West Indies.

If the Molasses Act had been enforced vigorously, the Yankee traders would have been badly hurt. Actually, little attention was paid to it by traders in any of the northern colonies.

The profit from the smuggling provided the means for paying for manufactured goods from England. English manufacturers were pleased that their New Eng-

e tightening of control, Britain's new colonial policy, was not only a change in laws but also change in law enforcement--an effort to enforce existing laws, raise revenue, and assert tain's authority.

165

Jean Baptiste Dutertre, "Histoire Generale des Antilles . . . ," Paris, 1667 (New York Public Library)

What does this picture show about the climate of sugar-producing areas?

Sugar is being manufactured on this French West Indian plantation, seen as it looked in the seventeenth century. Slaves are carrying sugarcane stalks to the place—in the right background—where the cane is pressed to produce juice. The juice is being piped to the stove—in the center— where the sweet liquid will be boiled until sugar forms.

land customers could afford to buy the products of English industry. For about thirty years Englishmen in the mother country made believe they did not see the smuggling of molasses and sugar.

A new attitude. By 1763, however, a change in outlook was beginning to occur in England on the ticklish matter of dealing with the colonies. The seemingly unpatriotic way in which vessels from New England and the middle colonies had steadily traded with the enemy during the French and Indian War angered Englishmen at home. In the midst of a war to the death with France, American trade with the French and Spanish seemed nothing less than treason.

In October, 1763, the English authorities ordered all customs officials—the men who collected the duties—to their posts in the colonies. Before, it had been customary to send substitutes or appoint American-born deputies who were as likely as not to wink at smugglers. The customs officers would enforce strictly the laws regarding colonial trade.

The Sugar Act. A major step in the effort to collect from the colonists was the passage of the Sugar Act in 1764. This law was an attempt to bring the Molasses Act up to date by making its provisions seem reasonable. The duty on foreign molasses was reduced, but the duty on sugar was increased.

The Sugar Act was aimed squarely at the illegal trade in sugar with the French islands, although it respected the dependence of the New England rum-distillers on molasses. This law was certainly going to be enforced!

Much was at stake. A Philadelphia merchant explained how the issue seemed to him in a letter he wrote to an English friend in April, 1764:

I think there is scarce anything you can do that may be hurtful to us, but what will be as much or more so to you. . . . What you get from us in Taxes you must lose in Trade. The Cat can yield but it's Skin. And as you must have the whole Hide, if you first cut Thongs out of it, 'Tis at your own Expence. The same in regard to our Trade with the Foreign West Indian Islands. If you restrain it in any Degree, you restrain in the same Proportion our Power of making our Remittances to you [that is, buying from you], [and] of course our Demand for your Goods.

#Ask students to examine this letter. Why, according to the merchant, would trade-restrictions hurt both the colonies and Britain?

the British view, if the trans-Appalachian West was closed to settlement, the need for and the ost of defending that area would be less.

Pontiac's war. If New Englanders, especially, were distressed by these new arrangements, the middle and southern colonies, especially, were aroused by a new Indian policy. As we have seen, by the terms of the settlement at the end of the French and Indian War, Britain acquired a vast region of western lands. This area required careful management.

Under a brilliant Ottawa Indian chief named Pontiac, a strong alliance of western tribesmen offered resistance to the advance of settlers. In the late spring of 1763, the well-organized Indians set upon and captured every British fort west of Fort Niagara except Detroit. The tribesmen fought fiercely not only to protect their land but to get revenge for severe mistreatment, including being cheated by fur traders and land speculators.

The Proclamation of 1763. The British then issued the now famous Proclamation of 1763, which proposed to end the Indian wars. It made the rich region west of the Appalachians a huge Indian reservation. The area was henceforth to be closed to settlers and also to land speculators.

The colonial governors were forbidden to give grants to land companies or to permit surveyors in the territory to stake out the land. Also, separate governments for East and West Florida were set up and the province of Quebec created in Canada.

The Proclamation of 1763 in short was intended to take care of controlling the trans-Appalachian region. Colonists were forbidden to enter the area, which was governed by commissioners in charge of Indian affairs. The British hoped that some or all of the West might become available

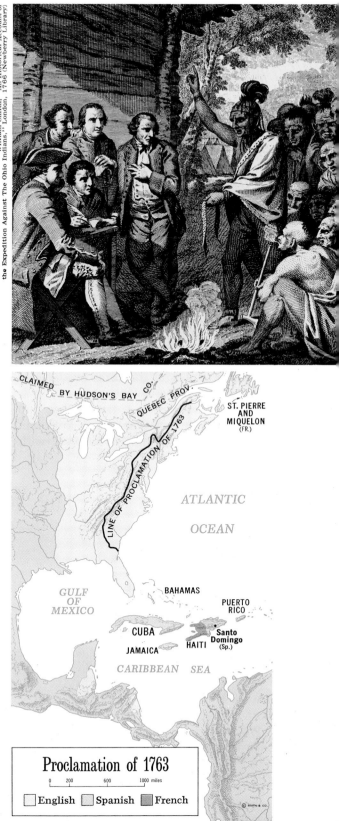

William Smith, "An Historical Account of the Expedition Against The Ohio Indians," London, 1766 (Newberry Library)

Above: An Indian leader in the trans-Appalachian West is giving English officials in 1764 a piece of his mind. The American artist Benjamin West sketched the drawing from which this picture was made.
Right: The Proclamation of 1763 in effect put a fence around desirable American land and said to the colonists, "Keep out!"

CLAIMED BY HUDSON'S BAY CO.
QUEBEC PROV.
LINE OF PROCLAMATION OF 1763
ST. PIERRE AND MIQUELON (FR.)

ATLANTIC OCEAN

GULF OF MEXICO
BAHAMAS
PUERTO RICO
CUBA
HAITI
Santo Domingo (Sp.)
JAMAICA
CARIBBEAN SEA

Proclamation of 1763
0   200   600   1000 miles

☐ English   ☐ Spanish   ■ French

the American view, the proclamation
pt the colonists from developing what
ey considered their land.

for *their* investment and profit rather than for the investment and profit of grasping colonial land companies.

You can see what was happening: in New England and the middle colonies traders who smuggled were irritated by the new policy of enforcing the Navigation Acts. In the middle and southern colonies the Proclamation of 1763 offended badly two groups of people. One was made up of men of property who speculated in land, and the other of settlers who were looking for an opportunity to help occupy the new region.

Nasty questions. On top of everything, the colonies were no longer accepting happily their position of dependence within the British Empire. Many a colonist must have echoed John Adams' sentiments of 1765. Adams was writing that there was "something exceedingly fallacious [that is, wrong-headed] in the commonplace images of mother country and children colonies. . . . Are we not brethren and fellow subjects with those in Britain . . . !"

\# What would happen if the English continued to enforce Parliament's laws and continued to make changes in them without consulting the colonies? What would happen if more and more colonists held ideas like those of Adams?

Neither the English nor the colonists were prepared in the early 1760's to answer the questions. Most Englishmen were probably unconcerned about what the answers would be. But a steadily increasing number of Americans must have sensed that upon the answers the very course of the future would depend.

---

1. Name three sources of wealth in the colonies in the 1750's. 2. What products came from American forests? What colonial industry depended on the forests? 3. Name a manufactured product made from an imported raw product. One made from a colonial raw product. 4. What two products came from the sea? 5. Name four farm products and tell where they were mainly produced. 6. Where did the southern colonies chiefly trade? The northern colonies? 7. Name the main provisions of the Navigation Acts. 8. What new policy did Britain adopt in 1763? In what ways did it carry out the policy?

The Workshop

The Shapers of Our World

Identify the following:

Ohio Company	Jeffrey Amherst
George Washington	James Wolfe
Fort Duquesne	Plains of Abraham
Fort Necessity	Treaty of Paris,
Albany Plan	1763
of Union	Molasses Act
Edward Braddock	Sugar Act
Battle of the	Pontiac
Wilderness	Proclamation
Louis Montcalm	of 1763

Adding to Your Vocabulary

Be sure you know the meaning of each of these terms:

federalism	indigo
militia	forge
privateering	staple-
naval stores	producer
bounty	smuggling
Yankee	customs
molasses	officials
"blue-water	duty
policy"	

#Ask students to keep these questions in mind as they prepare to study Chapter 9. Discuss whether or not the colonies by 1763 were too self-reliant to be treated as children of the mother country, England.

Thinking Things Through

After reviewing the boxed-in exercises within the chapter, see if you can answer these questions:

1. Why did most non-English groups tend to settle along the frontier region of the thirteen colonies rather than in the coastal regions?

2. A large school in Pittsburgh is called Duquesne University. Why is it so named?

3. Why do you think General Braddock had little respect for the Virginia militia? (Relate your answer to the ideas in John Adams' comments, given on page 168.)

4. Why was Pitt's "blue-water policy" particularly well suited to a small island nation such as Britain? What is the connection between Pitt's reasoning and the defeat of the Spanish Armada (page 66)?

5. How would you prove that because of the French and Indian War the colonists felt less need for British protection and, as a result, resented closer British supervision?

6. Why did some eighteenth-century Europeans argue that Britain's most valuable possessions in the New World were the southern colonies and the West Indian sugar islands?

7. Did the prosperity of Britain and its possessions depend upon British restriction of colonial manufacturing and encouragement of colonial production of raw materials? Defend your opinion.

8. Reread John Adams' statement reported on page 168. What events described in this chapter made such an opinion natural? Would such a statement have been made in 1700? Explain.

9. What were the principal causes of the colonists' dissatisfaction with the mother country by the year 1763? Explain the British point of view in each case. What new feeling on the part of the colonists made them more likely to complain than before?

Geography and History

1. What geographical area in North America was the prize which the French and the British wished to hold? Why did both have such an ambition? What were the results of the struggle between the two countries? Name the states that lie within the area today. How is it still a prize?

2. How did geography aid the French in protecting Quebec? How did the British overcome the French advantage?

3. Canada today may be called a country of two cultures. What are they? Account for the two.

4. Name the large area in North America Spain gained after the French and Indian War. With what other possessions on the continent was it joined?

5. Why was England eager to gain control of Florida?

The Research Center

1. Try to find a reproduction of Benjamin West's famous painting of the death of Wolfe at Quebec and bring it to show the class. This painting hangs in the rotunda of the Capitol, in Washington, D.C. Why do you think it is so honored?

2. Use reference books to identify the chief American centers today of (a) shipbuilding; (b) fishing; (c) rice, wheat, corn, and tobacco growing; (d) livestock raising; and (e) shipping. How do the locations of these centers today compare with those in the late 1700's?

3. Why, in the French and Indian War, did the French have stronger allies among the Indians than the English had? Your research should concern the treatment of the Indians by both English and French.

4. Read to the class sections of Longfellow's *Evangeline* dealing with the troubles faced by the Acadians. Can you name any similar groups of displaced persons in the world today?

Many of the questions in "Thinking Things Through" call for answers that are concise and factual, reasoning and analysis, or the statement and defense of a given point of view. Students, therefore, need not simply recite facts and decide once and for all which side was right.

169

(a)

(b)

(c)

(d)

(e)

(a) An aerial view of Boston, Massachusetts, today—a center of activity that sparked the American Revolution. The parklike area is the Boston Common (see page 98).
(b) This statue of a minuteman, in Concord, Massachusetts, helps keep alive the memory of the brave colonists who were ready to fight the British on an instant's notice.
(c) Two swords carried at the Battle of Concord—the one at the right by the commander of the minutemen.
(d) One of the lanterns that was hung in the tower of North Church in Boston to signal that the redcoats were coming.
(e) In 1774 colonial representatives met here, in Carpenters' Hall, Philadelphia, to discuss their troubles with England.
(f—next page) The front page of this Pennsylvania newspaper gave its frank opinion of Britain's Stamp Act.

e TIMES are
Dreadful,
Dismal
Doleful
Dolorous, and
DOLLAR-LESS.

(f)

of the STAMP

An Emblem of the Effects

O! the fatal Stamp

the pictures on p. 170 to introduce scenes of the American Revolution. Some students will be familiar
h aspects of the Revolution: minutemen, Paul Revere, Concord, Independence Hall, and the like.

CHAPTER 9

BICKERING WITH
THE MOTHER COUNTRY

view briefly the first signs of irritation between England and the colonies (the situations that resulted from
Navigation Acts, the Sugar Act, the French and Indian War, and the Proclamation of 1763).

DURING most of the half century before 1763, the British government, to a considerable extent, had been leaving Americans alone. Year after year a colonist might never see a representative of the king—except the officials sent to enforce the Navigation Acts.

Because immigration from England had long since stopped, the amount of contact between the colonists and the mother country—even by mail—had grown sparser with each passing year. Even the colo-

nial governors, who were appointed by the king, exercised their authority only lightly. They quickly realized that their salaries depended on the good will of the colonial legislatures. This fact kept them friendly.

In short, the colonists seemed almost free of the mother country, and at the same time they were enjoying a prosperity that steadily increased. In fact, they usually explained their prosperity as being the result of their freedom from England's apron strings.

Britain Uses a Firmer Hand in America

Anything that interfered with the colonists' liberty, then, was bound to annoy them. Possibly, they thought, the new English laws were only the beginning of other interferences with their freedom.

Opposite Views

British policies after the year 1763 were not designed to end the freedom of the colonists. They were based on other ideas.

sk how many students have ever talked in person with government representatives or officials.
nericans are much nearer government authority today than the colonists were.
scuss why this is so.

Paying the war debt. First, the cost of the French and Indian War had put a heavy burden on Englishmen in the mother country, hindering *their* prosperity. It seemed only right to the British lawmakers that the vigorous offspring in America pay
a part of the debt that had been acquired in defeating France in America.

Calming trans-Appalachia. Also, the region west of the hated line established by the Proclamation of 1763 had been the scene of conflict. Difficulties had arisen between traders and trappers, colonial frontiersmen and representatives of land companies, settlers and Indians, and Indians and Indians. If the British were to govern the trans-Appalachian area—by first bringing peace to it—they had to use firmness and even strong measures.

Only to irritate. The efforts of Parliament, Britain's legislature, to deal with the British debt and the control of the area beyond the Appalachians neither helped the British nor satisfied the colonists. And each action of the mother country seemed to people on this side of the Atlantic to be not part of a plan at all—but only a new irritation.

"Royal tyranny." For instance, in order to bring peace to the frontier, the British maintained even after 1763 the office of commander in chief—general of all the king's forces—in America. As the colonists saw it, the redcoats remaining in the colonies showed that the British were determined to make Americans toe the mark. The soldiers surely represented abuse of authority by the king—royal tyranny!

As time went on, the British government and the colonists questioned more angrily each other's purposes. In a little more than ten years, it became impossible for either side to feel kindly toward the other.

Trial and Error

Thoughtful Britons had long known that they might stir up dangerous troubles by trying to tax the American colonists. The proposal to do so had been made to a British prime minister some years earlier. He is said to have replied, "I will leave that for some of my successors, who may have more courage than I have."

The Sugar Act. Members of Parliament had acted boldly when they passed the Sugar Act in 1764 (see page 166). On its face the act was aimed simply at regulating trade. Actually, it was intended to raise *revenue*—money—too, something the mother country had never tried to do in the colonies before. The outcry was immediate: free people ought not pay taxes they did not themselves vote for.

Suddenly the colonists seemed united— a situation the French and Indian War had

Some stamps were sold already printed on paper, and some were sold separately. *Left:* A stamp in outline, on which you can see the word America and the value of the stamp. *Center and right:* The dark, oblong squares show where these stamps were attached to paper with tin or lead.

not been able to bring about. The British view, though, was expressed by an English official. He said that the 1764 law had allowed the rabble-rousers to oppose all orders from London "which don't square with their notions of the rights of the people."

The Stamp Act. Every responsible person in the colonies and England believed, however, that common sense would win out. Parliament decided that if the colonists would not accept willingly a revenue law disguised as a law to regulate trade, they should be taxed directly. Accordingly, it passed the Stamp Act in March, 1765, without much debate.

Under the Stamp Act's provisions, people had to buy revenue stamps and stick them on almost every kind of document issued in the colonies after it took effect. The list of documents, covering almost six printed pages, included such items as marriage licenses, calendars, newspapers, and pamphlets. The colonists objected, of course, to the nuisance as well as the expense of seeing to it that every legal document passing through their hands was on properly stamped paper.

A stamp act was already in force in England, however, and it did not seem unreasonable to the mother country to extend its provisions to the colonies. Further, the revenues acquired through the Stamp Act were to be set aside for the colonies themselves. The money raised would pay for their military defense.

The law was not to go into effect until November, 1765. But the news of it arrived quickly in the colonies. Opposition daily gained in force and fierceness—the way a small snowball, pushed down a hill, grows bigger and bigger and rolls faster and faster.

It was clear what the colonists were against. They were angry because they were being subjected to "taxation without representation."

Patrick Henry's words. In Virginia, Pat-

Patrick Henry Memorial Foundation

Patrick Henry vigorously opposing the Stamp Act in the House of Burgesses, on the ground that Parliament had no right to tax the colonists directly.

rick Henry brought a gasp to the hushed House of Burgesses when he uttered words sounding like treason: "Caesar had his Brutus [Brutus had stabbed Caesar to death], Charles the First, his Cromwell [Cromwell had had Charles beheaded], and George the Third——" He ended the sentence with "may profit by their example. If this be treason, make the most of it."

Everywhere the cry of protest was heard, and in little towns and big ones citizens made up their minds to resist the Stamp Act by rebellion if necessary. They organized themselves into groups called ## Sons of Liberty.

The Stamp Act Congress. In New York a Stamp Act Congress, called by Massachusetts, met in October, 1765. It was attended by representatives of nine colonies. This gathering of twenty-seven men was the most impressive intercolonial assembly

Library of Congress

In Boston and other towns, stirred-up Americans gathered to protest the Stamp Act. Here stamps are being burned in the cobblestone street.

ever held. It drew up a Declaration of Rights and Grievances, which was sent to the king.

Among the rights claimed was the "undoubted right of Englishmen, that no taxes be imposed on them but with their own consent." The group also asked for the repeal of the Stamp Act and announced that colonies would *boycott*, that is, not buy, British goods until it was repealed.

The Declaration of Rights described the members of the congress as "sincerely devoted with the warmest sentiments of affection and duty to His Majesty's person and Government." Outside the congress, though, the mood was blacker. Stamp agents were forced—often by violence or threat of violence—to resign. In Massachusetts a mob lost control of itself and sacked and burned the beautiful home of Lieutenant Governor Thomas Hutchinson. It was clear that the Stamp Act could not be enforced.

#Recall how English merchants were glad to avoid trouble over the Molasses Act (see pp. 165-166).

Moreover, the merchants of England put pressure on Parliament to repeal the Stamp Act. They were feeling keenly the effects of the American agreements not to import any English-made goods as long as the Stamp Act remained in force.

Repeal. The British government finally yielded to the pressure from English merchants. They feared not only that they would suffer further loss of trade but also that Americans would not pay debts already owed them. The Stamp Act was repealed—that is, it was withdrawn—in# 1766.

Benjamin Franklin, who happened to be in London while the repeal was being debated, gave witty and convincing testimony before the committee in Parliament dealing with the question. A member of Parliament who was anxious to amend—that is, change—the act rather than repeal it asked the great Philadelphian if he would make a suggestion.

Franklin replied, "I have thought of one amendment. . . . It is in that clause where it is said, 'that from and after the first day of November, one thousand seven hundred and sixty-five, there shall be paid,' etc. The Amendment I would propose is, for *one* read *two*, and then all the rest of the Act may stand as it does. I believe it will give nobody in America any uneasiness."

Franklin actually misled Parliament, causing members to think that the colonies were merely injured by the Stamp Act, not angered. In truth, the spirit of rebellion was already taking hold of them.

Although Parliament repealed the Stamp Act, it did not stop there. It stated again that it had the right to pass laws fully binding upon the colonies—"in all cases whatsoever." Did the right to pass laws for the colonies include the right to tax? The British held that it did.

Meanwhile, the colonists celebrated wildly the repeal of the Stamp Act. There were bonfires, parades, and public dinners.

174 ##By refusing to buy English goods, the colonists successfully used their economic power. The success of the boycott must have impressed Americans, for they used it again in 1768-1769 (see p. 176) and after 1774 (see p. 185).

In New York and elsewhere, the people raised statues to King George III and to William Pitt, hero of Englishmen everywhere, who had helped bring about repeal. British merchants rejoiced also.

"Champagne Charley." Pitt shortly afterward became prime minister again. The news brought pleasure to the colonists. But a serious misfortune struck the colonies as well as that faithful friend of the Americans: he became ill. The business of dealing with America fell to Charles Townshend, England's chancellor of the exchequer (an official like our Secretary of the Treasury).

A noted English author of the day, Horace Walpole, expressed a strong opinion of "Champagne Charley," as this sporting gentleman was sometimes called. He said, "[Townshend] had almost every great talent . . . if he had had but common modesty, common steadiness, common courage and common sense."

Duties on imports. Townshend, who took a stern attitude toward the colonies, had boasted that he knew how to get tax money out of the Americans painlessly. One of the colonists' objections to the Stamp Act had been that it was an "internal tax"—that is, it was collected *inside* the colonies.

Townshend planned an "external tax," one that would be collected at the American ports. The result of his planning was the Townshend Revenue Act, passed in 1767. It imposed duties—taxes—on all tea, glass, paper, lead, and paint imported into the colonies.

Although the main purpose of the act was to collect revenue, Parliament also had in mind increasing its control over the colonies. The money raised under the Townshend Revenue Act was to be used to pay the salaries of British officials in America and support the British army there. Since the colonial assemblies had previously paid the salaries, the new arrangement would make the officials less dependent on the wishes of Americans.

Writs of assistance. Parliament's intentions were shown by other Townshend acts, too. One of them set up a board of customs officials in Boston and provided it with vessels, money, and men to catch smugglers. Another authorized colonial courts to issue *writs of assistance*. These were papers which permitted British officials to search anywhere for evidence of failure to pay the taxes on imports. Another suspended the legislature of New York because it refused to provide food and lodging for soldiers stationed in the colony.

When news of Parliament's decisions reached the colonies, once again there were howls of anguish and outbreaks of disorder. The concern of leading citizens now took new forms: If articles can be taxed at the ports, how high will those grasping Englishmen in Britain force the taxes to go? If one assembly can be suspended, how safe is local government anywhere in America?

Some thoughts of John Dickinson. One # of the most learned men of that day was John Dickinson, of Pennsylvania, a lawyer who had taken a leading part in the Stamp Act Congress. He wrote a series of articles, called *Letters from a Farmer in Pennsylvania*, which appeared in colonial newspapers in 1767–1768. In them Dickinson said, "Let us behave like dutiful children, who have received unmerited blows from a beloved parent, but let us protest these new taxes which infringe upon American liberty."

Britain, Dickinson declared, could tax in order to *regulate trade* but not in order to collect revenue. "We are," he insisted, "only as much dependent on . . . Britain as a perfectly free people can be on another."

Colonial merchants, who had lost business on account of the Townshend Rev-

ccording to John Dickinson, what legitimate power did England have over the colonies? Ask
dents if they can tell whether Dickinson still considered himself a British subject.

175

enue Act, found Dickinson's arguments very convincing. Because they owned property, they were going to object to *any* plan of Parliament's to take from them the right to tax themselves. Angered by the Townshend Revenue Act, they joined in *nonimportation* agreements, agreements not to import English goods, to make English merchants once again force Parliament to repeal an unpopular law.

Hurting the pocketbook. The extent to which the American merchants were able to work together is remarkable. Between 1768 and 1769 imports from the mother country to the city of Boston were cut in half. Philadelphia's purchases from Britain dropped to one-third their former amount, and a similar effect was registered in all leading shipping centers. Both George Washington and Benjamin Franklin believed the opportunity was at hand to develop American manufacturing.

The fact that the colonists could unite in nonimportation agreements was an important sign of even fuller coöperation to come. The fact that the colonists cut down on using English-made goods foretold the development of even greater self-reliance. The fact that the British seemed unable to find a way of dealing with the colonies foreshadowed a dependence on anger and force rather than on reason.

A Time of Violence

There could be no doubt that many Americans who worked with their hands supported the colonial merchants, as did many rowdies in cities and towns. Many of the merchants, in fact, became worried, fearing that the dispute with the mother country was only an excuse for some colonists to take part in violence.

In Philadelphia, for instance, a large quantity of wine was stolen from British officers, who had seized it from smugglers. In a number of places British officials and informers were tarred and feathered or otherwise attacked.

The *Romney* incident. A serious crisis occurred in June, 1768. The British had sent to Boston the man-of-war *Romney* to back up the authority of the customs officials. This show of strength set the teeth of Bostonians on edge.

When John Hancock's sloop *Liberty*, carrying a cargo of Madeira wine, entered Boston Harbor, a customs searcher came aboard to inspect the ship's cargo. Hancock, a leading merchant and smuggler, had vowed not "to sell or to drink wine polluted by the payments of . . . duties." Locking the customs official in the ship's cabin, the *Liberty*'s crew began to land the illegal goods.

The *Romney* proceeded to seize Hancock's sloop. In the meantime a mob, learning about the capture of the *Liberty*,

A page from Dickinson's *Letters*, through which his arguments against the British tax policy spread from colony to colony.

New York Public Library

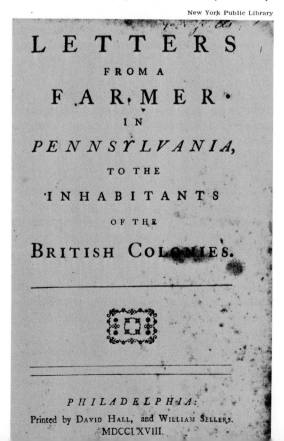

LETTERS

FROM A

FARMER

IN

PENNSYLVANIA,

TO THE

INHABITANTS

OF THE

BRITISH COLONIES.

PHILADELPHIA:

Printed by DAVID HALL, and WILLIAM SELLERS.
MDCCLXVIII.

#Notice that civil disorder often accompanied legitimate protest.

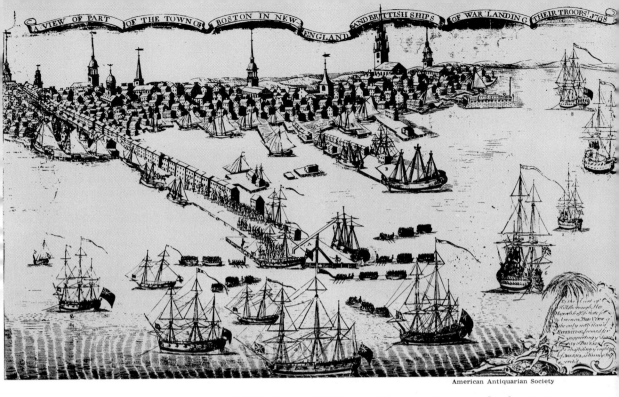

A VIEW OF PART OF THE TOWN OF BOSTON IN NEW ENGLAND AND BRITISH SHIPS OF WAR LANDING THEIR TROOPS! 1768

British ships in 1768 unload troops at the long wharf—seen at the left—in Boston Harbor. The smaller wharf at the right was John Hancock's. Ship No. 6 is the *Romney*.

hat does this scene suggest out British policy and ston's trade?

rushed to the customs offices and to the officials' houses. There they laid hold of the occupants and drove them out of the city.

The situation in the colonies was heating up rapidly, and the *patriots*—the colonists who supported the colonial side —had the advantage of vigorous support from the colonial newspapers. One enthusiastic American shouted: "The press hath never done greater service since its first Invention!" The columns of the papers were filled with grave warnings about how Britain was threatening the liberties of Americans.

Englishmen on the other side of the ocean—even some who only recently had been friends of America—were growing impatient. One English newspaper insisted that the time had come to teach those Americans "their Insignificancy" and to reduce the city of Boston to "a poor smuggling Village."

The landing of redcoats. In September,

1768, two regiments of British soldiers arrived in Boston to help keep order. Two other regiments were on the way. Sam Adams, John Hancock, and other leading patriots learned in advance of the decision to send troops and were prepared to fight to prevent the men from landing. But there was no general support for such action, and the British soldiers set up camp without difficulty.

The relationship between the colonies and the mother country was in a sorry state. Scarcely anybody on either side openly talked of war, but there were fewer and fewer signs that the differences were going to be adjusted satisfactorily.

Lull before the storm. All was not yet lost, though. In 1769 the British withdrew two regiments of redcoats, sending them to Nova Scotia. The remaining troops, weakened by the departure, were now open to attack by the Bostonians. One resident of Boston gloated, "The Soldiers must now

espite the gradual worsening of relations, conflict between England and the colonies did not ad to war in the 1760's. Radicals, like Adams and Hancock, were in a minority. Have dents consider the saying "Revolution is born of a few determined men."

Point out the closeness of farm and city life in colonial America.

In this watercolor drawing, made in 1768, British soldiers are encamped on Boston Common. The large house belonged to John Hancock, and some of his cows—despite the noise—relax at the left.

take care of themselves . . . for they are but a handful in comparison with the Sons of Liberty who could destroy them in a moment, if they pleased."

The moment, though, had not yet arrived. First, and most important of all, Parliament in April, 1770, repealed all the Townshend duties, except for the one on tea. (This duty was retained in order to # show that Parliament still claimed the right to tax the colonies.)

Second, business was good in England. Few people cared to interfere with it by stirring up new troubles with the American colonies.

Third, most Americans, also enjoying prosperity, were willing to accept a partial repeal of the Townshend duties rather than endure further violence. They also dropped their boycott of British goods. In short, on both sides sane voices prevented a blowup which could have had fearful results for all.

Golden Hill. Nevertheless, the British troops stationed in America continued to irritate the public. They were daily reminders of British "tyranny."

In New York City, in January, 1770, a brief clash occurred between citizens and soldiers which resulted in bloodshed. Sometimes called the Battle of Golden Hill, it followed an attempt of the British troops to cut down a "liberty pole." This was the name given to any tall mast having a cap or banner at the top that served as a rallying place for the Sons of Liberty.

Some very serious clashes took place the same year in Boston. There redcoats out alone were often subject to beatings. At least twenty of them had been knocked down and struck at various times. On one occasion a mob actually attacked troops marching in formation.

The "Boston Massacre." The commanding officer of the British troops sensed that the public was growing more and more upset. Further, unruly people, in particular, thought they could abuse the soldiers without limit.

On March 5, 1770, when a crowd began

#This duty, like the earlier Declaratory Act, was a gesture by which Parliament asserted its right to tax the colonies without fully exercising that right. Note that as a result, in 1770 the colonists did not object to the tax on tea.

to throw snowballs at a redcoat on guard at the customhouse—where import duties were collected—soldiers hurried to assist him. The captain in command of the men apparently believed that the mob was intending to seize the tax receipts stored there. He was unable to calm the crowd. It closed in on the soldiers and knocked one of them down. Then the word "Fire!" was heard, and British muskets responded.

Five colonists were killed. One of them, Crispus Attucks, a Negro, seems to have been the leader of the mob. Attucks and his fellow victims had become the first martyrs in the American struggle against Britain.

The acting governor of Massachusetts, Thomas Hutchinson, who knew street violence at first hand (since his house had been destroyed during the Stamp Act crisis), was forced to withdraw the troops. The Boston citizens became calmer, but the dangerous cry "To arms! To arms! To arms! Turn out with your guns!" had been heard in the streets of the city.

Men who were bent on keeping the embers of revolt alive would not rest. Word spread that the British were engaged in a large-scale effort to do away with the disloyal Americans. The terrible clash of March 5, 1770, came to be called the Boston Massacre, and the victims were public heroes.

John Adams, who would later play a large role in the American struggle against Britain, was one of two lawyers who undertook to defend Captain Thomas Preston. Preston, commander of the British troops at the customhouse, was charged with murder.

Adams, explaining why he was risking unpopularity in serving as counsel to Preston, spoke a powerful American principle at the trial: "It is of more importance to *the community that innocence should be protected than it is that guilt should be punished."

Independence National Historical Park Collection

The "Boston Massacre," a picture printed and sold by Paul Revere. Redcoats are firing from in front of the customhouse—right. The Old State House is in the center background.

Preston (and six other soldiers) in the end were freed. They owed their lives to the skill of their fearless American lawyers, who were severely criticized in the local newspapers.

1. What two facts explain British policies after 1763? 2. How did the colonists react to the Sugar Act? 3. Describe the Stamp Act, the colonial response to it, and the result of the response. 4. Give provisions of the Townshend acts and tell what results they had in the colonies. 5. Identify the *Romney* incident, and explain its seriousness. 6. Name three reasons why there was hope for avoiding further violence in the colonies in the early part of 1770. 7. Give an account of the "Boston Massacre." 8. What American principle was expressed by John Adams at the trial of Preston?

*A basic principle of American justice. Can students give examples that show how this
:inciple has been upheld or abused recently? (In the past few years some Supreme Court
ases have dealt with the subject.)

Patriots Fan the Fires of Resistance

The spirit of revolt, though, was already well seeded in the American colonies. We realize today that the British were already losing control of their possessions on the Atlantic seaboard. Moreover, a determined band of patriots was going to keep the seeds of revolt well nourished and well watered.

What is a rebel?

Rebel Sam Adams

One of the leading rebels was John Adams' older cousin Sam. Sam Adams apparently had a very winning personality. We know that in the early 1770's one friend built him a barn and another repaired his house. Still another outfitted him from head to toe in new clothes. A fourth provided him with some money.

Adams never openly approved of violence. But his opposition to wealthy men in Boston and to local leaders such as Hutchinson always put him on the side of the crowd. He sincerely believed that wealthy men in England were using the colonists for their own purposes and, if necessary, would establish complete control of them to achieve their ends.

Forming his forces. A skillful politician and always active in the cause of his fellow patriots, Sam Adams united the merchants —whom he distrusted but needed—with the farmers and artisans. One of the merchants was John Hancock, who became a leading patriot. Adams convinced him and many other businessmen that they would find advantages in opposing England.

Master propagandist. In political pamphlets, which he wrote with rare brilliance, Adams persuaded his followers that their very liberty depended on increasing their opposition to British policies. His success

at *propaganda*—that is, definite effort to influence opinion—has never been surpassed. He seemed always to be ahead of his supporters but never so far ahead that they could not follow him.

In the 1760's, when the troubles with Britain began, Sam Adams seems to have favored a separate legislature for America. Not long afterward he seems to have concluded that only complete separation from the mother country would be satisfactory. And the British—like clumsy checkers players—seemed unable to avoid giving him just the opportunity he could use to his advantage.

The *Gaspee*. Still determined to prevent smuggling, British officials had sent an armed vessel, the *Gaspee*, to see to the enforcement of the trade regulations. A few miles south of the city of Providence, Rhode Island, in June, 1772, the *Gaspee* ran aground on a sandspit while pursuing another vessel. That night men from Providence boarded the *Gaspee*, wounded its commanding officer, seized the crew, and set the ship afire.

The outraged British authorities vowed to leave no stone unturned in finding the culprits—who were well-known citizens of Providence. The men they were looking for were never caught, although there had been eight boatloads of them.

The efforts of the British to locate the guilty men aroused new resentments. This was because investigating officials sometimes carelessly made enemies by behaving in a high-handed way. The announcement that the Americans would be taken to England for trial—when they were caught— further stirred up the colonists.

The Committees of Correspondence. Sam Adams now persuaded the people of Bos-

#Why, in this instance, would Britain want to try Americans in England? (They thought that American jurors would decide in favor of fellow Americans, whether guilty or not.)

ton to appoint a committee to correspond with similar committees to be appointed in other towns in Massachusetts. The aim was to exchange colonial views on steps that might be required to protect the rights of the people against the actions of Britain.

The following year Virginia's House of Burgesses appointed a Committee of Correspondence to put itself in touch with other colonies for the purpose of sharing information about British plans. Four more colonies agreed to do the same. The Virginia leaders were Thomas Jefferson, Patrick Henry, and Richard Henry Lee.

At last, for the first time the most influential northern spokesmen and the most influential southern spokesmen were working together for a common purpose. Shortly they would work together in common action as well. The opportunity arose before long in still another crisis—ushering in the gravest period yet in American-British relations.

An invitation to tea. The crisis revolved around—of all things—tea, the most popular beverage in the colonies. A famous Swedish traveler commented that because American girls drank so much tea—with sugar—they often lost their teeth before they reached the age of twenty.

Because tea was popular, at low cost it was in great demand. A good deal of it was bought from Dutch traders and smuggled into the colonies. The legally imported tea came into America on ships of the British East India Company, formed by British traders. This organization was in serious financial difficulties in the early 1770's, partly because it had on hand a surplus of seventeen million pounds of tea.

In May, 1773, the British government decided it must help the East India Company. It permitted the company to send tea to America without paying first the usual duty in Britain. Further, the tea was to be placed in the hands of a picked group of American merchants for retail sale. Even with the Townshend duty, the tea would be cheaper in the colonies than smuggled tea from Dutch traders.

The British officials were sure the colonists would willingly buy the British tea. The East India Company would be helped financially, and in addition the colonists by their purchases would acknowledge Parliament's right to lay taxes on America. An extra but important benefit would be the damage that would be done to the smugglers.

Although the English calculated careful-

What does the fact that eight boatloads of Gaspee raiders could not be found suggest about the attitudes of the people of Providence?

The *Gaspee* burning in the waters off Providence, Roger Williams' town.

Rhode Island Historical Society

A rare drawing of the Boston Tea Party, made not long after it occurred in Boston Harbor. Observe the interested bystanders in the left background.

The Granger Collection

ly, they did not catch the colonial patriots napping. The patriots saw immediately that they must prevent the tea from being landed. They knew that if it was ever brought ashore, it would be snapped up by housewives and others looking for bargains. Such sales would mean the end of # the colonial refusal to pay the taxes levied by Parliament. Many merchants feared that if tea could be delivered to a favored few American merchants, other goods would also soon be marketed in the same unfair way.

A bad mistake. The East India Company appointed agents at the various American ports to receive the tea, but no protection was provided for them. Like the stamp agents, they found themselves exposed to threats in both words and actions. It was apparent that the British had blundered badly in their plan to help the East India Company.

The tea agents appointed in New York, Philadelphia, and Charleston were mindful of their own safety. Placing it ahead of duty to the king, they resigned their places. The shipments of tea to New York and Philadelphia were returned to England. The one sent to Charleston was stored in a

warehouse from which it was sold at auction a few years later.

The story in Boston was different. There Governor Thomas Hutchinson, who had had enough of the impudence of the patriots, made up his mind to defend the king's cause. The tea, he declared, was going to be landed (two sons and a nephew had been appointed agents). In due time, he figured, Sam Adams and his friends would have to yield. Hutchinson would never grant permission for that tea to be shipped back.

Tea Party. In challenging Sam Adams, # Hutchinson brewed not tea but terrible trouble. In late November, 1770, Adams called a meeting of the Committees of Correspondence of Boston and nearby towns in old South Church in Boston. There the men agreed to prevent the tea from being brought ashore.

On December 16, 1773, a group of fifty or sixty men dressed as Mohawk Indians met at the Green Dragon Tavern. From there they went aboard three ships of the East India Company tied up at Griffin's wharf and dumped the tea into Boston Harbor—three hundred forty-two chests of it. Shortly a popular song began:

##To the British the Boston Tea Party was a planned, hostile act. It could not be overlooked if Parliament was to preserve its authority in the colonies. Was there any way for either side to save face?

Rally, Mohawks! bring out your axes,
And tell King George we'll pay no
　　taxes on his foreign tea;
His threats are vain and vain to
　　think
To force our girls and wives to
　　drink His
　　vile Bohea [a kind of tea]!
Then rally, boys, and hasten on
To meet our chiefs at the Green Dragon.

Thousands of law-abiding Americans on shore watched the dumping of the tea, but not a finger was raised to prevent this destruction of private property. This fact shows how far resistance to royal authority had gone.

An Angry Parliament

When news of the Boston Tea Party reached the mother country in late January, 1774, the response was one of rage and shame. Even William Pitt, that old friend of America, condemned the violent act. Here in America the patriots were applauded in many places, but in some others their actions were severely criticized. A few towns disbanded their Committees of Correspondence.

Boston's punishment. But by their harsh punishment of the city of Boston, the British forced Americans to stop criticizing the actions of the "Indians" and to stand together. In March, Parliament passed a series of laws which became known in the colonies as the "Intolerable Acts."

The most dramatic of the new British laws ordered the port of Boston closed until the dumped tea had been paid for. Another provided that British soldiers were to be stationed in the colonies to put down disturbances.

Still another act directed that British officials accused of crime in carrying out British laws or in putting down riots be sent to England or another colony for trial. The idea was to protect officials who might get into trouble as a result of actions taken against the colonists. A fourth act said that town meetings could not be held in the state except with the permission of the governor.

The Quebec Act. Another law which many regarded as one of the "Intolerable Acts" was the Quebec Act, but it had no connection with the Boston Tea Party, as far as we know. It extended the boundaries of the province of Quebec to include all the land between the Ohio and Mississippi rivers. Land speculators of Virginia, Pennsylvania, Massachusetts, and Connecticut, who claimed rights in this vast region, were indignant.

The Quebec Act also granted Roman Catholics religious toleration in Quebec. This angered and alarmed prejudiced people in the seaboard colonies.

From the point of view of the mother country, the act would lead to better government in the territory acquired from France in 1763. Adequate provision for Quebec had not been made before. From the point of view of the colonists, the Quebec Act was the crowning example of British tyranny.

Colonial Unity

The colonists were aghast because the punishment given to Massachusetts was so severe and also because General Thomas Gage, Britain's commander in chief in America, was named governor there. Boston also felt keenly the loss of its trade, the main means of making a living there.

Support for Boston. Many inhabitants were made "wretchedly miserable," and for the first time in American history a city had to find means to provide public relief. But help in the form of supplies, food especially, came in huge quantities from the other colonies. Connecticut sent sheep, Pennsylvania flour, and the Carolinas rice. The Sons of Liberty in New York promised

id the "Intolerable Acts" prove the patriots' argument that parliamentary laws, if not subject
the approval of colonial assemblies, might result in tyranny? Note that Parliament's actions
ruck at political rights as well as at economic life.　　　183

to support Boston, if necessary, for ten years.

General Gage, who had been in America for a long time and knew it well (he was married to an American) at first was believed likely to be lenient. He soon showed that he meant business. When he enforced the unpopular laws, deep concern spread throughout the colonies. A demand for a meeting of colonial representatives soon developed.

First Continental Congress. Through the Committees of Correspondence the colonists decided to call together an intercolonial gathering to discuss the plight of the colonies. Known as the First Continental Congress, it met in Carpenters' Hall, Philadelphia, on September 5, 1774, and remained in session until October 26. Massachusetts and Virginia took the lead in calling the meeting, and every colony except Georgia sent a delegate.

Made up of wealthy men for the most part, the Continental Congress was a gathering which in general hoped to work out a

General Thomas E. Gage, who had been with Braddock in 1755 (see page 154) and who commanded British troops in America until 1775.

friendly settlement of difficulties. William Pitt in London said that the Congress was the "most honourable assembly of Statesmen since those of ancient Greeks and Romans."

The delegates. John Adams, one of those representing Massachusetts, saw the men at closer range. The delegates were "all strangers . . . not acquainted with each other's language, ideas, views, designs. They are, therefore, jealous of each other —fearful, timid, skittish."

More important, though, the colonial # leaders were coming together for the first time face-to-face. They were overcoming their local outlooks and narrow views. Said Patrick Henry, of Virginia, with his usual liveliness: "The distinctions between Virginians, Pennsylvanians, New Yorkers and New Englanders are no more. I am not a Virginian but an American."

A leading figure was George Washington. The richest of the planters, he had earlier advised a "go-slow" policy. Now in 1774 he was a Virginia delegate to the Continental Congress. Someone who knew him well described him as "a modest man, but sensible and speaks little—in action cool, like a Bishop at his prayers."

Even though Washington spoke less than some others, he was able to persuade his associates. He had the quality of integrity, that is, soundness of character, which other men recognize. In time of crisis it is absolutely necessary for successful leadership.

Washington had known when he went to Philadelphia that he had the support of fellow Virginians. His presence alone— even if his words were few—raised the spirits of the delegates. Being well known, he could help bring unity to the men from the various colonies.

There could be no question, though, that Sam Adams quickly became the most influential of the delegates. He seized with both hands his chance to press forward the patriots' purposes. "He eats little," Joseph Galloway, of Pennsylvania, observed, "sleeps little, drinks little, thinks much, and is most decisive and indefatigable [untiring] in the pursuit of his objects."

The political skills Sam Adams had learned and practiced in Massachusetts he now put to work on a larger stage for action. But not all his fellow delegates were ready to follow where he was heading: toward a complete breaking of ties with the mother country.

John Adams' work. In the end it was the other Adams, John, who wrote the most important measure passed by the First Continental Congress. This statement again denied that Parliament had authority to pass laws to govern the colonies without their consent. The Congress declared, furthermore, that the "Intolerable Acts" were not to be obeyed.

The First Continental Congress also agreed that the colonies would not import goods from the mother country after December, 1774. After September, 1775, they would not export goods to the mother country, either.

What was happening was that the colonists were at last shedding some of their feeling of dependence on the mother country. In fact, they wanted to be recognized as being equal to Englishmen in Britain.

The colonists had taken the bit in their teeth and had assumed authority formerly claimed by Parliament. However, nothing was said in the Congress about independence, and the response of Americans was still far from united. The leadership of the patriots, however, was firm, and that of the opposition was disorganized.

Arming. The patriots in New England #knew that when Parliament learned of the meeting of the First Continental Congress, it would take bold steps. Accordingly, they began to store arms and ammunition and prepare for the showdown with the mother country that was sure to come.

Brooklyn Museum

George Washington became commander of American forces in the struggle with Britain and, unlike Gage, kept his position. In this portrait, by Charles Willson Peale, he wears the commander's blue ribbon.

In Virginia, George Washington, accepting command of seven companies of militia, donned a uniform. Its colors, blue and buff, would soon be a symbol of the struggle of a people to be free and independent.

A Determined England

On the other side of the Atlantic, the talk, as the American patriots could guess, was about how to put down rebellious colonists. Britain's King George III had already declared, "The New England governments are in a state of rebellion, blows must decide."

Gage. General Gage, in Boston, asked for more troops, for he knew that if London ordered "blows" against Bostonians, Massachusetts would not be fighting alone. Gage must have realized the sense of what Edmund Burke, the great English orator,

‡Ask students to think about the probable British reaction to the actions of the First Continental ~~ongress. Why did the colonists begin arming themselves?

told Parliament: "This fierce spirit of liberty is stronger in the English colonies probably than in any other people of the earth."

The king's voice. Yet there was determination in the mother country, too. As the king expressed it: "The spirit of the British nation [is] too high . . . to give up so many colonies which she has planted with great industry, nursed with great tenderness . . . and protected and defended at much expense of blood and treasures."

Parliament, after a long and heated

Above: Surviving minutemen—in the foreground—withdraw after the first shots at Lexington.
Below: After being defeated at Concord, the redcoats retreat to Boston.

Connecticut Historical Society

debate on how to deal with the colonies, decided to declare Massachusetts in rebellion. The next step was to pass a law preventing it from trading anywhere but in Britain, Ireland, and the British West Indies and excluding its fishermen from Newfoundland. The law was shortly extended to apply also to other colonies.

Lord North. The British believed that if they could arrest Sam Adams and John Hancock and bring them to trial in England, they could end the revolt. Furthermore, Frederick, Lord North, the prime minister, and others believed still that Americans in general were envious of Boston and anxious to see its people taken down a peg or two.

The British should have known by this time that a plan to arrest and try Adams and Hancock in England would not work. Moreover, they should have known that the colonists would not be put in their place by a tactless man like Gage.

One British officer in America made a joking remark about what the authorities would have done if they had had their wits about them. He said, "[They] would have sent out . . . a Man of Fashion and Politeness, who would have complimented, entertained, flattered, and danced us all into good Humour."

But the British were in no mood to be pleasant. Their pride had been hurt when their authority had been so outrageously scorned. British soldiers were eager to see action against the troublemakers. "I am satisfied," an officer said, "that one active campaign, a smart action, and burning two or three of their towns will set everything to rights."

The march against Concord and Lexington. On April 15, 1775, Gage, acting on British orders, planned to seize the colonists' supply of arms at Concord, Massachusetts. The patriots, though, got wind of his plans and he changed the date. Meanwhile, the patriots remained sharply alert, determined to protect their leaders, Adams and Hancock, at Lexington and the arms they had collected at Concord.

The redcoats stationed in Boston were kept under constant watch. A well-known Boston silversmith and engraver, Paul Revere, arranged with others to inform the countryside when the English troops moved toward Lexington. As Revere later described it: "If the British went by water, we would show two lanthorns in the North Church steeple; and if by land, one as a signal."

Shortly before midnight on chilly April 18, 1775, Gage sent his men toward Lexington. Within a short time, two lanterns in the church steeple told that British soldiers were coming by water. Revere and William Dawes, a tanner, were on their way to alert the minutemen, a special group of American militiamen pledged to answer a call to arms instantly.

Revere, forty years old, was doing the work of a much younger man. He made his way across the Charles River under the very guns of the British ships, his oars muffled by an old petticoat.

Near Lexington, Revere found Adams and Hancock and helped them make their escape. As the men stole across the meadows at daybreak, Adams observed to Hancock, "What a glorious morning this is!" Then he added thoughtfully, and no doubt with a twinkle in his eye, "I mean for America."

"Disperse, ye rebels!" Just before daybreak the beating of drums brought the minutemen running to the Lexington village green—some seventy of them. The redcoats were approaching. Out of the ranks of the minutemen, it is said, came the confident voice of Captain John Parker: "Don't fire unless fired upon. But if they want a war let it begin here."

Out of the ranks of the redcoats came the order "Disperse, ye rebels!" Shots were exchanged, and as the minutemen with-

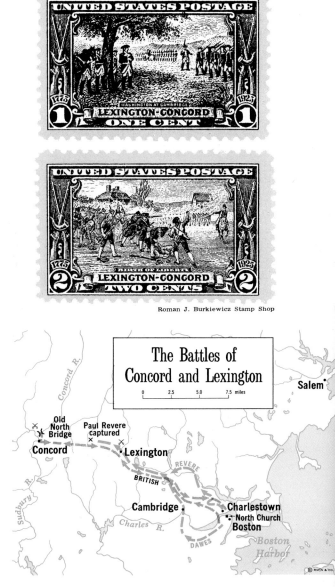

Roman J. Burkiewicz Stamp Shop

Above: American stamps issued on the one-hundred-fiftieth anniversary of the Battles of Lexington and Concord. *Below:* Follow the moves of the British and relate them to the picture on page 186.

drew, eight of their number lay dead and ten wounded.

The English soldiers then headed for Concord. Though they laid hands on some of the rebels' munitions there, most of the American supplies of arms had safely been

Why did Adams say it was "a glorious morning" for America? What other facts show that the
patriots knew what was at stake at Lexington?

carried elsewhere. Minutemen poured into Concord from every nearby town and village. They held the North Bridge against the enemy and succeeded in driving the British, by now exhausted, pell-mell back toward Boston.

The British were rescued from destruction by the arrival of relief units under the command of Lord Percy. Though saved from complete rout, they were annoyed all the way back to Charlestown by Americans who fired at them from behind stone walls and trees and from windows.

Riders carried news of the fighting throughout the colonies. In Kentucky a group of frontiersmen named one of their settlements after Lexington. Colonists everywhere were thrilled at the account of the American victory over the British.

Shortly a lady in Philadelphia would be writing an appealing letter to her friend, a British officer in Boston. In it she would say, "Nothing is heard now in our streets but the trumpet and drum; and the universal cry is 'Americans, to arms!' . . . The God of mercy will, I hope, open the eyes of our king that he may see, while in seeking our destruction, he will go near to complete his own."

The day for healing the break, as events quickly showed, had now passed. The colonists were in open rebellion.

---

1. Name two leading patriots and tell why each opposed the mother country. 2. Give the main facts about the *Gaspee* incident. 3. What steps did the colonists take afterward? 4. Describe the events that preceded and followed the Boston Tea Party. 5. Name two provisions of the Quebec Act and explain how it affected the colonists. 6. Tell what the First Continental Congress was, where it met and when, who its leaders were, and what it did. 7. Give the main facts about the Battles of Lexington and Concord.

The Workshop

The Shapers of Our World

Identify the following people, terms, and events, telling how each was related to the American Revolution.

Stamp Act
Patrick Henry
Sons of Liberty
Stamp Act Congress
George III
Charles Townshend
writs of
  assistance
John Dickinson
the *Romney*
Crispus Attucks
"Boston Massacre"
Sam Adams

John Hancock
Gaspee incident
Committees of
  Correspondence
Boston Tea Party
"Intolerable Acts"
Quebec Act
First Continental
  Congress
Lexington
  and Concord
Paul Revere
John Adams

Adding to Your Vocabulary

Show your understanding of these terms by using them in sentences which relate to the coming of the American Revolution.

boycott
sacked
exchequer
internal tax
external tax
nonimportation

unity
patriots
regiment
propaganda
tyranny

Thinking Things Through

After reviewing the boxed-in exercises within the chapter, see if you can answer the following:

Ask students to try to summarize the causes of the American Revolution. Discuss thoughtfully whether or not the Revolution could have been avoided. Some students might look into the history of Canada's relations with England for possible answers.

1. Why was it so difficult for the colonists to distinguish between taxation for revenue and taxation to regulate trade?

2. Samuel Adams performed a remarkable feat of organization. Why is it hard to unite farmers with merchants?

3. Why is it necessary for good public leaders always to be just far enough ahead of public opinion to lead it but never too far ahead to lose it?

4. Why was it a mistake for the British Parliament to repeal the Stamp Act? What did the colonists imagine the repeal meant?

5. Why do you think the British refused to accept the idea of "no taxation without representation"?

6. Review the king's role in the establishment of the colonies. How does this role help explain why there was so little royal control of the colonies before 1763?

7. Show how Britain by the time of the Quebec Act was learning to handle colonial problems—even though it was having serious difficulties with the colonies on the Atlantic seaboard.

8. Since the patriots were admittedly a small part of the colonial population, why in your opinion were they able to bring about such impressive results?

9. Review the various British acts that led up to Lexington and Concord. What special-interest groups were alarmed by each one? Why did the Stamp Act in particular damage British standing?

10. Why do you think the British reaction to the colonial demands of 1774 was different from the reaction at the time of the Stamp Act or the Townshend acts?

The Research Center

1. Obtain a copy of Longfellow's poem "Paul Revere's Ride" and read it to the class. Does it differ from the true account of the ride?

2. Two of Patrick Henry's most famous speeches were the one delivered to a group of Virginia leaders at St. John's Church in Richmond in March, 1775, and the one to the House of Burgesses at Williamsburg in May, 1785. Obtain copies of these speeches, read them to the class, and tell what rights Patrick Henry was referring to.

3. Consult with your local tax collector's office. What kinds of taxes are collected in your community? Are any of them excise taxes? If so, give some examples.

The Beginnings of Union

1. In 1754 representatives of some of the colonies wanted to form a union. Why? What was the union's name? What was the outcome of the plans for it? Why?

2. What event ten years later produced a stronger feeling of unity? How was it shown?

3. Why can the members of the First Continental Congress be spoken of as *Americans*, not English colonists?

4. Why was it difficult for the colonists to learn to act together instead of continuing to act separately?

5. Most of the colonists either brought English culture to the colonies or shared in it. What English ideas did they have which contributed to their wanting to become independent?

Your Opinion, Please

1. If you had lived in Boston in the early 1770's, would you have been likely to sympathize with the patriots? Why?

2. Have you ever been affected by propaganda? How? Have you ever used it? How?

completing the exercises in "The Beginnings of Union," students can trace British-American lations between 1754 and 1775, from the first efforts for union to the final open rebellion. hese activities are useful in organizing and reviewing the contents of Chapter 9.

189

(a) The Liberty Bell, now in Independence Hall, rang out in July, 1776, to celebrate American independence.
(b) A bronze statue of George Rogers Clark, a Virginian who receives credit for winning the West in the American Revolution.
(c) A portion of the completed Declaration of Independence.
(d) The inkstand in which men dipped their quill pens to sign the Declaration.
(e) A committee presents to the Second Continental Congress in 1776 its idea of what the Declaration should contain. John Adams stands at the left. The tall man at his right is Jefferson—the short one is Franklin.

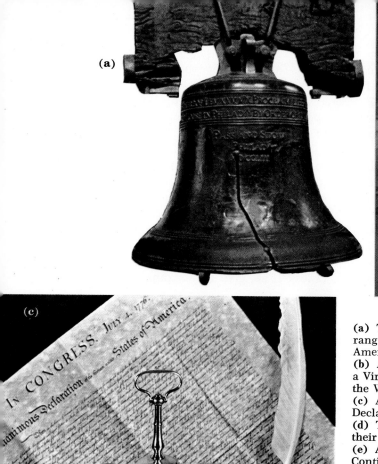

(f) A silver medal created
in 1776 to recall the beginning
of American independence.
(g) Paper money used by
Americans during the
War for Independence.
Paper money was often
considered unstable and
unreliable in value.

(f)

(g)

CHAPTER 10

FORGING THE AMERICAN REVOLUTION

int out that this chapter concerns a change in American opposition to England--a change from
en rebellion, aimed at protesting British laws, to a war aimed at winning American independence.

As the news of what had happened at Lexington and Concord spread through the colonies, the colonists could sense that they were heading toward war. The Second Continental Congress, called by the First just before it ended its sessions, gathered in Philadelphia in May, 1775, and held meetings through June of that year. Its members, this time including a delegation from Georgia, decided to try soft words with England one more time, still hoping to avoid a break.

The Second Continental Congress functioned as the colonies' central government throughout the war.

The Time to Patch Things Up Is Past

John Dickinson, a leading Pennsylvanian, presented and obtained the passage of what was called the Olive Branch Petition —signed by "your faithful colonists." It mentioned the hope that the colonists and the king might be at peace. Dickinson yet thought that the colonies could regain the affection of the mother country.

Ready to Fight

But thousands of other Americans had drawn a different conclusion. They had decided that England was not going to re-peal the laws punishing Massachusetts, remove the redcoats, and give up its claim to authority over the colonies. Only force would be able to achieve these far-reaching results. When news arrived in the late summer that George III had refused even ## to receive the Olive Branch Petition, the patriots were driven further into rebellion.

The Green Mountain Boys. Already the Second Continental Congress had decided that only a large and effective army could prevent disaster for America. When the Congress was opening in May, 1775, a rag-tag group of colonial volunteers known as

Discuss the action of George III in refusing the petition. Should he have accepted it? Would it

ve seemed that England gave in--surrendered--after the colonists used armed force?

191

Recall the role of Fort Ticonderoga in the French and Indian War.

Fort Ticonderoga today (see the map, page 195), in the rolling hills of New York State. What you see is a restoration, but a faithful one. The guns guarding it are the old ones of Revolutionary days.

Forward's Color Productions, Manchester, Vermont

the Green Mountain Boys had captured Crown Point and Fort Ticonderoga. These were at the northern tip of Lake George, on the road to Canada.

When the leader of the Green Mountain Boys, Ethan Allen, was asked by what authority he sought the surrender of Fort Ticonderoga, he is said to have replied loudly, "In the name of the Great Jehovah and the Continental Congress." Just imagine, the delegates to the Congress must have thought, how easy the fight would be if a properly led and properly trained army were in the field.

Washington in command. For leadership the delegates' attention turned naturally and easily to George Washington, the outstanding military man in America. He was the only one among them who had arrived in Philadelphia wearing a uniform. On his way north he had reviewed several companies of volunteers which had formed.

When Washington's name was proposed as commander in chief of the Continental army, he was elected unanimously, on June 15, 1775. Embarrassed by one of the speeches in his behalf, he quietly slipped out of the room in order not to hear.

John Adams, member of the Second Continental Congress, wrote to his wife about the choice. He said he was sure Washington's election would have a "great effect in cementing and securing the union of these colonies," which "the liberties of America depend upon, in a great degree." Abigail Adams later met Washington and paid him the compliment of saying that "the gentleman and the soldier look agreeably blended in him."

"Reluctant rebels." Still, most Americans were not yet ready to declare independence from Britain. Many wealthy Americans, particularly, hung back. They feared that the people who had threatened the stamp collectors, hurled tea into Boston Harbor, and burned the *Gaspee*, might now turn against *them*. But these troubled men had no strong leadership and no encouragement from the mother country.

At Bunker Hill. On June 17, 1775, two days after Washington was given command of the army, the first battle of the American Revolution took place in Boston —the Battle of Bunker Hill. (It was actually fought on Breed's Hill, nearby.)

The patriot troops were made up of men from the four New England colonies. They occupied the heights around Boston and were fortifying their positions in order to try to drive the British general, Thomas Gage, out of the city. Before they could fortify Breed's Hill, Gage struck.

192

#Note that Washington was <u>elected</u> commander in chief. Many colonial militias also elected their officers. Officers in the British army usually bought their commissions. What does that difference in procedure suggest?

After withstanding two heavy assaults, the patriots, having run out of ammunition, were pushed off Breed's Hill. They had suffered about four hundred casualties, but the British had suffered over a thousand. Almost half the number of redcoats engaged in the battle had been either wounded or killed. Gage wrote home that his losses were "greater than we can bear." The Americans knew they could stand up to their enemy.

In charge of Washington. When Washington arrived in Cambridge, Massachusetts, near Boston, on July 3, 1775, he took over a defeated but not discouraged patriot army. He spent about six months trying to organize the soldiers to the best advantage. Proud of his name, Washington may have recalled that the day was the twenty-first anniversary of his surrender to the French at Fort Necessity. He did not intend to be shamed by failing again.

As a slave owner, Washington at first disliked the idea of having Negro soldiers. In November, 1776, he ordered an end to the enlistment of Negroes. When the British began arming slaves, though, the Americans reversed themselves. Washington welcomed Negroes then, and over five thousand served as soldiers and sailors in the Continental forces at such places as Valley Forge and Saratoga.

Colored minutemen had already served at Lexington, Concord, and Ticonderoga.

One of them, Peter Salem, was hailed as a hero for having killed at Bunker Hill the British major John Pitcairn, whose men had fired on the patriots at Lexington.

The time for the British to destroy the # patriot army was before Washington could organize it. But they had made a change in generals, replacing Gage with General William Howe. Howe proved to be timid—often a fatal shortcoming in a general.

By the spring of 1776 Washington and his troops had been strengthened by supplies of cannon and ammunition captured at Fort Ticonderoga. These had been dragged part of the way to Boston on sleds drawn by oxen. The Americans had fortified Dorchester Heights, overlooking Boston (which, strangely, the redcoats had never taken). This move enabled Washington's forces to bring Howe's troops and fleet within reach of American guns.

Evacuation. The British withdrew from Boston before they could bombard the Americans or be bombarded. Sailing with them to Halifax, Nova Scotia, on March 26, 1776, were about a thousand Loyalists, Americans who remained loyal to the English king. They thought that already the British side had lost.

The rebels' military effort, though, still had no general purpose. The idea of independence continued to frighten many people—even those who could not be called Loyalists.

#How did British delay and the evacuation of Boston aid the rebel cause?

Digging trenches and dragging guns into place, patriots hastily fortify Breed's Hill on the night of June 16, 1776. At the left is the water of Boston Harbor.

The British Plans

The mother country was relying on the Loyalists—or Tories, as they were usually called in the South—to assert themselves and bring the colonies to their senses. In fact, the British thought that if they sent ships to the Carolinas, they would find so many Loyalists that they could keep those colonies from revolting.

The role of the Loyalists. But the rebels defeated the Tories in a battle at Moore's Creek Bridge (near Wilmington, North Carolina) in February, 1776. Over 850 Loyalist troops were captured by the rebels. This victory greatly strengthened the American cause. By the time a British fleet commanded by Sir Peter Parker and General Henry Clinton arrived, the chances for British success in North Carolina were slim.

Moving south to Charleston, South Carolina, the British fleet attacked the city in June, 1776. There it met a wall of resistance from Colonel William Moultrie and his six hundred brave militiamen.

Sheltered behind an incomplete fort (later called Fort Moultrie) made of palmetto logs, the rebels poured deadly fire on the British vessels in the harbor. The badly battered ships turned tail and later sailed toward New York, their commanders having suffered what Clinton called "great mortification."

South from Canada. The patriots were aware that they would require help against their powerful foe—even if twice it had been forced to flee. The French in Canada, of course, could be admirable allies—and the Americans hoped to have them on their side.

In late 1775 Americans led by General Richard Montgomery had attacked and captured Montreal, defended by Sir Guy Carleton's army. Montgomery and Benedict Arnold had tried to take Quebec, too,

but had failed, and Montgomery had been killed in the assault.

Arnold and his men had remained outside Quebec during the winter. When the spring of 1776 came, the British, superbly led by Carleton, forced them to turn southward again. Carleton chased Arnold's army as far as Lake Champlain.

Focus on New York. The British commander's move southward admirably suited British *strategy*, that is, their military planning. It had been decided that General Howe would bring his forces south from Halifax to New York, land, attack, and press northward along the Hudson River Valley. Howe and his men would then join Carleton's troops at Albany. The prize, of course, was the control of the whole of New York, for winning it would divide the colonies into two sections, cut off from one another.

The attack on New York City was a powerful one. The British army that General Howe headed was well trained and well disciplined. The British fleet commanded by Howe's brother—Admiral Richard Howe—consisted of more than 350 ships. It was to be used for transporting troops and blockading ports. Both the army and the navy were professional forces.

Washington, who realized what the English might be planning, had transferred part of his army from Boston to New York. The Americans, still insufficiently trained, took a position on Brooklyn Heights, overlooking the city. On July 2, 1776, General Howe came ashore on Staten Island, in New York Harbor. Not long afterward his brother arrived. General Howe headed for Long Island and toward Washington's army. The Americans were forced to retreat, and in September Howe occupied New York City.

An offer of peace. The Howe brothers had come not only to fight but to offer peace, too. Acting under the authority of Parliament, they were prepared to offer

Had the British dealt with the Continental Congress, they would have admitted its legality.

freedom and protection to Americans if they would again pledge allegiance to the king. But the Howes had orders not to deal with the colonies as such until the Second Continental Congress and the colonial armies had been disbanded.

Nothing came of the peace effort. Washington refused to receive a communication from General Howe because it was addressed to him as a civilian rather than as *General* George Washington.

e the pictures on p. 190 with the section below.

The Great Declaration

The effort at peacemaking failed chiefly because a major event had taken place in Congress: the adoption of the Declaration of Independence. This declaration would change the entire course of the struggle. And far beyond that result—although that was immense—it would change the course of history for the whole world.

Slowness. The movement for independence had begun in earnest just about the time the year 1775 was drawing to a close. Still, many moderate people were tending toward "kissing and making up" with the mother country.

The Quakers of Pennsylvania, for instance, deeply *pacifist* (opposed to violence) in their thinking, shunned war and knew that a drive for independence would lead to war. One patriot, in fact, complained that Pennsylvania was displaying the gentleness "of a Spaniel dog, that grows more fond in proportion to the ill usage he receives."

Furthermore, some Loyalists believed that a war would have a serious effect at home on relations between rich and poor and between colony and colony. Carter Braxton, of Virginia, for instance, predicted that as a result of open warfare "the continent would be torn in pieces."

What British and American plans are illustrated here?

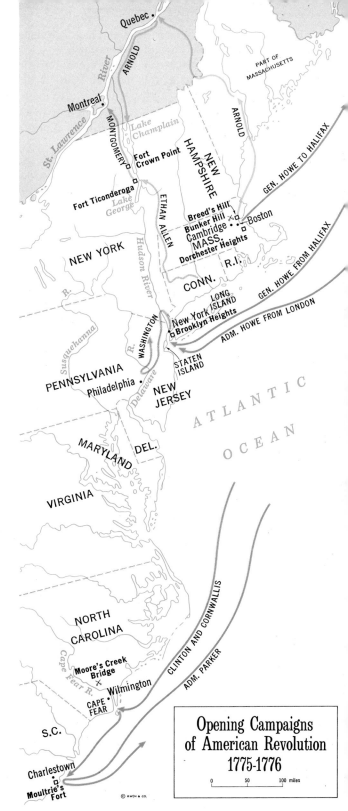

Opening Campaigns
of American Revolution
1775-1776

0   50   100 miles

Note the failure of the campaign in Canada, the British effort to control the southern coast, 1 the shifting of the battle to the Middle Colonies.

Yet the pressures for independence were very great. An army was in the field, fighting the king's soldiers. For what was it fighting? The answer, Independence, was inevitably heard more and more, though not yet loudly and clearly.

Tom Paine's *Common Sense*. Early in 1776 a pamphlet was published that made the argument for independence better than it had ever been made before. The pamphlet, called *Common Sense,* had been written by Thomas Paine, who had recently arrived in America from England.

Paine shocked many people by his words. For example, he called George III the "Royal Brute of Great Britain." Yet Paine's words were convincing, and they had widespread influence:

> Every thing that is right or reasonable pleads for separation. The blood of the slain, the weeping voice of nature cries, 'TIS TIME TO PART. Even the distance at which the Almighty hath placed England and America is a strong and natural proof that the authority of the one over the other, was never the design of heaven. . . .

Lee's proposal. Since many newspapers were also calling for independence, and since the army was begging for assistance that could come only through independence, the Second Continental Congress acted. On June 7, 1776, Richard Henry Lee, of Virginia, rose to propose that it adopt the resolution That these United Colonies are, and of right ought to be, free and independent States. . . .

Although John Adams quickly seconded the motion, some of the delegates, still hesitant, urged postponing a vote on the proposal. They won a brief delay.

Preparing the words. Finally, on July 2 the Congress approved Lee's resolution calling for independence. Meanwhile a committee had been formed to prepare a declaration of independence.

The committee—Thomas Jefferson, of Virginia; Benjamin Franklin, of Pennsylvania; John Adams, of Massachusetts; Roger Sherman, of Connecticut; and Robert R. Livingston, of New York—agreed on the declaration's general content. Then a subcommittee made up of Jefferson and Adams was chosen to put it in shape.

Jefferson and Adams. The actual final writing (see pages 701–702) was largely Thomas Jefferson's. Years later Adams told how this had come about: "Jefferson proposed to me to make the draught . . . I said, 'I will not.'

'You should do it.'

'Oh! no.'

'Why will you not? You ought to do it.'

'I will not.'

'Why?'

'Reason enough.'

'What can be your reasons?'

'Reason first__. You are a Virginian, and a Virginian ought to appear at the head of this business. Reason second__. I am obnoxious, suspected and unpopular. You are very much otherwise. Reason third __. You can write ten times better than I can.'

'Well,' said Jefferson, 'if you are decided I will do as well as I can.'

'Very well, when you have drawn it up we will have a meeting.'"

"The immortal Declaration," as later generations came to revere it, made separation from England the goal of the American Revolution. "We hold these truths to be self-evident:" it begins, "That all men are created equal. . . ." It does not say "all Englishmen"—it says "all men."

For history and the world. Because of the Declaration of Independence, the conflict raging between mother country and colonies took on a new meaning. It now encouraged the struggle of downtrodden men everywhere to be free.

The Declaration of Independence became in time a beacon light of hope for all humanity. When it was written, though, it

Have the class turn to the Declaration on pp. 701-702. What rights does Jefferson discuss? In his view, when is revolution justified? How can the Declaration of Independence be related to revolutions in modern times?

…y did Jefferson list such a wide range of …ges against the English king?

…was splendid propaganda, offering in its second part a list of twenty-eight charges of tyranny against George III.

The signatures. Congress debated Jefferson's Declaration on the afternoon of July 2, on July 3, and on part of July 4. It then approved the document "unanimously." John Hancock, as president of the Congress, signed it first, and other members affixed their names in a formal signing ceremony on August 2.

Some of the signatures were probably added later, for Congress seems to have made signing it a condition for a new member of Congress to take his seat. Copies of the Declaration of Independence were sent to all the *former* colonies.

Men began to measure the step they had taken. Even as the debate was taking place, John Adams was writing to his dear Abigail. He said, "I am well aware of the toil, and blood, and treasure, that it will cost us to maintain this declaration and support and defend these States. Yet through all the gloom I can see the rays of ravishing light and glory."

Some immediate effects. Having declared their independence, the Americans could form state governments, seek foreign aid, and create a national government. The fulfillment of the many other dreams they had would have to wait for the successful outcome of the war. Meanwhile they were sure that free and independent America would be, "with the blessing of the Almighty, great among the nations of the earth."

At Washington's headquarters in New York there was interest in the Declaration of Independence when news of its adoption arrived, but there was scarcely time to reflect upon it. The landing of General Howe on Staten Island was causing grave concern. Nevertheless, on July 9, in a hot summer's sun, Washington's brigades were drawn up in formation to listen to a reading of the Declaration.

Fort Ticonderoga Library

Americans rejoiced in the streets as news of the adoption of the Declaration of Independence was brought to them "live" from Philadelphia.

An observer said the words were received without any show of emotion, although three cheers were given. That night some soldiers, together with a crowd of civilians, pulled down the gilt statue of George III situated in lower New York and cut off its head. Later, bullets were made from the statue for the American army.

1. What move did the colonists make in 1775 to patch things up with England? What was the result? 2. Name the first battle of the American Revolution and tell what occurred. 3. On what group of southern colonists did the British rely? With what result? 4. How did Fort Moultrie get its name? 5. Account for the American campaign against Canada, 1775–1776, and describe the outcome. 6. What strategy did the British plan for the control of New York? 7. How did it work out? 8. By whom was the Declaration of Independence written, what did it contain, and on what day was it signed? 9. Name some immediate effects.

…fter proclaiming independence as a war aim, the Americans found it easier to get foreign …stance. Why? (Would foreign powers risk war with England to help the colonists modify …ish laws?)

The Rebels Rely on Pluck, Luck, and the French

Meanwhile the struggle to make independence real went on. Washington was terribly discouraged by the loss of New York (see page 194) and other points. Moreover, he found his ranks being constantly thinned by desertions and by the # departure for home of men who had completed their enlistments.

Reserves and Recoveries

Pushed out of New York, Washington and his forlorn troops fell back across New Jersey into Pennsylvania. They crossed the Delaware River at Trenton in December, 1776.

Enlisting the men. Washington was writing to his cousin at about this time, "Our only dependence now is upon the speedy enlistment of a new army. If this fails, I think the game will be pretty well up."

There was, it seemed, nothing now to prevent the British from occupying Philadelphia, too. The Second Continental Congress, aware of being a special target in case the British took the city, slipped away to Baltimore.

Low spirits. The spirits of the American people struck a new low. They sorely needed some encouragement. For a time it came chiefly from Tom Paine. He wrote, in one of a series of widely read pamphlets called *The Crisis:* "These are the times that try men's souls: The summer soldier and the sunshine patriot will, in this crisis, shrink from the service of their country; but he that stands it *now* deserves the love and thanks of man and woman."

Washington bore the brunt of severe criticism—the fate of generals when they are not winning. Moreover, his troops were still dwindling as enlistments expired. Washington knew that he must counterattack before January 1, 1777, when many more of his men were to go home.

Falling on the Hessians. From his encampment in Pennsylvania, Washington could gaze across at Trenton, New Jersey, and down at Bordentown. These places were held by some of the thirty thousand German troops hired by the British to help them fight the Americans.

Many, though not all, of the men came from the German state of Hesse-Kassel. Hence they were all usually called Hessians, which came to be a term of contempt that patriots uttered with a sneer. The Hessians had only scorn for the Americans—whom one of them called country clowns.

But the "country clowns" put one over on the Hessians. On Christmas night, 1776, when the Hessians were sleeping off the effects of some of the heaviest drinking ever seen in Trenton, Washington and his troops crossed the Delaware River. Under cover of darkness, the patriot army braved the ice, cold, and flooding waters to reach the other side and smash the Hessians. Their watchword described the situation: "Victory or Death!"

The surprise of the Germans was so complete that the American soldiers—the Continentals—had scarcely begun to fire on them when they surrendered. Almost a thousand German officers and men were captured, and valuable ammunition was seized. The Battle of Trenton was brought to a swift close, a mighty victory for Washington, who recrossed the Delaware. Greatly heartened, many Continentals decided not to leave the army, as they had planned, but to stay on and fight.

At dawn January 3, 1777, Americans under General Hugh Mercer opened battle with the surprised British just outside Princeton. Mercer was killed, and the outlook was bad until Washington—on horseback, center—rode up with the main forces. Mercer's son William painted this picture.

:ate Trenton and
nceton on the map
p. 201.

Cornwallis outsmarted. The British were very much upset by the turn of events. They sent General Charles Cornwallis hurrying from New York with reinforcements to attack Washington. The American commander in chief again moved across the Delaware to Trenton.

Cornwallis could have begun a battle immediately upon his arrival late on January 2, 1777. But he decided to wait until the next day—a terrible mistake, as he soon found out.

During the night Washington, sensing disaster, slipped out with his army and marched in the darkness to Princeton, New Jersey. There he met and destroyed a British unit and captured its supplies.

The British withdrew all but a few garrisons from New Jersey, which left it practically cleared of the enemy. One British officer moaned, "We have been boxed about in Jersey as if we had no feelings." As Washington and his army settled in at Morristown, New Jersey, for the winter, the British knew that the American rebellion was not going to be crushed quickly.

"Gentleman Johnny." Another critical turn came early in 1777, when the British tried to cut New England off from the rest of the colonies. The hopeful British commanding general was "Gentleman Johnny" Burgoyne. He had arrived to assist General Gage in 1775 and already knew the fierceness with which Americans could fight. "Gentleman Johnny" was both handsome and gifted—at writing plays.

Burgoyne had convinced the British that they would win in America if they adopted his plan to cut New England off from the rest of the colonies. The plan called for a three-way movement of troops. The main force, of not less than eight thousand men under his direct command, was to press southward from Canada, coming along Lake Champlain to Fort Ticonderoga and the upper Hudson.

Another force was to push eastward from Fort Oswego along the Mohawk Valley. General Howe, meanwhile, was to set out from New York and take control of the Hudson. Burgoyne and Howe were to meet at Albany.

te the importance of Trenton and Princeton in restoring colonial hopes after a year of astrous reverses. Although in March, 1776, the British evacuated Boston, throughout the t of that year Washington's army had to make one retreat after another.

#To explain this statement, use John Adams' belief that the American Revolution had been accomplished in the "hearts and minds of the people" before the war began.

It is not clear that the British could have
put down the rebellion even if their plan had been carried out successfully. New England might have been isolated for a time, but the patriots would have been far from finished. At any rate, the plan failed.

General Howe decided to capture Philadelphia first and then send only a portion of his troops up the Hudson to Albany. Burgoyne, meanwhile, had set forth from Canada with some crack English troops and some of the best German soldiers. He was able to capture Fort Ticonderoga, which the American general, Arthur St. Clair, simply could not defend for want of sufficient troops.

Effects of surrender at Ticonderoga. For the Americans the loss of Fort Ticonderoga (so dramatically won in 1775—see page 192) was a terrible blow. It seemed that the way for the British to capture Albany now surely lay open. But Burgoyne, though confident, was also having troubles. He had no less than six hundred wagons slowly—oh, so slowly—pulling his supplies through the wilderness.

Burgoyne's army had consumed its food

before it reached Albany. Hearing of grain and other supplies in Vermont, Burgoyne detached a force of Hessians and Tories to seize them. The soldiers that he sent out were surprised by American General John Stark and two thousand militiamen, including the Green Mountain Boys. In the Battle of Bennington, the Americans either killed or took prisoner the entire Hessian group of more than seven hundred men.

Heroic Herkimer. Meanwhile the British troops (including Hessians, Loyalists, and Indians), led by Colonel Barry St. Leger, pushed toward the Mohawk River and succeeded in laying siege to Fort Stanwix. An American of German ancestry, Nicholas Herkimer, and his men, who were marching to the relief of the fort, were ambushed near the town of Oriskany by an enemy force. Soon one of the bloodiest battles of the war followed.

Herkimer, though fatally wounded, had himself propped up against a tree, from where he directed the battle with his pipe clenched between his teeth. Another American force—of about a thousand men—under Benedict Arnold frightened the Indians in the British army so thoroughly that they deserted. St. Leger had no choice now but to return to Oswego.

The loss of Philadelphia. Burgoyne was determined to press on toward Albany—although his prospects were darkening because of events outside his control. If he was counting on help from New York, he was sadly mistaken. Troops under Sir Henry Clinton started up the Hudson but timidly turned back at the site of present-day Kingston, New York.

Howe, of course, was on his way not to join Burgoyne but to take Philadelphia. The idea was not a completely crazy one. He believed that the Loyalists around the city would be "so numerous and so ready to give every aid . . . in their power" that the rest of Pennsylvania could be easily conquered. Howe was sure that if he succeed-

General Herkimer gave his life to protect Fort Stanwix, the key to the Mohawk Valley.

Library of Congress

##What value would the capture of Philadelphia, the American capital, have for the British?

ed in this attempt, Maryland and New Jersey would fall to him, too.

Brandywine and Germantown. Before the end of September, 1777, General Howe's troops had sailed up Chesapeake Bay and had taken Philadelphia, the American capital. Washington and his men had tried to stop him outside the city, at Brandywine Creek, but they were thrown back and forced to retreat to Chester. They quickly recovered, though, and early in October they attacked the main body of the British army, which was encamped at the village of Germantown, Pennsylvania, just outside Philadelphia.

The assault, well planned but badly executed, failed. The Americans, caught in a blinding fog made worse by the smoke of battle, panicked and began to retreat. General Anthony Wayne wrote sadly, "We ran from Victory."

The Battles of Brandywine and Germantown, coming close together in 1777, greatly weakened Washington's forces. Despite strong American defenses around the city of Philadelphia, the Howe brothers, one of them moving by land and the other by sea, cleared the Delaware River area of resistance. Before 1777 had ended, the British controlled traffic on the river.

The gloom of the patriots—except the greatest Philadelphian, Benjamin Franklin—was thick. Then in Paris, Franklin, when told that Howe had taken Philadelphia, answered, "No, Philadelphia has captured Howe!"

Franklin must have meant that Howe would get little coöperation from the people of the city. He proved to be wrong. In fact, not only was Howe well received, but he also put the citizens to work with his soldiers building fortifications which made the city safe against a rebel attack.

Follow the British moves to capture the state of New York and to cut the colonies in two.

Campaigns of Late 1776 and 1777

0   25   50   75 miles

© RM&H & CO.

The fall of Philadelphia hurt patriot morale, further hindering Washington's efforts to recruit men, money, and supplies. Yet Washington kept his army together and prevented Howe from reinforcing Burgoyne. In the end, the army proved more important than the capital.

Into winter quarters. Actually, Washington's army was in no condition to launch an attack on Philadelphia. A week before Christmas, 1777, his ragged, exhausted men set up winter quarters in the drab hills of Valley Forge, some twenty miles outside Philadelphia.

Meanwhile, what was happening to Burgoyne? Howe had learned of the defeat at Bennington, but he had also discovered how strong Americans could be in the fighting around Philadelphia. The result was that he had decided he could not spare troops to aid "Gentleman Johnny."

Burgoyne was now aware that he probably was not going to receive help from Clinton, either. But crossing over to the west side of the Hudson River on September 13, he continued to push southward to Albany.

In September, 1777, Burgoyne and his troops met American forces under the overall command of General Horatio Gates. After a brief but fierce fight at an abandoned farm owned by a Mr. Freeman, the Americans were forced to withdraw. At the Battle of Freeman's Farm they had, though, inflicted very heavy losses on the British.

The rebel and redcoat soldiers for the next several weeks engaged in hit-or-miss skirmishes in the same vicinity. Suddenly this tense period was ended. Burgoyne, on October 7, 1777, took the offensive, but his army was thrown back to Bemis Heights—with heavy losses.

Brave Arnold. General Gates had hoped merely to defend his army from the enemy. But General Benedict Arnold suddenly rushed from his tent, mounted his bay horse, and led the cheering American troops in a headlong attack on the British force. An American officer was later to write, "Nothing could exceed the bravery of Arnold on this day."

Burgoyne's ranks melted away under the withering musket fire of the rebels, many of whom perched themselves in trees. A redcoat reported afterward that there was "seldom a minute's interval of smoke in any part of our line without officers being taken off by single shot."

Surrender at Saratoga. From Bemis Heights Burgoyne's army retreated to Saratoga. There, at the Battle of Saratoga, the British were surrounded by the Americans. Burgoyne's dreams were now lost. He had been let down by those who might have rescued him, and his ranks were now growing thinner hourly. He himself, he wrote, was "sunk in mind and body." On October 17, 1777, he surrendered his army with all its equipment as the American band played "Yankee Doodle."

The British troops were allowed to march off after handing over their arms. The men were to be returned to England "on condition of not serving again in North America during the present conflict." The Battle of Saratoga was a victory without parallel for the Americans. It has been called the turning point of the War for Independence.

In England Parliament demanded an explanation from Burgoyne. He told his hearers that he had learned two important things. The first was that the patriots had a powerful weapon in their boundless enthusiasm. The second was that the Loyalists in America could not be counted on for help. Never again did Burgoyne command an army.

The shame of Valley Forge. As the year 1778 opened, the American future was uncertain but by no means without promise. Exuberant patriots expected Washington to handle Howe as Gates had handled Burgoyne. But the American soldiers were suffering at Valley Forge as few fighting men have ever suffered—from a lack of support from their countrymen.

Washington reported to Congress on December 23, 1777, that about twenty-nine hundred of his men were "unfit for duty

#According to the usual military practice before the Revolution, ranks of soldiers exchanged regular volleys. The Americans changed these tactics--and alarmed the British--by having sharpshooters continually trying to pick off officers.

Commander in Chief Washington, astride a white horse, reviews his ragged soldiers, some barefoot in the snow.

Discuss why the home front often failed the army.

because they were barefoot and otherwise naked." General Wayne implored, "Not one whole shirt to a Brigade. For God's sake give us—if you can't give us anything else —give us linen that we may be Enabled to Rescue the poor Worthy fellows from the Vermin which are now Devouring them."

There is just one explanation for this shocking state of affairs: the American home front failed the troops. First, supplies were often taken away from the rebel army to be sold to more profitable markets, including the British army! Second, there was an incredible lack of transportation to Valley Forge. At the height of the soldiers' food and clothing shortages, teamsters went on strike because they said they could not afford to work for the low pay Congress had set.

Third, in November, 1777, Thomas Mifflin, of Pennsylvania, resigned as army quartermaster (the officer in charge of supplies and equipment). Congress then bungled by failing for three months to appoint a replacement.

Tragically, there was abundant food throughout the country, and the food shortage could have been avoided. Sadly, grafters and some merchants were profiting while the men who bore arms were made to feel forgotten.

The Turn of the Tide

What held the little American army together in the face of such grim conditions? ## First of all, the men were filled with what the Hessian commander called so well the "spirit of liberty." Such men do not mutiny.

Second, the strength of George Washington in the face of his men's suffering and in the face of his personal enemies' attempts to remove him held the tottering troops together. Third, in the midst of the crisis, a number of foreign officers arrived who helped train the patriot soldiers and who notably raised their spirits.

Steuben to the rescue. By springtime a new and optimistic outlook had developed at Valley Forge. One of the heroes of the

Despite the troubles of the Continental army, the question remains, How did an ill-equipped and often poorly trained army stand up to a much larger force representing the world's most powerful nation at that time?

What type of government did France have at the time? How did French aristocrats assist in their own downfall by aiding the colonial rebels? (The French Revolution broke out in 1789.)

Benjamin Franklin, whose plain dress contrasts sharply with the elegant clothing of French nobles and their ladies, appears at a French reception.

Old Print Shop

wonderful revival was the Prussian Baron Friedrich von Steuben, who arrived when things were at their worst. Steuben had volunteered his services to Washington.

A genial and tactful man, Steuben soon won the good will and even the affection of the American troops. From him they learned military discipline and the technique of drill—necessities for training a successful army. More than that, he taught the men how to use their bayonets better and how to charge upon the enemy.

Food, clothing, and some music. By springtime, 1778, an army was forming that could fight professionally. The supplies of clothing and food increased.

The scene was improved, too, by the arrival of the wives of some of the generals —for example, Mrs. Washington and Mrs. Nathanael Greene. They visited the sick and helped organize social events, including musicales and play-acting. As the weather warmed, the nightmare of neglect by the home front ended, even though victory was still far off.

The Treaty of Alliance and Friendship. Early May brought bright news from abroad that lifted morale as nothing else did. France had come to the side of America by signing the Treaty of Alliance and

Friendship at Paris in February. How had this marvelous turn of affairs come about?

A few months after the Declaration of Independence, Congress had appointed three representatives to go to France to seek help. They were Benjamin Franklin; Arthur Lee, of Virginia; and Silas Deane, of Connecticut.

Franklin was by far the most important of the three. Seventy years old, he had a ticklish job to do. Known personally better than any other American, he was to Frenchmen "the man who had drawn lightning from the skies"—a tribute to his experiments with electricity.

Benjamin Franklin's contribution. Franklin was well acquainted with human nature. Knowing that the French were fascinated by Americans, whom they regarded as a remarkable people living free of the restrictions in Europe, Franklin decided to play a role. He took off the wig he usually wore in Philadelphia and put on instead a fur hat—the headgear of a frontiersman. He wrote from Paris in a letter:

Figure me in your mind . . . very plainly dressed, wearing my thin gray straight hair, that peeps out under my only coiffure, a fine fur cap, which

#Point out that success in diplomacy, like victory in war, takes many months of preparation. What tactics did Franklin use in France? How do politicians still "play a role" in order to win support?

comes down my forehead almost to my spectacles. Think how this must appear among the powdered heads of Paris!

Franklin, a hero in France and cheered everywhere, used his popularity to advantage as a diplomat. But his shrewdness alone had not brought France to the side of the colonies. Ever since their disastrous defeat at British hands in the French and Indian War, the French had been looking for revenge. The revolt of England's colonies provided a glorious opportunity to find it at last.

The French, understandably, did not make an official move to aid America until they had news of some rebel military success. There was clearly nothing to be gained from supporting a *losing* cause. A *winning* cause was another thing.

When the news that Burgoyne had surrendered at Saratoga reached Paris in December, 1777, the French began to think of aiding the Americans actively. Franklin hurried them along by hinting that unless France provided help, the rebels would probably make up with Britain.

The French feared that if Britain and the colonies were brought back together, they might jointly attack the French West Indies. For this and other reasons, the treaty which the French agreed to in 1778 pledged them to help the Americans.

To many Americans the arrangement seemed amazing, for as we have seen, the French and the English-speaking people had long been fighting one another in the American wilderness. But now they were allies: each side needed the other for its own purposes. When word of the treaty of alliance with France reached George Washington, he declared: "I believe no event was ever received with more heartfelt joy."

Other European help. Spain, as another old-time enemy of Britain, could also be helpful to the colonists. The Spanish king, however, wanted to avoid encouraging the independence of the British colonies lest the idea of shaking off the crown spread to the Spanish colonies, too.

In 1779 the Spanish entered the American struggle against Britain anyhow. They were infuriated by the refusal of the British to turn over to them the valuable Mediterranean naval base of Gibraltar.

The Netherlands also helped the Americans, although Dutch military strength was limited. Old trade rivals of the English, the Dutch supplied military equipment to the patriots from the islands of the Dutch West Indies.

The angry English went to war against the Dutch in 1780, quickly destroyed Dutch shipping, and took over the Dutch East Indies. These defeats did not prevent the Netherlands from making a generous loan to America in 1782.

We see that England, beyond question the most powerful nation in the world, had enemies on every side. The American colo-

Franklin in his fur hat, seen here as he looked to admiring Frenchmen.

nies reaped the benefit. Possibly the most important result of the help foreign friends gave America was that England was forced to keep its powerful navy scattered around the world. It could not center it in American waters, where its full use against the rebellion could have turned the tide.

John Paul Jones. An important result of the French alliance was that American naval vessels, as well as privateers, could operate against England out of French ports. The naval hero of the patriots was Captain John Paul Jones. It was he who, on December 3, 1775, raised the first American flag on a naval vessel.

In 1777 Jones took command of the *Ranger,* a spanking new 18-gun ship built at Portsmouth, New Hampshire, and sailed it to France. From there, after the treaty with France went into effect, he conducted a daring raid on the British coast, setting fires at the water's edge.

The high moment of Jones's exploits came in September, 1779. Jones was then in command of a worn-out ship the French king had put at his disposal. Jones had renamed the ship the *Bon Homme Richard* (in honor of Benjamin Franklin, whose *Poor Richard's Almanack* had first won him fame as a printer).

While sailing his ship on a bold raiding expedition around the British Isles, Jones came upon the British warship *Serapis,* a larger vessel than his own. Undaunted, he sailed in close, lashed his ship to the *Serapis* to reduce the advantage of the enemy's guns, and launched a hand-to-hand attack with pistols, muskets, and knives.

Three and a half hours later, the battle —one of the bloodiest in naval history— ended by moonlight as the *Serapis* surrendered. The *Bon Homme Richard,* afire and leaking, was kept afloat for a time by the use of pumps. It sank later, after Jones and his men had boarded the *Serapis.*

When the battle was at its fiercest and Jones and his ship seemed doomed, the British commander asked the American if he was ready to give up. Bravely Jones replied, "I have not yet begun to fight."

The victory seemed, indeed, a triumph of David over Goliath. Because the battle took place in Europe, Jones was even more widely hailed in France than in the United States. His exploits did much to cement relations between France and the United States.

John Barry. Meanwhile, at home Washington's army was beginning to look ahead to new campaigns. It had been a long time since the rebels had won a victory on land. The last real cheering had been for Captain John Barry's courage in capturing in the lower Delaware River several transports with supplies headed for the British army at Philadelphia.

Barry, who had been a successful shipmaster and shipowner in Philadelphia before the war, ranks just below Jones among the naval heroes of the Revolution. He is remembered best for his victory at sea over two British vessels just before the fighting ended.

Indians in the struggle. But if Britain was to be defeated, it would have to be defeated on land. An American victory was dependent not only on the fighting of the two trained American armies but also on the efforts of American frontiersmen. In the War for Independence, the back country was the scene of sharp clashes which seemed to be matters of life and death.

Using their Indian allies, the British did not hesitate to seek the total destruction of Americans living beyond the edge of the older, settled areas. In 1778, for instance, British troops and their Indian allies burned and sacked Pennsylvania settlements along the banks of the Susquehanna River. The same year the brilliant Mohawk war chief, Joseph Brant, together with British soldiers, led a shameful massacre of Americans near Lake Otsego.

Along the frontier, particularly in Penn-

Why did Americans have trouble creating and maintaining a navy during the war? Discuss the role of privateers and explain what is meant by a naval blockade. Why did John Paul Jones operate in European waters?

hy did the Indians usually favor the British over e Americans? (Recall the Proclamation of 1763.)

sylvania, the settlers lived in constant dread of the Indians. In 1779 George Washington sent General John Sullivan to lay waste Iroquois land, which extended from Lake Ontario to the Susquehanna and from the Catskill Mountains to Lake Erie. Supported by other generals and their troops, Sullivan burned Iroquois villages and ripe fields. He succeeded in defeating the Indian and Loyalist forces near what is now Elmira, New York.

The defeated Indians were driven mercilessly toward Fort Niagara. The following winter, because of the terribly cold weather, hundreds of Indian families starved and froze to death. Although chased from the Susquehanna, Mohawk, and Allegheny river valleys, the Indians had not been wiped out, and the British continued to use them to advantage.

Clark in the old Northwest. At almost the same time, another kind of fighting was taking place in the old Northwest. The

Chicago Historical Society

Below: The *Bon Homme Richard*, left, attacks the *Serapis*, right. *Above:* John Paul Jones, commander of the American ship, though only 5 feet 6 inches in height, was a giant of the navy in the Revolution.

United States Naval Academy Museum (Photo by Stu Whelan)

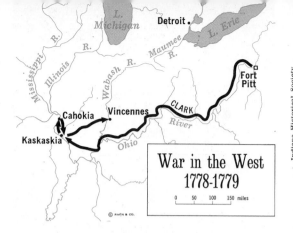

Above: Clark's route to Illinois and to Vincennes, in what is now Indiana. *Right:* Clark and his men arrive at Vincennes, after wading across flooded land.

hero from the rebel viewpoint was the young Virginia-born surveyor George Rogers Clark. He set out in 1778 to end once and for all the attacks by Indians who had been stirred up, apparently, by the British at Detroit.

At Detroit the English commander, Colonel Henry Hamilton, had earned an unenviable reputation as the "Hair Buyer." He got the name because, it was said, he paid a bounty to the Indians for every scalp they brought in.

Enthusiastically, Patrick Henry, governor of Virginia, backed up Clark's plan. It was aimed at conquering the entire territory north of the Ohio River and extending American control to the Mississippi. The former French villages (then held by the British) of Kaskaskia and Vincennes were to be captured.

Clark succeeded in seizing Kaskaskia on July 4, and Vincennes fell to another American force. But in December Hamilton attacked Vincennes and retook it. Learning of this turn of events, Clark and his men set out on an eighteen-day journey toward the settlement in early 1779. After brief resistance, they captured the British garrison there, including the "Hair Buyer."

But Clark never was able to move against Detroit. Despite his gallant exploits, the old Northwest remained in British hands. The simple truth was that American military strength was never sufficient to push the enemy out of the region. Also, the British made every effort to hold it because it was rich in furs and skins.

Final Stage

By the early summer of 1778, the war in the Northeast had reached a *stalemate,* a time when events had come to a standstill. An important explanation is that Sir Henry Clinton had replaced General Howe as commanding officer of all British troops in North America.

The Battle of Monmouth. Having been ordered to send troops to attack the French in the West Indies and the Spanish in Florida, Clinton withdrew the army from Philadelphia. He took it back to New York.

Clark's expedition helped direct American attention to the Ohio Valley. It strengthened American claims to this area at the peace conference following the war. What would have happened if this area had remained British instead of becoming American?

On the way the army barely managed to save itself from being routed by the Americans at Monmouth Courthouse, in New Jersey, in June, 1778. The Battle of Monmouth, as it is known, greatly heartened Washington, who was one of its heroes. He now moved his forces to White Plains, New York. There he watched Clinton's troops carefully, but he lacked the forces to attack. Part of his army, as we have seen, had had to be sent off to fight Indians.

Cornwallis again. Because of new orders from England, the scene of action in the war was then shifted to the southern colonies. Sir Henry Clinton was ordered to move south from New York in June, 1778. A timid battle-planner, he placed the actual southern operations in the hands of General Cornwallis, a man who already had a reputation for not being cautious enough.

British sea power. The British counted on their sea power to move their troops to their target, Savannah, Georgia. This sea power, they thought, would place at a disadvantage the American troops, who would have to move overland by the very poor roads available. The British also counted on the support of southern Loyalists, who they expected would be quite numerous.

Both British expectations were mistaken. They were to find out that although the French were never in control of the sea, they were able often to be in the right place when needed.

Further, Loyalists in the South proved to be far less numerous than expected. Indeed, because the back country supported well the patriots' cause in most places, the rebel army was well supplied and the British troops often were not.

The fall of Savannah and Charleston. Clinton's troops, including Hessians and Tories, took Savannah, Georgia, without difficulty on December 29, 1778. The Pole Casimir Pulaski was killed in defending the city.

The city of Charleston, South Carolina, also fell to the British—after a siege lasting several months—in May, 1780. The fall of Charleston was the severest single loss of the war. The American general, Benjamin Lincoln, was forced to surrender not only over five thousand men but also several ships and all his supplies.

As many Americans in Georgia and South Carolina were flocking to take again the oath of allegiance to the king, England's General Clinton was feeling very hopeful. In June he left for New York City, leaving Cornwallis in charge of all British troops in the South.

Peace rumors. Rumors spread that Congress was ready to make peace by agreeing to leave the two southernmost colonies in Britain's hand. But Congress passed a unanimous resolution stating, "This Confederacy is most sacredly pledged to support the liberty and independence of every one of its members."

The "Swamp Fox." Although fortune seemed now to smile on British efforts, patriots' resistance in the South was fierce. They engaged in what we now call *guerrilla* warfare—in which bands of men attack the enemy independently.

Fighters like Francis Marion, who earned fame as the "Swamp Fox" because of his cunning fighting in difficult surroundings, jabbed at the British and Tory troops day and night. Moreover, the rebels were heartened to know that they had not been abandoned or forgotten by Congress —or by George Washington.

In June some of Washington's forces under Baron Johann de Kalb—another brilliant foreign officer who had joined the rebel cause—arrived in North Carolina. They were soon strengthened by soldiers under General Horatio Gates, the "hero of Saratoga," who had been appointed by Congress to take General Lincoln's place.

Have students bring to class news of recent examples of guerrilla warfare. Why can guerrilla
rfare sometimes be more successful than traditional military operations? Why is guerrilla
rfare so difficult to combat?   209

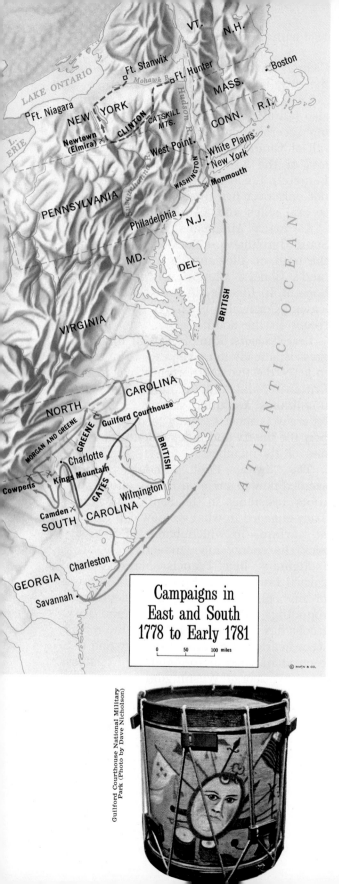

Campaigns in
East and South
1778 to Early 1781

0   50   100 miles

© RM'N & CO.

Use the map to review how England moved the war from the northern to the southern colonies.

At Camden. Under Gates the Americans marched directly against a British supply base at Camden, South Carolina, August 16, 1780. There they were met by redcoats reinforced by troops under Cornwallis. In the fierce Battle of Camden, the Americans were badly weakened by hunger and illness—and by their commander, General Gates, who made one mistake in judgment after another. They fought as well as they could, but then, dropping their weapons, they fled, leaving behind Baron de Kalb, fatally wounded.

Gates rode away, not stopping until he reached Charlotte, North Carolina, 60 miles away. Later he was removed from his command. Washington sent the former Quaker blacksmith from Rhode Island, Nathanael Greene, to head American forces in the South. Greene was a gifted leader of men who had long been denied full recognition because of petty jealousies.

Kings Mountain. By the time Greene arrived in the North Carolina–South Carolina region, Cornwallis had already begun to find things turning against him. At a ridge on the border between the Carolinas called Kings Mountain, in October, 1780, a force of patriot riflemen succeeded in capturing or killing 1100 Tory troops. The losses were a serious blow to Cornwallis, who was depending on the men.

When Greene took over in early December, he divided his troops into small, fast-moving units which could avoid destruction by slipping away quickly. In short, Greene used guerrilla methods, which had already proved successful in the South. Some of his troops were commanded by Daniel Morgan, a master of warfare.

It was against Morgan that Cornwallis

#Both Gates and Arnold were men for whom the war brought fame and then disgrace.
Left above: From June, 1778, to the end of the war, the South was the center of important campaigns. *Left below:* A drum carried by a North Carolina Revolutionary soldier.

sent one of his units. This was a mistake: in the desperate battle that developed at Cowpens, South Carolina, where once cows had grazed, the British were soundly beaten. Cornwallis admitted that he had suffered "a very unexpected and severe blow."

Guilford Courthouse. When at last Greene had received reinforcements, he met the British at Guilford Courthouse, in North Carolina, in March, 1781. Cornwallis forced the Americans to retreat, but he suffered over five hundred casualties. Despite this victory, he knew he had to get out of North Carolina.

Traitor Arnold. Where was Cornwallis to go? For a time he thought of joining Benedict Arnold, who was in command of British raiders in Virginia.

Arnold had committed the greatest treachery of the war. An immensely able soldier, he had felt mistreated by Congress and General Gates. Then, when he was given the command of Philadelphia, he lived so extravagantly—some thought he relied on corruption—that he was court-martialed. But George Washington trusted him still and in 1780 gave him the command of West Point, the military post that controlled the Hudson.

Arnold was no doubt egged on to betray his country by his pretty and extravagant wife, Peggy. His weakness as a man combined with his anger over real and imagined slights and his almost uncontrollable ambition led him to offer to turn over West Point to Sir Henry Clinton.

Arnold's deceitful plans fell apart when his British messenger, Major John André, was accidentally captured with telltale papers hidden in his shoes. The traitor Arnold escaped to British lines, where he was made a brigadier general. Almost immediately he was sent off to Virginia to fight fellow Americans.

The awful fact of Arnold's treason reached the public's ears just after the discouraging news of the defeat at Camden became known. But Arnold's treachery had little effect on the war. Although Arnold appealed to American soldiers to join him, none did. Soon events would make him seem foolish as well as wicked.

The Marquis de Lafayette. When Cornwallis raided Virginia and caused widespread disheartenment there, Washington responded by sending some regiments under the Marquis de Lafayette. Lafayette, a Frenchman of noble birth, had been overjoyed at the news of the outbreak of the American revolt. Leaving his family in France, he had arrived here in 1777 at the age of twenty and immediately had been made a major general.

Quickly becoming a close friend of Washington's, Lafayette served at Brandywine, where he was wounded, and endured the terrible winter at Valley Forge. Now he

Describe the strategy used by the Americans and the French, as shown here.

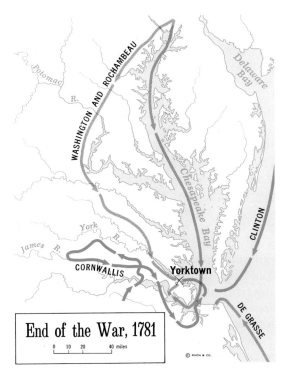

End of the War, 1781

0 10 20   40 miles

uring wars, governments often adopt policies that control or restrict aliens in the belief that   211
tizens can be trusted more than foreigners. What if Congress had adopted such a policy during
e Revolution? Compare Arnold and Lafayette.

John Trumbull painted this picture of the British surrender at Yorktown. General Benjamin Lincoln—center, on horseback— leads the Englishmen between the French troops at the left and his fellow Americans at the right.

was about to gain immortality in American hearts for his faithful service.

The end at Yorktown. Despite the arguments of General Clinton, Cornwallis in 1781 pulled his troops onto the peninsula which lies between the James and York rivers. On August 1 he arrived at Yorktown and began building strong fortifications.

Washington seized the opportunity. He had laid plans with Jean Baptiste de Rochambeau, commander of the French forces in America and a veteran of the French and Indian War, and with Admiral François de Grasse. De Grasse was the strong, towering man who commanded the French fleet in American waters.

At first a combined attack on New York had been arranged, but a change in the plan was made when De Grasse decided to sail into Chesapeake Bay. (The Americans could not control the movements of their powerful ally.) Lying in these waters, the French fleet could blockade Cornwallis. No supplies or troops could reach him.

Meanwhile, Washington and Rochambeau, under cover of secrecy, moved their men across New Jersey toward Yorktown. On the land as well as on the sea, Cornwallis was hemmed in. One of the patriot generals wrote to General Greene, "We have got him handsomely in a pudding bag."

The Battle of Yorktown began near the end of September. Cornwallis made a show of resistance while waiting in vain for Clinton to send a fleet to relieve him. When a fleet finally arrived, it was greeted with the news that Cornwallis, to end the bloodshed, had offered to surrender. He did so on October 19, 1781.

How it felt. Cornwallis himself could not bear to look at the ceremony of surrender. It was well he did not. An eyewitness reported, "The British officers in general behaved like boys who had been whipped at school. Some bit their lips; some pouted; others cried. Their round, broad-brimmed hats were well adapted to the occasion, hiding those faces they were ashamed to show."

Another eyewitness was in London the following month when Lord North heard the news. And how did he take it? Not

Locate Yorktown on the map on p. 211. What other colonial cities, studied earlier, were located near Yorktown? (Jamestown and Williamsburg.)
#Ask students to suggest why the British officers felt as they did.

n making a separate peace, a nation in effect andons its allies.

well. "He opened his arms, exclaiming wildly, as he paced up and down, 'O God! it is all over!'—words which he repeated many times under emotions of the deepest . . . distress."

The peacemakers. The British prime minister now was Lord Shelburne, who, unlike Lord North, thought it England's highest duty to cultivate America's friendship. In Paris, Benjamin Franklin, John Adams, and John Jay negotiated the peace treaty that officially ended the War for Independence. Having pledged in 1778 to make no separate peace, that is, none without France's consent, the men kept the French informed about their talks with the British.

Then one day John Jay learned that the French were secretly negotiating with the British to make a separate peace, that is, one without *our* agreement. The Americans were afraid that France wanted to make a territorial settlement which would divide the area west of the Appalachians between Spain and England and thus, as Franklin said, "coop us up."

Actually, the French were themselves hoping to come back to America. Possibly one day, they dreamed, they would acquire Spain's share of the American West.

The Treaty of Paris. The American treaty commissioners then went ahead and made a separate peace with England. The Treaty of Paris, signed in 1783, provided that England acknowledge American independence. It set the western boundary of the United States at the middle of the #Mississippi River and the southern one at 31° north latitude. (Spain received Florida.) It established the northern boundary

The United States 1783

0   200   400   600 miles

(Eagle) Bennington Museum, Bennington, Vt.
(Delegates) Henry Francis du Pont Winterthur Museum

Right above: Compare this map with the one on page 158. *Right center:* The eagle has been our national symbol since 1782, about when this model was made. *Right below:* An unfinished portrait of the American peace delegates in Paris. Left to right—John Jay, John Adams, Franklin, Henry Laurens, and Franklin's grandson William.

#Why did England prefer having Americans, instead of the French or Spanish, own the area rest of the Appalachians?

The British could have prolonged the war. Why did they make peace? (A longer war might have increased French and Spanish attacks on English colonies in other parts of the world.)

of the United States about where it is today. It gave Americans fishing rights at the Grand Banks, off Newfoundland.

The treaty also provided that Congress recommend to the American states that they pay for Loyalist estates seized during the war. It declared that prewar debts on both sides of the Atlantic would continue to be collectible. Further, it stated that the British would withdraw their fleets and troops from "every port, place, and harbour" in the former colonies.

Washington, "having now finished the work assigned me," as he told Congress, returned to civilian life—to his home at Mount Vernon. But alas, the "work" was only partially done.

A young aide of Washington's, Alexander Hamilton, who was himself a hero of Yorktown, was writing a close associate, "Peace made, my dear friend, a new scene opens. The object will be to make our independence a blessing. To do this we must secure our Union on solid foundations. . . . It requires all the virtue and all the abilities of our country."

Hamilton could have added that no people had ever had an opportunity like the one offered to independent America as the 1780's ran their course.

1. What two setbacks did Americans hand the British in late 1776 and early 1777? 2. Describe the three-way movement of troops planned by Burgoyne in 1777. 3. What was the outcome of the plan? 4. Tell how each part of the plan was carried out. 5. What was the significance of the Battles of Brandywine, Germantown, and Saratoga? 6. Name three ways in which the home front failed the American troops. 7. What held the American army together? 8. What contribution did Franklin make in the American Revolution? 9. Describe the most important American naval battle of the war. 10. Account for Clark's failure to take the old Northwest. 11. Give the important facts about the war in the South. 12. Describe the final battle of the war. 13. Give the provisions of the Treaty of Paris, 1783.

The Workshop

The Shapers of Our World

Identify each of the following:

Ethan Allen
George
 Washington
Bunker Hill
Loyalists
Benedict Arnold
Trenton
Princeton
Tom Paine
Richard
 Henry Lee

Benjamin
 Franklin
Charles
 Cornwallis
John Burgoyne
Nicholas
 Herkimer
Valley Forge
Saratoga
Baron von **Steuben**
Horatio Gates

Thomas Jefferson
John Paul
 Jones
John Barry
George Rogers
 Clark
Francis Marion
Nathanael Greene

treaty with
 France
Marquis
 de Lafayette
Kings Mountain
François
 de Grasse
Treaty of Paris

Adding to Your Vocabulary

Be sure you understand these terms:

back country
stalemate

strategy
mortification

Discuss the terms of the Treaty of Paris of 1783. Ask students to try to determine which parts of the treaty would cause future trouble. For a recent study of the peace conference, see Richard B. Morris, The Peacemakers (Harper & Row, 1965).

guerrilla   pacifist
 warfare   consternation
corruption

2. Would the writing of the peace treaty have been different if France had not been our ally?

Thinking Things Through

After reviewing the exercises in the chapter, try to answer these questions:

1. Why did most colonists think the patriot troops had won a victory at Breed's Hill even though they had been forced from it? What influence do you think this fighting had on the colonists who were undecided about revolting against England?

2. Why do you think the French residents of Canada did not revolt against British rule during the American Revolution? (Review the Quebec Act, page 183.)

3. Look at the signatures to the Declaration of Independence, shown on pages 702–703. Why did saying "Give me your John Hancock" become a popular way of asking someone to sign his name?

4. Why do you think the patriots waited so long to issue the Declaration of Independence? How did this document make the colonists choose sides in the American Revolution? What effect did the Declaration have on efforts to obtain foreign help?

5. When Cornwallis surrendered at Yorktown, the British band played a tune called "The World Turned Upside Down." Why was such a selection suitable?

6. Many historians regard the Battle of Saratoga as far more important than the Battle of Yorktown in the way the war turned out. Why?

7. In view of the aim of the War for Independence, why were countries like France and Spain willing to coöperate with the colonies in their venture?

Your Opinion, Please

1. Could the Americans have won the Revolution without the help of foreign countries? Explain.

The Research Center

1. The United States government maintains national historical parks named (a) Independence, in Philadelphia; (b) Minute Man, between Lexington and Concord; (c) Morristown, near Morristown, New Jersey; and (d) Saratoga, in New York. It also has national military parks at Guilford Courthouse, Kings Mountain, and Moore's Creek. Find out the difference between national historical parks, national military parks, and national monuments. Why does our government maintain all three? Explain the significance of each of the parks named above.

2. Find out what has happened to the Liberty Bell in the years since it rang to announce American independence.

Sharpening Your Map Skills

1. The English had the most powerful navy in the world in 1775. Look at the maps in this chapter and tell how the English used it to try to defeat the Americans during the Revolution. What successes did their use of the navy bring them? What setbacks did the navy suffer?

2. Compare the scales on the maps in this chapter. Which is largest, and which is smallest? How do you tell? Why are different scales used?

Geography and History

1. What part did weather play in the ## War for Independence? Give examples showing the effects on both the British and the Americans.

2. Why was the control of New York, Philadelphia, Boston, Charleston, and Savannah so important to both sides?

‡Note, for example, that some battles occurred during the winter, a departure from .aditional European military practice.

Part Three Workshop

Time and Change

1. What space of time is covered in Part Three? How many years? Decades?

2. Historians often use the word era to refer to a period of time in which a historical event or development affected people very deeply. What years do you think would be contained in the following eras: (*a*) the era of French power in America; (*b*) the era of the American Revolution?

3. What major changes came to the colonies in (*a*) 1763, (*b*) 1773, (*c*) 1783? What changes came to Britain in each of these years? Be sure to think not only of changes in government and boundaries but also of changes in attitudes.

Then and Now

1. There are many kinds of revolutions, and they have various causes. (*a*) Name some revolutions not aimed at changing governments. (*b*) When is a revolution in government justified?

\# 2. More than fifty countries have won their independence in the lifetimes of your parents. Some became independent through revolutions that were peaceful, and some through revolutions that were not. A class committee should investigate the causes of and methods used in movements that led to the independence of each of the following countries and report about them. Compare each revolution with our own.

a.	Canada	*d.*	Algeria
b.	Mexico	*e.*	Nigeria
c.	India	*f.*	Indonesia

3. Remnants of French culture may be found in the United States as well as in Canada. Eau Claire, Fond du Lac, Prairie du Chien, and De Pere are cities in Wisconsin. Find out what each name means.

Tell how these cities in Illinois got their names: Marseilles, Joliet, La Salle.

Three cities along the Mississippi River are St. Louis, in Missouri, and Baton Rouge and New Orleans, in Louisiana. What do these names mean? One or more students could do research and give a special report on French culture in present-day New Orleans or Quebec.

The Book Shelf

Freidel, Frank. *George Washington, Man and Monument.* New York: Grosset & Dunlap, Inc., 1965. (The life of the man who was "first in war, first in peace, and first in the hearts of his countrymen.")

Grant, Bruce. *American Forts, Yesterday and Today.* New York: E. P. Dutton & Co., Inc., 1965. (Descriptions and pictures of our historic defenses.)

Hagen, Harold K. *A History of American Fishing.* Chicago: Rand McNally & Co., 1967. (On the role of fishermen in American history.)

Hall-Quest, Olga W. *The Bell That Rang for Freedom.* New York: E. P. Dutton & Co., Inc., 1965. (The Liberty Bell.)

Martin, Joseph Plumb. *Yankee Doodle Boy.* New York: William R. Scott, Inc., 1964. (A young soldier's account of his adventures in the American Revolution.)

Russell, Francis, and eds. of *American Heritage* Magazine. *The French and Indian Wars.* New York: The American Heritage Publishing Co., Inc., 1962. (Includes stories of brave colonists.)

Wyman, Edgar P. *A History of American Forestry.* Chicago: Rand McNally & Co., 1967. (An account of an important American industry.)

\#These nations can be used to further a discussion of the results of revolutions. What problems come with independence? What sort of relations do these nations have with their former mother countries?

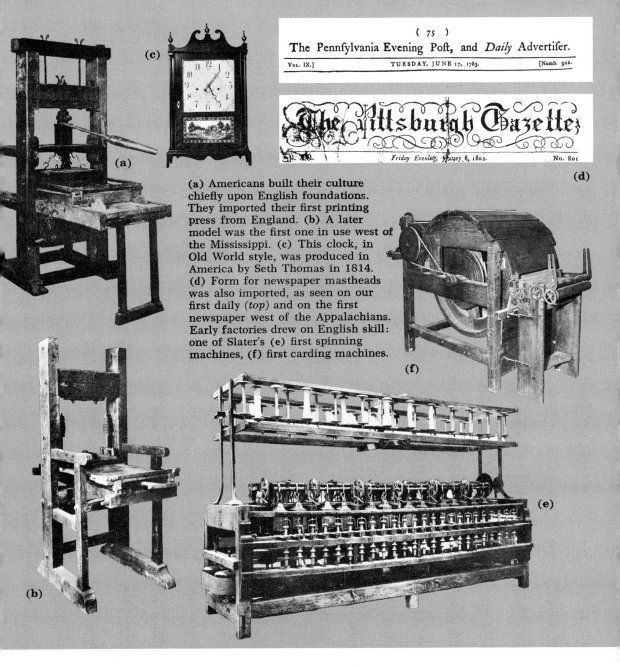

(75)

The Pennſylvania Evening Poſt, and *Daily* Advertiſer.

VOL. IX.]   TUESDAY, JUNE 17, 1783.   [Numb. 922.

The Pittsburgh Gazette

Friday Evening, January 8, 1802.   NO. 801

(a) Americans built their culture chiefly upon English foundations. They imported their first printing press from England. (b) A later model was the first one in use west of the Mississippi. (c) This clock, in Old World style, was produced in America by Seth Thomas in 1814. (d) Form for newspaper mastheads was also imported, as seen on our first daily (*top*) and on the first newspaper west of the Appalachians. Early factories drew on English skill: one of Slater's (e) first spinning machines, (f) first carding machines.

Part Four: SHAPING A NATION

After England accepted the independence of the colonies, Americans had to face a number of new problems. They literally had to shape a nation out of thirteen independent states. Efforts to establish a strong union, to maintain liberty, to defend the country from foreign enemies, and to develop its riches are the subjects of Part Four.

Part Four: SHAPING A NATION

Continued on facing page

A JUST AND BELOVED GOVERNMENT

Although James Madison served as Secretary of State and later as president of the United States, he was only average in both offices. But as the man with a design for a just and beloved government, he is immortal.

Madison was always more comfortable as a writer than as a public person, probably because he did not have the physical appearance that inspires confidence. He was short—only a little over 5 feet tall—and he weighed but 100 pounds. Washington Irving, the author, described him in 1812: "Jemmy Madison—oh, poor Jemmy, he is but a withered applejohn."

Time and Change Trace events that involve relations between the United States and foreign countries

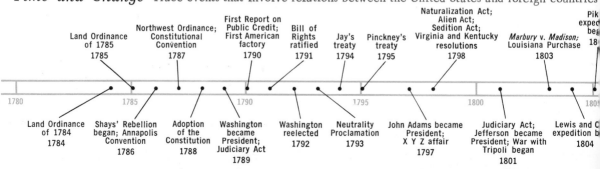

Land Ordinance of 1785 — 1785
Northwest Ordinance; Constitutional Convention — 1787
First Report on Public Credit; First American factory — 1790
Bill of Rights ratified — 1791
Jay's treaty — 1794
Pinckney's treaty — 1795
Naturalization Act; Alien Act; Sedition Act; Virginia and Kentucky resolutions — 1798
Marbury v. Madison; Louisiana Purchase — 1803
Pik expec beg 18

Land Ordinance of 1784 — 1784
Shays' Rebellion began; Annapolis Convention — 1786
Adoption of the Constitution — 1788
Washington became President; Judiciary Act — 1789
Washington reelected — 1792
Neutrality Proclamation — 1793
John Adams became President; X Y Z affair — 1797
Judiciary Act; Jefferson became President; War with Tripoli began — 1801
Lewis and C expedition b 1804

A Virginian, Madison was completing his education at the College of New Jersey (now Princeton) just as the American Revolution broke out. He observed—and learned much—as the British, like Humpty-Dumpty, had a great fall. When peace came in 1783, Madison was already determined that the United States must never be a Humpty-Dumpty.

Throughout the 1780's Madison's thoughts steadily matured. At the Constitutional Convention in Philadelphia in 1787, his were the compelling ideas which shaped the new United States Constitution.

Like Sam Adams, Madison had a "Love of Mankind." But he had come to some conclusions. "If men were angels," he wrote, "no government would be necessary.... In framing a government ... by men over men ... you must first enable the government to control the governed; and in the next place oblige it to control itself."

The completed Constitution seemed to satisfy only the first of these delicate requirements. And Madison, particularly, was dissatisfied. As a member of the first Congress, therefore, he introduced and pressed for the passage of the Bill of Rights. To this day it is the strongest shield protecting the liberties of the people.

With typical shyness Madison always refused credit for his monumental accomplishments. He emphasized that the Constitution "ought to be regarded as the work of many heads and many hands"—as it was. Yet this modest wisp of a man, close friend to Washington, Franklin, and Jefferson, towered among the architects of our republic.

GROWING PAINS OF THE YOUNG REPUBLIC

The Army and Navy Battle a Powerful Foe

The Union Gains in Pride and Strength

The Sections Glare Angrily at Each Other

Discuss Madison's view of men and governments. Do his ideas apply today?

The American bald eagle has been our national symbol since 1782, when the Great Seal of the United States was adopted. This is the face of the seal.

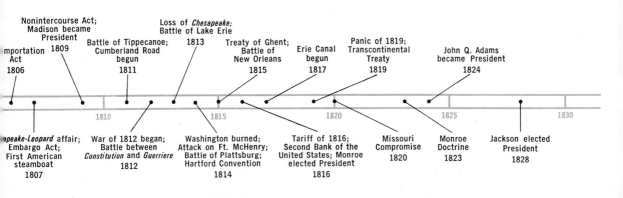

Nonintercourse Act; Madison became President 1809

...mportation Act 1806

Battle of Tippecanoe; Cumberland Road begun 1811

Loss of *Chesapeake;* Battle of Lake Erie 1813

Treaty of Ghent; Battle of New Orleans 1815

Erie Canal begun 1817

Panic of 1819; Transcontinental Treaty 1819

John Q. Adams became President 1824

...apeake-Leopard affair; Embargo Act; First American steamboat 1807

War of 1812 began; Battle between *Constitution* and *Guerriere* 1812

Washington burned; Attack on Ft. McHenry; Battle of Plattsburg; Hartford Convention 1814

Tariff of 1816; Second Bank of the United States; Monroe elected President 1816

Missouri Compromise 1820

Monroe Doctrine 1823

Jackson elected President 1828

1810   1815   1820   1825   1830

(a)

(b)

(a) Members of the Constitutional Convention vote on accepting the Constitution in 1787. Chairman George Washington stands on the platform.
(b) An American penny, minted in 1792.
(c) A reconstruction of a log-cabin school in the Northwest Territory— this one at New Salem, Illinois.
(d) Daniel Boone, one of the stouthearted frontiersmen who helped open up the American West for settlement.
(e) Boone's powder horn, a flask made of horn for carrying gunpowder.

(c)

(d)

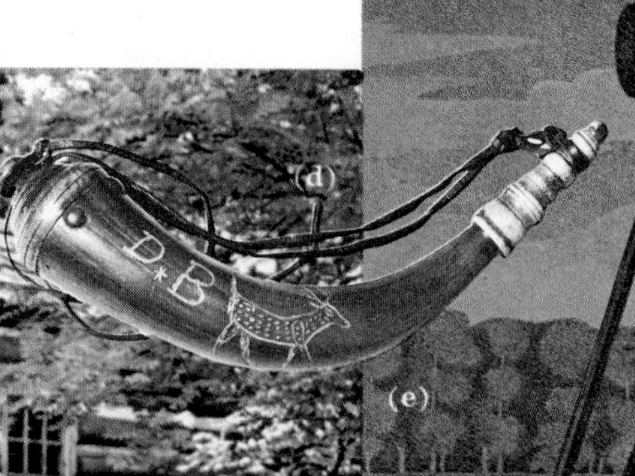

(e)

We the People *of the United States, in order to form a more perfect Union, establish justice,*

Article 1.

(f) The preamble—introduction—
to the United States
Constitution.

Have students refer to the page of pictures for clues to the concerns
of both the men who attended the Constitutional Convention and
those who led western settlement.

CHAPTER 11

FASHIONING A NEW GOVERNMENT

ter achieving independence, Americans had to face a number of new problems. Their efforts to over-
me these difficulties and to establish an effective national government are the subjects of this chapter.
ave students compare the situation of newly independent peoples in the world today with that of
mericans in the 1780's.

AMERICANS in 1783 sighed in relief that the fighting of the American Revolution was over. Their energies and emotions had had one purpose: winning the war. Yet a huge new effort was required to make the separate states work together in harmony now that there was no longer an enemy to unite Americans.

Benjamin Franklin, who always looked on the bright side of things, said he could see in America only "little discontents" and "domestic misunderstandings . . . of small extent." He was sure these would quickly disappear. Unfortunately, he was wrong.

Discuss why it is often easier to rally people against something than it is to get them to cooperate
organizing or building something.

Americans Shoulder the Burdens of Freedom

Actually, Americans faced dangerous challenges in the post-Revolutionary years. They had the satisfaction, though, of facing them as a "free and independent" people. The solutions they attempted were their own.

Suggest challenges faced by the new nation.

The Marks of War

All wars leave two kinds of marks on the country they touch. Some can be seen with the naked eye. These are results of the physical damage caused by the fighting it-self. The others cannot be seen. They are the changes in people's outlooks, thoughts, and even ways of life that wars bring about on the home front. Sometimes these do not show up until long after the fighting which causes them has ended.

Rubble and humans. The rebuilding of torn-up communities was faced first. Norfolk, Virginia, for instance, had been set afire first by the British and then by the patriots so that the British could not use it. New York City had been partially destroyed by two fires, one of which, possibly

The marks of war are evident in the world today. Students might suggest those attitudes,
oughts, activities, and situations--especially in their own country--which appear to be the
sult of either current or past wars. Which of the suggestions seem typical of every war?

set to hinder the British, had "reduced to beggary" thousands of the townspeople.

The redcoats, moreover, had sometimes singled out for attack the private property of patriots. Richard Stockton, for example, a signer of the Declaration of Independence, returned from the war to find his beautiful dwelling in New Jersey raided and his library burned.

Many of the personal sorrows of war are the same in every time and place. Those of the War for Independence were no exception: there were new widows, new orphans, and terrifying upsets in people's lives. Few Americans remained unaffected. Many people who had remained Loyalists sadly left the United States in 1783, sure that they could find no satisfactory place in the new country. They, too, were victims of the war.

A destruction of "aristocratic ways." But the chief casualty of the struggle was the earlier "aristocratic way of life" in the colonies. New democratic features of American life were beginning to appear. In part, the nature of the fighting itself produced this result. Around many a campfire at Valley Forge, for instance, both enlisted men and officers must have tried to keep themselves warm—without attention to differences in rank.

For another example, after a man had shared in the experiences and difficulties of army life, it was hard to deny him the vote later. The reason for not giving it to him—that he did not own enough property to qualify—seemed plainly unfair.

In part, too, the gradual disappearance of the "aristocratic way of life" grew out of conditions which became more marked as a result of the war. Skilled workmen, for example, had become scarcer than ever after many years of fighting and little new immigration. A new employer tended not to ask a man his religion or what country he was born in, lest he insult him.

In general, bowing and scraping before one's "betters" (a word commonly used in the eighteenth century) seemed to occur less after the war. The brave words of the Declaration of Independence somehow could not be ignored: "We hold these truths to be self-evident:—That all men are created equal . . . ."

The feeling that one man is as good as another gradually became widespread. Royall Tyler, the Revolutionary War soldier who gained fame as a playwright, wrote of America as the land—

> Where the proud titles of "My Lord!"
> "Your Grace!"
> To humble "Mr." and plain "Sir"
> give place.

Be sure that the meaning of <u>legal</u> and <u>social</u> is clear.

Legal and Social Changes

The break with England also had given Americans an opportunity to write *state constitutions*—documents containing the main principles according to which the states were to be governed. In them the people received more control over their state governments than they had had over their colonial governments. They also provided that people could follow the religion they preferred, and they could say and print what they wished. Most of the constitutions guaranteed persons accused of crimes the right to trial by jury. In other words, people were to enjoy freedom of religion, freedom of speech, freedom of the press, and protection against being unjustly imprisoned.

End of primogeniture. State laws recognized some democratic advances already under way. For example, the arrangement known as primogeniture (prī′ mṓ jĕn′ ĭ tūr) was done away with. Under it in a number of colonies, especially in the South, a man's eldest son alone inherited his father's property, a European practice copied here. Primogeniture was most unfair to children who were not firstborn males. Gradually

#Why did many of the new state constitutions contain a number of provisions for the protection individual rights? Consider what attitudes toward government power are revealed in these state constitutions.

disappearing anyhow, it was ended in all the states.

A limited abolition of slavery. On large plantations in the "Tidewater South," Negro slaves continued to labor without a change in their condition. Slavery, however, had been *abolished*, or ended, in Pennsylvania in 1780. Later Massachusetts, Connecticut, Rhode Island, New York, and New Jersey followed the example of Pennsylvania. But in the northern states slavery had never flourished or been widespread.

Distributing Loyalist property. Although Loyalists' estates were seized in a number of states, they were not all divided into small lots for sale to people who had no land. Usually the estates fell whole into the hands of speculators or other profiteers. Sometimes the results were astonishing. One observer wrote in 1777, "Men who could scarcely maintain their families before the war now live in splendor . . . raised to immense wealth."

Disestablishment of religion. In 1776 every colony except Pennsylvania and Rhode Island had an *established church*. This was a church which each taxpayer helped support whether he was a member of it or not. In New England it was the Congregational church, the main church organization, which placed complete religious authority in the local congregation, led by its minister. In the South the established church was the Church of England (see page 65).

Because the head of the Church of England was the English monarch, it was considered patriotic to *disestablish*—withdraw government support from—the king's church. The southern legislatures eagerly took this important step. Much pressure for disestablishment of the Church of England came, too, from leaders of other religious groups who had long resented having to support a church that was not their own.

Historic St. Luke's Restoration, Smithfield, Va.

St. Luke's Church, in Smithfield, Virginia, was built about 1632. Its members belonged to the established Church of England until about the end of the eighteenth century.

In New England, where the majority of the people were Congregationalists, the disestablishment of the Congregational church did not come right away. In Massachusetts, for instance, it did not occur until 1833.

But a legal landmark that still towers over the early period of our history was the Virginia Statute of Religious Freedom, largely the work of Thomas Jefferson. Men like Patrick Henry and George Washington had wanted to place all Christian churches on an equal footing and let them share equally in government support. Jefferson, on the other hand, wanted a complete *separation of church and state*, that is, a cutting of the ties between churches and government. Jefferson finally had his way.

The eighteenth-century language of the Virginia law which resulted speaks clearly even today: "No man shall be compelled to frequent or support any religious worship, place or ministry whatsoever, nor shall be enforced, restrained, molested, or burthened in his body or goods, nor shall otherwise suffer on account of his religious opinions or beliefs. . . ." In time these principles came to be accepted by every state.

In Jefferson's time, separation of church and state meant primarily ending government financial support of churches and removing religious qualifications for officeholding. Discuss what issues have arisen in our time over the idea of separation of church and state.

223

Note that the family pictured has no wagon. Discuss why this situation was typical.

On foot and horseback, taking their animals with them, these Americans were hopefully moving west, seeking land of their own and new opportunities for themselves and their children.

A fresh thrust westward. Still another hopeful result of the war was a new *mobility,* or trend toward movement, of the population. All wars tend to make it easier for people to pull up their roots and relocate their homes. Moreover, soldiers, shifted from point to point, have opportunities to see unfamiliar places and often decide to settle in them when the fighting is over. The lands west of the Appalachians proved particularly attractive, offering many possibilities to people who were eager to improve themselves.

George Washington expressed the idea this way, "Let the poor, the needy, and the oppressed of the Earth and those who want land, resort to the fertile plains of our western country . . . and there dwell in peace." The *Massachusetts Sentinel* in 1785 published the lines:

\# Where happy millions their own fields possess,
No tyrant awes them, and no lords oppress.

In short, the acquisition by the United States in 1783 of the area extending to the Mississippi had opened wider than ever before one of the choicest of freedoms. Freedom of opportunity was this golden prize.

1. Describe two kinds of marks war leaves on a country. 2. What are two reasons that account for the disappearance of the "aristocratic way of life" in the young United States? 3. Name three rights given people in state constitutions. 4. Give one example of the democratic advances made under state laws. 5. What people were not affected by democratic changes in the United States? 6. What is the relation today between government and churches in our country? Who early favored such a relation? 7. How did the American Revolution affect the mobility of the people?

\#Discuss the concept of land ownership as a protection against tyranny. Take up whether the idea applies in the present-day United States. Why would the viewpoint expressed by the Massachusetts Sentinel be common among Americans in the 1780's?

ar in mind that the Declaration of Independence did not guarantee a union of the thirteen states.
view the New England Confederation of 1643 and the Albany Plan of 1754 and discuss why they
led. Point out the problems of achieving unity in certain new countries today.

The First Union of States Proves Too Weak

As the United States began its history as an independent country, Americans relied heavily on the idea that it already stood alone in the history of mankind. An American of French parentage named Crèvecoeur (krěv′ kûr′) expressed this belief in a widely read series of articles which he called *Letters from an American Farmer*.

In the letters Crèvecoeur pointed out that the "race now called Americans" had been formed from people who had come from many different lands. "Here," he said, "individuals of all nations are melted into a new race of men."

But the new American states had not yet learned to conduct their affairs jointly. Thomas Paine, that old friend of America, was saying in 1783, in one of the last of his great pamphlets, "Our great national character depends on Union of the States."

Thomas Jefferson felt this way, too. He was writing in a letter from Paris in 1785, "The interests of the States ought to be made joint in every possible instance, in order to cultivate the idea of our being one nation."

The Articles of Confederation

The question, then, was, How is a union of the states to be brought about? In the past Americans had shown that they were better at waging war than at putting their government in order. In June, 1776, Congress had appointed a thirteen-man committee to draw up a constitution under which the country could govern itself.

Dickinson's role. The work of writing the constitution had fallen chiefly upon the shoulders of John Dickinson, of Pennsylvania. He had aimed to write a set of rules which would create a strong central government without clipping too much the power of the individual states. His task had required great tact, because the patriots, who were about to break loose from the strong government of Britain, had not wanted a similar strong one of their own. #

The states in control. Dickinson called the government he planned "a firm league of friendship." His blueprint, known as the Articles of Confederation, set up something like an alliance among the states. The states were superior to the national government, which was almost entirely dependent upon them.

The Articles of Confederation could not go into operation until all the states had approved, or *ratified*, them. Ratification was not completed until 1781—when the war was over. Probably the delay was fortunate, because the Articles did not provide for a government strong enough to wage war successfully.

Furthermore, at the start of the war the public was not very willing to accept a demanding government. The Second Continental Congress, despite the good will and authority it enjoyed, met much resistance from the states when they were asked for men and money.

The western lands. It took five years to obtain ratification of the Articles of Confederation. The chief reason for the delay was a dispute over land. Maryland insisted it would not approve the new frame of government until all the states with old charter claims to western lands surrendered them to the new national government. These states were New York, Virginia, the Carolinas, Georgia, Massachusetts, and Connecticut.

Other "landless" states, particularly Pennsylvania, joined Maryland in the de-

ecause many Americans equated strong government with tyranny, great pains were taken to
quire unanimous approval of almost every major government action. (Note the Confedera-
n.) Discuss whether it is practical to try to base a government on unanimous support.

225

Western Land Claims

0 100 200 300 400 miles

BRITISH

TO MASS.

Claimed by Virginia, given up 1784

Claimed by Va., Conn., and N.Y., given up 1784-1785

Claimed by Va., Conn., and N.Y., given up 1785-1786

Given up 1800

Claimed by Va. and N.Y., given up 1784

Claimed by Va. and N.Y. Became state of Ky., 1792

Claimed by N.C., given up 1790

Claimed by S.C. and Ga., given up 1802

Claimed by Spain to 1795

NEW YORK

N.H.

MASS.

CONN. R.I.

Claimed by N.Y. and Mass.

PENN.

N.J.

MD. DEL.

VIRGINIA

NORTH CAROLINA

SOUTH CAROLINA

GEORGIA

SPANISH

Mississippi River

Ohio R.

SPANISH

© RAND & CO.

This set an important precedent: unorganized lands were to be held by the central government.

Show how the western land claims of the states were based on colonial charters.

mand. Land speculators in Pennsylvania believed it might be easier to get their hands on western acres if there was national rather than state control of them.

In 1784 Virginia broke the deadlock by giving up its western territories, "preferring the good of the country to every object of smaller importance." The other states later followed Virginia's example and then ratified the Articles of Confederation.

Power of the states. The delay in ratification had involved much more than the dispute over land. Another issue was the large and difficult question of how much power the states ought to give up to the national government.

The Articles of Confederation, as we have seen, emphasized the authority of the states. The delegates to the Congress established by the Confederation were even paid, not by the national government, but by the state governments, which could call them home whenever they wished. In the Congress—which had only one house— the vote on legislation was taken by states rather than by individual members. Each state had only one vote, although it could

Above: One of the first tests of the states' willingness to place the good of the whole country ahead of their own came in the dispute over land claims. *Below:* Settlers soon moved onto the rolling farmland seen here, in present-day Ohio but once claimed by Virginia and New York.

Indiana University Library

send not fewer than two and not more than seven delegates to the Congress.

No single executive. Under the Articles there was no executive chosen to carry out the laws. There was, instead, the "Committee of the States," which only became active when the Congress was not in session. The committee had one member from each state and required the agreement of nine members in order to make any decision.

The powers of the Congress. The Articles gave the Congress some important powers. It could (1) make war and peace and raise an army; (2) make treaties and alliances; (3) settle disputes between states, establish state boundaries, and admit new states; (4) borrow money; and (5) establish post offices.

But the national government under the Articles had no muscle: the powers not specifically granted to the national government were kept by the states. This source of weakness was a terrible drawback, because it meant that the Congress could neither tax individual citizens nor regulate trade between the states.

Why is the power to tax vital to a government?

Unloved and Unrespected

From the time the Confederation was established, a number of thoughtful Americans recognized that it could not work successfully. Alexander Hamilton frankly said of the new government, "It is neither fit for war or peace." He wrote, "We must have a Government, with more power. We must have a Bank.... We must have an Administration [that is, an executive] distinct from Congress, and in the hands of single men [that is, not committees]."

Some brakes on action. But although a number of proposals to reorganize the central government were made, circumstances were not right for a change. First and foremost, as a result of the struggle with the mother country, Americans

had developed a respectful fear of *all* government. The farther away from their own state the control of affairs was exercised, the more distrustful they became.

Second, there was still much petty jealousy and rivalry among the sections of the country. John Adams, for instance, was writing as if it were holy truth, "New England must produce the heroes, the statesmen ... or America will make no great figure for some time."

A lack of energy. Though there were barriers to improving the Articles, the fact remained that a weak government could command respect neither at home nor abroad. The Confederation showed its lack of strength as early as 1781, when the Congress was unable to provide troops to put down an uprising of veteran Pennsylvania regiments.

When some of the soldiers proceeded to the national capital—which was then Philadelphia—members of the Congress, in session there, were afraid of being attacked! Congress, declared a member from North Carolina, was "responsible for every thing, and unable to do any thing, hated by the public creditors, insulted by the Soldiery and unsupported by the citizens."

In dealing with the rest of the world, America under the Articles was pitiable. Chiefly because of a lack of salary, Robert R. Livingston resigned as Minister of Foreign Affairs in 1782, although he remained in office another year. Not until 1784 was his successor—John Jay—chosen.

Before Jay took office, however, the Netherlands, which had just signed a treaty of friendship and trade with the United States, sent an envoy to take up his duties here. Not only was there no Minister of Foreign Affairs to greet him, but also there was no one on hand in the government who could read the Dutch language.

On top of everything, since the Congress of the Confederation could not hold ses-

ve students indicate the factors which cause a government to be respected (<u>a</u>) by the people
o live in the country, and (<u>b</u>) by the governments of foreign countries. Compare the interna-
nal reaction to the thirteen states in the 1780's with that to newly independent countries today.

227

sions when fewer than nine states were represented, it often did not meet at all! Sometimes as few as three states had representatives at the capital.

Financial troubles. A particularly tragic fact was that the Confederation could not solve the country's money problems. The heavy foreign and domestic debt could not be paid without taxation, and the government established by the Articles could not tax the people.

An amendment to the Articles, which would have permitted a tax on goods imported into the country, was defeated when Rhode Island voted against it. (The Articles could be amended only by unanimous vote.)

The failure of the national government to put its treasury in order was not caused by a lack of gifted men. Robert Morris, of New York, who was Superintendent of Finance, was a wizard in money matters. Sometimes known as the financier of the Revolution, he persuaded the Congress to charter a bank. The result was the establishment of the Bank of North America in 1781, which, however, proved to be too small.

General lack of interest. The Congress time and again issued warnings to the states. Jefferson wrote to James Madison on February 20, "We have sent [a warning] today. If it fails, it seems as well we should all retire "

The public at large seemed not to care whether the Congress met or not. Many were suspicious of it—seeming to think it had and would use the power of a tyrant. In fact, Alexander Hamilton wrote that some people regarded the Congress as though its members were "annually chosen by the Emperor of Morocco, and sent over to enslave us."

What made Americans so foolish? Hamilton believed that they had an uncontrolled "rage for liberty." He knew, as did others, that the most difficult of all tasks for free people is to learn how to balance a love of liberty against a need for order.
#Discuss whether this attitude is still held.

Solid Achievements

Despite its obvious shortcomings, however, the government set up by the Articles of Confederation wrestled hard and successfully with some of the pressing problems of the day. Its most lasting achievement was its arrangement for governing and settling western land. To this we turn now.

Note how settlers followed valleys and passes in crossing the mountains.

Long before the Revolution and during it, large enough numbers of men and women were moving into the West to permit Kentucky and Tennessee to become the first new states west of the Appalachians.

Western Settlement 1769-1796

0   70   140 miles

Filling the new lands. The movement of Americans westward had continued with fresh force after the War for Independence ended. The push of people into new lands could be observed almost everywhere from North to South.

In 1783 the population of the state of Vermont—which was then regarded by some people as "west"—had reached about 80,000. From 1769 on, what is today Tennessee was being settled, chiefly by people from Virginia and North Carolina.

The Wataugans. Two popular leaders of the Tennessee pioneers were James Robertson and John Sevier, both Virginians. They settled the area near the Watauga River in the southeastern part of present-day Tennessee and created a settlement near Nashville, which was founded by Robertson in 1780.

At one point the Wataugans decided to form a state of their own, calling it Franklin, in honor of Benjamin Franklin. Sevier appointed himself its governor.

The Kentuckians. The experience of the early Tennesseans was matched in adventure by the experience of those who lived in Kentucky. There the leader was Richard Henderson, a former judge from North Carolina. He organized the Transylvania Company—a group of land speculators—to settle the Kentucky region with the aid of Daniel Boone. In 1775 the first permanent settlers of Kentucky moved onto the company's land.

Kentucky, claimed by both Virginia and North Carolina, was torn by disputes. Some Kentuckians wanted it to join Spain —and in this way share in the use of the Mississippi River, then under Spanish control. Others thought it should be a part of the United States.

Still others, like Daniel Boone, favored independence, saying that the demand for statehood was "intirely against the voice of the people at Large." Congress "sat on its hands" for a long time and did nothing

Filson Club

This fort, the beginning of Boonesboro, Kentucky, was built by Boone as a protection against Indians in 1775, the year the Revolution began.

about the western lands. Moreover, it seemed to choose to take no part in the conflicting claims and hopes of the people living on them.

Jefferson's Land Ordinance of 1784. Plainly, however, the United States had a choice to make. It could allow the seaboard states to send settlers to the newer lands, which would then become dependent on the states. Or it could simplify matters once and for all by setting rules for forming new states.

The Congress finally decided to establish rules. It began by providing for settlement in the area known as the old Northwest, or the Northwest Territory. This was the domain north of the Ohio River, made of land turned over by states to the central government. #

The man chiefly responsible for the plan adopted by the Congress was Thomas Jefferson. He was chairman of a Congressional committee to draft a law, or *ordinance*, for governing all land acquired by the national government.

Stress the importance of Congress' taking action to organize the western lands. (Settlers are
…ore readily attracted to an area for which there is an orderly process for settlement than
…ey are to one where they are entirely on their own.)

229

#Illustrate the survey system by showing students a legal description of a piece of real estate.

Collection of Charles F. Adams, Dover, Mass. (Frick Art Reference Library)

The earliest portrait of Thomas Jefferson, painted two years after the Ordinance of 1784, which he wrote, and ten years after the immortal Declaration of Independence.

Jefferson proposed that the Northwest Territory be divided into ten districts, each to become a state in time. He even chose names for the districts, including such melodious ones as "Dolypotamia," "Assinisippia," and "Metropotamia." Also, he proposed that slavery be prohibited in the entire area after 1800.

The Land Ordinance of 1784 passed by the Congress neither provided for the names Jefferson had suggested nor included the provision about slavery. But it remains one of Jefferson's noble achievements. Jefferson had paved the way for the development of the West, not by land speculators, but by actual settlers who would govern themselves.

As Jefferson had proposed, the ordinance provided that the Northwest Territory be divided into ten districts. Each district was to form a government when its population reached 20,000. When the number of people in a district equaled the number of free persons in the smallest of the original states, it could hold a constitutional convention and ask to become a state.

Selling sections. Having laid down general principles for governing the Northwest Territory, the Congress in 1785 passed another land ordinance providing for the sale of the land. According to it, the Northwest Territory was to be surveyed into square *townships*, 6 miles long on each side. Each township, consisting, therefore, of 36 square miles, would be divided into thirty-six *sections*, each numbered. Each section would be 1 mile long on each side—that is, it would occupy 1 square mile, or 640 acres.

Look at the diagram on the next page and observe how regular and planned the pattern of settlement was. This regular pattern was later repeated throughout our Middle West and West, for other land was divided up as the Northwest Territory was. Today as one flies over the old Northwest and other parts of the country similarly laid out, the farming regions give the impression of being a huge checkerboard.

The Land Ordinance of 1785 was very specific: Four sections of land in each township were to be set aside for the use of the United States government. And one (always Section Number 16) was to be reserved for the support of public schools. The smallest purchase of land that could be made at auction was to be one section, or 640 acres. The price was to be not less than one dollar an acre.

Before 1785, as we have seen, land was free or almost free. But by 1785 the Congress was grasping anxiously at every source of money. From time to time in the years that followed, the smallest acreage that could be bought and the price per acre were reduced. Not until 1862, however, when the United States passed the Homestead Act, would land once again be made free or almost free for actual settlers.

230 ##Let students discuss the desirability of giving free land to settlers. Are there reasons why requiring purchase is better? Indicate places in the present-day United States where free government land is available to settlers (Alaska, for example).

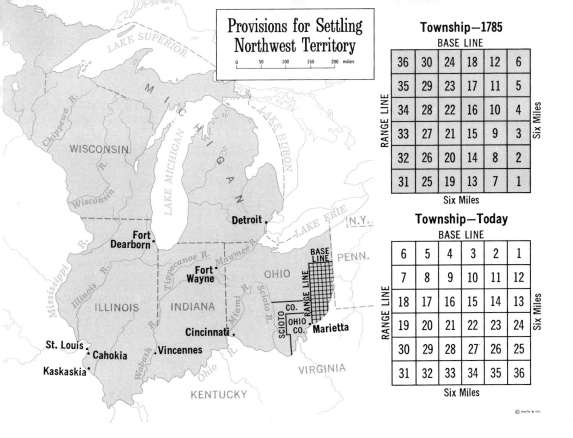

Provisions for Settling Northwest Territory

0   50   100   150   200 miles

Township—1785

BASE LINE

36	30	24	18	12	6
35	29	23	17	11	5
34	28	22	16	10	4
33	27	21	15	9	3
32	26	20	14	8	2
31	25	19	13	7	1

RANGE LINE — Six Miles

Six Miles

Township—Today

BASE LINE

6	5	4	3	2	1
7	8	9	10	11	12
18	17	16	15	14	13
19	20	21	22	23	24
30	29	28	27	26	25
31	32	33	34	35	36

RANGE LINE — Six Miles

Six Miles

© RAND & CO.

Speculators. It should be observed that the Land Ordinance of 1785 required that a prospective farmer have, at the very least, $640 in cash. Such a sum was well beyond the reach of most Americans. The **result was that several land companies** were formed by speculators.

The companies aimed to acquire large **tracts of western land at low cost and then** sell small parcels of it to farmers. The speculators would make a profit and the farmers would obtain land at a price they could afford.

The most important of the companies were the Ohio Company—not related to the old colonial company of the same name—and the Scioto (sī ō' tō) Company. Both were named by their promoters for the rivers on which their tracts of land were located. The Congress was persuaded to make this land available (see the map above) to the companies for less than ten cents an acre.

Compare the Ohio and Scioto companies with the London, Plymouth, and Massachusetts Bay Companies.

Above: All of the first forty-eight states of our country—except Texas and the original thirteen—entered the Union in the way set up by the Northwest Ordinance. *Below:* The seal of the Ohio Company. The Latin words mean "peace and trade." What do the symbols mean?

"George Mercer Papers" (Darlington Library, University of Pittsburgh)

PAX ET COMMERCIUM

##Consider the effect of the slavery limitation in the Ordinance of 1787 on future controversies over slavery in the territories.

In Ipswich, Massachusetts, the first settlers prepare to leave for Ohio. Ipswich was the home of the Rev. Mr. Cutler, who bought from Congress nearly two million acres of western land for development. Cutler's church is in the background.

Henry Howe, "Historical Collections of Ohio, Vol. II, Cincinnati, 1888

A leading figure in promoting the Ohio Company was the Reverend Manasseh Cutler, a remarkable man. In addition to being a clergyman, he was a soldier, explorer, and scientist. He also practiced as a physician at one time and was one of the first American doctors to vaccinate people against smallpox.

A quick result of granting land to the land companies was the need for governing the Northwest Territory. The Ordinance of 1784, passed by the Congress to provide government for the area, had never been carried out because the settlers required were lacking.

The Northwest Ordinance. Expecting the land companies to bring considerable numbers of people into the region, the Congress passed the third of its great ordinances—the Ordinance of 1787, or Northwest Ordinance. It provided for governing the Northwest Territory as a single unit by means of a governor, a secretary, and three judges—all to be appointed by Congress.

When 5000 free adult male inhabitants had settled in any one part of the Northwest Territory, they were to form a "territory." Every man owning at least 50 acres of land was to have the right to vote for the members of a territorial legislature. These voters were also given the power to choose a delegate to the Congress, who might engage in discussion but who could not vote.

The Northwest Territory was to be divided into not fewer than three or more than five states. As soon as a territory had 60,000 inhabitants, it was to be admitted to the Union "on an equal footing with the original States in all respects whatever." The Ordinance of 1787 was ever after the basis for the entrance of new states into the Union.

Other very important provisions of the ordinance prohibited slavery within the Northwest Territory and directed the beginning of free public education. These measures have remained special reminders of the enlightened opinions of the men of the Confederation.

The decimal system of money. Thomas Jefferson, whose mind was exceptionally

#Note that even when a territory had 60,000 inhabitants, its attainment of statehood depended upon the approval of Congress. Cite the long Congressional delay in the case of Hawaii. Stress the equality of new states with the old--the original thirteen states could not dominate.

inventive, played the chief part during the period of the Confederation in creating the system of money we use to this day. Based on the *decimal* system—its units are decimal fractions of 100—it is even now being copied by other nations. Jefferson wrote:

> The most *easy ratio* of multiplication and division, is that by ten.... If we adopt the Dollar for our unit, we should strike four coins, one of gold, two of silver, and one of copper, viz. [as follows]:
> 1. A golden piece, equal to ten dollars:
> 2. The Unit or Dollar itself, of silver:
> 3. The tenth of a Dollar, of silver also:
> 4. The hundredth of a Dollar, of copper.

Jefferson also proposed two other familiar coins we use today, the half-dollar and the quarter.

Bad times in the 1780's. Despite the clever system of money and the Bank of North America, though, the 1780's were not prosperous for most Americans. The wartime boom in business collapsed soon after the peace treaty of 1783 was signed. France withdrew the special trading privileges it had given Americans in the French West Indies, and the British cut our trade in the British West Indies.

Ambitious merchants were looking for new markets. In 1784 a group of businessmen, probably including Robert Morris, sent a ship out of New York Harbor on its way to open trade in China. Shrewdly, they named the vessel the *Empress of China.* Its return cargo of silks and teas and cheap cloth proved to be very profitable.

The "China trade" had been opened, but it had had only a modest beginning. The growth of international trade would be steady but slow. In fact, in 1785 the United States as a whole, and New England especially, was in the grip of a bad business *depression,* or "slump." Jobs were scarce, and people had little money.

##Have students give examples of depression and inflation at other times in our history. What about today?

Public Unrest

A chief cause of the bad times in 1785 was the serious shortage of money. Farmers were especially hard hit: even in good times they had had very little hard cash. They and other debtors—that is, people who owed money—often demanded that their states issue paper money, even though it had no gold or silver backing it up. Whenever such paper money appears in large quantities, its value drops quickly.

Effects of money shortage. The ways of dealing with the money shortage varied from place to place. In some places debtors called for laws requiring *creditors*—people who lent money—to accept land or even crops in repayment of debts. In some instances, debtors pressed their state legislatures for *stay* laws. These were acts putting off, or staying, the collection of debts.

Naturally, there were differing effects, also. In South Carolina and New York, paper money was issued without the backing of gold or silver. But because the amount was carefully controlled, it did not quickly fall in value.

In Rhode Island and North Carolina, too much unbacked paper money was issued. It quickly fell in value, and *inflation* set in. ## Inflation occurs when a large amount of money is in circulation and too few goods are available. Inflation forces prices up.

Anger in Massachusetts. The struggle between creditors and debtors reached the breaking point in Massachusetts. There widespread unemployment had come about as a result of the closing of trade with the West Indies. The loss of this business had brought hard times to the distilling, that is, the liquor-making, industry. It had also hurt shipping activities of all sorts.

In the interior of the state, many farm mortgages were foreclosed. In those days one could be imprisoned for failing to re-

ake sure that students understand the relationship between paper money and gold in the 18th and
th centuries. Confidence in the interchangeability of the two kept the value of paper on a par
th that of gold. What backs our paper money today? Can it be exchanged for gold or silver?

233

pay debts. The number of debtors in prison rose sharply between 1785 and 1786. Nevertheless, Massachusetts officials turned a deaf ear to the loud pleas for paper money.

Consequently the hard-pressed debtors decided to use force to prevent the courts, generally harsh on those who owed money, from bringing them to trial and sentencing them to prison. In fact, mobs in a number of Massachusetts towns prevented the courts from sitting in session.

Shays' Rebellion. The most famous leader of the misguided farmers was thirty-nine-year-old Captain Daniel Shays, a wounded hero of the Revolution. In 1786 he and his followers forced the court at Springfield, Massachusetts, to adjourn— that is, to cease sitting.

The governor of Massachusetts declared the Shaysmen to be outlaws and appointed General Benjamin Lincoln to go after them with a militia. Shays' little band was scattered. Shays himself fled to Vermont, and what we call Shays' Rebellion was over. Nobody was punished for taking part in it.

Shays' rebels were a pitiful group. Lack-ing uniforms, they wore sprigs of evergreen in their hats to identify themselves. Lacking guns, they carried clubs cut from hickory trees. They aroused much public sympathy for themselves. Baron von Steuben, the old drillmaster of the Revolutionary army, concluded, "When a whole people complains . . . something must be wrong."

1. What relation existed between the states and the national government under the Articles of Confederation? 2. Name two disputes that delayed ratification of the Articles. 3. Identify three major sources of weakness in the government under the Articles. 4. Give two reasons for Americans' unwillingness to remove them. 5. Name three instances in which the central government showed its weakness. 6. Give the provisions of the Land Ordinances of 1784, 1785, and 1787. 7. Name two ways of dealing with the postwar money shortage in the country. 8. What were the cause and outcome of Shays' Rebellion?

Necessity Leads to Writing a Constitution

Many Americans decided that representative government itself had failed. Noah Webster, who later became famous for his dictionaries and spellers, was even willing to have a king rule him again. He was
writing, "I would sooner be the subject of the caprice [that is, the whim] of one man, than to the ignorance and passions of the multitude."

From Mount Vernon George Washington was warning, "Commotions of this sort, like snow-balls, gather strength as they roll, if there is no opposition in the way to divide and crumble them."

Sneered At

Property owners in every state trembled and wondered. Had the American Revolution been fought in order to allow mobs to triumph? Was the hour at hand to strengthen the national government? How would Americans regain the confidence they once had in their ability to manage their affairs successfully?

Foreign disrespect. Abroad, especially in western Europe, the United States was for the most part held in contempt. An exam-

Shays' Rebellion was a threat to the propertied classes because it struck at the sanctity of contracts. If personal debts could be canceled by mob action, then all debts, mortgages, etc., could be wiped out. The rebellion made the need to revise the Articles apparent.

England was unwilling to give its former colonies the respect due independent states.

Fort Detroit in 1794, one of the trading posts which the British refused to leave after the American Revolution, although it and the others were on American land. British ships are seen in the foreground.

ple is the editorial that appeared in a London newspaper shortly after John Adams arrived in 1785 to take up his position in England as United States minister there. It read, "An ambassador from America! Good heavens, what a sound! The Gazette surely never announced anything so extraordinary before."

It was not an easy matter to represent an upstart nation abroad. At one public reception the English king turned his back on Adams, and on Jefferson, who had come over from Paris to pay Adams a visit. Only a strong government can command respect for its representatives abroad—its diplomats. And the solution to a number of America's problems depended on work only diplomats could handle.

Denied the northwest posts. A most stubborn issue was the British refusal to get out of the trading posts in the old Northwest. (They were supposed to do so after the peace treaty of 1783 was signed.) The continued presence of the British there prevented American use of the Great Lakes.

Further, the continued British alliance with Indian friends in the old Northwest prevented Americans from taking over the profitable fur trade there. The British occupation also tended to prevent the westward movement of Americans into the Great Lakes region.

The British excused their behavior by stating that America had not lived up to the terms of the treaty of peace, either. They said that we had not restored property taken from Loyalists or paid debts owed to Britons.

Refused navigation of the Mississippi. American relations with Spain were just as unfriendly as those with Britain. The Spanish had never recognized United States possession of the area south of the Ohio River. Our ally in the War for Independence, Spain was as determined to hem Americans in as was Britain, our enemy.

In 1783 the Spanish had gained East and West Florida (see page 213). The next year Spain limited American shipping on the lower Mississippi River and taxed American exports passing through New Orleans.

The Spanish action caused especially

Review the terms in the Treaty of 1783 that were previously noted as sources of trouble. Show why the central government could not require the states to live up to the terms of the treaty.

grave concern in Kentucky and Tennessee. You can see why from the map on page 228. Farmers living there could send their goods to market most easily down the Mississippi. The only other way would be to transport them over the Appalachian Mountains, which was too expensive.

Jay's efforts. The western farmers want-
ed their government to take action to help them. John Jay, especially chosen to represent the United States, and the Spanish minister to the United States attempted to *negotiate*—arrange through discussion—a settlement. The Spaniard tried hard to win Americans to his side. He showered attention on Mrs. Jay, and he even sent George Washington a splendid donkey upon hearing that the General was raising mules at Mount Vernon.

Jay was sympathetic to the demands of eastern merchants, who were afraid of losing Spanish trade, and decided he would not press Spain for shipping rights on the Mississippi. The westerners were outraged. They wished that the national government were strong enough to open the Mississippi River for them *and* force Spain to trade with the United States.

French schemes. Relations with our ally, France, were only slightly more friendly than those with Britain and Spain. France allowed our ships to carry on a very limited trade in the French West Indies. But France had plans, too. Since it hoped to keep the United States weak, it worked to prevent the new country from expanding westward. Only in this way could the French ever again establish themselves in North America—a dream they had clung to after 1763, when they were pushed out by the British.

Need for a stronger government. To even the ordinary citizen it was clear that our ability to solve problems in our relations with strong European powers depended on a stronger national government. By its performance at home, such a government could win respect abroad.

The rulers of Europe, unsympathetic with people who had rebelled against a monarch, did not want the American government to succeed without a king. The United States could expect no help from them. Sometimes they seemed like vultures ready to pounce on a helpless victim.

Early steps toward a stronger government.

Forward Steps

The movement to strengthen the Confederation had long been under way. Almost from the beginning people had been referring to the new country as a "Monster with Thirteen Heads."

The leadership of Washington. Among those who saw that the nation must be strong or be nothing was Washington. When the war ended, he went home to his beloved Mount Vernon, above the Potomac River.

To his old comrade, Lafayette, the General wrote, "I have not only retired from all public employments, but I am retiring within myself. . . . I will move gently down the stream of life, until I sleep with my fathers." But a truer view was that of the French minister to the United States. He wrote home, "It will be useless for him [Washington] to try to hide himself and live the life of a private man; he will always be the first citizen of the United States." Washington was shortly in the thick of things.

A meeting at Mount Vernon. Some members of the Virginia legislature were concerned about the navigation of the Potomac River. A meeting was called in 1785, which was held at Washington's home. There an agreement between Virginia and Maryland was reached for regulating traffic and trade on the river, which was their common boundary.

The Annapolis Convention. The success of the Mount Vernon conference encouraged the Virginia Assembly. It planned a

##In the 1780's the Americans were alone in diplomatic circles for two reasons. First, their ideas of government were contrary to those of the European monarchies. Second, their government had too little power to be either feared or courted.

Mount Vernon, Washington's beloved home on the Potomac River, as it looked in 1785.

larger meeting to be attended by more states and to deal with the problems connected with trade between the states. The outcome was the Annapolis Convention, which met in Annapolis, Maryland, in September, 1786.

Drama at Philadelphia

It was a disappointment that only five states sent representatives. James Madison, of Virginia, a young friend and neighbor of Jefferson's, and Alexander Hamilton, of New York, were the leaders of the Annapolis Convention. The conference lasted only a short time because so few people attended it. But it issued a call for a convention to meet in Philadelphia on the second Monday of the following May.

The purpose of the convention—officially, at least—was to revise the Articles of Confederation, not to write a new frame of government. The Congress of the Confederation approved the call as being the "most probable means of establishing in these states a firm national government."

Getting ready. The scene in Philadelphia on Sunday, May 13, 1787, was memorable. George Washington, a delegate from Virginia, arrived in the afternoon. The first thing he did after taking up lodgings with Mr. and Mrs. Robert Morris was to call on Benjamin Franklin. Some of the great heroes of the Revolutionary era were coming together to try again to solve America's problems.

#Consider how important George Washington's presence was to the success of the convention.

Thomas Jefferson was in Paris, but his mind was on the doings in Philadelphia. When he learned who the convention delegates were, he wrote that they appeared to be able men, "so that I hope Good from their Meeting. Indeed, if it does not do good it must do Harm, as it will show that we have not Wisdom enough among us to govern ourselves."

Not until May 25 were enough delegates on hand to begin what is now called the Constitutional Convention. By then seven states had sent their men. Within a few weeks afterward, all the states except Rhode Island were represented.

Altogether there were fifty-five delegates, including some of the ablest men in America, well acquainted with public affairs. Eight of the men had signed the Declaration of Independence, two had signed the Articles of Confederation, and seven had attended the Annapolis Convention. Three had served as president of the Congress. It must have meant much to the delegates to be meeting in Independence Hall, where the Declaration of Independence had been adopted and signed eleven years earlier.

George Washington in the chair. The most important of the people present was # George Washington. Without his active support the meetings had only little hope of success. Franklin's support was also necessary, although in 1787 he was too old to take a leading part in the discussions.

At the first session Washington was elected president of the convention. Somewhat reserved in manner, he was perfect in this role. As the president, he could not make speeches and he had to be neutral in public on the subjects discussed. When ballots were taken, however, he could leave his chair and vote as a representative from Virginia.

Because James Madison and some other members made notes of the proceedings, which were later published, we know now

nless the states were willing to surrender some of their powers to the central government or to are certain powers with it, there was no way to improve upon the Articles of Confederation. ote that most delegates wanted to strengthen the central government.

For a discussion of the motives and beliefs of the men at the Constitutional Convention, see Richard Hofstadter, <u>The American Political Tradition</u> (Vintage, 1954), Chapter 1.

how the delegates argued and how the arguments went. In 1787, though, the public was in the dark, because the meetings were secret.

The delegates—later called the Founding Fathers—knew the importance of the convention. Washington is said to have declared as the meetings began, "If to please the people, we offer what we ourselves disapprove, how can we afterwards defend our work? Let us raise a standard to which the wise and honest can repair [that is, look up]; the event is in the hand of God."

The Virginia Plan. On May 29 Governor Edmund Randolph, of Virginia—described by one of his colleagues as possessing "a most harmonious voice . . . and striking manners"—opened the "main business." He introduced what has come to be known as the Virginia Plan, or the large-state plan, prepared by the Virginia delegates. Although Randolph's name is connected with the plan, it contained many of the ideas of Madison, who dominated the convention behind the scenes.

The Virginia Plan provided for a national legislature of two houses. Members of the lower house it proposed would be elected by qualified voters, and members of the upper house would be chosen by men in the lower house. This new legislature would have vastly greater powers than the Continental Congress had enjoyed.

The Virginia Plan had three other notable provisions. The number of representatives a state would have in both houses would be determined by *the size of its population.* In the Congress of the Confederation, all *states*, you will recall, had been represented equally. Furthermore, the plan also provided for a national *executive*— an official to carry out the laws—and a national *judiciary*, that is, a national system of courts.

As discussions of Randolph's proposal began, it was clear that it was not a revision of the Articles of Confederation. Randolph had opened the way to an entirely new *kind* of government.

In the following weeks some important changes in the plan were made. One gave responsibility for electing members of the upper house to the state legislatures instead of to qualified voters. Another gave the executive a veto over laws passed by the new legislature. Observe how men of the American Revolution, who had placed so much blame on George III, were unwilling to give power to any one man.

The New Jersey Plan. On June 15 another proposal—the New Jersey (or small-state) Plan—was introduced by William Paterson, of New Jersey. He was described as "one of those kind of men . . . who never speaks but when he understands his subject well."

Paterson spoke for those delegates who feared the creation of a strong national government. He was aiming only to patch up the Articles of Confederation.

Paterson's plan contained a proposal that treaties and acts of the Congress be the supreme law of the states. In emphasizing the states, he showed that he favored a weak national government. Like many others from the small states, he was worried that in a new arrangement of government based on population, the small states might be swallowed up by the large states. (The large states were New York, Massachusetts, Pennsylvania, North Carolina, and Virginia.)

A heated debate then began between the delegates favoring the small-state plan and those for the large-state plan. Despite the keen argument, almost everyone seemed to agree that the Articles had to be dropped —they could not simply be overhauled.

The Great Compromise. A settlement of the disagreement between those favoring the Virginia Plan and those favoring the New Jersey Plan was finally arranged by the Connecticut delegates. Often called the

#Indicate clearly the compromises that took place. Explain the positions of both large and small states and of both North and South. For example, the North wanted slaves counted for taxes but not for representation. And taxes on exports were feared by the South.

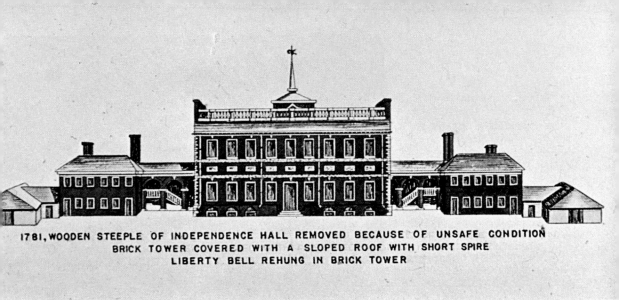

1781, WOODEN STEEPLE OF INDEPENDENCE HALL REMOVED BECAUSE OF UNSAFE CONDITION
BRICK TOWER COVERED WITH A SLOPED ROOF WITH SHORT SPIRE
LIBERTY BELL REHUNG IN BRICK TOWER

mpare a recent photo of Independence Hall with this cture. Why is this building "shrine of liberty"?

The State House in Philadelphia, now called Independence Hall, as it looked in 1787. Today maintained by the national government, it is the place where the Declaration of Independence was signed, where the Second Continental Congress met, and where the Constitution was written and signed.

Great Compromise—a *compromise* being a settlement in which each side yields something it wants—or the Connecticut compromise, it took into account the views of both the large and the small states.

The agreement reached provided that the legislature still be made up of two houses. But in the lower house representation was to be based on population, and in the upper house all states were to be represented equally. (This legislature became our Congress, consisting of a House of Representatives and a Senate.)

Another part of the Great Compromise was the decision to count three-fifths of a state's slaves as inhabitants in electing members to the House of Representatives. (Southern delegates wanted to count all of them.) Direct taxes (taxes based on a state's population) by the new government would be levied on the same basis.

Controlling foreign trade. Another dispute grew out of the fear of southern delegates especially that the central government might be able to pass unwelcome navigation acts. Still another compromise re-

sulted: the central government would have unlimited power over foreign trade, but a tax on *exports* was forbidden forever. Furthermore, the power of Congress to interfere with or abolish the slave trade would not go into effect until 1808.

"Supreme law of the land." The question of the control of the new national government over the states was also a source of trouble. The New Jersey Plan suggested the solution. It would have made Congressional laws and treaties the "supreme laws of the States." The delegates now changed the phrase to the "supreme law of the land" # and used it to refer to the new frame of government they were writing.

#Emphasize the significance of this wording.

The Accomplishment

Our United States Constitution (see ## pages 704–726)—the finished work of the delegates—offered a masterly solution to the question of the relationship between the central and state governments. It gave to Congress the power "to lay and collect taxes" and "to regulate commerce with

Because students frequently refer to the Constitution throughout the year, it has been placed the Appendix, where it can be found easily. The helpful clause-by-clause commentary companying the Constitution clarifies the formal wording and gives additional information.

239

On the official flag of the
president of the United
States, the eagle, encircled
by stars representing the
fifty states, is centered on
a field of dark blue.
Compare this design with the
one shown on page 219.

Office of the President, The White House

foreign nations, and among the several states." Also, it could "raise and support armies"—powers the Congress of the Confederation had lacked.

In addition, the Constitution gave Congress the power to pass any other laws which may be "necessary and proper" to carry out its stated powers. In time, for example, Congress was able to pass laws calling for duties on imports, provide charters for banks, and arrange for drafting men into military service.

On the other hand, all the powers not listed as belonging to the national government remained with the states. These powers have been taken to include, among others, provisions for educating children, building roads, and protecting health and safety.

Federalism. The splendid balance between the powers of the central government and the powers of the states was a special feature of the Constitution. It # created a far better *federal* system of government than had existed under the Articles of Confederation.

The word federal describes a central government which divides and shares authority with the states. The national government takes charge of all problems affecting the whole country and leaves it up to the states to control strictly local questions.

The presidency. One of the most remarkable decisions of the Constitutional Convention was the one taken to make the chief executive an important figure. At first the delegates thought that the President ought to be elected by the new Congress. But soon they decided that such a practice would be bad, because the man chosen might become a mere servant of Congress.

The *presidency*—the office of President —was fully discussed. Among the issues raised were: How long should a man serve? Should he have control over questions of war and peace? Should he have a salary?

An especially important question was, How should the President be chosen? When it was agreed that the choice should be made by the people, the question arose, Should he be chosen directly or indirectly?

In giving an answer, the delegates were influenced by the viewpoint of their times.

#Help students see the difference between a federal system of shared power and a centralized
system--as in France. Indicate why the "necessary and proper" clause has been called the
Elastic Clause, and discuss the changing roles of the national government and the states.

They were convinced that "the people" could not be trusted, that they were likely to be excitable and therefore unreliable in their judgments. The President, the convention decided, must be elected indirectly. In a way, the delegates were attempting to protect the people from themselves!

The electoral college. As finally worked out, the Constitution provided that the President be chosen not by the people or the Congress or the state legislatures. He was to be chosen by a group of officials called electors, to be selected as the legislatures wished. The number of electors that represented each state was to be equal to the combined number of its Senators and Representatives in Congress.

When the electors met (forming the *electoral college*), each would vote for two men for President, one of whom had to be an inhabitant of a state different from the elector's. The man receiving the majority of votes would become President. The man receiving the next largest number would become Vice-President. As we shall see shortly, this arrangement did not work out well and had to be changed (see the Twelfth Amendment, pages 721-722).

The Constitution fixed the term of the President at four years, with no limit on the number of terms he might serve. Later a limit on the number of terms was set by a Constitutional amendment (see the Twenty-second Amendment, page 725).

Procedure for ratification. The Constitutional Convention had achieved far more than many Americans had thought possible. It had set out to amend the Articles, but it had created a new frame of government. It had established the United States as a *republic*, a country governed by representatives chosen by the people. The Founding Fathers had provided that the new federal government would begin to operate when *nine* states had ratified the Constitution. No one state could stand in the way. (You will recall that the Articles

could be changed only by consent of *all* the states.)

The delegates arranged that special state conventions, rather than the state legislatures, be elected to reject or ratify the finished Constitution. It was believed that in this way the people's wishes could be expressed most fully.

"We, the people...." When the Constitution was being completed, a *preamble,* or opening statement, was composed to begin the document (see page 704). It contains the majestic words "We, the people of the United States, in order to form a more perfect Union, establish justice, insure domestic tranquillity, provide for the common defense, promote the general welfare, and secure the blessings of liberty to ourselves and our posterity, do ordain and establish this Constitution for the United States of America."

The words of the preamble should be memorized by every American, for they are the noblest of all statements of the meaning of our government. The stirring words "We, the people" have come to be taken as an expression of the wish of the Founding Fathers that the national government rest solidly on the consent of the whole people.

Franklin's judgment. As the Constitutional Convention ended and as members heard the finished document read for the last time, the aged Benjamin Franklin asked for the floor. What he had to say were words of common sense. He was not sure that the new Constitution was going to be a flaming success. But, he said,

I doubt ... whether any other Convention we can obtain may be able to make a better Constitution. For when you assemble a number of men to have the advantages of their joint wisdom, you inevitably assemble with those men, all their prejudices, their passions, their errors in opinion, their local interests, and their selfish views. From such an

‡The principal problem of ratification was how to get the states to accept a reduction of their powers. It was feared that state legislatures might reject the new Constitution. Note that the new Constitution went into effect for only those states that ratified it.

Assembly, can a perfect production be expected? It therefore astonishes me ... to find this system approaching so near to perfection as it does; and I think it will astonish our enemies, who are waiting with confidence to hear that our councils are confounded like those of the Builders of Babel; and that our States are on the point of separation, only to meet hereafter for the purpose of cutting one another's throats.

#Note the different uses of the word Federalist.

The Ratification Fight

People in favor of the Constitution— who were soon being called Federalists— organized the ratification campaign skillfully. Between December and January the states of Delaware, Pennsylvania, New Jersey, Georgia, and Connecticut ratified the Constitution.

Afterward ratification proceeded more slowly, because the people opposing the Constitution — called Antifederalists — were beginning to be well organized, too. But before June, 1788, was over, Massachusetts, Maryland, South Carolina, and New Hampshire had ratified.

The call for a bill of rights. Massachusetts accepted the new government with a recommendation for a series of amend-ments—a bill of rights—to be added to the Constitution. Such a bill of rights would protect the *civil liberties* of the individual against future action by the federal government. Such civil liberties include freedom of speech, press, and religion, the right to trial by jury, and guarantees against cruel and unusual punishments and unreasonable searches and seizures.

In 1791 the first ten amendments to the Constitution, written chiefly by Madison, were ratified (see pages 719–720). Called the American Bill of Rights, they assure Americans of rights necessary to all people who call themselves free.

New Hampshire's ratification was especially important because it meant that nine states had accepted the Constitution, putting it into effect. Nevertheless, until Virginia and New York, two powerful, large states, ratified the Constitution, the new government would be greatly handicapped. In both states the Federalists and Antifederalists were almost equally divided.

Virginia's acceptance. In Virginia, Patrick Henry, long a popular figure, was opposed to the Constitution. He and others criticized the document especially for its lack of guarantees of individual freedom,

Left: John Jay, a New York lawyer and a graduate of King's College, was a strong supporter of the Constitution. *Right:* George Clinton, another New York City lawyer, who at first keenly opposed the new Constitution.

New York Historical Society

New York Historical Society

The FŒDERALIST, No. 10.

To the People of the State of New-York.

AMONG the numerous advantages promised by a well constructed Union, none deserves to be more accurately developed than its tendency to break and control the violence of faction. The friend of popular governments, never finds himself so much alarmed for their character and fate, as when he contemplates their propensity to this dangerous vice. He will not fail therefore to set a due value on any plan which, without violating the principles to which he is attached, provides a proper cure for it. The instability, injustice and confusion introduced into the public councils, have in truth been the mortal diseases under which popular governments have every where perished; as they continue to be the favorite and fruitful topics from which the adversaries to liberty derive their most specious declamations. The valuable improvements made by the American Constitutions on the popular models, b~~ ~~ncient and modern, cann~~~~~~~~~ly

The beginning and end of the tenth *Federalist* paper, one of seventy-seven essays written by Alexander Hamilton, James Madison, and John Jay. These essays favored a strong national government to correct the weaknesses of the Articles of Confederation. First published as articles in New York newspapers, they were signed with the name "Publius."

"New York Packet," Nov. 23, 1787 (New York Public Library)

therefore, we behold a republican remedy for the diseases most incident to republican Government. And according to the degree of pleasure and pride, we feel in being Republicans, ought to be our zeal in cherishing the spirit and supporting the character of Fœderalists.

P U B L I U S.

as men in Massachusetts had.

By a very slim margin, Virginia's convention ratified the Constitution on June 25, 1788, after proposing amendments. Many delegates assumed, as they voted to ratify, that George Washington would be elected the first President, and this idea influenced them.

The struggle in New York. The leader of the Antifederalists in New York was the popular governor, George Clinton. Clinton, like other opponents of the Constitution elsewhere, feared, among other things, being "left out" if the new government had no place for him. He knew the power he was commanding as chief executive of a large state, but he felt uncertain about his future career.

##Selections from The Federalist might be used to give students an experience with primary sources.

In time Clinton discovered that there could be a position for him after all in the new national government. He became one of the early Vice-Presidents.

The movement for ratification was greatly aided in New York by a brilliant series of newspaper articles written by Alexander Hamilton, John Jay, and James Madison. These essays, known as *The Federalist*, were widely read. ##

New York finally ratified the Constitution by the close vote of 30 to 27 on July 26, 1788. Many of the New York delegates apparently thought that because of their criticism of the Constitution, a new national convention would shortly be called.

Though North Carolina and Rhode Island still had not accepted the Constitution, the Congress of the Confederation decided its services could come to an end. On September 13, 1788, it called for the new Congress to meet on the first Wednesday in March, 1789. The members of the electoral college, meanwhile, were to name a President in February.

What had now been achieved? No one could say for sure. One notable fact was that as the states ratified the Constitution, they held great parades—"federal processions," as they were known. In the Philadelphia procession held on the Fourth of July, 1788, was a float drawn by ten white horses. Called the "New Roof, or Grand Federal Edifice," it consisted of a dome supported by thirteen pillars, ten complete and three unfinished. (They represented the fact that at the time three states had not yet ratified the Constitution.)

On top of the dome was a figure standing for plenty, and around the base of the "Edifice" were the words "In Union the Fabric stands firm." A report of the day tells us that when the procession ended, the "New Roof" was taken back to Independence Hall. There for days crowds gathered around it in admiration.

Show why ratification of the Constitution by New York and Virginia was important to the other states economically, politically, and geographically. North Carolina ratified in November, 1789, and Rhode Island finally ratified in May, 1790--over a year after Washington's inauguration.

Relate the comments below to the aims stated in the preamble to the Constitution. Can individual citizen actually sense their roles in shaping their country's destiny?

What were these people celebrating? Some scholars have said they were rejoicing because they looked forward to prosperity. Others have said these Americans were sensing that they had taken a giant step on the long road free men have traveled toward successful self-government. We can never know for certain what they were thinking.

Perhaps some Philadelphians looked at "The Grand Federal Edifice" as they would at a new house of their own, wondering what joys and sorrows would unfold inside it. One thing we are certain about: the people in 1788 knew that hard work lay ahead before the new "Edifice" would be fully serviceable.

The bricklayers of Philadelphia, marching in the procession, carried a banner that bore a timely motto. It would have been fitting for all Americans: "Both Buildings and Rulers are the Work of our hands."

1. Describe the difficulties Britain, Spain, and France caused the United States after 1783. 2. What meetings led to the Constitutional Convention? 3. State the aim of the Constitutional Convention, and tell where the meetings were held. 4. Describe the Virginia and New Jersey plans. 5. What were the terms of two compromises that were made? 6. Contrast the relation between states and the central government established by the Constitution with that established under the Articles. 7. How was the President originally elected? For how long? What changes were later made? 8. Name two groups that formed over the question of ratifying the Constitution. What side did each group take? 9. On what grounds did Massachusetts oppose the Constitution? How was its objection met?

Many activities and questions in this Workshop are designed to show the relation of certain proposals, events, and decisions to

The Workshop

the student's own life. Note especially the activities in "The Research Center" and the questions concerning the Constitution.

The Shapers of Our World

Identify each of the following and tell what role each played in the first years of the independent United States:

Virginia Statute of
    Religious Freedom
John Dickinson
Articles of
    Confederation
Robert Morris
Wataugans
Land Ordinance
    of 1784
Land Ordinance
    of 1785
Northwest
    Ordinance
Daniel Boone

Shays' Re-
    bellion
the northwest
    posts
John Jay
Annapolis Con-
    vention
Virginia Plan
New Jersey Plan
Founding Fathers
Bill of Rights
The Federalist
Constitutional
    Convention

Adding to Your Vocabulary

Be sure you know the meaning of these words and phrases:

state con-
    stitutions
primogeniture
established church
separation of
    church and state
mobility
ratify
executive
ordinance

depression
creditor
inflation
negotiate
judiciary
compromise
federal
republic
preamble
civil liberties

Understanding Pictures

1. Look at the face of the Great Seal of the United States, shown on page 219.

Consider that just as we are guided to some extent by our past, the men of the Congress and the Constitutional Convention were influenced by their colonial and European pasts. Many of them were well versed in the ideas of leading European thinkers.

What is the eagle carrying? Explain what those symbols represent. The dollar bill carries both faces of the seal. What symbols are shown on the back face?

2. You saw another seal on page 231 and also on other pages of this book. How do the various seals that have been used in the American past throw light on United States history? If historians in the future were to select seals to illustrate history in our time, what ones do you think they might choose?

3. Three of the illustrations on page 217 are connected with printing. What special importance do printing and printed materials have in a democratic country? What relationship was there between the establishment of schools and the development of the printing industry in America?

The United States Constitution

1. Read carefully the preamble to the Constitution (page 704). What does it accomplish? What do you think "general welfare," "a more perfect Union," the "blessings of liberty," and "our posterity" refer to? How do you explain the fact that the preamble begins with "We, the people of the United States" instead of with "We, the authors of the Constitution"?

Be sure to memorize the preamble.

2. The Constitution itself is divided into seven main sections called articles. What subjects do Articles 1, 2, and 3 deal with?

3. Who are your United States Senators? What requirements does the Constitution set for a person who seeks a Senate seat?

4. How many members does your state send to the House of Representatives in Congress? What requirements does the Constitution lay down for members of the House?

5. Who may become President?

6. How may we amend the Constitution?

7. How many amendments have been ## added to the Constitution? When were the first ten added? The most recent one?

8. Read Article 6, Clause 2. What is the Constitution called there? How does this clause recall the difficulties that the American people experienced under the Articles of Confederation?

The Research Center

1. When did the state you live in come into the Union? If you live in any state besides one of the first thirteen, find out what procedure it followed in gaining admission. Was your state formerly a part of an organized territory? If so, what one? When was it organized?

2. If you live in a state that was made from part of the old Northwest, find out how the provision in the Northwest Ordinance about public education affected it.

3. If you live in a state where the land is divided into townships and sections, find out what township you live in. Is there a township government? What does it do?

Sharpening Your Map Skills

1. Look at the map on page 226. On what basis did the states make the claims shown there? What states had no claims? Why? The area that was ceded to the national government by the states became the public domain. What present-day states were carved out of it?

2. Find on the map on page 231 the boundary that gave the United States government difficulty after the Revolution. What does the map tell you about the problems Americans had in removing the British from the area? About the problems Spanish control of the Mississippi caused Americans?

Consider that although the United States has changed greatly since 1787 (in size, population, ver, and responsibilities), the Constitution has been changed very little. Show how the astic Clause" has made relatively few amendments necessary.

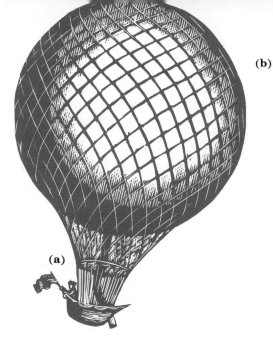

(a)

(b)

(c)

(a) The balloon that lifted a man from Philadelphia to a town in New Jersey in 1793, on the first such flight in the United States. From Independence Hall, Washington had watched it go up.
(b) The carved wooden figure of a navigator, used as a sign over a shop in Massachusetts in the early 1800's.
(c) A leather fire bucket for use in case of fire in Washington's home.
(d) Washington's coach, which was powered by four horses. (e) Martha Washington, the first First Lady.
(f) The rear of Mount Vernon in 1792.

(d)

(e)

(f)

(g) A stained-glass window in Christ Church, Philadelphia, showing the congregation in 1790. Robert Morris is in the center of the front row, and the President and his wife, at the left in the second row, are by Betsy Ross and Alexander Hamilton.

(g)

CHAPTER 12

THE FIRST YEARS UNDER PRESIDENTS

review briefly the sections of Chapter 11 about the weaknesses of the Articles of Confederation and about e ways in which the Constitution corrected these weaknesses. Show that the first leaders of the new public were men who had become prominent during the Revolutionary era.

To the surprise of no one, George Washington was the people's choice for the presidency. He himself had no desire for further public service. In fact, he thought it unfair that he be asked again to leave Mount Vernon. "[T]he great Searcher of hearts is my witness," he said, "that I have no wish which aspires beyond the humble and happy lot of living and dying a private citizen on my own farm."

iscuss why the selection of Washington as President was crucial to the success of the new government.

The People Put Washington in Charge Again

However, the "New Roof"—as the Constitution was being called in many places—required Washington's powerful influence. And many of Washington's friends kept insisting to him that he become the first President. Alexander Hamilton, a brash but brilliant young man, saw clearly the need to have Washington at the head of the new government.

Hamilton wrote to the General, "I feel a conviction [that is, I am sure] that you will finally see your acceptance to be indispensable [necessary]. . . . I am not sure that your refusal would not throw everything into confusion. . . . I think circum-stances leave you no option [choice]." Or as a newspaper reporter in Philadelphia stated, "[T]hirteen staves and ne'er a hoop will not make a barrel."

Shaping the Presidency

Washington, in coöperation with Congress and the federal courts, would be the hoop. But remember, no one knew how the three separate branches of government—the executive, legislative, and judicial—would work. The first *administration*, that is, the first group of men officially responsible for the operation of the government,

what ways was the government of the United States a new type of political system? What idelines did Washington have for "shaping the presidency"? Ask students to identify present actices of our government that began during Washington's presidency.

247

Fine Arts Collection, Seamen's Bank for Savings, New York

The newly elected President arrives at the corner of Wall Street, in New York City, April 29, 1789, having crossed the Hudson on a boat which met him on the New Jersey side of the river.

#Washington is our only president to be elected unanimously. How did this help unify the country?

settled: the chief executive would be called President of the United States of America. A Senator from Pennsylvania said, "This is his title of office, nor can we alter, add to, or diminish it without infringing [trespassing on] the Constitution."

The same Senator, William Maclay, wrote in his diary, "I entertain no doubt but that many people are aiming with all their force to establish a splendid court with all the pomp of majesty. Alas, poor Washington, if you are taken in this snare!"

Relations with fellow citizens. In his residence in New York, then capital of the United States, once a week—on Tuesdays—Washington held an afternoon reception for men. He would stand before the fireplace, clad in a black velvet suit, wearing shoes with silver buckles and a dress sword in a white leather sheath which hung at his side.

As the name of each visitor was announced (loudly, because the President had become quite deaf), he would bow—having decided that the dignity of his office forbade shaking hands. Although the Washingtons gave regular dinners, the President also made it a practice never to accept invitations to dine out, and he never returned a visit.

Dealings with Congress. The President's relations with Congress, as well as with citizens, had to be established. On one occasion, Washington rode in his coach to Federal Hall, the Capitol—then in New York City—to obtain "advice and consent" about a proposed Indian treaty.

The Senators criticized the treaty. Their understanding of the provision in the Constitution that they share the treaty-making power with the President was that they should give him "advice and consent." Washington was furious at the criticism, which he took personally. He departed angrily.

To this day no other chief executive has

had to find out for itself. It had to deal with all kinds of public issues, large and small.

Washington, elected President by a unanimous vote of the electoral college, took office in 1789, becoming head of the first administration. John Adams was chosen as Vice-President. Washington and Adams were inaugurated in New York City amid stirring celebrations.

A proper title. One of the first questions —the answer to which we take for granted today—tells us how hard it was to start a new government. It was, How does one refer to the President? A Senate committee, for example, thought up this title for him: "His Highness the President of the United States of America, and Protector of their Liberties."

The name sounded to many people too much like one they might use for a king. Yet never before had there been a President, and it took time to become accustomed to one.

At last the question about the title was

##Discuss some of the social customs surrounding the presidency today. What ceremonies go along with the inauguration (speeches, receptions, etc.)? How is the President addressed in conversation (Mr. President)?

England's system, for example, the prime minister and cabinet ministers engage in debate in Parliament. In our system, cabinet members may testify in Congress but they do not share in debates.

entered into an argument with Senators on the floor of the Senate chamber. Provisions of the Constitution, which had seemed so clear and simple to the Founding Fathers at the Philadelphia convention, sometimes worked out strangely (or not at all) in practice.

Relations with governors. And what would happen when the President visited outside of New York State? Was the governor of the state being visited expected to turn out to greet the President, or was the President to make a formal call on the governor?

In the fall of 1789, Washington went on a trip to New England. When he was in Massachusetts, Governor John Hancock, pretending to be ill, refused to pay Washington a courtesy visit. He thought the President ought to call on him. Hancock, seeing that Washington made no move to do so and discovering that the chief executive was being cheered everywhere, recov-

ered overnight. The next day he called on the President.

Some Favorable Conditions

So the process of establishing new customs and procedures went, step by step. Americans were fortunate in having as their President a man so generally admired as George Washington was. Perhaps "revered" is a better word.

A popular hero. After Washington's death, a fellow Virginian, in a speech of praise, would call him "first in war, first in peace, and first in the hearts of his countrymen." Long before his death, too, Washington occupied the highest place in American affections.

As early as 1777 a writer in the *Pennsylvania Journal*, a newspaper, had expressed this esteem: "Had he lived in the days of idolatry [that is, when people prayed to idols], he had been worshipped as a god."

Was it wise of the Washingtons to have such formal receptions as pictured here?

One of the First Lady's receptions in New York City in 1789, before the capital was located in Philadelphia. Beautifully dressed, she stands on a platform at the left, while the President—in the center background—mingles with the guests.

Sympathetic associates. Washington as
President enjoyed a number of advantages in addition to the public's respect. First, he had the active help of the important men who had been members of the Philadelphia convention or who had otherwise promoted the Constitution. To take only one example, James Madison, already renowned as the "Father of the Constitution," was a member of the House of Representatives from Virginia.

Altogether there were eighty-one men in the first Congress (twenty-two Senators and fifty-nine members of the House of Representatives). Of these, fifty-four had either taken part in writing the Constitution or had campaigned and voted for it at the ratifying conventions in the states—or both. All the members of Congress wanted to see the new government succeed, and their energies and intelligence were directed to that end.

A calm time. A second advantage—the phrase "piece of luck" may be better—was that 1789 was a year without an important crisis. Although various foreign problems existed, they were not pressing ones. Moreover, business conditions were getting better. The unrest of farmers, recently seen in New England especially, had vanished.

An acceptable government. Yet another advantage was that the new Constitution strengthened—it did not originate—an already deep American devotion to representative government. This love had long been developing in the colonial assemblies and in the Continental Congresses. The new government gave the people a means of expressing their wishes that in general was both familiar and agreeable to them.

Links with the past. Americans in 1789, furthermore, did not see that they had made a sharp break with the past. It did not appear odd, for example, that President Washington should put William Jackson, the former secretary of the Continental Congress, on his staff as secretary.

Also, some of the departments in the executive branch of the government which had existed under the Confederation—the postal service, for instance—continued in the new government.

Men Around the Chief

The use of heads of the executive departments as a group of official advisers for the President was not provided for in the Constitution. The Constitution simply states (see page 714) that the President "may require the opinion . . . of the principal officer in each of the executive departments, upon any subject relating to . . . their respective offices. . . . " Yet by 1793 these men as a group were beginning to be called the Cabinet, and they were enjoying positions of honor because they had the special trust and confidence of the President.

Hamilton. The most important Cabinet appointment Washington made was that of Alexander Hamilton, of New York, who was named Secretary of the Treasury. Hamilton was only thirty-four years old. A leader in the movement to strengthen the Articles of Confederation, as we have seen, Hamilton, like Robert Morris, was a wizard with money. He used every ounce of his rare skill to make Washington's administration succeed.

Jefferson. Another major appointment was that of the Virginian Thomas Jefferson as Secretary of State. He was responsible chiefly for taking care of foreign affairs. Jefferson had been minister of the United States to France. Like some other Virginians, he had been only lukewarm about the new Constitution because it had lacked a bill of rights. But he knew its shortcomings would be corrected and that the government from then on would be the one provided by the Constitution.

Jefferson wrote a friend shortly after the new frame of government was adopted. He

##The Cabinet was really created during Washington's first administration. As in other government matters, there was little experience to go on. What qualities do you think Washington looked for in making Cabinet appointments? How does a President choose his Cabinet today?

said, "[A]ll of us going together, we shall be sure to cure the evils of our new Constitution before they do great harm." Jefferson generally looked on the bright side of things, and he believed that in America there were two powerful forces to rely upon: "good sense and a free spirit."

Edmund Randolph. To Edmund Randolph, also of Virginia, whose large-state plan had been used in determining representation in Congress, Washington gave the post of Attorney-General. This office was provided for in the Judiciary Act of 1789, one of the first pieces of legislation passed by Congress. That law also created our system of federal courts—at the head of which was placed the Supreme Court.

General Knox. For department heads Washington selected some men who had served in the government of the Confederation. He chose as Secretary of War his old associate and artillery chief in the American Revolution, Henry Knox, of Massachusetts. Knox had been head of the War Department under the Articles of Confederation. Only thirty-nine years of age in 1789 and weighing nearly 300 pounds, he had placed the cannon in position at the Battle of Yorktown.

In the post office. Washington named Samuel Osgood, of Massachusetts, to head the postal service. Osgood, who had at first opposed the Constitution, had been a director of the Bank of North America (see page 228) and a treasury official of the Confederation. By choosing a man like Osgood, Washington was hoping to gain the support of other citizens who had also been Antifederalists.

Chief Justice John Jay. As Chief Justice (chief judge) of the Supreme Court, Washington chose John Jay, of New York. Washington no doubt wanted Jay close by, for he relied on him frequently for decisions in many governmental matters. The Supreme Court was not immediately the dignified body it later became. Jay even

ran for the governorship of New York while continuing to serve as Chief Justice!

Well-balanced choices. The new administration had drawn upon both northerners and southerners, and its members were experienced, eager, and youthful men. Just as important, despite the fact that most of the officials were Federalists, it had sought the loyalty of men who had somewhat unwillingly offered their support to the Constitution.

George Washington, unlike modern Presidents, did not have in mind laws he hoped Congress would enact. After all, he had not "run" for the presidency as presidential candidates do today. There were no political parties as we know them, and no platforms. Feeling his way in a brand-new

The President—right—wearing a black velvet suit, has a conference with his Cabinet. From left to right are: Knox, seated; Jefferson; Randolph, his back turned; and the handsome Hamilton.

American Museum of Natural History

situation, the President relied for advice on those he had placed around himself.

Madison. One of Washington's mainstays was his fellow Virginian James Madison. Their friendship was natural because Madison, too, believed that the Constitution could make a strong America.

Hamilton's Program

The one who came to the fore most quickly, however, was Alexander Hamilton. Hamilton was personally ambitious # and both able and anxious to offer advice. For some time he appears to have considered himself a kind of prime minister, making himself responsible for pressing a series of laws upon Congress.

Years later people would say that Hamilton tried to take powers which were not properly his. But it is well to remember that a description of the relations between the President's advisers and members of Congress had not been written down or agreed upon anywhere. Hamilton, for instance, thought that as Secretary of the Treasury he ought to be able to appear personally in Congress to present his ideas.

Being the most vigorous member of the Cabinet, Hamilton had the field pretty much to himself until March, 1790. At that time Jefferson returned from Paris to take up his position as Secretary of State. Jefferson, too, had ideas about how the new government should be conducted, and he did not hesitate to express them.

The man's vision. Meanwhile, though, Hamilton had taken important steps to strengthen the government. He recognized that men who owned property would have to be persuaded that it was to their advantage to support the Constitution with enthusiasm. They would have to be shown that if the government of the United States prospered, it would be more respected abroad than it was then. Respect abroad, they well knew, would lead to new opportunities for American trade. And at home, too, a strong government able to encourage business would be helpful to men of wealth wanting to invest their money profitably.

What could Hamilton do to win the support of businessmen for the new government? In a series of reports to Congress, he laid out a program for the country. His proposals have ever since been regarded as brilliant, even by opponents. In January, 1790, he presented his first Report on the Public Credit.

Assumption of the debts. Hamilton's first report dealt with money. In it, Hamilton called for the *assumption*, that is, the taking over, of the entire foreign and domestic debt owed by the United States under the Articles of Confederation. The understanding was that this debt would be paid in full by the new federal government. Such a step, Hamilton thought, would immediately prove to the world that Americans were an honorable people.

The debt, totaling about $77,000,000, had been run up in winning and strengthening independence. The new government could have refused to pay it, using as an excuse the fact that it had been acquired under a government that was no longer in existence.

Hamilton's first report did not stop with the plan for paying the national debt. It included taking over, too, *state* debts. In insisting on paying debts the states had run up, Hamilton was being especially cunning. He knew that a number of states had not paid off their debts because they had been unwilling to tax their people to do so.

Hamilton further wanted to pay off the debts with money from national taxes. He would in this way quickly establish the control of the national government over the use of such taxes.

Bank of the United States. Hamilton's second report called for the establishment

##Review briefly how Americans raised money for the War for Independence. Discuss how the carrying out of Hamilton's financial program increased the power and prestige of the national government both at home and abroad.

Columbiana Collection, Columbia University

A portrait of Alexander Hamilton at the age of twenty-three, painted by Charles Willson Peale, probably for Hamilton's wife, Elizabeth.

of a Bank of the United States. This bank would handle the money affairs of the government, including keeping on deposit the funds of the federal government itself.

In his plans for the bank, Hamilton provided that bank stock could be bought by private individuals. Men with funds to invest would be delighted with such an opportunity, he thought. Surely, said Hamilton, these investors would want the new government to succeed. Not only would their country be much better off because of its success, but also the value of their bank stock would increase.

Excise taxes. To raise tax money, Hamilton proposed *excise taxes*—direct taxes —on certain goods. Hamilton's program included also a system of *tariffs*, or duties on imports. These would produce money— as well as protect American manufactured goods from competition with European-made items.

An industrial America. Hamilton devoted an entire report to the subject of the de-velopment of industry, in which he had a keen interest. In his Report on Manufac-tures, presented to Congress in December, 1791, Hamilton predicted that the United States would one day be an industrialized country. He said that he believed Ameri-cans should develop factories because these could provide many of the supplies needed in time of war as well as peace.

Hamilton was also of the opinion that if a large number of Americans entered in-dustry, the home market for the products of our farms would be enlarged. Hamilton was aiming to make America more truly than ever a "land of opportunity."

To accomplish his purpose, Hamilton would give government itself a large role in business. He expected the federal gov-ernment to provide grants of money, or # *subsidies*, to help infant industries get started. He also was in favor of encourag-ing immigration to help man and "woman" the factories and of paying handsome re-wards for useful inventions.

The active hand of government. In the America Hamilton foresaw, the hand of the federal government would constantly be affecting the lives of the people. How-ever, he had little faith in the people's ability to solve their own problems. He once said, "The voice of the people has been said to be the voice of God; and how-ever generally this . . . has been quoted and believed, it is not true in fact. The people . . . seldom judge or determine right."

Americans were living still in an age when farming was the principal way to make a living. People thought mainly about agriculture and about selling farm goods. As a result, many of Hamilton's pro-posals ran into stiff arguments.

Dispute over state debts. Paying state debts, many Americans insisted, was quite different from paying the national debt. Some states had already paid their debts. Their people would resent keenly being taxed to pay the debts of other states

at features of Hamilton's program have become part of the economic policy of our govern-
nt? Discuss the idea of <u>subsidies</u>. Ask students to give examples of how federal funds, like
sidies, are used to aid new or important industries.

253

which, they believed, had ignored or dodged their financial obligations.

One of the men who spoke out strongly against the assumption of state debts was James Madison. He did not want Virginians—who had been gradually paying off their state debt—to have to help pay debts of other states, too, particularly those of Massachusetts and South Carolina.

Hamilton's answer was that Massachusetts and South Carolina had borne an unusually heavy burden of fighting during the American Revolution. Paying their debt, therefore, could not be considered unreasonable by true patriots.

Disagreement over national debt. The idea of paying off the national debt in full also aroused opposition. This is why. Years before, when the Continental Congress began to acquire the debt, it did so by borrow-
ing money through selling *bonds* to the people. These bonds—papers promising that the government would repay the loans with interest—gradually fell in value in the years that followed. The reason was the general belief that the United States would never redeem them, that is, pay them off.

The speculators. During the period of the Articles of Confederation, speculators often had been able to buy the bonds of the government practically for nothing. These speculators had been gambling that at some time in the future the bonds would be redeemed at the value printed on them. Hamilton's plan to pay the debt seemed to them like a dream come true.

Moreover, when word of Hamilton's intentions spread, speculators rushed into the back country to purchase bonds held by people who had not heard of the new plan to redeem them. It was said that speculators and other get-rich-quick types were drawn to the bonds like "crows round a carcass."

There is no doubt that the speculators tended to be located in or near the larger cities, like Boston, New York, and Philadelphia. Therefore the people of chiefly one section of the country—the North—were going to profit at the expense of the whole country. To James Madison, especially, it seemed unjust for things to turn out that way.

Some effects on politics. The disagreement which developed over paying the national debt in full had an important effect on politics. The Federalists, who had been united since 1787, began to break into two groups. One group, largely though not entirely from the North, favored Hamilton's program. The other group, almost entirely southern, opposed it.

Jefferson's arrival. At first Madison was the leader of the southern group. But Jefferson, older and more experienced, took it over when he arrived on the scene —fresh from Paris—in the spring of 1790. He had come back to take up his post as Secretary of State.

The fate of Hamilton's program hung in the balance. At the height of the argument that spring, an epidemic of influenza and pneumonia spread throughout the country. President Washington himself fell ill in May. For a time it was feared that he would die. Hamilton, who counted heavily on Washington's great influence to win votes for his program in Congress, was especially alarmed.

Hamilton and Jefferson. Early in the following month, though, the President, recovering, went on a fishing trip for a few days off the coast of New Jersey. In his party were Hamilton and Jefferson—the leaders of the two groups beginning to appear as political parties.

We probably shall never know what the two men talked about. It would be a good guess, though, that they talked politics. A modern biographer has written of Hamilton on that trip. Here is his comment: "Perhaps as he [Hamilton] watched Jefferson land one whopper after another,

Which groups seemed to benefit more from Hamilton's program--farmers or manufacturers, debtors or creditors, southerners or northerners? In what ways did they benefit? Use these questions to review Hamilton's program.

The lonely site of what was to become the new capital, Washington, as it looked in 1794, when an English artist painted it. A few buildings and some boats may be seen in the center background near what looks like a bend in the Potomac River.

at were the reasons for
lding the capital here?

he began to consider the possibility of baiting his hook for the Secretary of State himself."

Clearly, if Hamilton's program was to pass Congress, Hamilton would have to have the support of the Virginia members. So far he had succeeded only in driving Madison, one of the leaders of the Virginians, into fierce opposition. Hamilton's chance for success appeared to rest with Jefferson, who had not yet taken a firm stand on Hamilton's proposals.

Not long afterward Jefferson, on his way to keep an appointment with Washington, met Hamilton on the street. Hamilton, Jefferson later wrote, was showing the effects of worry over his program. He was looking downcast beyond description, with "even his dress uncouth & neglected. He walked me backward and forward before the President's door for half an hour," painting a picture of how the Union itself might break up if his program failed to pass Congress.

A deal. The effect on Jefferson was marked. The next day he, Madison, and Hamilton had dinner together. The two Virginians used the occasion to name their price for ending southern opposition to the plans for paying the state debts. It was: the permanent capital of the United States had to be located on the banks of the Potomac River.

Hamilton was happy to strike a bargain. In exchange for many southern votes for his program, he rounded up enough northern votes to insure the new location of the capital.

Since Pennsylvania votes for paying the debts were among those required, it was agreed that the temporary capital would be located at Philadelphia for ten years. (New York City had counted on remaining the capital. It had, in fact, spent a considerable amount of money to make federal officeholders feel comfortable.)

The deal stuck, despite doubters. For a long time many thought that once Philadelphia was the seat of government, it would remain so for good. George Washington's influence was great, however, and he hoped to see the capital located on the Potomac—the river he loved so much. Not until 1800—the year after his death—was the government moved to Washington, D.C.

Farmers against the "moneyed interests." The passage first of the bill to pay the na-

scuss the idea of bargaining in reaching agreements and passing laws in the United States.
sider, for example, the deal between Hamilton and Jefferson. (Do students today think of
hington, D.C., as being southern?)

255

tional debt and second of the bill to pay the state debts opened a deep wound in American political life. Already there were people who were saying that the farmers were going to be squeezed dry by the "moneyed interests," almost as if farmers were just so many milk cows.

Hamilton did not worry about the people's opposition to the program he favored. He believed firmly that they should have laws which were good for them, even though the laws pinched them badly.

Argument over the bank. Another argument arose over whether or not the Bank of the United States should be established. By the time Hamilton issued his report on it, the government had moved to Philadelphia. There in the City of Brotherly Love, Hamilton hoped to establish the only bank in the country with a federal charter.

But already suspicions were being aroused. Most important of all, the old fear of too much government control was growing. Also, farmers thought that the new bank would lend money chiefly to people in business and manufacturing.

Nevertheless, the bill to establish a bank passed by an overwhelming vote. Senator Maclay, who strongly opposed the measure, wrote, "Mr. Hamilton is all-powerful, and fails in nothing he attempts."

Washington could not quickly make up his mind to sign the bank bill. Because Madison, whom he greatly respected, was against it, the President sought the opinions of others as well before deciding.

"Strict construction." One of the men he consulted was Jefferson. Jefferson sent the President a written reply. In it, he took a position that afterward came to be called the *strict construction* of the Constitution. (The word construction here means the act of construing, or interpreting.)

According to Jefferson's strict construction, Congress had no authority under the Constitution to create a bank. On the other hand, Jefferson knew that such an un-

"Fleet's Pocket Almanack," 1791, Collection of I. S. Seidman, New York

A page from a pocket almanac published in 1791, listing government officials and their salaries. What are the salaries of the President and Vice-President today?

bending idea of the power of Congress as his could be fatal to the new government. He advised the President, therefore, that although the organizing of the bank could not be justified, the President ought to accept the bill out of "a . . . respect for the wisdom of the legislature."

"Loose construction." Hamilton was much more sure of how he felt than Jefferson was. He said that for every power listed in the Constitution as belonging to Congress, Congress had additional power to pass suitable laws to put the listed one into effect. This additional power is called *implied power* because it is implied in

#Explain the terms "strict construction" and "loose construction" and discuss their meaning. Use a specifically listed power of Congress (Article I, Section 8, Clause 3 is a good one for this purpose) and show how the Elastic Clause operates.

the Constitution rather than stated specifically. Hamilton's view came to be known as the *loose construction* of the Constitution.

Congress' power to issue money, therefore, carried with it, Hamilton said, an implied power to establish a bank. Hamilton said the government may pass whatever laws it regards as "necessary and proper" (see Article 1, Section 8, Clause 18, page 711).

In later times the papers containing the conflicting opinions about the United States bank were made public. Long before then, however, these opinions had been recognized as two views of how the federal government should work. Meanwhile, Washington took the advice to accept the judgment of Congress, and he signed the bank bill.

The Rise of Political Parties

Hamilton behaved like the cat who has swallowed the canary. As a matter of fact, however, he had reached the peak of his accomplishments—although he did not know it at the time. The argument about the bank had united his opponents.

The Republicans. Hamilton's opponents were calling themselves the Democratic-Republicans or just Republicans. Meeting together once in a while, they were the beginning of a political party. And why should we not organize? they must have thought. A group—which came to be called Federalists—had been formed to support almost anything that Hamilton proposed.

Jefferson became the leader of the Republicans. A former governor of Virginia, he had had so many unpleasant experiences with politicians that he wanted to avoid disputes. He was, though, a man who held deep beliefs for which he was willing to fight. In an age when political speeches were less important than the

written word, he was a master of the written language. This fact made what he said unusually influential.

Although Jefferson did not openly attack Hamilton's money policies, he did not approve of Hamilton's program for paying debts. He thought that a debt—private or public—was a curse, not a blessing, and that it should be paid off as soon as possible. Being devoted to farming, he saw no reason for catering to businessmen.

Above all, Jefferson was against encouraging manufacturing. (How different is the outlook of the leaders of the new nations in our own day. They seem to accept without question the idea that they must strengthen industry as soon as possible.)

Jefferson knew, needless to say, the importance of manufactured goods. "But," he said, "let our workshops remain in Europe." He firmly believed that those who work the soil are superior to those who do not, and he had a powerful fear of the growth of cities. In a now-famous sentence he wrote, "The mobs of great cities add just so much to the support of pure government as sores do to the strength of the human body."

Jefferson disliked industry because he thought it weakened men's character not to be working as farmers. But also he was concerned over what the growth of industry could lead to. He wrote Madison in 1787, "When they get piled up upon one another in large cities, as in Europe, they shall become corrupt as in Europe, and go to eating one another as they do there."

In the summer of 1791, Jefferson and Madison took a trip from Philadelphia to Lake George, in New York State, and then through New England and back to Philadelphia. They were on a vacation, but they must have made valuable contacts with local politicians who shared their suspicion and fear of what Hamilton was planning. Jefferson and Madison, in short, were spreading their political influence.

Make sure that students do not confuse the federalists and the Federalists. The two groups are not always the same. For example, James Madison, "the father of the Constitution" (a federalist in that sense), was later a leader of the Republicans, the opponents of the Federalists.

257

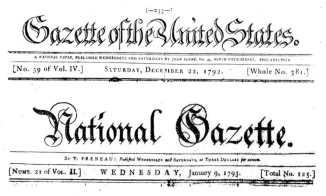

Library of Congress

Do newspapers today support political parties? I can students check? (Editorial pages, headlines.

The pro-Hamilton *Gazette of the United States*—above—called itself a national newspaper. As you can see, it was not a daily. In this issue on the Saturday before Christmas, 1792, it was continuing its attack on Jefferson. Freneau's paper—below—published on the same days as its rival and costing subscribers three dollars a year, not only criticized Hamilton but in this issue spoke sharply about the danger of "worshipping" the President.

Newspaper warfare. Hamilton and *his* supporters began to grow openly unfriendly to Jefferson, and the contest between the two men showed up in articles in the newspapers. Two papers in Philadelphia seemed to exist only to argue with one another. One of them, the *Gazette of the United States,* supported Hamilton, and the other, the *National Gazette,* supported the views of Jefferson.

The *National Gazette*'s editor was a splendid poet, Philip Freneau (frĕn nō′), who had known Madison when they were both undergraduates at the College of New Jersey (now Princeton). In the fashion of that day, the editors of both papers were supported by friends in the government. Jefferson gave Freneau a position as translator in the Department of State. Hamilton saw to it that the editor of the *Gazette of the United States* received valuable contracts to do public printing.

Two "sides," therefore, developed in the new government. The central issue between them apparently was, What kind of country ought the United States to be?

Hamilton had more stomach for the battle than Jefferson. Jefferson, in fact, told Washington one morning after breakfast in February, 1792, that he intended to retire as Secretary of State at the end of Washington's term as President.

Effects in the Cabinet. Naturally, Washington was terribly distressed by the news, and he would not hear of Jefferson's leaving the Cabinet. He persuaded the Virgini-

This drawing of a low-domed building won a contest in 1792 for the best design for the new Capitol in Washington. It became the model for the building and brought to its creator a prize of five hundred dollars and a city lot.

Library of Congress; United States Capitol Historical Society

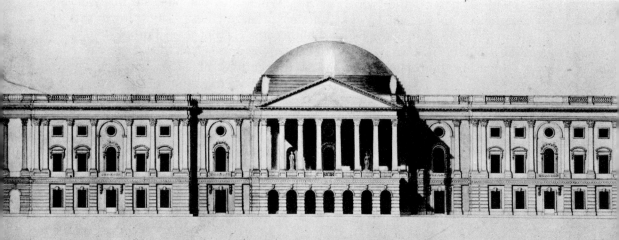

an to remain, but not before Jefferson had expressed opposition to Hamilton's program in blunt language. Washington now knew at first hand how deep-seated was the quarrel between his chief Cabinet officers.

Jefferson pinned his hopes on the forthcoming presidential elections. If Washington would agree to continue as President, the people, in whom Jefferson had unbounded confidence, would be able to try to elect Congressmen who would resist Hamilton's schemes.

Jefferson thought the fate of the new government itself still depended on George Washington. He told the President: "The confidence of the whole Union is centered n you. . . . North and South will hang together if they have you to hang on."

A second term. After a period of making up his mind, Washington agreed to accept the clear will of the people. He and Adams were reelected in 1792. Washington refused to become involved in the charges and countercharges which Hamilton and Jefferson—and their followers, too—were hurling at one another. He convinced Jefferson that Hamilton could be con-

trolled best if Jefferson remained in office "to keep things in their proper channel, and prevent them from going too far."

The President handled Hamilton with equal consideration, being respectful of the work the Secretary of the Treasury had done. The credit of the United States, Washington said, had been raised from a desperate low point to "the highest pitch."

---

1. What customs and procedures did the first President set? 2. Name four members of Washington's first Cabinet and tell what each did. 3. Describe the proposals Hamilton made in his first and second reports on the public credit. 4. Identify two predictions Hamilton made which came true. 5. What arguments did Hamilton's proposals stir up? 6. Account for the movement of the national capital to Washington, D.C. 7. How did Jefferson's understanding of the Constitution differ from Hamilton's? 8. What important effect did the differences between Hamilton and Jefferson and their followers have on American politics?

---

se views--Jefferson's or Hamilton's--came closer to describing the development of the United States?

War Abroad Sharpens the Conflict at Home

The quarrel between the Republicans and the Federalists was influenced greatly by events taking place in Europe. Over these, Americans, of course, had no control.

In the Cockpit of the World

Hamilton and the Federalists greatly admired Britain. They believed that despite the troubles of the past, the time had come to recognize that close relations with the British could bring about the growth of trade on which American prosperity depended. Hamilton, of course, kept in mind

that his own plans would not work well unless commerce was brisk.

Jefferson and the Republicans, on the other hand, had a deep affection for France. Jefferson cared little for the British, calling them once those "rich, proud . . . animals . . . on the other side of the [English] Channel."

Bloody revolution. The French Revolution, which had broken out shortly after Washington first became President, affected Americans deeply. They felt forced to take sides in that great event.

The revolution was the result of a long

period of growing dissatisfaction in France with the way the king and his officials governed. A highlight was the storming of a hated prison fortress, the Bastille, by the Parisian street mob on July 14, 1789. They released the prisoners it held.

News of the attack on the Bastille burst upon the United States like a bombshell. Frenchmen, it seemed to people in America, had struck their blow for liberty as we had in 1776. Remembering the aid France had given us in the days of the American Revolution, most Americans were happy for the French people.

Joy in America. Jefferson might have been speaking for all his countrymen when he wrote Lafayette in 1790. He said, "Wherever I am, or shall be, I shall be sincere in my friendship to you and to your nation."

Americans showed their enthusiasm in a number of ways. They sang French songs and followed events in the French Revolution as closely as possible. The most wildly enthusiastic people changed street names to honor French heroes. When the leaders of the French Revolution adopted the slogan "Liberty, Equality, Fraternity," the cry was taken up here.

This enthusiasm was shaken after January, 1793, when the French Revolution entered a new and bloody stage. Its leaders had arrested and then beheaded King Louis XVI and Queen Marie Antoinette and many other aristocrats.

Most Americans keenly disapproved of these murders. Yet Jefferson wrote, "The liberty of the whole earth was depending on the issue [that is, the outcome] of the contest, and was ever such a prize won with so little innocent blood." Many people, though, watched events in France with increasing alarm.

Meanwhile, the monarchs of Europe, feeling sympathy for the French king and queen, had turned their wrath against the French people. By the spring of 1793,

Britain, the Netherlands, and Spain were among the countries that had gone to war against France.

Some consequences. What would be the effects of the war in Europe on the United States? Even though the strength of the United States as yet weighed almost nothing in international affairs, our country had to have a policy.

Many of the Federalists advised entering the war on the side of the European countries against the leaders of the French Revolution and their followers. A defeat of the French, they thought, would discourage supporters of the French here in America. Hamilton himself wanted not war with France but simply continued peace with Britain. He always had in mind that his financial program depended on maintaining smooth relations with the British.

Jefferson, too, was guided by what he thought would be best for America. As he and other Republicans saw things, it would do the United States no good if the Spanish and the English, especially, joined together and were successful against France. Spain and England both had possessions in North America, and they might become bold enough to threaten us directly. By aiding France, Jefferson thought, we would be helping to weaken the very countries which could endanger us here in America.

Neutrality Proclamation. President Washington refused flatly to take either the English side or the French side. On April 22, 1793, he issued his Neutrality Proclamation. This memorable statement was to remain for the next hundred years an important part of our policy toward other countries—our *foreign policy.* In it Washington advised that the United States follow a policy of *neutrality,* that is, of not favoring any one European power or group of powers.

Washington's warning to "adopt and pursue a conduct friendly and impartial"

Discuss how Hamilton, Jefferson, and Washington--each "guided by what he thought would be best for America"--proposed different policies for the United States to follow in the war between France and the monarchies of Europe.

e that neutrality did not mean isolation--it meant <u>not</u> taking sides. Washington wanted the U.S. to ..ntain trade and friendly relations with all nations but to stay out of European wars.

.toward the countries of Europe at war did not prevent us from coming very close to war with England. In 1794 the relations between the United States and Britain were as strained as they had been at any time since the outbreak of the War for Independence.

The northwest posts. The reason was that Britain had still failed to withdraw its troops from the posts in the old Northwest. It had agreed to do so in the Treaty of Paris of 1783. The British troops in those garrisons continued to be allied with the Indians so they could control the fur trade. They stirred up the tribesmen frequently to prey on Americans, who were just beginning to settle the Northwest Territory.

Impressment of seamen. Furthermore, since Britain and France were at war in Europe, the British tried to prevent supplies from reaching their enemy. As a result, British naval vessels halted on the seas American ships bound for French ports. Many members of the crews were then seized—"impressed" was the word used—and forced into the British navy.

Americans were furious. In Congress a group of Jeffersonians supported a law to suspend all trade with Britain until it halted its impressment of American seamen. Hamilton, too, was aroused. After all, even if a government was financially sound, what did it amount to if it could not protect its citizens?

Nevertheless, Congress took no action against Britain on account of the almost equally warlike activities of France. The French had no strong navy with which to fight Britain. They tried to weaken the British by seizing American ships in the French ports in the Caribbean—ships which might carry goods to England.

Attempts to Keep Peace

The Federalists in Washington's administration took a step to try to head off a possible anti-British action by the Republicans. They sent John Jay, Chief Justice of the Supreme Court, to England to try to settle some of the difficulties with the mother country.

Jay's mission. Republican newspapers immediately launched a severe personal attack on Jay. The chief charge was that he was a widely known friend of Britain's and would not propose anything which would not please its people.

Actually, the United States was in a poor position to deal with powerful foreign powers. We were militarily weak. Yet we were not wholly helpless. We could threaten to join the countries in Europe then organizing themselves to protest British practices on the high seas.

But an unbelievable thing had happened to prevent us even from taking this action. Alexander Hamilton had told the British minister in Philadelphia that under no circumstances would the United States make such a move! The minister promptly reported this fact to his government, taking from Jay one ace in the hole he might have tried to use.

A representation of what happened when the English impressed sailors on a United States vessel. The Americans were forced to leave their ship and board the British vessel.

..pressment and the old ..thwest caused trouble until ..r the War of 1812.

GENERAL GEORGE WASHINGTON.
Reviewing the Western army at Fort Cumberland the 18ᵗʰ of octobᵣ

Henry Francis du Pont Winterthur Museum

President Washington reviews militiamen after he called out troops from Maryland and other states to enforce a federal law.

There is no excuse for Hamilton's action. By way of explanation, though, it must be said that he did what he did because he was concerned that upsetting American relations with Britain would upset American trade. Such an outcome would interfere with his program. (Not until 1925 was the fact that Hamilton had held the conversation with the British minister revealed. Can you imagine what the Jeffersonians—the followers of Jefferson—would have said if they had known?)

Jay's treaty. The result of Jay's difficult mission to Britain was Jay's treaty, of November, 1794. In the treaty the British promised again to get out of the northwest posts. This time they kept their word, but they still were to be allowed to carry on the fur trade on American soil and trade with the Indians.

In addition, Americans would now be permitted to trade with the British in the West Indies—although they were not to send a ship with a cargo capacity of any more than 70 tons. Also, certain goods, sugar and cotton, for example, could not be carried in American ships.

However, the treaty said nothing about the seizure of American ships and seamen and nothing about paying for slaves carried off by the British during the American Revolution. As a result, the treaty was angrily attacked in many places in the United States as being a "surrender" to Britain.

Further, an event in Ohio especially added to the treaty's unpopularity. In Au-

Why did Jay sign a treaty before forcing England to make more concessions? Would more concessions from England have prevented criticism of the treaty? Discuss the difficulties of negotiating treaties between strong and weak nations.

gust, 1794, the American general "Mad Anthony" Wayne had given some of the Indians being aided by the British a solid drubbing at the Battle of Fallen Timbers. If we can stand up to our tormentors in this way, Jay's critics asked, why is our victory not recognized in bargaining with Britain?

On the frontier the opposition to Federalist policies had grown keener earlier in the year, making Jay's treaty seem to many there like the last straw. The reason was the so-called Whisky Rebellion. The farmers of western Pennsylvania had refused to pay the excise tax on whisky.

The President called on the militia of several states to suppress the rebellion. At the head of the 15,000 troops was Alexander Hamilton—a fact that Jefferson's supporters used to advantage. The Jeffersonians had a field day criticizing Jay's work and the Washington administration for finding it acceptable.

Our relations with Spain proved to be much more agreeable than those with the mother country. In 1795 Spain switched sides in Europe—from the side of England to the side of France. It had become important for the Spanish to protect themselves against the day when England might be free to turn on them and thrash them. The Spanish would then find the friendship of the United States very handy—especially since much Spanish territory adjoined that of the United States.

Pinckney's work. The result was that Thomas Pinckney, the American minister in Spain, was able to conclude in 1795 a very favorable treaty with the Spanish. ## This document, known ever since in America as Pinckney's treaty, unlike Jay's treaty, was approved unanimously by the Senate.

Pinckney's treaty opened the Mississippi River to free, that is, unhindered, navigation on it by Americans. Also, Americans acquired the valuable right—for a three-year period—to use without charge warehouses at New Orleans for goods awaiting later shipment to markets elsewhere. Spain furthermore agreed to keep in check Indians under their control who had been attacking Americans.

Lastly, the Spanish agreed to set the boundary of West Florida at 31° north latitude, where, since 1783, we had been claiming it belonged (see the map on page 213). This treaty shows that European troubles sometimes worked to the advantage of the United States.

> 1. What view of the war between France and other European countries did the Federalists take? The Republicans? 2. What stand did Washington take? 3. Name two reasons for bad feeling between the British and Americans. 4. Tell why Jay was sent to Britain and what he accomplished. 5. Give the main facts about the Whisky Rebellion. 6. State the provisions of the Pinckney treaty.

Were the Spanish concessions to the United States a sign of Spanish friendship for the United States? Discuss.

The Torch of Leadership Passes Smoothly

As Washington prepared to retire from the presidency in 1796, there was pressure on him, especially from Hamilton and his people, to seek the office once again. Washington's response was typical of him: "[I]f principles instead of men are not the steady pursuit of the Federalists, their cause will soon be at an end." Besides, Washington did not see why John Adams, who was then the Vice-President, would not be a perfectly satisfactory President for the young United States.

Discuss Washington's response to those who urged him to run for a third term. Note that by refusing to run, he established the two-term tradition. Franklin D. Roosevelt (1932-1945) is the only President to be elected to more than two full terms.

263

Adams in the White House

In the presidential election of 1796, Adams was chosen President. He won a *majority*, that is, more than half, of the electoral votes. Although Adams was a Federalist, Thomas Jefferson, having the second largest number of electoral votes, became Vice-President. So it happened that the country had a President of one party and a Vice-President of another.

An unbearable situation might have arisen if John Adams had died in office and Jefferson had succeeded him. But death did not remove a President until after—long after—the system of electing our chief executive had been changed (see pages 721–722).

Washington's Farewell Address. Before Washington departed for his home in Mount Vernon, he issued a Farewell Address to the American people, which Alexander Hamilton had helped him prepare. The address was not spoken, as it would be today. It was published in the *American Daily Advertiser,* a Philadelphia newspaper, and in other papers.

At the time, the chief purpose of the message was to tell the people that the President had decided definitely not to run again. But the President's additional words for years afterward influenced Americans. Among them these became famous: "It is our true policy to steer clear of permanent
alliances with any portion of the foreign world."

Washington did not mean that we must keep ourselves *isolated*—separated—from the rest of the world. He meant that Europe—which he had chiefly in mind—had interests and concerns of its own which it would be unwise for us to become involved in. Washington was apparently advising that the storm in Europe must blow itself out without damaging the new republic by its backlash.

It is said that on the day John Adam took the oath of office, March 4, 1797, hi hands trembled uncontrollably. He knev how difficult it would be to take Washing ton's place.

Reporting to Abigail. Adams, of course took pride, as all Americans could, in th fact that the changeover from one Presi dent to another was happening peacefully Such an event was new in man's history Adams expressed his pride this way in letter he wrote to his beloved wife, Abi gail: "The sight of the sun setting.. and another rising (though less splendid) was a novelty."

As Adams began his administration, h longed to have Abigail at his side. She wa still in Massachusetts, preparing to joi him at the President's house in Philadel phia. That dwelling was furnished onl with what Washington had left behind "There is not a chair fit to sit in," Adam wrote, and "The beds and bedding are in woeful pickle."

Adams soon had more important wor ries. He was confronted with a crisis i foreign affairs. The French refused to re ceive our new minister, Charles Cotes worth Pinckney, of South Carolina, be cause, for one reason, they were angry a our failure to deal strongly with the Brit ish. Adams appointed a commission t talk with the French, made up of Pinck ney; John Marshall, of Virginia; and El bridge Gerry, of Massachusetts.

The X Y Z affair. Nothing good came o the discussions the Americans held i 1797 with representatives of the Frencl government in Paris. The French spokes men—there were three of them—wer identified only as "X," "Y," and "Z." "X made the startling request for a bribe o $240,000 to smooth the way to reopenin; regular diplomatic relations betweer France and the United States. Whe pressed to give his answer, Pinckne shouted, "It is No! No! Not a sixpence!

##It is often difficult to find a capable man for an office that has just been held by a strong, popular leader. Why? Ask students to think of well-known leaders in the world today who face the problem of finding able men to succeed them.

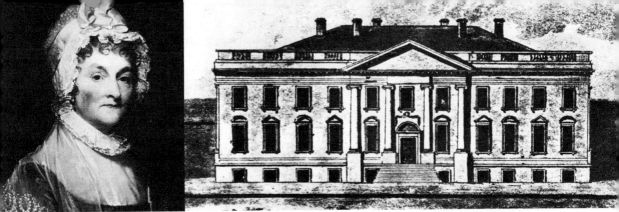

(Left) Abigail Adams Historical Society; (Right) Charles William Janson, "The Stranger of America," 1807 (United States National Park Service)

Left: Abigail Smith Adams, the first President's wife to live in Washington. Mrs. Adams had upheld her husband's Revolutionary activities and was his constant helpmate.
Right: The President's house as it looked when the Adamses moved in.

"Hail, Columbia!" When the word reached the United States of the insult to the Americans, the public response was as strong as Pinckney's. A popular slogan of the time was "Millions for defense but not one cent for tribute." In the outburst of patriotism that followed, the first of our great patriotic songs was born: "Hail, Columbia!"

The song was the work of Joseph Hopkinson, who tried, he wrote, to arouse "An *American spirit*." Its best-known lines are:

Hail! Columbia, happy land!
Hail! ye heroes, heaven-born band,
Who fought and bled in freedom's
cause . . . .

Hopkinson could see how fiercely anti-French the Federalists had become and how anti-British the Republicans were. He wanted his song to stir both groups, he wrote not long afterward, "for both were American."

War Fever

A war against France would have been popular with a great many Americans—especially the Federalists. Immediately, a campaign for military preparation began. It was led by Hamilton, even though he was out of the government. Some people thought it would be a good idea to bring Washington out of retirement and make him the military leader.

But Adams decided that he did not want to take advantage of war fever in the United States to take the country into a conflict. He considered such a war as unnecessary as it would be costly. He wanted to be reelected President in 1800, but not by supporting friends in his own party who might take advantage of war abroad to destroy liberties at home.

Attack on civil liberties. The liberties, or freedoms, that were threatened were civil liberties—especially, freedom of the press and freedom of speech. In 1798 the Federalists in Congress brought about the passage of the Naturalization Act of 1798. This law aimed to slow down the granting of citizenship to foreigners. Many of the newcomers tended to become followers of Jefferson. The new law stretched the *period of naturalization*—in which foreigners became citizens—from 5 to 14 years. #

Another law contrary to the spirit of our Constitution was known as the Alien Act, passed in 1798 also. In this law Congress gave the President authority unheard of. He could order to leave the country any alien—foreigner—who, in his opinion, was "dangerous to the peace and safety of the United States."

ote that laws are sometimes used for partisan purposes. The laws mentioned on pp. 265-266
re really aimed at suppressing the followers of Jefferson. What might have happened if laws
ainst "foreigners" had been passed during the War for Independence?

265

This unbelievable grant of power was intended to squelch criticism of the Adams administration. Some Federalists intended using the law to deport, that is, send out of the country, some Republican newspaper editors—and others—who happened to have been born abroad!

A third law that invaded civil liberties was the Sedition Act, also enacted in 1798.

\# It forbade, among other things, "false, scandalous, and malicious" remarks—spoken or written—about the President or Congress. The victims of this shameful attack on freedoms of speech and press were also chiefly Republican editors.

The outcry against the three laws was loud and in the end effective. Within a few years they were either repealed or allowed to run out. Adams himself was never enthusiastic over them, acknowledging that the Republicans possessed "a difference of sentiment on public measures," not a lack of patriotism.

Resolutions in Virginia and Kentucky. It was Jefferson and Madison who, in 1798, became the leaders of an attack on the laws. They were the authors of what came to be remembered as the Virginia and Ken-

\#\# tucky resolutions, passed by the legislatures of Virginia and Kentucky. The resolutions stated that the Alien and Sedition acts were contrary to the Constitution and said the offending acts might "drive these States into revolution and blood."

A stubborn man. Nevertheless, the hero of the critical years at the close of the eighteenth century was not Jefferson or Madison, but Adams. Learning finally that the French would receive a minister from the United States, Adams took steps to send one. The outcry of the Federalists was loud and furious. But Adams had his way—and peace between France and the United States continued.

Adams, a giant of the American Revolution, himself believed that sending a minister to France instead of calling for war was the best act of his life. Though his fellow Federalists fumed, they were powerless to force him to do other than what he regarded as right.

Choosing Jefferson

As the year 1800 rolled around, the President found himself under heavy attack from other Federalists. Meanwhile, Thomas Jefferson was the Republicans' candidate for the presidency.

A fierce fight. The campaign was hotly fought. Republican newspapers said that the country had had enough of "the . . . monarchs of Braintree [Adams' birthplace in Massachusetts] and Mount Vernon," and that it was time to start anew.

The Federalists' assault on Jefferson was equally vigorous. A clergyman even accused the Virginian of "having robbed a

\#\#These resolutions signified the beginning of the long struggle over state rights.

The first wing of the Capitol—the north one—which was completed in 1800. Observe the coaches and the "buggy."

> I Pray Heaven to Bestow
> The Best of Blessings on
> ✦ THIS HOUSE ✦
> and on All that shall hereafter
> Inhabit it. May none but Honest
> and Wise Men ever rule under This Roof!
>
> NOV. 2, 1800
> JOHN ADAMS

The hope and prayer of John Adams about the future of the White House, written to his wife when he arrived there in 1800 and now read by visitors from all over the world.

How does this inscription present a challenge to the American voter?

widow and fatherless children of an estate" which he, Jefferson, was legally responsible for as a trustee.

Years before, Abigail Adams had said of Jefferson in admiration: "He is one of the choice ones of the earth!" That was in the period when Adams was representing the United States at London and Jefferson was the American minister at Paris. In 1800 she no longer had kind words for the man who was her husband's rival.

While the excitement of the presidential campaign was mounting, Adams supervised the moving of the government to "the Federal City" on the Potomac. In the first letter ever written from the new presidential mansion in Washington, he wrote of his deepest hope—to Abigail, of course. He said, "I pray heaven to bestow the best of blessings on this house, and on all that shall hereafter inhabit it. May none but honest and wise men ever rule under this roof."

Franklin D. Roosevelt, elected President in 1932, had Adams' words carved over the fireplace in the State Dining Room of the White House. Foreign officials, especially, are often entertained there.

A tie vote. The returns from the election of 1800 showed that Jefferson was tied with Aaron Burr, of New York, for the presidency. Each had received seventy-three votes in the electoral college, with Adams running third. Burr, like everyone else, knew that those who voted for him meant him to be Vice-President. But he refused to yield the top prize without a fight.

Consequently, in accordance with the Constitution, the House of Representatives had to decide who would be President. A long, angry battle took place there that did not end until Inauguration Day was almost at hand.

The House chose Jefferson to be President. Under the Constitution's provisions Burr became Vice-President, because he had the second largest number of votes.

The Twelfth Amendment, added to the Constitution in 1804, prevents men of the same party from being tied again. To see how, read the amendment, on page 721.

Hamilton's influence. The tie vote between Jefferson and Burr had been broken through the influence of none other than Alexander Hamilton—to whom Federalists had turned for guidance. Hamilton despised Burr as a man lacking in sound character. He has, Hamilton declared, "no principle, public or private."

Hamilton had no affection for Jefferson, either. He wrote, "If there be a man in the world I ought to hate, it is Jefferson." Yet Hamilton threw his support to him, saying "the public good must be paramount to [above] every private consideration."

The new President. On March 4, 1801,

#

The Founding Fathers had not provided for all the problems of the new republic when they wrote the Constitution. Emphasize that the amending process is one of the ways of adapting the Constitution to changing needs.

267

The election of 1800 brought not only a change in administration but also a change in the political party in power. That these changes were accomplished peacefully is an important point.

the Republicans had a day of rejoicing they would long remember. A huge crowd followed joyfully as their man Jefferson, accompanied by military units, came to the Senate chamber to take the oath of office.

Meanwhile, a new anthem was being sung in Philadelphia. Written by the artist Rembrandt Peale, it was called "The People's Friend":

Devoted to his country's cause,
The Rights of Men and equal Laws,
    His hallow'd pen was given:
And now those Rights and Laws to save,
From sinking to an early grave,
    He comes, employ'd by Heaven.

What joyful prospects rise before!
Peace, Arts and Science hail our shore,
    And thro' the country spread:
Long may these blessings be preserv'd,
And by a virtuous land deserv'd
    With JEFFERSON our head.

Three pictures on the wall. Adams, feeling deserted by the people, did not even attend the ceremony. He had left Washington for home early that morning.

Adams could not know, of course, that when Jefferson moved into the President's mansion in Washington, one of his first acts was to hang three pictures on his bedroom wall. One was of Washington, another of Adams, and a third of himself. The Presidents were beginning to make up a national roll of honor—despite fierce battles between political parties and men.

---

1. Who became our second President? Our second Vice-President? 2. What did Washington's Farewell Address mean? 3. Describe the X Y Z affair. 4. Name three laws passed in Adams' administration that attacked civil liberties. 5. What opinion of the laws did Jefferson and Madison express? How? 6. Give the main facts about the election of 1800.

The Workshop

The Shapers of Our World

Tell how each of the following contributed to putting the new government of the United States on a firm footing:

George Washington
Washington's
    Farewell Address
Alexander Hamilton
Thomas Jefferson
Judiciary Act
    of 1789
Edmund Randolph
Bank of the
    United States
Neutrality Proclamation
    of 1793

Henry Knox
John Jay
Jay's treaty
    of 1794
Battle of
    Fallen Timbers
Whisky Rebellion
Pinckney's treaty
    of 1795
election of 1792
election of 1796
John Adams

James Madison
Virginia and
    Kentucky resolutions

X Y Z affair
election of 1800
Samuel Osgood

Adding to Your Vocabulary

Be sure you know these terms:

administration
electoral college
Cabinet
Supreme Court
excise tax
tariff
subsidy
bonds
speculator
"strict construction"

implied power
"loose construction"
foreign policy
neutrality
impressed
majority
isolated
naturalization
sedition
alien

The Federalists and the Republicans represented opposing views of government. In the next chapter students will find out what the Republicans did about Federalist policies and how Jefferson put the Republican philosophy into practice.

hat western settlers wanted at New Orleans was the right of deposit--that is, the right to mporarily store goods without paying special taxes or fees.

Thinking Things Through

After reviewing the chapter with the help of the boxed-in exercises, see if you can answer these questions:

1. Why do you think Americans of 1789 were so quick to resent any suggestion that the presidency might resemble a royal court?

2. How do you explain the fact that most of the men elected to the first Congress originally supported ratification?

3. Why was the name "Federalist" a suitable one for a person supporting Hamilton's program?

4. Compare the arguments at the Constitutional Convention over the powers of the central government *versus* those of the state governments with arguments about the meaning of the Constitution between Federalists and Democratic-Republicans.

5. Why do new nations today always encourage the development of industry, no matter what the cost?

6. Review the workshop for Part Three. How can it be said that the French Revolution of 1789 was an example of the fact that the shots at Lexington and Concord were "heard round the world"?

7. What lesson can be learned from our difficulties with Britain and France over the role of neutrals and over trading with nations at war?

8. Why do you think Washington used a large force headed by a Cabinet member to put down the Whisky Rebellion? Compare that uprising with Shays' Rebellion. What does the comparison tell you about the power of the central government under the Articles of Confederation compared with that of the central government under the new Constitution?

9. Why was the right to store goods at New Orleans so important to western settlers?

10. How might John Adams have used the war fever in the country to insure re-election in 1800? How do you account for the fact that Presidents are usually re-elected when the country is at war?

The Research Center

1. Make a scrapbook of famous historical expressions, such as "I've just begun to fight," "Give me liberty or give me death," and "Millions for defense but not one cent for tribute." Find out with what event each is connected and how these events affected our nation. Add to the scrapbook throughout the year.

2. Investigate the method of electing our President and Vice-President. How has the Founding Fathers' idea of the electoral college been largely ignored in recent years? Why? How does the Twelfth Amendment protect us from the situation that developed in the election of 1800?

3. Use reference books to learn about the Cabinet today. How many Cabinet positions are there? Who occupies each? What are the principal duties of each member of the Cabinet? Can you think of any national problems not assigned to any member of the Cabinet that you feel require attention?

Presenting Information

1. Let one student be a Federalist Senator from the state of Massachusetts and another a Democratic-Republican Senator from South Carolina. Let each tell why Jay's treaty should be ratified or rejected.

2. Write a letter a western farmer might have sent to a friend in New Hampshire telling why Pinckney's treaty was so important to him.

3. Hold a meeting of Cabinet members in the Washington administration. Possible subjects that might be discussed are the Bank of the United States and paying the state debt. Represent both the Hamiltonian and the Jeffersonian viewpoints.

(a)

(b)

(a) A painting of American ground squirrels by John James Audubon, the most popular American nature artist of the early 1800's.

(b) The Stars and Stripes is raised in New Orleans as that city and the huge area called the Louisiana Purchase become American.

(c) Thomas Jefferson as he looked when he was President.

(d) The wax seal which Jefferson used to fasten the envelopes of his letters.

(e) A telescope owned by Jefferson.

(f) The speedometer Jefferson had on his carriage.

(c)

(d)

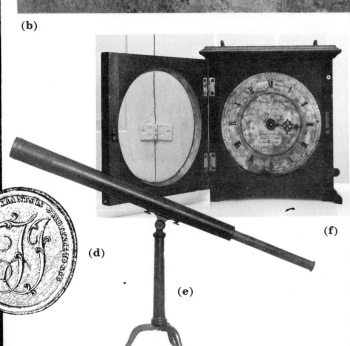

(f)

(e)

(g) Jefferson and his Cabinet—James Madison, Secretary of State, is seated at the left. The President is seated at the right, in the foreground.

(g)

CHAPTER 13

JEFFERSON AND HIS FRIENDS AT THE HELM

is chapter covers the period from the inauguration of Jefferson to the beginning of the War of 1812. What sident besides Jefferson held office during these years? What new territory was added to the United States? an interested student to report on Jefferson's many scientific activities.

WHEN Thomas Jefferson and his fellow Republicans came into power in 1801, the new government was established soundly and growing more surefooted every day. The presidency was already becoming the center of political attention in the nation.

Jefferson had given an advance copy of his inaugural address (the one delivered on taking office) to the editor of *The National Intelligencer,* a Washington newspaper. Before the swearing-in ceremony in the Senate chamber was over, little boys outside were selling copies of *The Intelligencer* on the street. It contained the full text of the speech Jefferson had just uttered. This "scoop," remarkable for its day, made newspaper history. #

ow do newsmen today get advance information on the speeches of public officials? ention the press release.)

The Republicans Find Victory Is Limited

The public interest in the inaugural address also marked the beginning of a new era in the relationship between the President and the people. A President was recognized to be more than a spokesman for the party in power—in this case the Republican party. He was the one person who could speak for the whole nation. After George Washington's terms as President, nobody had been sure that any other man could do this.

New People and New Outlooks

The words that Jefferson uttered in his inaugural were addressed to the whole American people. "Every difference of opinion," he said, "is not a difference of principle. . . . We are all Republicans, we are all Federalists." He meant that every American supports our system of government, based on representation by the

view briefly the differences between the Federalists and the Republicans. What changes in vernment could Jefferson have been expected to make? Ask students to offer evidence that ferson viewed his job as President as more than that of a party leader.

271

Charles McIntosh, "Flora and Pompona,"
London, 1829 (Henry E. Huntington Library)

Wine grapes and an apricot—two of the fruits
Jefferson introduced into the United States
because of his interest in farming and plants.
He also brought the olive tree to America.

people—despite disagreements sometimes about methods and means of doing things.

A democratic style. Jefferson was an agreeable host. Twice a year—on New Year's Day and the Fourth of July—he invited the public to be his guests. The new President wanted to make sure no one would accuse him of trying to act like a king—something people had said of Washington.

In greeting visitors, Jefferson did not recognize any difference based on rank. "All persons when brought together in society [that is, in social relations]," he said, "are perfectly equal, whether foreign or domestic, titled or untitled, in or out of office." Jefferson, furthermore, was the first President to shake hands. Washington, you will remember—and Adams—had only bowed.

Despite the burdens of his office, Jefferson spent as much time as possible at Monticello. There he could carry on the scientific experiments he took pleasure in. There he could also enjoy gardening.

"No occupation is so delightful to me as the culture of the earth," the President said, "and no culture comparable to that of the garden." But despite his affection for science and farming, he could not devote all his time to them. He once wrote that the exciting times in which he had happened to be born had forced him to play his part in life chiefly on "the boisterous [that is, rough] ocean" of politics.

Discuss Jefferson's ideas of democracy. Give examples of his faith in the democratic process.

Jefferson wanted a strong Cabinet, but he knew that he alone was responsible for all the actions of his administration. If Cabinet officers had too much authority, he said, the government would have more than one head, "drawing sometimes in different directions."

The Madisons. The President appointed as Secretary of State James Madison, the friend younger than himself who had become his faithful associate. A woman who once saw them at work said, "I do believe father never loved son more than Mr. Jefferson loves Mr. Madison."

Madison and his wife, Dolley, became familiar figures at the President's house. Not only did Madison often visit there, but also Mrs. Madison served as hostess for the President, because he was a widower.

Jefferson had two daughters who could not be with him. They were rearing young families back at Monticello, Jefferson's house in Virginia. So a messenger often sped to Mrs. Madison, bearing a note beginning: "Thomas Jefferson begs Mrs. Madison to take care of female friends expected...."

Economy in government. As Secretary of the Treasury, Jefferson appointed Albert Gallatin, also a man who had previously worked closely with him. A Swiss by birth, he spoke English with a French accent. Having lived in America in the region of the Pennsylvania backwoods, he understood the interests of frontiersmen.

Gallatin, reversing the idea which Hamilton had made popular—that "a public debt is a public blessing"—tried to lower the national debt. He succeeded despite the fact that he also obtained the repeal of the hated whisky tax. The decrease in governmental spending was chiefly the result of cuts in money for the army and navy. Jefferson and his followers believed that a large army and navy—instead of preventing—tended to cause wars.

Jefferson and his Cabinet were able to

#How did Jefferson's belief in "economy in government" limit the powers of the government? Use Gallatin's program as an example of Republican principles being put into practice. What conditions seemed to justify Jefferson's effort to reduce the debt and the army and navy?

reduce the national debt, but they were less successful in carrying out their other ideas about the government. They learned *that those who criticize the acts of men in office—as they had—are sometimes unable or unwilling to do differently when they themselves are in power.

Politics, the Law, and Marshall

The struggle between the Republicans and the Federalists came to be waged in courtrooms rather than in legislatures. It # is not just an accident that the law courts became the center of attention.

Because many Americans were on the move and much land was changing hands, people were everlastingly disputing over claims to land. Furthermore, the number of American businesses had grown so rapidly that new kinds of lawsuits and larger numbers of cases than ever before were brought into court. Legal questions arose over the collecting of debts, over bankruptcies, over wills, and over the making or breaking of contracts.

Usually state courts were friendly to local people, or at least not unfriendly. The judges were usually well known and liked.

Angry Jeffersonians. The federal courts were another matter. Not only were their judges often out-of-state people—"foreigners"—but they were also always Federalists, because they had been appointed in the two Federalist administrations. The federal judges often made speeches to the juries which today would be called political speeches. Moreover, it seemed to many that these judges were especially harsh on people in debt and people who had become bankrupt.

Because the Jeffersonians regarded the Federalist judges as political enemies, they angrily attacked the federal courts. This attack had mighty results.

The "midnight judges." The first result was that Jefferson and the Republicans decided to seek the repeal of a law they blamed for the troubles. The law was the Judiciary Act of 1801, passed by Federalist Congressmen just before they went out of office.

The act, which increased the number of federal courts, had been misused—so the Jeffersonians thought—by John Adams. He had named Federalists to fill the newly created judgeships. Because these appointments were made in the closing days of his administration, the new judges were known as the midnight appointees.

The inviting library at Monticello, Jefferson's home in Virginia. Many of the volumes lining the walls are lawbooks which he used before the Revolution, when he practiced law.

Mike Roberts

#As a result, federal judges cannot be removed because of the unpopularity of their decisions.

But how could Republicans bring about repeal of a law that would remove federal judges from their positions? The Constitution makes it quite clear that all federal
judges "shall hold their offices during good behavior."

The Supreme Court. The United States Supreme Court, the highest court in the land, did not yet enjoy a high reputation. So far it had not contributed in important ways to the new government. John Jay had resigned as Chief Justice in 1795 to become governor of New York, saying that the Supreme Court lacked "energy, weight, and dignity."

The Supreme Court did not even meet in a building of its own. It held its sessions in the office of the Clerk of the Senate—a part of what is today the north wing of the Capitol. In 1801, before Jefferson was inaugurated, John Marshall, of Virginia, accepted the office of Chief Justice. He believed it would afford him time to complete a biography of George Washington, whom he greatly admired.

The Chief Justice. The public did not greet Marshall's appointment with enthusiasm. Jeffersonians were furious because they had hoped to appoint one of their own party to this choice position.

Marshall was known to have a mind as keen as a steel trap, but he also liked jokes and enjoyed leisure. A tall, lean man with a dark complexion and with eyes that often flashed with kindliness, Marshall looked somewhat older than his forty-five years. He had a gangling gait and dressed carelessly, a habit that possibly came from his rearing on the Virginia frontier.

Jefferson seems never to have guessed how powerful an opponent Marshall would become. If he had, it is doubtful if he would have invited the new Chief Justice to administer the presidential oath to him in 1801.

Marbury v. *Madison.* The interesting court case of *Marbury* v. *Madison* provided

Virginia State Library

John Marshall as he looked a few years after his appointment as Chief Justice. His expression suggests how important his role was in the serious work of helping build a strong national government.

the first opportunity for Marshall and Jefferson to test one another. These are the facts: William Marbury was a forty-one-year-old resident of Washington. One of John Adams' "midnight appointees," he had been named a justice of the peace for the District of Columbia.

Although the Senate had approved the appointment of Marbury, Jefferson told Secretary of State James Madison not to deliver to Marbury the paper permitting him to take over his judgeship. (The sending out of such documents is a duty of the Secretary of State. It is because he has this responsibility and others like it that he is not called Secretary of Foreign Affairs. That name would suggest that his duties are concerned solely with foreign affairs.)

Marbury asked the Supreme Court to order Madison to issue the proper document. For this reason the case of *Marbury* v. *Madison* came before the Court in 1803.

Marshall was a skillful politician as well as a strong Federalist and an able judge.

Rejected at the polls in 1800, the Federalist party kept its principles alive by having Federalists appointed to federal judgeships. Judges, though striving to be impartial, often reflect a political philosophy in their decisions.

He knew that if he granted the court order which Marbury wanted, Madison would probably ignore it. Such an act would embarrass the Supreme Court and rob it of any standing it had. And if he refused to grant the order, he would be doing exactly what the Republicans wanted.

The decision. Marshall shrewdly took neither step. He decided that Marbury was entitled to the order but that the Supreme Court did not have authority, or *jurisdiction*, in the case and so could not issue it.

Why? Because the Constitution says (see page 716) that the only cases that may begin in the Supreme Court are those "affecting ambassadors, other public ministers and consuls, and those in which a state shall be a party." These conditions did not apply to the case of *Marbury* v. *Madison*.

Why had Marbury come to the Supreme Court for the order? Because a section of the Judiciary Act of 1789 said he could. Marshall said that the Judiciary Act, therefore, conflicted with the Constitution and was unconstitutional, that is, not authorized by it.

Judicial review. The Supreme Court in this decision had set an important precedent. It had taken for itself the right to say whether or not a law passed by Congress was constitutional. This right is called *judicial review*.

Jefferson was furious. The Constitution, he said, had become "a mere thing of wax," to be twisted and shaped as the judges liked. But what choice did he have? The principle of judicial review made the judicial branch of government equal in strength to the other two branches. It had the effect also of limiting the powers of both Congress and the President.

---

1. What two special roles did a President have by 1801? 2. Name two members of Jefferson's Cabinet. 3. What idea did his Secretary of the Treasury have? 4. Name two reasons why there were numerous court cases in Jefferson's first term. 5. Who were the "midnight appointees"? 6. Give the main facts concerning the *Marbury* v. *Madison* case. 7. What important precedent did John Marshall set? What effect did it have?

The Country Doubles Its Size in a Flash

A triumph Jefferson had in foreign affairs a little later in 1803 helped him overcome his disappointment over *Marbury* v. *Madison*. The drama of this victory began in some of the royal courts of Europe. It ended with a land deal for Americans which has never been surpassed by any other anywhere in the world.

The Louisiana Purchase

The principal figure of the story was Napoleon Bonaparte, who had recently become head of France. Considering himself a successor of the great kings of his country's past, he wanted high honors, too.

Napoleon's scheme. One thing he could do, Napoleon thought, would be to regain a French empire on the American continent. If only Spain could be persuaded to return Louisiana (see page 158) to him, his plans would be well under way.

A swap with Spain. The Spanish king, Don Carlos IV, made a deal in 1800 with Napoleon. Napoleon, whose armies had just conquered the Italian peninsula, would give up a small part of Italy in return for Louisiana.

view the importance of New Orleans to Americans living west of the Appalachians. Would
poleon have to control New Orleans to build an empire in North America? How would
ericans have reacted if New Orleans had been transferred from Spain to France?

Old Print Shop

Toussaint L'Ouverture, shown here in a pose fitting the successful leader of a revolt.

Don Carlos congratulated himself on the splendid bargain he had made. Florence, the incomparably beautiful city where Michelangelo, Galileo, and Amerigo Vespucci had once lived and labored, is in the region he acquired.

Today we can ask how Florence could be compared with a domain that extended from the Gulf of Mexico to Lake Superior and for a thousand miles westward. Nevertheless, on October 1, 1800, the deal was closed by the signing of a treaty between Napoleon and the Spanish king.

Santo Domingo. The following year Napoleon (now Emperor Napoleon) felt free to start work on the building of an empire in the New World. The center of its defense was to be the island of Santo Domingo (see the map, page 158). Half of it belonged to France, and half to Spain. The French portion supplied much of Europe's sugar, coffee, and cotton. It was to be dependent on Louisiana for its supply of grain and other provisions.

L'Ouverture's uprising. But Napoleon's glowing dream turned into a nightmare. The island of Santo Domingo, where the lives of Negro slaves were especially harsh, was plunged into one of the bloodiest slave rebellions in history. The leader was a remarkable slave named Toussaint L'Ouverture, whose rise to power somewhat resembled Napoleon's own. L'Ouverture in 1801 seized control of the entire island, established a constitution, and claimed the right to rule and to name his successor.

Napoleon responded like a tiger attacked. He sent to the island ten thousand troops under one of the best of his generals, Charles Leclerc. Leclerc was the husband of Napoleon's lovely sister, Pauline. The island became a charred battlefield. Leclerc was unable to crush the rebellion, even though L'Ouverture was captured and sent to France, where he died in prison.

Meanwhile, Jefferson had kept his eyes on events in the West Indies. He knew that if Napoleon reestablished the French empire in the New World there would be new troubles for the United States. One of the goals of Jefferson's administration, therefore, was to prevent France from taking over Louisiana.

Concern in the United States. In 1801 rumors began to reach the United States that Spain was handing Louisiana back to the French. The new minister of the United States to France was Robert R. Livingston. Secretary of State Madison instructed him to try to find out if there was any truth in the rumors and to attempt to stop the deal between Spain and France.

Flabbergasted negotiators. Early in 1803 James Monroe was sent to Paris to help Livingston in his negotiations. Monroe and Livingston were instructed to offer up to $10,000,000 for New Orleans and West Florida, which were believed to be included in Louisiana.

About the time Monroe was departing for Europe, word reached Paris from Santo Domingo that Leclerc was dead. On hearing the news, Napoleon gave up his hope of creating an empire in the New World.

To the utter astonishment of Livingston and Monroe, the French offered them the whole of Louisiana—not just New Orleans —for $15,000,000. (They did not obtain West Florida.) Going beyond their instructions, but guessing that they would be backed up by Jefferson, the Americans quickly accepted.

The Americans were aware, of course, that Napoleon had some reason for selling Louisiana in addition to his disappointment. They saw quickly that France was renewing its old struggle with England and that it could be useful for the French to be friends with Americans again. Once more, rivalries in Europe were creating advantages for the United States.

When news of the purchase of Louisiana reached the United States, Americans were greatly excited. Many regarded it as a guarantee of the nation's future greatness. They were pleased also because France seemed to be showing again the warm friendship for us it had shown during the American Revolution.

Some arguments. There were some Americans, though, who thought the Louisiana Purchase might be a threat to the Union. They asked, Will not the new region be a magnet, constantly attracting hardy men and women away from the older states? Will not these states be weakened as a result?

Opponents of the purchase also argued that it was unconstitutional for the United States to acquire new territory. They made Jefferson squirm, for they were offering the very argument he had used in advising Washington about approving the United States bank. This was that whatever is not

How did the location of New Orleans affect its growth and prosperity?

A painting of New Orleans made just after the Louisiana Purchase. The forest shows how close to the city the wilderness still was. New Orleans prospered, as the eagle said it would. By 1810 it was one of the ten largest cities in the country.

UNDER MY WINGS EVERY THING PROSPERS

The boundaries of the Louisiana Purchase were not finally agreed upon until long after the United States obtained it. Observe how much of the territory now part of the United States was still held by Spain in 1803.

plainly provided for in the Constitution is prohibited by it (see page 256).

But Jefferson was not troubled very long. He simply would not be performing his duty as President, he concluded, if he allowed the golden opportunity to obtain Louisiana to pass by. He held uppermost in his mind the advantages that the infant United States would gain.

No one could say for sure how large the new territory was. It extended roughly from the Mississippi River to the Rocky Mountains. In acquiring it, Jefferson dou-

bled the land area of the United States. How fitting it was that Jefferson—the farmers' friend—was responsible for buying these millions of acres of some of the richest farmland in the world.

Jeffersonian democracy. Yet the President had his mind upon more than farming itself. He also was thinking of a vast America pressing westward toward the Pacific. He believed that the larger America was, the more easily an individual could obtain land of his own—something Jefferson considered necessary for good citizenship.

#The Louisiana Purchase illustrates the problem of applying principles to practice. How did the Louisiana Purchase conform to Jefferson's strict-constructionist views of the Constitution? How did it go along with his hope for a nation of landholding, farming citizens?

Jefferson thought that men who owned property would cast their votes with particular care in order to protect what they owned. He, therefore, hoped always to have not only an America that consisted of contented farmers, living democratically, but also an America that would be strong in its government. His ideas and dream ever afterward have been known as Jeffersonian democracy.

The Journey of Lewis and Clark

Jefferson, in fact, was eyeing the land lying west of the Louisiana Purchase. Just before he sent Monroe to Paris to help Livingston, he asked Congress for a sum of $2500 for the exploration of the Far West.

The plan. The money would pay the expenses of an army officer and a party of about a dozen men. The request was granted, and Jefferson appointed his private secretary, Meriwether Lewis, as the officer in command.

The purposes. Jefferson had two particular reasons for wanting an expedition to explore the land all the way to the Pacific. For one thing, he was curious to find out about the features of the vast area and about the Indians living there.

For another, the President wished to give the United States an advantage in its rivalry with England for the fur trade of the region then called the Oregon Country. If Americans could discover an overland route to the Oregon Country, the United States would be in a favored position to control that trade.

While the preparations for the trip were going forward, Louisiana became part of the United States. Jefferson now could instruct Lewis to tell the Indians there that they would find Americans to be "faithful friends and protectors." Jefferson, in short, had caught a glimpse of an America extending from "sea to shining sea," and Lewis would prepare the way.

The explorers. Lewis, who for years had wanted to undertake a mission such as the one Jefferson had in mind, chose as his companion William Clark. Clark, a lieutenant in the army, was the younger brother of George Rogers Clark. Like all the members of his family, William had red hair, and the Indians of Louisiana would know him as "Red Head."

Lewis and Clark were certainly well matched. In asking Clark to join the expedition, Lewis invited him to have a part in "its fatigues, its dangers and its honors. . . . [T]here is no man on earth with whom I should feel equal pleasure in sharing them as with yourself." The friendship of Lewis and Clark became deeper as the years passed and as they came to know each other under all kinds of conditions.

First leg. The explorers and their party spent the winter of 1803–1804 in southern Illinois, where they raised the American flag. In beginning the first part of their journey across Louisiana, Lewis and Clark and their men set out in the spring of 1804 to follow the Missouri River to its source.

The party's experiences were fascinating, frightening, and exhausting. As the men made their way westward, there must have been times when they laughed together at the thought that France had given up such valuable land. And there could have been times when they wept over the fact the United States had bought it.

Dangers like snakes and wild animals were rarely absent. Also, the men had to face the terrible heat of the summer (Clark wrote one day in June that "the Thermometer stood at 96 above 0," making "the men becom verry feeble.")

On the other hand, the beautiful scenery the explorers saw was thrilling, especially the sunsets and the mountains. And the variety of fish they could catch was beyond belief.

Each day was a new challenge. The members of the expedition, for example,

Trace the route of Lewis and Clark on the map on p. 278. Indicate the progress they made
ar by year until their return to St. Louis in 1806. What states were created from the areas
ey explored?

279

Students will enjoy reading selections from the Journal of Lewis and Clark edited by Bernard De Voto (Houghton Mifflin Co., 1963).

Patrick Gass, "Journal of the Voyages and Travels of a Corps of Discovery," Philadelphia, 1811 (Newberry Library)

Three pictures from a journal kept by one of the men who accompanied Lewis and Clark. The top sketch gives a sample of why the expedition was so exciting. The drawing below that shows Lewis and Clark building a shelter in the wilderness. The third of the sketches shows the action as an angry bear trees one of the men.

were probably the first non-Indians to encounter the grizzly bear. Clark wrote of one of them, "It was a most tremendious looking anamal, and extreemly hard to kill, notwithstanding he had five balls through his lungs . . . he swam more than half the distance across the river to a sand-bar, & it was at least twenty minutes before he died."

Among the Mandan. In late autumn the expedition arrived at the villages of the Mandan Indians in present-day North Dakota. There Lewis and Clark, having traveled 1600 miles, decided to spend their second winter. So far things had gone well, but they were now at the edge of an area they knew nothing about.

As they set forth again in April, 1805, Lewis wrote to Jefferson, "We do not calculate on completing our voyage within the present year." To his diary Lewis confided that they were "about to penetrate a country at least two thousand miles in width, on which the foot of civilized man had never trodden."

Sacajawea. On their journey into the strange territory, the explorers were accompanied by a remarkable Indian girl, Sacajawea (a name that means "Canoe Pusher"). She was a Shoshone Indian whose people lived in the region toward which Lewis and Clark were traveling (see the map on page 278). Carrying strapped to her back her youngster, nicknamed Pomp (which in Shoshone means "eldest son"), she was a striking figure, setting the pace in endurance and courage.

A critical moment. By midsummer of 1805, the party had reached the Great Falls of the Missouri and had passed around them. Then for a time they were at the end of their travels by water. As they made their way overland, they nervously eyed the changed appearance of the landscape: they faced the foothills of the Rockies. The Indians of the area seemed to disappear—to the dismay of Lewis and

#A statue of Sacajawea now stands in Statuary Hall in the national capital. Ask students to look up the major Indian peoples who lived in the region explored by Lewis and Clark. How did Indians contribute to the success of the expedition?

Lewis and Clark and their party as they arrived at the Columbia River. Accustomed though they were by then to the splendors of the American West, they were thrilled with the awesome beauty of what is now our Pacific Northwest.

United States Information Service

Clark, who wanted to obtain horses from them.

With the Shoshone. The Americans badly needed horses and other help. The country they were in was unmapped and wild. Moreover, who could show them a pass through the mountains? It is no wonder that when Clark fell ill of a fever at this critical time, a kind of panic spread among the men.

At last, though, the expedition entered the country of Sacajawea's people, the Shoshone. The Shoshone proved to be admirable hosts, and Sacajawea helped to smooth the meeting between her people and the Americans.

The Indians were poor but generous. Lewis reported, "An indian called me . . . and gave me . . . a piece of fresh salmon roasted . . . this was the first salmon I had seen and perfectly convinced me that we were on the waters of the Pacific Ocean."

The Pacific at last. Obtaining horses from the Shoshone, Lewis and Clark and their sturdy men crossed the continental divide and came into the valley of the Clearwater River. They then floated down the Columbia River to the Pacific Ocean, which they reached in November, 1805. They had crossed the continent by navigating two of its great rivers, the Missouri and the Columbia.

Oregon. At the present site of Astoria, in what is now Oregon, they built Fort Clatsop, spending the winter of 1805–1806 encamped there. In the spring of 1806 the expedition set out at last for home. Dividing into two groups so that the men might cover more ground in their exploration (see the map, page 278), they reached St. Louis in September. Having by now been given up as lost, they were met by astonished people who gave them an unusually lively welcome.

Pike's Expeditions

Jefferson applauded the exploits of Lewis and Clark, as did the entire country. But the two explorers were not long alone in the sun of public popularity. The President, a man who seems to have fixed his gaze westward, was sending other explorers into the unopened part of America.

Like Henry the Navigator, Jefferson inspired discovery—but with a difference. Whereas Henry had aimed to spread Christianity and government by a king, the President's aim was to spread representative government and the blessings of freedom.

In the Mississippi Valley. One of the most daring of the men Jefferson sent to explore in the unknown portions of the

Why did Lewis and Clark take their expedition beyond the area of the Louisiana Purchase? Their travels in the Oregon Country--claimed at the time by England--served later as a basis United States claims in that area.)

Major Z. M. Pike, "An Account of Expedition to the Sources of Mississippi . . . ," Philadelphia, 1810 (Illinois State Historical Library)

A portrait of Zebulon Pike, painted by Charles Willson Peale. Pike and his men braved snow and cold in trying to reach the top of the mountain in Colorado known today as Pike's Peak.

West was Lieutenant Zebulon Montgomery Pike. Only twenty-six years old in 1805, he was chosen that year to head an expedition to find the source of the Mississippi River. Pike and his men set forth from St. Louis in August, but before they had completed their mission, winter began.

Establishing a winter base at the Falls of St. Anthony, near present-day Minneapolis, Pike—with twelve of his men—traveled northward in the snow on sleds. He reached the upper Mississippi and what he thought—mistakenly—was the source of the river. Finding the British flag flying over a trading post, he made the British there run up the Stars and Stripes instead. He and his men then turned south and were back in St. Louis on the last day of April, 1806.

Facing down the Pawnee. In July of the same year Pike was sent out again—this time to explore the headwaters of the Arkansas and Red rivers. Pike and his party met angry Pawnee Indians, but Captain

Pike (he had by now been promoted) was a bold man and stood his ground. He told the Indians that "the young warriors of his great American Father were not women to be turned back by words." He later wrote, "[I]t would have cost them at least one hundred men to have exterminated us."

Climbing in the Rockies. Pike and his band proceeded up the Arkansas, glimpsing the Rocky Mountains and reaching the present-day site of Pueblo, Colorado. Although snow was on the ground, Pike and three of his companions decided to climb the great peak which now bears his name. Badly equipped, they were not successful in their attempt.

Returning to Arkansas and exploring the head of the Arkansas River, Pike and his men now traveled south—on foot—in search of the Red River. Turning up in Spanish territory—in present-day New Mexico—they were soon practically prisoners of the commanding Spanish general. They were treated well, although all of Pike's papers were taken from him.

Pike stored in his memory the details of his stirring journey and published an account of them in 1810. Within a very few years, an edition of his work was published in England, and the book was translated into French, Dutch, and German. Europeans were keenly interested in the American West. And why not? The West was truly the scene of some of man's most heroic struggles with raw nature.

1. What deal did Napoleon make with the Spanish king in 1800? 2. Describe Napoleon's plan for establishing an empire in the New World. 3. How was his plan upset? 4. Sum up the main facts about the Louisiana Purchase. 5. Tell what is meant by "Jeffersonian democracy." 6. Give two reasons why Jefferson wanted the land to the Pacific explored. 7. Name three explorers of the land and describe their routes.

##News of these expeditions was sensational. But were the discoveries of any immediate use? Did they prove to be more important in the future? (Remember that the explorers returned with information about plants, animals, and natural features.)

Review some of the problems the United States had had with foreign powers--impressment and violation
neutral rights, for example. Why was it essential for the United States to maintain its neutral rights and
reedom to trade with all nations? Why did France and England refuse to respect American neutrality?

Americans Decide to Defend Their Rights

Abroad President Jefferson faced some unusual events, too—and with a totally inadequate navy. Africa's north coast was one of the places where problems developed that demanded American attention. Note the Barbary powers on the map below.

The Barbary Pirates

Along the North African coast, pirates of the Barbary powers—Algeria, Tripoli, Tunis, and Morocco—seized foreign ships and crews passing through the Mediterranean Sea. They then demanded a high ransom for the release of the captured men.

The attacks by the pirates represented a serious threat to America. First of all, they interfered with our trade—which we badly needed. Second, they were insults to the American flag, which challenged the new nation keenly.

War with Tripoli. In 1795 we had signed a treaty with Algeria in which we had agreed to pay an annual sum of "protection money" as a price for being let alone. A year or so later we had made a similar arrangement with Tripoli. But this treaty did not please the ruler of Tripoli, and in 1801 he declared war on the United States.

Jefferson was a man of peace. But he had long realized that the Barbary pirates could be dealt with only by force. He sent warships to North Africa. In the fighting that followed there were several American heroes.

Decatur's raid. One of the most adventurous was a young lieutenant, Stephen Decatur. In 1804 Decatur made a spectacular raid inside the port of Tripoli. He recovered the United States frigate *Philadelphia*, which had been captured earlier, and set it afire. Now it would no longer be useful to the enemy.

Settlement. Just when the United States Navy vessels in the Mediterranean were preparing an assault on Tripoli, peace was arranged. Under the treaty which resulted, prisoners were exchanged and we paid a ransom of $60,000. For several years thereafter we continued to pay some tribute. Not until 1816 did we finally stop.

By fighting, the United States had won new dignity, for it was the first nation to stand up to the Barbary pirates. Furthermore, the naval actions had helped train a group of young officers whose skills shortly would be needed against old enemies, the British.

Britain Against France

Like Washington and Adams before him, Jefferson had to concern himself with war in western Europe. The overall fact from which the United States could not escape was that England and France were ##

The home bases of the Barbary pirates. The words "to the shores of Tripoli" in the song of the Marine Corps recall the role of the marines in fighting the pirates.

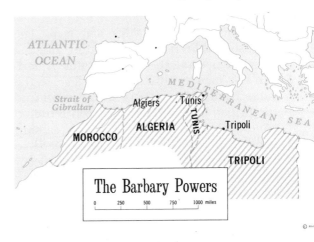

The Barbary Powers

Jefferson inherited some problems in foreign relations. When war broke out in Europe, did it matter much to our foreign policy whether Federalists or Republicans were in office? What, for example, was the effect of Jefferson's "economy in government" on the country's military power?

engaged in a struggle to the death—and we were caught between them.

The fighting between the two countries, which had begun in 1793, broke out afresh in 1803. Because they were playing for keeps, both needed as many soldiers as they could get. As large numbers of French and English farmers became soldiers, France and England often had to depend upon the products of American farms. For this reason, both countries were sometimes willing to allow American merchant vessels and ships of other neutral countries to enter European waters. At other times they would not permit it.

Blockades. The war in Europe heated up as Napoleon, the French leader and military genius, conquered much of western Europe. Because the English lacked the means to stop his conquest on land, they decided they would starve him out by using their vast navy to blockade the European continent.

When the British announced their plans in 1806, the French replied that they would blockade the British Isles. The English responded by requiring that all neutral ships proceeding toward a blockaded port first stop at a British port to obtain a license and pay a fee. The French then announced, in December, 1807, that they would seize any neutral ship which arrived at a continental port after stopping to obey British regulations.

American victims: ships and men. The English and French orders mainly affected the chief neutral, the United States. American ship captains often felt helpless. In the years from 1803 to 1812, the French and the British captured about fifteen hundred American vessels. However, if a ship could run the blockades, profits were so high that a shipowner—like a land speculator or any other gambler—was willing to risk much to make a "killing."

The heaviest burden was borne, however, not by the shipowners but by the sea-

men. They might be seized, or impressed, and forced into the British navy to serve for the duration of the war. The practice of impressment was, to Americans, an outrageous violation of the dignity of the United States. We must understand, though, what lay behind it.

Explanations, if not excuses. The British desperately needed men to man their ships. Yet the conditions of life in the Royal Navy were fearful. Admiral Horatio Nelson, the English hero in the struggle with Napoleon, declared that a seaman's lifespan averaged only forty-five years. And was it any wonder? The food aboard ship was dreadful. Conditions of living were a constant threat to health. Punishment was common and often took the form of flogging, that is, whipping.

It was a hardy young man, indeed, who would *volunteer* for service in the Royal Navy. As a result, the problem of obtaining crews was solved chiefly by impressing able-bodied men wherever they could be found.

Sometimes men were released from prisons on condition that they help man the fleet. Sometimes gangs working along the British waterfront would simply capture men by brute force and take them to sea.

As the British felt their situation growing more critical after 1803, they used even more desperate measures. Their ships would stop merchant ships, no matter what country's flag they were flying, and seize crewmen to serve in the king's navy.

The only possibility of escape for a Briton, once he had been impressed, was death or desertion. Death came often because the rate of disease was high.

The deserters. The chief opportunity to desert presented itself in foreign ports, where it was possible to "jump" to American vessels anchored there. The wages on American ships were far better than on British naval vessels, to say nothing of the treatment of seamen, which was also far better. And when an American ship reached a home port, it was fairly easy and quick for an Englishman to be naturalized—to become an American citizen.

As the British grew frantic for men, they searched for deserters from the service. If they found a Briton aboard an American vessel, they did not hesitate to lay hold of him—kicking and screaming—and drag him back to service for England. Frequently they were not very careful to make sure they had a *British* seaman.

Also, the British refused to recognize that United States naturalization proceedings might have made a man born in Britain an American citizen. The argument they used was, Once an Englishman, always an Englishman.

Interference with trade. Besides impressing seamen on American ships, the British offended the United States in another way. Beginning in 1805, they seized American ships carrying on trade between France and the West Indies.

British vessels sometimes even invaded American home waters to perform their mischief. At one time New York Harbor was practically blockaded by two British ships. Years later a midshipman aboard one of them told what they were up to:

> Every morning at daybreak, we set about arresting the progress of all the vessels we saw [that is, stopping them], firing off guns to the right and left to make every ship that was running in heave to, or wait until we had leisure to send a boat on board 'to see' in our lingo, 'what she was made of [that is, to examine its cargo].' I have frequently known a dozen, and sometimes a couple of dozen, ships lying a league or two off the port, losing their fair wind, their tide, and worse than all their market . . . sometimes the whole day, before our search was completed.

The *Chesapeake* and the *Leopard*. But undoubtedly the worst insult to Americans occurred off the coast of Virginia on June 22, 1807, when the United States war ves-

ny were the ships so se before firing began?

Off our eastern coast the British warship *Leopard* (left) opens fire on the American *Chesapeake*.

Mariners Museum, Newport News, Virginia

sel *Chesapeake* set sail for the Mediterranean. In its crew were four men who, the British insisted, were deserters from a British man-of-war. Scarcely had the vessel sailed out of sight of the American shore when it was hailed (a seamen's word meaning "greeted") by the British warship *Leopard*.

The commander of the *Chesapeake*, thinking the British wanted letters carried to Europe, allowed the *Leopard* to come alongside without first preparing to fire his guns. When he learned that the British commander wanted to search the *Chesapeake* for the sailors who were supposed to be deserters, he properly refused.

Before the American crew could prepare for action, the British opened fire, killing three men and wounding eighteen, including the American commander himself. To prevent further bloodshed, the *Chesapeake* surrendered. A British searching party then came aboard the American ship and removed the four men they were looking for.

When at last the *Chesapeake* limped home and the episode became known, Americans were aroused as they had not been since the X Y Z affair. Possibly for the first time many of them felt a deep national loyalty, or patriotism. Americans were so united in their deep shame that undoubtedly they would have been willing to go to war.

Fighting Without Firing

President Jefferson was aware of the people's feelings, but, like Adams before him, he was determined to have peace. Besides, he knew that war could severely hurt the infant republic. He detested the abuse of American rights as much as anyone, but he knew that the country still lacked strength to do anything about the outrages committed against it. Yet the President had to do *something*. What?

Nonimportation. In 1806 Jefferson had obtained from Congress the passage of the Nonimportation Act. This law forbade the entry into American markets of certain goods manufactured by Britain. Some people had opposed the act because they believed stronger measures should be taken. The Virginian John Randolph, for example, shouted angrily, "What is it? A milk-and-water bill! A dose of chicken-broth."

Embargo. It turned out that Randolph was right. After the *Chesapeake-Leopard* affair, nobody could deny that mild measures had failed. Accordingly, at the end of December, 1807, Congress passed the Embargo Act. Under it the United States put a stop to *all* trade with *all* foreign countries.

Americans felt that this law would show both the French and the British that they could not trifle with Americans. The United States had no military power, but it had commercial power, Americans thought. In short, they would keep trying to influence enemies by peaceful means.

Unfortunately, the effect was felt most keenly by Americans, not by Europeans. Our trade was simply not as important to Europeans as Jefferson and some of his fellow Republicans thought it was. Only the linen industry in Ireland suffered since it was almost entirely dependent upon American flax and flaxseed.

Backfire. Americans suffered considerably as a result of the stoppage of trade. Federalist newspapers no doubt magnified some losses in order to embarrass the Republican administration. Nevertheless, the lack of a market for cotton ruined many planters, and the disappearance of a market for western farm produce badly hurt many western farmers.

The shipping towns were hurt especially. More than five hundred ships were tied up in New York alone, and two hundred in Savannah. Salem, Massachusetts, established soup kitchens to feed twelve hundred people every day.

##Why did the embargo prohibit "all trade with all foreign countries"? (To make enforcement easier. Otherwise, ships could get false papers to clear American ports; the government could not control their trade.) What groups in America suffered because of the embargo?

y was it said that grass grew in
streets of commercial towns
ng the embargo?

A wharf in Salem, Massachusetts, after the Embargo Act.
Forbidden to leave American ports, ships were tied up and left idle
here and at other wharves for over a year.

The truth was that our powerful enemies could not be affected by such a method as the embargo. In fact, the British may
have been helped more than they were
hurt by the law. After the American Revolution, Americans had become keen competitors, and it was now illegal for Yankees
to be trading anywhere in the world.

Jefferson never (even at the very end of
his life) gave up his belief that in time the
embargo would have brought the desired
results. But by 1809 Americans had run
out of patience. Congress responded by re-
pealing the Embargo Act, and Jefferson
signed the repeal on March 1, 1809—three
days before he went out of office.

Nonintercourse. In place of the Embargo Act, Congress enacted quickly a strange
new kind of law, the Nonintercourse Act.
It provided that trade be reopened with all
the nations of the world except England
and France. It permitted the President to
begin to trade with either of these two
powers if it stopped violating our rights as
a neutral country.

Madison's Turn

Jefferson, following the example set by
George Washington, would not allow him-
self to be considered for a third term as
President. His successor in the White
House in 1809 was Secretary of State
James Madison. Madison, therefore, be-

came the third Virginian to be president of
the United States.

Madison, who had had a hand in the
measures taken against Britain by
Jefferson, had no new ideas on the subject.
Nor did members of the Federalist party.
Madison's election indicated a continued
public faith in the Republicans rather
than an expectation of new policies.

A depressed President. On Inauguration
Day, Madison, who was only 5 feet tall,
was a pale and trembling man. A lady who
was a friend of Mrs. Madison's and of the
new President's contrasted their behavior
at the inaugural ball. This friend wrote:

[Dolley Madison] looked a queen. She
had on a pale buff-colored velvet, made
plain, with a very long train, but not the
least trimming, and beautiful pearl
necklace, earrings, and bracelets. Her
head dress was a turban of the same colored velvet and white satin (from Paris)
with two superb plumes, the bird of paradise feathers. It would be *absolutely
impossible* for any one to behave with
more perfect propriety than she did. Un-
assuming dignity, sweetness, grace. Mr.
Madison, on the contrary, seemed spirit-
less and exhausted. While he was standing by me, I said, "I wish with all my
heart I had a little bit of seat to offer
you." "I wish so too," said he, with a
most woe-begone face, and looking as if
he could hardly stand.

anged conditions require changed policies. Economic boycotts had worked against England
ore the Revolution. But the Embargo and Nonintercourse acts failed. How did the failure
w that while the United States was independent of England, it was dependent on foreign trade?

New York Historical Society

Dolley (sometimes incorrectly spelled "Dolly") Madison, the blue-eyed, black-haired wife of the fourth President. She was a Quaker and very popular and influential because of her friendliness.

Embarrassments. Madison needed all the strength he had, because he faced tough problems. When the Nonintercourse Act expired in 1810, Congress replaced it with another. It permitted the President to reopen trade with both Britain and France. If either country stopped interfering with American neutral rights, the United States would reward it by stopping trade with the other. What a way to obtain the good behavior of one's tormentors!

On top of everything, the President was embarrassed personally by a trick of Napoleon's. Napoleon caused Madison to believe that the French had canceled their orders concerning neutral trade. Overjoyed, the President reopened trade with France and closed that with Britain. But the French # had fooled the Americans, and Madison had to admit that the situation of American shipping was as bad as ever.

Stirred-up Indians. Gradually, however,

#How does this show the difficulty of enforcing a kind of partial embargo?

Britain seemed to be more treacherous than France. All the old wounds suffered during the American Revolution seemed to be opening again. In the old Northwest, the Indians were active with tomahawks and scalping knives.

The evidence was, as Andrew Jackson put it, that secret agents of Britain were keeping the tribesmen stirred up against the Americans. A newspaper in Kentucky asked if Congress was going to "treat the citizens of the *Western country* as they have treated the [impressed] seamen for eighteen years." That is, was the United States going to continue to ignore the crimes committed against Americans?

Harrison at Tippecanoe. In 1811 General William Henry Harrison, governor of the Indiana territory, inflicted upon the Indians at Tippecanoe River (see the map, page 231) what he considered a stunning defeat. The leader of the Indians was Tecumseh, although he was not present. He and his brother, the Prophet, had created an Indian confederation made up of tribes of the old Northwest and also of those along the Gulf of Mexico. Americans believed that if war came, these tribesmen, bribed by the English, would ravage the frontier regions and massacre the women and children.

A growing feeling. The United States was turning fiercely anti-British. Merchants in ports along the eastern seaboard, who were especially hurt by the loss of trade, seemed ready to take strong measures against the former mother country.

In the South a fall in the prices of hemp, cotton, and tobacco made it seem that England would have to be punished. Was it not England's fault that the ports of Europe were closed?

No matter where one looked or listened, England—the old enemy of other days—seemed at fault. But how could the United States—without a navy—wage war against England? The answer appeared clear: attack it on land by seizing Canada.

Canada within reach. A leading newspaper in Cincinnati printed a warning to England. It said that unless the British ended their interruption of American trade and their impressment of our American youths, "the most valuable of all her colonies [Canada] will be torn from her grasp."

Observe two important facts. First, the desire to invade Canada was not aroused mainly so the United States could possess new land, but so it could punish England. Second, even though westerners lived a great distance from the sea, they were ready to fight for seamen.

There was also a widespread feeling that in spite of a deep desire for peace, we had to fight a war to save the nation's self-respect. Our rights would be respected, many Americans thought, only when we earned respect through success in battle.

The War Hawks. Some of the people who held the view that Americans should fight were fairly young westerners who had recently arrived in Congress. One was Henry Clay, of Kentucky; another was John C. Calhoun, of South Carolina; and still another was Felix Grundy, of Tennessee. Clay was immediately elected Speaker of the House, and Calhoun and Grundy became members of the powerful House Committee on Foreign Affairs.

Because President Madison was a weak leader, the control of things, to an unusual degree, fell into the hands of the Congressmen. All fiery orators, they acquired the name "War Hawks." They were different from the older generation of leaders—of which Madison was an example. The older generation preferred writing to speaking in public and believed—as Adams and Jefferson had shown—that to keep peace is not necessarily a disgrace.

By the beginning of 1812 preparations for war were under way, though in England there were signs that changes in policy might be made to please Americans. Nonintercourse was causing English factories to close and the price of food to rise.

Too late. It is sometimes said that if there had been a telegraph cable across the Atlantic in 1812, war would not have come. On June 16, 1812, the British announced the repeal of their restrictions on American trade. Just two days later, Congress, not knowing about the announcement, declared war on Britain.

The reasons. In asking Congress to declare war, Madison listed four main reasons. They were (1) the impressment of American seamen, (2) the violation of our rights on the sea, (3) the blockade of American ports, and (4) the British interference with our seaborne commerce.

General Harrison, in front of the chair, is seen here in a meeting with Indians in Vincennes, Indiana, in 1810. Harrison was appointed by John Adams as the first governor of the Indiana territory. The General, who held the office until 1812, was expected to deal with the tribesmen, who naturally opposed the settlement of the old Northwest.

"The Life of Major-General William Henry Harrison . . . ," Philadelphia, 1840 (New York Public Library)

Probably few Americans desired war, but to many the nation's honor seemed at stake. Madison had believed he could bring about a peaceful solution to the troubles, but he failed to get it and Congress forced war upon him.

The British had been sure that the United States would not go to war over the impressment of seamen. But the United States did go to war over impressment. Then the British believed that when the Americans learned about the repeal of the trade regulations, they would quickly halt the war. This did not occur.

Gamely but unhappily the British decided they would have to fight in the New World again. As a London newspaper said, "We cannot fear a war with any power in the world . . . but it is not unmanly to say, that we regret the sad necessity . . . of carrying the flame and devastation of war to a part of the world which has not seen a hostile foot for thirty years."

Unready for war against a mighty enemy, Americans faced it with a very small army, an overconfident Congress, and a downcast President. We can appreciate why one Jeffersonian, upon hearing of the declaration of war, wrote grimly to the Secretary of State, "May God send you a safe deliverance."

1. In what two ways did the attacks by Barbary pirates affect the United States? 2. How did Jefferson deal with the attacks? 3. In what two ways did the British anger Americans before the War of 1812? 4. Describe the worst insult Americans received. 5. Name three laws passed by Congress to meet the situation of the United States, and tell what each provided. 6. State a number of reasons that explain why Americans were more bitter toward Britain than toward France. 7. Give two explanations of the westerners' desire to invade Canada. 8. Madison asked Congress to declare war on Britain for what four reasons?

Point out that at this time in American history, a change of characters takes place. Men such as Clay,

The Workshop

Calhoun, and Webster begin to take over the stage from the last of the Revolutionary leaders.

The Shapers of Our World

Tell what role each of the following played in our country's early history:

James Madison
Albert Gallatin
John Marshall
Judiciary Act
   of 1801
Marbury v. *Madison*
Napoleon Bonaparte
Toussaint L'Ouverture
Robert Livingston
James Monroe
Meriwether Lewis
William Clark

Sacajawea
Zebulon Pike
Barbary pirates
Stephen Decatur
Chesapeake
Nonimportation Act
Embargo Act
Nonintercourse Act
William Henry
   Harrison
Henry Clay
John C. Calhoun

Adding to Your Vocabulary

Be sure you know the meaning of the following:

inaugural
portage
blockade

judicial review
flogging
generation

Thinking Things Through

After reviewing the boxed-in exercises, prepare to discuss the following questions:

1. Do you think Jefferson's and Gallatin's idea of large armies and wars is correct? Defend your answer.

2. Review the decision in *Marbury* v.

#Does this remark indicate that the United States was prepared for war? Was the country unified when it entered the war? Ask students to anticipate some of the problems that bothered the government during the war. These problems will be considered in Chapter 14.

Madison. Why do you think many Americans feel that the Supreme Court is the most powerful branch of our government?

3. We are told that the expression "grass is growing in the streets of the cities" was heard during the years 1807–1809. Can you tell why?

4. Both England and France issued orders to block our shipping routes before the War of 1812. But most Americans blamed Britain more than France for their difficulties. Why?

5. How was Madison affected after the War of 1812 began by some of the measures to save money his friend Jefferson had taken?

6. What two very important reasons for war against Britain were omitted by Madison in his message to Congress in 1812?

7. Why would the failure of Jefferson to purchase Louisiana have been "political suicide" for his party?

8. Jefferson once said that if the French held on to New Orleans, "we must marry ourselves to the British fleet and nation." What did he mean?

9. Reread the author's description of some Jeffersonian beliefs and practices. Compare these with some of the Federalist ideas. Is it right to speak of the election of 1800—as many people do—as having been a "revolution"?

Maps and Graphs Tell a Story

1. Using the scale of the map on page 278, tell how far Lewis and Clark and Pike traveled in exploring the area west of the Mississippi. About how long did these journeys take? Compare the time the Lewis and Clark trip west took with that of (*a*) an automobile, (*b*) a modern airplane.

2. Make bar graphs comparing each of the following: (*a*) the total area (in square miles) of the United States in 1803 *versus* the number of square miles in the Louisiana Purchase; (*b*) the total area (in square miles) of the United States today *versus* the area of the Louisiana Purchase; (*c*) the total population of the United States in the most recent census *versus* the populations of the states made from the Louisiana Purchase.

What Should the Nation Do?

1. The year is 1811. Debate the following: *Resolved,* That the United States should declare war on France. At the close of the debate, have each of the listeners write a paragraph telling which side won and why.

2. Present a round-table discussion of the Louisiana Purchase or judicial review or the *Chesapeake-Leopard* affair by three Democratic-Republican Senators and three Federalist Senators. Let each Senator represent a different section of the country.

The Seeds of Democracy

1. Prepare a panel report on Thomas Jefferson and his varied work. Discuss the meaning of Jeffersonian democracy. Be sure to tell what Jefferson considered his main achievements—they are identified on his tombstone.

2. Jefferson, like Washington, served in the presidency for two terms only. How do you explain why both men believed that the chief executive should serve no longer? Read the Twenty-second Amendment. When was it added to the Constitution? Find out why.

dents who like to draw could prepare political cartoons concerning some of the issues that ided Federalists and Republicans. Use cartoons to show public reaction to the activities England and France.

291

(a) Near Little Falls, New York, boats pass through the Erie Canal, the man-made passage between Albany and Buffalo, New York. (b) and (c) *Left:* Isaac Hull, commander of the American ship *Constitution*. *Right:* The *Constitution*—left—pounding the British vessel *Guerrière*. (d) The opening bars of the national anthem—the first printed copy. (e) Philadelphians joyfully celebrate the Fourth of July in the year 1819.

(f) This eagle, bearing the brave words of an American captain in the War of 1812, later decorated a ship's prow (its front).

(f)

CHAPTER 14

How do the pictures on pp. 292-293 suggest the growing sense of unity among the American people?

GROWING PAINS OF THE YOUNG REPUBLIC

iew briefly American disputes with England and France before the outbreak of the War of 1812. ntion the Jeffersonian attitude toward defense and our lack of readiness for war in 1812. What did United States hope to accomplish by declaring war on England?

A week after Congress declared war in 1812, Napoleon—at the peak of his power—turned his army against Russia. He planned to make the whole of Europe his own.

It upset the British that they would have to take men from the main fighting in Europe in order to engage the Americans. # And because this additional war seemed to them outrageously unnecessary, they were determined to thrash their cousins in the New World.

nphasize that at the beginning of the War of 1812, England was already involved in a European war.

The Army and Navy Battle a Powerful Foe

In the face of its angry opponent, the United States was not even united. A Federalist in Massachusetts, who probably was like most Federalists, angrily referred to the hostilities as "this wicked and foolish war."

Many Federalists opposed the war especially because they believed that a Republican administration had brought it on. Others had close personal and business ties with England, and they feared endangering them. Those who lived in New England's port cities and towns, particularly, were simply afraid—afraid of British na-

val power. All Americans recalled with respect how in 1801 the ships of Britain's Admiral Lord Nelson had stood off the coast of Denmark and bombarded the city of Copenhagen.

Getting Started

Of course many Americans were afraid because they knew how badly armed our country was. The Republicans had long been reducing the size of the army and navy. Now we had declared war on the most powerful nation in the world!

his war message Madison listed British violations of American neutral rights as the chief cause the war. Yet the section of the country that depended most on shipping gave the least support the war. Discuss reasons why this was so.

293

#Why did the United States have an unprepared and poorly led army at the start of the War of 1812? Discuss the American distrust of a large standing army in peacetime.

Unsatisfactory leadership. When the fighting began, the United States had only 7000 men in the regular army—although Congress had authorized 35,000. The military leadership of the country was woeful. The Secretary of War, William Eustis, was a likable physician who had cared for the wounded at Bunker Hill. He resigned before the year 1812 was over, which was a good thing, because everyone could see how little he knew about military matters.

The senior officer of the army, Major General Henry Dearborn, inspired hardly any more confidence than Eustis. Dearborn had also started his career as a doc-

tor, but he had given up medicine for politics. If Dearborn had once had ability, it was now gone, and he often seemed to be unaware of the world about him.

A third figure of importance who had little to contribute to military success was William Hull, a fifty-nine-year-old hero of the American Revolution. Hull was persuaded by President Madison to accept a commission as a brigadier general. Madison sent him to take over a force ordered to Detroit.

Disaster at Detroit. Hull was expected to march from Detroit into what is now Ontario and capture the area. The War

The campaigns of the War of 1812 were scattered widely, as this map shows. What was each side trying to do?

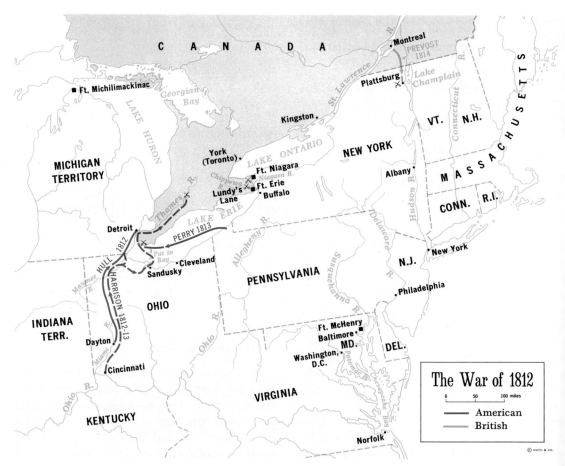

The shipyard in Philadelphia seen here turned out most of the warships Americans used in the War of 1812. Among them were the *Constitution,* the *Chesapeake,* and the *President.* Each had more guns on a single deck than any other frigate of the time.

Atwater Kent Museum

Department thought that the numerous Americans living there would rise up against the British at the first sight of the Stars and Stripes. The American plan for winning the war was summed up in the slogan "On to Canada!"

Disregarding the British troops and the Indians in back of him, Hull set out for Canada on July 12, 1812. As he did so, the British quickly captured Forts Dearborn (on the site of present-day Chicago) and Michilimackinac. The able English general, Isaac Brock, moving westward from Fort Niagara to Detroit, cut Hull off from his base. This gave Hull no choice but to surrender.

An uninspired army. New disasters followed. General Dearborn, in command of troops marching out of Plattsburg, on Lake Champlain, toward Canada, could not inspire his men to go all the way with him.

Election in wartime. While discouraging events were occurring in the military campaigns, the election of 1812 took place— the first presidential election in wartime. James Madison was reelected, winning over DeWitt Clinton, the most powerful political figure in New York State.

Clinton, in many ways the forerunner of a modern type of political leader, tried to "carry water on both shoulders." That is, he told Federalists that he would stop the war quickly and at the same time assured Republicans that he would wage it more diligently than Madison.

Some Victories at Sea

The Americans seemed helpless to carry out the plans they had made to take Canada. But they won some notable successes at sea.

Three beautiful ships. The navy had only three frigates—named appropriately

iscuss the importance of holding a presidential election during times of national crisis--even ring an unpopular war. What does this action reveal about the strength of American democracy? w does it allow criticism to continue along with the orderly process of government?

295

In what ways could the small United States Navy challenge British sea power during the War of 1812?

The 44-gun *Constitution* finishes off the 38-gun *Guerrière*. So badly crippled was the British ship that the Americans blew it up instead of capturing it.

the *United States*, the *President*, and the *Constitution*. These vessels were superior to those of the British both in design and in number of guns carried. The American navy owed much to the skill of the ship builder Joshua Humphreys.

Humphreys had designed vessels which were powerful enough to fight ship for ship against any others in the world and fast enough to run away if necessary. He had shrewdly recognized that it would be many years before the United States could have as many ships as our possible enemies.

Able sailors. The crews of the American ships were men who had gained fighting experience in the war against Tripoli. Against them were British crews often made up of unwilling men who had been impressed into service or men who underestimated the Americans.

The *Constitution* and the *Guerrière*. For reasons like these, in the first year of the fighting, the Americans achieved some astounding naval victories. Off Halifax, Nova Scotia, on August 19, 1812, the *Constitution* sent the British *Guerrière* to the bottom of the ocean. Almost 30 percent of the *Guerrière*'s 272-man crew was killed or wounded.

On December 29 the *Constitution* sank the *Java* off the coast of Brazil. The *Constitution*'s victories heartened Americans at a low point in the war.

"Old Ironsides." The ship itself became a symbol of America. Years later, when there was a proposal to scrap it, the New England writer Oliver Wendell Holmes was greatly upset at the idea. He paid tribute to "Old Ironsides" in lines which are now famous:

> Ay, tear her tattered ensign down!
>   Long has it waved on high,
> And many an eye has danced to see
>   That banner in the sky;
> Beneath it rung the battle shout,
>   And burst the cannon's roar;—
> The meteor of the ocean air
>   Shall sweep the clouds no more!

296   American naval victories provided exciting news, since the small American navy was really no match for British sea power. But the victories at sea had little effect on the outcome of the fighting in North America.

Capture of the *Macedonian*. In October, 1812, the *United States*, four days out of the port of Boston, captured the British warship *Macedonian* after a brilliant display of American marksmanship. There were stunning victories, too, for the American sloops *Hornet* and *Wasp*.

British Power

Triumphs like these showed that American sailors were inferior to none in the world. The overwhelming power of the British on the seas, nevertheless, soon showed itself.

Brave Lawrence. The *Chesapeake*, apparently going to be a "bad-luck" ship, was defeated in 1813 by the fine British craft the *Shannon* off the coast near Boston. The American crew was led by Captain James Lawrence, a brave man who suffered somewhat from his lack of experience with both his ship and his crew. The capture of the *Chesapeake* was made memorable by Lawrence's dying words, spoken as British sailors boarded his vessel, "Don't give up the ship!"

The loss of the *President*. Much later, in early 1815, the gallant ship the *President* ran aground and was captured as it fled past British blockading vessels off New York Harbor. Stephen Decatur, its captain —the hero of the war with the Barbary pirates (see page 283)—had no choice as the Royal Navy vessels closed in upon him. He later reported gravely, "I deemed it my duty to surrender."

Harrison in defeat. The news from the fighting on land was not good, either. General Harrison, the hero of Tippecanoe (see page 288), had tried to reinforce Hull at Detroit. He and his 1000 men were beaten back—weakened by the effects of severe winter weather and the difficulty of transporting enough food and supplies.

Captain Perry's miracle. Meantime, a remarkable operation was taking place on Lake Erie. There Captain Oliver Hazard Perry was building a small fleet out of fir trees felled in the nearby forest with the efforts of many ship carpenters.

Although Perry knew that he needed 740 officers and sailors, he launched his little navy of nine small schooners and a captured British ship with only 490 men. Most of them were soldiers or frontiersmen or others who had never before been on a ship. Among them were many Negroes.

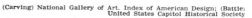

Left: A wood carving of Perry which in 1822 decorated a ship named for him. *Right:* Perry in the Battle of Lake Erie transfers the flag to a place of safety on another ship.

(Carving) National Gallery of Art. Index of American Design; (Battle) United States Capitol Historical Society

On September 10, 1813, at Put in Bay (see the map, page 294), Perry and his ships attacked a British squadron which had also been built hastily. After the fierce battle that followed, Perry could make a thrilling report to his superiors in Washington: "We have met the enemy and they are ours."

Americans had gained control of the Great Lakes. Now General Harrison was ready to move against the British again. In short order, the enemy were in full retreat from Detroit. The Americans pursued them into Canada, defeating them in the Battle of the Thames. The Indian chieftain Tecumseh fell in the struggle. (After Tecumseh's death and the defeat of the British soldiers who were the Indians' protectors, Indian attacks in the Northwest # Territory were ended.)

British successes. The fighting was still far from over. In December, 1813, the British crossed the Niagara River into United States territory and captured Fort Niagara. Moreover, they stirred up the Indians there against the local people. The British were having some revenge for the fires set by Americans in several Canadian towns, including York (present-day Toronto).

In Europe in the spring of 1814, England's long war against France was ending at last. Napoleon, his power broken, was forced to give up his throne. The hour had now come which the English had been waiting impatiently for. They transferred some of their victorious armed forces from Europe to the New World and went after the Americans.

The first step the British took was to ## blockade the coast of the United States. The second was to conduct hit-and-run naval and military attacks on the seaboard cities.

The burning of Washington. One of these assaults was launched in August, 1814, from Chesapeake Bay against the city of Washington. Washington was al-most defenseless in the face of a powerful British invasion. American soldiers and hundreds of Washington residents fled across the bridge leading from the District of Columbia into Virginia.

Two days before the enemy arrived, President Madison had to leave the city, hoping to join the military commander of the Chesapeake Bay area. Dolley Madison, alert and unafraid, remained behind in the White House almost until the British entered the city on August 24. She managed to save many official papers.

When at the last minute the First Lady was being urged to hasten her departure, she insisted on first saving a portrait of George Washington painted by Gilbert Stuart. There was not even time to remove the framed picture from the wall, so she ordered the frame to be broken and the precious canvas removed. Only then did she take flight.

The Madisons, now separated by this national disaster, wandered in the Virginia woods along the Potomac River for three days. (The President seems to have spent one night in a hen house.) In some way they finally found each other again.

Meanwhile, the British put the torch to the Capitol and then swept toward the White House. There they threw the handsome furniture, only recently delivered by cabinetmakers, into a pile in the parlor. Obtaining a live coal from a nearby tavern, they set the pile aflame.

The fires the British lighted in the city made the skies glow. In addition to the White House and the Capitol, they burned the Navy Yard buildings and most of those housing the other government departments. The following day a hurricane dealt Washington another cruel blow, although the heavy rains which accompanied the storm put out the flames.

Before the British finally withdrew, their commanding officer, Admiral Sir George Cockburn, stopped at a newspaper office.

Flames shoot out from buildings in Washington as the British attack it. All the records in the Capitol were lost because the men in charge of them were serving in the army and there was nobody to save them. This woodcut was made in 1814.

Library of Congress

There he had his men destroy all the C's in the type case, "so that," he explained, "the editors cannot any longer abuse my name."

Attack on Fort McHenry. The British ships that had landed the invaders now rejoined the main fleet, which was getting ready to attack Baltimore. English troops went ashore to try to take Fort McHenry. Their way was blocked by felled trees and other obstacles, so they decided to await the outcome of the bombardment of the fort from the sea.

It turned out that because of the shallow water, the heavier ships could not come close enough to hit the fort. And the fort was able to withstand successfully the shellfire from the lighter vessels. The next morning the British withdrew their soldiers. Their navy departed soon afterward.

"O say, can you see . . .?" As the sun rose on that September day in 1814, a young lawyer from the District of Columbia, Francis Scott Key, saw the Stars and Stripes still fluttering in the breeze. He immediately composed a poem which began:

O say, can you see, by the dawn's early light,
What so proudly we hailed at the twilight's last gleaming?
Whose broad stripes and bright stars, through the perilous fight,
O'er the ramparts we watched were so gallantly streaming!

Key set the words down on paper later that morning and rewrote them in a hotel in Baltimore that night. His wife's sister, who lived in Baltimore, was so delighted with the poem that she took it to a printer, who struck off handbills bearing it and distributed them. "The Star-Spangled Banner" gradually became known and appreciated throughout the country, and it was adopted as the national anthem.

American Recovery

In the year 1814 the burning of the city of Washington was uppermost in everyone's mind. President Madison's reputation sank to a new low—if *any* was left.

Englishmen at first applauded the destruction of the American capital. Then many felt ashamed, as many Americans felt ashamed of what their soldiers had done in York.

The events in Washington and Baltimore, despite the drama they contained, were of little military importance. The influential developments were occurring elsewhere. They resulted from the success of a new crop of American army officers.

Discuss why the British planned hit-and-run raids on coastal cities rather than the capture and occupation of territory. What kind of military operations have the greater effect--attacks against the opposing army or those directed at the civilian population?

The bombs are "bursting in air" as the British attack Fort McHenry—the building flying the American flag. In this land view of the battle, you can see the fruitless bombarding of the fort by the massed British ships.

Triumphs under Brown and Scott. On July 3, 1814, General Jacob Brown, a Pennsylvanian of Quaker ancestry, captured Fort Erie on the Niagara River. Next, one of Brown's officers, Winfield Scott, of Virginia, won the Battle of Chippewa—on the Chippewa River. Later in the month, Brown and Scott outfought a superior British force at Lundy's Lane, a village on the Canadian side of Niagara Falls.

A decisive moment in the war came in the following month when a splendid English army marched from Montreal to Lake Champlain. The aim was to cut New England off from the rest of the Union—a plan that could have resulted in disaster for America.

The work of Macdonough. The advancing British troops considerably outnumbered the American forces, which were located at Plattsburg, New York. But the struggle with the enemy occurred on water, not on land. Thomas Macdonough, only thirty-one years old, the commander

of the American ships on Lake Champlain, made a hard, seesaw battle finally turn his way. The British withdrew, leaving the United States in clear control of Lake Champlain.

The Peacemakers

Even while Americans were discovering fresh military ability and strength, diplomats were making efforts to end the war through negotiations. Early in the fighting the Russians had made a fruitless effort to bring peace by offering to *mediate*. That is, they had suggested that they act as a go-between to help settle the differences. At last, in the summer of 1814, American spokesmen arrived to commence peace talks at the town of Ghent, in Belgium.

Personalities. The American peacemakers were men of considerable standing. One was John Quincy Adams, the son of John Adams, who had had long experience in international affairs. A second was Hen-

#Summarize the American position at the opening of peace negotiations. Were the Americans working from a position of strength or from one of weakness? Compare negotiations to end the War of 1812 with those that ended the War for Independence.

ry Clay, whose all-night card games and frequent cigar-smoking told of a new kind of American politician—the shrewd and hard-living westerner.

Another was Albert Gallatin. Sometimes his warm and pleasing personality would help heal the effects of disagreements among the American peace delegates.

The men were strong personalities who often quarreled among themselves. Adams at one point wrote acidly in his diary about his fellow peacemakers, "They sit after dinner and drink bad wine and smoke cigars, which neither suits my habits nor my health, and absorbs time which I cannot spare."

Instructions. The Americans had instructions to insist that the British government meet certain conditions. It must stop impressing our seamen, respect the rights of neutrals on the high seas, and pay for the damages inflicted before and during the war. The American negotiators were told also to try to obtain Canada.

Having helped send Napoleon into exile, the British for their part hoped to deal firmly with America, too. The *London Times* was saying, "Our demands may be couched in a single word—Submission!"

English conditions. The English were planning to insist on the permanent possession of all the American territory they might be occupying at the end of the war. They were also going to ask that a part of Maine be added to Canada. Besides, they would demand that much of the old Northwest be opened up to allow the English to trade freely there.

The defeat by Macdonough, however, had stung the British to the quick. So had the retreat from Baltimore. Both made the British territorial demands in America seem beyond achieving.

When the Americans and Englishmen sat down to talk, the stiff demands on both sides disappeared. The simple truth was that the ending of the war between France and England had removed the outstanding disputes between the United States and # Britain.

Settlement. The treaty that was finally agreed upon—known as the Treaty of Ghent—did not even mention the reasons that had led to the war. But it brought peace. It provided that commissions of American and English experts try to settle some of the issues still open.

Jackson on the move. While the peace was being negotiated, American soldiers were having the greatest triumph of the war. In 1814, with a force of devoted frontiersmen, Andrew Jackson, a major general in the Tennessee militia, battled in Alabama a powerful confederacy of Creek Indians. The Creek (see page 8) were friends of the British. In March, 1814, Jackson forced the tribesmen to surrender.

The Battle of New Orleans. Then, believing that the British would try to use a Spanish base in Florida to stage a military operation northward, Jackson marched in and seized it. Having done this, he pressed on toward New Orleans. There he awaited the arrival of what proved to be 8000 crack British veterans of the war in Europe.

Among the British troops were Scotsmen in kilts, infantry wearing coats of scarlet, and riflemen clad in cloaks of green. Arrayed against the Europeans was

John Quincy Adams—center—an American peacemaker, shakes hands with the chief British representative in Ghent on December 24, 1814.

Discuss what influence the Battle of New Orleans might have had on the peace negotiations.

General Andrew Jackson, commanding near the American flag, leads his men—left, in blue—in forcing back the redcoats, who are making a vigorous attack in the Battle of New Orleans. In the foreground are the waters of the Mississippi.

Jackson's smaller army of militiamen, sailors, and even pirates.

In the battle that soon began, the Americans carried the day brilliantly, inflicting over two thousand casualties on the enemy. Among Jackson's soldiers, eight were killed and thirteen wounded.

The Battle of New Orleans took place on January 8, 1815, two weeks after the treaty of peace was signed in Ghent. It produced another great national hero—Andrew Jackson.

Ever afterward Jackson's name and the victory at New Orleans would be connected in the minds of Americans. The statue of Jackson on a horse that today stands in Lafayette Square across the street from the White House was cast from British guns captured in the battle.

The tremendous triumph lifted the sagging spirits of Americans. A Federalist historian wrote years later that it enabled Madison and his fellow Republicans to say, "[W]e can hide our shame for the moment in the smoke of Jackson's victory . . . why we can drag the country into a belief that it has been a glorious war!"

The Hartford Convention. The Federalists, more and more as time went on, opposed the war and the Republicans' handling of it. In December, 1814, a disgraceful Federalist meeting took place at Hartford, Connecticut.

Each of the New England states of that time—Massachusetts, Rhode Island, Connecticut, Vermont, and New Hampshire—sent representatives. They came with anger in their hearts. Against the war and President Madison, they even talked of the need for New England to withdraw

#Pride in the victory at New Orleans contributed to the feeling of national unity. Most Americ took the outcome of this battle to be typical of the progress of the entire war. Discuss whether or not their view of the War of 1812 was correct.

from the Union. For everything wrong they particularly blamed the Presidents from the state of Virginia.

The delegates to the Hartford Convention, as the gathering came to be called, passed a resolution about the presidency. It stated that the country must not permit itself to choose a President from the same state twice in a row. In another resolution the convention declared that a state must be allowed to resist as unconstitutional any law it believed interfered with the liberties of its people. The New Englanders, you see, were thinking of the Embargo Act, the bad effects of which they were still feeling.

\# The Federalists who went to Washington to present the resolutions passed by the Hartford Convention arrived just as word of the Treaty of Ghent reached the city. The men were glad to sneak out of town practically unnoticed.

> 1. Name three reasons why Federalists opposed the War of 1812. 2. Identify three American war leaders and describe them. 3. What two setbacks discouraged Americans at the beginning of the war? 4. What part of the American war plans failed? 5. Name three American frigates and tell what victories two achieved. What fame did the third one win? 6. Describe Perry's accomplishments on Lake Erie. 7. What two steps did the British take in 1814 to end the war in America? 8. Describe the circumstances in which Dolley Madison saved Washington's picture. In which our national anthem was written. 9. What was the significance of the Battle of Plattsburg? 10. Describe the Treaty of Ghent. 11. What made Jackson a national hero? 12. What two resolutions were passed by the Hartford Convention?

\#The Hartford Convention brought about the end of the Federalist party (see pp. 309-310).

The Union Gains in Pride and Strength

Although the country had come close to disaster in the War of 1812, it gained strength from the experience. Many citizens were now aware that they must never again be careless of the nation's defenses.

Out of the costly experience came a stronger patriotic feeling toward America than had ever existed before. The war had produced "The Star-Spangled Banner" and "Old Ironsides"—both rich reminders of love of country. It had created one of the most magnetic heroes in our history, Andrew Jackson. It had even seen the appearance for the first time of the name "Uncle Sam" to stand for the United States.

After the war was over, Americans were relieved to turn again to the problems of internal growth. In a short while the country had become different from what it had been only a few years earlier.

The Coming of Factories

The amazing development of manufacturing was one change. With the United States cut off by the war from the manufactured products of Europe, factories here found an excellent market for their goods.

American manufacturing began with the establishment of a cotton factory in Pawtucket, just north of Providence, Rhode Island, in 1790. It was the remarkable work of Samuel Slater, recently arrived from England. Slater had been an apprentice in the cotton factory of a neighbor and friend in Britain. There he had become familiar with some of the machinery that was beginning to speed up the production of cotton cloth.

Slater left his native country for the

The War of 1812, though by no means a great success, had important results. Americans not only felt increased national pride but also saw the need for more industry and better transportation. Note examples of these attitudes in this section.

#The British did not want their skilled workers to leave England and set up factories in other countries. Discuss why not. (Bear in mind that the British had discouraged manufacturing in the American colonies.)

United States in 1789. He had been attracted by the advertisements of state legislatures seeking experts in the machine weaving of textiles, that is, the manufacturing of the various kinds of cloth. It had been necessary for him to slip away in disguise, because anyone with the knowledge # he had was forbidden to emigrate.

Slater's excellent memory. Slater found employment quickly in the United States, where he was told to build a cotton mill like the one he had recently left. Bit by bit in 1790 he reproduced from memory the superb machines of the master craftsmen of England, making them run on water power from the Pawtucket Falls. The era of the factory in America had begun.

Slow but steady acceptance. Yet the call for American manufactured goods did not sweep the country overnight. A traveler in the area of Philadelphia in 1805 wrote that a considerable quantity of stockings was being made there by machine. But, he said, the demand for them was so small that the owners of the factories had to spend two days a week trying to sell their products. "They lose one third of their time in endeavoring to sell what they make in the other two thirds."

Americans had not even begun to adjust themselves to the abundance of goods that factories could turn out. They were still accustomed to dealing with craftsmen who made to order, as they were needed, shoes, cabinets, clothing, or other products.

By the time of the War of 1812, though, considerable advances had been achieved in producing goods by machine. Slowly the style of American living changed. Farmers, for example, worked the land largely as their fathers had, but they were giving up making nails in wintertime by the light and heat of the fireplace. Their wives and daughters were still churning milk into butter by hand, but spinning wheels had disappeared from wide use by 1820 or so.

By 1820, too, farmers no longer made their own beer and whisky at home. By 1830 they were no longer themselves curing and tanning the animal hides from which some of their clothing was made.

New opportunities. Along with making life easier in America, the coming of industry seemed to bring new opportunities for all people here. It was stated reliably in 1815, "One half of our wealthy men, over 45 years of age, were once common day laborers or journeymen [that is, artisans], or otherwise very humble in their circumstances when they began [in] the world."

Slater's cotton mill, in Rhode Island, in part perched on stilts at the left. The Pawtucket Falls—right—provided the water power needed to run his machines.

Old Slater Mill Museum

Winter in Brooklyn, New York, about 1817, when the roads were also the streets and when animals and people moved about with equal freedom.

The Growth of Cities

Another change was that more and more there was a tendency for people to live in cities. Between 1790 and 1820 the number of Americans living in communities of 2500 or more increased from 5 percent to over 7 percent of the total population.

The leaders: New York and Philadelphia. In 1800 the leading cities were Philadelphia and New York, in that order. By 1810 New York had become the largest urban center, clearly outstripping Philadelphia, which had occupied that position during the last fifty years of the eighteenth century.

Baltimore. The third-ranking city in 1810, Baltimore, owed its position to resourceful businessmen. They had shrewd-ly made the grain and tobacco trade of Virginia and Maryland flow through their city. Baltimore's population, which had been 26,514 in 1800, rose to about 45,500 in 1810.

Boston. Before Philadelphia and then New York outgrew it, Boston had been the leading city of the country. But it did not grow as rapidly as its rivals did. Nevertheless, Boston, the fourth largest city both in 1800 and in 1810, remained a trading center. It drew to itself the finished industrial products of the rest of New England.

New Orleans and Charleston. In 1810 the cities that ranked fifth and sixth in size were in the South. They were Charleston, South Carolina, and New Orleans. New Orleans, known sometimes as the Crescent City because it developed along a crescent-shaped bend in the Mississippi River, was on the verge of great growth.

Discuss the reasons for the growth of cities. Have students discuss location, resources, and ·cal effort as factors that explain why the communities listed above became the leading ·ties in the early United States.

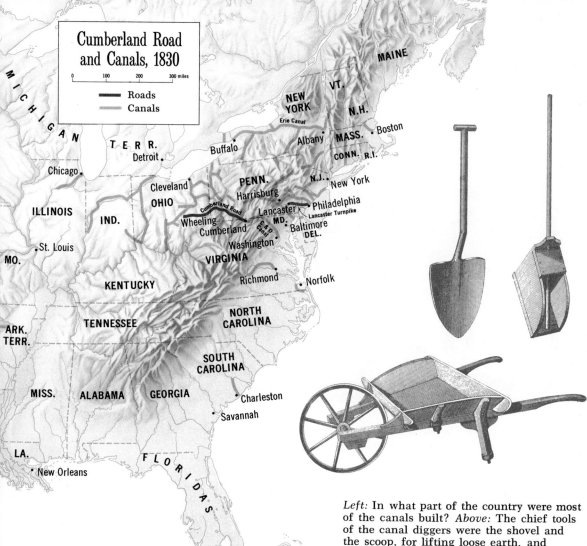

Cumberland Road and Canals, 1830

0 100 200 300 miles

— Roads
— Canals

Left: In what part of the country were most of the canals built? *Above:* The chief tools of the canal diggers were the shovel and the scoop, for lifting loose earth, and the wheelbarrow, for hauling it off.

"Rees' Cyclopedia" (New York Public Library)

Movement of People and Goods

A third change in the United States was in the way people transported goods. The successful trip of the steamboat *Clermont* on the Hudson River in 1807 had solved at last the problem of providing speedy and efficient river transportation of freight.

Steamboat traffic. On the Ohio and Mississippi rivers, steamboats shortly were carrying a steady flow of farm products—as well as sugar and cotton grown in the lower South—toward New Orleans. In fact, in some years in the 1830's and 1840's, New Orleans surpassed New York in the total volume of trade it handled.

Turnpikes. The serious problem of land transportation also called for a solution. The ability to move people and freight from one part of the country to another cheaply and rapidly might well determine how large the United States could grow.

Before 1812 Americans had built a considerable number of *turnpikes*—that is, toll roads. They were frequently privately owned, and the profits they made went to the stockholders of the companies that

Consider that rivers and canals were important shipping arteries because land transportation was so unsatisfactory. Not until the building of the railroads did the United States begin to have good land transportation--despite the turnpikes.

took the financial risk of constructing them.

One of the best-known—and best-built—roads was the turnpike between Philadelphia and Lancaster, Pennsylvania, completed in 1794. Built by the Philadelphia and Lancaster Turnpike Road Company, it was made of crushed stone laid 18 inches deep in the middle and 12 inches at the sides. The slope insured good drainage.

Roads built with private money, however, were often inferior. If the foundations, or beds, were poor, the roads were likely to wash out or collapse in time.

A French traveler had described the general situation in President John Adams' lifetime:

> Such portions of the roads as are bad and muddy, are filled up with trees, placed near each other; when they sink into the ground others are laid upon them. Over small brooks, bridges are thrown, which consist of boards, placed on two beams, laid along the banks of the brook. These boards frequently rot, and remain in this condition for months.... We have passed several such bridges, with great danger to our horses, from the bad condition of the boards.

Gallatin's proposal. In a report Albert Gallatin issued in 1808, he stated that the federal government would have to take a hand in aiding transportation. His report as a whole was never acted upon, but the federal government in 1811 began to build the Cumberland Road.

The Cumberland Road. Known also as the National Road, by 1818 the Cumberland Road was opened for traffic between Cumberland, Maryland, and the Ohio River city of Wheeling, Virginia. Constructed of crushed stone, it followed in part the Indian path that George Washington and later General Braddock's wagon train had followed.

Experience in wartime. The War of 1812 had proved thoroughly the unsatisfactory state of American roads. It had been almost impossible to move soldiers by land either to the Canadian border or southward. The situation had been made worse by the British blockade of the Atlantic seacoast. This move had practically wiped out the coastal shipping that had helped in transporting people and goods. The country was forced to rely increasingly on roads, which, being overused, more than ever before revealed how very poor they were.

Canals. At the time Americans were beginning to seek better roads, they also began to construct canals. At the end of the War of 1812, less than 100 miles of canals had been built. There were good reasons for this slow pace: first, canals required a very large outlay of money, and second, they had not proved profitable.

The *Clermont* (center), the steamboat which successfully traveled up the Hudson River from New York City to Albany. Built by Robert Fulton, it moved with power provided by a steam engine that turned large paddle wheels on each side of the boat. An artist of the time drew this picture.

Mariners Museum, Newport News, Va.

#Trace the route of the Erie Canal on a map. Point out how this waterway opened the Great Lakes region to settlement. What cities prospered because of the canal?

"Clinton's Big Ditch." A significant move was made by the state of New York in 1817 when it approved the construction of the Erie Canal and agreed to finance it. It was to run between the cities of Albany and Buffalo, a distance of 364 miles. (The longest canal built previously had extended less than 30 miles from beginning to end.)

The Erie Canal, a monument to the determination of New York's governor, De Witt Clinton, was at times laughingly called Clinton's Big Ditch. But as section by section opened before its completion in 1825, and as it showed immediate profits, the laughter turned to respect. Other communities everywhere rushed wildly into the building of canals, too.

An Estimate of Things

The changes in the ways Americans made a living and transported themselves and their goods gave the country an air of national pride. A citizen of the city of Charleston, in a speech celebrating a Fourth of July, said with satisfaction, "The War has given strength and splendor to the chain of the Union. Every link exhibits the lustre of the diamond. Local feelings are absorbed in the proud feelings of being an American."

Naturally, the people were interested in what went on in Europe and in the development of foreign trade. But mostly they were taken up with their own problems, which were those of a growing country.

In facing the future, Americans recognized that there ought to be a feeling of loyalty to their nation. But they also recognized that the country was made up of three sections—North, South, and West— each with somewhat different aims and needs. The business of national politics was to try to patch up differences of opinion without disturbing harmony within the country as a whole.

1. What two symbols of American patriotism were produced during the War of 1812? 2. Name three important changes in this country in the early 1800's. 3. State the main facts about the establishment of the first factory in the United States. 4. Name the six largest American cities in 1810. 5. Give the main facts about the construction of the Cumberland Road and the Erie Canal.

Summarize the section above by having students note the striking changes that occurred in American life—in industry, in cities, and in transportation.

The Sections Glare Angrily at Each Other

The needs of American industry, which was concentrated in the North—in New England especially—led Congress to take appropriate steps. These steps were not fully acceptable in other parts of the country.

Aid to Industry

Immediately after the War of 1812, British manufacturers began to flood the American market with their goods. British factory owners thought it would be a good time to strangle at birth the "infant" indus-# tries of the United States.

A protective tariff. Congress answered with a tariff law—the Tariff of 1816—the cries for protection that came from American factory owners. It placed a duty on manufactured goods shipped into the United States. The tax raised the cost of foreign-made products and in that way "protected" American industry. A chief argument made in favor of the law was that

308 ##America's new, developing factories often charged more for products than did their well established competition in England. Without a tariff to raise the cost of foreign-made products, many claimed, buyers would prefer cheaper foreign products to expensive American ones.

the United States would be stronger in time of war if it could become independent of foreign manufacturers.

Southern opposition. A number of Congressmen, chiefly southerners, opposed the law. They said it would keep the cost of manufactured goods high but would do nothing to raise the price of farm products.

Nevertheless, in general, all sections of the country were willing, for the time being, to support a protective tariff. Many people believed that once American industries were firmly established, the tariff would be repealed.

The second Bank of the United States. A new bank, too, was made necessary by events. The charter of the first Bank of the United States had expired in 1811. As a result, the number of state banks increased. They issued bank notes—that is, currency—without proper control, a dangerous practice.

Western opposition. Madison, who had fought against the first Bank of the United States tooth and nail, felt after the war that a second one, also to be in the East, was absolutely necessary. Many westerners did not want great financial power, such as the Bank could exercise, to be located so far from their reach. Nevertheless, Congress in 1816 granted a charter to the second Bank of the United States.

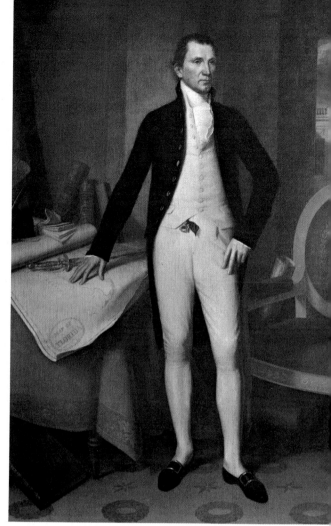

New York City Hall Art Collection

James Monroe as he looked when he was President—the fourth one who had come from Virginia.

Republican Sweep

Both the passage of the Tariff of 1816 and the chartering of the second Bank in the same year would have delighted Alexander Hamilton. (He had been killed in a duel in 1804.) The Federalists, of course, were saying that the Republicans had stolen *their* program.

But the Federalists were not able to take political advantage of the fact that their opponents appeared to have adopted Hamilton's ideas. The Federalists had been disgraced by their treasonable role at the

Hartford Convention. For the election of 1816 they were hard put to find a candidate to unseat the Republicans' man—whoever he might be. The Republicans, of course, were claiming credit for the "victory" over the mother country in the War of 1812 and for the general prosperity.

James Monroe. The Republicans named as their candidate in 1816 James Monroe, still another Virginian. Fifty-eight years old, he had enjoyed a career that went back to the era of the American Revolution.

tress that after the War of 1812 many Americans, flushed with the spirit of nationalism, were ling to sacrifice certain sectional interests for the sake of building a stronger nation. Note t the tariff was expected to help the country become self-sufficient.

In 1816 he even seemed old-fashioned. He still wore knee-length pantaloons, although many American men were wearing trousers by then.

By his very appearance Monroe reminded Americans of a time they were proud of. His victory over the Federalist candidate, Rufus King, was fortunate. The nation sorely needed a man like Monroe to knit together a country beginning to feel more sharply its sectional differences.

Appeal to all. Keenly aware of the feeling of New Englanders against having another President from Virginia, Monroe chose as his Secretary of State John Quincy Adams, of Massachusetts. And in his inaugural address, the President spoke of the American people as "one great family with a common interest."

Monroe and the First Lady spent a part of the year 1817 furnishing the rebuilt White House. Their taste showed a wish to be elegant and practical at the same time—desirable in a flourishing republic.

A Virginia Senator described the completed work: "The quality . . . very much resembles that of a private gentleman's. . . . There is only one room splendidly furnished [the Blue Room, used for diplomatic receptions] . . . designed to impress upon foreign ministers a respect for the Government, which may have a valuable influence upon our foreign relations."

"General satisfaction." The reopening of the White House to the public on New Year's Day in 1818 added to the people's sense that the country was doing well. A leading Washington newspaper reported "It was gratifying once more to salute the President of the United States with the compliments of the season in his . . . residence, and the continuance of the . . . custom has given . . . general satisfaction."

Two jolts. But two unfortunate developments badly disturbed the calm. The first was a serious business depression, generally known as the Panic of 1819. It was caused by unwise speculation in western land and careless policies of the second Bank of the United States in making loans, especially in the South and West.

Second, the production of tobacco and cotton had been suddenly expanded to supply the markets in Europe. When the demand for these products dropped off all at once, thousands of farmers suffered.

The people did not blame President Monroe for the troubles which befell the nation. But southerners and westerners generally tended thereafter to be increasingly suspicious of the second Bank of the United States, located in Philadelphia.

Many Americans viewed the North as the home of the "money power." As a result, some bad feeling developed between the North on the one hand and the South and West on the other. This feeling was not going to be easily smoothed over.

The Admission of Missouri

Another unhappy development also foretold continuing difficulties. Like the Panic of 1819, it, too, grew out of the westward movement of Americans. It began in this way: in 1818 the Missouri territory, a part of the Louisiana Purchase, applied for admission as a state.

The Minerva clock, which was presented to the White House by President Monroe. Seen today on the mantel in the Blue Room, it takes its name from the figure representing the Greek goddess of wisdom.

#Louisiana had already been admitted as a state in 1812.

Corcoran Gallery of Art

The House of Representatives as it looked about the time of the debate on slavery caused by Tallmadge's proposal and the heated discussion of the Missouri Compromise.

w many Senators were there in 1819?

Tallmadge's suggestion. The following year, Representative James Tallmadge, Jr., of New York State, proposed in Congress that no new slaves be taken to Missouri after it was admitted to the Union. Also, he wanted all children born to slaves already in Missouri to be freed when they became twenty-five years of age. In this way slavery would eventually be wiped out there.

Tallmadge said slavery was evil. He and other northerners were determined to keep it out of the region that was being opened up on the western side of the Mississippi River.

The heart of the question. The proposal opened a public debate on slavery that went on until 1820. At stake was the even balance in the Senate between free states, where there were no slaves, and slave states. Because there were eleven slave and eleven free states, another free state would give the North an advantage in the Senate. Already the slave states could be outvoted in the House.

Jefferson's alarm. Clearly the issue of slavery was in the national spotlight for the first time. Jefferson, who was spending the last years of his life at Monticello, in Virginia, said that the "momentous question [of slavery]" stirred him and terrified him. The raising of the issue, he said in words now famous, was "like a fire bell in the night."

Many southerners were beginning to feel that they must defend themselves. They were coming to be afraid of northern control of the Union itself.

A compromise. The furious and far-reaching debate on the admission of Missouri called forth speeches by the leading figures in Congress. At last, in 1820 a settlement of differences (see page 239) was agreed to. As we shall see, it was the first in a series of compromises that were made ## on the slavery question.

According to the compromise, Missouri was to be admitted to the Union as a slave state and Maine was to be admitted as a free state. There would, therefore, be twelve free states and twelve slave states, and the balance in the Senate would be maintained.

In addition, a line would be drawn

In the Missouri Compromise, as in the Northwest Ordinance of 1787, Congress declared ether a territory was open or closed to slavery. The power of Congress to pass laws about very was to be questioned in the growing sectional dispute.

across the Louisiana Purchase along the parallel 36° 30′. North of it slavery would be forever forbidden—except in Missouri. The line became the southern boundary of the new state.

President Monroe somewhat unwillingly signed the bill containing the Missouri Compromise, as it was called. He believed that it was unconstitutional to limit the spread of slavery. On the other side, Adams, the Secretary of State, believed it wrong to compromise on slavery, which he regarded as a sin of man against man.

What did each side gain in the Missouri Compromise? What, on the other hand, did each give up?

The United States, 1821

0   100   200   300   400 miles

Free States — Free Terr. — Slave States — Slave Terr.

BRITISH

UNORGANIZED TERRITORY

MICHIGAN TERRITORY

MAINE 1820

VT. 1791

N.H.

NEW YORK

MASS.

CONN.   R.I.

PENN.

N.J.

ILL. 1818   IND. 1816   OHIO 1803

MD. DEL.

MO. 1821

VIRGINIA

KENTUCKY 1792

NORTH CAROLINA

36°30′

TENN. 1796

ARKANSAS TERRITORY

S.C.

MISS. 1817   ALA. 1819   GEORGIA

SPANISH

LA. 1812

FLORIDAS

© RMSN & CO.

Who won? At the time the Missouri Compromise was being worked out, most northerners believed that the South had got a much better bargain than the North. The vast area of land that would be free consisted for the most part of grassland which most people thought would never prove suitable for agriculture. In fact, map-makers called much of the land between the Missouri River and the Rockies the Great American Desert.

A Statement to the World

Despite the costly depression in 1819 and the angry dispute over the Missouri question, Monroe was reelected in 1820. In the electoral college he received every vote but one. One elector cast a blank ballot, declaring that the honor of a unanimous election should remain George Washington's alone.

The overwhelming victory for Monroe was a result of the fact that the old political parties—Republican as well as Federalist—were breaking up. They plainly were unprepared to face the difficult new issues which were arising. Only Monroe, a hero of other days, had support—largely personal—in all sections of the country.

In his relations with foreign countries, Monroe was as careful as he was in affairs at home. He served well Americans' growing sense that theirs was a nation that could have an influence in the world.

The revolt of the Spanish colonies. An opportunity for America to assert itself came after Spain's colonies in the New World revolted against their mother country beginning in 1810. These included the present-day country of Mexico as well as countries in Central and South America. At first the Spanish made no move to regain their possessions, for they were busy with the war against Napoleon in Europe.

Acquiring the Floridas. But after Napoleon's defeat in 1815, the expanding

Why was the number of slave states so vital to the slaveholding South? (Outvoted in the House by the more populous North, the South hoped to keep an equal voice--a veto power--in the Senate by maintaining an equal number of slave and free states.)

United States kept a keen eye on develop-ments in Spanish America. Secretary of State Adams arranged in 1819 an agree-ment with Spain called the Transconti-nental Treaty. By it America obtained East and West Florida. In addition, arguments over where the western boundary of the Louisiana Territory belonged were settled. It had not been definitely located in 1803.

Reasons for concern. Although by the terms of the treaty Spain gave up some of its land in North America, Americans were afraid the Spanish would try to regain their other New World colonies.

The United States had several excellent reasons for wanting to keep European powers from undertaking such recon-quests of American land. The first and most important reason was military: Euro-pean armies in the New World could be a direct threat to the United States.

Second, we sympathized with the Latin American people, who, like ourselves, had freed themselves of the control of a Euro-pean country. Third, the United States ex-pected a larger share of the trade of the newly independent countries than we had been permitted to have when they were possessions of Spain.

Britain's interesting offer. The British hoped for a share in the same trade. In ad-dition, they wanted to make profitable in-vestments in the new countries.

In the summer of 1823 the British acted to head off a possible invasion of the New World. They invited the United States to join with them in a warning against any European military expedition which might threaten the newly independent countries.

The offer of Britain to have the United States act jointly with it was very flattering to us. President Monroe and his advisers carefully discussed whether we should ac-cept or not. Monroe even consulted with former presidents of the United States.

Words of wisdom. Jefferson's advice was to seize this good chance to stand with

Museum of Fine Arts, Boston

John Quincy Adams at
the age of twenty-eight,
in a portrait painted by John Singleton
Copley. Young Adams, son of the second
President and Abigail, became
a Boston lawyer like his father
before entering politics.

Britain. He felt sure that if we had the mother country "on our side we need not fear the whole world." Madison agreed heartily with his dear friend that the time had come to reach out for the hand of the old enemy England.

The advice that prevailed with Monroe, however, was that of the Secretary of State, John Quincy Adams. Adams saw no reason why we should involve ourselves in a declaration *with* Britain. He reasoned, If we are going to make a declaration against European intervention in America, why not make it ourselves, alone? That way, it would apply to England just as much as it would to any other powers of Europe.

Adams, a persuasive man, convinced his associates of the correctness of his argu-ments. Monroe, in his annual message to Congress on December 2, 1823, expressed the policy, which was agreed upon.

ow how the Monroe Doctrine was another example of the growth of national feeling. Compare
Monroe Doctrine and Washington's views on foreign relations. How did both envision an
ependent role for the United States in world affairs?　　313

Why was England willing to have the Monroe Doctrine enforced?

A message from the President. Monroe's statement contained four main points:

First, the New World was not open to future colonization.

Second, the United States did not favor the establishment in the Americas of government by kings and queens.

Third, the United States would not interfere with European colonies already in existence in North and South America.

Fourth, the United States would not involve itself in European affairs which did not concern the New World.

The effects. In 1823 the bold declaration to the powers of Europe made very little impression. In those days the utterances of an American President were not listened to everywhere in the world, as they are today.

The Russian minister in Washington, in fact, was told by his government that "the document in question [Monroe's message] ... merits only the most profound contempt." Years later, when America acquired the military strength to enforce its policies, the words would be heeded well. By then Monroe's statement would be re-
ferred to as the Monroe Doctrine.

New Political Winds

As the election of 1824 approached, a number of men strong in their own sections of the country wanted to be President. All were Republicans.

"Harper's Bazaar," March 18, 1871 (Library of Congress)

"The Adams Papers," Massachusetts Historical Society

Above: On January 8, 1824, before the unpleasantness of the election of that year, the Adamses gave a ball to celebrate the anniversary of the Battle of New Orleans. Jackson, then a Senator, stands in the center, and his host, Secretary of State Adams, at the far right. *Below:* John Quincy Adams' ticket to a celebration of the anniversary of the Declaration of Independence. (A "collation" may have been something like a buffet supper in our time.) The words printed in a circle are a quotation from his father's writings.

#Note that the Monroe Doctrine is not a part of international law but merely a statement of the policy of the United States. What would have happened if England had disagreed with this policy? Is the Monroe Doctrine still applicable to Latin America?

efer to the Twelfth Amendment to the Constitution (pp. 721-722). How did this amendment apply the situation in the election of 1824?

The candidates. John Quincy Adams, the candidate from New England, believed that he deserved the honor because he was Secretary of State. All the Virginia Presidents—except Washington—had served in that office before stepping up to the White House.

Other candidates were Henry Clay, of Kentucky, who had strong support in the West, and Andrew Jackson, of Tennessee, who rivaled Clay as a western favorite. In the South the able Secretary of the Treasury, William Crawford, and John C. Calhoun, Secretary of War, had many backers. (After Crawford suffered a crippling stroke in 1823, his chances were doomed.)

Settling the election in the House. No candidate had sufficient strength outside his own section to overwhelm all his rivals. When the returns were in, Jackson had 99 electoral votes and Adams, 84. Clay ran fourth. Since no candidate had a majority of electoral votes, that is, more than half the total number cast, in accordance with the Constitution, the House of Representatives decided the issue. In the contest in the House, Clay, after a long deadlock, threw his support to Adams and made him the winner.

The rage of the Jackson men. Jackson and his followers were furious. Jackson had won the most electoral votes. Why, then, had he not been chosen in the House of Representatives?

When Adams announced that his choice for Secretary of State was Henry Clay, the cry of the Jacksonians went up even more loudly. "Bargain and corruption," they shouted in outrage.

The diligent Mr. Adams. But Adams' father, John Adams, rejoiced at his beloved "Johnny's" election. He wrote his son touchingly upon hearing the news, "The multitude of my thoughts, and the intensity of my feelings are too much for a mind like mine, in its ninetieth year."

The new President was keenly aware of the anger among many Americans that the manner of his election had produced. With admirable frankness he told his fellow citizens in his inaugural address, "[I am] less possessed of your confidence . . . than any of my predecessors."

John Quincy Adams worked as hard as any President has ever worked. He rose usually between four and six and took a walk around the Capitol, returned to the White House, made the fire, read the papers, and had breakfast. Then he was ready for the day and the ceaseless round of visitors.

In the summertime the President went swimming in the Potomac River daily at daybreak. On one occasion when he went out in a little boat that sank, he almost did not make it back to shore. He wrote in his diary, "My principal difficulty was in the loose sleeves of my shirt, which filled with water and hung like two fifty-six pound weights upon my arms."

Yet Adams simply could not combine his energy and his experience to become a popular and successful President. To many of his countrymen he seemed to be out of step with his time.

A new taste. The public appeared now not to be wanting their chief executive to be a man of thought—as Adams was. They were attracted rather to the man of action. The vast job of building the country seemed to require a boldness that ought to be typified by the President himself.

Unable to find a candidate strong in every part of the country, the old Republican party had begun to break up. One important group, including many of Jefferson's former supporters, western frontiersmen, and craftsmen of the cities, had started calling themselves Democrats. Their leader was Andrew Jackson.

The four years of Adams' presidency were used by the Democrats as a kind of four-year-long campaign to put their man into the White House in 1829. On Election

»mpare the elections of 1820 and 1824. Which factors showed the influence of nationalism; lich indicated sectionalism? Note that by 1824 Jefferson's old Republican party included men many different points of view.

Day in 1828 they had their triumph as Andrew Jackson overwhelmed Adams, seeking reelection. Adams would not attend "Old Hickory's" inauguration—just as his father had refused to attend Jefferson's.

The inauguration of a hero. Jackson came into the White House accompanied by the thunderous cheers of Americans who were celebrating the election of a *people's* President. If they were not clear in their minds about what they wanted him to do for them, it did not matter. For the moment they were enjoying the idea that the "aristocrats" had been thrown out of power.

Jackson's inaugural celebration became a mob scene as crowds pushed through the gates of the White House to catch a glimpse of the man of the hour. Women fainted, and china and crystal glasses were trampled upon. People in muddy boots stood on the silken chairs. It is said that the milling public was finally lured out of the mansion only when tubs of punch were placed on the lawn.

Jackson, meanwhile, had been taken to a nearby inn to await the end of the celebrating. The hero of New Orleans was now the hero of Washington.

Jackson was always a man of perfect self-confidence. But surely during that long and noisy afternoon he must have wondered to himself what the people expected of him. How could he ever prove worthy of such a welcome? Could he be in peacetime the idol he had been in war?

1. Name two important measures passed by Congress in 1816. 2. What two jolts disturbed Americans in 1819? 3. State the main facts about the Missouri Compromise. 4. What public debate did the compromise open? 5. How did we gain the Floridas? 6. Give three reasons for issuing the Monroe Doctrine. 7. State the four main points of the Doctrine. 8. Describe the election of 1824. 9. What attracted American people to Andrew Jackson?

Why are military heroes often popular as presidential candidates? Ask a student to look up generals other than

The Workshop

Jackson who became President. What preparation for holding public office does military service give?

The Shapers of Our World

Tell how each of the following contributed to developing either a strong national feeling or a strong sectional feeling:

William Hull
"Old Ironsides"
Oliver Hazard Perry
William Henry
  Harrison
James Madison
Dolley Madison
Thomas Macdonough
John Quincy
  Adams

Monroe Doctrine
Hartford Convention
Samuel Slater
Clermont
Cumberland Road
De Witt Clinton
James Monroe
Tariff of 1816
second Bank of
  the United States

Francis Scott Key
Henry Clay
Treaty of Ghent
Andrew Jackson

Panic of 1819
Florida treaty
Missouri Compromise

Adding to Your Vocabulary

Be sure you know the meaning of these terms:

sloop
turnpike
depression
speculation
idol
rival

mediate
senior officer
nationalism
sectionalism
casualty

To summarize political changes in the United States, discuss the elections of 1800 and 1828. Why were both referred to as revolutions? Compare Jefferson and Jackson in terms of their political beliefs and their concepts of the presidency.

Thinking Things Through

After reviewing the boxed-in exercises in the chapter, see if you can answer these questions:

1. Since violations of our sea rights were the main cause of the War of 1812, why did the section of our country most dependent on trade most oppose the war?

2. How did the Battle of New Orleans change the viewpoint of most Americans concerning the war?

3. How did the Hartford Convention help destroy the Federalist party?

4. Review the circumstances leading to the declaration of the War of 1812. How would modern communications have affected both the outbreak of the fighting and its close?

5. Reread the second resolution passed by the Hartford Convention. What were the delegates saying about our federal government and the relation of the states to the central government?

6. How do you account for the fact that Madison fought against the first Bank of the United States but supported the second?

7. Discuss Federalist opposition to the Louisiana Purchase and the Democratic-Republican support of the tariff and the United States Bank as they show how parties change their views over the years.

8. Only the two Presidents from the Adams family failed to win reelection in the early years of our republic. Explain this fact by comparing the elections of 1800 and 1828.

9. Discuss the stanzas of "The Star-Spangled Banner." How do they show the progress of the battle being fought when it was written?

The Research Center

1. Report to the class on the careers of Simón Bolívar and José de San Martín. Compare their struggles for military vic-

tory with those of George Washington.

2. Choose one of the republics of Latin America and present a report on its fight for independence. You might also tell about its first years of freedom and about how American democracy was tried abroad. How was this attempt another example of the fact that the shots of Lexington and Concord were "heard round the world"?

3. Prepare a bulletin-board display on Virginia, "Mother of Presidents." Refer to the chart on page 727 in order to include all the chief executives from the "Old Dominion." You might show some pictures of their homes and some indicating their greatest accomplishments.

How do you account for the fact that so many of our early Presidents came from Virginia? Discuss the idea of the delegates to the Hartford Convention that no two Presidents in succession should come from the same state.

4. Report on the life of Tecumseh.

Presenting Information

1. Imagine yourself as a reporter at Jackson's inauguration in 1829. Write a news account describing the scene for your paper, which is published in New Hampshire and which supported John Quincy Adams for the presidency.

2. Dramatize a Cabinet meeting of the Monroe administration. Discuss the Monroe Doctrine. Be sure to represent both viewpoints mentioned in the chapter.

3. John Adams and Thomas Jefferson died within five hours of each other on July 4, 1826. Write a letter either man might have sent to the other shortly before his death. How do you think a person who had watched developments since the American Revolution would have viewed the condition of the Union in 1826?

4. Ask your music teacher to play some examples of songs of the canal era. Perhaps the class could sing some of them.

ere is value in looking forward and backward from the vantage point of the late 1820's. Show by that time the United States had become firmly established. Show also that the conditions ch led to the eventual breakup of the Union were already apparent.

Part Four Workshop

Then and Now

1. What American explorations today can be compared with those of Pike and of Lewis and Clark in (a) purposes, (b) accomplishments, and (c) source of support?

2. What parts of the Constitution were written in 1787? What has been added since then? When was the most recent addition made?

3. Contrast George Washington and the President today in (a) dress, (b) receiving the public, (c) dealing with Congress.

4. How many Senators and members of the House of Representatives were there in 1789? How many are there today? How many men does your state send to Congress? Why? How many does the largest of the states send?

5. Compare the national debt in 1789 and today. How was the first one acquired? What accounts for our present-day debt?

6. What rights guaranteed in the Bill of Rights are often mentioned in the news today? Why? Why are they guaranteed?

7. What improvement or improvements in transportation today will students read about in the future as people now read about the steamboat, the Cumberland Road, and the Erie Canal?

8. What efforts to keep peace did the United States make before the War of 1812? What is our country doing today to promote peace?

Time and Change

Look at the time line on pages 218–219 and answer the following questions about the years covered there:

1. What important change or changes did Americans make in (a) their government, (b) the size of their country, (c) the way they produced goods, (d) the way they moved goods and people?

2. What two important statements were made about the role of the United States in world affairs?

3. What steps were taken which showed the growing strength of the young republic?

4. What plans were made and carried out to make the country stronger and more prosperous in the future?

5. When in the period did the Federalists flourish? Why did they disappear?

The Book Shelf

Beard, Charles A., and Beard, William. *The Presidents in American History* (rev. ed.). New York: Julian Messner, Inc., 1965. (Their biographies.)

Donovan, Frank. *Mr. Madison's Constitution.* New York: Dodd, Mead & Co., Inc. 1965. (The story of the creating of the supreme law of the land.)

————. *Mr. Monroe's Message.* New York: Dodd, Mead & Co., Inc., 1963. (Discusses the Monroe Doctrine.)

Douty, Esther. *Under the New Roof.* Chicago: Rand McNally & Co., 1965. (Biographies of five patriots of our young republic.)

Kornwolf, James D. *A History of American Dwellings.* Chicago: Rand McNally & Co., 1967. (About outstanding houses and kinds of architecture in America from colonial times to the present.)

Lomask, Milton. *John Quincy Adams.* New York: Farrar, Straus & Giroux, Inc., 1965. (Tells about the sixth President.)

Smith, Irene. *Washington, D.C.* Chicago: Rand McNally & Co., 1964. (Describes the history and layout of the city.)

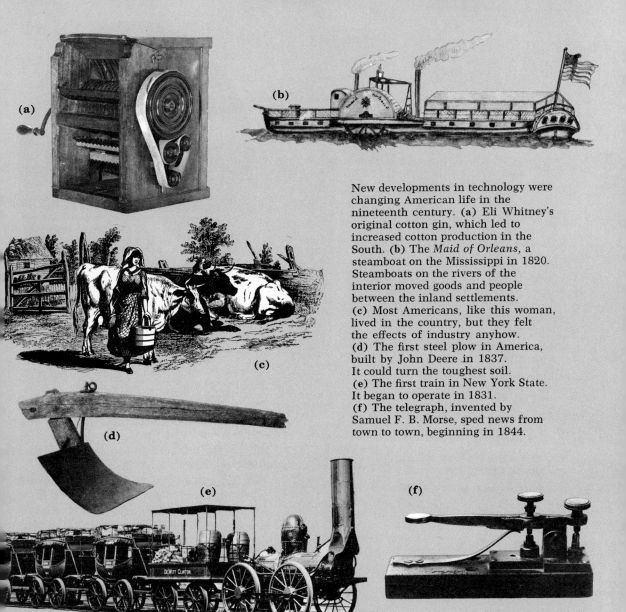

New developments in technology were changing American life in the nineteenth century. (a) Eli Whitney's original cotton gin, which led to increased cotton production in the South. (b) The *Maid of Orleans,* a steamboat on the Mississippi in 1820. Steamboats on the rivers of the interior moved goods and people between the inland settlements. (c) Most Americans, like this woman, lived in the country, but they felt the effects of industry anyhow. (d) The first steel plow in America, built by John Deere in 1837. It could turn the toughest soil. (e) The first train in New York State. It began to operate in 1831. (f) The telegraph, invented by Samuel F. B. Morse, sped news from town to town, beginning in 1844.

Part Five: SECTIONAL SQUABBLING

te that seemingly unrelated developments in technology are often connected. For example, the cotton
and the steamboat were both vital to the cotton producers in the South, and the steel plow and the
road were important to the farmers of the West.

Part Five:
SECTIONAL SQUABBLING

Continued on facing page

H. Clay

"'THE UNION IS MY COUNTRY"

Henry Clay was once the most famous American from west of the Appalachians. In Kentucky, where his home was, he owned slaves and lived like a king. A dashing figure, he also had the simple manner of one who has grown up close to nature. Even when he was old, it is said, he still recited each night before going to bed, "Now I lay me down to sleep. . . ."

A lady who knew "Harry of the West," as he was often called, once said: "Henry Clay was made for action—not rest." His life showed how right she was. Elected to the Sen-

Time and Change

Point out that the national debate over slavery intensified after 1848.

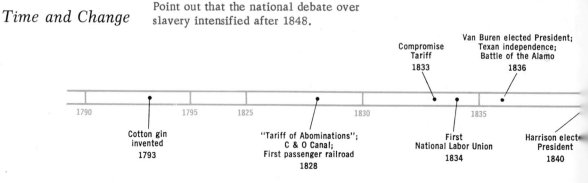

Cotton gin invented 1793

"Tariff of Abominations"; C & O Canal; First passenger railroad 1828

Compromise Tariff 1833

First National Labor Union 1834

Van Buren elected President; Texan independence; Battle of the Alamo 1836

Harrison elected President 1840

1790   1795   1825   1830   1835

te in 1810, he gave up his seat there for a
while to run for a place in the House of Representatives. He explained that he preferred
the . . . turbulence [that is, the hubbub] of a
lower house to the solemn stillness of the
Senate."

Yet neither love of action nor love of
noise (he was sometimes also known as the
noisy Mr. Clay) explains this man's lasting
reputation. He is remembered for having been
master of the art of political compromise—
that is, of getting rivals to give as well as take
in their disputes on public questions. Three
times—in 1821, in 1833, and in 1850—he had
an important hand in persuading the North
and the South to settle their most serious
disagreements.

Clay also worked as hard as any other
man ever has to make himself the president
of the United States. Three times he ran for
the office and was defeated. In a mood of sour
grapes, he finally decided "I'd rather be right
than be President."

From 1810 on Clay pushed hard for the
United States to go to war against England
because he thought the safety of the nation
required it. At heart, though, he was a man
of peace. As Secretary of State he argued for
friendship among the nations of the New
World.

But he always returned to the task of arguing for friendship among the sections of
the United States. In the closing days of his
career, he summed up his constant plea in
words that have never been forgotten. He
told his fellow Senators, "*I know no South, no
North, no East, no West*, to which I owe any
allegiance. . . . The Union . . . is my country."

THE RISE OF ABRAHAM LINCOLN

The Parties Face the Slavery Issue

The "Final Settlement" Is Quickly Reopened

The Union Splits at the Sectional Seams

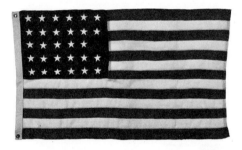

The United States flag in 1846, when twenty-nine states made up the Union.

In what ways did Henry Clay represent a new style in American politics? Compare him with earlier political leaders.

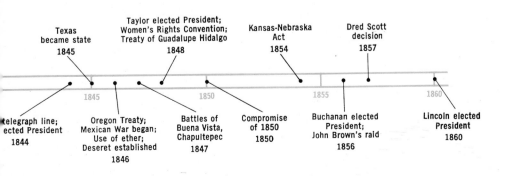

Telegraph line; elected President 1844

Texas became state 1845

Oregon Treaty; Mexican War began; Use of ether; Deseret established 1846

Taylor elected President; Women's Rights Convention; Treaty of Guadalupe Hidalgo 1848

Battles of Buena Vista, Chapultepec 1847

Compromise of 1850 1850

Kansas-Nebraska Act 1854

Buchanan elected President; John Brown's raid 1856

Dred Scott decision 1857

Lincoln elected President 1860

(a) Andrew Jackson, here wearing his general's uniform, won the presidency largely because of his successful military career.
(b) The "President's March," which is played at public appearances of the chief executive, came into use about 1828.
(c) Senator Daniel Webster, strong supporter of the Union, as he looked in 1835.
(d) Jackson's banjo.
(e) A campaign poster for the winning candidate in the presidential election of 1840.
(f) Washington, D.C., in 1833—the domed Capitol in the background at the right, the White House at the left.

(g) The mail stage, which made regular trips between New York and Boston in the early 1800's, advertised for passengers to take the rough and long trip.

(h) Jackson's admirers printed this poster supporting "Old Hickory" for the presidency.

COMMERCIAL MAIL STAGE,
☞ IN THIRTY-NINE HOURS,
From Boston to New York,
☞ CARRYING ONLY SIX PASSENGERS.

Runs by the way of Worcester, Stafford Springs.

Hartford, Middletown, New-Haven to New-York.....Leaves Boston every day at 1 o'clock. P. M.—arrives at Hartford at 7 o'clock, A. M.—arrives at New-Haven 3 o'clock P. M.—arrives at New-York, 6 o'clock, A. M.

Returning......Leaves New-York for Boston

every day at half past six o'clock, A. M.—leave New-Haven at 10 o'clock, P. M.—leave Hartford half past 2 o'clock, A. M.—arrives at Boston half past 11 o'clock. P. M.—arrives Thirty-nine hours, it being seven hours sooner than ever performed before.

The Proprietors solicit the Patronage of the Public, and pledge themselves that every care

Fare to be paid in Boston, New Haven and New-York.

☞ For Seats apply at the Stage Office, Exchange Coffee-House, entrance in C—

☞ For Seats in the Accommodation Stage, apply as above.

BOSTON, February, 1815.

Jackson Forever!
The Hero of Two Wars and of Orleans!
The Man of the People!
HE WHO COULD NOT BARTER NOR BARGAIN FOR THE
PRESIDENCY!
Who, although "A Military Chieftain," valued the purity of Elections and of the Electors, MORE than the Office of PRESIDENT itself! Although the greatest in the gift of his countrymen, and the highest in point of dignity of any in the world.
BECAUSE
It should be derived from the
PEOPLE!
No Gag Laws! No Black Cockades! No Reign of Terror! No Standing Army or Navy Officers, when under the pay of Government, to browbeat, or
KNOCK DOWN
Old Revolutionary Characters, or our Representatives while in the discharge of their duty. To the Polls then, and vote for those who will support
OLD HICKORY
AND THE ELECTORAL LAW.

(g)

(h)

CHAPTER 15

THE INDELIBLE STAMP OF JACKSON

What do the pictures on pp. 322-323 suggest about the democracy, prosperity, internal development, and national feeling of the United States in the 1830's?

THE election of Andrew Jackson brought to the White House a remarkable self-made man. Jackson, known as Old Hickory, was the first American President born in poverty. He had been on his own since the age of fourteen, when his mother had died. Although he had made the law his career and prospered in it, he had been drawn to military service.

By the time of the War of 1812, Jackson, who as a boy had been captured by the British in the American Revolution, was known as a splendid soldier. As we have seen, his performance at New Orleans had strengthened that judgment. His brief service as a Senator from Tennessee had not been extraordinary, but already the possibility of electing him to the presidency had occurred to some of his friends.

Jackson himself at first expressed some doubts about his abilities. But not being modest, he came to believe otherwise.

Review the election dispute of 1824 among Jackson, Adams, and Clay. How was Jackson more politically skillful than Adams?

A Hero in War Becomes a Hero in Peace

After his defeat in the election of 1824, Jackson had been angry. Though he had declared over and over again that he was "no politician," he proved himself to be an excellent one. A man who often acted on impulse, he also could plan a political step with the care he used in preparing a military campaign.

Friends and Enemies

"Old Hickory," age sixty-one, was the oldest President yet elected. He seemed older to people than he was because, living

in a time before important advances in medicine had been made, he ailed a great deal.

Moreover, Jackson was a lonesome and sad man because his beloved wife had just died. She had been a victim, he never ceased to say, of the slanders she had had to endure during the fierce campaign that won him the presidency.

An impression. An English actor who visited Jackson at the White House described him this way:

As viewed on horseback, the General is a fine soldierly, well-preserved old

Why is it that strong personalities often have a knack for making many friends--and many enemies? How did Jackson's frontier-military background contribute to his sometimes stormy relations with other persons?

323

gentleman with a pale, wrinkled countenance, and a keen clear eye, restless and searching.... Both the wife and sister of an English officer of high rank ... observed to me, in speaking of the President, that they had seldom met a person possessed of more native courtesy, or a more dignified deportment.

Some personal traits. Although many regarded Jackson as a friend of the people, he never permitted others to be familiar with him. But he was warmhearted and straightforward. Above all else, he was seemingly a man without personal fear.

Nothing showed this trait better than the upsetting occasion in 1835 when a madman fired two pistols at Jackson while Jackson was at the Capitol. It was the first attempt to take a President's life in our nation's history. Jackson, fortunately unharmed and unruffled, lifted his cane as if it were a club and took out after his attacker, who was quickly caught by others.

"Throw the rascals out!" By then Jackson had shown immense talent as a President. Chiefly, he had made it clear that a chief executive must not be timid about using the great power at his disposal.

Jackson's first move had been to remove from office large numbers of jobholders appointed by previous Presidents. It was generally accepted that because "one man is as good as another," a victorious party might remove officeholders previously appointed by its defeated opponents.

Jacksonians believed that the public ## would benefit from a change of officeholders from time to time. This change would prevent the development of a permanent group of such persons, who after a while would be out of touch with the people.

"Throw the rascals out!" became the cry, as Jacksonians went after the old jobholders. Jackson's own supporters were appointed in their places.

Spoils. The system of punishing one's opponents and rewarding one's supporters

Jackson's wife, Rachel, who was savagely criticized because she was mistaken in believing she had been divorced from her former husband.

became known as the spoils system. It took its name from the slogan of a New York politician: "To the victor belong the spoils!" He was using the word spoils to refer to political jobs as if they were booty taken in war.

Jackson's first year in office was filled with concern over appointments. One of them produced a crisis that keenly affected the whole of his term.

Pretty Peggy O'Neale. The crisis began when the President chose as his Secretary of War John H. Eaton, of Tennessee, who had early supported him for the presidency. Eaton had married for the second time shortly before "Old Hickory's" Inauguration Day. Eaton's new bride was Peggy O'Neale, a beauty whose father was an innkeeper in Washington.

Eaton had taken lodgings at O'Neale's place upon becoming Senator in 1818. When Jackson also arrived in Washington as Senator, he, too, rented rooms there. He wrote Mrs. Jackson about the O'Neales. Peggy, he said, "plays the piano delightful-

##Discuss Jackson's views about officeholding. Are Jackson's practices still followed today in finding men for government jobs? (Discuss the appointment and civil service systems used today for nonelective offices.)

#Have students be on the lookout for other disputes between Jackson and Calhoun.

Jackson entered the White House grieving deeply over Rachel's death and thinking the honor of the office empty without her.

Ladies' Hermitage Association

ly, and every Sunday evening entertains her . . . mother with sacred music to which we are invited."

Presidential outrage. Peggy O'Neale, alas, had acquired a bad reputation, and as Eaton's wife she was snubbed by the wives of the other members of the Cabinet. Jackson was outraged at the treatment accorded her. Not only did he regard her as a friend he must protect, but also he remembered how his wife, Rachel, had suffered from similar personal abuse and slander of character.

Loyalty to Rachel's memory—as well as to Eaton, a long-time friend—prompted Jackson's strong stand. The President even broke with his wife's niece Emily, whom he loved dearly and who was serving as his hostess in the White House. He sent her back to Tennessee because she ignored or insulted Mrs. Eaton.

Culprit Calhoun. Jackson early made up his mind that the chief cause of what came to be called the Eaton Malaria was Vice-President John C. Calhoun. The Presi-

dent's fury at Calhoun was skillfully kept hot by the new Secretary of State, Martin Van Buren. Van Buren, a New Yorker, was gracious in his manners and a master of polite conversation. Some thought he was an "apple polisher."

It did not improve Calhoun's standing # with Jackson when the President found out that Calhoun had once severely criticized him. Jackson and Calhoun practically stopped having anything to do with one another—a low point in relations between a President and his Vice-President.

Van Buren's interests. Because Van Buren was a widower with four grown sons, he could pay attention to Mrs. Eaton without causing his family to object. At the same time, by his courtesies to her, he could gain the favor of the President. Van Buren had set his heart on becoming Jackson's "heir apparent"—that is, his personal choice as successor in the White House.

Cabinet shifts. Jackson reorganized his Cabinet to end the apparently senseless dispute caused by Peggy O'Neale, and he named Van Buren the United States minister to Britain. Nothing pleased the "Little Magician"—as Van Buren was sometimes called—more than this appointment. It would keep him off the scene in the party battles ahead. Afterward he could return, undamaged by the trouble, to await the call of the people to the presidency.

Calhoun, however, had other thoughts. Van Buren's appointment had to be confirmed, that is, approved, by the Sen- ## ate. Calhoun's friends arranged that there would be a tie when the votes were counted on the motion to confirm the appointment. Because Calhoun was the Vice-President and therefore the presiding officer of the Senate, he would have the deciding vote.

Calhoun enjoyed the satisfaction of voting no, laughing to a friend: "It will kill him, sir, kill him dead. He will never kick, sir, never kick." Van Buren was not confirmed.

an Buren went to England, since he was appointed when the Senate was not in session. When Senate reconvened and rejected his appointment, he had to return to the United States.

Corcoran Gallery of Art

John C. Calhoun, handsome graduate of Yale College, statesman of South Carolina, and the chief nullifier.

Resignation. Calhoun, realizing that he himself could never hope to be Jackson's "heir apparent," resigned as Vice-President in 1832. (Calhoun remains to this day the only man who ever voluntarily gave up the
second highest office in the land.) Back home in South Carolina, he was reelected to the United States Senate, and he was quickly in the center of events again in Washington.

The Nullification Crisis

Calhoun had already set the stage for the next act of his battle with Jackson. The issue this time was the tariff.

The unwanted tariff. In 1828 Congress had passed a high tariff nicknamed the Tariff of Abominations—"the tariff of spites." It had been tinkered with so much by scheming Congressmen that no section of the country was satisfied with it.

Southerners felt themselves especially injured by the "Tariff of Abominations"— in fact, they felt injured by all protective tariffs. As a section, the South was now almost completely dependent on other parts of the country and on England for its manufactured goods. Southerners were sure that the cost of these products would be lower if there were no tariff.

Protest. For his home state, South Carolina, Calhoun in 1828 wrote a protest against the tariff passed that year. In his paper he said that the tariff made southerners "the serfs of the system—out of whose labor is raised, not only the money paid into the Treasury, but the funds out of which are drawn the rich rewards of the manufacturer[s]. . . . Their encouragement is our discouragement."

What did Calhoun propose? That people recognize the right of any state to declare unconstitutional any laws passed by the national government. This was the same idea that Madison and Jefferson had proposed in the Virginia and Kentucky resolutions (see page 266).

Calhoun warned that unless the administration took steps to remedy the "wrong" done by the Tariff of 1828, South Carolina would have no choice but to *nullify* it. That is, South Carolina would declare the tariff, which was a law passed by Congress, to be null and void—of no effect within the borders of South Carolina.

Senate debate. At the time that Calhoun was expressing his views, South Carolinians, like the rest of their countrymen, were waiting to see what Jackson would do about Calhoun's protest. Even though Jackson did not mention the question of nullification, it came to the front anyhow. It arose in 1830 in a roundabout way, in connection with a Senatorial debate on another subject.

The debaters soon got off their subject

##Explain the reasoning behind the theory of nullification. Why did Calhoun feel that a state could legally void an act of Congress? Show how the practice of nullification could return the central government to its weak situation under the Articles of Confederation.

and turned their argument into one on how strong the Union should be. As he defended the right of nullification, Senator Robert Y. Hayne, of South Carolina, took the side of those who wanted a federal government with limited powers. He reminded his northern associates that at the Hartford Convention, New Englanders had argued for nullification.

Webster's reply. When Hayne had finished speaking, Daniel Webster, of Massachusetts, took the floor to answer him. Webster was already famous for being the best speaker in the Senate. A fellow lawyer in admiration had described him when he (Webster) was in his twenties: "His language is correct, his gestures good, and his delivery slow . . . and distinct. . . ."

Now at the age of forty-eight, Webster was at the height of his powers. His reply to Hayne is today one of the most famous orations in American history. As a defense of the Union, it remains unequaled.

In brief, Webster's argument was that nullification was a first step toward breaking up the Union. He ended with the stirring words which, for many generations afterward, schoolboys and schoolgirls had to learn by heart:

When my eyes shall be turned to behold for the last time the sun in heaven, may I not see him shining on the broken and dishonored fragments of a once glorious Union. . . . Let their last feeble and lingering glance, rather, behold the gorgeous ensign of the Republic, now known and honored throughout the earth, still full high advanced, its arms and trophies streaming in their original lustre, not a stripe erased or polluted, nor a single star obscured, bearing for its motto no such miserable interrogatory [that is, question] as 'What is all this worth?' nor those other words of delusion and folly 'Liberty first and Union afterward'; but everywhere, spread all over in characters of living light, blazing on all its ample folds, as they float over the sea and over the land, and in every wind under the whole heavens, that other sentiment, dear to every American heart—Liberty *and* Union, now and forever, one and inseparable!

#

Webster, drawn up to his fullest height, answers Hayne, seated at left center, left of the Senator with his hand on his chin. Calhoun stands at the far left.

Faneuil Hall, Boston (Photo by George M. Cushing, Jr.)

We no longer speak such flowery language as Webster used. But "Webster's Reply to Hayne," as this address was called, stirred Americans of that day as no other had. It seemed to express a sentimental feeling about the Union that many people were beginning to develop but could not themselves express. It has been said that Webster's reply played a very large part in helping to make the states into a firm Union.

Dinner-party festivities. But Webster's vigorous speech did not settle the question of nullification. On April 15, 1830, at a dinner celebrating Jefferson's birthday, the Jacksonians listened to the toasts prepared for the occasion. Jackson realized that most of them seemed to take the part of the states against the federal government. When his turn, as the leading guest, arrived, he rose and spoke these words: "Our Union: it must be preserved."

Silence fell upon the gathering: the President had left unmistakably clear how he stood on the leading question of the moment. Eyes now turned to Calhoun, whose hand had fairly trembled as he listened to Jackson's words. A good speaker with a quick tongue, Calhoun then offered *his* toast: "The Union: next to our liberty, the most dear."

A threat. Jackson had given his warning to those who might dare to nullify a law of the federal government. He said further to a Congressman from South Carolina who was homeward-bound: "Tell them [the nullifiers] from me that they can talk and write resolutions and print threats to their hearts' content. But if one drop of blood be shed there in defiance of the laws of the United States, I will hang the first man of them I can get my hands on to the first tree I can find."

Null and void. South Carolina put Jackson—and the Union—to the test shortly after Congress passed the Tariff of 1832. Jackson signed the bill, which provided for a lower tariff than the one in 1828—but a protective tariff, nevertheless.

The Palmetto State—as South Carolina is sometimes called—promptly declared both the Tariff of 1828 and the Tariff of 1832 null and void. South Carolina made plain that if the federal government tried to collect duties there after February 1, 1833, the state would no longer regard itself as in the Union. The South Carolinians counted on the support of other southerners, but no other state followed their example.

Jackson was already talking of leading an army against the nullifiers. The President told an old friend who had been with him at the Battle of New Orleans: "If this thing goes on, our country will be like a bag of meal with both ends open. Pick it up in the middle or endwise, and it will run out. I must tie the bag and save the country."

Breaking the logjam. As February 1, 1833, drew nearer, people became calmer. Although Congress passed a bill giving Jackson power to use force to execute the law, the President was willing to compromise. So were the South Carolinians. The result was the Compromise Tariff of 1833, under which import duties would be gradually reduced over a period of ten years.

A judgment. Both sides claimed victory, and in a sense both sides were right. On the one hand, it was established that laws passed by Congress must be obeyed unless they are repealed (by Congress) or declared unconstitutional by the Supreme Court. On the other hand, the South Carolinians *had* forced Congress to replace the tariff law that they regarded as harmful to them.

The strong action planned by Jackson has been remembered ever since. It has become a standard against which the Presidents who have come after him measure their performance in moments of serious national dispute.

According to Jackson nullification meant defying, not simply limiting, federal authority. Emphasize why both Jackson and the South Carolinians could claim victory in the nullification cris

The first Bank of the United States, whose location in the East—in Philadelphia—helped turn Jackson against it.

War on the "Monster"

Jackson was involved with the wealthy men of the Northeast at almost the same time he was opposing the planters of South Carolina. The reason was the second Bank of the United States. According to the Democrats, the Bank was a "monster" out to destroy the prosperity of "little people" everywhere.

Some reasons. Jackson appears to have brought with him into the White House a deep hatred of the Bank—the B.U.S., as it was frequently called. Like many westerners, he was suspicious of all banks.

This feeling was once natural. Banks did not perform the variety of useful services they provide today. Like the European banks they were modeled on, they were chiefly places which loaned money—and there was no control over them by the public. Westerners were often in difficulties with their banks because they needed money, and money was scarce on the frontier. It was easy to blame the B.U.S. for the shortage.

The B.U.S. was run by twenty-five directors, only five of them required to be chosen by the president of the United States. Moreover, Jackson knew that most members of the board of directors were against him personally. They may even have used the influence of the Bank to work against his election!

Nicholas Biddle. The president of the Bank was Nicholas Biddle, who reached that high position in 1823, when he was only thirty-seven years old. No matter how Biddle tried to satisfy Jackson, he could not change the President's blind hatred of the "monster."

The plan to recharter. In 1832 the Bank's charter still had four years to run before it needed to be renewed. But Henry Clay and Daniel Webster—opponents of Jackson—convinced Biddle that 1832, a year of presidential election, was the best possible time to obtain a new charter.

kson's actions in the Bank war and the nullification crisis helped him appear as the champion he people against the privileged classes. Note his victory in the election of 1832.

Clay had made his own plans: he would run for the presidency on a platform favoring rechartering the Bank. He thought that he could win the election easily because Jackson was against a new charter. But Clay's plan misfired. Public opinion seemed to support Jackson's position, not his own.

A veto. The Bank, said Jackson, was unconstitutional. Besides, he argued, he was president of all the people. In his opinion, the second Bank of the United States was organized to aid only "the rich and the powerful." Jackson vetoed the recharter bill as Clay's supporters jeered. And on Election Day Jackson's defeat of Clay was overwhelming.

"Pet banks." Jackson's second term as President had scarcely begun when he de-#cided to kill the Bank even before its charter had run out. He did this by withdrawing government funds deposited in the B.U.S. and placing them in banks chartered by states. The particular ones he chose became known as pet banks. The President vowed: "I will never recharter the United States Bank, or sign a charter for any other bank, so long as my name is Andrew Jackson."

It must be said that Jackson was no expert on matters of banking and money. Yet he had a way of knowing what the majority of the people wanted, and he became their hero.

"King Andrew the First"

Because of his frail health and because he was so involved in battles in Congress and with individuals, Jackson rarely left the city of Washington. But in the summer of 1833 he toured New England and New York and was received with thunderous enthusiasm.

The applause of the public. People who could recall other memorable visits observed that only Washington and Lafay-ette had been cheered as hard in Boston as Jackson was. At Harvard College the President was given the honorary degree of Doctor of Laws.

The newspapers tried to paint Jackson as a folksy man—which he was not. The stories that were circulated, though, tell us how warmly the people felt toward this chief executive.

It was said, for example, that the scholars at Harvard amused themselves by addressing Jackson, the old Indian fighter, as "Doctor." It was also reported that someone leaned over and whispered to the President as he received his sheepskin scroll, "You must give 'em a little Latin, *Doctor!*" And the President immediately obliged with: "*E pluribus unum,* my friends."

The rise of the Whigs. Jackson had "the people" behind him. His enemies, however, frequently attacked him because they regarded him as high-handed. It was popular among these opponents to refer to him as "King Andrew the First" and to compare him with that other tyrant George III.

People who were against Jackson called the Democrats "the Tories," too. That, of course, made *them* "the Whigs," the name of the party in England that had weakened the power of the king. By 1834 members of the anti-Jackson group were beginning to be known generally as Whigs. Shortly they would make up a new political party.

The great Weed. The brilliant leader of the Whigs was Thurlow Weed, of New York. He became so skillful at party management that he is remembered as the first national-party boss.

The members. The Whigs attracted to their ranks men who did not approve of Jackson's attack on the second Bank of the United States. They also drew persons who favored *state rights,* especially the right of states to decide when a federal law was unconstitutional. Such people disapproved of the way the President had acted on the nullification issue. Further, Whigs were men

Note that the Whig party originated as the opposition to Jackson. Which groups eventually joined the Whigs? Use the Whigs as an example of a political party formed by men who come from many regions and hold differing points of view.

at was the cartoonist trying ay about Van Buren?

An anti-Jackson cartoonist in 1833 showed Jackson *(center)* trying hard to catch up with Henry Clay *(front)* but stumbling over the Bank issue. The little figure behind the President is Martin Van Buren.

owning considerable property who looked down upon the backwoodsmen and "little people" among the President's followers.

The Whigs also appealed to the handful of men who could imagine the kind of America that industry could make. These men were able to foresee the day when internal improvements—canals, roads, and, shortly, railroads—would enable goods and people to move with ease across the country.

Leaders on the horizon. A number of young men of outstanding ability joined the Whigs. One was Horace Greeley, whose *New York Tribune,* especially its weekly edition, was the first American newspaper to be read in all parts of the country. A second was William H. Seward, also of New York, who became one of the first important politicians to join the antislavery movement. A third was Abraham Lincoln, of Illinois, a young man in his twenties in Jackson's time.

The year 1836. The careers of the three young Whigs were only beginning in the 1820's and 1830's. But as early as 1836 the power of their new party—the Whig party—could be felt. In the election of 1836, the three Senators who most controlled Whig affairs—Clay, Calhoun, and Webster—

were solidly against the Democrats' candidate, Martin Van Buren.

The Whigs, however, did not have a man strong enough to win in all sections. They hoped to name a number of candidates powerful enough in their local regions to prevent Van Buren from winning a majority in the electoral college. Then the election would be thrown into the House of Representatives, as had happened in the election of 1824. In that event, the Whigs thought, they could combine all the candidates' strength behind a single candidate in the House and defeat the Democrats.

1. Describe the personal characteristics of Jackson. 2. Give the main facts about the difficulties over Mrs. Eaton. 3. Name two Cabinet members that were affected. 4. What dispute did Calhoun arouse in 1828? 5. Tell what positions Hayne, Webster, and Jackson took in it. 6. State what each side in the dispute accomplished. 7. Name two reasons why Jackson opposed the second Bank of the United States. 8. Identify four kinds of people who joined the Whig party.

mphasize this point. Students rarely think of Lincoln as a political figure much before the il War. Help them see that outstanding Americans were active over periods of history, not during their times of prominence.

Van Buren Wins His Chance and Muffs It

Martin Van Buren upset the plans, winning the election as a result of Jackson's strong backing. As Jackson, feeble and ill, retired to his beloved house, the Hermitage, in Tennessee, he had the satisfaction of seeing the people support his candidate and his ideas of government.

A Deep Depression

Although he was a successful politician, # Van Buren was not able to fill the huge boots left behind by the "Hero of New Orleans." Van Buren had the strong backing of Democrats in the eastern part of the country, who felt greatly indebted to him for helping to build their party. But frontiersmen never felt comfortable with him. Davy Crockett spread the story that the President wore a tight corset and used perfume—which was untrue.

Blamed. Van Buren's reputation as a dandy hurt him in many rural communities, but the depression of 1837 hurt him even more. This terrible business disaster fell upon the country almost as soon as Van Buren became President. Naturally, the people blamed him for their difficulties.

Inherited trouble. Because he was Jackson's man, Van Buren was not in a position to blame the money policies "Old Hickory" had used. But many people believed the destruction of the B.U.S. had removed the one force in the country which might have controlled the unchecked issuance of paper money by the state banks.

Furthermore, in 1836 Jackson had issued what was called the Specie Circular. His aim had been to cut down the wild speculation in land—that is, the buying of property in the hope that it would increase in value without fresh effort by its owner.

The Specie Circular had announced that the federal government would accept only *specie*, that is, gold or silver, in payment for public land.

The effect of the circular on the frontiersmen was serious. Always short of gold and silver, they found themselves more strapped for money than ever.

In the East the Specie Circular also created a shortage of specie, as the available supply gradually left circulation and found its way into the federal treasury. By May, 1837, there was a severe depression, which resulted in widespread unemployment. Jackson's money policies appeared to be the cause.

Van Buren wrote to Jackson of the difficulties the bad times produced. Jackson urged "The Little Magician" not to repeal the Specie Circular, as many were urging him to do.

In the end Van Buren followed the advice of the "Hero of New Orleans." And people linked Van Buren in their minds with the most unpopular step Jackson had taken. This stand caused his popularity to drop even lower—if that was possible!

The subtreasuries. Van Buren believed that the issuance of paper money by the "pet banks" had helped to bring on the depression by making speculation too easy. The federal government, he decided, ought to withdraw its funds even from the "pet banks." It should keep them in the vaults of the United States Treasury—called subtreasuries—located in various cities.

The removal of federal money from the "pet banks" meant that these banks could no longer provide the services to individuals they had given before. What Van Buren was suggesting was that the federal government ought to be involved as little as

##Before this, the government had accepted paper money in payment for public land. Sales of land had climbed from $2,623,000 in 1832 to $24,877,000 in 1836--figures which indicate the high degree of speculation during the 1830's.

possible in the business affairs of private individuals. We had not yet come into an era in which the federal government took responsibility for its citizens' welfare.

The Whigs disagreed sharply with the President. Daniel Webster, for instance, said that he could hardly believe that he was living in America. "I see schemes of public policy proposed [he had in mind, of course, Van Buren's subtreasury plan] having for their object the convenience of Government only, and leaving the people to shift for themselves."

Van Buren had his way, however. In 1840 the Independent Treasury Act, which set up branches of the United States Treasury, was passed. The Whigs, furious at this last step of the Jacksonians, bided their time. In 1840, they were sure, they would capture the White House.

Electing "Old Tip" and Tyler, Too

The Whigs had learned much about politics from the Jacksonians. Taking a lesson from them, they found themselves a hero. He was General William Henry Harrison, the victor of the Battle of Tippecanoe in 1811 (see page 288), now almost seventy years old. His running mate was John Tyler, of Virginia, and their slogan, which meant nothing but which rhymed, was "Tippecanoe and Tyler, too."

The Whigs declared that their man was a simple, God-fearing farmer who "would strike his plough into the soil of corruption at Washington, and turn it to the light of the sun." "Martin Van Ruin," on the other hand, they said, was an extravagant, fancy gentleman who was robbing the treasury to pay for champagne and other luxuries.

"Log Cabin and Hard Cider." The supporters of Van Buren struck back hard. A leading charge against Harrison was that he was crude. A Baltimore newspaperman friendly to Van Buren said of "Old Tip": "Give him a barrel of hard cider and settle a pension of two thousand a year on him, and my word for it, he will sit the remainder of his days in a log cabin."

Unexpectedly, this simple political insult gave the Whigs the opportunity they needed. They were delighted to boast that their man Harrison was the "Log Cabin and Hard Cider" candidate.

Campaign frolic. Within a short time the most rollicking campaign in American history was on. Van Buren was ridiculed as "Van, Van, a used-up man" who proposed for workingmen "fifty cents a day and French soup." The Whigs, for their part, stood for "two dollars a day and roast beef." Harrison and Tyler were pictured by the Whigs as simple souls who lived in log cabins and who could understand well the aims of the common man.

for examples of this
e of campaign in
sent-day American
itics.

Whigs stage a barbecue
for their candidates
in 1840, featuring
the symbols
of their campaign.

Library of Congress

For the first time the country was treated to huge election parades. Cannon accompanying them were frequently fired, and torchlights were used to light the way at night. The expression "Keep the ball rolling" originated during this campaign. Huge victory balls were rolled through the streets. One group of Harrison supporters rolled a huge paper ball from Kentucky to Baltimore, where a convention of young Whigs was being held. The cry was "Keep the ball rolling to Washington."

Neither Harrison nor Tyler lived in a log cabin—and they never had. Harrison's house in North Bend, Ohio, had twenty-two rooms and was covered with clapboard. The Harrisons, like Tyler, had a Virginia background, and their heritage was "aristocratic." Harrison's father had signed the Declaration of Independence and had been Speaker of the House of Delegates in the Virginia House of Burgesses. Furthermore, Harrison did not drink hard cider.

But Thurlow Weed, the Whig leader, had recognized the value of the log cabin as a symbol which would draw votes. His scheme worked splendidly. "Old Tippecanoe" was elected by a wide margin.

A brief presidency. General Harrison was the oldest chief executive ever inaugurated and the last to have been born a British subject. Wearing no gloves or overcoat in the freezing weather, he rode a white horse up Pennsylvania Avenue to the Capitol to take the oath of office.

Harrison was "as tickled with the Presidency as a young woman with a new bonnet." His two-hour inaugural address, which Daniel Webster had helped him prepare, was the first ever circulated to some parts of the country by railroad. The fact that the people of Philadelphia were able to read about the inauguration the same day it took place was an important sign of change in America.

The President was almost immediately overwhelmed by people seeking office. Harrison, worried also by Henry Clay, who could scarcely hold back his desire to control the President, quickly suffered in health. He caught a cold, and a month after taking the oath of office he was dead, the first President to die in office.

Chief executive by accident. At his home in Williamsburg, John Tyler was immediately notified of the awful event. As the city of Washington prepared for its first presidential funeral, Tyler hurried to assume the role of tenth chief executive.

As Tyler was the first Vice-President to move up to the White House under such circumstances, many of the people expressed doubt that he was entitled to be called President. Some thought he was

The vice-presidency has been called a forgotten job--a dead end for an ambitious politician. Why is this view inaccurate? Have a student study how the vice-presidency has changed over the years and find out how many Vice-Presidents have become President.

only Acting President. Others said he was Vice-President–Acting President. When he left office in 1845, many referred to him as the Ex–Vice-President.

Tyler paid no attention to people who did not consider him President. He refused even to accept mail addressed in any way that would suggest that his powers or dignity were less than those of the president of the United States.

Former President John Quincy Adams wrote in his diary, "I paid a visit this morning to Mr. Tyler, who styles himself President . . . and not Vice-President acting as President. . . ." Adams noted also that some would question "whether the Vice President has the right to occupy the President's house, or to claim his salary."

But no one succeeded in the argument that Tyler's right to be in the White House was any different from the rights of a man elected to the office. Tyler, therefore, set an example for the orderly continuation of government at those sad and sometimes tragic times when a **President dies during his term.**

Advice to the Cabinet. Tyler, completely frank in his personal relations, soon made it clear that he was not going to be controlled by the men around him. He told the Cabinet straightforwardly: "I shall be pleased to avail myself of your counsel and advice. But I can never consent to being dictated to as to what I shall or shall not do. . . . When you think otherwise, your resignations will be accepted."

Originally a Democrat, Tyler had broken with the party because he did not approve of Jackson's leadership and had become a Whig. The Democrats regarded him as "Turncoat Tyler." The Whigs did not accept him, either, because on many issues he was in sympathy with the ideas of the Democratic party.

Clay's challenge. The Whigs in Congress tried in 1841 to establish a new Bank of the United States. But when the bill creat-

ing it reached Tyler, he vetoed it. Angered by the veto, the entire Cabinet—with the exception of Daniel Webster—resigned. They were being egged on by Henry Clay. Webster, the Secretary of State, did not want to break off his work on a treaty with England, which he hoped to complete soon.

Tyler, however, refused to knuckle under to Clay and the other Whigs. The only Whig proposal the President signed was the tariff bill of 1842. Clay and his friends took what pleasure they could in referring to the President among themselves as "His Accidency."

Clay irritated the President shamelessly. Nevertheless, he also recognized some of America's new needs in the age that was now beginning. He vigorously supported the building of roads and canals paid for by the federal government out of the surplus money produced by the tariff. These internal improvements, he said, would succeed in tying the sections together.

Tyler, like others reared in the southern states along the Atlantic seaboard, was not enthusiastic about the measures. In general, these southerners did not see how their section of the country could benefit from roads and canals.

Clay hoped that the year 1844 might see him elected to the White House at last. Then he would get busy. Bold new measures were required to deal with the growing problems the expanding country was beginning to face.

---

1. What was the purpose of the Specie Circular? What was its effect?   2. Describe Van Buren's plan for storing federal money.   3. How did he carry it out?   4. Give the main facts about the election of 1840.   5. How did Tyler anger the Whigs?   6. What needs of America did Clay foresee?

ᴾoint out that Clay thought in terms of the nation as a whole. He expected the tariff to protect ᴸthern manufacturers from European competition and the roads and canals to help westerners their farm products to market.

335

The Nation Accepts New Aims, Outlooks, and Hopes

Some of the new problems developed out of what is called Jacksonian democracy. "Jacksonian democracy" is a term which describes a way of living, a way of reshaping America for a better future, and a way of conducting political affairs. We shall look first at how people lived in Jackson's time.

A Way of Living

Life in the America of Jackson's day differed far more from that of Jefferson's time than life in the America of Jefferson's day had differed from that of colonial times. The main way of making a living in the colonies, you will recall, had been farming.

As it used to be. The farming had included the raising of food crops as well as the growing of staples. Farmers had raised food crops largely for themselves and their families. This kind of agriculture—called *subsistence agriculture*—lasted well into the beginning of the nineteenth century. It was still important in Jefferson's administrations, when nine out of ten Americans earned their living from the soil.

Jefferson's world. The ease with which land could be acquired gave farmers in the early years of our country a sense of liberty and opportunity which was the envy of Europeans. The kind of nation which Jefferson hoped to see develop was one in which people would not rival, fear, or envy one another. The term "Jeffersonian democracy" meant a nation of small farmers, each proud to have his own farm. Cities and city people were not favored and were to be tolerated—on a small scale— # only when absolutely necessary.

The importance of the merchants. Even

in Jefferson's day, however, a change was taking place. The merchants were also becoming important. In backwoods communities as well as in coastal cities, they had made their appearance.

A traveler in western Pennsylvania in 1806 wrote of the general stores there. They were places, he said, where one could find "both a needle and an anchor, a tin pot and a large copper boiler, a child's whistle and a pianoforte . . . a glass of whisky and a barrel of brandy."

Through the merchants the farmers not only found the manufactured goods they needed. Also, the merchants created places for marketing farm goods. As a result, farmers were able to raise crops for a profit, not merely for subsistence.

But farm life still shaped merchant life. Merchants sold chiefly what the farmers wanted and required. Not yet were merchants in the cities deciding the fashions and the interests of America—both rural and urban.

Seeking a profit. By Jackson's time merchants in the cities had become powerful

Figure out what percentage of the population was urban in 1790 and in 1840.

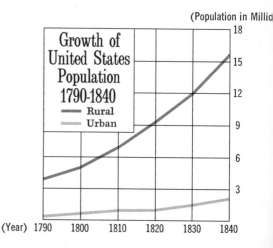

Growth of United States Population 1790-1840
— Rural
— Urban

(Population in Millions)

(Year) 1790 1800 1810 1820 1830 1840

#Cities, for example, were necessary in trade--as markets for farm products.

people, and those in rural regions reflected their wealthier city cousins. Merchants gave the nation new characteristics. Americans became a people always on the lookout for new *enterprises*—that is, new undertakings—that might make a profit.

A range of activities. Because the activities of merchants sharply affected life in the United States, Jackson's time became vastly different from the earlier days of the Republic. Merchants sent ships bearing the American flag and carrying all kinds of cargoes from Boston, New York, Philadelphia, Baltimore, and New Orleans to the other ports of the world.

Many merchants invested their money in factories, having learned from England's experience that such investment opened a road to wealth. They provided new jobs for thousands and drew people away from the farms. As the old settled rural life began to disappear, city life, long scorned, became common for more people all the time.

The new problems that resulted could not all be solved overnight, but they could not be ignored, either. Many of them, however, became very serious before solutions were sought.

Effects on people. Cities changed not only the look of America but people, too. City life made people conscious of every hour and minute of the day and of the need to be able to read and to be well informed. It also brought home to them the advantages—and the disadvantages—of living close to others.

America was still largely agricultural in Jackson's time. But no one could deny that American life was being changed by the influences of the cities and merchants, whose interest in profits was so catching.

Getting Ahead Better

In its effect on Americans' ideas of themselves and the future, the period between 1820 and 1840 was strong. It was a

Cincinnati Art Museum

A customer checks his long, hand-written bill in a country store in 1840. Observe how the goods were displayed.

time in which people discovered better opportunity than ever for everybody—except Indians and slaves—to get ahead in the world. This is why the years have sometimes been called the age of the common man.

A larger America. One major reason why America by the 1830's was an ideal place for the people to advance was that

ave students list the ten largest cities in the United States in 1820 and the ten largest in 1850 ee pages 730-731). Discuss reasons for the differences in the lists. What had caused the owth of each of the cities?

337

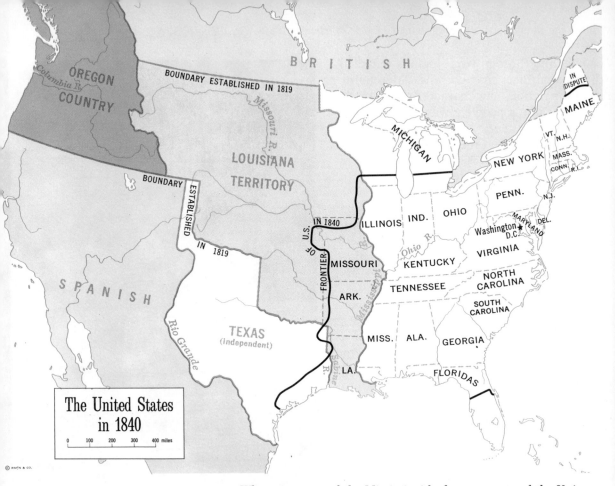

The United States in 1840

0   100   200   300   400 miles

© RAND M°N & CO.

What areas east of the Mississippi had not yet entered the Union as
states in 1840? What areas now part of the United States still
belonged to European countries?

the country's size was growing by leaps and bounds. Between 1803 and 1837 ten new states entered the Union: Ohio, Louisiana, Mississippi, Indiana, Illinois, Alabama, Maine, Missouri, Arkansas, and Michigan. Another half dozen would be admitted by 1850. Surely an ambitious man with skills and talents could put them to good use in a country expanding at such a rate.

"Loose-footedness." Men were freer in the United States than elsewhere and were not chained by the past or by government. Every man was "loose-footed"—an interesting term first coined and used in the age of Jackson.

The eyes of visitors. The American be-

came a restless individual always on the go, always trying to better himself. Foreigners saw this clearly, because the spirit they found was so different from that in their homelands. A French traveler here, Alexis de Tocqueville (tŏk´vĭl), wrote:

> In the United States a man builds a house in which to spend his old age, and he sells it before the roof is on; he plants a garden and lets it [that is, rents it] just as the trees are coming into bearing; he brings a field into tillage and leaves other men to gather the crops; he embraces a profession and gives it up; he settles in a place, which he soon afterwards leaves to carry his changeable longings elsewhere.

#According to Alexis de Tocqueville, what seemed interesting about Americans? Why would a person buy a house and then sell it "before the roof is on"? How is continual moving about still characteristic of American life?

The wharves of Boston in 1840, when the city was the third largest in the country. Foreign trade as well as American industry drew people and goods to Boston and to other United States ports.

Bob Amft

An Austrian visitor in America put it this way: "A man, in America, is not despised for being poor in the outset . . . but every year which passes, without adding to his prosperity, is a reproach to his understanding or industry [that is, a criticism of his good sense or willingness to work]."

A materialistic people. The age of Jackson, besides making it easier for a man to rise in the world, encouraged people to place great value on *material* things, that is, physical possessions. An Englishman who toured America in the 1830's wrote: "[A] large house, fine furniture, and costly dresses for the female portion of the family . . . seem the first objects of every man's ambition."

New Paths in Politics

Jacksonian democracy left permanent marks on the way we conduct our political affairs. In "Old Hickory's" day more Americans were voting than ever before.

Democracy. In the age of Jackson, Americans believed in the equality of men —even though this equality did not generally extend to Indians and Negroes. For the first time, therefore, government was likely to respond immediately to public demands—that is, to be democratic.

To many people the word democracy still meant something like "rule by the mob." For the older, well-established classes of people, democracy was a dangerous thing. In fact, these people were worried about the possible effects of allowing the "common man" to have the vote, or the *suffrage*. They regarded the spread of the suffrage as a serious threat to the republic.

An end to aristocratic notions. Aristocratic feelings, however, had long been gradually disappearing. The Constitution itself, for example, forbade the creation by the federal government of titles of nobility. Moreover, in 1792 it was decided that United States coins would not bear a likeness of George Washington because he was still living. In European countries having kings, it was a typical aristocratic practice to honor these rulers in such a way while they were alive.

The nominating convention. The greater participation of the citizens in government in the years between 1820 and 1840 led to some unusual developments. One was the holding of national nominating conventions to choose presidential candidates. The clumsy system provided for in the Constitution had proved too indirect. The public wanted a fuller share in choosing its leaders.

oint out that qualifications for voting and officeholding were determined by the states. Over e years many states had changed their requirements so that more people could participate in litical life. Which groups still did not have the vote in 1840?

San Jacinto Museum of History

Davy Crockett in the hunting clothes he wore
in his native Tennessee, with some friends.

#Why did frontiersmen seem to distrust professionals and look down on formal schooling?
Davy Crockett, who served in Congress in the 1830's. Crockett liked to boast of how he earlier had handed down decisions as a judge even though he could scarcely write his own name.

"My judgments were never appealed from," Crockett wrote in his *Autobiography*, "and if they had been they would have stuck like wax, as I . . . relied on natural born sense, and not on law learning to guide me; for I have never read a page in a law book in all my life."

Colorful officeholders. There was also a clowning quality in some politicians, particularly westerners, which would not have been acceptable earlier. There was, for instance, Representative "Sausage" Sawyer, from Ohio. He would sit at the Speaker's desk in the House of Representatives munching his sausages, caring not a bit for the dignity a legislative body ought to have.

There was also very heavy drinking in the Senate and House cloakrooms. There even were brawls between Congressmen on the floor of the House, one of which led to the firing of a revolver.

As the older "aristocratic" gentlemanliness disappeared, bragging and self-praise

In the early years of the Republic, candidates for the presidency were selected in a *caucus*, or a meeting of members of Congress. By the 1820's this method seemed wrong. "King Caucus," as it was called, was on its way out.

By the 1830's party nominating conventions were making their appearance. A delegate to a nominating convention was chosen locally to attend the convention, often with advance knowledge of whom he was supporting.

Preferred men. We have already seen how Jackson used the spoils system to fill positions in the government service. Closely related to the idea of the spoils system was the idea that educated men were somehow less valuable people than uneducated ones.

This attitude became widespread in Jackson's time. It was illustrated well by

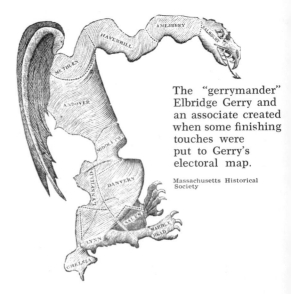

The "gerrymander"
Elbridge Gerry and
an associate created
when some finishing
touches were
put to Gerry's
electoral map.

Massachusetts Historical
Society

Have a committee report on presidential-nominating conventions. One person could report on early conventions, another on important results of recent conventions, another on methods of se lecting delegates, etc. (Magazines published around the time of an election are good sources.

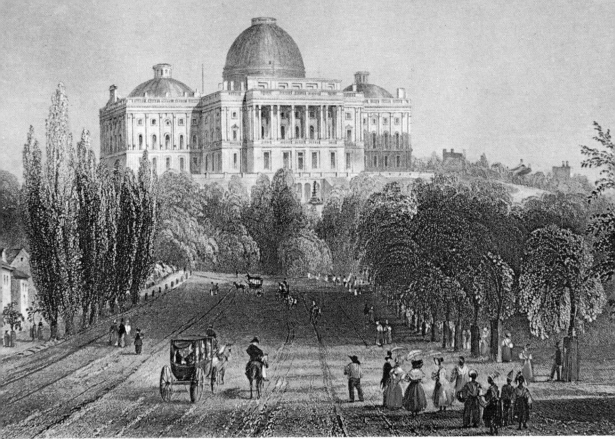

Kiplinger Collection; United States Capitol Historical Society

The Capitol as it looked in the 1830's. Its stately appearance fitted its role as the center of the legislative branch of the developing national government. Notice the dirt road.

became typical of politicians' statements about themselves. Also, politicians were less likely to try to hide their personal aims and ambitions than previously.

Logrolling. The first of two regrettable practices that had already arisen in legislatures was *logrolling*. That was the practice in which representatives voted by advance agreement for one another's bills.

Thomas Jefferson, writing in 1817, explained that the name logrolling came from "the term of the farmers for their exchanges of aid in rolling together the logs of their newly-cleared grounds."

Gerrymandering. The other unfortunate practice was called *gerrymandering*. The term means making the lines of an electoral district so irregular that one party acquires more legislative representatives

than it would otherwise be able to have.

The name comes from the work of Elbridge Gerry, who reshaped the electoral map of Massachusetts. A friend, seeing it, sketched a head, wings, and claws on the misshapen district and declared, "That will do for a salamander." "No," shouted a witty bystander: "Gerrymander!"

Lobbying. Still another practice which developed in the 1820's and 1830's was *lobbying*. This term means pressuring for the passage of certain bills by men who are not legislators. The word comes from the fact that lobbyists—men engaged in lobbying—used to wait in the lobby of a legislature in order to buttonhole the legislators. The word lobbying appears to have been used for the first time in the year 1832.

ote that logrolling, gerrymandering, and lobbying seem to go on in legislatures behind the
enes--away from public notice. How does this fact help explain public reaction to these
actices?

The age of Andrew Jackson seems today to have been a kind of bridge linking America in the days of the Founding Fathers with our country today. Americans in the age of Jackson were finding new ways to carry on politics and new ways to deal with one another in business affairs. But above all else, they were developing a higher opinion of human possibilities.

This age recognized the worth of the *individual*. Americans were taking steps to increase the opportunities open to every person regardless of the station in life in which he had been born.

A famous historian, George Bancroft, who knew Jackson and his time well, explained some years after these events "Old Hickory's" importance in the life of the country.

The secret of his greatness is this: ... he shared and possessed all the creative ideas of his country and his time; he expressed them with dauntless intrepidi-

ty [that is, with unbending courage]; he enforced them with an immovable will; he executed them with an electric power that attracted and swayed the American people.

Few war heroes have had, like Jackson an opportunity to labor as brilliantly in peacetime as they had in wartime and to serve their nation's highest ideals.

1. To what three things does Jacksonian democracy refer? 2. What group of people were leaders in colonial America? 3. Name the group that became powerful in Jackson's time. 4. In what three ways did city life change Americans? 5. In the age of Jackson some Americans were not affected by the belief in the equality of man. Who were they? 6. Name six ways in which the age of Jackson affected the way we conduct our political affairs.

The Workshop

The Shapers of Our World

Tell what role each of the following had in the years between 1828 and 1840:

spoils system	Henry Clay
Peggy O'Neale	Nicholas Biddle
Eaton	election of 1832
John C. Calhoun	"pet banks"
Martin Van Buren	Whigs
"Tariff	B.U.S.
of Abominations"	Specie Circular
Webster-Hayne	individual
debate	John Tyler
subtreasury system	Jacksonian
"Tippecanoe and	democracy
Tyler, too"	Davy Crockett
Compromise Tariff	equality of men
of 1833	

Adding to Your Vocabulary

Show that you know the meaning of these words by using them in sentences describing the age of Jackson.

specie	subsistence
slander	agriculture
deportment	material things
dignified	suffrage
"heir apparent"	caucus
nullify	lobbying
party boss	gerrymandering
state rights	logrolling

Thinking Things Through

After reviewing the boxed-in exercises in the chapter, answer the following:

As a culminating activity, ask students to write a newspaper article about America in 1840, representing the views of a foreign correspondent writing for a European newspaper. The article should tell how Americans lived, what they valued, and what their future seemed to hold.

me students might want to begin a historical catalog of American clothing styles. Study the pictures
this book for changes in men's and women's fashions since colonial times.

1. Why did Van Buren's appointment as ambassador to England have to be approved by the Senate?

2. Reread the statements of Webster, Jackson, and Calhoun about the Union and liberty. How does the Webster view combine the feelings of both Jackson and Calhoun?

3. Why were westerners usually distrustful of banks? What groups in the United States today are also suspicious of banks?

4. Consider both the old Democratic-Republican idea of strict interpretation of the Constitution and strong state government *and* the Federalist idea of loose interpretation and strong central government. What two major actions of Jackson seemed to place him on both sides of this issue? Why do you think he put himself in such a position?

5. Why was Jackson greeted so warmly in New England?

6. Why did the Whig party seem to be established on a shaky foundation? What two major groups in the Whig party directly opposed each other?

7. During prosperous times Presidents are rarely defeated for reelection. During depressions they rarely win reelection. Using the elections of 1836 and 1840 as examples, explain why.

8. Why was it so difficult for Van Buren to take forceful action when the panic of 1837 developed?

9. In his heart Clay was a nationalist, and Tyler, on the other hand, was a product of sectionalism. Prove this statement.

10. How did the principles of Jacksonian democracy appeal to immigrants and native-born Americans alike?

Presenting Information

1. Organize a round-table discussion on the B.U.S. See that the various sections and groups in the country in 1832 are represented. The main point of the discussion should be Jackson's veto of the charter in 1832.

2. Describe to the class, on the one hand, the advantages of living on a farm in the 1830's and, on the other hand, the advantages of city life in the same period.

3. Have a committee bring in a report on lobbying today, identifying the chief lobbyists in Washington and telling what they lobby for.

Many cities, companies, and labor unions have lobbyists who work at your state capital or perhaps in Washington, D.C. Invite one of these people to come to your class and tell about his work.

4. Draw some political cartoons based on events in Jackson's career as President that might well have appeared in a Whig newspaper.

Your Opinion, Please

1. Can Americans today be said to have as high a regard for democracy as the Jacksonians seemed to have? Defend your answer.

2. What would have happened if South Carolina had been allowed to nullify the Tariff of 1832? Describe a likely chain of events.

any of the questions in "Thinking Things Through" can be used to show how complex
merican politics really is. They also reveal important political principles: Why, for
:ample, are American political parties made up of men having differing points of view?
hat value do political debate and disagreement have for the country as a whole?

(a) A slave market in 1853 in Richmond, Virginia. Slaves in the older states of the South were often sold for work on the new western lands.

(b) A cotton plant, the symbol of the crop that became the mainstay of the South and that helped fasten slavery on the region.

(c) The iron horse frightens a live one in this painting, done in 1859.

(d) An advertisement of a slaveholder in St. Louis for his runaway slaves.

(e) A lesson from McGuffey's *First Reader*, one of a series most children used, beginning in the 1850's.

$200 REWARD.

Ran off from the subscriber on Thursday morning, 14th inst, one Negro Woman, named Rittea or Henrietta Jones, with her three children, Martha, Sarah and James. The woman is large and fleshy, of a dark complexion and very sullen countenance; the oldest daughter, Martha is six years old, the second Sarah is 4, and the son James is 2. The children are of a lighter color than their mother.

The husband of Rittea, Nicholas Jones, is a free dark mulatto about thirty-five years old, slightly spotted with the small-pox, about 5 feet 8 or 9 inches high, and quite impertinent when spoken to. Said Nicholas had a white man at Alton, to carry his family to Carlinville Ill. in a two horse box wagon, covered with white linen or cotton.

I will give One hundred dollars for the delivery of Nicholas in St. Louis, if taken out of the State, or fifty dollars if apprehended in it, or the latter sum if confined in any Jail in the United States, so that I can get him. I will also give One hundred dollars for the delivery of Rittea and her children, in St. Louis, if taken out of this State, or fifty dollars if apprehended in it, or the same sum if confined in any Jail in the United States so that I can get them. In addition to the above reward all reasonable expenses will be paid by me.

JOHN FINNLY.

St. Louis, Mo.

P. S. Since the above was written I have been informed that Nicholas, his wife and three children were seen at L. N. Ransom's boarding house, at Springfield Ill., on yesterday morning.

Springfield October 18th, 1841.

(d)

LESSON XLIV.

laid	lamb	where	fol-low
rule	what	fleece	ev-er-y
that	harm	school	wait-ed
love	made	ea-ger	ap-pear
sure	snow	Ma-ry	a-gainst
bind	white	gen-tle	an-i-mal
near	laugh	a-fraid	ling-er-ed
went	makes	teach-er	pa-tient-ly

MA-RY'S LAMB.

MA-RY had a lit-tle lamb,
Its fleece was white as snow,
And ev-er-y where that Ma-ry went,
The lamb was sure to go.

(e)

possible, show a copy of McGuffey's st Reader to the class. Why did it come important for everyone to have ability to read?

CHAPTER 16

THE FACTORY HAND AND THE SLAVE

roduce the chapter by having students interpret the pictures on pp. 344-345: new states entered the ion, cotton production moved west, and railroads became increasingly important. The railroad was ymbol of both northern industrialization and the westward movement.

WHEN the age of Jackson ended, Americans as a whole shared many new goals and hopes. It has been said that, proud of their nation, they were beginning to look at the rest of the world through red, white, and blue eyeglasses.

But also, all Americans were aware that they lived in particular sections of the country and that these sections differed much from one another. It was clear that each section had its own needs. These needs helped decide one section's relationships to other sections and to the entire country.

Northerners Hear the Hum of the Machine

The North, which was made up of New England, the Middle Atlantic states, and the old Northwest, was the first section which felt the effects of industrialization. By the 1830's it was being shaped chiefly by the steady growth of manufacturing.

The greatest result of the industrial development was that goods for consumers —household goods, clothing, and gadgets of almost every description—could be produced in large quantity. After a while this production, increasing annually, would change people's lives beyond imagination.

The American way of living in time would fascinate people everywhere in the world and make them envy it.

The Role of the Northwest

The first effect of the growth of industry in the North was the movement of people to factories or mill towns to work for wages. A gradual downward trend in farming in New England and in parts of the Middle Atlantic states explains why some farmers there took work in factories.

sk students to review the history and major characteristics of New England, the Middle lantic states, the South, and the old Northwest. Point out that section names change; example, the old Northwest has become known as the Middle West.

#Stress the importance of
transportation to the farmers
of the old Northwest.
A wheat farm in Illinois about 1855. Some wheat raised on America's rich farmlands was already being consumed in England, where the farmers were not able to raise large enough crops.

A flood of grain. A major cause of the decrease in farming in the Northeast was the opening of the Erie Canal in 1825. # This canal made it convenient for the first time for farmers of the old Northwest to reach the eastern markets with their grain. Their crops, produced on more fertile and cheaper land than that in the East, could undersell the products of eastern farms.

As the demand for wheat and corn grew, new farming country was opened up west of the Mississippi. Iowa became a state in 1846, and Minnesota in 1858.

Advantages for manufacturers. Although some factories were established in the old Northwest, the chief business there was the growing of grain. The manufacturers of the East were pleased. They had a local labor supply of displaced eastern farmers and a market for their goods in the West.

In 1836 a Senator explained on the floor of the Senate the relationship which had developed between the Northeast and the old Northwest. He stated, "The old States now supply nearly all the wants of the farmers of the [Ohio] Valley of the West, and hence its prosperity wonderfully promotes the welfare of the older States of the Union."

The Working People

The factories of the Northeast seemed at first to offer a chance for excitement rather than the opportunity to become wealthy. The men and women attracted sometimes learned soon that they were exchanging one kind of boredom for another.

The craftsmen's fate. Many a craftsman gave up his independence in order to take a job in a mill or factory. We cannot even guess today how many quickly felt a terrible loss of pride. Of course, many handicraftsmen had no choice, because they were forced out of business by the competition from factories.

Emphasize the growing ties between the manufacturer in the Northeast and the farmer in the Northwest. Show how the railroads cemented these ties (see the maps on pages 362 and 426).

A good artisan made an entire product himself, often with a skill it took a lifetime to acquire. Factory owners were having practically the same work performed more cheaply and quickly in separate tasks—and each task was being done by a more or less unskilled person.

Whitney's discovery. An inspired teacher and tinkerer, Eli Whitney, of Massachusetts, had made an important discovery which led to the loss of work by craftsmen. In 1798 Whitney had obtained a contract with the government to deliver ten thousand muskets. To manufacture them, he had planned to try an idea he had picked up from watching a mint in Connecticut stamp out large numbers of coins, each one alike.

Whitney spent a year tooling up his musket factory for the purpose of stamping out runs of *interchangeable parts.* That is, each gun barrel was exactly the same as all the other barrels, each trigger was the same as all the other triggers, and so forth. When Whitney had assembled five hundred muskets, he put on a demonstration before President John Adams and Vice-President Thomas Jefferson. He took apart ten weapons, scrambled the parts, and then assembled them again—to the utter amazement of the nation's leaders looking on.

Whitney was demonstrating the principle on which *mass production*—production in quantity—of goods depends. This is the making of parts according to a single standard, so that factory products may be put together quickly and easily. Custom-made products (each of which is made separately)—the pride of craftsmen—were on their way out.

"Homework." Factories, however, did not spring up everywhere overnight. For a long time the "homework" system continued to be profitable. An Englishwoman traveling in Massachusetts in 1836 described how it operated.

The shoemaking at Lynn is carried on almost entirely in private dwellings ... [because] the people who do it are almost all farmers or fishermen likewise.... When a Lynn shoe manufacturer receives an order, he issues the tidings [that is, he announces the fact]. The leather is cut out by men on his premises; and then the work is given to those who apply for it; if possible, in small quantities.... The shoes are brought home on Friday night, packed off on Saturday, and in a fortnight or three weeks are on the feet of dwellers in all parts of the Union. The whole family works upon shoes during the winter; and in the summer, the father and sons turn out into the fields, or go fishing.

In general, the "homework" system did not produce goods as well as the factory system, and sooner or later it disappeared entirely. This was because, first, factory owners could easily supervise and control their workers. And, second, the various steps in manufacturing could be completed with less wasted motion when they were all performed under one roof.

Factories were at first built near the sites of waterfalls, which produced the power to run machines. But sometimes it was not possible to establish a factory near *both* water power *and* a labor supply.

An ironworks in Pennsylvania in 1840. Far larger than the colonial forges, plants like this grew into today's giants.

Historical Society of Pennsylvania

The Waltham girls. A factory owner sometimes had to be clever to attract factory "hands"—a common term which suggests how seldom working people were thought of as individuals with recognizable faces. One of the most famous factories, with an excellent supply of hands, was established at Waltham, Massachusetts, in 1813 (see the map, page 362).

The Waltham establishment employed girls as if it were a boarding school and they were the students! A man who lived in the 1830's, when the Waltham system flourished not only in Waltham but in other New England towns as well, described how it came about.

> There was here no such pauper class as that from which the English mills were supplied, and the factories were to be recruited [that is, had to employ workers] from respectable families. By the erection of boarding-houses at the expense and under the control of the factory; putting at the head of them matrons of tried character and allowing no boarders to be received except the female operatives [workers] of the mill; by . . . regulations for the government of these houses; by all these precautions, they gained the confidence of the rural population, who were no longer afraid to trust their daughters in a manufacturing town.

The author pointed out, moreover, that a career in a factory was no handicap to marriage. A girl could, he said, look forward to assuming the "higher and more appropriate responsibilities of her sex."

Transplanted families. Another, more usual method of obtaining workers was to hire entire families. This meant herding fathers, mothers, and children into poorly lighted, poorly ventilated buildings which often broke their health and spirit.

Frequently the families lived in houses owned by the company which ran the factory in which they worked. Usually they could not choose to live elsewhere. The rent was subtracted from their wages.

The labor of children. Boys and girls quickly lost the bloom and joy of childhood in the factories. One outspoken critic of child labor was a carpenter named Seth Luther. Writing in 1832, Luther described the "whipping rooms" where young children were lashed with cowhide straps in the factory owners' efforts to make them produce goods faster.

Luther urged anybody who doubted his statements to visit the "prisons in New England, called cotton mills." There one would see "instead of rosy cheeks, the *pale, sickly, haggard* countenance of the ragged child." According to Luther, a visitor might see "the child taken from his bed at four in the morning, and plunged into cold water to drive away his slumbers and prepare him for the labors in the mill."

Unhappy lives. By the 1840's even the Waltham system had lost its glamour. The cheerful girls had been replaced by less happy ones. They were working thirteen hours a day in the summertime and from sunup to sundown in the winter.

In the 1840's the young ladies had to be at the mill at five o'clock in the morning. At seven they were given breakfast, for which they could take thirty minutes. At noon they were allowed another thirty minutes for eating their meal. "But within this time they must hurry to their boarding houses and return to the factory, and that through the hot sun or the rain or the cold," wrote a visitor.

Also, the girls worked in a room with the windows closed. The air was very damp and filled "with cotton filaments and dust, which, we are told, are very injurious to the lungs."

Furthermore, the visitor noticed, "the young women sleep upon an average six in a room three beds to a room. There is no privacy, no retirement, here. It is almost impossible to read or write alone, as the parlor is full and so many sleep in the same chamber."

By 1850 the Waltham system had come to an end. Factory help—adult males and females as well as children—was now readily available. A new source was the immigration from Ireland, which began in the late 1840's.

Labor's Self-Protection

Laboring people were early aware that they had to protect themselves from the evils of factories. They began to organize unions to bargain with their employers.

Earliest unions. The first unions were made up of highly skilled workers who banded together for companionship and sometimes to provide life-insurance benefits for members. Some groups of craftsmen had formed unions in the eighteenth century. These were tailors, printers, carpenters, and shoemakers.

A national organization. In the 1820's and 1830's the various organizations of craftsmen began for the first time to join together to form city-wide unions. The next step was for the city-wide unions themselves to join together. In 1834 delegates from six cities formed the National Trades' Union—the first national union in the country.

Laboring people were now recognizing that their problems were common from one part of the North to another. They were ready to fight for what they regarded as their rights.

Hurdles and barriers. For the most part, though, unions had only slight success. They had to battle against laws which discouraged union organization.

Unions also had to struggle against a general unwillingness of skilled Americans to regard themselves as workingmen. Workingmen who were skilled preferred to consider themselves small businessmen. They were slow to see that they might have much in common with other workingmen who happened to be less skilled.

A damaging depression. The depression

ote the rural setting this factory.

The American artist Winslow Homer painted these New England mill girls— who had been reared on farms—going to work, lunch in hand.

Collection of Mrs. Stephen C. Clark, New York (Francis G. Mayer)

# of 1837 (see page 332) killed off the Na-
tional Trades' Union. Jobs had become
scarce, and union dues were difficult to
collect. Men fought with each other over
available work. In short, laboring people
lost whatever willingness to coöperate with
each other they had acquired. Further, factory owners, who would lose money if unions forced higher wages, could always be
counted on to fight unions. Labor unions
grew slowly at a time when industry was
developing rapidly.

Idealists and Reformers

Side by side with the establishment of
unions, some people were trying to bring
about reforms—changes for the better—
that would help remove the evils of rapid
industrialization. These evils included not
only the new dangers to health but also the
threat to people's happiness that factory
work could mean.

One of the best-known reformers was a
Briton, Robert Owen. Owen, after establishing a model village for workers in his
textile mills in Scotland, came to the
United States in 1824.

New Harmony. The following year, with
his son Robert Dale Owen, Owen established the community of New Harmony,
Indiana. There he planned to settle twenty-
four hundred people who badly needed
help, making them happy and useful again.

The experiment did not work, although
many outstanding people, including James
Monroe and John Quincy Adams, were interested in its success. But the idea of
creating "perfect" communities for human
beings did not die.

Brook Farm. Schemes for reforming
America were everywhere, it seemed. Ralph
Waldo Emerson, the influential New England writer, said in 1840: "We are all a
little wild here with numberless projects
of social reform. Not a reading man but
has a draft of a new Community in his
waistcoat pocket." It was at Emerson's
house that he and a group of brilliant
friends laid plans for an ideal community,
Brook Farm, to be located at West Rox-
bury, one of the suburbs of Boston.

Those who joined Brook Farm were expected not only to improve their minds but
to raise their own food as well. Nathaniel
Hawthorne, the author, wrote that on the
very first day he arrived, a pitchfork was
thrust into his hands. Pupils in school, too,
had to do some of the manual labor of the
community.

Because some of the most thoughtful
Americans of the day were members of
Brook Farm or interested in it, there are
many accounts describing life there. One
man wrote of a lively Brook Farm party he
attended, at which his cousin was wearing
"a pretty Creole dress made of handker-
chiefs from the West Indies." He wrote

##What can be learned from
experiments like Brook Farm--
even though they do not succeed?

The model community of Brook Farm in 1846, one year before it was
abandoned. The farmhouse—second from left—was the first building.

also of the everyday clothing of the Brook Farm schoolboys—bright-colored chintz blouses and "little round . . . caps with tassels."

Although the leaders of Brook Farm had the best of intentions, the community failed because it lacked money. Further, "ideal" communities like Brook Farm were unsuited to a rapidly growing and changing America. Industrial development was bringing problems in American life, but they could not be solved if people ran away from them and tried to start over.

Many Americans, of course, welcomed industrialization. By the 1840's they were excited by what it could mean to the country's future. They agreed with the magazine writer who had declared, "Other nations boast of what they are or have been, but the true citizen of the United States exalts [that is, proudly lifts] his head to the skies . . . [over] what the grandeur of his country is going to be."

Some people in the 1840's were sure that they would see a golden age come to pass for America in *their* lifetime. A great number of such men and women worked for the reform of particular evils in order to speed up the arrival of this golden age. These reformers scarcely overlooked any trouble or wrong suffered by Americans. Like master surgeons they hoped to cut out evils at their roots and in this way make America stronger and healthier.

Women's rights. Some reformers labored for new attitudes toward the rights of women. At the Women's Rights Convention held in Seneca Falls, New York, in 1848, the ladies gathered passed a resolution which began, "We hold these truths to be self-evident:—That all men *and women* are created equal. . . ."

The rights of children. A cry was also being raised against child labor, even though factories were only in an early period of development. Alexander Hamilton had defended the employment of young people in industry. He had written, "Children are rendered [made] more useful by manufacturing establishments than they would otherwise be."

Now that the damaging effects of the employment of children at an early age could be seen and judged, a new idea was appearing. It was that our country was more in need of educated young people than of young people worn out by hard work before they reached their teens.

Horace Mann and education. The main developer of the idea of educating boys and girls was Horace Mann, who in 1837 became secretary of the newly organized board of education in Massachusetts. During his term in office he established the first teacher-training school in his state at Lexington. He also became the great defender of the rights of children.

Mann understood the power of education in the age of Jackson. His beliefs apply to our time as well. He said:

> Education . . . is a great equalizer of the conditions of man,—the balance wheel of the social machinery. . . . I mean that it gives each man the independence and the means by which he can resist the selfishness of other men.

Mann was beginning the long and difficult work of convincing his fellow Americans that every boy and girl is entitled to a free public education. This means one paid for by the people through taxes. Up to then, education had been a privilege open only to young people whose parents could afford private schooling or those who received it as a form of charity.

Dorothea Dix and the mentally ill. The mentally ill also had a vigorous sympathizer, the newspaperwoman Dorothea L. Dix, of Boston. Miss Dix had served as a private teacher to the children of William Ellery Channing, one of the most famous ministers of Boston. She discovered her life's work one dreary Sunday when she found

Have students list the conditions in America that nineteenth-century reformers wanted to change.   351
Compare this list with one of the changes demanded by reformers in our time.   Do any of the
reforms started in the 1840's still affect Americans?

insane people herded together, almost deserted, in an unheated room in a prison she visited in Cambridge, Massachusetts.

Miss Dix became so aroused that she began to investigate conditions of the insane in the jails and poorhouses of Massachusetts. Then she wrote a now-famous report to stir the consciences of the state legislators. She began, "I tell what I have seen." What had she seen? She had seen insane people imprisoned "in *cages, closets, cellars, stalls, pens! Chained, naked, beaten with rods*, and *lashed* into *obedience!*"

Miss Dix's efforts won for her a national reputation. But help for poor and mentally ill people generally continued to come not from governments but from private citizens and organizations.

A crusade against liquor. Still other reformers wanted to put an end to the evil of unlimited drinking. These people believed that such use of alcohol robs any man of his dignity and that he spends money on drink which he should spend on his family. They thought also that heavy drinking interfered with the success of democracy, in which sober people must continuously make important decisions.

Although the crusade against alcohol found many supporters, some people said that outlawing whisky was an invasion of a man's private life and denied him the "pursuit of happiness." Nevertheless, Neal Dow, of Portland, Maine, led a campaign for many years to put through his state legislature a bill prohibiting the sale of intoxicating drinks.

A Maine law in 1846 declared the sale of liquor illegal. A stronger law was finally passed in 1851. Known as the Maine Liquor Law, it became a model for similar acts in other states and communities.

A rich variety. Other enthusiastic reformers worked to prevent cruelty to children and animals or to give people greater opportunities for higher education. Still others worked for world peace or to shorten the workday or to improve conditions in the prisons. The variety was endless.

The factory system, then, more and more gave northerners their characteristic outlook. First of all, the great amount of manufactured products hinted at a better —and easier—life for all. This created enthusiasm for what tomorrow might be like.

Second, the seemingly unlimited need for factory workers gave northerners the feeling that their section was a place of opportunity for people from the farm and from Europe alike. Factories themselves were considered improvements in a community, creating progress.

And third, the various evils that factory life led to stirred people up not only to fight them but also to want to correct other wrongs. As some of America's drawbacks were removed before their very eyes, northerners developed an unlimited faith in what a free people could accomplish.

In time the greatest of all reform movements, with the most far-reaching results, was the drive to end slavery. In order to understand the antislavery, or *abolitionist*, movement, we must turn our attention to the South and its culture.

1. In what section of the country did industry first develop? 2. Name two effects of the growth of industry on people. 3. What three parts of the country made up the North? Explain the decrease in farming in two of them. 4. How was the drop in farm production in one part of the country made up elsewhere? 5. Name the important contribution Whitney made to industry. 6. For what two reasons did manufacturing in homes disappear? 7. Describe the Waltham system. 8. How did working people try to protect themselves? 9. Name two ideal communities that were established in the United States. 10. Name eight reforms that people tried to bring about.

#Reformers are not always admired by those around them, especially because they often seem to be criticizing their friends and neighbors and traditional ways of doing things. In the end, how does the country benefit from the often lonely struggle carried on by reformers?

Southerners Proudly Enthrone King Cotton

The story of the South in the first half of the nineteenth century was closely connected with the raising of cotton. The growth of population in Europe and in the American North and the ability to manufacture cheap cloth in both places made it profitable to raise cotton. The demand for cotton seemed without limit.

The Contribution of the Gin

In the United States the only kind of cotton that it paid to raise was the so-called sea-island kind, which grew on the islands off the shores of Georgia and South Carolina. It had smooth, black seeds and long fibers, or *staples*, which could be picked off easily.

Another type of cotton, the so-called short-staple cotton, had short fibers and sticky green seeds that were very difficult to remove. It was grown on a small scale in parts of the South. A slave could clean only about 1 or 2 pounds a day—hardly enough to make the cultivation of short-staple cotton worthwhile.

Whitney's invention. But the cultivation of the short-staple kind was suddenly made profitable by the work of Eli Whitney, who, you remember, also discovered the idea of interchangeable parts. Whitney invented a machine, or gin (that is, an engine), which could quickly clean large quantities of short-staple cotton.

The cotton gin today seems simple enough. A roller containing metal teeth caught a boll of cotton and pulled it through a wire mesh, leaving the seeds on the other side. A brush revolving against the roller removed the cotton lint, which later was spun into the all-important cotton thread.

Whitney made his invention in 1793. By the opening of the nineteenth century its effect already could be seen. The cultivation of cotton had spread inland from the coastal islands of the South.

So we trace to Whitney both the cotton gin, which completely changed southern life, and mass production, which formed the basis of modern industry and greatly affected life in the North. Although the cotton gin proved to be attractive to southern planters, they paid little attention to Whitney's other discovery. Why bother with industry when cotton raising was so profitable? Unlike northerners, southerners failed to industrialize their section of the country.

A far-reaching result of the spread of cotton growing was that the South extended and defended Negro slavery. In doing so, it raised some of the gravest problems in our entire history as a nation.

Into new lands. The first step in the spread of cotton cultivation was the west-

Notice the fairly steady increase in cotton production that took place after the cotton gin came into use.

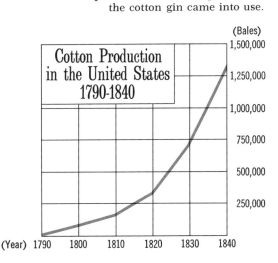

Cotton Production in the United States 1790-1840

me the southern states that entered the Union after Whitney's invention. In which of them s cotton the main crop? On the graph above, note the rapid increase in cotton production er 1820. (By that time western lands were being opened to cotton production.)

353

ward movement of southerners. Their aim was to search for good land on which to grow their "white gold"—as cotton was sometimes proudly called. The soils of Virginia and Maryland had been exhausted because of the heavy cultivation of tobacco over a long period. That is, they had lost their fertility.

Planters looking for new land found a broad southwestern region where cotton would grow. It was an area with rich soil stretching from central Alabama into Mississippi and Texas.

By the early 1820's settlers were moving across the Mississippi River into Texas. Their need for field hands—slaves who worked in the fields—became enormous. The effect of this situation on the South was remarkable.

A changed opinion. Southerners who hated slavery began to give up the idea that the slaves could be freed. Besides, any criticism of slavery came to be regarded by planters as an attack on their right to grow cotton and earn a living.

Southerners felt the need to defend slavery at the very time the spirit of Jacksonian democracy was capturing national attention. Amid so much talking about freedom, slavery seemed more than ever a denial of the flaming words of the Declaration of Independence, "All men are created equal."

Angry defense. The planters' arguments in defense of slavery were vigorous. A common one was that slaves lived more healthfully and happily than Irish workingmen in the North.

Southerners said, too, that people who wanted to do away with slavery were only troublemakers. Northerners who opposed slavery, the planters said, were pretending to be better than they were. They were simply trying to forget their own guilt for having taken part in the slave trade that brought the slaves to America. One southern poet wrote:

They drag the Negro from his
    native shore,
Make him a slave, and then his
    fate deplore;
Sell him in distant countries,
    and when sold,
Revile [criticize] the buyers,
    but retain the gold.

Despite the bold verses, slavery weighed heavily on the consciences of many southerners—even those who did not own any bondsmen. They knew slavery was wrong, and they hoped and prayed that a way might be found to end the terrible curse.

The Peculiar Institution

Southerners developed the habit of not mentioning slavery by name but of calling it the peculiar institution. They talked of their "hands" or their "servants" rather than of their "slaves." If a slave knew a craft, it was usual for his owner to refer to him as "my cabinetmaker" or "my shoemaker." Also, slaves might be referred to as "my people" or "the force."

An inside view. But no words could hide the nature of slavery. Frederick Douglass, a slave who ran away and later became a distinguished leader of his freed people, wrote about what it was like to be a slave.

The slave is a human being, divested [stripped] of all rights—reduced to the level of a brute—a mere 'chattel'.... In law, the slave has no wife, no children, no country, and no home. He can own nothing, possess nothing, acquire nothing, but what must belong to another. To eat the fruit of his own toil, to clothe his person with the work of his own hands, is considered stealing. He toils that another may reap the fruit ... he eats unbolted meal, that another may eat the bread of fine flour; he labors in chains at home, under a burning sun and biting lash, that another may ride in ease and splendor ... he is sheltered only by the wretched hovel, that a master may dwell

354   #Note the difficulty of squaring slavery with democratic ideals. Many farmers in the South held democratic political views but feared that if slavery were abolished, they would have to compete with the freedmen economically.

in a magnificent mansion; and to this condition he is bound down as by an arm of iron.

Some effects. The effect on the slave was to make him so dependent on his master that his ambition, will, and self-respect were destroyed. Then the master often regarded him as shiftless and lazy and in need of stern control.

Some differences. Slavery differed in the various parts of the South. It was naturally most widespread in the newer, western portions of the South where cotton lands were being opened up. Because slaves escaped more easily from planters there than from eastern owners, they were guarded more closely in newer portions of the South than in older ones.

Furthermore, if a southerner owned only one or two slaves, he worked side by side with them in the field and was likely to treat them well. If a man owned several hundred slaves, he might have an overseer, who was often brutal in handling them, especially the ones who tried to run away. A Mississippian expressed a widely held idea when he said of overseers, "They are as a class a worthless set of vagabonds."

Some slaves were under almost constant supervision, while others rarely saw their owners. For instance, some might work on rice plantations in the South Carolina swamps, where only about once a year they were visited by the owners, who might live in Charleston. Or sometimes slaves would be hired out to a town or city and live almost as if they were freedmen.

The routine in the field. A day on a plantation began just before sunrise, when a bell or horn was sounded. The day ended when the sun set. There was always some-

"Harper's Weekly" (Library of Congress)

Right: These pictures of the life of a field slave on a cotton plantation were drawn by an artist for a popular magazine in the nineteenth century. He shows the summons at dawn, the bosses looking on, and the various kinds of seasonal work.

here did slaves work, besides in the fields
large plantations?

The same artist who created the illustrations on page 355 also did this one of "ration day" (*left*), when food was given out to slaves for use in their own homes, and one showing a happy time among the slaves.

thing for a slave to do—morning or afternoon and in every season. When it rained, there were tasks to be performed indoors. One planter wrote his father in Connecticut, "There is no lying by, no leisure, no long sleeping season such as you have in New England."

Slaveholders could seldom make their Negro slaves absolutely obedient—and disobedience brought waste. Sometimes in order to encourage slaves to work well, a master would assign each one ground to till as his own. The slave could keep the proceeds of the crop he raised on it.

Opposition. Slaves learned how to avoid work on their jobs. It was not unusual to find rocks or wood in the bottom of a cotton basket containing the results of a day's labor in the field. They might help at weigh-in time to hide a day of loafing.

Masters understood the situation. Loafing was only one way in which slaves fought back against the harshness of slavery. They also stole, damaged crops, injured livestock, and destroyed tools and machinery. This day-by-day resistance was no less real than the open revolts which had little chance of success because slaves were outnumbered and outgunned.

A famous southern magazine, *De Bow's Review*, to which almost every planter subscribed, ran an article about this opposition. It contained the opinion that "Every attempt to force a slave beyond the limit that he fixes himself as a sufficient amount of labor to render [give] his master . . . only tends to make him unprofitable, unmanageable . . . and a curse. If you pro-

tract [lengthen] his regular hours of labor, his movements become . . . slower."

The lash. Unquestionably the continuation of slavery depended on the power of the master to punish his slaves. Frequently the punishment for something serious was whipping, although it had to be given with care because it could injure a slave and reduce his value. He was, after all, a piece of property his master wanted to protect.

Other punishment. Of course there were other forms of punishment. Sometimes a master put a slave into a jail on his plantation. Sometimes he clapped chains and irons on a poor wretch who had broken a rule. Sometimes a "misbehaving" slave had to wear an iron collar—occasionally with a bell attached. Sometimes slave owners shamed slaves who were "bad." One way, for instance, was to force a male victim to do work usually performed by women.

On the other hand, many masters treated their slaves with kindness. There were the natural ties of affection that developed among people dependent upon one another as slave owners and slaves were. Laws in every slave state forbade the teaching of reading and writing to bondsmen. But many slaves learned to both read and write —with the knowledge and sometimes the help of their owners.

The breaking up of families. One of the greatest griefs of slave life was that slave families were sometimes cruelly broken up so that each slave might be sold separately. This happened usually when a master died and his property was sold at auction for the benefit of his heirs. Sometimes, how-

What were the worst aspects of slavery in the United States? Consider the effects on both the slave and the slaveholder.

any non-slaveholders hoped to own slaves eventually. And although the planters were a minority, they re the strongest political and social force in the South.

ever, a master willingly bought a slave who had married one of his slaves.

In order to help make his life bearable, a slave often pretended to accept his situation, using quick laughter and a meek or carefree tone. But these outward appearances could be deceiving, and they were often misunderstood.

One southerner in the 1850's, for example, wrote of the bondsmen, "I love the simple . . . slave, with his . . . mirth, his swagger, and his nonsense. I love to look upon his countenance shining with content . . . I love to study his affectionate heart." Many slave owners believed that their slaves had the minds of children and could not think or act independently.

The urge to escape. Most slaves felt keenly about their hard lives. One said the fields he worked seemed to stretch "from one end of the earth to the other."

Nevertheless, it was hard to escape to freedom. Once in a while a slave would hide for a while in a nearby swamp or forest, but he usually would be successfully hunted down or would surrender as a result of hunger. An organization of Quakers and others in areas nearest the cotton-growing states helped some slaves to escape. They took the fleeing Negroes to Canada, where there was no slavery.

Harriet Tubman. The operation of the underground railroad, as the organization was called, was not as widespread as has been thought. It was a way of helping slaves to escape by passing them from "station" to "station"—often houses—on the way to Canada or another safe place.

An important Negro heroine of this method of fleeing was Harriet Tubman. She had been guided only by the light of the North Star in her journey from a plantation in Maryland to freedom. Later this "Moses" of her people returned to the South from time to time on trips to lead, it is said, numerous others out of bondage.

Slave hunters with dogs searched in the mountains and forests for runaway slaves, whom the slave owners considered bad Negroes. Under laws called slave codes, enacted by state legislatures, a slave had to have a pass to be off his plantation. Patrols could search slave cabins for slaves from other plantations without passes.

Turner's revolt. Acts of violence against slaveholders and their property were always a threat—which made many southerners constantly fearful. One of the most famous of the slave revolts occurred in 1831 in Virginia, led by the slave Nat Turner. Turner's mother, it was said, could hardly bear the thought that her child would be a slave like her, and she had to be prevented from killing him at birth.

Turner grew up to become a preacher of recognized ability. He organized a murderous attack on homes in Southampton County, Virginia. Before he and his band were finished, about one hundred sixty men of both races had been killed. Turner was finally caught and executed, but the South never forgot his bloody attack.

Some figures. There is a commonly held belief that the South in 1860 was filled with vast plantations and numerous Negro slaves. This idea was created by movie writers and novelists. In fact, only a very few people in the entire South in 1860 owned as many as five hundred slaves.

It should be remembered, too, that most southerners were not slaveholders. There were 1,600,000 families in the South in 1860, and of these only about 400,000—one family out of every four—owned slaves. And 30 percent of the slave-holding families owned only one slave.

Nevertheless, even if only a few southerners profited from slavery directly, the whole South was tied to the cruel arrangement. Cotton cultivation gave the region the product it sent to market. Out of the profits, southerners could pay for the goods they imported from elsewhere.

Some southerners were discouraged

In most areas escape was nearly impossible. It meant walking hundreds of miles through stile, unfamiliar country. Slaves who made it usually depended on the help of free Negroes the North.

when they saw that surplus money in their part of the country was used to expand cotton growing, not to build factories. Almost all the factory goods they bought came from outside the South—from the North and from Britain.

A critical judgment. One famous southern critic of slavery pointed out:

> We want Bibles, brooms, buckets and books, and we go to the North . . . we want furniture, crockery, glassware and pianos, and we go to the North; we want toys, primers, school books, fashionable apparel, machinery, medicines, tombstones, and a thousand other things, and we go to the North for them all. Instead of keeping our money in circulation at home, by patronizing our own mechanics, manufacturers, and laborers, we send it all away to the North, and there it remains; it never falls into our hands again.

Furthermore, he wrote:

> We have no foreign trade, no princely merchants, nor respectable artisans. . . . In comparison with the free states we contribute nothing to literature . . . and inventions of the age.

It was clear as the years of the nineteenth century passed that the culture of people in the South was becoming different from that in the free states. Europeans looking toward America as a land of promise or expecting to become immigrants sensed quickly that there was no welcome place for them in the land of slavery.

Slavery, then, was shaping the outlook of southerners as surely as the factory was shaping the outlook of northerners. The South was holding fast to the present, terribly afraid of any kind of criticism or change. More and more, southern life was being modeled on aristocratic life in western Europe, which was already dying.

Increasingly, southerners felt that they were a separate nation within the United States. Already John C. Calhoun was saying that it was "difficult to see how two people as different and hostile [as opposed as southerners and northerners were] can exist together in one common union."

Abolition

One source of bad feeling between the North and the South was the antislavery movement. Part of the reforming in the North, it owed its strength to some striking personalities.

The leaders in the early history of the movement were Quakers. They believed that all men are equal before God and that therefore master and slave stand on the same footing—neither being superior to the other.

Benjamin Lundy. Benjamin Lundy, a New Jersey Quaker, was one of the first to voice antislavery feelings publicly. Having moved to Virginia at the age of nineteen, he had come into close contact with the trade in slaves, and it disgusted him. He was never to forget the horror of what he had seen.

In later years as a businessman in Ohio, Lundy organized the Union Humane Society to help slaves. Soon, traveling thousands of miles on foot, he was devoting all his time to promoting the abolition of slavery. He proposed the idea of colonization, that is, the freeing and settlement of Negroes somewhere outside the United States. Lundy established one of the first newspapers devoted entirely to the antislavery cause.

William Lloyd Garrison. By the time Lundy died in 1839, William Lloyd Garrison was being listened to. His paper *The Liberator* appeared in print for the first time just a few months before the outbreak of Nat Turner's revolt. Garrison expressed in these words his firm intention to fight slavery: "I am in earnest . . . I will not retreat a single inch—*and I will be heard.*"

#How does Calhoun's statement show the growth of sectional feeling? What were the results of such an attitude? What was happening to the old nationalistic ideas of Clay and Webster?

Many southerners considered Garrison's writings responsible for Turner's attack.

The planters were easily disturbed in the 1830's because Mexico had abolished slavery in 1829, and in 1833 the British ended it in their possessions. Garrison added to the anxiety of southern slaveholders by opposing every plan for the colonization of Negroes. He argued instead for the immediate freeing of all slaves in the United States.

James G. Birney. A few powerful individuals who preached antislavery ideas were born in the South—into slaveholding families. One was James G. Birney, of Kentucky, a planter in Alabama. He had tried to persuade those who were writing Alabama's first constitution to provide for the gradual freeing of slaves.

In 1834 Birney himself freed his slaves, and soon afterward he became a leader in the American Anti-Slavery Society, a national organization. In 1840, when the Liberty party was organized urging the abolition of slavery, Birney became its presidential candidate.

The Grimké girls. Two South Carolina sisters left their mark on the antislavery movement, too. They were Sarah and Angelina Grimké. As a child, Sarah had felt slavery to be a wrong. She was known to smuggle ointment to slaves on her father's plantation who had been whipped. She was terribly put out when her mother gave her a girl slave as a present for her sixteenth birthday.

Gradually Sarah—and Angelina—entered the stirring antislavery movement. Sarah's splendid gifts as a speaker made her much in demand among women's groups. These often were groups organized to talk about the rights of women, although they were called such polite names as "sewing circles" or "reading societies."

Theodore Weld. In 1838, when she was already known nationally, Angelina Grimké was married to an abolitionist minister

"Gleason's Pictorial," May 3, 1851 (New York Public Library)

Wendell Phillips, who often wrote antislavery articles for *The Liberator*, speaks against slavery in the Boston Common.

from Connecticut, Theodore Dwight Weld. Weld was greatly influenced by the enthusiasm for reform of his day. In the 1820's he was the best-known spokesman for the anti-liquor cause in the western part of New York State.

From the beginning of the 1830's on, Weld gave his energy to the antislavery movement. In Huntsville, Alabama, in 1831, he converted James G. Birney.

Weld's activities were so widespread and effective that he is regarded by many people as the most influential of the abolitionists. He was a very modest man, though, who never spoke in the presence of representatives of eastern newspapers. Nor would he allow his speeches to be printed. The result was that he did not receive nearly the same amount of publicity as others did—like Garrison.

Weld was greatly affected by Charles Stuart, an English abolitionist whom he had met as a young boy. Weld absorbed some of Stuart's saintly enthusiasm for freeing slaves, a fact that shows how the movement for abolition in Europe was

##Colonization was costly and unworkable. By the 1830's most slaves had closer ties to America than to Africa. To some, colonization seemed to be a plan for removing free Negroes from the South, not for ending slavery.

influencing the one in America. Angelina and Theodore Weld named one of their sons Charles Stuart.

The work of former slaves. Negro abolitionists were important, also. Orators like Frederick Douglass and Sojourner Truth moved audiences with recitals of the wrongs of slavery. They also showed that Negroes were equal in ability to any other people. Samuel Cornish and John Russwurm began publication of the first Negro newspaper, *Freedom's Journal.*

Some hesitation. The American campaign for abolition would in time swallow up all the other reform movements. It became itself a revolutionary force which would not end until it had done its work. Nevertheless, northerners were by no means completely won over by abolitionist arguments. Many regarded the reformers simply as cranks or people who were not practical. Many workmen thought that

freeing the slaves would be the same as opening doors to rivals for their jobs.

Furthermore, because the Constitution protects property, people thought that it also protected *slave* property. Garrison angered millions of Americans when he called the Constitution—which had become a revered document—"an agreement with hell."

1. Name three reasons for the development of cotton cultivation in the South. 2. What was the far-reaching effect on the region?   3. Describe the differences in the treatment of slaves in the South. 4. Describe Nat Turner's revolt.   5. What percent of southern families owned no slaves?   6. Describe the effect of slavery on the outlook of southerners.   7. Name six antislavery leaders and describe their work.

#In what ways did the Constitution seem to recognize slavery? (Review the 3/5 compromise.)

Railroads and Immigrants Change the North

The differences in outlook between the North and the South were sharpened by two other important developments. Their effects by the end of the 1840's were far-reaching.

The Iron Horse

The first development was the building of railroads. The earliest ones were the products of English experiments.

Slowly gathering steam. The idea of building railroads quickly crossed the Atlantic. As early as 1813, Oliver Evans, an American favoring railroads, was making prophecies. He wrote, "I do verily believe that . . . carriages propelled by steam will be in general use . . . traveling at the rate of . . . 300 miles a day."

But enthusiasm for rail transportation

did not develop quickly. One Boston editor thought that a railroad from Boston to Albany would prove to be "as useless as a railroad to the moon." People still largely relied on canals.

Start of a race. On July 4, 1828, Charles Carroll, the last living signer of the Declaration of Independence, lifted a spade near Baltimore to begin work that resulted in the Baltimore and Ohio Railroad. The Baltimore and Ohio became the first passenger railway in the country.

On the same day, just outside Washington, D.C., President John Quincy Adams was turning the first spadeful of earth to begin the Chesapeake and Ohio Canal (see page 306).

The race was on between canals and railroads. By the 1840's the railroads were gaining in the number of miles covered. By

Why were immigration and transportation important to the growing industries of the North? Note that while the North and the South were drawing apart, the North and the West were coming closer together.

the end of the 1840's, the era of canal-building was at an end.

In the early 1830's steam power was introduced as a means of moving trains on the Baltimore and Ohio Railroad, fulfilling Evans' prophecy. Until then the cars had been drawn by horses. Thereafter the iron horse, as the steam locomotive was naturally called, spread its influence widely.

Active construction. The first building of railroads, though, was not according to a definite plan. A celebrated engine named for De Witt Clinton pulled a train on a road that connected Albany and Schenectady, New York, in 1831. In 1833 a 136-mile line was completed between Charleston and Hamburg, South Carolina, the longest railroad in the world at that date. No line connected New York and New Haven at a time when New Haven and Hartford were already linked.

The nation enjoyed the excitement of building new lines. Thousands of people invested their money in this construction. Today we cannot imagine the feeling of satisfaction which overtook a town when the first train pulled in, bearing people, mail, goods—and ideas—from elsewhere.

A stirring rivalry among the leading cities eager to be in touch by rail with other main cities made the 1840's and 1850's a time of almost furious railroad-building. Finally nearly every city and town was linked to the rest of its section and to the entire country through rail connections.

But gradually single lines extending over great distances were created. The Baltimore and Ohio had been built to Wheeling, in Virginia, by 1853. The New York Central, reaching at last from New York City to the Great Lakes, consisted of many small roads built piecemeal between 1831 and 1853, when it was established.

In 1836 a rail line was planned and begun from New York to Lake Erie—the Erie Railroad. It was to pass across several hundred miles and link New York with the West. When it was finished fifteen years later, it was hailed as the "Work of the Age."

In 1846 the great Pennsylvania Railroad was organized. Twelve years later the first passenger train ran the entire length of the line, from Philadelphia to Pittsburgh—and carried the first smoking car.

Noticeable results. By the beginning of the 1850's, the varied and extraordinary effects of railroads could be seen. First, surplus products were being shipped readily from one part of the country to another where they might be sold. Second, Americans, who had always been "on the move," moved faster and farther than ever before. Land near railroad junctions rose enormously in value as businesses sought locations near the freight depots.

Third, coal deposits for the first time could be used to advantage because iron ore could easily be shipped to them for the manufacture of iron. Fourth, the nation as a whole began to find a new meaning for the term "on time," which indicated the

A train pulls into the first depot, or railroad station, in Philadelphia. The passenger cars looked much like stagecoaches and therefore were simply called coaches.

Historical Society of Pennsylvania

361

growing importance of the self-control industrial people must acquire.

Fifth, railroads greatly stimulated the building of factories in the North, because goods and markets were brought together. Without railroads factories could not have continued to grow in number and prosper.

Newcomers at the "Golden Door"

A second major development of the 1840's was increased immigration. As factories multiplied, the poor, the unfor-

tunate, and the adventurous people of Europe were attracted to the North. Two shattering events on the other side of the Atlantic added to the number of immigrants coming to America.

Famine in Ireland. The first was the "Great Hunger" in Ireland in 1845, caused by the failure of the Irish potato crop. Reading about the famine and its horrors chills the blood.

When disease was added to the misery of the Irish in the spring of 1847, they began a headlong flight to America. An

In what section of the country were most of the railroads located in 1850? What cities were railroad terminals? How does the map help explain why New York City doubled its population between 1840 and 1850?

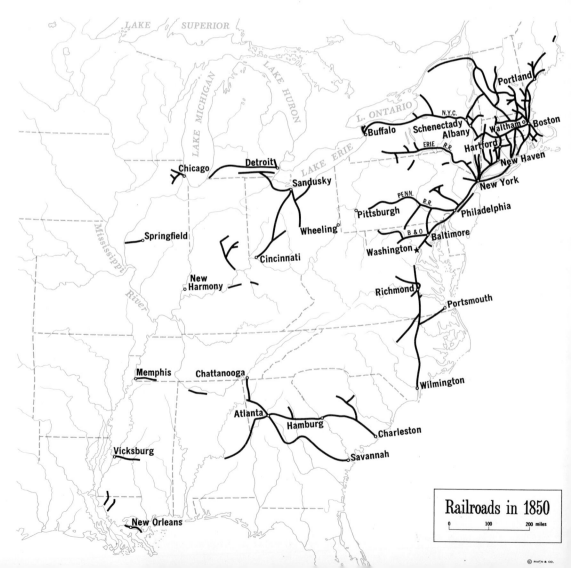

Railroads in 1850

0   100   200 miles

A large group of Irish immigrants arrive with all their possessions in New York Harbor in 1847. By then oceangoing steamboats were rapidly driving out the sailing vessels—the packets and clippers—which had made the American flag familiar throughout the world.

y could America
dily absorb large
nbers of immigrants?

official report from Ireland said, "All with means are emigrating, only the utterly destitute are left behind, and enfeebled labourers." In 1847 over 105,000 Irish men and women came to these shores. In 1848 the number was even greater.

Settlers in the city. Although the Irish immigrants were almost always farmers, they became city dwellers in the United States. Usually they remained in the American ports where they landed—Boston, New York, Philadelphia, Baltimore, and others—because they did not have the money to go farther and purchase land. They found out that although they lived in slums and worked chiefly with picks and shovels (they helped to build the first railroads), their children would "have it better."

Often people harshly and sometimes violently opposed Irish immigration because the Irish were Catholic and because some were paupers. But in a few years the Irish were strengthening the North by working in the factories, building railroads, and helping police and govern the great cities.

German refugees. A second event in Europe also pushed to our shores a large number of German immigrants. This was the failure in their homeland of an uprising in 1848 against their king, which had aimed to establish the beginnings of democratic government. The "forty-eighters," as they were often called, included professional men as well as farmers.

The German immigrants, having more money than the Irishmen, settled not only in the bigger cities of the East but also on farms throughout the midwestern states. They brought with them a driving ambition for a better way of living and a love of freedom that had been deepened by their personal experiences.

Sharpened Sectional Differences

The railroads and the immigration, then, were having an important effect on the North. Combined with the reform movements and the beginning of industry,

ve a group of students report on the conditions in Ireland and Germany that gave rise to ligration. What contributions did the Irish and German immigrants make to American ture? Where did Irish and German emigrants go other than to America?

they were helping to make a new way of life.

The South was following a different
path by the 1840's. Fewer railroads were built in the South than in the North because the need was not so great and the money required was not so easily obtained. As we have seen, immigrants, seeking a new start, generally stayed out of the South.

The single-crop South. While the North was developing a culture that offered people various kinds of opportunities, the South was gambling everything on the growing of cotton. The South remained almost entirely dependent on the North for providing its grain, for its insurance, and for most of its manufactured supplies.

Leaning on England. On the other hand, southerners held England in *their* grip, because the English factories required their cotton. A magazine published in Britain stated in 1851, "Suppose America wishes to bully us, to make us abandon Canada or Jamaica for example, she has no need to go to war. She has only to stop the export of cotton for six months, and the whole of our manufacturing counties are starving or in rebellion."

The tie to England—made of cotton thread—gave southerners a feeling of self- # confidence and power which northerners had not yet felt. But northerners could take pleasure and satisfaction in the fact that, after all was said and done, theirs were the *free* states.

---

1. Identify four of the first American railroads. 2. For what reason was "through traffic" difficult on early railways? 3. Name five ways in which railroads affected Americans. 4. What two events in Europe caused an increase in the number of immigrants coming to America? 5. In what ways was the South dependent on the North? How did England depend on the South?

The Workshop

The Shapers of Our World

The author describes changes in the early nineteenth century that helped give each of the sections of the country its own characteristics. Tell how each of the following contributed to this result:

Eli Whitney
Waltham system
National Trades'
  Union
Robert Owen
Brook Farm
Horace Mann
Dorothea Dix
William Lloyd
  Garrison

Benjamin **Lundy**
Maine liquor law
"peculiar institution"
underground railroad
potato famine
  of 1845
Harriet Tubman
Nat Turner
Quakers
Theodore Weld

Frederick Douglass
James G. Birney
the Grimké sisters
cotton gin

Baltimore and Ohio
  Railroad
"forty-eighters"

Adding to Your Vocabulary

Be sure you know these terms:

mill
interchangeable parts
mass production
custom-made

reform
prohibition
field hand
abolition

Understanding Pictures

1. Look at picture *a* on page 344. What does the presence of the children suggest

about the effect of slavery on families?

2. What main idea does the artist who painted picture *c* express? What symbols did he use? Now look at the picture on page 349. How is its message similar to that of picture *c*?

3. Compare the pictures of workers shown on pages 347 and 355. What similarities do you see? Differences? How did the lives of the workers differ?

4. The scene shown in the picture on page 363 has been repeated with variations many, many times in American ports. What shows that the immigrants came to this country to start a new life?

Thinking Things Through

After reviewing the boxed-in exercises in the chapter, answer these questions:

1. What problems did a worker have when he no longer produced an entire product himself and instead simply produced one part over and over again?

2. Why do you think Americans in the early 1800's were willing to accept bad working conditions?

3. Why is it true that during hard times, when workingmen most need the help of unions, unions have greater difficulty in getting members than in any other periods?

4. Why is the education of all Americans necessary for living in a democracy?

5. Why did immigrants from Europe tend to avoid settling in the South?

6. Why did antislavery ideas take hold so slowly, even though the Declaration of Independence long ago had said, "All men are created equal"?

7. Why are transportation and the location of raw materials so vital to the development of any industry?

The Art of Discussion

1. Organize a panel discussion of reforms in the early 1800's. Each participant should describe one of them.

2. Let the class be a state legislature trying to decide what reform movements should be encouraged by legislation. Give examples of some possible laws.

3. Discuss the situation of workingmen in the 1830's. One student could represent a factory owner, another a worker, and another a union organizer.

4. Ask a group of students to report on the contributions of recent immigrants to American life. If you know some recent immigrants in your community, invite them to tell you about their groups' culture and about their life in the United States. Afterward discuss what you learned.

History in Your Community

1. Coöperate with your local Negro History Week committee by helping with their program and by preparing materials for your school bulletin board. Report on some special part of Negro history, drawing upon books suggested in the list on page 412.

2. Organize a field trip to a local factory. Follow the production of one item from raw material to finished product. Ask a representative of the factory to tell about working conditions in the factory. Write a description of what you saw and compare it with what is said in the chapter about working conditions in the early 1800's.

Maps and Graphs Tell a Story

1. Look at the line graph showing cotton production on page 353. During what decade did the greatest increase in production take place? The smallest?

2. The ten largest cities in the United States in 1850 were New York, Philadelphia, Boston, Baltimore, Cincinnati, New Orleans, St. Louis, Pittsburgh, Louisville, and Albany. From looking at the map on page 362, can you see any good reason for the growth in population of these cities?

Dramatize the problem of immigration to the South: Have students write a letter that a German immigrant might have sent to a Mississippi planter, telling why the newcomer settled in the West instead of in the cotton-growing South.

(a) The poinsettia plant, named for Joel R. Poinsett, minister to Mexico in th 1820's who introduced it to Americans.
(b) A wagon train on the Oregon Trail.
(c) A California Indian, seen in a history book of 1839.
(d) The bowie knife, a tool of American frontiersmen.
(e) The Alamo, where a few Texans battl a Mexican army.

(a)

(b)

(c)   **(d)**   **(e)**

(g)

(f) The Lone Star flag of the state of Texas.
(g) The Bear flag of California which flew in 846. The symbols live on in the present state flag.

(f)

the pictures on pp. 366-367 to introduce the three as that are discussed in this chapter.

CHAPTER 17

THE PUSH TO THE PACIFIC

is chapter resumes the story of westward expansion: the settlement of Oregon and of California, Texas, other lands acquired from Mexico. Westward expansion brought new states into the Union and inten- ed the slavery issue.

E VEN as northerners and southerners were facing problems created by their cultures, other Americans were still taming the western wilderness and exploring its secrets. Once again they were reaching for land that was under a flag not their own. Their purposes and their hopes varied. But in common they seemed to believe that personal courage could make every obstacle disappear.

Discuss the idea of natural limits to American expansion. In theory what were these limits?

America Expands Toward Its Natural Limits

In the West people were meeting many of the conditions which two centuries earlier other pioneers had found along the eastern seaboard. They were also about to run into some conditions which no American had ever before faced.

The Oregon Country

The region that we now call the Pacific Northwest was a center of attention by the 1840's. Americans had first heard of the Oregon Country, as it was then called, in 1788 when Robert Gray and John Kendrick, of Boston, were in the area of Vancouver Island.

Astor's company. Gray, in 1792, was the first American to sail into the mouth of the Columbia River. Not many years later, when the fur traders were just beginning to push up the Missouri River, a vessel rounded South America to retrace the route Gray had traveled. That ship was owned by the American Fur Company, organized by John Jacob Astor in 1808. In 1811 Astor established Astoria, a trading post, at the mouth of the Columbia.

The voyage laid a basis for the claims of Astor's company and of the United States to the Pacific Northwest. The British also claimed the region on the basis of a sea captain's visit there.

d westward expansion follow definite, gradual stages of settlement? (Stress that Americans at to the Pacific coast before filling in the western area nearer to the Mississippi. They ce regarded the grasslands as the Great American Desert.)

Joint occupation. After the War of 1812 ended, the United States and Britain # agreed—in 1818—to occupy the Oregon Country jointly. Under this arrangement, British and American citizens were both to enjoy use of the Columbia River Valley.

Ten years later the agreement was renewed for an unlimited time, although either side could end it after a year's notice. The United States, it appeared, would wait patiently for a suitable time to lay sole claim to the vast, rich region.

A Boston teacher. One of the people who pressed for making the Oregon region entirely ours was a Boston schoolteacher named Hall Jackson Kelley. Kelley was an unlikely person to leave a mark as a bold adventurer in the American forest. Nevertheless, he had read the *Journal* of Lewis and Clark with great enthusiasm.

Kelley himself could only dream of succeeding in the perilous Oregon Country. He was unable to organize a colonizing expedition. Yet he was able to interest an ice merchant of Cambridge, Massachusetts, named Nathaniel Wyeth. Nat Wyeth was said to have invented every important tool used in the ice business.

Wyeth's work. Wyeth organized a company to develop the resources along the Columbia River. Sending his heavy possessions by boat, he started overland for the Pacific Northwest from Boston in 1832. But his supplies never reached him, and he returned with only a few of his party.

In 1834 Wyeth again set out on the journey west, this time accompanied by some missionaries and scientists. He set up a trading post on the Snake River, calling it Fort Hall. He also established Fort William at the mouth of the Willamette River.

Although Wyeth's business efforts along the Columbia were a failure, he kept Americans aware of the importance of the Oregon Country. Fort Hall in time became a place where settlers stopped on their way to the Northwest.

The British in the Oregon Country were even better served by Dr. John McLoughlin, who represented the Hudson's Bay Company, an English fur-trading firm in what is now Canada. McLoughlin was a man with a fierce temper, but he was able to establish excellent relations with the Indians. It was he who gave shelter to the first American missionaries who arrived in the Pacific Northwest.

The Whitmans. One of the most famous of the missionaries was Dr. Marcus Whitman, of New York State. Whitman, thirty-two years old in 1834, had practiced medicine for a time in Canada. In 1834 he and his brother were operating a sawmill in their hometown. He decided to answer a call for Protestant missionaries to work among the Indians in Oregon.

After making a trip to the Oregon Country to look over the land, Whitman went back east to prepare for his important work. While home he acquired a wife, who was in the small, brave party he took west with him in 1836. Narcissa Whitman, one of the first non-Indian women to come into the Pacific Northwest, had courage equal to her husband's.

Within a short time the Whitmans' cheerfulness began to disappear, but they never lost their braveness. They held on despite many hardships and irritations.

By the early 1840's a steady stream of immigrants was arriving from the East. Dr. Whitman, on a trip home in 1842–1843, tried without success to persuade the Secretary of War to build a road on which wagons could be moved along the route to the Oregon Country. Whitman returned to Narcissa little dreaming of the fate that lay ahead of them.

In 1847 the doctor-missionary was unable to halt a measles epidemic brought in by the immigrants. The children of the new arrivals who contracted the disease and were treated by Whitman generally recovered. The disease almost invariably

##Remember that Spain and France had used missionaries to help extend their colonial frontiers. In the United States, however, there had been little missionary activity among the Indians until the 1830's, when Protestant clergymen responded as part of their interest in reform causes.

A close-up of a group which made the exhausting trip to California, drawn from life by an unknown artist about 1850. Other wagons go ahead of and follow this one.

Chicago Museum of Science and Industry

proved fatal to Indian children. The Indians, in their grief, felt keen anger and resentment. In blind rage they slew the Whitmans and twelve others.

De Smet. The Jesuit missionary Pierre Jean De Smet began his work of organizing missions in the Oregon Country seven years before the Whitmans were killed. In the six years of his work with the Indians there, he set up several missions himself and aided other Catholic missionaries in founding more. A friend to the Indians, he helped settle difficulties between them and also between the tribesmen and the settlers over who owned the land.

The grand trail. The path that led to the Pacific Northwest became famous throughout the world as the Oregon Trail (see the map on page 370). It started at Independence, Missouri. In 1845 the editor of the Independence newspaper described a sight he had seen.

Even while we write, we see a long train of wagons coming through our busy streets; they are hailed with shouts of welcome by their fellow voyagers, and, to judge from the pleased expression on every face, it "all goes as merry as a marriage bell." On looking out at the passing train, we see among the foremost a very comfortably covered wagon, one of the sheets drawn aside, and an extremely nice looking lady seated inside very quietly sewing; the bottom of the wagon is carpeted; there are two or three chairs, and at one end is a bureau, surmounted by a mirror; various articles of ornament and convenience hang around the sides—a perfect prairie boudoir [that is, bedroom]. Blessed be women!

The same newspaperman made an estimate "that not less than two or three thousand people are congregating [that is, gathering] at this point previous to their start upon the broad prairie which will be on or about the 10th of May." Starts would be made by latecomers until June, when the heat would begin to be so great that travel on the Plains would be hindered.

The dangers on the Oregon Trail were enormous. People who survived a journey along it inevitably passed the graves—often fresh ones—of those who could not stand the hardships of the trip.

The Donner party. One of the grimmest stories in the history of the entire American frontier occurred on a branch of the Oregon Trail. It concerns a party led by the Donner brothers, which in 1846 followed the Oregon Trail to what is now Wyoming. Then, dividing into two groups, the smaller one took a well-known route to California and the other struck out by a little-known route thought to be shorter.

Early snows marooned the larger Donner band in the Sierra Nevada, and a terrible winter of suffering followed. Only half the party survived the ordeal. They did so

have students trace the Oregon Trail on current road maps.   Ask them to estimate the driving
me required for a trip from Independence, Missouri, to Portland, Oregon, today.   What hard-
ips did settlers bound for Oregon in the 1840's have to face that travelers today can avoid?

369

There is a monument to the Donner party located on Route 40, the main transcontinental highway that crosses the Sierras between California and Nevada. Some students may have seen it.

only because they ate the bodies of those who did not. We must wonder whether the lady who seemed so comfortable in her carpeted covered wagon ever made it safely to Oregon and how comfortable she was at the end of her journey.

The magnet of land. The Americans who made the trip to the Oregon Country crossed 2000 miles of land, including prairie, Great Plains, and mountains. They were drawn to the Oregon Country by what had always attracted frontiersmen: a glimpse of better land and a chance for improving themselves and their families. Even the prospect of a hair-raising trip across the continent against heavy odds could not dim such bright dreams.

By the time John Tyler left the White House in 1845, about five thousand Americans were living in the Oregon territory

What states were formed from the Oregon Country?

Compare this map with the one on page 278. What change or changes can you find? *Inset picture:* A heavy-duty Conestoga wagon, the chief means of transporting goods and people west before the railroads.

(Wagon) National Gallery of Art, Index of American Design

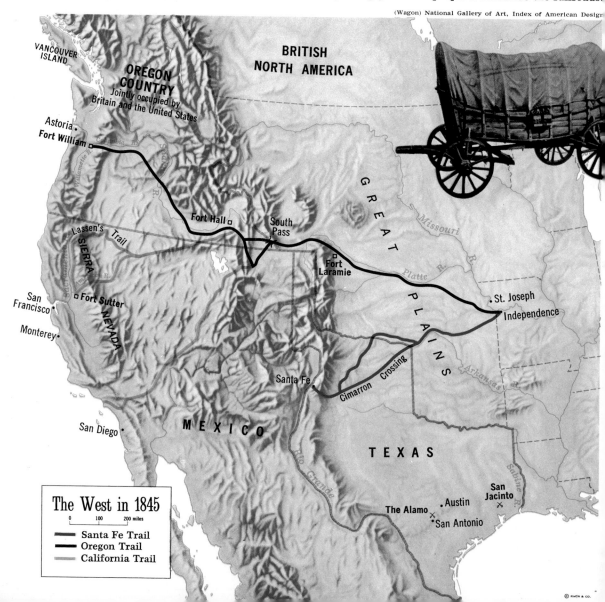

The West in 1845

| 0 | 100 | 200 miles |

— Santa Fe Trail
— Oregon Trail
— California Trail

south of the Columbia River. They looked forward to the day when the land they had settled on would be fully a part of the United States.

California also lured easterners. It, too, satisfied the dreams of farmers. After safely reaching California, a thirteen-year-old girl who had lived through the terror of the Donner disaster wrote a cousin in Illinois. She said, "It is a beautiful country. It ought to be a beautiful country . . . to pay us for our troubles in getting to it."

California

California, which had once been a part of the Spanish empire and then had become part of the independent country of Mexico, had never been more than a kind of distant outpost. When Americans began to go to California, they went around South America as traders and merchants hoping to sell their goods to Mexicans or to Indians.

Junípero Serra. Much of the development accomplished in California was the work of the Spanish priest Junípero Serra. In 1769 he founded the San Diego Mission, the first of nine he established.

For fifteen years Serra served as a missionary to the Indians, Christianizing large numbers of them. Through his efforts European cattle were brought to California and European methods of farming were introduced. The Spanish heritage which shows itself in California today was handed down in large part through Serra's efforts.

Putting it on the map. Like the Oregon Country, California had its American boosters, who shouted its good points in books and pamphlets (and often in letters sent back home). The most important publication was a book by Richard Henry Dana entitled *Two Years before the Mast*, which boys still read today.

In the book Dana told about his experiences when he spent the years from 1834 to 1836 aboard a vessel that sailed from Boston around South America. After visiting California ports, it turned homeward again. Enthusiastic about the glorious land he saw, Dana wrote, "In the hands of an enterprising people, what a country this might be!"

Another leading figure in making California well known was the merchant Thomas O. Larkin, who had established a business in Monterey in 1832. Larkin, whose children were the first born in California of parents who had both come from the United States, was appointed a United States agent in California in the 1840's. He was especially instructed to stir up the American residents in California to seek its annexation by the United States.

"General" Sutter. By 1845 about seven hundred Americans were living in California, most of them in the Sacramento Valley. The leader of the people in this area was John A. Sutter. He had been born in Germany, had served in the Swiss army, and in 1845 was a Mexican subject.

Sutter's huge estate, located where the American and Sacramento rivers join, became richly productive. Indians had helped clear the land. They had also dug irrigation ditches and built a fort. Usually called General, Sutter, who was a kindly little man, welcomed warmly new settlers to the Sacramento Valley. His place there became a center for Americans who hoped one day to free themselves from the rule of Mexico.

New Mexico

The area known now as New Mexico and Arizona, a second part of Mexico, was not a place where Americans had been welcomed before Mexico became independent in 1821. You will recall that Zebulon Pike was captured by the Spanish when he entered New Mexico in 1806 (see page 282).

Serra's missions stretched north of San Diego, spaced about one day's journey apart. Today, because of the restoration work of the last fifty years, the California missions are well-preserved historical sites.

In 1821 an American named William Becknell took a load of goods into Santa Fe and sold it at a profit. This trip began the extensive Santa Fe trade, although some traders had moved goods along the same route earlier.

The Santa Fe Trail. It was not long before merchants gathered at a central location like Independence, Missouri, and then, traveling together, covered the distance of about 800 miles to Santa Fe. Some of the men made a great deal of money. In general, though, the trade on the Santa Fe # Trail was important chiefly because it drew American attention to New Mexico. Later, people thought of New Mexico as an area to add to the Union.

Kit Carson's contribution. A man who became a popular hero, Kit Carson, also helped to open up New Mexico. Carson had served as guide to the first expedition of young John C. Frémont, which had explored the Southwest. When this region later became American land, about sixty thousand Americans were already living there.

Texas

A third portion of Mexico in which Americans settled was Texas. The United States had claimed Texas as part of the Louisiana Purchase but had given up the claims in 1819. That year, in a treaty with Spain the United States had rounded off the Louisiana boundary (see the map on page 370). Our negotiators had not insisted on any land west of the Sabine River. Ever afterward many westerners condemned President James Monroe for having accepted the treaty.

Immigrants from the States. Both John Quincy Adams and Andrew Jackson tried to buy Texas, but the Mexican government was not interested in making a deal. Meanwhile, Americans in considerable numbers were moving into Texas, welcomed by the government of Mexico. It gave huge grants of land to colonists like Stephen Austin if they agreed to bring in their families and become Roman Catholics. By 1836 the population of Texas was estimated to be between 25,000 and 30,000.

Difficulties with Mexico. In time conflicts arose between the Texans and the Mexican authorities. Each group was trying to take advantage of the other. The Texans wished to shake themselves free of the control of Mexico. The Mexicans hoped to add to their government's treasury by taxing the foreigners—the Americans in Texas.

Americans in Texas came to resent the requirement that they be Roman Catholics, even though they knew about it when they received Texas land. Being cotton growers, Texans who had brought slaves to their new settlements were also concerned because Mexico had forbidden slavery after 1829.

Another serious blow was the fact that a dictator named Santa Anna had arisen in Mexico. He appeared to want to take from the Texans what they considered to be their rights.

Under Sam Houston. In 1835 the Texans rose in revolt, led by Sam Houston, who had been one of Jackson's brave men in the War of 1812. The Mexican general Santa Anna was determined to beat the Texans into submission.

Heroes at the Alamo. With five thousand Mexicans, Santa Anna attacked an old mission in San Antonio called the Alamo. Inside were fewer than two hundred Texans. As the siege began on February 23, 1836, Lieutenant Colonel William B. Travis, commander of the rebels, boldly wrote a message to the "outside world." It was addressed "To the People of Texas & all Americans in the World." Travis wrote:

> I call on you in the name of Liberty, of patriotism & everything dear to the American character, to come to our aid,

Discuss whether or not the Texas revolt and the American Revolution can be regarded as basically similar movements. What caused the lack of understanding between Americans and Mexicans in Texas?

with all dispatch. . . . If this call is neglected, I am determined to sustain myself as long as possible & die like a soldier who never forgets what is due to his own honor & that of his country—*Victory or Death.*

No aid came, and thirteen days later, March 6, the Texans had perished to the last man. Among those who died there were James Bowie, inventor of the bowie knife, and Davy Crockett, his famous coonskin hat neatly arranged at his side. There is no completely reliable figure for the number of Mexicans who died in the fight, but it was probably around six hundred.

Revenge at San Jacinto. Texans would never rest until the killings at the Alamo were avenged. An opportunity came on April 21, 1836, at San Jacinto, when General Houston's small Texas army attacked Mexican soldiers. Screaming "Remember the Alamo!" so loudly that it was heard above the din of battle, the Texans struck. It is said that many of the enemy fell to their knees terror-stricken, protesting in the only English that they knew, "Me no Alamo."

Santa Anna himself was discovered and taken prisoner the next morning. Wearing a faded blue jacket and red slippers, he identified himself to his captors as a lowly private. But when his own soldiers saw him and shouted "El Presidente! El Presidente!" his disguise was over.

Houston resisted the strong efforts of his supporters to kill Santa Anna. Instead, he forced a very scared Santa Anna to sign agreements to take the Mexican troops out of Texas, give Texas its independence, and make peace.

The Lone Star Republic. After Santa Anna had been released, though, he insisted that the arrangements he had agreed to while a prisoner could not bind him. Nevertheless, he and the other Mexicans made no further efforts to win back the rebel-

General Sam Houston, the leader of the Texans in their fight for independence from Mexico.

lious Texans. In 1836 the Americans in Texas declared it independent, calling it the Lone Star Republic.

The Texans knew that their new republic would have to be annexed by the United States if they were ever to be safe against efforts by the Mexicans to reconquer the territory.

Argument over annexation. The United States was in a mood to acquire new territory, yet there were difficulties in acquiring Texas. The fact is that southerners like John C. Calhoun were urging the annexation of Texas in order to have another slave state in the Union. On the other hand, abolitionists were insisting that Tex-

eview the slavery question in terms of the effect on the Senate of adding new states to the ion. If Texas had been divided into a number of states, would the North have been more lling to have it annexed?

as must stay out of the Union because it permitted slavery.

Texas, in short, was a "hot potato" in American politics. President Jackson, though personally in favor of annexation, did nothing about the matter. Before he went out of office in 1837, he recognized the independence of Texas—that is, he formally acknowledged the existence of the Lone Star Republic. He further agreed to exchanging diplomatic representatives.

Independent Texas also had diplomatic relations with France and England. England was especially interested in the fate of Texas. How useful it could be for England, a cotton-manufacturing country, to tie itself by treaty to a cotton-growing country! In such a case, Texas would have the advantage of the military protection of England. Its anxious days would be ended.

Unwilling to see Texas allied with Britain, the United States did not hesitate to act. In fact, England's influence in North America—even to defend Americans in Texas—would be a violation of the Monroe Doctrine.

In April, 1844, Calhoun, who had become Secretary of State, submitted to Congress a treaty providing for the annexation of Texas. Once again it was defeated, since it was still regarded by many northern Congressmen as simply a means of extending slavery.

Taken into the Union. President Tyler, however, wished to receive credit in history for bringing Texas into the Union before he retired from the presidency in 1845. He believed that if the country delayed in taking action, Texas might fall into the hands of England or France.

It was done: in 1845 the Senate and House passed a resolution admitting Texas as a state. This joint resolution required only a simple majority. A treaty would have required a two-thirds majority—which earlier it had proved impossible to obtain. The antislavery forces were fu-

rious. One of them said angrily, "The real object of the annexation is the protection of slavery."

The State of Deseret

The area that later became Utah also was being occupied in the period of the 1840's. The driving force behind its settlement was provided by a religious movement as powerful in encouraging colonization as any in the seventeenth century. Its founder was Joseph Smith, the son of a poor Vermont family, who had been born in 1805.

The Mormons. Smith stated that an angel of the Lord had revealed important secrets to him. He had been told to look for a set of gold plates on which there was writing in a strange language. Smith said he found them in a cave on a hillside in New York.

A method was provided for Smith to translate the plates, which contained the *Book of Mormon*. The *Book of Mormon*, published in 1830, contains the teachings of a new religion.

Under Smith the Church of Jesus Christ of Latter-Day Saints—whose members are commonly called Mormons—was created. In the face of keen opposition to the Mormons, the zeal of Smith's followers was remarkable. Smith himself had aroused the anger of his neighbors by saying that he had been divinely chosen to reveal the one true religion.

Early struggles. After leaving New York, the Mormons tried to establish themselves in Ohio. But the depression of 1837 hurt them badly. So the little band proceeded to Missouri—to the neighborhood of Independence, from which they were brutally expelled in 1838. They then went to Illinois, where they tried to put down roots at the little river town they called Nauvoo.

Again the community was hostile to the Mormons, although it tolerated them. As

For a detailed account of the Mormon migration see, Billington, Ray A. "Best Prepared Pioneers in West," American Heritage (October, 1956), p. 20.

they became more numerous, they received considerable support—from politicians anxious to have their vote.

The slaying of Smith. But trouble—serious trouble—was about to break out. The number of Mormon women was greater than the number of men, perhaps because women were easier to convert to the new religion. Joseph Smith was said to have received in 1843 a new revelation—that he should practice *polygamy*, that is, have more than one wife. Non-Mormons were furious at Smith, and many Mormons also turned sharply on him.

Smith smashed the printing press belonging to Mormons who opposed him, forcing the local officials to throw him into the jail at nearby Carthage, Illinois. There a mob seized Smith and his brother and killed them. Smith became a martyr to the Mormon cause.

Brigham Young's leadership. Two years later Brigham Young became the leader of the Mormons. Young was also a New Englander. He was by trade a glazier (that is, one who sets glass in windows), a house painter, and a carpenter. He had been a farmer, too. Above all, though, he possessed that combination of iron will and common sense which important leaders have.

Young was aware that relations between the Mormons and the Gentiles (as the non-Mormons were called) were growing worse. He decided he must lead his people to a new location or see them destroyed. In freezing weather in the early part of 1846, Young guided his followers across the Mississippi River. The great migration of Mormons was on.

At the Great Salt Lake. Young, "the Lion of the Lord," led the first wave of Mormons into the Salt Lake Valley on July 24, 1847 —a day ever since celebrated by the Mormons as Pioneer Day. The view they saw from a high place above the valley was awe-inspiring. High overhead were the glo-

Map below: The Mormons followed the route shown on the map, not in a single group but in a number of small ones. Young led the first band. Picture below: The original copy of the Book of Mormon, which contains Mormon teachings.

Church of Jesus Christ of Latter-Day Saints

The Mormon Migration

0   100   200 miles

© RMÉN & CO.

Columbia R.

OREGON COUNTRY

Snake R.

South Pass

Fort Laramie

Missouri R.

Council Bluffs

Nauvoo

Carthage

Great Salt Lake

Fort Bridger

Salt Lake City

Fort Kearny

Platte R.

Independence

MEXICAN TERRITORY

Arkansas R.

TEXAS

Mississippi

rious snow-capped peaks of mountains, and to the north and west lay the glistening Great Salt Lake.

The first years. But the land itself was forbidding. Before anything could be grown on it, irrigation had to be undertaken. The suffering in the first winter was terrible, for there was a lack of food. Moreover, there was no lumber, and wood had to be brought from great distances. When the first blasts of winter came, not everybody had proper shelter. Fortunately the weather that year was mild.

The faith of the people, though, could not be shaken. Young returned east to round up more migrants, whom his followers had even found in Europe. Young urged his people, "Come immediately and prepare to go West, bring with you all kinds of choice seeds, grains, vegetables, fruits, shrubbery, trees, and vines—anything that will please the eye, gladden the heart or cheer the soul of man."

Success came only slowly. The years 1847–1849 were the Mormons' "starving

Above: Members of one party of Mormons find a stream and a good place to rest on their migration west. *Below:* A beehive—a Mormon symbol—ornaments a staircase post in the Brigham Young home in Salt Lake City today. Another one sits atop the cupola

376 The beehive, the Mormon symbol for hard work and industry, appears today on Utah's state seal.

time"—which could be compared with Virginia's long before (see page 79). The pioneer band of Mormons was "reduced to the necessity of . . . living upon the hides of animals which they had previously made use of for roofing their cabins, but which were now torn off for food."

Making the desert bloom. Young's talent as an organizer showed itself in the crisis. He established the community on a coöperative basis: the individuals were taught to aid each other rather than struggle against each other. The land was divided equally.

Water, which was scarce, was divided justly so that the limited supply could serve as many people as possible. Later a visitor to the Mormon colony reported what he saw there.

> The irrigating canals, which flow before every door, furnish an abundance of water for the nourishment of shade trees, and the open space before each building, and the pavement before it, when planted with shrubbery and adorned with flowers, will make this one of the most lovely spots between the Mississippi and the Pacific.

"The State of the Honeybee." The Mormons continued to grow in number. They gave their colony the name State of Deseret. Its area included present-day Utah, a corner of California, and a piece of Wyoming. "Deseret" was a word coined in the

Book of Mormon, meaning "honeybee." Although the name was dropped in a few years, the beehive remains an inspiring Mormon symbol.

At this point let us think for a moment about what the West was like in the 1840's. In the western Oregon Country, Americans were finding an environment something like the one that they had known—with plentiful rainfall and an abundance of trees. A serious problem, though, was England's continued interest in the region.

In California, many Americans were enjoying prosperity and steadily increasing numbers. In New Mexico, Americans were tolerated by Mexicans. In the State of Deseret, Mormons wished only to be safe from interference as they worked out their problems of survival.

---

1. On what grounds did both Americans and British claim the Oregon Country? 2. Give the main facts about the Whitmans in the Oregon Country and the Donner party. 3. Name three parts of Mexico in which Americans settled. 4. For what three reasons did Texans revolt? 5. How did they win their independence? 6. Describe the events that led up to the establishment of the State of Deseret.

---

sure students understand that Texas was part of the U.S. before the war with Mexico.

President Polk Carries On a War with Mexico

The annexation of Texas to the United States had not succeeded in ending trouble with Mexico. In fact, the difficulties became more and more severe. They finally caused war, which affected the later history not only of Texas and California but also of the land in between.

When Tyler went out of office in 1845,

he was a man unloved by the people or the political parties. As you remember, the Whigs could not get along with him or he with them. And the Democrats would not claim him because he had gone over to the Whigs. So in 1844 both the Whigs and the Democrats looked for a candidate who could unite party members of all opinions.

The "Dark Horse" Chief

The Whigs chose Henry Clay as their presidential candidate. The Democrats named James K. Polk, of Tennessee. Polk was a "dark horse"—that is, at the beginning of the convention that nominated him he was not thought of as having a chance.

During the campaign, the Whigs made believe they had never heard of Polk before, using as a slogan "Who is James K. Polk?" The people answered the question on Election Day: he was the president of the United States!

Earlier career. Polk, who had been Speaker of the House of Representatives, had been persuaded by Andrew Jackson to leave Congress in order to run for the governorship of Tennessee. (It is unusual today for a person holding a national elective office to leave it to seek a state office, but it was a familiar practice until about the mid-1800's.) A Whig critic of Polk referred to him as Jackson's "chief cook and bottle-washer."

Actually, Polk was a hard-working man who exhausted himself so badly as President that he lived only a few months after his term was over. The First Lady was also a model of correctness.

"The Presidentress." Mrs. Polk followed politics very closely, and she was frequent-ly referred to with respect as "The Presidentress." An English visitor described her as a "very handsome woman. Her hair is very black and her dark eyes and complection remind one of the Spanish donnas." Her husband could not have got along without her.

Although Polk was not as well known as some other members of the Democratic party, he was a man of firmness. Just forty-nine years old—the youngest President to take office up to that time—Polk promised shortly after his inauguration that he would not seek a second term.

Polk and the First Lady were deeply interested in American history. To many a White House affair, Dolley Madison—crowding eighty years of age—would be invited, a reminder of the early days of the presidency. At Polk's inauguration Mrs. Polk carried a fan bearing imprinted on its silk the names and portraits of our eleven Presidents, beginning with Washington and including her husband.

Ideas of national growth. But devotion to the past did not interfere with Polk's bold handling of foreign affairs. The problems he confronted grew out of the West.

Polk had run on a platform which called for acquiring both Oregon and Texas. Texas came into the Union, as we have seen, shortly before Polk became President.

Obtaining all of Oregon. Almost immediately after Polk entered the White

This is the fan Mrs. Polk carried at her husband's inauguration. A likeness of Jackson—fifth from the right—can be recognized. Already Americans regarded their Presidents as an important part of their history.

Polk Home, Columbia, Tennessee

House, he took steps to end the joint occupation with Britain of the Oregon Country. Although many people had hopes of seeing the entire Oregon area American, diplomats expected to have to compromise with Britain in setting the boundary line. Britain finally proposed dividing the land at the forty-ninth parallel of north latitude. This boundary was accepted by the United States in a treaty in the late spring of 1846.

Eyes on California. California also seized the President's attention—and that of the whole country. Late in 1844 a confidential report reached Washington that Mexico was willing to sell it to the United States. This excited the interest of Polk, and after he became President he took steps to send a diplomatic representative to negotiate with Mexico.

Meanwhile, though, a new government had taken over in Mexico, and it refused to receive the United States negotiator. Many Americans thought that this was shabby treatment and that Mexico ought to be severely punished.

At the same time, a group of Spanish-speaking Californians, with the help of a number of Americans, were trying to stir up a rebellion against Mexican rule of the territory. The American army officer John C. Frémont, supposedly on an exploring expedition, attempted to help push their plans along. But he made so many Californians angry with his meddling that the plans were dropped. He withdrew from the scene for the moment.

The Bear Flag Republic. In June, 1846, Frémont returned to California and joined forces with a group of American settlers who had proclaimed their own government. It became known as the Bear Flag Republic. This name came from its flag, a white cloth with a strip of red flannel along the lower edge. On the white background appeared a bear looking at a red star and the words "California Republic."

Hostilities South of the Border

War, meantime, had broken out between the United States and Mexico. The main cause was a long-standing dispute over where the southern boundary of Texas belonged. Americans were saying it lay along the Rio Grande, and the Mexicans were insisting that it belonged along the Nueces River.

Forces at the Rio Grande. In January, 1846, Polk ordered General Zachary Taylor's forces to Texas to take up positions on the Rio Grande. Early in May the President made up his mind to send a message to Congress asking for a declaration of war against Mexico.

Shooting at last. Polk was impatient, knowing that a strong force commanded by General Taylor glared across the Rio Grande at Mexican soldiers, who glared back. The President was anxious to begin war at once, but the Secretary of the Navy insisted that the Mexicans must make the first move. It came on April 24, 1846, when the Mexicans crossed the Rio Grande. In a skirmish which followed, sixteen Americans were killed or wounded. At this, the Battle of Palo Alto, the Mexican War began.

A young Whig Congressman from Illinois, Abraham Lincoln, regarded the United States as having been in the wrong in entering the war. He would not accept the Polk administration's assertion that American blood had been shed on American soil. He demanded to know exactly the ## spot on American soil on which the blood had been shed. No one could tell him.

Polk took active charge of the Mexican War, and he carried it on with skill—military and diplomatic. To him an honorable peace meant obtaining for the United States all the Mexican land lying between Texas and the Pacific Ocean.

Taylor as the general. The command-

Lincoln's "spot resolutions" showed that some Americans questioned the reasons for the exican War. Ask students to explain how the Mexican War was related to the growing ctional controversy over slavery.

379

The Mexican War was a training ground for young officers who later assumed commands in the Civil War. For example, both Grant and Lee served in the Mexican War.

ing officer in the field, Zachary Taylor, was sixty-one years old—a splendid soldier, although not very good at planning campaigns. He had done most of his fighting against Indians in a career that was now forty years old. Because he did not like to march in a dress uniform, much preferring to wear shirt-sleeves, he was called by his men "Old Rough and Ready."

Polk hoped to have the American soldiers capture important places on the Mexican border and then allow the Mexicans to make peace on American terms. One plan was to march on Monterrey, in Mexico, capture it, and proceed to Mexico City.

The plan did not go as well as Polk had hoped. First of all, Taylor after a hard fight accepted the surrender of Monterrey and allowed the Mexican garrison there to get away without being pursued. Second, Taylor was too poorly equipped and supplied to make the hard march into the mountains on the road to Mexico City.

Annexing California. Meanwhile, however, outside the principal scene of the fighting, the United States was acquiring New Mexico and California. New Mexico fell easily. From Fort Leavenworth, Kansas, in the early summer of 1846, Colonel Stephen W. Kearny set forth for Santa Fe. With no source of supplies and with only enough food to reach his destination, Kearny confidently pressed ahead. Santa Fe fell without a fight, and Kearny claimed it for the United States.

On instructions from the President, Kearny now moved to California. However, his services were not needed there. Commodore John D. Sloat, commander of the Pacific squadron of the United States Navy, took Monterey, California, in July, 1846. Retiring shortly afterward, Sloat was replaced by Commodore Robert F. Stockton, who completed the conquest of the California region. By the time Kearny arrived, the area was in American hands. Polk's territorial aims had now been

achieved. The war might have ended if Mexico had been willing to admit to its people that it could not recover the lost territory. But no nation—even against hopeless odds—will yield its lands without a struggle.

General Winfield Scott. Polk needed a better general than Taylor. At that time the best American military man was Winfield Scott—a veteran of the War of 1812 (see page 300). Polk, however, did not get along well with Scott, who was often a difficult man, enjoying his own firm opinions more than seemed necessary. Besides, Scott was a Whig and was being mentioned as a possible presidential candidate. In this respect he was as displeasing to Polk as to Taylor, who was also a Whig, being advertised as a successor to Polk.

Strategy. Putting politics aside, Polk and Scott worked out a military plan. Troops under Scott's command would gather south of Tampico (see the map on the next page). From there they would be shipped by the navy to Veracruz. Veracruz would be captured and made into a base for further operations. From Veracruz the troops would head for Mexico City.

Meanwhile, Taylor's forces were weakened considerably when some of his soldiers were transferred to Scott's command. Taylor grew stubborn and moved his troops—many of them new soldiers—into exposed positions south of Monterrey. Santa Anna thought this American advance gave him his chance. He would march against Taylor and destroy him. Then he would turn and proceed against Scott without fear of being attacked from the rear.

"Hero of Buena Vista." Learning about the Mexican march toward him, Taylor saw that he was needlessly risking his men. So he moved them back to the village of Buena Vista and made ready for Santa Anna. The Americans were severely pounded in the battle which followed, but Taylor rallied his men. Among the heroes

#Note that Scott's route was much the same as the one Cortés had used many years earlier. Why did Mexico keep on fighting despite the many victories won by the Americans? Discuss the idea of national honor.

f the Battle of Buena Vista, which took place in February, 1847, were the "Missis-sippi Rifles," under the command of a outhern planter named Jefferson Davis.

Although the Mexicans greatly outnum-bered the Americans, they were slowly pushed back. They could have recovered and carried on the fight the next day, but their appetite for battle had been dulled. They were gone when the sun rose the fol-lowing morning.

Taylor fired off a message to Washing-ton which announced a gigantic victory. Ever afterward he would be known among his grateful countrymen as the "Hero of Buena Vista." #

The capture of Mexico City. Santa Anna now hurried back to defend Mexico City. He was none too soon. Scott had been wag-ing a brilliant campaign after seizing the city of Veracruz.

First Scott crushed a Mexican force led

The main campaigns of the only war the United States has ever fought with an American neighbor—one about which its citizens had divided opinions.

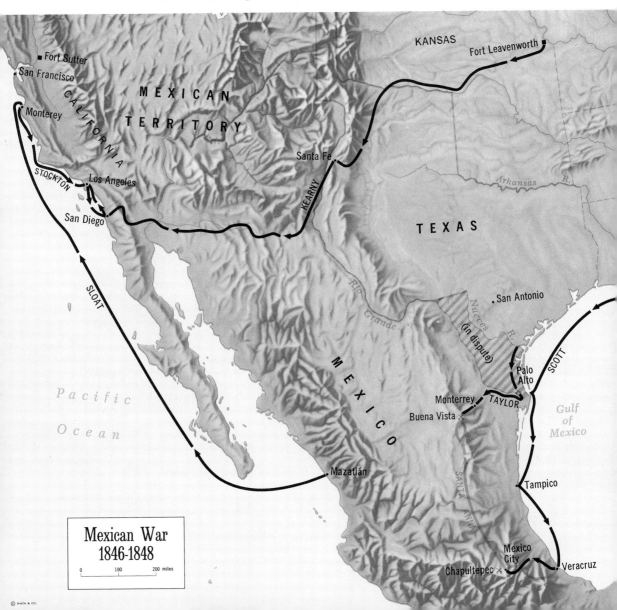

Mexican War
1846-1848

0   100   200 miles

against him by Santa Anna. Then he inflicted a terrible defeat on the Mexicans before Mexico City. The final step was a furious hand-to-hand struggle with bayonets on the hill of Chapultepec (chä pōol'- tå pĕk'), at the western outskirts of the Mexican capital. The Aztec Indians used to call it the "Hill of the Grasshoppers."

At the top of Chapultepec, which was about 200 feet high, was the building that housed the cadets of the National Military Academy of Mexico. These youths, wearing trim gray uniforms and caps with blue tassels, rather than surrender, fought to the death. Altogether, about two thousand Mexicans were killed or wounded.

The Mexicans have never forgotten the
event, which they regard as a massacre.

More than a century later President Dwight D. Eisenhower visited Chapultepec and expressed the hope in the presence of the president of Mexico that bygones would be bygones.

On September 14, 1847, the American troops entered Mexico City—"the halls of Montezuma." Many Americans proudly compared our army's triumph with that of the Spanish conquistadors of the 1500's.

Scott rode into the center of the city on a magnificent bay charger. The band played "Hail, Columbia," "Washington's March," "Yankee Doodle," and at the end "Hail to the Chief." The sight was so splendid, it is said, that even the defeated people looking on cheered.

The tense atmosphere after the capture

What states were formed from the land acquired from Mexico?

Look at this map and then at the one on page 370. What large and small areas of land did we acquire between 1845 and 1853?

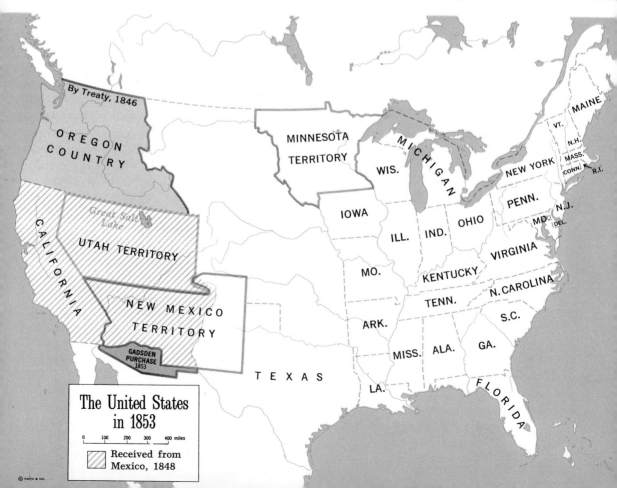

By Treaty, 1846

OREGON COUNTRY

MINNESOTA TERRITORY

MICHIGAN

MAINE

VT.

N.H.

WIS.

NEW YORK

MASS.

CONN. R.I.

Great Salt Lake

CALIFORNIA

UTAH TERRITORY

IOWA

ILL. IND. OHIO

PENN.

N.J.

MD. DEL.

MO.

VIRGINIA

KENTUCKY

NEW MEXICO TERRITORY

TENN.

N. CAROLINA

GADSDEN PURCHASE 1853

ARK.

S.C.

TEXAS

MISS. ALA. GA.

LA.

FLORIDA

The United States in 1853

0   100   200   300   400 miles

Received from Mexico, 1848

© RAND & CO.

General Winfield Scott, on the bay (brown) horse at the right, rides with his men into the public square of Mexico City, before the Cathedral of Mexico. The Aztecs used to listen to Montezuma speaking here.

Chicago Historical Society

of Mexico City was made more bearable by a change in the Mexican government. A new group of men had come to power willing to make peace with the United States.

Trist's treaty. It so happened that a peace commissioner appointed by Polk was traveling with Scott's army. The man, Nicholas P. Trist, was chief clerk of the Department of State. Trist did not accomplish anything at first, and Polk somewhat impatiently called him back to Washington. The news of the recall reached Trist just as he was beginning his negotiations. He went ahead with them anyhow.

The result was a treaty in 1848—the Treaty of Guadalupe Hidalgo. In it the Mexicans promised to turn over to the United States California and all the land they had owned between California and Texas. They also acknowledged the Rio Grande as the southern boundary of Texas. The United States agreed to pay to Mexico the claims of its citizens against Mexico and also a sum of $15,000,000.

The immense addition of territory provided by the Treaty of Guadalupe Hidalgo all but filled out the present-day southwestern boundary of the United States. The boundary was completed in 1853 by the Gadsden Purchase, named for the South Carolinian who negotiated it with Mexico. This deal obtained for us for $10,000,000 the Gila River region which today makes up the southern portion of New Mexico and Arizona.

Polk was angry with Trist for ignoring instructions. But there was nothing he could reasonably do except submit the treaty to the Senate for ratification. Polk knew that many supporters of slavery wanted to annex all of Mexico and open it to the spread of slavery. This would have caused a fight with the antislavery people, which Polk wanted to avoid. The Treaty of Guadalupe Hidalgo was ratified.

Presidential pettiness. Polk, showing smallness, punished Trist for disobeying orders by refusing to permit him to be repaid for his expenses. Toward Scott Polk was also unfriendly. Instead of permitting "Old Fuss and Feathers," as Scott was called, to have a triumphal parade, Polk had him brought before a military commission investigating the way in which the war had been carried on.

1. Name the man who was elected President in 1844, identify his party, and tell on what platform he had run. 2. How were his two aims accomplished? 3. What was the main cause of the Mexican War? 4. In what places did fighting occur? 5. Give the terms of the Treaty of Guadalupe Hidalgo.

all of Mexico had been annexed, the United States would have become a colonial power owning a large foreign population. How would such a move have been different from previous westward expansion? When did the United States first acquire colonies?

Gold in California Pulls People Westward

The Mexican War and the struggle over Texas brought a huge domain of new territory under the American flag. Furthermore, the movement of Americans westward was reaching huge proportions. Only a generation earlier the poet William Cullen Bryant had written of

> The continuous woods
> Where rolls the Oregon,
>   [that is, the Columbia River]
> and hears no sound,
> Save his own dashings . . . .

Now the quiet had ended, and the push of people going west was growing.

Discovery at a Sawmill

No event in the history of the West has stirred up more interest than the discovery of gold in California in 1848. One morning in January one of "General" Sutter's men, James W. Marshall, noticed pea-size flecks of bright metal in water where a sawmill was being built. The location was about 40 miles from Sutter's fort. He wrote later about picking up some of the ore (see page 68). "It made my heart thump. I was certain it was gold."

An unkept secret. Marshall rushed off to tell Sutter. They agreed to keep the discovery secret until they could complete the mill. But so exciting a fact as the finding of gold would not remain concealed. "Gold fever" in a short time struck the entire country, and before long the word was "Ho! for California."

The rush. Thousands of Americans climbed into wagons and were off—often without skills, physical endurance, or proper equipment. Some went overland in covered wagons, discovering more often than not that they had carried too much of the wrong kind of baggage with them.

Some of the gold seekers traveled by sea around South America to California. Others, less patient, chose a water route which would short-circuit the long voyage. They sailed the 2200 miles from New York to Panama and then undertook a dangerous journey across the Isthmus of Panama.

Those who died of cholera and fevers were many, but perhaps they were luckier than those who merely fell ill and could not continue. These pitiful people had to listen to the chattering of monkeys and parrots and hope to avoid the vultures, which were overhead—waiting hopefully.

Many men, therefore, never made it to the goldfields, and, of course, very few ever made a lucky strike or, as they also said, "hit it lucky." A Vermont preacher who was living in Monterey, the capital of California, wrote in his diary of what happened when word of the gold strike was proved.

> My messenger, sent to the mines, has returned with specimens of the gold; he dismounted in a sea of upturned faces. As he drew forth the yellow lumps from his pockets and passed them around among the eager crowd the doubts which had lingered till now, fled. . . . The blacksmith dropped his hammer, the carpenter his plane, the mason his trowel, the farmer his sickle, the baker his loaf, and the tapster his bottle. All were off for the mines, some on horses, some on carts, and some on crutches; and one went in a litter.

The majority of the gold seekers were more disappointed than we can imagine, but some found unbelievable wealth. Considering the low wages of eastern workers, the miners generally made fair profits.

Have the class read some of the writings of Mark Twain and Bret Harte about life in the mining camps. In what ways did the California gold rush affect the westward movement?

Los Angeles County Museum

A hopeful miner pans for gold in California during the rush in 1850.

Vigilance committees. However, the people who remained in California had to live amid shocking lawlessness. Local government was simply not prepared to handle the large numbers of people who poured into the territory.

To meet the situation, groups known as *vigilance committees* organized for self-protection. The members, of course, were "taking the law into their own hands," and innocent people no doubt were often punished by excited and unruly vigilantes. But though they lasted for a long time, these committees gradually gave way to orderly self-government.

Effects Elsewhere

A chief result of the rush to the gold-fields was that California gained large numbers of permanent settlers. Some eighty thousand gold seekers arrived there in 1849 alone. The energetic miners set

#Note that the gold rush had many unanticipated effects.

up schools in their camps, and newspapers and theaters followed. In time the miners were replaced by less colorful yet necessary farmers and merchants, who continued the work of settling and developing California.

But California was not alone in being directly affected by the rush. All the other settled regions of the West were involved. #

Suppliers of food and clothing. Oregon, which for some years sold wheat to California, profited sufficiently to stand on its own feet. In 1859 Oregon was admitted to the Union as the thirty-third state.

The State of Deseret began to prosper, too, as a result of the gold rush. At first news of the discovery presented a challenge to Brigham Young—Mormons wanted to leave their colony and head for California. Because the Mormons lived at the halfway point on the way to California, they often sold—at prices far too high, it was said—goods needed by "gold rushers."

By providing food and clothing, the Mormons kept alive untold numbers of people on the way to the diggings. The Mormons also received many California-bound migrants into their church. Others stayed in the State of Deseret and helped found non-Mormon communities in Utah. The gold rush, in short, may have made possible the survival of the Mormon colony. In 1850 Deseret was organized as the Utah territory. (Utah did not become a state, though, until the century was almost ended.)

Background events. These momentous developments gave the map of the United States a new appearance and thrilled Americans to the core. As is the case in every era, however, hidden in the background were other major events that created little general excitement but would in time vitally affect people's lives.

We can note only a few. In 1844 government surveyors in the hills west of Lake Superior beheld for the first time the Mesabi Range—the greatest deposit of iron in the world. The same year, Samuel F. B.

at problems result from large-scale migrations of people? What happens to the inhabitants of area receiving a huge influx of new residents? Students might compare and contrast the move-t of people to California after 1848 with the movement there in the 1950's and 1960's.

385

Morse built the first practical telegraph line, stringing it from Baltimore to Washington, D.C.

Two years later announcement was made of the successful use of ether as an anesthetic—by a Massachusetts dentist, Dr. William T. G. Morton. The same year, the first baseball game we have record of was played at Hoboken, New Jersey, between two teams from New York, the Knickerbockers and the New Yorks. (The New Yorks won, 24 to 1.)

Most important, the leadership of the country was taking a new turn. You will recall that in 1810 the arrival of Clay, Calhoun, and others marked the beginning of a new generation of leaders. Now in the 1840's *that* generation was beginning to leave the scene, too.

End of an era. Nothing symbolized the passing of the older generation better than the death of John Quincy Adams in the House of Representatives. After his service as President, he had been elected in 1831 to the House of Representatives. There he served until 1848, seemingly in judgment of everything that Congress did. On February 21, 1848, Adams, in his eighty-first year, suddenly slumped in his chair in the House. Only two days later he moaned hi last words, "This is the last of earth. I am content."

Both houses of Congress immediatel adjourned. The front door of the Whit House was draped in black. The body la in state in the rotunda of the Capitol.

A military funeral was held, attended b the President, the Vice-President, member of the Cabinet, the Supreme Court, an Congress. President Polk wrote in his di ary, "It was a splendid pageant."

Polk could not know that Adams' funer al brought to a close an age, just as surel as a period ends a sentence. It would be a long, long time before the nation's politica leaders were again as united as they wer that February day when they bade farewel to "Old Man Eloquent."

1. Describe the discovery of gold in California. 2. By what two routes did the gold seekers go to California? 3. What benefits did the gold rush bring to Oregon and the State of Deseret? 4. Name four important nonpolitical events in the years 1844–1848.

The Workshop

The Shapers of Our World

Tell how each of the following contributed to filling out the area that made up the first forty-eight states.

Robert Gray
John Jacob
  Astor
Marcus Whitman
Oregon Trail
Donner party
Junípero Serra

Gadsden Purchase
John Tyler
Brigham Young
James K. Polk
Henry Clay
Bear Flag
  Republic

Thomas Larkin
John A. Sutter
Stephen Austin
Santa Anna
Sam Houston
Battle of
  San Jacinto
Rio Grande

Lone Star
  Republic
Zachary Taylor
Stephen W. Kearny
Winfield Scott
Treaty of
  Guadalupe Hidalgo

Adding to Your Vocabulary

Be sure you know the meaning of these terms:

Have students select persons listed in "The Shapers of Our World" and indicate what they think each person would have considered the most important thing he had ever done. Require students to justify their answers.

e Gila River Valley was one of few natural breaks in the western mountains. It was desired as a
ible route for a railroad to the Pacific coast.

nnexation   coöperative
ecognize   "dark horse"
esolution   acquiring
olygamy   vigilance

Thinking Things Through

After reviewing the boxed-in exercises n the chapter, answer these questions:

1. What was the main argument of the Mexican government against carrying out he treaty signed by Santa Anna at San acinto?

2. In what ways may Brigham Young nd Captain John Smith be compared? Compare the characteristics of the settlers f Deseret and Jamestown.

3. Why was Polk politically clever in he campaign of 1844 to call for the annexation of both Texas and Oregon?

4. Polk wanted the United States to increase in size. How does that explain his ittitude toward Mexico?

5. John Quincy Adams, Clay, and Webster had all passed from the stage of American history by 1852. What idea about the United States and its future also passed from the stage for a time with the death of these three men?

The Research Center

Use reference books to prepare reports on the following subjects:

1. Why did the United States pay ten million dollars for a small valley in 1853, when not long before it had paid only fifteen million dollars for all the land acquired in the Treaty of Guadalupe Hidalgo?

2. Present pictures or drawings of the several flags that have flown over Texas and California. Tell about the events connected with the various claims to the regions.

3. Four students should represent Serra,

Whitman, De Smet, and Young. Have each write a description of the physical features of the area where he did his missionary work. With what early colonists can the men be compared? How?

4. Present a discussion in the United States Senate of the Texas annexation. Be sure to include varying views of the proposal, such as those of the southern Democrats and the northern Whigs.

5. Report on the Donner expedition.

Sharpening Your Map Skills

1. Look at the map on page 370 and compare it with the one on pages 542–543. What present-day states are in the area owned by Mexico in 1845? What new state—once part of Mexico—had joined the Union in that year?

What parts of the country were settled by the people who traveled along the trails shown on the map on page 370? What large area did these people pass up?

2. Before 1959 it was correct to say that the United States had acquired by 1853 all the land making up its states. Look at the latest map of the country, on page 382, and explain why the statement is no longer true.

3. What was the highest-priced land that the United States had acquired by 1853? When was it turned into states? (Use the tables on pages 728 and 729.)

Your Opinion, Please

1. In Mexico today Americans sometimes meet people who still have ill feeling toward the United States because of the Mexican War. What would you say if someone expressed such feeling to you?

2. Mexico needed money in the 1840's. Why do you think it did not sell California to the United States at a good price?

ch of the gold-rush towns exist today? Discuss what factors enabled some mining towns to
ive and caused others to become ghost towns.

(a)

(b)

The Butcher.

(c)

(a) Harpers Ferry, the town on the Potomac Ri[ver] where John Brown tried to stir up a slave revolt. (b) A butcher in New York City sold meat in the 1840's at a little stand in a crowded street, where other merchants also sold food. (c) Young Abe Lincoln prepares himself to be a grown-up. (d) The bare little log cabin where Lincoln was born in 1809, the year Madison became President. (e) The stovepipe hat Lincoln often wore as President. (f) The title page of the first edition of *Uncle Tom's Cabin.*

(f)

(e)

(d)

UNCLE TOM'S CABIN;

OR,

LIFE AMONG THE LOW[LY]

BY

HARRIET BEECHER STOWE.

VOL. I.

BOSTON:
JOHN P. JEWETT & COMPAN[Y]
CLEVELAND, OHIO:
JEWETT, PROCTOR & WORTHINGTON.
1852.

(g) In the 1840's this baker made early-morning rounds in New York City in his cart, meeting his customers more than halfway

mpare the methods of marketing
ods shown here and on p. 388 with
se of present-day retailers.

(g)

CHAPTER 18

THE RISE OF ABRAHAM LINCOLN

1850 Clay, Calhoun, and Webster grappled once more with the problem of sectional compromise. But
ir "final settlement" was only temporary. The North and the South continued to drift apart, and the
w generation of political leaders--Lincoln, Douglas, Davis--had to face the slavery issue squarely.

Politics in the United States from 1848 on was greatly affected by the westward movement of people into the newly opened lands. Along with their personal belongings, men carried with them to their new homes their affection for particular political parties.

The two parties—the Whigs and the Democrats—were really loose organizations interested chiefly in local issues. But people developed loyalties to either the Whigs or the Democrats, and often they considered belonging to a certain party a matter of family pride.

y do national parties often avoid clean-cut stands on controversial issues?

The Parties Face the Slavery Issue

People belonging to the Whig party usually moved westward with the migrants from New England. Democrats, in general, flowed from Virginia in a southwesterly direction, through Missouri and into Texas. These transplanted people voted for their old parties in their new communities. As a result, voters in one part of the country felt closely tied to those in another.

Voters also were linked together by national issues on which special groups could agree. For example, the protective tariff was supported by iron manufac-

turers in Pennsylvania as well as by sugar planters in Louisiana. Moreover, businessmen or farmers in Massachusetts, for instance, usually favored the same solutions to problems as businessmen or farmers in, let us say, Illinois.

Sometimes public issues held together people of different groups. For instance, Jackson's attack on the Bank of the United States attracted the enthusiastic support of small businessmen everywhere in the country and of farmers in a great many regions.

certain parts of our country still considered predominantly Democratic or predominantly
ublican? What groups are believed to have definite party loyalties? Discuss some of the
sons why a person may regularly support one political party.

#Why did a well-known general seem a better candidate than a well-known politician? Note that the Whigs had also run a general in 1840.

Choices for President

The challenge to politicians was to unite as many of the various groups and interests in the country as possible. To do this, they had to find presidential candidates with wide appeal, which often meant men who had not taken clear stands on the major issues. It became more difficult to find such people as it became tougher and tougher to dodge the issues.

Until the 1840's northern and southern politicians had been able to make useful compromises with each other when they disagreed. We shall see now how compromise became increasingly difficult—and finally impossible.

A Whig general. The Mexican War had brought little glory to the Democrats. Both of the heroes of the fighting, Taylor and Scott, turned out to be Whigs. In 1848 the Whigs selected Taylor to lead them in the presidential campaign.

At first Taylor was unwilling to run, but he became convinced that Polk was out to damage his reputation, and he decided to accept the Whig offer. Many Whigs believed they had in "Old Rough and Ready" a hero who could do for them what Jackson had done for the Democrats.

The divided Democrats. The Democrats were not in agreement in 1848. One might have thought that the victory over Mexico with a Democratic President in the White House would have united the Democrats in addition to making them proud. But the process of arranging peace had resulted in stirring up the antislavery feeling of northern Democrats.

The trouble had begun on a very hot day in August, 1846. Representative David Wilmot, of Pennsylvania, had risen in the House of Representatives to propose what has ever since been remembered as the Wilmot Proviso. It stated simply that slavery was to be forever barred from the

Collection of I. S. Seidman, New York

The banner of the candidates who won the election in 1848. Notice the various appeals to the voters' patriotism.

territories that might be acquired from Mexico. The language Wilmot used was the same as that in the Northwest Ordinance of 1787. He appeared to be calling for a "Southwest Ordinance."

The response of southerners was immediate, for they had been struck at the heart. John C. Calhoun expressed his section's feelings: "The present scheme of the North is that the South shall do all the fighting and pay all the expenses, and they to have all the conquered territory." The storm signals were flying.

Although southern Democrats opposed the Wilmot Proviso, northern members of the Democratic party supported it. The Democrats were split so badly that they could not agree on a candidate for the presidency at the convention of 1848.

The Free-Soilers. An antislavery group of Democrats withdrew from the party and nominated former President Martin Van

##Note that in national politics the dispute was over the expansion of slavery, not over the existence of slavery in the South. Why did Calhoun nevertheless see the Wilmot Proviso as a threat to slavery itself?

Buren, who became the head of a party calling itself the Free-Soil party. The Free-Soilers stood against any extension of slavery into the territories or the admitting of any new slave states.

A Democratic general. The remaining Democrats finally nominated General Lewis Cass, of Michigan. Cass had seen service in the War of 1812. The son of a blacksmith, Cass never forgot the struggles of poor men, even when he became governor of the Michigan territory and then Secretary of War under Jackson.

Cass contributed an important idea to solving the problem of whether there should be slavery in the territories. He suggested that *popular sovereignty* was the only means of dealing with this tough issue. Popular sovereignty meant allowing the voters in a territory to decide if they wanted to be admitted to the Union as citizens of a free or a slave state.

Taylor in the White House. Taylor won the election by a good margin, bringing the Whig party back into the White House. His victory at the polls was helped by the fact that Van Buren took from Cass about three hundred thousand Democratic votes. The slavery question was beginning to decide the outcome of elections.

The new President, a little man who had such short legs that he had to be helped to mount a horse, chewed tobacco continually. Although other former soldiers had become chief executives, Taylor was the first regular-army man elected to the office.

Mrs. Taylor, an invalid, had not wanted her husband to run, feeling that as an army wife she had already done her fair share of moving about the country. When she finally joined him at the White House, she never appeared at public dinners or other occasions. Taylor appreciated the sacrifices she had made for his career. He once said to Jefferson Davis, his son-in-law, "You know my wife was as much of a soldier as I was."

The Compromise of 1850

Taylor's idea of dealing with the question of freedom or slavery in the new territories was straightforward. He prodded the people of California and New Mexico to ## apply for admission to the Union as states. It was clear that both would enter as free states.

Southerners were flabbergasted, especially because Taylor was one of their own. They did not realize that he was simply taking a national rather than a sectional view of things in telling the territories to seek statehood as soon as possible.

Tempers rose in the South. Southerners expected California and states made from the area called New Mexico to come into the Union as free states finally. But they were angry because Taylor was hurrying things too much. Southerners took the position that if California was admitted as a free state, the South deserved something in return.

California. California acted quickly on the President's suggestion. Its population was reaching 100,000, and it wished to join the Union as a free state. It chose and sent to Washington two Senators and two Representatives.

The bad feeling between the North and the South became keener. Southern legislatures passed resolutions threatening all kinds of serious steps if the North did not change its ways.

Many southerners were enraged because northerners, despite fugitive-slave laws, were protecting runaway slaves from recapture. People of the South had already become very angry because many northerners were ready to accept the Wilmot Proviso. These northerners were even calling for the end of the slave trade in the District of Columbia. The buying and selling of slaves near the Capitol had long been a disgraceful sight.

California and Texas are the only two states (except for the original thirteen) to have entered the Union without first passing through the territorial stage. Emphasize that the admission of California as a free state upset the balance in the Senate between free and slave states.

Anger in Congress. When Congress gathered in December, 1849, tempers on both sides were boiling. Southerners were vowing to protect their "peculiar institution" everywhere the flag flew. This meant that they wanted to be able to take their slaves into the territories if they chose to. They had decided to maintain the balance in the Senate by keeping California out of the Union if necessary. They knew, also, that to do so might mean closing the door to the gold of California and to its rich trade.

The disagreement between northerners and southerners was so great that it seemed impossible even to elect a Speaker of the House of Representatives. Sixty-three ballots were required before agreement was reached. By that time it can be said that the members had only worn themselves out—they had not ironed out their differences.

The view of the chief executive. Taylor, himself a slaveholder, gradually became convinced that the southerners were to blame for the very serious difficulties. Upon learning that southern leaders wanted to spread slavery by moving the boundary of Texas west at the expense of New Mexico, he acted. He sent troops to guard the Texas–New Mexico border.

A group of southern Whigs told the President they believed that army officers would not fire on citizens of Texas. Taylor replied that in such a case he himself would take command of the army. If he found men in rebellion against the Union, he would hang them with less hesitation than he had hung "deserters and spies in Mexico"! Such language reminded Americans of Jackson during the nullification crisis.

Three old Senators. The strained scene now shifted to the Senate. The men who had been there since the 1830's were together for the last time. Because of the silver-tongued oratory they provided, their years in the Senate have been referred to as America's Silver Age.

Henry Clay, of Kentucky, seventy-three years old, had been elected to the Senate again after several years away from Washington. He probably had made up his mind that he was not going to be President after all. (When he had learned of his defeat in 1844, he and Mrs. Clay, desperately disappointed, had wept in each other's arms.)

Clay was so ill that he had to be aided in walking up the steps of the Capitol. Yet the old war hawk of 1812 wanted to make one more stab at saving the Union. "I implore . . ." he said, "that if the . . . sad event of the dissolution [breakup] of the Union shall happen, I may not survive to behold the sad and heart-rending spectacle."

John C. Calhoun, of South Carolina, was also still in the Senate. Sixty-eight years old, he was racked by tuberculosis, and he coughed constantly. His hair, once bushy and brown, now hung gray and stringy over his forehead. His eyes still gleamed from sunken sockets, though the face was very thin.

The third of the giants in the Senate was Daniel Webster, of Massachusetts, also sixty-eight years old. He was not as skillful in managing legislation as Clay or as convincing a leader as Calhoun. But no one could match his splendid gifts as a public speaker. Once he had been so handsome and commanding in appearance that he had won the nickname "the god-like Daniel." Now he was also ill, suffering from being unable to sleep, and he was taking a good deal of medicine.

Some younger men. In addition, newcomers to the Senate were on hand, forming their own views. One of them was Stephen A. Douglas, of Illinois. A small man, only 5 feet 4 inches tall, he was already known as the Little Giant. He had a strong face, out of which looked piercing deep-blue—almost violet-colored—eyes. He made such an impression that he was

#Bear in mind that Clay and Webster were strong nationalists and intensely devoted to preserving the Union in the face of sectional conflict. Recall previous sectional compromises in which Clay had a hand.

called in a compliment "a steam-engine in britches."

Another of the powerful men present was William H. Seward, of New York. Forty-eight years old, he still looked boyish. His hair was straw-colored now, but once it had been red. His nose was huge, like an eagle's beak, and it made his chin seem even smaller than it was.

When Seward spoke, he read from a prepared manuscript—in an age when most successful politicians talked from notes. Seward was using to good advantage the spreading public habit of regularly reading newspapers. His words were not meant merely for Senators' ears—they were meant to be *read* throughout the country.

Clay at work again. The man who became the miracle worker for the cause of the Union was Henry Clay. Taylor and many other Whigs did not trust him because they thought he had only returned to the Senate in order to make another bid for the presidency. He had to act with all the cleverness he had developed over many years as a legislator and a compromiser.

In arranging a compromise this time, Clay faced the fact that there was no new slave state to offer to the South to balance the free state of California. But he knew southerners would be willing to accept a vow that their property would be protected.

The proposals. What Clay accomplished has come to be known as the Compromise of 1850. It began as three Congressional bills. One would admit California as a free state and allow the territories of New Mexico and Utah to decide for themselves whether they would become free states or slave states.

The Senate chamber as it looked about the time the Compromise of 1850, which Clay had proposed, was being debated.

New York Historical Society

##In John F. Kennedy's <u>Profiles in Courage</u> (Harper & Row, 1961), students will find an account of the crisis Webster faced in deciding to support the Compromise of 1850.

A second bill would adjust the boundary line between Texas and New Mexico. Although Texas would be made smaller, its state debt would be paid by the federal government. The third bill would abolish the slave trade in the District of Columbia.

\#　The set of proposals did not have smooth sailing. President Taylor was against it. Why should he agree to a deal to bring California into the Union? Anyone who was against California's admission without conditions, he said, was a traitor.

Calhoun was opposed to the compromise, because, he thought, the South had already given up enough to northerners. "If the South is to be saved," he wrote, "now is the time."

The debate on the bills was dramatic. Clay, Calhoun, and Webster were about to cross swords for the last time. Their political differences had become personal differences, too. Once after Calhoun's twenty-year-old niece was greeted affectionately by Henry Clay, she rushed off with evident joy to tell her uncle. "Oh," she burst out, "I have been kissed by the great Mr. Clay!" "Amelia," warned Calhoun, "don't you put your trust in that old man."

When Clay presented his proposals, he showed that he had lost little of his magical powers as a speaker. He had come, he said, to plead for the Union. His plan, he insisted, was reasonable. Only unreasonable men would refuse to accept it.

Calhoun's last stand. Calhoun's turn was next. He was now so ill that he looked like "a fugitive from the grave." Wrapped in a heavy cloak, he glared at his fellow Senators. When his turn to speak came, he was too weak to perform. A member from Virginia read his words to the hushed Senate and galleries, which were completely filled.

He, too, loved the Union, Calhoun said, but northerners were destroying it by continually stirring up the slavery question. They must now stop. If they would not, he said, it was time for the South to "part in peace." Calhoun returned to his boardinghouse, his body worn-out, his mind excited by the knowledge that the speech had made a deep impression.

The Seventh of March Speech. On March 7, 1850, Webster's hour came. Not many in the Senate audience knew that on the previous day Webster had called on Calhoun. Webster had no doubt greeted his old friend with the gay words he had often spoken to him: "How do the men of '82 stand on their pins?" (He had been referring to the fact that both of them were born in 1782.)

Calhoun was desperately ill. He had wanted to be present to hear Webster, but he was too near death ever to appear in the Senate again.

Webster's plea—always known afterward as the Seventh of March Speech—was for compromise, something Calhoun had turned down. Webster began with words which generations of students would memorize and remember all their lives: "I wish to speak today, not as a Massachusetts man, nor as a Northern man, but as an American, and a member of the Senate of the United States. . . . I speak today for the preservation of the Union. 'Hear me for my cause.'"

Two deaths. Webster's arguments were convincing, but he could not influence enough Senators to take his side—for compromise. The deadlock seemed unbreakable. Just then, death took the strongest opponents from the scene, and things changed remarkably. Calhoun was gone by the end of March, 1850. President Taylor died in July.

Taylor's passing was the result of an illness that seems to have begun after he returned home from long Independence Day ceremonies. His funeral was a military display. It was said that all eyes were on Old Whitey, the faithful horse that had carried Taylor safely through the Mexican War.

\#Analyze Clay's compromise proposals. What did they offer the North? How was the South supposed to gain? Compare Clay's attempt to get each side to yield something with Calhoun's view that the South had already yielded too much.

Webster—standing at the
right—speaks in the
Senate on March 7, 1850.
Vice-President Fillmore
—framed between the
draperies—presides.
Though Calhoun was not
there, the artist
showed him—fourth man
from the left, second
row—listening angrily.

Trustees of Dartmouth College
(Hopkins Center Art Galleries)

With the help of Fillmore. Millard Fillmore, of New York, the Vice-President, became the new President. He had no military glamour and little of the fighter in him. Fillmore quickly put himself on the side of Webster and Clay. By now Clay was completely exhausted, and the leadership of the fight for compromise fell to Douglas.

Finally enough votes were obtained to pass the series of bills. The Union was saved. What made the Compromise of 1850 a compromise was that northerners gave up the idea that slavery definitely would *not* go into the new territories. Southerners gave up their idea that slavery could go *everywhere*.

The arrangement. As finally passed, the Compromise of 1850 was chiefly what Clay had proposed the previous January. California was admitted as a free state. States from the territories of New Mexico and Utah were to be admitted as slave or free states according to the wishes of their people. Texas was paid $10,000,000, and its boundary was fixed where it is today. Slave trading in the District of Columbia

was ended forever. A stricter fugitive-slave act replaced an older law. #

In general, the public was not enthusiastic about the Compromise of 1850, but it was relieved. The firebrands in both the North and the South thought it was a "surrender." In Massachusetts, when Webster resigned from the Senate to join Fillmore's Cabinet as Secretary of State, many were very pleased. His successor was Charles Sumner, whom we shall shortly meet again. Sumner was against the Compromise of 1850.

1. What was the Wilmot Proviso? How did the South regard it? 2. Name three presidential candidates in 1848, and tell to what party each belonged. 3. Who was elected President? 4. Identify five important United States Senators in 1850, and tell what state each represented. 5. What was the occasion of Webster's Seventh of March Speech? 6. State the provisions of the Compromise of 1850.

The stricter fugitive-slave law put the power of the federal government on the side of those king the return of runaway slaves. To many northerners the law seemed to force the North help the South maintain slavery.

#Was it realistic to suppose that the Compromise of 1850 was the "final settlement" of the slavery questio
Which groups, North and South, refused to compromise? Did compromise settle or merely put off for a
time the slavery problem?

The "Final Settlement" Is Reopened

Large numbers of Americans both in the North and in the South felt that there would be no more trouble over whether territory would be slave or free. The matter had been settled once and for all. Senator Douglas pledged himself "never to make another speech on the slavery question." President Fillmore held the opinion that the compromise was "a final settlement" of the problem.

The Kansas-Nebraska Bill

The presidential campaign of 1852 showed the effect of the Compromise of 1850 on American politics. The politicians tried hard not to reopen the wounds just closed. When the Democrats met in their nominating convention, they were unable to agree on any of the famous men in the party. They chose instead a "dark horse" candidate, as they had eight years earlier. Their man was Franklin Pierce, of New Hampshire. Their slogan was "We Polked 'em in '44; we'll Pierce 'em in '52."

The Whigs once again chose as their candidate a military hero, naming this time General Winfield Scott, of Virginia. Many southerners shied away from Scott because he was friendly with Senator Seward and because he had failed to lend his support to the Compromise of 1850.

Pierce was very acceptable to southerners. Indeed, many northerners called him a "doughface," a term of that day meaning a northern man with a southern point of view.

The ordinary Pierce. Pierce, unfortunately a man who did not have very much natural ability as a leader and who often drank too much, was easily elected. His inauguration was for him a sad occasion as well as a political triumph. A few weeks earlier, he and Mrs. Pierce had had the horrifying experience of seeing their eleven-year-old son killed in a railroad accident before their very eyes.

Mrs. Pierce, the daughter of a former president of Bowdoin College, in Maine, did not attend the oath-taking ceremony. Besides being grief-stricken, she hated Washington and had long wished that her husband would leave public life.

Pierce was a graduate of Bowdoin. While enrolled there, he met a fellow student, Nathaniel Hawthorne, who later became a famous writer. As long as they both lived, Pierce and Hawthorne remained close friends. In 1852 Pierce's campaign biography, which introduced him to the public as a presidential candidate, was written by Hawthorne.

The meddling of Douglas. Pierce was not able to deal with the storm that broke before his administration was over. This storm was the result of the ambitions of the Democrat Stephen A. Douglas. The "Little Giant" had recently promised never to talk again on the subject of slavery in the territories. Yet he not only spoke on it, but he also stirred up a hornet's nest of trouble concerning it. The storm he began did not end until slavery had been destroyed altogether.

Douglas, who hoped one day to be President, favored neither barring slavery from the territories, which many northerners wanted, nor protecting it everywhere, something many southerners wanted. He supported the principle that when each territory was ready to become a state, it should vote for a constitution in favor of slavery or for one against it. According to the Compromise of 1850, this was what

396 Review the proposals for solving the problem of allowing slavery in the territories: (1) the view
that slaves should be regarded as property, (2) the Wilmot Proviso, (3) extension of the 36° 30'
line, (4) popular sovereignty. Which was favored by those who opposed the spread of slavery?

states made from the territories of Utah and New Mexico were to do.

Popular sovereignty. In 1854 Douglas, who was then serving as chairman of the Senate Committee on Territories, was anxious to see the lands west of Missouri and Iowa organized. That is, he wanted them opened to settlement. Look at the map on page 382 and you will see that this area was not included in the territories acquired from Mexico. It had been a part of the Louisiana Purchase. Douglas proposed settlement on the basis of popular sovereignty (see page 391).

Americans everywhere gasped. They thought that the Missouri Compromise had already settled the fate of slavery north of the line 36°30′ (see pages 311–312)—by barring it.

The pull of ambition. What was Douglas up to? It was said that he never drew a breath without imagining himself in the White House one day. He hoped, it now appeared, to gain support in the South for his presidential candidacy by appearing to open to slavery land long closed to it.

"If the people want slavery," Douglas declared, "they have a right to it, and if they do not, it should not be forced on them. The determination as to whether a new state shall be slave or free depends not upon the north or south, but upon the people themselves."

Douglas no doubt had other reasons for introducing the Kansas-Nebraska bill. He apparently hoped that when a transcontinental railroad was built, Chicago, in his home state, would be the city at its eastern end. For this to be accomplished, the Indians on the Great Plains would have

Pierce—in a top hat—rides to his inauguration at the Capitol in Washington on March 4, 1853, where he delivered an inaugural address he had painstakingly learned by heart.

"Illustrated News," March 12, 1853 (Franklin Pierce House, Concord, New Hampshire)

to be pushed aside. They could be moved only if the territory was settled.

The passage of the Kansas-Nebraska bill in 1854, as you can see on the map on this page, made it possible for slavery to enter the Kansas and Nebraska territories. These included what are now Kansas, Nebraska, Montana, the Dakotas, and parts of Colorado and Wyoming. Douglas was confident that settlers there would never vote for slavery. He would be able, therefore, to say to the people of the North that his proposal had not harmed the cause of freedom.

A howl of criticism. But Douglas misunderstood badly the attitude of northerners. They were not willing to let time prove him right—as, no doubt, it would

have. Douglas failed to foresee what would happen after the bill passed in 1854. He thought that, following its passage, the slavery issue would die down again. On the other hand, it was livelier than ever.

Throughout the North there were meetings at which Douglas was sharply criticized. In so many places was a dummy representing Douglas burned that he himself said he could have traveled from Boston to Chicago by the light of the fires.

The rise of the Republicans. Many of the people against the Kansas-Nebraska Act now formed their own political groups. In the beginning, they called themselves simply Anti-Nebraska Democrats. Then some of them began to call themselves Republicans in honor of the party of Jefferson,

Left: A statuette of Stephen A. Douglas, author of the Kansas-Nebraska Act. *Right:* How long had the United States owned the land affected by the law? In the 1820's eastern Indians had been moved there because it was considered worthless. Now they would be moved again.

Illinois State Museum

Kansas and Nebraska Territories, 1854

0   100   200   300 miles

The Republican party began as a kind of third party and in a short time grew into one of the two major political parties. Why was it able to do so?

Jackson, Michigan, was one of the places where people met in 1854 to form a new political party, a privilege of democracy.

Republican National Committee

who, you will remember, had helped ban slavery in the Northwest Territory.

The new Republican party, which was formed at meetings in Ripon, Wisconsin, and elsewhere in the old Northwest, grew rapidly in numbers and strength. It absorbed thousands of northern Whigs, whose own party had died out because it could no longer appeal successfully in both North and South. The Republicans also attracted Free-Soilers, who wanted to join their strength to a larger organization. It drew antislavery Democrats who were disgusted with Douglas.

Bleeding Kansas

Meanwhile, Kansas itself became the center of national attention. Both the free-soil (that is, antislavery) supporters and the slavery supporters were determined to win Kansas territory for their side. This meant making certain that the "right people" moved into it.

In the East a Massachusetts organization began looking for "colonists" for Kansas whose opinions would be antislavery. In various parts of the South a similar movement was under way to find "colonists" who would be for slavery.

Rival governments. The first elections held in Kansas territory did not indicate that most of the settlers were—as Douglas had thought—antislavery. The reason was that when elections were held, hundreds of proslavery Missourians swarmed over the border into Kansas and cast ballots. As a result, Kansas had a proslavery delegate to Congress and a proslavery territorial legislature. Outraged, the antislavery settlers of Kansas elected their own legislature and their own governor.

President Pierce was weak and did nothing to end what was clearly a civil war in Kansas. He enraged abolitionists when he personally assisted in the return of a slave, Anthony Burns, from Boston to Virginia.

The attack on Lawrence. The conflict in Kansas became a bloody one. In May, 1856, a band of Missourians known as Border Ruffians sacked the free-soil town of Lawrence, destroying its printing press and terrorizing the people. A favorite boast of any "Border Ruffian" was that he could "scream louder, jump higher, shoot closer, get drunker at night and wake up soberer in the morning than any man this side of the Rocky Mountains."

John Brown's acts. A violent abolitionist named John Brown determined to seek revenge. The father of twenty children, in 1855 he gave up even trying to support his

Kansas became the testing ground for the concept of popular sovereignty. Voting alone did not settle sectional differences. Why is it often difficult to hold fair and meaningful elections in areas that are newly organized and settled?

family, devoting his time to battling slavery. In 1856 he and his sons descended upon Pottawatomie Creek in Kansas, raided there a tiny proslavery settlement of four families, and killed five people in cold blood. Brown's explanation was that the murders had been "decreed by Almighty God, ordained from eternity."

The proslavery people, up in arms, then seized Brown and his band and beat them. Next they turned on the Browns' hometown of Osawatomie, proposing to wipe it off the map. The raiders numbered about 250, whereas there were 40 townspeople in Osawatomie. In the skirmish that followed, there were casualties on both sides and the town was burned.

A caning in the Senate. "Bleeding Kansas," as that unhappy territory came to be called, was a center of national attention. The mounting fury led indirectly to a shameful occurrence in the Senate. There in May, 1856, Senator Charles Sumner delivered a speech which was an insulting attack on Douglas, on South Carolina, and on one of South Carolina's Senators, Andrew Pickens Butler, who was absent at the time.

Two days later Butler's nephew, Representative Preston S. Brooks, strode into the Senate chamber, found Sumner at his seat, and beat him unconscious with a cane. Brooks immediately became a hero to many southerners. Thoughtful people in both North and South wondered if there was not some way to bring an end to the spreading violence.

Other political effects. But the stormy events in Kansas were having an even more upsetting effect on politics. Nothing showed this better than the election of 1856.

That year the Republicans chose a presidential candidate who made a good showing at the ballot box. Considering the fact that the party had only recently been founded, this was remarkable. It can be

explained by the rapid spread in the North of the idea that there must be *no further spread of slavery.*

The Republicans made the principle of opposing the spread of slavery the main purpose of their party. They had other important planks in their platform, including a call for the construction of a transcontinental railroad and for federal aid for other internal improvements.

The Republicans had a program which appealed to farmers, workingmen, some businessmen, and some immigrants. But the plea for the non-extension of slavery was the one which tied together all the various members of the party.

The "Pathfinder of the West." The candidate of the Republicans was John C. Frémont, the "Pathfinder of the West." His geographical discoveries had made him the best-known American of the day abroad, and he was a hero to millions of people in this country.

The bachelor Buchanan. The Democrats once again looked for—and found—a man who, by straddling on the slavery issue, could win votes in both the North and the South. In short, they ran another "doughface" like Pierce. He was James Buchanan, of Pennsylvania. Buchanan defeated Frémont easily, despite the Republicans' catchy slogan "Free soil, Free men, Frémont and victory."

Buchanan was a perfect symbol of his party. He looked vigorous and strong but was in fact ailing and weak. His eyes were of different colors—one blue, one hazel—and he squinted. To cover scars on his neck, which were a result of surgery, he wore a high white collar. He also wore a long black dress coat, to which he had grown accustomed during his service as United States minister to England.

Buchanan was a formal man, and there were few who called him by his given name. Even his niece, Harriet Lane, who faithfully served as his First Lady because

#The rapid growth of the Republican party showed the increased opposition to the extension of slavery. How did the Republican platform depart from the old idea that to have national appeal political parties should straddle the fence on controversial issues?

he was a bachelor, always addressed him as "Mr. Buchanan" in public. Buchanan suffered from heart trouble, although the fact was not widely known. In the nineteenth century matters like the President's health were not discussed in the press as they are today.

Buchanan's inaugural address on March 4, 1857, provided a tip-off on his policies. He expressed the hope that the slavery question would soon cease to keep the nation stirred up. He knew that the United States Supreme Court was about to decide an important case. Although he did not say so, he was aware of what the decision was going to be.

The Dred Scott case. Two days after Buchanan's inauguration in 1857, the Supreme Court decision came. It grew out of the situation of Dred Scott, a slave. These are the facts in the case: Scott, born in Missouri, was taken by his owner to the state of Illinois and then into what became Minnesota. When Scott was taken back to Missouri, he claimed his freedom on the ground that his residence in free territory (the old Northwest) had made him free.

The first court to hear the case was in Missouri. It upheld Dred Scott, saying that he was entitled to his freedom. The Missouri supreme court, to which the case was then taken, overruled the lower court's decision. The case then went to the United States Supreme Court.

The Supreme Court justices decided against Scott by a vote of 6 to 3. Chief Justice Roger B. Taney (tô′nĭ) wrote an opinion in which he said that Negroes were not citizens of the United States. Taney also said that Dred Scott was not a citizen of Missouri and had no right to bring a suit in its courts.

Furthermore, the Chief Justice went on, the federal government cannot take property—in this case, a slave—from a citizen "without due process of law." (This expression means "without proceedings in court.") Therefore, Taney said, the Missouri Compromise, which did this, was unconstitutional and void—even though it had been the law of the land for thirty-seven years. ##

The immediate effect of the Dred Scott decision was to strike a blow at the developing Republican party. If slavery could go anywhere slave owners wanted it to go, then the chief Republican plank—no further extension of slavery—was meaning-

#Why did Taney go beyond the decision in Scott's case to declare the Missouri Compromise unconstitutional? The case could have ended without the added opinion.)

A poster that appeared in Philadelphia after the Dred Scott decision, advertising a meeting of protest called by abolitionists.

Lincoln University Library

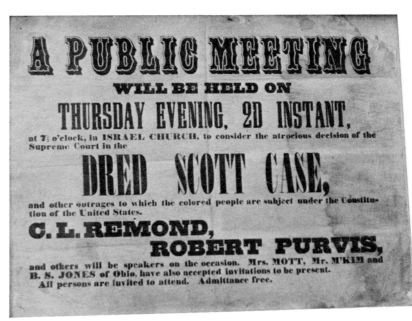

A gathering of antislavery men in Topeka, Kansas, in 1855. Notice the guns. Even before the proslavery people had drawn up their constitution, these individuals had acted to make Kansas free—but without success.

less. The Republican party might just as well disband.

Popular sovereignty in operation. What would happen to the idea of popular sovereignty if it was brought before the Supreme Court? No one, of course, could say. Kansans were still fighting over popular sovereignty. Buchanan took a hand in trying to bring peace to Kansas by getting people to hold a convention to write a state constitution. The free-soil men, however, refused to take part in the elections to such a convention. They said that the proslavery forces had rigged them.

As a result, the proslavery people drew up a constitution which would make Kansas a slave state. The free-soil people at once called it a fraud.

A year later, in 1858, the governor of the Kansas territory called for the election of a territorial legislature. The governor, a Mississippian, tried hard to see that the voting was honest. The result was a victory for the free-soil group. The free-soil legislature promptly turned down the state constitution written by the proslavery people.

You can see what the struggle in Kansas was doing to the principle of popular sovereignty. It was making a joke of it. Clearly the majority of the Kansans were anti-slavery. Senator Douglas had no choice except to speak out against the proslavery constitution.

The Senator against the President. The "Little Giant," a widower, had recently married Adele Cutts, a grandniece of Dolley Madison. This marriage brought him important family connections. When his home became a center of Washington's social and political life, his hopes for the presidency rose. Yet the path to the White House was not easy—it never is. President Buchanan had decided to present the pro-slave Kansas constitution to Congress in order to bring Kansas into the Union as a slave state.

Douglas became frantic. The fact that popular sovereignty had not worked would be clear to everyone.

To save himself from defeat at the hands of the voters of Illinois, Douglas had to criticize Buchanan and battle against the proslavery constitution on the floor of the Senate. There is an old rule in American politics: no politician can further his career by attacking a President who belongs to his own party. Douglas was putting that rule to the test.

The Illinois Senator presented his views to the President directly, in the White

#To what extent should a President command the loyalty of members of his own party? Should disputes within a party be carried on in public or in private? Why did the break between Buchanan and Douglas become public?

House. Their conversation began without harsh words, but gradually it became more heated. Buchanan explained why he was going to support the proslavery constitution, and Douglas explained why he thought Buchanan must turn it down.

When the furious Douglas told Buchanan that he would publicly oppose him, the President stood up and uttered a harsh warning. He said, "Mr. Douglas, I desire you to remember that no Democrat ever yet differed from an Administration of his own choice without being crushed. Beware of the fate of Tallmadge and Rives." (Years before, Jackson had brought to an end the careers of these men, who had opposed him.) "Mr. President," said Douglas, stomping from the office, "I wish you to remember that General Jackson is dead!"

In the Senate Douglas opposed the Kansas constitution with all his might. But he could not persuade enough of his fellow Senators to follow him. Finally a compromise was arranged in the House of Representatives which provided for submitting the constitution again to the voters of Kansas—who voted it down.

The price. Douglas paid a high price for his stand. The Democratic newspapers turned on him. So did many of his friends. Of course, the Republicans would not accept him, either. They could not honor the man who had introduced the Kansas-Nebraska bill.

Republicans were, in effect, reminding Douglas of another old rule of politics: a man who breaks with his own party does not win favor with the opposition. Douglas, who hoped to unite the Democrats and make himself President, found himself the symbol of a terrible break in their ranks.

---

1. Name and describe the two presidential candidates in 1852, identify each one's party, and tell who won the election. 2. Who proposed the Kansas-Nebraska bill? What did it contain? 3. What effects did the passage of the bill have in the North? 4. Describe events in the Kansas territory following the Kansas-Nebraska Act. 5. State the main purpose of the new Republican party. 6. Describe the man who became President in 1856. 7. Give the main facts in the Dred Scott case. 8. What difficulty developed between Douglas and the President?

The Union Splits at the Sectional Seams

Douglas had to run for reelection to the Senate in 1858. The Democrats of Illinois were pleased to have such a strong candidate. The Republicans found a Senatorial candidate too. He was a tall, gangling lawyer named Abraham Lincoln, who practiced in Springfield, Illinois.

A Race for the Senate

Then forty-nine years old, Lincoln was a likable and ambitious politician. People who knew him—and he had made friends throughout the state—enjoyed his warm humor (he was a born storyteller.) His physical strength was enormous, and his shrewd judgment commanded respect.

An unsuccessful politician. So far Lincoln's success as a vote getter had been limited. From 1847 to 1849 (see page 379) he had served in Congress—without making a name for himself.

Lincoln had been losing interest in politics when the repeal of the Missouri Compromise aroused him again. It enabled him to pull together in his mind his experi-

ow did Douglas' hopes for the presidency depend on the outcome of his race for the Senate 1858? Why are local victories very important to a politician who hopes to become President? at is the connection between local and national politics?

403

ences to form an idea of how the slavery issue ought to be dealt with.

Lincoln owed much to his two heroes, Thomas Jefferson and Henry Clay. Of Jefferson's work he said, "I have never had a feeling politically that did not spring from the sentiments of the Declaration of Independence." Lincoln admired Clay chiefly for his skill at compromise.

Position on slavery. Having learned lessons from the careers of Jefferson and Clay, Lincoln came to his point of view on the slavery issue. He understood well that keeping fellow human beings in bondage is a terrible wrong, because "all men are created equal." But he was also aware that only in the territories would it be possible to prevent the growth of slavery. Therefore he did not concern himself with slavery where it already existed. However, he felt strongly that it must not be allowed to spread into new areas which shortly would be entering the Union.

When Douglas heard that Lincoln had been nominated as his opponent, he declared, "I shall have my hands full. He is the strong man of his party—full of wit, facts, dates—and the best stump speaker, with his droll ways and dry jokes, in the West."

"A house divided...." In accepting his nomination, Lincoln made his position clear. Many thought his words were foolish or that the country was not yet ready to hear them. He said, "'A house divided against itself cannot stand.' I believe this government cannot endure permanently half slave and half free. . . . It will become all one thing, or all the other." Years later

\# Lincoln said he was prouder of these words than of any others he ever spoke.

Douglas' belief. Douglas belittled the idea that the country could not continue to live half free and half slave, as it had since 1775. "I go," said Douglas, "for the principle of the Kansas-Nebraska bill, the right of the people to decide for themselves."

Lincoln and Douglas represented in their views the two differing opinions most frequently expressed by northerners.

The nation followed the Senatorial campaign in Illinois attentively, because Douglas was one of the most famous politicians of the day. Douglas rode about the state in a private railroad coach. (Sometimes Lincoln was an ordinary passenger riding on the same train that pulled Douglas' car.)

Public debates. Lincoln had to put himself in the public eye if he wished to defeat the "Little Giant." He therefore challenged his opponent to a series of debates. Douglas accepted the challenge.

The debates—seven in all—were held over a period of months from the late summer of 1858 into the fall. They were part of one of the most fateful Senatorial campaigns in American history.

Questions and answers at Freeport. A high point was the debate at Freeport, Illinois. There Lincoln called attention to what he thought was a contradiction in Douglas' support of both popular sovereignty and the Dred Scott decision. Standing before fifteen thousand people, Lincoln asked Douglas what appeared to be a very difficult question: If slave owners can take their slaves everywhere, even into free territory, how can people have a chance to vote slavery up or down?

Douglas did not hesitate in his answer. Despite the Dred Scott decision, he said, slavery could not exist a minute in a given area unless the local people wanted it and were willing to protect it.

The outcome. When the "Little Giant" won reelection, many believed his seemingly clever answer at Freeport had turned the trick. But his words had violently angered southerners, who had been encouraged to think that under the Dred Scott decision they could carry slavery everywhere. Douglas' chances of winning the support of the South for the Democratic nomination in 1860 had been seriously hurt.

"McClure's Magazine," Oct., 1896 (Illinois State Historical Library)

The fifth Lincoln-Douglas debate, being held at Knox College, Galesburg, Illinois. In their series of debates, the Senator and his challenger covered the state.

The Election of 1860

During the campaign of 1858, when Lincoln had been asked how he thought he was going to fare, he had replied: "You can't overturn a pyramid; but you can undermine it; that's what I've been trying to do." He had badly damaged Douglas' political future.

Democratic-party handicaps. In the next two years the fact that the Democrats could not lead the country became clear. Everyone could see that Buchanan lacked the imagination and energy to be a good President. Further, Douglas, the other important man in the party, no longer appealed to its southern members.

The depression of 1857, moreover, had been particularly bad for the iron industry of Pennsylvania, whose spokesmen sought a higher tariff as a remedy. Buchanan, himself a Pennsylvanian, proved to be unresponsive. This made many northerners say that the President was simply a puppet of southerners, who did not want to raise the tariff.

Southerners also were beginning to feel desperately that more and more they had to defend themselves. In defiance of the Fugitive Slave Law, northerners were protecting runaway slaves. What made things worse was that slave owners, despite their complaints, knew that slavery was wrong.

Uncle Tom's Cabin. Furthermore, a number of books were serving to make slavery a real—and terrible—thing, even for the millions who were not interested in national politics. The most famous book of all was *Uncle Tom's Cabin,* which had appeared in 1852. Its author was Harriet Beecher Stowe, the daughter of one of the best-known antislavery preachers in New York.

When Mrs. Stowe began her novel, she had had very little experience as a writer and was almost entirely without firsthand knowledge of slavery. But she had a powerful urge to write, and her hatred of slavery was fierce. Her success lay in her ability to draw memorable characters and to tell a heartrending tale. Somehow she managed to produce an unforgettable story.

Before the end of 1852, about 300,000 copies of the book had been sold, and the great printing presses were running day and night to keep up with the demand. Within a short time *Uncle Tom's Cabin* was translated into many of the other languages of the world. As a play it was seen by millions, who wept over Uncle Tom's sad fate and about Little Eva and Topsy.

The spreading popularity of *Uncle Tom's Cabin* came at a time when there was a growing fear of a slave rebellion in the South. Southerners had never forgotten Nat Turner's deeds (see page 357). In

hat were the weaknesses of the Democratic party as it approached the election of 1860? Why
the party try to avoid a clear-cut stand on the question of slavery? Would popular sovereignty
ve been acceptable to party members?

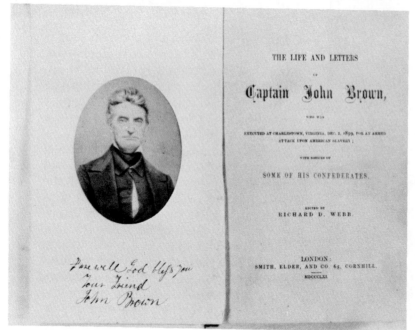

THE LIFE AND LETTERS
OF

Captain John Brown,

WHO WAS

EXECUTED AT CHARLESTOWN, VIRGINIA, DEC. 2, 1859, FOR AN ARMED
ATTACK UPON AMERICAN SLAVERY;

WITH NOTICES OF

SOME OF HIS CONFEDERATES.

EDITED BY

RICHARD D. WEBB.

LONDON:
SMITH, ELDER, AND CO. 65, CORNHILL.
MDCCCLXI.

Fare well God bless you
our friend
John Brown

The frontispiece and title page of a book about John Brown and some of his friends. What is the date of publication?

1856 slave unrest seemed to be particularly noticeable, and the talk of uprisings was widespread.

The raid at Harpers Ferry. In such inflamed circumstances, which appeared to continue on and off for several years, John Brown in 1859 made a new move. He had been making plans to do more than merely fight slavery in Kansas. Now he wanted to attack it in one of its strongholds: Virginia.

Brown planned to attack the federal arsenal at Harpers Ferry, Virginia. He aimed to obtain weapons with which to arm the slaves. After a long period of preparation, on October 16, 1859, he struck.

Quickly Brown captured the arsenal and a rifle factory nearby. Some of his men moved out into the countryside to seize slave owners as hostages. One of them was Colonel Lewis Washington, great-grand-nephew of George Washington. Brown knew that the colonel owned a dress sword that the first President was supposed to have received from the Prussian king, Frederick the Great. Brown put on the sword the day he captured the colonel.

Bloodshed. But Brown and his band overreached themselves. Shots were fired, the people of Harpers Ferry began to organize, and, most important, marines under Colonel Robert E. Lee arrived from Washington. Ten raiders died in the struggle (including two of Brown's sons), and four Harpers Ferry men and one marine lost their lives. In the end Brown was captured in a fire-engine house where he had held out until it was impossible for him to resist any longer.

John Brown was tried, declared guilty of treason and murder, and hanged on December 2. His last words to his executioner were "Be quick!" Some thought he was disposed of with indecent haste—although his crime was, of course, very serious.

Brown had looked forward to becoming a martyr. He wanted no prayers to be said at his funeral. Rather, he asked that "my only religious attendants be poor little, dirty, ragged, bareheaded and barefooted Slave boys and girls led by some grayheaded Slave Mother."

Contrary judgments. The North made Brown, a man whose miserable life was at

How did Uncle Tom's Cabin and John Brown's raid focus national attention on the dispute between the North and the South? Why were southerners outraged by them even though they had no proof that most northerners agreed with Harriet Beecher Stowe and John Brown?

last over, into a success. James Russell Lowell, the great poet of the abolitionists, wrote of his execution:

The shadows of his stormy life that
   moment fell apart;
And they who blamed the bloody hand
   forgave the loving heart.

The southern reaction was one of furious indignation. The *Richmond Enquirer* published these opinions:

The Harper's Ferry invasion has advanced the cause of Disunion more than any other event . . . since the formation of the Government. . . . The heretofore most determined friends of the Union may now be heard saying, "if . . . our peace is disturbed, our State invaded, its peaceful citizens cruelly murdered . . . by those who should be our warmest friends . . . *and the people of the North sustain* [that is, approve of] *the outrage*, then let disunion come.

High stakes. The presidential election of 1860 offered the nation a chance to find the national leader skillful enough to meet the difficulties. There is no question that the spirit of suspicion between northerner and southerner was now turning into open unfriendliness.

Nevertheless, the Union was a proud and precious inheritance to millions in both sections of the country. Most politicians on both sides still thought that more was to be gained by defending the Union and seeking ways to heal it than by widening the split. Moreover, throughout the country most Americans would have considered as wild any idea of breaking up the Union. They would have thought it even wilder to go to war with each other.

At the end of April, 1860, the Democrats met to choose their presidential candidate. It seemed to Senator Douglas that his turn to run had come at last. But would the party give him the nomination? We have seen the troubles which he had got himself and the country into—chiefly because of his ambitions.

A divided convention. The Democratic nominating convention met in Charleston, South Carolina, where people already were talking of leaving the Union. In this atmosphere, Douglas was hardly acceptable. The words he had used to answer Lincoln in the debates of 1858 now came back to haunt him.

Slavery men in South Carolina wanted the party to stand for protecting slavery in the territories. They said that they would live by the Dred Scott decision, which declared that slave property could be taken anywhere in the country. Douglas was stuck with his view that slavery could not exist in any place where the local people would not defend it.

Although Douglas had the support of more than half the delegates to the nominating convention, he lacked the two-thirds required in those days to win the nomination. The southern Democrats opposing Douglas walked out of the convention when their platform was not adopted. The convention ended without nominating anybody.

The failure of the delegates to name a candidate shows that the North and the South had at last reached the point of no compromise. Later the Democrats met again, this time in Baltimore—and Douglas was nominated because the southern firebrands had bolted (that is, walked out) and were not present to oppose him. These Democrats held a meeting of their own and chose as their man Senator John C. Breckinridge, of Kentucky. Breckinridge believed that Congress should not interfere with slavery in the territories.

The convention in Chicago. In May the Republicans gathered for their convention in the city of Chicago. Among a number of prominent candidates was William H. Seward. He regarded a breaking between North and South as unavoidable. He

Lincoln grew a beard shortly after his election (see p. 410).

said the country was on the verge of an "irrepressible conflict."

Unquestionably many friendly eyes were also on Abraham Lincoln. The reputation he had gained from his debates with Douglas had been strengthened by a speech he had delivered the previous February at a college in New York. It is known as the Cooper Union speech.

The visit to Cooper Union. In early 1860 Lincoln was very anxious to travel east to visit his son Robert, a student at Phillips Exeter Academy, in New Hampshire. Robert had failed the entrance examination to Harvard College and was spending the year in study in preparation for taking the examination again.

Being low on funds, Lincoln grabbed at an unexpected invitation which came to him to speak in New York City for a two-hundred-dollar fee. Arrangements were made for the address to be delivered at Cooper Union Institute, a recently opened college.

While he was in New York, Lincoln rode up Broadway Street to the studio of Mathew B. Brady, a photographer, who took his picture. This picture, shown at the right, was shortly reproduced in hundreds of publications.

That night Lincoln made his speech. An ungainly man, dressed in an ill-fitting suit, he was not impressive at first. His voice was very high-pitched as he began. The distinguished audience was sometimes restless when he could not be heard. Fortunately, whenever Lincoln's voice did not carry to the rear of the hall, by arrangement an old friend raised a silk topper on a cane as a signal.

The argument Lincoln offered was familiar: "Wrong as we think slavery is, we ## can yet afford to let it alone where it is . . . but can we, while our votes will prevent it, allow it to spread into the national Territories, and to overrun us here in these free states? If our sense of duty forbids

Cooper Union Museum

The picture Brady took of Lincoln in New York on the day of the Cooper Union speech, February 27, 1860, when Lincoln was still clean-shaven.

this, then let us stand by our duty, fearlessly and effectively."

One eyewitness reported, "For an hour and a half he held the audience in the hollow of his hand." The cheers when the speech was over echoed and reechoed throughout the hall—and then gradually among Republicans across the country.

Everybody's second choice. Lincoln knew what his chances were in Chicago. He knew the delegates had him in mind as their second choice. If the front-runners—including Seward—knocked each other out, the men of the convention would turn to him. Lincoln wanted the nomination badly, saying to a friend, "The taste *is* in my mouth a little." On the third ballot it happened as he hoped it would. Lincoln, in Springfield, the Illinois capital, received the news of his nomination by telegraph, excused himself, and took the message to his wife, Mary Todd Lincoln.

##Point out that Lincoln pledged repeatedly not to interfere with slavery where it already existe Why, then, did southerners view the election of Lincoln as a threat to slavery? What were the reasons for southern fears?

stress that the Republicans
appealed to a number of
groups. This helps to explain
the continuing strength of the
party after the Civil War.

New York City as it looked
about the time Lincoln
spoke there. The Hudson is
at the left and the East River
at the right. A city of over
a million people in 1860,
New York had long been
the largest American city.

Museum of the City of New York

Already Lincoln's mind must have been on victory in the forthcoming election, for the Democrats were dividing their strength and opening the door to him. Moreover, still another party was in the field, led by John Bell, of Tennessee. Calling itself the Constitutional Union party, it, too, was after Democratic votes. Bell and his people hoped to attract both northerners and southerners willing to place their love of the Union above the issue of slavery.

In addition to profiting from the division among their opponents, the Republicans had the advantage of an attractive platform. It appealed to businessmen with a promise of a higher tariff and to farmers with a promise of free land. It made immigrants happy with a promise that there would be no limits on the admission of foreigners to the United States. And it pleased many people with a promise of a railroad to the Pacific.

In accordance with the custom of that day, Lincoln made no campaign speeches, although Douglas did. Lincoln felt strongly that his position on the leading question—the extension of slavery—was already clear. He believed that if the voters had not listened to him before, they would not listen to him now.

Election Day brought Lincoln victory. This is how the popular vote went:

Lincoln	1,866,452
Douglas	1,375,157
Breckinridge	849,781
Bell	589,581

Largely, it was a sectional vote. Lincoln carried every state in the North except New Jersey. He had a clear majority in the electoral college, getting 180 electoral votes to 123 for his three opponents combined. Nevertheless, he won only 40 percent of the popular vote. Breckinridge took eleven of the fifteen southern states, Bell gained three others, and Douglas carried only one state—Missouri.

Secession. The election of Lincoln was a signal to the fire-eaters of the South. They regarded the President-elect as an unpolished westerner. How could *he* be a leader? Surely he would soon be completely controlled by the antislavery crowd, and the South would be threatened more than ever. Now was the time to get out of the Union.

The burden of dealing with the South would be Lincoln's, as Buchanan appeared to do little more than wait impatiently for his time as President to run out. There were only a few in 1860 who knew well the iron in Lincoln's soul. One of these was William Herndon, his law partner for over sixteen years.

Billy Herndon—as he was always called—wrote of Lincoln to a Massachusetts

##

Note that Lincoln won more electoral votes than all his opponents combined. Also, candidates taking the most extreme stands on slavery--Lincoln and Breckinridge--together polled about 60 percent of the vote. What does this suggest about popular feeling on the slavery issue?

In 1860 victory went to the Republicans, a party that had made no effort to attract southern votes. Did Lincoln's election prove Calhoun's fears about the growing minority status of the South?

Senator: "When on justice, right, liberty, the government and constitution, union, humanity, *then you may all stand aside;* he will rule then and no man can move him, no set of men can . . . and you mark what I say."

As Lincoln prepared his inaugural address, he had Herndon pull out for his reference copies of four documents. These were the United States Constitution, Andrew Jackson's proclamation against nullification, Webster's reply to Hayne, and Henry Clay's speech in defense of the Compromise of 1850. In the popular style of the day, Lincoln also grew a beard in the weeks before the journey to Washington.

Farewell to Springfield. Lincoln was sad as he made ready to leave Springfield, where he had "passed from a young to an old man," married, and buried a son. He took a last, wistful look at the worn shingle outside his office, turned slowly to Billy, and said: "Let it hang there undisturbed. Give our clients to understand that the election of a President makes no change in the firm of Lincoln and Herndon. If I live I'm coming back some time, and then we'll go right on practising law as if nothing had ever happened."

So it was that just before his fifty-second birthday, the "Rail-Splitter"—one of the youngest of our Presidents—went forth to the White House. There was hope but not confidence that he could save the Union from destruction.

---

1. Contrast Lincoln's and Douglas' views on slavery in 1858. 2. Lincoln asked Douglas what important question in a debate? What was the effect of the answer? 3. Give the main facts about *Uncle Tom's Cabin* and the raid on Harpers Ferry. 4. Who were the candidates in the presidential election of 1860? 5. Name two advantages the Republicans enjoyed. 6. How did the South feel about Lincoln's election?

By 1860 the South had lost its former powerful position in the federal government. What could have been

The Workshop

done to quiet southern fears about the future? (Secession was by no means the only alternative.)

The Shapers of Our World

Sectionalism led to a critical situation in 1860. Tell how each of the following contributed to the crisis:

Wilmot Proviso
Free-Soilers
popular sovereignty
Zachary Taylor
Compromise
  of 1850
Seventh of March
  Speech
Millard Fillmore
Charles Sumner
Kansas-Nebraska Act
Cooper Union speech

Franklin Pierce
Stephen A. Douglas
"bleeding Kansas"
John Brown
John C. Frémont
James Buchanan
Dred Scott case
Freeport debate
Harriet Beecher
  Stowe
John C.
  Breckinridge

Adding to Your Vocabulary

Show you know the meaning of these words by using them to describe events discussed in this chapter.

sovereignty
fugitive
firebrand
"doughface"
bolted

transcontinental
sacked
due process
plank
secession

Thinking Things Through

After a review of the boxed-in exercises in the chapter, dig deeper into the causes of secession by answering these questions:

1. Why has it been said that a political

Students might sum up the matter of slavery in the territories by preparing a series of maps showing the status of slavery in the United States in 1820, in 1850, and in 1854. How would the map have changed in 1857 if the Dred Scott decision had been enforced?

...arty that tries to please everyone pleases ...o one? Use the Whig party as an example in your answer.

2. Why was the South so fearful of the admission of California as a free state?

3. Many of the younger members of Congress were opposed to the Compromise of 1850, and most older Senators and Representatives favored it. Why?

4. Why did many Americans feel that the Compromise of 1850 could be regarded as a "final settlement"?

5. What was the basic weakness of the Democratic party in the 1850's? How did the Pierce and Buchanan administrations show this weakness?

6. Why was even popular sovereignty unconstitutional according to the Dred Scott decision?

7. Why did the Republican party concern itself only with the extension of slavery in the territories?

8. Why can an unknown person in a political contest gain more benefit from taking part in public debates than a better-known opponent?

9. What two events contributed most to the defeat of Douglas in the election of 1860?

10. How was it possible for Lincoln— with only 40 percent of the popular vote— to have a majority of the electoral vote in 1860?

The Seeds of Democracy

1. Compromise is one of the techniques of democracy. Why? Name five well-known compromises in American history and tell what each accomplished.

2. What steps were taken in creating the Republican party? Why is the formation of a new political party an example of democracy at work?

3. Find out how United States Senators were elected at the time of the Lincoln-Douglas debates. What change has taken place in this procedure since then? How? Why?

The Art of Discussion

1. Present a round-table discussion of admitting California to the Union in 1850. Express the views of Clay, Webster, Calhoun, and others, such as abolitionists.

2. Present a second panel discussion on the lives of the Presidents of the 1850's. Why did not some of the men of great ability become President?

The Research Center

Use reference books and books listed on page 412 to prepare reports on the following subjects:

1. The Lincoln-Douglas debates: Where were they held? What did the debaters talk about? What presidential candidates debated publicly in 1960?

2. The early life of Abraham Lincoln: What is known about his boyhood? What education did he have? What profession did he follow? What political experience did he have before 1860? What was his view of slavery?

3. The Supreme Court: How many justices are there? How are cases brought before it? What kinds of cases does it hear? On what basis does it make its decisions?

Your Opinion, Please

1. "The democratic act of compromise broke down in the United States in the late 1850's." What does this mean? What do you think should have been done to prevent the breakdown? Why?

2. It is sometimes said that men do not make events, but that events make men. Do you agree? Defend your answer by telling what you think would have happened if Lincoln had been killed before his first inauguration—as had been feared.

...dents who like to write might express the ideas of the period by writing (1) an editorial for an ...litionist newspaper on John Brown's death, (2) a description by a Kansas farmer of "bleeding ...sas," or (3) a letter from a South Carolina planter to a friend in Boston, supporting secession.

411

The events of Part Five can be grouped according to these categories: (1) the impact of Jackson and Jacksonian ideals, (2) the growth of industry and the spread of agriculture, (3) the expansion of the country, and (4) the triumph of sectionalism.

Part Five Workshop

Time and Change

Look at the time line on pages 320–321 and answer these questions:

1. What period of years is included there? With what years do the chapters in Part Five chiefly deal?

2. What five important technological improvements are named in the time line? What areas of American life did they affect?

3. What three changes in the size of the United States occurred?

4. What two arrangements concerning slavery in the territories were made? What did they provide for?

5. What three events showed the dissatisfaction of Americans with their situations? What action did they take?

6. What two things happened which had a particularly strong effect on the lives of slaves?

7. Were the Presidents between 1837 and 1860 strong or weak chief executives? Explain.

Reaching to the Present

1. Review the term "loose-footed," used in Chapter 15. How does the expression apply to Americans today?

2. How are presidential candidates chosen today? When was this method first used?

3. How is lobbying carried on today? Logrolling?

The Book Shelf

Coit, Margaret L. *Andrew Jackson.* Boston: Houghton Mifflin Co., 1965. (A biography.)

Cross, Helen Reeder. *Life in Lincoln's America.* New York: Random House Inc., 1964. (How Americans worked, played, and traveled in the years 1800–1865.)

Hobart, Lois. *Mexican Mural; the Story of Mexico, Past and Present.* New York: Harcourt, Brace & World, Inc., 1963. (The history and geography of our neighbor.)

Horgan, Paul. *Citizen of New Salem.* New York: Farrar, Strauss & Giroux, Inc., 1961. (About Abraham Lincoln.)

Johnson, Dorothy M. *Some Went West.* New York: Dodd, Mead & Co., Inc., 1965. (The story of women pioneers in the West.)

Keating, Bern. *Zebulon Pike, Early America's Frontier Scout.* New York: G. P. Putnam's Sons, Inc., 1965. (Describes the journeys of the discoverer of Pike's Peak.)

Latham, Jean Lee. *The Retreat to Glory; the Story of Sam Houston.* New York: Harper & Row, Publishers, 1965. (About the Texas hero.)

Mingay, G. E. *From a Foreign Viewpoint.* Chicago: Rand McNally & Co., 1967. (Contains descriptions of what European tourists saw.)

Severn, Bill. *Frontier President.* New York: Ives Washburn, Inc., 1965. (The life of James K. Polk.)

Smith, Fredrika Shumway. *Frémont; Soldier, Explorer, Statesman.* Chicago: Rand McNally & Co., 1966. (Describes the career of the "Pathfinder of the West.")

Wise, Winifred E. *Woman with a Cause.* New York: G. P. Putnam's Sons, Inc., 1965. (A biography of Harriet Beecher Stowe.)

The abolitionists were one of a number of groups of determined reformers in American history. Why have some historical periods been more productive of reform movements than others? Have students discuss whether or not Americans are now in a period of reform.

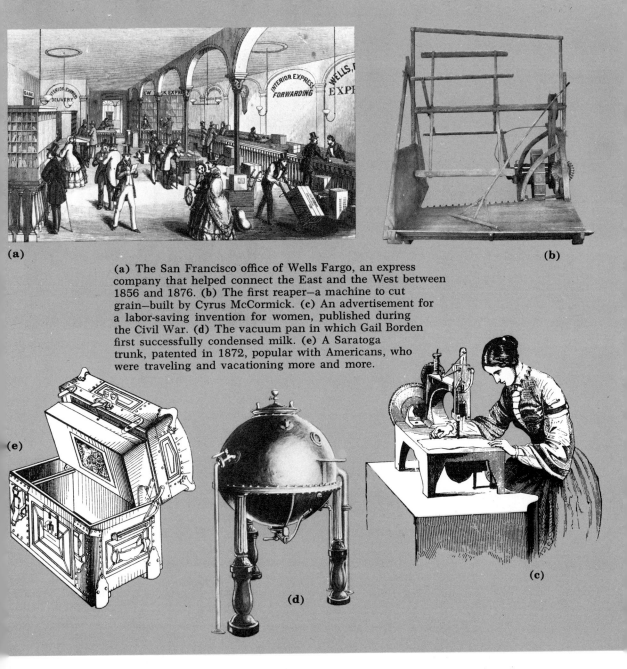

(a) The San Francisco office of Wells Fargo, an express company that helped connect the East and the West between 1856 and 1876. (b) The first reaper—a machine to cut grain—built by Cyrus McCormick. (c) An advertisement for a labor-saving invention for women, published during the Civil War. (d) The vacuum pan in which Gail Borden first successfully condensed milk. (e) A Saratoga trunk, patented in 1872, popular with Americans, who were traveling and vacationing more and more.

Part Six: BROTHERS IN CONFLICT

The items and scenes shown above became common in the North around the time of the Civil War and before long were typical of the whole United States. The reaper, the sewing machine, and the vacuum pan all played important parts in the Union war effort (see p. 425).

Part Six:
BROTHERS IN CONFLICT

Why can it be said that men of this era had to find brand-new solutions to some long-standing problems?

A. Lincoln

ALL THE WORLD WAS WATCHING

Public men no longer dress as Abraham Lincoln did during the Civil War, wearing stovepipe hats, black shawls, and beards. But Lincoln will always be in style for Americans.

Tall and lanky, Lincoln had many of the good points we are proud to think Uncle Sam himself has. He was astonishingly strong, not only in body but also in spirit. He was a sad man who could feel the suffering of other people as if it were his own. Still he liked jokes and laughed easily, for he understood that life can be funny as well as painful.

On the frontier of Kentucky, where he was born in 1809, Lincoln learned courage and endurance. He needed both, for when he

Time and Change

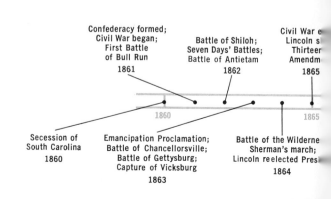

Confederacy formed;
Civil War began;
First Battle
of Bull Run
1861

Battle of Shiloh;
Seven Days' Battles;
Battle of Antietam
1862

Civil War e
Lincoln s
Thirteer
Amendm
1865

1860   1865

Secession of
South Carolina
1860

Emancipation Proclamation;
Battle of Chancellorsville;
Battle of Gettysburg;
Capture of Vicksburg
1863

Battle of the Wilderne
Sherman's march;
Lincoln reelected Presi
1864

eached the White House, he faced problems no American before had had to wrestle with.

By 1860 Lincoln had thought deeply about what the aim of government should be. He had come to the conclusion that government must "do for a community of people whatever they need to have done, but cannot do at all, or cannot do so well for themselves. . . ."

The most helpless "community of people" was made up of the slaves. For them Lincoln opened the rocky pathway to freedom. He changed what was at first a war to save the Union into a war also to extend democracy. He will shine forever as the "Great Emancipator."

The weapon Lincoln himself used best was the English language, of which he was a master. Because of his skill with words, he became not just an able military leader, but a convincing teacher whose ideas and ideals all Americans could understand and accept.

Lincoln taught that the terrible Civil War could lead to better opportunities for all men. He told a group of soldiers: "It is not merely for today, but for all time . . . that we should perpetuate [preserve] for our children's children this great and free government. . . . I happen temporarily to occupy this big White House. I am a living witness that any one of your children may look to come here as my father's child has."

Lincoln never forgot that all the world was watching to see if the glorious American experiment in self-rule would succeed. He bravely took upon himself the burden of saving—as "the last best hope of earth"—the *United* States of America.

The American bald eagle, bearing a slogan that might have been Lincoln's.

Lincoln once said, "As I would not be a slave, so I would not be a master. This expresses my idea of democracy. Whatever differs from this, to the extent of the difference, is no democracy." Discuss his view of democracy and his role as President in light of this.

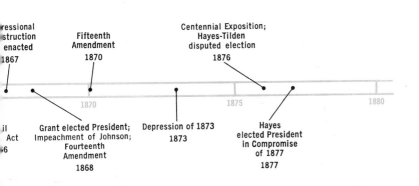

ressional
struction
enacted
1867

Fifteenth
Amendment
1870

Centennial Exposition;
Hayes-Tilden
disputed election
1876

1870   1875   1880

il
Act
66

Grant elected President;
Impeachment of Johnson;
Fourteenth
Amendment
1868

Depression of 1873
1873

Hayes
elected President
in Compromise
of 1877
1877

(a)

(a) Many soldiers in the Civil War were only fifteen or sixteen years old. This is a Georgia boy, one of the very young southerners who lost their lives.
(b) A Negro youth in the Union army—one of many.
(c) Another boy soldier, a northerner, painted in oil by Winslow Homer, a popular nineteenth-century artist.
(d) General Ulysses S. Grant's saddle. **(e)** The mess kit General Robert E. Lee used throughout the war.
(f) The Confederate flag flies over Fort Sumter, at Charleston.

(b)

(c)

(d)

(e)

(f)

(g)

[s]ome ways the Civil War was more like total war [of] the twentieth century than it was like the Revolu- [tion]. Industrial power and modern transportation [were] of key importance, and therefore the capture [of c]ities and railroad centers was as vital as the [dest]ruction of bodies of troops.

CHAPTER 19

THE COUNTRY IN FLAMES

[Sec]ssion presented Lincoln with a crisis unlike any other in our history. Have students keep in mind the [foll]owing questions: Was war caused by a single, dramatic, unexpected event? Or was it the result of a [seri]es of moves and countermoves by each side? Why, finally, did secession lead to war?

PRESIDENT-ELECT Abraham Lincoln took a roundabout way to Washington. The journey took eleven days. In every place the train stopped, he made a speech to the people who had gathered at the station to hear him.

Few people had Lincoln's command of the English language. His words, which could move an audience deeply, were simple and direct. For example, he said at Indianapolis, Indiana:

> If the union of these States, and the liberties of this people, shall be lost, it is but little to any one man of fifty-two years of age [that is, like himself], but a great deal to the thirty millions of people who inhabit these United States, and to their posterity [that is, to those who come after them] in all coming time. It is your business to rise up and preserve the Union and liberty, for yourselves, and not for me.

Lincoln was using his opportunities to win support for whatever policies (he did not reveal them) he was going to propose as the new President. He was taking advantage of the magnetic quality he knew # he possessed.

Lincoln Faces the Problem of Secession

A powerful man, nearly 6 feet 4 inches tall, Lincoln dressed carelessly. Most of his height was in his legs, and it was not until he stood up that people realized how tall he was. When he walked with his head forward and his hands clasped behind his back, he seemed to be a gangling man with little physical grace. Some people thought there was something comical or even undignified about his loose-jointed gait.

But the President made a lasting impression on people who saw him. Although all of us today think we know what his face looked like—mainly from seeing the Lincoln penny—those who knew him

417

were sure no photograph did him justice. One of his secretaries later wrote, "Lincoln's features were the despair of every artist who undertook his portrait."

Lincoln's look was grave. But when he began to speak, his face seemed to come alive—"the eyes began to sparkle, the mouth to smile . . . so that a stranger would have said, 'Why, this man, so angular and somber a moment ago, is really handsome.'"

Nevertheless, the country's problems called for something far more than an unusual manner in its President. They called for wisdom and courage and forethought that no ordinary man could have been expected to possess in large enough amounts.

The Confederate States of America

In the time between Lincoln's election in 1860 and his inauguration, shattering events took place. Lincoln had always made it clear to southerners that he would not seek to free the slaves. He was, after all, a Republican, not an abolitionist. But some of the most vigorous and powerful southern spokesmen firmly believed that the South had been doomed by Lincoln's election.

South Carolina's leadership. The first state to express ideas about going out of the Union was South Carolina—where such talk had been heard since the late 1820's. The South Carolinians believed that under Lincoln the northerners and the northern point of view on slavery would control the federal government. They feared that the South could never again capture the White House because Presidents, it seemed, could be elected without any southern support whatsoever.

The South Carolinians were no doubt also influenced by the fact that the population of the free states was increasing faster than that of the slave states. And it seemed

clear that no new slave states would ever come into the Union. The most recent states—California, Minnesota, and Oregon —were all free.

After it was known that Lincoln was to be the new President, South Carolina called a meeting which voted unanimously on December 20, 1860, to *secede*. That is, all the men attending it agreed that the state would leave the Union.

Meeting at Montgomery. People in other parts of the South were also saying that the time had come for their states to secede. Within six weeks of South Carolina's action, six more states announced that they were leaving the Union. These were Georgia, Florida, Alabama, Mississippi, Texas, and Louisiana. On February 4, 1861, representatives from the seceding states met in Montgomery, Alabama, to form a government.

The constitution. The delegates spent five weeks drawing up a constitution and choosing officers. The finished product was modeled on the United States Constitution. But the southerners made what they considered improvements.

The president of the new government was to serve for six years and not be eligible to run for the presidency again. Protective-tariff laws were forbidden. So was legislation providing money for internal improvements.

Although the African slave trade was prohibited, the protection of slave property was, of course, provided for. Further, in any territories which the new government might control, slavery was to be permitted without interference.

The delegates wanted the new constitution to be easier to amend than the United States Constitution. They, therefore, provided that the agreement of two-thirds rather than three-quarters of the states was to be required.

Jefferson Davis. So was formed the Confederate States of America—as a rule

##What southern needs did the Confederate constitution appear to satisfy? Why was it modeled on the United States Constitution? Ask students to find out what the Confederate constitution did about the sovereignty of the states and the right of secession.

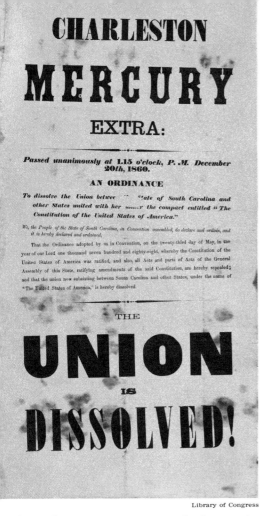

This is the way a newspaper in the largest city in South Carolina announced the state's secession, which had been decided in Columbia.

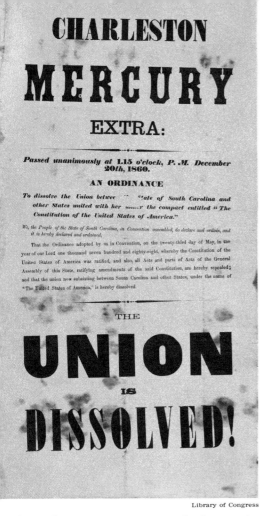

CHARLESTON MERCURY

EXTRA:

Passed unanimously at 1.15 o'clock, P. M. December 20th, 1860.

AN ORDINANCE

To dissolve the Union between State of South Carolina and other States united with her under the compact entitled "The Constitution of the United States of America."

We, the People of the State of South Carolina, in Convention assembled, do declare and ordain, and it is hereby declared and ordained,

That the Ordinance adopted by us in Convention, on the twenty-third day of May, in the year of our Lord one thousand seven hundred and eighty-eight, whereby the Constitution of the United States of America was ratified, and also, all Acts and parts of Acts of the General Assembly of this State, ratifying amendments of the said Constitution, are hereby repealed; and that the union now subsisting between South Carolina and other States, under the name of "The United States of America," is hereby dissolved.

THE

UNION IS DISSOLVED!

called simply the Confederacy. Jefferson Davis, of Mississippi, was chosen as president. Many regarded him as the perfect man to be head of the southern cause. Said one fire-eating South Carolinian with delight, "The man and the hour are met." This judgment was not correct, although Davis had previously had a brilliant career.

A graduate of West Point, Davis might have made an excellent military commander, for he had had an outstanding record in the Mexican War. But as a civilian leader, he showed himself to be a stubborn man who was not able to work easily with others.

#How would compromise at this point have shown the power of the secessionists?

Efforts to patch things up. Not all the slave states joined the seven seceded states. Only cotton-growing states went out of the Union. The others watched and waited. Perhaps there would be a compromise after all.

President Buchanan himself offered only weak leadership. He had taken an oath to defend the Constitution, yet in the crisis he did practically nothing. A number of frantic, last-minute efforts, however, were made to find a way to save the Union.

The House of Representatives appointed a committee of thirty-three to see if there was not something that could still be tried. The Senate appointed a committee of thirteen with a similar purpose.

Senator John J. Crittenden, of Kentucky, proposed in Congress on December 18, 1860, what seemed to be a reasonable and simple solution. He would revive the old Missouri Compromise line of 36° 30′ (see pages 311–312) and protect by constitutional amendment slavery in the territories south of it. Lincoln's advice was to turn down Crittenden's proposal, and therefore it failed. #

Another who tried to bring about a last-ditch settlement was former President John Tyler. He served as head of a peace convention called at the request of the Virginia legislature. The uncheerful gathering, made up mostly of men who had held important positions in government, met in Washington early in February, 1861. Nineteen former governors were present. But the conference was a failure. Tyler himself later became a Confederate.

A gloomy inauguration. Lincoln, against his wishes, entered Washington secretly and under heavy guard. Because there were warnings of a possible assassination plot against him, Lincoln had changed his published travel schedule.

On Inauguration Day President Buchanan called for Lincoln at a Washington hotel. The two men came out arm in arm

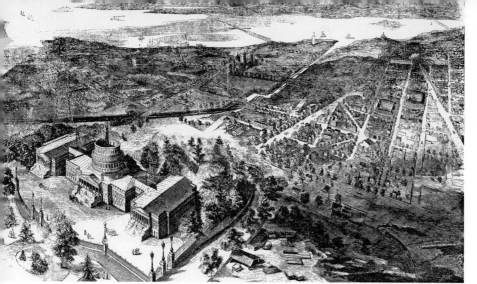

and rode together down Pennsylvania Avenue for the swearing-in ceremony. The day was black and cloudy, seeming to resemble the mood of the nation.

In front of the Capitol, where the oath taking was to occur, ten thousand people had assembled. As Lincoln gazed out upon them, he saw a sea of black silk hats. Seated behind him on the platform was Stephen A. Douglas, who wanted to show that men of all parties were rallying around the new President.

Chief Justice Taney, now eighty-four years old, stepped forward to administer the oath of office. Lincoln was the ninth President he had sworn in. Taney's hands trembled noticeably.

Lincoln, his left hand on the open Bible, repeated after Taney the sacred oath to "preserve, protect, and defend the Constitution of the United States." Thousands in the audience must have wondered how he intended to carry out his solemn promise.

A friendly plea to the South. The inaugural address which Lincoln pulled from his pocket had been most carefully written. Throughout the country anxious men and women crowded around newspaper offices waiting to find out the new President's views as they came from Washington on the telegraph.

The tone in which Lincoln spoke was one of friendliness to the states which had seceded. But he was direct in his message, making clear that no state could lawfully leave the Union. "Physically speaking," he declared, "we cannot separate. . . . A husband and wife may be divorced, and go out of the presence, and beyond the reach of each other; but the different parts of our country cannot do this."

War, the President said, could not provide the answer to the problems the country faced. After dreadful losses on both sides, he said, the fighting would come to an end. But the questions which had caused the disagreements in the first place would still remain to be settled.

Lincoln appealed to his fellow countrymen to take their time and to seek a just and peaceful solution to the terrible situation they faced. "We are not enemies, but friends," he emphasized. Yet he also gently warned them that he meant business. "You have no oath registered in Heaven to destroy the government, while I have the most solemn one to 'preserve, protect, and defend' it."

The address was widely praised. The New York Tribune declared, for example, "To twenty millions of people, it will carry tidings, good or not . . . that the federal government of the United States is still in existence, with a Man at the head of it."

#In the weeks before Lincoln's inauguration, seven states formed the Confederacy, troops seized federal property in the South, and compromise attempts failed. Why did Lincoln refrain from threatening to use force to retake federal property and end what he considered a rebellion?

Fort Sumter

Lincoln's address did not bring the seceded states back into the Union. In fact, shortly after the inauguration, representatives of the Confederacy came to Washington, seeking recognition as if they were diplomats from a foreign country. The new Secretary of State, William H. Seward, prepared to negotiate with them.

Lincoln had not yet worked out his plans, but dealing with the Confederacy as a foreign power was not among them. He thought of the seceded states as being in rebellion against the United States.

Seward's advice. Seward, who had tried hard to win the Republican nomination for the presidency in 1860, wanted to be the "power behind the throne" in the Lincoln administration. Seward regarded Lincoln as a "Simple Susan" in great need of help. The Secretary of State thought that to do nothing about the Confederacy would be best—that the seceded states would recognize they had made a mistake and rejoin the Union.

Lincoln knew that such a scheme would never work. Secessionists were not going to return unless they were forced to. Already a southern Senator had said, "This Federal Government is dead. The only question is, whether we will give it a decent . . . burial."

Standing fast. In the South the seceded states had taken possession of the federal

t out the impor-
e of the border states.

From this map the questions faced by Lincoln in his first weeks in office are clear: Upon which states can I depend to help me to preserve the Union? Which states are "on the fence"?

The United States April, 1861

0 100 200 300 400 miles

Union
Confederacy
Border States

arsenals located within their boundaries. In South Carolina, federal troops had withdrawn to Fort Sumter, a federal arsenal on an island in the harbor of Charleston, South Carolina.

Confederates said that the federal troops who had taken refuge there must get out. The Lincoln administration naturally wanted the soldiers to stay at Fort Sumter and hold on to the federal property. Any withdrawal might suggest that the government at Washington was not capable of defending the Union.

The commanding officer of Fort Sumter was Major Robert Anderson. A Kentuckian by birth, Anderson sympathized with the Confederates. He was saying the time had come to leave the fort. This was also the opinion of the commander of the United States Army, General Winfield Scott.

Federal decision. Anderson and his men needed supplies. The federal ships bearing them would have to pass within the range of Confederate guns. Earlier, President Buchanan had sent a relief ship, but it had retreated under Confederate fire. What would Lincoln do?

Lincoln had pledged himself in his inaugural address to hold federal "property and places"—which included Fort Sumter. This meant he had to send relief. The governor of South Carolina was informed that an expedition would be on its way. Ander-

son was also told that supplies were coming and that the President was entirely confident that the Major would act "as becomes a patriot and soldier."

Confederate action. Despite his personal feelings, Anderson knew what his oath as a federal soldier meant. He prepared his guns for firing on Confederates. Anderson's old friend from West Point days, General Pierre G. T. de Beauregard, a native of New Orleans, offered Anderson and his men a chance to leave the fort unharmed. Anderson turned it down.

Beauregard opened fire on Fort Sumter an hour after receiving Anderson's reply. It was then April 12, 1861. When the Confederates fired, the Civil War began. Tragically, brothers were going to fight brother to the death.

For over a day Confederate artillery pounded Fort Sumter. Since Sumter's defenders could not hold out without reinforcements, they surrendered—on April 14. The relief expedition, delayed by a severe storm and weakened by the absence of some necessary vessels, could do little more than take the men away from Fort Sumter. They were moved to New York.

Americans throughout the North were stunned and angered by the Confederate attack. The Stars and Stripes had been fired upon! Everywhere, it seemed, mass meetings were held to pass resolutions in

Buchanan had tried to send food to Fort Sumter early in 1861 on the *Star of the West* (inset), but gunfire had kept the ship from docking. Here the men holding the arsenal see the attack.

"Battles and Leaders of the Civil War," The Century Co., 1884

nphasize the strategic and psychological
ortance of Virginia's secession.

upport of the Union and the Constitution
nd to shout cheers for both. As if on signal, flags flew from thousands of flagpoles
and church steeples throughout the northern states. This outburst of patriotism
clearly showed the people's devotion to the
Union. The firing on Fort Sumter had
united the North.

Ready to Fight

The long line of events beginning with
he Kansas-Nebraska Act would now take a
new turn. A prominent New Yorker wrote
n his diary that the "intolerable brag and
bluster . . . of the South has driven us
. . . to assert our own rights." On the other
hand, a southern newspaper declared,
"Alas! It is becoming not a question of
secession and treason, but a question of
our own and our children's freedom." Both
sides prepared to fight.

The call for volunteers. The day following the fall of Fort Sumter, Lincoln called
for seventy-five thousand volunteers to
serve in the Union army for three months.
His call was quickly answered. Many believed that the war would be short because
the rebels would be easily thrashed.

One of the first songs of the war, which
was published shortly after the attack on
Fort Sumter, was entitled "Take Your Gun
and Go, John." Another song had verses
which included the patriotic lines:

> Stand up for Uncle Sam, my boys,
> For he has stood by you.

The Confederacy, too, issued a call to
arms—which southerners hastened to answer. The number of volunteers was so
great at first that the government could not
arm and equip them all and had to turn
many away.

Lee's hard choice. In addition, more
states made the difficult decision to get out
of the Union. Virginia—except for its
western part, present-day West Virginia—

Robert E. Lee in 1846. The artist who painted
this portrait after the Civil War copied an
earlier picture but put Lee in a general's uniform.

voted to secede. North Carolina, Arkansas,
and Tennessee also seceded. Virginia
seized the federal arsenal at Harpers Ferry
and the large navy yard at Norfolk.

Through the secession of Virginia, the ##
Confederacy gained the services of its
greatest general, Robert E. Lee. Lee, who
had attended West Point on an appointment obtained for him with the help of
John C. Calhoun, was offered the command of the Union's forces. After searching his soul, he refused it and resigned his
commission in the United States Army.

Lee wrote his old chief, Winfield Scott,
"Save in the defense of my native State I
never again desire to draw my sword." A
few days later he became commander of
the forces of Virginia.

The South, too, soon had songs to stir
the blood. Within a few months, southerners were singing "The Bonnie Blue Flag,"
"Maryland! My Maryland!," and various
versions of "Dixie." Thousands would
sing, with sincerity, especially words like:

> In Dixie land I'll take my stand
> To live and die in Dixie.

e Union and Confederate armies were made up mostly of volunteers. But both sides--the
federacy in 1862 and the Union in 1863--passed conscription laws that authorized drafting
for military service (see pp. 442-443).

423

The Opponents

Underneath the excitement people were thinking about what the actual fighting would be like. The balance between the sections seemed very uneven. There were 23 states with a population of 22,000,000 in the North. The South had 11 states with a population of about 9,500,000—including over 3,600,000 slaves. The North would be able to replace even heavy losses on the battlefield—the South would not.

Nevertheless, the southerners were fighting for their independence, on their own soil. This gave them great heart for the battles ahead. It also meant that they had the advantage of waging a defensive war—a war in which the enemy must come to them.

Military plans and costs. Jefferson Davis saw the possibility of establishing well-defended strong points along the Mason-Dixon line, to the Ohio River and then to the Mississippi River. The North, the Confederacy's leaders believed, could not carry out attacks strong enough to smash into the Confederacy. Furthermore, they thought, if the Union's forces blockaded southern ports, the British and the French would surely interfere—in order to guarantee themselves a supply of cotton.

General Scott's plan for the North to follow was a bold one. It came to be called the "anaconda policy"—after the large snake which crushes its victims. The plan was to capture Richmond, the Confederate capital, hold the loyal border states (Delaware, Maryland, Kentucky, and Missouri), gain control of the Mississippi, and blockade the Confederacy. When this ring of iron had been placed around the Confederacy, the vast man power of the North would be hurled against the defenders with overwhelming force.

Both sides would learn much about what neither figured on: the terrible cost a

victory for one side or the other would involve. Furthermore, some other things had not been fully recognized.

The South's army, to give a main example, had better generals than the North's at the start of the war. Many southern youths aiming at careers in public service had been attracted to the United States Military Academy at West Point for their education and had become army officers. The best of them were already well known.

Lincoln, on the other hand, had to shift his generals around a great deal before he found "the right man for the right place." The time thus lost cost much in lives and equipment.

The role of northern industry. But most important, the North's growing industries were a powerful ally of the Union soldiers. They were able in time to produce—and replace—the supplies needed to fight a modern war.

By the 1850's manufacturing establishments were mushrooming in Massachusetts, especially, and in Rhode Island, Connecticut, along the Erie Canal, and in the growing cities of the West. These cities included Pittsburgh, Cincinnati, Chicago, and St. Louis.

The quantity of goods the factories could turn out aroused confidence in northerners. Before the war was over, for example, the Cooper and Hewitt Iron works, at Trenton, New Jersey, was producing all the gun-barrel material for the Union army.

Already some areas were specializing in certain products. Western Pennsylvania was producing iron. Massachusetts was making boots and shoes and textiles. Connecticut had become a center for the manufacture of small metal products, like clocks, guns, and other hardware items.

A number of fairly recent inventions helped account for northern industrial development. These inventions were increasing in number every year—like a roller

At first the military position of the Confederacy seemed similar to that of Washington's army during the Revolution--defensive, aiming to wear down the enemy's will to fight. Discuss why the two situations were really different. (Stress geographical and technological factors.)

The Fort Pitt Ironworks at Pittsburgh, Pennsylvania, seen from the Monongahela River. Northern factories like this one expanded during the Civil War and strengthened the Union side.

coaster going faster and faster. From 1790 to 1811 an average of 77 patents were registered each year at the United States Patent Office. In the ten years from 1841 to 1850, however, 6460 patents were granted. In the ten years before the Civil War, they totaled 25,250.

Many of the inventions and discoveries were immediately useful in manufacturing processes. As a result, they directly affected the northern war effort.

Goodyear's work. One of the most important discoveries, by Charles Goodyear in 1844, was the *vulcanization* of rubber—that is, the toughening of it by heat and chemicals. This made it available for tires, waterproof boots and coats, and thousands of other things. Inflatable balloons, for instance, could now be raised by Union troops to look at Confederate positions.

Howe's sewing machine. The development of the sewing machine by Elias Howe —it was patented in 1846—made possible the mass production of clothing and shoes. As its use spread, women no longer had to make their families' clothes by hand.

Sewing machines made it possible to manufacture uniforms and shoes for the Union army. By the time of the attack on Fort Sumter, seventy-four companies were building these machines—the best known being the firm of Isaac M. Singer.

Over thirty-eight hundred companies were already engaged in the manufacture of ready-made clothing. Many of these changed over easily to the production of military goods.

The preserving of food. Inventions to help in the processing of food also aided the side of the North. By the middle of the nineteenth century, for example, canning was replacing older methods of preserving meat with salt. In 1856 Gail Borden, a New Yorker who had joined Stephen Austin's colony in Texas, was granted a patent "on a process of evaporating milk in vacuum."

Borden opened a plant for processing milk in 1858. He was just in time to provide a very important and easily transported food for the northern troops in the field.

McCormick's reaper. A new invention which affected agriculture also did much for the northern war effort. This was the mechanical grain reaper. The man who was chiefly responsible was Cyrus McCor-

ote that these inventions and discoveries had important effects on civilians as well as the army. nsider, for example, that mass production of shoes, men's clothes, canned goods, and other ms was to bring about far-reaching changes in American life after the Civil War.

mick, a native of Virginia, who in 1832 built a reaper that was an improvement on the one his father had made. He is said to have told his father, "In Virginia the reaper is a luxury ... across the mountains [the Appalachians], I think it is a necessity. Anyway, I'm going to find out."

McCormick was right. He made his fortune in Chicago, where he built a plant to manufacture reapers. When the Civil War # came, reapers made it possible for the North to have a large enough supply of

grain without interrupting campaigns to send soldiers home at harvesttime. Reapers helped make possible the enormous advantage the North had over the South in feeding both civilians and men in uniform.

Importance in the war. In 1861, then the sources of the North's manufacturing strength were already present. Businessmen, Congress, and President Lincoln developed ways of harnessing this strength to take care of the needs of the Union.

The railway lines and steamboats. The

Its railroad network, much heavier than the one in the South, enabled the Union to move the goods and men necessary for victory more easily than the Confederates could

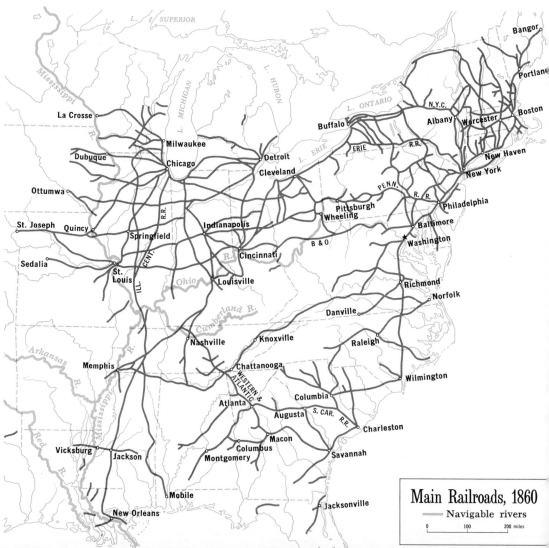

Main Railroads, 1860
— Navigable rivers

0   100   200 miles

A stagecoach carrying mail and passengers crosses an unsettled part of the West on its way from St. Louis to San Francisco, a distance of about 3000 miles. The Pony Express later carried the mail.

expanding railroad system of the North (as you can see on the map on page 426) also played a vital role in the war effort. It was able to handle the men and equipment required for victory.

Railroads were already the backbone of the North's transportation system. By 1860 the Pennsylvania, Baltimore and Ohio, New York Central, and Illinois Central railroads were the chief carriers of goods and the army's supplies.

In the West steamboats made the Mississippi, the Ohio, the Cumberland, the Arkansas, and the Red rivers noisy, productive, and fascinating. In 1860 there were sixteen hundred steamboats on the Mississippi and about nine hundred on the Ohio. But the railroads were playing the chief role in linking the parts of the country—particularly of the North—together.

The lines of communication. Also helping to bind the country together was a network of telegraph lines. When the revolutionary invention that led to them became usable for the first time, there was a rush to create telegraph companies. Scores were formed. By the time of the Civil War, two had become standouts: the American Telegraph Company, in the East, and Western Union, in the West. Because the telegraph was used mainly to speed the movement of goods, the North, as a trading section, had greater use than the South for this modern miracle.

Express lines. Express companies were also cementing the country together—and

int out to students that the North had more east-west railroad lines than the South. As a lt, the old Northwest was closely tied to the Northeast and did not have to rely on the sissippi River as an outlet for its products.

427

filling a somewhat greater need in the North than in the South. The best known was Wells Fargo (Wells, Fargo & Company). Like its smaller competitors, it carried letters, packages, and money safely and rapidly. The Post Office Department did not yet carry parcel post or registered mail, by which money is often transported today.

Another advantage. The way in which the railroads, telegraph lines, steamboats, and express companies had developed, therefore, gave the North an advantage over the South. Through these channels would flow the endless stream of men, goods, news, and military orders that were necessary for winning the war.

Europe's response. At the beginning of every war there are bad guesses and judgments about how events will turn out. The Confederacy suffered several disappointments because of some mistaken ideas.

\# The most important setback was the behavior of the European countries on whose support southerners had counted. Although the Union came close to war with both Britain and France, it remained at peace with them. Moreover, European diplomats firmly held to the rule that the American states had only one government —the one at Washington, D.C.

The countries of Europe refused even to receive diplomatic representatives from the Confederacy. As a result, the Confederates were never able to make a plea for foreign help of any kind.

A flaw of government. Almost as important as the failure to be recognized abroad was the way in which the Confederate government itself worked at home. The Confederacy, whose leaders believed in state rights, was based on the idea that the states were more important than the central government. Through its officials, therefore, each state argued with the officials at the capital in Richmond that its defense required the presence of its own soldiers. An effect was that the Confederates were never able to create powerful armies made up of men drawn from all over the South.

---

1. State four reasons for South Carolina's secession. 2. What were two of the efforts made to save the Union? 3. Describe the events that led to the firing on Fort Sumter. 4. Name the effects the firing had on the North and the South. 5. Describe the Confederacy's and the Union's plans for the war. 6. Sum up the advantages and disadvantages of both sides. 7. Name five inventions which aided the North. 8. In what respect was the Confederacy's form of government a handicap to its war effort?

##Why might it be said that the same force that disrupted the Union eventually wrecked the Confederacy?

A Bloody War Rages Across the Land

General Scott had been relieved of his command before the Civil War began. "Old Fuss and Feathers," then seventy-five years old, had been injured in a fall and could stand only with difficulty. He had completed his service to the nation. The army was now entrusted to General Irvin McDowell, a career officer who had never before had command of troops.

The Opening Clash

On a beautiful Sunday late in July, 1861, General McDowell and about 30,000 men and boys—largely untrained—met a somewhat smaller number of Confederates. The southerners—also largely untrained—were under the command of

General Beauregard. The scene was Manassas Junction in Virginia, near Bull Run Creek—about 30 miles from Washington.

First Bull Run. The North's aim was to throw open the road to the new Confederate capital of Richmond. "On to Richmond" was the cry shouted by impatient northerners. Many people—including even Congressmen—who lived in Washington rode south into Virginia in their carriages in order to see the fun.

The Union troops seemed, as expected, to be on their way to victory at what became the first Battle of Bull Run. But southern troops under General Joseph E. Johnston brought help to Beauregard's men. Also, Confederate troops under General Thomas J. Jackson held fast. A fellow officer gave him his name for history, "Stonewall," when he shouted above the noise of the battle, "There is Jackson standing like a stone wall!"

Embarrassing retreat. As the Confederates pressed their advantage, the Union troops fled back toward the city of Washington. They and the panic-stricken sightseers quickly filled up the roads. The Confederates made no attempt to follow them.

Lincoln, in the White House, had heard the first news—that the Union troops were winning—and had left to go for a carriage ride. Not long afterward a messenger was sent to take him word of the true result and to hurry him back to his desk.

Lincoln and the North now knew that the war would not be over quickly. One of the volunteers wrote not long afterward, "I had a dim notion about the 'romance' of a soldier's life, etc. I have got bravely over it since."

Too much confidence. If Bull Run had the effect of throwing cold water on the northerners, its effect on the Confederates was just the opposite. It gave them overconfidence. Jefferson Davis, who had arrived in time to witness the end of the battle, had telegraphed his Secretary of War that 15,000 Confederates had crushed 35,000 Federals. The word spread in the South that one southerner could defeat two northerners! Many southern soldiers left for home. They had decided they would not be needed.

The appointment of McClellan. The defeat of the Union soldiers—sometimes also called the Blues, from the color of their uniforms—at the first Battle of Bull Run brought prompt action from Lincoln.

"Battles and Leaders of the Civil War," The Century Co., 1884

"Stonewall" Jackson, Virginia graduate of West Point, and the cap he wore in the war.

hat ways is morale, or a sense of well-being, important to a modern army?
he industrial age are wars usually decided by the spirit of the fighting men
y the material advantages of the armies?

He appointed as general in chief of the Union army a thirty-four-year-old fellow Illinoisan, George B. McClellan.

McClellan, who had performed brilliantly as a cadet at the United States Military Academy at West Point, had had a splendid record as a captain in the Mexican War. Short in build and somewhat conceited, he was already known as the Young Napoleon of the West. By commanding the # Army of the Potomac—as the Union army in the East was called—he hoped to become a great national hero.

Hammer Strokes in the West

The nation waited—sometimes impatiently—for McClellan to get his army into shape. Meanwhile the war was going on in ## the West.

The development of Grant. There another man was rising to leadership. He was Ulysses S. Grant, also from the state of Illinois. His aim was to gain control of the Mississippi, which was held by the South.

Grant had been an outstanding horseman at West Point and had done well at mathematics, but he had shown only a mild interest in military life. Like many other generals in the Civil War, he had learned much about the art of warfare during the Mexican War.

After the Mexican War, Grant had been assigned to California. There awful loneliness and homesickness had led him to drink very heavily, and he had been forced to resign his commission. Later, shifting from one occupation to another, he could not even support his family as well as he should have.

When the Civil War came, Grant reentered the service—as a brigadier general. Not an impressive man or a particularly colorful one, he nevertheless had a strong will and other qualities that made soldiers follow him confidently.

On the Cumberland and the Tennessee.

Grant first became a national figure in early 1862. At that time he undertook to open the Mississippi River—which the Confederates held—by advancing up the Tennessee and Cumberland rivers, through Kentucky and into Tennessee. Defending these states was Confederate General Albert Sidney Johnston.

Working together with Rear Admiral Andrew H. Foote, Grant in February 1862, captured Fort Henry, on the Tennessee River, and Fort Donelson, on the Cumberland River. At Fort Donelson Grant earned the nickname "Unconditional Surrender," because he would offer the enemy no terms except unconditional ones.

Having won control of Kentucky and western Tennessee, Grant turned south to join the army under Union General Don Carlos Buell, which was pressing on the city of Nashville. General Johnston, who had been trying to defend Nashville, then moved south to take up headquarters at Corinth, Mississippi. There General Beauregard, coming from Virginia, joined him.

Grant moved his army to Pittsburg Landing, a stopping place for boats on the Tennessee River about 30 miles northeast of Corinth. The General had no idea he would be attacked there.

The church called Shiloh. Johnston and his men, however, had been steadily approaching. The powerful army struck Grant's men near a little log church called Shiloh. It gave its name to the terrible battle that was fought there on Sunday, April 6, 1862.

Taken by surprise, Grant's army reeled under the enemy's blows during the first day. Grant himself had recently been injured in a fall from a horse and had a painfully swollen ankle. But he was with his men in the thick of the fight. The fierce struggle, fought in part in a heavy downpour, lasted two days.

Shiloh was one of the bloodiest battles of the entire war. Each side lost more than

##What part did the West play in the war plans of the Union? What would the capture of the Mississippi River system do to the Confederacy? How did Grant's victories advance the Union's plans?

Above left: The Battle of New Orleans—
Confederate guns on the shore fire at Union
ships, which fire back. *Above right:*
A Confederate soldier, a "Louisiana Tiger."
Below: Follow the campaigns.

10,000 men, killed or wounded. Johnston
himself was killed—to be succeeded by
Beauregard. The Confederates retreated
into Mississippi.

There was much criticism of Grant for
the heavy Union losses. A friend of Lincoln's came to the President to say that
Grant ought to be removed. But Lincoln
replied, "I can't spare this man; he fights."

The capture of New Orleans. Meanwhile, during the time when Grant was
moving up the Tennessee and Cumberland
rivers, Commodores David G. Farragut
and David D. Porter were preparing a naval expedition to capture New Orleans.
The Confederates strengthened defenses
near that southern city, and the Union fleet
met heavy bombardment. Nevertheless, on
April 25, 1862, New Orleans came into
Union hands, and the United States flag
was raised there.

The Civil War cost 618,000 American lives--more
than all the other wars in our history combined.

The Civil War in the West, 1861-1862

0   100   200   300 miles

——— Grant	▓▓▓ Bragg
– – – Buell	– – – Beauregard
･･･ Farragut & Porter	••• A. S. Johnston

Seesaw in the East

Lincoln had his mind on the war in the East. There, along the banks of the Potomac River, McClellan was still training and drilling his army of a quarter million. The best and worst of "Little Mac's" personal traits were showing—both his skill as an organizer and his vanity.

A slow general. Complicating the situation was the fact that McClellan did not respect his commander in chief, the President. McClellan regarded Lincoln as a bumbling fool. Lincoln held McClellan's military ability in high regard. But he grad-

Follow McClellan's route on this map and turn back to it when you read on page 434 about Lee's later moves.

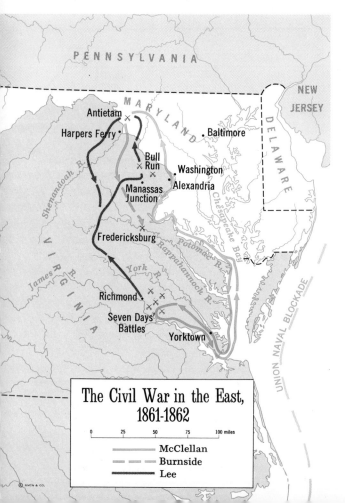

The Civil War in the East, 1861-1862

0   25   50   75   100 miles

——— McClellan
- - - Burnside
——— Lee

ually lost patience with the General's apparent unwillingness to get the army into action against the enemy. Concluded Lincoln, "He has got the 'slows.'"

McClellan, despite constant prodding, did not move his well-trained army until April, 1862. Even then he did not budge until he had received a command to do so from Lincoln.

Into the peninsula. In order to capture Richmond, McClellan planned to head for that city by way of the peninsula, a marshy area about 15 miles wide between the James and York rivers. Richmond lies on the northern side of the James.

At Yorktown McClellan's army met the Confederates—or the Grays—under General Joseph E. Johnston and forced them to retreat. They pulled back toward Richmond, pursued by the Union forces.

The Confederates were greatly aided, however, by the bold moves of "Stonewall" Jackson in the Shenandoah Valley. His attacks on Union forces were planned to make the North fear for the safety of the city of Washington. This, the Confederates hoped, would keep Lincoln from sending McDowell with help for McClellan.

A new Confederate commander. During the peninsula campaign, Confederate leader General Johnston was badly wounded. The command of his army was passed to Robert E. Lee, often affectionately called Marse Robert by those who knew him.

Lee was a gentle man who had not been in favor of secession and who years earlier had freed the few slaves he owned. He had a knack for keeping high the spirits of his men. In part this was because he did not like to strut in his uniform or take advantage of his authority.

Lee was determined that the Confederates would not remain on the defensive at Richmond. Every man who could be spared was called to the southern capital.

The Seven Days' Battles. On June 26, 1862, the enlarged Confederate army, un-

Wagon trains of the Army of the Potomac retreat toward the James and Potomac rivers during the savage fighting in the Seven Days' Battles.

der Lee's leadership, lashed out at the Union forces only a few miles from Richmond. This was the beginning of a fierce, week-long struggle known as the Seven Days' Battles. In it Lee had the help of his famous cavalry leader, General A. P. Hill, and of General James Longstreet. Gradually, at great cost to the Confederates, the Union forces were rolled back, though not destroyed, and Richmond was saved. The peninsula campaign was over.

Two mistakes. Lincoln could wait no longer to act. He appointed as McClellan's superior officer General Henry W. Halleck, who had been Grant's chief in the West. Halleck's nickname was "Brains." Lincoln needed a man of brains, but he also required a man of energy.

You can imagine Lincoln's disappointment when Halleck at first could not seem to tear himself loose from his duties in the West. The President had to send him a wire reading, "I am very anxious—almost impatient—to have you here." At last, on July 1, 1862, Halleck succeeded McClel-lan, making Washington his headquarters.

Lincoln quickly found that he had made a very bad mistake. In fact, he had made two. He had also appointed General John Pope to command a part of the Army of the Potomac. Pope had been a critic of "Little Mac." Lincoln had chosen him in hopes he could silence the Congressmen who were calling for more vigorous military leadership. Pope, though, was disastrously defeated by Lee at the second Battle of Bull Run, August 29 and 30, 1862.

The President was beside himself. A few weeks before, Union soldiers had been just outside Richmond. Now the great Army of the Potomac had been pushed back and the city of Washington itself appeared to be threatened.

The return of McClellan. Lincoln once again turned to "Little Mac"—but with only slight confidence—to take over the Army of the Potomac. Lincoln's reason for entrusting the army to him again was, "If he can't fight himself, he excels in making others ready to fight."

‡Halleck had written books on military planning. His talents were those of the office, not the battlefield. In the war his early reputation came from the victories won by officers, like Grant, under his command. Later, however, Halleck was an able chief of staff.

The Commander in Chief is seen here visiting McClellan at the General's field headquarters on October 3, 1862, just after Antietam.

Turning Point

Meanwhile, Lee had pressed forward across the Potomac River. He hoped to capture arms and ammunition at Harpers Ferry. You will recall—as he did—that he had been there before (see page 406).

Lee's chief plan was to invade the border of Maryland and cut the railroad lines to Washington. He wanted to obtain supplies and to remove the war from Virginia's soil during the harvest season. He hoped possibly to persuade Maryland to join the Confederacy.

Antietam. Luck now ran with McClellan. A copy of Lee's orders fell into his hands, and "Little Mac" was excited. He declared, "Here is a paper with which, if I cannot whip Bobbie Lee, I will be willing to go home." McClellan caught Lee's outnumbered troops at Antietam Creek, in Maryland, on September 17, 1862. Nearly 3000 Confederates were killed, and over 9000 were wounded. The Union forces suffered almost equally. Unable to stand up against such a murderous assault, Lee retreated across the Potomac.

But once again McClellan failed at a critical moment: he did not order his men to pursue the Confederates. They escaped across the Potomac—to fight again another day.

Effect abroad. The Battle of Antietam was important because it showed that the Union had the military strength to defeat the Confederates. Before the news of this federal triumph reached Europe, England and France had been planning to try to bring the Union and the Confederacy to peaceful terms. Afterward, Europeans knew the Union itself could end the war.

The Emancipation Proclamation. Antietam also enabled Lincoln to strike a hard blow at the southern "aristocrats." He announced that beginning January 1, 1863, all slaves in areas still in rebellion would be ever afterward free people. When that day arrived, the President issued the Emancipation Proclamation, carrying out his intention.

The making of such an announcement had long been in Lincoln's mind. After the Battle of Antietam, he felt he could go ahead with it.

The Emancipation Proclamation was a *military* measure—as well as one for the welfare of human beings. Lincoln hoped that it would weaken the southerners' war effort because it would take property from them. It was not intended to produce a slave uprising—although many Confederates charged that this was its purpose.

Importance. The immediate effect of the proclamation on slavery was slight, because it applied only to states at war with the Union. Yet it served notice on the en-

#Discuss the importance of the Emancipation Proclamation. What was the proclamation supposed to accomplish? Why did Lincoln include some but not all the areas where slavery existed?

ire country that the fate of slavery would no longer be in the hands of the states but in those of the federal government. Furthermore, the proclamation was another milestone in the development of American democracy. It made clear that the great words of the Declaration of Independence —especially, "all men are created equal"— continued to have life and meaning.

A change in purpose. By the time the Emancipation Proclamation went into effect, it was clear that the war would deeply affect the relationship between the races in the United States. The struggle, which had begun as an effort to save the Union, was becoming also a war for the freedom of slaves.

As late as August 22, 1862, Lincoln had written to Horace Greeley, editor of the *New York Tribune:*

My paramount [that is, chief] object in this struggle is to save the Union, and is not either to save or to destroy slavery. If I could save the Union without freeing *any* slave I would do it; and if I could save it by freeing *all* the slaves I would do it; and if I could save it by freeing some and leaving others alone, I would also do that.

By the beginning of 1863, many Negroes understood that the Civil War had a new purpose. Many had doubted earlier that the promise to free the slaves would ever be put into effect.

In Boston, for example, the distinguished former slave Frederick Douglass waited with increasing impatience and disappointment as the day and evening of January 1 passed with no word from Washington. Then the telegraph began to click

Slaves freed by the Emancipation Proclamation join some Union forces. These migrants had left their owners, but many loyal slaves remained behind in the only homes they had known.

out the stirring news, and people streamed in shouting, "It's coming! It's on the wires!"

Negro soldiers in blue. Negroes began to be enrolled in the Union army after the Department of War authorized their recruitment in the summer of 1862. The first official Negro regiment was under the command of T. W. Higginson of Boston. It was known as the First South Carolina Volunteers.

Another Negro unit—and one which saw very heavy action—was the Fifty-fourth Massachusetts Volunteers. Its commander was a Boston abolitionist, Colonel Robert G. Shaw. Shaw fell in battle on July 18, 1863, leading his troops against Fort Wagner, a Confederate post guarding Charleston Harbor.

By 1865 about 180,000 Negroes had seized the opportunity to help fight for their people's freedom. Twenty-one Negroes earned the Congressional Medal of Honor for bravery.

Still in Virginia

Lincoln knew that McClellan had to go —once and for all—when that general failed to pursue Lee after Antietam. The President had seen enough of the "slows." Another West Pointer, General Ambrose E. Burnside, now replaced McClellan. Some of the men of the Army of the Potomac vowed that they would serve none but their old commander. But "Little Mac" urged them to "stand by General Burnside as you have stood by me."

Now Burnside. Burnside was a likable man whose bushy side-whiskers and mustache set him apart—and added the word sideburns to our language. But he himself was aware that he lacked the qualities required for supreme command.

Fredericksburg. Taking hold of the Union army in northern Virginia, Burnside decided to lead it across the Rappahannock River at Fredericksburg. From there he would drive on toward Richmond. When he reached Fredericksburg in late fall 1862, however, he found Lee—with "Stonewall" Jackson and James Longstreet —already dug in on the heights facing the Union troops. Shortly, on December 13, a total of 200,000 men joined in deadly battle. The Confederate soldiers were greatly outnumbered.

The Union forces attacked fiercely. Their spirits, unfortunately, were low because McClellan, their favorite, was no longer in command and they lacked confidence in Burnside. They suffered roughly 12,000 casualties before Burnside withdrew them across the river. If Lee had pursued Burnside, the Union army might have been destroyed.

"Fighting Joe." Once more Lincoln had to change generals. This time he chose one of Burnside's officers, General Joseph Hooker, who went by the nickname "Fighting Joe."

Now Hooker made preparations. Confidently he told some of his officers, "My plans are perfect, and when I start to carry them out, may God have mercy on General Lee, for I will have none."

Chancellorsville. But Hooker was no equal to his words when the test came. In April, 1863, he, too, went across the Rappahannock to search for the Confederates and to advance on Richmond. At Chancellorsville, Virginia, he engaged the Confederates under Lee in a fierce battle.

Lee split his army in two, giving one part to "Stonewall" Jackson and leading the other himself. The two Confederate forces then outflanked Hooker's men and after three days of fighting sent them sprawling across the river again in defeat.

The North lost 17,000 men at Chancellorsville. Lincoln was pacing up and down in his office, waiting for news, when the word of the disaster reached him. He could only exclaim, "My God! My God! What will the country say! What will the country

436   ##Political pressures also forced Lincoln into this desperate search for a general who would eng[...] in decisive actions. Radicals in the Republican party wanted immediate victory, and some Democrats called for an end to the war.

say!" So another Union campaign had failed, and thousands of families had received the awful word from the Department of War: "Your son has died in action."

The South, too, was being faced with losses of men it could not afford. At Chancellorsville "Stonewall" Jackson was fatally wounded—accidentally, by his own troops—and shortly afterward died. Jackson, a deeply religious man, had demanded iron discipline among his troops. Yet they made him their hero. Abraham Lincoln had not yet found a general who could win, and Jefferson Davis would not again find a general like Jackson.

Beginning of the End

How badly the South would need its best military talent was shown in the next few months. In Richmond, Jefferson Davis, his Cabinet, and Lee decided on an invasion of Pennsylvania. Lee hoped to accomplish at least three things: (1) divide the North and hasten the end of the war; (2) seize badly needed food supplies; and (3) by his success bring foreign assistance to the side of the South.

Meade in charge. Beginning in the middle of June, 1863, Lee began to move his army across the Potomac River. With him were Longstreet and A. P. Hill, but he missed Jackson badly.

The Union army was situated at Frederick, Maryland. Lincoln had removed Hooker and had given the command to General George G. Meade. An able military man but not a superior one, he inspired respect among his men, although not blind loyalty. He had a hot temper (he was known as the old snapping turtle) which held people at a distance.

The Battle of Gettysburg. As Lee's army moved toward the town of Gettysburg, Pennsylvania, his advance force met Meade's advance force. The date was July 1, 1863. The Battle of Gettysburg, the bloodiest battle ever fought on this continent, was about to begin. For three days it raged, as Meade's men held off brave Confederate attacks.

Pickett's charge. The high point of the attacks came on July 3. Troops led by the South's General George Pickett were ordered to cross a rolling plain that separated the central Union position from that

Pickett's charge, in the early afternoon of July 3, 1863, from a sketch made at the time. The lines of Confederates are seen in the center. Southern soldiers examine their tattered flag.

"Battles and Leaders of the Civil War," The Century Co., 1884

of the Confederates. The 15,000 Confederates in Pickett's charge—as it was ever afterward known—moved forward with their shining bayonets fixed. As they approached within range of the Union guns on Cemetery Ridge, they met a withering fire. When it stopped, not a single mounted officer was left. Staggering numbers of Pickett's men had been killed or wounded.

Lee met the stunned Pickett to offer him the comforting words "Your men have done all that men could do; the fault is entirely my own." Whatever was in Lee's mind we do not know, of course. But he may have recognized that the victory which so far had been escaping the Union's grasp was never going to be his, either. Possibly deep down he had always felt this.

A poor judgment. On the night of July 4, Lee's men began an orderly retreat in a drenching downpour. They could not know

The final campaigns of the war in both the East and the West.

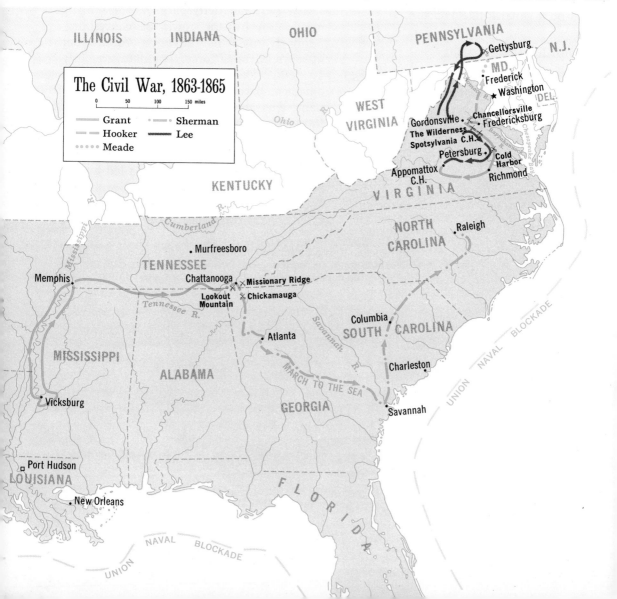

Civil War soldiers did not spend all their time fighting.
Left: Northerners receive welcome letters and newspapers from home.
Right: Confederates have some fun throwing snowballs.

that they were falling back from the northernmost point the Confederates would reach in the entire war. Each side had lost between 23,000 and 28,000 men.

Meade could have chased Lee and destroyed his army, but to Lincoln's unspeakable annoyance, he allowed Lee to return to Virginia. Somehow Meade had thought his task to be merely one of driving the invader out of the North—not of crushing the enemy.

Lincoln asked Meade, "Do you know, general, what your attitude toward Lee for a week after the battle reminded me of?"

"No, Mr. President," Meade answered. "What is it?"

Replied Lincoln, "I'll be hanged if I could think of anything else than a woman trying to shoo her geese across a creek."

But Lincoln kept Meade in his post.

The immortal Gettysburg Address. The following November 19, Lincoln attended the dedication of the Union cemetery at Gettysburg. The main speaker was Edward Everett, earlier a Massachusetts Senator and a president of Harvard College. His address lasted two hours.

Then the President spoke, uttering exactly ten sentences which will be remembered forever. They expressed—better than anyone else has ever expressed—what America stands for and what the Civil War was being fought to preserve. "We here highly resolve," the President said, "that these dead shall not have died in vain; that this nation, under God, shall have a new birth of freedom, and that government of the people, by the people, and for the people, shall not perish from the earth."

The long-winded Senator sent Lincoln a message not long afterward. "I should be glad if I could flatter myself," he wrote, "that I came as near the central idea . . . in two hours as you did in two minutes."

Vicksburg. On the same Fourth of July in 1863, when the Battle of Gettysburg was going on, the Union was gaining full control of the Mississippi River again. This very important event was the result of a series of bold moves. At the start of 1863, a Union army under General William Starke Rosecrans had taken a terrible mauling in defeating a Confederate army near Murfreesboro, Tennessee. But "Old Rosy's" army had slowly recovered and finally was able to help capture the city of Chattanooga.

How do Lincoln's words show that he looked upon the war as a struggle to maintain representative government? Lincoln viewed the United States in a world context as the oldest, most important representative democracy--"the last, best hope of earth."

National Archives

Ulysses S. Grant, a West Pointer who had left the army and had come back to be the general Lincoln was looking for.

he had allowed them to combine their strength.

On July 4, 1863, after a fierce and costly siege, Vicksburg fell to Grant.

"Unvexed to the sea." A few days later, when Port Hudson, another Confederate fortress, fell, the Mississippi was no longer in southern hands and the Confederacy was cut in two. Now Abraham Lincoln could write words which became famous: "The Father of Waters again goes unvexed [that is, unhindered] to the sea."

Chickamauga. After Vicksburg Rosecrans advanced south of Chattanooga, chasing Confederates under Braxton Bragg. But General Bragg surprised him at Chickamauga, where the Union army was saved only by General George H. Thomas, who held like a rock. Thomas has been remembered as the "Rock of Chickamauga."

The Confederates now bottled up the northerners in Chattanooga and tried to starve them into surrender. Generals Grant and Sherman came to the rescue from Vicksburg, breaking the siege. In the Battle of Lookout Mountain–Missionary Ridge, late in 1863, Grant, Thomas, Sherman, and Hooker teamed up and defeated Bragg.

While waiting for the freeing of the Tennessee River, Union military planners had kept their eyes on the Mississippi. After Farragut's capture of New Orleans and his advance up the Mississippi in the spring of 1862, only Vicksburg remained as a Confederate stronghold on the river. If it could be taken, the Mississippi River would be in northern hands.

To take the city, Grant, with 20,000 men, crossed the river below Vicksburg, cutting himself loose from his supply line. # Operating brilliantly in enemy territory, he defeated, one after the other, Confederate forces that could have crushed him if

1. Describe the first battle of the Civil War. 2. Which northern war aim did Grant try to carry out in early 1862? 3. To what extent had the aim been carried out by April 25, 1862? 4. Tell the purpose of and describe McClellan's peninsula campaign. 5. What important effect did the Battle of Antietam have abroad? 6. State three results of the Emancipation Proclamation. 7. Name Lee's three reasons for invading Pennsylvania. 8. On what occasion did Lincoln deliver the Gettysburg Address? 9. Tell how Union forces finally gained control of the Mississippi.

#The daring and success of Grant in the West were the main reasons for his rise to the command of the whole army. Grant, like Sherman and Sheridan, represented a new group of generals who led Union forces in the last phase of the war.

Blow upon Blow Pummels the South

The recapture of control of the river by the Union and the defeat of Lee at Gettysburg foretold that the end of the war would not be a happy one for the Confederacy. Time was running out for it.

Dixie's Home Front

On the southern home front a number of serious problems had already appeared. They grew worse as the war continued.

Financial troubles. Possibly the most serious problem was financial. The Confederate government did not tax the people enough to pay the cost of the war. Failing to tax its citizens, it had to seek loans. But since the Confederacy was without diplomatic recognition and had poor financial backing, only one foreign bank was willing to lend the South money.

Because there was a heavy demand for gold and silver, coins disappeared from circulation as southerners hoarded and concealed both metals. The Confederacy issued huge quantities of paper money, which was worth less and less as time passed. Counterfeiting was very easy, and many fake bills were printed in the North and pushed into circulation in the South to weaken the Confederate currency further.

Wild prices. As the value of the currency went down, prices rose like skyrockets. By 1864 in Richmond, for instance, shoes were selling at $125 a pair, potatoes at $25 a bushel, and bacon at $9 a pound. Before the war was over, more and more people had to obtain goods through barter—that is, by swapping—because there was a lack of enough acceptable money.

Serious shortages. Life was also made more difficult in the South by shortages of most of the necessary goods. Wool was scarce from the start of the war. Salt—especially necessary for preserving meat—was almost completely unavailable by 1865. (Remember that refrigeration as we know it had not yet been developed.) There was also a shortage of many drugs and medicines.

A lack of factories. In addition to the need to supply the general population, there were huge requirements for uniforms, shoes, arms, and ammunition for the troops in the field. Having built few industries, the South was at a definite disadvantage. The Confederate government was forced to establish its own manufacturing plants—not all of which were well managed.

The distribution of some goods was

Southerners who, in February, 1864, were forced by the lack of food and other supplies in the Confederacy to make an uncomfortable trip to a Union commissary—a place where such things were available.

affected by the jealousy of the states. North Carolina, for instance, had a considerable number of cotton mills, but its governor kept the cloth they produced for the use of its own soldiers.

Inadequate rail system. When the Civil War broke out, southern railroads consisted of a large number of short lines which were poorly linked together. No one seems to have recognized the important part a railroad network could play in the war. As a result, not only were the lines not improved, but also they were allowed to become run-down.

Gradually the railroads became a bottleneck in the movement of southern soldiers and supplies. Many skilled railroad men disappeared into the army. Those who were northerners living in the South simply went home. As the destruction of the railroads by the Union armies increased southerners could repair main lines only by tearing up branch lines to get rails.

No navy. The lack of a navy or merchant fleet was a severe handicap the Confederacy never overcame. The South could not lift the North's blockades and open the way to imports from abroad. At one point in 1862, the Confederates succeeded in doing damage to Union vessels with an armored steamship, the *Merrimac*. Off the Virginia coast, however, it met a Union ship clad in iron, the *Monitor*. The duel that followed did not lead to victory for either side. But the Union blockade remained unbroken.

Uninspiring civilian leaders. The South never developed civilian leaders as good as its military leaders. The men Davis chose for his Cabinet had only ordinary ability. They lacked the influence in the Confederacy that Lincoln's Cabinet members enjoyed in the North.

Davis himself, far from having the common touch which was one of Lincoln's outstanding qualities, had an icy manner. He was always sure his judgments were better

than anybody else's. Moreover, he meddled unnecessarily in military affairs.

Fear of the slaves. On top of everything, southerners lived with the terrible fear of a slave uprising. Mrs. Mary Chestnut, a South Carolinian, kept a fascinating diary during much of the war. On the very day that the guns were booming in the attack on Fort Sumter, she was writing:

> Not by one word or look can we detect any change in the demeanor [that is, conduct] of these Negro servants. You could not tell that they even heard the awful roar going on in the bay, though it has been dinning in their ears night and day. People talk before them as if they were chairs and tables. They make no sign. Are they stolidly stupid? or wiser than we are; silent and strong, biding their time?

In March, 1865, ignoring fear, the Confederate congress passed a bill to permit the arming of Negroes. This, of course, was a last-ditch step, for it meant the South would hurl into the final battles the very property it was fighting to protect!

Toward Surrender

In spite of the turning of the tide, a weariness with the fighting had begun to take hold in the North by the middle of 1863. There were no longer enough volunteers, and Congress had passed draft laws.

The laws applied unevenly to the population. A man might escape military service by finding and paying for a substitute. For $300 one could avoid army duty altogether. Almost 87,000 men got out of doing service by paying the sum required. Almost 118,000 northerners found substitutes for themselves.

New York's draft riots. A week after northerners heard what was to them the glorious news of victories from Gettysburg and Vicksburg, riots occurred in New York City in protest against the draft. Mobs

The *Merrimac*, a Confederate ironclad vessel—center —fires on the smaller Union *Monitor*—right. The *Monitor* is returning fire with guns mounted on a revolving turret in the center of its flat deck.

from the poorer sections of the city roamed the streets looting and burning and shouting "Down with the rich!" A number of people were killed, including especially Negroes, targets of strong racial feeling.

The new lieutenant general. Lincoln made a long-awaited move early in 1864. He appointed General Grant—whom he had never met—to be lieutenant general in charge of all the United States forces. Grant went east to report to the President. A famous editor described the new commander in these words:

> He had a cigar in his mouth, and rather the look of a man who did, or once did, take a little too much to drink ... a slightly seedy look, as if he was out of office and on half pay, nothing to do but hang around, a clear blue eye and a look of resolution [that is, determination] as if he could not be trifled with. ... He does not march, nor quite walk, but pitches along as if the next step would bring him on his nose.

Lincoln's welcome to Grant was warm and plain: "I'm glad to see you, general."

Final plans. Plans were now made to smash the Confederates. Grant would move south toward Richmond to attack Lee. General William Tecumseh Sherman, who had replaced Grant in the West, would move in a southeasterly direction from Chattanooga, Tennessee, into Georgia, and take Atlanta. Another army under General Benjamin F. Butler was scheduled to force its way south to Richmond up the south bank of the James River.

The Wilderness. Grant's troops greatly outnumbered Lee's, but the nature of the terrain (that is, land features) helped the Confederates. Grant's men marched into a stretch of woods, called the Wilderness, where, on May 5, 1864, Lee attacked them in the Battle of the Wilderness.

The losses of life were tremendous. Grant lost more than 17,000 men. But instead of retreating, he advanced under cover of the night. At last Lincoln had a man who dared to stand up and fight.

Spotsylvania and Cold Harbor. Like a pair of bloody giants, the armies slugged away at each other. At Spotsylvania Court House and Cold Harbor, near Richmond, two ferocious battles were fought, leaving more thousands dead. The men on both sides awoke each morning wondering if they would live to see the sunset.

How many soldiers must have asked, as one lieutenant did, "Why is it that 200,000 men of one blood and tongue, believing as one man in the fatherhood of God and the universal brotherhood of man, should in

443

'ry to find the qualities that made Grant a good soldier. How did he compare with other ion generals in background, experience, appearance, and willingness to fight?

the nineteenth century of the Christian era
be thus armed with all the appliances of
modern warfare and seeking one another's
lives?"

Petersburg. Grant had said at Spotsylvania, "I . . . propose to fight it out on this
line if it takes all summer." But now he
changed his plans. He moved his troops
from before Richmond and aimed for Petersburg. If he could capture the railroad
leading from there to Richmond, he could
cut Lee off from his supplies.

Lee arrived at Petersburg ahead of
Grant, a fact which for the moment saved
Richmond. But the clock was running down
for Lee. He could not replace his losses,
and he was short of supplies.

Lee attempted to draw off some of
Grant's men by sending a force northward
toward Washington. The force was beaten
back—as Lincoln himself watched. That
was the last time the capital of the Union
was threatened.

Sherman's march. Meanwhile, in 1864,
at about the same time the Wilderness
campaign was beginning, General Sherman set forth from Chattanooga toward
Atlanta. Four months later he captured the
city. Nevertheless, he had not destroyed
the Confederate army. He decided not to
wait any longer. First practically destroying Atlanta by burning it, he and his
men set out on a bold march to the sea.

Sherman, who at the outbreak of the
war had been Superintendent of Louisiana
State Seminary (now Louisiana State University), instructed his troops not to injure
civilians unnecessarily. But they disobeyed
orders and pillaged and looted without
conscience. Not only did Sherman's men
destroy public buildings and raid farmhouses for horses and other livestock,
but they lived off the land. That is, groups
of soldiers called bummers systematically
rounded up food and supplies for the Union troops from the land through which
they marched.

American Heritage Publishing Co.

Adam Link, one-hundred-two-year-old veteran of
the American Revolution, in 1864. As a youth
he had witnessed the start of the nation, and
in his old age he rejoiced to see it reunited.

On December 22, 1864, Savannah fell to
Sherman. Behind him lay a 50-mile stretch
of Georgia utterly ruined. Sherman, a modern general in that he realized how important civilian feeling could be, said sadly,
"To realize what war is, one should follow
our tracks."

Sherman now continued into South Carolina and North Carolina—to Raleigh—
meeting practically no opposition. His men
continued to burn and pillage.

The fall of Richmond. In the spring,
moreover, Petersburg fell to Grant. On
April 3, 1865, Richmond also surrendered.
A few days later Lincoln visited the plundered Confederate capital. Negroes gathered around him wherever he went. He
had already become known as "The Great
Emancipator."

The Appomattox meeting. Lee could not
escape defeat. Grant wrote him, "The results of the last week must convince you of
the hopelessness of further resistance." On
April 9, 1865, General Lee surrendered
near Appomattox Court House, a small
town in Virginia.

The scene—after all the bloodshed—

##What did Sherman mean by this statement? Sherman, perhaps more than any other soldier,
444   realized the destructive nature of modern warfare. Why did his march bring injury to civilians
as well as to soldiers?

was a simple one. Grant, almost forty-three, still had the look of a quite young man. Modestly, he wore a private's uniform to which had been fastened on the shoulders the three stars of his rank.

Lee, riding his faithful horse Traveler, wore a brand-new general's uniform and carried a bejeweled sword of honor. The war had aged Lee badly: his hair and his beard had turned white.

Grant's greeting to Lee was pleasant. He began, "I met you once before, General Lee, while we were serving in Mexico." After a few minutes the simple terms of surrender were arranged: the defeated soldiers were to sign pledges not to fight any more, and then they would go home. They could keep their horses and side arms.

Grant and Lee saluted, and Lee rode off to tell his troops, "Men, we have fought through this war together. I have done the best I could for you. My heart is too full to say any more."

Grant had stopped his men from cheering Lee's surrender at Appomattox Court House, saying, "The rebels are our countrymen again." But, in fact, the scene was opening on struggles that were just as angry as wartime battles even though they were not fought by men in uniforms. All eyes turned to the city of Washington for guidance. There Lincoln was beginning a second term in office.

The Fallen Commander in Chief

In 1864, as Sherman was nearing Atlanta, the presidential election was held. Lincoln's unsuccessful Democratic rival was none other than General McClellan.

Lincoln's hopes. As Lincoln took the oath of office again, he was thinking of how to make peace in the war between brothers. When he delivered his second inaugural address on March 4, 1865, the end of the fighting was in sight. He said:

Grant and Lee meet in the McClean house at Appomattox Court House. After their talk Grant sent food to Lee's soldiers, and Grant's officers looked up old friends and classmates among the Confederates, including Longstreet, who had attended Grant's wedding.

Appomattox Court House National Historical Park

With malice [that is, bad will] toward none; with charity for all; with firmness in the right, as God gives us to see the right, let us strive on to finish the work we are in; to bind up the nation's wounds; to care for him who shall have borne the battle, and for his widow, and his orphan—to do all which may achieve and cherish a just, and a lasting peace, among ourselves, and with all nations.

Death at the theater. But Lincoln himself did not live to "finish the work." On April 14—Good Friday—1865, Abraham and Mary Lincoln went to Ford's Theater in Washington to attend the comedy *Our American Cousin.* The Grants, who were to have been with them, begged off because the General's wife was going to visit their children in New Jersey.

The President and the First Lady arrived at about 8:30 P.M. The play had been on for three-quarters of an hour. The band struck up "Hail to the Chief," the audience clapped, and the play resumed.

At a few minutes after ten, John Wilkes Booth, a famous actor grieving deeply over the South's defeat, entered the President's box and fired one shot. Mrs. Lincoln screamed, and then all was confusion in the theater. Booth made his escape by jumping to the stage and by riding away on his horse. The President, critically wounded, was carried to a house across the street from the theater. There he died the following morning, as his doctors stood by helplessly.

The nation mourned now as it had never mourned before. The people had just begun to appreciate the wisdom and humanity of the President. And in mourning the martyred Lincoln, many everywhere were in fact grieving for themselves. Jefferson Davis, in a touching tribute, said of Lincoln's passing, "Next to the destruction of the Confederacy, the death of Abraham Lincoln was the darkest day the South has known."

1. Name seven causes of difficulties in the South during the Civil War. 2. State the three final plans Union leaders made to defeat the Confederacy. 3. What success did the North have in carrying them out? 4. Where and when did Lee surrender? 5. Give the main facts about the murder of President Lincoln.

The Workshop

The Shapers of Our World

Tell what role each of the following played in the outcome of the Civil War:

Jefferson Davis
Crittenden
  Compromise
Fort Sumter
Pierre T.
  Beauregard
Robert E. Lee

Charles Goodyear
Elias Howe
Isaac M. Singer
Cyrus McCormick
"Stonewall" Jackson
Albert Sidney
  Johnston

George B.
  McClellan
Ulysses S. Grant
John Wilkes Booth
Battle of Shiloh
David G. Farragut
the Seven Days'
  Battles
First Bull Run
Battle of Antietam
James Longstreet
Gettysburg

Battle of
  Chancellorsville
Emancipation
  Proclamation
Vicksburg
the *Monitor* and
  the *Merrimac*
William T. Sherman
Appomattox
  Court House
Forts Henry
  and Donelson

##Discuss whether or not it was reasonable, at the end of the war, to assume that Lincoln would have been as successful in restoring the Union as he had been in maintaining it?

Adding to Your Vocabulary

Be sure you know these words:

gait

malice

processing

reaper

secede

grave

vulcanization

Thinking Things Through

After reviewing the boxed-in exercises in the chapter, answer these questions:

1. Why do incoming Presidents rarely announce their plans until they actually take office?

2. How did the 1860 election show the loss of southern political power?

3. Why did Lincoln, being a Republican President-elect, have to advise against the Crittenden Compromise?

4. Why did some people think it not fitting for Chief Justice Taney, who handed down the Dred Scott decision, to give the oath of office to Lincoln?

5. Why was the Civil War fought in the South rather than in the North?

6. Why did Lincoln not make the Emancipation Proclamation apply to the border states?

7. Why do some historians consider the blockade of the South the most effective "weapon" of the Civil War?

8. What one idea lay behind each of the following: (a) the Virginia and Kentucky resolutions; (b) the calling of the Hartford Convention; (c) Calhoun's statement of nullification; and (d) the secession of southern states? Compare the responses of Jackson, Buchanan, and Lincoln.

History Through the Arts

1. Dramatize for the class some of the following incidents of the Civil War: (a) Lee's refusal to accept command of the Union forces; (b) Lincoln's meeting with McClellan after the Battle of Antietam or with Meade after the Battle of Gettysburg; (c) a Confederate cabinet meeting after the fall of Atlanta; (d) Lee at Appomattox.

2. Sing some of these famous songs of the war: "The Battle Hymn of the Republic," "Bonnie Blue Flag," "The Battle Cry of Freedom," "Dixie," "Tenting on the Old Camp Ground," and "Just before the Battle, Mother."

What do the songs tell you about the belief in being right both sides had? How do the songs show the suffering of a civil war?

3. Read Walt Whitman's "O Captain, My Captain!" Julia Ward Howe's "Robert E. Lee," and Father Abram Ryan's "Furl Thy Banner."

Sharpening Your Map Skills

1. What were the aims of the Union campaigns shown on the map on page 431?

2. What was McClellan trying to do in the peninsula campaign, shown on the map on page 432? What was Lee attempting in the Seven Days' Battles?

3. Looking at the map on page 438, tell: (a) about how far Lee advanced into Union territory; (b) what he had in mind in the invasion; (c) what war aims the map indicates the Union forces carried out.

Your Opinion, Please

1. How might the course of the Civil War have been changed if the Confederates had followed up their victory at the first Battle of Bull Run by attacking Washington? If Lee had been pursued after the Battle of Gettysburg?

2. Why would Jefferson Davis deeply grieve over the death of Abraham Lincoln?

3. The Civil War continues to fascinate Americans, and they wonder how it could have happened to them. What did they learn from it?

There have been many different points of view about the Civil War. To help students begin to appreciate this difference of opinion, have them explain how a Confederate and a Unionist might have reacted to the results of the war.

(a)

(b)

(c)

(a) Americans enjoy the one-hundredth
birthday of their independence at a fair
held in Philadelphia in 1876.
(b) The hand and torch of the Statue of
Liberty, which were displayed at the
fair before the completed statue
was placed in New York Harbor.
(c) A campaign lantern of 1876, showing
the face of Rutherford B. Hayes, who won
the presidency. (d) Hayes bought this
brass door knocker in 1882
for his home in Fremont, Ohio.
(e) The Capitol in 1871, soon after the
dome was completed (see page 420).

(d)

(e)

(f) A fashionable parlor in New York City about 1875.

ter the Civil War did Americans
m to become more concerned
h public display--with fairs,
blicity, and fashionable houses--
n in the past? (Use the pictures
pp. 448-449.)

CHAPTER 20

UNITING THE STATES AGAIN

Lincoln had to master unprecedented crises during the war, his successors had to face similarly serious
tters following it. Why did reuniting the nation seem almost as difficult as preserving the Union?
at questions had the war settled?

THE Civil War had settled the question of whether the Union could be broken up by secession. The question Americans now asked was, What price will the states of the Confederacy have to pay before they can have "business as usual" again with the rest of the country?

Often the southerners believed that the crushing military defeat they had suffered —including the loss of billions of dollars' worth of slaves—had been punishment enough. Widows, orphans, and injured ex-soldiers—to say nothing of the destroyed property—were reminders everywhere of how heavy the penalty for them already #
had been.

#Compare the losses of northerners and southerners. Both sides suffered greatly.

Two Presidents Try to Bind Up the Wounds

Possibly most southerners were simply anxious to get on with the physical rebuilding of their section of the country. In some places everything that can make life worth living had been wiped out.

The Wreckage

A witness described the scene along the line of Sherman's march into South Carolina. He said it looked "like a broad black streak of ruin and desolation—the fences all gone; lonesome smoke stacks, sur-

rounded by dark heaps of ashes and cinders, marking the spots where human habitations [dwelling places] had stood."

The former planters. Planters who had been wealthy in 1861 were reduced to beggary by 1865. A keen observer wrote, for example, of Charleston, South Carolina, that "luxury, refinement, [and] happiness have fled... and poverty is enthroned there." The reunions of tattered soldiers with their penniless families produced scenes that, it was said, "would draw pity from a stone."

449

ided in war, the North and South remained for a time divided in reconstruction. Have stu-
ts consider the different, often opposing attitudes toward procedures for reuniting the states.

Many southerners hoped that they could put things back together pretty much as they had been before the disaster. But of course, life could never be the same again. The freeing of the slaves had made that fact certain. Yet former masters were as unprepared as the former slaves for the day of emancipation.

The former slaves. In some places in the South, the freedmen stayed on at their plantations for a while after the war and worked as always. After all, poor as the slave quarters might be, they *were* "home." Besides, where could the freedmen go?

Many former slaves—as well as white people—were supported by a new system of farming called *sharecropping*. Under it a landowner would assign a piece of his land to a man and loan him money for seed and other supplies so that the soil could be worked. At harvesttime the owner would "share" the crop.

Other ex-slaves viewed the granting of freedom as an end to the need to work. Some seem to have wandered about alone or in groups. Many, of course, wandered in search of relatives separated from them through sale. Undoubtedly some freedmen stole to keep alive.

Still other ex-slaves, when the "day of jubilee" came, made their way to the cities or joined in the general westward movement of southerners. Many looked upon their freedom as an opportunity for self-improvement—even though there were practically no ways to accomplish it.

Lincoln's Extended Hand

The Civil War left on both sides smoldering fires of hatred and hopes for vengeance that lasted for years. The North had lost about 360,000 men—the South, about 258,000. The wounded northerners numbered an additional 275,000—and the southerners, at least 100,000. The victorious section had not suffered the destruction of property the defeated one had—because the war had been mainly fought in the South. Nevertheless, the financial cost of the Union effort was staggering.

As a result, in the days after Appomattox, northerners responded as expected. Yes, they seemed to say, Dixie will be restored to the Union and in time forgiven, but first its people must be made humble.

The work of planning for political reconstruction, that is, the restoration of the

This destruction was caused by a fire.

The ruins brought by war: a burned-out part of Richmond, Virginia, capital of the Confederacy, photographed in April, 1865.

Library of Congress

Confederate states to the Union, was, it had seemed at first, the task of the President. Already Lincoln had taken some steps. His terms to the South—which he had issued in a proclamation on December 8, 1863—had been remarkably generous, considering how fiercely the war was being fought.

The 10-percent plan. Lincoln had said that all Confederates who swore loyalty to the United States would be pardoned. In any former Confederate state a new state government could be formed when 10 percent of those eligible to vote in 1860 had taken oaths of allegiance to the Constitution. The federal government would then recognize it. What the President had hoped to find was a group of people in each former Confederate state who would create a loyal government.

Objections in Congress. But many members of Congress had not been satisfied with Lincoln's ideas. They had proposed a harsher plan of reconstruction. Their plan would have placed military governors in districts made up of ex-Confederate states. These generals would have been in charge of the procedure for reconstruction.

In each of the states a convention would have to be called by voters who could take an oath that they had never voluntarily supported the Confederacy. The convention would then be expected to cancel the state's approval of secession and also to abolish slavery.

Regarding the bill as too severe, President Lincoln had refused to sign it. The group in Congress seeking to take over the task of reconstruction had sharply criticized Lincoln for his refusal, but they had let the matter rest for the time.

Lincoln, who had believed the Confederate states had never actually been *out* of the Union, had hoped to bring the seceded states back into their "proper relation with the Union." At the time of his death, an answer to how to handle the defeated South could no longer be put off.

Andrew Johnson, the Vice-President who became President through the death of Lincoln.

Library of Congress

Johnson Under Fire

The North first of all had to decide whether or not the ex-Confederates were ready to play their part in the Union again. There were differing opinions about this. General Grant, who toured the states of Dixie late in 1865, thought that on the whole southerners were accepting their defeat.

A well-known northern newspaperman, however, had an opposite view. He wrote, "The war feeling here is like a burning bush with a wet blanket wrapped around it. Looked at from the outside, the fire seems quenched. But just peep under the blanket and there it is, all alive, and eating, eating in."

The southern Negroes became the No. 1 problem for the North and the South to tackle. About 500,000 Negroes had fled their masters, and 135,000 of them were serving in the Union army when the war ended. It seemed unjust to return any of these men to slavery. Something more than the Emancipation Proclamation was required to free *all* the slaves, because some were not affected by it—for example, those in Missouri and the border states.

The Thirteenth Amendment. The freeing of *all* the slaves was the work of the "Radical Republicans" in Congress. They received this name because they were fiercely antislavery and unready to forgive

e a student do a brief report comparing the aftermath of the Civil War with that of other
dern "total wars"--World War I and World War II, for example. In view of the conditions
t have followed other modern wars, was reconstruction after the Civil War harsh or lenient?

the Confederates. It was these men who introduced into Congress what became the Thirteenth Amendment to the Constitution. Its provision was simple: slavery in the United States was banished forever.

#

The amendment was quickly ratified by the required number of states—three-fourths—and went into effect on December 18, 1865, a glorious Christmas present for about four million Negroes.

The fate of freedmen. Nevertheless, the gift of freedom found most Negroes homeless and without work. They would need help in order to prosper as free people.

The codes. The southern governments responded to the problems of the freedmen not in new ways, but in old ones. Southern legislatures passed laws, or codes, to control the activities of the freedmen and especially to prevent trouble between the races. These codes regulated labor contracts (a freedman in South Carolina, for instance, needed a special license to work at anything but farming).

The laws also stated the terms on which Negroes could sue in court (in Alabama, for example, they could not testify against anybody but Negroes). The laws generally forbade Negroes to carry arms.

A Negro could be arrested and fined in Mississippi if he was a vagrant—that is, without any visible means of support. If he could not pay his fine—and very few could —he could be hired out by the sheriff until he had worked off the money he owed.

The postwar codes were often old slave codes with only minor changes. Today it is easy to pass judgment on the southerners who enacted them. They were faced with the necessity for maintaining law and order, and they did so according to their experience. Furthermore, they needed workers to help maintain life itself, even though they had no money to pay wages.

The man in the White House. Andrew Johnson, who, as the Vice-President, became President after Lincoln's assassina-

tion, was not the right man to help the freedmen adjust to their new conditions. He lacked both sympathy and tact.

Born in North Carolina in poverty, Johnson had early in his life moved to Tennessee. With the help of friends, he had gone far. He had stepped up from membership in the state legislature to the United States House of Representatives, to the governorship of his state, and then to the United States Senate. In 1864 he had become Lincoln's running mate and been elected Vice-President.

Johnson had never been opposed to slavery, but he had never stopped hating the southern planters who had ignored or snubbed him in the early years of his career. His strong feeling fitted with his opinion of how the war had been started. On one occasion President Johnson told a visiting delegation from Virginia, "You know perfectly well it was the wealthy men of the South who dragooned [forced] the people into secession."

A revealing change. Johnson changed the Lincoln plan of reconstruction, but not in any important way. Of course, the southern states now had to ratify the Thirteenth Amendment. But one addition Johnson made revealed something about his past life: certain rich southerners had to ask him personally for special pardon.

Like Lincoln, Johnson had not thought of trying to get revenge on the South. In fact, considering the terrible cost of the war in life and money, there was surprisingly little punishment of the Confederate civil leaders. Only Jefferson Davis was imprisoned—and he was released in less than two years.

The southern state governments, however, did not do all that was expected of them. They abolished slavery by accepting the Thirteenth Amendment. However, they made no provision for any freedmen to vote, despite Johnson's urging.

Ready or not? Nevertheless, in Decem-

"Vanity Fair," 1872 (Granger Collection)

This cartoonist's drawing of a severe-looking Sumner appeared in a magazine of 1872.

which were set tightly, he had from the beginning of his public career been defending the underdog. As a young man he had worked hard to obtain laws for free public education.

Stevens was ill in 1865, and he knew he might not live to see the end of reconstruction. But he made up his mind to devote his remaining years to punishing the ex-Confederates—he called them traitors.

The Congressman's plan was to take the public lands of the seceded states and divide them among former slaves. Stevens did not believe, as many did, that a freedman who talked of wanting to own "forty acres and a mule" was only daydreaming. Stevens saw clearly that without a helping hand the newly freed Negroes could not make the best use of their freedom.

Charles Sumner. Another important Radical Republican was Charles Sumner, of Massachusetts. You will recall that before the Civil War he had been beaten severely on the floor of the Senate (see page 400). In contrast to Stevens, who was a rough-and-tumble politician, Sumner had been educated at Harvard College and had somewhat the manner of a dandy.

Sumner was as interested in seeing justice done to the Negro as Stevens was. Negroes, he said, should take part in the government of the states in which they lived. Only in this way could they as Americans have a share in American democracy.

Ben Wade. Still another leading Radical Republican was Benjamin F. Wade, of Ohio. Wade, a coarse man who was often loud in his arguments, had had a large part in the antislavery movement before the war. From 1864 on, he had been attacking presidential reconstruction, even calling it anti-American.

Wade, like other Radicals, had had hopes that Johnson would be easier to work with than Lincoln had been. Disappointed, he was soon saying that Johnson was either "a knave or a fool."

ber, 1865, when the southern Congressmen began to arrive in Washington to take their seats, Johnson was ready to accept them. In his opinion, the reconstruction of the Union was by that time complete.

The Radical Republicans, who were determined to help the freedmen and who gradually came to control Congress, were outraged. And Congress, irritated with the way reconstruction seemed to be working under the President's leadership, decided to take charge of it themselves.

Thad Stevens. The leaders of the Radical Republicans were strong-willed men led by a courageous Pennsylvania Representative, Thaddeus Stevens. A stern man of seventy-four who spoke through lips

Part of the problem was that although Congress had many powerful leaders, Johnson had led to include them in his planning for reconstruction.

What worried Wade—besides Johnson's failure to help the Negroes—was the *political* effects of allowing the southern members of Congress to take their seats. Since slavery had been wiped out and since a slave no longer could be counted as only three-fifths of a person, the South would have more seats than ever in Congress. If the southerners—all Democrats—returned to Congress, Republicans would be outvoted. The defeated people in the war # might then be able to have their way in Congress.

High stakes. Like other Radical Republicans, Wade realized that the Republican party itself was at stake. The Radicals, we see, therefore were guided by both a desire to do justice to the Negro and a hope of protecting the Republican party.

Furthermore, various laws affecting the country's prosperity had been passed during the Civil War, although the Radicals and the Republicans in general had not agreed concerning all of them. A number of Congressional acts had raised the tariff, established a new national banking system, and provided for the building of a transcontinental railroad. One law, the Homestead Act, had made it possible for farmers to obtain 160-acre plots of western land—homesteads—free of charge.

The laws could not have been passed if the southern states had remained in the Union. Their Senators and Representatives would have voted against them.

Possibly, the Radicals thought, if the Democrats should gain control of Congress, the laws would be repealed or seriously changed. A young French newspaperman was in Washington in the late 1860's. He understood clearly why the Radicals felt the way they did about giving southern Congressmen seats again. He wrote:

> When anyone has for four successive years joined in such a struggle as that which the United States has seen . . .

[he wishes] not to lose the dearly bought fruits of so many personal sacrifices. When the war ended, the North was concerned not to let itself be tricked out of what it had spent so much trouble and perseverance to win.

The Joint Committee. The first thing the angry Radicals did when Congress met in December, 1865, was to prevent the seating of Representatives from the southern states. A second step was to create a Joint Committee of Fifteen—made up of Republicans and Democrats from both the Senate and the House of Representatives. Its aim was to consider all proposals about reconstruction and to make recommendations concerning them to Congress.

The following April the Joint Committee of Fifteen issued a report. It stated that the states of the former Confederacy were not entitled to self-government until the civil rights—the basic American rights—of all their citizens were guaranteed.

A protecting hand. Already Congress, through the Radical Republicans, was acting to change the nature of reconstruction. Moreover, it was taking control of reconstruction out of the President's hands.

In February, 1866, the Radicals tried to put an end to the southern codes regulating Negroes. Also, recognizing that the Negroes needed help in facing the future, they passed a bill to increase the powers of the Freedmen's Bureau. This was an organization which had been set up during the war simply to help feed, clothe, and establish schools for Negroes. Now it was even given the power to protect Negroes against people who threatened or frightened them.

A stern veto. Johnson vetoed the bill, being unwilling to allow military force to be used in peacetime. He disapproved of it also because southern Congressmen were not present in Congress when it was passed. Further, he simply did not think that the United States Constitution al-

##This committee consisted of six Senators and nine Representatives and was dominated by Thaddeus Stevens (see p. 453).

edmen by the thousand sought
ortunities to obtain education.
Freedmen's Bureau operated
four thousand elementary
ools and over one hundred
anced-training schools for
roes.

A New England schoolteacher
who went to Mississippi to
help educate the freedmen
works with a primary class
in Vicksburg in 1866.

"Harper's Weekly,"
June 24, 1866 (Library of Congress)

owed the use of federal funds for the sup-
ort of unfortunate people—which the
reedmen were. Johnson came to regard
he Radicals as traitors because, he said,
hey were standing in the way of the resto-
ation of the Union.

Civil rights. Congress passed the bill
ver Johnson's veto. It also enacted a civil
ights bill in April, 1866, which Johnson
etoed, but which became a law in the
ame way. The Civil Rights Act stated that
ll persons (except Indians, who were not
axed) born in the United States were citi-
ens of the United States. As such they
ere entitled to all the privileges of citizen-
hip no matter what local laws might say.

The Fourteenth Amendment. The final
reak between the President and Congress
ame in June, 1866. At that time Congress
assed and submitted to the states for
atification what became the Fourteenth
Amendment to the Constitution. Adopted
n 1868, it added to the Constitution the
main provisions of the Civil Rights Act.
That is, it provides that all persons born or
naturalized in the United States are citi-
ens of the United States and of the states
where they live. As citizens, the amendment said, they are entitled to the equal
protection of the laws.

The amendment canceled the "three-
fifths clause" of the Constitution (see page
239). It provided a penalty for any state
which denied the vote to Negroes. It also
said that former Confederates who had
held federal or state offices could not hold
office again unless pardoned by Congress.

Johnson publicly urged the southern
states not to ratify the Fourteenth Amendment. Only Tennessee ignored his advice
and ratified it. Congress rewarded Tennessee by allowing it to reenter the Union.

1. Compare the loss of Union lives in
the Civil War with the loss of Confederate lives. 2. Tell about Lincoln's
plan for restoring the ex-Confederate
states to the Union. 3. What does the
Thirteenth Amendment provide? 4.
Describe the laws that were made in the
South to control the freedmen. 5.
Name three reasons why the Radicals
opposed the return of ex-Confederates
to Congress. 6. What two steps did the
Radicals take when Congress met in
1865? 7. Describe two laws that Congress passed over Johnson's veto. 8.
What does the Fourteenth Amendment
provide?

e students read and study the Fourteenth Amendment (see pp. 722-723). It did away with
Dred Scott decision of 1857, which had held that Negro slaves were not citizens. Section 2
he amendment has never been enforced.

Congress Has Its Way in the South

In the meantime the 1866 Congressional-election campaign was beginning to get under way. New bitterness was felt when Johnson entered the contest against the Radical candidates who were running for reelection.

A Dirty Campaign

Late in the summer, the President traveled westward from Washington on a speaking tour to defend his views. He made many speeches, mostly of a rabble-rousing sort. Sometimes when he attacked the Radicals, he seemed not to care about his own dignity or that of his office.

Wild charges. His opponents, the Radicals, also waged a rough and sometimes vulgar campaign. They called the President a drunkard. They wildly accused him of various misdeeds, even of being involved in the killing of Lincoln.

Northern feeling. The Radicals found it got them support to tell the voters of the North that Johnson wanted to let the former Confederates off scot-free. The reason is easy to see. The cost of saving the Union had been dreadful for almost every northern community. Thousands of widows and orphans and disabled veterans knew personally what the price had been. None could bear to hear that all their sacrifices might have been in vain.

In the election the Radical candidates # for Congress rolled up a huge victory, giving the Radicals control of the new session. Not only were they going to have their own way, but also they were going to even the score with Johnson. They would no longer care about his opinion of their bills. Now they could easily pass them over his vetoes.

Radical Reconstruction

In March of 1867, the Radicals put through a bill containing *their* plan of reconstruction. It came to be known as the Congressional plan. Later laws changed it somewhat, but its main terms remained.

According to the plan, the old Confederacy, with the exception of Tennessee, was divided into five military districts. Each of the districts was placed under a military commander with troops. The commanders were given wide powers to maintain peace and protect life and property. They were also under instructions to prepare their districts for self-government once again by enrolling the voters—including Negroes. The ex-Confederates in certain groups named in the Fourteenth Amendment were denied the vote.

A state would be ready to apply to Congress for readmission to the Union when it had taken various steps. First, a convention in each ex-Confederate state would have to draw up a new constitution acceptable to Congress. Then this constitution would have to be ratified by the people. After that a state legislature would be elected, which would have to ratify the Fourteenth Amendment.

The law was so stern that even after following these steps, a state would not be automatically readmitted. It would have to wait until enough states had ratified the Fourteenth Amendment to put it into effect. In this way Congress hoped to guarantee the vote to Negroes.

Johnson vetoed the bill, regarding the whole arrangement as outrageous and unconstitutional. Nevertheless, it was passed over his veto. In the South there was much

456   ##Note that not all southern whites or all ex-Confederates were denied the vote--only those who before the war had taken an oath to support the United States and then had gone against that oath by joining the Confederacy. Even they were eventually pardoned.

anger over the Congressional plan. Many southerners said that Congressional reconstruction had reduced the states to the condition of mere "conquered provinces." But there seemed no way out.

The new governments. Congressional reconstruction brought a remarkable change to the South. In the new state governments, Negroes for the first time voted and held political office. So did many white people who were poor and whose needs the planters had never looked out for in the old days.

Carpetbaggers and scalawags. The leaders of the so-called Radical state governments came from two groups of white people. These were the "carpetbaggers" and the "scalawags."

The carpetbaggers quickly arrived on the scene from the North. They got their nickname from the kind of valises made of carpet in which they carried their belongings, in accordance with the style of the day. Many of the carpetbaggers were selfish men planning to take advantage of the Negroes and of southern difficulties in general. On the other hand, some of the carpetbaggers were sincere reformers who

A traveler carrying the kind of satchel for which carpetbaggers were named.

Chicago Museum of Science and Industry

hoped to help the freedmen overcome the hardships they were experiencing.

The scalawags were southern businessmen and former planters. No one knows for sure how this nickname, meaning "scamp" or "rascal," got its start. The scalawags became Republicans. The Republican party, they believed, stood for the kinds of laws concerning business from which they could benefit.

Slowly the carpetbaggers became more powerful than the scalawags. They won Negroes, especially, to their side because they worked with them more closely and easily than the scalawags did.

Some readmissions. By midsummer in 1868, seven states—Alabama, Arkansas, Florida, Georgia, Louisiana, North Carolina, and South Carolina—had done what was expected of them. And since the Fourteenth Amendment had been ratified, they were readmitted to the Union. Virginia, Texas, and Mississippi were not readmitted until 1870. (By then the country had also ratified the Fifteenth Amendment, specifically granting the vote to Negroes. Congress required ratification of this amendment as an added proof of loyalty.)

The new governments ended laws calling for imprisonment for debt and abolished property qualifications for voting and for holding office in those states where they existed. They also built public schools for *all* to attend. Attempts were made to integrate schools, but only in South Carolina, Louisiana, and Mississippi.

The role of the Negroes. The years from 1868 to 1877 have sometimes been called the Era of Black Reconstruction, because Negroes supposedly played a large part in southern governments. Actually, it is wrong to think that Negroes held a main position in southern governments during these years. Only in South Carolina was the number of Negroes in the lower house of the legislature greater than the number of whites. Very few Negroes were elected

By 1868, just over a year after Congressional reconstruction began, most southern states had been restored to the Union.

457

The first Negro Congressmen in the United States. At the left is Senator Hiram R. Revels, of Mississippi, a minister and teacher.

to the highest offices. None was elected governor.

In South Carolina there were two lieutenant governors who were Negro, and there was a Negro judge in the state supreme court. Mississippi, Louisiana, and Florida had Negro lieutenant governors and superintendents of education.

Fourteen Negroes were elected to the United States House of Representatives, six coming from South Carolina. Naturally all did not serve at the same time.

Two Negroes, both from Mississippi, became members of the United States Senate. They were Hiram R. Revels and Blanche K. Bruce. Revels, a free Negro from North Carolina, had studied at Knox College, in Galesburg, Illinois, and had become a minister. He had recruited Negro soldiers for the Union army during the war, and then he had entered the service as a chaplain of a Negro regiment. His place in the Senate in 1871–1872 had last been held by Jefferson Davis.

Blanche Bruce was probably the greatest of the Negro politicians of that period. He had a long career in the public service after his Senatorial term was over. Once he was considered for a Cabinet post.

How well did the Radical state governments do? It is hard to judge because the answer depends on the point of view. The idea that men who had recently been slaves should be taking important parts in government made many southerners shudder with rage. To these men the Radical legislatures seemed to be more than failures—they appeared to be disasters.

It was hard to make distinguished legislators out of inexperienced and uneducated people. On the other hand a leading northern politician said, "The colored men who took their seats in both Senate and House did not appear ignorant or helpless. They were as a rule studious, earnest, ambitious men whose public conduct . . . would be honorable to any race."

Increased cost of government. Under the Radical governments public spending and taxes were high. A few illustrations suggest what happened within a very few years. Louisiana's public debt in 1868 was $17,347,000. And four years later it was $29,619,000. Alabama's debt amounted to $8,355,000 in 1869. Five years later it was $25,500,000. However, the debt in Mississippi increased scarcely at all.

Necessary spending. It should be kept in mind that most of the huge expenditures voted by the state legislatures went for rebuilding parts of the South damaged in the war. Railroads had to be repaired or constructed with public funds because there was too little private money available. Levees had to be restored. Schools had to be put up.

Furthermore, the number of people on which funds were being spent was larger by five million than it had been before the war. The reason was that previously, as slaves, Negroes had had very little of the benefit of public spending.

Corruption. There were many examples of corruption in the Radical state governments. In South Carolina the presiding officer of one of the branches of the legislature lost a thousand-dollar bet, and the legislature promptly voted the money to pay him back. In Arkansas the repair of a $500

#In other words, debts increased partly because state governments were providing new services and therefore had to meet new costs.

oridge cost $9000. The printing bill for the state of Florida in 1869 was for more money than had been spent for the entire state government in 1860.

An explanation. And yet there was an explanation. Corruption was then widespread *throughout* the United States. It was not found only in the South. The increased responsibilities taken on by government made necessary public contracts involving large sums of money. Politicians had more favors to sell than ever before. As city and state budgets all over the country grew, the amount of money to be used could not be easily watched.

In New York City the political leader, "Boss" Tweed, and the mayor—and their cronies—took such huge sums from the city that the total may never be known. Possibly they stole $100,000,000! There were many examples of political fraud elsewhere, too. What went on in the Radical legislatures, then, was not unusual.

The Ku Klux Klan. Although members of the two races were able to govern side by side in the South, the bad feeling between them was often great. Between 1867 and 1869 thousands of southerners banded together to frighten Negro voters and end Negro influence in Radical governments.

A cartoon by Thomas Nast, published in a national magazine in the early 1870's.

"Harper's Weekly," Oct. 24, 1874 (Library of Congress)

The best-known organization opposed to the Negroes' taking part in politics was the Ku Klux Klan. Its members carried on a campaign of terror against the freedmen which included beating, tarring and feathering, and murder.

Impeachment

While far-reaching events were bringing great changes to the South, the struggle between the President and Congress came to a sorry stage. Johnson and his friends believed that the Congress which had carried out reconstruction was an illegal body. They said it could not legislate lawfully unless there were members from the former Confederacy seated in its ranks. Some of Johnson's friends were even urging him to dissolve Congress by force and call for new elections.

Tying the President's hands. The Radicals in Congress acted to head off any such plan. First, they reduced Johnson's power as commander in chief over the army—by saying the President could only give his orders to the army through the general of the army. This was General Grant, who was thought of as a Radical Republican.

Second, the Radicals passed a law saying that the President could not remove from office, without obtaining the Senate's consent, any official whose appointment the Senate had approved. This act was intended to prevent the President from removing Edwin Stanton—also regarded as a Radical—from his position as Secretary of War. (Many years later the Supreme Court held the act unconstitutional.)

Johnson may sometimes have lacked dignity, but he did not lack self-respect. He struck back at the Radicals. For example, he dismissed the district commanders in the South who appeared to be sympathetic to the Radical governments.

Fight over the Department of War. Then in August, 1867, the President suspended

459

Secretary Stanton from office and appointed in his place General Grant, believing that Grant would coöperate with him. The Senate was not in session at the time. When it met later in the year, it refused to accept Stanton's removal.

Grant, not wanting to be caught in a fight between the President and Congress, stepped aside. Johnson then made a seri-
ous mistake. He publicly criticized Grant, the hero of the Union and the most popular man in the North.

The President seemed now to be hopelessly in difficulty with the Radicals. He appointed another general, Lorenzo Thomas, to be Secretary of War, and Stanton would not step aside to allow Thomas to take the office!

Accusations. The Radicals declared that Johnson was violating the law they had passed requiring Senate approval before an appointed official could be dismissed. Having made up their minds on this point, they decided to try to remove Johnson from office.

The first step in the proceedings, in accordance with the Constitution, was to *im-*
peach the President—that is, to accuse him. This the House of Representatives did, in February of 1868. The various charges which the Radicals brought against the President dealt mainly with his attempt to remove Stanton.

But no doubt the real cause of the impeachment was that the President had aimed to reconstruct the seceded states on his own. He had done so, the Radicals charged, "in the interests of the great criminals who carried them into the rebellion." They declared, furthermore, that Johnson "did attempt to bring into disgrace, ridicule, hatred, contempt and reproach the Congress of the United States."

Trial in the Senate. Although the House of Representatives has the power to impeach a United States official, his trial must be held in the Senate. There, on

"Harper's Weekly," March 14, 1868 (Library of Congress)

Looking worn and thin, Stevens (*center*) reads the charges against Johnson on March 14, 1868.

March 5, 1868, Johnson's trial began. The presiding officer was the chief justice of the United States, Salmon P. Chase, of Ohio. The leaders of the prosecution included Thaddeus Stevens. He was so ill, however, that a Massachusetts man, Benjamin F. Butler, took over as prosecutor.

Johnson was defended by the United States Attorney-General, who resigned from the Cabinet to undertake the defense. The President never appeared at the trial in person—a final dishonor he was spared.

The President's supporters, in general, were men who looked to the future. They could see that the presidency itself was about to be dragged through the mud and were not going to let this happen.

The outcome. When the vote was finally taken, Johnson was saved from being put out of office by one vote. Seven Republicans broke with their party to cast ballots for acquittal and so save the presidency from disgrace.

Senator Lyman Trumbull, of Illinois, one of the men who voted against the removal of Johnson, explained his position. He said, "Once set the example of im-

##Emphasize that "impeach" means to bring charges against an official; it does not mean to remove him from office. Johnson was impeached--that is, the House brought formal charges against him, and the Senate held the trial. But he was not convicted and so remained in office

beaching [and removing] a President for what, when the excitement of the hour shall have subsided, will be regarded as insufficient cause, and no future President will be safe who happens to differ with a majority of the House and two-thirds of the Senate on any measure deemed by them important."

The trial served as a kind of safety valve or the nation, allowing the overheated steam of national politics to escape at last. Not many Americans thought that Ben Wade, who, as president of the Senate, would have succeeded Johnson, would be a particularly good chief executive. Fewer still thought that Ben Butler would make a good Secretary of State—a position Wade had intended to give him.

Cooled tempers. In fact, many Radicals, despite their irritation with Johnson, were glad, when the dramatic trial was over, that they had not removed him from office

When their anger cooled, they took pleasure in looking forward to having a *real* President in the White House. During the summer of 1868, the Republican national convention nominated General Grant. Johnson did not have to be removed. Now he could be ignored!

---

1. Describe the Congressional plan of reconstruction. 2. What change did Congressional reconstruction bring to Negroes in the South? 3. Tell what two kinds of leaders appeared in the South. 4. Tell what the new southern state governments accomplished. 5. What explains the corruption in the state governments? 6. Describe two Congressional laws which helped bring about the impeachment of Johnson. 7. Who impeached the President? Who tried him?

---

e Presidential Succession Act of 1792 was still in effect.

The Sections Bury the Hatchet at Last

The move to make Grant President had begun during the Congressional attack on Johnson. Republicans who opposed Johnson believed they would have in Grant a man they could both respect and control— although it is impossible to do both.

Grant had little enthusiasm for accepting the nomination, but he became convinced it was his duty to do so. He wrote only a brief acceptance note to the Republican party, and he hardly campaigned at all. However, he won by a good margin over the Democrats' choice, Horatio J. Seymour, the governor of New York.

The Hero at the Top

Despite Grant's high reputation as a military hero, he was unfit by training or personality to be President. The public,

though, sometimes shows a blind confidence that a war hero can lead it in civilian life, too. In selecting Grant for the White House, the people did neither him nor themselves a favor.

Bad appointments. Grant, in setting up his administration, seems to have consulted no one, not even his beloved wife, Julia. His Cabinet choices were not good. He rewarded with posts personal friends who had no talent for their positions. The chief qualification of the Secretary of War, for instance, was that he had been Grant's neighbor in Illinois.

The one able man in the official family was the second man Grant chose to be Secretary of State, Hamilton Fish, a brilliant lawyer from New York. The first Secretary of State, a friend of Grant's, had been so poor at his work that he had had to be re-

iew other occasions when war heroes were chosen as presidential candidates. How were
nt's problems as President the result of his lack of civilian training, his personality, and
many personal friends?

461

moved almost immediately. When it was suggested to Grant that he appoint the distinguished diplomat and historian John L. Motley to be Secretary of State, he refused. The reason that Grant gave was, "He parts his hair in the middle, and carries a single eyeglass!"

Grant filled his household with relatives. Present most of the time was Mrs. Grant's father, Frederick Dent. A southern Democrat, Grandfather Dent gave endless interviews to newspapermen, often saying his son-in-law was a Democrat at heart.

The Fifteenth Amendment. Because Negroes had been denied the vote in some parts of the South—despite the presence of Radical governments there—Congress acted very early in Grant's administration. In February, 1869, it passed and sent to the states for ratification what became the Fifteenth Amendment to the Constitution.

The Fifteenth Amendment provided that no citizen shall be denied the vote "on account of race, color, or previous condition of servitude." So was completed the great series of Civil War amendments to the Constitution. The Thirteenth had granted freedom to the slaves, the Fourteenth had guaranteed them citizenship, and the Fifteenth had assured them that the right to vote could not be withheld because of race. All three contributed a great deal to American democracy.

Revival of the Democrats. The difficulties of reconstruction were not ended. Negroes often met with violence in trying to exercise their rights. Congress felt obliged to pass a Force Act, carrying heavy penalties for violations of the Fourteenth and Fifteenth amendments. Nevertheless, the Congressional elections of 1870 showed that the Democratic party was being revived in the South and that Negroes were frequently not being allowed to vote.

The Radicals were furious at this turn of things. In 1871 they passed the Ku Klux Klan Act, intended to prevent members of the Klan from terrorizing the freedmen.

Amnesty. Radical reconstruction, however, was over by 1872 in many places. Under a law passed that year, amnesty—that is, legal forgiveness—was granted to all former Confederates (except some of those who had held the highest rank). They could now, once again, vote and hold office. Congress in 1872 also allowed the Freedmen's Bureau to go out of existence.

A number of things account for the change in the attitude of Congress. First, the Radicals were dying off or being retired. Thaddeus Stevens had died in 1868. His tombstone bore words that had been the guiding motto of his life, "Equality of Man before his Creator." Benjamin Wade had lost his Senate seat in 1868. Charles Sumner had had a fierce argument with Grant and thereafter lost his influence. It is said that Grant used to shake his fist angrily in the direction of Sumner's house whenever he rode past.

Of course, new leaders were arising. But as we shall see, they made no efforts to continue the work of providing equality as well as freedom for the former slaves.

Besides, other problems were beginning to rise: what to do about the tariff, how to improve the methods of appointing certain governmental officials, and how to regulate the railroads. The *whole* country would have to face these issues squarely. It would have to forget the past and face the future. In order to take care of other developing needs, the northerners began to forget about the Negro and the completion of his emancipation.

The Liberal Republicans. Because of Grant's ready ear for friends, some of the most alarming frauds ever committed in the federal government took place right under the President's nose. One effect of the corruption was that a group of Republican reformers broke away to run their own candidates in 1872. A leader of these Liberal Republicans, as they called them-

Why did popular interest seem to shift by the 1870's to issues other than reconstruction of the South? How much did the Radical program, like the earlier abolition movement, depend on strong-willed men to make the public aware of the issues involved?

An artist showed Greeley crying with joy after his nomination, "By George! I've got it!"

elves, was Carl Schurz, a remarkable politician from Missouri. Not many years before, he had been a German immigrant unable to speak English well.

Candidate Greeley. The Liberal Republicans nominated for President Horace Greeley, the famous editor of the *New York Tribune*. The nomination of Greeley to run against Grant, who was chosen again by the rest of the party, was a terrible mistake.

Greeley's appearance did not win people's confidence. He let his hair grow long and allowed it to flow around his face. Usually he wore boots with one trouser leg stuffed inside and the other out. And he went about wearing a white suit and huge white hat and carrying a green umbrella.

A second term. The Democrats, still suffering as the "party of the Rebellion," felt that they had to go along with Greeley as their choice, too. They were afraid of splitting the opposition to Grant and so handing him easy reelection.

#He died within a month after the election.

Greeley, though, was quickly hurt by the many articles he had written attacking the Democrats—which had appeared in the past in the *Tribune*. The campaign # became a nightmare for him.

The nation was in a mood to stay with Grant. The "savior of the Union" won a second term by a very large margin.

The Radicals' loss of influence. Grant knew that only a few people in the North wanted to continue the Radical program of bearing down on the South. Besides, many prosperous northern businessmen, looking for places to invest their money, turned their eyes toward the South, which required a great deal of help. But they hesitated to put their money there because they regarded the Radical governments as being financially shaky. The businessmen were ready to say, as one of them did, "Now let the South alone."

It is probably safe to say that many Negroes wanted to be left alone, too. More and more, also, the carpetbaggers and the scalawags disagreed about the policies the Radical governments ought to follow. The scalawags gradually withdrew from taking part with carpetbaggers and freedmen in the governing of southern states.

By 1876 the Radical Republicans still controlled only South Carolina, Louisiana, and Florida. The Radicals stayed in office in those three states chiefly because federal troops remained there yet. In other southern states Democrats were once again in charge.

A Deal for the Presidency

The presidential election of 1876 was one of the hardest fought in American history. It produced the severest crisis in the nation since 1860.

Hayes, of Ohio. The Republicans that year chose Rutherford B. Hayes, the governor of Ohio, as their standard-bearer. An honest man with a good war record, he had

lly when a political party splits during an election year, it loses the election. In 1872, ever, President Grant--despite the Liberal Republican movement--was reelected by an whelming margin.

463

earned a reputation as a reformer—that is, as a person favoring clean politics.

The burden of "Grantism." The Governor's reputation stood him in good stead because the Republicans—and the country —were suffering from a terrible lack of public honesty. Grant's own reputation had continued to be hurt by all the greed and dishonesty. To the President's everlasting shame, the corruption had come to be known as Grantism.

A particularly distasteful scandal resulted when it was learned that the profits from building the first transcontinental railroad had gone into the pockets of the few who were insiders. Furthermore, it was shown that bribes to members of Congress had resulted in covering up the fraud.

This bold cheating had taken place before Grant became President, but it had involved many prominent Republicans. Among them had been a Congressman from Ohio, James A. Garfield, who would shortly be president of the United States.

Other scandals touched Grant more closely because they brought disgrace to men he himself had appointed. It was learned, for example, that the Secretary of War, William Belknap, had taken bribes from traders at Indian posts. And Grant's own secretary, General Orville Babcock, was involved with a group of men who were cheating the government of large sums of money.

The long depression. Hayes' nomination was welcomed by many people throughout the country, who were not only angry over the corruption in high places but who also suffered in the depression of 1873. That depression, one of the longest in American history, dragged on into the 1880's before better times returned. Meanwhile, many banks had closed their doors, costing depositors their life's savings. Thousands were unemployed, a situation resulting in untold suffering. Farmers were badly hurt, too, as prices for crops hit record lows.

Tilden, of New York. The Democrats were licking their chops as they looked forward to the election. They had been out of the presidency for twenty years. They thought they could win by talking to voters about the twin issues of corruption and depression. Meeting in St. Louis, they chose as their man the governor of New York, Samuel J. Tilden.

Tilden, nicknamed "Whispering Sammy," was a bachelor who worried too much about his health. A gifted leader, however, he had a wide following of friends who admired his record as a defender of honesty in government. Tilden's fame was based on his having smashed the Tweed Ring in New York (see page 459).

The campaign was loud and hot. The Republicans over and over again tried to hide Grant's failures by calling the Democrats the party of disloyalty. Real Americans, they urged, should "vote as they shot." Hayes washed his hands of any connection with Grant's policies and practically promised to restore self-rule to the South —that is, to pull out the federal troops.

Disputed returns. The campaign was exciting, but the argument over the returns was even more so. The question of who had won the election raged for weeks. On the basis of the popular votes cast, Tilden was clearly the winner, having received about 260,000 more than Hayes.

A total of 185 electoral votes was required to elect a President. Tilden had 184 sure votes, and he needed only one more to be declared the winner. In dispute were 20 electoral votes, 19 of them in the South— in South Carolina, Florida, and Louisiana. These were the states that still had Radical Republican governments.

In each of the three states, two rival boards of election officials—one Democratic and one Republican—reported returns. The Democratic boards declared that Tilden had won. The Republican boards said that Hayes was the winner.

#The other disputed electoral vote came from Oregon. In order to win, Hayes needed all twenty disputed votes. The problem was to decide which sets of returns to accept.

A photograph of the dressed-up guests at a reception given for the Hayeses at their home in Ohio on September 14, 1877. Some of the lanterns strung around the porch may have been like the one seen on page 448.

"Frank Leslie's Illustrated Newspaper," Oct. 6, 1877 (Rutherford B. Hayes Library)

Who was to decide which returns to accept? Finding the answer severely tested the people's method of electing a President. The Constitution offered no guide.

A solution. Congress came up with an answer early in 1877. It decided to appoint an electoral commission consisting of fifteen members. Seven of them would be Democrats and seven would be Republicans. The fifteenth was expected to be Supreme Court Justice David Davis, of Illinois, who belonged to neither party. Davis was believed to be as neutral as any man who could be found.

The decision. At the last minute, however, Davis could not serve, because he had accepted an appointment to a seat in the Senate. The man who took his place in the Supreme Court was Joseph P. Bradley, of New Jersey.

The decision was now Bradley's to make. There is some evidence that he intended to choose Tilden but that at the last minute he changed his mind under heavy pressure from fellow Republicans. Hayes was given every one of the disputed electoral votes. A few weeks later he took office.

A secret bargain. In order to gain Democratic support for the settlement of the disputed election, the new administration had made a deal behind the scenes. It had promised the Democrats that immediately after Hayes' inauguration, the last of the federal troops would be withdrawn from the South. The new President would appoint a southerner to his Cabinet, and he would aid the South in obtaining internal improvements, particularly railroads.

"Put aside the bayonet." Hayes came into office, then, as the result of a compromise—the Compromise of 1877. Possibly # it was as important in preserving the Union as the Compromises of 1820 and 1850 had been. The new President wrote in his diary shortly after taking the presidential oath of office, "My policy is trust—peace, and to put aside the bayonet."

Some, not all, of the Compromise of 1877 was put into effect. The troops were withdrawn as promised. Hayes appointed to his Cabinet a Tennessean, David M. Key —to be the Postmaster General. The South got some, but not all, of the internal improvements that had been promised. It had especially wanted a railroad.

The North and the South were at last finding it possible to work together again. Northern Republicans, turning to new activities, had lost interest in helping the freedmen. Negroes would for a long time be robbed of their right to vote and be discriminated against.

Nevertheless, the Fourteenth and Fifteenth amendments to the Constitution would be lasting results of Radical reconstruction. One day they would take on, as we shall see, the full meaning their authors, the Radical Republicans, intended them to have.

In 1877 another era of American history was about to begin. The fair held in Philadelphia in 1876 to celebrate the one hundredth anniversary of the Declaration of Independence hinted at what that era might hold. The theme of the fair was power—a fairly new idea to most Americans.

One of the exhibits was the Corliss steam engine, the greatest steam engine ever built. On the opening day President Grant and Emperor Dom Pedro, of Brazil, turned it on. Although it was said to weigh 1,700,000 pounds, it worked very quietly, generating enough power to run all the other machinery on exhibition.

Another outstanding feature of the fair was the telephone, recently invented by Alexander Graham Bell. Visitors, struck dumb, were delighted to hear the human voice transmitted over wires.

Still another exhibit which drew much attention was the huge hand and torch of the Statue of Liberty. The mammoth statue, a gift of the French people, was still being made by sculptors in France. The only part of it that had been completed was the uplifted hand and torch.

Unfinished business. Somehow these attractions of the Centennial Exposition told much about the United States one hundred years after its birth. The people were on their way to becoming masters of engineering and industrialization. Yet the fact that there was only a piece of the Statue of Liberty seemed to say that the work of building democracy in America was still far from finished.

---

1. State the content of the Fifteenth Amendment. 2. What two things in 1872 showed a change in the thinking of the Radical Republicans? 3. State three new problems that Americans faced in the 1870's. 4. Name the presidential candidates in 1872. Who was elected? 5. Describe the election of 1876 and the Compromise of 1877. 6. Name two lasting results of Radical Republicanism.

The Workshop

Compare the Compromise of 1877 with the Compromises of 1820 and 1850. Compromise always exacts some price. Evaluate the Compromise of 1877 in terms of its contributions and costs.

The Shapers of Our World

Tell what part each of the following played in the reconstruction period:

10-percent plan
Thirteenth Amendment
Andrew Johnson
Thaddeus Stevens
Charles Sumner
Benjamin F. Wade
Radical Republican
Freedmen's Bureau
Fourteenth Amendment
carpetbagger
scalawag
Ku Klux Klan
Compromise of 1877
Fifteenth Amendment
"Boss" Tweed
Edwin M. Stanton
Liberal Republican
Horace Greeley
"Grantism"
Samuel J. Tilden
Rutherford B. Hayes
Alexander Graham Bell

Adding to Your Vocabulary

Be sure you know these words:

harecropping   impeach
nabitation   amnesty
beggary   corruption
vagrant   transcontinental
dragooned

Thinking Things Through

After a review of the boxed-in exercises in the chapter, see if you can answer these questions:

1. After the Emancipation Proclamation, why was the Thirteenth Amendment necessary?

2. Why was the South poorly prepared to begin rebuilding its wrecked property and industries?

3. Why is political corruption often widespread after a war?

4. What are the special problems a new President faces if he follows a great and popular President in office?

5. What role did Congress have in policy-making during the Civil War? What role was it determined to have during the reconstruction period?

The Seeds of Democracy

1. Explain why the Thirteenth, Fourteenth, and Fifteenth amendments and the Civil Rights Act of 1866 were milestones in the development of democracy in the United States.

2. Read Article 1, Section 2, Clause 5 and Section 3 of Clause 6 in the Constitution, pages 705–707. Why is the power to impeach and try officials necessary in a democracy?

Presenting Information

1. Stage the last day of the trial of Andrew Johnson. Give final arguments for both the prosecution and the defense.

2. Student "reporters" who represent both southern and northern newspapers should interview classmates taking the parts of Thaddeus Stevens, Charles Sumner, Robert E. Lee, and Andrew Johnson. The subject of the interviews: reconstruction of the South. The questions should be of the "Meet the Press" kind.

3. Prepare newspaper editorials contrasting northern and southern views about the Freedmen's Bureau and its work.

The Research Center

1. Choose from these topics for oral reports: (a) the Ku Klux Klan, (b) Robert E. Lee's life after the Civil War, (c) the life of Frederick Douglass, (d) the Grant administration, (e) Horace Greeley, (f) the Tweed Ring, (g) the Centennial Exposition in 1876.

2. At the present time new jobs and business opportunities are growing at an extraordinary rate in the South. Using reference books, magazine articles, and other materials, prepare a bulletin-board display showing the development of the "new South" since the Civil War.

3. Find out all you can about Booker T. Washington. What advice did he have for Negroes? Why did some Negro leaders come to regard his advice as misguided? (Possibly you can read Washington's autobiography, *Up from Slavery*.)

Your Opinion, Please

1. Would the Radicals have had a much more difficult time in gaining control of reconstruction policies if Lincoln had lived?

2. What reconstruction policy or policies do you think should have been used after the Civil War?

3. Why did the country accept the results of the election of 1876 when it appeared that the real winner had lost?

Many countries have had civil wars. Have a student compare the American Civil War and its aftermath with another civil war. Have him emphasize especially the causes and lasting effects of the conflicts.

Part Six Workshop

Reaching to the Present

1. Since 1861 no state has seceded or attempted to secede from the Union. What does the Civil War have to do with this fact?

2. Amendments are added to the Constitution when the people discover a situation that requires changes in the set of basic laws on which the federal government is founded. What situations after the Civil War led to the Thirteenth, Fourteenth, and Fifteenth amendments? Did they correct the situations?

3. What is the most recent civil rights act passed by Congress? What does it provide for?

4. After the Civil War Robert E. Lee advised against feelings of bitterness between Americans that might result from it. Did people follow his advice? Explain.

5. The Centennial Exposition of 1876 celebrated the first hundred years of American independence. What are some of the happenings of those years that Americans could look back on with pleasure? With sadness?

Time and Change

Look at the time line on pages 414–415 when necessary in order to answer these questions:

1. How did the Civil War affect: (a) the slave owners, (b) the slaves, and (c) northern industry?

2. How did the presidencies of Jackson and Lincoln affect the way Americans looked upon the highest office in the land? What change did Grant's presidency cause in the way Americans regarded him? Why?

3. Which political party was strengthened by the Civil War? Weakened?

The Book Shelf

Catton, Bruce, and eds. of *American Heritage* Magazine. *The Battle of Gettysburg*. New York: American Heritage Publishing Co., Inc., 1963. (Describes the turning point in the Civil War.)

Davis, Burke. *Appomattox; Closing Struggle of the Civil War*. New York: Harper & Row, Publishers, Inc., 1963. (About the last days of the war.)

Goldman, Peter. *Civil Rights; the Challenge of the Fourteenth Amendment*. New York: Coward-McCann, Inc., 1965. (The story of the Negro's fight for his civil rights.)

Hunt, Irene. *Across Five Aprils*. Chicago: Follett Publishing Co., 1964. (About the life of a family during the Civil War.)

Kane, Harnett T. *A Picture History of the Confederacy*. New York: Lothrop, Lee & Shepard Co., Inc., 1965. (An account of the southern fight in the Civil War.)

McCarthy, Agnes. *Worth Fighting For; a History of the Negro in the U.S. during the Civil War and Reconstruction*. New York: Doubleday & Co., Inc., 1965. (About Negroes in one of the most trying periods in American history.)

Meltzer, Milton (ed.). *In Their Own Words; a History of the American Negro, 1865–1916*. New York: Thomas Y. Crowell Co., 1965. (Letters, articles, speeches, and quotations.)

Toppin, Edgar A. *Contributions of American Negroes*. Chicago: Rand McNally & Co., 1967. (A survey of the accomplishments of Negroes throughout American history.)

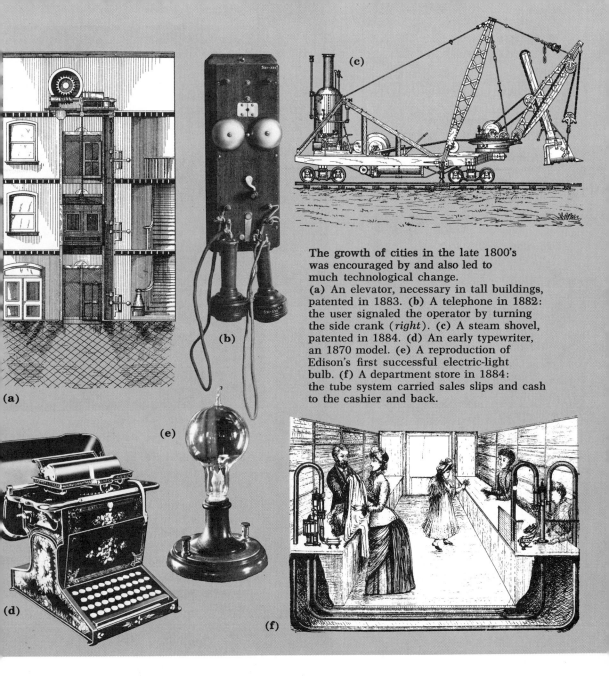

The growth of cities in the late 1800's was encouraged by and also led to much technological change.
(a) An elevator, necessary in tall buildings, patented in 1883. (b) A telephone in 1882: the user signaled the operator by turning the side crank (*right*). (c) A steam shovel, patented in 1884. (d) An early typewriter, an 1870 model. (e) A reproduction of Edison's first successful electric-light bulb. (f) A department store in 1884: the tube system carried sales slips and cash to the cashier and back.

(a)

(b)

(c)

(d)

(e)

(f)

Part Seven: THE TESTING OF DEMOCRACY

The technological change illustrated here may seem commonplace to students today, but it was far from that in the late nineteenth century. All the inventions named appeared most frequently in cities: the steam shovel was used to dig holes for the foundations of tall buildings, for example. The typewriter became vital to carrying on business. The tube system (f) was used for years--well into the twentieth century.

Solving the problems of the late 1800's tested
the ability of American democracy.

Part Seven:
THE TESTING OF DEMOCRACY

Continued on facing page

A "DOCTOR" TO THE TROUBLED CITIES

Jane Addams, who was the daughter of well-
to-do parents in rural Illinois, spent much of
her life dealing with the problems of the poor
in the great city of Chicago. There she became world famous for establishing Hull
House, a social-service organization to aid
those men, women, and children who lacked
advantages.

Time and Change

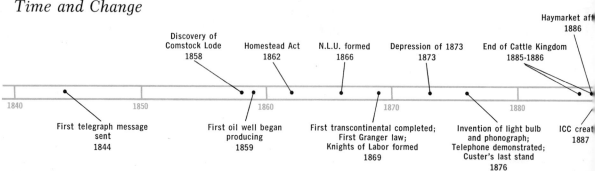

Haymarket aff
1886

Discovery of
Comstock Lode
1858

Homestead Act
1862

N.L.U. formed
1866

Depression of 1873
1873

End of Cattle Kingdom
1885-1886

1840   1850   1860   1870   1880

First telegraph message
sent
1844

First oil well began
producing
1859

First transcontinental completed;
First Granger law;
Knights of Labor formed
1869

Invention of light bulb
and phonograph;
Telephone demonstrated;
Custer's last stand
1876

ICC creat
1887

...e Addams stirred Americans' interest in
...lping unfortunate individuals.

Born on the eve of the Civil War, Jane Addams died in 1935, the year Congress passed the first social-security law. Her life, therefore, spanned the busy years in which America was building industry faster than any other nation ever had. At the same time, desperate problems were being created for millions of urban people who found it difficult to adjust to the great changes industrialization was bringing.

At first Jane Addams set out to study medicine, but she soon gave up the idea. She became, instead, a "doctor" to the troubled cities, by trying to mend the damaged lives of some of their people and by facing the needs of the poverty-stricken.

By working amid people in want and by writing about them for the larger public, Jane Addams helped educate Americans about the nature of poverty. She taught, for instance, that the reason the poor generally do not save money is not that they are spendthrifts but that they do not have enough cash to spare. She taught that the unemployed usually are not lazy or shiftless but are only the victims of circumstances altogether beyond their control.

In her endless labors Jane Addams also concerned herself with the crusades for women's rights, for world peace, and for better race relations. But her chief accomplishment was in turning the light on the people unfavorably affected by the industrial age. In doing this, she awakened the conscience of fellow Americans about the needs of the underprivileged—a conscience that has never gone to sleep again.

The bronze Statue of Freedom which has stood atop the dome of the Capitol in Washington, D.C., since 1863.

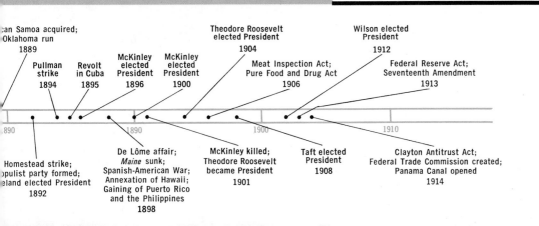

American Samoa acquired;
Oklahoma run
1889

Pullman strike
1894

Revolt in Cuba
1895

McKinley elected President
1896

McKinley elected President
1900

Theodore Roosevelt elected President
1904

Meat Inspection Act;
Pure Food and Drug Act
1906

Wilson elected President
1912

Federal Reserve Act;
Seventeenth Amendment
1913

1890   1890   1900   1910

Homestead strike;
Populist party formed;
Cleveland elected President
1892

De Lôme affair;
Maine sunk;
Spanish-American War;
Annexation of Hawaii;
Gaining of Puerto Rico and the Philippines
1898

McKinley killed;
Theodore Roosevelt became President
1901

Taft elected President
1908

Clayton Antitrust Act;
Federal Trade Commission created;
Panama Canal opened
1914

(a)

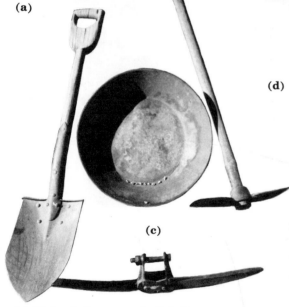

(d)

(c)

(b)

(a) Plains Indians on a buffalo hunt, a
painting by George Catlin, an American artist
who greatly admired the tribesmen and traveled
widely in the West to see and paint them.
(b) A cast-iron hitching post, made in
New York City by the Ornamental Ironworks
about 1860. Before the automobile, such posts
lined the streets of American cities, and
there were many water tanks for thirsty horses.
(c) Tools of California gold miners in 1849—
a shovel, a pan, a pick, and a pick head.
(d) A cowboy ropes a longhorn, painted by
Charles M. Russell, who arrived in Montana
in 1871, later becoming the "cowboy artist."

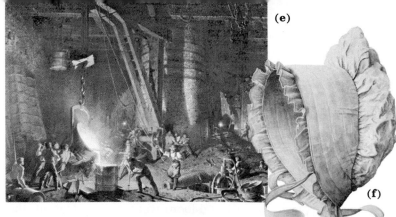

(e) A foundry at the time of the great development of industry in the late 1800's: melted metal is being cast into molds.
(f) A sunbonnet, protection against sun and wind, worn by a woman pioneer on the Great Plains in the 1890's.

What part might the foundry shown above have played in producing items pictured on p. 472?

CHAPTER 21

COAST-TO-COAST CHANGES

This chapter is concerned with many of the changes that occurred in the United States following the Civil War. Students will read about developments in manufacturing, transportation, communication, mining, and ranching. Point out that these developments affected all areas of American life.

WHEN the Civil War ended, the United States was very rapidly turning into one of the mighty industrial nations of the world. Northern industry, which had begun to develop before the war, was greatly enlarged to meet the requirements of the Union army (see pages 424–426). Even more important, however, a change in people's thinking helped encourage the building of factories.

In earlier days people had commonly believed that the only useful, productive work was farming. Now it was becoming accepted that the surest way for a community to grow wealthy was by the development of manufacturing.

Masterful Men Create Giant Industries

The far-reaching change in attitudes toward industry in less than fifty years resulted from a number of things. Among them was the realization that the United States was rich in natural resources. Further, there was money for investment, and Americans were hard-working, inventive people who could build on a foundation of European technology. The change was also aided by the demands of American customers and the vigorous leadership of some adventurous individuals.

The expansion of American industry after 1865 affected almost every imaginable product, from cotton cloth and boots and shoes to canned foods and locomotives. But it was the development of *new* industries that provided the foundation for the enormous industrial growth of the United States. #

King of Steel

The first and most important of the new industries was the one producing steel. In 1866 a new method of making steel by re-

Review the reasons for the industrial growth of the United States. What industries had been developed in the United States by the time of the Civil War? What had the Civil War revealed about the power of a section having a varied industrial and agricultural economy?

473

moving impurities from the melted iron was patented, changing the iron industry completely. A number of unusually imaginative businessmen were able to take advantage of the new process.

Andy in Scotland. The most successful of these men was Andrew Carnegie, who as a boy had come to America from Scotland. When Andy was twelve years old, his father lost his job as a hand-loom weaver because the factory he worked in began using machine looms to do his task.

Perhaps the experience impressed Andy with the importance of machines in general. He never forgot his father's coming home after trying to find employment and saying to Mrs. Carnegie, "Well, Andra, I canna get nae mair work."

When the Carnegies came to America, they settled in Pennsylvania. Almost immediately Andy got a job as a bobbin boy in a cotton mill. His chore was to see that the looms were kept supplied with thread. His pay was $1.20 a week.

On the way up. Always keeping his eye on the chance to improve himself, Carnegie gradually made himself a success in business. He became a messenger in the Pittsburgh telegraph office. In almost no time he learned to be a telegraph operator simply by watching others do the work. He became one of the best in the country.

Sixteen years old then, Carnegie wrote home to a favorite cousin in Scotland, "I have got past delivering messages and have got to operating. I am to have four dollars a week now and a good prospect of soon getting more." He was on his way.

In the telegraph office, Carnegie met regularly an official of the Pennsylvania Railroad named Thomas Scott. Scott took a liking to Andy and hired him to be his private secretary—at $35 a month.

The year was 1853. Carnegie remained with the Pennsylvania Railroad until 1865, having succeeded Scott as head of the Pennsylvania's western division.

From Scott Carnegie learned many business techniques. Most important, Scott showed Carnegie how to invest his savings. On Scott's advice Carnegie bought shares in the Pullman Company, which built sleeping cars for the Pennsylvania Railroad. With the profits from this investment, he bought stock in an oil company. Rapidly his fortune increased.

Out of the railroad business. Carnegie left railroading in order to enter the iron and steel industry. A first step was to buy the Keystone Bridge Company, which manufactured iron bridges. (He was sure that the day of wooden railroad bridges was over.)

Next Carnegie traveled in Europe and became a close friend of Sir Henry Bessemer, who, with William Kelly, an American, had produced steel by the new method. After 1873 the manufacture of steel became the only business in which Carnegie actively engaged. He was following the policy, he said, "of putting all his eggs in one basket, and then watching the basket."

Rails for sale. Carnegie first built a huge plant—the J. Edgar Thomson Steel Works—close to Pittsburgh. Shrewdly he named it for the president of the Pennsylvania Railroad, hoping to get orders for steel rails from that line. He did.

Carnegie knew very little about the technical details of making steel. But he had a genius for finding the right kind of employees. He once said in a joke that his tombstone ought to say "Here lies the man who was able to surround himself with men far cleverer than himself."

The assistance of Frick. One of the people Carnegie hired was Henry Clay Frick. Frick became Carnegie's chief assistant in 1889. He was a cold and somewhat unbending man who guarded against wastefulness in Carnegie's plants.

Frick had been in the coke business. Coke, which is coal that has been burned without oxygen, is an ideal fuel for smelt-

In what ways did Carnegie's success result from a combination of skill and good fortune? Ask students to decide what things seemed most important in explaining Carnegie's success.

Left: The J. Edgar Thomson Steel Works in 1875, the first American plant to produce steel in large quantities by the new Bessemer method.
Right: Carnegie, one of the first "big businessmen" in the country.

ing iron. When burned with iron ore, it produces the intense heat required to make high-grade steel. Naturally Frick's operations had already brought him close to Carnegie, who had become his best customer. Now they were joined, and they became a powerful combination.

Carnegie's business became so successful that in the year 1900 alone its profits amounted to $40,000,000. The following year Carnegie sold out to a group that had formed the United States Steel Corporation. He personally received for his share of the company a total of $225,000,000.

Others copied Carnegie's methods of production and management, and these imitators were often very successful. But Carnegie deserves the prime credit for bringing post–Civil War America into the "age of steel."

Using his riches. After Carnegie retired, he devoted his life to writing and to charities. He was especially interested in building libraries, improving education, and seeking ways of keeping international peace. He gave a fortune away. He once wrote: "The man who dies ... rich dies disgraced."

Ask students to try to think of international or internal developments that help explain the variations shown on the graph.

In what years did the greatest increases in steel production occur?

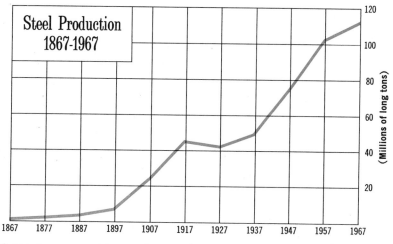

Steel Production 1867-1967

(Millions of long tons)

1867 1877 1887 1897 1907 1917 1927 1937 1947 1957 1967

Be sure students understand that Carnegie prospered in part because he combined under one ownership many of the operations needed in steelmaking. Use Carnegie's joining with Frick as an example of such combination.

Lord of Oil

Another figure who rose to be a maker of industrial America was John D. Rockefeller, born in upper New York State. His father was an easygoing man who earned money by selling patent medicines. John, a deeply religious boy, took both his interest in religion and a certain sternness from his mother. He was fascinated by profit-making and determined to have a career in business.

Rockefeller's start. Living in Cleveland, Ohio, John found a job for $3.50 a week with the firm of a merchant. Like Carnegie, Rockefeller kept his eyes open for opportunity. Like Carnegie, he had great faith in the virtue of thrift and the advantages of not-too-risky investments.

Rockefeller went into business with a young Englishman to trade in grains and meats. During the Civil War the business did very well, for foodstuffs of all kinds were in great demand not only for the Union army but for Europe, too.

The story of petroleum. By the time the Civil War was over, Rockefeller's keen eyes had already spotted the growing importance of petroleum. To see what he saw, it is necessary to look briefly at the history of oil in America.

In western Pennsylvania, oil had always floated on the surface of a branch of the Allegheny River (see page 151). Accordingly, this branch became known as Oil Creek. Medical fakers, often posing as "Indian healers," used to skim the oil off the surface, put it in bottles, and sell it to ailing people.

One of the most famous of these patent medicines was sold as "Seneca Oil"—a "cure" for rheumatism. Another "medicine" was peddled by a Dr. Samuel Kier under the name "Kier's Rock Oil."

It was not as a "medicine" that oil became a valuable product, but as a lubricant

American Petroleum Institute

Kier's Rock Oil was wrapped in paper showing an ailing traveler being helped by a friendly passerby who gives him the "medicine."

for machinery and a fuel for lamps. But how could anyone get enough of it?

"Drake's Folly." George H. Bissell, a New York lawyer long interested in oil chemistry, hit upon the idea of drilling into the earth in the area near Oil Creek. He arranged for "Colonel" E. L. Drake, a conductor on the New Haven Railroad, to do the work.

When Drake arrived in Titusville, Pennsylvania, to begin his task, the local people thought he was crazy. But oil started flowing at "Drake's Folly," as it quickly came to be known, in August, 1859, amounting to twenty-five barrels a day.

Overnight an oil rush was on. The area around the oil well, once a sleepy rural region reached by a few poor roads, was changed. New towns sprang up as people flocked in to try their luck at drilling. Most of them—like the forty-niners—"went bust," but a few struck it rich.

Emphasis on refining. Rockefeller followed developments in the oil fields and watched with growing fascination as oil refineries began to appear in Cleveland. He quickly recognized that the profit was

Have a student collect information and illustrative material on the petroleum industry and report to the class. (See "The Research Center," Exercise 2, p. 493.) Use the report to show the importance of changes in technology and business organization in a particular industry.

greater and more reliable in the refining of oil than in its production.

A fruitful combination. Rockefeller (only twenty-three years of age) had considerable savings now. He found in a man named Samuel Andrews an expert who had invented an inexpensive process for refining oil. Also, he added to his firm a very able young Cleveland businessman, Henry M. Flagler. So was created in 1867 the company of Rockefeller, Andrews & Flagler.

Within a few years the new business, though no bigger than some others in Cleveland, was being run more carefully. Rockefeller was a stickler for details, and he could not bear to see any wastefulness.

Standard Oil. Realizing that oil would be widely used in industry, Rockefeller in 1870 turned his company into a larger concern, the Standard Oil Company of Ohio. Standard quickly bought other oil-refining companies and took over their customers. It is said that in 1870 there were twenty-five independent producers of oil in Cleveland. Two years later there were only five: Rockefeller's company had acquired the other twenty!

By 1875 the power of the Standard Oil Company led to its gaining control of the largest refineries in New York and Philadelphia. Those in Baltimore and Pittsburgh also passed into Standard's grip. The last holdouts were the refiners near Titusville, where the oil boom had started.

So at thirty-eight years of age, Rockefeller had become the commanding figure in the oil industry. The Standard Oil Company had almost a *monopoly*—that is, almost complete control—of the oil-refining factories of the country. Rockefeller's wealth and influence became awesome.

Branching out. At the same time that Rockefeller was buying out other oil refineries, he was also aiming to get control of the suppliers and distributors of oil. For example, he purchased the pipelines and the tank cars through which oil went to refineries. He built factories for manufacturing his own barrels. He pioneered in chemical research that led to such everyday by-products of oil as paraffin, vaseline, and even insecticides.

The trust. But Rockefeller's most talked-about business contribution was the *trust*. This was the legal arrangement by which a company—in this case the Standard Oil Company—controlled the various corporations that were part of it.

To Rockefeller the trust meant new power to make his operations more successful than ever. To the general public, however, the trust became a feared symbol of monopoly.

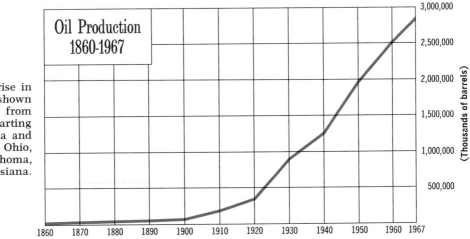

Oil Production 1860-1967

The rise in oil production shown here resulted from an oil boom starting in Pennsylvania and spreading to Ohio, Texas, Oklahoma, and Louisiana.

trust was formed when the stock of various corporations was placed in the hands of a single group of stockholders called trustees. The original stockholders received "trustee certificates" in return for their stock.

477

Tamers of Electricity

A commodity which changed life just as remarkably as oil was electricity. In the days when Carnegie and Rockefeller were first making their names and fortunes, electricity was still a plaything.

Franklin's kite. In an experiment with a kite, Benjamin Franklin had earned international applause in the eighteenth century by proving that lightning and electricity are the same. In 1831 an English scientist, Michael Faraday, had shown that man can generate electricity by spinning a magnet around a wire. He had revealed the secret of the dynamo.

"What hath God wrought?" Electricity was applied in a practical way for the first time in communication. Using known scientific principles, Samuel F. B. Morse —a portrait painter—ran a telegraph line from Baltimore to Washington. He obtained from Congress the money to pay the expenses. On May 24, 1844, he tapped out his now-famous first message, "What hath God wrought?"

Edison, the "wizard." The person who alone played a larger part than any other in harnessing electricity was Thomas Alva Edison. He was sometimes called the wizard of Menlo Park—the town in New Jersey in which he performed some of his most important experiments.

Like Morse, Edison did not discover new scientific principles, but he had a remarkable skill in putting to work the principles others had found. Though he lived until 1931, Edison's most important inventions were made in the 1870's and 1880's.

The electric light. The most famous of Edison's creations was the electric-light bulb. Edison had quickly seen the chief problem in making an incandescent lamp —as the light bulb was known at first. It was to find a filament (the thread within the glass bulb) which would burn for more than just a few hours. In October, 1879, Edison announced that he had been able to get a cotton thread covered with carbon to glow for over forty hours.

Always seeking perfection, Edison was not satisfied. He began a worldwide hunt for a better material for the filament. He even tried the whiskers of a red-haired man. By the time his bulb was patented in 1880, he had discovered that a certain kind of bamboo gave the best results.

In no time electric light became the rage for homes and businesses. Its advantages were plain. It gave a steady, dependable light of even brightness. Moreover, it could be turned on and off easily.

People could stay up later at night, and the days became fuller and more productive as a result of electric lighting. The demand for electricity could barely be satisfied by the power stations which had to be built at a furious pace. In 1882 there were only thirty-eight in the country, and in 1898 there were about three thousand.

The current and appliances. Edison was an excellent manager of his inventions. In 1878—the year after he invented the phonograph—Edison formed the Edison Electric Light Company. It controlled the main patents for Edison's electric-light bulbs and set standards for local companies which provided electricity.

The electrical industry—including the companies which sold current and those which sold equipment—had not even existed before the Civil War. By the end of the 1880's, it was a big business.

Telephone's Bell

Another powerful new industry based on a single invention was the telephone industry. The telephone first appeared in public at the Centennial Exposition of 1876 (see page 466). It was the thrilling work of Alexander Graham Bell, a teacher of deaf-mutes. He had created an instru-

How did the inventions of the late 1800's provide a basis for the material things of modern American life? What things in use today were introduced during this period? How did one invention lead to another?

ment which caused the Emperor Dom Pedro of Brazil (a visitor to the exposition) to shout as he put it to his ear, "My God! It talks!"

Early opposition. The first telephone naturally did not reproduce the voice as faithfully as one today does. Moreover, at first it seemed a ridiculous gadget to many. People made fun of it, saying that no one could get *them* to shout into a metal box.

Mark Twain, the author of *The Adventures of Tom Sawyer*, was one of these people. He stated firmly that he would not have a telephone "at any price." But in a short time, he had changed his mind and had had one installed and connected with the local newspaper office. His phone is said to have been the first one ever placed in a private home.

The switchboard. A major technical breakthrough came when central switchboards were created. They ended the requirement that each telephone must be connected with others directly. By 1885 switchboards had come into general use and were being connected with one another, increasing the range of telephone conversations.

The "Hello girls." In those days and until the 1930's, it was necessary in many places to tell the operator at "central" the number of the telephone one was calling. At first the operators were boys, but they were early replaced by girls, who were less likely to swear at the customers. For many years these girls were popularly known as Hello girls.

The Bell Telephone Company was founded in 1877 and was well managed from the start. Early its leaders saw the advantages in leasing, not selling, telephones and telephone lines to subscribers. The Bell people were fortunate, too, because they won a patent suit. A court upheld their claim to having the sole right to manufacture phones.

Service across the country. The American Telephone and Telegraph Company, made up of the various telephone systems joined together, made possible telephone and telegraph service across the nation.## People could telephone from town to town beginning in 1879.

In 1880 eighty-five communities had centrals. By the time of the presidential campaign of 1896, the Republican candidate, William McKinley, could remain at home and take care of his business over long-distance phones.

The new United States which was developing was a country being knit together more tightly than ever before. People in almost any part of it were in contact with those in almost any other part—either by telegraph or by telephone. Americans throughout the country could now respond

How did the telephone ...d the growth and the ...ge-scale organization ...business?

"Hello girls" at central in New York City about 1888: the young women are using a switchboard to make connections between telephone lines. Notice the plain wooden chairs and the bare electric-light bulbs.

American Telephone and Telegraph Co.

immediately to news and other information.

More truly than ever before, Americans could have a *national* outlook and *national* feelings.

A Nation of Factories

Before the Civil War the amount of textile manufacturing had indicated how prosperous a country was. After the war the amount of steel produced each year told the story of how strong a country was.

In the United States steel production rose in a short time. In 1867 the country was producing 19,643 tons every year. Before the century ended, the figure had reached more than 10,000,000 tons—a greater amount than was manufactured in any other country in the world.

Spreading influence. Much of the steel went into the building of other factories and into the machines which made those factories hum. In the decades after the Civil War, factories multiplied many times over. A man writing in 1880 reported in wonderment that within a period of thirty years, the factories were engaged in

the manufacture of boots and shoes, of watches, musical instruments, clothing, agricultural implements, metallic goods generally, fire-arms, carriages and wagons, wooden goods, rubber goods, and even in the slaughtering of hogs.

Each year, it seemed also, new and better methods of production were established. Americans, unlike many other peoples, became accustomed to accepting novel and unfamiliar methods of doing things. One early expert on how to manage factories stated what appeared to be a rule: "The usual way of doing things is always the wrong way."

Attracting customers. Manufacturers were constantly seeking fresh methods of informing the people about the many new products that were available. One of these methods was advertising.

The rise of the advertising industry aroused in people a desire for goods that they either had not known about at all or that they had not known they wanted. In 1875, a leading magazine reported: "The preparation and planning of advertisements of all sorts have assumed the proportions of [become like] a business by itself, to which the entire time and thought of a number of men are devoted."

The results. The effect of all these developments on Americans was increasingly clear. Above all, people grew accustomed to the rapid rate of technological change (see page 6). They began to feel that science and technology could provide a better answer each year to almost every human need—with a new machine, a new gadget, or a new medicine.

Moreover, Americans were pleased because most of them could enjoy more and more comforts than any other people. They talked proudly of the American standard of living, which steadily marched upward.

That standard of living can be measured by the total of goods and services of all kinds available to consumers. In 1870, for each person in the United States the nation produced $165 worth of goods and services. In 1880 the total came to $186, and in 1890 it was $204. In 1900 it amounted to $231. Today it stands at more than $3000.

---

1. What are four things that account for the remarkable development of manufacturing in the United States? 2. Name four large industries that developed after the Civil War and identify the person who was the leading figure in each. 3. In which industry was the first trust formed? How? 4. Name one method by which manufacturers gained customers. 5. What effect did the growth of industry have on the American standard of living?

##Discuss the role of advertising in American business. How does it increase production and create jobs? Why has advertising become more and more important over the years?

Transcontinentals Cement the Nation

The railroad, as we know, had already played an important role in helping unite the American people. This role became even bigger in the years after the Civil War as the country saw a very large-scale growth of rail transportation.

A stirring new chapter in the story of the railroad was the building of the first transcontinental. It caught the imagination of the public the way triumphs in space capture it today.

"A Work of Giants"

An interest in making real the dream of "linking the oceans" had developed after the discovery of gold in California in 1848. Congress first acted to reach this goal in 1862, when it established the Union Pacific Railroad Company. The U.P., as it was called, was given the right to build a road from Omaha, a town in the territory of Nebraska, to the eastern boundary of California. Meanwhile, a company named the Central Pacific (the C.P.) was instructed to build a line eastward from Sacramento, California, to meet the Union Pacific.

Federal money. To make the undertaking successful—and to spur it on—Congress provided subsidies of money to the railroad companies. They were figured in this way: $16,000 a mile in the level country east of the Rockies—$48,000 a mile in the rugged country of the mountains themselves—and $32,000 a mile between the mountain ranges. The federal government also gave the companies generous tracts of land along the paths of the lines.

The feeling then was that without federal aid, private businessmen would not be able to undertake the mammoth task. William T. Sherman, the Civil War general, said that the building of a transcontinental railroad would be "a work of giants." He added, "Uncle Sam is the only giant I know who can grapple the subject."

Putting down the rails. The heroes of building the railroads were the thousands of workingmen. Some were farm boys recently arrived from Ireland. Others were farm boys brought from China.

To build a transcontinental, two rail-laying gangs—one on each side of the new track—walked in front of a railroad car. They threw a pair of rails to the ground—one on each side of the rail ties which were already in place. Then two groups of five men, one group working on either side, would set the rails in place.

An observer of the work wrote:

A transcontinental-railroad track takes shape on the bare, treeless Great Plains.

Great Northern Railway

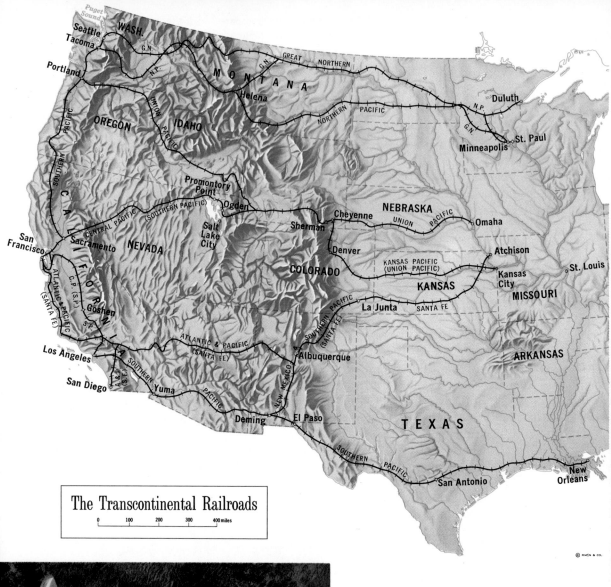

The Transcontinental Railroads

0   100   200   300   400 miles

© RAND & CO.

The Pacific Railroad ground broken January 8th 1863 and completed May 8th 1869

Stanford University Museum

Above: Measure the distance covered by one of the transcontinentals. *Left:* The golden spike that Leland Stanford, the governor of California, drove on May 10, 1869, to finish the first railroad linking the East and the West. (The date on the spike is incorrect.)

The chief of the squad calls out 'Down' in a tone that equals the 'Forward' to any army. Every 30 seconds there came that brave 'Down,' 'Down,' on either side of the track. They were the pendulum beats of a mighty era; they marked the time of the march and its regulation beat.

Obstacles. Sometimes there was trouble with the Indians through whose territory the roads ran. One group of tribesmen, the Shoshone (see page 8), was quieted by a "treaty" negotiated on the spot by an officer of the C.P. He told the story: "We gave the old chiefs a pass each, good on the passenger cars, and we told our men to let the

On the map above, point out some of the cities that prospered because of their location on the major rail lines. With the exception of James Hill's Great Northern, all of the railroads shown above received federal land grants.

 common Indians ride on the freight cars whenever they saw fit."

Sometimes there were fearful snow-storms—in the mountains, especially. At one time 15 feet of snow buried the roadbed. Five giant locomotives were required to push a snowplow through 30-foot snowdrifts.

The race to the end. Despite everything, by the summer of 1868 the C.P. had laid tracks across California and was preparing to continue across Nevada. The U.P. had passed the most difficult point in the Rockies and was pressing to the west from Sherman, Wyoming. A race was on to see which would complete its task first.

The competition became so fierce that the engineers worked far ahead of the construction crews, selecting the sites for roadbeds. At one point the U.P. engineers were surveying ahead almost to the California border, and the C.P. people were looking over areas well east of Ogden, Utah.

Before the race was over, prepared roadbeds ran parallel to one another for great distances! When they had the opportunity, the rival crews did their best to destroy their opponents' roadbeds—even occasionally using explosives.

The "wedding." In Washington, D.C., the place where the two lines were to join was finally agreed upon. It was the tiny town of Promontory Point, 6 miles west of Ogden, Utah. With impressive ceremony, the last spike—a gold one—was driven into place a little after noon on May 10, 1869, as the country "listened in" on telegraph lines. To celebrate the event, the railroaders sent President Ulysses S. Grant and his Secretary of State rings inscribed "The Mountain Wedding: May 10th 1869."

A fantastic development followed the completion of the transcontinental railroad. Places which had been mere "shack towns" or had not even existed earlier became lively trade centers: Kansas City,

Missouri; Denver, Colorado; Cheyenne, Wyoming; Helena, Montana; Portland, Oregon; and St. Paul and Minneapolis, Minnesota, were among many others. Moreover, in a few years there was hardly a town in the West not reached by a railroad, as "feeder" lines were built to nearly all communities.

Through the Southwest

The chief engineer of the Union Pacific had predicted that three transcontinental railroads would soon be needed. Before many years there were four.

The Southern Pacific. One of them was the Southern Pacific Railroad. It developed out of a branch of the Central Pacific. Established in 1864, it was the high achievement of Collis P. Huntington. The map on page 482 shows that it extended across the American Southwest as far east as New Orleans and as far north as Oregon.

The Santa Fe. Another of the great trunk railroads in the Southwest was the Atchison, Topeka & Santa Fe. It was built along the old Santa Fe Trail of Spanish days (see page 372).

A Pennsylvanian, Cyrus Holliday, was the promoter of the Santa Fe (as the name of the railroad was abbreviated). Holliday sent colonizing agents as far as Russia to seek settlers to live near his new railroad.

To the Pacific Northwest

A transcontinental was constructed in the Pacific Northwest, too. It was called the Northern Pacific Railroad.

The Northern Pacific. Under the act of Congress which created it in 1864, the Northern Pacific was to run from a point on Lake Superior to or near to Portland, Oregon. Its construction, as you can see on the map at the left, was a forbidding task. When the Civil War ended, work was begun in earnest. The company of Jay

he Southern Pacific went through an area of the Gadsden Purchase--along the route originally
posed for it.
483
Vhy did the railroad companies want settlers to live near their lines?

Use the Great Northern to show the role of railroads in the development of the West. Hill realized that his railroad would profit only if the area through which it passed was settled and prosperous.

The track-laying crews who built the Great Northern by working from the east and west meet on January 6, 1893, near what is now Scenic, Washington, in the Cascade Mountains. They are about to set the final spike.

Cooke, a wealthy Philadelphian, invested much of the money needed for it.

A business depression in 1873 caused Jay Cooke and Company to fail. The completion of the railroad was slowed by the resulting financial difficulties. Not until the 1880's did the line reach Portland—through the use of a local railroad's tracks.

Hill's Great Northern. Still another transcontinental was the Great Northern Railroad. Built between Lake Superior and Puget Sound—without government land grants—it was the distinguished work of a Canadian named James J. Hill. Born in 1838, he lost an eye early in his life because of the accidental shooting of an arrow. Full of energy and ideas, he established himself in St. Paul and from there built a vast railroad empire.

During the depression of 1873, Hill had acquired a small bankrupt line, the St. Paul and Pacific. People had laughed at Hill and called his investment Hill's folly. They seemed to have good reason, because the farmers of Minnesota, the railroad's customers, had suffered fearfully in the depression. Moreover, the crops they were able to grow had been badly damaged by a terrible plague of grasshoppers.

A little bit of luck. But good luck was on Hill's side. The grasshoppers went away in 1877, and the wheat crop of Minnesota

was excellent. Before the harvest season was over, Hill was seeking additional locomotives and freight cars to carry it.

Gradually adding to his line, Hill in 1889 formed the Great Northern Railroad. So successful was he that when the depression of 1893 drove the other transcontinental railroads into bankruptcy, Hill continued to prosper.

Attracting settlers. Hill made efforts to help obtain settlers along the route of the Great Northern. With great imagination and vigor, he encouraged farmers and ranchers to come to the land along his line.

Hill even sent agents to Europe to help persuade Scotsmen, Englishmen, Norwegians, and Swedes to settle in America. Because the land of the Great Plains is dry, he carried on experiments in dry farming—farming requiring little water—to improve its productivity.

1. Name five railroad companies that were formed during the building of the transcontinental railroads in the second half of the nineteenth century. 2. In what two ways did the federal government encourage the lines? 3. What difficulties did the workers face? 4. Describe the effect the railroads had on the trans-Mississippi West.

Railroads did not make all their profits from freight and passenger traffic. They also sold or rented land and leased their mineral rights--often making money in these ways from the land granted to them by the federal government.

An important point. Individual miners could profit as long as precious metals were near the surface, but
veins of ore deep in the earth required a heavy investment in equipment--more than an individual could
afford. (Mining, like the making of goods, was changed by the machine age.)

New Rushes Pull People to Western Mines

The railroads made it possible to enter easily some regions of the West which several generations of migrants had passed by. These regions included the mountain areas of present-day Nevada, Colorado, Arizona, Idaho, Montana, and Wyoming.

Strike After Strike

What drew people in droves to places ignored earlier was a series of gold and silver rushes like the one that had filled California in 1849. The first of these began with a lucky strike in 1858 in the Pike's Peak section of Colorado.

At Pike's Peak. The news of the strike near Pike's Peak spread like wildfire. All during the following winter there was activity in scores of towns in California and the Mississippi Valley, as well as in the East. A man in a Missouri town wrote, "The streets are full of people buying flour, bacon, and groceries, with wagons and outfits, and all around the town are little camps preparing to go West."

In no time thousands of people were competing fiercely with one another to make lucky strikes. Denver and other little camps became cities overnight.

The Colorado boom quickly ended. Ores of precious metals were present, but for the most part they could not be dug out by individuals. Removing them required methods and equipment which only companies with large amounts of money could afford. Colorado would become largely an agricultural state.

Like the sound of a chain of firecrackers going off, though, new mining "booms" were heard in rapid succession. Soon after the Colorado rush was over, the prospectors shifted their equipment and their hopes to Nevada, at that time a part of the Utah territory. At first it was gold which drew men there. But soon it was silver that made them rich—a few, anyway.

The Comstock Lode. In the Washoe Mountains of Nevada, a band of miners in 1858 found the richest silver deposit in history. It was called the Comstock Lode,

Denver in 1864—
hardly touched by the
Civil War, then in its
last year "back East."

State Historical Society of Colorado

being named for Henry Comstock, a miner who bragged much about the discovery—although it was not actually his.

The Comstock Lode was responsible for the mushroom-like growth of Virginia City. Almost overnight the town hummed with activity. Transportation to bring in supplies for thousands of people and to carry out the precious metals had to be arranged. The comforts of life—theaters, schools, banks, hotels, and a thousand other conveniences—had to be created.

There were hundreds of other claims i Nevada, but only a dozen of them prove profitable. For the owners of these, course, life was completely changed. The lived like kings.

Between 1860 and 1880 the Comstoc Lode and other finds in Nevada yielded or valued at over three hundred million do lars. And in 1864 Nevada was admitted t the Union. But the ore deposits had bee played out by 1880, and people in Nevad were in difficulties. They could not easil

What states in the West owe their beginning at least in part to th discovery of minerals? How were many of the western Indians affected

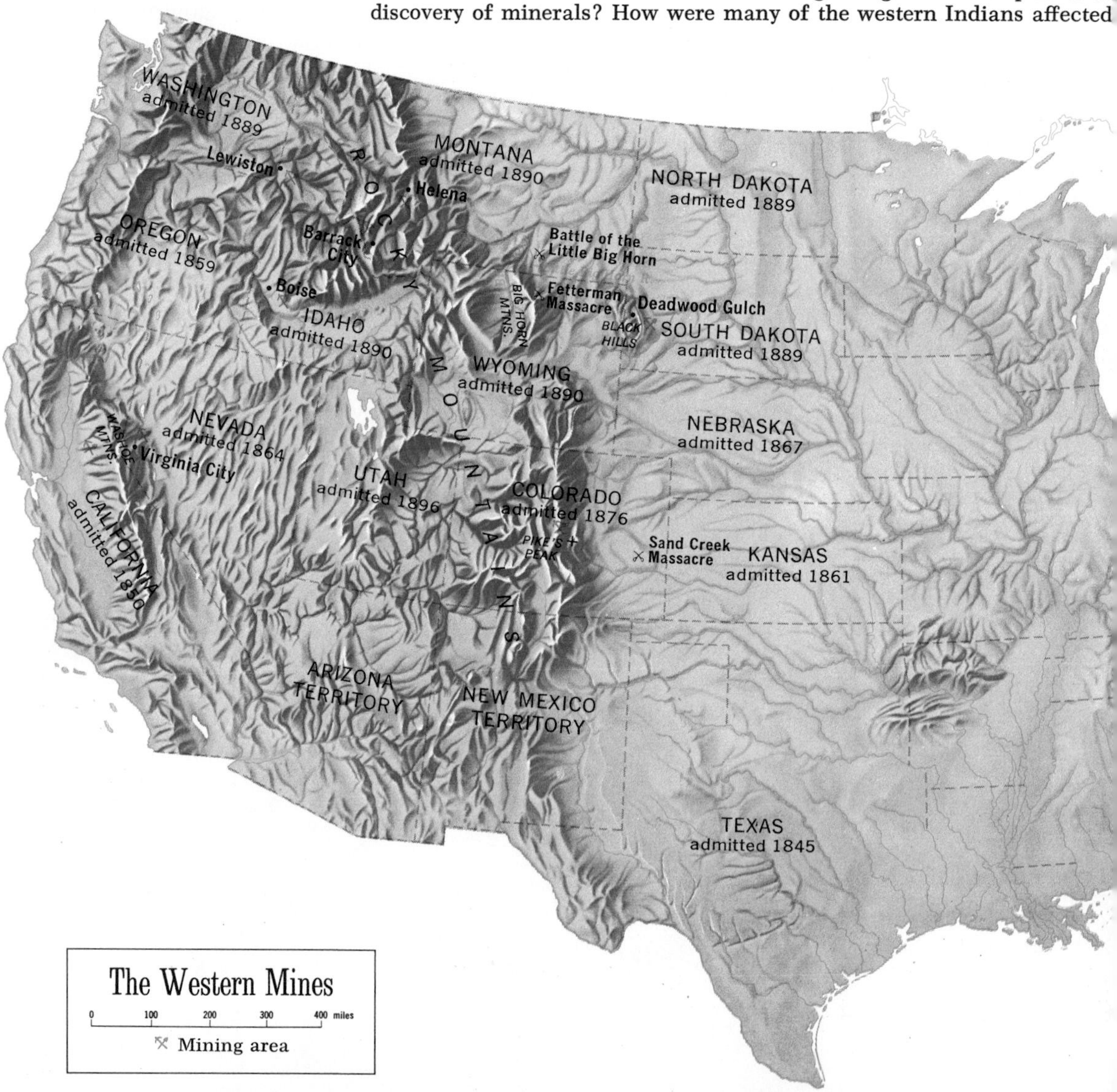

The Western Mines

0   100   200   300   400 miles

⋉ Mining area

hift to farming, because the land there
vas not well suited to it.

In Idaho and Montana. Before the Civil
Var was ended, gold booms occurred in
daho and Montana. Both places were part
f the territory of Washington, but quickly
hey were made separate territories. In Ida-
o the leading towns were Boise and Lew-
ston. In Montana they were Helena and
arrack City.

The mineral finds in these places were
ot as rewarding as those in other areas.
ut when the Montana supply of gold bean to run thin, some wealth continued
o flow from copper and silver deposits.

Near Tucson. A boom story also unfold-
d in the western part of the New Mexico
erritory. There gold and silver had been
iscovered near Tucson before 1860. The
esulting activity in that region led to its
eing organized separately as the Arizona
erritory. When the ores were gone, a dis-
overy of copper supported the miners.

Deadwood Gulch. No other booms oc-
urred until 1874, when gold was found in
he Black Hills, in the southwestern part of
he Dakota territory. The land there had
een given to the Sioux (soo) Indians. The
own which became the center of the strike
vas Deadwood Gulch. Within a short time,
owever, Deadwood Gulch joined Virginia
City and other boom places as a ghost
own, full of memories of a brief but glo-
ious time.

The Defeat of the Indians

The results of all the fascinating discov-
ries can be measured in the millions of
lollars' worth of precious metals removed
rom the earth. They can also be measured
n their effect on the Indians.

Blood on the Plains. The Plains Indians,
vhose lands were invaded by the miners,
ived in bands of a few hundred people,
ach band under a chief. With only bows
nd arrows, the Plains Indians for a time

were able to stand up against the advancing settlers. The settlers relied on muzzle-
loading guns, to which they had to feed
bullets one by one—difficult on horseback.

The miners could not destroy the Indians by burning their crops and villages.
Many of the tribesmen were nomads who
did not depend on these things. Only after
the Colt six-shooter and the repeating rifle
—weapons that could be fired rapidly and
repeatedly—came into general use did the
newcomers have an advantage.

The Chivington massacre. Conflict arose
first in Colorado. The rush there had
brought miners to the very area which the
Arapaho and Cheyenne Indians had been
promised would be theirs forever.

A terrible slaughter of the tribesmen—
never to be forgotten—took place in Colorado on the night of November 28, 1864.
Colonel John M. Chivington, of the Colorado militia, fell upon five hundred Cheyenne Indians sleeping in a reservation and
destroyed them. Ignoring the pleas of
Chief Black Kettle, Chivington's men
knifed and scalped some of their victims,
including women and children, and beat
and crippled others. Chivington's massacre
ended Indian resistance in that part of
the country.

The Sioux War. Between 1865 and 1867
the struggle of the Indians to hold on to
their land in spite of the miners' advances
moved to the Dakota territory. The fighting
which inflamed the region is known as the
Sioux War. The outbreaks were a result of
news of the Chivington massacre and the
trespassing of miners on the hunting
grounds of the Sioux Indians.

In one tragic event late in 1866, about a
hundred United States soldiers under Captain W. J. Fetterman were ambushed and
slain by Sioux Indians. The leader of the
raid was the clever Chief Red Cloud.

The Chivington and Fetterman massa-
cres did not cancel one another out. But
they drew the attention of people every-

scuss the injustice done to the Indians during the settlement of the West. How could it have
n avoided or the Indians treated more fairly? What problems were caused by the reservation
em? Have students begin work on Exercise 1 in "The Research Center" (p. 492).   487

where to the need to find a new policy for dealing with the Indians in the West. In the late 1860's officials in Washington asked for the assistance of the churches in bringing about peace with the Indians.

The plan failed because churchmen as well as other Americans did not understand the problems involved. By treaties arranged with the western Indians in the late 1860's, the northern Plains tribes were sent to live on reservations in the Black Hills region of the Dakota territory. The southern Plains Indians were to be located on land in the western part of Oklahoma.

In the Black Hills. One of the final wrongs that the tribesmen suffered was inflicted in 1875. At that time thousands # of American gold seekers were permitted to pour into the Black Hills territory which had been promised to the Indians. This invasion was almost more than the Sioux could bear. Chiefs Sitting Bull and Crazy Horse began preparations for war, collecting supplies on the Little Big Horn River.

"Custer's last stand." Colonel George A. Custer, a West Pointer whose great-grandfather had been a Hessian officer in the American Revolution, was in charge of the American troops sent to fight the Indians. At the Battle of the Little Big Horn, in June, 1876, he foolishly led his entire command of 264 soldiers to their death. The struggle there has been ever after remembered as Custer's last stand.

Nevertheless, the strength of the United States was overwhelming. By the end of the next year, Indian fighting was over. Chief Sitting Bull had fled to Canada. His people had no choice but to ask for peace.

The buffalo. One of the leading reasons for the defeat of the Plains Indians was the killing off of the buffalo. When the Civil War ended, it was estimated that there were fifteen million of them living on the plains west of the Mississippi. The huge, shaggy buffalo completely supported the Indians. They provided food, clothing,

Woolaroc Museum, Bartlesville, Okla.

Chief Sitting Bull, Sioux medicine man who helped prepare for the battle with Custer.

tenting—everything. Even their droppings, when dried, were useful as fuel.

The first stages in wiping out the buffalo came when the building of the Union Pacific divided the animals into two herds —one on the north side of the tracks and one on the south side. Then a tannery in Pennsylvania discovered that buffalo hides could be used for leather. The price for a buffalo skin became established at from $1.00 to $3.00.

Wasteful slaughter. Then "sportsmen" began to appear in the West. Taking advantage of the new kinds of rifles produced during the Civil War, they began to organize hunting parties. They usually "hunted" from railroad trains moving past the buffalo herds. One estimate has it that over three million buffalo were brutally slain by such hunters between 1871 and 1874.

The building of the western railroads also took a heavy toll of buffalo life. Hunters were hired to clear the animals off the

Recall the difficulties faced by the Aztecs and Incas in their contacts with the Spanish in the 1500's. Compare United States and Spanish relations with the Indians. What were the major differences? Why? Consider the part differing technologies played in both relationships.

right-of-ways and to provide meat for the gangs of railroad workers. One of the tireless killers of buffalo was the handsome William F. Cody, always remembered as Buffalo Bill.

By 1875 the market for buffalo hides had become so oversupplied that the price for a skin fell to 65¢. By 1880 the southern herd had practically disappeared. The northern herd lasted a little longer, but the building of the Northern Pacific Railroad doomed it, too.

1. Name six present-day mountain states whose earliest settlers were largely miners. 2. Where was the first lucky strike made? 3. Where was the richest silver deposit in history found? 4. What are ghost towns? Name two of them. 5. Describe the Chivington massacre. 6. Tell two results it had. 7. Give an account of events in the Black Hills territory in 1875. 8. Name a main reason for the defeat of the Plains Indians.

Cowboys and Cattle Take Over the Plains

By the year 1903 only thirty-four buffalo remained of the millions there had been a few years earlier. The "woolly West" had disappeared—and with it a valuable resource which had supported thousands of Indians also vanished.

When the tribesmen were gone from the railroads' right-of-ways and the Great Plains were clear of buffalo, the land was put to a new use by the cattle industry. The Plains became the home of cowboys, of longhorn cattle roaming freely, and of dusty, noisy cow towns. The region became known as the Cattle Kingdom.

North from Texas

The new cattle industry began to grow after the Civil War. The Texas ranchers were able to reach the eastern markets more easily than earlier because the rail lines extended beyond the Mississippi.

The first cattle were not outstanding, for the animals had not yet been bred to bring out the qualities most advantageous for the production of beef. Gradually the ranchers learned how to produce larger and tastier beasts.

The northern grass. A special reason for the improvement of the cattle was the dis-covery that grass on the northern Plains was good food for the animals. In the wintertime, when the winds there blew snow into drifts and exposed the soil sufficiently, the herds could feed even after blizzards. Moreover, the deep ravines offered protection for the cattle in the very worst weather.

The long drive. By the early 1860's the long drive from Texas to the north each winter was a regular feature of the cattle business. The cattle traveled along several well-established trails (see the map on page 490).

Cow towns. The creation of a shipping point at Abilene, Kansas, in 1867 especially encouraged Texans to make the long drive to take their cattle north. This great cattle market, located along the Kansas-Pacific Railroad, began the colorful era of the cow towns.

A number of such marketing towns were established in time along the trails of the long drive—Wichita, Ellsworth, and Dodge City, Kansas, among others (also shown on page 490). It is estimated that between 1866 and 1888 more than six million head of cattle were driven north to winter on the Great Plains. Afterward they were shipped to market by railroad.

what ways did the railroad make the Cattle Kingdom possible? Ask a student to look into pects of modern cattle raising: methods of feeding and shipping, of grading beef, and of rforming other related tasks in which changes have occurred.

489

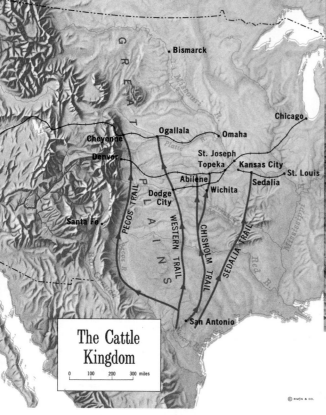

The Cattle Kingdom

0   100   200   300 miles

Old Print Shop

Left: The long drives leading to marketing centers made Americans beefeating people. *Above:* Texas longhorn cattle—developed from a Spanish breed—in a prize herd in 1881.

Why did the drives move north, not south and east to the Gulf ports?

Home on the Range

As the Cattle Kingdom boomed, some features of ranching became part of the legend of the West. First of all, there was the staggering size of the operation. A ranch might be said to include a million acres or more, since the owner's animals roamed widely over an enormous distance.

A second feature of ranching was the cowboy, whose task was the management of the animals. Cowboys' skill as horsemen was equaled only by that of the Plains Indians at their best.

With saddle and lasso. The cowboy sometimes seemed larger than life—as he does today in the westerns (novels, movies, and TV) which exaggerate his activities. But although his work could be exciting, it was also demanding. Moreover, much of it was not at all glamorous.

For his dangerous life a cowboy needed, to be sure, extra strength and courage. He also required saintly patience to endur the endless days and nights of outriding— that is, circling around and around th herd. Sometimes he prevented cattle fror straying and rustlers from stealing an mals. He also saw to it that nesters—farm ers—did not keep the cattle from reachin water holes.

In addition, cowboys had to be able t shoe horses, nurse sick animals, and some times assist at the birth of calves. Cowboy also had to be masters of the rope. Thi skill enabled them to corral (herd togeth er) straying longhorns and to hold calve so that they might be branded.

Brands were the only means of identify ing beasts that wandered freely over grea distances. The law in Texas was that brand had to be "a large and plain mar. branded on the left side of the back behin the shoulder." The busiest—and no doub the noisiest—time of the year occurre each spring when the new calves wer dragged to the fire to be marked.

Discuss why Americans have made so much of the legend of the cowboy, when in fact the cow boy era was merely a brief episode in our history.

The outfits that cowboys wore were not really meant for showing off. The clothing was made of horsehide or buckskin so it would wear out less quickly than cotton cloth. Also, it would resist cactus thorns far better.

Moreover, the broad-brimmed hat served to protect the cowboy from the hot sun, the drenching rain, and the mud from flying hooves that so often followed the rain. And the handkerchief around the neck, which could be quickly raised over the nose, offered protection against the clouds of dust a herd could raise in the summer.

Occasionally the cowboys got into fights in the cow towns, but not nearly as often as some television shows indicate. For the most part, they were too anxious to rest from their heavy labors to spoil occasional days off with violence.

"Boom-and-bust." By the beginning of the 1880's, the Cattle Kingdom had become very prosperous. The wealthiest of the cattle ranchers were popularly called cattle barons. Each owned hundreds of thousands of head of cattle. They spent their money lavishly and adorned themselves with diamond rings.

But before the 1880's were over, the cattle boom had ended. First of all, the open range of the Great Plains became overcrowded with animals—"overstocked" was the expression.

Second, despite the long drive's advantages in feeding and marketing cattle, it was not reliable. The animals could not be cared for properly, and the weather could be dangerous, particularly for the calves. Also, animal diseases passed easily from one beast to another under the conditions of the open range. Moreover, it was hard for ranchers to improve the breeds unless they could fence in the cattle.

Toward disaster. The year 1885 saw the beginning of a terrible slump in the cattle business. Prices fell because of the enormous supply of animals. The grass—despite the vastness of the Great Plains—was not sufficient to feed them all.

On top of everything else, the winter of 1885–1886 was fearful. The snows were so heavy that the grass was completely covered and stayed covered. Never had such blizzards been seen or heard of. In the spring, 85 percent of the animals that had been exposed to them lay dead.

Left: Branding irons used to make identifying marks on western cattle—valuable property to be protected. *Below:* Another painting by Russell: cowboys racing for grub at the chuck wagon—a high point of any day.

(Branding Irons) "Steelways" Magazine, published by American Iron and Steel Institute; (Cowboys) Montana Historical Society

Unfortunately, the following summer was hot and dry. Because of a drought, the grass did not grow thickly enough to feed the animals that had survived. As a result, they were in poor condition when the winter of 1886–1887 began.

That winter was even more severe than the previous one. It completed the work of destroying the Cattle Kingdom. The shocking sight when spring came brought pangs of conscience to the ranchers whose animals had either perished or were limping about on frozen legs.

The cattle industry revived in a few years. But cattle no longer roamed the open range. Ranchers kept their herds on private pasturelands where the animals could be sheltered and fed properly.

On the northern Great Plains new developments were now occurring. Speaking in Minnesota in 1902, James J. Hill made a prediction: "Churches and schools will be erected where now bands of cattle and sheep roam; not that cattle and sheep are not all right, but farms are better."

The fabulous region which recently had been the home of Indians and buffalo and then of cowboys and longhorn cattle was about to change again. The new occupants would be farmers, for whose use Jefferson had purchased the area in the first place. These farmers would produce the food to feed city people and factory workers whose contributions Hamilton had had so much hope for. The visions of these two Founding Fathers were about to come alive.

---

1. What connection was there between the transcontinental railroads and the development of the Cattle Kingdom? 2. Name four cow towns. 3. What were two outstanding features of ranching? 4. Describe the work of the cowboy. 5. Give three reasons for the ending of the Cattle Kingdom.

Some students might work on a pictorial chart showing major inventions, the names of the inventors, the year of each

The Workshop

invention, and lists of changes that occurred in the economic or social and political life of the nation because of each

The Shapers of Our World

Tell how each of the following helped change the "face" of the country:

Andrew Carnegie
Henry Bessemer
John D. Rockefeller
E. L. Drake
Samuel F. B. Morse
Thomas A. Edison
Alexander
    Graham Bell
"Hello girl"
Jay Cooke

Union Pacific
    Railroad
Central Pacific
    Railroad
James J. Hill
Comstock Lode
"Custer's last
    stand"
Sitting Bull

Adding to Your Vocabulary

Show your understanding of the changes discussed in the chapter by using these words in sentences:

natural resource
investment
coke
smelting
monopoly
corral
longhorn
ghost town

trust
filament
patent
outriding
range
nester
baron

The Research Center

1. Present a panel discussion of one of the western Indian tribes. Describe its culture, its contact with Americans moving west, and what became of it. Report on the Dawes Act and some of the present-day

Write newspaper articles covering "Drake's Folly," the Centennial Exposition, the completion of the first transcontinental railroad, life at Virginia City, Nevada, and an interview with a "cattle baron" after the winter of 1886-1887.

nsider how many industries use steel as a basic material in their products. Also, steel is a vital
.erial in the weapons and other equipment of modern warfare.

lans financed by the federal government
o aid American Indians.

2. Present a program about the growth
f American industry. Report on (a) particular industries, (b) their origins, and (c) their growth. Show some pictures indicating changes in the methods of production, including those resulting from automation.

Some questions that should be answered: Has there been an increase in the number of workers? Was retraining of these people necessary? What was the effect of automation on the demand for the goods produced? Were other industries affected?

3. Your local Chamber of Commerce will help you obtain information about the industries in your community. What influenced them to locate there? What is your community or state doing to attract new industries?

4. Many new American industries are products of improved technology and were unknown when your parents were in school. Prepare for a parents' night a program about some of these new industries. Illustrate your presentation with pictures.

5. Find out what songs were popular (a) among the early settlers of the West, and (b) among the cowboys. Ask your music teacher to help you learn some of them.

Thinking Things Through

After reviewing the boxed-in exercises in the chapter, answer these questions:

1. What lesson about achieving success in business can be learned by studying the Carnegie-Frick connection?

2. Why are the profits of a large company in a particular industry often greater than the combined profits of many smaller companies?

3. Why is the steel production of a country a measure of its position as a world power?

4. Why were railroads one of the most successful means of promoting settlement of the West?

5. Can you tell why any government policy of giving the Indians land in the West would eventually not be respected by many of the settlers who moved to areas beyond the Mississippi?

6. Why was the ending of the Cattle Kingdom a sure sign that the frontier was disappearing?

7. On page 729 find the dates when Colorado, Idaho, Montana, North and South Dakota, Utah, Washington, and Wyoming entered the Union. Why did all these states come into the Union at about the same time?

Your Opinion, Please

1. The settlers in Colorado and the Dakotas thought of the Indians as dangerous savages. What do you think the Indians thought of the settlers?

2. American farmers have always had a name for being friendlier than city people to strangers. Do you think this is true? Explain.

pare maps showing transportation in the United States in 1900. Show major railroads, high-
s, canals, and navigable rivers. Compare these maps with some showing American trans-
ation in 1800 and others showing transportation in the 1960's. Discuss how improved trans-
ation has affected business, political affairs, and personal lives.

(a)

(b)

(c)

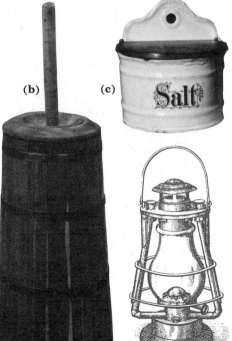

(d)

(a) An American farm scene in the second half of the 1800's. (b) A butter churn: the handle, attached to a dasher, was moved up and down until butter formed from the cream. (c) A salt box of the kind that hung on kitchen walls. (d) A kerosene lantern, a boon to farmers, invented in 1883. (e) Prairie dogs, native to the Great Plains, at the entrance to their burrow. Though they are members of the ground-squirrel family, their shrill bark led to their name.

(e)

(f) A settler and his son "open" a farm in the Platte River Valley—possibly in Nebraska—in 1873.

pictures on pp. 494-495 can be
d to help students understand some
he features of American farming
he late 1800's. Note that the
a pictured on the right is almost
eless.

(f)

CHAPTER 22

PLOWMEN AND WORKINGMEN

his question can be used to introduce the chapter. Relate the problems of the farmer to the growth of ustry in the United States. Help students see how developments in manufacturing and in farming were ated. How did these developments change the lives of most Americans?

FARMERS, who had always been the most numerous of our citizens, faced new and puzzling conditions after the Civil War. Americans as a whole still believed that Jefferson had been right when he wrote, "Those who labor in the earth are the chosen people of God . . . ." Yet there had begun to be talk about a farm problem. What had happened to Jefferson's vision # of America as a nation of farmers?

ow the area commonly called the Great Plains on a map of the present-day United States.

Farmers Break the Sod of the Plains

At the time that the veterans of the Civil War left the army and the navy, "free" land acted as a magnet drawing thousands of them westward. They and others who were raising families began the postwar years full of high hope.

"Free" Homesteads

The passage in 1862 of the Homestead Act was largely responsible for the remarkable westward movement. Under this law any citizen who was the head of a family and over twenty-one years of age was entitled to have 160 acres of land practically free. However, he had to live on it continuously for five years.

Victory. The Homestead Act ended a long campaign to make "free" land available to American farmers. It finally won enough support in Congress after a long struggle in which many interested groups had taken part.

Ruined dreams. The Homestead Act led to disappointment as well as to good for ## those who had obtained land under it. First, some of the very best farmland did not go to farmers. It was acquired by land speculators.

Second, farmers in the East looking for

Another example of a law's having unintended effects. Why was it difficult for some Americans take advantage of the cheap land offered through the Homestead Act? Which groups might ve opposed this law?

better land soon realized that they needed money to be able to move themselves and their families west. Few had enough.

Third, workingmen saw that it was not easy to drop their tools, take up those of the farmer, and, without previous experience, "make a go" of farming. People rarely changed their trades.

Early in the 1870's farming people from the states bordering the Mississippi River began to obtain land on the Great Plains. This vast stretch of territory had been bypassed by the travelers moving west on the Oregon Trail. They had regarded it as a useless country suitable only for nomadic Indians and buffalo. Now Americans prepared to tackle it for farming.

A New Environment

In settling on the Great Plains, the farmers had to face—and solve—problems which they had never before dreamed of. Only slowly did they discover answers to them.

The fence problem. The first puzzle that confronted the settlers was finding a way to build fences in a grassland area which had no timber. Fences were important on the Great Plains because they protected a farmer's land from animals, especially cattle and sheep.

What was needed was a fencing material that was both plentiful and cheap. Bringing in lumber by rail or wagon was far too expensive. In 1870 it was estimated that a wooden fence around a 160-acre farm would cost about $1000. Of course such a sum was beyond the wildest thoughts of most any western farmer.

A rivalry developed among people who were attempting to find a suitable material for fences. A great variety of things were tried—including several kinds of hedges.

A pot of gold and great personal satisfaction would reward the man who found the right material. He turned out to be an Illinois farmer and cattle rancher named Joseph F. Glidden.

Barbed wire. In enclosing his own farm, Glidden made use of and improved on an idea he had picked up at a county fair in 1873. It was to string from post to post two strands of wire twisted in such a way that every few inches there was a sharp, mean barb. He was granted a patent on his barbed wire in 1874.

Glidden soon was manufacturing his invention and selling it for a few cents a pound. At first he hired young boys to put the barbs onto the wire. Later his firm used automatic machines for the same purpose. Tens of millions of pounds of barbed wire were sold within the next few years.

The water problem. A second problem farmers on the Great Plains faced was to find adequate water. Except in a very few locations there simply is not enough rainfall in the region for the inhabitants to farm as people do east of the Mississippi.

Barbed-wire fences similar to this one provided cheaper and more permanent protection against trespassing than the older, wooden ones. The unwelcome trespassers were mostly cattle and sheep. American industry made possible the large-scale production of the barbed wire.

Kansas State Historical Society

Threshing grain on the Plains: The wagon (*left*) brought wheat to the thresher (*center*). The motor (*right*) provided power through the belt.

And when it does rain, much of the water, instead of soaking into the ground, is forced by the tight sod to run off.

Also, the rivers on the Great Plains are shallower than more easterly ones, making it difficult to use them for irrigation. Moreover, the usual high winds there greatly speed up the rate of evaporation of water.

Pioneers who thought that wells could be dug quickly on the Great Plains to provide water were sadly mistaken. The underground water in the region is several hundred feet below the surface. It was necessary to use machines to dig wells. And then the question became how to bring the water to the surface. The "old oaken bucket" reeled on a cord could not be used to bring up water from such depths.

Windmills. By the early 1870's technology was solving the water problem, at least in part. Windmills—long in use in the eastern part of the United States and in the Netherlands—were adapted to the need. Taking advantage of the wind, a windmill provided the power necessary to bring up the underground water from considerable depths.

The cost of digging wells was as high as $2.00 a foot—again, beyond the reach of most farmers. As a result, for a long time very few could afford wells, let alone wind-mills. Not until near the end of the nineteenth century could most farmers afford both wells and the windmills that made them usable.

Dry farming. Meanwhile farmers discovered the value of dry farming. They carefully broke the ground after rain fell in order to preserve every possible drop of water. Of course, to perform this work on a large-sized farm, machines to turn the soil were needed.

New types of machinery. By the 1870's, also, many kinds of farm machines had been invented or vastly improved and were being produced in quantity. The most important was James Oliver's chilled-iron plow—introduced in 1877—an improvement on an older one created early in the century. The importance of Oliver's plow was that it was made of specially prepared iron strong enough to make a clean furrow in the tough sod of the Great Plains.

Many other machines became available to help farmers manage with work forces no larger than their own families. The machines included grain drills for planting seeds in rows, plows that farmers could ride on, and threshing machines that separated wheat from chaff and bagged the grains of wheat.

Yet the machines were expensive. A

ow were the problems of farming in this new environment overcome? Which of the improvements discussed above had to be manufactured? (Use this point to show how the growth of manufacturing and changes in farming were related.)

497

Compare the house and lands above with those shown on pp. 220, 226, 388.

The sod house—larger than most—of a Kansas farmer and his family. For lack of a barn, the buggy (under the windmill) and the farm machinery are without cover. Notice: not a tree or bush is in sight.

farmer could afford them only if he made a profit on his farm. And usually it was profitable only if he had machines! Like mountain climbers on slippery slopes, farmers made progress upward only slowly.

Sometimes the farmers failed completely, especially those on the plains of western Kansas and Nebraska. A Kansas newspaper editor described a pair of farm wagons he saw pass through his town in the 1890's. The men who drove it, he said, had given up "only after a ten years' hard vicious fight . . . which had left its scars on their faces, had bent their bodies, had taken the elasticity from their steps. . . . They had such high hopes when they went out there; they are so desolate now."

The sod houses. Some of the most distressing experiences of all took place in the northern part of the Great Plains. There for a time people lived in houses made of soil and grass—sod houses. These were built of squares of turf piled one on top of another. A man in Kansas wrote in 1877:

At first these sod houses are unplastered . . . such a house is somewhat cold in the winter, as the crevices [that is, the spaces] between the sods admit some cold air; so some of the houses are plastered with a kind of "native lime," made of sand and a very sticky native clay. This plaster is very good unless it happens to get wet.

The people who live in sod houses, and, in fact, all who live under a dirt roof, are pestered with swarms of bed bugs.

You don't have to keep a dog to have plenty of fleas, for they are natives too and do their best to drive out the intruding settlers. . . .

Another nuisance here is what people call "Kansas itch," which attacks nearly everybody within a short time after arrival here; few are immune.

Grasshoppers. Nothing, though, seemed to keep newcomers from the dry grasslands—not even the visits of grasshoppers. These chewing insects would arrive in swarms thick enough to blot the sun from sight. They would eat everything that grew above ground and then go to work on the vegetables that were underground. They often weighed down so heavily the few trees that grew that the limbs were snapped off the trunks.

498 #Note that farmers on the Great Plains used a new technology to remove many natural obstacles that for a time at least had seemed beyond man's control. How might the farmers struggle have affected their outlook? Why did the settlers continue to come--despite all the difficulties?

The grasshoppers even ate clothing, the wooden handles of farm tools, and whatever food might be inside farmhouses. The year 1874 was especially horrible. That year the 'hoppers covered the entire Great Plains from early summer until frost.

Severe weather. The unfamiliar features of the Great Plains weather could also be discouraging. The heat in the summer was sometimes almost unbearable. In the winter the fierce blizzards often were fearful. And a moist, warm breeze called the chinook often melted the snow overnight and caused floods. The wind was named for the fact that it blows from the west across the Plains from the direction of the Chinook Indians (see page 8). Further, the ice storms were often disastrous.

A rich "breadbasket." But the farmers were a hardy lot, and in time they made permanent homes on the Great Plains. They turned the new land into one of the richest "breadbaskets" in the world. Because of it, the United States was able in 1876 to produce about 309,000,000 bushels of wheat. Twenty years later the figure stood at only slightly less than 523,000,000 bushels.

The Oklahoma run. Steadily, new settlers came to the West, willing to brave the dangers and accept the disappointments. Nothing proves this fact better than the way in which a section of Oklahoma was opened to settlement at noon on April 22, 1889. The area was the home of seventy-five thousand Indians of various tribes, who had been moved from the eastern part of the country to reservations on the supposedly worthless land. Now much of this land would be taken.

As April 22 approached, thousands upon thousands of people poured into the adjoining region and waited at the border. Some came on horseback, some by wagon, some by train. At the hour that had been set, a pistol shot announced that the "run" was on. Thousands of men and women rushed madly across the line to stake their claims.

The excitement of the settling of Guthrie, Oklahoma, is probably only hinted at in this eyewitness account:

Left: A farm family living on the fringe of the Great Plains—see the trees—sweep up and burn thousands of grasshoppers in 1875. *Right:* A close-up of the greedy insect whose relatives covered the Plains.

te that the whole family d to share in the work.

(Burning Grasshoppers) Kansas State Historical Society; (Close-up) American Museum of Natural History

Which of the lands shown on the map below are still controlled by Indian tribes?

Left: Moccasins worn by Plains Indians.
Below: The area into which the Oklahoma run was made belonged to the Cherokee, tribesmen who had been forced out of Georgia in the winter of 1838–1839.

Unlike Rome, the city of Guthrie was built in a day. To be strictly accurate in the matter, it might be said that it was built in an afternoon. At twelve o'clock on Monday April 22nd, the resident population of Guthrie was nothing; before sundown it was at least ten thousand. In that time streets had been laid out, town lots staked off, and steps taken toward the formation of a municipal government. At twilight the camp-fires of ten thousand people gleamed on the grassy slopes of the Cimarron Valley, where, the night before, the coyote, the gray wolf, and the deer had roamed undisturbed.

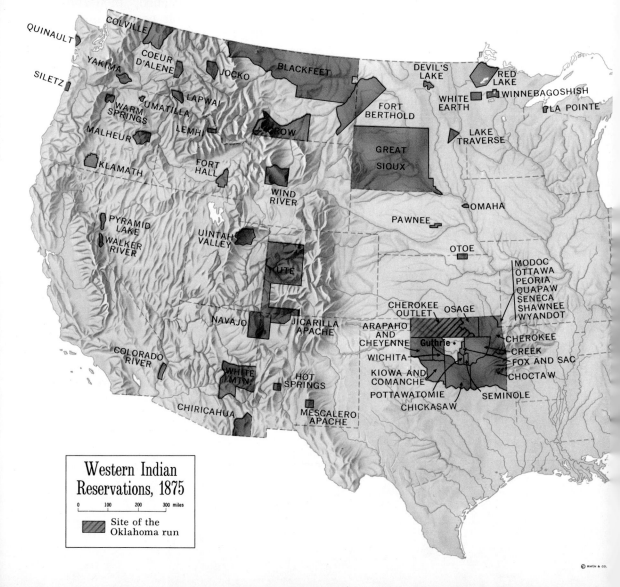

Western Indian Reservations, 1875

0   100   200   300 miles

Site of the Oklahoma run

Settlers rush pell-mell into the newly opened Oklahoma land. This painting is by John Noble, an artist who took part in the run.

"Down on the Farm"

After the excitement of owning a farm had died down, the labor of turning it into a home began. The routines were the same in most parts of the country.

Of course, today it is almost impossible to recapture a sense of what life "down on the farm" was like in the nineteenth century. But the word work sums it up very well. It is said that any boy or girl brought up on a farm who later moved to a city never complained of hard work there.

The chores. For the farmer himself, the day's labor began before dawn with the milking of the cows in the barn. It ended after dark with the milking of the cows in the barn. Taking care of those animals was the farmer's unchanging chore every day of his life.

Other chores were seasonal. In the winter a farmer cut ice from any nearby lake or stream and stored it for use in the summer. In the springtime he manured and plowed his fields and sowed seed. In the summer, while his crops were growing, he took care of them, built fences, and worried about the weather. In the fall he butchered, harvested, and prepared his produce for market.

Work animals. To accomplish many of these tasks and scores of others, the farmer depended on power furnished by horses and mules. Sometimes when a great deal of strength was required, but not speed, he relied on oxen.

The horse, often affectionately known

Have a group of students present a discussion of farm life in the United States today. How does it differ from what is described on pp. 501-502? What things help explain the differences? Is farm life today much different from city life?

Milking time on an American farm in 1903. After the family had done this chore, the milk was stored in a cool place. The cream that rose to the top was collected and later churned. The skim milk could be used for making cottage cheese.

Kansas State Historical Society

as Old Dobbin, was the farmer's "best friend." Beginning about 1850, horses made possible the use of certain farm machinery. After 1870 steam tractors and threshers were coming into use. But horses —and mules—were busy until about 1915, when gasoline engines began to replace them. (Even so, as late as 1920 there still were over twenty million work animals on the farms of America.)

The children. The farmer also leaned heavily on the labor of his children—and only occasionally on a hired man. The children helped according to their age and ability. Young ones fed the chickens or churned the milk into butter or tended the new kittens. (Cats were useful in keeping the barns free of mice.) Older boys chopped wood or painted the barn or pitched hay into the loft. Older girls cleaned house or washed dishes or pitched in to nurse a sick member of the family.

The working wife. Possibly no one worked as hard as the farmer's wife. When she was not picking berries or preserving food or baking bread and cake, she was sewing a patch on a pair of pants. When she was not doing her share to bring in the harvest, she was looking after an ailing calf. When she was not scrubbing clothes over her tin washboard, she was turning out ice cream or doing cross-stitching on a

Sunday dress or making a quilt for the new baby's cradle.

The farmer and his family, of course, increasingly obtained "store-bought" goods. Nevertheless, barrels, brooms, clothing, furniture, and a hundred other items long were made at home. Much of this home manufacturing continued until well after the nineteenth century was over. Items were dropped from the list only as income started to rise and factory-made goods had been improved until they were clearly better than the handmade ones.

Lonely lives. Yet comforts came very slowly. It was a lucky farm family that had tap water in the house. And even luckier was the one that had the regular companionship of another family. The loneliness of much farm life, particularly on the Plains, where distances were so great, is unimaginable. When problems arose, people had no one to talk them over with.

Bad Times

By the 1870's the Plains farmers were very unhappy and bewildered. They found themselves struggling to find ways of marketing crops and paying for supplies.

Complaints. Although industries and banks and railroads appeared prosperous at that time, farming was in a slump. The

#Point out the length of time it took for tractors to replace work animals on most farms. Discus[s] why old ways continue despite improvements in technology.

farmers, moreover, were angry. They believed they worked harder and under worse conditions than anybody else in the country. They asked why they were not sharing in the general prosperity. They thought that somehow they were being cheated.

One of the spokesmen for the farmers was a brilliant writer, Hamlin Garland. He stated their complaint: "Men and women alike labor unendingly in the fields. Yet their reward is nothing more than a dreary present and a . . . hopeless future."

Foreign wheat. While farmers in many parts of the United States felt bowed down, those on the Plains who grew wheat and corn probably suffered worst. An important reason was that crops grown in foreign countries were rivaling more and more those grown here. In particular, Canada, Australia, Argentina, and sections of Russia were becoming prosperous wheat-growing regions.

The competition became especially keen after the development of steamship lines and railroads made it easy to ship goods from one part of the world to another. The price of grain in the United States was bound to be forced down when world supplies were greater than the demand.

Between 1870 and 1897 agricultural prices fell steadily. Sometimes farmers found it cheaper to burn the corn they raised for fuel than to ship it to market.

The "enemy." Made miserable by their difficulties and disappointments, farmers tried to fix the blame. As a result, the railroads became the "enemy." It is easy to understand why.

The western farmers had to use the railroads to get their crops to market. They were unhappy because they could rarely choose between railroads. Whichever line ran through the nearest town had all the local shipping.

Railroad rates. Farmers were hurt also by the fact that railroads were often corruptly run. Management frequently pocketed the money the lines made instead of buying new equipment for them or keeping them in good repair.

To replace the money which crooked officials had taken, the railroads borrowed more and more. And then, in order to pay back their growing debts and the interest on them, the lines naturally raised their rates. Farmers believed that railroads set rates as high as they thought they could.

Railroads understood how to prevent farmers from combining against them. They played one group of farmers against another. Frequently they gave better rates to the large shippers of crops than to the small ones. Although the rates posted in freight yards were there for all to see—and to pay—a large shipper secretly received a *rebate*, or rake-off.

A defense. The railroad owners, of course, defended themselves. They pointed out that if it were not for the railroads, most farmers could not exist at all. And they denied that the rates were too high. The president of the Union Pacific, for example, asked, "What would it cost for a man to carry a ton of wheat one mile? What would it cost for a horse to do the same? The railway does it at a cost of less than a cent."

The view of the states. What happened when the farmer turned to his state for help in protecting his rights? He found that, in general, government officials sympathized with the railroads.

The railroad pass. The lack of sympathy with the farmers resulted in part from the fact that the railroads every year distributed railroad passes to countless public officials—governors, legislators, judges. These passes, sometimes worth hundreds of dollars a year, were bribes, however much they might be described as "gifts" or "courtesies." As bribes, they succeeded in preventing action against the railroads.

Moreover, the general belief among Americans that government must not in-

int out that although the farmer had long considered himself more independent than the city
rker, he was in reality extremely dependent upon others--to get his products to market, to
nish loans for land and equipment, to make the tools and machinery he needed, etc.

503

National Grange Association

Grange meetings have been held continuously in this building—near Minneapolis, Minnesota—since 1873, when No. 398 was organized. Kelley was a native of Minnesota.

The Grange. The farmers were able to achieve these slight gains because they at last had begun to organize themselves. This was a result of the work of a clerk in the Department of Agriculture, Oliver Hudson Kelley.

Kelley had a keen eye for the bleakness and boredom of farm life—especially in the West. He therefore created for farmers and their wives a national organization to fill their spare time with social activities. It had a fancy name—the National Grange of the Patrons of Husbandry. (Patrons of husbandry were people concerned with the raising of crops and animals.)

At first the Grange, as it came to be called, grew very slowly. But as prices for farm products fell in the 1870's, the membership lists began to grow rapidly. By 1874 over a million and a half farm couples were enrolled.

The Grange showed farmers how much political power they had when they stood together. In fact, the laws passed in the states to regulate railroads and grain elevators were known as Granger Laws.

The regulation of the railroads and the grain elevators was an outstanding achievement, but its effects were limited. The owners of the businesses concerned tried to prove that regulation was illegal. They argued in court that they conducted *private enterprises* which could not be controlled by the public. (By "private enterprises" is meant businesses run for profit by private individuals with their own money.)

Supreme Court decisions. In a notable decision in 1877, the United States Su-# preme Court declared that the states *could* regulate grain elevators, railroads, ferries, gristmills, and so forth. The Court said that these businesses, though private, had important effects on the "public interest." The Granger Laws established a pattern for a vast regulation of private businesses of all kinds in the years that followed.

terfere with the freedom of businessmen also worked against help for the farmers. The fear of government control which had developed during the struggle with the mother country in the 1770's had been strengthened during the age of Jackson. It was generally felt that wrongs such as those which injured the farmers would *automatically* right themselves. To tinker with them, it was said, would only make things worse.

Control by the states. Nevertheless, between 1869 and 1874 some laws regulating railroads were passed by the state of Illinois. Within the next few years the legislatures of Iowa, Minnesota, Wisconsin, Missouri, and Nebraska enacted similar laws. Such attempts to control the railroads—also, generally, the grain elevators (places for storing grain)—called for creating commissions. These had power to forbid rebates, the issuance of railroad passes, and other abuses.

#Discuss whether or not railroads were simply private enterprises. Point out that many western railroads had accepted government aid in the form of land grants and subsidies.
##The case referred to is Munn v. Illinois.

or examples of other regulatory commissions, see pp. 575 (FTC), 638 (SEC), and 640 (NLRB).

Nine years after the decision of 1877, however, the Supreme Court seemed to change its mind—at least about the railroads. It decided that a state could not regulate a railroad line which ran in more than one state, because such a railroad was engaged in *interstate commerce*. Under the provisions of the Constitution, only Congress can regulate interstate commerce. Since all important railroads ran in more than one state, the decision meant an end to railroad regulation by the states.

The ICC. Congress now took steps. In 1887 it created the Interstate Commerce Commission, a body of five men with the power to regulate railroad rates. For a long time the ICC was not permitted to regulate railroads fully, but the establishment of the commission proved to be a landmark in American history. In the twentieth century *regulatory commissions* like the ICC would be set up in many other fields.

The farmers, therefore, had had a hand in bringing about an important change in American life. They had led the federal government to accept responsibility for maintaining the just treatment of citizens by private enterprise.

> 1. Tell what the Homestead Act provided. 2. Name three disappointments connected with it. 3. Identify two problems farmers on the Great Plains had and tell how they were solved. 4. What farm implement was most important for the farmers? Why? 5. Describe the Oklahoma run. 6. Name some abuses which the Granger Laws tried to correct. 7. Tell the purpose of the ICC.

view efforts to organize unions during the age of Jackson (see pp. 349-350).

New Unions Aim to Help Working People

Laboring men had problems, too. They, also, were caught up in changes to which they had to adjust. From the start, however, they were in a different position from that of the farmers. Farmers long had had a reputation for being nature's noblemen. Workingmen were scorned, chiefly because they lived in cities, depending closely on others and owning no land.

Background Conditions

The opportunity to organize did not come easily to unskilled factory workers. They were increasingly ignored by the skilled workers, who looked down upon them.

The unskilled immigrant. One reason was that the unskilled from the 1840's on were usually immigrants, often only recently arrived. Their foreign ways, often including a foreign language or accent, made many Americans feel superior. Also, skilled Americans had the feeling that as "master craftsmen" they had earned privileges they did not need to share easily with anybody, particularly newcomers.

Newly arrived immigrants were at a disadvantage as workers. Often they had to agree to conditions of employment that were terrible. The men very frequently hoped to send money back to the old country to bring other members of their families here. Consequently, some immigrants seemed more interested in merely having jobs than in the conditions of work. Possibly these circumstances slowed down the growth of labor unions in the 1850's.

Local strikes. But some important strikes took place, too. For instance, the shoemakers in Massachusetts called one in order to win higher wages. Among the twenty thousand strikers were many women. The fierceness of this strike and others indicated the strength that labor would possess once it was organized.

The Civil War years. When the Civil War came, working people responded to Lincoln's first call for volunteers—just as other northerners did. Yet not all working-men thought alike about abolishing slavery. Some feared that the freeing of the slaves could lead to a loss of their own jobs. In 1860 a large number of unions favored making compromises with the South.

Nevertheless, many workingmen sensed that as long as Negro slavery existed, it acted as a drag on the wages and working conditions of all who labored. If one # group of men could be held down, all others could be, too.

In general, however, workingmen felt imposed on as the fighting continued. First of all, they began to think of themselves as victims of the draft. The law provided that a man with the necessary money could pay for a substitute to go into the army for him. Workingmen had no money for such purposes.

As a result, workers were more burdened by the fighting than the wealthy people were. Furthermore, though prices rose during the course of the fighting—owing to various shortages of civilian goods—wages tended to remain where they were.

A loss of personal pride. What deeply hurt the workingmen, too, was that more and more were losing a sense of their own worth as individuals. Mere numbers on a payroll, they could be fired and replaced overnight. They were just "factory hands" who were a part of a "labor market."

Lagging in the race. Besides, at the end of the war, some Americans had become or were on the way to becoming very wealthy. The enormous growth of industry, as we have seen, was creating new millionaires. But laboring men saw themselves falling behind their fellow citizens in the race for improvement.

Removing Evils

When the war was over and labor leaders were once again at their task of organizing working people, they seemed more than ever determined to succeed. The situation of the laboring man appeared worse than ever.

The N.L.U. The first big success that workingmen had was the creation of the National Labor Union in 1866. It linked together in one organization all skilled and unskilled workers in the country, regardless of race, religion, or nationality.

Nevertheless, the N.L.U. opposed strikes on the ground that they hurt the working man himself most of all. The N.L.U. recommended instead that disputes be settled through *arbitration*—that is, by the decisions of impartial committees acting as judges. The N.L.U. proposed that the federal government form a Department of Labor—in the same way that it had created a Department of Agriculture in 1862.

The work of Sylvis. The N.L.U. for a time had a splendid leader in William H. Sylvis, the son of a wagon maker. Sylvis was himself a skilled ironworker from Pennsylvania. He once said of the N.L.U., "I hold it more dear than I do my family or my life."

Far in advance of his time, Sylvis called for an eight-hour day and for ending the tenement-house evil. He expressed support of "the sewing-women and daughters of toil in this land." He died in 1869, when he was only forty. Without Sylvis at its head, the N.L.U., which was largely a one-man creation, went downhill rapidly.

The Knights of Labor. The first national union which survived for more than only a few years was the Noble and Holy Order of the Knights of Labor. Formed in 1869, its very name suggested the importance workingmen attached to upholding their dignity. It referred to them as noble knights.

Compare the organization and the objectives of the National Labor Union with those of the Knights of Labor. How did the two unions differ in their reasons for opposing strikes? Ask students to account for the short-lived success and rapid decline of these organizations.

Uriah S. Stephens. The leader of the Knights of Labor was a remarkable Philadelphia garment cutter, Uriah S. Stephens. As a young man he had studied briefly to be a minister, and he was an excellent public speaker. He had also traveled widely in the West Indies, South America, and California. His journeys had given him an idea of the world that workingmen generally did not have.

To be a member. Stephens and the six men who helped him found the Knights decided that their organization would take as members all wage earners, skilled or unskilled. The only people who were not allowed to join were liquor dealers, lawyers, bankers, professional gamblers, and stockbrokers.

Secrecy. Because a man might lose his job if his employer found out that he was a member of a labor union, the Knights of Labor was a secret organization. For a long time, in any public notice it was referred to in this way: * * * * *. It was therefore sometimes called the Five Stars. Not until 1881 was some of the secrecy abolished.

Feeling about strikes. Stephens, who enjoyed the title of "Grand Master Workman," preached that all men are brothers and should be against calling strikes. To many, his kindly ideas did not seem practical. In fact, in the very years when the Knights were being established, some bloody labor disputes were occurring.

The depression of 1873. In 1873 a terrible depression brought very great suffering to thousands of workingmen. As the 1870's passed, the conditions faced by factory labor seemed worse than ever and more hopeless. It was said that in New York City alone, 25 percent of the workers were unemployed. All the leading cities had soup kitchens where a small amount of food kept poor people alive. In 1874 thousands of homeless men tramped the streets.

A time of violence. In the face of this disaster, it is little wonder that violence

Granger Collection

The Brotherhood of Locomotive Firemen of North America, a union of railroad workers, advertised itself with this poster in 1885. #

broke out. It occurred on the railroads and in the coalfields. Before it was over, troops had to be called to control it.

The first strike on the railroads began on the Baltimore and Ohio in July, 1877. It followed an announcement by the line that wages were to be cut—for the fourth time in seven years. Before long, as wage reductions were announced by other railroads, strikes were spreading from line to line across the country.

In Pittsburgh, striking railroad men seized control of the trains. Because the

507

What impression does this advertisement try to give about labor unions? (Study the various sets.) What public feeling about unions was this poster supposed to remedy?

local authorities tended to sympathize with the workingmen, soldiers had to be sent from Philadelphia to try to put down the distrubance.

When the soldiers arrived at the scene, a battle with the strikers began in which the troops fired their weapons. About twenty-five of the workingmen were killed, and many others were wounded.

Enraged now, the strikers rushed to nearby gun shops, grabbed weapons, and went after the troops. Driving the soldiers out of town, the strikers, joined by others who were unemployed, took over railroad # properties and burned and looted them. Order was not restored until the president of the United States dispatched federal troops to Pittsburgh.

The Molly Maguires. In the coalfields of Pennsylvania at the same time, violence was also breaking out. There a group of Irish immigrants known as the Molly Maguires was trying to negotiate a labor settlement with the coalfield operators. The Molly Maguires were a secret organization ready to engage in assault, arson, and murder against unfair mineowners.

The "Mollies" flourished for many years. The group was finally exposed and broken up, and many members paid with their lives for the crimes they had committed.

The tragic events at Pittsburgh and the activities of the Molly Maguires aroused the leaders of industry. However, instead of studying these outbreaks of violence to find out why they occurred, businessmen made up their minds to crush all labor organizations. They regarded them as groups aiming to destroy law and order.

Workingmen throughout the country thought they were badly misunderstood. They believed they had to organize to end abuses they could not resist as individuals.

The "truck system." One particularly outrageous practice in many industries was the so-called truck system. Under it an employer forced his workers to buy things they needed at a company store which he owned. He often charged 10 or 20 percent more than retail stores customarily did. The employer made sure his employees bought at his store by paying them not in money but in coupons, or script, which could be used only in the company store.

Sometimes, also, manufacturers paid their workers in the products they made. A cigar-producing firm in Cincinnati, for instance, gave its men two boxes of cigars a week. On their days off they had to peddle them, usually by going from saloon to saloon, to make a few dollars to put food on the table at home.

Dangers to health. There were still other evils, too—ones which did not always show their effects immediately. These included working conditions which could injure the health of men and women. For example, dust of various kinds, the products of industrial processes, helped cause dreaded lung diseases like tuberculosis and silicosis. For those who worked in quarries, there was stone dust to breathe in. For textile workers, there was lint. For brass workers and iron molders, there were metal filings.

Industrial accidents. Moreover, factories were, in general, badly lighted and poorly ventilated. Working in such places made people less alert than usual. They therefore more easily became victims of industrial accidents that could involve the loss of eyes or limbs or other permanent disablement. And anyone who could not work as well as expected was easily replaced.

Why? Why did people accept these conditions of work? The answer is that they had no real choice.

A person who had a job was glad to obey the rules his employers set. If he went out on a strike, his place would probably be quickly filled by a willing strikebreaker—commonly called a scab.

The Knights' luck. The Knights of Labor in the 1880's were gaining members by

...eaps and bounds. But this was not be-...ause unskilled factory hands, who needed ...elp, were joining. Actually, the Knights ...were simply benefiting from some success-...ul local strikes. Sometimes these would ...roduce small but strong organizations of ...workers. Rather than disband after their ...uccess, they would join the Knights.

Terence V. Powderly. Uriah S. Stephens ...esigned as Grand Master Workman in ...879. He was replaced by Terence V. Pow-...lerly, of Carbondale, Pennsylvania.

Powderly, like Stephens, believed that ...he future of working people lay in avoid-...ng strikes. He said they should become ...nvolved in coöperative activities—that is, ...n purchasing and operating their own ...nines, factories, and railroads.

Not all members of the Knights of Labor ...greed with Powderly. The Knights were ...urt by their disputes over his views on ...trikes and coöperative business activities.

But even more damaging was the fact ...hat many members of *trade unions*—that ...s, organizations taking in the workers ...rom one craft only—hesitated to join the ...Knights. This was because skilled workers ...lid not want to be in an organization ...where they would be outnumbered by un-...skilled workers. Besides, a trade union de-...cided who could enter its craft. Its mem-...bers did not want to give up this privilege ...to the Knights.

The American Federation of Labor. As a ...result, beginning in 1881, leaders of trade ...unions began to form a "union of unions." ...Soon this became the American Federation ...of Labor, usually known as the AFL.

There were three main differences be-...tween the Knights and the AFL. The mem-...bers of the Knights were individuals, even ...though they were organized in local chap-...ters or lodges. The members of the AFL ...were *unions*, not individual workers.

Second, the AFL was concerned solely ...with skilled workers. Only such workers ...belonged to trade unions.

Third, the local chapters that made up the Knights existed to serve and strength-en the national organization. The AFL, on the other hand, was intended to serve and strengthen the member unions.

Gompers, of the cigar makers. The lead-ers in forming the AFL were the cigar makers. They worked under particularly bad conditions. Often they manufactured their product in tenements where the hours seemed endless and the sun never shone.

Samuel Gompers, an English-born cigar maker of Dutch-Jewish background, be-came president of the New York cigar makers in 1874. Only twenty-four years old, he was to devote his whole long life to organizing unions and improving the con-ditions of workers. After taking a leading part in creating the AFL, he became its main leader and remained so until his death in 1924.

As a young boy sitting at a worktable rolling cigars, Gompers had listened to dis-cussions of politics by the older men. Sometimes they had chipped in to pay one worker to read books or pamphlets to them (to make up for the wages he had lost). Gompers had often got this assignment.

The material Gompers had read dealt frequently with revolutionary proposals for solving some of labor's problems. But these proposals had only convinced Gom-pers that the way to improve the condition of workers was *not* to seek such solutions. He became a hardheaded, practical man, supporting measures he thought were rea-sonable and possible.

For example, in 1886 the AFL began to demand an eight-hour day. It was several decades more before the eight-hour work-ing day became general, but by then argu-ments for it no longer seemed ridiculous.

Strikes and agreements. The AFL did not hesitate to support a strike when all else had failed. But to prevent strikes, it arranged that employers sign agreements, or *contracts*. In them, wages, hours, and

...ote that the AFL differed from earlier unions both in organization and in philosophy. What ...e the results of Gompers' policy of forming <u>trade unions</u> aimed only at improving wages, ...rs, and working conditions?

509

working conditions were agreed upon. It was hoped that arranging these contracts would iron out disputes over hours and wages without upsetting the lives of employers and employees alike.

There was a brief rivalry between the Knights and the AFL both over members and over the leadership of workers. But by the 1890's, the membership of the AFL was growing and that of the Knights going down. Apparently the AFL's blunt dependence on contracts and its frank acceptance of the strike as a weapon appealed to the skilled workers. Nevertheless, it provided no help for unskilled workers.

Murder in Haymarket Square. A terrible event that hastened the downfall of the Knights was the Haymarket affair of 1886. In that year some unions in Chicago went on strike for an eight-hour day—against the wishes of the Knights' Powderly. They soon had the support of a group of *anarchists*—that is, people who favored getting rid of all government, by violence.

In the rough-and-tumble clashes between strikers and police which followed, several strikers near the McCormick reaper works were shot. To protest the shooting, the anarchists held a rally in Haymarket Square. The crowd was smaller than expected. Near the end of the meeting, the police arrived and a bomb was hurled. Who threw the bomb no one has ever found out, but a number of men were killed by the blast and in the rioting which followed.

Eight men were finally found guilty of the crime, and four were hanged. The State's attorney had shouted to the jury, "Convict these men, make examples of them, hang them, and you save our institutions." The judge was not impartial. All in all, we realize today that the accused men did not receive a fair trial.

The public view. The Knights of Labor got a bad and undeserved black eye from the Haymarket affair. The public chose to think that any labor organization or labor dispute was likely to bring on a bloody revolution.

Trials of Strength

In the next few years big businessmen opposed more than ever the workers' efforts to improve their conditions. De-

The scene of the bombing in Haymarket Square, once an open-air market.
Policemen stand around the spot, holding back the crowds.
The anarchists' speakers had used the wagon as a platform.

Chicago Historical Society

out that in both cases the strikers were refus-
wage cuts--not trying to increase wages.

scriptions of two strikes in particular tell
us how things were going.

Trouble at Homestead. The first of them
took place at the Carnegie Steel Company's plant in Homestead, Pennsylvania, in
1892. The Amalgamated Association of
Iron, Steel, and Tin Workers had gone on
strike, refusing to accept a wage cut which
Henry Clay Frick, Carnegie's assistant, was
trying to force upon them. Frick responded
by attempting to smash the union—an
old one which had existed in the steel industry for years.

Frick closed the Homestead plant to
the strikers, creating a *lockout*, and hired
three hundred "detectives" to guard the
strikebreakers who were brought in to
make steel. A battle developed between the
"detectives" and the steelworkers. After
hours and hours of fighting, the "detectives" retreated and fled the town. Order
was finally restored by the state militia.

The power of the striking union, never
very great, had been broken. There would
not be another union agreement with the
Homestead plant for forty-five years.
Hundreds of the union members were
locked out for good. Moreover, they were
blacklisted—that is, their names were reported to other employers, who would refuse to hire such "troublemakers."

The struggle in Pullman. A strike at the
Pullman Palace Car Company, a manufacturer of railroad sleeping cars, in 1894 had
different issues but a similar outcome. Beginning in 1880, this company had created
a "model" town for its employees.

The town, named Pullman, built just
south of Chicago, was clearly no paradise.
The rents were 20 to 25 percent higher
than in the nearby city of Chicago. If a
worker chose to live somewhere else, he
might find he was not employed any longer
by the Pullman Company.

The company made high charges for
other services, too. These included the
supplying of water and gas and the run-

Chicago Historical Society

A cartoonist in 1894 expressed in this way
his idea of the hold the railroad unions had.
The man is Eugene V. Debs, who was jailed
during the Pullman strike.

ning of company stores where food and
clothing were for sale.

The Pullman employees were furious at
their employer. Their anger boiled over
during the depression of 1893. The firm
laid off 3000 men—out of a work force of
5800. The wages of those who were kept
on were cut as much as 40 percent. At the
same time, the company refused to reduce
the rents in Pullman.

When the Pullman men finally went out
on strike, they had the support of the
American Railway Union—a newly organized union of railroad employees. It refused to handle trains with Pullman cars.

By the summer of 1894, the strike had
become so widespread that the railroad
system of the whole country was upset.
George Pullman flatly refused to arbitrate.
In the end the railroad operators persuaded the federal government to help.

White House intervention. Using the ex-
cuse that the mails were being held up,
President Grover Cleveland sent troops to
Chicago to stop the violence caused by the

at was the attitude of the government toward labor disputes like those at Homestead and
lman? Discuss whether or not government policy had any effect on early unions. How
es government policy affect unions today?

Why was it difficult for farmers and laboring people to join together as a powerful force in politics? Together they made up a majority of the American people.

strike and guarantee uninterrupted mail service. Clearly, the United States Army was being thrown against the workingmen —resulting in a very lopsided contest.

The hardships which people who worked with their hands endured—or believed they endured—seemed unreasonable in America, the "Promised Land." Henry George, an American who carefully studied American life, expressed their complaint in a book published in 1879 called *Progress and Poverty*. He wrote:

We plow new fields, we open new mines, we found new cities; we drive back the Indian and exterminate the buffalo; we girdle the land with iron roads and lace the air with telegraph wires; we add knowledge to knowledge, and utilize [use] invention after invention. . . yet it becomes no easier for the masses of our people to make a living. On the contrary, it is becoming harder. . . . The gulf between the employed and the employer is growing wider.

Our natural resources were abundant and our form of government was admired throughout the world. But was the good life to be only for the few who could make it to the top? Could our problems be solved in the democratic way—by elections and by compromise among men of good will? In the thirty years or so after the Civil War, neither plowmen nor workingmen were sure the answer would be yes.

1. Describe the first big success workingmen achieved.   2. Name two instances of the breaking out of violence among workingmen in the 1870's.   3. What helped cause it?   4. Name three complaints workingmen had about employers.   5. What three main differences were there between the Knights of Labor and the AFL?   6. How did the AFL try to prevent strikes?   7. Describe the Haymarket affair, the trouble at Homestead, Pennsylvania, and the struggle in Pullman.

A special activity: Have a group of students dramatize a hearing before the Interstate Commerce Commission in the 1890's. Take up the

The Workshop

matter of railroad rates for hauling grain. Have students represent the points of view of the railroads, farmers, flour millers, and consumers

The Shapers of Our World

Tell what part each of the following had in the struggle of the farmers and workingmen in the second half of the nineteenth century to improve their situations in American life:

Homestead Act	Interstate Commerce
Great Plains	Commission
Joseph F. Glidden	National Labor
James Oliver	Union
Oklahoma run	Knights of
Oliver Hudson	Labor
Kelley	Uriah S.
Granger Law	Stephens
Pullman strike	Molly Maguires

"truck system"   AFL
Terence V.   Samuel Gompers
    Powderly

Adding to Your Vocabulary

Show your understanding of the problems of the farmers and laborers by using these words in sentences:

sod	slump
barbed	rebate
wire	grain
dry farming	elevator
threshing	private
chaff	enterprise
chinook	bewildered

512   Have students discuss the ideal relationship between employer and worker in the factory system. What is the responsibility of the employer to the worker? Of the worker to the employer? Of the government to both?

a student to look into the work of the branch of the Department of Labor or the Department of Agri-
ure in your area. In what ways does each of these agencies try to serve the public?

nterstate
  commerce
egulatory
  commission
rbitration
ontract

scab
trade union
coöperative
anarchist
lockout
blacklist

Thinking Things Through

After a review of the boxed-in exercises
n the chapter, answer these questions:

1. How do the problems of the farmers
n the Great Plains help you understand
he difficulties farmers in some of the
underdeveloped countries today have in in-
reasing their output of food?

2. In the early years on the Great Plains,
vhy was the school year short and the
vacation period long?

3. Why were the railroads so important
o the western farmers of the late 1800's?
Compare the need for them then with the
need of earlier western settlers for other
nternal improvements.

4. How is it possible for the Supreme
Court to reverse itself, that is, change its
mind? What does this fact tell you about
he problems involved in interpreting the
Constitution?

5. Why have workingmen usually been
against unlimited immigration?

Presenting Information

1. Ask a coin collector to show the class
ome of the coins used in the period discussed in the chapter.

2. Prepare posters that might have been
used by a western railroad to describe the
advantages of settling on land along it.

3. Draw up some handbills which an
owner of a Boston textile mill might have
distributed at the dock as groups of immigrants landed after their voyage from
Europe. Point out the advantages of working in the factory.

4. If there is a Four-H club or a Future

Farmers of America club in your community, collect some of its literature and display it in the classroom. Discuss it.

5. Ask a spokesman for a union in your
community to come to your class and tell
you about its activities.

6. Collect and exhibit pictures of inventions which have enabled a decreasing
number of farmers to produce enough food
for a growing population.

7. How did activities that led to violence hurt the chances labor had for public
support?

8. What belief about government helped
to keep the federal government from aiding farmers in the 1870's and early 1880's?

9. Why is the establishment of the ICC
called a landmark in American history?

10. Write a letter from an early member of the American Federation of Labor
to a fellow employee telling him his union
should join the AFL.

11. Write a letter a factory worker in
the 1870's might have sent to tell a cousin
on a farm how his life would be changed
if he came to work in the factory.

12. Dramatize a Grange meeting in the
late 1800's. Discuss the various concerns
the members of the organization had.

Expanding Your Learning

Have a committee prepare a large wall
map of the United States showing the
name of each state, the date of its admission to the Union, its nickname, and its
state flag. Have students in the class tell
the origins of each flag.

Your Opinion, Please

Why was it difficult for the anarchists
to receive a fair trial after the Haymarket
affair? What responsibility do Americans
have to see that people charged with crimes
receive justice, no matter what the charges
and the circumstances?

answering this question, students should consider whether or not different times and conditions
l for different interpretations of the Constitution. This matter of changing interpretations is   513
he heart of one of the leading political issues of our time.

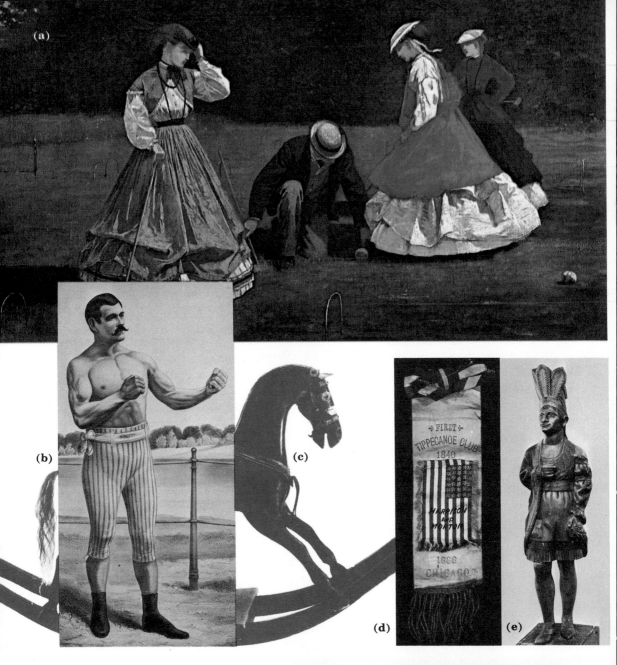

(a) Playing croquet in the 1860's—the first outdoor game that both men and women could play. (b) John L. Sullivan, heavyweight boxing champion in 1882. (c) A boy's toy in the late 1800's. (d) A campaign ribbon boosting Benjamin Harrison—winner of the presidental race in 1888—and his running mate. (e) One of the wooden Indians that decorated the fronts of cigar stores, tobacco being considered a gift of the tribesmen. (f) An iron weather vane featuring a famous trotter pulling a sulky in the 1870's. (g—next page) The 9:45 pulls into a Connecticut town in 1867.

(g)

ne of the pictures on the op-
ite page show that the people
he cities had time for amuse-

CHAPTER 23

ments--including spectator sports.
Above: The railroad station will
change this village into a city.

NEW NEEDS AND OLD POLITICS

cuss with the class the meaning of this title. New times automatically mean that new needs arise, which
n require new legislation. "Old politics" refers to old attitudes of lawmakers and old ways of looking at
ditions which clearly call for new attitudes and new ways.

THE cities of the United States, which had always been mainly a rural country, grew in an amazing way after the Civil War. Out of a population of 31,500,000 in 1860, about six million people—one person in every five—had lived in urban communities. In 1860 there had been only sixteen places in the country with populations of more than 50,000, and only one city—New York and its suburbs—had contained more than a million inhabitants.

Out of a 76,000,000 population in 1900, about thirty million people—almost one person out of every two and one-half—lived in cities. There were seventy-eight places with populations of over 50,000, and four of them contained—with their suburban areas—a million or more people.

the activities under "Graphs Tell a Story," p. 533. See also pp. 730-731.

Ballooning Cities Reshape American Life

What had been responsible for the remarkable blossoming of cities and city living? The most important cause was the increase in farm production, resulting, as we have seen, from the settlement of the Great Plains and a wider use of farm machinery. Fewer farmers than ever before were needed to feed an increasing number of Americans.

A second cause was the vast number of new jobs in the new factories. These attracted men and women who for one reason or another were not satisfied with farm life.

A third cause was the huge increase in the amount of railroad-building. Because railroads could haul people and goods quite easily over great distances, they made it possible for city people to be fed and clothed properly. Horses and boats would have been unable to do this for a large population.

hasize that both industry and improved transportation--products of an advancing tech-
zy--helped cause the growth of cities. Point out that the increase in farm production
nues today, even though there are fewer farmers than ever before.

A chain store proudly advertises its role in refreshing the railroa
passengers who stop at a station lunchroom in one of the growing citie

Above: The artist had a good sense of humor.

Urban Influence

As the cities grew in size and number, certain changes appeared in American life. Not all of them showed up everywhere, but they were general enough to be easily seen.

New ideas. First of all, city people need for success a special alertness. This fact helped make cities the centers of new ideas —political, artistic, and social.

Magnets for ambitious people. Second, the cities attracted a steady stream of newcomers from the farms and from abroad. Often these people were among the most able and most ambitious of all Americans. Third, because many businesses were located in cities, cities became places where people might get ahead much faster than on farms. In cities men and women coul make names and fortunes for themselves

Richer living. Fourth, in the urban area were good opportunities for meeting othe people and for making life fuller an better. In a city of a half-million people for example, enough interested person could be found to support a library, an a museum, a theater, or a ballet troupe.

Further, women particularly were abl to find in the cities the companionshi they had only rarely enjoyed on the farm They could attend shows or social gathe ings or simply travel to other parts of tow to visit relatives—or public libraries. The could have the pleasure of shopping i stores with a wider variety of goods tha they had ever dreamed of.

Department stores, for example, becam

Ask students what they like about city life and what they dislike. What advantages of cities named here are now available outside cities because of technological change?

common throughout the country. R. H. Macy and Company, which had opened in New York in 1858, was one of the pioneers. Mail-order houses, bringing the latest of goods into even isolated rural communities, also developed. The firm of Montgomery Ward, which began in Chicago in 1872, was the first.

The larger and larger quantity of goods ed to an increasing amount of rivalry among retail merchants to find purchasers. This was one reason for the creation of chains of stores—that is, groups of branch stores, all under one management, in various parts of the country.

The first of the chains was formed in the grocery business in the late 1860's. It adopted the name "The Great Atlantic and Pacific Tea Company." As its branches spread to almost every city, it became familiar to millions as simply the A & P.

Another chain specialized in articles priced at five and ten cents. It was begun by Frank W. Woolworth, a farm lad from New York State, whose favorite game as a boy had been "playing store." Woolworth's first store opened in Lancaster, Pennsylvania, in 1879. At his death forty years later, his company owned over a thousand "five-and-tens" located throughout the United States and Canada.

A chance for more education. Fifth, the cities also offered new educational opportunities. Schools were more numerous in populous localities than in areas of scattered population. In addition, city schools could be readily supervised. Standards could be more easily maintained in them than in one-room rural schoolhouses.

Moreover, fairly large communities had the means for enforcing the laws making school attendance compulsory. The establishment of the College of the City of New York in 1849 and its rapid growth after the Civil War showed that it was possible to develop even free *higher* education.

Changed families. Sixth, the cities also changed enormously the old ways of family living. The space in city dwellings, usually small in comparison with farmhouses, limited the size of families. Therefore, city parents often had fewer children than farm parents and could spend more time and money on them.

The mother of a city family became an even more important person than she would have been on the farm. Since her husband was away from home most of the day, she often had to make family decisions on her own.

Wider personal freedom. Seventh, the cities greatly strengthened the spirit of personal freedom. Young people in a city learned quickly that it was easier there than on the farm to leave home in order to "try their luck." Besides, they found there a greater variety of job opportunities and possible marriage partners.

Spectator sports. Finally, the cities provided more excitement to fill leisure time than ever before. One reason was the development of spectator sports—that is, athletic contests in which people were simply yelling bystanders rather than participants. Keen loyalties to baseball players or men who boxed developed among fans.

Women in the cities enjoy a wide range of shopping—and occasionally a sale.
Clarence P. Hornung, "Handbook of Early Advertising Art," Dover Publications, 1956

The first championship game in baseball (see page 386) is being played here between the New Yorks and the Knickerbockers at Hoboken, New Jersey, in 1846. This was the beginning of today's Major League baseball.

In 1869 the first professional baseball team was formed—the Cincinnati Red Stockings. Seven years later the National League was organized, and the American League was begun in 1900. In time baseball became known as the national pastime, and its stadiums were favorite gathering places for leisure hours.

In 1882 John L. Sullivan, "the Boston strong boy," became the first modern heavyweight champion. Professional boxing never approached baseball in popular appeal, but it created a new kind of public hero—the triumphant athlete. Moreover, it often provided a quick rise to fame and riches for children of poor parents.

A Refuge for Newcomers

A chief source of strength for the cities before 1900 was the immigration from Europe. Between 1820 and 1930 over sixty-two million people left their homes in Europe and went to other continents. About thirty-two million of them came to the United States, bringing various languages, ways of doing things, and outlooks with them. It seems safe to guess that many of the brightest and most ambitious Europeans were among those who left their native lands.

The "old immigration." The newcomers who came to America before the Civil War are today referred to as the old immigration. They came here in the largest numbers in the 1850's, having left homelands chiefly in northern and western Europe—England, France, the Low Countries, Germany, and Scandinavia. Also, a very large group of immigrants arrived from Ireland after the failure of the potato crop there in 1845 (see page 363).

Why they came. People came to the United States for many different reasons.

#This paragraph provides another opportunity to emphasize that American culture has been enriched by the contributions of many immigrants and for that reason is called plural. Some of these countries had long sent people here; Americans were used to this immigration.

A great many Germans who wanted political freedom—like Carl Schurz, for example—fled to American shores in 1848 or shortly afterward. For a long time they took pride in being referred to as forty-eighters. Other people came for other reasons, including the scarcity of opportunities to make a living in Europe.

Samuel Gompers, who arrived here in 1863, wrote in his autobiography that he had learned as a child to sing joyfully a song entitled "To the West." He said it expressed the feeling of most English wage earners. Gompers also wrote that Andrew Carnegie many years later told him that he, too, had known the song and that it had inspired his own father to come to America. The words go:

> To the west, to the west, to
> the land of the free
> Where mighty Missouri rolls
> down to the sea;
> Where a man is a man if
> he's willing to toil,
> And the humblest may gather
> the fruits of the soil.
> Where children are blessings
> and he who hath most
> Has aid for his fortunes
> and riches to boast.
> Where the young may exult
> and the aged may rest,
> Away, far away, to the
> land of the west.

The "new immigration." The opportunities for personal freedom, better jobs, and better homes continued to attract people to America after the Civil War—and still do. But two changes in immigration occurred after 1880. First, more immigrants than ever came to America (as you see on the graph on page 520). Second, they came from countries of eastern and southern Europe instead of northern and western Europe. Among them were Italians, Greeks, Poles, and Russians (including Jews).

The people of the "new immigration" differed greatly in ways and languages from the northern and western Europeans. These differences led to much bad feeling on the part of earlier arrivals living in the new land.

Help from city machines. The only people who seemed interested in helping the immigrants were the bosses of the city political machines. These machines were usually corrupt, but they provided the downtrodden newcomers with many badly needed services. A local machine might find jobs for a political party's faithful supporters, take care of hospital bills, or arrange for necessary legal help. To very poor families it might donate turkey baskets at Thanksgiving and supplies of coal during the winter.

Sometimes local politicians sponsored boat rides or "June walks" (outings in the park). These offered welcome relief from the summer's heat for young people and older ones alike.

The best-known machine was Tweed's Tammany Hall, which controlled New York City (see page 459). Like many other

Cartoons like this one helped destroy Boss William Marcy Tweed.

Albert Bigelow Paine, "Thomas Nast: His Period and His Pictures," Harper & Brothers, 1904

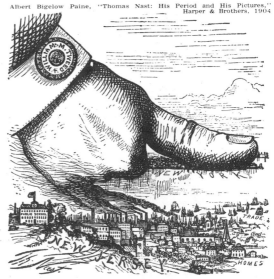

UNDER THE THUMB.

cuss the motives "Boss" Tweed had in
ping the newcomers in the cities.

519

such organizations, it held its power by winning votes through the favors it could distribute.

Feelings about the old country. Understandably many immigrants longed for the easy acceptance they had known "back home." This feeling kept alive a certain affection for the old country—a fact that American politicians often kept in mind as they sought support for various foreign policies.

Of course, sometimes immigrants were appealed to by politicians who knew they could make themselves popular by attacking the old country. For instance, Irishmen were delighted to hear anti-British talk, for they blamed Britain for their troubles. And after years of persecution in Russia, Jewish voters rejoiced to hear anti-Russian opinions. Politicians were quick to recognize, however, that immigrants were more interested in improving their lot in America than in hearing about their former countries.

Comforts and Discomforts

Mingled together in every urban com
munity were the exciting advantages o
living close to large numbers of other peo
ple—and all the terrible disadvantages
Each city dweller had to decide for himsel
if the advantages and disadvantages ba
anced each other.

The electric trolleys. A lucky event tha
made the modern-type city livable, as w
have seen (page 478), was the discovery
of new uses for electricity. One of the
most important of these was to furnish
power for trolley cars. After the trolley firs
appeared in 1887, in Richmond, Virginia
a network of electric wires hung over the
streets of every major city.

Before the electric trolley car was devel
oped, the usual vehicle for transporting
people had been the horse-drawn car—li
by oil at night and dirty, smelly, and some
what uncertain. Trolleys were such an im

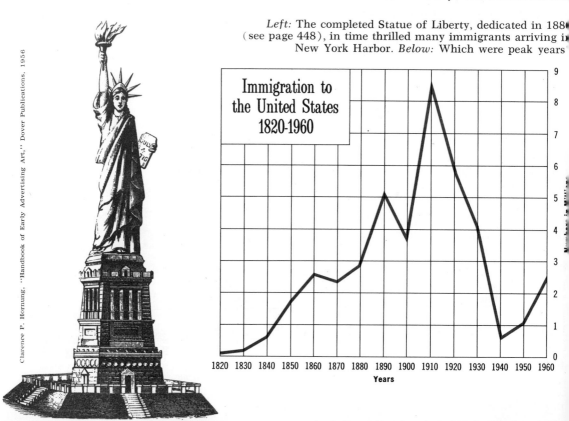

Left: The completed Statue of Liberty, dedicated in 188
(see page 448), in time thrilled many immigrants arriving i
New York Harbor. *Below:* Which were peak years

Immigration to
the United States
1820-1960

Years

Clarence P. Hornung, "Handbook of Early Advertising Art," Dover Publications, 1956

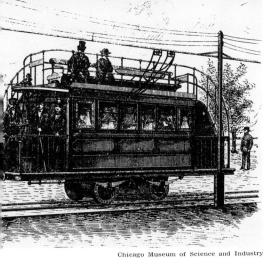

Electric streetcars changed the looks of city streets. Overhead wires provided the power.

provement that they helped make city life attractive to millions. They carried people swiftly to their work in the business districts of the cities, where many then completed on elevators—also made possible by electricity—the journeys to their jobs.

The electric els. In the largest cities, elevated railroads—els—were built to carry huge numbers of passengers daily. At first run by steam power, they, too, were eventually electrified.

Sights, sounds, and odors. There were also many shortcomings to city life. In 1880 a famous educator discovered that more than half the city children entering the first grade had never seen a sheep or a robin. They had not seen the ordinary implements used in farming, and they could not tell one kind of tree from another.

The city dwellers became accustomed to new kinds of noises and odors. In place of the owl's screech at night, they heard the clang of fire engines or the comings and goings of neighbors. Instead of the aroma of new-mown hay, they often inhaled the smoke that poured from factory chimneys.

Bad sanitation. As early as 1880 the Bureau of the Census was reporting that the rivers near most major cities were being polluted by wastes from manufacturing and by raw sewage. Philadelphia, to cite

Left: An example of technological change. Observe the clothing of the people--and the canes.

one example, poured wastes into the Delaware River, from which it also drew some of its water supply.

Also, the sanitation measures within the cities were not good. It was reported of Philadelphia, for instance: "The custom almost universally practiced of turning sink-and-slop water on the ground allowing it to flow across the sidewalks, and stagnate [stand] in the street-gutters, has such a pernicious [bad] influence upon the atmosphere that one feels an indescribable sense of relief in going to the park or moving out of town."

Public-health problems. By the beginning of the twentieth century, the major cities in the United States had created departments of public health. But before they were established, thousands of people had died of diseases. The greatest of these killers was tuberculosis, often a disease of poverty and undernourishment—and crowded living. The life expectancy of a baby boy born in 1890 in a large American city was forty-four years. One born on a farm could expect to live ten years longer.

Disease was not the only cause of this difference in life expectancy. The more rapid pace of life in the cities produced strains that seemed to wear people out. There were industrial accidents, as well, which annually caused much suffering. Furthermore, in the cities there were dangers of physical harm from fire and from thieves and other prowlers.

---

1. Name three reasons for the rapid growth of cities after 1860. 2. List eight changes in American life produced by the increasing number of cities. 3. Name some reasons why immigrants came to America before 1880. 4. What two changes took place in immigration after 1880? 5. Describe the comforts and discomforts of city life in the late nineteenth century.

k how our water resources are being polluted today and what is being done about the pollu-
. The subject is so important that taking some time to discuss it is worthwhile.
sk which of the problems have been solved and which are still with us.

#Students should also be reminded at once that Jefferson wanted the United States to be a nation of farme[rs,]
something it definitely was not going to be, as the growth of cities showed.
##This paragraph sums up the meaning of "old politics" in the title of this chapter.

Party Battles Yield Uninspiring Leaders

Most of the special needs of city dwellers —as well as of farmers and working people generally—were not being met by national leaders in the late nineteenth century. Politicians had generally grown up to believe that people are governed best when they have as little government as possible.
This old idea had been a favorite one of Thomas Jefferson's.

In the late nineteenth century, however, the belief worked against trying new ways of dealing with growing American problems (which were often city problems). Such things as helping underprivileged people, preventing unemployment, and cleaning up filthy rivers were more and more calling for attention.

The Men at the Top

The problems of urban America had come to stay, but no political leader in Washington was quick to tackle them. Almost all the Presidents had rural or small-town backgrounds. They did not respond easily to the country's new requirements.

Rural viewpoints. The Presidents, moreover, did not think of their office as the place that should produce new ideas in government. Congress, the Presidents believed, ought to pass without much encouragement whatever laws the country might require. But an overwhelming number of Congressmen had been farm boys—like the Presidents. Moreover, in Congress there were far more seats filled by representatives from rural districts than from urban ones.

Even if the Presidents and Congressmen had been more farseeing, the nation as a whole was not yet ready to be concerned with the personal problems of individuals.

Some of the worst human suffering in America's history, as we have seen, had been caused by the depression of 1873. Yet it would have seemed foolish for anyone to say the federal government ought to help the people hurt by financial disaster.

The lobby. Congress had fallen into the habit of passing out special favors to groups that could lobby (see page 341) for them. This had produced widespread dishonesty in public office.

The bribe. The bribing of public officials became an ordinary thing. Collis P. Huntington, one of the owners of the Southern Pacific Railroad, put it bluntly to one of his employees: "If you have to pay money to have the right thing done, it is only just and fair to do it."

Dealing with Warmed-over Topics

By the middle of the 1870's, many Americans were beginning to talk of the dangers to freedom in a government in which political favors were for sale. Reform—bringing an end to corruption in government—became a lively topic for discussion. The time had come, it appeared, to see to it that politicians placed the good of the public above their own.

But the political subjects Americans usually talked about seemed far away from the problems of day-to-day living which most people experienced. And even on such subjects no one seemed to be saying much that was new or different.

Hayes, of Ohio. A Republican, Rutherford Hayes, who became President in 1877, had been nominated because of his record as a reformer in Ohio (see pages 463–464). Early in his administration he decided to take over from the politicians

The fact that the nation was not concerned with the personal problems of individuals may be strange to students, since today the nation is quick to respond when disaster strikes a group.

Compare the garments worn by Fanny and Lucy Hayes with those worn by women and young girls today. President and Mrs. Hayes introduced the custom of rolling Easter eggs on the White House lawn.

Rutherford Hayes' only daughter, Fanny. *Right:* Fanny's mother, Lucy, the first President's wife to hold a college degree. Since she never served liquor, she was jokingly called Lemonade Lucy.

Rutherford B. Hayes Library

in Congress the power to appoint and remove important public officeholders.

Hayes had a serious disadvantage. The office of President had been soiled badly by the impeachment of Andrew Johnson and the trial that almost removed him. Then corruption under Grant had brought the office even lower. A decent man of high intelligence, Hayes made Congress recognize the dignity of the presidency again.

Angering the working people. In 1877 it was Hayes who called upon federal troops to bring order to the railroad dispute on the Baltimore and Ohio Railroad (see page 508). Laboring people never forgot Hayes' action, believing it showed that the President was opposed to their aims.

Upsetting the farmers. Farmers were made equally unhappy by Hayes. They declared that his money policies had resulted in a fall in the prices of their crops.

Moreover, the farmers were beginning to object to the high tariff, which was another result of Republican policy. They had formerly supported it.

Businessmen continued to argue for the tariff. It would, they said, protect them—and American workingmen—from competition from Europe's factories, or from "cheap labor."

To many farmers it seemed wrong to have to buy manufactured goods protected from foreign competition while having to sell unprotected farm goods. Why, they asked, should manufacturers' prices be kept high but not the prices for crops?

Cheap money and dear. The farmers' ideas about money sprang from the country's experience during the Civil War. Then the Department of the Treasury had issued paper bills known generally, from the color on one side, as greenbacks.

When the war ended, most businessmen wanted to be able to turn in these greenbacks for gold and silver. Farmers, however, had hopes that the greenbacks would continue to circulate. They could benefit. Many had enlarged their farms during the war by buying new land when money was cheap—that is, when the government's printing presses were turning out greenbacks as needed.

important idea: How a person fills an office creates or destroys respect for it. The presidency is the highest office in the land, and its dignity should be preserved.

What two groups were displeased with Hayes? Why? What group was pleased? Why?

These farmers had usually borrowed money to make their purchases. How could they ever pay back their loans if money suddenly became dear—that is, if the government allowed only money backed by gold and silver to circulate?

In the argument between farmers and businessmen over the right policy, the businessmen won. Congress finally provided that beginning on January 1, 1879, the Treasury would begin once again redeeming greenbacks with gold and silver.

When Hayes' term was almost over, he could take credit for having won some brave fights, particularly with Congress. But because he had seriously angered both the working people and the farmers, the Republican party made no effort to renominate him.

The Republican convention of 1880, which met in Chicago, was one of the stormiest ever held. One group in the party, known as the Stalwarts, was ready to nominate for a third term its hero, General Grant, fresh from a trip around the world. Another Republican group, the Half-Breeds, was for James G. Blaine.

Garfield, a dark horse. Neither of the front runners was chosen. Finally, on the thirty-sixth ballot political lightning struck James A. Garfield, of Ohio, who became the Republican party's choice. Garfield was a Half-Breed, and to satisfy the Stalwarts the convention nominated Chester A. Arthur, of New York, to be Vice-President.

Garfield's association with a Union Pacific scandal did not make people trust him. But he was more acceptable to a larger number of his party's politicians than any other man.

The Democrats selected as their candidate another Union hero—of the Battle of Gettysburg. He was General Winfield Scott Hancock. Not only did he bear a famous name, but he could quiet those Republicans who still said the Democratic party was the party of former Confederates.

In the campaign Garfield made something of the fact that he had been born in a log cabin—he was the last President able to make such a statement truthfully. Garfield also voiced ideas about money policies which delighted businessmen.

Moreover, Garfield expressed his hope that there might be a reform of the method of choosing public officials. He said that merit ought to be the main reason for selecting men for public office. In general, though, nothing in Garfield's position on the leading questions of the day set him apart from others in his party.

Squeaking in. On Election Day the ticket of Garfield and Arthur won by fewer than ten thousand popular votes out of about nine million cast. The day for the Democrats to recapture the White House was coming closer. But it had not yet arrived.

Garfield appointed James G. Blaine as Secretary of State. In advance, Garfield had made Blaine promise he would not run for the presidency in 1884. Garfield explained, "I do not propose to allow myself nor anyone else to use the next four years as the camping ground for fighting the next presidential battle."

Fighting within the party. Blaine tried to influence President Garfield to hurt Senator Roscoe Conkling, the Stalwarts' leader. Garfield named one of Conkling's enemies in New York to be collector of customs in the port of New York.

Conkling struck back. He and the other Senator from New York resigned their places in the Senate and sought reelection. Until 1913 members of the Senate were elected by their state legislatures. Conkling, therefore, was trying to have the legislature at Albany, New York, give him back his Senate seat and in that way show up the President.

Conkling was playing with fire, and he knew it. He, like Tallmadge and Rives before him (see page 403), was ignoring an unwritten rule about attacking a President.

##This would be a good time to refer to the Seventeenth Amendment to the Constitution, p. 72 The difficulty that arose between Garfield and Conkling did neither man nor his party any good. Emphasize that it was caused by naming someone displeasing to Conkling for a job in New York

rom one's own party.

Tragedy in Union Station. While Conking was waiting for the state legislature o act, a tragic event occurred. On July 2, 881, an insane, disappointed office seeker hot the President in the back as he stood n Union Station in Washington. The assassin shouted as he fired his gun, "I am a Stalwart and Arthur is President now." The country was stunned.

The shooting of Garfield turned the national spotlight on the problem of finding a better way of choosing men for federal obs. In the few weeks that Garfield had been President, he had been hounded day and night by men trying to obtain political positions. Garfield himself had written in his diary, "My day is frittered away with he personal seeking of people when it ought to be given to the great problems which concern the whole country."

The President lasted through the summer as an invalid. His suffering ended with his death, near the end of September. He lived long enough to know that the New York legislature did not reelect Conkling.

Arthur as President. When Arthur replaced the dead President, the people had little confidence in his honesty, and they knew nothing of his ability. Ex-President Hayes had written on learning that Garfield had been wounded, "The death of the President at this time would be a national calamity."

However, Arthur proved better than had been foreseen, although he was not an outstanding chief executive. His friend Conkling did not take charge of things, as people had expected. But Arthur appointed many Stalwarts to jobs simply because they were Stalwarts. Blaine, of course, resigned as Secretary of State almost immediately—and prepared to run for the White House in 1884, regarding himself as freed from his promise to Garfield.

Arthur's personal style. Chester Arthur liked to dress well and to entertain lavishly. Mrs. Blaine, who had a thorough knowledge of the White House, said that in 1882 he bought twenty-five new coats.

Arthur had the White House redecorated completely in the style which was fashionable then. A newspaper reported early in 1882 that "twenty-four wagon loads of furniture and other household articles [from the White House] were sold at public auction." Over seventy-five years later, another President—Harry S Truman—tried to restore to the White House its original furnishings. He said, "That auction was one

painting shows
eavy furnishings
elaborate appear-
of the homes
e well-to-do
e time.

James A. Garfield and his family in their living room. From left to right: James Rudolph, Mary (Mollie), the President, his wife, his mother, Abram, Harry Augustus, and Irvin McDowell, named for General McDowell. Observe the lighting.

Western Reserve Historical Society

Arthur lived in the days before sports clothes.

President Arthur (*foreground*) enjoys both a fishing trip and posing for the now-famous photographer Mathew Brady or one of his assistants.

of the most outrageous things that ever happened to the White House."

Dealing with frauds. Arthur vigorously went after the criminals who took part in the so-called Star Route frauds in the Post Office Department. This was a scandal connected with some private contracts for the delivery of mail. But the public was still not convinced that the new President was all he should have been.

Civil service reform. The time was ripe to reform the civil service. Already some steps had been taken to begin the changes necessary to avoid a mass turnover of public officeholders after each election. Most important, people were realizing that although Americans like to think that in a #democracy any man can fill any job, this is not the case in fact.

Certain positions, requiring skilled individuals, should not depend on politics. Moreover, a man performing routine duties ought not to have to rely for his job on the friendship of a politician who happens to be in power.

In 1883 Congress passed and Arthur gladly signed a bill creating a Civil Service Commission made up of representatives of both parties. Its task was to take charge of the writing and giving of examinations to test on a fair basis the qualifications of applicants for federal jobs.

Thereafter the number of federal positions that by law could only be filled from the lists of those who had passed the test gradually increased. Today only about a thousand positions in the entire federal civil service are filled by the President without drawing from the lists.

Rebuilding the navy. During Arthur's presidency and under his active leadership, the strength of the United States Navy was revived. For years the navy had been in such a condition that it was no longer a fighting force. Some people had even said it was no stronger than it had been on the eve of the War of 1812.

The navy began to build modern, steel-clad vessels. Americans could now compare their fighting ships with those of the English and the French.

1. Name two reasons why there was little interest in city problems in the late nineteenth century. 2. How did President Hayes cause bad feeling among working people and farmers? 3. Tell what Congress did about redeeming greenbacks. 4. Name the presidential candidates in 1880 and tell who won. 5. How did Arthur become President? 6. What was the purpose of the Civil Service Commission?

#Review the origin of this idea, recalling who had begun the practice of throwing public officeholders out of office after an election for political reasons (see p. 324).
##Civil service employees cannot be removed because an administration changes.

Ugly Issues Begin to Rear Their Heads

By 1884 Arthur had become an acceptable President, but he had not won admirers among the American people. Furthermore, the leaders of his party did not feel grateful enough to him to want to nominate him for a term of his own. It had not yet become the practice for a party automatically to nominate for President a man who had reached the White House because of the accident of death. Tyler, Fillmore, and Andrew Johnson had been turned down by their parties in the same way.

Instead of Arthur, the Republicans in 1884 nominated James G. Blaine—the Plumed Knight, an admirer called him. However, many Republicans had decided that it was time to have a general cleanup of political corruption. They simply could not support Blaine, who as a member of the House of Representatives had done political favors for an Arkansas railroad. These reforming Republicans, who were called Mugwumps (from an Indian word meaning "big shot"), waited to see if they could support the Democratic choice. It turned out that they could.

Cleveland and Harrison

The Democrats' choice was a huge, burly man named Grover Cleveland, who had become well known within just a few years. He had been elected mayor of Buffalo, New York, in the year Garfield was assassinated, and he had been chosen governor of New York the following year.

Still a bachelor, Cleveland had been involved in a personal scandal when a young man. He had been accused of being the father of a son born to an unmarried woman. But in his public life he was beyond criticism of character.

A low-level campaign. The campaign was one of the roughest fought in the whole nineteenth century. Among the things that were brought into it were Blaine's public reputation and the scandal connected with Cleveland.

Democrats back again. On Election Day the voters chose Grover Cleveland—the first Democrat to be elected President since Buchanan had been elected in 1856. The new President felt very kindly toward the outgoing chief executive, Chester Arthur, who gave a splendid Inauguration Day luncheon for Cleveland. Cleveland's entrance into office was celebrated that night by one of the largest and most crowded inaugural balls in history—and the first ever lighted by electricity.

A young First Lady. Before Cleveland's term was over, he became the first President to be married in the White House. His bride—the wedding was in 1886—was Frances Folsom, then twenty-two years old, the daughter of a deceased law partner of Cleveland's. Cleveland had been the legal guardian of "Frank," as he called his bride (he had bought her first baby carriage), and had supervised her bringing-up with loving care.

The young First Lady established the policy of holding receptions in the White House on Saturday afternoons. In that way young ladies who worked during the rest of the week might be greeted by her and might shake her hand. As many as six thousand people came to these receptions —a sign of the Clevelands' personal popularity and of the growing number of working girls.

Reform and politics. Cleveland, a courageous man who believed a public official bore a heavy burden of personal responsi-

ave the class look at the chart on p. 727, which lists the Presidents and shows the party of ch one. Ask why there had been so many Republican Presidents. (Students can connect the ge number of them with the northern victory in the Civil War--Democrats were discredited.)

527

bility, lacked the imagination he needed to help solve the problems of the day. The only program to which he was deeply devoted was civil service reform.

But Cleveland found himself caught between the men who had supported him as a reformer and the Democratic politicians who were hungry for jobs. In the end he could not resist the Democratic politicians. He enraged his Mugwump supporters by dismissing thousands of jobholders simply because they were Republicans.

A vetoing President. Yet Cleveland could show backbone, too. A memorable example was his veto of a pension bill under which any veteran of the Civil War who had served ninety days would be provided with a pension.

This veto took special courage because
Cleveland was not himself a veteran. Also, the organization of former Union soldiers called the Grand Army of the Republic was a powerful political force, and it wanted this law badly.

Cleveland did not hesitate to veto a large number of bills introduced by Congressmen to aid favored veterans of their districts. One veteran claimed he deserved help because he was suffering from an eye disease which he blamed on diarrhea he had had in the army twenty years earlier! A widow whose husband was killed in a fall from a ladder in 1881 said the accident was caused by a slight wound in his leg suffered in 1865!

The tariff tangle. Cleveland also showed great strength of character in the way he handled the tariff question. Whether or not there was a protective tariff affected the profits of big business and the prices the ordinary consumer paid for the goods he needed. At an earlier period (see page
##308) the tariff had been created to help establish manufacturing. In the 1880's the tariff had become a wall behind which, many Democrats charged, manufacturers were needlessly keeping their prices high.

Library of Congre

Thomas Nast, the cartoonist, shows Clevelan guarding the Treasury while pension bil he vetoed litter his office floo

The Democrats argued that the tari ought to be lowered. Would it not be bette they asked, if the prices of manufacture goods were reduced through a lowering o rates—even though the duties collecte would also be reduced?

Cleveland in 1887 decided to act on hi personal belief that the tariff rates wer too high. In an unheard-of step he devote his entire annual message to Congress t calling for a reduction in the tariff.

Cleveland knew that trying to chang the tariff would hurt his chances of win ning another term in the White House. Ye he told one of his advisers, "What is th use of being elected or reelected, unles you stand for something?" In his messag he boldly called the tariff an unjust form of taxation for the benefit of a few.

The tariff reformers were delighted. On of them said of the message, "It clears th air like a thunderstorm on a sultry day.

A failure. But the tariff bill which re sulted—and which provided for moderat cuts—did not pass in Congress. The fierc opposition of businessmen in many part of the country had its effect. One manufac

##Review the discussion on p. 308. In the 1880's the industries which had been in their infanc 1816 had grown up, and it had been shown that American industry could produce very well in t of war (see p. 424).

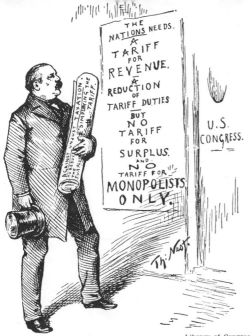

The sign held reads: THE NATION'S NEEDS. A TARIFF FOR REVENUE. A REDUCTION OF TARIFF DUTIES BUT NO TARIFF FOR SURPLUS. AND NO TARIFF FOR MONOPOLISTS ONLY. The box reads: U.S. CONGRESS.

Library of Congress

Cleveland, who had a huge surplus in the Treasury, is seen here favoring a tariff cut.

urer correctly predicted, "This thing will kill Cleveland [so far as his reelection might be concerned]."

Tippecanoe's grandson. In the election of 1888, Cleveland, though renominated by his party, faced stiff opposition from a Civil War veteran—Benjamin Harrison, Senator from Indiana. Harrison was the grandson of "Old Tippecanoe." He easily won the Republican nomination after Blaine withdrew as a possible candidate.

Harrison ran on a platform that was boldly in favor of a protective tariff. Cleveland defended his plea for a cut in the tariff. Mudslinging was a feature of this campaign, too. For example, Cleveland was accused of mistreating his wife.

When the returns were in, Harrison was the winner because of the number of electoral votes he had piled up. Cleveland, however, had one hundred thousand more popular votes than his opponent. It now seems clear that bribery of voters in New York, Rhode Island, Ohio, and Indiana gave those states—and the whole election —to the Republicans.

Misunderstanding the results. Harrison

Discuss the meanings of "tariff for revenue" and "no tariff for monopolists only."

was a religious man who read the Bible regularly and held a daily prayer service in his library. When he met the head of the Republican party, Matt Quay, a Pennsylvanian, he could not help saying, "Providence has given us the victory."

Quay, who knew how Indiana and New York had wound up in the Republican column, had an answer later in private. He said he supposed that Harrison "would never know how close a number of men were compelled to approach the gates of the penitentiary to make him President."

The "millionaires' Cabinet." Harrison's Cabinet choices strongly suggested that a number of deals had been made to insure support for him in the party. James G. Blaine was in the Cabinet—back again as Secretary of State. Another member was John Wanamaker, a wealthy dry-goods merchant from Philadelphia.

So prominent were businessmen in the new official family that it was often referred to as the millionaires' Cabinet. And presiding over the Senate as vice-president of the United States was Levi P. Morton, of Indiana, one of the leading bankers of the country.

Although Harrison had the best of intentions, he was not equal to the demands of the presidency. Perhaps—in spite of his Civil War heroism—he was simply a very timid man. It is said, for instance, that the President and the rest of his family were afraid to touch the electric-light switches recently installed in the White House. After the engineer left in the afternoon, the bedrooms there were kept dark and the lights in other rooms were kept burning until he arrived again the next morning.

Spending the surplus. Congress allowed the surplus of money from the high tariff to pile up. It then voted to spend so much money that it came to be known as the Billion-Dollar Congress—the first in our history. Among the laws the Republican-controlled group passed were those expand-

w out the opinions of members of the class concerning mudslinging in campaigns.
k how Cleveland could win more popular votes than Harrison but lose the election. Review
act that the number of a state's electors equals the number of its representatives in Congress.

ing the navy and providing new pensions
for war veterans and their families.

New laws. In 1890 Congress pushed
through the highest tariff ever. The man
who proposed it and worked harder than
anyone else to get it accepted was a representative from Ohio, William McKinley.

\# The rates set under the McKinley Tariff
were so high that western farm people
were especially angered. They foresaw that
the cost of manufactured goods would be
forced higher than ever.

To quiet the criticism from the West,
Congress passed an act in 1890 providing
for the purchase of more silver than before.
The silver-mine owners had persuaded
farmers that this would raise farm prices,
and the farmers had influenced Congress.

\#\# Another law aimed at pleasing the farmers was the Sherman Antitrust Act, also
passed in 1890. It was supposed to end the
kind of monopolies which farmers had
long blamed for helping keep the prices of
manufactured goods too high.

Disappointment and revolt. Clearly, Congress was failing to meet the needs of
farmers well enough. It was ignoring completely other large groups of people.

In 1890 a revolt began. It affected the
elections to the House of Representatives.
The Republicans, who had controlled the
House after 1888, were badly defeated,
and the Democrats took charge.

The Democrats had no program of action and no new leaders. They seemed to
be elected simply because of widespread
disappointment over the record made by
their rivals.

A Nation with Troubles

In 1892 the Republicans renominated
Harrison, and the Democrats once more
chose Grover Cleveland to carry their banner. Compared with some of the campaigns that had gone before, this one
was clean and gentlemanly. The torchlight

Chicago Historical Society

Americans already took pride in doing nothing
on a small scale: this Ferris wheel at the
world's fair of 1893 was the largest ever built

parades and the huge rallies were largely
absent. Perhaps, even though many public
problems were still being ignored, political
campaigns were beginning to be thought
of as more than a form of entertainment.

During the summer of 1892, Carrie Harrison fell mortally ill. Cleveland, out of respect for her, did very little campaigning.
Just before the election the First Lady
died. By then the President seemed to have
lost interest in victory.

Gigantic triumph. The size of Cleveland's victory was astonishing—the most
overwhelming election triumph since Lincoln's in 1864. The Republicans had suffered a greater defeat than in 1890.

As Cleveland accepted the applause of
his admirers, he declared, "We must hear

\#\#A trust was created when control of a number of rival corporations was put in the hands of a
single group of stockholders. The trust then would control the market and could raise prices
if it wished. After the Sherman Antitrust Act, other monopolies were formed, however.

above victorious shouts, the call of our fellow countrymen to public duty."

Depression. Hardly had the Clevelands returned to the White House when troubles of all kinds broke out. The most serious was the depression of 1893.

As the depression's effects spread, banks closed, causing untold grief for thousands of depositors. Factories shut down, bringing terrible suffering to countless families.

World's fair. In the same year, the Columbian Exposition opened in Chicago—marking the beginning of the fifth century since Columbus first arrived in the New World. The magnificence of that world's fair (which had among its exhibits the first skyscraper) showed the kind of achievement the country was capable of. The breadlines and the soup kitchens and the long lines of unemployed men contrasted sharply with the boastful impression created in Chicago.

Troops as strikebreakers. We have already heard of the Pullman strike of 1894 (see pages 511–512). At that time Cleveland's idea of what to do was to send federal troops to protect the mails. In other words, he placed the power of the national government on the side of the railroads. The troops broke the strike.

Laboring people, in general, were angry, especially at those who had advised Cleveland to take such an action. The chief adviser had been the Attorney-General, formerly a lawyer for one of the railroads.

Cleveland continued to believe in tariff reduction—something he had promised in his recent campaign to try to bring about. But the Democrats in Congress were unable to accomplish much.

A tariff bill *was* passed that provided for some reductions, but it was changed in the Senate in such a way that many of the new tariff rates were higher than ever. Cleveland was angry. He attacked the legislation as a breaking of faith with his party.

A proposal turned down. One section of the new tariff bill provided for a small income tax, one that hardly touched most Americans. Cleveland himself was opposed to the tax, and the following year the Supreme Court declared it unconstitutional. The Court said it was a direct tax on personal property, something forbidden by the Constitution. (The Sixteenth Amendment, added to the Constitution in 1913, gave Congress the right to tax all kinds of incomes.)

A proposal ignored. Neither the President nor Congress provided aid for the unemployed. America had not yet arrived at the day when it would regard its people—

only was Coxey arrested because his men walked on the ss of Capitol Hill, but he was put in prison for a while.

In May, 1894, an army of unemployed men led by Jacob S. Coxey marched to the Capitol, in Washington. Here policemen force the crowds back as Coxey's men walk four abreast.

UPI

its human resources—as its most precious possession.

One of the most exciting new ideas to help the unfortunate was presented in an interesting manner. It came from Jacob S. Coxey, a successful businessman from Massillon, Ohio. Coxey suggested that unemployed men be put to work building roads and that this public-works program be paid for by the federal government.

In May, 1894, Coxey led an "army" of unemployed to the Capitol in Washington to try to influence Congress to pass the "Good Roads bill." The efforts of "Coxey's army" failed. Coxey himself was arrested for invading the Capitol grounds.

The fact that there were several new Presidents between the administrations of Hayes and Cleveland seemed to have little effect on the country. Except for differences in looks and character, the chief executives could easily have been interchangeable.

But noises were being heard in the distance—from farmers tired of being ignored, from workingmen bearing too much of the burden of industrial develop-

ment, and from immigrants and Negroe who were resentful of their treatment Above all, cities were producing problem affecting the whole country—which re quired new kinds of leaders and new kind of solutions.

Shortly our Presidents would become better known than ever before. Their per sonalities and stories about them and thei families would interest many Americans Political parties—as well as the chief execu tives—would stand for programs of action The dull, do-nothing days of politics in the 1870's, 1880's, and early 1890's would be ended.

1. Name the presidential candidates in 1884, describe the campaign, and tell who was elected. 2. Name two instances in which Cleveland showed strength of character. 3. Who ran for the presidency in 1888? Who won it? 4. Describe the McKinley Tariff. How did Congress quiet its western critics? 5. Give the main facts about the election of 1892. 6. Name four important events in the four years that followed.

Work on the first exercise under "The Research Center," p. 533, should be begun early, when students are studying about

The Workshop

cities of the past. The sec exercise under the same he could be carried out when exhibit is complete.

The Shapers of Our World

Tell how each of the following contributed well or poorly to the life of Americans in the late 1800's.

John L. Sullivan
Cincinnati Red
  Stockings
Tammany Hall
Rutherford
  B. Hayes
greenback
James G. Blaine

Stalwart
  and Half-Breed
James A. Garfield
Chester A. Arthur
Roscoe Conkling
Mugwump
Civil Service
  Commission

Grover Cleveland
Grand Army of
  the Republic
Benjamin Harrison
Billion-Dollar
  Congress

McKinley Tariff
Sherman
  Antitrust Act
depression
  of 1893
Jacob S. Coxey

Adding to Your Vocabulary

Be sure you know the meaning of the following words or expressions:

mail-order house
higher education

city machine
boss

##How do Americans today show their interest in the President and his family? How are the fami affected by the attention they receive from the public?

"old
    immigration"
"new
    immigration"
spectator sport

el
dark horse
polluted
stagnate

The Research Center

1. Organize a bulletin-board campaign to advertise the attractions of your community or area. Include pictures, programs, newspaper articles, and advertisements.

2. List the problems your community faces today. Then present a panel discussion dealing with one of them. Discuss the problem and its origin and then make suggestions for solving it.

3. Plan to present for your class or a parents' night an "I Am an American Day" program. Tell about the conditions which attracted some immigrant groups to your community or state. What problems did they face? Did the community help them? How? Give individual reports on immigrants who have made significant contributions to the United States.

4. Report on the steps immigrants are required to take to become American citizens. How have the requirements been changed over the years? Invite a recently naturalized citizen to talk to the class.

Understanding Political Cartoons

1. Look at the political cartoon on page 519. What symbols did Thomas Nast use in it? What message does he give readers?

2. Review the major political campaigns mentioned in the text. Draw a political cartoon for either a Democratic or a Republican newspaper, calling attention to an important issue. Use symbols—especially the elephant and the donkey, which Nast originated.

3. Bring to class some present-day political cartoons and study them. What is the secret of drawing good cartoons?

Thinking Things Through

After reviewing the boxed-in exercises in the chapter, answer these questions:

1. Why were immigrants of unusual ## ability often attracted to America, even though they could probably have made a satisfactory living in their own countries?

2. What experiences in our early history made Americans suspicious of "too much government"?

3. How would you answer Collis P. Huntington's argument for giving bribes to public officials?

4. Why was it safer for politicians of the 1870's and 1880's to talk of warmed-over topics than of new ones?

5. Why must a country that hopes to become a world power have a strong navy?

6. How do you explain the fact that the Democrats elected their presidential candidate in 1884—for the first time in twenty-eight years?

7. Review the word logrolling (see page 341). How was logrolling involved in the passage of the act to purchase silver in 1890, the Sherman Antitrust Act, and the McKinley Tariff?

8. This chapter might have been called "New Problems but Old Answers." Why?

Graphs Tell a Story

1. Prepare two pie graphs, the first showing the percentage of people living in urban communities in 1850 and the second to give the same information for 1900.

2. On an outline map of the United States, locate the sixteen cities of the United States that had populations of over 50,000 in 1860. Then on another outline map locate the seventy-four cities in the same rank in 1900.

Display the map and the graphs you prepared for Exercise 1 on the bulletin board. What do you notice about the locations of the cities?

#Students will be able to name the opportunity to get ahead, which the United States continued to offer to individuals of unusual ability (in spite of the problems named in the chapter). In answering the next question, students may think of colonial experiences with Britain.

533

全軍艦 (a)

(b)

94

(c)

(d)

(a) Two ships in the naval expedition of Matthew C. Perry, which opened up trade with Japan in 1854. (b) The insignia of artillerymen in the Spanish-American War. (c) A canteen used by a soldier in the war. (d) The flag of Hawaii, islands annexed by the United States in 1898, which now form the "Aloha Oe" state. (e) An American artist's idea of the Battle of San Juan Hill in 1898. (f) Mark Twain, an American author.

(f)

(e)

(g) The United States Navy played a large role in the war with Cuba. This is its emblem.

(h) A coal-oil lamp of the kind that lighted many American homes in the late 1800's and early 1900's.

(g)

(h)

The coal-oil lamp was long used in rural areas after cities enjoyed electricity.

CHAPTER 24

DRUMBEATS AT HOME AND ABROAD

The title refers to the facts that Americans fought the Spanish-American War in the period discussed in this chapter and that people at home became quite excited over events preceding and during that war and over other things as well--the election of 1896, for example.

FOR most Americans the 1890's were anything but the "gay nineties" which have sometimes been celebrated on television and in the movies. While girls in the music halls were dancing the cancan and sweethearts could ride a "bicycle built for two," there was serious unrest among farmers and workingmen. Nor was the period a time of peace. The country became involved in a mean war.

Some of the pictures on p. 534 suggest new relations Americans had with the rest of the world.

Farmers Take to the Warpath for Remedies

In the last years of the nineteenth century, the unrest among farmers and workingmen deeply affected America. As we have seen, it had long been in the making.

A New Party

After the Granger movement failed to meet the needs of farmers in the 1870's (see page 504), a new kind of organization called an alliance developed. In alliances farmers joined together to work for entire programs of help for themselves. By the year 1890, they had as members millions of farmers in both North and South.

Relations with workingmen. By that time many farmers hoped that they could join their strength to that of laboring men. They hoped to link together "the millions who till the soil" and "the millions who consume the products of [farm] labor."

Actually the complaints of the farmers were generally of little concern to workingmen. The grumbling was over low prices for crops, high costs of shipping, steep interest rates on mortgages, and a federal government deaf to pleas for help.

The birth of the Populists. By 1890 some farmers were talking of founding a new party to take care of their needs. Two

#Ask what the workingmen's complaints were. (Low wages, long hours, bad working conditions, etc.) The workingmen were no more interested in the farmers' difficulties than the farmers were in the things workingmen complained of. However, the farmers knew they needed some support.

535

#Again students should be reminded that in a democracy people have the right to form new political parties--a right not permitted in a dictatorship. See also pp. 398-399.

years later it was formed at St. Louis and was called the Populist party—that is, the People's party. The Populists caused a stir # in America that no other new party—often called a third party—had ever caused.

A candidate for President. In the election of 1892 James B. Weaver, of Iowa, became the Populists' candidate for President. Weaver, a former Union general, had white hair and a fatherly manner. Also, he was a convincing, fiery orator.

Proposals. The platform Weaver ran on contained many ideas that the farmers' alliances had been discussing for years. It called for the unlimited coinage of silver to increase the supply of money in circulation. It favored the direct election of Senators, thinking this would give Americans a fuller hand in their national legislature. (At that time, the state legislatures were choosing Senators, in accordance with the Constitution.)

In addition, the Populists called for government ownership of the railroads and other public utilities like the telegraph companies. Their platform also demanded an end to the ownership of land by foreigners and the creation of postal-savings banks.

The party platform advocated, too, the secret ballot (which was considered a protection of the people's control of their affairs) and single terms for the President and Vice-President. In an appeal for the votes of laboring men, the Populists went on record in favor of the eight-hour day.

Colorful leaders. In addition to Weaver, the Populists had many lively spokesmen who could use colorful language. One of them was Mrs. Mary Elizabeth Lease, the "Pythoness [female snake] of Kansas," according to her enemies.

Mrs. Lease, the mother of four children, had lived in Kansas since 1883. She had been an eyewitness to much of the suffering she proposed to find a remedy for. In 1890 alone she had delivered over 150 public addresses.

Another leader from Kansas was Jerry Simpson. He has always been remembered as Sockless Jerry Simpson. This is because when his opponent in a Congressional election was described as a man who wore silk socks, *Simpson* was billed as a man who wore none at all!

A fourth outstanding Populist was Ignatius Donnelly, who was known as the sage of Nininger after the town in Minnesota he came from. He was a gifted public speaker who could charm his audiences.

Arousing concern. The Populists as a whole were never as extreme as certain party members may have sounded or as the eastern newspapers and magazines sometimes described them. But because the party members blamed all their troubles on the bankers and on the "moneyed interests" generally, they aroused anger

Photography was often poorer in the late 1800's than it is now. Among the men of that time, beards and mustaches were popular.

Jerry Simpson—in shirt sleeves on a warm day— enthusiastically presents the Populists' view in Harper, Kansas, in 1892.

Kansas State Historical Society

and fear among many citizens. Valuing law and order, these people believed the Populists were threatening them.

Grover Cleveland, the Democratic nominee, won the election. He defeated President Harrison. Weaver, the Populists' candidate, came in third, having run remarkably well. The depression of 1893 (see page 531), which fell upon the country as Grover Cleveland began his second term, encouraged the Populists for 1896. Cleveland, who had little use for their ideas and did not hesitate to say so, became for the Populists a new symbol of the "enemy" in the East.

The Excitement of '96

As Cleveland's second term drew to an end, the mood of the American people in many places was ugly. More and more the question of freely coining silver was receiving public attention. The farmers, especially, had become convinced that such a policy would bring prosperity to them and the whole nation.

McKinley, the "gold man." When convention time came in 1896, the Republicans nominated the chief author of the tariff of 1890, William McKinley, of Ohio. The Republican platform supported solidly the continued use of gold to back the paper money of the country.

Many workingmen were pleased with the naming of McKinley as a candidate for the presidency. Years before, as a young lawyer he had defended a group of strikers in court. Because strikers received very little public sympathy, his action earned him the undying gratitude of laborers.

The push for silver. The strong stand on gold that the Republicans took encouraged the Democrats who supported silver. They thought that they could choose the man *they*—rather than the "gold Democrats" like Cleveland—wanted.

The unlimited coinage of silver had be-

Granger Collection

The two "Bills": A cartoon supporting McKinley for President in 1896. The "Bill" at the left is the protective tariff of 1890.

come the aim of thousands, maybe millions, of Americans. This was not because most Americans understood all about money and currency—they did not. It was because "free silver" sounded to many dissatisfied people like a cure worth trying for whatever was wrong in American life.

When the Democrats met in their national convention in July, 1896, feeling was running higher among party members than at any other time since 1860. The men who, like the Populists, wanted the unlimited coinage of silver soon took charge.

William Jennings Bryan. The Democrats' most convincing call for "free silver" was a remarkable speech delivered by William Jennings Bryan, a former Congressman from Nebraska. Bryan was a handsome man with a clear, musical voice, and his words carried without seeming effort to the farthest corners of the convention hall. Moreover, he had prepared his

The cartoon above shows the Republican candidate arm in arm with the McKinley Tariff of 1890 (see p. 530), which greatly pleased American businessmen. Because of this, McKinley had the support of workingmen as well as that of businessmen.

537

address with the utmost care. And because he had already used parts of it here and there in the South and West, he knew how deeply moved his audience would be.

"Upon a cross of gold." As Bryan reached his last words, the delegates were on their feet, jumping up and down and cheering wildly. "You shall not press down upon the brow of labor this crown of thorns," he shouted. "You shall not crucify mankind upon a cross of gold." Possibly no other political convention has ever witnessed such excitement.

Almost immediately a move was on to make Bryan the Democrats' presidential candidate. No one could stop him, and he was nominated easily.

What to do? When the Populists met later in July, they gloomily studied what had happened to their hopes as a result of Bryan's nomination. The most thoughtful of them realized that the silver question was their best issue. Yet they also saw that it offered a solution to only one of a long list of problems the country faced.

The Populists wondered what they were to do. Should they support the Democratic candidate, Bryan, because he agreed with them about silver? Or should they name one of their own men—who would accept their total program? Many of the Populists realized that if they accepted Bryan, they would have to give up all their other proposals for reform. Some rhyme published the previous year expressed their fear:

O, come into my party, said the
  spider to the fly.
Then he sharpened up his pencil
  and winked the other eye.
The way into my party is
  across a single plank—
You can take it from your platform,
  the rest can go to—blank.

The Populists finally decided to back Bryan. Many farmers who since the 1870's had waited for a candidate to carry out Populist ideas felt sick at heart. They saw

A cartoonist of the 1890's showed William Jennings Bryan as a "Paul Revere" of the Populists, riding out to stir up the voters.

Call attention to the straw hats, the pitcher of water, and the garden flowers.

McKinley speaks to an attentive crowd from a small, carpeted platform on his front porch.

Ohio Historical Society

that they were going to be captured by the Democrats, the way a spider takes a fly.

A fiery campaign. Bryan made his campaign one of the most vigorous in our history, sometimes giving as many as thirty-six speeches a day. He set a new style for presidential campaigns. In fact, he introduced the modern presidential campaign, in which the candidate himself plays the chief part, which was not the case earlier. Everywhere there were brass bands and hoopla, because the Democrats were beating the drums of a crusade—a crusade for silver coinage.

Bryan's magic on the speaker's platform seemed to be having a favorable effect. The Republicans tried to influence the voters equally by making large outlays of money. Threats were also used to try to make people vote for McKinley. Many employees, for example, were told that they would be fired if Bryan won.

McKinley, deeply devoted to his wife, Ida, who suffered from a form of epilepsy, did not tour the country because he would not leave her side. From his home in Canton, Ohio, he carried on a "front-porch" campaign, greeting delegations of politicians who traveled to Canton from various parts of the country. Some of the visitors

sang for the candidate a popular campaign tune, "We Want Yer, McKinley, Yes, We Do."

The winner. The outcome in November was a clear-cut victory for McKinley. In general, the agricultural regions of the South and West supported Bryan, and the industrial areas of the East went for McKinley. But the Republican candidate also carried important farming states in the Middle West, including Iowa, Minnesota, and South Dakota.

Some explanations. What had happened? First of all, workingmen generally had not voted for Bryan. Some may have been frightened by Republican threats. But most of them probably had been more afraid of inflation, which the unlimited ## coinage of silver could have led to. Many people must have been influenced by the campaign slogan, "Good money never made times hard." To millions of Americans, "good money" was money backed by gold.

Effects in the long run. Although many farmers were disappointed over the results of the election, and although the Populist party was dead, the Democratic campaign of 1896 had not been completely wasted. It had called attention to the need for some far-reaching reforms which neither the Republican nor the Democratic party had yet brought about.

An unlooked-for result was that Bryan became the most popular Democrat of his time. In each of the next four elections after that campaign, he was a candidate for his party's presidential nomination.

Although McKinley did not possess great talent, he was solidly dependable. As the country became more and more prosperous during the last part of 1896 and the beginning of 1897, the Republicans claimed the credit. They even succeeded in

raising the tariff to the highest point in history—without drawing a public outcry.

1. Describe the Populist platform in 1892. 2. Name four Populist leaders. 3. What party's presidential candidate was elected? Who was he? 4. Name the main issue and the two party nominees in the presidential election of 1896, and tell what each party stood for. 5. Who won the election? For what reasons? 6. Describe the effects of the election.

Students need to understand what imperialism is because of its importance in history.

Americans Look Far Beyond Their Borders

Before McKinley had been long in office, the nation became involved in international activities it felt it could not escape. They go by the name of *imperialism*. The word means the acquiring by a country of possessions outside its boundaries—in short, building an empire.

Reasons

Imperialism was greatly encouraged in the United States by several conditions. Two of them were connected with the growth of American industry. Many raw materials required by American factories —rubber, tin, and bauxite, to name only a few—came from parts of the world which could be made into colonies. Moreover, industrialists were constantly searching for new places in which to sell the endless variety of goods the factories were producing.

European examples. Third, nations found themselves rivaling one another for power —which they measured by the number and size of their overseas possessions. Britain, having been the first nation in the world to industrialize, had had a big head start in acquiring overseas possessions. By

the end of the nineteenth century, its flag flew in every quarter of the globe. But close behind in the contest were both France and Germany.

A self-assigned "burden." A fourth important reason for imperialism was a disturbing new attitude toward race. By the late nineteenth century many Europeans were saying that introducing other peoples of the earth to European civilization was the "white man's burden," which he could not escape. The English made much of being the bearers of the heavy "burden."

The notion attracted Americans, too. One man declared that the United States should join other nations in the work of "subduing [conquering] the world, in order to make mankind free."

A foretaste: the purchase of Alaska. Of course, Americans had long been reaching out into the rest of their continent and the world. In 1867 the United States had acquired Russian America—that is, Alaska —by buying it from Russia. William Seward, the Secretary of State who arranged the purchase, had dreamed of the expansion of the United States into the Caribbean and the Pacific Ocean, too.

#The United States was interested in obtaining possessions outside its boundaries for a time, but
540 imperialism has never been a characteristic of the United States as a nation.
##Students can find out the size of Alaska--now our largest state--by turning to p. 728.

flag marks Alaska,
ther Hawaii, another
rto Rico, etc.

Uncle Sam happily tries
placing the Stars and
Stripes on various spots
on the globe—a
cartoonist's idea of the
viewpoint of American
imperialists in
the late 1800's.

"Rocky Mountain News,"
May 15, 1898

Eyes on the Caribbean

The Caribbean Sea area had long drawn the close attention of Americans. Much of the interest centered on the island of Cuba. For one thing, its location at the entrance to the Gulf of Mexico made it important to Americans. For another, it was the "world's sugar bowl."

As long as Spain, a weak country, possessed Cuba (see page 158), there was no danger. But other European powers eyed the Spanish possession with envy. And until the United States was strong enough to enforce the Monroe Doctrine, we could not be sure England or France would not make a move to take the island.

Offer to buy. When the United States tried to purchase Cuba in 1848, the offer was rudely turned aside by the Spanish government. A spokesman for Spain declared, "Sooner than see the island transferred to any other power, they [the Spanish authorities] would prefer seeing it sunk into the ocean."

A shocking event. In 1868 a rebellion broke out in Cuba. The Grant administration was badly tempted to become involved in it—in the hope of separating the island from Spain. During the revolt a rebel Cu-

ban vessel, the *Virginius*, was seized by the Spanish navy. Fifty-three of its passengers and crew were taken to Cuba and shot. Americans were deeply shocked, and only the most skillful diplomacy prevented war between the United States and Spain.

The move to annex. The Grant administration was busy elsewhere in the Caribbean, too. It arranged for the United States to annex both the Danish West Indies and the Dominican Republic. But in both cases the Senate turned down the treaties of annexation. (In 1917 the United States purchased the Danish West Indies from Denmark and renamed them the Virgin Islands.)

The Pull of the Pacific

The Pacific Ocean area was also inviting to Americans. First, it was the pathway to Asia, particularly China. There trade had been attracting Americans since the earliest days of the United States. Although this trade was never very large, its possible future growth was always in people's minds. And second, the people living on Pacific islands were non-Christians in the main. For this reason, Christian missionaries considered areas of the Pacific as choice places for their work.

ne United States did not want to have a strong power in possession of Cuba, since it is the
est island in the West Indies. Britain already held many smaller islands there.
The Virgin Is., shown but not named on the map on p. 553, lie east of Puerto Rico.

542 Insets are used here in order to show the forty-eight original states in greater detail. The relief makes it easier to pick out the physical regions of the United States. From west to east these are: Coast Ranges, Central Valley, Cascades and Sierra Nevada, Great Basin,

The United States

0 50 100 200 miles	

🐾 1,000,000 and over
◉ 500,000 to 1,000,000
◎ 50,000 to 500,000
○ 0 to 50,000

<u>WASHINGTON</u> - National Capitals
<u>Madison</u> - Secondary Capitals

lorado Plateau, Rocky Mountains, Great Plains, Great Central Lowland, Ozark Highland
d Ouachita Mountains, Gulf-Atlantic Coastal Plain, Appalachian Highland. We have not
ed smaller regions here or on the map.

543

Norfolk Museum of Arts and Sciences

彼理上陸斯

Commodore Perry and one of his men sketched by a Japanese artist who saw them come ashore from their ships, anchored in Tokyo Bay.

Convenient ports. The early interest in gaining a foothold in the Pacific seemed to develop naturally. It had always been necessary for whalers and traders to have other ports there at which water and supplies—including coal later—could be taken aboard.

Perry in Japan. In a famous episode in our history, Commodore Matthew C. Perry and his expedition of black American ships visited Japan in 1853–1854. He was able to persuade the Japanese to sign a treaty of trade and friendship with the United States. Under this treaty several ports were opened to American sailors.

Dividing Samoa. In 1878 the United States was given, by a treaty, the privilege of using a harbor on Samoa—a name for a group of islands (see the map on page 553) in the southern Pacific. Because Germany and Britain received similar rights, there was danger of a clash among the three countries. In 1889 a conference arranged for the three powers to rule Samoa jointly. Ten years later Britain gave up its claim, and the United States and Germany agreed to divide the islands between them.

The Hawaiian Islands. Americans were more deeply interested in the Hawaiian Islands than in any other territory in the Pacific. These beautiful tropical lands were a source of sandalwood, useful in trading with China, as well as a place at which travelers could refresh themselves.

As early as 1842, Daniel Webster, then Secretary of State, had declared that the United States did not intend to acquire the islands. However, he had gone on to say we would not allow any other country to do so. In other words, we were practically extending the Monroe Doctrine to include these prize Pacific islands.

An effort to annex Hawaii by treaty in 1854 was defeated in the Senate. The reason was that the treaty provided for Hawaii's immediate statehood, which many Senators were opposed to. In the years that followed, Hawaii became—like Cuba—a very important producer of sugar. The United States agreed in 1875 to import Hawaiian sugar and other Hawaiian products duty free (without collecting duties on them), and the islands at once began to prosper.

Pearl Harbor. When the treaty was renewed in 1887, the United States asked for the right to use Pearl Harbor, on Oahu, one of the Hawaiian Islands, as a naval and coaling base. The request was granted. In spite of this favor, in 1890 Congress passed a tariff that was highly unfavorable to the Hawaiian sugar industry, which suffered as a result.

A spunky queen. American settlers on the islands who owned sugar plantations there found themselves in trouble. The

##This statement shows that the American navy was growing in size, as was American trade; both naval ships and the merchant marine--vessels engaged in commerce--needed coaling base particularly in the Pacific. The naval base the United States obtained was Pearl Harbor.

As her picture shows, the queen was a handsome woman and one proud of her heritage.

Hawaiians blamed them for the depression the islands were in. One who especially disliked the Americans was Queen Liliuokalani (lē-lē′oo-ō-kä-lä′-nē). In 1891 this strong-willed and very proud woman followed her weak brother on Hawaii's throne.

A brief rebellion. The American sugar growers decided that the only way to save their property was to bring Hawaii under the Stars and Stripes. Protected by troops from an American naval vessel, they rebelled against "Queen Lil" in 1893 and overthrew her government. Actually, they did little more than surround her palace.

Within a few days the United States recognized the new government of the islands, which was established by the rebels. Nevertheless, a treaty to annex Hawaii was halted by President Cleveland. Cleveland was clearly upset over the way in which the Hawaiian government had been overthrown. He even tried to restore Liliuokalani to her throne.

In 1897, when McKinley was in the White House, a new treaty of annexation was presented to Congress. Again it was turned down—this time by the Senate.

But soon the feeling of the country about owning colonies changed completely. Moreover, new events suddenly tied together American ambitions in the Pacific and the Caribbean.

Daughters of Hawaii, Queen Emma's Summer Palace

Above: Liliuokalani, ruler of Hawaii for three years and writer of the song "Aloha Oe."
Below: The islands now making up the 50th state.

1. Name four reasons for the growth of imperialism in the United States. 2. What land did the United States acquire in 1867? How? 3. Give two reasons for American interest in Cuba. 4. Name an area President Grant tried to annex which the United States later bought. 5. Account in two ways for American interest in the Pacific. 6. How did the United States gain part of Samoa? 7. Describe our relations with Hawaii between 1842 and 1897.

Hawaiian Islands

e class would probably enjoy listening to a recording of "Aloha Oe." The greeting "aloha" her "hello" or "farewell") has passed into the English language now that Hawaii is our fiftieth te. One student might report on the early history of the Hawaiian Islands.

A Quick War Frees Cuba

A series of stirring episodes began in 1895 in Cuba. There a revolt which had been smoldering for more than twenty-five years suddenly burst into flame. The United States could not ignore the outbreak, for Americans were affected seriously by the upsetting of trade that resulted. The United States was Cuba's largest market for sugar and tobacco.

"Cuba Libre!"

The leaders of the revolt in Cuba were young men who had lived and traveled in the United States. They took advantage of hard times on their island to try to throw off Spain's rule at last. Their cry became "Cuba Libre!"—"a free Cuba!"

Rebels in action. The *insurrectos*, or rebels, skillfully used Cuba's rugged country for their purposes. They hid in the mountains, and from there small groups attacked targets like sugar plantations or mills and set fire to them.

Many Cubans sympathized with the *insurrectos*. As a result, the rebels could not be found when the Spanish soldiers came looking for them.

Weyler's method. Beginning in 1896 the Spanish determined to crush the rebellion and restore law and order to the island. It sent to Cuba a stern general, Valeriano Weyler.

Weyler's policy was to herd the people from the sugar plantations into camps surrounded by barbed wire. Then he could destroy the plantations, which provided the rebels' food and arms. In this way, Weyler hoped he would deny the rebels the supplies on which they depended.

But the plan backfired and caused terrible suffering. The camps, lacking in proper sanitation, became pestholes that invite disease. The victims—especially wome and children—died by the hundreds thousands.

Noisy newspapers. By the beginning 1897, American interest in Cuba was keer A leading reason was the way America newspapers—New York newspapers, espe cially—were reporting the events in th struggle between the rebels and Spain.

By the 1890's newspapers were for th first time being read widely by the public There were several reasons for this nev American habit.

One was the low cost of *newsprint—* that is, cheap paper made from wood pul A second was the development of typeset ting machinery and of the rotary press which made possible the rapid printing o large numbers of newspapers. A third wa the invention of a way to print photo graphs. A fourth was the general improve ment in communications and transporta tion, which speeded up the handling o news. A fifth was the growth of the adver tising industry (see page 480), which ha found the newspapers useful in reachin possible customers.

Yellow journalism. To attract the atten tion of the new mass-reading public, som newspapers practiced what came to b called yellow journalism. Yellow journal ism included the use of big headlines, eye filling pictures, stories exposing scandals and gossip. The name came from "The Yel low Kid," a character in a popular comi strip appearing in the *New York World*.

The *New York World* and the *New Yor Journal*, the leading "yellows," were en gaged in a fierce circulation war—that is a hot rivalry for readers. The Cuban situa tion was made to order for them. Each

#The first four reasons given for the new American habit have to do with technological change Emphasize that the reading of newspapers is a desirable habit for people of a democracy, who need to keep informed about what is going on in order to make wise decisions.

ublished wilder accounts than the other bout the war in Cuba.

The papers were best at giving accounts f *atrocities*—that is, of shockingly cruel leeds. A favorite villain was General Weyler, or, as he was frequently called, Butcher" Weyler.

Sympathy. The picture Americans got of he desperate situation of the Cuban people appealed strongly to their sympathy. Our people felt that the unfortunate Cuans deserved help simply because they vere fellow human beings. Americans also hought Cuba was a place which should enjoy the benefits of American democracy.

Patience at the White House. President McKinley was unwilling to become inolved in a war in Cuba. Nevertheless, he strongly criticized Weyler's policy there. The President hoped that new officials in Spain would make the changes necessary o end the rebels' fighting. Throughout the year 1897 he practiced patience.

A critical letter. Then unexpected happenings dashed the hope for a peaceful setlement. The first event was a foolish blunder by Dupuy de Lôme, a Spanish diplomat in Washington. In December, 1897, he wrote a letter to a friend in Havana, Cuba, in which he criticized President McKinley sharply. The letter was stolen from a Havana post office and turned over in early 1898 to a reporter for the *New York Journal.*

Shortly a translation of the letter appeared in every newspaper in the United States, arousing much resentment toward Spain and strengthening the rebels in Cuba. De Lôme, of course, resigned his post immediately.

"Remember the *Maine!*" Relations between the United States and Spain had hardly settled down again when they were rocked by another serious event. This one occurred in the harbor of Havana (see the map on page 550). The United States' prized new battleship *Maine*, visiting Cuba to protect American citizens there, was torn apart by an explosion on February 15, 1898.

Not only was the vessel destroyed, but also 260 sailors lost their lives. The people of the United States were stunned. Not since the summer day in 1881 when Garfield was shot had the country known such a moment of gloom.

The question on everyone's lips was, Has Spain attacked the United States? No one yet could answer—in fact, nobody knows to this day. But the yellow newspapers swiftly formed an opinion. The *New York Journal* said in a headline, "The warship *Maine* was split in two by an enemy's secret infernal machine." Everywhere the cry went up "Remember the *Maine!*" calling to mind the cry of sixty-two years before, "Remember the Alamo!"

The Assistant Secretary of the Navy. The pressure on McKinley to take steps now increased. One of the most excited of those who called for action was a young hot-blood named Theodore Roosevelt, who was Assistant Secretary of the Navy.

Roosevelt wrote to a friend, "I would

The *New York Journal* reports its explanation of the blowing up of the *Maine.*

"New York Journal," Feb. 17, 1898 (Library of Congress)

NAVAL OFFICERS THINK THE MAINE WAS DESTROYED BY A SPANISH MINE.

serve the newspaper headline. The one quoted Col. 2, Paragraph 2, was in a different issue.

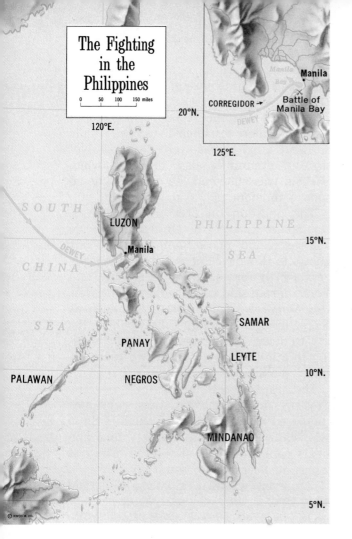

The Fighting in the Philippines

0   50   100   150 miles

120°E.

20°N.

CORREGIDOR →

125°E.

Manila

Battle of
Manila Bay

DEWEY

SOUTH

CHINA

SEA

LUZON

Manila

PHILIPPINE

SEA

15°N.

DEWEY

SAMAR

PANAY

LEYTE

NEGROS

10°N.

PALAWAN

MINDANAO

5°N.

Above: Manila Bay, entrance to the city the
Spanish founded nearly four hundred years ago,
is about 40 miles long and 35 miles wide.
Scene of the Battle of Manila—shown below—it
is guarded by the rocky island of Corregidor.

Cowlitz County Historical Museum

#Yellow journalism may have had something
to do with fostering this idea.

give anything if President McKinley woul
order the fleet to Havana tomorrow." Bu
McKinley told a friend, "I don't propose t
be swept off my feet. . . . The country ca
afford to withhold its judgment and no
strike an avenging blow until the truth i
known."

Getting ready. Businessmen, still recov
ering from the depression of 1893, did no
want war. They believed that Spain coul
be influenced to begin the necessary re
forms in Cuba without the use of force. Bu
other people put great pressure on th
President to ask Congress to declare wa
on Spain. Early in March the House o
Representatives passed a bill providin
$50,000,000 for the "national defense."

In addition to pushing for war, Theo
dore Roosevelt had made plans. He ha
played a part in bringing about the ap
pointment of Commodore George E. Dew
ey as commander of the Asian Squadron o
the United States Navy. Roosevelt was no
overlooking the fact that Spain had posses
sions in the Pacific as well as in the Carib
bean. He sent Dewey instructions early i
1898 that if war broke out, Dewey was t
begin attacking the Philippine Islands
which belonged to Spain.

The idea of adventure on distant soi
was attractive to many Americans. Mor
youths rushed to enlist in the army in 189
than rushed to Alaska, where gold had jus
been discovered.

es were important in
tary plans through the
World War. After
mechanized equip-
replaced them.
ard Wood was born
e year Lincoln was
ted President.

Colonel Leonard Wood as
en by Frederic Remington,
an American artist of that
day who was both a painter
and a sculptor.

Into Battle

Despite the fact that because of American protests the Spanish had agreed to
change their policy in Cuba, Congress declared war on Spain on April 25, 1898.
The United States made clear, however,
that it had no intention of annexing Cuba.

Dewey at Manila. Commodore Dewey
had been waiting in the British colony of
Hong Kong. He now set forth to prevent
the Spanish naval force from leaving the
Philippine port of Manila (see the map on
page 548). At midnight on April 30, 1898,
Dewey's ships slipped past the Spanish
guns on Corregidor Island, in Manila Harbor. For unexplained reasons the Spanish
did not fire.

Proceeding, the Americans met a Spanish force lying at anchor in the harbor. As
the sun rose, Dewey calmly issued an order
to Charles Vernon Gridley, the commander
of the flagship, *Olympia:* "You may fire
when you are ready, Gridley."

Less than two hours later three of the
Spanish vessels were afire. At 7:35 A.M.
the *Olympia* signaled to the other American ships to break off the fighting so that
their crews could have breakfast. Before
lunch the American squadron had closed
in and smashed the Spanish shore batter-
ies. By sunset the United States Navy was
anchored off the city of Manila as safely as
in peacetime.

The Rough Riders. Despite much dis-
comfort, some soldiers found the war an
adventure. A unit which attracted much
publicity was a mounted regiment, the
First United States Volunteer Cavalry. It
came to be known as the Rough Riders. An
army surgeon, Leonard Wood, was the
commanding officer.

But the regiment's second-in-command
drew far more public attention than Wood.
He was Theodore Roosevelt, who, with the
rank of lieutenant colonel, had left the
comfort and safety of Washington for the
thick of the battle.

The army and navy. The United States

ng Kong may be seen on the map on p. 680; students can see there how close it was to the
ppines. The British obtained the island by a treaty with the Chinese in 1842. Hong Kong
an excellent harbor. The island's name means "fragrant harbor."

Sampson and Schley were in charge of blockading Cuba. Schley's late arrival allowed the Spanish to reach Santiago de Cuba. Schley then guarded Cervera, and Sampson took over the blockade.

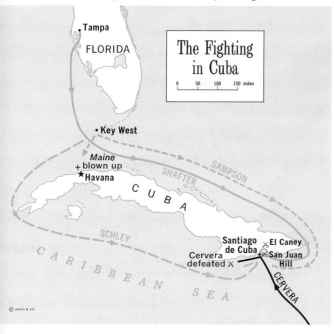

American forces in Cuba had the advantage of being closer to home and supplies than the ones in the Philippines.

troops which were being assembled and trained would be transported to Cuba by ship. But first the seas would have to be made safe. The task of the navy, therefore, was to locate and destroy the Spanish fleet of Admiral Pascual Cervera, which had left Europe for Cuba on April 29.

For some time Cervera's ships could not be found. Meanwhile, many people living in the major cities along our Atlantic coast greatly feared that they were about to be hammered by Cervera's guns.

Admiral William T. Sampson, who commanded the American Atlantic Fleet, was ready for Cervera in the Caribbean. Another American naval officer, Commodore Winfield S. Schley, was stationed off Virginia to cut off the Spanish ships.

However, the Spanish fleet managed to slip past the waiting Americans and sail safely into the harbor of Santiago de Cuba. Upon learning this, the United States Navy blockaded the port and bottled up Cervera.

The American army of 17,000 soldier could then be shipped from the mainlan to Cuba. It was under the overall comman of General William R. Shafter. Weighin 300 pounds, he was handicapped i fighting in an expedition overseas.

The first United States troops wen ashore in Cuba on June 22 just east of th city of Santiago. Another landing followe shortly. The army's first aim was to cap ture the city in order to place guns on it heights and pound Cervera's fleet.

El Caney. Two fortified Spanish posi tions blocked the American advance. On was at El Caney. The bloody eight-hou battle which developed there revealed t the American troops that the Spanis were no pushovers. The enemy had th advantage of being able to use a smoke less powder, which concealed their guns

At San Juan Hill. The other strong poin to be taken was San Juan Hill. There, o July 1, about 8000 American troops i thick underbrush were kept under murder ous Spanish fire for hours.

About midday a force of Rough Rider under Theodore Roosevelt found itsel pinned down before a height known after ward as Kettle Hill—because sugar kettle were found there. Roosevelt's men, sup ported by some Negro soldiers, worke their way through tall grass up to the to of the hill. They discovered that the enem had fled.

A hero. Within a short time San Jua Hill itself was taken. Theodore Roosevel was given credit for its capture and wa ever afterward called the hero of San Jua Hill.

The end of the Spanish fleet. The Span ish now helped the Americans—but not o purpose. Five days after San Juan Hill wa taken by the Americans, Admiral Cerver received orders to move his fleet out o Santiago Harbor. He himself believed tha his brave ships would be destroyed by th Americans. He was right.

Before the day was over, all of Cervera's ships had surrendered or been either run aground or destroyed. It was a glorious Fourth of July in 1898: Admiral Sampson offered the United States the Spanish fleet as a birthday present.

Having lost their ships, the Spanish could not reinforce their troops in Cuba. They could not win the war. On July 17, 1898, Santiago surrendered. The Spanish flag, which had flown over the city for 385 years, was hauled down for the last time. The Star-Spangled Banner went up in its place as the band played "Hail, Columbia." With the surrender of Santiago, all Cuba fell.

Puerto Rico. The following day, July 18, the Spanish ambassador in Paris asked the French government to use its influence to help bring about a truce. The same day the United States instructed General Nelson A. Miles to go to the island of Puerto Rico (see the map, page 553) and raise the American flag there.

There had never been a very active anti-Spanish movement in Puerto Rico, but the American troops were warmly welcomed anyhow. A leading citizen may have expressed the feelings of his people when he said simply, "We are glad that the United States is to be our country."

Annexation of Hawaii. At about the same time, American forces were arriving in the Philippines to help hold the city of Manila. Amid all this excitement Hawaii was finally annexed, also in July, 1898. The United States was now a nation with far-reaching interests in the Caribbean and Pacific. ##

Peace and Its Aftermath

On August 12 the United States and Spain agreed to make peace. The Spanish gave up Cuba and promised to yield Puerto Rico and an island in the Pacific (this was Guam) as war damages. It was agreed that American troops would remain in Manila until a treaty of peace was signed and that we would pay Spain $20,000,000 for the Philippines.

The end of the Spanish-American War came none too soon for the Americans. Not only had the casualties (men killed and wounded) been heavy in Cuba—about 10 percent of the troops engaged—but also disease had taken a very heavy toll. Malaria, dysentery, and yellow fever had caused a great deal of suffering.

United States troops land in Cuba in June, 1898, arriving in small boats from the transport that brought them to Cuban waters.

Cowlitz County Historical Museum

James Cardinal Gibbons (*center*), of Baltimore, Maryland, gives the benediction in a service in Washington honoring Admiral George Dewey, a hero of the war in the Philippines. President McKinley stands at the left.

Filipino fighters. It turned out that the Philippines were not at all easy to bring under control, either. Rebel Filipinos under a determined leader, Emilio Aguinaldo, battled tooth and nail against the United States forces. He and his men caused military losses considerably greater than those which had been inflicted in the Spanish-American War itself.

A new outlook. By the time the peace treaty with Spain was ratified in 1899, a remarkable change had occurred in American thinking. The *Washington Post* was declaring, "The guns of Dewey at Manila have changed the destiny of the United States." It went on to say that the United States had now become a country with an empire. The *Philadelphia Record* was expressing the opinion "We have entered upon our career as a world power."

McKinley, who had given in only under great pressure to the Americans who wanted war, now accepted the ideas of those who thought the country ought to own colonies. The question of what to do about the Philippines, however, required an answer. At one point the President said, "If old

Gibbons was the second American to be named a cardinal of the Roman Catholic church.

Dewey had just sailed away when he smashed the Spanish fleet, what a lot of trouble he would have saved us."

Then, as McKinley thought over the question, he decided that the United States had only one choice: to annex. Moreover, public support for keeping the islands was considerable.

A Senator from Indiana declared that American troops must remain in the Philippines. This is the language he used:

> Fellow-Americans, we are God's chosen people.... We cannot fly from our world duties. . . . We cannot retreat from any soil where Providence has unfurled our banner; it is ours to save that soil for liberty and civilization.

Against imperialism. Of course, not everyone held those notions. All along, many Americans had said that the Filipinos were as much entitled to decide their future for themselves as Americans had been in 1776. A group calling itself the American Anti-Imperialist League had been organized. Its members included such outstanding people as Mark Twain and Andrew Carnegie.

These people had also presented their views bluntly:

> We regret that it has become necessary in the land of Washington and Lincoln to reaffirm [that is, to say again] that all men, of whatever race or color, are entitled to life, liberty, and the pursuit of happiness. . . . We insist that the subjugation [conquest] of any people is 'criminal aggression' and open disloyalty to the . . . principles of our government.

Effect of the treaty. The peace treaty was ratified before the American public ever had an opportunity to decide whether to have overseas possessions or not. By only a stroke of the pen Spain gave up its possessions in the New World and the Pacific. As a result, the United States became one of the great powers of the world.

#Call attention to this quotation from the Declaration of Independence. "Aggression" is defined on p. 648. Doubtless the reference is to the conquest of the Philippines, where Aguinaldo led Filipino guerrilla warfare against Americans. Stress the American right to free speech.

Above: In 1901 the Pan-American Exposition in Buffalo, New York, honored all the New World republics. *Below:* The territorial gains.

The election of 1900. In the election of 1900, there was something of a debate over imperialism. The Republicans, renominating McKinley (and naming Theodore Roosevelt as their candidate for Vice-President), defended the acquiring of colonies. The Democrats, choosing Bryan again, declared, "No nation can long endure half republic and half empire."

The great victory for McKinley did not show public approval of imperialism. It seems to have been simply a victory for people who wished to leave things as they were. Besides, McKinley promised to continue the "full dinner pail." This appealed to millions of working people, who were enjoying prosperity.

Toward self-government. As Americans turned back to daily problems at home, they lost interest in overseas colonies. Cuba, as the United States had promised, was granted its political independence.

In the next few years Congress made step-by-step arrangements for the Philippines, Puerto Rico, and Hawaii to move toward self-government. The Supreme

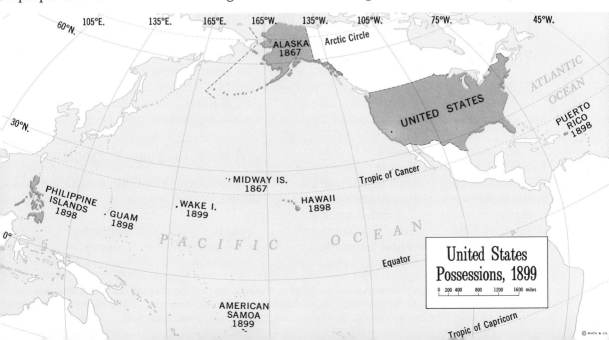

Court said in a series of decisions, however, that the new possessions were not covered by provisions in the Constitution of the United States. Many Americans understood by this that the possessions would not be granted statehood.

Assassination. McKinley had just begun his second term when he went to Buffalo, New York, to attend the Pan-American Exposition early in September, 1901. On September 5 as he stood in one of the buildings greeting the public in a receiving line, a national tragedy struck. A mentally disturbed man with a burning hatred of kings and presidents fired a concealed revolver at McKinley and fatally wounded him.

As the man was seized, the gentle McKinley's words were "Don't let them hurt him." Early on the morning of September 14, the President died—the third chief executive to be assassinated in a little more than thirty-five years.

The Vice-President became the new President—Theodore Roosevelt, the Rough Rider. In his hands would lie the responsibility for directing America in its new role as a world power.

Only the day before McKinley was shot he made a speech at Buffalo. In it he said that Americans must learn to live in the modern world, where the telegraph, the cable, and fast trains and ships had wiped out distance between nations. "Isolation [that is, deliberate political separation from the rest of the world]," he declared, "is no longer possible or desirable."

Most Americans had not yet given thought to the meaning of the statement. They saw in their new President only a symbol of themselves—youthful, energetic, confident.

---

1. How did the Cuban revolt of 1895 affect the United States? 2. Name five things that, by the 1890's, accounted for increased reading of newspapers in the United States. 3. What effect did certain newspapers have on America's relations with Spain? 4. Name two events that led directly to the Spanish-American War. 5. Where did the fighting in the war take place? 6. Describe the peace treaty signed in 1898. 7. How did Theodore Roosevelt first become President?

##Ask why McKinley said it was no longer possible. (Having world possessions would naturally cause the United States to take a bigger part in world affairs.)

The Workshop

The Shapers of Our World

Tell how each of the following contributed to arousing new American interests and an awareness of a new kind of future.

Populist party	Matthew C. Perry
James B. Weaver	Samoa
William McKinley	Queen Liliuokalani
William Jennings	Pan-American
Bryan	Exposition, 1901
election of 1896	Valeriano Weyler
Alaska	yellow journalism
Danish West Indies	Dupuy de Lôme

the *Maine*	William
Theodore Roosevelt	T. Sampson
George E. Dewey	election of 1900
Rough Riders	Anti-Imperialist
Emilio Aguinaldo	League

Adding to Your Vocabulary

Be sure you know the meaning of these terms:

public	episode
utility	newsprint
imperialism	rotary press

A good test for this chapter would be to give students an outline map of the world and ask them to name on it the possessions the United States gained in the last half of the nineteenth century and to write beside each name the date when the possession was acquired.

subduing   atrocity
foretaste   isolation
annex   alliance

Thinking Things Through

After a review of the boxed-in exercises in the chapter, answer the following:

1. Why is it so difficult for third parties to organize and become successful?

2. Examine the Populist platform of 1892. Why was it said to contain something to please all reformers?

3. Why did the Populists support Bryan in 1896 instead of nominating their own candidate?

4. In what way was the imperialism of 1898 a revival of the spirit of expansion of James K. Polk's time?

5. Why were many Americans opposed to the idea that the United States should acquire colonies?

6. Why was it considered a sure sign of world power when a country acquired colonies? Why were industrialized countries at an advantage in obtaining overseas possessions?

7. Compare the feelings among Americans in 1898 with those after the War of 1812. In what ways were they similar? Different?

Presenting Information

1. Imagine yourself as "Queen Lil," who voluntarily lived "in exile" in her palace after the revolution in Hawaii in 1893. Write a letter to President Cleveland describing the revolution and telling why the United States should oppose annexation of Hawaii.

2. Have each of seven students portray a different person mentioned in the chapter, describing but not identifying her or him. Let other members of the class guess the identities by quizzing the portrayers. A total of five questions may be asked about each person described, and only answers of yes and no may be given.

Discovering for Yourself

1. Find out what kind of government Spain had in 1898. Compare the Spanish and the American governments of that day. Why are conditions like those Weyler created in Cuba especially unacceptable to people who prize democracy?

2. Collect some front-page headlines of today. Do they describe the most important stories in the papers? Explain. Is yellow journalism practiced today? Give some examples.

Your Opinion, Please

1. Could a "front-porch" presidential campaign like McKinley's in 1896 be successful today? Explain.

2. What would have happened if Congress had declared war in 1898 and McKinley had stood for peace?

3. What responsibility do newspapers and other news agencies have in presenting information to the public?

4. Was the American declaration of war against Spain justified?

5. Theodore Roosevelt is said to have stated several times in the 1890's, "This country needs a war." Are wars ever necessary?

6. How does the expression "white man's burden" show ignorance about the differences between races?

This question should remind students that only Congress can declare war. McKinley would have had no choice but to go along with Congress, no matter how he felt about its decision. Question 6 (last on the page) is important: The expression implies that the white people are superior to those of other races, an idea that scientists today do not accept.

555

(a) A view of the Panama Canal, opened in 1914. The ship is in the Pedro Miguel (pē′drō mǐ gěl′) Locks, near the Pacific entrance. (b) Theodore Roosevelt and his family. Quentin—leaning on his father—was killed in the First World War. (c) The latest style in women's shoes in 1897. (d) Woodrow Wilson, a scholar President, wearing the robe of a Doctor of Philosophy while he was president of Princeton University.

(a)

(b)

(c)

(d)

(e) The sign of the Pure Food and Drug Administration, which developed after a law was passed in 1906 to protect American food and drugs. (f) An electric table lamp with a fancy shade—of dragonfly design—made in 1904.

...e students study the photographs showing ...odore Roosevelt and Woodrow Wilson. ...ough they were very different in person... ...y and style, both men are usually con... ...red among the nation's greatest Presidents. ...y both illustrated the spirit of the ...ressive period.

FDA (e)

(f)

CHAPTER 25

A NEW DAY OF REFORM

...ew the proposals for reform made by the Populists in 1892 (see p. 536). This chapter deals with the ...rms of the <u>progressives</u>--reformers of the early 1900's. Have students compare Theodore Roosevelt ...Woodrow Wilson both as Presidents and as reformers.

ON the evening of the day following President McKinley's funeral, Theodore Roosevelt, the new chief executive, sat with friends at dinner in the home of his sister in Washington. Almost forty-three years old, the youngest President so far in American history, he had a strange worry —not about the present, but about the ...en as President, Roosevelt still took boxing lessons.

future. How could he pass his time after he had finished McKinley's term as President, had been elected to one of his own, and still was barely fifty years old?

By this concern Roosevelt showed what millions of Americans knew well. He was a man of restless energy for whom life could never offer enough challenges.

"T. R." Presides in the Progressives' Era

As a boy Theodore Roosevelt had suffered from a frail body racked by asthma. Only by working hard and using great willpower had he grown into healthy manhood. He always believed that he owed his recovery to the vigorous outdoor life he had led.

Roosevelt developed a love of what he regarded as manly sports—boxing and big-game hunting. Possibly by taking part in these activities he was really trying to overcome a deep fear of being puny and weak.

A Powerful Personality

Roosevelt brought to the White House considerable and varied experience. He had come into the world in New York City —the first President born in a big city. As a young man, he had spent some time in the Dakotas, where he had learned to ap-## preciate America's beauty and natural resources. Before becoming McKinley's Assistant Secretary of the Navy, he had been

...Much of Roosevelt's work as President was directly related to personal experiences earlier in ...lifetime. His life in the Dakotas impressed him with the need for conservation of natural ...urces; his work in state and local government made him interested in reform.

"Teddy" Roosevelt—right—
enjoys a trip to the
mountains of the West. His
companion—next to him—
is John Muir, an American
naturalist, explorer,
and writer.

Underwood & Underwood

a member of the New York legislature, a federal civil service commissioner, and police commissioner in New York City. After the Spanish-American War, he had become governor of New York.

Strong views. As the governor, "T. R.," as he was often called, had revealed a deep-seated interest in reform—of taxation, of the civil service, of city affairs, and of the state legislature. With typical frankness he had said, "I think I have been the best Governor within my time, better than either [Grover] Cleveland or [Samuel J.] Tilden."

A fascinating family. President Roosevelt and his family filled the White House. He had six children—Alice, the oldest (often called the Princess), Theodore, Jr., Kermit, Ethel, Archibald, and Quentin (who was only four years old in 1901). Along with the respected First Lady—an excellent horsewoman—they gave the White House a joyfulness it had not recently known.

A love of action. "T. R." inspired in his family his burning love of action. He wrote one of his children, "I always believe in going hard at everything. My experience is that it pays never to let up or grow slack and fall behind."

Supporter of conservation. Roosevelt's lifelong affection for the outdoor life was his trademark. Because of it, he developed

what was called the *conservation* movement, one of the most popular programs of his administration. Its aim was to bring about the conservation, or wise use, of natural resources.

The movement had begun in the 1890's as a result of the heavy cutting down of America's remaining forest. In 1891 timberland in various parts of the country and in Alaska had been placed under the control of the federal government.

As President, "T. R." gave control of the forest lands to the Department of Agriculture. He also called a national conservation conference to give publicity to the effort to save America's natural resources from wasteful use—and misuse.

"T. R." believed that the destruction of animals and of forests was part of a terrible selfishness of people which creates much of the misery in our civilization. Yet somehow he never seemed to see anything unusual in his active interest in conservation on the one hand and his own love of big-game hunting on the other.

Social Evils

Roosevelt's strong personality quickly made an impression on American life. The disturbing problems created by the growth of industry after the Civil War became his special concern.

#More important than Roosevelt's official actions in support of conservation--setting aside forest lands, etc.--was the fact that he focused public attention on the conservation movement. Discuss how the President stirs public interest in things today.

A nation out of balance. Anyone could see that the efforts made to spread the country's influence in the world had not been matched by efforts to improve conditions at home. There were too few rich people and too many poor people in the United States. Some Americans were especially unfortunate. Among them were children who worked at an early age, Negroes almost everywhere in the country, slum dwellers in the cities (especially immigrants), and factory workers.

Growing concern. Beginning in the 1890's, people began to develop a great conscience about the suffering of fellow Americans. This public conscience in time influenced city, state, and federal governments. The results came to be called the *progressive movement.* It was an effort by many writers, politicians, professors, and humanitarians to improve American life through private and governmental activities. Above all, these reformers—these *progressives*—believed that better laws could make better lives. But they did not all agree about what the laws ought to be.

Progress and Poverty. One of the forerunners of the reformers (see page 512) was Henry George. Gifted with a keen mind and a talent for writing, George wrote a book which caused a great stir in the years that followed its publication in 1879. Called *Progress and Poverty*, it dealt with the painful question of why there was so much want in a country capable of producing plenty.

Soon after George had directed attention to the glaring shame of America's widespread poverty, others took up the subject. They often gained publicity by writing articles for national magazines. Like newspapers, magazines were just beginning to attract readers by the millions.

Muckraking. The articles in these magazines informed and aroused the public about an amazing variety of evils, of which poverty was only one. The writers, who came to be called *muckrakers*, sometimes turned out books, too, or collected their articles and published them as books.

How the Other Half Lives. A writer who described the terrible slums in large American cities was Jacob Riis. Born in Denmark, he was a police reporter for New York newspapers. His descriptions of tenement houses earned him the friendship of Theodore Roosevelt. Riis took his reader to "see" a tenement in a book he named *How the Other Half Lives,* published in 1891.

Be a little careful, please! The hall is dark and you might stumble over the children pitching pennies back there. Not that it would hurt them; kicks and cuffs are their daily diet. They have little else. Here where the hall turns and dives into utter darkness is a step, and another, another. . . . You can feel your way if you cannot see. . . .

All the fresh air that ever enters these stairs comes from the hall-door that is forever slamming, and from the windows of dark bedrooms that in turn receive from the stairs their sole supply of the elements God meant to be free. . . .

That was a woman filling her pail by the hydrant you just bumped against. The sinks are in the hallway, that all the tenants may have access—and all be poisoned alike by their summer stenches. Hear the pump squeak! It is the lullaby of tenement-house babes. In summer, when a thousand thirsty throats pant for a cooling drink in this block, it is worked in vain.

The Woman Who Toils. Two women of means, Marie Van Vorst and Mrs. John Van Vorst, sisters-in-law, published in 1903 a book entitled *The Woman Who Toils.* They had masqueraded as working girls in order to gather material for writing about women in industry. One of them had obtained a job as a shoe cleaner in a boot and shoe factory. She described the work she had learned and what it did to a girl's hands as follows:

Read other passages from How the Other Half Lives. Compare conditions in present-day city ums with those described by Riis. Ask students to account for the similarities and differences. escribe present government attempts to eliminate slums.

Point out that large-sc meat-packing was a re tively new industry. I merly city people bou, their meat directly fro butchers who did their own slaughtering.

After the Civil War the Union Stock Yards in Chicago became a center to which cattle were shipped by railroad to supply a growing meat industry.

I dipped my forefinger in a glass of hot soap and water, water which soon became black as ink. I passed my wet, soapy finger all around the boot's edge, from toe to heel. This loosened, in the space between the sole and vamp [that is, the top part of the shoe], the sticky dye substance on the leather and particles of so-called "dirt". . . .

When my employer had left me I observed the woman at my side: an untidy, degraded-looking creature, long past youth. Her hands beggared [that is, defied] description; their covering resembled skin not at all, but a dark-blue substance, leatherlike, bruised, ingrained. . . . Her nails looked as though they had been beaten severely. One of her thumbs was bandaged.

"I lost one nail; rotted off."

"Horrible! How, pray?"

"That there water; it's poison from the shoe-dye. . . ."

I don't believe the shoe-dye really to be poisonous. I suppose it is scarcely possible that it can be so; but the constant pressure against forefinger nail is enough to induce disease.

The Jungle. Using his knowledge of the Chicago stockyards, Upton Sinclair, a youthful reformer who had written stories to pay his way through college, wrote a frank novel called *The Jungle*. Published in 1906, it seemed to scream on every page

for reform in meat-packing. Here is a sample of the content:

There were some jobs that it only paid to do once in a long time, and among these was the cleaning out of the waste-barrels. Every Spring they did it, and in the barrels would be dirt and rust and old nails and stale water—and cart load after cart load of it would be taken up and dumped into the hoppers with fresh meat, and sent out to the public's breakfast. Some of it they would make into "smoked" sausage—but as the smoking took time, and was therefore expensive, they would call upon their chemistry department, and preserve it with borax and color it with gelatine to make it brown. All of their sausage came out of the same bowl, but when they came to wrap it they would stamp some of it "special," and for this they would charge two cents more a pound.

The Bitter Cry of the Children. John Spargo, a reformer who had been born in England, wrote about the conditions under which children worked in the sweatshops. (These were small factories where working conditions were unfair and unsanitary.) His book, published also in 1906, was called *The Bitter Cry of the Children*. In it he described a talk he had on one occasion with a little girl named Marie outside a flax mill in Paterson, New Jersey. He said she

#Other interesting food additives were formaldehyde in pork and beans--to act as a preservative --and copper sulfate in canned peas--to make them look green.

See the comments about Jane Addams in the opening to Part Seven (pp. 470-471).

claimed "thirteen years, though she was smaller than many a child of ten."

If my little Paterson friend was thirteen, perhaps the nature of her employment will explain her puny, stunted body. She works in the "steaming room" of the flax mill. All day long, in a room filled with clouds of steam, she has to stand barefooted in pools of water twisting coils of wet hemp. When I saw her she was dripping wet, though she said that she had worn a rubber apron all day. In the coldest evenings of winter little Marie, and hundreds of other little girls, must go out from the superheated steaming rooms into the bitter cold in just that condition. [It is] no wonder that such children are stunted and underdeveloped!

Devoted men and women. Attacking the various shames of the "land of opportunity" was the work of people in all walks of life. Of course, government had both money and power to throw into the fight, but private individuals played a huge part.

Jane Addams, in Chicago, was one of the best known of them. Thousands of poor people, especially immigrants, found at Hull House—which she had the leading part in establishing—some of the help they could not find elsewhere. At this community center they were given legal, medical, and educational assistance and offered many kinds of recreation.

Another humanitarian was Moorfield Storey, a Boston lawyer who worked valiantly for the rights of Indians and Negroes. He helped found the National Association for the Advancement of Colored People in 1908 and was long its president.

Right: **Within twenty-five years the Union Stock Yards had expanded enormously. (a)** Two views of a meat-packing plant located there. **(b)** Cutting up beef. **(c)** Cooking meat for packing. **(d)** Barreling meat.

Chicago Historical Society

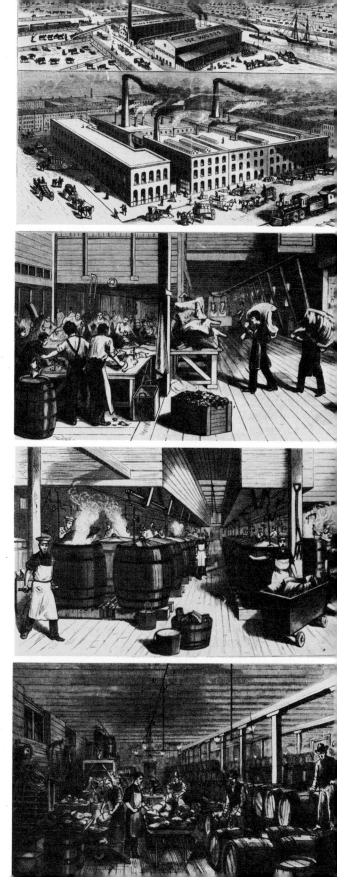

Attack on Big Business

One evil—the growing and uncontrolled power of big business—particularly drew the attention and energy of the President. (As we have seen, that energy was very great.) "T. R." was determined that government must find a way to provide a square deal, as he called it, for all people in the United States.

Winning a big case. Very early in his administration the President made up his mind to break up into smaller parts a company he believed had too much control over the country's railroads. This was the Northern Securities Company, operated by some of the leading bankers in the country. It fought back savagely. But finally in 1904 the Supreme Court decided that the President was right: the company would have to be broken up. "T. R." rejoiced. He considered this triumph one of his great achievements.

Other lawsuits. Later Roosevelt took legal action against other large combinations of businessmen in various industries. He brought lawsuits against the meat-packing companies (popularly called the Beef Trust), against the Standard Oil Company, and against the American Tobacco Company.

However, the circumstances were not as dramatic as in the Northern Securities case. But the effect was important, because it warned big businessmen that they could not do as they pleased.

Roosevelt did not seek to destroy big business. Rather, he was making an effort to establish a better balance between its power over the public and the right of government to protect all the people.

Handling the coal operators. Roosevelt sometimes used the power of his office to help laboring people. Very early in his administration he was faced by a strike in the hard-coal industry. The leader of the striking mine workers was an able young man named John Mitchell. Mitchell had succeeded in winning a great deal of public sympathy by drawing attention to the low wages of miners and the terrible working conditions in the mines.

The mineowners had proved to be very stubborn. At first they would not coöperate with the President in seeking a settlement —refusing even to talk with Mitchell. The President lost no time in telling them that if necessary he would call upon the United States Army to operate the mines.

As a result of Roosevelt's action, the strike was settled: the miners won a nine-hour day, a 10-percent wage increase, and other demands. This action was one of the most important a President had ever before taken in a labor dispute.

A Changing Outlook

The progressive movement gradually brought about changes in the viewpoints of courts in the United States, and also of Congress, although reformers experienced disappointments with both. In a number of states, laws to remove evils were passed. However, this legislation was not immediately accepted as constitutional.

An early setback. For example, in 1884 New York passed a law prohibiting the manufacture of cigars in tenement houses. The stated purpose of the law was to protect public health. Actually, the aim was to improve living conditions in the slums.

The state court decided that the law was unconstitutional. The court held that even a law for protecting health must not interfere with the personal liberty of people to work when and where they please.

New immigrants or other unskilled workingmen and -women actually could not make such a choice. If they did not work where their employer said they must, they did not work at all. And if they did not work, they did not eat.

##One reason why Roosevelt took action was to help the public--winter was approaching, and many people might have to go without fuel if the strike continued. Give examples of recent presidential action to end strikes harmful to the public interest.

Above: The situations of families working in "flats" like this in New York tenements helped arouse reformers. *Right:* Conditions on the outsides of such places were also bad.

The overworked bakers. The Supreme Court of the United States also took the position that the New York court had. In a 1905 case that is now famous, it declared unconstitutional a law which said bakers may not work more than sixty hours a week. The Court said that the law interfered with a man's right to make a contract. In this instance it interfered with his willingness to agree to work as long as he liked each week.

Clearly the workingman required some kind of protection. In bargaining over the conditions of his work, he did not have the power of his employer—who could fire him on the spot and replace him overnight. The courts would have to be convinced their old opinions were no longer right.

Women in laundries. A changed idea appeared in a case in Oregon in 1908. The state legislature there had passed a law making it illegal for a woman to work more than ten hours a day in a laundry. The Oregon court studied the New York decision and said it did not apply to the Oregon law. It declared that it was necessary to offer women special protection "in order to preserve the strength and vigor of the race."

Louis D. Brandeis. The lawyer defending Oregon's law was Louis D. Brandeis, a brilliant attorney from Boston. Brandeis had long believed that government must take a hand in protecting citizens. Later he became a member of the Supreme Court and played a part—with others—in changing the way the Court judged such laws.

Purer foods and drugs. Congress, like the Supreme Court, responded to abuses in American life. It enacted a number of laws which tried to correct some particularly glaring evils.

563

is important for students to understand how Supreme Court interpretations can change over the years. The cases discussed above are <u>Lochner</u> v. <u>New York</u>, 1905, and <u>Muller</u> v. <u>Oregon</u>, 1908.

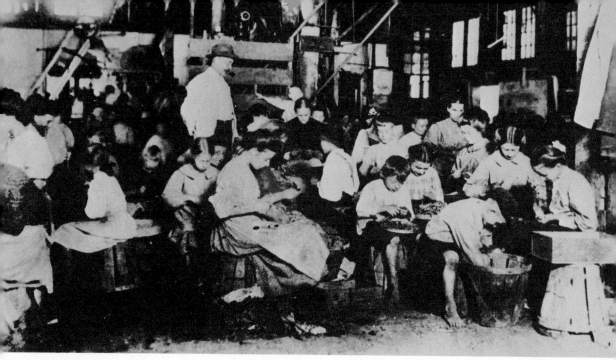

Women and children at work in a plant in New York City at the turn of the century. Supervised by a foreman—standing—they are cutting green beans, to be canned and eaten by Americans.

One of these laws, the Meat Inspection Act, provided for federal inspection of meat. It was passed in 1906, despite the widespread opposition of meat-packers. Another, also passed in 1906, was a Pure # Food and Drug Act to control the distribution of medicines and food.

Neither the Meat Inspection Act nor the Pure Food and Drug Act ended all the problems it was supposed to. Nevertheless, these laws were important first steps in protecting Americans from being the victims of careless handling or manufacture of food and drugs.

Brakes on improvements. Despite the serious problems which the progressives had pointed out, the amount of corrective legislation passed by Congress was small. First of all, many of the situations could be dealt with only by the state and local governments.

Second, President Roosevelt himself feared that the exposures of evils in the magazines would lead to a "revolutionary feeling." The President was especially afraid that wrongful attacks might be made on honest men, and that a result could be harm to the country.

Corruption in Government

No evil in American life drew more attention than the widespread corruption in state and city governments. We have already seen how rapidly cities grew in number and size after the Civil War.

Why? To provide for the variety of needs of people in cities—water, transportation, police and fire protection, gas and electric service—required huge sums of money. For this reason, it gave many opportunities for crookedness to city officials looking for bribes in exchange for giving out jobs and contracts for public works. As a result, most of the major cities produced "bosses" who had almost complete control of the city government.

The Shame of the Cities. Lincoln Steffens

#Ask a student to report on recent activities of the Food and Drug Administration.
##Bosses held their power by controlling blocs of votes and by being able to grant jobs to their supporters.

...n his book *The Shame of the Cities,* published in 1904, described, for example, ...ow Christopher Magee controlled Pittsburgh from 1882 to 1899:

> Boss Magee's idea was not to corrupt the city government, but to be it; not to hire votes in councils, but to own councilmen; and so, having seized control of his organization, he nominated cheap or dependent men for the select and common councils [that is, the city's governing bodies]. Relatives and friends were his first recourse [that is, the ones he turned to immediately], then came bartenders, saloon-keepers, liquor dealers, and others ... who were ... dependent ... upon maladministration of the law [that is, misgovernment].

The role of businessmen. Many businessmen played a central part in corrupting public officials. They were constantly looking for "benefits" to buy. In addition to such things as contracts to provide for city services, these "benefits" might include, for example, a lowered tax rate or the closing of a street to make room for an expanding factory.

"Golden Rule" Jones. Gradually people began to listen to individuals who wished to reform the cities. Reformers became mayors in a number of places. They set standards for city government which have remained to the present.

One of the most famous of these reformers was Samuel "Golden Rule" Jones, of Toledo, Ohio. His nickname came from the fact that in his machinery-manufacturing plant he posted a card bearing the golden rule as a guide for the treatment of the employees.

As mayor of Toledo from 1897 to 1904, Jones established civil service in the chief city departments. He also introduced a minimum wage—that is, a wage that was the least an employer could pay—and the eight-hour day for city employees. He set up the city's first kindergartens and its first public playgrounds and golf courses. He also sponsored free concerts.

The city manager. Under the influence of reform movements, many cities stopped electing their chief officials and instead hired them under contracts. In this way a city could obtain a *city manager,* and his employer expected him to do his job fairly and honestly.

The Wisconsin idea. The slow improvement in city governments influenced the quality of state government. A leading figure in the reform of state government was Robert La Follette, who became governor of Wisconsin in 1900. The three chief

...view the laws of your state ...at regulate the employment ...young people.

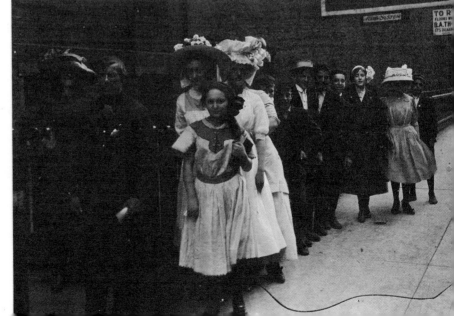

Boys and girls—right—line up in Chicago in 1911 to obtain the work permits they are required to have in order to take jobs in factories.

Chicago Historical Society

"Backyards," a painting of a slum in New York City in the early twentieth century, by the American artist John Sloan.

points in his program of government became famous as the Wisconsin idea.

It included (1) the nomination of state officials by a state primary election—that is, nominations were to be made by the voting public, not chiefly by bosses in the rooms of their clubhouses; (2) a reform of taxation so that the burden would fall more equally on the people; and (3) regulation of the railroads. This regulation meant, among other things, an ending of the free-pass system, which encouraged dishonesty (see page 503).

\# **Tools for democracy.** The Wisconsin idea was changed and improved in many

parts of the country. In some places, in addition to the *direct primary*, either the *initiative* or the *referendum*—or both—was adopted.

The initiative allowed voters, by petitioning, to place on the ballot proposals they wanted to have made into law. The referendum provided an opportunity for voters to express their wishes about proposed laws. In a few places the *recall* was adopted, making possible the removal (that is, the recall) of public officials considered to be unsatisfactory.

Progressives everywhere supported the secret ballot as another safeguard against

#Which of the political practices described here are found in your state? Give examples of recent referenda, etc., on the local or state level. Does your state have a sales tax? An income tax?

the corruption of government. In some states, women were granted the right to vote—still another democratic advance.

Popular election of Senators. In one of the most important progressive moves, steps were taken toward the election of Senators directly by the people. By the year 1910 or so voters in some states were being allowed to name their choices for Senators. In other states, the legislatures were still choosing Senators, as the Constitution provided The Seventeenth Amendment to the Constitution (see page 723) was a result of the efforts of the progressives. Added in 1913, it provided for the direct election of Senators.

1. Describe Theodore Roosevelt's life before he became President. 2. Describe one of his most popular programs. 3. Name five writers who called attention to the evils that had developed in American life. 4. Give the titles of two muckraking books and tell who wrote them. 5. Name four lawsuits Roosevelt brought to check the power of big business. 6. Describe his handling of a strike by miners. 7. Give the main points of the Wisconsin idea. 8. In what five ways did progressives help voters take part in their government more directly than before?

e how many of the Populist proposals for political reform were adopted (see also p. 536).

The People See Bold Leadership and Weak

The reputation Theodore Roosevelt enjoyed as a man of action was strengthened by the building of the Panama Canal. It was an accomplishment that made Americans proud of their engineering and medical skills. Also, though, it brought them much criticism for the way they handled the necessary negotiations with Colombia, the South American country that owned Panama.

Digging the Big Ditch

The United States had long wanted to construct a waterway through the Isthmus of Panama. The purpose, of course, was to connect the Atlantic and Pacific coasts in order to shorten the journey between them. But there had been one difficulty and delay after another.

In 1879 a French company had begun what proved to be an unsuccessful attempt to build a canal. After the United States acquired islands in the Caribbean and in the Pacific, Americans decided that their own country would have to undertake the

task. People could see how much easier it would be to protect the new possessions if naval vessels could move back and forth swiftly between the Atlantic and Pacific oceans.

Two choices. Two routes for a canal seemed to be possible—one across the Isthmus of Panama, the other across Nicaragua. The first was the shorter of the two proposed routes, but it would be the more difficult to build.

The spokesmen for the French company that had failed in its own efforts to construct a canal urged the United States to build in Panama. The French company asked $109,000,000 for its equipment and rights.

Bargain offer. The United States officials decided that the price was too high—that $40,000,000 would be about right—and turned seriously to the idea of building in Nicaragua. The response of the French company was immediate. Its spokesmen said that it would sell the equipment and rights for $40,000,000.

A helpful volcano. The French company

ecause of a treaty signed in 1914, the United States still has the right to build a canal
ough Nicaragua. Some students might report on recent proposals to build a new canal
ough Central America or to widen the present one.

567

#The Colombians had been offered $10,000,000 and wanted at least $25,000,000. They did not think it right that the United States would pay the French company four times as much as Colombia would receive

also carried on a campaign to persuade the members of the United States Senate to accept a Panama route rather than a Nicaragua one. Luck played into their hands: Mount Pelee, a volcano situated on a Caribbean island off Nicaragua, erupted, causing a terrible loss of life. It spewed forth, it was said, enough earth to fill up the proposed Nicaraguan canal.

The supporters of the Panama route then rushed to say that the whole of Nicaragua was more likely to have volcanoes than Panama. A representative of the French company placed on each Senator's desk a Nicaraguan postage stamp showing a smoking volcano in the middle of Lake Nicaragua. The Senators were persuaded, and in June, 1902, Congress enacted a bill that provided for building a *Panama* canal.

Colombian stubbornness. But permission to build the canal had to be obtained from Colombia, because Panama was its possession. And Colombia refused to sign a proposed treaty under which the United

States would acquire the canal zone i wanted. The reason for the refusal was that the sum of money to be paid to the South American country by the United States seemed too small.

The Panama Canal not only shortened the distance between the Atlantic and the Pacific but also strengthened the position and influence of the United States in the Caribbean area. *Above:* The Nicaraguan postage stamp each Senator received

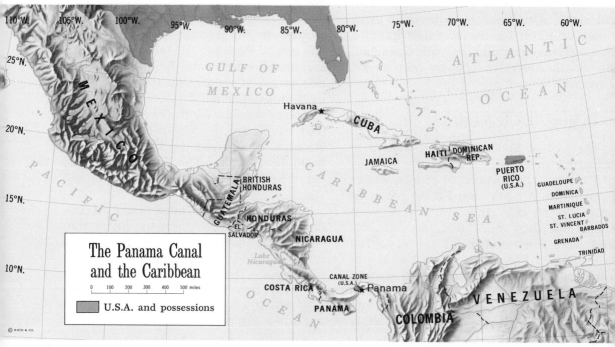

The building of the Panama Canal made Americans very sensitive about conditions in the entire Caribbean area. As a result, when Caribbean countries were threatened by revolution or when they could not pay their foreign debts, the United States frequently stepped into their affairs.

Theodore Roosevelt was beside himself with anger when the Colombian senate turned down the proposed treaty. He declared that the United States was being "held up" by the Colombians.

A revolt made to order. With the coöperation of the French canal company, a group of Panamanians was able to cook up a successful revolt for independence from Colombia. The United States hastened to *recognize* the independent Panama—that is, to establish diplomatic relations with it. And a lawyer for the French company turned up as Panama's ambassador to the United States!

The new ambassador quickly arranged a treaty under which the United States agreed to pay Panama what it had previously offered to give Colombia. In return, the United States received the use of a zone in Panama 10 miles wide.

Unhappily, along with the Panama Canal Zone, the United States gained the deep hatred of many Latin Americans. "T. R." himself boastfully admitted in a public speech in 1911, "I took the Canal Zone." In 1921 the United States made a gift of $25,000,000 to Colombia. Many understood it as a way of saying "The United States is sorry."

Superhuman labors. The building of the Panama Canal, begun in 1904, took ten years. The engineers and their men risked fevers and other dangers in digging the big ditch. Before it was completed, the steam shovels had removed about 211,000,000 cubic yards of earth.

Moreover, before the work ended, medical teams had found ways to wipe out two dreaded diseases in that part of the world: yellow fever and malaria. The leader of this remarkable work was William C. Gorgas, of the United States Army Medical Corps, who had earlier conquered yellow fever in Havana.

Political Stumbling

Theodore Roosevelt was elected President on his own in 1904. His Democratic-party opponent had been a colorless New York judge, Alton B. Parker. On election night Roosevelt announced that he would not seek renomination in 1908. He kept his word.

Taft, of Ohio. "T. R." had so much influence with the Republican-party leaders that in 1908 he practically chose his successor to the White House. The man was William Howard Taft, easygoing and

y means of a system of locks,
ship passing through the
anama Canal is raised more
an 80 feet above sea level
d then lowered again on
e other side.

A steam shovel bites into the tough earth as American workers build the Panama Canal. The task, involving the removal of millions of cubic yards of earth and rock, demanded an advanced technology.

Underwood & Underwood

Granger Collection

Underwood & Underwood

#Taft's huge vote really showed the public's high regard for "T. R."--not its feeling for Taft.

agreeable, from Ohio, weighing well over 300 pounds.

Handpicked. Taft had served as governor of the Philippines and then as Secretary of War. "T. R." liked him very much, and the Roosevelts and the Tafts were often in each other's company. One night early in 1908, after dining together at the White House, the two families went to the library to talk. There the President sat down, closed his eyes, and teased the Tafts.

Seeming to peer into the future, "T. R." sang in the manner of a fortune-teller: "I see a man standing before me weighing about 350 pounds. There is something hanging over his head. I cannot make out what it is; it is hanging by a slender thread. At one time it looks like the Presidency—then again it looks like the Chief Justiceship."

"Make it the Presidency!" Mrs. Taft shouted.

"Make it the Chief Justiceship!" said Taft more calmly.

Taft was completely sincere in his statement. (So was Mrs. Taft in hers.) Many years later Taft did become chief justice of the United States—the only man who has ever held the two highest offices in the land.

But for the moment it was to be the presidency. Taft's opponent in the election of 1908—running for the third time—was William Jennings Bryan.

Despite the blessing of "T. R." and a huge electoral vote, Taft from the start had a hard time of it. Unsure of himself, he was something like Van Buren—an able lieutenant who felt uneasy when called upon to take the captain's place (see page

Above: This cartoon, published in 1904, shows the popular Roosevelt towering above everybody else at the Republican National Convention in Chicago that summer. *Below:* Roosevelt poses in a steam shovel during a trip he made in 1906 to see for himself how the Panama Canal was coming along.

like Roosevelt, Taft did not know how to use lic opinion as a political weapon.

332). Taft once said that whenever he heard the words "Mr. President" uttered in his presence, he turned around to see if Roosevelt was there.

Touching the tariff. Taft's first mistake, as he tried to satisfy a group of reformers in his party known as Progressive Republicans, was dealing with the tariff. These reformers believed that tariff rates were too high and that the time had come for reducing them. Taft carried out a campaign promise when he called a special session of Congress to meet to discuss the question.

The Senate, which was controlled by spokesmen for eastern big business, left the tariff rates high. This greatly displeased most farmers, who believed that such rates kept the price of manufactured goods too high. Being mainly Republicans, they had expected help from Taft. They now blamed him for not receiving it.

Angry Progressives. Taft, anxious to keep the good will of the eastern members of his party, called the new tariff the best that the Republicans had ever passed. This angered the Progressive Republicans, who had been working for tariff reduction.

A public impression. Taft ran into trouble on conservation, too. He actually removed from public sale more land which contained timber, coal, and oil than "T. R." had done in a similar period of time. But because of mistakes, Taft's efforts caused people to decide that he was a tool of big business, ready to turn over the nation's natural resources to greedy people.

Split-up of friends. "T. R." was off on a hunting trip in Africa and a tour of Europe as Taft began his administration. He had told Taft, "You blessed old trump, I have always said you would be the greatest President, bar only Washington and Lincoln, and I might . . . strike out the exception!" Privately, though, "T. R." had said of his successor, "He's all right; he means well and he'll do his best. But he's weak."

Underwood & Underwood

William Howard Taft (*center*), who won the presidency in 1908, had served with credit as the first governor of the Philippines and then as Roosevelt's Secretary of War. Here he inspects the Panama Canal in 1907.

By the time Roosevelt returned from Europe in 1910, he was convinced that the policies he had begun were not being carried on. He no doubt was itching to get back into politics.

At first Taft apologized to "T. R." for the way things were going. He seemed never to have recovered from the idea that Roosevelt was still the President. He wrote to Roosevelt, "I have had a hard time. I have been conscientiously trying to carry out your policies, but my method of doing so has not worked smoothly."

By the following year, however, trouble had developed between the old friends. In a speech in Boston Taft attacked Roosevelt —and Roosevelt was calling Taft a scoundrel, a fool, and a blackguard.

npare Taft's political difficulties with those of Presidents Van Buren and Andrew Johnson. Dis-
whether or not the successor of a very strong or popular leader usually has special problems.

Chicago Historical Society

A campaign poster for Theodore Roosevelt
in the presidential race of 1912.

By 1910 "T. R." was making speeches in support of Progressive Republicans. It seemed clear to Taft that Roosevelt was going to run for the presidency again. The President said, "If you were to remove Roosevelt's skull now, you would find written on his brain '1912.'"

As the presidential election of 1912 approached, it looked as if the Taft Republicans were in trouble. The Progressive Republicans seemed determined to run their own candidate.

La Follette. The man who appeared likely to be the Progressive candidate was Senator Robert M. La Follette, of Wisconsin. Some of the reforms he had supported in his home state had become attractive to Americans in many parts of the country.

La Follette's popularity continued to grow, but early in 1912 he collapsed while delivering an important speech. Many Progressives became convinced that they must find another candidate. Of course, some were sure that Theodore Roosevelt would be available.

A few weeks after La Follette became ill, "T. R." announced: "My hat is in the ring" —meaning that he was available to be nominated. The Taft forces knew they would have a fight on their hands. And it would be some time before Taft and Roosevelt spoke to one another again.

Republican party breakup. The Republican convention met in Chicago. It proceeded to name Taft as its choice to head the party. "T. R." declared that the Taft people had stolen from *him* the votes which renominated their man.

Roosevelt's supporters now left the Republican party and formed their own, calling a separate convention. They chose Theodore Roosevelt to be their candidate. As the wildly cheering delegates shouted "Teddy, we want Teddy!" he accepted the nomination. The delegates paraded around singing "Onward, Christian Soldiers."

Bull Mooses. The party of "T. R." and his followers, the Progressive party, was nicknamed the Bull Moose party. This name grew out of one of Roosevelt's remarks on the eve of the convention, "I feel as fit as a bull moose."

"T. R." held before his enthusiastic supporters a vision of an America where nobody would be unemployed or poor. The Progressive-party platform called for many laws. Among them were special ones protecting women and children and providing for health insurance, inheritance and income taxes, farm relief, and woman suffrage. In its day the platform seemed quite revolutionary—it made many old-fashioned people gasp in horror.

1. Describe the events which led to the building of the Panama Canal by the United States. 2. What two advances in medicine resulted from the digging of the canal? 3. How did Roosevelt help Taft to become President? 4. What was the first mistake Taft made? 5. Name the candidates for the presidency in 1912. 6. What did the Progressives stand for?

He said this because the leadership of the Republican convention was in the hands of Taft supporters who refused to seat many of the Roosevelt delegates. (Out of 254 contested seats, only 19 were given to Roosevelt delegates.)

Reforming Reaches a Peak Under Wilson

While the Republicans were being split between those who wanted Taft and those
who wanted "T. R." back, the Democrats
were holding their convention. They knew
they had a chance to take advantage of the
deep split among the Republicans. What
they needed was a new standard-bearer.
Again, William Jennings Bryan was working hard for the nomination.

A Professor in Politics

But the Democrats at last chose as their
candidate the governor of New Jersey,
Woodrow Wilson. Wilson had been president of Princeton University before he became governor. And before that he had
been a professor, writing and teaching
about government.

His longtime goal. Wilson, born in Virginia in 1856, had been educated for a career as a lawyer. But his real ambition, he
had said, was to make his mark in politics.

Wilson never liked the work of a lawyer
and gave it up to teach in college. But he
never gave up his goal of succeeding as a
politician. For a while he thought he could
satisfy his desire to influence people by
teaching and by writing books and articles
on government. However, he finally decided that such activities could not fulfill
what he called his "longing to do immortal
work."

Wilson began to attract national attention about the time "T. R." became President. At Princeton he led a fight for what
he considered to be a more democratic
kind of student organization than already
existed. This fight—largely unsuccessful
—in the end led him to leave his university. He became a leader in the world of
politics because he expressed the needs and
hopes of so many Americans.

The "new freedom." Wilson's campaign
had one leading idea. It was that the country needed new laws to help people who

Wilson was nominated on
e forty-sixth ballot--partly
cause Bryan shifted his
pport to him.

In 1896 Woodrow Wilson—
far left—attended a family
gathering in Columbia, South
Carolina. His wife, Ellen,
holds their younger daughter, Eleanor, and their
older daughter, Margaret,
sits on the steps.

UPI

Taft may have been happy because the burden of the presidency could be set aside. He had written to a brother in 1911, "I am not very happy in this renomination and reelection business. I have to set my teeth and go through with it.... But I shall be willing to retire and let another take the burden."

Taft rides happily to the Capitol with President-elect Wilson on Inauguration Day in 1913.

were trying to get their feet on the bottom rung of life's ladder. He felt sure such laws should do something about reducing the control of big business over the country.

Wilson called the program he stood for the new freedom. Those who listened to him could tell that he admired the simpler world that had existed fifty years earlier. They believed that although he knew he could not turn the clock back to those days, he would hope to recapture some of their spirit.

Roosevelt's platform. In the campaign of 1912 "T. R." also talked about the evils of big business. Yet he would not rely on # breaking up big business, he said, but rather on government regulation of it.

Victory for the Democrats. Although Wilson—an excellent speaker—was well received, very likely it was not his ideas so much as the split in the Republican party that won him the presidency on Election Day. He captured only 42 percent of the vote, but in the three-cornered contest it was enough. Roosevelt was next, and Taft ran a poor third, carrying only two states.

A Variety of Results

A new kind of President took office on March 4, 1913. A scholarly, thoughtful man, full of high ideals and uplifting words, Woodrow Wilson had reached the goal he had set for himself as a mere youth.

Aided by a skillful Texan, Colonel Edward M. House, Wilson soon began to deal with some of the problems which had concerned people since the 1890's. In his inaugural address, he described what he thought had happened to America:

The great Government we loved has too often been made use of for private and selfish purposes, and those who used it had forgotten the people. . . . There has been something crude and heartless and unfeeling in our haste to succeed and be great. Our thought has been 'Let every man look out for himself.'

A new tariff. Wilson shortly made clear in a far-reaching series of proposals what he wanted to do. The first thing was to re-

574 #Note this difference in Roosevelt's and Wilson's views on big business: Roosevelt did not want to break up the trusts; he wanted to regulate them. Wilson, on the other hand, wanted to put an end to the trusts.

duce the tariff. The cost of living had risen sharply after 1897. There was a widespread belief that high prices—which hurt poor people more directly than anyone else—would drop if the tariff were less "protective." Like Taft, Wilson called a special session of Congress to deal with lowering it.

To emphasize how strongly he felt—and to take advantage of his great gift as a public speaker—he went before Congress personally to present his case. This was the first time since Thomas Jefferson's day that a president of the United States had communicated with the national legislature in any way but in writing.

Wilson's leadership brought results. Congress passed a sharply lowered tariff—reduced for the first time since the Civil War. It was a great personal victory for the President. He said proudly, "I have had the accomplishment of something like this at heart ever since I was a boy."

A new banking system. But Wilson did not rest after the tariff was lowered. He was ready to move also against the control over money and banking held by a few financial centers in the East. In short, he was attacking the great bankers of New York City.

After many delicate discussions, Congress passed the Federal Reserve Act before the end of 1913. It provided for dividing the United States into twelve banking districts, which were to have considerable power over the money and credit policies of banks. Now, for the first time since Jackson, the country had a banking system able to meet its needs.

New controls over big business. Before Wilson's term of office ended, a variety of new laws had been enacted. One of them, passed in 1914, created the Federal Trade Commission. The purpose of the FTC was to keep an eye on the methods used by big corporations in carrying on their business.

Another attempt to control big business was the Clayton Antitrust Act, also passed

Music Division, Library of Congress

The outside of the sheet music for a happy song Americans sang in the early 1900's.

in 1914. One of its chief provisions was that labor unions could not be prosecuted for being "conspiracies."

Other new beginnings. Congress also passed laws to control child labor and the number of hours worked by railroad employees, to provide easier loans for farmers, and to improve conditions aboard American merchant ships. These laws showed that the government was capable of taking care of particular problems in our country.

President Wilson was widely praised for his leadership. He liked to think, though, that what he had been able to bring about was the result of vigorous public support. In a way he was right. After so many years of talking about reform, people felt that the time had come to stop talking, and act.

By Wilson's time the laws that were passed seemed far less revolutionary than those some people had wanted in the early

Iave students find out which Federal Reserve district they live in. Where is the district's
eral Reserve bank located? Which of the banks in your community belong to the Federal
erve system?

575

part of Theodore Roosevelt's administration. The program of Wilson's "new freedom" completed the progressive work begun under Roosevelt's "square deal."

What had been accomplished, aside from the passage of a number of reform laws? Most important, the progressives had helped Americans through the trying years in which the rural United States had become industrialized. The horse-and-buggy days were ending, and the day of the automobile was beginning. The number of miles of railroad track in use was already decreasing, and the air age was getting under way. A once-simple world was being changed faster than most people liked.

Collier's was a popular magazine of the beginning of this century. It stated in its issue of January 24, 1914, "Fifty years from now the future historian will say that the ten years ending about January 1, 1914 was the period of the greatest . . . advance made by this nation in any decade."

No one questioned this judgment. Americans were confident that the country was making progress. Wasn't that, after all, the reason for the name "*progressive* period"? It was no wonder that a popular song of the day was the carefree tune "In the Good Old Summertime."

But before 1914 was over, a less carefree song was being heard—"I Didn't Raise My Boy to Be a Soldier." The work of removing evils in the United States, so well begun, was being interrupted by events far from our shores.

---

1. Give the main facts about Wilson's career before he became President. 2. Why was he elected President in 1912? 3. What kind of tariff was passed after he became President? 4. Name three laws aimed at controlling banking and big business which were enacted under Wilson's leadership.

Every age has its reformers. Ask students to indicate what the concerns of present-day reformers are. How do the conditions they are

The Workshop

working to change compare with those of the progressive period? What is the current attitude of the public toward reform?

The Shapers of Our World

Tell how each of the following contributed to the labeling of the years between 1900 and 1914 as the progressive era:

progressive movement	Seventeenth Amendment
Progress and Poverty	Pure Food and Drug Act
Jacob Riis	Meat Inspection Act
Upton Sinclair	Edward M. House
Jane Addams	Bull Moose party
Northern Securities case	Woodrow Wilson
Louis D. Brandeis	Federal Reserve System
Robert La Follette	"new freedom"
"square deal"	William C. Gorgas
Lincoln Steffens	William Howard Taft

Adding to Your Vocabulary

Use the following words to show your understanding of this chapter:

racked	direct primary
trademark	recall
conservation	referendum
muckrakers	city manager
tenement	isthmus
defied	malaria
sweatshops	yellow fever
initiative	

Thinking Things Through

After a review of the checkup exercises, answer the following questions:

1. What was the contribution of the

muckrakers to the forming of public opinion in their day? Why was this opinion so important?

2. How did Roosevelt's idea of the role of government concerning business and labor compare with Cleveland's, McKinley's, and Wilson's?

3. How do the referendum and the initiative transfer a part of legislative power directly to the people?

4. Why did other Latin American countries—not just Colombia—distrust the United States after the Panama revolt?

5. Taft's administration was responsible for more progressive legislation than Theodore Roosevelt's. Even so, people accused him of being unfaithful to progressive ideas. Why?

6. Compare the platforms of the Progressive party in 1912 and the Populist party in 1892. What similarities are there? What differences?

7. Why is a split in a political party a sure cause of defeat in an election? Name two presidential elections whose outcomes illustrate your answer.

8. Why was Wilson more successful than Taft in winning a reduction in the tariff?

9. What was the basic contribution of the progressives to American life?

Democracy's Continuing Growth

1. What groups of Americans were especially in need of help in the late nineteenth century? Why were they unable to look out for themselves? Why were their situations a blot on democracy's record in the United States?

2. What steps were taken that aimed to help members of the unfortunate groups?

3. How did the Wisconsin idea contribute to the growth of democracy?

4. Why are the direct primary, the initiative, the recall, and the referendum called tools for democracy?

5. Explain how the Sixteenth and Seventeenth amendments showed that American democracy was still growing.

Sharpening Your Map Skills

1. An American warship, the *Oregon*, was at San Francisco when the Spanish-American War broke out. It took 71 days to make the trip around Cape Horn to the war scene.

On a globe measure the distance the *Oregon* traveled from San Francisco to Cuba. Then measure the distance it would have traveled if the Panama Canal had been open to ships in that year. How many miles would the use of the canal have saved? How much time would have been saved?

2. Look at the map on page 568. A vessel entering the canal today from the Pacific side travels in what direction to reach the Caribbean?

Your Opinion, Please

1. What is your opinion of the way the United States obtained the Panama Canal Zone? Do you think that the results justified the method used?

2. Do you think that the American respect for the individual person was undermined in the progressive era by the need to protect the public?

3. What would the framers of the Constitution have said about the Sixteenth and Seventeenth amendments?

What is the proper role of government in a largely urban, industrialized society? What is the   577
per balance between individual freedom and the needs of the community? These remain
ic questions in our time.

##Crops, particularly wheat, are raised, especially in the

Part Seven Workshop

northern Great Plains. L: stock is also raised.

Reaching to the Present

1. How did the United States gain possession of: (*a*) Alaska and Hawaii, (*b*) the Philippines, (*c*) Puerto Rico, and (*d*) the Panama Canal Zone? Describe the relationship of each to the United States today. Do these various relationships bring credit to Americans? Explain.

2. Name some city problems today which existed in the progressive era. Which ones were solved? How? Name some new city problems. What is being done to solve both the new ones and the remaining old ones?

3. Compare the President in the White House today with Theodore Roosevelt and Woodrow Wilson in feeling about reform. What reforms has the present chief executive brought about? What ones is he working for?

4. What kinds of farming are there on the Great Plains today? Were the problems people in that region had in the late nineteenth century finally solved? How? What new problems have arisen in this century? How are they being solved?

Time and Change

Review the time line on pages 470–471 and answer these questions:

1. Part Seven covers what century or centuries? What years? What decades?

2. Identify the following changes that took place in the period: (*a*) two in the means of communication, (*b*) one in lighting, (*c*) one in the method of electing United States Senators, (*d*) two affecting public health, (*e*) two in the way big business was treated by the federal government, (*f*) three in life on the Great

Plains, and (*g*) three in the ownership o: islands in the Caribbean and the Pacific

The Book Shelf

Adams, Andy. *Trail Drive; a True Narrative of Cowboy Life*, ed. Glen Rounds From the author's *Log of a Cowboy* New York: Holiday House, 1965. (A story of a cattle drive from Mexico to Montana in the 1880's.)

Arnold, Pauline, and White, Percival. *How We Named Our States*. New York: Criterion Books, Inc., 1966. (Tells how the state names and nicknames developed.)

Burlingame, Roger. *Out of Silence into Sound*. New York: The Macmillan Co. Publishers, 1964. (A biography of Alexander Graham Bell.)

Cooke, David C. *Apache Warrior*. New York: W. W. Norton & Co., Inc., Publishers, 1963. (The struggle of the Apache to resist the onrush of white settlers.)

Durham, Philip, and Jones, Everett L. *The Negro Cowboys*. New York: Dodd, Mead & Co., Inc., 1965. (The contributions of Negro cowboys in the building of the West.)

Fanning, Leonard M. *Titans of Business*. Philadelphia: J. B. Lippincott Co., 1964. (Seven biographies of well-known American businessmen.)

Gies, Joseph. *Stars of the Series; a Complete History of the World Series*. New York: Thomas Y. Crowell Co., 1964. (Covers the World Series of baseball in detail.)

Veith, Ilza, and Zimmerman, Leo M. *American Medicine*, Bks. 1 and 2. Chicago: Rand McNally & Co., 1967. (The development of American medicine.)

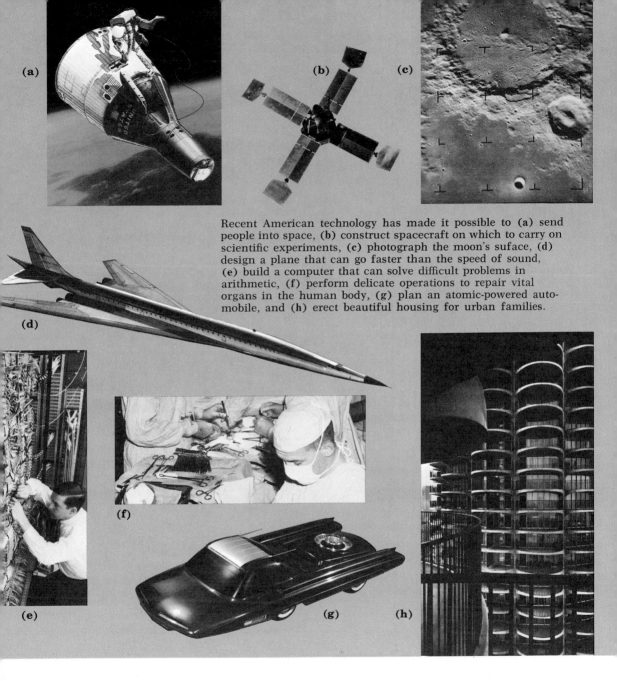

Recent American technology has made it possible to **(a)** send people into space, **(b)** construct spacecraft on which to carry on scientific experiments, **(c)** photograph the moon's suface, **(d)** design a plane that can go faster than the speed of sound, **(e)** build a computer that can solve difficult problems in arithmetic, **(f)** perform delicate operations to repair vital organs in the human body, **(g)** plan an atomic-powered automobile, and **(h)** erect beautiful housing for urban families.

Part Eight:
This opening illustrates achievements of technology which are current or which will be shortly. The plane is a supersonic one.

IN DEFENSE OF FREEDOM

Picture e shows part of the intricate insides of a computer; f, a complicated operation in Houston, Texas; g, a model of a forthcoming car; and h, Marina Towers in Chicago, the circular apartment buildings which give the residents the circular balconies seen here.

This part tells about two world wars and two wars limited to Asia.

Part Eight:
IN DEFENSE OF FREEDOM

Continued on facing page

Have students find on the time line the years when fighting in defense of freedom occurred.

WITH A MIGHTY INHERITANCE

The defense of freedom has always been the chief business of American patriots. In the twentieth century serious threats from abroad have made this task far heavier than in the past. The perils have had to be met by the sacrifices and often the lifeblood of patriots in uniform—GI's.

The grim work of the GI's has taken them to every continent and into every climate. Twice they have struggled to hold back the tide of aggression in Europe, three times in Asia. They stand on duty today at Amer-

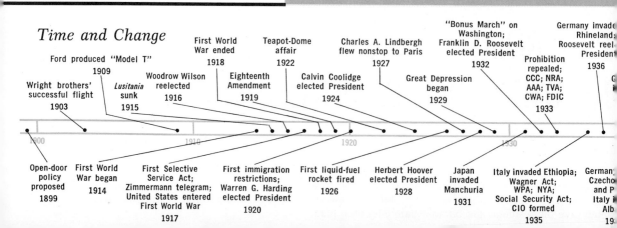

Time and Change

Wright brothers' successful flight
1903

Ford produced "Model T"
1909

Lusitania sunk
1915

Woodrow Wilson reelected
1916

First World War ended
1918

Eighteenth Amendment
1919

Teapot-Dome affair
1922

Calvin Coolidge elected President
1924

Charles A. Lindbergh flew nonstop to Paris
1927

Great Depression began
1929

"Bonus March" on Washington; Franklin D. Roosevelt elected President
1932

Prohibition repealed; CCC; NRA; AAA; TVA; CWA; FDIC
1933

Germany invade Rhineland; Roosevelt reel President
1936

1900   1910   1920   1930

Open-door policy proposed
1899

First World War began
1914

First Selective Service Act; Zimmermann telegram; United States entered First World War
1917

First immigration restrictions; Warren G. Harding elected President
1920

First liquid-fuel rocket fired
1926

Herbert Hoover elected President
1928

Japan invaded Manchuria
1931

Italy invaded Ethiopia; Wagner Act; WPA; NYA; Social Security Act; CIO formed
1935

German Czecho and P Italy Alb
19

can outposts stretching around the world.

There is no single typical GI, for GI's come from every race and from every part of the country. They are the sons of poor parents and of those who are well-to-do. They were born in the city as well as on the farm.

General Douglas MacArthur, an outstanding commander of American troops in three wars, proudly offered this judgment of the GI: "When I think of his patience under adversity [that is, when things go badly], of his courage under fire, and of his modesty in victory, I am filled with an emotion of admiration I cannot put into words."

Yet in spite of bravery and devotion, fighting men alone do not and cannot keep a free people free. This the people must do themselves. The GI's cannot do more than fend off the enemies from without.

General Dwight D. Eisenhower, another triumphant leader of GI's, once talked of the defense of freedom in this way. He said it is not to be compared to the winning of a game—with the victory recorded forever in history. Freedom has its life in the hearts, the actions, the spirit of men and so it must be daily earned and refreshed—else like a flower cut from its life-giving roots, it will wither and die."

So, when the GI goes forth into battle, as sometimes he must, he is the best-equipped fighter in the world. His countrymen provide him with the finest supplies they can obtain. But also he is armed with a mighty inheritance. It is the habit of living in freedom, which Americans long ago learned to prize and improve upon steadily—and which they intend to keep, whatever the cost.

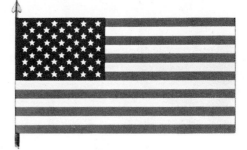

The fifty-star flag—representing the original thirteen states and the others added throughout the nation's history.

Discuss what it means to "live in freedom," something Americans too often take for granted because they are accustomed to it.

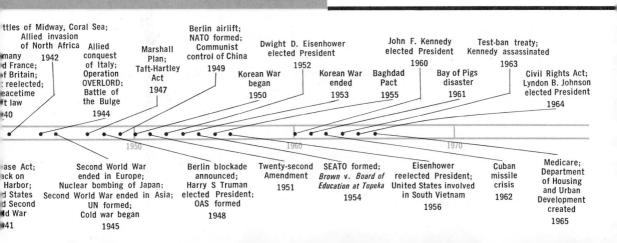

ttles of Midway, Coral Sea; Allied invasion of North Africa
1942

many
d France;
f Britain;
reelected;
eacetime
ft law
40

Allied conquest of Italy; Operation OVERLORD; Battle of the Bulge
1944

Marshall Plan; Taft-Hartley Act
1947

Berlin airlift; NATO formed; Communist control of China
1949

Korean War began
1950

Dwight D. Eisenhower elected President
1952

Korean War ended
1953

Baghdad Pact
1955

John F. Kennedy elected President
1960

Bay of Pigs disaster
1961

Test-ban treaty; Kennedy assassinated
1963

Civil Rights Act; Lyndon B. Johnson elected President
1964

1950   1960   1970

ase Act;
ck on
Harbor;
d States
Second
d War
41

Second World War ended in Europe; Nuclear bombing of Japan; Second World War ended in Asia; UN formed; Cold war began
1945

Berlin blockade announced; Harry S Truman elected President; OAS formed
1948

Twenty-second Amendment
1951

SEATO formed; *Brown v. Board of Education at Topeka*
1954

Eisenhower reelected President; United States involved in South Vietnam
1956

Cuban missile crisis
1962

Medicare; Department of Housing and Urban Development created
1965

(a)

(b)

(a) Ships of the United States fleet passing through the Strait of Magellan (see page 30) on the trip around the world planned by Theodore Roosevelt in 1907. (b) The Democrats used this truck to drum up votes for Woodrow Wilson in his second presidential campaign, in 1916. (c) A poster which helped stir Americans' patriotism and sell Liberty Bonds in the First World War.

VOTE FOR WILSON AND MARSHALL SEABURY AND McCOMBS

FOR PRESIDENT

WOODROW WILSON

WOMENS BUREAU
DEMOCRATIC NATIONAL COMMITTEE

WHO BROKE THE MONEY TRUST?
WHO KEEPS US OUT OF WAR?
WHO STANDS FOR THE 8 HOUR DAY?
WHO EXTENDED THE PARCEL POST?
WHO GAVE THE FARMER RURAL CREDITS?

VOTE FOR WILSON
PEACE WITH HONOR
PROSPERITY
PREPAREDNESS

Our Daddy is fighting at the Front for You—
Back him up— Buy a United States Gov't Bond of the
2nd LIBERTY LOAN
of 1917

(c)

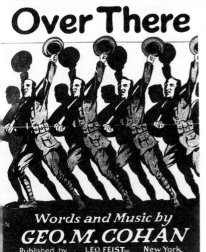

Over There

Words and Music by
GEO. M. COHAN
Published by · LEO. FEISTᵢₙc. New York

(d)

(e)

(d) More than two million copies of this rousing marching song were sold, and its composer won a gold Congressional Medal.
(e) Each honorably discharged American soldier received a button like this after the war.

Each of the illustrations on pp. 582 and 583 indicates American involvement in or concern with foreign affairs. Expand on the concept of the United States as an active world power.

CHAPTER 26

WAGING WAR "OVER THERE"

is chapter focuses on foreign affairs from 1900 to 1919. Included are comments on American policies in in America and in Asia as well as a thorough account of our nation's role in the First World War. As y read the chapter, students should consider whether or not Americans carried the reform spirit of the gressive period into their relations with the rest of the world.

AMERICANS of the progressive years— even those whose lives were hard—felt safe from foreign enemies. Bounded on both the north and the south by countries which did not threaten it, and on the east

and the west by wide oceans, the nation seemed protected. America was like one of those great European castles of the Middle Ages, surrounded by a moat which no enemy could cross.

how changes in technology have made natural features--mountains, oceans, etc.--meaningless tective barriers.

The Nation Prospers Without Alliances

The United States' geographical location had long had a marked influence on its relations with other countries. Americans came to believe that this location made it possible for them to stay out of the struggles of the Old World.

Looking Across the Atlantic

The Founding Fathers—especially Washington—had warned their fellow citizens against becoming involved in conflicts in Europe. (Nobody dreamed that we would ever be involved in war in Asia.)

Thomas Jefferson had expressed a deep

wish of the people in his first inaugural address. He had proposed that Americans encourage "peace, commerce, and honest friendship with all nations, entangling alliances with none." The Monroe Doctrine (see page 314) had also stated a popular desire in its pledge that the United States would not take part in the international affairs of the European countries.

Because of their seemingly safe location, in short, Americans were sure that they needed no alliances with other countries of the world. They believed that they could live in isolation—that is, take little part in the affairs of other nations.

Briefly review the history of United States relations with European countries. Discuss whether not the United States was ever able to stay out of major European struggles. (Consider our empts to avoid involvement in the Napoleonic wars, for example.)

A beginning republic. The policy of isolation was an excellent one for a weak republic struggling to live in a world of warring kings. Even when the United States became stronger, Americans thought it best to stay out of European troubles, at least not to form alliances in Europe.

An older republic. By the end of the nineteenth century, the foreign policy of the United States—the policy it carried out in dealing with other countries—was still like that of Washington, Jefferson, and Monroe. Nevertheless, a person did not have to be very clever to see that a good many changes were taking place.

One change was the vast growth of international trade, the effects of which were felt on the farms as well as in the factories. The farmers of the Middle West, for example, liked to think they had turned their backs on Europe forever. Actually they depended on the whole world for their markets, and they were quickly affected by whatever went on "over there"—in Europe.

A second change was the growth of a red-hot feeling of *nationalism*—that is, deep patriotism and a desire to make the country more powerful. In 1898–1899 this nationalism had led the United States to acquire overseas possessions.

A change in outlook. As a result of the two developments, the nation—very slowly —began to change its attitude toward its relations with other countries. Theodore Roosevelt, especially, saw that isolation was no longer satisfactory. He said, "I wish that all Americans would realize that American politics is world politics; that # we are and that we shall be involved in all great questions [in the world]."

Reaching into the World

In their relations with Latin America, Americans saw best how deeply they were involved in world affairs. Cuba especially drew their attention.

To the utter surprise of the European countries, the United States kept its promise to give independence to Cuba. But first the American government made Cuba agree to certain special arrangements.

Cuba was to sell or lease to the United States places for naval and coaling stations where American ships could stop for repairs and refueling. (The chief station became Guantánamo naval base.) The United States was to keep the right to take action in Cuba to preserve order and protect the independence of the island.

Involvement in Cuba. In 1906 a revolution brought a call from Cuba for United States troops to help restore order. "T. R.," who was President then, sent the troops, but he was angry that he had to do this. He feared that his action would convince people in South America that we wished to interfere in their affairs. Unfortunately, in the next few years the United States felt forced to act in a number of Latin American countries.

An international policeman. Many Latin Americans, naturally, were displeased over the role that the "big brother" to the north was playing. In their view the United States was bullying them. The United States, however, believed that it had to be the "policeman" of the Latin American countries, arguing that Latin Americans were not able to manage their affairs by themselves.

The "policeman" had become so strong by 1904 that it would not allow some European nations to try to collect debts the Dominican Republic owed them. (The Dominican Republic occupies the eastern half of Hispaniola.) The United States declared, however, that it would collect the money for them. The aim of President Roosevelt, of course, was to prevent any European power from gaining a foothold in the New World.

But the Latin American nations did not appreciate the conduct of their "big

##In 1934 the United States formally gave up its right to intervene in Cuban affairs. This action was part of an attempt during Franklin D. Roosevelt's presidency to overcome the bitterness that many Latin Americans felt toward the United States.

ance, Germany, Russia, and Japan each had
lusive trading rights in parts of China.
brother." In time they became outraged
by his viewpoint. They maintained that
the Monroe Doctrine had been changed.
Formerly its purpose had been to keep
European countries out of the New World.
Now, they said, it was being used to excuse
United States interference in Latin American affairs.

The open-door policy. Toward Asia, too,
the United States had begun to develop a
new policy. In 1899 it had urged the countries that had won trading privileges in
parts of China to agree to allow all nations
to trade equally there. This became known
as the *open-door policy*.

Americans had long kept their eyes on
trade with China. The tremendous population of China suggested a possible huge
market for American goods. Furthermore,
many American missionaries were hoping
that hundreds of millions of Chinese would
become Christians.

When Russia and Japan seemed to be
making moves into the northern part of
China at the beginning of the twentieth
century, the United States was greatly
concerned. It was even more worried when
war broke out in 1904 between Russia and
Japan. If one of those countries beat the
other badly, it might then feel strong
enough to seize a piece of China.

Helping end a war. Because the United
States wanted to prevent a loss of Chinese
territory, Americans worked for a settlement to end the war before either Russia
or Japan was a clear winner. Theodore
Roosevelt served as a *mediator*—that is, a
go-between—in ending the war. For his
work he became in 1906 the first American
to win the Nobel Peace Prize.

The white fleet's journey. Roosevelt, trying hard to play one power off against
another in East Asia, decided that Japan
was growing too strong. As a result, in
1908 he sent the United States fleet—the
great white fleet—on a "good-will trip"
around the world.

Underwood & Underwood

President Roosevelt (*center*) meets with two
Russian delegates (*left*) and two Japanese
representatives at a conference he called at
Portsmouth, New Hampshire, in 1905 to bring
peace between Russia and Japan.

The President aimed especially to show
Japan and other powerful countries that
this country had a strong navy. In effect,
he was saying to the world that the United
States hoped to remain at peace with other
nations but was not afraid of any of them.

Making up with Britain. The United
States depended heavily in Europe on a
growing friendship with Britain. The two
countries had at last put aside their old
anger at one another, having discovered
it was to their advantage to coöperate.

Because Britain had the largest navy in
the world and the American navy was
growing steadily, the United States felt
doubly safe. Nevertheless, it was disturbing
for Americans to hear that the European
powers were all trying to build better armies
and navies than their neighbors. A misstep
could lead to war.

The most thoughtful Americans realized
that the United States had little to fear
from a war in Europe. But they suspected

Note a major difference between American policies in Asia and in Latin America. In Asia
United States tried to balance one power against another, but in Latin America it dominated
airs. Ask students to account for this difference.

585

that if Britain should be beaten in such a war, then we might be directly involved. For in that case the victorious country— and it would likely be Germany—might take over British possessions in America, something the Monroe Doctrine forbade.

Some disarmament conferences. To help keep peace in the world, the United States was willing to take a number of measures —but not to enter into alliances with other countries to stop wars. Twice, in 1899 and 1907, the United States took part in international conferences in the Netherlands. These meetings were intended to control the movement among the countries of Europe to rearm. The gatherings accomplished practically nothing.

"Dollar diplomacy." When Taft became President in 1909, he did not take as active a part in foreign affairs as "T. R." had. But he was no less devoted to defending American interests. His administration is known as the one that first used *"dollar diplomacy."*

"Dollar diplomacy" meant the spreading of American influence in the world without using force. American bankers were encouraged to loan money to governments and persons in various parts of the world in order to gain friends for America.

1. What policy in foreign affairs had the young United States carried out? 2. Name two changes which gave the country a new outlook on its foreign policy. 3. Describe the relations between the United States and the Latin American countries in the early twentieth century. 4. What was the open-door policy and how did it develop? 5. Tell about the policy President Taft began.

Wilson Seeks a World Safe for Democracy

But despite the activities of their country in world affairs, most Americans in the early part of the twentieth century did not give much deep thought to these matters. People busy wiping out the evils the progressives had pointed out could not believe foreign relations were important. President Woodrow Wilson did not even mention them in his first inaugural address.

Furthermore, millions of immigrants had left European countries for America because of persecution, a lack of opportunity, and compulsory military service. To them, having anything to do with Europe seemed downright wrong.

Troubles in Mexico

In 1913, just as Woodrow Wilson was taking office, trouble broke out across the southern border of the United States. A revolution two years before in Mexico had overthrown a government that had been in power for more than thirty years.

Opposing a dictator. In the fierce struggle that followed the revolution, a cold-blooded man of violence, Victoriano Huerta (wĕr′tä), had risen to power in Mexico. In 1913 Wilson refused to recognize him, considering him a dictator. Said the President, "I am going to teach the South American republics to elect good men!" Wilson was saying that the United States was setting itself up as a kind of judge of the leaders of other countries.

Wilson continued to criticize Huerta, calling him a desperate brute and demanding that he get out of the Mexican government. When words alone seemingly did not affect him, the United States allowed Huerta's rivals for power in Mexico to receive weapons.

Compare Wilson's refusal to recognize the Huerta government with the American refusal to recognize the Communist government that took over China in 1949. What is the importance of nonrecognition? Discuss its effectiveness as a form of criticism.

Underwood & Underwood

Left: The ruins in Columbus, New Mexico, after Pancho Villa and his men had raided it. An American soldier stands guard on the ground where the Commercial Hotel had stood and where six Americans had died. *Right:* General Pershing beside his automobile on his expedition to Mexico.

Many Americans were disturbed. Some who had invested money in Mexico believed that the President could be influenced to recognize Huerta in order to protect their property. They were mistaken.

Pancho Villa on the loose. Huerta finally lost his position as head of the Mexican government—and the trouble seemed at an end. But the Mexicans were torn by new difficulties.

Huerta was followed in office by Venustiano Carranza, who called himself a reformer. Carranza could not handle his right-hand man, a bandit named Pancho Villa. Villa showed his feeling toward the United States by killing seventeen Americans in a raid into New Mexico.

Pershing on the chase. Wilson acted immediately. He ordered General John J. Pershing to take American soldiers into Mexico and punish Villa. Although Pershing came close to capturing Villa, the expedition in a short time became really a wild-goose chase. In January, 1917, Wilson, facing more serious problems with Germany, withdrew Pershing and his men.

Explosion in Europe

Wilson's experience with Mexico was his first taste of the difficulties caused by foreign affairs. He was soon struggling with unforeseen events across the Atlantic Ocean, too.

The great powers of western Europe by 1914 had for 35 years been building up their military power in a furious rivalry with each other. Several times it had appeared that war was about to break out. Europe seemed like a powder keg as the year 1914 opened. President Wilson's chief adviser, Colonel Edward M. House, said: "It only needs a spark to set the whole thing off."

A royal assassination. The spark was provided in 1914, in the little town of Sarajevo, in Bosnia (see the map, page 593). On June 28 the Austrian archduke Franz Ferdinand and the archduchess, who were visiting there, were assassinated by a visiting Serbian patriot—who deeply hated the Austrians.

Bosnia, which is part of present-day Yugoslavia, belonged to Austria. Serbians hoped to form a Slavic state in southern Europe by taking over Bosnia and other territory belonging to Austria. Their hopes were fulfilled to an extent when Yugoslavia was created at the end of the war.

Theodore Roosevelt speaks in 1915 at an army officers' training camp. Criticizing Wilson's neutrality, he favored # joining the Allies.

The fiery furnace. A month later Austria declared war on Serbia, and Austria's ally, Germany, followed suit. Russia came into the war on the side of Serbia, and France, a member of an alliance with Russia, did also. When German soldiers marched toward France, they began to cross neutral Belgium. Britain then entered the war on the side of France.

It was now early August, 1914. The First World War had begun. Before it ended in November, 1918, the fighting had spread to 30 countries, and over eight million men had died in action or of wounds. More than twenty-one million wounded men lived, although as many as one-third were permanently disabled.

Most Americans at first thought that the fighting in Europe was none of their business. As they watched the European nations slip into war, most rejoiced that this country had made no alliances with European countries. As a Chicago newspaper put it, "Peace-loving citizens of this country will now rise up and tender [give] a hearty vote of thanks to Columbus for having discovered America."

A position of neutrality. Most Americans probably favored the Allies—as France, England, and Russia were called. Yet President Wilson urged Americans to be neutral in their thinking as well as in their actions. (This was hard to do. Wilson himself burst out at one point, "England is fighting our fight.")

The blockade and the submarine. Bu whatever hopes the President had that the war would not touch this country were soon gone. Britain established a nava blockade of Germany, which meant that neutral ships—particularly American ones —would be stopped on the high seas. The British often forced a ship that had been stopped by its navy to go to the neares port, because it could not be inspected or the spot.

The suspicion developed in some places in the United States that Britain was trying to use the war to hurt American trade. To a great many Americans the situation seemed like the one in the years before the War of 1812. Wilson himself felt very close to James Madison—the other Princeton graduate who as President had faced the problem of how to remain neutral in a world at war.

The Germans, too, were interfering with American commerce. They were using submarines in order to sink ships taking goods to England. Under the old rules of warfare a ship stopped at sea would have been boarded and searched. But submarines are easily destroyed by the shots of enemy ships. They rely for their own safety on hit-and-run attacks. Once a submarine fires its torpedoes, it flees.

From the beginning of the submarine attacks, government officials in Washington held their breath. The day would surely come when the Germans would sink an

##Compare the attempts of the United States to remain neutral in the First World War with its attempts to do the same during the period before the War of 1812. In what ways was the world status of the United States in 1914 different from what it had been in the early 1800's?

American vessel. The Department of State warned the German government that the United States would hold it responsible for whatever happened.

Some American lives were lost on British ships that were sent to the bottom of the sea. The Germans warned that Americans sailed on Allied vessels only at their own risk. But Wilson boldly declared that Americans could travel anywhere—even on the ships of warring countries.

The sinking of the *Lusitania.* Then a terrible disaster occurred. On May 7, 1915, the British passenger liner *Lusitania*, traveling off the Irish coast, was struck by a German torpedo. The vessel sank within a few minutes, carrying 1198 people with it—128 of them Americans. It was one of the greatest sea disasters in history.

The Germans said that the ship had been sunk because it was carrying ammunition and, therefore, had lost the protection it would have had as an unarmed ship. The *New York Times* demanded that the United States inform the Germans that they "shall no longer make war like savages drunk with blood." And the *New York*

Tribune declared, "The nation which remembered the sailors of the *Maine* will not forget the civilians of the *Lusitania!*"

But Wilson hoped to quiet the nation. "There is," he said calmly, "such a thing as a man being too proud to fight."

Those words "too proud to fight" were seized upon by the President's enemies, who said he was afraid to fight. Theodore Roosevelt (whose youngest son would later be killed in action in the war) was especially angry.

German promises. For almost two years diplomatic notes went back and forth between the United States and Germany. In the end Germany agreed to be responsible for the loss of American lives aboard the *Lusitania* and to pay a sum of money as damages. Meanwhile it had promised that passenger liners would not be sunk by submarines without warning and without protecting the lives of the passengers.

The following year a German submarine sank another unarmed ship—this time a freight vessel—also causing a loss of American lives. The United States again was aroused.

Below: The *Lusitania*, photographed in late 1914. *Right:* The warning that appeared in New York newspapers before the ship sailed.

(Ship) UPI; (Warning) Cunard Line

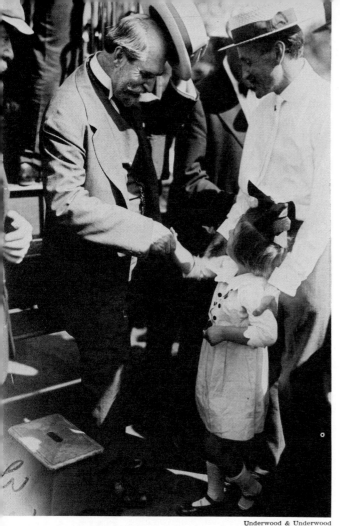

Underwood & Underwood

Charles Evans Hughes, campaigning for the presidency in 1916, steps down from his railroad car to greet an admirer at Red Wing, Minnesota.

Wilson informed Germany that if it continued to carry on submarine warfare in reckless fashion, the United States would be forced to break diplomatic relations. # Germany seemed to pledge that it would thereafter respect human life aboard freight-carrying ships—as well as aboard passenger ships.

Preparing the country. At first Wilson was against taking any steps to prepare the United States for war, for fear he might make America seem less neutral. By 1916, however, he had changed his mind. He declared, "America cannot be an

##"T. R." was willing to run, but the Republican party regulars would not have him. ostrich with its head in the sand. America cannot shut itself out from the rest of the world. . . . Do you want the situation to be such that all the President can do is write messages to utter words of protest?"

"He kept us out of war." But Wilson avoided involving the United States in the fighting. In 1916 he ran for reelection on the popular slogan "He kept us out of war." His rival was Charles Evans Hughes— whose slogan was "America first and America efficient." Hughes, the last major American politician to wear a beard, had stepped down from his position as a justice of the Supreme Court to accept the Republican nomination.

Wilson received the support of many progressives who thought his administration had accomplished some good things. "T. R." and many of his Bull Moose followers, however, had gone back to the Republican party. The result was a very close election—so close, in fact, that Hughes went to sleep on election night thinking that he had been elected President! But Wilson won the office, for a second time.

Thoughts for the future. In 1916 Wilson began to think that America might be able to lead the world along a new road to peace. He said, "The interests of all nations are our own also. We are partners with the rest. What affects mankind is . . . our affair as well as the affair of the nations of Europe and of Asia."

The President spoke of his hope that every nation could have its own land and that the territory of small countries might be as well respected as that of large ones. Yet even though Wilson was thinking of the future, he realized that the United States might have to fight in the war.

Trying to end the bloodshed. At the close of 1916, Wilson made an effort to bring together the two warring sides in Europe to discuss stopping the fighting—without success. The truth of the matter was that

#Note that Germany seemed anxious to keep the United States out of the war. To do so, the Germans were willing for a time to restrict the activities of their submarines. Why were they concerned about the United States?

the Allies were losing the war. For that reason it was a poor time to try to get the Germans to quit fighting.

Failing to end the war, Wilson in January, 1917, made a plea for a settlement in which neither side would triumph—a "peace without victory," he called it. He also asked for a "league—a union—of nations" to help make possible coöperation among peoples. These were new ideas to most countries.

The Kaiser's risk. Meanwhile the German government, headed by a ruler called the Kaiser (kī′zər), was making plans. He and his military advisers believed that the Allies were tottering and that a push in 1917 would end the war. To bring about the finish, they intended to go back to submarine warfare that was not limited by the promises they had made. The Kaiser knew that in following such a course of action he would be risking a declaration of war by the United States.

The Zimmermann telegram. Arthur Zimmermann, German Secretary of Foreign Affairs, telegraphed the German spokesman in Mexico City to seek an alliance with Mexico if war with the United States broke out. Zimmermann told his man to offer the Mexicans as bribes the states of New Mexico, Arizona, and Texas.

The publication of the Zimmermann telegram on March 1, 1917, caused much excitement in the United States. The feeling ran especially high in the Middle West, where many people had felt that the war did not concern Americans.

Announcement by Berlin. On January 31, 1917, the German ambassador in Washington informed the United States government that Germany was withdrawing its promise to guard against sinking unarmed vessels. The United States, though, would be allowed to send one ship a week to Europe. The Germans would keep hands off that vessel provided it was carefully marked and did not carry war supplies.

A break in relations. The President broke off diplomatic relations with Germany, but he said he could not believe that the German government would carry out unrestricted submarine warfare. Germany, nevertheless, went ahead with its plans. Between February 3 and April 1, its submarines sank eight American vessels. Before February was over, the President had asked Congress for authority to arm American freight-carrying vessels.

A group of Senators whom Wilson angrily criticized attempted to block passage of this bill. Their argument was that it would be better for America to have "peace at any price" than to take part in a shooting war. But Wilson won out.

Asking Congress to act. Wilson now called Congress into special session. Before both houses sitting together, the President on April 2, 1917, asked the members to recognize that war had been "thrust" upon the United States. He said we would be

ent in secret code, the Zimmermann message was intercepted and decoded by the British, who passed the information on to the Americans.

Americans drafted for service line up at one of the army camps.

UPI

fighting "for the rights of nations great and small and the privilege of men everywhere to choose their way of life. . . . The world must be made safe for democracy."

Some reasons why. The American people as a whole were not really prepared to fight for such high aims as Wilson expressed. They were, however, furious at Germany for the loss of American lives on the high seas and for the boldness of the Zimmermann proposal. Moreover, they had been shocked over the cruel way the Germans had marched into tiny Belgium.

Most Americans probably accepted, also, the idea of being joined with England and France—the underdogs in the war. They probably believed, too, that if Germany won the war the United States would be seriously threatened. Above all, Americans wanted the defeat of Germany.

But the public was not bloodthirsty. It hoped that the war would in the long run become an aid to world peace by being a "war to end war."

For all these reasons, the country was united behind the President. On April 6, 1917, Congress declared war on Germany.

The Doughboys in France

At the time of the declaration of war, the United States Army contained only a few more than two hundred thousand men. Our air strength consisted of 55 planes that were mainly out-of-date and 35 pilots. The navy was being rebuilt. Our factories were not organized to produce materials for a full-scale war.

The draft. But the country quickly began the task of meeting the requirements of war. In May, 1917, the first Selective Service Act in American history was passed. By fall the first of over three million draftees had entered the service. Over four million men would finally serve in the army, and more than half a million in the navy.

The most popular song of the day was the snappy tune "Over There." Written by a stage star, George M. Cohan, its words stirred the nation:

> Over there—over there—
> Send the word, send the word
>   over there—
> That the Yanks are coming, the
>   Yanks are coming,
> The drums rum-tumming ev'rywhere . . . .

Pershing in command. The commanding general of the United States troops in Europe was John J. Pershing. He was a handsome West Point graduate who had a determined-looking jaw which seemed the very symbol of the nation's iron will.

When Pershing and his staff left for Europe, he was under strict orders to keep the United States troops a separate fighting unit. This meant that American soldiers were not merely to be assigned to the British and French armies to replace the heavy losses they were suffering.

Never before had the United States prepared for war on such a scale and so quickly. It poured into the war not only man power but also huge quantities of food and other supplies.

Hoover's work. Wilson appointed Herbert Hoover, a mining engineer who earlier had organized relief for Belgium, to develop a food-saving program. The nation cut down on its eating of meat and bread and taught itself not to waste food. Many Americans learned for the first time how to grow their own vegetables as they raised "war gardens," sometimes on their front lawns.

To make sure that supplies were delivered to the men on the battlefields, the American army put forth enormous effort and energy. In France it built wharves and piers and laid over a thousand miles of railroad track.

The first American soldiers went into action before October, 1917, was over. By the end of the year, United States troops

##"Food will win the war," became a wartime slogan. Efforts were also made to save fuel. For example, daylight saving was introduced to cut down on the need for electricity during the work day. "Gasless" Sundays saved gasoline and oil, and "heatless" Mondays saved coal.

s a result, Russia (the U.S.S.R. after 1917) k no part in the peace conference.

were arriving in France at a rate of about fifty thousand a month.

About half a million American men were in France by May, 1918, and their numbers were increasing daily. General Pershing found himself under very heavy pressure to place additional soldiers into battle.

By the spring of 1918, Russia had withdrawn from the war. A revolution there had overthrown the ruler, and shortly Communists had taken charge. The Germans now were free to transfer their eastern troops to the west, facing France. They organized a drive on the city of Paris to end the war quickly.

At that point Pershing went to see the French commanding general. He declared, "I am here to say that the American people would consider it a great honor for our troops to be engaged in the present battle. . . . All that we have are yours."

As a result, an American unit was given a position to defend outside Paris. (One of the officers in charge of planning the defense was Colonel George C. Marshall. As we will see, in a later war he would become an American hero.)

Cantigny. At Cantigny (kän tē nyē′), near Paris, the Americans drove out the

UPI

Above: One of the women who took jobs in factories to help win the war.
Below: Where Americans fought in the war.

IRELAND

BRITAIN

NORTH SEA

NETHERLANDS

+ LUSITANIA
SINKING
MAY 7, 1915

ATLANTIC

OCEAN

English Channel

Strait of Dover

Calais

Ghent • Antwerp
B·ELGIUM
Brussels

Armentières

GERMANY

The First World War
in 1918

0 20 40 60 80 100 120 miles

Cantigny

Somme R.

Oise R.

Sedan

LUXEMBOURG

ALLIES' LINE IN NOV. 1918

BELLEAU
WOOD

ARGONNE
FOREST

Metz

Versailles • Paris

LIMIT OF GERMAN ADVANCE

Château-
Thierry

Marne

St.
Mihiel

FRANCE

Rhine R.

Seine R.

© RMSN & CO.

Germans, although they suffered fearful casualties. They had their first taste of the horror of trench warfare—in which row after row of men dug themselves into the ground and faced each other in bloody battle.

Château-Thierry and Belleau Wood. Meanwhile, American units had succeeded in helping the French meet a German advance at Château-Thierry (shă tō′ tē ərē), 56 miles from Paris. American marines just east of Château-Thierry captured a forest less than 2 square miles in size,

known as Belleau (bĕl′ō) Wood. The Germans had covered the area with machine gun nests.

The raw courage of the marines in overrunning the German troops—crack troops at that—cost dearly. Almost five thousand Americans were killed or wounded.

Still hoping to bring about the end of the war, the Germans struck the Allied line in a savage attack along the Marne River. Over 85,000 American troops helped the French fight back the attack and clear the enemy from the region.

Street barricades in Château-Thierry as American soldiers battled in 1918 to check the German advance at this town on the Marne River.

Smithsonian Institution (Photo by Henry B. Bevil)

He Did. (Cartoon) Library of Congress; (News of Armistice) UPI

Left: "He did."
Right: Doughboys in France—members of Company M, Sixth Infantry Regiment, Fifth Division—cheer the news of the armistice.

St. Mihiel. But the killing and the dying were far from done. An American army of 550,000 men under Pershing took charge of the front near St. Mihiel (săN mē yĕl′) early in September and sent the Germans into a retreat.

The attack of the doughboys, as the Americans were affectionately called, was supported by about eight hundred planes—spotting targets for the field guns and engaging in strafing and bombing. This was the first battle in history in which air power played a large role.

The Argonne Forest. Before September, 1918, was over, United States forces were driving ahead to cut a railroad which was a supply line of the German forces. They had to slash their way through the difficult Argonne Forest. In doing so, they suffered 120,000 casualties—one for every ten men.

The victory in the Argonne Forest brought the end of the war into sight. Victories elsewhere for the British and the French made it clear to the Germans that they should prepare for final defeat.

Armistice at last. On November 6, 1918, the German government, at Berlin, asked for an armistice—a cease-fire. When the guns finally fell silent on November 11, the United States had suffered 279,000 casualties, of which 49,000 had been killed.

1. Describe the difficulties Wilson had with Mexico. 2. Tell how the First World War began. 3. In what ways was the American situation in the first years of the war like that before the War of 1812? 4. Identify the candidates in the election of 1916. Who won? With what slogan? 5. What was the result of the Zimmermann telegram? 6. When and why did the United States declare war on Germany? 7. Name five battles in which Americans took part.

te that the Germans asked for an armistice based on Wilson's Fourteen Points (see p. 596). The es were never enthusiastic about the Fourteen Points, but their war weariness led them to accept armistice on that basis. They also insisted that Germany pay them war damages.

The United States Turns Down the League

The Americans had by no means won the war for the Allies. But without American help the Allies would not have been able to roll the Germans back.

The Fourteen Points

After Germany's defeat England's chief interest was in seeing to it that the German navy was taken away so that Germany could never again threaten the safety of Britain. France wanted most to make sure that the German army would never again be strong enough to break into French territory. Both England and France wanted to make Germany pay dearly for the terrible loss of life and property the war had caused.

Convincing the German people. Woodrow Wilson had other ideas. He wanted to avoid a peace which would be so full of revenge that Germany would only wait its turn to "get even." From the beginning of the war, he had tried to make it clear that the German people should not be punished for the deeds of their government.

Wilson's stand pleased many Germans, of course. Having thrown out the Kaiser, they believed they had done all that could be expected of them. Wilson had emphasized that they need not fear either severe punishment or the loss of their overseas possessions.

For a peaceful world. But Wilson had never got the Allies to agree with him.
\# Moreover, the President had never found out how much support he had at home for his peace plans. He announced his program to Congress in January, 1918. It became known as the Fourteen Points.

The Fourteen Points included a call for an end to secret diplomacy—that is, un-announced alliances between countries. They also provided for a cutting down of armaments, freedom of the seas for all nations, and the right of various peoples to have their own governments.

The final point—the fourteenth—was the one closest to the President's heart. It asked for a "league of nations" which would guarantee both the territory and the independence of all nations, "great and small . . . alike."

An honored figure. Wilson never had Congress' or the Cabinet's approval for his Fourteen Points. They were his alone.

The President's plans were made public at a time when the world was eager to hear what his war aims were. He quickly became for millions of people everywhere, here and abroad, a symbol of hope for a peaceful world.

\#\#"League" equals "alliance."

Peace at Last

But the leaders of the victorious European countries did not entirely agree with Wilson's proposals. They regarded him as a man who was not at all practical. They could see no guarantee for the safety of their countries in what he was proposing. Like millions of other Europeans, they felt keenly a need to seek revenge from the Germans. Finally, they were keenly jealous of Wilson's great popularity in Europe.

When Germany asked for peace on the basis of Wilson's Fourteen Points, however, the Allies were as ready to end the war as the Germans. Unbelievable as it may seem, the French had had 6,161,000 soldiers killed or wounded, Britain 3,190,000, and Germany 7,143,000.

The Big Four. Wilson quickly made up his mind to go to Europe to help in the

\#Since Wilson wanted his Fourteen Points to influence the making of the peace treaty with Germany and since the Senate had to approve the treaty, this was a serious omission.

writing of a peace treaty. In Paris, France, he joined David Lloyd George, prime minister of Britain, and the representatives of France and Italy in conferences to decide the fate of Germany. (Italy had joined the Allies in 1915.)

The French member of the group was Georges Clemenceau (klĕm ən sō′), a man of seventy-seven who hated Germany with all his heart. (As a young writer he had covered Andrew Johnson's impeachment trial for a Paris newspaper.) Clemenceau respected Wilson's views, but he thought the President was too idealistic.

A warm reception. Nevertheless, Clemenceau and the other members of the Big Four also knew that the American President was a beloved hero of the French people. The reception Wilson had received in Paris had been amazing. Like giant waves the cheers had rolled through the streets of Paris, "Vive, Wil-son! ['Long live Wilson!'] Vive, Wil-son! Vive, Wil-son!"

Wilson had made the creation of the League of Nations his main aim. He had persuaded the other leaders in Paris to establish the League even before they got down to the business of writing a peace treaty. When at last the Covenant of the League—that is, its charter—was approved, Wilson said, with unashamed pleasure, "A living thing is born."

Opponents at home. Wilson had failed, however, to consider his opponents at home—especially in the Senate. They continued to argue for America's isolation from Europe. The League of Nations, they said, was an "entangling alliance" (see page 583).

Actually the League's purpose was to help keep the peace of the world. To do this, the League might need to propose military and naval action. One provision in the charter—Article X—made the members of the League promise to protect each other against attacks by other countries.

Arguments. Americans who were against

UPI

Wilson is welcomed in London by a crowd gathered to see him as he arrives on his way to Paris.

the League declared that it would take over ## important powers of Congress in matters of war and peace. They hesitated, too, to believe that a world organization for peace could keep us out of war by preventing wars from starting.

Wilson came home once during the many months in which the peace treaty was being written. He saw that his ideas were going to face stiff opposition. Yet he continued to argue that the treaty of peace itself would be in danger if the United States did not accept the League.

The Treaty of Versailles. The completed treaty was signed in the Hall of Mirrors at Versailles (vĕr sī′), just outside Paris. On the one hand, the treaty followed the

Ask the class what powers the critics of the League of Nations had in mind. (The power of ongress to declare war and the power of the Senate to approve or disapprove treaties.) It was ticle X which aroused the most opposition to the League in the United States.

597

wishes of the European members of the Big Four. Germany was made smaller and # was stripped of its colonies and its army and navy. (Later it was told to pay a huge bill for war damages.)

On the other hand, the men had followed as closely as they could many of Wilson's Fourteen Points. The treaty provided for the League of Nations, whose members would help protect each other. Also, a number of new countries were formed. Their peoples, now become self-governing, had formerly been ruled by the Russian, Austro-Hungarian, and Turkish emperors.

Despite the fact that Wilson had once called for "peace without victory," he had become sure that Germany must be severely dealt with. He now said, "We must not forget what our soldiers fought for, even if it means that we may have to fight again." (He was thinking of a possible future German war of revenge.)

Home again in July, 1919, Wilson almost immediately went in person to the Senate to present the treaty for approval. When he entered, two Senators failed even to rise out of courtesy to the President.

Stubborn Senators. The most powerful—and the ablest—of the Senators against Wilson was Theodore Roosevelt's close friend Senator Henry Cabot Lodge, of Massachusetts. Lodge envied Wilson his place as a leading figure of the world. Like Wilson, Lodge was a "scholar in politics." He did not trust Democrats, and especially he did not trust Wilson.

Another opponent with considerable influence was Senator William E. Borah, of Idaho. Borah called the President "Britain's tool—a dodger and a cheater." Borah spoke for a considerable number of people who were angered by the strong anti-German foreign policy the United States had been following.

A stubborn President. While in Paris Wilson had fallen ill with a fever. Some-

how he did not seem the same after he was up and about again. He was cross with his associates. Gone was his smiling, self-confident manner (some had thought it cocky).

When the President presented the treaty to the Senate, he seemed ill. But he quickly perked up, for he was sure he was expressing the hopes and wishes of the people. He believed they were in back of him and his ideas.

Many of Wilson's friends and warm supporters wanted the President to accept a compromise about the membership of the United States in the League of Nations. They wanted him to agree that we would# not go to war even to defend another country unless Congress approved. The President, however, remained stubborn. The Senate, he said, must accept the Covenant the way it was written.

A fateful trip. By the end of the summer of 1919, the doughboys were coming home from Europe. The American people were preparing for peace with the same enthusiasm they had shown in going to war. They were tired of war and of European problems. If the President was going to have the United States join the League of Nations, he would have to act fast.

Against the advice of doctors, Wilson decided to go on a speaking tour in the Middle West and West to win support for the treaty. It would have been a hard trip even for a younger man in the best of health.

"When this treaty is accepted," the President said in Ohio, "men in khaki will not have to cross the seas again." In Indiana he told an audience, "If it is not to be this arrangement, what arrangement do you suggest to secure the peace of the world? It is a case of put up or shut up."

The crowds which turned out to see the President grew larger and friendlier as the trip proceeded. But the daily speaking and traveling wore him out.

##In other words, they wanted Wilson to compromise about Article X of the Covenant of the League, which had become part of the peace treaty. Wilson believed that the League would be powerless without Article X, and for that reason he held fast to his position.

Clemenceau, with the drooping mustache, is opposite the man in the chair with back turned. Lloyd George also faces the man in the chair.

The signing of the Treaty of Versailles in the Hall of Mirrors: Wilson holds a newspaper. Clemenceau sits at his right, and David Lloyd George is at Clemenceau's right.

Imperial War Museum, London

Late in September, after speaking in Pueblo, Colorado, the President went to bed and spent a terrible night. His doctor begged him to cancel the remainder of his trip. Wilson refused. He was afraid that Senator Lodge and others would call him a quitter. Moreover, he thought the success of the Treaty of Versailles depended on his own public-speaking appearances.

But Mrs. Wilson persuaded the President that he must give up. A few days later, back in Washington now, Wilson fell unconscious—the victim of a stroke.

A leaderless land. Never before had the country suffered from having a disabled President at a critical moment in its his-

tory. As Wilson slowly recovered, the public gradually learned the truth: he was partially paralyzed and unable to speak properly.

The country was leaderless. For weeks the President could not perform the duties of his office at all. For over seven months he did not meet with his Cabinet. The nation was stunned.

Turned down by the Senate. The Senate went on with its business. After much discussion and harsh words, it refused in November, 1919, to approve the peace treaty. Senator Borah called this action "the greatest victory since Appomattox."

The chief blame for the failure of the

Americans were made aware for the first time that the Constitution made no provision for taking care of the situation they now found themselves in. The President would never again be able to carry out his duties, but he did not resign, and he lived until 1924.

tions must be shared equally by Wilson and Lodge. But the sufferers were the American people and, in the end, the other people of the world.

##the responsibilities of world leadership. They seemed to be against making any change in America's role. They felt they had enough to do at home. They did not care to worry about the rest of mankind.

Wilson said of his fellow Americans, "They will have to learn now by bitter experience just what they have lost. . . . We had a chance to gain the leadership of the world. We have lost it."

New tunes. American soldiers by then had returned from Paris, had held a victory parade down Fifth Avenue in New York, and were back in civilian clothing. Their serious business having been done, they turned to lighter things again. They were soon singing, for example, a new song which asked, "Five-foot two, eyes of blue, has anybody seen my girl?"

The words of some of the most popular songs after the war seemed to tell us that nonsense was to take the place of thought. One of the tunes, for instance, praised "Barney Google with his goo-goo-googly eyes." Another favorite was called "Yes, We Have No Bananas."

These songs and others like them helped mark a new era in this country. In it most Americans turned away from concern over foreign problems without ever trying to find out their possible effects.

---

1. What different ideas did England, France, and Wilson have concerning what to do about the defeated Germany? 2. Name five proposals Wilson made. 3. What two arguments were used in the United States against the President's main proposal? 4. Describe the Treaty of Versailles. 5. Name two Senators who opposed American approval of the treaty. 6. What action was taken on the treaty? Why?

Exercise 1 under "Your Opinion, Please," is an excellent one to

The Workshop

use in discussing the feelings of Americans after the First World War.

The Shapers of Our World

Tell how each of the following did or did not contribute to making the United States a leader in world affairs.

Guantánamo
  naval base
open-door policy
Russo-Japanese
  War
Victoriano Huerta
Venustiano
  Carranza
Pancho Villa
John J. Pershing
Belleau Wood

doughboy
November 11, 1918
Argonne Forest
Fourteen Points
David Lloyd
  George
Woodrow Wilson
Sarajevo, Bosnia
Lusitania
Charles Evans
  Hughes

the Kaiser
Arthur Zimmermann
Herbert C. Hoover
Cantigny
Château-Thierry
George Clemenceau

League of Nations
Article X
Treaty
  of Versailles
Henry Cabot Lodge

Adding to Your Vocabulary

Show your understanding of the chapter by using these words:

isolation
entangling
  alliance
trench warfare
nationalism

mediator
"dollar diplomacy"
tender (*verb*)
armistice
efficient

Some of the men or things named under "The Shapers of Our World" obviously had nothing to do with making the United States a world leader, except indirectly. Pershing had a direct role, however, as did Wilson, in spite of the failure of the United States to join the League.

Thinking Things Through

After reviewing the boxed-in exercises in the chapter, discuss the following:

1. Why did the acquisition of colonies after the Spanish-American War make the affairs of Asia thereafter a concern of the American people?

2. Why was Roosevelt alarmed when European countries threatened to use force to collect debts in the Caribbean area?

3. Why do you think Wilson's criticism of Huerta had little effect?

4. Why was it almost impossible for Germany to carry on submarine warfare and at the same time to accept Wilson's demands?

5. Why was Hughes' resignation from the Supreme Court a most unusual step?

6. What was the meaning of Wilson's "peace without victory" statement?

7. Why did Zimmermann offer New Mexico, Arizona, and Texas as bribes for Mexican participation in the First World War?

8. A popular remark said to have been made by an American officer when the troops landed in France in 1917 was "Lafayette, we are here." What did he mean?

9. Wilson called the war a war to "make the world safe for democracy." What did *he* mean?

The Research Center

1. When and under what circumstances did Veterans Day originate? In its honor prepare a program or a display in your school. Your local American Legion can provide material.

2. The Tomb of the Unknowns is located in Arlington National Cemetery. Prepare a report about this monument and what it signifies.

3. Create a display of newspaper headlines that might have appeared in your hometown paper or papers showing the course of the First World War from 1914 to 1918.

4. Obtain a copy of John McCrae's poem "In Flanders Field" and read it to the class. Explain what it says about war.

5. Present a display of materials relating to the First World War. Uniforms, weapons, and old newspapers and pictures can be shown. Friends or relatives might have items to lend.

6. Bring to class recordings or sheet music of some of the songs popular during the time of the First World War. How do they compare with popular songs today?

7. Interview people who lived during the years of the First World War and ask for their impressions of life then. Publish their remarks in your school magazine.

Maps and Graphs Tell a Story

1. On an outline map of Europe, show the Allies in blue, the Central Powers in red, and the neutral countries in green. Save this map in order to compare the information it presents with the same information about the Second World War.

2. Using the map on page 593, tell: (*a*) how close the Germans came to Paris, (*b*) where most of the battles were fought, (*c*) how close to England the *Lusitania* was when sunk.

3. Make a graph showing how the American casualties compared with those of Britain, France, Russia, and Germany.

Your Opinion, Please

1. Why do people often become tired of reform movements after a war and seem to want only to be left alone?

2. Should Wilson have compromised on the matter of American admission to the League of Nations? Explain.

3. If Americans could have known that there would be a Second World War, would they have joined the League of Nations?

ᵗWilson was referring to the fact that Germany and Austria-Hungary were ruled by emperors. ᴇrmany and Austria-Hungary were opposed to the democracies--the United States, Britain, ᴵd France--and were as a result threatening democracy.

(a) A poster advertising a performance by two leading American circuses, which were joined in 1919. Circuses became popular in the United States in the late nineteenth century.
(b) So did automobiles. This is the "Model T" Ford in 1909. It combined all the latest features.
(c) Rudolph Valentino, a movie idol of thousands of Americans in the 1920's, in one of his romantic roles.

THE RINGLING BROS AND BARNUM & BAILEY COMBINED SHOWS

BIG NEW ANIMAL CIRCUS
NOW ADDED TO THE GREATEST SHOW ON EARTH

(a)

(b)

(c)

(d) The small, light plane in which Charles A. Lindbergh made the first nonstop flight across the Atlantic Ocean.

The pictures on the opposite page and above suggest the pleasures Americans sought in amusements in the 20's and two new means of transportation which changed American life. The 1909 Ford was much higher than recent models of cars are and required running boards for passengers to step on. The horn was just outside the driver's seat.

CHAPTER 27

A TIME OF FASTER LIVING

Automobiles and airplanes both helped make the 1920's a time for faster living. Automobiles not only moved people more quickly from one place to another than before but also made them more aware of what was going on in areas other than their own, adding to their sense of faster living.

As Americans turned back to peacetime ways after the First World War, they could see how different life was from what it had been when "T. R." was President.

In fact, changes had become so common that change itself was now something to get used to. It was said, "To stay where you are here, you must keep moving."

This section deals with the development of cars and planes and with the important results.

Americans Take to the Road and the Air

Improvements in American transportation alone were staggering. Within a few years, beginning around the start of this century, the nation was made over by the gasoline engine.

Behind the Steering Wheel

At the opening of the war, the automobile was already reshaping American life. In the year 1900 there had been only eight thousand motorcars in the entire country —most of them owned by rich people. By 1915 there were two and a half million, and they were not in the hands of wealthy families only.

Henry Ford's work. One motorcar genius was Henry Ford, whose name became a synonym throughout the world for the word automobile. Henry Ford foresaw that the automobile could be not only a toy for the wealthy but also a force for freeing the "little man" from being tied down to one place.

Selden's patent. Ford drew heavily on the experience of others. One of these people was George B. Selden, who had applied in 1879 for the first patent ever issued anywhere on a gasoline-type engine attached to a carriage. Selden managed to delay until 1895 the actual issuance of his patent in order to protect it until the public was

Call attention to this tremendous increase in just fifteen years. A student might try to find out how many automobiles are owned in a single large city or state today. Many people who are by no means wealthy or even moderately well-off think that cars are necessities.

Ford Motor Company

Part of the assembly line at the Ford plant in 1914: a body is being dropped on a chassis.

#Compare assembly-line production with work b a craftsman, in which one man does everything.

when he brought out his "Model T" in 1908. By the time he stopped producing that model in 1927, he had manufactured fifteen million cars. Moreover, the price of a "Model T" had dropped from $850 in 1908 to $290 in 1924.

Ford's factory in Highland Park, Michigan, could in 1914 assemble an automobile in 93 minutes. By means of a conveyor belt, unskilled men could perform operations which, put together, added up to the complicated process of automobile-building.

Some rivals. In time more elegant automobiles appeared—like the Chevrolet and the Dodge—which for a time took away Ford's market. But the "Model T," which people called a flivver or a Tin Lizzie, for a long time held the nation's affection.

Effects: good and bad. The automobile changed American business life. The increase in the number of automobiles from 8,226,000 in 1920 to 23,122,000 by 1929 was alone bound to have powerful effects. By the 1920's the automobile industry—if one counts the value of its products—was the most important American industry. The quantities of rubber, glass, leather, copper, aluminum, and other valuable items which it consumed were enormous.

ready for his invention. Meanwhile, however, there were other "horseless carriages" on the way, including Ford's.

In 1896 Ford ran his "autocycle" in Detroit. It had the advantage of being lighter than any of its rivals—weighing only 500 pounds. Further, Ford learned much from Ransom E. Olds, who manufactured the "merry Oldsmobile" from 1899 on. Olds was the man who first used mass production in the automobile industry.

The "Model T." Ford applied the principle of mass production to the manufacture of low-priced cars. "I will build a motor car for the great multitude," he promised

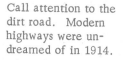

Call attention to the dirt road. Modern highways were undreamed of in 1914.

A pleasant ride in the country is spoiled by an *un*lucky horseshoe. This drawing was made in 1914.

Old Print Shop

The Wrights' plane on its first flight. Orville, lying down, pilots it. Wilbur, running alongside, shows how close to the ground it is.

Even more important, though, the automobile brought countless changes in the way Americans lived. No longer did people have to dwell near their places of employment. Parts of the country which were less prosperous than they used to be—New England and parts of the South, for instance—became tourist centers. Farmers were no longer separated from the rest of the world. Young people developed new dating habits as they found they had more freedom of movement than ever before.

Automobiles, moreover, caused an increase in crime and were as much to blame for deaths and crippled bodies as wars. They also led to the building of highways which often spoiled the countryside's beauty.

Toward the Sky

Before 1903 many men had dreamed of flying like birds. People had risen in balloons, and they had gone through the air in gliders which had been pushed off hilltops. But flying as we know it today awaited Wilbur and Orville Wright.

The Wrights' flight. Late in 1903 the Wright brothers reported from Kitty Hawk, North Carolina, that they had remained aloft in their airplane for 12 seconds. Their flight, they said, had been the first "in which a machine carrying a man had raised itself by its own power into the air in free flight . . . and had finally landed without being wrecked."

The Wrights succeeded because they had discovered how to keep a plane stable —that is, keep it from rolling and pitching in the air. They had found out that the secret was to make a portion of the wing of the plane go up and down.

Plane designers. Other men were also experimenting with "flying machines." One was Edson Gallaudet, of Connecticut. He quit college to continue tinkering with aircraft. Later he established the first airplane-manufacturing company.

Another airplane designer was Glenn Curtiss, of New York, who had started his career as a manufacturer of motorcycle engines. He became the chief rival of the Wrights in producing airplanes.

Hard to believe. Nevertheless, who, unless he had actually seen a plane fly, would believe such flight was possible? Although by 1905 the Wrights had flown distances up to 24 miles, many people in both Europe and America were asking, Are they fliers or liars? In the meantime, though, despite a terrible toll in lives, men—and women—*were* flying planes.

Military aviation. The value of planes for military use was clear from the beginning. The First World War showed some of the things they could do—spot artillery, drop explosives (or propaganda pamphlets), and photograph military targets.

During the war, by an enormous effort the country had succeeded in producing over 12,000 planes and training the necessary number of pilots. The war in the air produced notable heroes, including especially Lieutenant Eddie Rickenbacker. A former automobile-racing driver, he was the top United States ace, having shot down 22 German planes.

Shrinking distances. After the war men of the Army Air Service showed what was possible with air travel and transportation. In 1922, for example, Lieutenant James H. Doolittle became the first person to fly across the American continent in less than a day. He made it from Florida to California, with one stop, in 21 hours and 20 minutes. The following year two other lieutenants, John Macready and Oakley Kelley, spanned the continent for the first time on a nonstop flight.

The navy as well as the army was practicing with airplanes. In 1922 it launched the first aircraft carrier. A naval officer, Lieutenant Commander Richard E. Byrd, and his pilot, Floyd Bennett, in 1926 were the first men to fly over the North Pole.

"Lucky Lindy"

The most publicized flier of all time, however, was Charles A. Lindbergh. He flew nonstop from New York to Paris in the first solo flight ever made across the Atlantic Ocean, becoming a giant hero.

A prize of $25,000. Lindbergh, the son of a former Minnesota Congressman, was an experienced flier in 1926, when he began to think about a trip across the Atlantic. He had his eyes on the $25,000 offered by a New Yorker to the first aviator to cross the ocean nonstop from or to New York.

The *Spirit of St. Louis*. A new engine had recently been developed capable of carrying a plane on such a long journey—3300 miles. A group of businessmen in St. Louis to whom Lindbergh had gone had agreed

Lindbergh's craft, damaged by a crowd on his arrival in France, is wheeled out after being repaired.

UPI

Enthusiastic Irishmen greet Amelia Earhart Putnam as she completes the first transatlantic flight made alone by a woman.

to back him by helping him buy and equip a suitable plane. He named it the *Spirit of St. Louis.*

By May Lindbergh was ready, though he had to wait for the weather to become favorable. While waiting, he checked his plane over and over again, trying to make it as light in weight as possible.

On May 19, 1927, Lindbergh got word unexpectedly in New York that the weather over the North Atlantic had cleared. He decided to get ready to leave on his flight the next morning.

"Well, I did it." Lindbergh took off in the rain, heading toward his goal. He carried no radio and no parachute. Twenty-seven hours later he swooped down low over some fishing boats and shouted, "Which way is Ireland?" He got no answer, but he was on the right course.

A little more than six hours after that, Lindbergh landed at Paris. Wildly cheering crowds awaiting his arrival rushed forward to greet him—and to tear souvenirs from his airplane. His first words to the United States ambassador who met him were, "Well, I did it."

Within the day Lindbergh became an international hero. His handsome boyishness and modesty were very appealing to millions of people. Americans found in him proof than an individual who makes up his mind can, even in the busy industrial age, triumph on his own against heavy odds. Wherever Lindbergh went, he was cheered as "Lucky Lindy."

"Lady Lindy." After Lindbergh's success many other daring pilots cut new paths in the sky. These included women as well as men. One of the most accomplished of the women pilots was Amelia Earhart, the wife of a New York book publisher. She was sometimes known as Lady Lindy.

The airlines. After Lindbergh's memorable trip, airplanes became a recognized means of transportation. In 1927, 8661 passengers traveled by air. In the following year, the number jumped to 47,800. By the end of 1928, there were 48 established air routes—covering a combined distance of 20,000 miles.

In 1930 United Air Lines was formed from a number of lines, and so a transcontinental air route was created. A rival was formed later the same year, afterward called TWA. A third great system brought together a number of small airlines mostly in the southern part of the country. It was called American Airways, later American Airlines.

In addition to these three giant airlines, there was a jumble of smaller lines. The resulting demand for planes was large, and by 1929 about seventy-five hundred machines were being made each year.

1. What contribution did Henry Ford make to the automobile industry? 2. Describe the good and the bad results automobiles had. 3. Tell the reason for the success of the Wright brothers. 4. What military and peacetime advantages came from the development of aviation? 5. Describe Lindbergh's flight. 6. How old is our oldest transcontinental air route?

sk students to name some major airlines today, both domestic and foreign. Some students
y be able to bring maps to class showing some commercial airline routes, but a map that
ws a great many of them is likely to become a hopeless jumble of crisscrossing lines.

607

The Nation Mixes Play with Its Problems

The changes that were remaking American culture could be upsetting to people as well as exciting. Many felt great uncertainty about the years ahead. They seemed to say, "Whatever the future holds, let's enjoy ourselves *now*." A popular expression was "It's later than you think." And so the nation played as it had never played before.

The new means of transportation gave Americans—ahead of all other people—a new feeling of physical freedom. Before, most Americans probably had lived out their lives without ever traveling more than 25 or 30 miles from the places where they had been born.

The Attempt at Prohibition

But Americans in the 1920's did not seek pleasure without self-control. They tried to live without alcoholic beverages. The movement to stop the use of intoxicating drink—*prohibition*—began before the Civil War. It gained new force during the First World War.

Some explanations. The most important reason for the new strength of the movement probably was the organizing of the supporters of prohibition. These reformers often seemed to be men and women who were afraid of the way the growing cities were rapidly changing old ways. Saloons, hangouts especially of newcomers who settled in urban areas, were typical of cities. A good way to show anger at the changes coming to America, it appeared, was to attack the saloons.

Another reason, no doubt, was that drunkenness had become a more serious problem than ever before. Moreover, to make things worse, drinking did not go well with the use of the automobile, which was becoming common. A slogan which was often heard at the time went, "Alcohol and gasoline don't mix."

Third, many people believed that cutting down on the use of liquor might reduce the bad feeling between races that developed in some parts of the country. A widely held view was that such feeling boiled to the surface and led to violence among people who had drunk too much.

Fourth, during the First World War it was often felt that when grain was being saved to send to Europe, it ought not be wasted to make alcoholic drinks. Fifth, most people wanted to keep liquor away from the military training camps.

The Eighteenth Amendment. The variety of influences leading to prohibition came together in 1917 to produce the Eighteenth Amendment. This forbade "the manufacture, sale, or transportation of intoxicating liquors." In 1919, when three-fourths of the states had ratified the amendment, it was added to the Constitution.

Did it work? It is hard to judge the effects of prohibition. During the prohibition period, savings-bank deposits and the sales of soft drinks and candy increased. Moreover, the drinking of milk and fruit juices also became more common than earlier. Friends of prohibition explained these happy developments as being the results of closing the saloons.

Others had different explanations. These changes, they said, were due chiefly to the growth of prosperity, to changes in the food and health habits of the people, and to the increasing influence of advertising.

Getting around the law. Prohibition was unpopular, especially in the cities, and it was therefore hard to enforce. Many ways

##Ask what slogan or slogans today deal with the same idea. ("If you drive, don't drink.") The Volstead Act of 1919 was passed to carry out or enforce the amendment (see pp. 723-724). The Eighteenth Amendment was repealed by the Twenty-first (see p. 725).

Left: Before prohibition Carry Nation fought saloons, smashing them with a hatchet. *Right:* Mary Pickford—earliest, best-loved movie star.

of avoiding it were developed. First of all, there was bootlegging—the selling of liquor which had been smuggled into the country or had been manufactured in illegal stills.

Second, there was the misuse of doctors' prescriptions (doctors were able to prescribe liquor for "medical purposes"). Third, there was widespread home brewing of alcoholic beverages—sometimes known as moonshine or bathtub gin.

A new kind of highway robber made his appearance during the prohibition period: the hijacker. He would waylay a bootlegger's trucks, knowing that his victims could not turn to the police for help.

Prohibition seems to have greatly encouraged lawlessness. It was said that oftentimes a policeman would gladly direct a person to a speakeasy—an illegal saloon—where liquor was being sold. On one occasion thousands of bathers at Coney Island in New York cheered a rum-running vessel (a ship smuggling liquor) as it escaped from a government ship.

Organized crime. The rewards for smuggling liquor to the "thirsty" were so great that prohibition failed because it could not be enforced. The most widely known bootlegger was Al "Scarface" Capone, a gangster, or member of a band of criminals, who operated in the Chicago area. When rivals tried to cut in on Capone's territory, gang wars resulted.

Capone's career and others like it showed how dishonest some local officials were and how prohibition broke down the enforcement of law and order. Seemingly, a local chief of the bootleggers was everywhere "in" with the police.

The Movies

A favorite way for people to play in the 1920's was by attending motion pictures. The movies, which had been developing for some time, became the rage then.

In the years after the Civil War, a New England physician, Oliver Wendell Holmes, had begun to study photographs of people

his and other methods of committing crimes continued after the prohibition period came to an
d. Organized crime also continued after the 1920's and early 1930's. <u>Above</u>: Mary Pickford,
led America's sweetheart, was the first American movie queen.

609

walking, caught at various points in their strides. He had been trying hard to improve the artificial limbs being supplied to the wounded veterans.

Edison's patent. A number of other experiments had also taken place, leading at last to a patent in 1893 for Thomas A. Edison. Edison's patent had been on a camera—the Kinetoscope—capable of "taking a large number of photographs of a moving object in such a manner that any two successive pictures are almost identical in appearance."

The five-cent shows. The earliest movie theaters showed merely scenes of action. People were willing to pay to see such marvels. The films were shown in stores fixed up with screens and folding chairs. Because the admission charge was five cents, these theaters were called nickelodeons. By 1908 probably every town in the United States could boast of having at least one.

The first hit. The earliest picture with a plot, called *The Great Train Robbery*, appeared in 1903. But it was several years before technology made movies anything more than photographed stage plays.

Gradually the use of such camera techniques as the close-up, the fade-out, and even slow motion helped create a truly new form of art. The first motion picture that used these techniques well was produced on the eve of the First World War. Called *The Birth of a Nation*, it dealt with the reconstruction period of American history. Because the film showed Negroes in an unfavorable light, it damaged the relations between races in this country. Not only, therefore, was this picture very unfortunate, but also it showed the power of this new means of communication.

Stars. Movies were within a few years producing new heroes and heroines—stars —whose doings became everybody's business. And the wilder these doings were, the more widely they were reported. Clara Bow, for instance, was referred to through-out the country as the "It" girl. She, along with seven red Chow dogs, whose color matched her hair, liked to whiz down Hollywood's Sunset Boulevard in her flaming red convertible.

The "dream man" for millions of flappers in the twenties was Rudolph Valentino. When he died suddenly in 1926 many were injured in the crush of the thousands who tried to attend his funeral.

The World of Sport

Spectator sports were bringing pleasure to millions of Americans in the 1920's and were helping to fill leisure time. Moreover these sports were producing a new kind of public hero that rivaled the Greek gods of the ancient world.

The prize ring. Prizefighting became a sport which even well-educated people enjoyed. The first fight to bring a return of over a million dollars at the box office took place in 1921. It was a match between Jack Dempsey and a French war veteran, Georges Carpentier. Five years later Dempsey lost his world's heavyweight title to Gene Tunney, a handsome ex-sailor. At least 120,000 people saw this bout.

The "national pastime." Baseball, called the national pastime, also attracted crowds of spectators. It suffered greatly in the public eye as a result of the World Series of 1919. At that time some dishonest players fell into the hands of gamblers and fixed the scores of games. But before long the sport was as popular as ever.

The greatest baseball figure of his time was George Herman "Babe" Ruth, who had come out of the slums of Baltimore. As the hard-hitting right fielder of the New York Yankees, he drew millions of fans through the turnstiles of Yankee Stadium, in New York, and other ball parks where he played.

The high point of Babe Ruth's career came in 1927, when he hit 60 home runs in 154 games, still baseball's proudest

#Ask the students if they think moviemakers have a responsibility in presenting information, as newspapers and other news agencies do (see Question 3, Col. 2, p. 555).
##Basketball, the only sport originating here, has the disadvantage of being an indoor game.

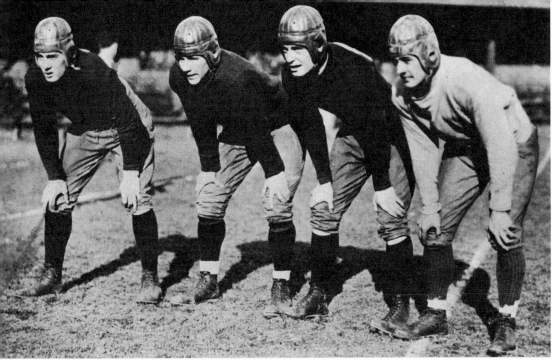

record. The following year the Yankees paid Ruth a salary of $80,000 for his services, more than the president of the United States received then. When someone pointed this out to Ruth, he said, "Well, I had a better year."

The gridiron. Football had its heroes, too. None won greater fame than the young men in the backfield of the University of Notre Dame's team in 1924. They were nicknamed the Four Horsemen. Just as well known was Harold "Red" Grange, a ball carrier for the University of Illinois, whom many regarded as a one-man team.

Golf, tennis, horse racing, and swimming all had their stars. It was a time of champions.

Women athletes. Women, too, captured headlines on the sports pages of newspapers. Helen Wills, called Little Miss Poker Face, was an international celebrity after winning the United States women's tennis championship at the age of seventeen. In 1926 Gertrude Ederle became the first woman to swim across the English Channel, beating the men's speed record for this feat by almost 2½ hours.

Above: The "Four Horsemen"—(*left to right*) Don Miller, Elmer Layden, Jim Crowley, Harry Stuhldreher. *Below:* Helen Wills in action.

men athletes and movie stars and public figures like Amelia Earhart called attention to the position of women in American culture, in which they were freer than in many other cultures. The stars of sports and screen satisfied the public desire for heroes and heroines.

Out of the Radio Set

The radio was one of the most important of all instruments for spreading an interest in sports. It made it possible for millions everywhere to follow descriptions of the great sporting events and make believe they were present. Never before had so many people shared in the excitement of athletics performed by others. Radio, though, also brought many other advantages to countless Americans.

Rapid growth. The radio for home use was a development of the 1920's. In 1907 an American, Lee De Forest, patented the vacuum tube on which radio transmission is based. On November 2, 1920, the Westinghouse Electric Company opened at East Pittsburgh, Pennsylvania, the first commercial radio station, KDKA, just in time to broadcast the election returns.

Within two years three million listening sets were in operation. By 1929 sets could be found in 40 percent of American homes.

Nationwide networks. Using long-distance telephone lines to send broadcasts throughout the nation, the Radio Corporation of America was able to create the National Broadcasting System in 1926. The following year the Columbia Broadcasting System was organized.

As the number of radio stations increased, it became necessary to prevent them from broadcasting on each other's wavelengths. Congress created the Federal Radio Commission to regulate the stations.

At first every radio set had earphones, and only one person at a time could listen to it. But shortly the Stromberg-Carlson Company brought out the first loudspeaker. Within a few years this company ran away with the field in radio sales.

Popular programs. What was being heard on radio? In 1922 the first commercial (which happened to be a "plug" for a real-estate company) was heard on New York's station WEAF. Within a few years radio broadcasting had become big business.

Certain programs won national popularity: "The A & P Gypsies," "The Happiness Boys," "Roxy and His Gang," the "Salada Tea Timers," and many others. Each fall the World Series was broadcast play-by-play. News bulletins were delivered breathlessly.

Because of radio, music could be heard in almost every home at almost any hour. The crooning voice of Rudy Vallee, for instance, brought this good news to millions of women listeners: "I'm Just a Vaga-

The grandmother was part of this American family, as she was in the 1880's (see p. 525), but she seldom is now in today's smaller homes and apartments.

The influence of the loudspeaker on the American home.

LIFE, March 4, 1926
(Warshaw Collection)

dy, born in 1873, wrote "St. Louis Blues" in 1914. es are slow and mournful.

W. C. Handy, left foreground, "father of the blues," when he taught band in a college in Normal, Alabama, between 1900 and 1902. He has autographed the picture.

ond Lover." Guy Lombardo and his orchestra played for millions "the sweetest music this side of heaven."

As the sounds of new tunes ("It Ain't Gonna Rain No More," "I'm Always Chasing Rainbows," and countless others) spread across the country, dancing became more popular than ever. Dance studios sprang up to teach the new steps—including the Charleston—to old and young like.

The sound of jazz. Another important influence radio had on music was to spread the exciting sound of jazz. Jazz developed out of a variety of musical forms. One of these, called ragtime, first appeared in the 890's. It had rhythms which combined march time with an irregular beat.

The blues were another source of jazz. They are a type of music featuring a blue note—a slightly flat tone that a singer or instrumentalist strikes or sings gently.

The blues began among the Negro population, being especially popular in Memphis and New Orleans. A noted artist of the form was W. C. Handy, whose "Memphis Blues" and "St. Louis Blues"

became very popular. Through the influence of brass bands, playing what was called Dixieland jazz, the power of jazz became recognized by the 1920's. Paul Whiteman, one of its masters, called it the folk music of the machine age. Louis Armstrong, the trumpet player often called the greatest of jazz musicians, helped make the 1920's the "jazz age."

The New Household

The freeing of women from some of the drudgery of housekeeping helped create leisure time for a large part of the population. In the 1920's foods prepared in factories were common on the American table. And year after year factory canning contributed to more varied meals, with "less work for mother." Commercial laundries made possible an end to "washdays" and the long, long hours spent over the washboard and the ironing board. The American living room became far less a center of life than it had once been. Recreation and entertainment more than ever before took place outside the home.

t the class discuss how the work of keeping house has been further lightened today. One It has been that more women now work outside their homes than ever before.
adio and television have kept homes centers of entertainment to some extent.

The flapper. If grandmothers were pleased at the good fortune of their daughters, they were often shocked at the behavior of their granddaughters. Unmarried girls no longer were expected to be accompanied by older adults when they were out on dates with young men. Girls wore lipstick and rouge as a matter of course, something only actresses and "fast ones" had done before.

Women emphasized boyishness in their looks. They bobbed their hair, often getting it cut in men's barber shops. Sometimes they bleached it or dyed it. They shortened their skirts and rolled their stockings, which made it easier for them to drive automobiles and to dance and play.

Also, the straight figure became the ideal, and women dieted to become as skinny as possible. F. Scott Fitzgerald, a leading writer of the 1920's, wrote that the perfect flapper was "lovely and expensive and about nineteen."

The rising divorce rate. As modern American life made the members of families seem less dependent on one another, the rate of divorce increased. In 1900 there was not quite one divorce for every 100 persons. But by 1928 the rate had almost doubled. In the 1920's there was only one chance in five or six that any particular marriage would succeed.

The falling birthrate. Another fact of the period that could be measured was the birthrate. The yearly rate in 1900 had been over 32.3 for each 1000 of the population. By 1920 it had fallen to 27.7. Some gloomy people even said that the population would finally decrease to the point where it would disappear altogether.

The Pressure of Advertising

The enjoyment of leisure was for most Americans greatly affected by the way they spent their money. In this "task" Americans were greatly aided—or pushed—by the advertising industry.

Catching the eye. Producers of goods for sale have always advertised their wares. But the catchy pictures and slogans accompanying ads became more and more important in the 1920's. By then the public

This flapper was a center of attention when she went for a stroll in the park.

LIFE, Aug. 20, 1925
(Warshaw Collection)

NICHOLAS
for BOYS and GIRLS
1920

Left: A cover of one of the most popular magazines ever published for young people. The clothing is in the style of the time. *Right:* One of the cleverest advertisements.

#Ask if this practice is common today. (Today it is often seen in TV commercials.)

Trade Mark Reg U S Pat Of
Time to Re-tire?
(Buy Fisk)

tions which carried them were entering illions of homes each week or month.

Certain slogans became household expressions because they were repeated over and over. One for an automobile tire, showing a little boy ready for bed, asked, "Time to re-tire?" One for a French perfume declared, "It costs a little more but milady deserves the best." It is said that the use of advertising doubled the amount of the florist business.

It became common for actors and actresses and athletes to endorse (approve) certain products, being paid by advertisers to lend their names to what was being sold. Sometimes even the royalty of Europe were said to like certain goods. In seeking purchasers, advertisers appealed to people's vanity—their desire to look younger, richer, or more worldly than they were.

A sure way to sell a product was to be able to say readers ought to have it because their neighbors had it. "Keeping up with the Joneses" became the goal of millions of Americans.

A big business. Products were sometimes advertised to make a special appeal to particular customers—to children, homemakers, working women, or factory workers. Business firms spent one and one-half billion dollars for advertising in the year 1927.

In advertising their products, some companies made claims for them that were either half-truths or actually dishonest. "Truth in Advertising" associations and "Better Business Bureaus" were formed to protect the public from being misled.

1. Give five reasons for the strength the movement for prohibition gained during the First World War. 2. What were three ways in which prohibition was avoided? 3. What was the importance of *The Birth of a Nation*? 4. Name three sports which captured national attention during the 1920's. 5. What new means of communication developed in the 1920's? On what was it based? 6. Name at least three changes in American culture resulting from an increase in the number of factories and from improved transportation.

k students to bring to class advertisements from magazines. Ask what desire of the reader ad appeals to. (Some people say everybody has four desires--he craves love, praise, new iences, and security--and that advertisers today appeal to each desire.)

Fear Leads to a Wave of Intolerance

Beneath the playfulness and the exciting novelty of the 1920's, there were some distressing signs, too. One of these was intolerance toward *minorities*—groups of people whose race, religion, or national background differs from that of the majority of Americans.

Immigration Restriction

For many years there had been criticism of unrestricted immigration into the United States. Labor unions especially had wanted to cut down on this flow of people.

The claims. One claim frequently heard about immigration was that war-torn Europe was about to dump new millions of people onto American shores to be looked after by those here. A second claim was that many recent arrivals were disloyal people who "ought to go back where they came from."

Nevertheless, the main reason for the feeling against immigrants was, sadly, intolerance. Those coming to this country continued to be largely from southern and eastern Europe. Many were Jews, to whom some Americans were unfriendly.

The time had come, said a Congressma from Minnesota in 1920, to pass "a genu ine 100 percent American immigratio law." What he meant was a law that woul limit the number of new arrivals and favo immigrants from the British Isles an northern Europe.

New laws. The laws passed in the 1920 accomplished what the Congressman ha wanted. The result was that before th 1920's were over, immigration to Americ had been severely cut down. In defendin this legislation, the president of the Unite States said in 1923, "America must be ke[American." By this he seemed to mea that minorities would not be welcomed.

The Ku Klux Klan

About the same time, a powerful an dangerous effort arose to keep control c the country in the hands of "native, white and Protestant" people. A leader in the e[fort, often violent, was the Ku Klux Klan– a new organization formed in 1915, usin the name and methods of the old post–Civ War Klan. The Klan was against Negroe Catholics, and Jews.

#Jews are a religious group, not a racial or national one.

Ellis Island ceased being an immigration station in 1954

Immigrants like these were the targets of restricted immigration. The are passing through the receiving station at Ellis Island, where most newcomers arrived.

UPI

mericanism" is defined as devotion to the
ed States and its ideals, customs, etc.

The Negro as a target. The Negro was
specially singled out for persecution by
he Klan. He was, according to that organ-
zation, "simply racially incapable of un-
erstanding, sharing or contributing to
mericanism." This poison of intolerance
pread as Negroes moved from the rural
outh into cities throughout the nation.

The use of violence. In its work the Ku
lux Klan killed, mutilated, flogged, tarred
nd feathered, and even branded its vic-
ims. Setting itself up as a judge of "Amer-
canism," the Klan—through its leader—
xplained the meaning of the word. Amer-
canism is, he said, "a thing of the spirit
. . [and] few aliens can understand that
pirit."

The nation as a victim. It has been esti-
nated that by the mid-1920's the Klan's
nembership was four million. The nation
hat so recently had been preaching about
he need to make the world safe for democ-
acy was a victim of this undemocratic
invisible government."

The "Red Scare"

See Exercise 11,
Col. 1, page 623.

One of the reasons for fear and intolerance in America was a revolution in Rus-
ia, resulting in the establishment of Communist ("Red") rule. Most Americans did
not know the details of events there, where
men called Bolsheviks had overthrown the
government, killed the czar and his family,
and placed themselves in power. But people
here saw themselves threatened by the
violence on the other side of the world.

Strikes and bombs. One effect of the Russian Revolution was a widespread "Red
scare" in which many Americans thought
they saw Communists at every turn. Their
fear increased when a general strike in
Seattle—that is, a work stoppage by every
union—tied up the city. It grew greater
when most of the police of Boston went on
strike in 1919, leaving the city's streets
without protection except from volunteers.

Underwood & Underwood

One of the thousands
of Ku Klux Klansmen who paraded
in a celebration of the Fourth of July
at Long Branch, New Jersey, in 1924.

President Wilson called this strike a crime
against civilization.

Still another development that contributed to the "Red scare" was a terrifying
outbreak of violence by *anarchists* in the
United States. (They believed that all government is bad and must be destroyed.)
Several places were bombed, including the
home of the Attorney-General of the United
States. Bombs were also sent through the
mails to some leading Americans—among
them John D. Rockefeller, the oil king.

Actions against foreigners. The "Red
scare" became so very widespread between
1919 and 1920 that the Attorney-General
rounded up and arrested thousands of
foreigners. Some of them were sent out
of the country for reasons which would
be very difficult to defend.

Negroes were far from being aliens--most were descended from men and women who came to
erica in the seventeenth and eighteenth centuries. Let students discuss the fact that Americans
o are intolerant of aliens forget that their ancestors were once in that group.

The Sacco-Vanzetti case. No single event of the "Red scare" attracted more attention than that involving Nicola Sacco and Bartolomeo Vanzetti. These men were tried in April, 1920, for the robbing and murdering of the paymaster of a shoe factory in South Braintree, Massachusetts.

Sacco, a shoemaker, and Vanzetti, a fish peddler, were anarchists. Throughout their trial and the years in which their case was appealed, many believed that the men were being "railroaded" to their execution on very flimsy evidence. Their defenders argued hard that two "innocent" men were being sent to their death not because they were murderers, but because they were # Italian anarchists.

Innocent or guilty? Those who insisted that Sacco and Vanzetti had been tried by a prejudiced judge were probably correct, but one or both of the men may have been guilty. A special committee appointed by the governor of Massachusetts and headed by the president of Harvard University declared Sacco and Vanzetti to be "guilty beyond a reasonable doubt."

Yet the case made many Americans ashamed, and they thought hard about ##some of their prejudices. Vanzetti was quoted as saying with pride, "Never in ou full life could we hope to do such wor for tolerance, for justice, for man's unde standing of man, as now we do by a accident."

Worldwide interest. The Sacco-Vanzet case gave many Americans a new caus to fight for. Moreover, it showed the powe ful interest in United States affairs whic the rest of the world had developed.

Before this century began, most Eu ropeans had not even known the name o the president of the United States—excep for Lincoln. They had not known much o anything about American politics. But a the day for the execution of Sacco an Vanzetti—August 23, 1927—drew neare there were demonstrations all over th world. Most were staged in the effort t bring about a delay in the punishment.

Often a really shattering event tha finally affects people deeply passes almos unnoticed at the time it occurs. One even like this, taking place at the height of th interest in the Sacco-Vanzetti case, wa the firing of the first liquid-fuel rocket i 1926. The genius responsible was Rober H. Goddard.

##Stress that "prejudice" comes from "prejudge."

Men and women in Sydney, Australia, demonstrate in 1926 in behalf of the two doomed Americans. (The first letter of the word let is missing.)

UPI

24

Goddard's rocket promised to have a very long range. Americans were uninterested.

Goddard was a professor of physics at Clark University, in Worcester, Massachusetts. There in fifteen years of research he developed the basic theories of rocket propulsion, including the first practical automatic device for steering rockets.

Unbelievable as it may seem, Goddard could obtain no support for his work from the United States government. He moved his experiments to New Mexico after the Worcester Fire Department objected to them.

UPI

Robert H. Goddard, "father of the modern rocket," demonstrates a model he made in 1924.

1. Give three reasons for the opposition in the 1920's to unrestricted immigration in the United States. 2. What was the result of the opposition? 3. Describe the Ku Klux Klan of the 1920's. 4. Give the main facts in the Sacco-Vanzetti case.

ss that Americans in the 1920's were not looking for strong Presidents.

Prosperity Survives Two Weak Presidents

The 1920's were a period of general prosperity. The quantity of goods and services he country was producing had increased greatly since the prewar years. The value of all these goods and services in 1929 averaged about $850 for every person in he United States. The figure had risen more or less steadily since 1922.

Hardly a day passed that saw no new gadget or gimmick or fad to claim a part of a family's income. And what a consumer could not afford to buy directly out of his pocket, he could pay for on the installment plan. In other words, he could pay for it little by little—a stated sum each week or each month.

Not everyone was really prosperous. Farmers and workingmen, for instance, went through some difficult times. But millions now could hope to share in the country's abundance. Year by year Americans had brighter hopes for a better life.

Harding, of Ohio

A remarkable effect of all these developments was that politics did not seem to produce leaders as able as those in business and industry. In the 1920's, moreover, the public appeared to be satisfied to have Presidents who did not raise unpleasant subjects—like distress on the farms and the unsatisfied hopes of laboring men and minorities.

In 1920 the Republicans nominated as their choice for President Warren G. Harding, a Senator from Ohio. They picked Calvin Coolidge, the governor of Massachusetts, to be the Vice-President.

A Republican party member explained, in part, why Harding was chosen. He said, "Harding is no world-beater. But he's the best of the second-raters."

Actually, Harding had been chosen by

ese made up a very large group of Americans. Though goods and services were increasing quantity, people with low incomes could buy few of them. Nevertheless, industry was gradly increasing everybody's opportunity for a better standard of living.

\# a group of party politicians who knew they could easily manage him. The blunt truth is that Harding did not have the ability or character to be a satisfactory President.

Harding's Democratic opponent was also an Ohioan, Governor James M. Cox. His running mate was Franklin D. Roosevelt, of New York.

The League question. Much of the campaign centered around the question of whether or not the United States ought to join the League of Nations. Harding's position was clear: no. "We seek no part in directing the destinies of the Old World," he said. "We do not mean to be entangled." Cox at first supported joining the League, but his enthusiasm later weakened.

Harding had the ability to make high-sounding speeches without saying much that was important. Nevertheless, he won the election.

"Normalcy." Harding had talked of a need to "return to normalcy." "Normalcy" was a word he coined and never defined, but it seemed to mean a return to earlier, simpler days. The public, though, was not expecting the kind of presidency that he provided.

First of all, Harding had no plans and no ideas for the country. Although he had long been in government, he did not know how he ought to deal with public problem. He told a secretary, for instance, "I can make a . . . thing out of this tax problem . . . I listen to one side and they seem right and then . . . I talk to the other side an they seem just as right, and here I am where I started."

Scandal upon scandal. Within a short time the country heard of scandals and dishonesty in the executive branch of the government which could not be compared with any others in American history. The most outrageous is remembered as the Teapot Dome affair. It took place in 1922 although it did not become public until 1924.

The villain in this scandal was the Secretary of the Interior, Albert B. Fall, of New Mexico. Fall had persuaded the President to transfer to his department the control of certain oil deposits that the navy relied on. One of them was a deposit—reserve—in Wyoming called Teapot Dome. Having acquired control of the reserves, Fall granted secret leases to private oil companies to drill on them. Fall had taken bribes from the oil companies involved. In time he was sent to prison for his crime. Very serious charges of bribe taking

Robert Todd Lincoln was born in 1843. A lawyer, he was Secretary of War under Garfield and Arthur.

In May, 1922, a hundred thousand people witnessed the dedication of the Lincoln Memorial, in Washington. Among them (*left to right*) were Coolidge, Chief Justice Taft, Harding, and Lincoln's son Robert Todd Lincoln (see page 408).

Underwood & Underwood

were also made against Attorney-General Harry M. Daugherty. Although Daugherty escaped jail, the public was shocked that the chief law-enforcement officer of the land had misbehaved so badly.

Death in San Francisco. Harding was spared the public embarrassment that these scandals would have brought him. In June, 1923, he had left Washington for a tour across the country and to Alaska. The President had seemed to be in failing health, unable to sleep or relax. It is possible that he had had wind of the dishonesty in his administration.

Back in this country from Alaska, Harding died on August 2 of a stroke, after a week in bed. The citizens of the nation mourned the death of their handsome, playful President, unaware of the disasters which had probably caused him much grief in his last days.

Silent Calvin Coolidge

When Vice-President Calvin Coolidge received the news from San Francisco of Harding's death, he was visiting his father, a storekeeper in Vermont. As his father held the Bible, he took the oath of office by the light of a kerosene lamp. Later when asked about his feelings on reaching the presidency so unexpectedly, Coolidge replied, "I thought I could swing it."

Coolidge, sometimes called Silent Cal because he was a man of few words, represented in the public's mind the Yankee virtues of thrift, hard work, and a strong personal character. These qualities in the President were particularly welcome to Americans after the scandals of the Harding administration became known.

His rise to fame. But Coolidge was also a man who was not very original. He had come to national attention in 1919 when the policemen of Boston had gone on strike. As governor of Massachusetts, he had been very slow to act. But a statement

White House Collection

Mrs. Coolidge, a gracious First Lady, with her dog, often an uninvited guest at White House affairs, begging food from official company.

Review "What the Pilgrims stand for," p. 84. Our idea of the New Englander, or Yankee, still based in part on our ideas of the Pilgrims. ("Yankee" by extension is a term applied sometimes to any northerner, or to any American in a foreign country.)

621

he had made had pleased the people and won him the congratulations of President Wilson. Coolidge had said, "There is no right to strike against the public safety by anybody, anywhere, any time."

Coolidge's political appointments were, on the whole, excellent. Also, the warmth and dignity of the First Lady, Grace Coolidge, earned for the administration the friendship of many who disliked the President's sometimes icy manner.

Coolidge's sixteen-year-old son died of blood poisoning in 1924—the result of an infected blister he had raised playing tennis on a White House tennis court. His father wrote some time later, "When he went, the power and the glory of the presidency went with him."

The business ahead. Coolidge was elected President in his own right later that year by an overwhelming margin. His slogan was "Keep cool with Coolidge." Yet he aroused little enthusiasm. Well in advance, he announced he would not run again in 1928. Coolidge seems to have sensed that

the nation required stronger leadership than he was capable of providing.

Harding and Coolidge were Presidents who left few permanent marks on the country. But most Americans were not looking for strong guidance from the White House in the 1920's. They were busy enjoying new standards of taste and behavior set, not, as in the past, by a few politicians or ministers or editors, but by "the crowd." They were busy, too, trying to get used to technological change that was occurring at a faster rate than ever before. And the best thing they were getting used to was the idea that prosperity was here to stay.

---

1. What facts explain why Harding was nominated for the presidency by the Republicans in 1920? 2. Name the chief issue in the campaign and tell how Harding stood regarding it. 3. Describe Harding's presidency. 4. For what is Coolidge chiefly remembered?

The list and the questions under "The Shapers of Our World"

The Workshop

could be the basis of a test on Chapter 27.

The Shapers of Our World

In the 1920's Americans created the impression that they were trying to cover serious matters through playfulness. Which of the following showed the playfulness? How? Which indicated the serious side of life? How?

Henry Ford	Gertrude Ederle
"Model T"	Rudy Vallee
Wright brothers	Ku Klux Klan
Charles A.	Sacco-Vanzetti
Lindbergh	trial
Thomas A. Edison	Robert H.
Rudolph Valentino	Goddard
Jack Dempsey	Warren G. Harding

Eighteenth	Teapot Dome
Amendment	affair
Gene Tunney	Calvin Coolidge
Babe Ruth	

Adding to Your Vocabulary

Show your understanding of the "golden twenties" by using these words:

flapper	speakeasy
close-up	rum running
fade-out	radio network
prohibition	wavelength
bootlegging	jazz
moonshine	general strike
hijacker	

#Ask why the twenties should be spoken of as golden. (Because of the new developments in technology, the increased leisure, the new amusements, and the absence of war.) The period is also sometimes called the roaring twenties. (Because of the lawlessness, cars, and new style

Thinking Things Through

After reviewing the questions within the hapter, discuss the following:

1. By giving examples, show how Americans in the 1920's wanted to make hanges in their personal lives and at the ame time to turn the clock back to an arlier time in their national life.

2. How did the automobile, the airplane, he movies, professional sports, and the adio help to unify the American people?

3. What does the failure of prohibition how about the relationship between the nforcement and public approval of a law?

4. Why was it possible for an interest n spectator sports to develop in the 1920's ut not in the 1820's?

5. Why did labor groups tend to oppose nrestricted immigration?

6. How were the fear of aliens, the deire to restrict immigration, and the development of the Ku Klux Klan related to the ear of joining the League of Nations?

7. Why was it so difficult to insure a air trial for Sacco and Vanzetti?

8. In what way did Harding and Coolidge seem to fit in with the outlook of the American people during the 1920's?

9. The 1920's were a time of hero worhip. Why?

10. A campaign slogan in 1924 was Keep cool with Coolidge." How did this eem to show the average American citien's attitude toward serious problems?

11. Why is an organization like the Ku Klux Klan dangerous to a democracy?

The Research Center

1. Bring the class examples of advertisng of American products today and compare them with the advertisements shown n the chapter. Do advertisers today use ny of the methods of the 1920's? To whom do the advertisements you bring in ppeal? How?

2. Obtain recordings of song hits of the 1920's. Compare them with today's hits.

3. Play for the class Edward R. Murrow's recording "I Can Hear It Now . . . ," Vol. III: 1919–1932. Be sure you know the important facts about the life of each person speaking.

4. With the help of the home-economics teacher, prepare a picture display showing the fashions of the 1920's. Compare them with those of the "gay nineties" and today.

5. Present a report on the life of one leader of American industry discussed in the chapter, emphasizing his contributions to American culture.

6. On an outline map of the world, mark the locations from which the ancestors of each member of the class came. How does your map show that we are a "nation of immigrants"?

7. Arrange a field trip to a local factory to see an assembly line in action. Before making the trip, list the information you wish to obtain. Afterward, discuss what you found out.

8. Find out what restrictions on immigration the United States has at present and report on them.

9. Prepare reports on two trials of the 1920's: the Scopes trial and the Sacco-Vanzetti trial. Discuss the verdicts handed down and the importance of each trial.

Your Opinion, Please

1. In 1919 Coolidge made this statement about a strike of policemen in Boston: "There is no right to strike against the public safety by anybody, anywhere, any time." Do you agree? Explain.

2. What causes race prejudice? Religious prejudice? Prejudice against foreigners? How can these prejudices be overcome?

3. What would Thomas Jefferson have thought of American industrial development in the 1920's?

(a)

(c)

NRA MEMBER

(d)

(e)

U.S.

WE DO OUR PART

(f)

(a) Spring in Central Park
in New York—a bit of the country
in America's largest urban center.
(b) Food prices in 1933, in the
depths of the Great Depression.
(c) President Franklin Delano Roosevelt
in one of his "fireside chats"
with the American people.
(d) The emblem of one of the best-known
measures of Roosevelt's New Deal.
(e) The fruit that became a symbol of
hard times because unemployed people
sold it on street corners
in trying to make a living.
(f) Members of the Civilian Conservation
Corps, who were given temporary
work protecting land and forests—
one of Roosevelt's efforts
to fight the Great Depression.

(g) A design on one of the sacks of flour sent by Americans to help feed Belgians after the First World War.
(h) The Kansas state flower and the trademark of the Republican candidate in the presidential election of 1936.

(g)

(h)

CHAPTER 28

THE PROMISE OF A NEW DEAL

is chapter deals with the Great Depression and Franklin D. Roosevelt's efforts to bring about reforms in
merican life. Since the suffering during the depression arose because of conditions foreign to most stu-
nts today, the pictures in the chapter will be most helpful.

I N the 1920's the city more and more was influencing American life as a whole, and the problems of its people were begin-ning to come to the surface. No national figure, however, had yet tried to deal with these problems—or had been forced to.

view the meaning of "depression." (Business drops off, people lose their jobs, and prices fall.)

The Nation Falls into a Great Depression

Before the 1920's were over, city people were in the majority in the United States. In 1910 over 54 percent of all Americans had lived in towns of 2500 or less, but in 1930 only 44 percent lived in such rural communities. In the ten years between 1920 and 1930 the population of the ur-ban part of America increased 27 per-cent, while that of rural America grew by only 4 percent.

A Revealing Election

The presidential election in 1928 seemed to show how strongly Americans felt about the increasing importance of cities. Both the Democrats and the Republicans chose good men to head their tickets. But the differences between the backgrounds of the candidates had a startling effect on the election's outcome.

Al Smith, of New York. The Democrats that year nominated Alfred E. Smith, the governor of New York. He was only the second presidential candidate of a major party from a large city (see page 557).

Born on New York City's lower East Side, Smith had had a childhood different from childhoods of politicians born on farms and in small towns. He had never fished along the banks of a country stream, where a boy can feel close to nature. He had not become used to climbing to the highest branches of trees, where a boy can perch

Ask why people moved to the cities in the 1920's and what the condition of farmers was during
at time. (The questions will give students an opportunity to review the attractions of the cities
the twenties and the fact that farmers generally were not prosperous.)

Wide World

Al Smith jauntily waves his derby in a campaign appearance in Milwaukee, Wisconsin, in 1928.

#Students should recall the religious intolerance of the 1920's, already discussed.

brown derby and smoked cigars, seemed to millions of Americans to be a perfect representative of the city. Many of those millions thought of cities as dens of sin and corruption. As a result, Smith had a heavy burden to bear in the campaign.

Herbert Hoover, from Iowa. The Republicans nominated as their presidential candidate Herbert C. Hoover, originally of Iowa, who had been the Secretary of Commerce under Harding and Coolidge. He had been a farm boy, knowing both the hard work and the personal satisfaction of "doing chores." Born as poor as Smith, he had nevertheless been able to obtain an education at Stanford University, in California. He was grown up before he ever set foot east of the Mississippi.

Hoover became a millionaire mining engineer whose work took him to many parts of the world. During the First World War he gave up his career in order to organize relief for the Belgian people. After the armistice, as one of the best-known living Americans, he was ready for a political career in his own country.

The nation's feelings. The contest between Smith and Hoover showed how keenly city and country were battling one another. It brought to the surface much intolerance, some of it anti-Catholic.

On the other hand, there was in rural regions widespread respect for the governor of New York. The leading editor in the state of Kansas, a Republican, said of Smith, "There is not in American life today a clearer, stronger, more accurately working brain in any man's head than Al Smith's brain."

Aided no doubt by the country's prosperity, for which his party was given the credit, Hoover won handsomely. City problems would one day be regarded as especially important business of the nation. But that day had not yet come.

The voting returns. The vote showed that the country still had enough prejudice

himself and feel independent of the whole world.

On the other hand, Smith had known what it was like to live in a crowded tenement. This may have helped him develop sympathy for people who had to live in slums. He had learned to swim in the city's East River, already being polluted by factory and human wastes. This may have helped him see early some of the problems of an industrial nation.

Al Smith was a Roman Catholic, having served as an altar boy for many years at a local church. As he advanced in his public career, he joined Tammany Hall, New York City's powerful political machine. He also became a pioneer in calling for social improvements by government. And almost from its start, he opposed prohibition.

So it was that Al Smith, who wore a

##Republicans had also been in office between 1921 and 1929, when Hoover was inaugurated. Under Wilson the tariff had been lowered, but it had been raised again in 1922 and would be raised to the highest level ever in 1930. Many connected the tariff with the prosperity.

against Catholics to make even states which usually voted Democratic turn Republican. It also showed the great strength of the Democratic party in the big cities. Smith carried many of these former Republican strongholds. The children of the immigrants of the early 1900's were beginning to cast their ballots for candidates who knew the problems of cities, where most of them lived.

The Big Crash

When Coolidge left office, he told Americans that their prosperity was "absolutely sound." Many people said that American prosperity had now become permanent. The automobile business was excellent, which in turn made other industries, especially the steel industry, expand.

Down, down, down. But early in September, 1929, prices in the stock market, where stock in industries was sold, began to fall, possibly an indirect result of poor money conditions in Britain. The drop continued, until by early November stock prices had fallen to 50 percent of what they had been only a few weeks before.

Unemployment. The effect of the stock-market crash was felt in a very short time even by millions of people who did not own a single share of stock. Especially hard hit were workingmen in industry, because people who suffered losses in the stock market cut down their buying of factory goods. This resulted in many unsold products, and manufacturers were forced to lay off the employees who had produced them. At first thousands and then millions were thrown out of work.

The size of the disaster. Many of the people who were affected used up their life savings. Goods they had purchased on the installment plan were picked up by the stores that had sold them. Many families lost not only newly purchased goods but their homes as well—because they could

Herbert Hoover Presidential Library

President Hoover as he looked in 1931. Notice the stiff collar and the "ice-cream pants."

not meet mortgage payments. Sometimes the members of a family would sit in the street on their chairs and beds, with no place to go.

In fear and flight. The depression also hit agriculture very hard. Things could not have been worse. The widespread unemployment meant that in the cities people bought less food, for they were simply eating less. Tens of thousands of farmers, unable to pay off mortgages, lost their farms. Some merely took to the road in their old cars and with their families worked wherever they could—a day here, a month there.

On the sidewalks. Many of the unemployed in the cities took advantage of a gift of the International Apple Shippers' Association and sold apples from crates on the street corners. Anyone who wanted to

This paragraph shows how dependent on each other the people of this country (and other
untries) are. In an industrialized country, especially, what affects one large group of
ople or one large, important industry affects other groups and industries.

627

Call attention to the clothes, the few possessions, and the discouraged manner of the father.

These victims of the drought, having fled their Oklahoma farm, are headed for California.

Franklin D. Roosevelt Library

help them could buy an apple—for a nickel.

The world seemed upside down for Americans. Once they had been proud because many humble men and women had gone from rags to riches in the United States. Now they had to face the fact that millions had within a short time gone from riches to rags.

Searching for a Solution

Although Hoover was blamed for the depression (as Van Buren and Cleveland had been in their administrations), he struggled hard to straighten the country out. But what plans should he follow?

Voluntary coöperation. When the Great Depression, as it was called, first came, Hoover held conferences at the White House with heads of railroads and leaders of industry. He tried to persuade them not to fire employees and to go ahead with their programs of expansion. In short, his first step was to ask for the *voluntary* coöperation of businessmen.

Also, Hoover wired the governors and mayors in the United States to urge them to increase their spending on public construction. His idea was that the slack in private employment would be taken up by governmental employment.

Another step which the President recommended was a cut in income taxes. He hoped to increase the amount of money available to buy goods with and in this way cause a demand for factory products.

In deeper. The results Hoover hoped for did not come about. Businessmen cut their costs to the bone, trying to stay alive. States gave so much money for the relief of the unemployed that they could not pay for new public buildings.

Drought and dust. On top of everything, below-normal rainfall throughout the country produced a costly drought beginning in 1930. The drought brought further difficulties for farmers.

The drought also led to fearful dust storms in a wide area from Texas to the Dakotas, which came to be called the dust bowl. There the topsoil, blown by high

628   #Hoover was trying to improve conditions without getting the federal government to give direct aid to the unemployed. Business and government officials were to provide employment.
    ##Since comparatively few people paid income taxes then, the results were unsatisfactory.

winds, rose in huge clouds which some-times blotted the sun from view at high noon. The dust seeped through even the most tightly closed window. It ruined food that ordinarily would be considered well protected.

Idle wanderers. Many farmers and their families grimly left the damaged land—which, often, their grandfathers had ac-quired under the Homestead Act. They were not the only uprooted persons. Many young people hopped freight trains to "ride the rails" in search—they did not know where—of better opportunity. Sometimes a youth left home because he thought he was "one mouth too many" to feed.

Hundreds of thousands of jobless peo-ple with no other place to lay their heads slept in the parks or—if they were lucky—in abandoned factories, where it was warmer than outdoors. It is estimated that a million people—young *and* old—were "on the road" in 1931.

Hoover kept on saying that good times would return. The Democrats, of course, took advantage of the embarrassment of the Republicans when they could not im-prove business conditions.

Stubborn difficulties. In general, the Dem-ocrats did not yet have plans for dealing

with the depression which promised any better results than the Republicans had been able to bring about. Actually, neither party had realized so far that there were serious difficulties preventing the nation from recovering rapidly.

One of these difficuties was that the # income of the American people was too unevenly distributed. For example, in 1929 one-third of all personal income went to only 5 percent of the population.

Another difficulty was that a great spurt in technological change in factories had thrown many people out of work. Because at that time there was no unemployment insurance to tide the victims over until they could find other jobs, their suffering was immediate and direct.

A third difficulty grew out of the wide-spread belief that whatever benefited busi-ness benefited everybody. The rights of workingmen often were ignored altogether.

A fourth drawback was that many men and women, one way or another, were held back by the color of their skin. And in 1930 there were over twelve and a half million non-white people in this country—more than one out of every ten Americans.

Fifth, bad times in Europe and else-where in the world had caused a severe

almost total lack of
oney led Americans to
ve in miserable con-
tions like these. The
eather was cold.

Shacks like these served as
homes for men out of work
in every large American
city. Tragic slums
of this kind were
nicknamed Hoovervilles.

Franklin D. Roosevelt Library

Herbert Hoover Presidential Library

Lou Henry Hoover, a well-read First Lady, spoke several languages and liked science.

drop in trade among nations. The United States depended on this trade.

A calm public. In the face of their condition, Americans were patient and long-suffering. There were a few outbreaks of violence. Some farmers joined together to try to stop banks from foreclosing mortgages—that is, taking over their property for failure to pay debts. Some tried to barricade highways to prevent milk trucks from reaching the towns, hoping in that way to force a rise in milk prices. But mostly Americans simply waited for the sun to shine again.

The President's heavy burden. However, Hoover was more and more blamed for the nagging depression. People asked how such a gifted organizer could fail to find a way to end the crisis. He felt keenly the stings of this criticism. But lacking personal warmth and a "glad hand," he was never able to make Americans confident that he could end the depression.

Hoover found his only peace at a weekend retreat, Rapidan Camp, in Virginia. There he enjoyed especially his favorite sport of trout fishing. Mrs. Hoover also loved the out-of-doors. She was for many years active in the Girl Scout movement. The national officers of the Girl Scouts often met with her at the White House and at Rapidan Camp.

In 1930 the Republicans lost control of the House of Representatives for the first time since Woodrow Wilson's presidency. That year, also, Franklin D. Roosevelt, a Democrat, was elected to his second two-year term as governor of New York. He immediately became a favorite for presidential nomination by his party in 1932.

The question of direct relief. It was clear that the federal government was going to have to provide *direct* relief—money or jobs or both—to the victims of the depression. They had been depending on private charity, which had been considerable. People who had been able to help others had been very generous. But the burden was now far too great for private agencies.

Hoover, however, did not believe that giving direct relief was a proper role for the federal government. He, like others, was influenced by the fact that in almost all earlier depressions the government had allowed things to work themselves out.

The cities tried hard to relieve the suffering of their people. When city governments ran out of money, the states stepped in to help them.

New York, under the governorship of Franklin Roosevelt, took the lead in giving direct aid to the unemployed. Before long most of the other states were carrying on similar programs. But what would happen when they ran out of money?

Many Democrats in Congress were already declaring that the federal government would have to provide help. Franklin

#Americans cherished the ideals of self-reliance and independence that had been handed down from the time when the frontier was being pushed westward. Once Americans had been able to rely chiefly on their own efforts, but now, because of industry, conditions were different.

"Rainy Night," painted by Charles E. Burchfield during the depression, seems to express the feeling of Americans of the time.

D. Roosevelt made it known that he shared this belief. Hoover was ready to offer direct relief to businesses through loans, but he refused to allow direct aid to unemployed men and women.

The "Bonus Marchers." The relations between the President and the people reached a low point in the summer of 1932 in Washington, D.C. There about twenty thousand unemployed veterans of the First World War had gathered to seek the passage of a bonus bill. This would have granted them ahead of time a payment they had been promised when they were in the army.

Hoover ordered the army's Chief of Staff, General Douglas MacArthur, to get rid of the marchers. MacArthur and his troops, fully armed and in battle dress, advanced on the "Bonus Army" and scattered it with tear gas. MacArthur's soldiers then set fire to the unused government buildings in which the veterans had been living.

1. Describe the candidates and issues and tell who won the presidential election in 1928. 2. What early steps did the new President take to end the depression? 3. Name five difficulties that stood in the way of better times. 4. How did Hoover view the question of giving direct relief to people?

But in communities throughout the country, individuals fortunate enough to be working contributed money to funds to help those less fortunate. Churches helped as much as possible, as did local charities, but both the churches and the charities received less and less money.

Roosevelt Tries New Experiments

As the public turned away from Hoover, it began to be attracted to Governor Franklin D. Roosevelt. When he had spoken in April, 1932, of the "forgotten man," millions had felt he was speaking of *them*.

A Man with a Smile

As the presidential campaign of 1932 approached, Roosevelt appeared likely to be Hoover's opponent. Roosevelt's lack of respect for old ways of doing things, his willingness to try new ones, and his warm smile and manner seemed to be what the country needed.

The nomination. In the Democratic convention in June, at Chicago, Roosevelt had two chief rivals. They were Al Smith, who felt that this time he could win the election, and John Nance Garner, of Texas, the Speaker of the House of Representatives. However, the nomination of Roosevelt, skillfully planned, followed only a brief struggle.

Roosevelt flew to Chicago to accept the nomination in person, thereby breaking a custom as old as the political parties. "Let it be from now on the task of our party to break foolish traditions [that is, customs]," he said in his speech. He wound up by declaring, "I pledge you, I pledge myself, to a new deal for the American people." The words "new deal" became the name of Roosevelt's program, which was still not announced.

Overwhelming victory. During the campaign Roosevelt sometimes contradicted himself. While promising reforms which would be very expensive, he promised to cut federal costs. Nevertheless, he also pledged a repeal of prohibition (something that was accomplished in 1933). Most important, however, by his tireless energy he made Hoover seem weary and idle. On election night, as expected, Roosevelt won a stunning victory, capturing all but six states.

The making of the "Chief." What kind of man had the country sent to the White House? This question was in the minds of millions of people.

Roosevelt, an only child, had been born in 1882 in a mansion overlooking the Hudson River at Hyde Park, New York. His

Roosevelt's smile and handshake were valuable assets. His campaign song was "Happy Days Are Here Again."

The Democratic candidate warmly greets a West Virginia miner in his vigorous campaign for the presidency in the fall of 1932.

Franklin D. Roosevelt Library

show you when I get home

We leave here on the first of September, arriving in Hamburg on the second.

With a great deal of love,

I am your affectionate grandson Franklin D. Roosevelt

Hôtel und Kurhaus
ST. BLASIEN
Söd. bad. Schwarzwald
Stationen:
ALBBRUCK u. TITISEE.

St. Blasien, den 23ᵗᵉⁿ Aug. 1896

My dear Grandpapa,

We are having a lovely time in the Black Forest; I have just been trout-fishing but the fish would not bite, so I had to return empty-handed. Mr. Dumper and I got back last Tuesday from

Left: A part of a letter the future President, as a fourteen-year-old, wrote from Germany to his grandfather.
Right: Franklin Delano, aged fifteen.

father, a wealthy man, had then been fifty-four years old. His mother, twenty-eight years old, would live to see her boy in the White House.

The young Roosevelt had been taught only privately until he was fourteen years old. His tutors had given him a good grounding in French and German, and he had traveled widely abroad. As a youth he had seen more of the world than any previous President (except John Quincy Adams) had seen all his life.

Marriage. Shortly after his graduation from Harvard, he wed in 1905 a distant cousin, Eleanor Roosevelt. Her "Uncle Ted," then the president of the United States, went to New York for the event.

Personal suffering. After being a member of the New York State legislature, Franklin Roosevelt, as we have seen, served as Wilson's Assistant Secretary of the Navy. Then a terrible personal tragedy struck him while he was vacationing with his family in Canada.

Roosevelt awoke one morning to find that he had a burning temperature and that his legs were paralyzed. He had contracted polio. With the help of baths at Warm Springs, Georgia, he gradually regained his health. But he never was able to walk again without help.

Until almost the end of his career as President, Roosevelt never publicly mentioned the fact that he was crippled, and no newspaper or magazine did, either. Most Americans were not aware of his handicap until after his death. Extraordinary arrangements were always made for his convenience and safety wherever he happened to be.

Roosevelt seemed to have developed a keener feeling for unfortunate people because of his illness. Moreover, having survived a dread disease, he developed a manner which appeared to say, "Things can only get better." As a close associate said of him in admiration, "The guy *never* knows when he is licked."

Son of wealthy parents, Roosevelt had received advantages which helped fit him for the role of President in a time when the United States became deeply involved in world affairs.

Ask how this disease has been eliminated or practically eliminated.

Inaugural words. Roosevelt delivered his inaugural address on the Capitol steps before thousands who braved windy weather to be there. He heartened them and the millions who listened on the radio. Within the next few days he received almost five hundred thousand letters of appreciation.

Roosevelt's words were a simple call for courage and a promise of vigorous leadership. "This great nation," he declared, "will endure as it has endured, will revive and will prosper." And he then added words which have become famous: "So first of all let me assert my firm belief that the only thing we have to fear is fear itself."

Trial and Error

"F. D. R.," as the new President was often called, was willing to experiment. If one plan did not work well, he turned to another without becoming downcast. A Republican Senator wrote soon after the inauguration, "We have exchanged for a frown in the White House a smile."

The Cabinet. Immediately after Roosevelt took office, the city of Washington came alive not only with new men but also with new ideas. The Cabinet, made up of unusually able people, included ex-Senator Cordell Hull, of Tennessee, as Secretary of State and Henry A. Wallace, of Iowa, a former Republican, as Secretary of Agriculture. As Secretary of Labor, Roosevelt chose the first woman to sit in a President's Cabinet, Frances Perkins, of New York.

Getting close to the people. The most important first step that Roosevelt took was to close all the banks in the country for four days. His immediate purpose was to have experts examine the records of the banks in order to make sure that only the sound ones reopened. In typical blunt words he told the people on the radio, "I can assure you that it is safer to keep your money in a reopened bank than under the mattress."

Roosevelt's use of the radio for what he called fireside chats put him in closer touch with the people than any other President had ever been. He almost always began his broadcast cheerily with, "My friends . . . ." Then he would explain plainly and simply what he proposed to do about whatever problem was before the nation.

The role of Eleanor Roosevelt. A great source of strength for the President was Mrs. Roosevelt. She provided him with an extra set of eyes and ears. Whenever she returned from one of her frequent trips, Roosevelt would want to hear every detail she could recall. She later wrote, "That I became, as the years went by, a better and better reporter and a better and better observer was largely owing to the fact that Franklin's questions covered such a wide range. I found myself obliged to notice everything."

Some Americans thought that Mrs. Roosevelt meddled too much in affairs that were not her business. Actually she was concerning herself with problems which had not yet forced themselves on the attention of the general public. These included the plight of the Negroes and other Americans who lacked advantages.#

Mrs. Roosevelt's love of people and sympathy for them made her famous and brought her the respect of the entire world. In her speeches and writing she was able to express her deep feeling about human suffering. She wrote, for example, about a house she visited in the West Virginia coal-mining country:

There were six children in the family, and they acted as though they were afraid of strangers. I noticed a bowl on the table filled with scraps, the kind that you or I might give to a dog, and I saw children, evidently looking for their noon-day meal, take a handful out of that bowl and go out munching. That was all they had to eat.

Mrs. Roosevelt, who set
a new pace for a First Lady,
visits a coal mine
in Ohio in 1935.

Wide World

As I went out, two of the children had gathered enough courage to stand by the door, the little boy holding a white rabbit in his arms. It was evident it was a most cherished pet. The little girl was thin and scrawny and had a gleam in her eyes as she looked at her brother. Turning to me she said: "He thinks we are not going to eat it, but we are," and at that the small boy fled down the road clutching the rabbit closer than ever.

Unemployment-relief program. The New Deal was a combination of restored confidence among the people and many imaginative methods of dealing with the nation's problems. The first group of the laws passed were *recovery* measures, to lift the nation out of the depression. Others were reforms—chiefly ways of preventing depressions in the future.

The first of the recovery tasks which could not wait was the feeding of millions of unemployed people and their families. Roosevelt proposed to do this by granting federal money to the states. He appointed a social worker, Harry Hopkins, of New York, to carry out this program of relief.

Hopkins had a sharp sense of what was required in the huge task, which nobody had ever performed before. He chose some

exceptionally good men to help him with the program. To head the work in Missouri, for instance, he appointed a respected local politician named Harry S Truman.

At the time the relief program began, it was hoped that its work would be necessary only for a short time. But by the end of the year, it was clear that unemployment would not be ended quickly. From the start Hopkins had believed strongly in putting men to work for their relief checks rather than in giving them money outright. He persuaded the President as the year 1933 was coming to a close that the administration ought to try *work relief* as a way of helping the unemployed.

As a result of Hopkins' advice, the President created a Civil Works Administration (CWA). Hopkins, its head, soon was in charge of finding jobs for about four million men—almost as many as had been in military uniform during the First World War. Many of the jobs were simply "made work," such as raking leaves in the parks and restoring public buildings so they could be used for adult-education classes.

Through the CWA about a billion dollars was poured into circulation, and a slight improvement in business resulted. But "F. D. R." was criticized for his "ex-

It is important to make a distinction between the two kinds of measures, or laws, passed.
isting the recovery laws on the chalkboard (using the abbreviated names) will be helpful.

#The WPA erected public buildings, built or improved public parks, and laid sidewalks and thousands of miles of roads.

WPA workers building a dike in an effort to hold back a spring flood.

travagance." An old Texas word, boondoggle, came into use to describe public work that seemed to be needless. Many businessmen, feeling safer in 1934 than in 1932, were finding fault with the President for "wasting money on boondoggling."

The WPA. By the spring of 1935, Con-# gress replaced direct relief with the Works Progress Administration (WPA) and provided almost one and a half billion dollars to run it. Harry Hopkins was put in charge.

The WPA enrolled over eight million people before it was ended in 1943. Because it aimed to spend its funds on wages rather than materials, many of its projects seemed wasteful. But the WPA contributed greatly to improving the appearance of America. It constructed a thousand airports throughout the land, built or rebuilt over a hundred thousand public buildings, laid a half million sewers, and improved thousands of parks and school grounds.

"We do our part." Businessmen also received help. The most outstanding was that provided in the National Industrial Recovery Act—usually called the NRA— passed in the late spring of 1933. The NRA allowed businessmen in a particular industry to write a "code of fair competition" for themselves. Such a code would estab-

lish fair prices, set minimum wages (the lowest wages that can legally be paid), and otherwise regulate business.

A general code was prepared for use until each industry made its special arrangements. It called for a minimum wage of 30¢ or 40¢ an hour and no more than 35 or 40 working hours a week.

The NRA came into existence with rallies and parades all over the country. The slogan it adopted was "We do our part." Businesses coöperating with their industry's code displayed a sign featuring a blue eagle. For a time, it was not only a splendid emblem of American strength and purpose but also a symbol of the spirit of the entire New Deal.

Aid for youth. Young people, representing, of course, the future of the nation, were especially singled out for help by the New Deal. An early move of the President's in 1933 was to bring about the creation of the Civilian Conservation Corps.

The CCC took unemployed young men —in the end, over two and a half million of them passed through its ranks—and put them to work in the forests and on soil-conservation projects. They planted millions of acres of trees, stocked streams with over a billion fish, fought forest fires,

636 The CWA had provided direct relief to the unemployed, although those aided had been assigned to various federal projects. The WPA, on the other hand, was a work-relief program from the outset. Its aim was to give work that would make men feel useful, besides providing income.

and battled pests like grasshoppers and gypsy moths. Members of the CCC received only part of their small wages. The rest of the money was sent home to their needy families.

In June, 1935, the President established the National Youth Administration. During the eight years the NYA was in existence, it found jobs in their schools for over six hundred thousand college youths and over a million and a half high school students. They aided teachers in various ways, assisted in laboratories, checked books in and out of libraries, and performed other useful tasks. The small sum of money a student could earn each month helped him to remain in school.

NYA funds were distributed through the states. The director of the NYA said that its best state administrator—also its youngest—was Lyndon B. Johnson, in Texas. Appointed when he was not yet twenty-seven years old, Johnson had known poverty himself. He brought great sympathy as well as energy to his job.

Help for farmers. The farmers also received help. The most important came to them through the Agricultural Adjustment Act of May, 1933. This act aimed to raise farm prices by reducing the amount of farm goods produced.

Under the AAA, farmers were to be paid a subsidy, or grant of money, for cutting their production of wheat, cotton, corn, hogs, rice, tobacco, and milk. The cost of the subsidy was to be met by a special tax paid by those who *processed*, or treated, these commodities—for one example, the owner of a mill that turned wheat into flour. Of course, the tax was passed along to the consumers in the form of higher prices.

A sad fact was that the AAA aided the bigger farmers especially. What help was there for the small farmers, desperately trying to save their farms? And what about the sharecroppers?

For such people the help came only slowly—and indirectly. Funds to help some farmers came in 1934 through the Federal Farm Mortgage Corporation, a government agency. Through the Resettlement Administration, a small number of farmers were moved to better land. (Starting out with high hopes, the RA at first had planned to move 500,000 families. In the end, however, it moved fewer than 4500.)

The hand of the Court. The laws providing for the NRA and the AAA were the chief recovery measures passed in "F. D. R.".'s first administration. But both were declared unconstitutional.

The NRA was declared unconstitutional in 1935. The particular case that brought about this decision—often called the sick-chicken case—involved a New York poultry company which had violated the NRA code for the live-poultry industry. The company had sold diseased chickens and had violated the industry's wages-and-hours agreement. The Court said that Congress in setting up the NRA had given to businessmen the right to make laws about wages and hours. Under the Constitution Congress alone may make laws.

In 1936 the Supreme Court stated in the case of the AAA that the processor's tax was a method of taking money from one group of people for the benefit of another. This is unconstitutional, the Court said, because the Constitution states that taxes may be levied only to promote the "general welfare."

---

1. Give the main facts about the early life of the successful candidate in the presidential election in 1932. 2. Name three members of the new Cabinet. 3. Name two important recovery laws passed in Roosevelt's first administration and tell what they provided and what happened to them.

Ask why bigger farmers benefited. (They possessed more land than the smaller farmers, and
y not only could afford to cut down their production, but they also received larger subsidies
cause they could leave more land untilled than the smaller farmers could.)

637

Permanent Changes Alter the Country

The Supreme Court decisions stunned Roosevelt. It seemed to him that the Court was claiming a right to paralyze the recovery efforts of the New Deal.

Bold New Arrangements

The President took no steps immediately, however. Possibly this was because the *reform* laws passed during his administration were not declared unconstitutional by the Supreme Court.

The Wheeler Dam on the Tennessee River, begun in 1933 and completed in three years, helps prevent floods and produces power. The lake behind it occupies over 67,000 acres.

Tennessee Valley Authority

Banks and stock exchanges. Some of the most important reforms these laws made dealt with abuses by banks and people who sold stocks and bonds. One law which was passed in 1933 not only prohibited banks from making unsafe investments with their depositors' money but also provided for the Federal Deposit Insurance Corporation. The FDIC insured up to $2500 each deposit in a member bank— one that subscribed to it. (The plan worked so well in protecting deposits against losses in bank failures that the amount of protection was gradually increased over the years.)

Another early step of Roosevelt's first administration was to arrange for the supervision of the stock market. Countless Americans believed that the stock crash had caused the depression. In 1934 Congress established the Securities and Exchange Commission to keep a close eye on the stock-and-bond business.

The TVA. Still another great reform measure was the creation of the Tennessee Valley Authority in May, 1933. The TVA set up a powerful three-man board of directors to plan for the entire Tennessee River region.

There were a number of reasons for wanting to develop the Tennessee Valley. Most important, in this region of about 41,000 square miles, three million people lived—for the most part—in unnecessary poverty. In the springtime floods often overran the land, bringing added misery.

It was clear that a system of dams on the Tennessee River could not only control the river but also help generate great amounts of electricity cheaply. This electricity could work a miracle in the area.

The TVA did its work so successfully

Stress that the TVA, like the creations of some other reform laws, became a permanent part of American life.

Dams Built in the
1930's

0   100   200   300   400 miles

ome students may have visited
e dams shown here and can
escribe them to the rest of the
lass.

Today the TVA alone affects the lives of over five million people,
and the other dams built during the depression
affect many, many more.

that it is today a model for river projects like it throughout the world. A series of dams on the Tennessee River created a 9-foot channel 630 miles long which was quickly busy with water-borne traffic.

The TVA has done more than control floods and generate electric power. It has taught the farmers of the region better ways of managing the land. It has built recreational lakes, maintained wildlife farms, helped control malaria, and been responsible for many other improvements.

Other dams. In the West the Bonneville and the Grand Coulee dams were constructed on the Columbia River. The Hoover Dam, authorized in Hoover's ad-

ministration, was built on the Colorado. These, too, have had a beneficial influence on the lives of the people affected by them.

Protection for the land. Land conservation was one of the chief activities of the New Deal. For example, to deal with the "dust bowl," the President ordered that a shelter belt of trees be planted on the Great Plains. The aim was to break the stiff winds there, hold the soil tighter, and draw moisture. Although there were many jokes about the millions of little trees, they stand today as mighty reminders of Roosevelt's boldness.

Encouragement of working people. A major group of neglected Americans was

Ask what New Deal measures were concerned with conserving natural resources. (Besides the
eation of TVA and the action affecting the "dust bowl," students can name forming the
CC.) The AAA had provided that untilled soil was to be sown to grass to make it more fertile.

639

Lewis argued for industry-wide unions because certain industries--like the one manufacturing automobiles--employed unskilled workers as well as skilled, and craft unions were not suitabl

John L. Lewis, magnetic president of the CIO, is on hand as members of a union sign an agreement.

Wide World

made up of laboring people. To them the New Deal brought many advantages. Under the NRA, labor's right to *bargain collectively*, that is, to arrange for wages and hours with employers, was strengthened. But when wages did not go up, labor grew restless. The letters "NRA," many workingmen said, stood for "National Run Around."

Wagner's work. Meanwhile, Senator Robert F. Wagner, of New York, the immigrant son of a janitor, was becoming a leading spokesman for labor. Wagner believed that the right to bargain collectively was not enough. Workingmen, he said, could not organize successfully unless certain unfair practices of employers were ended. He introduced a bill to bring this about.

Roosevelt was slow to see Wagner's point of view. But in July, 1935, he signed the National Labor Relations Act, generally called the Wagner Act. It created a strong National Labor Relations Board to make sure that employees have the right to bargain collectively with their employers. Among other duties, the National Labor Relations Board supervised factory elections that decided which union would represent the workers in bargaining with employers.

Forming the CIO. The drive to organize workingmen was encouraged by a split in the AFL (see page 509). The result was two great labor organizations in keen rivalry. A partial cause of the split was the Wagner Act's encouragement of large unions made up of all the workers in an industry. The AFL, being composed of craft unions only, opposed such organizations.

The head of the United Mine Workers, John L. Lewis, whose bushy eyebrows and rich command of English were his trademarks, favored developing industry-wide unions. Under his leadership a group was formed within the AFL: the CIO, the Committee for Industrial Organization (later the Congress of Industrial Organizations). It encouraged the creation of industry-wide unions. Later the CIO broke away from the AFL.

For big business there were advantages in dealing with one big union in an industry rather than with a number of craft unions. But business leaders saw also that in a clash with labor one industry-wide union could more easily tie up an entire industry than separate craft unions could.

Struggles between employers and employees. Fierce struggles took place as some factory owners tried to keep union organizers off their premises. But employers

#Contrast collective bargaining with individual bargaining. Workingmen were in a much strong position when collective bargaining was a right and when the Wagner Act enforced that right.

##Although the two organizations separated in 1937, they merged in 1955 to form the AFL-CIO.

fought a losing battle, as workers organized in one big company after another.

In the automobile industry the United Automobile Workers successfully used the sit-down strike as a weapon. (In such a strike, workers remained inside their plants and refused either to work or to leave.) In the end, they gained recognition. The refusal of state and federal governments to use force against the sit-down strikers —a result of the Wagner Act—marked an important change in labor's place in American life.

Roosevelt developed a reputation as being a friend of labor leaders like Walter Reuther, of the United Automobile Workers, and Sidney Hillman, vice-president of the CIO. But though sympathetic, the President never agreed with them entirely.

In 1940 fewer than 30 percent of all nonagricultural working people were organized in unions. Nevertheless, the number of union people totaled almost nine million—over three times as many as when Roosevelt had taken office in 1933.

Social Security. In 1935, also under Roosevelt's leadership, Congress, after a long debate, passed another reform measure, the Social Security Act. It provided for old-age pensions, for unemployment insurance, for the care of dependent mothers and children, for aid to the blind and the crippled, and for certain public-health services.

There was much opposition to the law. Nevertheless, many saw it not only as an effort to do what several western European countries were already doing but as the beginning of protection "from the cradle to the grave." Harry Hopkins thought the law ought even to provide for sickness and health insurance.

The passage of the Social Security Act established a new idea in American life. It was that people may call on the country as a whole to protect them against the damaging effects of the bad breaks and the ups and downs of life. For Roosevelt the word conservation applied not only to the natural resources of the country but to its *human resources*—to people—too.

As the year 1936 approached, prosperity had still not returned. But few questioned that the American outlook on what the job of government ought to be had greatly changed. Some people said that the changes were bad for the country—that many of the old-fashioned ways of doing, or *not* doing, things were better.

A Sweeping Reelection

In 1936 the Republicans nominated Alfred M. Landon, the governor of Kansas, as their presidential candidate. Landon was no match for Franklin Roosevelt, who was renominated by the Democrats.

Many wealthy people were greatly op-

e cars, loudspeakers,
d industry the men
orked in all developed
cause of technological
ange.

A union loudspeaker car
plays a role during a
sit-down strike
in an automobile plant
in Flint, Michigan.

Wide World

posed to Roosevelt. Some called him simply "that man" or "that man in the White House," as if pronouncing his name would burn their tongues. Roosevelt enjoyed teasing these people, some of whom were fellow Harvard graduates.

In the campaign Landon's emblem was the sunflower, the Kansas state flower. The Democrats declared, "Sunflowers die in November." On Election Day (in November) Roosevelt won the electoral vote of every state except Maine and Vermont. No President in over a hundred years had known such an overwhelming victory.

Attack on the Supreme Court. Now, at the height of his popularity, "F. D. R." decided to reform the Supreme Court. Fearing that the Court might wreck the New Deal, he struck at it. He proposed to appoint a new Justice for every one who did not retire

A cartoonist showed how Congress felt about the attack on the Supreme Court.

Jay N. Darling from the "Des Moines Register"

from the Court after he had reached seventy years of age. However, no more than six new ones were to be appointed.

The response to the plan was unfavorable throughout the country. Moreover, many of Roosevelt's own party opposed what they regarded as a shocking attack on the "Nine Old Men," as the Court was often called.

Roosevelt's proposal was defeated after a long battle in Congress. Within a short time, however, because of deaths and retirements the President was able to make a number of appointments of Justices whose views he believed were like his own. But after his Supreme Court plan, he never again had such solid support as before from either the public or the Democratic party.

"One-third of a nation . . . ." Roosevelt started his second term in snowy weather on January 20, 1937. He was the first President to take the oath of office under the provisions of the Twentieth Amendment (ratified in 1933), which changed the date of inauguration from March 4.

In the days of the Founding Fathers, it had taken weeks or even months for a new President or Congress to gather after being elected. Now only a few days were required. A new administration could begin its work without delay.

The President's second inaugural address was a statement of concern because the country, blessed with great resources, still had so many people living in poverty. In words which became famous "F. D. R." said, "I see one-third of a nation ill-housed, ill-clad, ill-nourished."

Setting wages and hours. Although much support was expressed for whatever reform measures might be required, only one more important New Deal law was passed. This was the Fair Labor Standards Act of 1938. Under it Congress established a minimum# wage of 40¢ an hour (since raised considerably) and a maximum 44-hour working

The minimum wage has been raised considerably, and the number of working hours lowered.

Left: Lawyer William Henry Hastie, a Roosevelt appointee as a federal judge. *Right:* Secretary of Labor Frances Perkins, woman Cabinet member.

week (later lowered to 40 hours). Also under it, the labor of children below the age of sixteen, except on the farms, was forbidden.

New Deal Democracy

Before New Deal reforms were completed, war broke out in Europe and Asia. We shall never know for sure whether or not Roosevelt's measures would have brought an end to the depression if they had not been interrupted by the war. As late as 1939 almost nine and a half million people were still unemployed, and well over four billion dollars was being spent on various programs of relief.

Results were far from being what Americans had hoped for. Nevertheless, as the editors of a British magazine stated it, "Mr. Roosevelt may have given the wrong answers to many of his problems. But he is at least the first President of modern Americans who has asked the right questions."

Effects on the presidency. The mark

Roosevelt left on the nation is permanent. First, he made the office of President once again a source of ideas, action, and hope.

Results for individuals. Second, Roosevelt made service in government what it had not been for a long time—a career for young men of talent seeking to help their country. Also, he made Americans feel close to their government. This he did in two ways. One was by letting them know that the leaders in Washington cared about their problems enough to try to solve them. The other was by making them fully aware of and keeping them informed about public issues.

Roosevelt was the first President to use the radio in carrying out his duties and the first to appear on television. (He was televised by the National Broadcasting Company at the opening of the New York World's Fair on April 30, 1939.)

New paths. Third, Roosevelt introduced the idea that in the United States no individual should ever again want for the necessities of life.

ask what the magazine writer meant. (He was referring to Roosevelt's giving attention to the problems of people unemployed in a time when the United States was largely a nation of cities and when industry and not farm work normally provided most employment.)

Fourth, we have seen that "F. D. R." placed a woman in the Cabinet for the first time. He also appointed the first Negro to be a federal court judge—William Henry Hastie, of Knoxville, Tennessee.

Fifth, Roosevelt was the first chief executive to work for public housing. What he did was the beginning of the urban-renewal programs that were carried out by later administrations.

Sixth, Roosevelt was the first President to visit Hawaii and South America. He established a Good Neighbor policy toward the people and countries of Latin America and announced that he was against interfering in their affairs.

A faith in democracy. Roosevelt, finally, never allowed his countrymen to forget that no matter how difficult problems might be, they could be solved in democratic ways. Democracy was for him not just a word but the best guarantee that people will achieve a good life.

\#

Above all, "F. D. R." was the first President able to convince his countrymen that democracy could both solve our problems and be a stirring faith to guide us in a dangerous and threatening world. He once said, "We Americans of today—all of us—we are characters in the living book of democracy." He encouraged the people to believe that the stories in that book could always have happy endings.

---

1. Name three reform laws of Roosevelt's first administration and tell what each accomplished. 2. How were working people encouraged in 1935? 3. Describe the CIO. 4. What advantage and disadvantage did businessmen see to having to deal with one large union in an industry? 5. Describe Roosevelt's plan for the Supreme Court. 6. Name seven changes that Roosevelt brought to American life.

#Roosevelt's appointing a Negro as a federal judge was one of his ways of putting

The Workshop

democracy into practice, since Negroes were general[ly] passed over.

The Shapers of Our World

Describe the part each of the following had in the effort to bring about "recovery and reform" during the 1930's.

Alfred E. Smith
Tammany Hall
Herbert C. Hoover
Great Depression
Franklin D.
 Roosevelt
"Bonus Army"
New Deal
Cordell Hull
Henry A. Wallace
Frances Perkins
Eleanor Roosevelt
Harry Hopkins

Social Security Act
Alfred M. Landon
Twentieth
 Amendment
CIO
John L. Lewis
TVA
CCC
Wagner Act
NRA
AAA
WPA
NYA

Adding to Your Vocabulary

Use the following words to show your understanding of the suffering in the Great Depression.

political machine
polluted
direct relief
intolerance
drought
"dust bowl"
"ride the rails"
work relief

polio
tutor
boondoggle
processed
collective
 bargaining
human
 resources

Thinking Things Through

Review the boxed exercises in the chapter and then answer these questions:

##Roosevelt called attention to the fact that in a democracy people could, through laws and othe[r] methods, bring about desirable changes and so take care of their problems themselves. Emphasi[ze] his faith in democracy and his ability to strengthen other Americans' faith in it.

1. Why did Al Smith think he would have been a winner in 1932?

2. What was there about Smith which seemed to have distressed rural voters?

3. Taxes are often raised during a time of inflation. Why?

4. What idea of Hoover's made it difficult for the people to receive direct help in the depression?

5. Explain how such measures as public-works projects and payment of the veterans' bonus could help in fighting the depression.

6. How did our high-tariff policy contribute to our trade difficulties during the depression?

7. Compare the "Bonus Army" of 1932 with Coxey's Army of 1894 (see page 532). What was the chief aim of each group? What was the view of the administration in each case?

8. How was Hoover's public image affected by the episode involving the "Bonus Army"?

9. How did the Great Depression force Americans to face some of the problems they had formerly ignored?

10. What was the reasoning behind such plans as the NRA and the AAA?

11. What reforms or changes did "F. D. R." make which are accepted as important parts of American life today?

Your Community and You

1. Invite a representative from your local Social Security office to come to your class and tell you what your family should know about Social Security. Ask other classes to hear him with you.

2. Collect pictures of some of the buildings, roads, sidewalks, parks, and recreation projects that were built in your community by the WPA and the PWA (Public Works Administration).

3. Ask someone from a local bank to tell the class in what ways banks are safer

places for keeping money than in the days before the Great Depression.

Presenting Information

1. Write a letter that a farmer in the "dust bowl" might have written to a friend in the East describing the conditions on his farm during the drought years of the early 1930's.

2. As a resident of the Tennessee Valley, write a letter to a friend in another part of the United States telling him what advantages the TVA has brought to you.

3. Imagine that you are a small businessman of 1929. Compose some entries for your diary corresponding to the important events between 1929 and 1936. Be sure each entry shows your feeling about the event described.

4. Prepare a chart of New Deal reform and recovery measures. List for each the difficulty it aimed to remove, the remedy proposed, and the results.

5. Collect pictures of the early 1930's which show the hardships Americans endured then.

6. Compare the depressions of 1837, 1873, and 1893 with that of 1929.

7. Present a panel discussion of the various measures of the New Deal and their relation to urbanization.

8. Draw political cartoons which might have appeared in Democratic or Republican newspapers in any of the three presidential elections mentioned in this chapter.

Your Opinion, Please

1. If you had been alive in 1937, how do you think you would have felt about Roosevelt's plan to change the Supreme Court?

2. What do you think was Franklin D. Roosevelt's main contribution to his country during the Great Depression?

w did the Democratic defeat in 1928 prepare the way for a Democratic victory in 1932? Com-
e the way Roosevelt and Lincoln campaigned for the presidency during a period of crisis. Why
both men fail to tell the voters exactly what they planned to do about the crises they faced?

(a)

(b)

(a) Paratroopers practice jumping on training maneuvers in the Second World War. (b) Five-star General Dwight D. Eisenhower in his "dress blues" (full-dress uniform). (c) A poster vividly recalling the attack on Pearl Harbor. (d) *Top:* A Democratic emblem in the presidential campaign in 1940. *Bottom:* A matching Republican one for the same year. (e) Secretary of War Henry L. Stimson picks the first number in the national drawing to determine which men registered in the fall of 1940 should be drafted first.

...we here highly resolve that these dead shall not have died in vain...

(c)

REMEMBER DEC. 7th!

(e)

AGAIN IN '40

(d)

LIFE BEGINS IN '40

(f) Dictators Adolf Hitler, of Germany, and Benito Mussolini, of Italy, were friends and partners in the Second World War.

e the pictures on pp. 646-647 to point out that ing the 1940's the effects of war came closer n ever before to the lives of most Americans-- m leading generals to the man on the street.

CHAPTER 29

TOPPLING THE AXIS DICTATORS

view the historical trends in American foreign relations before studying the Second World War. Show w disillusionment with the results of the First World War affected American thinking. What changes in e American attitude toward world affairs did the Second World War help bring about?

T HE coming of a new war in Europe halted the huge task of reconstructing American life which President Franklin D. Roosevelt had so dramatically undertaken. In the years immediately after the First World War, there were moments when people believed that wars were a thing of the past. But by the middle of the 1930's, their hopes were vanishing. The world again faced war—what the great Englishman Winston Churchill fittingly called the "renewal of the curse."

In Europe and in Asia War Makers March

The man most responsible for disturbing the peace in Europe was an insanely cruel German leader, Adolf Hitler. Hitler, who wanted revenge for the Treaty of Versailles (see pages 597–598), gathered together and inspired a group of strong-armed Germans. These men began to wear uniforms that included brown shirts.

Hitler's Nazis

The Brown Shirts—later known as the Nazis (nä'tsēz)—followed the ideas in a book Hitler wrote while he was in prison in 1923. Called *Mein Kampf* ("My Struggle"), it was anti-Jewish, anti-democratic, and full of statements about the need for Germany to expand.

Violating Versailles. By the 1930's Hitler's violent speeches and wild promises appealed to millions of Germans. A month after Roosevelt's inauguration, Hitler became chancellor—the top official—of Germany. In a short time he was no longer only an unreasoning man preaching that war is good but a man in power ready to disturb the peace.

Going against the Treaty of Versailles,

Nazis professed to believe that democracy was dangerous, that representative government was a aud run for the benefit of politicians and their hidden allies, and that ordinary men could not free. They attacked supposed internal enemies and called for a struggle for national glory.

647

Jay N. Darling from the "Des Moines Register"

Above: The way many Americans felt about a second involvement in European troubles.
Below: Hitler proudly sees his soldiers parade.

Dever from Black Star

#Hitler's plans were so aggressive and outrageous that at first they seemed hardly believable.

Hitler in 1936 sent his soldiers to the Rhineland—German territory west of the Rhine River. (The treaty had provided that no army would ever be placed there.) Although this move was part of Hitler's scheme of *aggression*—violation by force of the rights of other countries—no nation moved to stop him.

The world's response. There was worldwide concern, though. What could be done to prevent Hitler from carrying out his outrageous plans? On the tenth anniversary of its entry into the First World War, the United States had made a treaty with France known as the Pact of Paris. The two countries had agreed that they would not turn to war to settle their problems in foreign affairs.

In a short time many other nations of the world had also accepted the terms of the treaty. But it did not answer the question of how to stop a country like Germany that *would* go to war to achieve its goals.

Many people in the nations of Europe—as well as in America—believed the answer to halting Hitler lay in *collective security*—that is, the joining together of countries threatened by an aggressor. But the memory of the First World War was so recent that millions in those nations shied away from the thought of another bloody fight.

Besides, the Europeans were not united strongly enough to face their enemy. And although the United States had played an important part in defeating Germany in 1918, it refused to join in plans for collective security.

The isolationists. The reason Americans did not take part was the powerful influence of American isolationists. These men and women, both inside and outside Congress, believed that the United States need not and must not involve itself in European affairs.

The isolationists felt that since the world had plainly not been "made safe for democracy" by the First World War, another war

##Discuss whether or not isolationism seemed to be traditional American foreign policy.

UPI

w does this scene show
terror of modern war?
A child stands in a shell hole—center—in the splintered ruins of a city
in North China after a Japanese bombing in December, 1937.

would also be useless. Besides, when the Europeans had proved unwilling or unable to repay their debts from the First World War, many Americans had regarded them as ungrateful.

Only a few people in America argued that European affairs were our affairs, too. Only a few could see that if Germany overran Europe and defeated England, it might take over British possessions in the New World. Then the United States would be forced to fight over such a violation of the Monroe Doctrine.

The Men of Japan

In Asia, Japan had also begun to build up its army, navy, and air force. Beginning in 1931, the Japanese army invaded China, its neighbor, and seized an area called Manchuria (see the map on page 666).

The United States regarded this act as an interference with the open-door policy (see page 585) and a threat to world peace. An expanding Japan could threaten the safety of American possessions in the Pacific region and also those belonging to countries friendly to the United States.

Treaties without teeth. In 1921 the United States had joined with other countries in a series of treaties aimed at keeping peace in the Pacific area. But the treaties had no teeth in them—that is, they did not contain arrangements for dealing with aggression. Moreover, the United States would not promise to use its armed forces in case trouble broke out in Asian waters.

The aggressors linked. When Japan invaded China, breaking the peace in Asia, and when Hitler's troops marched into the Rhineland, the treaty arrangements of the 1920's were shown to be empty words. Moreover, in 1936 Germany and Italy (like Germany governed by a dictator—Benito Mussolini) joined together in an alliance. It became known as the Rome-Berlin Axis, after the capital cities of the two countries.

The Axis countries punished those among their own people who dared to speak out against their governments' programs. In Germany the ruling group that demanded such total obedience was the Nazi party, and in Italy it was the Fascist (făsh′ĭst) party. In Japan, whose leaders were joined with Hitler and Mussolini, it was a group of military men.

ese countries joined with Japan to form the Anti-Comintern Pact--that is, they tried to
ear before the world as the leading opponents of communism.

In May, 1936, posters announce to crowds in Rome "Mussolini has won!"—meaning that Italian troops have trampled on weak Ethiopia.

The Nation's Path

In the 1930's Congress indicated the American public's hope of staying out of war. A number of the laws it passed aimed to preserve our neutrality.

Neutrality laws. These laws were intended to prevent some of the situations which Americans thought had taken the United States into the First World War. They forbade the shipment of arms and munitions to countries engaged in war. They limited the making of loans to warring nations. They prevented Americans from traveling on ships owned by countries at war.

President Roosevelt was not happy about the neutrality laws. They took away from the chief executive so much power over the country's conduct of foreign affairs. But Roosevelt was not yet ready to try to persuade Congress—which was controlled by men favoring a policy of isolation—to repeal them. He needed Congressional support for New Deal laws, and he did not want to anger the legislators.

Congress was willing to spend money for national defense. But it was convinced that the United States must not become involved in the trouble in Europe. This set idea suited the dictators perfectly.

A dangerous neighbor. Beginning in 1938, Hitler's neighboring nations fell one by one under the attack of the Nazi army and air force. For example, early in 1938 the Nazis swallowed Austria. In September of the same year, they annexed a part of Czechoslovakia. In the spring of 1939, they seized another part of that defenseless country, which then disappeared from the map of Europe.

Italy in the act. Meanwhile Mussolini had also been busy. His troops had invaded Ethiopia, in East Africa, in 1935, conquering it after a one-sided struggle. In 1939 the Italians grabbed Albania.

The Japanese "new order." The Japanese war makers were active, too. In 1938 Japan announced it was ready to establish a new

On the map on p. 651, locate the countries attacked by Germany and Italy. Was each of the countries attacked considered strong or weak? Ask why the Axis leaders believed that expansion and victory in war were the only ways to make a nation strong.

order in Asia. Its slogan was "Asia for the Asiatics," but it really meant "Asia for the Japanese." The United States was aware that if Japan's program succeeded, the open door in China would be closed.

The "quarantine speech." Roosevelt was convinced that the freedom and peace of 90 percent of the people of the world were being endangered by the other 10 percent. In a speech delivered in Chicago in 1937, he compared the rapid flow of lawlessness through the world with an epidemic.

"When an epidemic of physical disease starts to spread," he said, "the community approves and joins in a quarantine of the patients in order to protect the health of the community against the spread of the disease."

"Deaf ears." Many people took seriously the President's call for joint action with other countries. But the general effect of the speech was disappointing. Roosevelt said the meaning of his address had fallen "upon deaf ears."

The attack on Ethiopia began a series of aggressions by both Italy and Germany which led to the results shown here and to a global war.

Expansion of Germany and Italy 1935-1940

0   100   200   300   400 miles

Germany and conquests

Italy and conquests

#Use the neutrality laws as an example of how a law or a government policy sometimes has an unintended effect.

Congress, it now appears, was lagging somewhat behind the opinions of many American citizens and newspaper editors. By the middle of 1939, many people were thinking that it was time to review the neutrality laws. The opinion was growing that the laws were actually *un*-neutral.

The truth was that Germany was arming itself to the teeth while Britain and France, which were weak, were prevented by our laws from buying American arms. So one # effect of the laws was to aid the very countries that threatened the peace.

When Roosevelt tried to obtain a change in the neutrality laws in the summer of 1939, he failed to budge Congress. Isolationist leaders declared that there was no danger of our becoming involved in the European war.

German soldiers parade through a Dutch village after the swift fall of the tiny Netherlands.

The push into Poland. On September 1 1939, Hitler sent his troops storming into Poland. Having promised earlier to come to the aid of the Poles if their country was invaded, Britain declared war on Germany France, having also pledged such help joined Britain.

A move by Congress. Like most Americans, Roosevelt hoped that the war would not involve the United States. One way to keep America out of it, of course, was to help the countries that were fighting the Germans. At last, despite continued opposition from isolationists, Congress repealed the law forbidding the sale of arms and munitions. The hand of the President had been freed to aid the victims of aggression.

Within a short time after the start of the war, Germany and the Soviet Union had succeeded in smashing Poland and dividing it between them. Then the fighting seemed to let up for a while.

The fall of western Europe. But the period of quiet was only temporary. In the spring of 1940, Hitler's mighty war machine moved into high gear. In April it invaded Norway and Denmark, overcoming them in a few weeks. In May, just as the tulips were blooming, the Netherlands and Belgium fell before the Nazi divisions. By the time June was over, France had surrendered and its leaders had signed a humiliating peace treaty.

Just before the French stopped fighting, Germany was joined by Italy in its attack on France. Roosevelt was outraged. In a now-famous speech delivered in Virginia, he said about Italy's action, "On this 10th day of June, 1940, the hand that held the dagger has struck it into the back of its neighbor."

Arms for Britain. More and more Americans had now become aware that their safety was threatened by the dictators of Europe. Nevertheless, they hoped they could find a way to keep the United States at peace. One solution to the terrible prob-

##Why was Germany able to defeat so many countries so rapidly? (Germany had motorized armored divisions and a modern air force.)

Franklin D. Roosevelt Library

In the critical year of 1940, "F. D. R." campaigns in his home state for a third term.

#Point out that other countries are usually greatly interested in the outcomes of American elections.

Roosevelt seems to have been deeply divided in his own mind as to whether he wanted another term in the White House. But about the time France was overcome in May, he decided to seek the office once more.

Since 1796, when George Washington refused a third term, there had been a tradition—or unwritten rule—that a President does not run a third time. Now Roosevelt was going against that tradition, feeling that the Axis would benefit if he did not run.

The Republicans—as well as some Democrats—attacked the President for his breaking of the no third-term tradition. But actually this seemed to most people less important than the fact that the country was threatened by the events in Europe and Asia. The Republicans nominated a Wall Street lawyer, Wendell L. Willkie.

Like Roosevelt, Willkie thoroughly believed the United States could not isolate itself from the world. Like Roosevelt, he favored all possible aid to Britain—short ## of joining in the war.

The excellent campaign Willkie waged was not good enough to overcome the confidence the public as a whole had in Roosevelt. In November "F. D. R." became the first third-term President in American history.

lem of what to do was to give England the weapons it required.

The British were desperately trying to survive the fierce Nazi drive against them. A huge British army of four hundred thousand men was caught in a military trap at Dunkerque, in northern France, just after the French surrender. Its only chance of escape was across the English Channel. By gathering together hundreds of small vessels for the trip across the water, the British succeeded in pulling their men back to safety. But the army's weapons were lost.

Roosevelt met the critical British situation by making the United States the chief supplier of arms and other material to Britain. The United States, he said, had to become the "arsenal of democracy."

A third campaign for "F. D. R." In the summer of 1940, when Britain was under fearful air attack from German bombers and Hitler seemed about to invade, the United States was getting ready to hold a presidential election. The Axis leaders, who regarded Roosevelt as their enemy, hoped he would not run again and so would be out of their way.

---

1. What kind of ideas did Hitler set forth in *Mein Kampf*? 2. How did Hitler break the Treaty of Versailles? What did the rest of the world do then? 3. Tell how and when the Japanese aggression began in Asia. 4. Give the provisions of the neutrality laws. 5. Name eight European countries that Germany conquered between 1938 and June, 1940, and two that Italy overcame. 6. What part did the Soviet Union take in the attacks? 7. What longtime tradition did Roosevelt break? How?

*Why would the Axis leaders probably have been disappointed whatever the results of the elections in the United States--even if Willkie had defeated Roosevelt? (Note that both candidates believed the United States had to aid Britain.)

653

A Sneak Blow Pulls America into Battle

During the campaign Roosevelt had shown boldness and, many thought, great political courage. He had given aid openhandedly to Britain.

Steps for Defense

In September of 1940, Roosevelt announced a deal with Britain. He had traded fifty overage navy ships, which the United States could spare, for long leases on a chain of bases in British territory in the New World. Roosevelt called the deal "a far-reaching act of preparation for continental defense in the face of grave danger."

The draft. Furthermore, guided by the President, Congress passed the first peacetime draft law in American history. There seemed little time to lose. Enacted in September, 1940, it registered 16,400,000 men in October.

That same month Japan entered into a treaty with the Axis countries, further strengthening both. Now there was a Rome-Berlin-Tokyo Axis. Already Germany had swallowed up five more European countries, including Greece.

As the United States strengthened itself for whatever might come, it also followed a firm policy of not allowing Britain to lack arms or other supplies. A poll showed that more than half of all Americans were willing to aid Britain even at the risk of war. They knew that if Britain went under, too, the United States would have to face the enemies of democracy alone.

Lend-lease. In keeping with public feeling, the Roosevelt administration proposed to sell or lend to Britain whatever ships, planes, or guns it needed in its death struggle. Roosevelt's idea was worked out in the Lend-Lease Act of March, 1941.

Under this law the President could rent, sell, exchange, lease, or even give war materials to any country whose defense he thought necessary to the defense of the United States.

The country now stopped talking about "all aid short of war." A few days after the Lend-Lease Act was passed, "F. D. R." was saying, "Ours is not a partial effort. It is a total effort. . . . Our country is going to play its full part."

Convoying the goods. Other steps were soon taken. First, in order to guarantee the safe delivery of our aid to Britain, the United States began to provide naval convoys. These were groups of naval vessels that accompanied the cargo ships across the ocean and guarded them against submarine attacks.

Second, the United States arranged with Denmark to occupy Greenland in order to set up air and naval bases there. These would provide better protection for Allied ships in the North Atlantic.

Third, before the spring of 1941 was over, American naval vessels were keeping a close lookout on the waters of the New World. They were not going to allow the Nazis to gain any kind of advantage in the Americas.

Britain threatened by invasion. Despite the efforts of the United States, the British seemed doomed to face a Nazi invasion. Their prime minister, Winston Churchill, had heroically rallied his people after the retreat at Dunkerque as they awaited the Battle of Britain—a series of heavy Nazi air attacks. He had said to them, "I have nothing to offer [you] but blood, toil, tears, and sweat."

Hitler's unbelievable turnabout. After the air attacks the British prepared to defend

 ##Lend-lease was the first large-scale foreign-aid effort of the United States--a way of providi goods instead of loans to foreign countries. How does lend-lease compare with recent America foreign-aid programs?

President Roosevelt and
Prime Minister Churchill
discuss in their meeting
the provisions of the
Atlantic Charter.

their homeland inch by inch against a German invasion. But Hitler did a very foolish thing. To the world's amazement, he did not try to invade Britain after the heavy German bombing. Instead, in June, 1941, he turned his powerful army against his recent ally, the Soviet Union. Sure that his troops could conquer that country in a short time, he had decided to wait before finishing off Britain. That decision was a supreme turning point in the war.

Help for the Soviets. The United States immediately agreed to send lend-lease supplies to the Soviet Union. Americans and Soviets were now strangely tied together by a common enemy, the Germans.

The Atlantic Charter. In August, 1941, the President and Prime Minister Churchill met on the high seas off Newfoundland. There they framed what came to be called the Atlantic Charter.

The Atlantic Charter contained plans for the postwar world. It called not only for destroying tyrants but also for a system of international coöperation to prevent people like Hitler from committing lawless acts in the future. It made it clear that the English-speaking peoples intended to stand together shoulder to shoulder against an enemy who meant to destroy both of them.

Roosevelt later described how the British and American crewmen had joined together in a religious service on the deck of the royal battleship that had brought Churchill to the meeting. He said:

There was their own ship's complement [that is, officers and men] with three or four hundred bluejackets and marines from American ships . . . completely intermingled, first one uniform and then another uniform. The service was conducted by two chaplains, one English and one American. . . . They had three hymns that everybody took part in, and a little ship's altar was decked with the American flag and the British flag. . . . The point is, I think everybody there, officers and enlisted men, felt that it was one of the great historic services. I know I did.

Why was the attack on the Soviet Union "before finishing off Britain" a turning point of the war? (It forced Hitler to divide his armies and fight on two fronts.) What had Germany done in a similar situation in the First World War?

Tokyo's Trickery

While the United States was making efforts to help halt the Nazis, the Japanese were also laying plans. Like their Axis partners, they had grown cockier after the fall of France in 1940. Ambitious Japanese military leaders were influencing their countrymen to believe that they could conquer whatever part of eastern Asia they wanted.

Into Indochina. The Japanese felt even more confident after the Nazi attack on the Soviets. In late 1940 they invaded northern Indochina (see the map on page 666), then owned by France. In July, 1941, they poured troops into the rest of Indochina. France, of course, was in no position to halt the invasions of its possession.

Where would Japan strike next? Most people believed that it would continue to expand in Southeast Asia—in Thailand, the Malay Peninsula, the Netherlands East Indies, and the Philippines. There the Japanese could obtain some of the vital materials that their war machine required —rubber, tin, and above all, oil.

The United States watched the Japanese expansion in Asia with great concern. In 1940 it had offered lend-lease supplies to China.

Talks in Washington. Americans knew that war with Japan could only be avoided by the most skillful diplomacy. Unfortunately, conversations being carried on between Secretary of State Cordell Hull and the Japanese ambassador in Washington during much of 1941 were having no success at all.

The United States made clear its wishes. These included withdrawal of the Japanese from Indochina and their pledge to remove their army from China. Also, Hull wanted to know what Japan's course of action would be if we became involved in war in Europe. On all of these matters the Americans received no satisfaction.

As the talks in Washington dragged on and on, they seemed to get nowhere. The United States saw it as a bad sign when in October a general and former war minister, Hideki Tojo (hē'dĕ kē' tō'jō), became prime minister of Japan. Known as the Razor because of the keenness of his mind, he showed impatience with the continuation of the conversations taking place between Hull and the Japanese ambassador in Washington.

We now know that even before Tojo took office, the Japanese had come to a decision about the United States. They had planned to attack the American naval base at Pearl Harbor, Hawaii, on December 7, 1941, if the talks had not brought results by November 25. To help in the talks, the Japanese government sent a special ambassador to Washington, Saburo Kurusu (sä bōō'rō kōō rōō' sōō).

The threat of Japan. Sure that the Nazis were going to win the war in Europe, Japan had no reason to think that it would not be victorious in Asia. As a result, the proposals Kurusu handed to Hull practically asked for an American surrender. On November 24 Roosevelt was informing Churchill, "I am not very hopeful and we must all be prepared for real trouble, possibly soon."

Roosevelt could not know, of course, that a Japanese naval force would leave its home waters the following day on a deadly mission. Time was now running out for keeping peace.

United States experts had been able to break (discover the key to) the code the Japanese used in secret messages passed between Tokyo officials and their representatives in other capitals. American leaders knew, therefore, that the Japanese were planning to strike somewhere. It was generally believed that the blow would fall on the British and Dutch possessions in Asia.

##Though Americans knew that some kind of attack was coming, they did not think Japan would attack American territory. And if an American base were to be attacked, the Philippines seemed a more likely target than Pearl Harbor, which was about 4000 miles from Japan.

ortunately, because port facilities and many
l-storage tanks were not destroyed, the base
uld continue operations.

Pearl Harbor and After

Sunday, December 7, 1941, began as a
beautiful day at the United States naval
base of Pearl Harbor, where American
ships were riding at anchor. But at 7:55
A.M. a fleet of Japanese dive-bombers appeared in the sky and began their carefully planned attack. Less than two hours
later it was completed. Five battleships had
been sunk and three others had been badly
damaged. A number of smaller vessels
also had been either sunk or badly hit.

The Japanese were overjoyed at their
success. A sailor of Japan wrote in glee,
"An air attack on Hawaii! A dream come
true! What will the people at home think
when they hear the news? . . . I can see
them clapping their hands and shouting
with joy!"

For Americans the disaster meant deep
sorrow and fierce anger. More than twenty-
four hundred navy people had been killed

Jay N. Darling from the "Des Moines Register"

Above: A cartoon printed one year after the attack on Pearl Harbor.
Below: Smoke billows at the naval base after the Japanese blow.

Library of Congress

and more than eleven hundred wounded. In this sudden sneak attack the fleet had suffered the worst defeat in American history.

"To absolute victory." The following day President Roosevelt went before Congress and asked it to recognize that from the moment of the attack the United States and Japan had been at war. His tone was calm as he declared, "Always will our whole nation remember the character of the onslaught against us. No matter how long it

The U.S.S. *Arizona*, one of three battleships sunk at Pearl Harbor, goes under after being struck, carrying over eleven hundred men with it.

Wide World

may take . . . the American people in their righteous might will win through to absolute victory." With only one nay, Congress passed the declaration the President had requested.

The isolationists' idea that the United States was not threatened by the warmaking nations had now been proved false. The people quickly recognized what they faced as Germany and Italy declared war on America.

Europe first. The United States immediately had to plan on fighting a vast, worldwide war. The American military chiefs saw, however, that no matter how angry at Japan the people were, good sense demanded that they focus on destroying the European Axis first. This way they could take advantage of the fact that Britain and the Soviet Union still remained unconquered.

Surrender in the Philippines. Nevertheless, the United States could not be idle in the Pacific. There we—and Britain and the Netherlands—suffered terrible defeats even after the attack on Pearl Harbor.

Lacking the air and sea support they needed, American and Filipino troops in the Philippines were forced to surrender to the Japanese on May 6, 1942. In the "Death March" which followed, the captives died like flies. There were an estimated twenty-five thousand victims of the march and of the cruel treatment afterward. Among the United States prisoners taken was General Jonathan "Skinny" Wainwright. He had hauled down the flag after reporting "with broken heart and head bowed in sadness but not in shame" that his men could hold out no longer.

"I shall return." The American commanding general in the Philippines, Douglas MacArthur, meanwhile had been rescued by a submarine on orders from President Roosevelt. Upon landing in Australia MacArthur declared, "I came through and I shall return." The words "I shall re-

ANT A VICTORY GARDEN

OUR FOOD IS FIGHTING

GARDEN WILL MAKE YOUR RATIONS GO FURTHER

Posters like this urged Americans to support the men at the front (see page 592).

In what ways did the home front help in the war effort?

turn" became a battle cry, suggesting a pledge the United States meant to fulfill.

More Japanese victories. Meanwhile the United States island outposts of Guam and Wake Island also had fallen to invading Japanese forces. And the British had lost their island of Hong Kong and their powerful base of Singapore, in Malaya. Shortly Burma and the Netherlands East Indies were also seized by the enemy (see the map on page 666).

1. What two steps were taken in 1940 to help in the defense of the United States? 2. Describe the Lend-Lease Act. 3. Name three other moves the United States made to help defend itself or to aid the Allies. 4. What decision of Hitler's was a turning point in the war? 5. Describe the Atlantic Charter. 6. Give the main facts about the attack on Pearl Harbor. 7. Name eight places in Asia or in the Pacific that Japan seized after 1940.

Victory Everywhere Rewards the Allies

For a time in the spring of 1942, it seemed impossible to stop the Japanese advance. And Australia appeared to be next on Japan's list of countries to conquer. But an Allied counterattack now began.

Success on the Seas

The spearhead of this counterattack was formed by the surviving aircraft carriers of the United States Navy. They were under the overall direction of Admiral Chester W. Nimitz, who had been rushed to Pearl Harbor to take over the naval command after the attack on December 7. His work was to stop the flow of Japanese men and supplies along the enemy lines.

At the Coral Sea. On May 7 and 8, 1942 —in the Battle of the Coral Sea—the # Americans heavily battered a Japanese force headed for Port Moresby, in New Guinea (again see the map on page 666). This was the first upset in the unbroken string of Japanese victories.

Off Midway. The triumphant American navy, feeling the satisfaction of revenge, was greatly aided by being able to read Japan's secret radio messages. In early June it won another tremendous victory, the Battle of Midway, in the central Pacific. This battle was a turning point in the war, because it prevented the Japanese from pushing toward the Hawaiian Islands and taking them. Moreover, in sinking four

The Battle of the Coral Sea showed the power of planes and submarines in regular naval battles. In surveying the events of the Second World War, consider how the widespread use of new weapons changed the nature of war.

During the war Churchill held up two fingers in a "V for Victory" sign. This was America's V.

Japanese aircraft carriers, the United States Navy dealt a particularly heavy blow to Japan, which lost as a result nearly all its best-trained navy pilots.

The struggle ahead. The Battles of the Coral Sea and Midway stopped Japan's advance in Pacific waters. But complete victory was as yet some years away. It was still necessary to root the Japanese troops out of the territory into which they had broken and to roll the Japanese war machine back to its home islands.

In the Atlantic. In the meanwhile the war was being hotly fought in the Atlantic. The German submarines active there were bent on sinking as many cargo ships as they could in order to prevent supplies from reaching the British and the Soviets.

The Germans had discovered that submarines greatly increased their power to sink ships by traveling together in groups —or as they were called, wolf packs. But having decided to help the Allies, Americans found ways of detecting and destroying the subs. Furthermore, by 1943 the United States was able to build ships faster than the subs could sink them.

Progress on Land

Both the British and the Soviets felt hard-pressed by the Nazis in 1942. They pleaded with the United States to open a second front in order to draw off some of the German strength from their own embattled forces.

The Americans wanted to help by sending a small force across the English Channel into France. But Winston Churchill persuaded them to invade North Africa instead. Crack German troops were only 75 miles from Egypt and were preparing to take the "land of the Pharaohs"—and shortly the Suez Canal.

Action under Eisenhower. Late in 1942 American and British forces made landings in North Africa at three places—at Oran and Algiers, in Algeria, and at Casablanca, in Morocco. The troops were under the overall command of General Dwight D. Eisenhower.

Eisenhower had been sent earlier in the year to England to report on how the United States should conduct its part of the war in Europe. When he had presented his report to General George C. Marshall, the senior United States general in Washington, Marshall had said to him, "I certainly do want to read it. You may be the man who executes it. If that's the case, when can you leave?" A few days later, Eisenhower had been appointed Supreme Commander of American forces in Europe.

The Allies at first suffered very heavy losses in North Africa as the Germans and Italians resisted fiercely. But American and British sea and air power gradually made the difference. In May, 1943, the last of the Axis troops fighting in Africa surrendered.

A call for unconditional surrender. As in the Pacific, victory in the European war was still far away, but the enemy had been slowed down. Moreover, in the middle of

Ask students to describe the contributions made by each of the armed services and by each of the major Allies to final victory over the Axis powers.

The Second World War in Europe and N. Africa 1941-1945

0 100 200 300 400 500 miles

→ Allied invasion routes
→ German invasion routes

Map labels: ATLANTIC OCEAN, NORTH SEA, Leningrad, Moscow, London, BATTLE OF THE BULGE, Berlin, Cologne, Remagen, Bastogne, Paris, Stalingrad, BLACK SEA, Anzio, Rome, Casablanca, Oran, Algiers, MOROCCO, ALGERIA, Tunis, TUNISIA, LIBYA, Bengàsi, Tobruk, El Alamein, EGYPT, Cairo, SUEZ CANAL, MEDITERRANEAN SEA

© RMTN & CO.

Notice the two places from which Allied forces launched the gigantic attacks on Europe. In addition to the courage and sacrifices of the troops, industrial strength and technological achievement helped bring victory in the end.

January that same year, President Roosevelt and Prime Minister Churchill had met in Casablanca, Morocco. In addition to making detailed war plans, they had announced their war aim. It was "unconditional surrender."

The end of Mussolini. The Allies' military plans were quickly unfolded. In July American and British forces invaded the island of Sicily, a part of Italy. It fell after thirty-

United States Department of the Army, Office of the Chief of Military History

Discuss why the Allies demanded unconditional surrender. (Review the meaning of the phrase.)

Eisenhower visits a group of paratroopers just before they board their plane to take part in the first assault in the invasion of Europe.

eight days of fighting. An important result was that the Italian dictator, Benito Mussolini, resigned and fled for safety. The Italians were eager to switch to the side of the Allies, but the Germans quickly sent troops to fight against the invasion.

The capture of Rome. The Allies then had to battle the Germans on Italian soil. The fighting was hard and the progress slow. Late in January, 1944, the Allies hoped to speed things up by landing behind the German battle line at Anzio. But not until May did they make noticeable forward movement. Rome fell on June 4, 1944.

The Invasion of Europe

Two days later—D day—the Allied invasion of Europe across the English Channel took place at last. The work of preparing and leading it had fallen to Eisenhower. His tactful manner, often accompanied by a warm grin, helped smooth over many disagreements among Allied leaders.

The amount of planning that had been done for Operation OVERLORD—the code name given to the invasion—staggers the imagination. One huge advantage had been that the American shipyards, having built enough cargo vessels to beat the submarine danger, could be turned to building the thousands of landing craft required. (There were enough of these ships to put ashore in the first forty-eight hours of the invasion 107,000 troops, 14,000 vehicles, and 14,500 tons of supplies.)

At last, by June, 1944, all seemed ready. As Eisenhower inspected his troops in England for the last time, he said of them, "If their fighting is as good as their training, God help the Nazis!"

Gambling on the weather. But the weather turned foul on June 5, when the ships were ready to pull out across the choppy waters of the English Channel. Some had already set out and had to be called back. Better weather was expected the next day.

Eisenhower wondered if he should gamble or not. He was afraid that if the weather turned bad again, the first wave of men—even if they gained a foothold— would be driven off the beaches. Also, planes would be handicapped and follow- up troops would be unable to land. Another general described the scene at headquarters when "Ike"—as Eisenhower had been affectionately called since his West Point days—made his decision:

Compare Eisenhower and Grant. What personal qualities did each have? How did both rise quickly to prominence as generals during wartime and as public figures afterward? (See also p. 685.)

The silence lasted for five full minutes while General Eisenhower sat on a sofa before the book case which filled the end of the room. . . . Finally he looked up, and the tension was gone from his face. He said briskly, "Well, we'll go!"

The Germans, of course, knew an invasion was coming, but its time and place— June 6, on the coast of Normandy, in France—took them by surprise. Hitler ordered his generals to hurl the invaders into the sea. But it was too late. The casualties among the American and British forces were very high. They succeeded, though, in creating small beachheads on the French coast so they could land more men and supplies. These areas were soon linked together and gradually widened.

A flood of troops. A total of just 176,000 men acted as the spearhead for the invasion. By July 2, 1,000,000 Allied troops were beginning to fan out over French territory.

A pounding from the skies. The preparation for the invasion had included massive air attacks on Germany aimed at drawing German planes into battle and destroying them so they could not interfere with the invasion. After the invasion the Allied troops, of course, required air protection. In addition to the planes which supplied it, there were heavy Allied bombers that pounded industrial targets, especially the great oil and chemical factories.

Slowly German production fell and the German spirit sagged. It is estimated that a million Germans were killed or wounded by the air attacks and that eight million lost their homes. The upset in the cities and towns was beyond description.

Of course, the price in Allied lives and planes was extremely high. Britain lost

ny must an invasion force first
cure a beachhead?

Medical Corpsmen and soldiers pour out of landing craft
at Normandy, June 12, 1944.

An American GI gazes at the Cathedral of Cologne, Germany, which stands amid the ruined city.

about twenty-two thousand aircraft, and the United States about eighteen thousand. Together, they lost about eighty thousand airmen—a loss evenly divided between them.

Retreat into the fatherland. By the end of August, 1944, the German army was retreating into Germany itself. It had suffered heavy blows at the hands of General George S. Patton, whose armored units had not only struck hard at the German lines but also raced around them.

The freeing of Paris. As the Nazis prepared to defend their fatherland, France had been cleared of the enemy, or in the

#Why did German leaders also fear that Germany would face another harsh peace?

language of that time, liberated. Some o the greatest excitement of the war was fel in the city of Paris on August 25. On tha day French soldiers marched as victoriou men into their capital, and the Germar garrison there surrendered.

The next day, France's General Charles de Gaulle, who in the darkest days oi French defeat had never given up hope oi victory, entered the city. From a headquarters in London, he had organized the "Free French" to fight for the recovery oi France's honor. Now the moment of recovery had arrived, and Frenchmen went wild with joy.

German anger at Hitler. Most Germans knew that their "number was up." But their leaders fought on with blind fury, certain that severe punishment awaited them as war criminals—that is, as men responsible for having caused the war.

As the Allies tore into Germany—and as the Soviet Union's troops, having fought back the German invasion, pushed westward into the eastern part of Germany— the anger of some Germans against Hitler grew. He narrowly missed being killed in July, 1944, by a bomb a German officer had hidden in a plot to assassinate him.

The Bulge. Before the Germans gave up, they undertook—in December—a last great effort against the Allies. Their drive was aimed at cutting off all the attacking armies in the North and taking huge stores of Allied supplies. Some Germans talked of being in Paris by Christmas. The word to the troops was, "Everything is at stake!"

The Germans succeeded in making a huge bulge in the Allied lines. But the Battle of the Bulge, as it was called, did not accomplish the German aim. The Germans at one point tried to capture a place named Bastogne (bàs'tôn′y`). It was held by an airborne division under the command of a youthful brigadier general, Anthony C. McAuliffe. When the Germans demanded surrender and informed the

##What did German leaders hope to gain from this last great effort? Why did Eisenhower want to maintain an even line for the western Allied advance? (Note the costs of this battle. See p. 665.)

Americans that their situation was hopeless, McAuliffe sent a one-word response: "Nuts!"

The Battle of the Bulge cost the Germans 120,000 casualties and the Americans 77,000, including 8000 who lost their lives. It was a terrible sacrifice of men and materials, and Hitler had only succeeded in delaying the outcome.

Across the Rhine. Now the Allies pressed on toward the Rhine River (see the map on page 661). Early in March, 1945, the Americans captured the beautiful city of Cologne (kŏ lōn').

The following day, through a stroke of luck, which can sometimes turn the course of a battle more surely than the genius of generals, the Americans crossed the Rhine. The Germans had been blowing up the bridges across the river. But a huge explosive charge on the one at Remagen had failed to go off, and the Americans seized their chance to cross the river.

Within a few hours Americans were pouring into Germany. As the Allies neared Berlin, Hitler committed suicide.

Meeting the Soviets. The Soviets by now were deep inside Germany, too. The Americans might have taken Berlin ahead of them, but Eisenhower ordered the troops of his command to meet them in central Germany. This action angered some people, who foresaw that the Soviet Union, one of our allies in the war, would be troublesome in the postwar days.

The end of Nazi Germany. V-E Day (or Victory-in-Europe Day) was May 8, 1945. On that day Germany surrendered all of its armed forces unconditionally. In the streets of cities in Europe and America, millions of people cheered the news that "it" was at last "over" in Europe. Eisenhower congratulated the men and women of his command. "You have," he said, "confused, defeated, and destroyed your savagely fighting foe."

Massacre of the Jews. The victory over Germany resulted in the uncovering of some of the most shameful deeds in all human history. The Allied soldiers found prison camps—called concentration camps—where starving Jewish men, women, and children had been penned up. The Nazis had also operated gas chambers where Jews and other Nazi opponents had been heartlessly put to death. In a brutal drive against the Jews, not only in Germany but in the conquered countries as well, Hitler and his men had wiped out an estimated *six million human beings*.

V-E Day in New York City—
a joyous scene that was
repeated in every city
in the country.

Finishing the Work

Now two of the Axis nations had fallen. The work of defeating Japan was already well under way. However, few believed on # V-E Day that V-J Day was close at hand, too.

The Solomons. In the summer of 1942, the United States Navy and some marine units had opened a campaign against Japan. They had landed in the Solomon Islands to take them from the Japanese.

The fighting was fierce, and not until the late winter was Guadalcanal (see the map below) taken—after a terrible battle.

Island by island. The pattern had by this time been established for the American campaign in the Pacific. It would be a program of island-hopping that usually involved first, heavy naval shelling, then bloody landings, and finally costly hand-to-hand fighting.

Sometimes the invasion force was the army, sometimes it was the marines, and sometimes it was a combination of both

What facts of geography made the war in the Pacific difficult?

The Pacific theater of war, where over 41,000 Americans lost their lives— about 12 percent of the 321,999 who died in the Second World War.

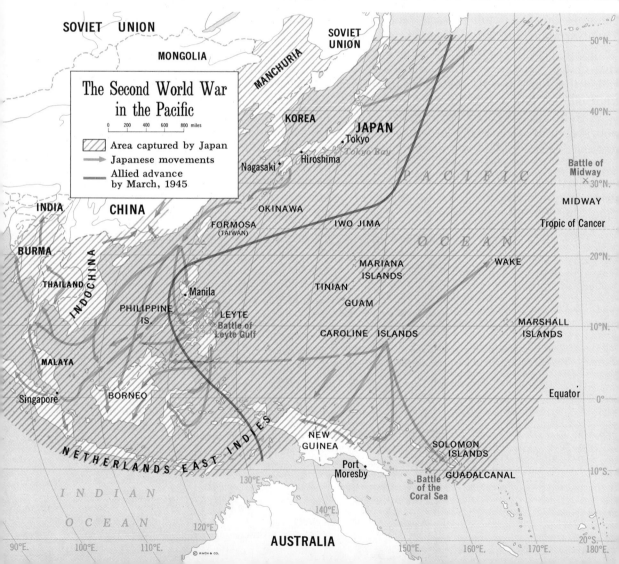

The Second World War in the Pacific

0   200   400   600   800 miles

▨ Area captured by Japan
→ Japanese movements
── Allied advance by March, 1945

Left: A GI at Guadalcanal. *Right:* Americans return to the Philippines in October, 1944, and begin the costly fight to reach Manila.

By the beginning of 1944, as the United States took the Marshall Islands and began to smash at the Marianas, Japan was beginning to reel.

The United States Navy rapidly turned the Pacific into an American lake. While gaining this control, its submarines took a terrible toll of Japanese shipping, which made food and other supplies exceedingly scarce throughout the areas held by Japan.

As the year 1944 went on, it was clear that America would win the final victory over Japan. However, the enemy was still guarded by a string of very strong bases.

In September, having taken the Marianas, the Americans landed on some of the Caroline Islands. Our men now were ready to attack the Philippines.

MacArthur's return. On October 20 troops under General MacArthur landed on Leyte (lā′tē) Island, in the Philippines. He had returned as he had promised he would—with six hundred ships and a quarter of a million men.

Facing disaster, the Japanese threw against the invaders most of what remained of their fleet. The result was the Battle of Leyte Gulf—the greatest naval engagement in history. In it the badly hurt

Japanese lost whatever chance they might still have had to win the war.

The land fighting in the Philippines went much more slowly. By early March, 1945, MacArthur was back on Corregidor (see the map on page 548), where he ordered his troops, "Hoist the colors and let no enemy ever haul them down." But the fighting there did not end until July.

Bloody Iwo Jima. Before that, however, the United States had engaged the Japanese in battle nearer their home islands. In February, 1945, United States Marines had landed on the little volcanic island of Iwo Jima (ē′wō jē′mȧ). There they had quickly become involved in the toughest battle in marine history: in the first fifty-eight hours of the struggle, they had suffered over five thousand casualties.

The Japanese had raked the invaders with gunfire from strong positions on Mount Suribachi. In a heroic operation the marines had finally battered their way to the top of the mountain and planted the American flag there. Yet several more weeks passed before Japanese resistance on Iwo Jima came to an end.

Okinawa. Now Japan's "house of cards" was falling. On April 1, 1945, the United States invaded the island of Okinawa

The struggles for Iwo Jima and Okinawa seemed to confirm American fears that the invasion Japan itself would be very costly. This point should be kept in mind as students consider American decisions for ending the war.

General Douglas MacArthur, back in the Philippines, surrounded by some of the Filipinos his forces freed from Japanese control.

(ō'kĭ nä'wȧ). It is only 352 miles from the main islands of Japan. By May the only Japanese still fighting were holdouts in caves. In numbers of American casualties suffered, the winning of Okinawa was the costliest victory of the war.

Attempt to destroy the navy. The Japanese were now aware that they could not halt the American advance unless they somehow could destroy the United States Navy. In a last-ditch effort they organized squadrons of suicide planes loaded with explosives to crash on American vessels. These caused very heavy damage.

The death of the Commander in Chief. As the war was reaching its final stages in April—both in Europe and in the Pacific—Franklin D. Roosevelt died suddenly of a stroke in Warm Springs, Georgia. Less than four months earlier he had begun his fourth term as President.

Mrs. Roosevelt cabled the sad news to her sons serving in the battle zones: "Darlings: Pa slept away this afternoon. He did his job to the end as he would want you to do."

Though he was mourned the world over by all free men who understood what was at stake in the war, the grief over Roosevelt's death was especially great in England. Churchill later wrote that on receiving the news, he sat speechless for a full five minutes. "I felt," he said, "as if I had been struck a physical blow."

Harry S Truman, of Missouri, the Vice-President, now the President, announced that the country's war policies would be continued. When Germany surrendered less than a month later, he said in an address from the White House, "I only wish that Franklin D. Roosevelt had lived to witness this day."

A last warning. In July Truman traveled to Germany, and there he and the other leaders of the war against the Axis laid final plans to overcome Japan. A result of the conference was a last warning to Japan to surrender or face "utter and prompt destruction." The Japanese government chose to ignore the warning, little realizing what would happen next.

The fire of a thousand suns. In close secrecy a group of American scientists—and foreign scientists exiled from their native lands—were at work harnessing the power contained in one type of the metal uranium. They aimed to create an atomic bomb. After spending over two billion dollars and several years in preparation, they were ready at last to test it on July 16, 1945.

No one was absolutely sure the new bomb would work. But it was exploded as planned at Alamogordo, New Mexico, as hundreds of scientists watched in awe at a safe distance. As the giant explosion sent up a mushroom-shaped cloud and

How did the success of the atomic bomb change the American estimate of the cost of defeating Japan? How did it affect earlier agreements among the Allies? For example, was Soviet aid in the Pacific still thought necessary to defeat Japan?

gave off the light of a thousand suns, they realized that a new era in history had suddenly opened.

Truman learned of the successful explosion while he was in Germany. He ordered the use of the new weapon against Japan.

On August 6, 1945, shortly after midnight, a B-29 "Superfortress" plane carrying an atomic bomb took off from Tinian Island, in the Marianas. Reaching the city of Hiroshima (hě rôsh′mä), in Japan, at 8:00 A.M., it dropped its deadly burden from a height of 31,600 feet. The bomb exploded about 2000 feet above the city with a force of 20,000 tons of TNT, the most powerful explosive previously known.

The destruction was enormous: over 80 percent of the buildings were destroyed, and nearly 17 percent of the ones remaining were badly damaged. But worst of all, between seventy and eighty thousand people were killed, and as many more were wounded.

Aboard the *Missouri*. When similar destruction was rained on the city of Naga-saki (nä′gȧ sä′kě) three days later, the Japanese decided to surrender. The end of the war in the Pacific came formally on September 2, 1945, in Tokyo Bay. There General MacArthur took charge of proceedings aboard the battleship *Missouri* (chosen in honor of the President). A Japanese diplomat described his first glimpse of the "Big Mo," as the ship was known, in his official report to the Japanese emperor:

> The huge 45,000 tonner towered high above the rest of the proud squadron. High on the mast there fluttered in the wind the Stars and Stripes. This was the same flag that was hoisted on the White House on the fateful day of the Pearl Harbor assault. The same flag was unfurled in Casablanca, Rome, and Berlin, commemorating each time the victorious entry of the American forces. Indeed, it was this flag that has lighted the marching step of America's destiny on to shining victory. Today this flag of glory was raised in triumph to mark the Big Day.

Amid the skeletons of buildings, a man gazes at the rubble of Hiroshima after the explosion of the first terrible atomic bomb.

United States Department of the Army

Two Japanese officials signed the surrender document, along with representatives of the victorious powers. Present for the United States, among others, was General Wainwright, just released from a Japanese prison.

As Americans rejoiced that on land, on sea, and in the air the Allies were victorious everywhere in the world, President Truman spoke to the nation over the radio. # He said:

It was the spirit of liberty which gave us our armed strength and which made our men invincible [unconquerable] in battle. We now know that that spirit of liberty, the freedom of the individual, and the personal dignity of man, are the strongest and toughest and most enduring forces in all the world. . . . And so on V-J Day we take renewed faith and pride in our way of life.

Democracy's work is never done. But after the Axis threat had been completely removed, few people could have guessed the kind of road the United States would have to travel in the postwar world.

1. Tell how American shipbuilding, the Allied invasions of North Africa and Italy, D day, and the Battle of the Bulge helped end the war in Europe. 2. What happened to Hitler and Mussolini? 3. What group of human beings within their own country and countries they conquered was a special target of the Nazis' hate? How were these people treated? 4. What was V-E Day? 5. Tell the main facts about the American drive in the Pacific, beginning in the summer of 1942 and ending with the taking of Okinawa. 6. How was Japan itself attacked? 7. Describe the surrender of Japan on September 2, 1945.

The Workshop

The Shapers of Our World

Identify the following by telling the role each had in bringing about the rise and fall of the Axis dictators.

Adolf Hitler
Pact of Paris
Rhineland
Manchuria
Nazi
Poland
Ethiopia
Benito Mussolini
Dunkerque
Wendell L.
   Willkie
Winston
   Churchill
Lend-Lease Act

Hideki Tojo
Saburo Kurusu
Douglas MacArthur
Chester W. Nimitz
Dwight D.
   Eisenhower
George C. Marshall
D day
George S. Patton
Charles
   de Gaulle
Battle of the Bulge
V-E Day
V-J Day

Pearl Harbor
Atlantic Charter
Harry S Truman
Cordell Hull

Iwo Jima
Okinawa
Hiroshima

Adding to Your Vocabulary

Use the following words to show your understanding of the events of the Second World War.

aggression
collective security
arsenal
atomic

convoy
beachhead
Fascist
concentration camp

Thinking Things Through

Discuss the following questions with your classmates.

To make the transition to Chapter 30, have students try to describe the road the United States would have to travel in the postwar world. What were the major problems resulting from the war?

1. Compare the causes of the First and Second World Wars. What relation can you see?

2. Why did the Pact of Paris prove worthless in keeping peace? How was it related to the thinking of people during the 1920's?

3. Give some examples of difficulties Americans faced before entering the First World War which led them to seek neutrality laws before the Second World War.

4. Why has the relationship in the Second World War between Britain and the United States on the one hand and the U.S.S.R. on the other been called the strange alliance?

5. The Nazis in Germany fought to the last, whereas the Japanese gave up before their homeland was invaded. Why?

6. Compare the principles of the Atlantic Charter with Wilson's Fourteen Points. What similarities in war aims are found in both?

7. How did technology make isolation old-fashioned?

8. What great mistake did Britain and France make when Italy invaded Ethiopia? When Germany broke the Treaty of Versailles by marching into the Rhineland? Account for these mistakes.

Presenting Information

1. Conduct a discussion of the type which might have taken place in the House of Representatives during 1939 on the subject of the enactment of a peacetime draft. Present the viewpoints of isolationists as well as of others. Finally, vote on the draft question.

2. Debate the subject, *Resolved*, That during wartime presidential elections should be postponed. Use the election of 1944 as the basis for the debate.

3. Make a chart listing the major battles in the Pacific and Atlantic theaters of war and their results.

4. Conduct a "Who Am I?" quiz. Members of the class should portray some of the famous personages of the Second World War.

5. Listen to the recording "I Can Hear It Now: 1933–1945," featuring the voice of Edward R. Murrow.

The Research Center

1. Prepare a panel discussion of activities on the home front during the Second World War. Discuss expanding defense production, food and gas rationing, the sale of war bonds, price controls, shortages, and drives for obtaining scrap iron and other materials. Perhaps you can find examples of posters, rationing stamps, and bond certificates to display.

2. Find out what methods Mussolini and Hitler used to obtain control of their countries and how they kept control. What lessons may be learned from a study of these methods?

3. Prepare reports on these subjects in relation to the Second World War: (*a*) the contributions of the United States Marines or the United States Army, (*b*) the work of the United States Air Force, (*c*) the service given by the United States Navy and the Seabees, and (*d*) the role of the women's units of the armed forces.

Your Opinion, Please

1. Some people have felt that the war with Japan could have been ended without the dropping of the atomic bomb. Do you agree? Explain.

2. Why did so many Americans favor the British position in the Second World War when before the First World War their sympathies were divided between Britain and Germany?

3. Why do you think American voters were willing to violate the two-term tradition for Presidents in both 1940 and 1944?

(a) A piece of clothing torn from a person fleeing over the Berlin Wall from Communist East Germany to free West Germany. (b) The symbol of the United Nations. (c) Negro Americans demonstrate for their civil rights. (d) The United States explodes an atomic bomb in Nevada in 1952.

(a)

(b)

(c)

(d)

(e) The sign President Harry S Truman kept on his desk. (f) Lyndon B. Johnson's Texas hat. (g) One of the silver calendars John F. Kennedy gave his closest advisers in the Cuban missile crisis. The dark figures mark the critical days.

(e)

(f)

(g)

the students to tell why they think each picture on p. 672 was chosen to introduce this chapter. Ask how President Truman's sign (above) showed his idea of the responsibility of his office.

CHAPTER 30

BUILDING THE GREAT SOCIETY

view the meaning of "society" before beginning this chapter, which is about the efforts Americans are king to improve life for all people in this country. The chapter discusses foreign affairs as well.

ALWAYS in the past, after Americans had fought in a war they had been able to turn their energies and thought to peacetime ways again. But even before the Second World War ended in 1945, a new international competition had developed, this time between the United States and the U.S.S.R. Americans gradually realized that they could not count on the Soviets to help make a peaceful world.

A Rivalry Turns into a Cold War

The keen rivalry between the United States and the Soviet Union quickly came to be called the cold war. This was a way of saying it was different from an unlimited shooting war, or hot war.

Yalta and San Francisco

The stage for the cold war was set at what proved to be the last meeting of the Big Three—Roosevelt, Churchill, and Joseph Stalin, the Soviet leader. This conference was held early in 1945 in the little town of Yalta, on the Black Sea.

Seemingly a bargain. At the Yalta meet-ing the Soviet Union agreed to enter the fighting against Japan within two or three months after the surrender of Germany. In return, the Soviets received a promise that certain Asian territory they had lost in previous wars would be returned. They also obtained the right to occupy part of Korea.

At the time, the Japanese were still fighting tooth and nail for every inch of land they gave up. For this reason Roosevelt thought he had made a good bargain.

Zones for Germany. Arrangements were made to rule the defeated Germany by dividing it into four zones—to be occupied

int out that the Second World War was still going on and that the Soviet Union so far had given Allies no help in the Pacific--help that had long been awaited. Nobody then was sure the mic bomb would work, and it was feared that Soviet assistance would be needed to defeat Japan.

separately by the victorious Allies: the United States, Britain, France, and the Soviet Union. Berlin itself, deep inside the Soviet zone, was divided among these four powers. Churchill and Roosevelt failed to see to it that a corridor—or pathway—was established through the Soviet zone for traveling to and from the city.

A promise of free elections. The Big Three agreed that Poland and other liberated countries of eastern Europe would have aid in establishing "governments responsible to the will of the people." By this it was understood that governments would be set up in accordance with the wishes of the people as expressed in elections.

Unexpected turns. But the agreements made at Yalta were turned within a very short time into disagreements. The belief spread among some Americans that the Soviet Union had "put one over" on the United States. What had happened?

First of all, the atomic bombs used against Hiroshima and Nagasaki had ended the war against Japan far more quickly than anyone had dared to hope.

A cartoon showed the unhappy relation of the satellites to the ventriloquist Stalin.

THE BUSY VENTRILOQUIST.

The Soviet Union had hastily entered the fighting after the first bomb had fallen. By the time Japan surrendered five days later, the Soviets could claim that their country was one of the victorious powers in Asia. Because of the Yalta agreements, it could take control of important areas in Asia with practically no sacrifice on its part.

Second, the Soviets ignored the agreements about Poland and other countries in eastern Europe. They made these countries become Communistic.

Because such nations then usually followed the wishes of the Soviet rulers, they began to be called satellite countries—in orbit around the Soviet Union. Each satellite was, like the Soviet Union, ruled by a Communist party which maintained an iron hand over the people.

The Communists. The goal of Communists has always been to control the world. They gain and keep their power in any country by destroying the freedom of the people. When it suits their purposes, they do not hesitate to ignore international agreements. Immediately after the Second World War, the political leaders of the Western countries worked hard to convince the Communist leaders that aggression would not be tolerated.

Forming the UN. But despite a chilling of the hopes for a peaceful postwar era, millions of people were encouraged by the creation of a new world organization of nations. This was the United Nations Organization—today called simply the United Nations (UN). It grew out of a meeting of the leaders of many countries which began at San Francisco in April, 1945.

The power of veto. The Charter of the United Nations was much like that of the League of Nations, although some of the provisions to which American isolationists had objected (see page 597) were removed. One example was their great fear that the United States might be dragged

Joseph Stalin, Soviet dictator, died in 1953. Nikita Khrushchev was the next Soviet leader to gain world prominence.

…uests (in foreground) ttend a UN meeting. hrough earphones mericans can hear nterpreters translate a oviet speech, for xample, into English. See Exercise 2, column 1, p. 697.)

The Security Council chamber of the UN, as seen from the public gallery. A Norwegian architect designed it, and Norway furnished most of it. The mural shows man's efforts to rise from a past of war and slavery to a future of peace and freedom.

United Nations

into military action against the wishes of Americans.

Peace-keeping arrangements. The UN Charter set up a Security Council and a General Assembly. The Security Council was to be the executive branch of the organization. Because of it the United Nations, unlike the League, could call for international police action against nations guilty of aggression. But each of the five main powers—the United States, the Soviet Union, Britain, France, and China— received at America's demand the power to veto proposals it disapproved of.

The Assembly was to consist of representatives of the fifty nations that signed the Charter. It was to be free to make and discuss proposals about keeping peace among nations. Its role, in short, would be to serve as a "town meeting of the world."

When the Charter was signed on June 26, 1945, President Truman told the delegates: "The Constitution of my own country came from a convention which—like this one—was made up of delegates with many different views. . . . When it was adopted, no one regarded it as a perfect document. But it grew and developed and expanded. And upon it was built a bigger, a better, a more perfect union."

Clouded hopes. The increasing friction between the Soviet Union and the United States handicapped the UN from the beginning. In its differences with the Soviet leaders, the United States acted as the leader of the free countries of the world.

The bad feeling between the Communist and Free worlds produced far-reaching results. In 1946 Winston Churchill speaking at Fulton, Missouri, warned that an "iron curtain" had descended across Europe. Truman sat listening on the speaker's platform as Churchill went on to say, "From what I have seen of our Russian friends and allies during the war, I am convinced that there is nothing they admire so much as strength, and there is nothing for which they have less respect than for weakness, especially military weakness."

#The beginning of a gigantic foreign-aid program.
Ask for a report on foreign aid carried on today.

President Truman signs a bill giving aid
to Europe after the Marshall Plan won
acceptance in the United States.

Harry S. Truman Library

The High Hand of Aggression

At first the American people in general were not ready to accept such a dark view as Churchill's. But events in a number of parts of the world soon convinced them he was right.

By patience and courage—but without turning the cold war into a hot war— President Truman and his administration adopted a policy of trying to "contain" the Soviet Union. This meant that the United States would act to stop Communist aggression whenever it occurred. The American planners early recognized that the struggle would be a long drawn-out duel and that the results would often be hard to measure.

Aid to Greece and Turkey. The containment policy was first carried out in 1947, when it appeared that Communists might gain control of Greece and Turkey. President Truman went before Congress to obtain the money necessary not only to strengthen the Greek and Turkish armed # forces but also to help the two countries in other ways.

Truman explained, Ideas such as communism "are nurtured [fed] by misery and want. They spread and grow in the evil soil of poverty and strife. They reach their full growth when the hopes of a people for a better life have died. We must keep that hope alive."

The Marshall Plan. Such a viewpoint led directly to adopting the greatest program of aid in all history. It was proposed in 1947 by and named for Secretary of State George C. Marshall—the Marshall Plan. He proposed to all European nations, including the Soviet Union, that they draw up plans for rebuilding their factories, railroads, and other sources of making a living.

For its part, the United States would pay most of the bill. The aim was to make Europe—badly torn up in the war—self-supporting again by 1951.

The European countries—except the Soviet Union and its satellites—responded immediately and with enthusiasm. In a period of three years, the United States spent twelve billion dollars on the program. The results were successful beyond even the wildest dreams of the planners. Not only did western Europe begin to enjoy a prosperity it had never known before, but also the appeal of communism to western Europeans dropped off noticeably.

Technical help. Similar aid became a leading weapon elsewhere in the cold war against communism. Truman in 1949 announced a program to give expert technical assistance to areas of the world still not industrialized. A leading purpose was to help battle poverty, on which communism might flourish.

The success of the Marshall Plan was,

##The class should be well aware that an advanced technology is a characteristic of American culture. Americans have had not only the know-how but also the money to give technical help to peoples whose cultures have not included the technology Western nations enjoy.

of course, a stunning blow to the Soviet Union. Moreover, that country was shaken especially by the creation of the West German Republic, or West Germany. To form this new government, the Western powers had joined together the American, British, and French zones of divided Germany.

The blockade of Berlin. The Soviets decided to seek revenge. In 1948 they took advantage of the location of West Berlin inside East Germany to deny the Western powers passage to the city on German highways and railroads. The Soviet aim was to force the Western powers to either get out of Berlin or abandon the idea of the West German Republic.

Truman, a peppery ex-Senator from Missouri, was not going to be pushed around by the Soviets, and the American people were solidly behind him. He set up an airlift in which transport planes carried into West Berlin the huge quantities of food and fuel it required.

The mighty fleets of planes that thundered in and out of the city day and night for months offered the world a new show of American power. The Soviets finally gave up the blockade as a failure.

Within a short time West Germany was taking part in the Marshall Plan and enjoying good times. A comparison of the prosperity of West Germany with that of ## East Germany (under Soviet occupation) was startling.

NATO. The Berlin blockade, as a Soviet threat to western Europe, stirred countries there to band together against future Soviet military moves. In April, 1949, the United States joined eleven of them in signing the North Atlantic Treaty. Later the twelve were joined also by Greece, Turkey, and West Germany. For the first time since the alliance of 1778 with France, the United States had promised military action in advance of trouble.

The agreement created the North Atlantic Treaty Organization (NATO), which was to provide all the members with a defense against Soviet aggression. Late in 1950 General Eisenhower, not long before made the president of Columbia University, took a leave of absence to organize the Supreme Headquarters of the Allied Powers in Europe (SHAPE).

This step in the direction of collective security (see page 648) appeared at last

what the feelings of the
ing West Germans must
e been as they watched
plane.

A group of young people in West Berlin stand on a war-damaged building in October, 1948, to watch the airlift. A United States Air Force plane flies overhead after depositing a cargo of coal.

Wide World

#Review American relations with China, considering especially the open-door policy (p. 585).
##Be sure students know the difference between the two Chinas today. Taiwan is shown on p. 680.

to mark an end to isolationism. And the step appeared to have been taken none too soon, for in 1949 two new developments strengthened world communism.

The fall of China. The first was the surrender of China to Chinese Communist armies under the shrewd leadership of Mao Tse-tung (mä'ŏ dzŭ' dŏong'). Mao's troops fought against the troops of Generalissimo Chiang Kai-shek (jḛ äng' kī'shĕk'), who was trying to keep the country from becoming Communist. By the end of 1949, Chiang Kai-shek and his Nationalist government had fled to the island of Taiwan (tī wän'), leaving Mao in control of mainland China.

Most Americans were shocked at what had happened in China. Some blamed Truman for not having given aid which might have slowed down the Communist advance. The important fact was that the United States, after trying so long to maintain the open door in China (see page 585), had now stood by and watched the door slammed shut.

For some years the leader of Nationalist China busily trained his troops on Taiwan, which was protected by the United States Navy. He looked forward to returning to the Chinese mainland one day in order to free it from the Communists. Few Americans believed, however, that he would ever succeed.

An atomic bomb for the U.S.S.R. The second new and discouraging development of 1949 was the subject of a very unexpected announcement by President Truman: "We have evidence that within recent weeks an atomic explosion occurred in the U.S.S.R." Most people had thought that

Troops attached to NATO practiced a rapid takeoff in an American transport plane to be sure that they could move anywhere fast if necessary.

Werner in "The Indianapolis Star"

The Chinese on Taiwan (Formosa) were placed under the protection of Uncle Sam.

the Soviet Union would not have a workable atomic bomb until 1952 or even 1955.

The word that the Soviets had "the Bomb"—coming so closely after the fall of China—made Americans feel especially insecure. They took comfort in the fact that the United States had both a stockpile of atomic bombs and the air strength to deliver them to enemy targets.

In the Hills of Korea

As the 1940's came to an end, then, communism had been only partially contained. In Europe it seemed to be in retreat. But in Asia it was on the march. Could Communist aggression be halted there?

President Truman had a chance to deal with that question in June, 1950, when difficulties arose in Korea. Korea was a divided country, half of it being under a Communist government, half of it under a free government. It was split along the 38th parallel of latitude (see the map on page 680). This was a line drawn in 1945 to mark the boundary of the Soviet occupation zone in Korea. Now Communist forces from North Korea were invading South Korea, hoping to gain control of the whole country.

MacArthur in command. Under orders from Truman, General MacArthur immediately sent United States weapons from Tokyo to help the South Korean defenders. The United States asked for approval of its action from the UN and obtained it. The UN then called upon its member nations to help the Republic of Korea push back the armed attack.

For the first time in history, the strength of many nations was being drawn together to put an end to aggression, although most of the soldiers proved to be Americans. General MacArthur was placed in command of the United States troops sent to Korea and of the UN forces as well.

UN triumph. In the first part of the war that followed, the North Koreans poured south before the UN forces could build up their strength. Since pushing the North Koreans back mile by mile would mean losing large numbers of men, MacArthur planned to land behind the enemy lines at the port of Inchon, near Seoul (sōl). Then he would "pinch off" the peninsula at its "waist." Seoul—in South Korea—had been captured by the North Koreans. The move, skillfully conducted by the United States Navy and Marines, seemed to take the Communists completely by surprise.

When the United Nations troops easily retook Seoul a short time later, the Korean War seemed about over. The North Korean army was breaking up as a fighting force and was fleeing north toward the 38th parallel.

The United Nations then had an important decision to make. Should the fleeing North Koreans be chased across the 38th parallel? The decision was made: the UN

The Soviet representative was absent from the Security Council meeting when the matter came
. Have the class follow on the map on p. 680 the events in the Korean War described here and
ter. Civilians as well as soldiers endured great hardships in the struggle.

679

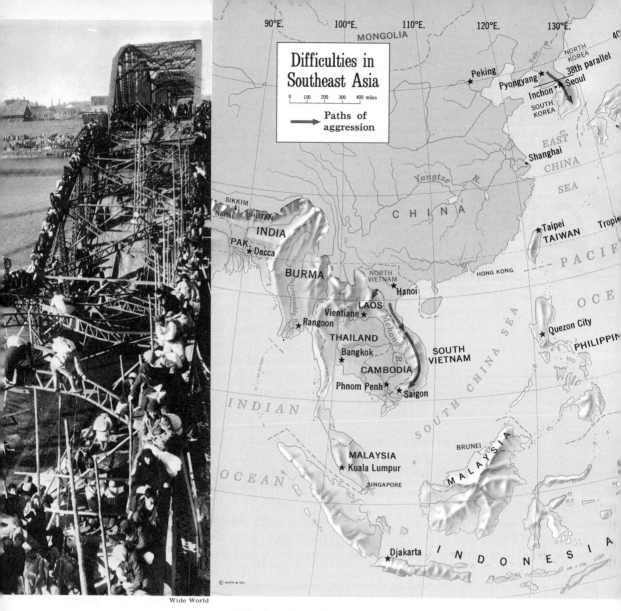

Left: Caught in the war in Korea, civilians crawl over a shattered bridge at Pyongyang in late 1950. *Right:* The new centers of aggression.

forces would press forward. By the end of October in 1950, the city of Pyongyang (pyûng yäng), the capital of North Korea, had surrendered.

The entrance of the Chinese. The northward march of the United Nations forces was suddenly halted at the end of November by a serious turn of events. The Chinese Communists had entered the war in very large numbers.

The American troops, in pulling out of the trap into which they had fallen, underwent a fierce attack in bitter-cold weather. Our men retreated, suffering as few Americans have ever suffered in battle. Weapons and food froze, and there were terrible casualties from frostbite.

The retreat stunned the American people, but they did not become discouraged. A Marine Corps general, in words which

#

#The Communist Chinese early began an internal hate campaign against the United States, the leader of the Free World. China's ambitions to overrun its neighbors have been resisted chiefly by our country, though other nations have helped some, as in the Korean War.

…became famous, declared that his men were not retreating at all. "We are merely attacking in another direction," he said.

The firing of MacArthur. As the Chinese forces pressed forward, they recrossed the 38th parallel and recaptured the South Korean capital of Seoul. General MacArthur argued hard that the United States should bomb Chinese bases in Manchuria.

The military chiefs in Washington said no. They declared that an attack on Chinese territory would lead to large-scale war with China. Such an involvement by the United States, they feared, would leave the Soviet Union free to do whatever it wanted to do in Europe and elsewhere

General MacArthur continued to repeat in public his point that the fate of communism in Europe would be decided in Asia. He wanted to win totally in Korea. "There is," he declared, "no substitute for victory."

Finally Truman decided to act. On April 11, 1951, he removed MacArthur from his command, saying it was his duty to keep civilian control over military decisions.

Meanwhile, the American Eighth Army had halted the Chinese advance, recrossed the 38th parallel, and recaptured Seoul. But the war did not end, and Americans watched impatiently as the fighting continued to produce a very heavy loss of life.

Peace talks at last. Finally, in June, 1951, a hint came that a settlement was possible. Negotiations between the two sides began in the following month.

1. Describe the agreements made at the Yalta Conference.   2. For what two reasons was the meeting disappointing? 3. Name the two main organizations in the United Nations. What does each do? 4. Give the main facts about the Marshall Plan.   5. Describe the episode of the Berlin blockade.   6. Tell what NATO is.   7. Name two events that strengthened world communism in 1949. 8. Give the main facts about the Korean War.

United Nations troops in Korea chase the enemy north of Seoul in May, 1951. The wall standing at the left is all that remains of a bombed building.

Wide World

Nagging Dangers Call for Public Patience

The Korean War naturally had a deep effect on American politics. Many people thought that the failure to end the war in Korea was proof that the Truman administration was "soft on communism."

The Communist Threat at Home

Already the idea about the administration's attitude toward communism was being used to advantage by a Senator from Wisconsin, Joseph R. McCarthy. McCarthy charged wildly that Communists and people in sympathy with their beliefs in the Department of State were shaping United States foreign policy.

"Smearing" the innocent. McCarthy made # one unproved charge after another, becoming a master at accusing innocent government servants—including even national heroes—without any proof. For example, in a speech in the Senate, McCarthy attacked as a traitor General George C. Marshall, the overall planner of the Allied victory in the Second World War.

Deep-seated effects. "McCarthyism," as the Wisconsin Senator's accusations came to be called, was felt in almost every walk of life. Actors and actresses were sometimes denied roles because of their political ties—or supposed political ties. Teachers in some instances felt less free than before to express their opinions.

Reasons for suspicions. Many Americans thought they had reason to believe that a conspiracy threatened the country. First, three court trials in the United States had indicated the presence of some disloyal Americans. Two of the trials had dealt with Alger Hiss, an official in the Department of State, who was convicted of lying about giving certain secret documents to Soviet officials.

A third trial had concerned a plan of some American Communists to send the Soviets the secret of how to make an atomic bomb. Two of these traitors, Julius and Ethel Rosenberg, were executed for their crime.

Second, the loss of China to Communists was, for most Americans, unexpected. Third, the bold efforts of the Soviet Union in many parts of the world to embarrass the United States and expand its own influence were a deep disappointment.

Political results. Many guessed that in the election of 1952 the Democrats would suffer for a number of reasons. These were the Korean War, the danger—real and imagined—of communism, and the uncovering of corruption in some high offices in Washington.

When President Truman had run in 1948 against Governor Thomas E. Dewey, of New York, the Republican choice, many

Ulysses S. Grant III (*left*) speaks in 1953 with Albert Woolson, the last surviving Union soldier of the Civil War, who had lived to see his country block aggression in Korea.

Sons of Union Veterans of the Civil War

Like the American Revolution veteran on p. 444, this old soldier is a tie with an earlier time and will help students develop a sense of chronology.

had also predicted the Democrats would lose. One of the issues had been the much-disputed Taft-Hartley Act of 1947—vetoed by Truman—which working people had declared hindered their union activities unfairly. But Truman's strength on Election Day had brought him and his party a stunning victory.

The chief executive had a down-to-earth, no-nonsense manner which appealed to millions of Americans. He appeared to enjoy being President, and no doubt he could have been renominated in 1952.

Under the Twenty-second Amendment, which had gone into effect in 1951, no President can serve more than two terms. However, Truman was eligible to run again even though he had been elected to a term of his own in 1948. The amendment, as you seen on page 725, exempted him.

"Ike" Eisenhower

Expressing the belief that after almost eight years in the White House he ought to lay down its burdens, Truman took himself out of the presidential race early in 1952. Adopting the campaign slogan "It's time for a change," the Republicans in their convention nominated as their candidate General Dwight D. Eisenhower. The packed galleries cheered "We like Ike."

The Democrats chose as their standard-bearer the witty, talented governor of Illinois, Adlai E. Stevenson. But Eisenhower, a beloved national hero, proved to be overwhelmingly popular, winning the election by a big majority.

Like Truman, Eisenhower had risen to the highest position in the land from a very modest start in life. He thought about it on his first day in the President's oval office in the White House. Later he wrote:

Remembering my beginnings, I had to smile. If my chances of walking into this room had been calculated when I

Wide World

"Ike" gives the wartime V sign as he greets crowds on one of his campaign trips in 1952.

was born in Denison, Texas, in 1890, they would have been approximately zero. And yet the homely old saw had proved to be true: in the United States any boy *can* grow up to be President.

The President's hand. During his campaign Eisenhower had promised the American people that he would go to Korea in order to end the war there as soon as ## possible. After his election and before his inauguration, he made his word good.

The end of battle. Nevertheless, the President was unable to get the Communists to take part in peace talks until he hinted that Americans would not hesitate to use nuclear weapons. At last in July, 1953, the Korean War came to an end. A line between North and South Korea was established about 30 miles north of the east end of the 38th parallel and a little south of it at the west end. The war had cost

Review "Ike's" career in the Second World War in connection with this. Use the map on
680 in discussing other troubles in Asia since the Korean War. Point out the areas that
e suffered from Communist aggression.   683

#Review the losses of life in the Civil War (p. 450). Stress the tragedy of casualties.

\# the United States about 140,000 casualties —including over 30,000 deaths—and $22,000,000,000.

The United States—and the United Nations—had not won the war, but they had forced the aggressors to halt their invasion. They had shown it was possible to stand up to the Communists and beat them back.

Wrestling with Khrushchev. Eisenhower had hardly been installed in office when an event of far-reaching importance occurred in the Soviet Union. This was the death in 1953 of Joseph Stalin, the dictator of the Soviets.

The man who took Stalin's place was Nikita Khrushchev (kroosh chôf′), a roly-poly longtime Communist. In an amazing address before leaders of his own country and of the satellites, Khrushchev criticized and condemned Stalin as a bloody-handed cutthroat who had abused his own people.

The United States took Khrushchev's words to mean that there was a chance of ending the cold war. Eisenhower fully realized that his reputation as a President might well rest on his ability to bring about a "just and lasting peace."

Many Americans thought that the hour had come to seek friendlier relations with the Soviets. The belief grew that the Soviet people were tired of spending so much money for arms and that they wanted to raise their standard of living.

In September, 1959, Khrushchev visited the United States. After touring the country and seeing some of its industrial and agricultural might, Khrushchev met with Eisenhower at Camp David, a presidential hideout in Maryland.

There the leaders of the two countries agreed that in the future disagreements between their nations "should be settled not by force but by peaceful means—by negotiations." Khrushchev remarked in a seemingly good-natured fashion, "Let us have more and more use for the short American word 'O.K.'"

While Khrushchev was here in 1959, he embraced Fidel Castro, of Cuba, at the UN

But the time was not ripe for a full settlement of the cold war. In early May, 1960, an American plane—a U-2—was shot down over Soviet territory while on a photographing mission. Khrushchev used the episode as an excuse to end his seeming friendliness toward the United States.

The Chinese-Soviet split. Khrushchev was undoubtedly influenced by a division that was gradually opening between the Soviet Union and Red China as each tried to gain leadership of the entire Communist movement. The split widened shortly after Khrushchev's visit to the United States. The Chinese expressed anger at the idea that a Communist leader like Khrushchev should be hobnobbing with a president of the United States.

The Soviets continued to push for advantages in Berlin, in the Middle East, and in Africa—wherever they found it

##Ask for a special report on this episode, which should include a discussion of Khrushchev's behavior toward Eisenhower, all the more insulting because "Ike" had been friendly during Khrushchev's tour of this country.

convenient and possible to operate. But the growing unfriendliness of China—their own neighbor—had the effect of cooling somewhat their desire for new moves against the United States and other Western countries.

Treaties for defense. Eisenhower's Secretary of State, John Foster Dulles, worked tirelessly to win collective security for the United States. Copying the idea of NATO, he arranged a series of defense agreements involving the United States throughout the world. He established defense arrangements with Korea and Nationalist China. He played an active part in promoting the Southeast Asia Treaty Organization (SEATO) in 1954 and the Baghdad Pact in 1955. America joined the first organization and supported the second. They tied us to nations of the Middle East and Asia. We were already joined with twenty-one countries of the New World in the Organization of American States (OAS), formed in 1948.

"Ike's" second term. During his presidency Eisenhower was ill three times. While on a vacation trip in 1955, he suffered a heart attack. He also underwent a serious intestinal operation and endured a mild stroke. But his recovery each time was remarkable.

In 1956 "Ike" decided that he was physically able to try for another term. Running against Adlai Stevenson for the second time, Eisenhower was easily reelected. He became the first Republican to serve two full terms since General Grant.

When Eisenhower went out of office in 1961, he was seventy-one years old—the oldest President in American history. He was followed, as fate would have it, by the youngest President ever elected.

#

##

##See the table of Presidents and Vice-Presidents on p. 727.

The Republican National Convention in 1956, in San Francisco, where "Ike" and his running mate, Richard M. Nixon, were renominated.

Gabriel Moulin Studios, San Francisco

In Kennedy's Thousand Days

The new President, John F. Kennedy, a graduate of Harvard, had been a hero of the Second World War. In the action in the South Pacific, he had shown unusual skill and bravery as the commander of P T boat 109. Shipwrecked as a result of enemy fire, he had courageously protected his men, avoiding capture until rescue came.

The road to the White House. After the war, Kennedy, a strikingly handsome man, was elected to the House of Representatives from his native state of Massachusetts. In 1953 he became a United States Senator.

When Kennedy decided to run for the presidency in 1960, it was generally said that his religion (he was a Roman Catholic) and his youth were severe handicaps. Kennedy took care of both issues in a masterly way.

\#   Recalling the fate of Al Smith (see pages 625–627), Kennedy appealed to people's sense of fair play. He said, "I refuse to believe that I was denied the right to be President on the day I was baptized."

Kennedy engaged in a series of televised debates with Vice-President Richard M. Nixon, the Republican candidate. In them Kennedy talked convincingly about the need to "get America moving again"—a crusade in which youthful energy could be a decided advantage.

Kennedy and Senator Lyndon B. Johnson, of Texas, his running mate, won the White House in November by the closest margin that had decided any presidential election in this century. Kennedy believed that the TV debates had made his victory possible.

A fresh approach. Kennedy appeared to bring a new style to the country's attempts to solve the serious problems it faced in foreign affairs. He acted as if he had made up his mind to try to settle the issues of the cold war. Nevertheless, he offered these words in his inaugural address as he began an administration destined to last only a thousand days:

> Let every nation know, whether it wishes us well or ill, that we shall pay any price, bear any burden, meet any hardship, support any friend, oppose any foe to assure the survival and success of liberty.

Kennedy's appointments. The President's Cabinet showed how democratic practices

Young Kennedy was only ten years old when he wrote this letter to his father. Students will find misspelled words.

In this letter, written in 1927, a Jack Kennedy then twelve years old made a case for himself

Kennedy Family

Left: Cuba became a Communist country at Uncle Sam's doorstep. *Right:* The Berlin Wall—center—divides East Berlin—right—from West Berlin—left.

had spread in the postwar years. For example, Kennedy chose as members of his official family two men of Jewish birth—Arthur J. Goldberg and Abraham A. Ribicoff. (Earlier Oscar Straus had served under Theodore Roosevelt, Henry Morgenthau, Jr., under "F. D. R.," and Lewis L. Straus under Eisenhower.)

Kennedy also selected for the first time for such high positions a man of Italian descent (Anthony J. Celebrezze) and one of Polish ancestry (John A. Gronouski, Jr.).

The Bay of Pigs. The new administration quickly faced a new turn in the cold war. A military dictatorship in Cuba had been overthrown as the result of a brilliant guerrilla campaign waged by Fidel Castro. Castro, who had become the Cuban leader, proved to be a Communist and fiercely opposed to the United States.

In April, 1961, a group of anti-Castro Cubans trained by Americans at Central American bases attempted to invade their homeland at the inlet named the Bay of Pigs. Expecting an uprising of the many non-Communist Cubans to help them, they were rudely disappointed when none oc-

curred. Kennedy refused to provide air protection for the invaders, and they were left to the mercy of the defenders of the Cuban coast.

Kennedy took full responsibility for the disaster. But he said privately that he should have known better than to rely on the "experts" in Washington. They had told him that the invasion, planned during the Eisenhower administration, could succeed.

The Berlin Wall. The Kennedy administration quickly recovered its balance and met with firmness new efforts by the Soviet Union to push the United States out of Berlin. The President made it clear to Khrushchev at a meeting in Vienna that the United States intended to stay in Berlin. Kennedy followed up his statement by increasing the number of American forces stationed in Europe.

The glaring differences between prosperous West Berlin and run-down East Berlin greatly annoyed Khrushchev. More and more, East Berliners were slipping into West Berlin and making their way to West Germany and freedom.

his discussion provides a fine opportunity to bring out that American culture is plural--enriched
contributions from people of many other nationalities and differing religions.
Review the history of Cuba, beginning with Spanish exploration.

In the summer of 1961, Khrushchev suddenly decided to seal up the "leak" by # building a wall across the entire border of East Berlin. The United States protested but with no results. Only through the use of force could the Berlin Wall be removed.

Nuclear testing. A widespread fear of nuclear war developed on both sides of the "Iron Curtain." In the United States considerable effort went into the building of air-raid shelters as many Americans prepared for the worst.

The Soviets' testing of nuclear weapons led some people to believe the U.S.S.R. had developed a successful anti-missile missile. (This would be a rocket able to knock out of the sky another one armed with a nuclear bomb and streaking toward enemy territory.) Such a defensive weapon would cancel out the possible effective use of our own intercontinental ballistic missiles (ICBM's), which are fitted with nuclear warheads.

The United States also tested nuclear weapons, despite much public opposition here and abroad. President Kennedy did not want to go ahead with the testing program but decided to anyway, saying, "In the absence of a major shift in Soviet policies, no American President—responsible for the freedom and safety of so many people—could in good faith make any other decision."

The Cuban missile crisis. A new development, even more dangerous than the nuclear testing, came to light in October, 1962. A U-2 plane flying over Cuba discovered the presence there of Soviet missile # sites capable of launching missiles which could destroy American cities.

After talking with his closest advisers, Kennedy decided to (1) demand that the Soviets pull their missiles out of Cuba, and (2) establish a naval blockade around the island to keep out all new weapons. In the meantime the United States armed forces went on "battle alert" throughout the world.

Mankind was clearly at the brink of nuclear war. But the Soviets decided not to push further. Some of their ships carrying dangerous cargoes to Cuba suddenly

It was during this visit that Kennedy told West Berliners, "Ich bin ein Berliner" ("I am a Berliner").

Crowds in West Berlin cheer President Kennedy—at left, in the car—as he visits the city in the summer of 1963.

UPI

stopped on the high seas and turned back. Dean Rusk, the United States Secretary of State, quietly remarked, "We're eyeball to eyeball and I think the other fellow just blinked."

Word now reached Kennedy from Khrushchev. The Soviet dictator said that if the United States would not invade Cuba, the Soviets would withdraw their missiles. Kennedy took him up on his offer, and after much discussion the terrible threat to the peace of the world ended.

The Cuban missile crisis was a dramatic turning point in the cold war. From then on, both sides—having faced the possibility of nuclear suicide—seem to have realized that they must do everything possible to avoid such a dangerous moment again.

A test-ban agreement. The following year, 1963, the United States and the Soviet Union signed a limited nuclear test-ban treaty. This treaty banned any but underground testing of nuclear devices. One purpose was to remove the dangers to health that can come from the exploding of nuclear weapons in the open. Another aim was to take a first step toward ending the growth of the "nuclear club"—that is, of the number of nations capable of making nuclear weapons. But France and Communist China soon after joined the "club." Progress in controlling the production of nuclear weapons was hardly noticeable.

A man on the moon. Some of the rivalry between the United States and the Soviet Union resulted in a fierce race to conquer outer space. Among Americans Alan B. Shepard, Jr., was the first in space; John H. Glenn, Jr., was the first to orbit the earth; and Edward H. White was the first to walk in space.

Both America and the U.S.S.R. carried on fantastically expensive engineering operations to put a man on the moon before the 1960's ended. They hoped not only to accomplish this feat but also to reach some of the planets.

National Aeronautics and Space Administration

Secured to the *Gemini 4* spacecraft, the American astronaut Edward H. White walks in space.

Nasty war in Vietnam. Meanwhile, the split between the Soviets and the Chinese became wider. And as the Chinese Communists spread their influence in Southeast Asia, the United States found itself faced by a new danger.

Communist forces, encouraged by Red China, were active in Laos, South Vietnam, and northern Thailand (see the map on page 680). In 1961 Kennedy and Khrushchev had agreed to make Laos neutral. But South Vietnam, formerly a French possession, was another matter. North Vietnam had already been taken over by Communists. The United States decided it would not allow South Vietnam to be overrun by Communists—many of whom were South Vietnamese.

Step by step Americans were drawn into large-scale fighting in South Vietnam. First, beginning in 1954, the United States provided a program of aid to the South Vietnamese. Then it found it had to send in military "advisers." As the North Vietnamese were spreading in ever-larger num-

Emphasize that American assistance to South Vietnam dates back to 1954. (This section on Vietnam is one of a number that provide excellent opportunities for activities designed around articles in newspapers and periodicals.)

689

Charles Bonnay, LIFE © 1966 by Time, Inc.

American troops in South Vietnam plan a helicopter mission into the mountains held by Viet Cong. These nimble aircraft can set down soldiers almost anywhere and can rescue them even from thick jungles.

concludes that a President does not mean what he says, we're finished."

A debate in the United States. Americans at home argued over whether the United States had any business to be fighting in South Vietnam. People who opposed the administration's policy said that if the United States was to carry on such large-scale fighting, Congress ought to declare war. They argued, too, that the United States might bring Red China into the fighting and possibly start a third world war.

Many critics demanded that the United States show its willingness to negotiate with the Communists. A series of determined efforts which aimed to make known that Americans wanted to end the war met with no response from "the other side."

One thing was certain: although the United States and its South Vietnamese allies were stuck in a cruel war, the United States showed no signs of abandoning the fourteen million South Vietnamese. Rusk put it this way: "Most [dictator] countries make a mistake about what a democracy will do at the end of the day." He said Hitler had made the same wrong judgment.

bers over South Vietnam's countryside, our country began to send troops in 1961. By the summer of 1966, the United States had between 250,000 and 300,000 men involved directly or indirectly in trying to stop the Communist enemy, the Viet Cong.

Secretary Rusk explained the United States' policy when he said, "It is most important that when the President says to
the North Vietnamese aggressors 'You're not going to have [South] Vietnam,' that he must be believed. If ever the other side

1. Name three reasons why "McCarthyism" developed in the United States. 2. Give the main facts about the election of 1952. 3. Name two important events that occurred in 1953. 4. What ended Eisenhower's attempt to be friendly with Khrushchev? 5. Tell what steps were taken for collective security in Eisenhower's presidency. 6. Describe two episodes involving Cuba which marked Kennedy's administration. 7. What new step did the Soviet Union take in Berlin? 8. Name and describe an agreement reached by the Soviet Union and the United States in 1963. 9. Tell how Americans became involved in a war in South Vietnam.

#Ask students to name instances when the United States has taken steps to stop aggression since the Second World War. (All have been examples of resistance to Communist aggression.)
##Ask why dictators misjudge democracies. (They pretend democracies are weak and indecisiv

A Rich America Aims to Improve Itself

Meanwhile, despite spending almost a hundred billion dollars for foreign aid and military assistance between 1945 and 1964, Americans at home were enjoying a remarkable prosperity. One measure of the success of the democratic way of life was being shown within the United States. In short, hand in hand with the defense of freedom abroad went efforts to improve American life at home.

Prosperous People

There were many ways of measuring the nation's prosperity. But one of the best was the growth from year to year of the total amount of goods and services produced in the country. In 1940 this total was about $101,000,000,000—averaging $761 for each person. In 1964 the total was over $622,000,000,000—or $3242 for each man, woman, and child.

Full employment. In the 1940's the goal of sixty million jobs for Americans in the postwar world had seemed wild. In 1965

almost seventy-four million Americans had jobs, and there were shortages of skilled workers in almost every field imaginable.

New industries. Not only did many of the old industries continue to prosper in the 1960's, but also a number of new ones appeared. The airplane industry, for example, contributed much to the country's prosperity. In 1940 there were 437 planes in commercial service, carrying passengers 119,000,000 miles and giving jobs to about twenty-two thousand people. In 1964 there were 1786 commercial planes flying regularly a distance of about 1,171,950,000 miles and employing nearly two hundred thousand people.

In 1940 the number of passengers was less than 2,500,000. Twenty-four years later the number was about 88,500,000. The changes this increase produced in the way people lived and the way businessmen conducted their affairs were immense.

Another industry which grew in an amazing fashion and deeply affected the daily lives of Americans involved *electron-*

k students to bring news-
per or magazine accounts
other uses of computers--
other sign of an advanced
chnology.

A business firm in Massachusetts—like many other companies— uses a computer to process accurately information needed in carrying on its work.

David F. Lawlor

based on electronics) were developed. These could keep business records, run factories automatically, or solve "impossible" mathematical problems for scientists.

The TV revolution. TV viewing remade the entertainment habits of American families. The television tube, long in development, was perfected in the ten-year period between 1930 and 1940. After 1945 it was sold commercially, and television quickly became the rage. Unbelievable as it may seem, by 1960 almost 88 percent of American households had television sets. More families had television sets than had bathtubs or showers, telephones, indoor toilets, or hot and cold running water.

For the first time millions of American families saw at almost the very instant it happened a national or an international event. Living rooms became places where families could not only see much nonsense but also become well acquainted with important public issues.

Jaques Lowe

President Kennedy, who suffered from an injured back, found it comfortable to sit in a rocking chair even at important discussions of the nation's problems.

ics. This is a branch of physics which is concerned with the use of radio tubes and other complicated electrical equipment.

Many electronic devices for military purposes appeared during the Second World War. After the war the electronics industry produced such things as high-fidelity record players and television sets for homes. Furthermore, high-speed calculating machines called computers (also

Unfinished Business: Civil Rights

From the 1950's on, no issue drew more deserved attention than the situation of the American Negro. Despite the Thirteenth, Fourteenth, and Fifteenth amendments to the Constitution, the Negro had been discriminated against by law and by custom in all parts of the country. He was, in short, a "second-class citizen" denied his civil rights. The attempts of organized Negroes and whites to arouse new concern over this blot on American democracy is known as the civil rights movement.

The desegregation of schools. The movement—really a very old one—got under way in earnest after a historic decision by the United States Supreme Court in 1954. In the case of *Brown* v. *Board of Education of Topeka*, the Court declared that separate (segregated) schools for Negroes and whites, found in many communities, were unconstitutional. Chief Justice Earl War-

##Ask what the heading means (students should review the three amendments named in the first paragraph below it). "Civil rights" are defined in Exercise 2, Column 2, p. 697. Discuss the meaning of "discrimination" as used here and why it is called a blot on democracy.

ren explained that segregation of this kind denies Negroes "the equal protection of the laws" guaranteed in the Fourteenth Amendment.

Using force. Step by step the courts and the office of the United States Attorney-General tried to carry out the changes made necessary by this decision. Too often force was required. President Eisenhower, for instance, called out federal troops to integrate (open to both Negroes and whites) Central High School in Little Rock, Arkansas, in 1957. In 1962 President Kennedy also called on federal power—to bring about the enrollment of a Negro student at the previously all-white University of Mississippi.

The work of Dr. Martin Luther King. The ray of hope revealed in the *Brown* decision led Negro leaders to take other actions to protest against segregation. Late in 1955 Negroes in Montgomery, Alabama, began to boycott busses (that is, they refused to ride on them) because Negroes and white people were seated separately on these vehicles.

Out of this successful effort appeared a leader who became world famous. He was the Rev. Dr. Martin Luther King, who had been born in the South and educated in the North. He preached a simple brotherly love and argued against the use of violence in the struggle for civil rights.

King's Southern Christian Leadership Conference and the Congress of Racial Equality (CORE) began a series of "sit-ins" in 1960 to end segregation in restaurants. "Sit-ins" and "lie-downs" by organized groups came to be familiar methods of nonviolent demand for Negroes' civil rights in many parts of the country.

The particular work of bringing together various civil rights groups for joint efforts was undertaken by the Student Nonviolent Coordinating Committee (SNCC, or "Snick"). Also, the National Association for the Advancement of Colored People (NAACP) helped organize Negroes and often provided valuable legal help.

The Negro employed a hopeful slogan, "Completely free by '63"—which was the one-hundredth anniversary of the Emanci-

Before policemen removed them, civil rights demonstrators blocked busy Pennsylvania Avenue in the nation's capital as a nonviolent means of calling attention to the Negro's continued drive for equality.

Wide World

pation Proclamation. But the wall of segregation did not come tumbling down that fast.

Extending the vote. Most thoughtful civil rights leaders recognized that no matter how many marches and "sit-ins" they staged, their best weapon in ending segre-

\# gation was the ballot. Congress was gradually won over to passing civil rights laws which could help insure the Negro the right to vote.

In 1964 Congress passed a Civil Rights Act setting penalties for any interference with a citizen's right to vote. The law was made even stronger in the Voting Rights Act in 1965. As southern Negroes began to vote in numbers, it seemed possible that what remained of legal discrimination would soon be brought to an end.

New Federal Tasks

The civil rights revolution was only a part of a much larger effort to make life richer and fuller for all Americans. Since New Deal days, Americans have come to believe more and more that certain kinds of advances in their standard of living depend on help from the federal government.

Known by various names. Under President Truman the effort to improve American life usually was called the Fair Deal. The movement continued under President Eisenhower—though it was not hastened

by him. Under President Kennedy it went by the name of the New Frontier. Nothing seems likely now to interrupt it.

The tragedy in Dallas. The course of our history is filled with unforeseen events. While on a political tour of Dallas, Texas, President Kennedy was assassinated on November 22, 1963. The accused killer was Lee Harvey Oswald, who was himself later shot by a bystander.

The senseless slaying of the young President cut tragically short the time of the Kennedys in the White House. Both the President and his lovely young wife, Jacqueline, had worked hard to encourage young people here and abroad to face the future with high spirits—even in a dangerous world.

Under Lyndon B. Johnson, of Texas. As the world was plunged into deep sorrow, Vice-President Johnson took over the presidency. Less than a year later he was elected in his own right by a large majority, over Senator Barry Goldwater, a Republican from Arizona. Senator Hubert H. Humphrey, of Minnesota, was Johnson's running mate.

Johnson, born in Johnson City, Texas, in 1908, was a product of rural hard times. As a boy he had tried to earn some coins by shining shoes in Johnson City. Later he had been on a road-construction gang as a day laborer. Still later, having decided to go to college, he had got a job as janitor

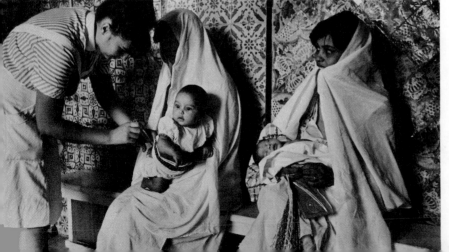

Discuss the benefits of the Peace Corps to countries like Tunisia, to the Corpsmen, and to our nation.

A Peace Corpsman—left— from Kansas City, Missouri, serves as a volunteer nurse in a clinic in the North African country of Tunisia

Peace Corps

to help pay his expenses. Afterward he had been a teacher.

"War on poverty." Although he had become a rich man by the time he was elected Vice-President, Johnson never forgot how it had felt to be poor. As President, he declared what he called unconditional war on poverty. By a series of programs, he proposed to win "total victory." He explained his purposes:

> We are not trying to give people more relief—we want to give people more opportunity. That is what the people want. They want education and training. They want a job and a wage which will let them provide for their family. Above all, they want their children to escape the poverty which has afflicted them. They want, in short, to be part of a great nation, and that nation will never be great until all of the people are part of it.

An educated nation. President Johnson called his proposals for far-reaching laws a plan for creating the Great Society. Its roots in the past were plain. As the President said, "Franklin D. Roosevelt and John F. Kennedy are gone. But our people still dream their dreams and we will carry on."

Johnson personally hoped he would be remembered as the "education President," because he was convinced that people would reach the goal of the Great Society more easily and quickly by being educated than in any other way. At the President's request Congress appropriated larger sums of money for educational purposes than ever before.

But, the President insisted, "We must seek an educational system which grows in quality as well as in size. This means better training for our teachers. It means preparing youth to enjoy their hours of leisure as well as their hours of labor."

The Peace Corps. A program begun in 1961 under Kennedy and continued by Johnson was the Peace Corps. This made it possible for Americans—mostly young

UPI

Robert C. Weaver, newly chosen Cabinet member, poses with the President early in 1966.

Americans—to live in foreign countries on invitation, serving as teachers or technical advisers.

"Medicare." A program which Democratic administrations had long worked for was "Medicare." A law finally passed in 1965 offered to people over sixty-five years of age a wide range of medical insurance. Its passage fulfilled a dream that this country would someday be rich enough to be able to afford medical care for older citizens. When a part of the law went into effect on July 1, 1966, a new day dawned for these Americans.

Recognizing urban needs. Achieving the Great Society meant facing the fact at last that Americans are an urban people. In ## 1965 Congress finally created a Department of Housing and Urban Development as a companion to the Department of Agriculture created more than a hundred years earlier. To be the head of the new department, Johnson chose Robert C. Weaver, the first Negro to hold a Cabinet post.

‡The number of Americans living in urban areas outnumbered those in rural areas for the first me in the census of 1920, and today more than 70 percent of our people are urban. Recall ith the class the long period during which urban needs were ignored.

The task for the Department of Housing and Urban Development is huge. As the population of the United States approaches 200,000,000 and more, our ability to house, feed, and transport people—living mainly in cities—will have to be improved. As President Johnson said, "In the remainder of this century urban population will double, city land will double, and we will have to build homes, highways, and facilities equal to all those built since this country was first settled. In the next forty # years we must rebuild the entire urban United States."

All historians who write the story of the American people to the latest moment must break off suddenly. They stop where the mystery of the future begins.

In facing the unknowns lying ahead, all Americans recognize that they require ## courage, strength, and an expectation that tomorrow will be better than today. These characteristics have always lighted the way for our countrymen.

But young Americans can have a special pleasure in gazing toward the misty future. They are able to believe that everything which happened before they were born was only a springboard for unimagined new triumphs. And they can hope by their own glorious achievements as men and women to make all the mighty heroes and heroines of the past seem like mere little people.

---

1. Name three signs of the nation's prosperity in the 1960's. 2. Give the main facts about the Negro's struggle for civil rights, beginning in 1954. 3. What help did Congress provide? 4. Name and describe four steps taken in the Kennedy and Johnson administrations to improve American life.

This Workshop and the one for Part Eight are longer than others, for Chapter 30 is extremely

The Workshop

important and the part worksho contains exercises requiring review of parts of the year's worl

The Shapers of Our World

Tell how each of the following helped make the years after the Second World War a period of crisis or rapid change:

Yalta Conference
Security Council
General Assembly
Marshall Plan
West German
  Republic
NATO
SHAPE
Hiroshima
U-2
SEATO
OAS
Arthur J. Goldberg
Fidel Castro

Brown v. *Board*
  of Education
  of Topeka
Martin Luther
  King
CORE
SNCC
NAACP
Civil Rights
  Act of 1964
Voting Rights Act
Great Society
Robert C. Weaver
Peace Corps

electronics
"Medicare"
John F. Kennedy
Mao Tse-tung
Chiang Kai-shek
Taiwan
cold war
Douglas MacArthur
Seoul
38th parallel
"McCarthyism"
Taft-Hartley Act

Bay of Pigs
"Iron Curtain"
Adlai E.
  Stevenson
Joseph Stalin
Nikita
  Khrushchev
ICBM
test-ban treaty
John Glenn
Lyndon B. Johnson
Viet Cong

Adding to Your Vocabulary

Master these words and be able to use them in talking about the people and things discussed in the chapter:

Communist   "nuclear club"

Do not overlook the activities under "The Growth of Democracy," pp. 697-698, and under "Then and Now" and "Looking Back on American History," pp. 699-700. Those under "Time and Change," pp. 698-699, emphasize particularly our foreign policy.

technical help   computer
free election   civil rights
hobnobbing   "sit-in"
nuclear   legal
    warhead   discrimination

The Research Center

1. Reread the discussion of Communists on page 674. Divide your class into groups to test each statement following the head "The Communists" by finding proof for it. Use as evidence as many examples as possible. Form a panel made up of a member from each group to present the information.

2. Find out and report what the present situations of the following are: NATO, SEATO, the UN, and the OAS.

3. In 1961 the United States and all the Latin American countries except Cuba agreed to join in the Alliance for Progress in order to help make the Latin American nations more prosperous. By using reference books and current publications, find out (a) what the Alliance has done, (b) the problems it has met, and (c) the results of its work.

Plan a Latin American day in your school. Display travel posters or posters you make representing the nations of South and Middle America. Show also articles made in those countries, and play recordings of Latin American music. Present the information about the Alliance for Progress in ways suitable for display, or prepare illustrated reports.

4. Prepare an illustrated report on one of the following subjects:
    a. American Space Achievements
    b. The Selection and Training
       of an Astronaut
    c. Peaceful Uses of Space Exploration
    d. My Favorite American Astronaut

5. Learn what has been done or is being done in your community to improve the situations of members of American minorities. What else needs to be done?

6. Find out what part of the current budget for the federal government is set aside for the national defense. What percentage of the total amount budgeted for federal expenses is it? What other item in the budget is related to defense? In what various ways is the money spent by the federal government obtained?

7. Find out what percent of the people in the United States today live in cities. How did President Johnson seek to meet the needs of city people? What problem did the growth of cities cause in the election of members to state legislatures? How is it being solved?

8. Invite a newspaperman from your community to tell the class about his experiences with the problem of freedom of the press. Find out the history of this problem in America. Look up the case of John Peter Zenger, the colonial publisher who was brought to trial in 1735 for statements which appeared in his paper. Report to the class, explaining what importance the outcome of the Zenger case had for the colonists and for the people of the United States.

The Growth of Democracy

1. How does the history of democracy in the United States show that self-improvement is a characteristic of democratic people?

2. In the United States "civil rights" are the rights of all persons to enjoy life, liberty, property, and protection of laws and to take part in government. These rights belong to Americans regardless of their race, religion, wealth, or the countries from which they or their ancestors came.

What steps have Negroes taken to win recognition of the fact that they have these rights? In what way was the failure to recognize their rights a blot on American democracy?

‡Be sure students understand the main reason for attempts at reapportionment: the fact that rban dwellers are often underrepresented in state legislatures. Discuss the objections to hanging this situation.

697

3. What is your idea of a good citizen in a democracy? How has technology made it easier than before for a person to do such things?

4. What is the special role of education in a democracy?

5. How did the Twenty-third and Twenty-fourth amendments (see pages 725–726) contribute to the growth of democracy?

Thinking Things Through

1. It is a principle of American law that any person be considered innocent until he is proved guilty. How did "McCarthyism" violate this principle?

2. In what way is "Medicare" an extension of the New Deal of Franklin Delano Roosevelt?

3. Why was the Twenty-second Amendment added to the Constitution?

4. Explain why both the Western countries and the Soviet Union hold parts of Berlin. Why do the Soviets want the Westerners out of the city?

5. What events discussed in the chapter show that the United States has given up isolationism?

6. How has today's technology made it more urgent than ever before for nations to live together peacefully?

Sharpening Your Map Skills

1. Look at the map on page 680 and locate, in relation to Red China, North and South Korea and North and South Vietnam. How far are Saigon and Seoul from the southern border of China? What other countries shown on the map lie along the same border? What danger do these countries face because of their locations?

2. What does the relief shown on the map tell you about difficulties in fighting a war in the Koreas or the Vietnams?

3. How much of South Vietnam lies in the tropics?

Your Opinion, Please

1. Why have Americans as a people always believed that tomorrow would be better than today?

2. Why must Americans today be more concerned about the foreign policy of the United States than ever before? How can they influence it?

3. Ask your parents what they think was the most important event between 1945 and 1966. How do you think you would answer this question when your children are your age?

4. What might have happened if help had not been sent to South Korea?

Part Eight Workshop

Time and Change

1. What change took place between 1918 and 1945 in the viewpoint of Americans about international organizations for collective security? What has been done since 1945 to provide such security?

2. Before the 1930's Americans generally believed that helping people who suffered under disadvantages was not the

work of the government. When and how was this belief changed?

3. Name the countries on our side in the First and Second World Wars. The main opponent of the United States in the cold war and in the wars in Korea and Vietnam. What accounts for changes?

4. In what parts of the world did Americans fight in the twentieth century? In each case why were they there?

##Students should recall that the belief was changed during the Great Depression and should remember some of the laws passed during "F.D.R.'s" presidency to aid people directly.

The teacher might divide these questions among the people in the class in order to provide individual work and cover all the material. Each question calls for thought and information.

5. The foreign policy of the United States has been changed since the Second World War to include giving much aid to foreign countries. Why? Name parts of the world that have received help. How is the Peace Corps part of our foreign policy?

6. Compare the foreign policy of Washington with the policies of Franklin D. Roosevelt, Dwight D. Eisenhower, Harry S Truman, John F. Kennedy, and Lyndon B. Johnson. What are the similarities? The differences? Account for them.

Then and Now

1. If George Washington could visit the president of the United States today, what changes would he see in the way the President conducts the nation's affairs? What things would be familiar to him?

2. If Thomas Jefferson could hear your panel discussion (next column) of the development of the United States as an industrialized country, what would he say?

3. If James Madison could read the United States Constitution today, what changes would he find in it? What do you think he would consider the most startling?

4. What changes would John C. Calhoun and Frederick Douglass find in the South today?

5. What characteristics of the United States today would especially please Alexander Hamilton? What might he disapprove of?

6. What change in American life would Al Smith particularly approve of?

7. If the reformers of the period between 1830 and 1850 lived today, what things that they worked for would they find done? What reforms in the twentieth century would astonish them?

8. If the first settlers of your community visited it today, what would strike them as strange or different?

9. Compare the activities of these First Ladies—Mrs. Madison, Mrs. John Adams, Mrs. Polk—with those of the First Ladies beginning with Mrs. Hoover. How do you account for the differences?

Looking Back on American History

1. How old is the United States? Compare its age with that of Greece, of Egypt, and of Nigeria. Would you say the United States is young, old, or middle-aged?

2. Write an essay on the development of democracy in the United States. Begin by naming the cornerstones of democracy laid in the English colonies and end with the present. Describe what you consider the main advances made through the years, and tell what you think still needs to be done. Finally, explain what democracy means to you.

3. Write a biography of one of the ## Americans who you think contributed most to the development of American democracy. Be prepared to defend your selection.

4. Present a panel discussion of the development of the United States as an industrialized nation. Include comments about these subjects: (a) ways of making a living in the English colonies and in the United States to about 1815; (b) the growth of industry before and during the Civil War; (c) the development of heavy industry; (d) changes in transportation; (e) the growth of cities; (f) the rapid technological change since 1880; and (g) effects of industrialization on Americans.

5. Write a history of the labor movement in the United States. Include a discussion of unions, important strikes, court decisions, and laws.

6. Prepare a program on the Negro in American history. Cover these periods: (a) 1619 to 1863; (b) 1863 to 1941; (c) 1941 to the present. Try to display pictures of outstanding American Negroes as part of the program.

7. All cultures are enriched by contacts with other cultures. Name as many groups

##This exercise and the one directly above it give you an opportunity to find out what the students have learned about democracy in the past year and what their attitudes are.

of people as you can who have contributed to American culture. Why is ours called a *plural* culture?

8. At what times in American history was sectionalism especially strong? Does it exist today? Explain.

9. What efforts to keep peace in the world has the United States made since Theodore Roosevelt's day? How successful have these efforts been?

10. What parts of American history are you especially proud of? Why?

11. Name the ten Americans who were not in politics who you think gave the greatest service to their country. Explain your choices.

12. Many memorials have been set up honoring the Americans who lost their lives in wars. What do you think would be the best memorial to them?

The Book Shelf

Bastert, Russell. *American Foreign Policy,* Bk. 1. Chicago: Rand McNally & Co., 1967. (Covers the years through 1865.)

Berman, Louis. *American Space Exploration.* Chicago: Rand McNally & Co., 1967. (An up-to-date discussion, with diagrams.)

Boardman, Fon Wyman. *History and Historians.* New York: Henry Z. Walck, Inc., Publishers, 1965. (About people who study and write history.)

Bowen, Joshua David. *The Struggle Within; Race Relations in the United States.* New York: W. W. Norton & Co., Inc., Publishers, 1965. (The reasons for race prejudice and for the Negro's protest against it.)

Cavanah, Frances. *Triumphant Adventure; the Story of Franklin Delano Roosevelt.* Chicago: Rand McNally & Co., 1964. (A biography.)

Clarke, Tom E. *The Big Road.* New York: Lothrop, Lee & Shepard Co., Inc., 1965. (A boy's life in the Great Depression.)

Heck, Bessie Holland. *The Hopeful Years.* Cleveland, Ohio: The World Publishing Co., 1964. (About an American family during the First World War.)

Hertel, Frank. *Sea Power in American History.* Chicago: Rand McNally & Co., 1967. (A historical treatment.)

Hirsch, S. Carl. *This Is Automation.* New York: The Viking Press, Inc., 1964. (About the use and control of automatic devices, including computers.)

Ruenheck, Wilbert H., and Flammer, Philip M. *A History of the U.S. Air Force.* Chicago: Rand McNally & Co., 1967. (The struggle to develop the United States Air Force.)

Shelton, William Roy. *Flights of the Astronauts.* Boston: Little, Brown & Co., 1963. (The first American and Soviet space flights.)

Sterne, Emma Gelders. *I Have a Dream.* New York: Alfred A. Knopf, Inc., 1965. (About the civil rights movement and its leaders.)

Terrell, John Upton. *The United States Department of Health, Education, and Welfare.* Des Moines, Iowa: Meredith Press, 1965. (About protecting American human resources.)

Trainor, Bernard. *A History of the U.S. Marines.* Chicago: Rand McNally & Co., 1967. (The contributions of the Marine Corps.)

Walters, Helen B. *Wernher Von Braun, Rocket Engineer.* New York: The Macmillan Co., Publishers, 1964. (Biography of an immigrant scientist who has contributed greatly to the American space program.)

Whittlesey, Susan. *U.S. Peace Corps; the Challenge of Good Will.* New York: Coward-McCann, Inc., 1963. (Describes the organization's purposes and work.)

Yates, W. Ross. *Democracy in the United States.* Chicago: Rand McNally & Co., 1967. (From colonial days until the present.)

A lasting, just peace would, of course, be the best memorial to these Americans.

Assign some of the books listed in "The Book Shelf" for special reports to the class.

APPENDIX

The Declaration of Independence

In Congress, July 4, 1776.

A Declaration by the Representatives of The United States of America, in Congress Assembled.

When, in the course of human events, it becomes necessary for one people to dissolve the political bands which have connected them with another, and to assume, among the powers of the earth, the separate and equal station to which the laws of nature and of nature's God entitle them, a decent respect to the opinions of mankind requires that they should declare the causes which impel them to the separation.

We hold these truths to be self-evident:—That all men are created equal; that they are endowed by their Creator with certain unalienable rights; that among these are life, liberty, and the pursuit of happiness. That, to secure these rights, governments are instituted among men, deriving their just powers from the consent of the governed; that, whenever any form of government becomes destructive of these ends, it is the right of the people to alter or to abolish it, and to institute a new government, laying its foundation on such principles, and organising its powers in such form, as to them shall seem most likely to effect their safety and happiness. Prudence, indeed, will dictate that governments long established should not be changed for light and transient causes; and, accordingly, all experience hath shown that mankind are more disposed to suffer, while evils are sufferable, than to right themselves by abolishing the forms to which they are accustomed. But, when a long train of abuses and usurpations, pursuing invariably the same object, evinces a design to reduce them under absolute despotism, it is their right, it is their duty, to throw off such government, and to provide new guards for their future security. Such has been the patient sufferance of these colonies; and such is now the necessity that constrains them to alter their former systems of government. The history of the present King of Great Britain is a history of repeated injuries and usurpations, all having, in direct object, the establishment of an absolute tyranny over these States. To prove this, let facts be submitted to a candid world.

He has refused his assent to laws the most wholesome and necessary for the public good.

He has forbidden his Governors to pass laws of immediate and pressing importance, unless suspended in their operation till his assent should be obtained; and, when so suspended, he has utterly neglected to attend to them.

He has refused to pass other laws for the accommodation of large districts of people, unless those people would relinquish the right of representation in the legislature—a right inestimable to them, and formidable to tyrants only.

He has called together legislative bodies at places unusual, uncomfortable, and distant from the depository of their public records, for the sole purpose of fatiguing them into compliance with his measure.

He has dissolved representative houses repeatedly, for opposing, with manly firmness, his invasions on the rights of the people.

He has refused, for a long time after such dissolutions, to cause others to be elected; whereby the legislative powers, incapable of annihilation, have returned to the people at large for their exercise; the State remaining, in the meantime, exposed to all dangers of invasion from without, and convulsions within.

He has endeavored to prevent the population of these States; for that purpose obstructing the laws for the naturalization of foreigners; refusing to pass others to encourage their migration hither, and raising the conditions of new appropriations of lands.

He has obstructed the administration of justice, by refusing his assent to laws for establishing judiciary powers.

He has made judges dependent on his will alone for the tenure of their offices, and the amount and payment of their salaries.

He has erected a multitude of new offices, and sent hither swarms of officers to harass our people and eat out their substance.

He has kept among us in times of peace, standing armies, without the consent of our legislatures.

He has affected to render the military independent of, and superior to, the civil power.

He has combined with others to subject us to a jurisdiction foreign to our constitutions, and unacknowledged by our laws; giving his assent to their acts of pretended legislation:

For quartering large bodies of armed troops among us;

For protecting them, by a mock trial, from punishment for any murders which they should commit on the inhabitants of these States;

For cutting off our trade with all parts of the world;

For imposing taxes on us without our consent;

For depriving us, in many cases, of the benefits of trial by jury;

For transporting us beyond the seas, to be tried for pretended offences;

For abolishing the free system of English laws in a neighboring province, establishing there an arbitrary government, and enlarging its boundaries, so as to render it at once an example and fit instrument for introducing the same absolute rule into these colonies;

For taking away our charters, abolishing our most valuable laws, and altering, fundamentally, the forms of our governments;

For suspending our own legislatures, and declaring themselves invested with power to legislate for us in all cases whatsoever.

He has abdicated government here, by declaring us out of his protection, and waging war against us.

He has plundered our seas, ravaged our coasts, burnt our towns, and destroyed the lives of our people.

He is at this time transporting large armies of foreign mercenaries to complete the works of death, desolation, and tyranny, already begun with circumstances of cruelty and perfidy scarcely paralleled in the most barbarous ages, and totally unworthy the head of a civilized nation.

He has constrained our fellow-citizens, taken captive on the high seas, to bear arms against their country, to become the executioners of their friends and brethren, or to fall themselves by their hands.

He has excited domestic insurrection amongst us, and has endeavored to bring on the inhabitants of our frontiers the merciless Indian savages, whose known rule of warfare is an undistinguished destruction of all ages, sexes, and conditions.

In every state of these oppressions we have petitioned for redress, in the most humble terms; our repeated petitions have been answered only by repeated injury. A prince whose character is thus marked by every act which may define a tyrant is unfit to be the ruler of a free people.

Nor have we been wanting in our attentions to our British brethren. We have warned them, from time to time, of attempts by their legislature to extend an unwarrantable jurisdiction over us. We have reminded them of the circumstances of our emigration and settlement here. We have appealed to their native justice and magnanimity; and we have conjured them, by the ties of our common kindred, to disavow these usurpations, which would inevitably interrupt our connections and correspondence. They, too, have been deaf to the voice of justice and of consanguinity. We must, therefore, acquiesce in the necessity which denounces our separation; and hold them, as we hold the rest of mankind, enemies in war, in peace friends.

WE, THEREFORE, the REPRESENTATIVES of the UNITED STATES OF AMERICA, in General Congress assembled, appealing to the Supreme Judge of the world for the rectitude of our intentions, do, in the name and by the authority of the good people of these colonies, solemnly publish and declare, That these united Colonies are, and of right ought to be, FREE AND INDEPENDENT STATES; that they are absolved from all allegiance to the British crown, and that all political connection between them and the state of Great Britain is, and ought to be, totally dissolved; and that, as free and independent states, they have full power to levy war, conclude peace, contract alliances, establish commerce, and to do all other acts and things which independent states may of right do. And, for the support of this declaration, with a firm reliance on the protection of Divine Providence, we mutually pledge to each other our lives, our fortunes, and our sacred honor.

JOHN HANCOCK.

The foregoing Declaration was, by order of Congress, engrossed and signed by the following members:—

New Hampshire.
JOSIAH BARTLETT,
WILLIAM WHIPPLE,
MATTHEW THORNTON.

Massachusetts Bay.
SAMUEL ADAMS,
JOHN ADAMS,
ROBERT TREAT PAINE,
ELBRIDGE GERRY.

Rhode Island.
STEPHEN HOPKINS,
WILLIAM ELLERY.

Connecticut.
ROGER SHERMAN,
SAMUEL HUNTINGTON,
WILLIAM WILLIAMS,
OLIVER WOLCOTT.

New York.
WILLIAM FLOYD,
PHILIP LIVINGSTON,
FRANCIS LEWIS,
LEWIS MORRIS.

New Jersey.
RICHARD STOCKTON,
JOHN WITHERSPOON,
FRANCIS HOPKINSON,
JOHN HART,
ABRAHAM CLARK.

Pennsylvania.
ROBERT MORRIS,
BENJAMIN RUSH,
BENJAMIN FRANKLIN,
JOHN MORTON,
GEORGE CLYMER,
JAMES SMITH,

GEORGE TAYLOR,
JAMES WILSON,
GEORGE ROSS.

Delaware.
CAESAR RODNEY,
GEORGE READ,
THOMAS M'KEAN.

Maryland.
SAMUEL CHASE,
WILLIAM PACA,
THOMAS STONE,
CHARLES CARROLL
    of Carrollton.

Virginia.
GEORGE WYTHE,
RICHARD HENRY LEE,
THOMAS JEFFERSON,

Resolved, That copies of the Declaration be sent to the several assemblies, conventions, and committees, or councils of safety, and to the several commanding officers of ... that it be proclaimed in ea... at the head of the army.

e Constitution of the United States

AND WHAT IT MEANS TODAY

set of basic laws on
overnment is founded,
It is printed in black,
h part comes a section
section will help you to
ution or the way it has

and the explanatory
for convenience. The
punctuation have been
reading.
e taken place in the United States and in our government since 1787, when the Constitutional Convention met in Philadelphia and wrote the Constitution. It has been in continuous use longer than any other written constitution in the world. As time passed and conditions changed, some parts of the Constitution went out of date. Some other parts have been set aside by amendments–additions or changes made after the original Constitution was adopted. These parts are in black like the rest of the Constitution, but in *italic* type.

---

ted States, want to bind the
than they were under the
/e want to set up fair laws.
vithin our nation. We want
gainst foreign enemies. We
rosperous and happy. And
this nation's people can be
/er. These are our purposes
for the United States of

lative Branch

s

slative powers herein
in a Congress of the
all consist of a Senate
tives.

All national laws must be made by Congress, not by any other part of the government. Even Congress cannot make any laws except those kinds that the Constitution gives it permission to make. Neither Congress nor anybody else can make certain kinds of laws that might harm the citizens. Congress is made up of two separate parts, or houses. These are the Senate, or upper house, and the House of Representatives, or lower house.

How Representatives Are Elected

SECTION 2, CLAUSE 1. The House of Representatives shall be composed of members chosen every second year by the people of the several states, and the electors in each state shall have the qualifications requisite for electors of the most numerous branch of the state legislature.

Members of the House of Representatives are elected in each state every two years. A Representative is elected for a two-year term. Any citizen whose state government permits him to vote for representatives in the state legislature must also be allowed to vote for members of the national House of Representatives. (Notice that this last rule really gives a state government the right to decide which of its citizens may vote for national Representatives.)

Who May Be a Representative

SECTION 2, CLAUSE 2. No person shall be a Representative who shall not have attained to the age of twenty-five years, and been seven years a citizen of the United States, and who shall not, when elected, be an inhabitant of that state in which he shall be chosen.

A person must be at least twenty-five years old before he can become a Representative. He must have been a United States citizen for seven years or more and must live in the state that elects him. These rules help to make sure that our laws are passed by mature persons.

Representatives and State Populations

SECTION 2, CLAUSE 3. Representatives *and direct taxes* shall be apportioned among the several states which may be included within this Union according to their respective numbers, *which shall be determined by adding to the whole number of free persons, including those bound to service for a term of years, and excluding Indians not taxed, three-fifths of all other persons.*

The number of Representatives that each state is entitled to send to Congress depends on the size of the state's population. (If State A, for instance, has twice as many people as State B, it may have, roughly, twice as many Representatives.) The amount of *direct taxes*—taxes handed over directly to the government by the taxpayer—which the national government collects from any state must also depend on the number of people in the state. But the Sixteenth Amendment, page 723, has changed this last rule as far as income taxes are concerned. Also, the long clause beginning "which shall be determined" is out-of-date, for there are no slaves or persons "bound to service" in this country any longer. Because of the Fourteenth Amendment, pages 722–723, all the people of a state, except its Indians who pay no taxes, are now counted in full to decide how many Representatives that state may have.

Taking the Census

The actual enumeration shall be made within three years after the first meeting of the Congress of the United States, and within every subsequent term of ten years, in such a manner as they shall by law direct. The number of Representatives shall not exceed one for every thirty thousand, but each state shall have at least one Representative; *and until such enumeration shall be made, the state of New Hampshire shall be entitled to choose 3; Massachusetts, 8; Rhode Island and Providence Plantations, 1; Connecticut, 5; New York, 6; New Jersey, 4; Pennsylvania, 8; Delaware, 1; Maryland, 6; Virginia, 10; North Carolina, 5; South Carolina, 5; and Georgia, 3.*

Congress may decide how the populations of the states are to be counted. But such a count, or *census,* must be made every ten years. Besides determining how many Representatives each state is entitled to have, the census gathers many other valuable facts about our people.

The Constitution rules that (1) the House of Representatives must have *not more than one member* for every 30,000 persons in the nation, but that (2) every state is entitled to *at least one member* no matter how small its population. If we still had one Representative for every 30,000 persons, the House would now contain more than 5000 members. To keep this from happening, Congress decided in 1929 that the House of Representatives should contain not more than 435 members. There is now one Representative for about every 400,000 persons. (You can find out how many Representatives your state is entitled to by dividing its population by 400,000.) In 1960 a number of states had fewer than 400,000 persons each, yet each of these states has one Representative in the House.

Filling Vacancies in the House

SECTION 2, CLAUSE 4. When vacancies happen in the representation from any state, the executive authority thereof shall issue writs of election to fill such vacancies.

When a state does not have all the Representatives in the House to which it is entitled—for instance, when a Representative dies or resigns—the state's governor must call for a special election to fill the vacancy.

Officers of the House, Impeachment

SECTION 2, CLAUSE 5. The House of Representatives shall choose their Speaker and other officers; and shall have the sole power of impeachment.

The House of Representatives elects its own officers, including the Speaker—that is, the chairman—the majority and minority leaders, the chaplain, and the sergeant-at-arms. Only the House has the right to *impeach* an official of the United States, that is, to accuse him of wrongdoing for which he may be tried and removed from his position.

The Senate

SECTION 3, CLAUSE 1. The Senate of the United States shall be composed of two Senators from each state, chosen *by the legislature thereof* for six years; and each Senator shall have one vote.

Each state has the right to send two Senators to Congress. (With fifty states, the Senate now contains one hundred members.) Each Senator serves for a six-year term and has one vote. In the Senate even the smallest state has as much power as the largest state.

Without this guarantee of equal power, the small states among the original thirteen might not have been willing to adopt the Constitution. They were afraid that the strong states would have too much power over them in the House, where the states with the most people had the most votes. Compare this section with Section 2, Clause 3, page 705.

Senators are not longer chosen by the legislatures of their states. Under the Seventeenth Amendment, page 723, adopted in 1913, United States Senators are now elected by the ordinary voters of their states, just as members of the national House of Representatives are.

When the Senators' Terms End

SECTION 3, CLAUSE 2. *Immediately after they shall be assembled in consequence of the first election, they shall be divided as equally as may be into three classes. The seats of the Senators of the first class shall be vacated at the expiration of the second year, of the second class at the expiration of the fourth year, and of the third class at the expiration of the sixth year, so that one-third may be chosen every second year; and if vacancies happen by resignation or otherwise during the recess of the legislature of any state, the executive thereof may make temporary appointments until the next meeting of the legislature, which shall then fill such vacancies.*

The three different classes of Senators ordered by this clause were intended only to get the Senate started. After the first four years of the Constitution Senators were no longer divided into classes; all Senators now have six-year terms. But because of this "staggering system," there is never more than one-third of the Senators who have just been elected— or reelected; one-third have served for two years, and one-third have served for four years. For this reason the Senate carries on its work without ever having a complete turnover in its membership.

The last part of this clause, describing how vacancies in the Senate were to be filled, has been changed by the Seventeenth Amendment, page 723.

Who May Be a Senator

SECTION 3, CLAUSE 3. No person shall be a Senator who shall not have attained to the age of thirty years and been nine years a citizen of the United States, and who shall not when elected be an inhabitant of that state for which he shall be chosen.

This clause names the requirements for becoming a Senator. Notice that the requirements for a Senator are more demanding than those for a Representative.

The Vice-President

SECTION 3, CLAUSE 4. The Vice-President of the United States shall be President of the Senate, but shall have no vote unless they be equally divided.

The vice-president of the United States serves as president of the Senate. That is, he serves as its chairman, in the same way that the Speaker serves as the chairman of the House of Representatives. The Vice-President is not a regular, elected member of the Senate. For this reason, he is not allowed to vote in the Senate unless his vote is needed to break a tie.

Other Officers of the Senate

SECTION 3, CLAUSE 5. The Senate shall choose their other officers, and also a President pro tempore, in the absence of the Vice-President, or when he shall exercise the office of the President of the United States.

The Senate chooses its other officers, for instance, its sergeant-at-arms and its chaplain. Because the vice-president of the United States sometimes is unable to serve as chairman of the Senate, the Senate chooses a Senator to be *president pro tempore*— president for the time being—who serves as the chairman in the absence of the Vice-President.

Impeachment Trials

SECTION 3, CLAUSE 6. The Senate shall have the sole power to try all impeachments. When sitting for that purpose, they shall be on oath or affirmation. When the President of the United States is tried, the Chief Justice shall preside; and no person shall be convicted without the concurrence of two-thirds of the members present.

Persons who are believed to have done serious wrongs as officials of the United States may be removed from office by the process called impeachment. Only the House of Representatives has the right to begin an impeachment, that is, make charges against a suspected official (Section 2, Clause 5, page 705). Only the Senate has the right to try the official after the House of Representatives has impeached him. In an impeachment, the official on trial is declared not guilty unless at least two-thirds of the total number of Senators who are present vote that he is guilty.

Ordinarily the president of the Senate presides at impeachment trials. But the chief justice of the United States must preside over the Senate when the president of the United States is being tried. It would not be fair to let the Vice-President preside then, for he would be the one to succeed to the presidency if the President were found guilty.

Punishment in Impeachment Trials

SECTION 3, CLAUSE 7. Judgment in cases of impeachment shall not extend further than to removal from office and disqualification to hold and enjoy any office of honor, trust, or profit under the United States; but the party convicted shall nevertheless be liable and subject to indictment, trial, judgment, and punishment, according to law.

If the Senate declares an impeached official guilty it can punish him in only one way, and that is by putting him out of office and forbidding him ever to hold another office in the national government. But this does not mean that a national official can commit crimes without severe punishment. After being put out of office, he can then be tried by a jury in a regular court. If the court finds him guilty, he can be punished like anyone else.

Members of Congress are never impeached. But they may be expelled by action of the house to which they have been elected. (*See* Section 5, Clause 2, this page.)

Elections to Congress

SECTION 4, CLAUSE 1. The times, places, and manner of holding elections for Senators and Representatives shall be prescribed in each state by the legislature thereof; but the Congress may at any time by law make or alter such regulations *except as to the places of choosing Senators.*

The legislature of each state has the right to pass laws deciding when, where, and how Senators and Representatives are to be elected. But Congress has the right to pass laws that change a state's election laws. One national law requires that secret ballots be used.

In every state the day for Congressional elections is the first Tuesday following the first Monday in November of even-numbered years (1966, 1968, and so on).

The last phrase of Clause 1 is not in effect. As a result of the Seventeenth Amendment, page 723, both Senators and Representatives are chosen by the same methods and in the same places.

Meetings of Congress

SECTION 4, CLAUSE 2. The Congress shall assemble at least once in every year, *and such meeting shall be on the first Monday in December, unless they shall by law appoint a different day.*

Congress must hold at least one meeting, or session, each year. This helps to guarantee that no executive can ever gain control of our government by putting an end to the work of our elected members of Congress. In 1933 the day for beginning each session of Congress

was changed to January 3 by the Twentieth Amendment, pages 724–725.

Rules of Congress

SECTION 5, CLAUSE 1. Each house shall be the judge of the elections, returns, and qualifications of its own members, and a majority of each shall constitute a quorum to do business; but a smaller number may adjourn from day to day and may be authorized to compel the attendance of absent members in such manner and under such penalties as each house may provide.

Each house of Congress has the right to decide whether its members were elected fairly and meet the requirements for members of Congress. A Senator or Representative who is newly elected can be kept from taking office if a majority in the house to which he was elected voted to keep him out.

A quorum is the number of members of a group that must be present before the group can do its official business. The Constitution says that a majority—half the members plus one—is the number needed to make a quorum in either house of Congress. But in practice, work may often be carried on without a quorum—provided that no member demands that those present be counted. When fewer that half the members of either house are present, that house may adjourn until the next day and may use penalties to force the absent members to attend.

More Rules of Congress

SECTION 5, CLAUSE 2. Each house may determine the rules of its proceedings, punish its members for disorderly behavior, and, with the concurrence of two-thirds, expel a member.

Each house has the right to make rules about its work and the actions of its members, and may punish its members for misbehaving. Each house has the right to expel any of its members by a two-thirds vote. This provides a way of discharging wrongdoers in Congress, much as impeachment weeds out officials who do wrong in other branches of the national government. (See Section 3, Clauses 6 and 7.)

Records of the Actions of Congress

SECTION 5, CLAUSE 3. Each house shall keep a journal of its proceedings, and from time to time publish the same, excepting such parts as may in their judgment require secrecy; and the yeas and nays of the members of either house on any question shall, at the desire of one-fifth of those present, be entered on the journal.

Each house of Congress must keep a separate record of what goes on at its meetings and must publish the record periodically. But the members may vote not to publish everything—that is, to keep some things secret. How each member votes on a particular question—whether yea (for) or nay (against)—is put into the record if one-fifth of the members who are present wish this to be done.

The Congressional Record, published for every day that Congress is in session, records the actions of both houses of Congress. At longer intervals, the House publishes *The House Journal,* and the Senate, *The Senate Journal.*

Adjournments

SECTION 5, CLAUSE 4. Neither house, during the session of Congress, shall without the consent of the other adjourn, for more than three days, nor to any other place than that in which the two houses shall be sitting.

During the period when Congress is meeting, neither house may suspend its meetings for more than three days unless the other house gives permission. Since the work of the two houses is closely related, neither house is allowed to move to another city unless the the other house agrees.

Pay and Privileges of Members of Congress

SECTION 6, CLAUSE 1. The Senators and Representatives shall receive a compensation for their services, to be ascertained by law, and paid out of the Treasury of the United States. They shall in all cases, except treason, felony, and breach of the peace, be privileged from arrest during their attendance at the session of their respective houses, and in going to and returning from the same; and for any speech or debate in either house they shall not be questioned in any other place.

Members of Congress are paid out of the United States Treasury. The amount of their pay is decided by law of Congress.

Members of Congress may not be arrested at meetings of Congress or on their way to or from those meetings—unless they are suspected of committing serious crimes or disturbing the peace. They may not be arrested or be punished for anything they may say in Congress except by the house of which they are members. These privileges, called Congressional immunity, allow members of Congress to say without fear of punishment what they believe is for the good of the country.

What the Members of Congress May Not Do

SECTION 6, CLAUSE 2. No Senator or Representative shall, during the time for which he was elected, be appointed to any civil office under the authority of the United States which shall have been created or the emoluments whereof shall have been increased during such time; and no person holding any office under the United States shall be a member of either house during his continuance in office.

Until his term has ended, no member of Congress may take any other job in the national government if that job was set up or the pay for that job was increased during the member's term. This rule helps to keep Congressmen from voting for good jobs for themselves. Furthermore, no person is allowed to become a member of Congress without first giving up any other national job that he may hold.

Bills for Raising Money

SECTION 7, CLAUSE 1. All bills for raising revenue shall originate in the House of Representatives; but the Senate may propose or concur with amendments as on other bills.

Either the Senate or the House of Representatives has the right to start most kinds of bills, but only the House may start a bill for raising money by taxes. But the Senate has the right to make amendments, or changes, in the tax bills begun in the House.

How Bills Become Laws

SECTION 7, CLAUSE 2. Every bill which shall have passed the House of Representatives and the Senate shall before it becomes a law be presented to the President of the United States. If he approve, he shall sign it; but if not, he shall return it with his objections to that house in which it shall have originated, who shall enter the objections at large on their journal and proceed to reconsider it. If after such reconsideration two-thirds of that house shall agree to pass the bill, it shall be sent, together with the objections, to the other house, by which it shall likewise be reconsidered; and if approved by two-thirds of that house, it shall become a law. But in all such cases the votes of both houses shall be determined by yeas and nays, and the names of the persons voting for and against the bill shall be entered on the journal of each house respectively.

This clause of the Constitution gives most of the method by which our nation's laws are made. Except for any tax bills (see Section 7, Clause 1), either the Senate or the House may write a bill proposing a new law. Suppose, for instance, that a bill is introduced in the Senate. If a majority of the Senators who are present vote against the bill, it dies in the Senate and does not become a law. But if a majority vote for it, it is then sent to the House of Representatives. Here, too, it either dies or is passed, depending on the vote of the majority. But very likely the House passes the bill only after having made amendments in it. If this is the case, it must then be sent back to the Senate to be voted on there in its amended form.

When both the Senate and the House have voted in favor of the bill, with its amendments, if any, it is sent to the president of the United States. He studies it and usually gets advice from some of his assistants. If he favors the bill, he signs it, and it then becomes an official law of the country—often called an Act of Congress. But if the President is against a proposed law, he *vetoes* the bill, that is, he refuses to sign it. He then sends the bill, usually accompanied by a written statement of his objections to it, back to the house in which it originated (in this supposed example, to the Senate).

Next, the Senate votes on the bill again, but this time the bill dies if less than two-thirds of the Senators present vote for it. When this occurs, the veto is "sustained." If two-thirds or more vote for the bill, it is passed in spite of the President's objection to it. This is called overriding the veto. When a veto is overridden, the name of each member of each house and the way he voted must be entered on the official record.

A bill repassed by the Senate over the President's veto is sent on to the House, still accompanied by the President's objections. Here the bill goes through the same process, and the President's veto either is sustained or is overridden by a two-thirds vote. If both houses override the veto, the bill becomes a law that is just as binding as if it had been signed by the President.

The rules for turning a bill into a law work the same way whether the bill begins in the Senate or in the House.

The "Pocket Veto"

If any bill shall not be returned by the President within ten days (Sundays excepted) after it shall have been presented to him, the same shall be a law in like manner as if he had signed it, unless the Congress by their adjournment prevent its return, in which case it shall not be a law.

If the President receives a bill passed by both houses and keeps it for ten days or more (not counting Sundays) without either signing it or vetoing it, it becomes a law without the need for Congress to do anything more about it. (The President sometimes does this when he does not want to take a stand either for the bill or against it.) But if Congress adjourns before the ten days are up and before the President has either signed or vetoed the bill, the bill dies. This is called the pocket veto.

By using his veto power, the President exercises one

of the checks and balances intended by the framers of the Constitution. So does Congress when it overrides a veto.

Other Actions of Congress

SECTION 7, CLAUSE 3. Every order, resolution, or vote to which the concurrence of the Senate and House of Representatives may be necessary (except on a question of adjournment) shall be presented to the President of the United States; and before the same shall take effect, shall be approved by him, or being disapproved by him, shall be repassed by two-thirds of the Senate and House of Representatives, according to the rules and limitations prescribed in the case of a bill.

Besides bills, there are other actions of Congress that take effect only after they have been approved by the President, or, if vetoed by him, have been repassed by two-thirds of both houses. These actions include "every order, resolution, or vote"—except a vote to adjourn Congress, which need only be passed by both houses of Congress.

The Laying of Taxes

SECTION 8, CLAUSE 1. The Congress shall have power to lay and collect taxes, duties, imposts, and excises, to pay the debts and provide for the common defense and general welfare of the United States; but all duties, imposts, and excises shall be uniform throughout the United States.

Congress may pass laws for collecting taxes of various kinds. It may do this for three purposes: (1) to pay the nation's debts, (2) to defend the nation against its enemies, and (3) to do whatever is necessary for the good of the people. If the national government had no power to tax, the nation could not meet its obligations and would soon fall to pieces.

All national taxes must be the same in all parts of the country. This rule keeps Congress from unfairly favoring or discriminating against any state or district.

The Borrowing of Money

SECTION 8, CLAUSE 2. To borrow money on the credit of the United States.

Congress has the power to borrow money for the use of the national government and promises to repay this money when it is due.

Foreign and Interstate Commerce

SECTION 8, CLAUSE 3. To regulate commerce with foreign nations, and among the several states, and with the Indian tribes.

Because of this clause, known as the Commerce Clause, Congress has passed laws to control trade (1) between this country and foreign countries (foreign commerce), and (2) between one state and another state (interstate commerce). These laws control the movements across national or state boundaries of persons, goods, and messages. These laws also control the facilities for international and interstate transportation and communication: ships, harbors, canals and navigable rivers, highways, railroads, bus lines, airlines, and telegraph, telephone, radio, and television systems.

Under the Commerce Clause, Congress encourages the commerce that means prosperity for our country and keeps the states from taxing goods sent in from other states. Congress can impose tariffs, or import taxes, on goods brought into this country, or can keep out goods—or undesirable persons—altogether. Throughout our country's history Congress has passed many laws based upon powers granted in this section.

Naturalization, Bankruptcy

SECTION 8, CLAUSE 4. To establish a uniform rule of naturalization, and uniform laws on the subject of bankruptcies throughout the United States.

Congress is empowered to decide which citizens of foreign countries may be naturalized—that is, which may become United States citizens—and how this may be done. A national bankruptcy law, which is the same for all parts of the country, helps to make sure of fair treatment for everybody to whom a person owes debts that he cannot pay.

Coinage, Weights and Measures

SECTION 8, CLAUSE 5. To coin money, regulate the value thereof and foreign coin, and fix the standard of weights and measures.

Congress controls the minting of money from metals and decides how much the coins shall be worth. It can set the value of foreign money in this country. By using its power to borrow money (see Section 8, Clause 2, page 709), Congress orders our paper money to be printed. Congress has set up the standards for measuring weights and distances. Much confusion is saved by having a pound, for instance, or a yard, exactly the same in all parts of the United States.

Counterfeiting

SECTION 8, CLAUSE 6. To provide for the punishment of counterfeiting the securities and current coin of the United States.

Congress passes laws ordering severe punishments

for persons who make false money or false government bonds and notes. Secret-service men in the Department of the Treasury protect us against counterfeiters.

Postal Service

SECTION 8, CLAUSE 7. To establish post offices and post roads.

Congress controls the postal system and the post offices for handling the mail and can build and maintain the roads over which the mail is carried. Over the years the Post Office Department has taken on additional functions besides delivering letters. It carries parcels and sells postal money orders.

Rights of Authors and Inventors

SECTION 8, CLAUSE 8. To promote the progress of science and useful arts, by securing for limited times to authors and inventors the exclusive right to their respective writings and discoveries.

Congress encourages this country's art, science, and industry by means of laws helping artists and inventors of various kinds. *Copyright laws* protect authors, composers, and artists from having their writings, music, paintings, and other works copied without payment. *Patent laws* protect in the same way those who invent or discover new and useful manufactured articles or valuable new methods in science and industry.

National Courts

SECTION 8, CLAUSE 9. To constitute tribunals inferior to the Supreme Court.

Congress sets up national courts that have less authority than the United States Supreme Court. Courts of appeals, district courts, and courts of claims are some of the different kinds of national courts.

Crimes at Sea, Crimes Against International Law

SECTION 8, CLAUSE 10. To define and punish piracies and felonies committed on the high seas, and offenses against the law of nations.

Congress rules what acts committed at sea are crimes and how they are to be punished. It may also make laws about crimes in which foreign countries or foreign citizens are involved.

Declarations of War

SECTION 8, CLAUSE 11. To declare war, *grant letters of marque and reprisal, and make rules concerning captures on land and water.*

Congress, and only Congress, has the power to declare war. But in the face of an attack by a foreign country, this country may need to use its armed forces even before Congress can act. The rest of this clause is about warfare carried on by private citizens; it is no longer allowed.

The Army

SECTION 8, CLAUSE 12. To raise and support armies, but no appropriation of money to that use shall be for a longer term than two years.

Congress may create an army for the United States and vote the money to pay for it. But Congress must not give the army at any one time more than enough for two years' expenses.

The Navy

SECTION 8, CLAUSE 13. To provide and maintain a navy.

Congress may create a navy for the United States and vote the money to pay for it.

Rules for the Armed Forces

SECTION 8, CLAUSE 14. To make rules for the government and regulation of the land and naval forces.

Congress may make the rules for our armed forces, which now include the air force.

Use of the Militia

SECTION 8, CLAUSE 15. To provide for calling forth the militia to execute the laws of the Union, suppress insurrections, and repel invasions.

Congress may rule how and when the militias—that is, the citizen-soldiers in the various states, now called the National Guard—are to be called to help the national government. The militias may be called on to enforce national laws, end rebellions, and drive out foreign enemies.

Control of the Militia

SECTION 8, CLAUSE 16. To provide for organizing, arming, and disciplining the militia, and for governing such part of them as may be employed in the service of the United States, reserving to the states, respectively, the appointment of the officers and the authority of training the militia according to the discipline prescribed by Congress.

Congress may organize the militias, furnish weapons to them, and make rules for those members of the militias who are in the service of the United States. Although the government of each state has the right to appoint the officers of its militia, it must train the militia as Congress directs.

The National Capital, Other National Property

SECTION 8, CLAUSE 17. To exercise exclusive legislation in all cases whatsoever over such district (not exceeding ten miles square) as may, by cession of particular states and the acceptance of Congress, become the seat of government of the United States; and to exercise like authority over all places purchased by the consent of the legislature of the state in which the same shall be, for the erection of forts, magazines, arsenals, dockyards, and other needful buildings.

Congress makes all the laws for governing the District of Columbia (containing the national capital— established in Washington). The capital is not under the control of any state or county government.

Congress also governs all other property belonging to the national government—post offices, national forests, etc.

Other Necessary Laws

SECTION 8, CLAUSE 18. And to make all laws which shall be necessary and proper for carrying into execution the foregoing powers and all other powers vested by this Constitution in the government of the United States, or in any department or officer thereof.

Besides the lawmaking powers specifically granted to Congress by the Constitution, Congress may make any other laws that are needed in order to carry out the orders in the Constitution. This clause is called the Elastic Clause because it can be stretched to fit the changing needs of the nation. But the Elastic Clause does not permit Congress to legislate without *any* restrictions. The Supreme Court and the other national courts have the power to rule out, as unconstitutional, any law of Congress which they consider not to be "necessary and proper" (see explanation of Article 3, Section 1, page 716).

The Slave Trade

SECTION 9, CLAUSE 1. *The migration or importation of such persons as any of the states now existing shall think proper to admit shall not be prohibited by the Congress prior to the year one thousand eight hundred and eight, but a tax or duty may be imposed on such importation, not exceeding ten dollars for each person.*

This clause made it possible to outlaw the bringing of slaves into the United States, beginning in 1808.

Habeas Corpus

SECTION 9, CLAUSE 2. The privilege of the writ of habeas corpus shall not be suspended, unless when in cases of rebellion or invasion the public safety may require it.

The national government is not allowed to take away anyone's right of habeas corpus except when great danger to the country makes this necessary. Habeas corpus gives a person accused of a crime the right to obtain a prompt hearing on the charges. It protects a person from arbitrary arrest or a long imprisonment without a hearing.

Bills of Attainder, Ex Post Facto Laws

SECTION 9, CLAUSE 3. No bill of attainder or ex post facto law shall be passed.

Congress must not pass any bill intending to punish one particular person—a bill of attainder. Congress must not pass any law that would punish a person for doing something that was not against the law at the time he did it.

Direct Taxes in Proportion to Population

SECTION 9, CLAUSE 4. No capitation or other direct tax shall be laid, unless in proportion to the census or enumeration hereinbefore directed to be taken.

Congress must not order any direct tax except in proportion to the populations of the various states as determined from the census count. An income tax is one kind of direct tax, but see the Sixteenth Amendment, page 723.

Export Taxes Forbidden

SECTION 9, CLAUSE 5. No tax or duty shall be laid on articles exported from any state.

Congress must not tax goods sent from one state to another or goods sent to other countries.

Ports and Port Duties

SECTION 9, CLAUSE 6. No preference shall be given by any regulation of commerce or revenue to the ports of one state over those of another; nor shall vessels bound to or from one state be obliged to enter, clear, or pay duties to another.

Congress must not give the ports of one state any advantage over the ports of another state. Congress must not tax goods being sent by water from one state to another state.

Accounting for Public Money

SECTION 9, CLAUSE 7. No money shall be drawn from the Treasury but in consequence of appropriations made by law; and a regular statement and account of the receipts and expenditures of all public money shall be published from time to time.

Money can be paid out of the Treasury only if an act of Congress gives permission. Statements showing how much money was received in the Treasury and how much was paid out must be published from time to time.

Titles of Nobility, Gifts

SECTION 9, CLAUSE 8. No title of nobility shall be granted by the United States; and no person holding any office of profit or trust under them shall without the consent of the Congress accept of any present, emolument, office, or title of any kind whatever from any king, prince, or foreign state.

The national government must not create noble rank for anybody. No national official may accept any gift, position, or title from any foreign government unless Congress gives its permission.

Actions Forbidden to the States

SECTION 10, CLAUSE 1. No state shall enter into any treaty, alliance, or confederation; grant letters of marque and reprisal; coin money; emit bills of credit; make anything but gold and silver coin a tender in payment of debts; pass any bill of attainder, ex post facto law, or law impairing the obligation of contracts, or grant any title of nobility.

State governments must not make treaties or pacts of union with foreign countries. State governments may not grant their citizens permission to fight against foreign countries, make coins or paper money for themselves, or allow anything but gold and silver coins to be used as legal money. These powers belong exclusively to the national government.

The state governments, like the national government, are forbidden to pass acts that punish people without giving them trials, to pass laws that would punish people for things they did that were not against the law when they did them, or to grant titles of nobility. State governments must not pass any laws that would de-

712

stroy the contracts by which people make legal agreements with one another.

Taxation by the States

SECTION 10, CLAUSE 2. No state shall, without the consent of the Congress, lay any imposts or duties on imports or exports, except what may be absolutely necessary for executing its inspection laws; and the net produce of all duties and imposts, laid by any state on imports or exports, shall be for the use of the Treasury of the United States; and all such laws shall be subject to the revision and control of the Congress.

States must not interfere with commerce by taxing goods entering or leaving their territory—except that they *may* charge fees for inspecting such goods. But any money the states collect as inspection fees must be paid into the Treasury of the United States. Congress has the power to change the inspection laws of any of the states.

Other State Actions Forbidden

SECTION 10, CLAUSE 3. No state shall, without the consent of Congress, lay any duty of tonnage, keep troops or ships of war in time of peace, enter into any agreement or compact with another state, or with a foreign power, or engage in war, unless actually invaded, or in such imminent danger as will not admit of delay.

Unless Congress gives permission, no state may do these things: (1) charge a tax on ships that enter its ports, (2) have its own army—except the militia—or navy in peacetime, (3) make treaties with other states or with foreign countries, (4) make war except when it has been invaded or is likely to be invaded. All these are powers that should be used only by the national government for the good of the whole country.

ARTICLE 2

The Presidency and the Executive Branch

Terms of the President and the Vice-President

SECTION 1, CLAUSE 1. The executive power shall be vested in a President of the United States of America. He shall hold his office during the term of four years and, together with the Vice-President, chosen for the same term, be elected as follows.

Our nation's laws are enforced, or executed, by the president of the United States. His term of office is four years. The Vice-President also has a four-year term.

The Presidential Electors

SECTION 1, CLAUSE 2. Each state shall appoint, in such manner as the legislature thereof may direct, a number of electors, equal to the whole number of Senators and Representatives to which the state may be entitled in the Congress; but no Senator or Representative, or person holding an office of trust or profit under the United States, shall be appointed an elector.

According to the Constitution, but not in actual practice nowadays, the President and the Vice-President are to be chosen by electors in each state. These electors are selected according to rules set up by the state legislatures. The electors from all the states form what is known as the electoral college, though they never meet as a single group. The number of electors in each state is equal to the number of that state's Senators and Representatives in Congress. Nobody who has any position in the national government may be an elector.

The election of the President and the Vice-President, both as it now is and as the writers of the Constitution intended it to be, is explained after the Twelfth Amendment, pages 721–722.

Duties of the Electors

SECTION 1, CLAUSE 3. *The electors shall meet in their respective states and vote by ballot for two persons, of whom one at least shall not be an inhabitant of the same state with themselves. And they shall make a list of all the persons voted for, and of the number of votes for each, which list they shall sign and certify and transmit, sealed, to the seat of the government of the United States, directed to the president of the Senate. The president of the Senate shall, in the presence of the Senate and the House of Representatives, open all the certificates, and the votes shall then be counted. The person having the greatest number of votes shall be the President, if such number be a majority of the whole number of electors appointed; and if there be more than one who have such majority, and have an equal number of votes, then the House of Representatives shall immediately choose by ballot one of them for President; and if no person have a majority, then from the five highest on the list the said House shall in like manner choose the President. But in choosing the President, the vote shall be taken by states, the representation from each state having one vote. A quorum for this purpose shall consist of a member or mem-*

bers from two-thirds of the states, and a majority of all the states shall be necessary to a choice. In every case, after the choice of President, the person having the greatest number of votes of the electors shall be the Vice-President. But if there should remain two or more who have equal votes, the Senate shall choose from them by ballot the Vice-President.

This clause did not work well in practice and was changed in 1804 by the Twelfth Amendment, page 721.

Election Day

SECTION 1, CLAUSE 4. The Congress may determine the time of choosing the electors and the day on which they shall give their votes, which day shall be the same throughout the United States.

Congress may decide on what day the electors are to be elected and the day when they are to cast their ballots for President and Vice-President. This day is the same in all parts of the United States. See the explanation of presidential elections following the Twelfth Amendment, pages 721–722.

Who May Become President

SECTION 1, CLAUSE 5. No person except a natural-born citizen *or a citizen of the United States at the time of the adoption of this Constitution* shall be eligible to the office of President; neither shall any person be eligible to that office who shall not have attained the age of thirty-five years and been fourteen years a resident within the United States.

Nobody may become President unless he is a citizen of the United States by birth, is at least thirty-five years old, and has lived in the United States for fourteen years or more.

Succession to the Presidency

SECTION 1, CLAUSE 6. In case of the removal of the President from office, or of his death, resignation, or inability to discharge the powers and duties of the said office, the same shall devolve on the Vice-President, and the Congress may by law provide for the case of removal, death, resignation, or inability, both of the President and Vice-President, declaring what officer shall then act as President, and such officer shall act accordingly until the disability be removed or a President shall be elected.

If the presidency becomes vacant, the Vice-President assumes the office. Congress has the right to decide

by law who becomes President when neither the President nor the Vice-President is able to serve. A law passed in 1886 ruled that when that happened, the members of the President's Cabinet should succeed to the presidency—in an order determined by the order in which the Cabinet posts were originally created. But in 1947 this law was changed, putting two other officials in line for the presidency ahead of any Cabinet members. The officials now in line for the Presidency, in order, are (1) the Speaker of the House of Representatives, and (2) the president pro tempore of the Senate.

The President's Salary

SECTION 1, CLAUSE 7. The President shall at stated times receive for his services a compensation, which shall neither be increased nor diminished during the period for which he shall have been elected, and he shall not receive within that period any other emolument from the United States, or any of them.

The President receives a salary, which must not be made either larger or smaller during his term of office. This rule keeps Congress from getting too much control over the President by threatening his income or trying to bribe him. His salary is now $100,000 a year, besides other sums for his expenses. He must not be given any other kind of salary by either the national or the state governments.

President's Oath of Office

SECTION 1, CLAUSE 8. Before he enter on the execution of his office he shall take the following oath or affirmation: "I do solemnly swear (or affirm) that I will faithfully execute the office of President of the United States, and will to the best of my ability preserve, protect, and defend the Constitution of the United States."

Before the President starts his term, he must make a solemn promise to perform his duties faithfully and to protect this country's form of government.

Military Powers, Pardons

SECTION 2, CLAUSE 1. The President shall be commander in chief of the Army and Navy of the United States, and of the militias of the several states when called into the actual service of the United States; he may require the opinion, in writing, of the principal officer in each of the executive departments, upon any subject relating to the duties of their respective offices, and he shall have power to grant reprieves and pardons for offenses against the United States, except in cases of impeachment.

The President is the commander in chief of the armed forces of the United States and of the militias when they are called into national service. He may order written reports from Cabinet officers about the work of their departments. He may pardon persons convicted of crimes against the national government or order their punishments to be delayed—but he may not do this for impeached government officials.

Treaties and Appointments

SECTION 2, CLAUSE 2. He shall have power, by and with the advice and consent of the Senate, to make treaties, provided two-thirds of the Senators present concur; and he shall nominate and, by and with the advice and consent of the Senate, shall appoint ambassadors, other public ministers and consuls, judges of the Supreme Court, and all other officers of the United States whose appointments are not herein provided for and which shall be established by law; but the Congress may by law vest the appointment of such inferior officers as they think proper in the President alone, in the courts of law, or in the heads of departments.

The President may make treaties with foreign countries, but at least two-thirds of the Senators present must approve a treaty before it becomes a law. He may appoint certain important officials only if the Senate approves his choices. But Congress may transfer, to the President, to his department chiefs, or to the courts, exclusive control over the appointment of less important officials.

Filling Vacant Positions

SECTION 2, CLAUSE 3. The President shall have power to fill up all vacancies that may happen during the recess of the Senate by granting commissions which shall expire at the end of their next session.

If positions become vacant when the Senate is not meeting, the President may appoint persons to fill them. These are temporary appointments which end at the close of the next session of the Senate.

In practice, the great majority of those who work for the national government are now appointed through the United States Civil Service Commission.

Other Duties of the President

SECTION 3. He shall from time to time give to the Congress information of the state of the Union, and recommend to their consideration such measures as he shall judge necessary and expedient; he may, on extraordinary occasions,

convene both houses, or either of them, and in case of disagreement between them, with respect to the time of adjournment, he may adjourn them to such time as he shall think proper; he shall receive ambassadors and other public ministers; he shall take care that the laws be faithfully executed, and shall commission all the officers of the United States.

The President must give Congress information about the condition of the country and suggest to Congress what he thinks Congress ought to legislate on. This information is called the State of the Union message. By custom, the President delivers such a message in a speech to Congress every January. He may call a special session of either house or both houses of Congress if there is an urgent need. He may end a session of Congress if the two houses cannot agree on time for ending. He receives representatives of foreign governments. It is his duty to make sure that the nation's laws are properly carried out. He signs official papers appointing persons to jobs in the national government.

Impeachments

SECTION 4. The President, Vice-President, and all civil officers of the United States shall be removed from office on impeachment for, and conviction of, treason, bribery, or other high crimes and misdemeanors.

The President, the Vice-President, or any civilian official of the national government must be put out of office if he has been impeached and found guilty of disloyalty to his country, of bribery, or of other crimes.

ARTICLE 3
The Supreme Court and the Judicial Branch

National Courts, National Judges

SECTION 1. The judicial power of the United States shall be vested in one Supreme Court, and in such inferior courts as the Congress may from time to time ordain and establish. The judges, both of the Supreme and inferior courts, shall hold their offices during good behavior, and shall at stated times receive for their services a compensation, which shall not be diminished during their continuance in office.

This, the third great branch of our national government, is the judicial branch, which has the task of judging cases and of explaining what our laws mean. The United States Supreme Court is at the head of the judicial branch. In addition there are other national courts set up by Congress, including courts of appeals, district courts, and courts of claims. The federal judges, including the Supreme Court justices, are appointed by the President, with Senate approval. These judges may hold their jobs as long as they live, unless they are impeached and found guilty. Their salaries cannot be lowered while they are in office.

One of the most important powers of the national courts, and especially of the Supreme Court, is not mentioned in the Constitution. This is their power to decide that certain national, state, and local laws are *unconstitutional*—that they are in violation of our Constitution. In this way, the national courts exercise one of the important checks and balances in our system of government.

Kinds of Cases Tried in National Courts

SECTION 2, CLAUSE 1. The judicial power shall extend to all cases in law and equity arising under this Constitution, the laws of the United States, and treaties made or which shall be made under their authority; to all cases affecting ambassadors, other public ministers, and consuls; to all cases of admiralty and maritime jurisdiction; to controversies to which the United States shall be a party; to controversies between two or more states; *between a state and citizens of another state;* between citizens of different states; between citizens of the same state claiming lands under grants of different states, and between a state, or the citizens thereof, and foreign states, citizens, or subjects.

The cases tried by the national courts are those concerning: (1) the Constitution and the nation's laws and treaties, (2) the representatives of foreign governments, (3) the laws controlling ships and sailors, (4) disagreements between our government and other governments or persons, (5) disagreements between states, (6) disagreements between citizens of different states, (7) disagreements in which citizens of the same state claim lands granted by different states, (8) disagreements between a state or its citizens and a foreign country or foreign citizens.

The out-of-date part of Clause 1 was changed by the Eleventh Amendment, page 720.

Jurisdiction of the Supreme Court

SECTION 2, CLAUSE 2. In all cases affecting ambassadors, other public ministers and consuls, and those in which a state shall be party, the Supreme Court shall have original jurisdiction. In all the other cases before mentioned, the Supreme Court shall have appellate jurisdiction, both as to law and fact, with such exceptions and under such regulations as the Congress shall make.

The Supreme Court has two kinds of jurisdiction—that is, authority to try cases. First, it can try new cases being brought to court for the first time, if those cases concern one of the states or a representative of a foreign government. This is the Supreme Court's *original jurisdiction.* Second, it can try cases again that have already been tried in lower national courts—but only if one of the parties in the case objects to the decision of the lower courts and appeals the case. This is the Supreme Court's *appellate jurisdiction.* After a case has been tried in the Supreme Court, there is no higher court to which appeals can be directed.

Trial by Jury for Criminal Cases

SECTION 2, CLAUSE 3. The trial of all crimes except in cases of impeachment shall be by jury; and such trial shall be held in the state where the said crimes shall have been committed; but when not committed within any state, the trial shall be at such place or places as the Congress may by law have directed.

Except for impeachment trials, all trials for crimes against national laws must be held before juries in the states where the crimes occurred. But if they took place outside of any state—at sea, for instance—then Congress can decide where the trials should be held.

Every citizen's right to a jury trial when he is accused of a crime keeps him from being punished unless a jury of his fellow citizens finds him guilty.

The Definition of Treason

SECTION 3, CLAUSE 1. Treason against the United States shall consist only in levying war against them, or in adhering to their enemies, giving them aid and comfort. No person shall be convicted of treason unless on the testimony of two witnesses to the same overt act, or on confession in open court.

Only these acts by a United States citizen may be considered treason: (1) making war against this country, and (2) helping this country's enemies. Nobody can be punished for treason unless two or more citizens both swear they saw him commit the same act of treason or unless he confesses in court.

The Punishment for Treason

SECTION 3, CLAUSE 2. The Congress shall have power to declare the punishment of treason, but no attainder of treason shall work corruption of blood or forfeiture except during the life of the person attainted.

Congress can pass laws ordering how treason is to be punished. But the families and descendants of a person found guilty of treason cannot be punished for his crime.

ARTICLE 4
The States and the Nation

Official Acts of the States

SECTION 1. Full faith and credit shall be given in each state to the public acts, records, and judicial proceedings of every other state. And the Congress may by general laws prescribe the manner in which such acts, records, and proceedings shall be proved, and the effect thereof.

Congress can force each state to respect the laws, records, and court decisions of all the other states. If the states did not respect each other's laws, the confusion would be unbearable.

Privileges of Citizens

SECTION 2, CLAUSE 1. The citizens of each state shall be entitled to all privileges and immunities of citizens in the several states.

Citizens of one state who move into or do business in another state have the same rights as the citizens who live in that state. (But a citizen who moves to another state must wait for a certain length of time before he may vote there.)

Fugitives from Justice

SECTION 2, CLAUSE 2. A person charged in any state with treason, felony, or other crime, who shall flee from justice, and be found in another state, shall, on demand of the executive authority of the state from which he fled, be delivered up, to be removed to the state having jurisdiction of the crime.

A person accused of a crime sometimes flees to another state to escape trial and punishment. If the governor of the state where the crime was committed requests it, the person sought may be returned. Sending fugitives from justice back for trial or punishment is called *extradition*. In practice, there is no way to force a state to extradite a criminal.

Runaway Slaves

SECTION 2, CLAUSE 3. *No person held to service or labor in one state, under the laws thereof, escaping into another, shall, in consequence of any law or regulation therein, be discharged from such service or labor, but shall be delivered up on claim of the party to whom such service or labor may be due.*

This clause has not been applied since the addition of the Thirteenth Amendment, page 722.

The Forming of New States

SECTION 3, CLAUSE 1. New states may be admitted by the Congress into this Union; but no new state shall be formed or erected within the jurisdiction of any other state, nor any state be formed by the junction of two or more states, or parts of states, without the consent of the legislatures of the states concerned as well as of the Congress.

New states may be added to the nation if Congress approves. But no new state may be made inside the boundaries of another state unless both Congress and the legislature of the state that would lose territory approve. No new state may be made out of the lands of two states without the consent of Congress and of the legislatures of both those states.

National Territory

SECTION 3, CLAUSE 2. The Congress shall have power to dispose of and make all needful rules and regulations respecting the territory or other property belonging to the United States; and nothing in this Constitution shall be so construed as to prejudice any claims of the United States, or of any particular state.

Congress can govern and decide what to do with national territories and other property. Here the word territories means lands that have not yet come under the government of any state.

Federal Guarantees to the States

SECTION 4. The United States shall guarantee to every state in this Union a republican form of government, and shall protect each of them against invasion; and, on application of the legislature, or of the executive (when the legislature cannot be convened), against domestic violence.

It is the duty of the national government to make sure that every state has and keeps a representative form of government—a government conducted by the people under a state constitution. It also has the duty to protect every state from being invaded by enemies. If the state asks the national government for help in stopping riots, the national government must give it.

ARTICLE 5

Amending the Constitution

The Congress, whenever two-thirds of both houses shall deem it necessary, shall propose amendments to this Constitution, or, on the application of the legislatures of two-thirds of the several states, shall call a convention for proposing amendments, which, in either case, shall be valid to all intents and purposes, as part of this Constitution, when ratified by the legislatures of three-fourths of the several states, or by conventions in three-fourths thereof, as the one or the other mode of ratification may be proposed by the Congress, provided *that no amendment which may be made prior to the year one thousand eight hundred and eight shall in any manner affect the first and fourth clauses in the Ninth Section of the First Article, and* that no state, without its consent, shall be deprived of its equal suffrage in the Senate.

The Constitution can be changed by amendments. An amendment can be proposed in either of two ways: (1) by the vote of two-thirds of the Senate and two-thirds of the House of Representatives, (2) by a special convention called together by Congress at the request of two-thirds of the state legislatures. After an amendment has been proposed, it is adopted as part of the Constitution if it is approved (1) by the legislatures of at least three-fourths of the states, or (2) by special conventions in at least three-fourths of the states. But no amendment can be adopted that would take away any state's right to have two Senators in Congress—unless the state gives its permission.

The clause beginning "that no amendment which may be made" was set aside by the passage of time and by laws passed in 1808.

It is possible but not easy to make changes in our Constitution—and our form of national government—when such changes are necessary. It is probably advantageous that the Constitution is hard to amend. Only those amendments really needed are likely to be adopted.

ARTICLE 6

The Supreme Law of the Land

The National Debt

CLAUSE 1. All debts contracted and engagements entered into before the adoption of this Constitution shall be as valid against the United States under this Constitution as under the Confederation.

In this clause the men who wrote the Constitution promised that the new United States government would pay the debts and carry out the agreements that had been made by the congress that acted under the Articles of Confederation.

National Laws Are Above State Laws

CLAUSE 2. This Constitution and the laws of the United States which shall be made in pursuance thereof, and all treaties made or which shall be made under the authority of the United States, shall be the supreme law of the land, and the judges in every state shall be bound thereby, anything in the constitution or laws of any state to the contrary notwithstanding.

Sometimes the Constitution, laws, and treaties of the United States provide for one thing and the constitutions and laws of the states provide for something else. When this happens, the Constitution, laws, and treaties of the United States must be obeyed, *not* the constitutions and laws of the states.

Oaths of Allegiance, Religious Tests

CLAUSE 3. The Senators and Representatives before mentioned, and the members of the several state legislatures, and all executive and judicial officers, both of the United States and of the several states, shall be bound by oath or affirmation to support this Constitution; but no religious test shall ever be required as a qualification to any office or public trust under the United States.

Members of Congress and the state legislatures and all other officials of the national and state governments must promise solemnly to uphold the Constitution and the form of government provided for by the Constitution.

Nobody who can meet the other requirements for holding a position in the United States government may be kept out of this position because of his religion.

ARTICLE 7

Adoption of the Constitution

The ratification of the conventions of nine states shall be sufficient for the establishment of this Constitution between the states so ratifying the same.

Done in convention by the unanimous consent of the states present the seventeenth day of September, in the year of our Lord one thousand seven hundred and eighty-seven and of the independence of the United States of America the twelfth. In witness whereof, we have hereunto subscribed our names.

(Thirty-nine delegates' signatures, headed by that of George Washington, follow.)

The Constitution was signed on September 17, 1787, by thirty-nine men sent to the Constitutional Convention from all the states except Rhode Island. As soon as special conventions in nine of the states had met and voted in favor of the Constitution, it was to go into effect in those states. Each state called a convention to vote on the new plan for national government. Within about nine months the conventions in nine states had voted to adopt the Constitution. By the middle of 1790, all the thirteen original states had voted in favor of it.

AMENDMENTS
TO THE CONSTITUTION
The Bill of Rights: *Amendments 1 to 10*

The First Congress began its meetings in 1789. Because many Americans felt that the Constitution did not guarantee enough liberties to the people and the states, twelve amendments were proposed in this First Congress. Ten of them were approved by the state legislatures and in 1791 became an official part of the Constitution. These first ten amendments have come to be known as the American Bill of Rights.

AMENDMENT 1.

Freedom of Religion, Speech, Press, Assembly, and Petition

Congress shall make no law respecting an establishment of religion, or prohibiting the free exercise thereof; or abridging the freedom of speech, or of the press; or the right of the people peaceably to assemble, and to petition the government for a redress of grievances.

Congress must not pass any laws that (1) make any religion the official religion of the country or keep people from following the religion they prefer, (2) forbid the people to say and print whatever they may choose, (3) keep the people from meeting together in a peaceable manner to talk about their government or keep them from making any rightful complaints to their government.

AMENDMENT 2.

The Right to Bear Arms

A well-regulated militia being necessary to the security of a free state, the right of the people to keep and bear arms shall not be infringed.

The national government must not interfere with the rights of the states to arm and drill their citizens in the state militia. This amendment does not guarantee that private citizens will be allowed to keep weapons for their personal use.

AMENDMENT 3.

Quartering Soldiers

No soldier shall in time of peace be quartered in any house without the consent of the owner; nor in time of war but in a manner to be prescribed by law.

In peacetime people must not be forced to take soldiers into their houses and give them room and board. Even in wartime people must not be forced to do this except according to laws passed by Congress.

AMENDMENT 4.

Searches and Seizures

The right of the people to be secure in their persons, houses, papers, and effects, against unreasonable searches and seizures, shall not be violated; and no warrants shall issue, but upon probable cause, supported by oath or affirmation, and particularly describing the place to be searched and the persons or things to be seized.

No national official may arrest or search a person, or search his home, or seize his belongings, unless a warrant—an official order from a judge—gives him permission to do so. No judge may give out such warrants unless he is sure that they are necessary to apprehend criminals.

AMENDMENT 5.

Rights of Those Accused of Crimes

No person shall be held to answer for a capital or otherwise infamous crime unless on a presentment or indictment of a grand jury, except in cases arising in the land or naval forces, or in the militia, when in actual service in time of war or public danger; nor shall any person be subject for the same offense to be twice put in jeopardy of life or limb, nor shall be compelled in any criminal case to be a witness against himself, nor be deprived of life, liberty, or property without due process of law; nor shall private property be taken for public use without just compensation.

No person may be tried in a national court for a serious crime unless a grand jury has examined the evidence and decided that the person ought to be tried.

The only persons *not* covered by this rule are those serving in the armed forces in time of war or other grave emergency for the nation. If a person has been tried for a crime and judged innocent, he can never be tried again for the same crime. No person may be forced to give evidence that will help to prove his guilt. No person may be executed, imprisoned, or fined except as a punishment after a fair trial. Private property must not be taken for public use unless the owner is paid a fair price for it.

AMENDMENT 6

Jury Trial in Criminal Cases

In all criminal prosecutions, the accused shall enjoy the right to a speedy and public trial, by an impartial jury of the state and district wherein the crime shall have been committed, which district shall have been previously ascertained by law, and to be informed of the nature and cause of the accusation; to be confronted with the witnesses against him; to have compulsory process for obtaining witnesses in his favor, and to have the assistance of counsel for his defense.

A person being tried for a crime in a national court must be tried promptly—and in public, where everybody can know what is being done to him. It is his right to have a jury of fair-minded citizens hear the evidence and decide whether he is innocent or guilty. These citizens must live in the district where the crime took place. The accused person must be told why he is being tried and must have a chance to see and hear those who give evidence against him. Witnesses who might prove that he is innocent can be forced to come to court and give their evidence. If the accused cannot pay for a lawyer, he has the right to one appointed by the court.

AMENDMENT 7.

Civil Suits

In suits at common law where the value in controversy shall exceed twenty dollars, the right of trial by jury shall be preserved, and no fact tried by a jury shall be otherwise reexamined in any court of the United States than according to the rules of the common law.

If a sum of money larger than $20 is involved in a lawsuit, the persons in the case may insist on a jury trial.

AMENDMENT 8.

Unreasonable Bail, Cruel Punishments

Excessive bail shall not be required, nor excessive fines imposed, or cruel and unusual punishments inflicted.

A person accused of a crime can get out of jail until his trial by handing over a sum of money to the court. This money, called bail, is returned to him if he comes to court to be tried when he is ordered to; if not, he loses his bail. National courts must not force accused persons to give unreasonably large amounts of bail.

A person tried in a national court and found guilty of a crime must not be punished by an unreasonably heavy fine or an unreasonably long prison sentence. He must not be punished in cruel or unusual ways—by being tortured or branded, for instance.

AMENDMENT 9.

Other Rights of the People

The enumeration in the Constitution of certain rights shall not be construed to deny or disparage others retained by the people.

It was not possible to list in the Constitution all the rights that United States citizens should have. There are other important rights that are to belong to the people even though the Constitution does not mention them.

AMENDMENT 10.

Powers Kept by the States or by the People

The powers not delegated to the United States by the Constitution, nor prohibited by it to the states, are reserved to the states respectively, or to the people.

The Constitution authorizes the national government to use certain powers and forbids the state governments to use certain powers. All other powers are to be kept by the states or by the people.

Amendments 11 to 24

AMENDMENT 11.

Suits Against a State (1798)

The judicial power of the United States shall not be construed to extend to any suit in law or equity commenced or prosecuted against one of the United States by citizens of another state, or by citizens or subjects of any foreign state.

No national court is allowed to try any case in which a state government is being sued by a citizen of another state or of a foreign country. Such a case must be tried in a court of the state that is being sued. This amendment changed a part of Article 3, Section 2, Clause 1, page 716.

AMENDMENT 12.

Presidential Elections (1804)

The electors shall meet in their respective states, and vote by ballot for President and Vice-President, one of whom, at least, shall not be an inhabitant of the same state with themselves; they shall name in their ballots the person voted for as President, and in distinct ballots the person voted for as Vice-President, and they shall make distinct lists of all persons voted for as President and of all persons voted for as Vice-President, and of the number of votes for each, which lists they shall sign and certify, and transmit, sealed, to the seat of the government of the United States, directed to the President of the Senate; the President of the Senate shall, in the presence of the Senate and House of Representatives, open all the certificates, and the votes shall then be counted. The person having the greatest number of votes for President shall be the President, if such number be a majority of the whole number of electors appointed; and if no person have such majority, then from the persons having the highest numbers, not exceeding three, on the list of those voted for as President, the House of Representatives shall choose immediately, by ballot, the President. But in choosing the President, the votes shall be taken by states, the representation from each state having one vote; a quorum for this purpose shall consist of a member or members from two-thirds of the states, and a majority of all the states shall be necessary to a choice. And if the House of Representatives shall not choose a President, whenever the right of choice shall devolve upon them, *before the fourth day of March next following*, then the Vice-President shall act as President, as in case of the death or other constitutional disability of the President. The person having the greatest number of votes as Vice-President shall be the Vice-President, if such number be a majority of the whole number of electors appointed, and if no person have a majority, then, from the two highest numbers on the list, the Senate shall choose the Vice-President; a quorum for the purpose shall consist of two-thirds of the whole number of Senators, and a majority of the whole number shall be necessary to a choice. But no person constitutionally ineligible to the office of President shall be eligible to that of Vice-President of the United States.

This amendment replaced Article 2, Section 1, Clause 3, pages 713–714, which had ordered the electors to vote for the President and the Vice-President on one ballot, without showing which person they wanted for each of the two positions. The person with the highest total of electoral votes was to be President, and the person with the next highest total was to be Vice-President. But serious problems arose because of a tie in the presidential election of 1800. The Twelfth Amendment was adopted to prevent such confusion later.

Although the Twelfth Amendment does not tell us how the President and the Vice-President are actually elected today, this is its meaning: The electors of each state meet in that state and vote for President and Vice-President. (Their votes are little more than a formality now.) Either the presidential or the vice-presidential candidate they vote for must live outside of the electors' own state. The electors must cast two separate ballots, one for President and one for Vice-President, and must record their votes on two separate lists. The lists from each state are sent to the United States Senate, where the votes are counted in the presence of the Senators and the Representatives. The presidential candidate with the most electoral votes becomes President if he has a majority of all the electoral votes for that office. If he does not have a majority, the House of Representatives chooses a President from among the three presidential candidates with the most electoral votes. But if the House of Representatives fails to choose a President by the time the new presidential term is to begin—now January 20 following the election, instead of March 4—then the man who was elected Vice-President acts as President.

The vice-presidential candidate with the most electoral votes becomes Vice-President if he has a majority of all the electoral votes for that office. If he does not, the Senate chooses a Vice-President from among the two vice-presidential candidates with the most electoral votes.

The Vice-President must meet the same requirements of age, citizenship, and residence as must the President.

The writers both of the original Constitution and of the Twelfth Amendment intended to have the President and the Vice-President chosen by small groups of men—the presidential electors—with greater wisdom and experience than the ordinary voters of the country had. However, the real power to choose the President and Vice-President has been taken away from the presidential electors and given to the ordinary voters. This change resulted from new customs.

The voters in each state vote for presidential electors who are known in advance to belong to one or another political party. These electors still follow the rules in the Twelfth Amendment, but they nearly always cast their ballots for the candidates belonging to their own political party. The result is that when a voter fills in his ballot on Election Day, he seems to be voting for an elector but is actually voting for the President and the Vice-President.

The day when presidential electors are to be elected by the voters is the first Tuesday after the first Monday in November of every fourth year—1968, 1972, 1976, and so on. Within a day or so everyone knows who the next President and Vice-President are to be, but the electors do not go through the ceremony of casting their ballots until about one month later.

AMENDMENT 13.

Slavery Forbidden (1865)

SECTION 1. Neither slavery nor involuntary servitude, except as a punishment for crime whereof the party shall have been duly convicted, shall exist within the United States or any place subject to their jurisdiction.

SECTION 2. Congress shall have power to enforce this article by appropriate legislation.

Nobody in the United States or its territories may be held in slavery. Nobody may be forced to work against his will except as a punishment for a crime after he has been tried in the courts and found guilty. Several amendments have *enabling acts* like Section 2. Compare their wording.

President Lincoln's Emancipation Proclamation of 1863 had ordered only the freeing of the slaves in the Confederate States. The Thirteenth Amendment freed all slaves in all states and territories.

AMENDMENT 14.

Restrictions on the States (1868)

SECTION 1. All persons born or naturalized in the United States, and subject to the jurisdiction thereof, are citizens of the United States and of the state wherein they reside. No state shall make or enforce any law which shall abridge the privileges or immunities of citizens of the United States, nor shall any state deprive any person of life, liberty, or property without due process of law, nor deny to any person within its jurisdiction the equal protection of the laws.

All persons born or naturalized in the United States and ruled by this nation's laws are citizens—citizens both of the United States and of the state they live in. (This amendment did away with the Supreme Court's Dred Scott decision of 1857, which had held that Negro slaves were not citizens.)

No state may take away the rights of United States citizens or take any person's life, freedom, or property

except according to law. All the laws of a state must affect everybody in the same way.

SECTION 2. Representatives shall be apportioned among the several states according to their respective numbers, counting the whole number of persons in each state, excluding Indians not taxed. But when the right to vote at any election for the choice of electors for President and Vice-President of the United States, Representatives in Congress, the executive and judicial officers of a state, or the members of the legislature thereof, is denied to any of the male inhabitants of such state, being twenty-one years of age, and citizens of the United States, or in any way abridged, except for participation in rebellion, or other crime, the basis of representation therein shall be reduced in the proportion which the number of such male citizens shall bear to the whole number of male citizens twenty-one years of age in such state.

A part of Article 1, Section 2, Clause 3, had ruled that only three-fifths of the Negro slaves in each state were to be counted when the number of Representatives which that state was entitled to send to Congress was being determined. But because of this section of the Fourteenth Amendment, Negroes were henceforth to be counted in full, like other citizens, in determining the number of Representatives. If a state kept any of its citizens who were entitled to vote from voting in national or state elections, that state's right to send members to the House of Representatives was to be cut down accordingly, as a penalty. This section was an attempt to force the southern states to let their Negro citizens vote. No state has ever been penalized for failing to do so.

SECTION 3. *No person shall be a Senator or Representative in Congress, or elector of President and Vice-President, or hold any office, civil or military, under the United States or under any state, who, having previously taken an oath as a member of Congress, or as an officer of the United States, or as a member of any state legislature, or as an executive or judicial officer of any state, to support the Constitution of the United States, shall have engaged in insurrection or rebellion against the same or given aid or comfort to the enemies thereof. But Congress may by a vote of two-thirds of each house remove such disability.*

According to this section, no person could ever become an official of the national government or a state government if he had ever held such office in the past and then had rebelled against the national government. But Congress could end this rule when two-thirds of the Senators and two-thirds of the Representatives voted to end it.

The effect of this section was to weaken the political power of the southern states and punish the leaders of the Confederacy. But the section is long since out-of-date. Congress gave back full political rights to most of the Confederate leaders in 1872 and to the rest of them in 1898.

SECTION 4. The validity of the public debt of the United States, authorized by law, including debts incurred for payment of pensions and bounties for services in suppressing insurrection and rebellion, shall not be questioned. But neither the United States nor any state shall assume or pay any debt or obligation incurred in aid of insurrection or rebellion against the United States, or any claim for the loss or emancipation of any slave; but all such debts, obligations, and claims shall be held illegal and void.

SECTION 5. The Congress shall have power to enforce by appropriate legislation the provisions of this article.

Under Section 4 the national government was ordered to pay back the money it had borrowed for the expenses of the Civil War. But neither the national government nor any state government was to be allowed to repay money that was borrowed by the Confederacy for fighting against the Union, or to pay slave owners for their slaves who had been set free.

AMENDMENT 15.

Negroes' Right to Vote (1870)

SECTION 1. The right of the citizens of the United States to vote shall not be denied or abridged by the United States or by any state on account of race, color, or previous condition of servitude.

SECTION 2. The Congress shall have power to enforce this article by appropriate legislation.

Neither the United States nor any state may keep a citizen from voting because of his race or color or because he was once a slave.

AMENDMENT 16.

The National Income Tax (1913)

The Congress shall have power to lay and collect taxes on incomes, from whatever source derived, without apportionment among the several states, and without regard to any census or enumeration.

Congress has the right to tax all kinds of incomes. The amount of money which the citizens of a state pay to the national government as income tax does not have to be in proportion to the population of that state.

In 1895 the Supreme Court ruled that the national government had no right to collect income taxes from the people of the states because such a tax was a direct tax and did not obey Article 1, Section 9, Clause 4, page 712. Eighteen years later, the Sixteenth Amendment superseded the Supreme Court's decision.

AMENDMENT 17.

Election of Senators by the People (1913)

CLAUSE 1. The Senate of the United States shall be composed of two Senators from each state, elected by the people thereof, for six years; and each Senator shall have one vote. The electors in each state shall have the qualifications requisite for electors of the most numerous branch of the state legislatures.

This clause changes Article 1, Section 3, Clause 1. See the explanation on pages 705–706.

CLAUSE 2. When vacancies happen in the representation of any state in the Senate, the executive authority of such state shall issue writs of election to fill such vacancies: Provided that the legislature of any state may empower the executive thereof to make temporary appointments until the people fill the vacancies by election as the legislature may direct.

CLAUSE 3. *This amendment shall not be so construed as to affect the election or term of any Senator chosen before it becomes valid as part of the Constitution.*

Clause 2 changes the last part of Article 1, Section 3, Clause 2, on page 706, which gave the governor of a state the right to appoint a Senator temporarily if one of that state's seats in the Senate became vacant while the legislature was not meeting. Under the present law, a vacancy in the Senate may be filled by the state's voters, who vote at a special election. Or, as more often happens, the governor has the legislature's permission to fill the vacancy by appointing a temporary Senator, and does so.

AMENDMENT 18.

Prohibition (1919)

SECTION 1. *After one year from the ratification of this article the manufacture, sale, or transportation of intoxicating liquors within, the importation thereof into, or the exportation thereof from the United States and all territory* subject to the jurisdiction thereof for beverage purposes is hereby prohibited.

SECTION 2. *The Congress and the several states shall have concurrent power to enforce this article by appropriate legislation.*

SECTION 3. *This article shall be inoperative unless it shall have been ratified as an amendment to the Constitution by the legislatures of the several states, as provided in the Constitution, within seven years from the date of the submission hereof to the states by the Congress.*

This amendment forbade the manufacture, sale, or shipment of intoxicating drinks, and it gave both to Congress and to the states the right to pass laws that would enforce it. In 1933 this amendment was repealed by the Twenty-first Amendment.

AMENDMENT 19.

Women's Voting Rights (1920)

CLAUSE 1. The right of citizens of the United States to vote shall not be denied or abridged by the United States or by any state on account of sex.

CLAUSE 2. Congress shall have power to enforce this article by appropriate legislation.

Neither the national government nor any state government may keep a woman citizen from voting merely because she is a woman. Congress may pass laws necessary to carry out this amendment.

AMENDMENT 20.

Terms of Office (1933)

SECTION 1. The terms of the President and Vice-President shall end at noon on the twentieth day of January, and the terms of Senators and Representatives at noon on the third day of January, of the years in which such terms would have ended if this article had not been ratified; and the terms of their successors shall then begin.

The President's and the Vice-President's terms in office end at noon on January 20 in the years following presidential elections—1969, 1973, 1977, and so on. Before this amendment was adopted, the President and the Vice-President did not take office until March 4. The terms of one-third of the Senators and all the Representatives end at noon on January 3 in the years with odd numbers—1967, 1969, 1971, and so on. The new terms for all these offices begin as soon as the old terms end.

This section of the amendment cut down the long delay that had previously occurred between the time of election of the President, the Vice-President, and the members of Congress and the time that they began doing the work for which the voters had elected them.

SECTION 2. The Congress shall assemble at least once in every year, and such meeting shall begin at noon on the third day of January unless they shall by law appoint a different day.

This section changes Article 1, Section 4, Clause 2, page 707, which ordered Congress to begin its meetings on the first Monday of December each year. Formerly the new Senators and Representatives that were elected to Congress in November did not actually begin their work until more than one year later. But under the Twentieth Amendment, Congress must meet at least once a year, beginning its meetings at noon on January 3 unless a law passed by Congress orders a different day.

SECTION 3. If, at the time fixed for the beginning of the term of the President, the President-elect shall have died, the Vice-President-elect shall become President. If a President shall not have been chosen before the time fixed for the beginning of his term, or if the President-elect shall have failed to qualify, then the Vice-President-elect shall act as President until a President shall have qualified; and the Congress may by law provide for the case wherein neither a President-elect nor a Vice-President-elect shall have qualified, declaring who shall then act as President, or the manner in which one who is to act shall be selected, and such person shall act accordingly until a President or Vice-President shall have qualified.

If the person elected President dies before January 20, when his term was to begin, then the person elected Vice-President becomes President. If no President has been chosen by January 20, or if the person chosen does not meet the Constitution's requirements for the presidency, then the newly elected Vice-President acts as President until a President who meets the requirements can be chosen. Congress may pass a law deciding what is to be done if neither the newly elected President nor the newly elected Vice-President can meet the requirements for the presidency that have been set up in the Constitution.

SECTION 4. The Congress may by law provide for the case of the death of any of the persons from whom the House of Representatives may choose a President whenever the right of choice shall have devolved upon them, and for the case of the death of any of the persons from whom the Senate may choose a Vice-President whenever the right of choice shall have devolved upon them.

Section 4 of the Twentieth Amendment permits Con-

724

gress to pass laws deciding what should be done if any of the candidates whom one or the other house of Congress might have chosen to be the President or the Vice-President should die. (See the Twelfth Amendment, page 721.)

SECTION 5. *Sections 1 and 2 shall take effect on the fifteenth day of October following the ratification of this article.*

Section 5 set the date on which the first two sections of this amendment were to go into effect after the amendment had been adopted by the states.

SECTION 6. *This article shall be inoperative unless it shall have been ratified as an amendment to the Constitution by the legislatures of three-fourths of the several states within seven years from the date of its submission.*

Section 6 of the Twentieth Amendment ruled how and when it was to be adopted as a part of the Constitution. This amendment has, of course, already been ratified by the several states.

AMENDMENT 21.

Repeal of Prohibition (1933)

SECTION 1. The eighteenth article of amendment to the Constitution of the United States is hereby repealed.

The Eighteenth Amendment, the "Prohibition Amendment," is repealed by this amendment.

SECTION 2. The transportation or importation into any state, territory, or possession of the United States for delivery or use therein of intoxicating liquors, in violation of the laws thereof, is hereby prohibited.

Any states, territories, or possessions of the United States that want to prohibit alcoholic liquors have the right to do so by laws of their own.

SECTION 3. *This article shall be inoperative unless it shall have been ratified as an amendment to the Constitution by convention in the several states, as provided in the Constitution, within seven years from the date of the submission hereof to the states by the Congress.*

This section ruled how and when the Twenty-first Amendment was to be adopted.

AMENDMENT 22.

Number of Terms for a President (1951)

SECTION 1. No person shall be elected to the office of the President more than twice, and no person who has held the office of President, or

acted as President, for more than two years of a term to which some other person was elected President shall be elected to the office of President more than once. But this Article shall not apply to any person holding the office of President when this Article was proposed by the Congress, and shall not prevent any person who may be holding the office of President, or acting as President, during the term within which this Article becomes operative from holding the office of President, or acting as President during the remainder of such term.

Nobody may be elected to the presidency more than twice. If any person serves for more than two years in place of an elected President, that person may himself be elected to the presidency only once.

This amendment was worded so that it did not apply to Harry S Truman, who was President when the amendment was proposed and adopted.

Because of the Twenty-second Amendment, the longest time that any person can serve as President is ten years—that is, not more than two years in completion of a predecessor's term plus two four-year terms as elected President.

SECTION 2. *This Article shall be inoperative unless it shall have been ratified as an amendment to the Constitution by the legislatures of three-fourths of the several states within seven years from the date of its submission to the states by Congress.*

This section ruled how and when the Twenty-second Amendment was to be adopted.

AMENDMENT 23.

Presidential Voting in the District of Columbia (1961)

SECTION 1. The District constituting the seat of Government of the United States shall appoint in such manner as the Congress may direct:

A number of electors of President and Vice-President equal to the whole number of Senators and Representatives in Congress to which the District would be entitled if it were a state, but in no event more than the least populous state; they shall be in addition to those appointed by the states, but they shall be considered, for the purposes of the election of President and Vice-President, to be electors appointed by a state; and they shall meet in the District and perform such duties as provided by the twelfth article of amendment.

The vote in presidential elections previously denied

to residents of the District of Columbia because it is not a state is made possible by this amendment. It creates and assigns to the District as many votes in the electoral college as are assigned to the state with the smallest population. At the present time this means three votes, because that is the number that Alaska has. The members of the electoral college from the District of Columbia, meeting in the District, cast their votes, along with members of the electoral college from the states, in accordance with the Twelfth Amendment of the Constitution.

SECTION 2.   The Congress shall have power to enforce this article by appropriate legislation.

Congress has the power to pass such laws as may be required to put this amendment into force.

This amendment is the first one ever passed that applies to a particular part of the country.

AMENDMENT 24.

Poll Taxes Forbidden (1964)

SECTION 1.   The right of citizens of the United States to vote in any primary or other election for President or Vice-President, for electors for President or Vice-President, or for Senator or Representative in Congress, shall not be denied or abridged by the United States or any state by reason of failure to pay any poll or other tax.

SECTION 2.   The Congress shall have power to enforce this article by appropriate legislation.

Neither the national government nor any state or local government may prevent any citizen from voting in national elections on grounds of his failure to pay a tax of any kind. Congress is empowered to enact laws necessary for the enforcing of this amendment.

Presidents and Vice-Presidents

NO.	NAME	BORN/DIED		YEARS IN OFFICE	POLITICAL PARTY	STATE	VICE-PRESIDENT
1	George Washington	1732	1799	1789–97	None	Va.	John Adams
2	John Adams	1735	1826	1797–1801	Federalist	Mass.	Thomas Jefferson
3	Thomas Jefferson	1743	1826	1801–9	Republican	Va.	Aaron Burr George Clinton
4	James Madison	1751	1836	1809–17	Republican	Va.	George Clinton Elbridge Gerry
5	James Monroe	1758	1831	1817–25	Republican	Va.	Daniel D. Tompkins
6	John Quincy Adams	1767	1848	1825–29	Republican	Mass.	John C. Calhoun
7	Andrew Jackson	1767	1845	1829–37	Democratic	Tenn.	John C. Calhoun Martin Van Buren
8	Martin Van Buren	1782	1862	1837–41	Democratic	N.Y.	Richard M. Johnson
9	William Henry Harrison	1773	1841	1841	Whig	Ohio	John Tyler
10	John Tyler	1790	1862	1841–45	Whig	Va.	
11	James K. Polk	1795	1849	1845–49	Democratic	Tenn.	George M. Dallas
12	Zachary Taylor	1784	1850	1849–50	Whig	La.	Millard Fillmore
13	Millard Fillmore	1800	1874	1850–53	Whig	N.Y.	
14	Franklin Pierce	1804	1869	1853–57	Democratic	N.H.	William R. King
15	James Buchanan	1791	1868	1857–61	Democratic	Pa.	John C. Breckinridge
16	Abraham Lincoln	1809	1865	1861–65	Republican	Ill.	Hannibal Hamlin Andrew Johnson
17	Andrew Johnson	1808	1875	1865–69	Republican	Tenn.	
18	Ulysses S. Grant	1822	1885	1869–77	Republican	Ill.	Schuyler Colfax Henry Wilson
19	Rutherford B. Hayes	1822	1893	1877–81	Republican	Ohio	William A. Wheeler
20	James A. Garfield	1831	1881	1881	Republican	Ohio	Chester A. Arthur
21	Chester A. Arthur	1830	1886	1881–85	Republican	N.Y.	
22	Grover Cleveland	1837	1908	1885–89	Democratic	N.Y.	Thomas A. Hendricks
23	Benjamin Harrison	1833	1901	1889–93	Republican	Ind.	Levi P. Morton
24	Grover Cleveland	1837	1908	1893–97	Democratic	N.Y.	Adlai E. Stevenson
25	William McKinley	1843	1901	1897–1901	Republican	Ohio	Garret A. Hobart Theodore Roosevelt
26	Theodore Roosevelt	1858	1919	1901–9	Republican	N.Y.	Charles W. Fairbanks
27	William Howard Taft	1857	1930	1909–13	Republican	Ohio	James S. Sherman
28	Woodrow Wilson	1856	1924	1913–21	Democratic	N.J.	Thomas R. Marshall
29	Warren G. Harding	1865	1923	1921–23	Republican	Ohio	Calvin Coolidge
30	Calvin Coolidge	1872	1933	1923–29	Republican	Mass.	Charles G. Dawes
31	Herbert Hoover	1874	1964	1929–33	Republican	Calif.	Charles Curtis
32	Franklin D. Roosevelt	1882	1945	1933–45	Democratic	N.Y.	John N. Garner Henry A. Wallace Harry S Truman
33	Harry S Truman	1884	——	1945–53	Democratic	Mo.	Alben W. Barkley
34	Dwight D. Eisenhower	1890	——	1953–61	Republican	N.Y.	Richard M. Nixon
35	John F. Kennedy	1917	1963	1961–63	Democratic	Mass.	Lyndon B. Johnson
36	Lyndon B. Johnson	1908	——	1963———	Democratic	Texas	Hubert H. Humphrey

The Continents

	AREA IN SQUARE MILES	POPULATION
World	57,280,000	3,237,000,000
Africa	11,685,000	290,200,000
Antarctica	5,100,000	Uninhabited
Asia	17,085,000	1,877,000,000
Oceania, including Australia	3,295,000	17,400,000
Europe	3,825,000	601,900,000
North America	9,420,000	289,700,000
South America	6,870,000	160,800,000

Area/Territorial Expansion: 1790 to 1960

ADDITION	DATE	GROSS AREA (LAND AND WATER) SQUARE MILES
Total, 1960 (excluding P.I.)[1]	———	3,680,084
United States	———	3,675,633[2]
Gadsden Purchase	1853	29,640
Mexican Cession	1848	529,017
Oregon	1846	285,580
Texas	1845	390,144
By treaty with Spain:		
Florida	1819	58,560
Other areas	1819	13,443
Louisiana Purchase	1803	827,192
Territory in 1790[3]	———	888,811
Alaska	1867	586,400
Hawaii	1898	6,424
Territories and possessions	———	4,451
Virgin Islands of the United States	1917	133
Panama Canal Zone	1904	553
American Samoa	1900	76
Guam	1899	212
Puerto Rico	1899	3,435
Miscellaneous Pacific Islands[4]	———	42

[1] The Philippine Islands (area 115,831 square miles), ceded by Spain in 1898, constituted a territorial possession of the United States from 1898 to 1946; they were granted independence as of July 4, 1946, becoming the Republic of the Philippines.

[2] Total area of the United States includes 3,548,974 square miles of land; 66,237 square miles of inland water; and 60,422 square miles of Great Lakes area not included in any state.

[3] Includes that part of the drainage basin of the Red River of the North, south of the 49th parallel, sometimes considered part of the Louisiana Purchase.

[4] Includes Howland, Baker, Midway, Wake, and certain other small islands.

Facts About the States

The number in front of each state name shows the order in which that state was admitted to the Union (or the order in which it adopted the Constitution, if one of the thirteen original states). The population figures for the states are 1965 estimates, and the numbers of representatives in Congress are based on the 1960 census.

NUMBER IN ORDER	NAME	YEAR OF ENTRANCE	AREA IN SQUARE MILES	POPULATION	REPRESENTATIVES IN CONGRESS
22	Alabama	1819	51,609	3,462,000	8
49	Alaska	1959	586,400	247,000	1
48	Arizona	1912	113,909	1,635,000	3
25	Arkansas	1836	53,104	1,889,000	4
31	California	1850	158,693	18,338,000	38
38	Colorado	1876	104,247	2,003,000	4
5	Connecticut	1788	5,009	2,752,000	6
1	Delaware	1787	2,057	494,000	1
27	Florida	1845	58,560	5,913,000	12
4	Georgia	1788	58,876	4,312,000	10
50	Hawaii	1959	6,424	710,000	2
43	Idaho	1890	83,557	702,000	2
21	Illinois	1818	56,400	10,584,000	24
19	Indiana	1816	36,291	4,914,000	11
29	Iowa	1846	56,290	2,783,000	7
34	Kansas	1861	82,264	2,251,000	5
15	Kentucky	1792	40,395	3,138,000	7
18	Louisiana	1812	48,523	3,480,000	8
23	Maine	1820	33,215	989,000	2
7	Maryland	1788	10,577	3,480,000	8
6	Massachusetts	1788	8,257	5,387,000	12
26	Michigan	1837	58,216	8,269,000	19
32	Minnesota	1858	84,068	3,613,000	8
20	Mississippi	1817	47,716	2,320,000	5
24	Missouri	1821	69,686	4,446,000	10
41	Montana	1889	147,138	717,000	2
37	Nebraska	1867	77,227	1,507,000	3
36	Nevada	1864	110,540	426,000	1
9	New Hampshire	1788	9,304	639,000	2
3	New Jersey	1787	7,836	6,587,000	15
47	New Mexico	1912	121,666	1,048,000	2
11	New York	1788	49,576	17,834,000	41
12	North Carolina	1789	52,712	4,877,000	11
39	North Dakota	1889	70,665	642,000	2
17	Ohio	1803	41,222	10,372,000	24
46	Oklahoma	1907	69,919	2,512,000	6
33	Oregon	1859	96,981	1,896,000	4
2	Pennsylvania	1787	45,333	11,511,000	27
13	Rhode Island	1790	1,214	897,000	2
8	South Carolina	1788	31,055	2,524,000	6
40	South Dakota	1889	77,047	711,000	2
16	Tennessee	1796	42,244	3,737,000	9
28	Texas	1845	267,339	10,669,000	23
45	Utah	1896	84,916	1,008,000	2
14	Vermont	1791	9,609	396,000	1
10	Virginia	1788	40,815	4,400,000	10
42	Washington	1889	68,192	3,051,000	7
35	West Virginia	1863	24,181	1,797,000	5
30	Wisconsin	1848	56,154	4,166,000	10
44	Wyoming	1890	97,914	355,000	1
..	District of Columbia	1791	69	810,000	..
	TOTALS		3,675,633[1]	193,850,000[2]	435

[1] Total area of the United States includes 3,548,974 square miles of land; 66,237 square miles of inland water; and 60,422 square miles of Great Lakes area not included in any state.

[2] Total 1965 estimated population of the United States includes 193,200,000 residents of the 50 states and the District of Columbia and 650,000 members of the armed forces overseas, not included in any state.

Metropolitan Areas in the United States with Populations of Over 1,000,000

METROPOLITAN AREA[1]	ESTIMATED POPULATION 1/1/1965	PRINCIPAL CITY	ESTIMATED POPULATION 1/1/1965
Atlanta, Ga.	1,230,000	Atlanta, Ga.	535,000
Baltimore, Md.	1,730,000	Baltimore, Md.	925,000
Boston, Mass.	3,499,000	Boston, Mass.	938,700
Buffalo – Niagara Falls, N.Y.	1,285,000	Buffalo, N.Y.	505,000
Chicago, Ill.	7,225,000	Chicago, Ill.	3,520,000
Cincinnati, Ohio	1,310,000	Cincinnati, Ohio	495,000
Cleveland, Ohio	2,250,000	Cleveland, Ohio	825,000
Dallas, Tex.	1,280,000	Dallas, Tex.	790,000
Denver, Colo.	1,035,000	Denver, Colo.	520,000
Detroit, Mich.	4,170,000	Detroit, Mich.	1,680,000
Houston, Tex.	1,490,000	Houston, Tex.	1,100,000
Kansas City, Mo.	1,140,000	Kansas City, Mo.	530,000
Los Angeles, Calif.	7,635,000	Los Angeles, Calif.	2,695,00
Miami – Fort Lauderdale, Fla.	1,500,000	Miami, Fla.	325,000
Milwaukee, Wis.	1,330,000	Milwaukee, Wis.	765,000
Minneapolis – St. Paul, Minn.	1,590,000	Minneapolis, Minn.	465,000
New York, N.Y.	16,550,000	New York, N.Y.	8,080,000
Philadelphia, Pa.	4,200,000	Philadelphia, Pa.	2,030,000
Pittsburgh, Pa.	1,955,000	Pittsburgh, Pa.	560,000
St. Louis, Mo.	2,195,000	St. Louis, Mo.	710,000
San Diego, Calif.	1,000,000	San Diego, Calif.	636,000
San Francisco – Oakland – San Jose, Calif.	3,805,000	San Francisco, Calif.	745,000
Seattle, Wash.	1,045,000	Seattle, Wash.	565,000
Washington, D.C.	2,485,000	Washington, D.C.	810,000

[1] Includes the city or cities proper and immediate suburbs.

Ten Largest Cities in the United States[1]

1790

1 Philadelphia, Pa. 44,092	4 Charleston, S.C. 16,359	8 Providence, R.I. 6,380
2 New York, N.Y. 33,131	5 Baltimore, Md. 13,503	9 Marblehead, Mass. 5,661
3 Boston, Mass. 18,320	6 Salem, Mass. 7,921	10 Gloucester, Mass. 5,317
	7 Newport, R.I. 6,716	

[1] Population figures include immediate suburbs.

	1820		**1850**		**1880**
1	New York, N.Y. 130,881	1	New York, N.Y. 619,241	1	New York, N.Y. 2,500,000
2	Philadelphia, Pa. 108,809	2	Philadelphia, Pa. 361,304	2	Philadelphia, Pa. 950,000
3	Baltimore, Md. 62,738	3	Boston, Mass. 202,166	3	Chicago, Ill. 590,000
4	Boston, Mass. 54,024	4	Baltimore, Md. 169,054	4	Boston, Mass. 550,000
5	New Orleans, La. 27,176	5	Cincinnati, Ohio 130,738	5	St. Louis, Mo. 400,000
6	Charleston, S.C. 24,780	6	New Orleans, La. 130,565	6	Baltimore, Md. 375,000
7	Washington, D.C. 20,607	7	St. Louis, Mo. 77,860	7	Cincinnati, Ohio 340,000
8	Salem, Mass. 17,014	8	Pittsburgh, Pa. 71,595	8	San Francisco, Calif. 290,000
9	Albany, N.Y. 12,630	9	Louisville, Ky. 51,375	9	Pittsburgh, Pa. 275,000
10	Richmond, Va. 12,067	10	Albany, N.Y. 50,763	10	New Orleans, La. 225,000

	1910		**1940**		*Estimated Population* **1965**
1	New York, N.Y. 6,500,000	1	New York, N.Y. 11,750,000	1	New York, N.Y. 16,550,000
2	Chicago, Ill. 2,475,000	2	Chicago, Ill. 4,550,000	2	Los Angeles, Calif. 7,635,000
3	Philadelphia, Pa. 1,950,000	3	Philadelphia, Pa. 2,850,000	3	Chicago, Ill. 7,225,000
4	Boston, Mass. 1,450,000	4	Los Angeles, Calif. 2,725,000	4	Philadelphia, Pa. 4,200,000
5	Pittsburgh, Pa. 930,000	5	Detroit, Mich. 2,325,000	5	Detroit, Mich. 4,170,000
6	St. Louis, Mo. 840,000	6	Boston, Mass. 2,250,000	6	San Francisco–Oakland–San Jose, Calif. 3,805,000
7	San Francisco–Oakland, Calif. 690,000	7	San Francisco–Oakland, Calif. 1,350,000	7	Boston, Mass. 3,499,000
8	Baltimore, Md. 675,000	8	Pittsburgh, Pa. 1,350,000	8	Washington, D.C. 2,485,000
9	Cleveland, Ohio 625,000	9	St. Louis, Mo. 1,300,000	9	Cleveland, Ohio 2,250,000
10	Cincinnati, Ohio 575,000	10	Cleveland, Ohio 1,250,000	10	St. Louis, Mo. 2,195,000

[1] Population figures include immediate suburbs.

INDEX
and Key to Pronunciation

A star (*) indicates a picture.

The Index includes page references to words pronounced in the text. Key to pronunciation: ā, as in āte; â, as in senâte; â, as in câre; ă, as in ăm; ă, as in finăl; ä, as in ärm; a̯, as in a̯sk; a̯, as in sofa̯; ē, as in ēve; ê, as in crêate; ĕ, as in ĕnd; ĕ, as in novĕl; ē, as in cindēr; ə, as in battlə; ī, as in īce; ĭ, as in ĭll; ĭ, as in charĭty; ō, as in ōld; ô, as in ôbey; ô, as in lôrd; ŏ, as in ŏdd; ŏ, as in cŏnnect; o͞o, as in fo͞od; o͝o, as in fŏŏt; oi, as in oil; ou, as in thou; ū, as in pūre; ŭ, as in ŭnite; û, as in ûrn; ŭ, as in stŭdy; u̯, as in circu̯s; N indicates the nasal tone, as in French, of the preceding vowel; g, as in go; th as in that; к, as in German ich.

presidential choice of Half-Breed group of Republicans, 524; as Secretary of State under Harrison, 529; withdraws as possible candidate in 1888, 529

Bonaparte, Napoleon, 312; bargain with Spain for return of Louisiana, 275–276; effect of decision to invade Russia, 293; effect of defeat on Americans, 298; L'Ouverture's uprising, 276; plan for Santo Domingo, 276; sale of Louisiana to United States, 276–278

Bonus March, 631

Book of Ser Marco Polo, 16, 17*, 18

Boone, Daniel, 220*, 229

Booth, John Wilkes, 446

Borah, William E., and League of Nations, 598, 599–600

Border Ruffians, 399

Boston: aerial view of, 170*; Battle of Bunker Hill, 192–193, 193*; "Boston Massacre," 178–179, 179*; British evacuation of, 193; establishment of first school, 143; fourth largest city in 1810, 305; landing of British troops, 177–178; punishment under "Intolerable Acts," 183; removal of settlers to, 89; results of the nonimportation agreements, 176; *Romney* incident, 176–177; support from other colonies, 183–184; third largest city in 1840, 339*

"Boston Massacre," 178–179, 179*

Boston Tea Party, 182–183

Bowie, James, 373

Braddock, General Edward, 154–155, 155*, 184, 307

Bradford, William, 81, 83

Brady, Mathew B., 408

Bragg, General Braxton, 440

Brandeis, Louis D., 563

Braxton, Carter, 195

Brazil, Magellan's voyage to, 30

Breckinridge, John C.: nomination for President by southern Democrats, 407; votes, 409

Brewster, William, 81, 83

Britain. *See* England; Great Britain

British East India Company, 181, 182

Brock, General Isaac, 295

Brook Farm, 350–351, 350*

Brown, John: capture and execution, 406–407, 406*; Kansas murders, 399; raid on Harpers Ferry, 406

Brown Shirts, 647. *See also* Nazis

Brown v. Board of Education of Topeka, 692–693

Bruce, Blanche K., 458

Bryan, William Jennings: and "cross of gold" speech, 537–538; defeat by McKinley, 553; defeat by Taft, 570; gains support of Populists, 538–539; seeks 1912 nomination, 573

Bryant, William Cullen, 384

Buchanan, James: clash with Douglas over proslavery Kansas constitution, 402–403; Dred Scott decision, 401–402; election to presidency, 400–401; failure to defend Union, 419; inactivity on request for tariff increase, 405; lack of imagination and energy, 405; marks time as term of office runs out, 409; sends relief ship to Fort Sumter, 422

Buena Vista, Battle of, 380–381

Buffalo, 36*, 488–489

Buffalo Bill, 489

Bulge, Battle of the, 661, 664–665

Bull Moose party: returns to the fold, 590; splits off from Republicans, 572. *See also* Republican party; Roosevelt, Theodore

Bull Run: first Battle of, 428–429; second Battle of, 433

Bunker Hill, Battle of, 192–193, 192*, 294

Burghers: as real rulers of New Netherland, 109; struggle against Stuyvesant, 110

Burgoyne, General John: Battle of Bennington, 200; Battle of Freeman's Farm, 202; defeat at Saratoga, 202, 205; explanation to Parliament, 202; plan to cut off New England, 199–200

Burke, Edmund, 185

Burma, fall of, 659

Burnside, General Ambrose E., 436

Burr, Aaron, tie election of 1800, 267

Butler, General Benjamin F., 443, 460, 461

Byrd, Richard E., first flight over North Pole, 606

CCC. *See* Civilian Conservation Corps

CIO. *See* Congress of Industrial Organizations

CORE. *See* Congress of Racial Equality

CWA. *See* Civil Works Administration

Cabeza de Vaca: crossing of North America, 35–36; route of, 37 (map)

Cabot, John, 26

Calhoun, John C.: candidacy for President, 315; failing health, 392; final appearance in Senate, 394; helps Lee obtain appointment to West Point, 423; O'Neale affair, 325; opposition to Compromise of 1850, 394; opposition to Van Buren, 331; reaction to proposal for Wilmot Proviso, 390; resignation from vice-presidency, 326; rise of the Whigs, 330–331; role in barring confirmation of Van Buren's ambassadorship, 325; sets forth doctrine of nullification, 326*; South Carolina declares Tariffs of 1828 and 1832 null and void, 328; urges annexation of Texas as slave state, 373–374; as War Hawk, 290; Webster-Hayne debate, 327–328, 327*

California: acts on Taylor's suggestion to apply for admission to Union, 391; admitted to Union, 395; American offer to purchase rejected by Mexico, 379; annexation of, 380; Bear Flag Republic, 379; cession to United States under Treaty of Guadalupe Hidalgo, 383; Clay's proposal for admission as free state, 394; discovery of gold, 384–385; effects of gold rush, 385; Junípero Serra, 371; southern desire to bar admission to Union, 392; Sutter's settlement, 371; vigilance committees, 385

Calvert, Cecilius (Lord Baltimore), 86*, 99–100, 100–101

Calvert, Sir George (Lord Baltimore), 99

Camden, Battle of, 210

Canada: American Revolutionary campaigns in, 194; American threat to invade, 288–289; influence of Jesuits, 54, 55. *See also* New France

Iron: importance in colonial commerce, 161; limitation on building of new ironworks, 165; Saugus Ironworks, 161*

Iroquois, 9*; American campaign against, 207; colonists at Albany seek treaty with, 154; defeat by French and Indian allies, 49; French treaty with (1667), 55

Isabella, queen of Castile, 19, 21

Isolationism: change brought about by growth of international trade and nationalism, 584; as chief plank in foreign policy of early republic, 583–584; influence of isolationists before Second World War, 648–649, 658

Italy: early monopoly of trade with the East, 17; entrance into First World War, 597; fall of Rome, 622; Fascist rise to power, 649; invasion of Ethiopia and conquest of Albania, 650; joins in attack on France, 652; joins Rome-Berlin Axis, 649; resignation and flight of Mussolini, 602

Iwo Jima, 667 (pronounced)

Jackson, age of: change from subsistence-agriculture economy, 336–337; changes in character of political life, 339–341; expansion of national boundaries, 337–338; expansion of opportunities, 337–339; and fear of governmental control of business, 504; growth of cities, 337; and recognition of individual worth, 342; rise of merchants, factories, 336–337; spread of democracy, 339

Jackson, Andrew, 288, 322*, 325*, 391, 403; attempt to buy Texas, 372; destruction of Bank of the United States, 329–330, 389; election to presidency in 1828, 315–316; inauguration, 316; introduction of spoils system to federal government, 324; loss of election to Adams, 315; money policies, 332–333; nullification crisis, 326–328; O'Neale affair, 324–325; personal popularity, 330–331; personal traits, 323–324; persuades Polk to run for governor of Tennessee, 373;

proclamation against nullification used by Lincoln in preparing first inaugural, 410; recognizes independence of Texas, 374; reorganization of Cabinet, 325; rise of the Whigs, 330–331; Specie Circular, 332; victor at Battle of New Orleans, 310–302, 302*. *See also* Jackson, age of; Jacksonian democracy

Jackson, Rachel (Mrs. Andrew), 323, 324*, 325

Jackson, Thomas J. (Stonewall): campaign in Shenandoah Valley, 432; death at Chancellorsville, 436–437; heroism at Bull Run, 429*

Jacksonian democracy, 354; defined, 336; changes in political life, 339–341

James, Duke of York, 111, 112, 113, 114

James I, king of England, 71, 81, 99

Jamestown, 64*; excavations, 76*, 77*; founding of, 72–74, 76; unloading of first Negroes in America, 140*

Japan: advance in Pacific slowed, 659–660; American island-hopping campaign, 666–667; atomic bombs fall on Hiroshima and Nagasaki, 669; attack on Pearl Harbor, 657–658, 657*, 658*; begins to establish "new order" in Asia, 650–651; builds up armed forces, 649; conquest of Philippines, Guam, Wake Island, Hong Kong, and Singapore, 659; "Death March," 658; invades Indochina, 656; invades Manchuria, 649; joins Rome-Berlin Axis, 654; peace talks in Washington, 656; Perry's expedition opens ports to American sailors, 544; Theodore Roosevelt acts as mediator to end war with Russia, 585; suicide planes, 668; surrender, 669–670

Jay, John, 242*; appointment as Chief Justice, 251; efforts to negotiate settlement of American navigation on Mississippi, 236; Jay's treaty, 262–263; mission to England, 261–262; named Minister of Foreign Affairs, 227; as one author of *The Feder-*

alist, 243; role in negotiating Treaty of Paris, 213

Jay's treaty. See Jay, John

Jazz, development of, 613

Jefferson, Thomas, 190*, 270*, 271*, 347, 398, 492; alarm at raising of slavery question, 311; American position in war between France and Spain, 284; appointment as Secretary of State, 250–251, 251*; candidate for President, 266–267; changes between time of Jefferson and age of Jackson, 336; *Chesapeake-Leopard* affair, 285–286; conflict with John Marshall, 274–275; and creation of American decimal system of money, 232–233; defines logrolling, 341; democratic style, 272; determination to keep peace, 286–287, 290; drafting of Land Ordinance of 1784, 229–230, 230*; election as Vice-President, 264; Hamilton's plea for support of his program, 254–255; home at Monticello, 274*; hopes for Constitutional Convention, 237; hopes for nation of farmers, 495; as idol of Lincoln, 404; impressment of American seamen, 284; inaugural address, 271–272; interest in science and farming, 272; as leader of Democratic-Republicans, 257; Lewis and Clark expedition, 279–281; Louisiana Purchase, 275–279, 278 (map); membership on Virginia Committee of Correspondence, 181; Nonimportation and Embargo acts, 286–287; opposition to industrialization, 258; Pike's explorations, 281–282; preference for least government possible, 522; pro-French sympathies, 259, 260; reaction to decision in *Marbury* v. *Madison*, 275; reduction of national debt, 272–273; refusal to seek third term, 287; Republican attacks on federal courts, 273–274; selection by House in tie election, 267–268; snubbing by George III, 235; and strict construction of Constitution, 256; urges stand with Britain to forbid European military expeditions to New